Analysis of Financial Time Series

WILEY SERIES IN PROBABILITY AND STATISTICS

Established by WALTER A. SHEWHART and SAMUEL S. WILKS

A complete list of the titles in this series appears at the end of this volume.

Analysis of Financial Time Series

Second Edition

RUEY S. TSAY

University of Chicago
Graduate School of Business

WILEY-INTERSCIENCE

A JOHN WILEY & SONS, INC., PUBLICATION

Published by John Wiley & Sons, Inc., Hoboken, New Jersey.
Published simultaneously in Canada.

Library of Congress Cataloging-in-Publication Data:

Tsay, Ruey S., 1951–
Analysis of financial time series/Ruey S. Tsay.—2nd ed.
p. cm.
"Wiley-Interscience."
Includes bibliographical references and index.
ISBN-13 978-0-471-69074-0
ISBN-10 0-471-69074-0 (cloth)
1. Time-series analysis. 2. Econometrics. 3. Risk management. I. Title.

HA30.3T76 2005
332′.01′51955—dc22

2005047030

Printed in the United States of America.

10 9 8 7 6 5 4 3

To my parents and Teresa

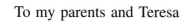

Contents

Preface

The subject of *financial time series analysis* has attracted substantial attention in recent years, especially with the 2003 Nobel awards to Professors Robert Engle and Clive Granger. At the same time, the field of financial econometrics has undergone various new developments, especially in high-frequency finance, stochastic volatility, and software availability. There is a need to make the material more complete and accessible for advanced undergraduate and graduate students, practitioners, and researchers. The main goals in preparing this second edition have been to bring the book up to date both in new developments and empirical analysis, and to enlarge the core material of the book by including consistent covariance estimation under heteroscedasticity and serial correlation, alternative approaches to volatility modeling, financial factor models, state-space models, Kalman filtering, and estimation of stochastic diffusion models.

The book therefore has been extended to 10 chapters and substantially revised to include S-Plus commands and illustrations. Many empirical demonstrations and exercises are updated so that they include the most recent data.

The two new chapters are Chapter 9, Principal Component Analysis and Factor Models, and Chapter 11, State-Space Models and Kalman Filter. The factor models discussed include macroeconomic, fundamental, and statistical factor models. They are simple and powerful tools for analyzing high-dimensional financial data such as portfolio returns. Empirical examples are used to demonstrate the applications. The state-space model and Kalman filter are added to demonstrate their applicability in finance and ease in computation. They are used in Chapter 12 to estimate stochastic volatility models under the general Markov chain Monte Carlo (MCMC) framework. The estimation also uses the technique of forward filtering and backward sampling to gain computational efficiency.

A brief summary of the added material in the second edition is:

1. To update the data used throughout the book.
2. To provide S-Plus commands and demonstrations.
3. To consider unit-root tests and methods for consistent estimation of the covariance matrix in the presence of conditional heteroscedasticity and serial correlation in Chapter 2.

4. To describe alternative approaches to volatility modeling, including use of high-frequency transactions data and daily high and low prices of an asset in Chapter 3.
5. To give more applications of nonlinear models and methods in Chapter 4.
6. To introduce additional concepts and applications of value at risk in Chapter 7.
7. To discuss cointegrated vector AR models in Chapter 8.
8. To cover various multivariate volatility models in Chapter 10.
9. To add an effective MCMC method for estimating stochastic volatility models in Chapter 12.

The revision benefits greatly from constructive comments of colleagues, friends, and many readers on the first edition. I am indebted to them all. In particular, I thank J. C. Artigas, Spencer Graves, Chung-Ming Kuan, Henry Lin, Daniel Peña, Jeff Russell, Michael Steele, George Tiao, Mark Wohar, Eric Zivot, and students of my MBA classes on financial time series for their comments and discussions, and Rosalyn Farkas, production editor, at John Wiley. I also thank my wife and children for their unconditional support and encouragement. Part of my research in financial econometrics is supported by the National Science Foundation, the High-Frequency Finance Project of the Institute of Economics, Academia Sinica, and the Graduate School of Business, University of Chicago.

Finally, the website for the book is:
`gsbwww.uchicago.edu/fac/ruey.tsay/teaching/fts2.`

RUEY S. TSAY

University of Chicago
Chicago, Illinois

Preface for the First Edition

This book grew out of an MBA course in analysis of financial time series that I have been teaching at the University of Chicago since 1999. It also covers materials of Ph.D. courses in time series analysis that I taught over the years. It is an introductory book intended to provide a comprehensive and systematic account of financial econometric models and their application to modeling and prediction of financial time series data. The goals are to learn basic characteristics of financial data, understand the application of financial econometric models, and gain experience in analyzing financial time series.

The book will be useful as a text of time series analysis for MBA students with finance concentration or senior undergraduate and graduate students in business, economics, mathematics, and statistics who are interested in financial econometrics. The book is also a useful reference for researchers and practitioners in business, finance, and insurance facing value at risk calculation, volatility modeling, and analysis of serially correlated data.

The distinctive features of this book include the combination of recent developments in financial econometrics in the econometric and statistical literature. The developments discussed include the timely topics of value at risk (VaR), high-frequency data analysis, and Markov chain Monte Carlo (MCMC) methods. In particular, the book covers some recent results that are yet to appear in academic journals; see Chapter 6 on derivative pricing using jump diffusion with closed-form formulas, Chapter 7 on value at risk calculation using extreme value theory based on a nonhomogeneous two-dimensional Poisson process, and Chapter 9 on multivariate volatility models with time-varying correlations. MCMC methods are introduced because they are powerful and widely applicable in financial econometrics. These methods will be used extensively in the future.

Another distinctive feature of this book is the emphasis on real examples and data analysis. Real financial data are used throughout the book to demonstrate applications of the models and methods discussed. The analysis is carried out by using several computer packages; the SCA (the Scientific Computing Associates) for building linear time series models, the RATS (regression analysis for time series) for estimating volatility models, and the S-Plus for implementing neural networks and obtaining postscript plots. Some commands required to run these packages are given in appendixes of appropriate chapters. In particular, complicated RATS programs used to estimate multivariate volatility models are shown in Appendix A of Chapter 9. Some Fortran programs written by myself and others are used to price simple options, estimate extreme value models, calculate VaR, and carry out Bayesian analysis. Some data sets and programs are accessible from the World Wide Web at http://www.gsb.uchicago.edu/fac/ruey.tsay/teaching/fts.

The book begins with some basic characteristics of financial time series data in Chapter 1. The other chapters are divided into three parts. The first part, consisting of Chapters 2 to 7, focuses on analysis and application of univariate financial time series. The second part of the book covers Chapters 8 and 9 and is concerned with the return series of multiple assets. The final part of the book is Chapter 10, which introduces Bayesian inference in finance via MCMC methods.

A knowledge of basic statistical concepts is needed to fully understand the book. Throughout the chapters, I have provided a brief review of the necessary statistical concepts when they first appear. Even so, a prerequisite in statistics or business statistics that includes probability distributions and linear regression analysis is highly recommended. A knowledge of finance will be helpful in understanding the applications discussed throughout the book. However, readers with advanced background in econometrics and statistics can find interesting and challenging topics in many areas of the book.

An MBA course may consist of Chapters 2 and 3 as a core component, followed by some nonlinear methods (e.g., the neural network of Chapter 4 and the applications discussed in Chapters 5–7 and 10). Readers who are interested in Bayesian inference may start with the first five sections of Chapter 10.

Research in financial time series evolves rapidly and new results continue to appear regularly. Although I have attempted to provide broad coverage, there are many subjects that I do not cover or can only mention in passing.

I sincerely thank my teacher and dear friend, George C. Tiao, for his guidance, encouragement, and deep conviction regarding statistical applications over the years. I am grateful to Steve Quigley, Heather Haselkorn, Leslie Galen, Danielle LaCouriere, and Amy Hendrickson for making the publication of this book possible, to Richard Smith for sending me the estimation program of extreme value theory, to Bonnie K. Ray for helpful comments on several chapters, to Steve Kou for sending me his preprint on jump diffusion models, to Robert E. McCulloch for many years of collaboration on MCMC methods, to many students in my courses on analysis of financial time series for their feedback and inputs, and to Jeffrey Russell and Michael Zhang for insightful discussions concerning analysis of high-frequency financial data. To all these wonderful people I owe a deep sense of gratitude. I am also grateful for the support of the Graduate School of Business, University of Chicago and the National Science Foundation. Finally, my heartfelt thanks to my wife, Teresa, for her continuous support, encouragement, and understanding; to Julie, Richard, and Vicki for bringing me joy and inspirations; and to my parents for their love and care.

RUEY S. TSAY

University of Chicago
Chicago, Illinois

CHAPTER 1

Financial Time Series and Their Characteristics

Financial time series analysis is concerned with the theory and practice of asset valuation over time. It is a highly empirical discipline, but like other scientific fields theory forms the foundation for making inference. There is, however, a key feature that distinguishes financial time series analysis from other time series analysis. Both financial theory and its empirical time series contain an element of uncertainty. For example, there are various definitions of asset volatility, and for a stock return series, the volatility is not directly observable. As a result of the added uncertainty, statistical theory and methods play an important role in financial time series analysis.

The objective of this book is to provide some knowledge of financial time series, introduce some statistical tools useful for analyzing these series, and gain experience in financial applications of various econometric methods. We begin with the basic concepts of asset returns and a brief introduction to the processes to be discussed throughout the book. Chapter 2 reviews basic concepts of linear time series analysis such as stationarity and autocorrelation function, introduces simple linear models for handling serial dependence of the series, and discusses regression models with time series errors, seasonality, unit-root nonstationarity, and long-memory processes. The chapter also provides methods for consistent estimation of the covariance matrix in the presence of conditional heteroscedasticity and serial correlations. Chapter 3 focuses on modeling conditional heteroscedasticity (i.e., the conditional variance of an asset return). It discusses various econometric models developed recently to describe the evolution of volatility of an asset return over time. The chapter also discusses alternative methods to volatility modeling, including use of high-frequency transactions data and daily high and low prices of an asset. In Chapter 4, we address nonlinearity in financial time series, introduce test statistics that can discriminate nonlinear series from linear ones, and discuss several nonlinear models. The chapter also introduces nonparametric

Analysis of Financial Time Series, Second Edition By Ruey S. Tsay

estimation methods and neural networks and shows various applications of nonlinear models in finance. Chapter 5 is concerned with analysis of high-frequency financial data and its application to market microstructure. It shows that nonsynchronous trading and bid–ask bounce can introduce serial correlations in a stock return. It also studies the dynamic of time duration between trades and some econometric models for analyzing transactions data. In Chapter 6, we introduce continuous-time diffusion models and Ito's lemma. Black–Scholes option pricing formulas are derived and a simple jump diffusion model is used to capture some characteristics commonly observed in options markets. Chapter 7 discusses extreme value theory, heavy-tailed distributions, and their application to financial risk management. In particular, it discusses various methods for calculating value at risk of a financial position. Chapter 8 focuses on multivariate time series analysis and simple multivariate models with emphasis on the lead–lag relationship between time series. The chapter also introduces cointegration, some cointegration tests, and threshold cointegration and applies the concept of cointegration to investigate arbitrage opportunity in financial markets. Chapter 9 discusses ways to simplify the dynamic structure of a multivariate series and methods to reduce the dimension. It introduces and demonstrates three types of factor model to analyze returns of multiple assets. In Chapter 10, we introduce multivariate volatility models, including those with time-varying correlations, and discuss methods that can be used to reparameterize a conditional covariance matrix to satisfy the positiveness constraint and reduce the complexity in volatility modeling. Chapter 11 introduces state-space models and the Kalman filter and discusses the relationship between state-space models and other econometric models discussed in the book. It also gives several examples of financial applications. Finally, in Chapter 12, we introduce some newly developed Markov chain Monte Carlo (MCMC) methods in the statistical literature and apply the methods to various financial research problems, such as the estimation of stochastic volatility and Markov switching models.

The book places great emphasis on application and empirical data analysis. Every chapter contains real examples and, on many occasions, empirical characteristics of financial time series are used to motivate the development of econometric models. Computer programs and commands used in data analysis are provided when needed. In some cases, the programs are given in an appendix. Many real data sets are also used in the exercises of each chapter.

1.1 ASSET RETURNS

Most financial studies involve returns, instead of prices, of assets. Campbell, Lo, and MacKinlay (1997) give two main reasons for using returns. First, for average investors, return of an asset is a complete and scale-free summary of the investment opportunity. Second, return series are easier to handle than price series because the former have more attractive statistical properties. There are, however, several definitions of an asset return.

Let P_t be the price of an asset at time index t. We discuss some definitions of returns that are used throughout the book. Assume for the moment that the asset pays no dividends.

One-Period Simple Return

Holding the asset for one period from date $t-1$ to date t would result in a *simple gross return*

$$1 + R_t = \frac{P_t}{P_{t-1}} \quad \text{or} \quad P_t = P_{t-1}(1 + R_t). \tag{1.1}$$

The corresponding one-period *simple net return* or *simple return* is

$$R_t = \frac{P_t}{P_{t-1}} - 1 = \frac{P_t - P_{t-1}}{P_{t-1}}. \tag{1.2}$$

Multiperiod Simple Return

Holding the asset for k periods between dates $t-k$ and t gives a k-period simple gross return

$$\begin{aligned} 1 + R_t[k] = \frac{P_t}{P_{t-k}} &= \frac{P_t}{P_{t-1}} \times \frac{P_{t-1}}{P_{t-2}} \times \cdots \times \frac{P_{t-k+1}}{P_{t-k}} \\ &= (1 + R_t)(1 + R_{t-1}) \cdots (1 + R_{t-k+1}) \\ &= \prod_{j=0}^{k-1} (1 + R_{t-j}). \end{aligned}$$

Thus, the k-period simple gross return is just the product of the k one-period simple gross returns involved. This is called a compound return. The k-period simple net return is $R_t[k] = (P_t - P_{t-k})/P_{t-k}$.

In practice, the actual time interval is important in discussing and comparing returns (e.g., monthly return or annual return). If the time interval is not given, then it is implicitly assumed to be one year. If the asset was held for k years, then the annualized (average) return is defined as

$$\text{Annualized}\{R_t[k]\} = \left[\prod_{j=0}^{k-1} (1 + R_{t-j})\right]^{1/k} - 1.$$

This is a geometric mean of the k one-period simple gross returns involved and can be computed by

$$\text{Annualized}\{R_t[k]\} = \exp\left[\frac{1}{k}\sum_{j=0}^{k-1} \ln(1 + R_{t-j})\right] - 1,$$

where $\exp(x)$ denotes the exponential function and $\ln(x)$ is the natural logarithm of the positive number x. Because it is easier to compute arithmetic average than geometric mean and the one-period returns tend to be small, one can use a first-order Taylor expansion to approximate the annualized return and obtain

$$\text{Annualized}\{R_t[k]\} \approx \frac{1}{k}\sum_{j=0}^{k-1} R_{t-j}. \tag{1.3}$$

Accuracy of the approximation in Eq. (1.3) may not be sufficient in some applications, however.

Continuous Compounding

Before introducing continuously compounded return, we discuss the effect of compounding. Assume that the interest rate of a bank deposit is 10% per annum and the initial deposit is \$1.00. If the bank pays interest once a year, then the net value of the deposit becomes $\$1(1 + 0.1) = \$1.1$ one year later. If the bank pays interest semiannually, the 6-month interest rate is $10\%/2 = 5\%$ and the net value is $\$1(1 + 0.1/2)^2 = \$1.1025$ after the first year. In general, if the bank pays interest m times a year, then the interest rate for each payment is $10\%/m$ and the net value of the deposit becomes $\$1(1 + 0.1/m)^m$ one year later. Table 1.1 gives the results for some commonly used time intervals on a deposit of \$1.00 with interest rate of 10% per annum. In particular, the net value approaches \$1.1052, which is obtained by exp(0.1) and referred to as the result of continuous compounding. The effect of compounding is clearly seen.

In general, the net asset value A of continuous compounding is

$$A = C\exp(r \times n), \tag{1.4}$$

where r is the interest rate per annum, C is the initial capital, and n is the number of years. From Eq. (1.4), we have

$$C = A\exp(-r \times n), \tag{1.5}$$

which is referred to as the *present value* of an asset that is worth A dollars n years from now, assuming that the continuously compounded interest rate is r per annum.

Table 1.1. Illustration of the Effects of Compounding[a]

Type	Number of Payments	Interest Rate per Period	Net Value
Annual	1	0.1	\$1.10000
Semiannual	2	0.05	\$1.10250
Quarterly	4	0.025	\$1.10381
Monthly	12	0.0083	\$1.10471
Weekly	52	0.1/52	\$1.10506
Daily	365	0.1/365	\$1.10516
Continuously	∞		\$1.10517

[a]The time interval is 1 year and the interest rate is 10% per annum.

Continuously Compounded Return

The natural logarithm of the simple gross return of an asset is called the continuously compounded return or *log return*:

$$r_t = \ln(1 + R_t) = \ln \frac{P_t}{P_{t-1}} = p_t - p_{t-1}, \tag{1.6}$$

where $p_t = \ln(P_t)$. Continuously compounded returns r_t enjoy some advantages over the simple net returns R_t. First, consider multiperiod returns. We have

$$\begin{aligned} r_t[k] &= \ln(1 + R_t[k]) = \ln[(1 + R_t)(1 + R_{t-1}) \cdots (1 + R_{t-k+1})] \\ &= \ln(1 + R_t) + \ln(1 + R_{t-1}) + \cdots + \ln(1 + R_{t-k+1}) \\ &= r_t + r_{t-1} + \cdots + r_{t-k+1}. \end{aligned}$$

Thus, the continuously compounded multiperiod return is simply the sum of continuously compounded one-period returns involved. Second, statistical properties of log returns are more tractable.

Portfolio Return

The simple net return of a portfolio consisting of N assets is a weighted average of the simple net returns of the assets involved, where the weight on each asset is the percentage of the portfolio's value invested in that asset. Let p be a portfolio that places weight w_i on asset i. Then the simple return of p at time t is $R_{p,t} = \sum_{i=1}^{N} w_i R_{it}$, where R_{it} is the simple return of asset i.

The continuously compounded returns of a portfolio, however, do not have the above convenient property. If the simple returns R_{it} are all small in magnitude, then we have $r_{p,t} \approx \sum_{i=1}^{N} w_i r_{it}$, where $r_{p,t}$ is the continuously compounded return of the portfolio at time t. This approximation is often used to study portfolio returns.

Dividend Payment

If an asset pays dividends periodically, we must modify the definitions of asset returns. Let D_t be the dividend payment of an asset between dates $t-1$ and t and P_t be the price of the asset at the end of period t. Thus, dividend is not included in P_t. Then the simple net return and continuously compounded return at time t become

$$R_t = \frac{P_t + D_t}{P_{t-1}} - 1, \qquad r_t = \ln(P_t + D_t) - \ln(P_{t-1}).$$

Excess Return

Excess return of an asset at time t is the difference between the asset's return and the return on some reference asset. The reference asset is often taken to be riskless such as a short-term U.S. Treasury bill return. The simple excess return and log excess return of an asset are then defined as

$$Z_t = R_t - R_{0t}, \qquad z_t = r_t - r_{0t}, \tag{1.7}$$

where R_{0t} and r_{0t} are the simple and log returns of the reference asset, respectively. In the finance literature, the excess return is thought of as the payoff on an arbitrage portfolio that goes long in an asset and short in the reference asset with no net initial investment.

Remark. A long financial position means owning the asset. A short position involves selling an asset one does not own. This is accomplished by borrowing the asset from an investor who has purchased it. At some subsequent date, the short seller is obligated to buy exactly the same number of shares borrowed to pay back the lender. Because the repayment requires equal shares rather than equal dollars, the short seller benefits from a decline in the price of the asset. If cash dividends are paid on the asset while a short position is maintained, these are paid to the buyer of the short sale. The short seller must also compensate the lender by matching the cash dividends from his own resources. In other words, the short seller is also obligated to pay cash dividends on the borrowed asset to the lender. □

Summary of Relationship

The relationships between simple return R_t and continuously compounded (or log) return r_t are

$$r_t = \ln(1 + R_t), \qquad R_t = e^{r_t} - 1.$$

If the returns R_t and r_t are in percentages, then

$$r_t = 100 \ln\left(1 + \frac{R_t}{100}\right), \qquad R_t = 100(e^{r_t/100} - 1).$$

Temporal aggregation of the returns produces

$$1 + R_t[k] = (1 + R_t)(1 + R_{t-1}) \cdots (1 + R_{t-k+1}),$$
$$r_t[k] = r_t + r_{t-1} + \cdots + r_{t-k+1}.$$

If the continuously compounded interest rate is r per annum, then the relationship between present and future values of an asset is

$$A = C \exp(r \times n), \qquad C = A \exp(-r \times n).$$

Example 1.1. If the monthly log return of an asset is 4.46%, then the corresponding monthly simple return is $100[\exp(4.46/100) - 1] = 4.56\%$. Also, if the monthly log returns of the asset within a quarter are 4.46%, −7.34%, and 10.77%, respectively, then the quarterly log return of the asset is $(4.46 - 7.34 + 10.77)\% = 7.89\%$.

1.2 DISTRIBUTIONAL PROPERTIES OF RETURNS

To study asset returns, it is best to begin with their distributional properties. The objective here is to understand the behavior of the returns across assets and over time. Consider a collection of N assets held for T time periods, say, $t = 1, \ldots, T$. For each asset i, let r_{it} be its log return at time t. The log returns under study are $\{r_{it}; i = 1, \ldots, N; t = 1, \ldots, T\}$. One can also consider the simple returns $\{R_{it}; i = 1, \ldots, N; t = 1, \ldots, T\}$ and the log excess returns $\{z_{it}; i = 1, \ldots, N; t = 1, \ldots, T\}$.

1.2.1 Review of Statistical Distributions and Their Moments

We briefly review some basic properties of statistical distributions and the moment equations of a random variable. Let R^k be the k-dimensional Euclidean space. A point in R^k is denoted by $\boldsymbol{x} \in R^k$. Consider two random vectors $\boldsymbol{X} = (X_1, \ldots, X_k)'$ and $\boldsymbol{Y} = (Y_1, \ldots, Y_q)'$. Let $P(X \in A, Y \in B)$ be the probability that $\boldsymbol{X}$ is in the subspace $A \subset R^k$ and $\boldsymbol{Y}$ is in the subspace $B \subset R^q$. For most of the cases considered in this book, both random vectors are assumed to be continuous.

Joint Distribution
The function

$$F_{X,Y}(\boldsymbol{x}, \boldsymbol{y}; \boldsymbol{\theta}) = P(X \le \boldsymbol{x}, \boldsymbol{Y} \le \boldsymbol{y}; \boldsymbol{\theta}),$$

where $\boldsymbol{x} \in R^p$, $\boldsymbol{y} \in R^q$, and the inequality "$\le$" is a component-by-component operation, is a joint distribution function of $\boldsymbol{X}$ and $\boldsymbol{Y}$ with parameter $\boldsymbol{\theta}$. Behavior of $\boldsymbol{X}$ and $\boldsymbol{Y}$ is characterized by $F_{X,Y}(\boldsymbol{x}, \boldsymbol{y}; \boldsymbol{\theta})$. If the joint probability density function $f_{x,y}(\boldsymbol{x}, \boldsymbol{y}; \boldsymbol{\theta})$ of $\boldsymbol{X}$ and $\boldsymbol{Y}$ exists, then

$$F_{X,Y}(\boldsymbol{x}, \boldsymbol{y}; \boldsymbol{\theta}) = \int_{-\infty}^{\boldsymbol{x}} \int_{-\infty}^{\boldsymbol{y}} f_{x,y}(\boldsymbol{w}, \boldsymbol{z}; \boldsymbol{\theta})\, d\boldsymbol{z}\, d\boldsymbol{w}.$$

In this case, $\boldsymbol{X}$ and $\boldsymbol{Y}$ are continuous random vectors.

Marginal Distribution
The marginal distribution of $\boldsymbol{X}$ is given by

$$F_X(\boldsymbol{x}; \boldsymbol{\theta}) = F_{X,Y}(\boldsymbol{x}, \infty, \ldots, \infty; \boldsymbol{\theta}).$$

Thus, the marginal distribution of $\boldsymbol{X}$ is obtained by integrating out $\boldsymbol{Y}$. A similar definition applies to the marginal distribution of $\boldsymbol{Y}$.

If $k = 1$, X is a scalar random variable and the distribution function becomes

$$F_X(x) = P(X \le x; \boldsymbol{\theta}),$$

which is known as the cumulative distribution function (CDF) of X. The CDF of a random variable is nondecreasing (i.e., $F_X(x_1) \le F_X(x_2)$ if $x_1 \le x_2$) and satisfies

$F_X(-\infty) = 0$ and $F_X(\infty) = 1$. For a given probability p, the smallest real number x_p such that $p \le F_X(x_p)$ is called the pth quantile of the random variable X. More specifically,

$$x_p = \inf_x \{x | p \le F_X(x)\}.$$

We use the CDF to compute the p value of a test statistic in the book.

Conditional Distribution

The conditional distribution of $\boldsymbol{X}$ given $\boldsymbol{Y} \le \boldsymbol{y}$ is given by

$$F_{X|Y\le y}(\boldsymbol{x}; \boldsymbol{\theta}) = \frac{P(\boldsymbol{X} \le \boldsymbol{x}, \boldsymbol{Y} \le \boldsymbol{y}; \boldsymbol{\theta})}{P(\boldsymbol{Y} \le \boldsymbol{y}; \boldsymbol{\theta})}.$$

If the probability density functions involved exist, then the conditional density of $\boldsymbol{X}$ given $\boldsymbol{Y} = \boldsymbol{y}$ is

$$f_{x|y}(\boldsymbol{x}; \boldsymbol{\theta}) = \frac{f_{x,y}(\boldsymbol{x}, \boldsymbol{y}; \boldsymbol{\theta})}{f_y(\boldsymbol{y}; \boldsymbol{\theta})}, \tag{1.8}$$

where the marginal density function $f_y(\boldsymbol{y}; \boldsymbol{\theta})$ is obtained by

$$f_y(\boldsymbol{y}; \boldsymbol{\theta}) = \int_{-\infty}^{\infty} f_{x,y}(\boldsymbol{x}, \boldsymbol{y}; \boldsymbol{\theta})\, d\boldsymbol{x}.$$

From Eq. (1.8), the relation among joint, marginal, and conditional distributions is

$$f_{x,y}(\boldsymbol{x}, \boldsymbol{y}; \boldsymbol{\theta}) = f_{x|y}(\boldsymbol{x}; \boldsymbol{\theta}) \times f_y(\boldsymbol{y}; \boldsymbol{\theta}). \tag{1.9}$$

This identity is used extensively in time series analysis (e.g., in maximum likelihood estimation). Finally, $\boldsymbol{X}$ and $\boldsymbol{Y}$ are independent random vectors if and only if $f_{x|y}(\boldsymbol{x}; \boldsymbol{\theta}) = f_x(\boldsymbol{x}; \boldsymbol{\theta})$. In this case, $f_{x,y}(\boldsymbol{x}, \boldsymbol{y}; \boldsymbol{\theta}) = f_x(\boldsymbol{x}; \boldsymbol{\theta}) f_y(\boldsymbol{y}; \boldsymbol{\theta})$.

Moments of a Random Variable

The ℓth moment of a continuous random variable X is defined as

$$m'_\ell = E(X^\ell) = \int_{-\infty}^{\infty} x^\ell f(x)\, dx,$$

where E stands for expectation and $f(x)$ is the probability density function of X. The first moment is called the *mean* or *expectation* of X. It measures the central location of the distribution. We denote the mean of X by μ_x. The ℓth central moment of X is defined as

$$m_\ell = E[(X - \mu_x)^\ell] = \int_{-\infty}^{\infty} (x - \mu_x)^\ell f(x)\, dx$$

provided that the integral exists. The second central moment, denoted by σ_x^2, measures the variability of X and is called the *variance* of X. The positive square root, σ_x, of variance is the *standard deviation* of X. The first two moments of a random variable uniquely determine a normal distribution. For other distributions, higher order moments are also of interest.

The third central moment measures the symmetry of X with respect to its mean, whereas the fourth central moment measures the tail behavior of X. In statistics, *skewness* and *kurtosis*, which are normalized third and fourth central moments of X, are often used to summarize the extent of asymmetry and tail thickness. Specifically, the skewness and kurtosis of X are defined as

$$S(x) = E\left[\frac{(X-\mu_x)^3}{\sigma_x^3}\right], \qquad K(x) = E\left[\frac{(X-\mu_x)^4}{\sigma_x^4}\right].$$

The quantity $K(x) - 3$ is called the *excess kurtosis* because $K(x) = 3$ for a normal distribution. Thus, the excess kurtosis of a normal random variable is zero. A distribution with positive excess kurtosis is said to have heavy tails, implying that the distribution puts more mass on the tails of its support than a normal distribution does. In practice, this means that a random sample from such a distribution tends to contain more extreme values. Such a distribution is said to be *leptokurtic*. On the other hand, a distribution with negative excess kurtosis has short tails (e.g., a uniform distribution over a finite interval). Such a distribution is said to be *platykurtic*.

In application, skewness and kurtosis can be estimated by their sample counterparts. Let $\{x_1, \ldots, x_T\}$ be a random sample of X with T observations. The sample mean is

$$\hat{\mu}_x = \frac{1}{T}\sum_{t=1}^{T} x_t, \tag{1.10}$$

the sample variance is

$$\hat{\sigma}_x^2 = \frac{1}{T-1}\sum_{t=1}^{T}(x_t - \hat{\mu}_x)^2, \tag{1.11}$$

the sample skewness is

$$\hat{S}(x) = \frac{1}{(T-1)\hat{\sigma}_x^3}\sum_{t=1}^{T}(x_t - \hat{\mu}_x)^3, \tag{1.12}$$

and the sample kurtosis is

$$\hat{K}(x) = \frac{1}{(T-1)\hat{\sigma}_x^4}\sum_{t=1}^{T}(x_t - \hat{\mu}_x)^4. \tag{1.13}$$

Under the normality assumption, $\hat{S}(x)$ and $\hat{K}(x) - 3$ are distributed asymptotically as normal with zero mean and variances $6/T$ and $24/T$, respectively; see Snedecor and Cochran (1980, p. 78). These asymptotic properties can be used to test the normality of asset returns. Given an asset return series $\{r_1, \ldots, r_T\}$, to test the skewness of the returns, we consider the null hypothesis $H_o : S(r) = 0$ versus the alternative hypothesis $H_a : S(r) \neq 0$. The t-ratio statistic of the sample skewness in Eq. (1.12) is

$$t = \frac{\hat{S}(r)}{\sqrt{6/T}}.$$

The decision rule is as follows. Reject the null hypothesis at the α significance level, if $|t| > Z_{\alpha/2}$, where $Z_{\alpha/2}$ is the upper $100(\alpha/2)$th quantile of the standard normal distribution. Alternatively, one can compute the p-value of the test statistic t and reject H_o if and only if the p-value is less than α.

Similarly, one can test the excess kurtosis of the return series using the hypotheses $H_o : K(r) - 3 = 0$ versus $H_a : K(r) - 3 \neq 0$. The test statistic is

$$t = \frac{\hat{K}(r) - 3}{\sqrt{24/T}},$$

which is asymptotically a standard normal random variable. The decision rule is to reject H_o if and only if the p-value of the test statistic is less than the significance level α. Jarque and Bera (1987) combine the two prior tests and use the test statistic

$$JB = \frac{\hat{S}^2(r)}{6/T} + \frac{(\hat{K}(r) - 3)^2}{24/T},$$

which is asymptotically distributed as a chi-squared random variable with 2 degrees of freedom, to test for the normality of r_t. One rejects H_o of normality if the p-value of the JB statistic is less than the significance level.

Example 1.2. Consider the daily simple returns of the IBM stock used in Table 1.2. The sample skewness and kurtosis of the returns are parts of the descriptive (or summary) statistics that can be obtained easily using various statistical software packages. Both SCA and S-Plus are used in the demonstration, where '`d-ibmvwewsp6203.txt`' is the data file name. Note that in SCA the *kurtosis* denotes excess kurtosis. From the output, the excess kurtosis is high, indicating that the daily simple returns of IBM stock have heavy tails. To test the symmetry of return distribution, we use the test statistic

$$t = \frac{0.0775}{0.024} = 3.23,$$

which gives a p-value of about 0.001, indicating that the daily simple returns of IBM stock are significantly skewed to the right at the 5% level.

Table 1.2. Descriptive Statistics for Daily and Monthly Simple and Log Returns of Selected Indexes and Stocks[a]

Security	Start	Size	Mean	Standard Deviation	Skewness	Excess Kurtosis	Minimum	Maximum
				Daily Simple Returns (%)				
SP	62/7/3	10446	0.033	0.945	−0.95	25.76	−20.47	9.10
VW	62/7/3	10446	0.045	0.794	−0.76	18.32	−17.14	8.66
EW	62/7/3	10446	0.085	0.726	−0.89	13.42	−10.39	6.95
IBM	62/7/3	10446	0.052	1.648	−0.08	10.21	−22.96	13.16
Intel	72/12/15	7828	0.131	2.998	−0.16	5.85	−29.57	26.38
3M	62/7/3	10446	0.054	1.465	−0.28	12.87	−25.98	11.54
Microsoft	86/3/14	4493	0.157	2.505	−0.25	8.75	−30.12	19.57
Citi-Group	86/10/30	4333	0.110	2.289	−0.10	6.79	−21.74	20.76
				Daily Log Returns (%)				
SP	62/7/3	10446	0.029	0.951	−1.41	36.91	−22.90	8.71
VW	62/7/3	10446	0.041	0.895	−1.06	23.91	−18.80	8.31
EW	62/7/3	10446	0.082	0.728	−1.29	14.70	−10.97	6.72
IBM	62/7/3	10446	0.039	1.649	−0.25	12.60	−26.09	12.37
Intel	72/12/15	7828	0.086	3.013	−0.54	7.54	−35.06	23.41
3M	62/7/3	10446	0.044	1.469	−0.69	20.06	−30.08	10.92
Microsoft	86/3/14	4493	0.126	2.518	−0.73	13.23	−35.83	17.87
Citi-Group	86/10/30	4333	0.084	2.289	−0.21	7.47	−24.51	18.86
				Monthly Simple Returns (%)				
SP	62/1	936	0.64	5.63	−0.35	9.26	−29.94	42.22
VW	26/1	936	0.95	5.49	−0.18	7.52	−28.98	38.27
EW	26/1	936	1.31	7.49	−1.54	14.46	−31.18	65.51
IBM	26/1	936	1.42	7.11	−0.27	2.15	−26.19	35.38
Intel	73/1	372	2.71	13.42	−0.26	2.43	−44.87	62.50
3M	46/2	695	1.37	6.53	−0.24	0.96	−27.83	25.80
Microsoft	86/4	213	3.37	11.95	−0.53	1.40	−34.35	51.55
Citi-Group	86/11	206	2.20	9.52	−0.18	0.87	−34.48	26.08
				Monthly Log Returns (%)				
SP	26/1	936	0.48	5.62	−0.50	7.77	−35.58	35.22
VW	26/1	936	0.79	5.48	−0.54	6.72	−34.22	32.41
EW	26/1	936	1.04	7.21	−0.29	8.40	−37.37	50.38
IBM	26/1	936	1.16	7.02	−0.15	2.04	−30.37	30.29
Intel	73/1	372	1.80	13.37	−0.60	2.90	−59.54	48.55
3M	46/2	695	1.16	6.43	−0.06	1.25	−32.61	22.95
Microsoft	86/4	213	2.66	11.48	−0.01	1.19	−42.09	41.58
Citi-Group	86/11	206	1.73	9.55	−0.65	2.08	−42.28	23.18

[a]Returns are in percentages and the sample period ends on December 31, 2003. The statistics are defined in eqs. (1.10)–(1.13). VW, EW, and SP denote value-weighted, equal-weighted, and S&P composite index.

SCA Demonstration

% denotes explanation.

```
input date, ibm, vw, ew, sp. file 'd-ibmvwewsp6203.txt'
% Load data into SCA and name the columns date,
% ibm, vw, ew, and sp.
 --
ibm=ibm*100 % Compute percentage returns
 --
desc ibm  % Obtain descriptive statistics of ibm

 VARIABLE     NAME     IS        IBM
 NUMBER OF OBSERVATIONS     10446
 NUMBER OF MISSING VALUES       0

                    STATISTIC      STD. ERROR     STATISTIC/S.E.
 MEAN                 0.0523          0.0161           3.2457
 VARIANCE             2.7163
 STD DEVIATION        1.6481
 C.V.                31.4900
 SKEWNESS             0.0775          0.0240
 KURTOSIS            10.2144          0.0479

                    QUARTILE
 MINIMUM            -22.9630
 1ST QUARTILE        -0.8380
 MEDIAN               0.0000
 3RD QUARTILE         0.8805
 MAXIMUM             13.1640

                       RANGE
 MAX - MIN           36.1270
 Q3  - Q1             1.7185
```

S-Plus Demonstration

> is the prompt character and % marks explanation.

```
> module(finmetrics) % Load the Finmetrics module.
> x=matrix(scan(file='d-ibmvwewsp6203.txt'),5)  % Load data
> ibm=x[2,]*100  % compute percentage returns
> summaryStats(ibm)  % obtain summary statistics

Sample Quantiles:
    min     1Q median     3Q   max
 -22.96 -0.838      0 0.8807 13.16

Sample Moments:
    mean   std skewness kurtosis
 0.05234 1.648   0.0775    13.22

Number of Observations:  10446
```

1.2.2 Distributions of Returns

The most general model for the log returns $\{r_{it}; i = 1, \ldots, N; t = 1, \ldots, T\}$ is its joint distribution function:

$$F_r(r_{11}, \ldots, r_{N1}; r_{12}, \ldots, r_{N2}; \ldots; r_{1T}, \ldots, r_{NT}; \boldsymbol{Y}; \boldsymbol{\theta}), \tag{1.14}$$

where $\boldsymbol{Y}$ is a state vector consisting of variables that summarize the environment in which asset returns are determined and $\boldsymbol{\theta}$ is a vector of parameters that uniquely determine the distribution function $F_r(.)$. The probability distribution $F_r(.)$ governs the stochastic behavior of the returns r_{it} and $\boldsymbol{Y}$. In many financial studies, the state vector $\boldsymbol{Y}$ is treated as given and the main concern is the conditional distribution of $\{r_{it}\}$ given $\boldsymbol{Y}$. Empirical analysis of asset returns is then to estimate the unknown parameter $\boldsymbol{\theta}$ and to draw statistical inference about the behavior of $\{r_{it}\}$ given some past log returns.

The model in Eq. (1.14) is too general to be of practical value. However, it provides a general framework with respect to which an econometric model for asset returns r_{it} can be put in a proper perspective.

Some financial theories such as the capital asset pricing model (CAPM) of Sharpe (1964) focus on the joint distribution of N returns at a single time index t (i.e., the distribution of $\{r_{1t}, \ldots, r_{Nt}\}$). Other theories emphasize the dynamic structure of individual asset returns (i.e., the distribution of $\{r_{i1}, \ldots, r_{iT}\}$ for a given asset i). In this book, we focus on both. In the univariate analysis of Chapters 2–7, our main concern is the joint distribution of $\{r_{it}\}_{t=1}^{T}$ for asset i. To this end, it is useful to partition the joint distribution as

$$\begin{aligned} F(r_{i1}, \ldots, r_{iT}; \boldsymbol{\theta}) &= F(r_{i1})F(r_{i2}|r_{1t}) \cdots F(r_{iT}|r_{i,T-1}, \ldots, r_{i1}) \\ &= F(r_{i1}) \prod_{t=2}^{T} F(r_{it}|r_{i,t-1}, \ldots, r_{i1}), \end{aligned} \tag{1.15}$$

where, for simplicity, the parameter $\boldsymbol{\theta}$ is omitted. This partition highlights the temporal dependencies of the log return r_{it}. The main issue then is the specification of the conditional distribution $F(r_{it}|r_{i,t-1}, .)$, in particular, how the conditional distribution evolves over time. In finance, different distributional specifications lead to different theories. For instance, one version of the random-walk hypothesis is that the conditional distribution $F(r_{it}|r_{i,t-1}, \ldots, r_{i1})$ is equal to the marginal distribution $F(r_{it})$. In this case, returns are temporally independent and, hence, not predictable.

It is customary to treat asset returns as continuous random variables, especially for index returns or stock returns calculated at a low frequency, and use their probability density functions. In this case, using the identity in Eq. (1.9), we can write the partition in Eq. (1.15) as

$$f(r_{i1}, \ldots, r_{iT}; \boldsymbol{\theta}) = f(r_{i1}; \boldsymbol{\theta}) \prod_{t=2}^{T} f(r_{it}|r_{i,t-1}, \ldots, r_{i1}, \boldsymbol{\theta}). \tag{1.16}$$

For high-frequency asset returns, discreteness becomes an issue. For example, stock prices change in multiples of a tick size on the New York Stock Exchange (NYSE). The tick size was one-eighth of a dollar before July 1997 and was one-sixteenth of a dollar from July 1997 to January 2001. Therefore, the tick-by-tick return of an individual stock listed on the NYSE is not continuous. We discuss high-frequency stock price changes and time durations between price changes later in Chapter 5.

Remark. On August 28, 2000, the NYSE began a pilot program with seven stocks priced in decimals and the American Stock Exchange (AMEX) began a pilot program with six stocks and two options classes. The NYSE added 57 stocks and 94 stocks to the program on September 25 and December 4, 2000, respectively. All NYSE and AMEX stocks started trading in decimals on January 29, 2001. □

Equation (1.16) suggests that conditional distributions are more relevant than marginal distributions in studying asset returns. However, the marginal distributions may still be of some interest. In particular, it is easier to estimate marginal distributions than conditional distributions using past returns. In addition, in some cases, asset returns have weak empirical serial correlations, and, hence, their marginal distributions are close to their conditional distributions.

Several statistical distributions have been proposed in the literature for the marginal distributions of asset returns, including normal distribution, lognormal distribution, stable distribution, and scale-mixture of normal distributions. We briefly discuss these distributions.

Normal Distribution

A traditional assumption made in financial study is that the simple returns $\{R_{it}|t = 1, \ldots, T\}$ are independently and identically distributed as normal with fixed mean and variance. This assumption makes statistical properties of asset returns tractable. But it encounters several difficulties. First, the lower bound of a simple return is -1. Yet the normal distribution may assume any value in the real line and, hence, has no lower bound. Second, if R_{it} is normally distributed, then the multiperiod simple return $R_{it}[k]$ is not normally distributed because it is a product of one-period returns. Third, the normality assumption is not supported by many empirical asset returns, which tend to have a positive excess kurtosis.

Lognormal Distribution

Another commonly used assumption is that the log returns r_t of an asset are independent and identically distributed (iid) as normal with mean μ and variance σ^2. The simple returns are then iid lognormal random variables with mean and variance given by

$$E(R_t) = \exp\left(\mu + \frac{\sigma^2}{2}\right) - 1, \qquad \text{Var}(R_t) = \exp(2\mu + \sigma^2)[\exp(\sigma^2) - 1]. \tag{1.17}$$

These two equations are useful in studying asset returns (e.g., in forecasting using models built for log returns). Alternatively, let m_1 and m_2 be the mean and variance of the simple return R_t, which is lognormally distributed. Then the mean and variance of the corresponding log return r_t are

$$E(r_t) = \ln\left(\frac{m_1 + 1}{\sqrt{1 + m_2/(1 + m_1)^2}}\right), \quad \mathrm{Var}(r_t) = \ln\left(1 + \frac{m_2}{(1 + m_1)^2}\right).$$

Because the sum of a finite number of iid normal random variables is normal, $r_t[k]$ is also normally distributed under the normal assumption for $\{r_t\}$. In addition, there is no lower bound for r_t, and the lower bound for R_t is satisfied using $1 + R_t = \exp(r_t)$. However, the lognormal assumption is not consistent with all the properties of historical stock returns. In particular, many stock returns exhibit a positive excess kurtosis.

Stable Distribution

The stable distributions are a natural generalization of normal in that they are stable under addition, which meets the need of continuously compounded returns r_t. Furthermore, stable distributions are capable of capturing excess kurtosis shown by historical stock returns. However, non-normal stable distributions do not have a finite variance, which is in conflict with most finance theories. In addition, statistical modeling using non-normal stable distributions is difficult. An example of non-normal stable distributions is the Cauchy distribution, which is symmetric with respect to its median but has infinite variance.

Scale Mixture of Normal Distributions

Recent studies of stock returns tend to use scale mixture or finite mixture of normal distributions. Under the assumption of scale mixture of normal distributions, the log return r_t is normally distributed with mean μ and variance σ^2 [i.e., $r_t \sim N(\mu, \sigma^2)$]. However, σ^2 is a random variable that follows a positive distribution (e.g., σ^{-2} follows a gamma distribution). An example of finite mixture of normal distributions is

$$r_t \sim (1 - X)N(\mu, \sigma_1^2) + XN(\mu, \sigma_2^2),$$

where X is a Bernoulli random variable such that $P(X = 1) = \alpha$ and $P(X = 0) = 1 - \alpha$ with $0 < \alpha < 1$, σ_1^2 is small, and σ_2^2 is relatively large. For instance, with $\alpha = 0.05$, the finite mixture says that 95% of the returns follow $N(\mu, \sigma_1^2)$ and 5% follow $N(\mu, \sigma_2^2)$. The large value of σ_2^2 enables the mixture to put more mass at the tails of its distribution. The low percentage of returns that are from $N(\mu, \sigma_2^2)$ says that the majority of the returns follow a simple normal distribution. Advantages of mixtures of normal include that they maintain the tractability of normal, have finite higher order moments, and can capture the excess kurtosis. Yet it is hard to estimate the mixture parameters (e.g., the α in the finite-mixture case).

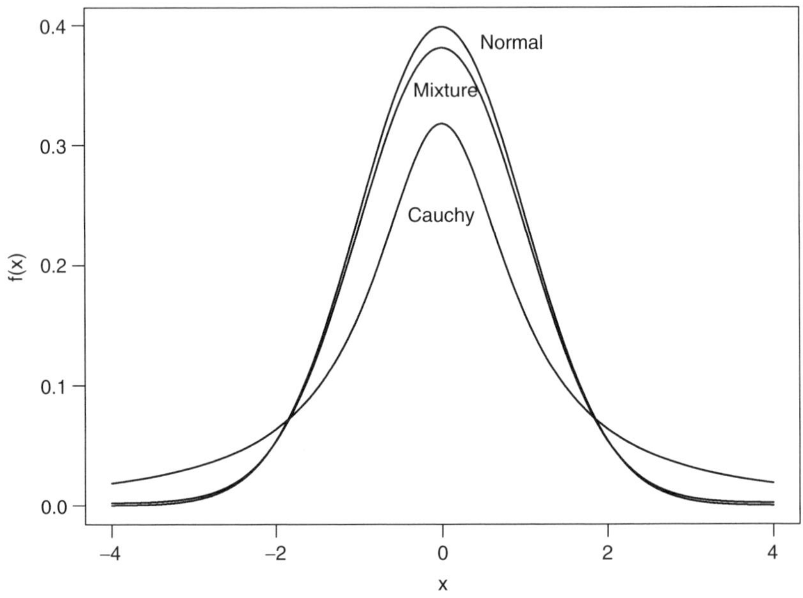

Figure 1.1. Comparison of finite mixture, stable, and standard normal density functions.

Figure 1.1 shows the probability density functions of a finite mixture of normal, Cauchy, and standard normal random variable. The finite mixture of normal is $(1 - X)N(0, 1) + X \times N(0, 16)$ with X being Bernoulli such that $P(X = 1) = 0.05$, and the density function of Cauchy is

$$f(x) = \frac{1}{\pi(1 + x^2)}, \qquad -\infty < x < \infty.$$

It is seen that the Cauchy distribution has fatter tails than the finite mixture of normal, which, in turn, has fatter tails than the standard normal.

1.2.3 Multivariate Returns

Let $\boldsymbol{r}_t = (r_{1t}, \ldots, r_{Nt})'$ be the log returns of N assets at time t. The multivariate analyses of Chapters 8 and 10 are concerned with the joint distribution of $\{\boldsymbol{r}_t\}_{t=1}^T$. This joint distribution can be partitioned in the same way as that of Eq. (1.15). The analysis is then focused on the specification of the conditional distribution function $F(\boldsymbol{r}_t|\boldsymbol{r}_{t-1}, \ldots, \boldsymbol{r}_1, \boldsymbol{\theta})$. In particular, how the conditional expectation and conditional covariance matrix of $\boldsymbol{r}_t$ evolve over time constitute the main subjects of Chapters 8 and 10.

The mean vector and covariance matrix of a random vector $\boldsymbol{X} = (X_1, \ldots, X_p)$ are defined as

$$E(\boldsymbol{X}) = \boldsymbol{\mu}_x = [E(X_1), \ldots, E(X_p)]',$$
$$\text{Cov}(\boldsymbol{X}) = \boldsymbol{\Sigma}_x = E[(\boldsymbol{X} - \boldsymbol{\mu}_x)(\boldsymbol{X} - \boldsymbol{\mu}_x)'],$$

provided that the expectations involved exist. When the data $\{\boldsymbol{x}_1, \ldots, \boldsymbol{x}_T\}$ of $\boldsymbol{X}$ are available, the sample mean and covariance matrix are defined as

$$\widehat{\boldsymbol{\mu}}_x = \frac{1}{T}\sum_{t=1}^{T} \boldsymbol{x}_t, \quad \widehat{\boldsymbol{\Sigma}}_x = \frac{1}{T-1}\sum_{t=1}^{T}(\boldsymbol{x}_t - \widehat{\boldsymbol{\mu}}_x)(\boldsymbol{x}_t - \widehat{\boldsymbol{\mu}}_x)'.$$

These sample statistics are consistent estimates of their theoretical counterparts provided that the covariance matrix of $\boldsymbol{X}$ exists. In the finance literature, the multivariate normal distribution is often used for the log return $\boldsymbol{r}_t$.

1.2.4 Likelihood Function of Returns

The partition of Eq. (1.15) can be used to obtain the likelihood function of the log returns $\{r_1, \ldots, r_T\}$ of an asset, where for ease in notation the subscript i is omitted from the log return. If the conditional distribution $f(r_t|r_{t-1}, \ldots, r_1, \boldsymbol{\theta})$ is normal with mean μ_t and variance σ_t^2, then $\boldsymbol{\theta}$ consists of the parameters in μ_t and σ_t^2 and the likelihood function of the data is

$$f(r_1, \ldots, r_T; \boldsymbol{\theta}) = f(r_1; \boldsymbol{\theta}) \prod_{t=2}^{T} \frac{1}{\sqrt{2\pi}\sigma_t} \exp\left(\frac{-(r_t - \mu_t)^2}{2\sigma_t^2}\right), \tag{1.18}$$

where $f(r_1; \boldsymbol{\theta})$ is the marginal density function of the first observation r_1. The value of $\boldsymbol{\theta}$ that maximizes this likelihood function is the maximum likelihood estimate (MLE) of $\boldsymbol{\theta}$. Since the log function is monotone, the MLE can be obtained by maximizing the log likelihood function,

$$\ln f(r_1, \ldots, r_T; \boldsymbol{\theta}) = \ln f(r_1; \boldsymbol{\theta}) - \frac{1}{2}\sum_{t=2}^{T}\left(\ln(2\pi) + \ln(\sigma_t^2) + \frac{(r_t - \mu_t)^2}{\sigma_t^2}\right),$$

which is easier to handle in practice. The log likelihood function of the data can be obtained in a similar manner if the conditional distribution $f(r_t|r_{t-1}, \ldots, r_1; \boldsymbol{\theta})$ is not normal.

1.2.5 Empirical Properties of Returns

The data used in this section are obtained from the Center for Research in Security Prices (CRSP) of the University of Chicago. Dividend payments, if any, are included in the returns. Figure 1.2 shows the time plots of monthly simple returns and log returns of International Business Machines (IBM) stock from January 1926 to December 2003. A *time plot* shows the data against the time index. The upper plot is for the simple returns. Figure 1.3 shows the same plots for the monthly returns of value-weighted market index. As expected, the plots show that the basic patterns of simple and log returns are similar.

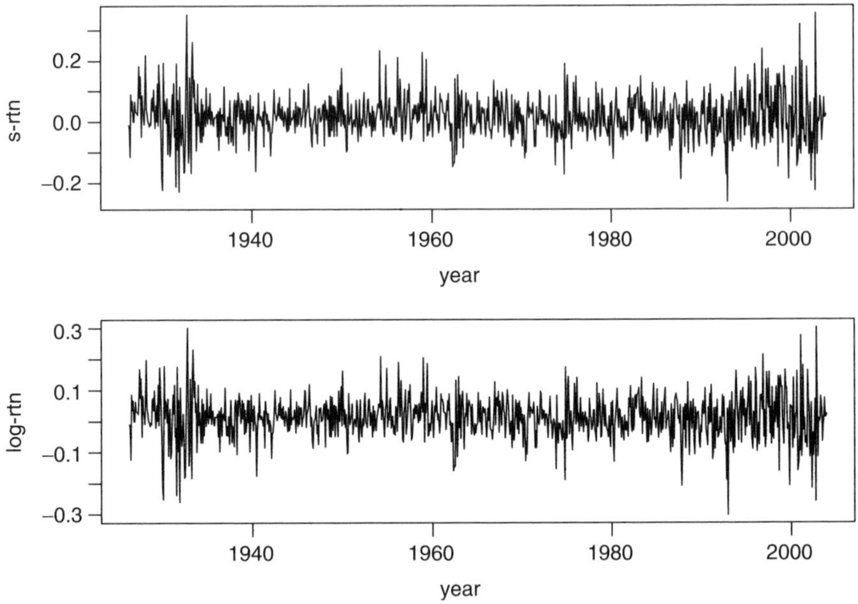

Figure 1.2. Time plots of monthly returns of IBM stock from January 1926 to December 2003. The upper panel is for simple returns, and the lower panel is for log returns.

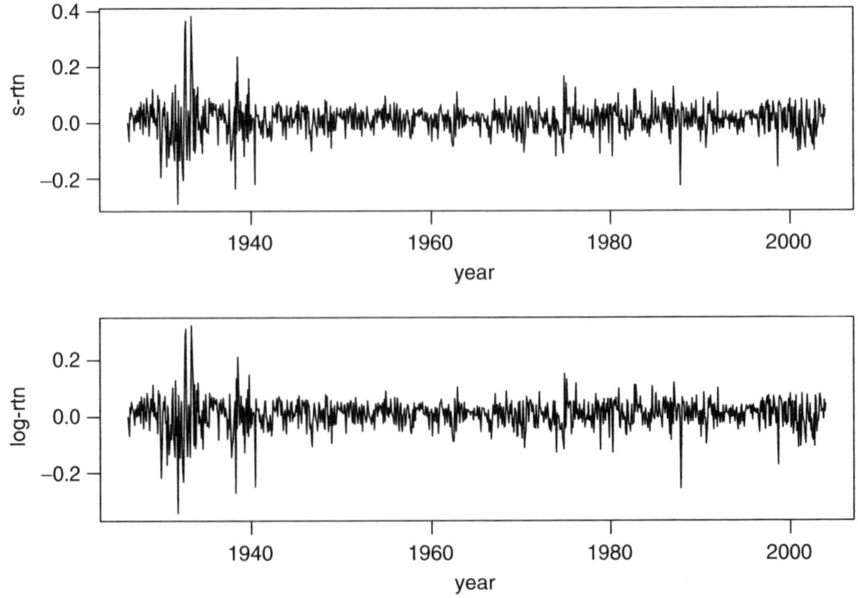

Figure 1.3. Time plots of monthly returns of the value-weighted index from January 1926 to December 2003. The upper panel is for simple returns, and the lower panel is for log returns.

Table 1.2 provides some descriptive statistics of simple and log returns for selected U.S. market indexes and individual stocks. The returns are for daily and monthly sample intervals and are in percentages. The data spans and sample sizes are also given in the table. From the table, we make the following observations. (a) Daily returns of the market indexes and individual stocks tend to have high excess kurtosis. For monthly series, the returns of market indexes have higher excess kurtosis than individual stocks. (b) The mean of a daily return series is close to zero, whereas that of a monthly return series is slightly larger. (c) Monthly returns have higher standard deviations than daily returns. (d) Among the daily returns, market indexes have smaller standard deviations than individual stocks. This is in agreement with common sense. (e) The skewness is not a serious problem for both daily and monthly returns. (f) The descriptive statistics show that the difference between simple and log returns is not substantial.

Figure 1.4 shows the empirical density functions of monthly simple and log returns of IBM stock. Also shown, by a dashed line, in each graph is the normal probability density function evaluated by using the sample mean and standard deviation of IBM returns given in Table 1.2. The plots indicate that the normality assumption is questionable for monthly IBM stock returns. The empirical density function has a higher peak around its mean, but fatter tails than that of the corresponding normal distribution. In other words, the empirical density function is taller and skinnier, but with a wider support than the corresponding normal density.

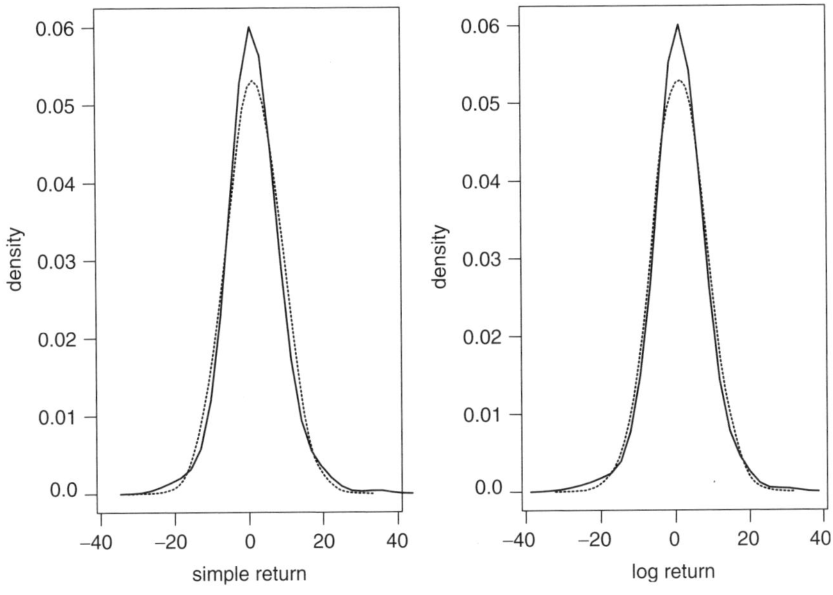

Figure 1.4. Comparison of empirical and normal densities for the monthly simple and log returns of IBM stock. The sample period is from January 1926 to December 2003. The left plot is for simple returns and the right plot for log returns. The normal density, shown by the dashed line, uses the sample mean and standard deviation given in Table 1.2.

1.3 PROCESSES CONSIDERED

Besides the return series, we also consider the volatility process and the behavior of extreme returns of an asset. The volatility process is concerned with the evolution of conditional variance of the return over time. This is a topic of interest because, as shown in Figures 1.2 and 1.3, the variabilities of returns vary over time and appear in clusters. In application, volatility plays an important role in pricing options and risk management. By extremes of a return series, we mean the large positive or negative returns. Table 1.2 shows that the minimum and maximum of a return series can be substantial. The negative extreme returns are important in risk management, whereas positive extreme returns are critical to holding a short position. We study properties and applications of extreme returns, such as the frequency of occurrence, the size of an extreme, and the impacts of economic variables on the extremes, in Chapter 7.

Other financial time series considered in the book include interest rates, exchange rates, bond yields, and quarterly earning per share of a company. Figure 1.5 shows the time plots of two U.S. monthly interest rates. They are the 10-year and 1-year Treasury constant maturity rates from April 1954 to March 2004. As expected, the two interest rates moved in unison, but the 1-year rates appear to be more volatile. Figure 1.6 shows the daily exchange rate between the U.S. dollar and

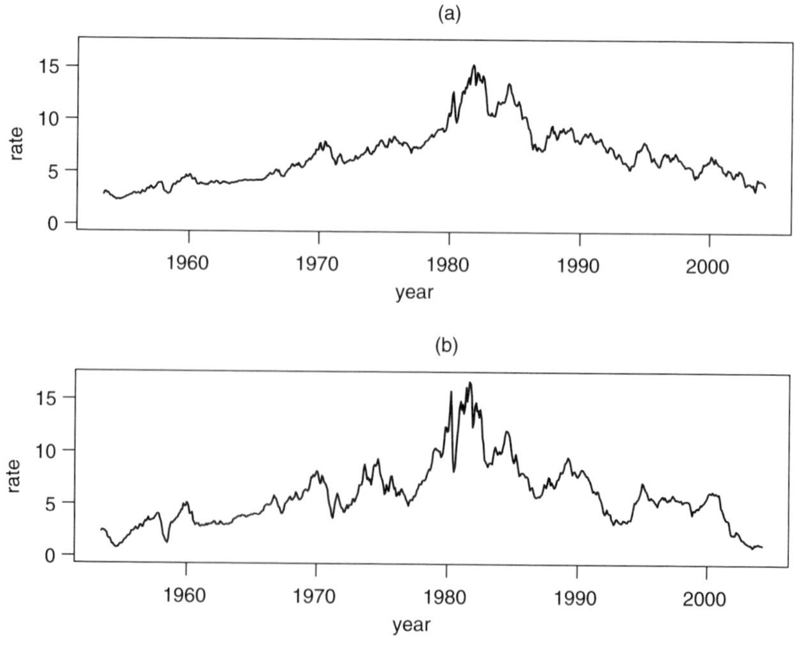

Figure 1.5. Time plots of monthly U.S. interest rates from April 1953 to March 2004: (a) the 10-year Treasury constant maturity rate and (b) the 1-year maturity rate.

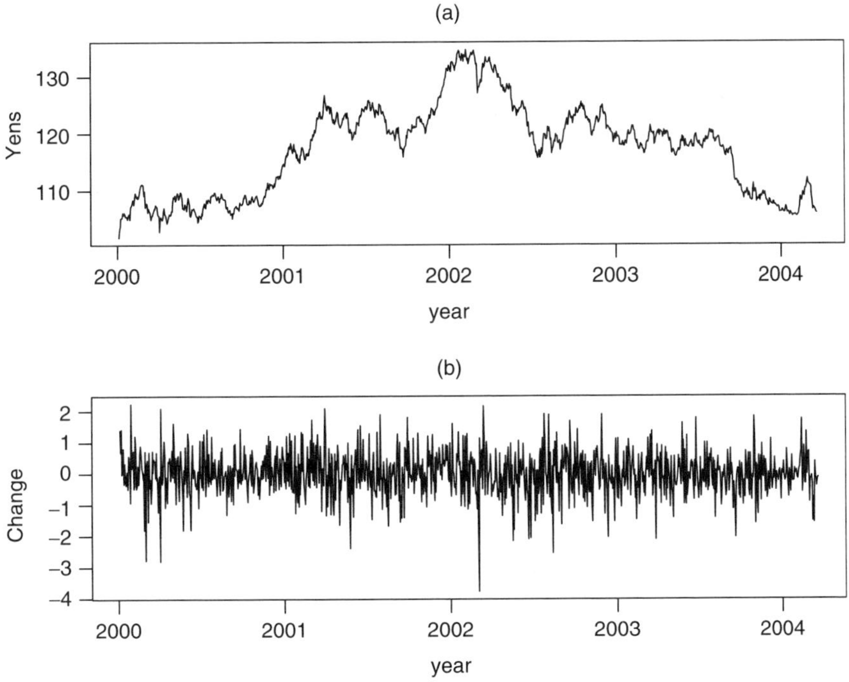

Figure 1.6. Time plot of daily exchange rate between U.S. dollar and Japanese yen from January 3, 2000 to March 26, 2004: (a) exchange rate and (b) changes in exchange rate.

the Japanese yen from January 2000 to March 2004. From the plot, the exchange rate encountered occasional big changes in the sampling period. Table 1.3 provides some descriptive statistics for selected U.S. financial time series. The monthly bond returns obtained from CRSP are Fama bond portfolio returns from January 1952 to December 2003. The interest rates are obtained from the Federal Reserve Bank of St. Louis. The weekly 3-month Treasury bill rate started on January 8, 1954, and the 6-month rate started on December 12, 1958. Both series ended on April 9, 2004. For the interest rate series, the sample means are proportional to the time to maturity, but the sample standard deviations are inversely proportional to the time to maturity. For the bond returns, the sample standard deviations are positively related to the time to maturity, whereas the sample means remain stable for all maturities. Most of the series considered have positive excess kurtosis.

With respect to the empirical characteristics of returns shown in Table 1.2, Chapters 2–4 focus on the first four moments of a return series and Chapter 7 on the behavior of minimum and maximum returns. Chapters 8 and 10 are concerned with moments of and the relationships between multiple asset returns, and Chapter 5 addresses properties of asset returns when the time interval is small. An introduction to mathematical finance is given in Chapter 6.

Table 1.3. Descriptive Statistics of Selected U.S. Financial Time Series[a]

Maturity	Mean	Standard Deviation	Skewness	Excess Kurtosis	Minimum	Maximum
Monthly Bond Returns: January 1952 to December 2003, $T = 624$						
1–12 months	0.47	0.36	2.43	12.67	−0.40	3.52
24–36 months	0.53	0.99	1.40	12.93	−4.90	9.33
48–60 months	0.53	1.42	0.62	4.97	−5.78	10.06
61–120 months	0.55	1.71	0.63	4.86	−7.35	10.92
Monthly Treasury Rates: April 1953 to March 2004, $T = 612$						
1 year	5.80	3.01	0.96	1.27	−0.82	16.72
3 years	6.21	2.86	0.89	0.81	−1.47	16.22
5 years	6.41	2.79	0.88	0.67	−1.85	15.93
10 years	6.60	2.73	0.83	0.42	−2.29	15.32
Weekly Treasury Bill Rates: End on February 16, 2001						
3 months	5.51	2.76	1.14	1.88	−0.58	16.76
6 months	6.08	2.56	1.26	1.82	−2.35	15.76

[a]The data are in percentages. The weekly 3-month Treasury bill rate started from January 8, 1954 and the 6-month rate started from December 12, 1958. Data sources are given in the text.

EXERCISES

1.1. Consider the daily stock returns of American Express (axp), Caterpillar (cat), and Starbucks (sbux) from January 1994 to December 2003. The data are simple returns given in the file `d-3stock.txt (date, axp, cat, sbux)`.

(a) Express the simple returns in percentages. Compute the sample mean, standard deviation, skewness, excess kurtosis, minimum, and maximum of the percentage simple returns.

(b) Transform the simple returns to log returns.

(c) Express the log returns in percentages. Compute the sample mean, standard deviation, skewness, excess kurtosis, minimum, and maximum of the percentage log returns.

(d) Test the null hypothesis that the mean of the log returns of each stock is zero. (Perform three separate tests.) Use 5% significance level to draw your conclusion.

1.2. Answer the same questions as Exercise 1.1 but using monthly stock returns for IBM, CRSP value-weighted index (VW), CRSP equal-weighted index (EW), and S&P composite index from January 1975 to December 2003. The returns of the indexes include dividend distributions. Data file is `m-ibm3dx7503.txt`.

1.3. Consider the monthly stock returns of S&P composite index from January 1975 to December 2003 in Exercise 1.2. Answer the following questions:

(**a**) What is the average annual log return over the data span?

(**b**) Assume that there were no transaction costs. If one invested \$1.00 on the S&P composite index at the beginning of 1975, what was the value of the investment at the end of 2003?

1.4. Consider the daily log returns of American Express stock from January 1994 to December 2003 as in Exercise 1.1. Use the 5% significance level to perform the following tests. (a) Test the null hypothesis that the skewness measure of the returns is zero. (b) Test the null hypothesis that the excess kurtosis of the returns is zero.

1.5. Daily foreign exchange rates (spot rates) can be obtained from the Federal Reserve Bank in Chicago. The data are the noon buying rates in New York City certified by the Federal Reserve Bank of New York. Consider the exchange rates between the U.S. dollar and the Canadian dollar, euro, U.K. pound, and Japanese yen from January 2000 to March 2004. (a) Compute the daily log return of each exchange rate. (b) Compute the sample mean, standard deviation, skewness, excess kurtosis, minimum, and maximum of the log returns of each exchange rate. (c) Discuss the empirical characteristics of the log returns of exchange rates.

REFERENCES

Campbell, J. Y., Lo, A. W., and MacKinlay, A. C. (1997). *The Econometrics of Financial Markets*. Princeton University Press, Princeton, NJ.

Jarque, C. M. and Bera, A. K. (1987). A test of normality of observations and regression residuals. *International Statistical Review* **55**: 163–172.

Sharpe, W. (1964). Capital asset prices: A theory of market equilibrium under conditions of risk. *Journal of Finance* **19**: 425–442.

Snedecor, G. W. and Cochran, W. G. (1980). *Statistical Methods*, 7th edition. Iowa State University Press, Ames, IA.

CHAPTER 2

Linear Time Series Analysis and Its Applications

In this chapter, we discuss basic theories of linear time series analysis, introduce some simple econometric models useful for analyzing financial time series, and apply the models to asset returns. Discussions of the concepts are brief with emphasis on those relevant to financial applications. Understanding the simple time series models introduced here will go a long way to better appreciate the more sophisticated financial econometric models of the later chapters. There are many time series textbooks available. For basic concepts of linear time series analysis, see Box, Jenkins, and Reinsel (1994, Chapters 2 and 3) and Brockwell and Davis (1996, Chapters 1–3).

Treating an asset return (e.g., log return r_t of a stock) as a collection of random variables over time, we have a time series $\{r_t\}$. Linear time series analysis provides a natural framework to study the dynamic structure of such a series. The theories of linear time series discussed include stationarity, dynamic dependence, autocorrelation function, modeling, and forecasting. The econometric models introduced include (a) simple autoregressive (AR) models, (b) simple moving-average (MA) models, (c) mixed autoregressive moving-average (ARMA) models, (d) seasonal models, (e) unit-root nonstationarity, (f) regression models with time series errors, and (g) fractionally differenced models for long-range dependence. For an asset return r_t, simple models attempt to capture the linear relationship between r_t and information available prior to time t. The information may contain the historical values of r_t and the random vector $\boldsymbol{Y}$ in Eq. (1.14) that describes the economic environment under which the asset price is determined. As such, correlation plays an important role in understanding these models. In particular, correlations between the variable of interest and its past values become the focus of linear time series analysis. These correlations are referred to as *serial correlations* or *autocorrelations*. They are the basic tool for studying a stationary time series.

Analysis of Financial Time Series, Second Edition By Ruey S. Tsay

2.1 STATIONARITY

The foundation of time series analysis is stationarity. A time series $\{r_t\}$ is said to be *strictly stationary* if the joint distribution of $(r_{t_1}, \ldots, r_{t_k})$ is identical to that of $(r_{t_1+t}, \ldots, r_{t_k+t})$ for all t, where k is an arbitrary positive integer and $(t_1, \ldots, t_k)$ is a collection of k positive integers. In other words, strict stationarity requires that the joint distribution of $(r_{t_1}, \ldots, r_{t_k})$ is invariant under time shift. This is a very strong condition that is hard to verify empirically. A weaker version of stationarity is often assumed. A time series $\{r_t\}$ is *weakly stationary* if both the mean of r_t and the covariance between r_t and $r_{t-\ell}$ are time-invariant, where ℓ is an arbitrary integer. More specifically, $\{r_t\}$ is weakly stationary if (a) $E(r_t) = \mu$, which is a constant, and (b) $\text{Cov}(r_t, r_{t-\ell}) = \gamma_\ell$, which only depends on ℓ. In practice, suppose that we have observed T data points $\{r_t | t = 1, \ldots, T\}$. The weak stationarity implies that the time plot of the data would show that the T values fluctuate with constant variation around a fixed level. In applications, weak stationarity enables one to make inferences concerning future observations (e.g., prediction).

Implicitly, in the condition of weak stationarity, we assume that the first two moments of r_t are finite. From the definitions, if r_t is strictly stationary and its first two moments are finite, then r_t is also weakly stationary. The converse is not true in general. However, if the time series r_t is normally distributed, then weak stationarity is equivalent to strict stationarity. In this book, we are mainly concerned with weakly stationary series.

The covariance $\gamma_\ell = \text{Cov}(r_t, r_{t-\ell})$ is called the lag-ℓ autocovariance of r_t. It has two important properties: (a) $\gamma_0 = \text{Var}(r_t)$ and (b) $\gamma_{-\ell} = \gamma_\ell$. The second property holds because $\text{Cov}(r_t, r_{t-(-\ell)}) = \text{Cov}(r_{t-(-\ell)}, r_t) = \text{Cov}(r_{t+\ell}, r_t) = \text{Cov}(r_{t_1}, r_{t_1-\ell})$, where $t_1 = t + \ell$.

In the finance literature, it is common to assume that an asset return series is weakly stationary. This assumption can be checked empirically provided that a sufficient number of historical returns are available. For example, one can divide the data into subsamples and check the consistency of the results obtained across the subsamples.

2.2 CORRELATION AND AUTOCORRELATION FUNCTION

The correlation coefficient between two random variables X and Y is defined as

$$\rho_{x,y} = \frac{\text{Cov}(X, Y)}{\sqrt{\text{Var}(X)\text{Var}(Y)}} = \frac{E[(X - \mu_x)(Y - \mu_y)]}{\sqrt{E(X - \mu_x)^2 E(Y - \mu_y)^2}},$$

where μ_x and μ_y are the mean of X and Y, respectively, and it is assumed that the variances exist. This coefficient measures the strength of linear dependence between X and Y, and it can be shown that $-1 \le \rho_{x,y} \le 1$ and $\rho_{x,y} = \rho_{y,x}$. The two random variables are uncorrelated if $\rho_{x,y} = 0$. In addition, if both X and Y are normal random variables, then $\rho_{x,y} = 0$ if and only if X and Y are independent. When the sample $\{(x_t, y_t)\}_{t=1}^T$ is available, the correlation can be consistently estimated by its sample counterpart

$$\hat{\rho}_{x,y} = \frac{\sum_{t=1}^T (x_t - \overline{x})(y_t - \overline{y})}{\sqrt{\sum_{t=1}^T (x_t - \overline{x})^2 \sum_{t=1}^T (y_t - \overline{y})^2}},$$

where $\overline{x} = \left(\sum_{t=1}^T x_t\right)/T$ and $\overline{y} = \left(\sum_{t=1}^T y_t\right)/T$ are the sample mean of X and Y, respectively.

***Autocorrelation Function* (ACF)**

Consider a weakly stationary return series r_t. When the linear dependence between r_t and its past values r_{t-i} is of interest, the concept of correlation is generalized to autocorrelation. The correlation coefficient between r_t and $r_{t-\ell}$ is called the lag-ℓ *autocorrelation* of r_t and is commonly denoted by ρ_ℓ, which under the weak stationarity assumption is a function of ℓ only. Specifically, we define

$$\rho_\ell = \frac{\text{Cov}(r_t, r_{t-\ell})}{\sqrt{\text{Var}(r_t)\text{Var}(r_{t-\ell})}} = \frac{\text{Cov}(r_t, r_{t-\ell})}{\text{Var}(r_t)} = \frac{\gamma_\ell}{\gamma_0}, \qquad (2.1)$$

where the property $\text{Var}(r_t) = \text{Var}(r_{t-\ell})$ for a weakly stationary series is used. From the definition, we have $\rho_0 = 1$, $\rho_\ell = \rho_{-\ell}$, and $-1 \leq \rho_\ell \leq 1$. In addition, a weakly stationary series r_t is not serially correlated if and only if $\rho_\ell = 0$ for all $\ell > 0$.

For a given sample of returns $\{r_t\}_{t=1}^T$, let $\overline{r}$ be the sample mean (i.e., $\overline{r} = \left(\sum_{t=1}^T r_t\right)/T$. Then the lag-1 sample autocorrelation of r_t is

$$\hat{\rho}_1 = \frac{\sum_{t=2}^T (r_t - \overline{r})(r_{t-1} - \overline{r})}{\sum_{t=1}^T (r_t - \overline{r})^2}.$$

Under some general conditions, $\hat{\rho}_1$ is a consistent estimate of ρ_1. For example, if $\{r_t\}$ is an independent and identically distributed (iid) sequence and $E(r_t^2) < \infty$, then $\hat{\rho}_1$ is asymptotically normal with mean zero and variance $1/T$; see Brockwell and Davis (1991, Theorem 7.2.2). This result can be used in practice to test the null hypothesis $H_o : \rho_1 = 0$ versus the alternative hypothesis $H_a : \rho_1 \neq 0$. The test statistic is the usual t ratio, which is $\sqrt{T}\hat{\rho}_1$, and follows asymptotically the standard normal distribution. In general, the lag-ℓ sample autocorrelation of r_t is defined as

$$\hat{\rho}_\ell = \frac{\sum_{t=\ell+1}^T (r_t - \overline{r})(r_{t-\ell} - \overline{r})}{\sum_{t=1}^T (r_t - \overline{r})^2}, \quad 0 \leq \ell < T - 1. \qquad (2.2)$$

If $\{r_t\}$ is an iid sequence satisfying $E(r_t^2) < \infty$, then $\hat{\rho}_\ell$ is asymptotically normal with mean zero and variance $1/T$ for any fixed positive integer ℓ. More generally, if r_t is a weakly stationary time series satisfying $r_t = \mu + \sum_{i=0}^q \psi_i a_{t-i}$, where $\psi_0 = 1, q$ is a non-negative integer, and $\{a_j\}$ is a Gaussian white noise series, then $\hat{\rho}_\ell$ is asymptotically normal with mean zero and variance $\left(1 + 2\sum_{i=1}^q \rho_i^2\right)/T$

for $\ell > q$. This is referred to as Bartlett's formula in the time series literature; see Box, Jenkins, and Reinsel (1994). For more information about the asymptotic distribution of sample autocorrelations, see Fuller (1976, Chapter 6) and Brockwell and Davis (1991, Chapter 7).

Testing Individual ACF

For a given positive integer ℓ, the previous result can be used to test $H_o : \rho_\ell = 0$ versus $H_a : \rho_\ell \neq 0$. The test statistic is

$$t\text{-ratio} = \frac{\hat{\rho}_\ell}{\sqrt{(1 + 2\sum_{i=1}^{\ell-1} \hat{\rho}_i^2)/T}}.$$

If $\{r_t\}$ is a stationary Gaussian series satisfying $\rho_j = 0$ for $j > \ell$, the t-ratio is asymptotically distributed as a standard normal random variable. Hence, the decision rule of the test is to reject H_o if $|t\text{-ratio}| > Z_{\alpha/2}$, where $Z_{\alpha/2}$ is the $100(1 - \alpha/2)$th percentile of the standard normal distribution.

In finite samples, $\hat{\rho}_\ell$ is a biased estimator of ρ_ℓ. The bias is on the order of $1/T$, which can be substantial when the sample size T is small. In most financial applications, T is relatively large so that the bias is not serious.

Portmanteau Test

Financial applications often require to test jointly that several autocorrelations of r_t are zero. Box and Pierce (1970) propose the Portmanteau statistic

$$Q^*(m) = T \sum_{\ell=1}^{m} \hat{\rho}_\ell^2$$

as a test statistic for the null hypothesis $H_o : \rho_1 = \cdots = \rho_m = 0$ against the alternative hypothesis $H_a : \rho_i \neq 0$ for some $i \in \{1, \ldots, m\}$. Under the assumption that $\{r_t\}$ is an iid sequence with certain moment conditions, $Q^*(m)$ is asymptotically a chi-squared random variable with m degrees of freedom.

Ljung and Box (1978) modify the $Q^*(m)$ statistic as below to increase the power of the test in finite samples:

$$Q(m) = T(T + 2) \sum_{\ell=1}^{m} \frac{\hat{\rho}_\ell^2}{T - \ell}. \tag{2.3}$$

The decision rule is to reject H_o if $Q(m) > \chi_\alpha^2$, where χ_α^2 denotes the $100(1 - \alpha)$th percentile of a chi-squared distribution with m degrees of freedom. Most software packets will provide the p-value of $Q(m)$. The decision rule is then to reject H_o if the p-value is less than or equal to α, the significance level.

In practice, the selection of m may affect the performance of the $Q(m)$ statistic. Several values of m are often used. Simulation studies suggest that the choice of $m \approx \ln(T)$ provides better power performance. This general rule needs modification in analysis of seasonal time series for which autocorrelations with lags at multiples of the seasonality are more important.

The statistics $\hat{\rho}_1, \hat{\rho}_2, \ldots$ defined in Eq. (2.2) is called the *sample autocorrelation function* (ACF) of r_t. It plays an important role in linear time series analysis. As a matter of fact, a linear time series model can be characterized by its ACF, and linear time series modeling makes use of the sample ACF to capture the linear dynamic of the data. Figure 2.1 shows the sample autocorrelation functions of monthly simple and log returns of IBM stock from January 1926 to December 1997. The two sample ACFs are very close to each other, and they suggest that the serial correlations of monthly IBM stock returns are very small, if any. The sample ACFs are all within their two standard-error limits, indicating that they are not significantly different from zero at the 5% level. In addition, for the simple returns, the Ljung–Box statistics give $Q(5) = 5.4$ and $Q(10) = 14.1$, which correspond to p-values of 0.37 and 0.17, respectively, based on chi-squared distributions with 5 and 10 degrees of freedom. For the log returns, we have $Q(5) = 5.8$ and $Q(10) = 13.7$ with p-values 0.33 and 0.19, respectively. The joint tests confirm that monthly IBM stock returns have no significant serial correlations. Figure 2.2 shows the same for the monthly returns of the value-weighted index from the Center for Research in Security Prices (CRSP), University of Chicago. There are some significant serial correlations at

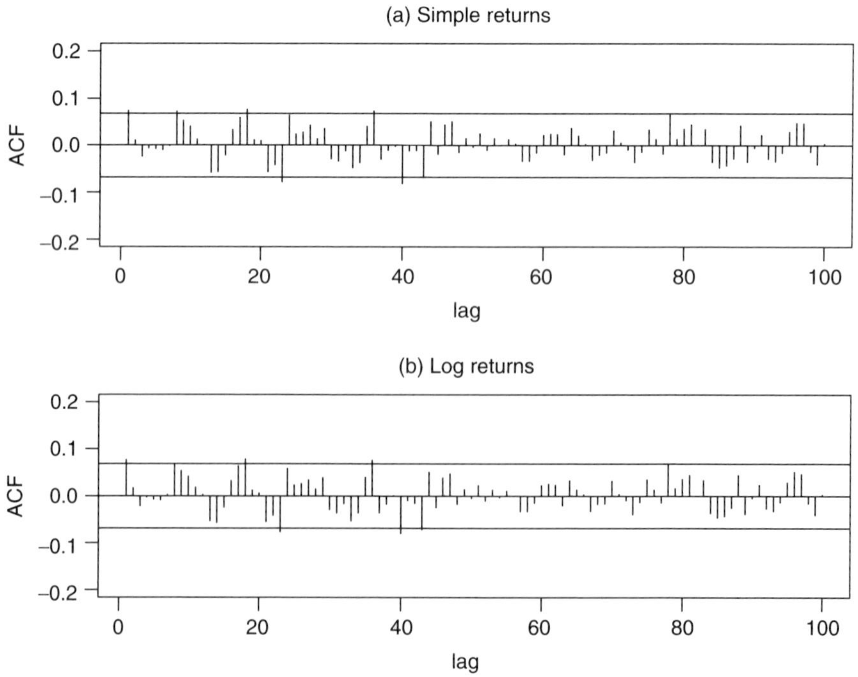

Figure 2.1. Sample autocorrelation functions of monthly (a) simple returns and (b) log returns of IBM stock from January 1926 to December 1997. In each plot, the two horizontal lines denote two standard-error limits of the sample ACF.

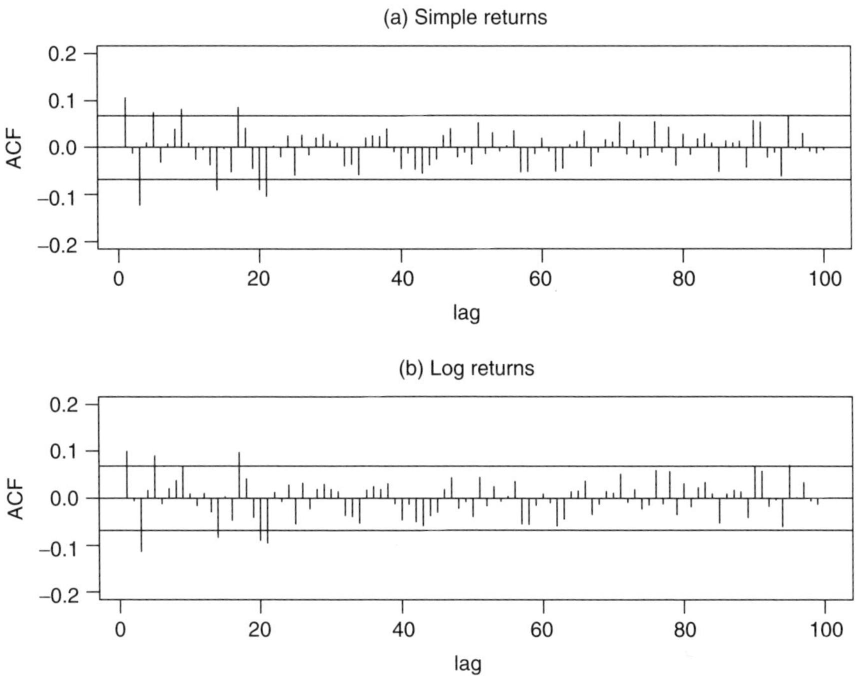

Figure 2.2. Sample autocorrelation functions of monthly (a) simple returns and (b) log returns of the value-weighted index of U.S. markets from January 1926 to December 1997. In each plot, the two horizontal lines denote two standard-error limits of the sample ACF.

the 5% level for both return series. The Ljung–Box statistics give $Q(5) = 27.8$ and $Q(10) = 36.0$ for the simple returns and $Q(5) = 26.9$ and $Q(10) = 32.7$ for the log returns. The p-values of these four test statistics are all less than 0.0003, suggesting that monthly returns of the value-weighted index are serially correlated. Thus, the monthly market index return seems to have stronger serial dependence than individual stock returns.

In the finance literature, a version of the capital asset pricing model (CAPM) theory is that the return $\{r_t\}$ of an asset is not predictable and should have no autocorrelations. Testing for zero autocorrelations has been used as a tool to check the efficient market assumption. However, the way by which stock prices are determined and index returns are calculated might introduce autocorrelations in the observed return series. This is particularly so in analysis of high-frequency financial data. We discuss some of these issues in Chapter 5.

SCA Demonstration

Output edited and % denotes explanation.

```
input ibm. file 'm-ibm2697.txt'   % Load data
 --
```

```
acf ibm. maxl 10.  % Compute 10 lags of ACF.

 NAME OF THE SERIES . . . . . . . . . .           IBM
 TIME PERIOD ANALYZED . . . . . . . . .   1  TO   864
 MEAN OF THE (DIFFERENCED) SERIES . . .        0.0142
 STANDARD DEVIATION OF THE SERIES . . .        0.0670
 T-VALUE OF MEAN (AGAINST ZERO) . . . .        6.2246

 AUTOCORRELATIONS  % ACF(lag 1 to 10), Standard error, Q(m)

   1- 10     .07  .01 -.02 -.01 -.01 -.01 -.00  .07  .05  .04
   ST.E.     .03  .03  .03  .03  .03  .03  .03  .03  .03  .03
    Q        4.8  4.9  5.4  5.4  5.4  5.5  5.5 10.2 12.6 14.1
 --
p=1-cdfc(5.4,5)    % Calculate p-value
 --
print p            % Print p-value

      .369
```

S-Plus Demonstration

Output edited and > denotes the prompt character.

```
> ibm=scan(file='m-ibm2697.txt') % Load data
> autocorTest(ibm,lag=5)         % Perform Q(5) test

Test for Autocorrelation: Ljung-Box

Null Hypothesis: no autocorrelation

Test Statistics:

Test Stat 5.4474
  p.value 0.3638

Dist. under Null: chi-square with 5 degrees of freedom
   Total Observ.: 864

> ibm=log(ibm+1)      % Convert into log returns
> autocorTest(ibm,lag=5)

Test Statistics:

Test Stat 5.7731
  p.value 0.3289

Dist. under Null: chi-square with 5 degrees of freedom
```

2.3 WHITE NOISE AND LINEAR TIME SERIES

White Noise

A time series r_t is called a white noise if $\{r_t\}$ is a sequence of independent and identically distributed random variables with finite mean and variance. In particular, if r_t is normally distributed with mean zero and variance σ^2, the series is called a Gaussian white noise. For a white noise series, all the ACFs are zero. In practice, if all sample ACFs are close to zero, then the series is a white noise series. Based on Figures 2.1 and 2.2, the monthly returns of IBM stock are close to white noise, whereas those of the value-weighted index are not.

The behavior of sample autocorrelations of the value-weighted index returns indicates that for some asset returns it is necessary to model the serial dependence before further analysis can be made. In what follows, we discuss some simple time series models that are useful in modeling the dynamic structure of a time series. The concepts presented are also useful later in modeling volatility of asset returns.

Linear Time Series

A time series r_t is said to be linear if it can be written as

$$r_t = \mu + \sum_{i=0}^{\infty} \psi_i a_{t-i}, \tag{2.4}$$

where μ is the mean of r_t, $\psi_0 = 1$, and $\{a_t\}$ is a sequence of independent and identically distributed random variables with mean zero and a well-defined distribution (i.e., $\{a_t\}$ is a white noise series). It will be seen later that a_t denotes the new information at time t of the time series and is often referred to as the *innovation* or *shock* at time t. In this book, we are mainly concerned with the case where a_t is a continuous random variable. Not all financial time series are linear, however. We study nonlinearity and nonlinear models in Chapter 4.

For a linear time series in Eq. (2.4), the dynamic structure of r_t is governed by the coefficients ψ_i, which are called the *ψ-weights* of r_t in the time series literature. If r_t is weakly stationary, we can obtain its mean and variance easily by using the independence of $\{a_t\}$ as

$$E(r_t) = \mu, \qquad \text{Var}(r_t) = \sigma_a^2 \sum_{i=0}^{\infty} \psi_i^2, \tag{2.5}$$

where σ_a^2 is the variance of a_t. Because $\text{Var}(r_t) < \infty$, $\{\psi_i^2\}$ must be a convergent sequence, that is, $\psi_i^2 \to 0$ and $i \to \infty$. Consequently, for a stationary series, impact of the remote shock a_{t-i} on the return r_t vanishes as i increases.

The lag-ℓ autocovariance of r_t is

$$\gamma_\ell = \text{Cov}(r_t, r_{t-\ell}) = E\left[\left(\sum_{i=0}^{\infty} \psi_i a_{t-i}\right)\left(\sum_{j=0}^{\infty} \psi_j a_{t-\ell-j}\right)\right]$$

$$= E\left(\sum_{i,j=0}^{\infty} \psi_i \psi_j a_{t-i} a_{t-\ell-j}\right)$$

$$= \sum_{j=0}^{\infty} \psi_{j+\ell}\psi_j E(a_{t-\ell-j}^2) = \sigma_a^2 \sum_{j=0}^{\infty} \psi_j \psi_{j+\ell}. \tag{2.6}$$

Consequently, the ψ-weights are related to the autocorrelations of r_t as follows:

$$\rho_\ell = \frac{\gamma_\ell}{\gamma_0} = \frac{\sum_{i=0}^{\infty} \psi_i \psi_{i+\ell}}{1 + \sum_{i=1}^{\infty} \psi_i^2}, \qquad \ell \geq 0, \tag{2.7}$$

where $\psi_0 = 1$. Linear time series models are econometric and statistical models used to describe the pattern of the ψ-weights of r_t. For a weakly stationary time series, $\psi_i \to 0$ as $i \to \infty$ and, hence, ρ_ℓ converges to zero as ℓ increases. For asset returns, this means that, as expected, the linear dependence of current return r_t on the remote past return $r_{t-\ell}$ diminishes for large ℓ.

2.4 SIMPLE AUTOREGRESSIVE MODELS

The fact that the monthly return r_t of CRSP value-weighted index has a statistically significant lag-1 autocorrelation indicates that the lagged return r_{t-1} might be useful in predicting r_t. A simple model that makes use of such predictive power is

$$r_t = \phi_0 + \phi_1 r_{t-1} + a_t, \tag{2.8}$$

where $\{a_t\}$ is assumed to be a white noise series with mean zero and variance σ_a^2. This model is in the same form as the well-known simple linear regression model in which r_t is the dependent variable and r_{t-1} is the explanatory variable. In the time series literature, model (2.8) is referred to as an autoregressive (AR) model of order 1 or simply an AR(1) model. This simple model is also widely used in stochastic volatility modeling when r_t is replaced by its log volatility; see Chapters 3 and 12.

The AR(1) model in Eq. (2.8) has several properties similar to those of the simple linear regression model. However, there are some significant differences between the two models, which we discuss later. Here it suffices to note that an AR(1) model implies that, conditional on the past return r_{t-1}, we have

$$E(r_t|r_{t-1}) = \phi_0 + \phi_1 r_{t-1}, \qquad \mathrm{Var}(r_t|r_{t-1}) = \mathrm{Var}(a_t) = \sigma_a^2.$$

That is, given the past return r_{t-1}, the current return is centered around $\phi_0 + \phi_1 r_{t-1}$ with standard deviation σ_a. This is a Markov property such that conditional on r_{t-1}, the return r_t is not correlated with r_{t-i} for $i > 1$. Obviously, there are situations in which r_{t-1} alone cannot determine the conditional expectation of r_t and a more flexible model must be sought. A straightforward generalization of the AR(1) model is the AR(p) model

$$r_t = \phi_0 + \phi_1 r_{t-1} + \cdots + \phi_p r_{t-p} + a_t, \tag{2.9}$$

where p is a non-negative integer and $\{a_t\}$ is defined in Eq. (2.8). This model says that the past p values r_{t-i} $(i = 1, \ldots, p)$ jointly determine the conditional expectation of r_t given the past data. The AR(p) model is in the same form as a multiple linear regression model with lagged values serving as the explanatory variables.

2.4.1 Properties of AR Models

For effective use of AR models, it pays to study their basic properties. We discuss properties of AR(1) and AR(2) models in detail and give the results for the general AR(p) model.

AR(1) Model

We begin with the sufficient and necessary condition for weak stationarity of the AR(1) model in Eq. (2.8). Assuming that the series is weakly stationary, we have $E(r_t) = \mu$, $\text{Var}(r_t) = \gamma_0$, and $\text{Cov}(r_t, r_{t-j}) = \gamma_j$, where μ and γ_0 are constant and γ_j is a function of j, not t. We can easily obtain the mean, variance, and autocorrelations of the series as follows. Taking the expectation of Eq. (2.8) and because $E(a_t) = 0$, we obtain

$$E(r_t) = \phi_0 + \phi_1 E(r_{t-1}).$$

Under the stationarity condition, $E(r_t) = E(r_{t-1}) = \mu$ and hence

$$\mu = \phi_0 + \phi_1 \mu \quad \text{or} \quad E(r_t) = \mu = \frac{\phi_0}{1 - \phi_1}.$$

This result has two implications for r_t. First, the mean of r_t exists if $\phi_1 \neq 1$. Second, the mean of r_t is zero if and only if $\phi_0 = 0$. Thus, for a stationary AR(1) process, the constant term ϕ_0 is related to the mean of r_t and $\phi_0 = 0$ implies that $E(r_t) = 0$.

Next, using $\phi_0 = (1 - \phi_1)\mu$, the AR(1) model can be rewritten as

$$r_t - \mu = \phi_1(r_{t-1} - \mu) + a_t. \tag{2.10}$$

By repeated substitutions, the prior equation implies that

$$\begin{aligned} r_t - \mu &= a_t + \phi_1 a_{t-1} + \phi_1^2 a_{t-2} + \cdots \\ &= \sum_{i=0}^{\infty} \phi_1^i a_{t-i}. \end{aligned} \tag{2.11}$$

Thus, $r_t - \mu$ is a linear function of a_{t-i} for $i \geq 0$. Using this property and the independence of the series $\{a_t\}$, we obtain $E[(r_t - \mu)a_{t+1}] = 0$. By the stationarity assumption, we have $\text{Cov}(r_{t-1}, a_t) = E[(r_{t-1} - \mu)a_t] = 0$. This latter result can also be seen from the fact that r_{t-1} occurred before time t and a_t does not depend on any past information. Taking the square, then the expectation of Eq. (2.10), we obtain

$$\text{Var}(r_t) = \phi_1^2 \,\text{Var}(r_{t-1}) + \sigma_a^2,$$

where σ_a^2 is the variance of a_t and we make use of the fact that the covariance between r_{t-1} and a_t is zero. Under the stationarity assumption, $\text{Var}(r_t) = \text{Var}(r_{t-1})$, so that

$$\text{Var}(r_t) = \frac{\sigma_a^2}{1 - \phi_1^2}$$

provided that $\phi_1^2 < 1$. The requirement of $\phi_1^2 < 1$ results from the fact that the variance of a random variable is bounded and non-negative. Consequently, the weak stationarity of an AR(1) model implies that $-1 < \phi_1 < 1$. Yet if $-1 < \phi_1 < 1$, then by Eq. (2.11) and the independence of the $\{a_t\}$ series, we can show that the mean and variance of r_t are finite; see Eq. (2.5). In addition, by Eq. (2.6), all the autocovariances of r_t are finite. Therefore, the AR(1) model is weakly stationary. In summary, the necessary and sufficient condition for the AR(1) model in Eq. (2.8) to be weakly stationary is $|\phi_1| < 1$.

Autocorrelation Function of an AR(1) Model

Multiplying Eq. (2.10) by a_t, using the independence between a_t and r_{t-1}, and taking expectation, we obtain

$$E[a_t(r_t - \mu)] = E[a_t(r_{t-1} - \mu)] + E(a_t^2) = E(a_t^2) = \sigma_a^2,$$

where σ_a^2 is the variance of a_t. Multiplying Eq. (2.10) by $(r_{t-\ell} - \mu)$, taking expectation, and using the prior result, we have

$$\gamma_\ell = \begin{cases} \phi_1\gamma_1 + \sigma_a^2 & \text{if } \ell = 0, \\ \phi_1\gamma_{\ell-1} & \text{if } \ell > 0, \end{cases}$$

where we use $\gamma_\ell = \gamma_{-\ell}$. Consequently, for a weakly stationary AR(1) model in Eq. (2.8), we have

$$\text{Var}(r_t) = \gamma_0 = \frac{\sigma^2}{1 - \phi_1^2}, \quad \text{and} \quad \gamma_\ell = \phi_1\gamma_{\ell-1}, \quad \text{for} \quad \ell > 0.$$

From the latter equation, the ACF of r_t satisfies

$$\rho_\ell = \phi_1\rho_{\ell-1}, \quad \text{for} \quad \ell \geq 0.$$

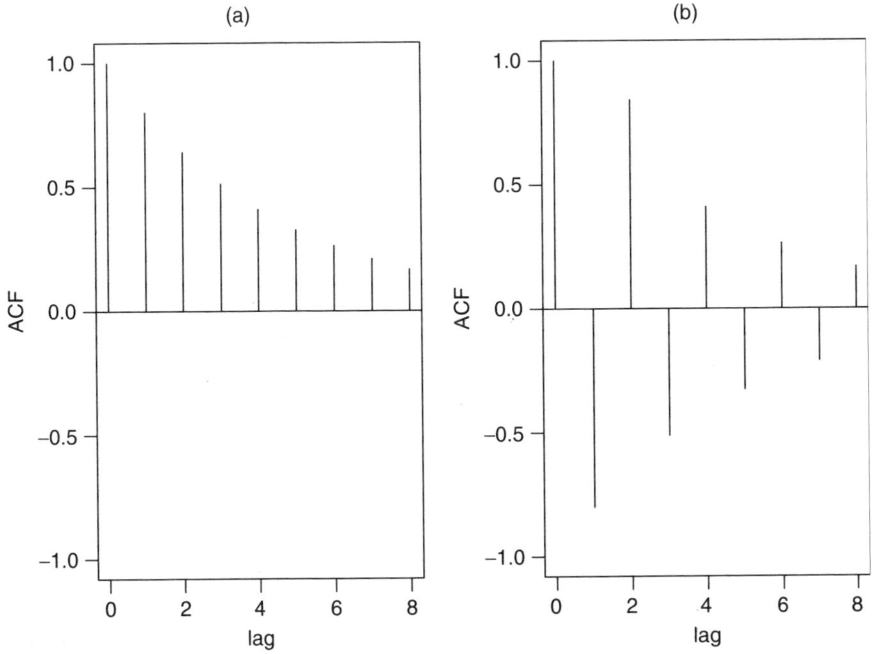

Figure 2.3. The autocorrelation function of an AR(1) model: (a) for $\phi_1 = 0.8$ and (b) for $\phi_1 = -0.8$.

Because $\rho_0 = 1$, we have $\rho_\ell = \phi_1^\ell$. This result says that the ACF of a weakly stationary AR(1) series decays exponentially with rate ϕ_1 and starting value $\rho_0 = 1$. For a positive ϕ_1, the plot of ACF of an AR(1) model shows a nice exponential decay. For a negative ϕ_1, the plot consists of two alternating exponential decays with rate ϕ_1^2. Figure 2.3 shows the ACF of two AR(1) models with $\phi_1 = 0.8$ and $\phi_1 = -0.8$.

AR(2) Model

An AR(2) model assumes the form

$$r_t = \phi_0 + \phi_1 r_{t-1} + \phi_2 r_{t-2} + a_t. \tag{2.12}$$

Using the same technique as that of the AR(1) case, we obtain

$$E(r_t) = \mu = \frac{\phi_0}{1 - \phi_1 - \phi_2}$$

provided that $\phi_1 + \phi_2 \neq 1$. Using $\phi_0 = (1 - \phi_1 - \phi_2)\mu$, we can rewrite the AR(2) model as

$$(r_t - \mu) = \phi_1(r_{t-1} - \mu) + \phi_2(r_{t-2} - \mu) + a_t.$$

Multiplying the prior equation by $(r_{t-\ell} - \mu)$, we have

$$(r_{t-\ell} - \mu)(r_t - \mu) = \phi_1(r_{t-\ell} - \mu)(r_{t-1} - \mu) + \phi_2(r_{t-\ell} - \mu)(r_{t-2} - \mu) + (r_{t-\ell} - \mu)a_t.$$

Taking expectation and using $E[(r_{t-\ell} - \mu)a_t] = 0$ for $\ell > 0$, we obtain

$$\gamma_\ell = \phi_1\gamma_{\ell-1} + \phi_2\gamma_{\ell-2}, \quad \text{for} \quad \ell > 0.$$

This result is referred to as the *moment equation* of a stationary AR(2) model. Dividing the above equation by γ_0, we have the property

$$\rho_\ell = \phi_1\rho_{\ell-1} + \phi_2\rho_{\ell-2}, \quad \text{for} \quad \ell > 0, \tag{2.13}$$

for the ACF of r_t. In particular, the lag-1 ACF satisfies

$$\rho_1 = \phi_1\rho_0 + \phi_2\rho_{-1} = \phi_1 + \phi_2\rho_1.$$

Therefore, for a stationary AR(2) series r_t, we have $\rho_0 = 1$,

$$\rho_1 = \frac{\phi_1}{1 - \phi_2},$$
$$\rho_\ell = \phi_1\rho_{\ell-1} + \phi_2\rho_{\ell-2}, \quad \ell \geq 2.$$

The result of Eq. (2.13) says that the ACF of a stationary AR(2) series satisfies the second-order difference equation

$$(1 - \phi_1 B - \phi_2 B^2)\rho_\ell = 0,$$

where B is called the *back-shift* operator such that $B\rho_\ell = \rho_{\ell-1}$. This difference equation determines the properties of the ACF of a stationary AR(2) time series. It also determines the behavior of the forecasts of r_t. In the time series literature, some people use the notation L instead of B for the back-shift operator. Here L stands for *lag* operator. For instance, $Lr_t = r_{t-1}$ and $L\psi_k = \psi_{k-1}$.

Corresponding to the prior difference equation, there is a second-order polynomial equation

$$1 - \phi_1 x - \phi_2 x^2 = 0. \tag{2.14}$$

Solutions of this equation are

$$x = \frac{\phi_1 \pm \sqrt{\phi_1^2 + 4\phi_2}}{-2\phi_2}.$$

In the time series literature, inverses of the two solutions are referred to as the *characteristic roots* of the AR(2) model. Denote the two solutions by ω_1 and ω_2. If both ω_i are real valued, then the second-order difference equation of the model can be factored as $(1 - \omega_1 B)(1 - \omega_2 B)$ and the AR(2) model can be regarded as an AR(1) model operating on top of another AR(1) model. The ACF of r_t is then a mixture of two exponential decays. If $\phi_1^2 + 4\phi_2 < 0$, then ω_1 and ω_2 are complex numbers (called a *complex conjugate pair*), and a plot of the ACF of r_t would show a picture of damping sine and cosine waves. In business and economic applications, complex characteristic roots are important. They give rise to the behavior of business cycles. It is then common for economic time series models to have complex-valued characteristic roots. For an AR(2) model in Eq. (2.12) with a pair of complex characteristic roots, the *average* length of the stochastic cycles is

$$k = \frac{2\pi}{\cos^{-1}[\phi_1/(2\sqrt{-\phi_2})]},$$

where the cosine inverse is stated in radians. If one writes the complex solutions as $a \pm bi$, where $i = \sqrt{-1}$, then we have $\phi_1 = 2a$, $\phi_2 = -(a^2 + b^2)$, and

$$k = \frac{2\pi}{\cos^{-1}(a/\sqrt{a^2 + b^2})},$$

where $\sqrt{a^2 + b^2}$ is the absolute value of $a \pm bi$.

Figure 2.4 shows the ACFs of four stationary AR(2) models. Part (b) is the ACF of the AR(2) model $(1 - 0.6B + 0.4B^2)r_t = a_t$. Because $\phi_1^2 + 4\phi_2 = 0.36 +$

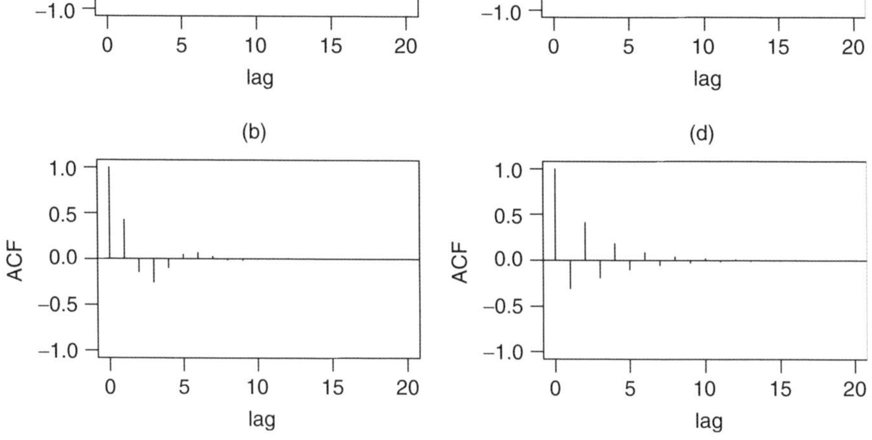

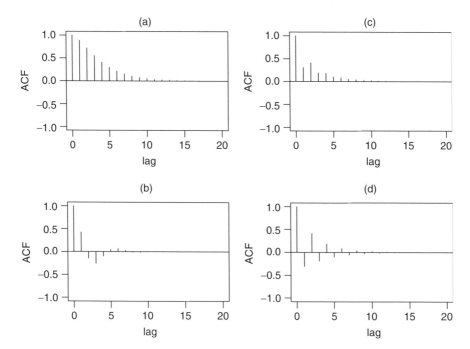

Figure 2.4. The autocorrelation function of an AR(2) model: (a) $\phi_1 = 1.2$ and $\phi_2 = -0.35$, (b) $\phi_1 = 0.6$ and $\phi_2 = -0.4$, (c) $\phi_1 = 0.2$ and $\phi_2 = 0.35$, and (d) $\phi_1 = -0.2$ and $\phi_2 = 0.35$.

$4 \times (-0.4) = -1.24 < 0$, this particular AR(2) model contains two complex characteristic roots, and hence its ACF exhibits damping sine and cosine waves. The other three AR(2) models have real-valued characteristic roots. Their ACFs decay exponentially.

Example 2.1. As an illustration, consider the quarterly growth rate of the U.S. real gross national product (GNP), seasonally adjusted, from the second quarter of 1947 to the first quarter of 1991. This series shown in Figure 2.5 is also used in Chapter 4 as an example of nonlinear economic time series. Here we simply employ an AR(3) model for the data. Denoting the growth rate by r_t, we can use the model building procedure of the next subsection to estimate the model. The fitted model is

$$r_t = 0.0047 + 0.35r_{t-1} + 0.18r_{t-2} - 0.14r_{t-3} + a_t, \quad \hat{\sigma}_a = 0.0098. \qquad (2.15)$$

Rewriting the model as

$$r_t - 0.35r_{t-1} - 0.18r_{t-2} + 0.14r_{t-3} = 0.0047 + a_t,$$

we obtain a corresponding third-order difference equation

$$(1 - 0.35B - 0.18B^2 + 0.14B^3) = 0,$$

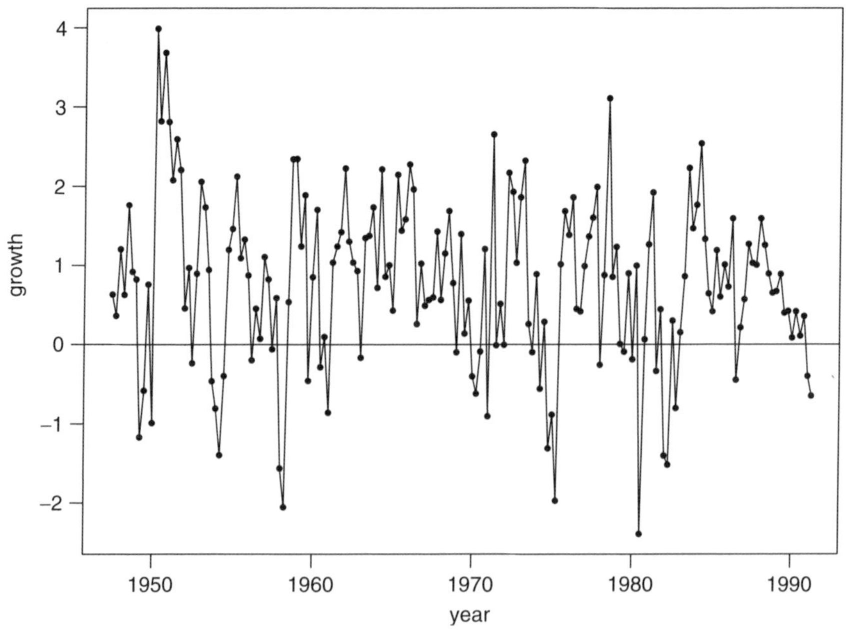

Figure 2.5. Time plot of the growth rate of U.S. quarterly real GNP from 1947.II to 1991.I. The data are seasonally adjusted and in percentages.

which can be factored as

$$(1 + 0.52B)(1 - 0.87B + 0.27B^2) = 0.$$

The first factor $(1 + 0.52B)$ shows an exponentially decaying feature of the GNP growth rate. Focusing on the second-order factor $1 - 0.87B - (-0.27)B^2 = 0$, we have $\phi_1^2 + 4\phi_2 = 0.87^2 + 4(-0.27) = -0.3231 < 0$. Therefore, the second factor of the AR(3) model confirms the existence of stochastic business cycles in the quarterly growth rate of the U.S. real GNP. This is reasonable as the U.S. economy went through expansion and contraction periods. The average length of the stochastic cycles is approximately

$$k = \frac{2(3.14159)}{\cos^{-1}[\phi_1/(2\sqrt{-\phi_2})]} = 10.83 \text{ quarters},$$

which is about 3 years. If one uses a nonlinear model to separate the U.S. economy into "expansion" and "contraction" periods, the data show that the average duration of contraction periods is about three quarters and that of expansion periods is about 3 years; see the analysis in Chapter 4. The average duration of 10.83 quarters is a compromise between the two separate durations. The periodic feature obtained here is common among growth rates of national economies. For example, similar features can be found for many OECD countries.

Stationarity

The stationarity condition of an AR(2) time series is that the absolute values of its two characteristic roots are less than one or, equivalently, its two characteristic roots are less than one in modulus. Under such a condition, the recursive equation in (2.13) ensures that the ACF of the model converges to zero as the lag ℓ increases. This convergence property is a necessary condition for a stationary time series. In fact, the condition also applies to the AR(1) model where the polynomial equation is $1 - \phi_1 x = 0$. The characteristic root is $w = 1/x = \phi_1$, which must be less than 1 in modulus for r_t to be stationary. As shown before, $\rho_\ell = \phi_1^\ell$ for a stationary AR(1) model. The condition implies that $\rho_\ell \to 0$ as $\ell \to \infty$.

AR(p) Model

The results of AR(1) and AR(2) models can readily be generalized to the general AR(p) model in Eq. (2.9). The mean of a stationary series is

$$E(r_t) = \frac{\phi_0}{1 - \phi_1 - \cdots - \phi_p}$$

provided that the denominator is not zero. The associated polynomial equation of the model is

$$1 - \phi_1 x - \phi_2 x^2 - \cdots - \phi_p x^p = 0,$$

which is referred to as the *characteristic equation* of the model. If all the solutions of this equation are greater than one in modulus, then the series r_t is stationary. Again, inverses of the solutions are the *characteristic roots* of the model. Thus, stationarity requires that all characteristic roots are less than 1 in modulus. For a stationary AR(p) series, the ACF satisfies the difference equation

$$(1 - \phi_1 B - \phi_2 B^2 - \cdots - \phi_p B^p)\rho_\ell = 0, \quad \text{for} \quad \ell > 0.$$

A plot of the ACF of a stationary AR(p) model would then show a mixture of damping sine and cosine patterns and exponential decays depending on the nature of its characteristic roots.

2.4.2 Identifying AR Models in Practice

In application, the order p of an AR time series is unknown and must be specified empirically. This is referred to as the *order determination* of AR models, and it has been extensively studied in the time series literature. Two general approaches are available for determining the value of p. The first approach is to use the partial autocorrelation function, and the second approach uses some information criterion function.

Partial Autocorrelation Function (PACF)

The PACF of a stationary time series is a function of its ACF and is a useful tool for determining the order p of an AR model. A simple, yet effective way to introduce PACF is to consider the following AR models in consecutive orders:

$$\begin{aligned}
r_t &= \phi_{0,1} + \phi_{1,1} r_{t-1} + e_{1t}, \\
r_t &= \phi_{0,2} + \phi_{1,2} r_{t-1} + \phi_{2,2} r_{t-2} + e_{2t}, \\
r_t &= \phi_{0,3} + \phi_{1,3} r_{t-1} + \phi_{2,3} r_{t-2} + \phi_{3,3} r_{t-3} + e_{3t}, \\
r_t &= \phi_{0,4} + \phi_{1,4} r_{t-1} + \phi_{2,4} r_{t-2} + \phi_{3,4} r_{t-3} + \phi_{4,4} r_{t-4} + e_{4t}, \\
&\vdots \quad \vdots
\end{aligned}$$

where $\phi_{0,j}$, $\phi_{i,j}$, and $\{e_{jt}\}$ are, respectively, the constant term, the coefficient of r_{t-i}, and the error term of an AR(j) model. These models are in the form of a multiple linear regression and can be estimated by the least squares method. As a matter of fact, they are arranged in a sequential order that enables us to apply the idea of partial F test in multiple linear regression analysis. The estimate $\hat{\phi}_{1,1}$ of the first equation is called the lag-1 sample PACF of r_t. The estimate $\hat{\phi}_{2,2}$ of the second equation is the lag-2 sample PACF of r_t. The estimate $\hat{\phi}_{3,3}$ of the third equation is the lag-3 sample PACF of r_t, and so on.

From the definition, the lag-2 PACF $\hat{\phi}_{2,2}$ shows the added contribution of r_{t-2} to r_t over the AR(1) model $r_t = \phi_0 + \phi_1 r_{t-1} + e_{1t}$. The lag-3 PACF shows the added contribution of r_{t-3} to r_t over an AR(2) model, and so on. Therefore, for

Table 2.1. Sample Partial Autocorrelation Function and Akaike Information Criterion for the Monthly Simple Returns of CRSP Value-Weighted Index from January 1926 to December 1997

p	1	2	3	4	5
PACF	0.11	−0.02	−0.12	0.04	0.07
AIC	−5.807	−5.805	−5.817	−5.816	−5.819
p	6	7	8	9	10
PACF	−0.06	0.02	0.06	0.06	−0.01
AIC	−5.821	−5.819	−5.820	−5.821	−5.818

an AR(p) model, the lag-p sample PACF should not be zero, but $\hat{\phi}_{j,j}$ should be close to zero for all $j > p$. We make use of this property to determine the order p. For a stationary Gaussian AR(p) model, it can be shown that the sample PACF has the following properties:

- $\hat{\phi}_{p,p}$ converges to ϕ_p as the sample size T goes to infinity.
- $\hat{\phi}_{\ell,\ell}$ converges to zero for all $\ell > p$.
- The asymptotic variance of $\hat{\phi}_{\ell,\ell}$ is $1/T$ for $\ell > p$.

These results say that, for an AR(p) series, the sample PACF cuts off at lag p.

As an example, consider the monthly simple returns of CRSP value-weighted index from January 1926 to December 1997. Table 2.1 gives the first 10 lags of a sample PACF of the series. With $T = 864$, the asymptotic standard error of the sample PACF is approximately 0.03. Therefore, using the 5% significance level, we identify an AR(3) or AR(5) model for the data (i.e., $p = 3$ or 5).

As another example, Figure 2.6 shows the PACF of the GNP growth rate series of Example 2.1. The two dotted lines of the plot denote the approximate two standard-error limits $\pm(2/\sqrt{176})$. The plot suggests an AR(3) model for the data because the first three lags of sample PACF appear to be large.

Information Criteria

There are several information criteria available to determine the order p of an AR process. All of them are likelihood based. For example, the well-known *Akaike information criterion* (AIC) (Akaike, 1973) is defined as

$$\text{AIC} = \frac{-2}{T}\ln(\text{likelihood}) + \frac{2}{T} \times (\text{number of parameters}), \qquad (2.16)$$

where the likelihood function is evaluated at the maximum likelihood estimates and T is the sample size. For a Gaussian AR(ℓ) model, AIC reduces to

$$\text{AIC}(\ell) = \ln(\tilde{\sigma}_\ell^2) + \frac{2\ell}{T},$$

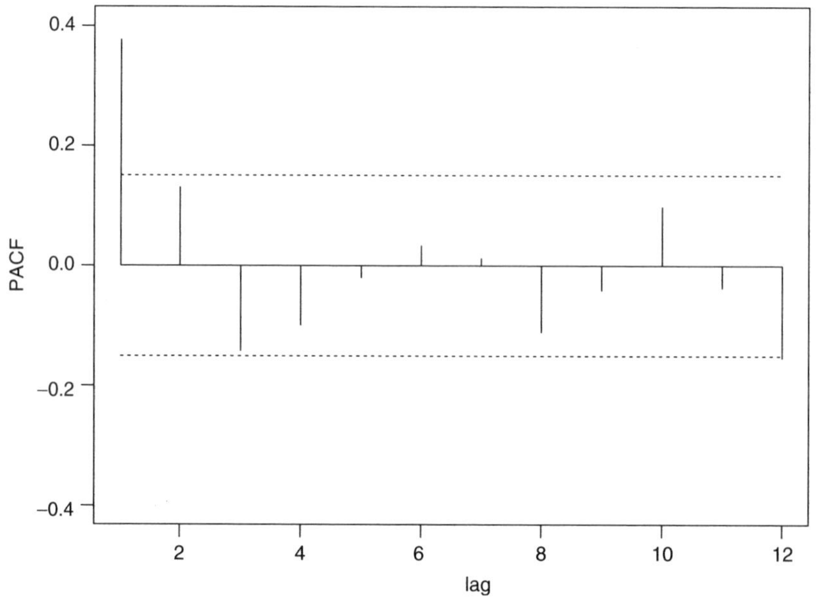

Figure 2.6. Sample partial autocorrelation function of the U.S. quarterly real GNP growth rate from 1947.II to 1991.I. The dotted lines give an approximate pointwise 95% confidence interval.

where $\tilde{\sigma}_\ell^2$ is the maximum likelihood estimate of σ_a^2, which is the variance of a_t, and T is the sample size; see Eq. (1.18). The first term of the AIC in Eq. (2.16) measures the goodness of fit of the AR(ℓ) model to the data whereas the second term is called the *penalty function* of the criterion because it penalizes a candidate model by the number of parameters used. Different penalty functions result in different information criteria.

Another commonly used criterion function is the (Schwarz) Bayesian information criterion (BIC). For a Gaussian AR(ℓ) model, the criterion is

$$\text{BIC}(\ell) = \ln(\tilde{\sigma}_\ell^2) + \frac{\ell \ln(T)}{T}.$$

The penalty for each parameter used is 2 for AIC and $\ln(T)$ for BIC. Thus, BIC tends to select a lower AR model when the sample size is moderate or large.

Selection Rule

To use AIC to select an AR model in practice, one computes AIC(ℓ) for $\ell = 0, \ldots, P$, where P is a prespecified positive integer, and selects the order k that has the minimum AIC value.

Table 2.1 also gives the AIC for $p = 1, \ldots, 10$. The AIC values are close to each other with minimum -5.821 occurring at $p = 6$ and 9, suggesting that an AR(6) model is preferred by the criterion. This example shows that different approaches for order determination may result in different choices of p. There is no evidence to suggest that one approach outperforms the other in a real application. Substantive information of the problem under study and simplicity are two factors that also play an important role in choosing an AR model for a given time series.

Again, consider the growth rate series of the U.S. quarterly real GNP of Example 2.1. The AIC obtained from the Finmetrics module of S-Plus also identifies an AR(3) model. Here the criterion value has been adjusted so that the minimum AIC is zero.

```
> gnp=scan(file='q-gnp4791.txt')
> ord=ar(gnp)
> ord$aic
 [1] 27.569  2.608  1.590  0.000  0.273  2.203
 [7]  4.017  5.992  5.826  7.523  7.822  9.581
[13]  7.398  8.943 10.912 12.895 14.298 16.279
[19] 18.100 20.050 22.007 23.436 25.378
> ord$order
[1] 3
```

Parameter Estimation

For a specified AR(p) model in Eq. (2.9), the conditional least squares method, which starts with the $(p+1)$th observation, is often used to estimate the parameters. Specifically, conditioning on the first p observations, we have

$$r_t = \phi_0 + \phi_1 r_{t-1} + \cdots + \phi_p r_{t-p} + a_t, \quad t = p+1, \ldots, T,$$

which is in the form of a multiple linear regression and can be estimated by the least squares method. Denote the estimate of ϕ_i by $\hat{\phi}_i$. The *fitted model* is

$$\hat{r}_t = \hat{\phi}_0 + \hat{\phi}_1 r_{t-1} + \cdots + \hat{\phi}_p r_{t-p}$$

and the associated residual is

$$\hat{a}_t = r_t - \hat{r}_t.$$

The series $\{\hat{a}_t\}$ is called the *residual series*, from which we obtain

$$\hat{\sigma}_a^2 = \frac{\sum_{t=p+1}^{T} \hat{a}_t^2}{T - 2p - 1}.$$

If the conditional likelihood method is used, the estimates of ϕ_i remain unchanged, but the estimate of σ_a^2 becomes $\tilde{\sigma}_a^2 = \hat{\sigma}_a^2 \times (T - 2p - 1)/(T - p)$. For illustration, consider an AR(3) model for the monthly simple returns of the value-weighted index in Table 2.1. The fitted model is

$$r_t = 0.0103 + 0.104 r_{t-1} - 0.010 r_{t-2} - 0.120 r_{t-3} + \hat{a}_t, \quad \hat{\sigma}_a = 0.054.$$

The standard errors of the coefficients are 0.002, 0.034, 0.034, and 0.034, respectively. Except for the lag-2 coefficient, all parameters are statistically significant at the 1% level.

For this example, the AR coefficients of the fitted model are small, indicating that the serial dependence of the series is weak, even though it is statistically significant at the 1% level. The significance of $\hat{\phi}_0$ of the entertained model implies that the expected mean return of the series is positive. In fact, $\hat{\mu} = 0.0103/(1 - 0.104 + 0.010 + 0.120) = 0.01$, which is small, but has an important long-term implication. It implies that the long-term return of the index can be substantial. Using the multiperiod simple return defined in Chapter 1, the average annual simple gross return is $\left[\prod_{t=1}^{864}(1 + R_t)\right]^{12/864} - 1 \approx 0.1053$. In other words, the monthly simple returns of the CRSP value-weighted index grew about 10.53% per annum from 1926 to 1997, supporting the common belief that equity market performs well in the long term. A \$1 investment at the beginning of 1926 would be worth about \$1350 at the end of 1997.

Model Checking

A fitted model must be examined carefully to check for possible model inadequacy. If the model is adequate, then the residual series should behave as a white noise. The ACF and the Ljung–Box statistics in Eq. (2.3) of the residuals can be used to check the closeness of $\hat{a}_t$ to a white noise. For an AR(p) model, the Ljung–Box statistic $Q(m)$ follows asymptotically a chi-squared distribution with $m - g$ degrees of freedom, where g denotes the number of AR coefficients used in the model. The adjustment in the degrees of freedom is made based on the number of constraints added to the residuals $\hat{a}_t$ from fitting an AR(p) to an AR(0) model. If a fitted model is found to be inadequate, it must be refined. For instance, if some of the estimated AR coefficients are not significantly different from zero, then the model should be simplified by trying to remove those insignificant parameters. If residual ACF shows additional serial correlations, then the model should be extended to take care of the those correlations.

Consider the residual series of the fitted AR(3) model for the monthly value-weighted simple returns. We have $Q(12) = 16.9$ with p-value 0.050 based on its asymptotic chi-squared distribution with 9 degrees of freedom. Thus, the null hypothesis of no residual serial correlation in the first 12 lags is barely not rejected at the 5% level. However, since the lag-2 AR coefficient is not significant at the 5% level, one can refine the model as

$$r_t = 0.0102 + 0.103r_{t-1} - 0.122r_{t-3} + a_t, \quad \hat{\sigma}_a = 0.0542,$$

where all the estimates are significant at the 5% level. The residual series gives $Q(12) = 17.2$ with p-value 0.070 (based on χ^2_{10}). The model is adequate in modeling the dynamic linear dependence of data.

SCA Demonstration

Output edited.

```
input vw. file 'm-vw2697.txt'
 --
tsm m1. model (1,2,3)vw=c+noise. % Model specification
```

```
 --
estim m1. hold resi(r1).

 SUMMARY FOR UNIVARIATE TIME SERIES MODEL --    M1
-----------------------------------------------------------
 VARIABLE  TYPE OF    ORIGINAL     DIFFERENCING
           VARIABLE   OR CENTERED

    VW     RANDOM     ORIGINAL     NONE
-----------------------------------------------------------
 PAR.  VAR.  NUM./  FACTOR ORDER CONS-    VALUE    STD     T
 LABEL NAME  DENOM.              TRAINT            ERROR  VALUE

 1 C         CNST    1      0    NONE      .0103  .0019   5.34
 2    VW     AR      1      1    NONE      .1041  .0338   3.08
 3    VW     AR      1      2    NONE     -.0103  .0340   -.30
 4    VW     AR      1      3    NONE     -.1204  .0338  -3.56

 EFFECTIVE NUMBER OF OBSERVATIONS . .              861
 R-SQUARE . . . . . . . . . . . . . .            0.025
 RESIDUAL STANDARD ERROR. . . . . . .  0.541903E-01
 --
acf r1. maxl 12.

 NAME OF THE SERIES . . . . . . . . . .               R1
 TIME PERIOD ANALYZED . . . . . . . . .    4  TO   864
 MEAN OF THE (DIFFERENCED) SERIES . . .         0.0000
 STANDARD DEVIATION OF THE SERIES . . .         0.0542
 T-VALUE OF MEAN (AGAINST ZERO) . . . .         0.0000

AUTOCORRELATIONS

1- 12   .01 .01 -.01 .03 .09 -.05 .01  .04  .08 -.00 -.03  .01
ST.E.   .03 .03  .03 .03 .03  .03 .03  .03  .03  .03  .03  .03
 Q       .0  .1   .2 1.0 7.4  9.3 9.3 10.6 15.8 15.8 16.8 16.9
 --
p=1-cdfc(16.9,9)  % Compute p value.
 --
print p

      .050
```

S-Plus Demonstration

Output edited and > is the prompt character.

```
> vw=scan(file='m-vw2697.txt')
> ar3=OLS(vw~ar(3))
> summary(ar3)

Call:
OLS(formula = vw ~ ar(3))
```

```
Residuals:
     Min      1Q  Median     3Q    Max
 -0.2845 -0.0259  0.0025 0.0288 0.3705

Coefficients:
               Value Std. Error t value Pr(>|t|)
(Intercept)  0.0103  0.0019     5.3314  0.0000
       lag1  0.1041  0.0339     3.0716  0.0022
       lag2 -0.0103  0.0341    -0.3016  0.7630
       lag3 -0.1204  0.0339    -3.5538  0.0004

Regression Diagnostics:

         R-Squared 0.0258
Adjusted R-Squared 0.0224
Durbin-Watson Stat 1.9890

> autocorTest(ar3$residuals,lag=12)

Test for Autocorrelation: Ljung-Box

Null Hypothesis: no autocorrelation

Test Statistics:

Test Stat 16.9367
  p.value  0.1520    % S-Plus uses 12 degrees of freedom.

> 1-pchisq(16.9367,9) % Calculate p-value using 9 df.
[1] 0.04971652
```

2.4.3 Goodness of Fit

A commonly used statistic to measure *goodness of fit* of a stationary model is the R-square (R^2) defined as

$$R^2 = 1 - \frac{\text{Residual sum of squares}}{\text{Total sum of squares}}.$$

For a stationary AR(p) time series model with T observations $\{r_t | t = 1, \ldots, T\}$, the measure becomes

$$R^2 = 1 - \frac{\sum_{t=p+1}^{T} \hat{a}_t^2}{\sum_{t=p+1}^{T} (r_t - \bar{r})^2},$$

where $\bar{r} = \left(\sum_{t=p+1}^{T} r_t\right)/(T - p)$. It is easy to show that $0 \le R^2 \le 1$. Typically, a larger R^2 indicates that the model provides a closer fit to the data. However, this is only true for a stationary time series. For the unit-root nonstationary series discussed later in this chapter, R^2 of an AR(1) fit converges to one when the sample size increases to infinity, regardless of the true underlying model of r_t.

For a given data set, it is well-known that R^2 is a nondecreasing function of the number of parameters used. To overcome this weakness, an *adjusted* R^2 is proposed, which is defined as

$$\begin{aligned}\text{Adj-}R^2 &= 1 - \frac{\text{Variance of residuals}}{\text{Variance of } r_t} \\ &= 1 - \frac{\hat{\sigma}_a^2}{\hat{\sigma}_r^2},\end{aligned}$$

where $\hat{\sigma}_r^2$ is the sample variance of r_t. This new measure takes into account the number of parameters used in the fitted model. However, it is no longer between 0 and 1.

2.4.4 Forecasting

Forecasting is an important application of time series analysis. For the AR(p) model in Eq. (2.9), suppose that we are at the time index h and interested in forecasting $r_{h+\ell}$, where $\ell \geq 1$. The time index h is called the *forecast origin* and the positive integer ℓ is the *forecast horizon*. Let $\hat{r}_h(\ell)$ be the forecast of $r_{h+\ell}$ using the minimum squared error loss function and F_h be the collection of information available at the forecast origin h. Then, the forecast $\hat{r}_k(\ell)$ is chosen such that

$$E\{[r_{h+\ell} - \hat{r}_h(\ell)]^2 | F_h\} \leq \min_g E[(r_{h+\ell} - g)^2 | F_h],$$

where g is a function of the information available at time h (inclusive), that is, a function of F_h. We referred to $\hat{r}_h(\ell)$ as the ℓ-step ahead forecast of r_t at the forecast origin h.

1-Step Ahead Forecast

From the AR(p) model, we have

$$r_{h+1} = \phi_0 + \phi_1 r_h + \cdots + \phi_p r_{h+1-p} + a_{h+1}.$$

Under the minimum squared error loss function, the point forecast of r_{h+1} given $F_h = \{r_h, r_{h-1}, \ldots\}$ is the conditional expectation

$$\hat{r}_h(1) = E(r_{h+1} | F_h) = \phi_0 + \sum_{i=1}^{p} \phi_i r_{h+1-i},$$

and the associated forecast error is

$$e_h(1) = r_{h+1} - \hat{r}_h(1) = a_{h+1}.$$

Consequently, the variance of the 1-step ahead forecast error is $\text{Var}[e_h(1)] = \text{Var}(a_{h+1}) = \sigma_a^2$. If a_t is normally distributed, then a 95% 1-step ahead interval forecast of r_{h+1} is $\hat{r}_h(1) \pm 1.96 \times \sigma_a$. For the linear model in Eq. (2.4), a_{t+1} is also the 1-step ahead forecast error at the forecast origin t. In the econometric literature, a_{t+1} is referred to as the *shock* to the series at time $t+1$.

In practice, estimated parameters are often used to compute point and interval forecasts. This results in a *conditional forecast* because such a forecast does not take into consideration the uncertainty in the parameter estimates. In theory, one can consider parameter uncertainty in forecasting, but it is much more involved. When the sample size used in estimation is sufficiently large, then the conditional forecast is close to the unconditional one.

2-Step Ahead Forecast

Next, consider the forecast of r_{h+2} at the forecast origin h. From the AR(p) model, we have

$$r_{h+2} = \phi_0 + \phi_1 r_{h+1} + \cdots + \phi_p r_{h+2-p} + a_{h+2}.$$

Taking conditional expectation, we have

$$\hat{r}_h(2) = E(r_{h+2}|F_h) = \phi_0 + \phi_1 \hat{r}_h(1) + \phi_2 r_h + \cdots + \phi_p r_{h+2-p}$$

and the associated forecast error

$$e_h(2) = r_{h+2} - \hat{r}_h(2) = \phi_1[r_{h+1} - \hat{r}_h(1)] + a_{h+2} = a_{h+2} + \phi_1 a_{h+1}.$$

The variance of the forecast error is $\text{Var}[e_h(2)] = (1+\phi_1^2)\sigma_a^2$. Interval forecasts of r_{h+2} can be computed in the same way as those for r_{h+1}. It is interesting to see that $\text{Var}[e_h(2)] \geq \text{Var}[e_h(1)]$, meaning that as the forecast horizon increases the uncertainty in forecast also increases. This is in agreement with common sense that we are more uncertain about r_{h+2} than r_{h+1} at the time index h for a linear time series.

Multistep Ahead Forecast

In general, we have

$$r_{h+\ell} = \phi_0 + \phi_1 r_{h+\ell-1} + \cdots + \phi_p r_{h+\ell-p} + a_{h+\ell}.$$

The ℓ-step ahead forecast based on the minimum squared error loss function is the conditional expectation of $r_{h+\ell}$ given F_h, which can be obtained as

$$\hat{r}_h(\ell) = \phi_0 + \sum_{i=1}^{p} \phi_i \hat{r}_h(\ell - i),$$

where it is understood that $\hat{r}_h(i) = r_{h+i}$ if $i \leq 0$. This forecast can be computed recursively using forecasts $\hat{r}_h(i)$ for $i = 1, \ldots, \ell - 1$. The ℓ-step ahead forecast

Table 2.2. Multistep Ahead Forecasts of an AR(3) Model for the Monthly Simple Returns of CRSP Value-Weighted Index with Forecast Origin of 858

Step	1	2	3	4	5	6
Forecast	0.0088	0.0020	0.0050	0.0097	0.0109	0.0106
Standard error	0.0542	0.0546	0.0546	0.0550	0.0550	0.0550
Actual	0.0762	−0.0365	0.0580	−0.0341	0.0311	0.0183

error is $e_h(\ell) = r_{h+\ell} - \hat{r}_h(\ell)$. It can be shown that for a stationary AR(p) model, $\hat{r}_h(\ell)$ converges to $E(r_t)$ as $\ell \to \infty$, meaning that for such a series long-term point forecast approaches its unconditional mean. This property is referred to as the *mean reversion* in the finance literature. For an AR(1) model, the speed of mean reversion is measured by the *half-life* defined as $k = \ln(0.5/|\phi_1|)$. The variance of the forecast error then approaches the unconditional variance of r_t.

Table 2.2 contains the 1-step to 6-step ahead forecasts and the standard errors of the associated forecast errors at the forecast origin 858 for the monthly simple return of the value-weighted index using an AR(3) model that was reestimated using the first 858 observations. The actual returns are also given. Because of the weak serial dependence in the series, the forecasts and standard deviations of

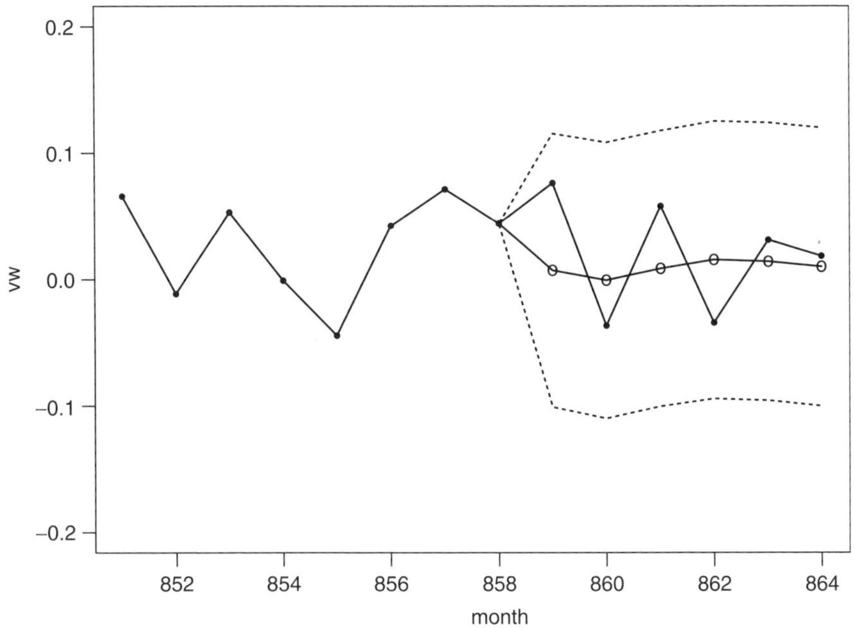

Figure 2.7. Plot of 1-step to 6-step ahead out-of-sample forecasts for the monthly log returns of the CRSP value-weighted index. The forecast origin is $t = 858$. The forecasts are denoted by ○ and the actual observations by black dots. The two dashed lines denote two standard-error limits of the forecasts.

forecast errors converge to the sample mean and standard deviation of the data quickly. For the first 858 observations, the sample mean and standard error are 0.0098 and 0.0550, respectively.

Figure 2.7 shows the 1-step to 6-step ahead out-of-sample forecasts and their two standard-error limits for the monthly log returns of value-weighted index. These forecasts are produced by the following AR(5) model:

$$r_t = 0.0075 + 0.103r_{t-1} + 0.002r_{t-2} - 0.114r_{t-3} + 0.032r_{t-4} + 0.084r_{t-5} + a_t,$$

where $\hat{\sigma}_a = 0.054$, which was built based on the procedure discussed earlier. For this particular series, the forecasts are close to the actual values that are all within the 95% interval forecasts.

2.5 SIMPLE MOVING-AVERAGE MODELS

We now turn to another class of simple models that are also useful in modeling return series in finance. These models are called moving-average (MA) models. There are several ways to introduce MA models. One approach is to treat the model as a simple extension of white noise series. Another approach is to treat the model as an infinite-order AR model with some parameter constraints. We adopt the second approach. As shown in Chapter 5, the bid–ask bounce in stock trading may introduce an MA(1) structure in a return series.

There is no particular reason, but simplicity, to assume a priori that the order of an AR model is finite. We may entertain, at least in theory, an AR model with infinite order as

$$r_t = \phi_0 + \phi_1 r_{t-1} + \phi_2 r_{t-2} + \cdots + a_t.$$

However, such an AR model is not realistic because it has infinite many parameters. One way to make the model practical is to assume that the coefficients ϕ_i satisfy some constraints so that they are determined by a finite number of parameters. A special case of this idea is

$$r_t = \phi_0 - \theta_1 r_{t-1} - \theta_1^2 r_{t-2} - \theta_1^3 r_{t-3} - \cdots + a_t, \tag{2.17}$$

where the coefficients depend on a single parameter θ_1 via $\phi_i = -\theta_1^i$ for $i \geq 1$. For the model in Eq. (2.17) to be stationary, θ_1 must be less than one in absolute value; otherwise, θ_1^i and the series will explode. Because $|\theta_1| < 1$, we have $\theta_1^i \to 0$ as $i \to \infty$. Thus, the contribution of r_{t-i} to r_t decays exponentially as i increases. This is reasonable as the dependence of a stationary series r_t on its lagged value r_{t-i}, if any, should decay over time.

The model in Eq. (2.17) can be rewritten in a rather compact form. To see this, rewrite the model as

$$r_t + \theta_1 r_{t-1} + \theta_1^2 r_{t-2} + \cdots = \phi_0 + a_t. \tag{2.18}$$

The model for r_{t-1} is then

$$r_{t-1} + \theta_1 r_{t-2} + \theta_1^2 r_{t-3} + \cdots = \phi_0 + a_{t-1}. \tag{2.19}$$

Multiplying Eq. (2.19) by θ_1 and subtracting the result from Eq. (2.18), we obtain

$$r_t = \phi_0(1 - \theta_1) + a_t - \theta_1 a_{t-1},$$

which says that, except for the constant term, r_t is a weighted average of shocks a_t and a_{t-1}. Therefore, the model is called an MA model of order 1 or MA(1) model for short. The general form of an MA(1) model is

$$r_t = c_0 + a_t - \theta_1 a_{t-1}, \quad \text{or} \quad r_t = c_0 + (1 - \theta_1 B)a_t, \tag{2.20}$$

where c_0 is a constant and $\{a_t\}$ is a white noise series. Similarly, an MA(2) model is in the form

$$r_t = c_0 + a_t - \theta_1 a_{t-1} - \theta_2 a_{t-2}, \tag{2.21}$$

and an MA(q) model is

$$r_t = c_0 + a_t - \theta_1 a_{t-1} - \cdots - \theta_q a_{t-q}, \tag{2.22}$$

or $r_t = c_0 + (1 - \theta_1 B - \cdots - \theta_q B^q)a_t$, where $q > 0$.

2.5.1 Properties of MA Models

Again, we focus on the simple MA(1) and MA(2) models. The results of MA(q) models can easily be obtained by the same techniques.

Stationarity

MA models are always weakly stationary because they are finite linear combinations of a white noise sequence for which the first two moments are time-invariant. For example, consider the MA(1) model in Eq. (2.20). Taking expectation of the model, we have

$$E(r_t) = c_0,$$

which is time-invariant. Taking the variance of Eq. (2.20), we have

$$\text{Var}(r_t) = \sigma_a^2 + \theta_1^2 \sigma_a^2 = (1 + \theta_1^2)\sigma_a^2,$$

where we use the fact that a_t and a_{t-1} are uncorrelated. Again, Var(r_t) is time-invariant. The prior discussion applies to general MA(q) models, and we obtain two general properties. First, the constant term of an MA model is the mean of the series (i.e., $E(r_t) = c_0$). Second, the variance of an MA(q) model is

$$\text{Var}(r_t) = (1 + \theta_1^2 + \theta_2^2 + \cdots + \theta_q^2)\sigma_a^2.$$

Autocorrelation Function

Assume for simplicity that $c_0 = 0$ for an MA(1) model. Multiplying the model by $r_{t-\ell}$, we have

$$r_{t-\ell}r_t = r_{t-\ell}a_t - \theta_1 r_{t-\ell}a_{t-1}.$$

Taking expectation, we obtain

$$\gamma_1 = -\theta_1\sigma_a^2, \quad \text{and} \quad \gamma_\ell = 0, \quad \text{for} \quad \ell > 1.$$

Using the prior result and the fact that $\mathrm{Var}(r_t) = (1+\theta_1^2)\sigma_a^2$, we have

$$\rho_0 = 1, \quad \rho_1 = \frac{-\theta_1}{1+\theta_1^2}, \quad \rho_\ell = 0, \quad \text{for} \quad \ell > 1.$$

Thus, for an MA(1) model, the lag-1 ACF is not zero, but all higher order ACFs are zero. In other words, the ACF of an MA(1) model cuts off at lag 1. For the MA(2) model in Eq. (2.21), the autocorrelation coefficients are

$$\rho_1 = \frac{-\theta_1 + \theta_1\theta_2}{1+\theta_1^2+\theta_2^2}, \quad \rho_2 = \frac{-\theta_2}{1+\theta_1^2+\theta_2^2}, \quad \rho_\ell = 0, \quad \text{for} \quad \ell > 2.$$

Here the ACF cuts off at lag 2. This property generalizes to other MA models. For an MA(q) model, the lag-q ACF is not zero, but $\rho_\ell = 0$ for $\ell > q$. Consequently, an MA(q) series is only linearly related to its first q lagged values and hence is a "finite-memory" model.

Invertibility

Rewriting a zero-mean MA(1) model as $a_t = r_t + \theta_1 a_{t-1}$, one can use repeated substitutions to obtain

$$a_t = r_t + \theta_1 r_{t-1} + \theta_1^2 r_{t-2} + \theta_1^3 r_{t-3} + \cdots.$$

This equation expresses the current shock a_t as a linear combination of the present and past returns. Intuitively, θ_1^j should go to zero as j increases because the remote return r_{t-j} should have very little impact on the current shock, if any. Consequently, for an MA(1) model to be plausible, we require $|\theta_1| < 1$. Such an MA(1) model is said to be *invertible*. If $|\theta_1| = 1$, then the MA(1) model is noninvertible. See Section 2.6.5 for further discussion on invertibility.

2.5.2 Identifying MA Order

The ACF is useful in identifying the order of an MA model. For a time series r_t with ACF ρ_ℓ, if $\rho_q \neq 0$, but $\rho_\ell = 0$ for $\ell > q$, then r_t follows an MA(q) model.

Figure 2.8 shows the time plot of monthly simple returns of the CRSP equal-weighted index from January 1926 to December 2003 and the sample ACF of the series. The two dashed lines shown on the ACF plot denote the two standard-error limits. It is seen that the series has significant ACF at lags 1, 3, and 9. There are

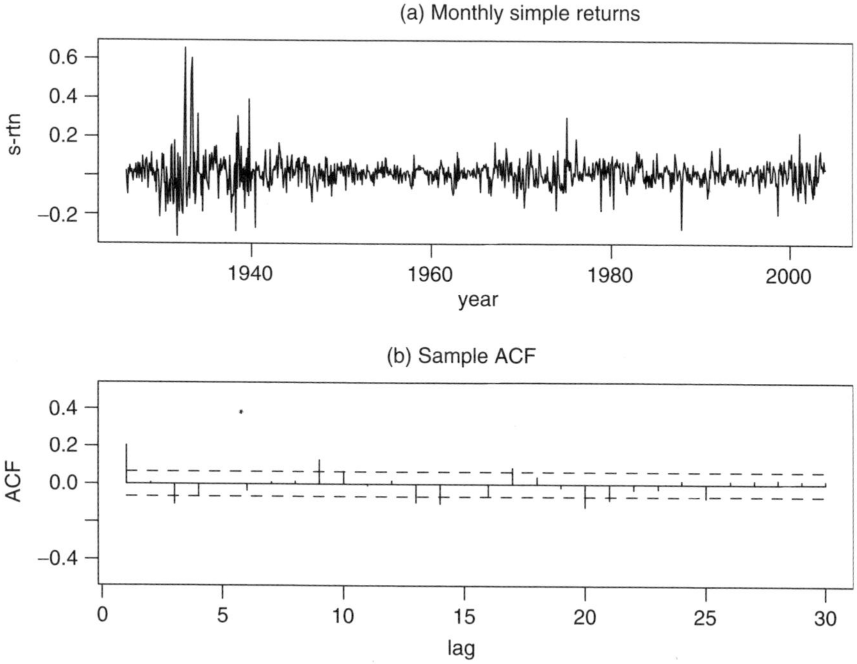

Figure 2.8. Time plot and sample autocorrelation function of the monthly simple returns of the CRSP equal-weighted index from January 1926 to December 2003.

some marginally significant ACFs at higher lags, but we do not consider them here. Based on the sample ACF, the following MA(9) model

$$r_t = c_0 + a_t - \theta_1 a_{t-1} - \theta_3 a_{t-3} - \theta_9 a_{t-9}$$

is identified for the series. Note that, unlike the sample PACF, the sample ACF provides information on the nonzero MA lags of the model.

2.5.3 Estimation

Maximum likelihood estimation is commonly used to estimate MA models. There are two approaches for evaluating the likelihood function of an MA model. The first approach assumes that the initial shocks (i.e., a_t for $t \leq 0$) are zero. As such, the shocks needed in likelihood function calculation are obtained recursively from the model, starting with $a_1 = r_1 - c_0$ and $a_2 = r_2 - c_0 + \theta_1 a_1$. This approach is referred to as the *conditional likelihood method* and the resulting estimates are the conditional maximum likelihood estimates. The second approach treats the initial shocks a_t, $t \leq 0$, as additional parameters of the model and estimates them jointly with other parameters. This approach is referred to as the *exact likelihood method*. The exact likelihood estimates are preferred over the conditional ones, especially when the MA model is close to being noninvertible. The exact method, however, requires more intensive computation. If the sample size is large, then the two types of maximum likelihood estimates are close to each other. For details of conditional and exact likelihood estimates of MA models, readers are referred to Box, Jenkins, and Reinsel (1994) or Chapter 8.

For illustration, consider the monthly simple return series of the CRSP equal-weighted index and the specified MA(9) model. The conditional maximum likelihood method produces the fitted model

$$r_t = 0.013 + a_t + 0.181a_{t-1} - 0.121a_{t-3} + 0.122a_{t-9}, \quad \hat{\sigma}_a = 0.0724, \qquad (2.23)$$

where standard errors of the coefficient estimates are 0.003, 0.032, 0.032, and 0.032, respectively. The Ljung–Box statistics of the residuals give $Q(12) = 15.0$ with p-value 0.091, which is based on an asymptotic chi-squared distribution with 9 degrees of freedom. The model appears to be adequate in modeling the linear dynamic dependence of the data. The exact maximum likelihood method produces the fitted model

$$r_t = 0.013 + a_t + 0.183a_{t-1} - 0.120a_{t-3} + 0.123a_{t-9}, \quad \hat{\sigma}_a = 0.0724, \qquad (2.24)$$

where standard errors of the estimates are 0.003, 0.032, 0.032, and 0.032, respectively. The Ljung–Box statistics of the residuals give $Q(12) = 15.2$ with p-value 0.086. This fitted model is also adequate. Comparing models (2.23) and (2.24), we see that, for this particular instance, the difference between the conditional and exact likelihood methods is negligible.

2.5.4 Forecasting Using MA Models

Forecasts of an MA model can easily be obtained. Because the model has finite memory, its point forecasts go to the mean of the series quickly. To see this, assume that the forecast origin is h and let F_h denote the information available at time h. For the 1-step ahead forecast of an MA(1) process, the model says

$$r_{h+1} = c_0 + a_{h+1} - \theta_1 a_h.$$

Taking the conditional expectation, we have

$$\hat{r}_h(1) = E(r_{h+1}|F_h) = c_0 - \theta_1 a_h,$$
$$e_h(1) = r_{h+1} - \hat{r}_h(1) = a_{h+1}.$$

The variance of the 1-step ahead forecast error is $\text{Var}[e_h(1)] = \sigma_a^2$. In practice, the quantity a_h can be obtained in several ways. For instance, assume that $a_0 = 0$, then $a_1 = r_1 - c_0$, and we can compute a_t for $2 \le t \le h$ recursively by using $a_t = r_t - c_0 + \theta_1 a_{t-1}$. Alternatively, it can be computed by using the AR representation of the MA(1) model; see Section 2.6.5.

For the 2-step ahead forecast, from the equation

$$r_{h+2} = c_0 + a_{h+2} - \theta_1 a_{h+1},$$

we have

$$\hat{r}_h(2) = E(r_{h+2}|F_h) = c_0,$$
$$e_h(2) = r_{h+2} - \hat{r}_h(2) = a_{h+2} - \theta_1 a_{h+1}.$$

The variance of the forecast error is Var$[e_h(2)] = (1+\theta_1^2)\sigma_a^2$, which is the variance of the model and is greater than or equal to that of the 1-step ahead forecast error. The prior result shows that for an MA(1) model the 2-step ahead forecast of the series is simply the unconditional mean of the model. This is true for any forecast origin h. More generally, $\hat{r}_h(\ell) = c_0$ for $\ell \geq 2$. In summary, for an MA(1) model, the 1-step ahead point forecast at the forecast origin h is $c_0 - \theta_1 a_h$ and the multistep ahead forecasts are c_0, which is the unconditional mean of the model. If we plot the forecasts $\hat{r}_h(\ell)$ versus ℓ, we see that the forecasts form a horizontal line after one step. Thus, for MA(1) models, mean-reverting only takes 1 time period.

Similarly, for an MA(2) model, we have

$$r_{h+\ell} = c_0 + a_{h+\ell} - \theta_1 a_{h+\ell-1} - \theta_2 a_{h+\ell-2},$$

from which we obtain

$$\hat{r}_h(1) = c_0 - \theta_1 a_h - \theta_2 a_{h-1},$$
$$\hat{r}_h(2) = c_0 - \theta_2 a_h,$$
$$\hat{r}_h(\ell) = c_0, \quad \text{for} \quad \ell > 2.$$

Thus, the multistep ahead forecasts of an MA(2) model go to the mean of the series after two steps. The variances of forecast errors go to the variance of the series after two steps. In general, for an MA(q) model, multistep ahead forecasts go to the mean after the first q steps.

Table 2.3 gives some forecasts of the MA(9) model in Eq. (2.23) for the monthly simple returns of the equal-weighted index at the forecast origin $h = 926$ (February 2003). The sample mean and standard error of the first 926 observations of the series are 0.0126 and 0.0751, respectively. As expected, the table shows that (a) the 10-step ahead forecast is the sample mean, and (b) the standard deviations of the forecast errors converge to the standard deviation of the series as the forecast horizon increases.

Summary

A brief summary of AR and MA models is in order. We have discussed the following properties:

- For MA models, the ACF is useful in specifying the order because the ACF cuts off at lag q for an MA(q) series.

Table 2.3. Forecast Performance of a MA(9) Model for the Monthly Simple Returns of the CRSP Equal-Weighted Index[a]

Step	1	2	3	4	5
Forecast	0.0140	−0.0050	0.0158	−0.0008	0.0171
Standard error	0.0726	0.0737	0.0737	0.0743	0.0743
Actual	0.0097	0.0983	0.1330	0.0496	0.0617
Step	6	7	8	9	10
Forecast	0.0257	0.0009	0.0149	0.0099	0.0126
Standard error	0.0743	0.0743	0.0743	0.0743	0.0748
Actual	0.0475	0.0252	0.0810	0.0381	0.0391

[a] The forecast origin is February 2003 with $h = 926$. The model is estimated by the conditional maximum likelihood method.

- For AR models, the PACF is useful in order determination because the PACF cuts off at lag p for an AR(p) process.
- An MA series is always stationary, but for an AR series to be stationary, all of its characteristic roots must be less than 1 in modulus.
- For a stationary series, the multistep ahead forecasts converge to the mean of the series and the variances of forecast errors converge to the variance of the series.

2.6 SIMPLE ARMA MODELS

In some applications, the AR or MA models discussed in the previous sections become cumbersome because one may need a high-order model with many parameters to adequately describe the dynamic structure of the data. To overcome this difficulty, the autoregressive moving-average (ARMA) models are introduced; see Box, Jenkins, and Reinsel (1994). Basically, an ARMA model combines the ideas of AR and MA models into a compact form so that the number of parameters used is kept small. For the return series in finance, the chance of using ARMA models is low. However, the concept of ARMA models is highly relevant in volatility modeling. As a matter of fact, the generalized autoregressive conditional heteroscedastic (GARCH) model can be regarded as an ARMA model, albeit nonstandard, for the a_t^2 series; see Chapter 3 for details. In this section, we study the simplest ARMA(1,1) model.

A time series r_t follows an ARMA(1,1) model if it satisfies

$$r_t - \phi_1 r_{t-1} = \phi_0 + a_t - \theta_1 a_{t-1}, \tag{2.25}$$

where $\{a_t\}$ is a white noise series. The left-hand side of Eq. (2.25) is the AR component of the model and the right-hand side gives the MA component. The constant term is ϕ_0. For this model to be meaningful, we need $\phi_1 \neq \theta_1$; otherwise, there is a cancellation in the equation and the process reduces to a white noise series.

2.6.1 Properties of ARMA(1,1) Models

Properties of ARMA(1,1) models are generalizations of those of AR(1) models with some minor modifications to handle the impact of the MA(1) component. We start with the stationarity condition. Taking expectation of Eq. (2.25), we have

$$E(r_t) - \phi_1 E(r_{t-1}) = \phi_0 + E(a_t) - \theta_1 E(a_{t-1}).$$

Because $E(a_i) = 0$ for all i, the mean of r_t is

$$E(r_t) = \mu = \frac{\phi_0}{1 - \phi_1}$$

provided that the series is weakly stationary. This result is exactly the same as that of the AR(1) model in Eq. (2.8).

Next, assuming for simplicity that $\phi_0 = 0$, we consider the autocovariance function of r_t. First, multiplying the model by a_t and taking expectation, we have

$$E(r_t a_t) = E(a_t^2) - \theta_1 E(a_t a_{t-1}) = E(a_t^2) = \sigma_a^2. \tag{2.26}$$

Rewriting the model as

$$r_t = \phi_1 r_{t-1} + a_t - \theta_1 a_{t-1}$$

and taking the variance of the prior equation, we have

$$\text{Var}(r_t) = \phi_1^2 \text{ Var}(r_{t-1}) + \sigma_a^2 + \theta_1^2 \sigma_a^2 - 2\phi_1 \theta_1 E(r_{t-1} a_{t-1}).$$

Here we make use of the fact that r_{t-1} and a_t are uncorrelated. Using Eq. (2.26), we obtain

$$\text{Var}(r_t) - \phi_1^2 \text{ Var}(r_{t-1}) = (1 - 2\phi_1\theta_1 + \theta_1^2)\sigma_a^2.$$

Therefore, if the series r_t is weakly stationary, then $\text{Var}(r_t) = \text{Var}(r_{t-1})$ and we have

$$\text{Var}(r_t) = \frac{(1 - 2\phi_1\theta_1 + \theta_1^2)\sigma_a^2}{1 - \phi_1^2}.$$

Because the variance is positive, we need $\phi_1^2 < 1$ (i.e., $|\phi_1| < 1$). Again, this is precisely the same stationarity condition as that of the AR(1) model.

To obtain the autocovariance function of r_t, we assume $\phi_0 = 0$ and multiply the model in Eq. (2.25) by $r_{t-\ell}$ to obtain

$$r_t r_{t-\ell} - \phi_1 r_{t-1} r_{t-\ell} = a_t r_{t-\ell} - \theta_1 a_{t-1} r_{t-\ell}.$$

For $\ell = 1$, taking expectation and using Eq. (2.26) for $t-1$, we have

$$\gamma_1 - \phi_1 \gamma_0 = -\theta_1 \sigma_a^2,$$

where $\gamma_\ell = \text{Cov}(r_t, r_{t-\ell})$. This result is different from that of the AR(1) case for which $\gamma_1 - \phi_1 \gamma_0 = 0$. However, for $\ell = 2$ and taking expectation, we have

$$\gamma_2 - \phi_1 \gamma_1 = 0,$$

which is identical to that of the AR(1) case. In fact, the same technique yields

$$\gamma_\ell - \phi_1 \gamma_{\ell-1} = 0, \quad \text{for} \quad \ell > 1. \tag{2.27}$$

In terms of the ACF, the previous results show that for a stationary ARMA(1,1) model

$$\rho_1 = \phi_1 - \frac{\theta_1 \sigma_a^2}{\gamma_0}, \qquad \rho_\ell = \phi_1 \rho_{\ell-1}, \quad \text{for} \quad \ell > 1.$$

Thus, the ACF of an ARMA(1,1) model behaves very much like that of an AR(1) model except that the exponential decay starts with lag 2. Consequently, the ACF of an ARMA(1,1) model does not cut off at any finite lag.

Turning to the PACF, one can show that the PACF of an ARMA(1,1) model does not cut off at any finite lag either. It behaves very much like that of an MA(1) model except that the exponential decay starts with lag 2 instead of lag 1.

In summary, the stationarity condition of an ARMA(1,1) model is the same as that of an AR(1) model, and the ACF of an ARMA(1,1) exhibits a pattern similar to that of an AR(1) model except that the pattern starts at lag 2.

2.6.2 General ARMA Models

A general ARMA(p, q) model is in the form

$$r_t = \phi_0 + \sum_{i=1}^{p} \phi_i r_{t-i} + a_t - \sum_{i=1}^{q} \theta_i a_{t-i},$$

where $\{a_t\}$ is a white noise series and p and q are non-negative integers. The AR and MA models are special cases of the ARMA(p, q) model. Using the back-shift operator, the model can be written as

$$(1 - \phi_1 B - \cdots - \phi_p B^p) r_t = \phi_0 + (1 - \theta_1 B - \cdots - \theta_q B^q) a_t. \tag{2.28}$$

The polynomial $1 - \phi_1 B - \cdots - \phi_p B^p$ is the AR polynomial of the model. Similarly, $1 - \theta_1 B - \cdots - \theta_q B^q$ is the MA polynomial. We require that there are no common factors between the AR and MA polynomials; otherwise the order (p, q) of the model can be reduced. Like a pure AR model, the AR polynomial introduces the characteristic equation of an ARMA model. If all of the solutions of the characteristic equation are less than 1 in absolute value, then the ARMA model is weakly stationary. In this case, the unconditional mean of the model is $E(r_t) = \phi_0/(1 - \phi_1 - \cdots - \phi_p)$.

2.6.3 Identifying ARMA Models

The ACF and PACF are not informative in determining the order of an ARMA model. Tsay and Tiao (1984) propose a new approach that uses the extended autocorrelation function (EACF) to specify the order of an ARMA process. The basic idea of EACF is relatively simple. If we can obtain a consistent estimate of the AR component of an ARMA model, then we can derive the MA component. From the derived MA series, we can use the ACF to identify the order of the MA component.

Derivation of the EACF is relatively involved; see Tsay and Tiao (1984) for details. Yet the function is easy to use. The output of the EACF is a two-way table, where the rows correspond to AR order p and the columns to MA order q. The theoretical version of the EACF for an ARMA(1,1) model is given in Table 2.4. The key feature of the table is that it contains a triangle of O's with the upper left vertex located at the order (1,1). This is the characteristic we use to identify the order of an ARMA process. In general, for an ARMA(p, q) model, the triangle of O's will have its upper left vertex at the (p, q) position.

For illustration, consider the monthly log stock returns of the 3M Company from February 1946 to December 1997. There are 623 observations. The return series and its sample ACF are shown in Figure 2.9. The ACF indicates that there are no significant serial correlations in the data at the 5% level. Table 2.5 shows the sample EACF and a corresponding simplified table for the series. The simplified table is constructed by using the following notation:

1. X denotes that the absolute value of the corresponding EACF is greater than or equal to $2/\sqrt{T}$, which is twice the asymptotic standard error of the EACF.
2. O denotes that the corresponding EACF is less than $2/\sqrt{T}$ in modulus.

Table 2.4. Theoretical EACF Table for an ARMA(1,1) Model[a]

	MA							
AR	0	1	2	3	4	5	6	7
0	X	X	X	X	X	X	X	X
1	X	O	O	O	O	O	O	O
2	*	X	O	O	O	O	O	O
3	*	*	X	O	O	O	O	O
4	*	*	*	X	O	O	O	O
5	*	*	*	*	X	O	O	O

[a] X denotes nonzero, O denotes zero, and * denotes either zero or nonzero. This latter category does not play any role in identifying the order (1,1).

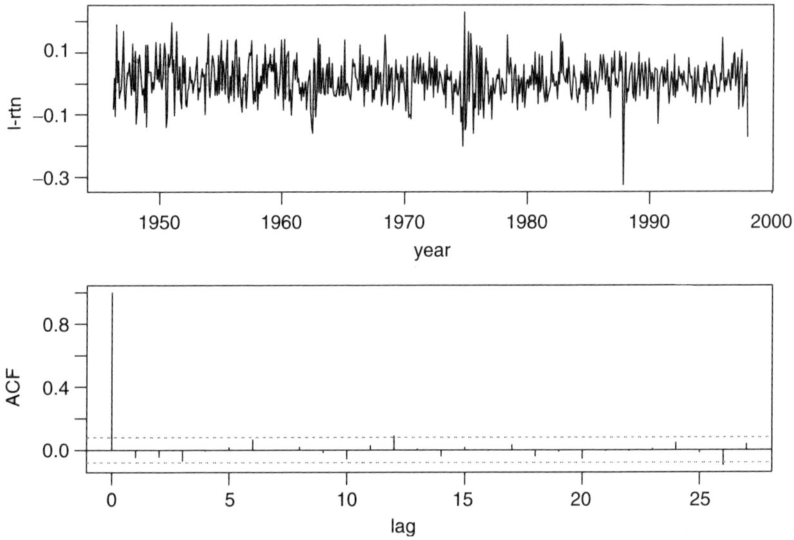

Figure 2.9. Time plot and sample autocorrelation function of the monthly log stock returns of 3M Company from February 1946 to December 1997.

Table 2.5. Sample Extended Autocorrelation Function and a Simplified Table for the Monthly Log Returns of 3M Stock from February 1946 to December 1997

Sample Extended Autocorrelation Function

MA Order: q

p	0	1	2	3	4	5	6	7	8	9	10	11	12
0	−0.05	−0.04	−0.07	−0.01	0.02	0.06	−0.00	0.02	−0.01	−0.06	0.03	0.09	0.01
1	−0.49	0.01	−0.06	−0.03	−0.00	0.06	0.01	0.01	−0.01	−0.05	0.02	0.08	0.02
2	−0.45	−0.18	−0.05	0.01	−0.02	0.06	0.03	0.02	−0.01	−0.00	0.01	0.05	0.05
3	−0.18	0.15	0.40	−0.01	−0.01	0.05	−0.00	0.03	−0.03	−0.00	0.00	0.02	0.05
4	0.42	0.04	0.39	−0.08	−0.01	0.01	−0.01	0.04	0.02	0.02	−0.00	0.01	0.03
5	−0.13	0.24	0.41	0.07	0.23	0.01	0.01	0.05	−0.03	0.02	−0.01	0.00	0.04
6	−0.07	−0.37	0.06	0.31	0.20	−0.09	0.01	0.06	−0.03	0.02	−0.01	0.00	0.03

Simplified EACF Table

MA Order: q

p	0	1	2	3	4	5	6	7	8	9	10	11	12
0	O	O	O	O	O	O	O	O	O	O	O	X	O
1	X	O	O	O	O	O	O	O	O	O	O	O	O
2	X	X	O	O	O	O	O	O	O	O	O	O	O
3	X	X	X	O	O	O	O	O	O	O	O	O	O
4	X	O	X	O	O	O	O	O	O	O	O	O	O
5	X	X	X	O	X	O	O	O	O	O	O	O	O
6	O	X	O	X	X	O	O	O	O	O	O	O	O

The simplified table clearly exhibits a triangular pattern of O's with its upper left vertex at the order $(p, q) = (0,0)$. The only exception is a single X in the first row, which corresponds to a sample EACF of 0.09 that is only slightly greater than $2/\sqrt{623} = 0.08$. Therefore, the EACF suggests that the monthly log returns of 3M stock follow an ARMA(0,0) model (i.e., a white noise series). This is in agreement with the result suggested by the sample ACF in Figure 2.9.

The information criteria discussed earlier can also be used to select ARMA models. Typically, for some prespecified positive integers P and Q, one computes AIC (or BIC) for ARMA(p, q) models, where $0 \le p \le P$ and $0 \le q \le Q$, and selects the model that gives the minimum AIC (or BIC). This approach requires maximum likelihood estimation of many models and in some cases may encounter the difficulty of overfitting in estimation.

Once an ARMA(p, q) model is specified, its parameters can be estimated by either the conditional or exact likelihood method. In addition, the Ljung–Box statistics of the residuals can be used to check the adequacy of a fitted model. If the model is correctly specified, then $Q(m)$ follows asymptotically a chi-squared distribution with $m - g$ degrees of freedom, where g denotes the number of parameters used in the model.

2.6.4 Forecasting Using an ARMA Model

Like the behavior of the ACF, forecasts of an ARMA(p, q) model have characteristics similar to those of an AR(p) model after adjusting for the impacts of the MA component on the lower horizon forecasts. Denote the forecast origin by h and the available information by F_h. The 1-step ahead forecast of r_{h+1} can easily be obtained from the model as

$$\hat{r}_h(1) = E(r_{h+1}|F_h) = \phi_0 + \sum_{i=1}^{p} \phi_i r_{h+1-i} - \sum_{i=1}^{q} \theta_i a_{h+1-i},$$

and the associated forecast error is $e_h(1) = r_{h+1} - \hat{r}_h(1) = a_{h+1}$. The variance of 1-step ahead forecast error is $\text{Var}[e_h(1)] = \sigma_a^2$. For the ℓ-step ahead forecast, we have

$$\hat{r}_h(\ell) = E(r_{h+\ell}|F_h) = \phi_0 + \sum_{i=1}^{p} \phi_i \hat{r}_h(\ell - i) - \sum_{i=1}^{q} \theta_i a_h(\ell - i),$$

where it is understood that $\hat{r}_h(\ell - i) = r_{h+\ell-i}$ if $\ell - i \le 0$ and $a_h(\ell - i) = 0$ if $\ell - i > 0$ and $a_h(\ell - i) = a_{h+\ell-i}$ if $\ell - i \le 0$. Thus, the multistep ahead forecasts of an ARMA model can be computed recursively. The associated forecast error is

$$e_h(\ell) = r_{h+\ell} - \hat{r}_h(\ell),$$

which can be computed easily via a formula to be given below in Eq. (2.34).

2.6.5 Three Model Representations for an ARMA Model

In this subsection, we briefly discuss three model representations for a stationary ARMA(p, q) model. The three representations serve three different purposes. Knowing these representations can lead to a better understanding of the model. The first representation is the ARMA(p, q) model in Eq. (2.28). This representation is compact and useful in parameter estimation. It is also useful in computing recursively multistep ahead forecasts of r_t; see the discussion of the last subsection.

For the other two representations, we use long division of two polynomials. Given two polynomials $\phi(B) = 1 - \sum_{i=1}^{p} \phi_i B^i$ and $\theta(B) = 1 - \sum_{i=1}^{q} \theta_i B^i$, we can obtain, by long division, that

$$\frac{\theta(B)}{\phi(B)} = 1 + \psi_1 B + \psi_2 B^2 + \cdots \equiv \psi(B) \tag{2.29}$$

and

$$\frac{\phi(B)}{\theta(B)} = 1 - \pi_1 B - \pi_2 B^2 - \cdots \equiv \pi(B). \tag{2.30}$$

For instance, if $\phi(B) = 1 - \phi_1 B$ and $\theta(B) = 1 - \theta_1 B$, then

$$\psi(B) = \frac{1 - \theta_1 B}{1 - \phi_1 B} = 1 + (\phi_1 - \theta_1)B + \phi_1(\phi_1 - \theta_1)B^2 + \phi_1^2(\phi_1 - \theta_1)B^3 + \cdots,$$

$$\pi(B) = \frac{1 - \phi_1 B}{1 - \theta_1 B} = 1 - (\phi_1 - \theta_1)B - \theta_1(\phi_1 - \theta_1)B^2 - \theta_1^2(\phi_1 - \theta_1)B^3 - \cdots.$$

From the definition, $\psi(B)\pi(B) = 1$. Making use of the fact that $Bc = c$ for any constant (because the value of a constant is time-invariant), we have

$$\frac{\phi_0}{\theta(1)} = \frac{\phi_0}{1 - \theta_1 - \cdots - \theta_q} \quad \text{and} \quad \frac{\phi_0}{\phi(1)} = \frac{\phi_0}{1 - \phi_1 - \cdots - \phi_p}.$$

AR Representation

Using the result of long division in Eq. (2.30), the ARMA(p, q) model can be written as

$$r_t = \frac{\phi_0}{1 - \theta_1 - \cdots - \theta_q} + \pi_1 r_{t-1} + \pi_2 r_{t-2} + \pi_3 r_{t-3} + \cdots + a_t. \tag{2.31}$$

This representation shows the dependence of the current return r_t on the past returns r_{t-i}, where $i > 0$. The coefficients $\{\pi_i\}$ are referred to as the π-*weights* of an ARMA model. To show that the contribution of the lagged value r_{t-i} to r_t is diminishing as i increases, the π_i coefficient should decay to zero as i increases. An ARMA(p, q) model that has this property is said to be invertible. For a pure AR model, $\theta(B) = 1$ so that $\pi(B) = \phi(B)$, which is a finite-degree polynomial. Thus, $\pi_i = 0$ for $i > p$, and the model is invertible. For other ARMA models, a sufficient condition for invertibility is that all the zeros of the polynomial $\theta(B)$ are greater than unity in modulus. For example, consider the MA(1) model $r_t = (1 - \theta_1 B)a_t$. The zero of the first-order polynomial $1 - \theta_1 B$ is $B = 1/\theta_1$. Therefore, an MA(1) model is invertible if $|1/\theta_1| > 1$. This is equivalent to $|\theta_1| < 1$.

From the AR representation in Eq. (2.31), an invertible ARMA(p, q) series r_t is a linear combination of the current shock a_t and a weighted average of the past values. The weights decay exponentially for more remote past values.

MA Representation

Again, using the result of long division in Eq. (2.29), an ARMA(p, q) model can also be written as

$$r_t = \mu + a_t + \psi_1 a_{t-1} + \psi_2 a_{t-2} + \cdots = \mu + \psi(B)a_t, \tag{2.32}$$

where $\mu = E(r_t) = \phi_0/(1 - \phi_1 - \cdots - \phi_p)$. This representation shows explicitly the impact of the past shock a_{t-i} $(i > 0)$ on the current return r_t. The coefficients $\{\psi_i\}$ are referred to as the *impulse response function* of the ARMA model. For a weakly stationary series, the ψ_i coefficients decay exponentially as i increases. This is understandable as the effect of shock a_{t-i} on the return r_t should diminish over time. Thus, for a stationary ARMA model, the shock a_{t-i} does not have a permanent impact on the series. If $\phi_0 \neq 0$, then the MA representation has a constant term, which is the mean of r_t (i.e., $\phi_0/(1 - \phi_1 - \cdots - \phi_p)$).

The MA representation in Eq. (2.32) is also useful in computing the variance of a forecast error. At the forecast origin h, we have the shocks $a_h, a_{h-1}, \ldots$. Therefore, the ℓ-step ahead point forecast is

$$\hat{r}_h(\ell) = \mu + \psi_\ell a_h + \psi_{\ell+1} a_{h-1} + \cdots, \tag{2.33}$$

and the associated forecast error is

$$e_h(\ell) = a_{h+\ell} + \psi_1 a_{h+\ell-1} + \cdots + \psi_{\ell-1} a_{h+1}.$$

Consequently, the variance of ℓ-step ahead forecast error is

$$\text{Var}[e_h(\ell)] = (1 + \psi_1^2 + \cdots + \psi_{\ell-1}^2)\sigma_a^2, \tag{2.34}$$

which, as expected, is a nondecreasing function of the forecast horizon ℓ.

Finally, the MA representation in Eq. (2.32) provides a simple proof of mean reversion of a stationary time series. The stationarity implies that ψ_i approaches zero as $i \to \infty$. Therefore, by Eq. (2.33), we have $\hat{r}_h(\ell) \to \mu$ as $\ell \to \infty$. Because $\hat{r}_h(\ell)$ is the conditional expectation of $r_{h+\ell}$ at the forecast origin h, the result says that in the long-term the return series is expected to approach its mean, that is, the series is mean-reverting. Furthermore, using the MA representation in Eq. (2.32), we have $\text{Var}(r_t) = \left(1 + \sum_{i=1}^{\infty} \psi_i^2\right)\sigma_a^2$. Consequently, by Eq. (2.34), we have $\text{Var}[e_h(\ell)] \to \text{Var}(r_t)$ as $\ell \to \infty$. The speed by which $\hat{r}_h(\ell)$ approaches μ determines the speed of mean-reverting.

2.7 UNIT-ROOT NONSTATIONARITY

So far we have focused on return series that are stationary. In some studies, interest rates, foreign exchange rates, or the price series of an asset are of interest. These series tend to be nonstationary. For a price series, the nonstationarity is mainly due to the fact that there is no fixed level for the price. In the time series literature, such a nonstationary series is called unit-root nonstationary time series. The best known example of unit-root nonstationary time series is the random-walk model.

2.7.1 Random Walk

A time series $\{p_t\}$ is a random walk if it satisfies

$$p_t = p_{t-1} + a_t, \tag{2.35}$$

where p_0 is a real number denoting the starting value of the process and $\{a_t\}$ is a white noise series. If p_t is the log price of a particular stock at date t, then p_0 could be the log price of the stock at its initial public offering (i.e., the logged IPO price). If a_t has a symmetric distribution around zero, then conditional on p_{t-1}, p_t has a 50–50 chance to go up or down, implying that p_t would go up or down at random. If we treat the random-walk model as a special AR(1) model, then the coefficient of p_{t-1} is unity, which does not satisfy the weak stationarity condition of an AR(1) model. A random-walk series is, therefore, not weakly stationary, and we call it a unit-root nonstationary time series.

The random-walk model has widely been considered as a statistical model for the movement of logged stock prices. Under such a model, the stock price is not predictable or mean-reverting. To see this, the 1-step ahead forecast of model (2.35) at the forecast origin h is

$$\hat{p}_h(1) = E(p_{h+1}|p_h, p_{h-1}, \ldots) = p_h,$$

which is the log price of the stock at the forecast origin. Such a forecast has no practical value. The 2-step ahead forecast is

$$\begin{aligned}\hat{p}_h(2) &= E(p_{h+2}|p_h, p_{h-1}, \ldots) = E(p_{h+1} + a_{h+2}|p_h, p_{h-1}, \ldots)\\ &= E(p_{h+1}|p_h, p_{h-1}, \ldots) = \hat{p}_h(1) = p_h,\end{aligned}$$

which again is the log price at the forecast origin. In fact, for any forecast horizon $\ell > 0$, we have

$$\hat{p}_h(\ell) = p_h.$$

Thus, for all forecast horizons, point forecasts of a random-walk model are simply the value of the series at the forecast origin. Therefore, the process is not mean-reverting.

The MA representation of the random-walk model in Eq. (2.35) is

$$p_t = a_t + a_{t-1} + a_{t-2} + \cdots.$$

This representation has several important practical implications. First, the ℓ-step ahead forecast error is

$$e_h(\ell) = a_{h+\ell} + \cdots + a_{h+1},$$

so that $\text{Var}[e_h(\ell)] = \ell\sigma_a^2$, which diverges to infinity as $\ell \to \infty$. The length of an interval forecast of $p_{h+\ell}$ will approach infinity as the forecast horizon increases. This result says that the usefulness of point forecast $\hat{p}_h(\ell)$ diminishes as ℓ increases, which again implies that the model is not predictable. Second, the unconditional variance of p_t is unbounded because $\text{Var}[e_h(\ell)]$ approaches infinity as ℓ increases. Theoretically, this means that p_t can assume any real value for a sufficiently large t. For the log price p_t of an individual stock, this is plausible. Yet for market indexes, negative log price is very rare if it happens at all. In this sense, the adequacy of a random-walk model for market indexes is questionable. Third, from the representation, $\psi_i = 1$ for all i. Thus, the impact of any past shock a_{t-i} on p_t does not decay over time. Consequently, the series has a strong memory as it remembers all of the past shocks. In economics, the shocks are said to have a permanent effect on the series. The strong memory of a unit-root time series can be seen from the sample ACF of the observed series. The sample ACFs are all approaching 1 as the sample size increases.

2.7.2 Random Walk with Drift

As shown by empirical examples considered so far, the log return series of a market index tends to have a small and positive mean. This implies that the model for the log price is

$$p_t = \mu + p_{t-1} + a_t, \tag{2.36}$$

where $\mu = E(p_t - p_{t-1})$ and $\{a_t\}$ is a white noise series. The constant term μ of model (2.36) is very important in financial study. It represents the time trend of the log price p_t and is often referred to as the *drift* of the model. To see this, assume that the initial log price is p_0. Then we have

$$\begin{aligned} p_1 &= \mu + p_0 + a_1, \\ p_2 &= \mu + p_1 + a_2 = 2\mu + p_0 + a_2 + a_1, \\ \vdots &\quad \vdots \\ p_t &= t\mu + p_0 + a_t + a_{t-1} + \cdots + a_1. \end{aligned}$$

The last equation shows that the log price consists of a time trend $t\mu$ and a pure random-walk process $\sum_{i=1}^{t} a_i$. Because $\text{Var}\left(\sum_{i=1}^{t} a_i\right) = t\sigma_a^2$, where σ_a^2 is the variance of a_t, the conditional standard deviation of p_t is $\sqrt{t}\sigma_a$, which grows at a slower rate than the conditional expectation of p_t. Therefore, if we graph p_t against the time index t, we have a time trend with slope μ. A positive slope μ implies that the log price eventually goes to infinity. In contrast, a negative μ implies that the log price would converge to $-\infty$ as t increases. Based on the above discussion, it is then not surprising to see that the log return series of the CRSP value- and equal-weighted indexes have a small, but statistically significant, positive mean.

To illustrate the effect of the drift parameter on the price series, we consider the monthly log stock returns of the 3M Company from February 1946 to December 1997. As shown by the sample EACF in Table 2.5, the series has no significant serial correlation. The series thus follows the simple model

$$r_t = 0.0115 + a_t, \quad \hat{\sigma}_a = 0.0639, \tag{2.37}$$

where 0.0115 is the sample mean of r_t and has a standard error 0.0026. The mean of the monthly log returns of 3M stock is, therefore, significantly different from zero at the 1% level. We use the log return series to construct two log price series, namely,

$$p_t = \sum_{i=1}^{t} r_i \quad \text{and} \quad p_t^* = \sum_{i=1}^{t} a_i,$$

where a_i is the mean-corrected log return in Eq. (2.37) (i.e., $a_t = r_t - 0.0115$). The p_t is the log price of 3M stock, assuming that the initial log price is zero (i.e., the log price of January 1946 was zero). The p_t^* is the corresponding log price if the mean of log returns was zero. Figure 2.10 shows the time plots of p_t and p_t^*

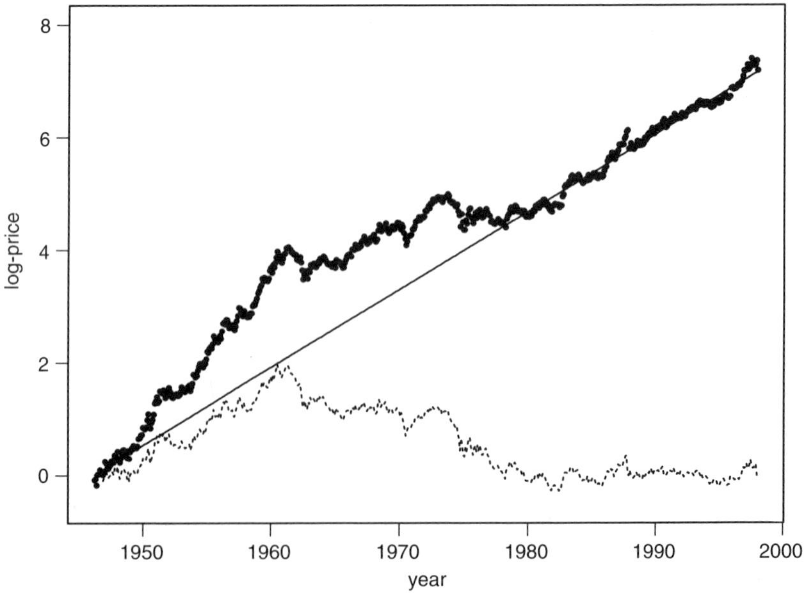

Figure 2.10. Time plots of log prices for 3M stock from February 1946 to December 1997, assuming that the log price of January 1946 was zero. The dashed line is for log price without time trend. The straight line is $y_t = 0.0115 \times t$.

as well as a straight line $y_t = 0.0115 \times t$. From the plots, the importance of the constant 0.0115 in Eq. (2.37) is evident. In addition, as expected, the slope of the upward trend of p_t is about 0.0115.

Finally, it is important to understand the meaning of a constant term in a time series model. First, for an MA(q) model in Eq. (2.22), the constant term is simply the mean of the series. Second, for a stationary AR(p) model in Eq. (2.9) or ARMA(p, q) model in Eq. (2.28), the constant term is related to the mean via $\mu = \phi_0/(1 - \phi_1 - \cdots - \phi_p)$. Third, for a random walk with drift, the constant term becomes the time slope. These different interpretations for the constant term in a time series model clearly highlight the difference between dynamic and usual linear regression models.

Another important difference between dynamic and regression models is shown by an AR(1) model and a simple linear regression model,

$$r_t = \phi_0 + \phi_1 r_{t-1} + a_t \quad \text{and} \quad y_t = \beta_0 + \beta_1 x_t + a_t.$$

For the AR(1) model to be meaningful, the coefficient ϕ_1 must satisfy $|\phi_1| \leq 1$. However, the coefficient β_1 can assume any fixed real number.

2.7.3 Trend-Stationary Time Series

A closely related model that exhibits linear trend is the trend-stationary time series model,

$$p_t = \beta_0 + \beta_1 t + r_t,$$

where r_t is a stationary time series, for example, a stationary AR(p) series. Here p_t grows linearly in time with rate β_1 and hence can exhibit behavior similar to that of a random-walk model with drift. However, there is a major difference between the two models. To see this, suppose that p_0 is fixed. The random-walk model with drift assumes the mean $E(p_t) = p_0 + \mu t$ and variance $\text{Var}(p_t) = t\sigma_a^2$, both of which are time dependent. On the other hand, the trend-stationary model assumes the mean $E(p_t) = \beta_0 + \beta_1 t$, which depends on time, and variance $\text{Var}(p_t) = \text{Var}(r_t)$, which is finite and time-invariant. The trend-stationary series can be transformed into a stationary one by removing the time trend via a simple linear regression analysis. For analysis of trend-stationary time series, see Section 2.9.

2.7.4 General Unit-Root Nonstationary Models

Consider an ARMA model. If one extends the model by allowing the AR polynomial to have 1 as a characteristic root, then the model becomes the well-known autoregressive integrated moving-average (ARIMA) model. An ARIMA model is said to be unit-root nonstationary because its AR polynomial has a unit root. Like a random-walk model, an ARIMA model has strong memory because the ψ_i coefficients in its MA representation do not decay over time to zero, implying that the past shock a_{t-i} of the model has a permanent effect on the series. A conventional approach for handling unit-root nonstationarity is to use *differencing*.

Differencing

A time series y_t is said to be an ARIMA$(p, 1, q)$ process if the change series $c_t = y_t - y_{t-1} = (1 - B)y_t$ follows a stationary and invertible ARMA(p, q) model. In finance, price series are commonly believed to be nonstationary, but the log return series, $r_t = \ln(p_t) - \ln(p_{t-1})$, is stationary. In this case, the log price series is unit-root nonstationary and hence can be treated as an ARIMA process. The idea of transforming a nonstationary series into a stationary one by considering its change series is called *differencing* in the time series literature. More formally, $c_t = y_t - y_{t-1}$ is referred to as the first differenced series of y_t. In some scientific fields, a time series y_t may contain multiple unit roots and needs to be differenced multiple times to become stationary. For example, if both y_t and its first differenced series $c_t = y_t - y_{t-1}$ are unit-root nonstationary, but $s_t = c_t - c_{t-1} = y_t - 2y_{t-1} + y_{t-2}$ is weakly stationary, then y_t has double unit roots, and s_t is the second differenced series of y_t. In addition, if s_t follows an ARMA(p, q) model, then y_t is an ARIMA$(p, 2, q)$ process. For such a time series, if s_t has a nonzero mean, then y_t has a quadratic time function and the quadratic time coefficient is related to the mean of s_t. The seasonally adjusted series of U.S. quarterly gross domestic product implicit price deflator might have double unit roots. However, the mean of the second differenced series is not significantly different from zero (see Exercises at end of chapter). Box, Jenkins, and Reinsel (1994) discuss many properties of general ARIMA models.

2.7.5 Unit-Root Test

To test whether the log price p_t of an asset follows a random walk or a random walk with drift, we employ the models

$$p_t = \phi_1 p_{t-1} + e_t, \tag{2.38}$$

$$p_t = \phi_0 + \phi_1 p_{t-1} + e_t, \tag{2.39}$$

where e_t denotes the error term, and consider the null hypothesis $H_o : \phi_1 = 1$ versus the alternative hypothesis $H_a : \phi_1 < 1$. This is the well-known unit-root testing problem; see Dickey and Fuller (1979). A convenient test statistic is the t-ratio of the least squares (LS) estimate of ϕ_1. For Eq. (2.38), the LS method gives

$$\hat{\phi}_1 = \frac{\sum_{t=1}^{T} p_{t-1} p_t}{\sum_{t=1}^{T} p_{t-1}^2}, \quad \hat{\sigma}_e^2 = \frac{\sum_{t=1}^{T} (p_t - \hat{\phi}_1 p_{t-1})^2}{T - 1},$$

where $p_0 = 0$ and T is the sample size. The t-ratio is

$$\text{DF} \equiv t\text{-ratio} = \frac{\hat{\phi}_1 - 1}{\text{std}(\hat{\phi}_1)} = \frac{\sum_{t=1}^{T} p_{t-1} e_t}{\hat{\sigma}_e \sqrt{\sum_{t=1}^{T} p_{t-1}^2}},$$

which is commonly referred to as the Dickey–Fuller test. If $\{e_t\}$ is a white noise series with finite moments of order slightly greater than 2, then the DF-statistic converges to a function of the standard Brownian motion as $T \to \infty$; see Chan and Wei (1988) and Phillips (1987) for more information. If ϕ_0 is zero but Eq. (2.39) is employed anyway, then the resulting t-ratio for testing $\phi_1 = 1$ will converge to another nonstandard asymptotic distribution. In either case, simulation is used to obtain critical values of the test statistics; see Fuller (1976, Chapter 8) for selected critical values. Yet if $\phi_0 \neq 0$ and Eq. (2.39) is used, then the t-ratio for testing $\phi_1 = 1$ is asymptotically normal. However, large sample sizes are needed for the asymptotic normal distribution to hold. Standard Brownian motion is introduced in Chapter 6.

For many economic time series, ARIMA(p, d, q) models might be more appropriate than the simple model in Eq. (2.39). In the econometric literature, AR(p) models are often used. Denote the series by x_t. To verify the existence of a unit root in an AR(p) process, one may perform the test $H_o : \beta = 1$ versus $H_a : \beta < 1$ using the regression

$$x_t = c_t + \beta x_{t-1} + \sum_{i=1}^{p-1} \phi_i \Delta x_{t-i} + e_t, \tag{2.40}$$

where c_t is a deterministic function of the time index t and $\Delta x_j = x_j - x_{j-1}$ is the differenced series of x_t. In practice, c_t can be zero or a constant or $c_t = \omega_0 + \omega_1 t$. The t-ratio of $\hat{\beta} - 1$,

$$\text{ADF-test} = \frac{\hat{\beta} - 1}{\text{std}(\hat{\beta})},$$

where $\hat{\beta}$ denotes the least squares estimate of β, is the well-known *augmented Dickey–Fuller* unit-root test. Note that because of the first differencing, Eq. (2.40) is equivalent to an AR(p) model with deterministic function c_t. Equation (2.40) can also be rewritten as

$$\Delta x_t = c_t + \beta_c x_{t-1} + \sum_{i=1}^{p-1} \phi_i \Delta x_{t-i} + e_t,$$

where $\beta_c = \beta - 1$. One can then test the equivalent hypothesis $H_o : \beta_c = 0$ versus $H_a : \beta_c < 0$.

Example 2.2. Consider the log series of U.S. quarterly gross domestic product (GDP) from 1947.I to 2003.IV. The series exhibits an upward trend, showing the growth of the U.S. economy, and has high sample serial correlations; see the left panel of Figure 2.11. The first differenced series, representing the growth rate of U.S. GDP and also shown in Figure 2.11, seems to vary around a fixed mean level, even though the variability appears to be smaller in recent years. To confirm the observed phenomenon, we apply the augmented Dickey–Fuller unit-root test to the log series. Based on the sample PACF of the differenced series shown in

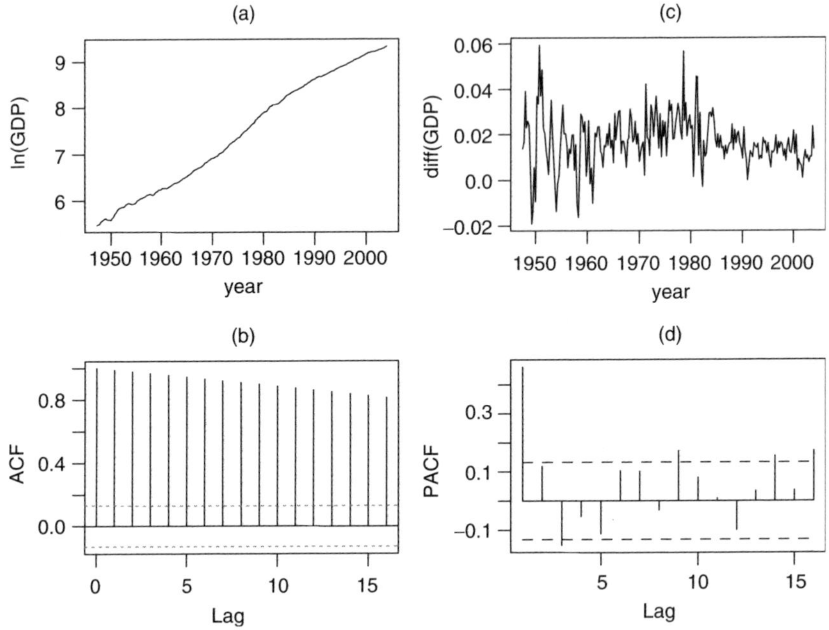

Figure 2.11. Log series of U.S. quarterly GDP from 1947.I to 2003.IV: (a) time plot of the logged GDP series, (b) sample ACF of the log GDP data, (c) time plot of the first differenced series, and (d) sample PACF of the differenced series.

Figure 2.11, we choose $p = 10$. Other values of p are also used, but they do not alter the conclusion of the test. With $p = 10$, the ADF-test statistic is -1.131 with p-value 0.7038, indicating that the unit-root hypothesis cannot be rejected. From the S-Plus output below, $\hat{\beta} = 1 + \hat{\beta}_c = 1 - 0.0006 = 0.9994$.

S-Plus Demonstration

Output edited.

```
> adft=unitroot(gdp,trend='c',method='adf',lags=10)
> summary(adft)

Test for Unit Root: Augmented DF Test

Null Hypothesis: there is a unit root
   Type of Test: t test
 Test Statistic: -1.131
        P-value: 0.7038

Coefficients:
           Value Std. Error t value Pr(>|t|)
    lag1 -0.0006  0.0006    -1.1306  0.2595
    lag2  0.3797  0.0679     5.5946  0.0000
```

```
   ...
   lag10  0.1798  0.0656     2.7405  0.0067
constant  0.0123  0.0048     2.5654  0.0110

Regression Diagnostics:

         R-Squared 0.2831
Adjusted R-Squared 0.2485

Residual standard error: 0.009498 on 214 degrees of freedom
```

As another example, consider the daily log series of the S&P 500 index from January 1990 to December 2003 for 3532 observations. The series is shown in Figure 2.12. Testing for a unit root in the index is relevant if one wishes to verify empirically that the index follows a random walk with drift. To this end, we use $c_t = \omega_0 + \omega_1 t$ in applying the augmented Dickey–Fuller test. Furthermore, we choose $p = 14$ because AIC selects an AR(13) model for the first differenced series. The resulting test statistic is -0.9648 with p-value 0.9469. Thus, the unit-root hypothesis cannot be rejected at any reasonable significance level. But the parameter estimates for the deterministic terms are not significantly different from zero at the usual 5% level. In summary, for the time period considered, the log series of the index contains a unit root, but there is no strong evidence of any time trend.

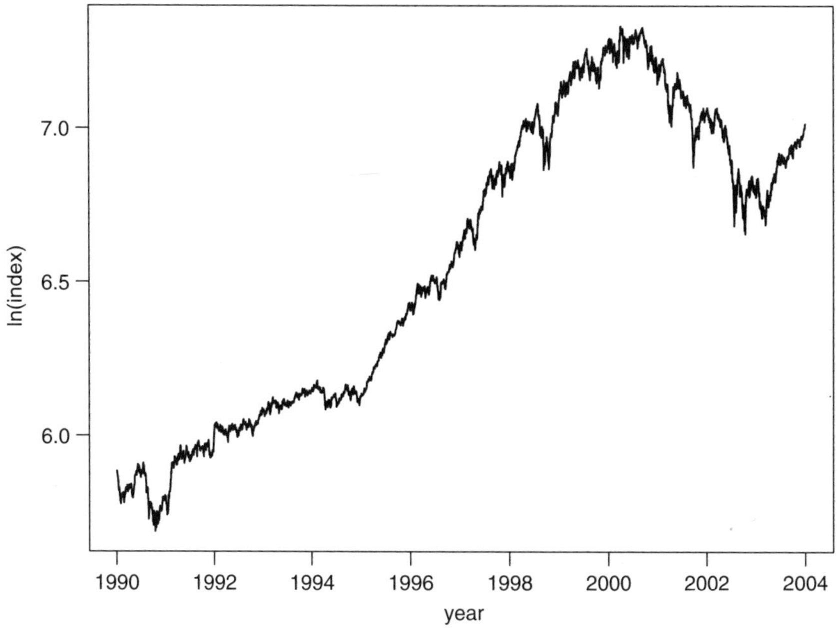

Figure 2.12. Time plot of the logarithm of daily S&P 500 index from January 2, 1990 to December 31, 2003.

S-Plus Demonstration

Output edited.

```
> adft=unitroot(sp,method='adf',trend='ct',lags=14)
> summary(adft)

Test for Unit Root: Augmented DF Test

Null Hypothesis: there is a unit root
   Type of Test: t test
 Test Statistic: -0.9648
        P-value: 0.9469

Coefficients:
           Value Std. Error t value Pr(>|t|)
    lag1 -0.0008  0.0008    -0.9648  0.3347
    ...
   lag14  0.0319  0.0169     1.8894  0.0589
constant  0.0056  0.0054     1.0316  0.3023
    time  0.0000  0.0000     0.4871  0.6262

Regression Diagnostics:

         R-Squared 0.0107
Adjusted R-Squared 0.0065

Residual standard error: 0.01049 on 3514 degrees of freedom
```

2.8 SEASONAL MODELS

Some financial time series such as quarterly earning per share of a company exhibits certain cyclical or periodic behavior. Such a time series is called a *seasonal time series*. Figure 2.13a shows the time plot of quarterly earning per share of Johnson and Johnson from the first quarter of 1960 to the last quarter of 1980. The data obtained from Shumway and Stoffer (2000) possess some special characteristics. In particular, the earning grew exponentially during the sample period and had a strong seasonality. Furthermore, the variability of earning increased over time. The cyclical pattern repeats itself every year so that the periodicity of the series is 4. If monthly data are considered (e.g., monthly sales of Wal-Mart stores), then the periodicity is 12. Seasonal time series models are also useful in pricing weather-related derivatives and energy futures, because most environmental time series exhibit strong seasonal behavior.

Analysis of seasonal time series has a long history. In some applications, seasonality is of secondary importance and is removed from the data, resulting in a seasonally adjusted time series that is then used to make inference. The procedure to remove seasonality from a time series is referred to as *seasonal adjustment*. Most economic data published by the U.S. government are seasonally adjusted (e.g., the growth rate of gross domestic product and the unemployment rate). In other applications such as forecasting, seasonality is as important as other characteristics of the data and must be handled accordingly. Because forecasting is a major objective of financial time series analysis, we focus on the latter approach and discuss some econometric models that are useful in modeling seasonal time series.

2.8.1 Seasonal Differencing

Figure 2.13b shows the time plot of log earning per share of Johnson and Johnson. We took the log transformation for two reasons. First, it is used to handle the exponential growth of the series. Indeed, the new plot confirms that the growth is linear on the log scale. Second, the transformation is used to stabilize the variability of the series. The increasing pattern in variability of Figure 2.13a disappears in the new plot. Log transformation is commonly used in analysis of financial and economic time series. In this particular instance, all earnings are positive so that no adjustment is needed before taking the transformation. In some cases, one may need to add a positive constant to every data point before taking the transformation.

Denote the log earning by x_t. The upper left panel of Figure 2.14 shows the sample ACF of x_t, which indicates that the quarterly log earning per share has strong serial correlations. A conventional method to handle such strong serial correlations

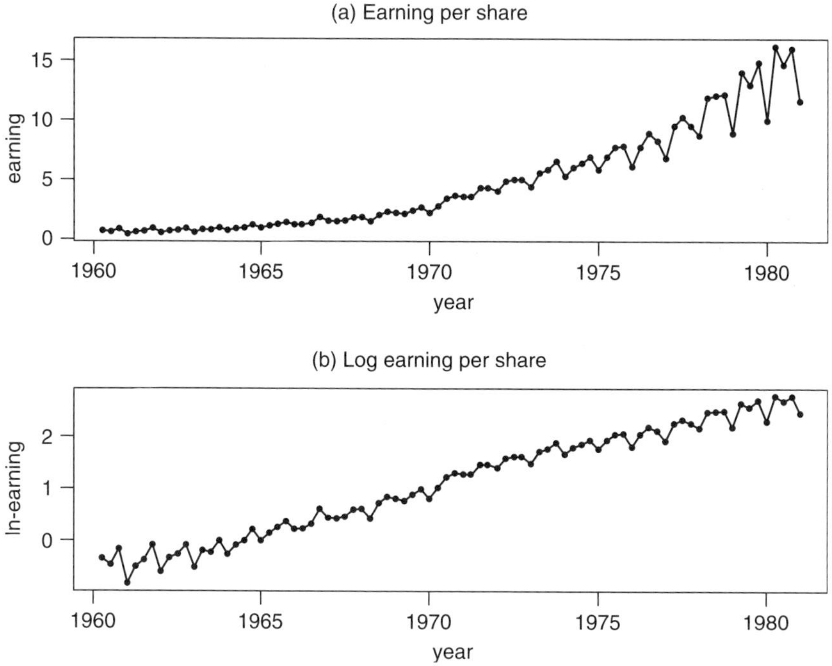

Figure 2.13. Time plots of quarterly earning per share of Johnson and Johnson from 1960 to 1980: (a) observed earning and (b) log earning.

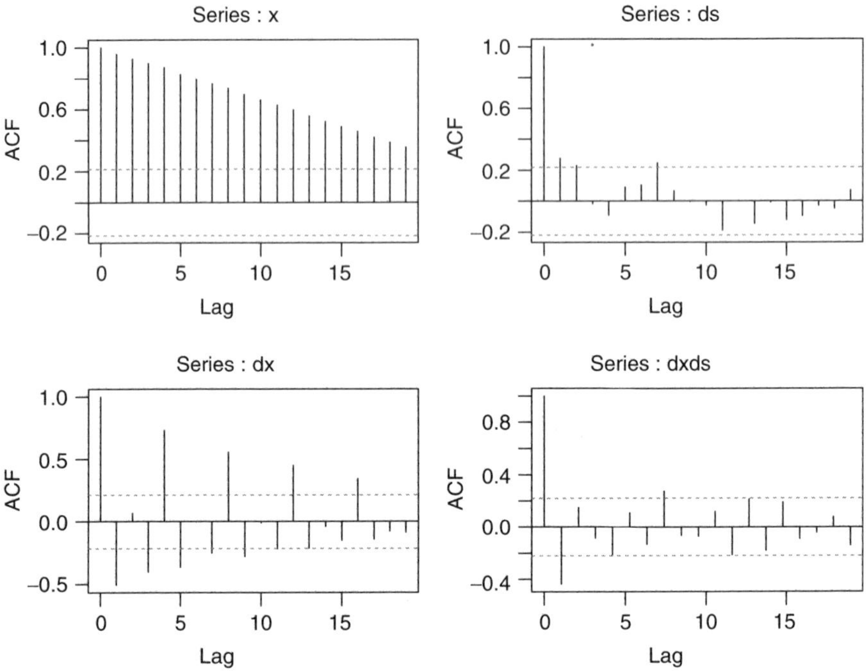

Figure 2.14. Sample ACF of the log series of quarterly earning per share of Johnson and Johnson from 1960 to 1980, where x_t is the log earning, dx is the first differenced series, ds is the seasonally differenced series, and dx ds denotes series with regular and seasonal differencing.

is to consider the first differenced series of x_t (i.e., $\Delta x_t = x_t - x_{t-1} = (1 - B)x_t$). The lower left plot of Figure 2.14 gives the sample ACF of Δx_t. The ACF is strong when the lag is a multiple of periodicity 4. This is a well-documented behavior of a sample ACF of a seasonal time series. Following the procedure of Box, Jenkins, and Reinsel (1994, Chapter 9), we take another difference of the data, that is,

$$\Delta_4(\Delta x_t) = (1 - B^4)\Delta x_t = \Delta x_t - \Delta x_{t-4} = x_t - x_{t-1} - x_{t-4} + x_{t-5}.$$

The operation $\Delta_4 = (1 - B^4)$ is called a *seasonal differencing*. In general, for a seasonal time series y_t with periodicity s, seasonal differencing means

$$\Delta_s y_t = y_t - y_{t-s} = (1 - B^s)y_t.$$

The conventional difference $\Delta y_t = y_t - y_{t-1} = (1 - B)y_t$ is referred to as the *regular differencing*. The lower right plot of Figure 2.14 shows the sample ACF of $\Delta_4 \Delta x_t$, which has a significant negative ACF at lag 1 and a marginal negative correlation at lag 4. For completeness, Figure 2.14 also gives the sample ACF of the seasonally differenced series $\Delta_4 x_t$.

2.8.2 Multiplicative Seasonal Models

The behavior of the sample ACF of $(1 - B^4)(1 - B)x_t$ in Figure 2.14 is common among seasonal time series. It led to the development of the following special seasonal time series model:

$$(1 - B^s)(1 - B)x_t = (1 - \theta B)(1 - \Theta B^s)a_t, \qquad (2.41)$$

where s is the periodicity of the series, a_t is a white noise series, $|\theta| < 1$, and $|\Theta| < 1$. This model is referred to as the *airline model* in the literature; see Box, Jenkins, and Reinsel (1994, Chapter 9). It has been found to be widely applicable in modeling seasonal time series. The AR part of the model simply consists of the regular and seasonal differences, whereas the MA part involves two parameters. Focusing on the MA part (i.e., on the model),

$$w_t = (1 - \theta B)(1 - \Theta B^s)a_t = a_t - \theta a_{t-1} - \Theta a_{t-s} + \theta\Theta a_{t-s-1},$$

where $w_t = (1 - B^s)(1 - B)x_t$ and $s > 1$. It is easy to obtain that $E(w_t) = 0$ and

$$\begin{aligned}
\mathrm{Var}(w_t) &= (1 + \theta^2)(1 + \Theta^2)\sigma_a^2, \\
\mathrm{Cov}(w_t, w_{t-1}) &= -\theta(1 + \Theta^2)\sigma_a^2, \\
\mathrm{Cov}(w_t, w_{t-s+1}) &= \theta\Theta\sigma_a^2, \\
\mathrm{Cov}(w_t, w_{t-s}) &= -\Theta(1 + \theta^2)\sigma_a^2, \\
\mathrm{Cov}(w_t, w_{t-s-1}) &= \theta\Theta\sigma_a^2, \\
\mathrm{Cov}(w_t, w_{t-\ell}) &= 0, \quad \text{for} \quad \ell \neq 0, 1, s - 1, s, s + 1.
\end{aligned}$$

Consequently, the ACF of the w_t series is given by

$$\rho_1 = \frac{-\theta}{1 + \theta^2}, \quad \rho_s = \frac{-\Theta}{1 + \Theta^2}, \quad \rho_{s-1} = \rho_{s+1} = \rho_1\rho_s = \frac{\theta\Theta}{(1 + \theta^2)(1 + \Theta^2)},$$

and $\rho_\ell = 0$ for $\ell > 0$ and $\ell \neq 1, s - 1, s, s + 1$. For example, if w_t is a quarterly time series, then $s = 4$ and for $\ell > 0$, the ACF ρ_ℓ is nonzero at lags 1, 3, 4, and 5 only.

It is interesting to compare the prior ACF with those of the MA(1) model $y_t = (1 - \theta B)a_t$ and the MA(s) model $z_t = (1 - \Theta B^s)a_t$. The ACFs of y_t and z_t series are

$$\rho_1(y) = \frac{-\theta}{1 + \theta^2}, \quad \text{and} \quad \rho_\ell(y) = 0, \quad \ell > 1,$$

$$\rho_s(z) = \frac{-\Theta}{1 + \Theta^2}, \quad \text{and} \quad \rho_\ell(z) = 0, \quad \ell > 0, \neq s.$$

We see that (a) $\rho_1 = \rho_1(y)$, (b) $\rho_s = \rho_s(z)$, and (c) $\rho_{s-1} = \rho_{s+1} = \rho_1(y) \times \rho_s(z)$. Therefore, the ACF of w_t at lags $(s - 1)$ and $(s + 1)$ can be regarded as the *interaction* between lag-1 and lag-s serial dependence, and the model of w_t is called a *multiplicative* seasonal MA model. In practice, a multiplicative seasonal model says that the dynamics of the regular and seasonal components of the series are approximately orthogonal.

The model

$$w_t = (1 - \theta B - \Theta B^s)a_t, \tag{2.42}$$

where $|\theta| < 1$ and $|\Theta| < 1$, is a nonmultiplicative seasonal MA model. It is easy to see that for the model in Eq. (2.42), $\rho_{s+1} = 0$. A multiplicative model is more parsimonious than the corresponding nonmultiplicative model because both models use the same number of parameters, but the multiplicative model has more nonzero ACFs.

Example 2.3. In this example we apply the airline model to the log series of quarterly earning per share of Johnson and Johnson from 1960 to 1980. Based on the exact likelihood method, the fitted model is

$$(1 - B)(1 - B^4)x_t = (1 - 0.678B)(1 - 0.314B^4)a_t, \quad \hat{\sigma}_a = 0.089,$$

where standard errors of the two MA parameters are 0.080 and 0.101, respectively. The Ljung–Box statistics of the residuals show $Q(12) = 10.0$ with p-value 0.44. The model appears to be adequate.

To illustrate the forecasting performance of the prior seasonal model, we reestimate the model using the first 76 observations and reserve the last eight data points for forecasting evaluation. We compute 1-step to 8-step ahead forecasts and their standard errors of the fitted model at the forecast origin $h = 76$. An antilog transformation is taken to obtain forecasts of earning per share using the relationship between normal and log-normal distributions given in Chapter 1. Figure 2.15 shows the forecast performance of the model, where the observed data are shown by the solid line, point forecasts are shown by dots, and the dashed lines show 95% interval forecasts. The forecasts show a strong seasonal pattern and are close to the observed data. Finally, for an alternative approach to modeling the quarterly earning data, see Section 11.7.

When the seasonal pattern of a time series is stable over time (e.g., close to a deterministic function), dummy variables may be used to handle the seasonality. This approach is taken by some analysts. However, deterministic seasonality is a special case of the multiplicative seasonal model discussed before. Specifically, if $\Theta = 1$, then model (2.41) contains a deterministic seasonal component. Consequently, the same forecasts are obtained by using either dummy variables or a multiplicative seasonal model when the seasonal pattern is deterministic. Yet use of dummy variables can lead to inferior forecasts if the seasonal pattern is not deterministic. In practice, we recommend that the exact likelihood method should be used to estimate a multiplicative seasonal model, especially when the sample

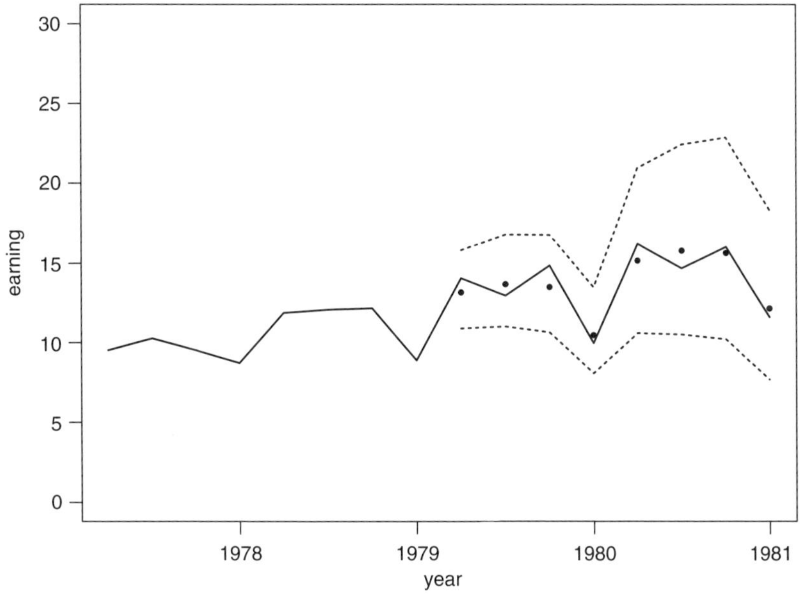

Figure 2.15. Out-of-sample point and interval forecasts for the quarterly earning of Johnson and Johnson. The forecast origin is the fourth quarter of 1978. In the plot, the solid line shows the actual observations, dots represent point forecasts, and dashed lines show 95% interval forecasts.

size is small or when there is the possibility of having a deterministic seasonal component.

Example 2.4. To demonstrate deterministic seasonal behavior, consider the monthly simple returns of the CRSP Decile 1 index from January 1960 to December 2003 for 528 observations. The series is shown in Figure 2.16a, and the time plot does not show any clear pattern of seasonality. However, the sample ACF of the return series shown in Figure 2.16b contains significant lags at 12, 24, and 36 as well as lag 1. If seasonal ARMA models are entertained, a model in the form

$$(1 - \phi_1 B)(1 - \phi_{12} B^{12}) R_t = c + (1 - \theta_{12} B^{12}) a_t$$

is identified, where R_t denotes the monthly simple return. Using the conditional likelihood method, the fitted model is

$$(1 - 0.25B)(1 - 0.99B^{12}) R_t = 0.0004 + (1 - 0.92B^{12}) a_t, \quad \tilde{\sigma}_a = 0.071.$$

The MA coefficient is close to unity, indicating that the fitted model is close to being noninvertible. If the exact likelihood method is used, we have

$$(1 - 0.264B)(1 - 0.996B^{12}) R_t = 0.0002 + (1 - 0.999B^{12}) a_t, \quad \tilde{\sigma}_a = 0.067.$$

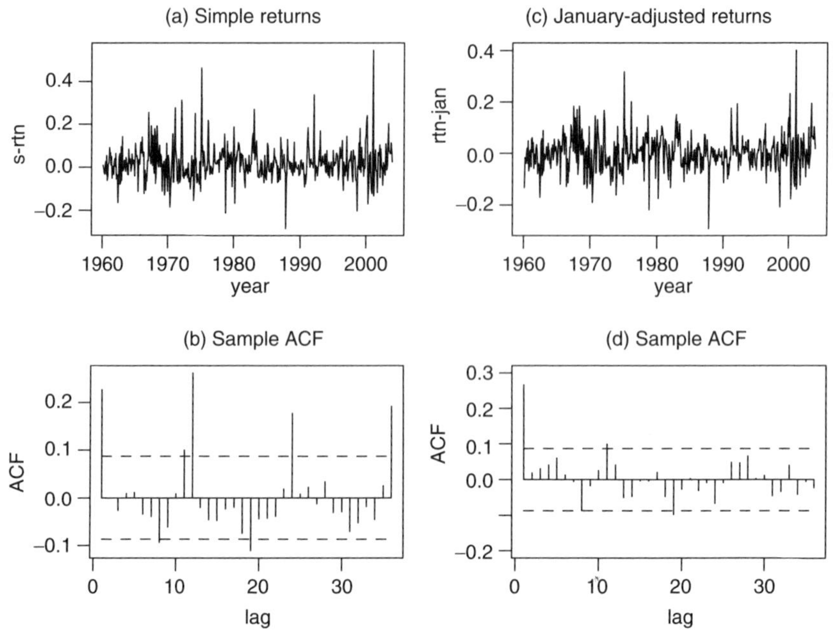

Figure 2.16. Monthly simple returns of CRSP Decile 1 index from January 1960 to December 2003: (a) time plot of the simple returns, (b) sample ACF of the simple returns, (c) time plot of the simple returns after adjusting for January effect, and (d) sample ACF of the adjusted simple returns.

The cancellation between seasonal AR and MA factors is clearly seen. This highlights the usefulness of using the exact likelihood method, and the estimation result suggests that the seasonal behavior might be deterministic. To further confirm this assertion, we define the dummy variable for January, that is,

$$\text{Jan}_t = \begin{cases} 1 & \text{if } t \text{ is January,} \\ 0 & \text{otherwise,} \end{cases}$$

and employ the simple liner regression

$$R_t = \beta_0 + \beta_1 \text{Jan}_t + e_t.$$

The right panel of Figure 2.16 shows the time plot and sample ACF of the residual series of the prior simple linear regression. From the sample ACF, there are no significant serial correlations at any multiples of 12, suggesting that the seasonal pattern has been successfully removed by the January dummy variable. Consequently, the seasonal behavior in the monthly simple return of Decile 1 is due to the *January effect*.

SCA Demonstration

Output edited.

```
tsm m1. model (1)(12)dec1=c1+(12)noise.
 --
estim m1. hold resi(r1)

 SUMMARY FOR UNIVARIATE TIME SERIES MODEL --    M1
 -----------------------------------------------------------
 VAR  TYPE OF   ORIGINAL    DIFFERENCING
      VARIABLE OR CENTERED

 DEC1 RANDOM     ORIGINAL     NONE
 -----------------------------------------------------------
PAR.   VAR.  NUM./  FACTOR  ORDER  CONS-    VALUE  STD    T
LABEL  NAME  DENOM.                TRAINT          ERROR  VALUE

1     C1      CNST      1      0    NONE   .0004  .0003   1.11
2     DEC1     MA       1     12    NONE   .9213  .0205  44.90
3     DEC1     AR       1      1    NONE   .2496  .0419   5.95
4     DEC1     AR       2     12    NONE   .9943  .0094 105.71

 EFFECTIVE NUMBER OF OBSERVATIONS . .            515
 R-SQUARE . . . . . . . . . . . . . .          0.207
 RESIDUAL STANDARD ERROR. . . . . . .   0.705662E-01
 --
estim m1. method exact. hold resi(r1)

SUMMARY FOR UNIVARIATE TIME SERIES MODEL --    M1
-----------------------------------------------------------
VAR.    TYPE OF   ORIGINAL    DIFFERENCING
        VAR.     OR CENTERED

DEC1   RANDOM     ORIGINAL     NONE
 -----------------------------------------------------------
PAR.   VARI.  NUM./  FACTOR ORDER  CONS-    VALUE  STD     T
LABEL  NAME   DENOM.               TRAINT          ERROR  VALUE

1     C1      CNST      1      0   NONE   .0002  .0002    .67
2     DEC1     MA       1     12   NONE   .9989  .0156 63.99
3     DEC1     AR       1      1   NONE   .2638  .0424  6.23
4     DEC1     AR       2     12   NONE   .9963  .0058 170.55

 EFFECTIVE NUMBER OF OBSERVATIONS . .            515
 R-SQUARE . . . . . . . . . . . . . .          0.283
 RESIDUAL STANDARD ERROR. . . . . . .   0.670734E-01
```

2.9 REGRESSION MODELS WITH TIME SERIES ERRORS

In many applications, the relationship between two time series is of major interest. The market model in finance is an example that relates the return of an individual stock to the return of a market index. The term structure of interest rates is another example in which the time evolution of the relationship between interest rates with different maturities is investigated. These examples lead to the consideration of a linear regression in the form

$$r_{1t} = \alpha + \beta r_{2t} + e_t, \tag{2.43}$$

where r_{1t} and r_{2t} are two time series and e_t denotes the error term. The least squares (LS) method is often used to estimate model (2.43). If $\{e_t\}$ is a white noise series, then the LS method produces consistent estimates. In practice, however, it is common to see that the error term e_t is serially correlated. In this case, we have a regression model with time series errors, and the LS estimates of α and β may not be consistent.

A regression model with time series errors is widely applicable in economics and finance, but it is one of the most commonly misused econometric models because the serial dependence in e_t is often overlooked. It pays to study the model carefully.

We introduce the model by considering the relationship between two U.S. weekly interest rate series:

- r_{1t}, the 1-year Treasury constant maturity rate.
- r_{3t}, the 3-year Treasury constant maturity rate.

Both series have 1967 observations from January 4, 1962 to September 10, 1999 and are measured in percentages. The series are obtained from the Federal Reserve Bank of St. Louis. Strictly speaking, we should model the two interest series jointly using multivariate time series analysis in Chapter 8. However, for simplicity, we focus here on regression-type analysis and ignore the issue of simultaneity.

Figure 2.17 shows the time plots of the two interest rates with the solid line denoting the 1-year rate and the dashed line the 3-year rate. Figure 2.18a plots r_{1t} versus r_{3t}, indicating that, as expected, the two interest rates are highly correlated. A naive way to describe the relationship between the two interest rates is to use the simple model $r_{3t} = \alpha + \beta r_{1t} + e_t$. This results in a fitted model

$$r_{3t} = 0.911 + 0.924 r_{1t} + e_t, \quad \hat{\sigma}_e = 0.538, \tag{2.44}$$

with $R^2 = 95.8\%$, where the standard errors of the two coefficients are 0.032 and 0.004, respectively. Model (2.44) confirms the high correlation between the two interest rates. However, the model is seriously inadequate as shown by Figure 2.19, which gives the time plot and ACF of its residuals. In particular, the sample ACF of the residuals is highly significant and decays slowly, showing the pattern of

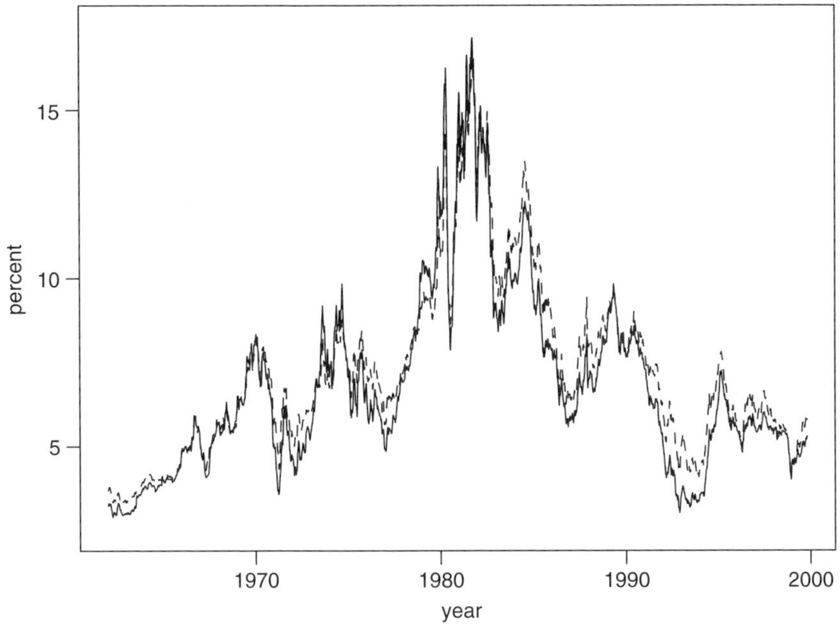

Figure 2.17. Time plots of U.S. weekly interest rates (in percentages) from January 4, 1962 to September 10, 1999. The solid line is the Treasury 1-year constant maturity rate and the dashed line the Treasury 3-year constant maturity rate.

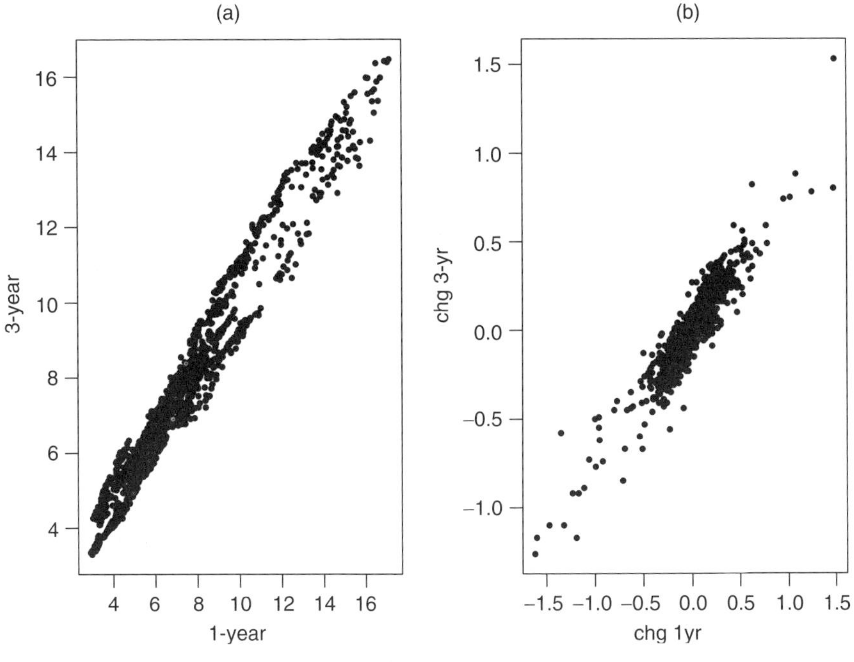

Figure 2.18. Scatterplots of U.S. weekly interest rates from January 5, 1962 to September 10, 1999: (a) 3-year rate versus 1-year rate and (b) changes in 3-year rate versus changes in 1-year rate.

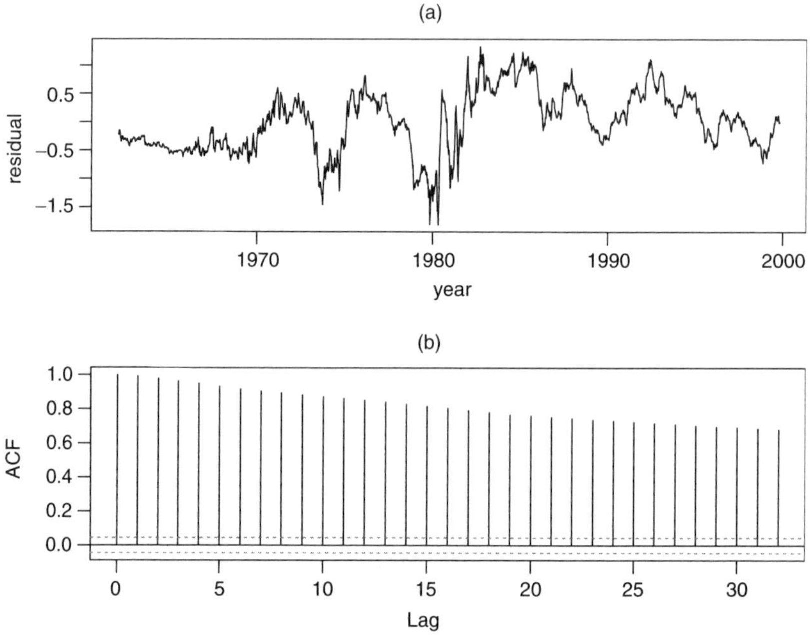

Figure 2.19. Residual series of linear regression (2.44) for two U.S. weekly interest rates: (a) time plot and (b) sample ACF.

a unit-root nonstationary time series. The behavior of the residuals suggests that marked differences exist between the two interest rates. Using modern econometric terminology, if one assumes that the two interest rate series are unit-root nonstationary, then the behavior of the residuals of Eq. (2.44) indicates that the two interest rates are not *cointegrated*; see Chapter 8 for discussion of cointegration. In other words, the data fail to support the hypothesis that there exists a long-term equilibrium between the two interest rates. In some sense, this is not surprising because the pattern of "inverted yield curve" did occur during the data span. By inverted yield curve, we mean the situation under which interest rates are inversely related to their time to maturities.

The unit-root behavior of both interest rates and the residuals of Eq. (2.44) leads to consideration of the change series of interest rates. Let

1. $c_{1t} = r_{1t} - r_{1,t-1} = (1 - B)r_{1t}$ for $t \geq 2$: changes in the 1-year interest rate;
2. $c_{3t} = r_{3t} - r_{3,t-1} = (1 - B)r_{3t}$ for $t \geq 2$: changes in the 3-year interest rate;

and consider the linear regression $c_{3t} = \alpha + \beta c_{1t} + e_t$. Figure 2.20 shows time plots of the two change series, whereas Figure 2.18b provides a scatterplot between them. The change series remain highly correlated with a fitted linear regression model given by

$$c_{3t} = 0.0002 + 0.7811 c_{1t} + e_t, \quad \hat{\sigma}_e = 0.0682, \tag{2.45}$$

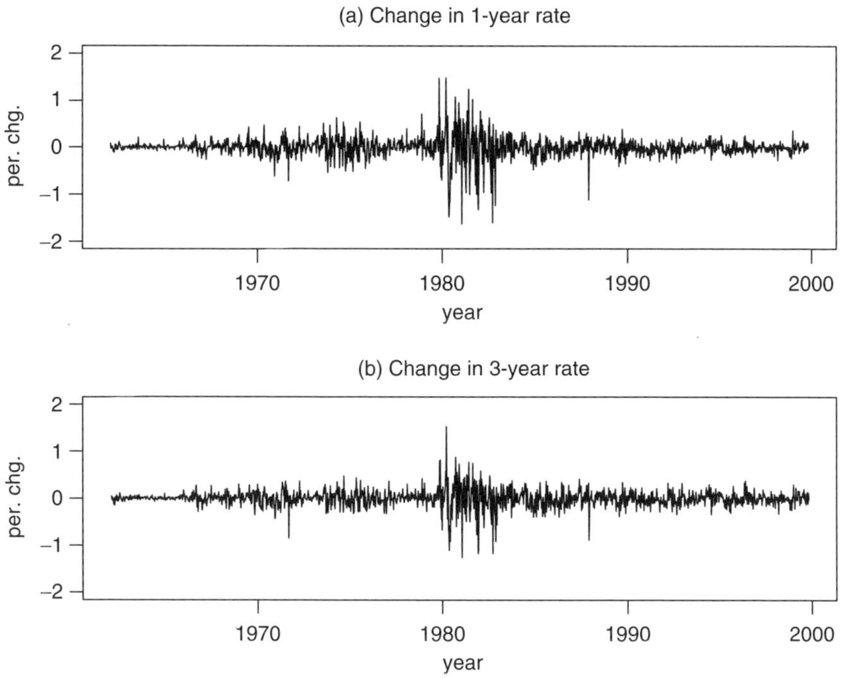

Figure 2.20. Time plots of the change series of U.S. weekly interest rates from January 12, 1962 to September 10, 1999: (a) changes in the Treasury 1-year constant maturity rate and (b) changes in the Treasury 3-year constant maturity rate.

with $R^2 = 84.8\%$. The standard errors of the two coefficients are 0.0015 and 0.0075, respectively. This model further confirms the strong linear dependence between interest rates. Figure 2.21 shows the time plot and sample ACF of the residuals of Eq. (2.45). Once again, the ACF shows some significant serial correlation in the residuals, but the magnitude of the correlation is much smaller. This weak serial dependence in the residuals can be modeled by using the simple time series models discussed in the previous sections, and we have a linear regression with time series errors.

The main objective of this section is to discuss a simple approach for building a linear regression model with time series errors. The approach is straightforward. We employ a simple time series model discussed in this chapter for the residual series and estimate the whole model jointly. For illustration, consider the simple linear regression in Eq. (2.45). Because residuals of the model are serially correlated, we shall identify a simple ARMA model for the residuals. From the sample ACF of the residuals shown in Figure 2.21, we specify an MA(1) model for the residuals and modify the linear regression model to

$$c_{3t} = \alpha + \beta c_{1t} + e_t, \quad e_t = a_t - \theta_1 a_{t-1}, \tag{2.46}$$

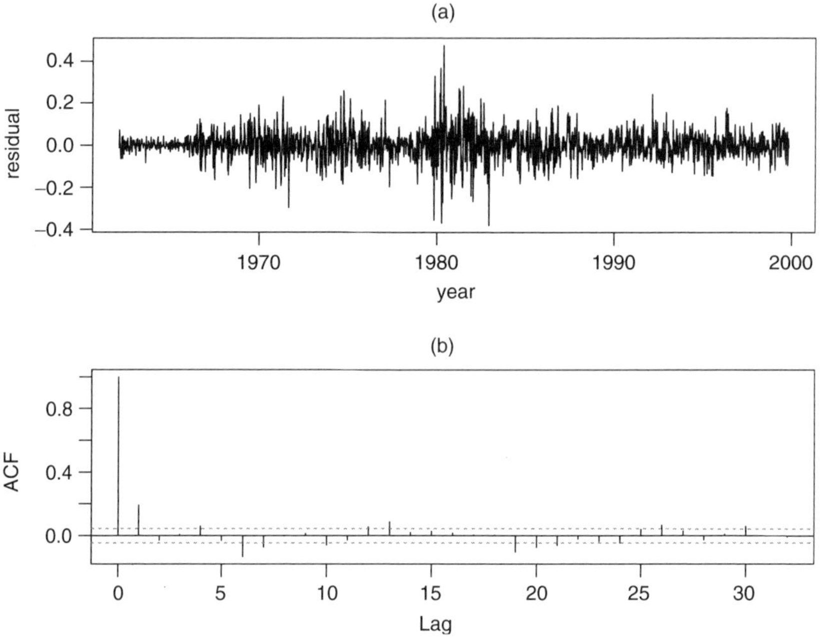

Figure 2.21. Residual series of the linear regression (2.45) for two change series of U.S. weekly interest rates: (a) time plot and (b) sample ACF.

where $\{a_t\}$ is assumed to be a white noise series. In other words, we simply use an MA(1) model, without the constant term, to capture the serial dependence in the error term of Eq. (2.45). The resulting model is a simple example of linear regression with time series errors. In practice, more elaborated time series models can be added to a linear regression equation to form a general regression model with time series errors.

Estimating a regression model with time series errors was not easy before the advent of modern computers. Special methods such as the Cochrane–Orcutt estimator have been proposed to handle the serial dependence in the residuals; see Greene (2000, p. 546). By now, the estimation is as easy as that of other time series models. If the time series model used is stationary and invertible, then one can estimate the model jointly via the maximum likelihood method. This is the approach we take by using the SCA package. S-Plus demonstration is given later. For the U.S. weekly interest rate data, the fitted version of model (2.46) is

$$c_{3t} = 0.0002 + 0.7824c_{1t} + e_t, \quad e_t = a_t + 0.2115a_{t-1}, \quad \hat{\sigma}_a = 0.0668, \quad (2.47)$$

with $R^2 = 85.4\%$. The standard errors of the parameters are 0.0018, 0.0077, and 0.0221, respectively. The model no longer has a significant lag-1 residual ACF, even though some minor residual serial correlations remain at lags 4 and 6. The incremental improvement of adding additional MA parameters at lags 4 and 6 to the residual equation is small and the result is not reported here.

Comparing the models in Eqs. (2.44), (2.45), and (2.47), we make the following observations. First, the high R^2 and coefficient 0.924 of model (2.44) are misleading because the residuals of the model show strong serial correlations. Second, for the change series, R^2 and the coefficient of c_{1t} of models (2.45) and (2.47) are close. In this particular instance, adding the MA(1) model to the change series only provides a marginal improvement. This is not surprising because the estimated MA coefficient is small numerically, even though it is statistically highly significant. Third, the analysis demonstrates that it is important to check residual serial dependence in linear regression analysis.

Because the constant term of Eq. (2.47) is insignificant, the model shows that the two weekly interest rate series are related as

$$r_{3t} = r_{3,t-1} + 0.782(r_{1t} - r_{1,t-1}) + a_t + 0.212a_{t-1}.$$

The interest rates are concurrently and serially correlated.

Summary

We outline a general procedure for analyzing linear regression models with time series errors:

1. Fit the linear regression model and check serial correlations of the residuals.
2. If the residual series is unit-root nonstationary, take the first difference of both the dependent and explanatory variables. Go to step 1. If the residual series appears to be stationary, identify an ARMA model for the residuals and modify the linear regression model accordingly.
3. Perform a joint estimation via the maximum likelihood method and check the fitted model for further improvement.

To check the serial correlations of residuals, we recommend that the Ljung–Box statistics be used instead of the Durbin–Watson (DW) statistic because the latter only considers the lag-1 serial correlation. There are cases in which residual serial dependence appears at higher order lags. This is particularly so when the time series involved exhibits some seasonal behavior.

Remark. For a residual series e_t with T observations, the Durbin–Watson statistic is

$$\text{DW} = \frac{\sum_{t=2}^{T}(e_t - e_{t-1})^2}{\sum_{t=1}^{T} e_t^2}.$$

Straightforward calculation shows that $\text{DW} \approx 2(1 - \hat{\rho}_1)$, where $\hat{\rho}_1$ is the lag-1 ACF of $\{e_t\}$.

In S-Plus, regression models with time series errors can be analyzed by the command `OLS` (ordinary least squares) if the residuals assume an AR model. Also, to identify a lagged variable, the command is `tslag`, for example, `y = tslag(r,1)`. For the interest rate series, the relevant commands are given below, where % denotes explanation of the command. □

```
> da=matrix(scan(file='w-gs1n36299.txt'),3)  %load data
> r1t=da[1,]
> r3t=da[2,]
> fit=OLS(r3t~r1t)      % fit the first regression
> summary(fit)
> c3t=diff(r3t)         % take difference
> c1t=diff(r1t)
> fit1=OLS(c3t~c1t)     % fit second regression
> summary(fit1)
> fit2=OLS(c3t~c1t+tslag(c3t,1)+tslag(c1t,1), na.rm=T)
> summary(fit2)
```

See the output in the next section for more information.

2.10 CONSISTENT COVARIANCE MATRIX ESTIMATION

Consider again the regression model in Eq. (2.43). There may exist situations in which the error term e_t has serial correlations and/or conditional heteroscedasticity, but the main objective of the analysis is to make inference concerning the regression coefficients α and β. See Chapter 3 for discussion of conditional heteroscedasticity. In situations under which the ordinary least squares estimates of the coefficients remain consistent, methods are available to provide consistent estimate of the covariance matrix of the coefficients. Two such methods are widely used. The first method is called heteroscedasticity consistent (HC) estimator; see Eicker (1967) and White (1980). The second method is called heteroscedasticity and autocorrelation consistent (HAC) estimator; see Newey and West (1987).

For ease in discussion, we shall rewrite the regression model as

$$y_t = \boldsymbol{x}_t'\boldsymbol{\beta} + e_t, \quad t = 1, \ldots, T, \tag{2.48}$$

where y_t is the dependent variable, $\boldsymbol{x}_t = (x_{1t}, \ldots, x_{kt})'$ is a k-dimensional vector of explanatory variables including constant, and $\boldsymbol{\beta} = (\beta_1, \ldots, \beta_k)'$ is the parameter vector. Here $\boldsymbol{c}'$ denotes the transpose of the vector $\boldsymbol{c}$. The LS estimate of $\boldsymbol{\beta}$ and the associated covariance matrix are

$$\hat{\boldsymbol{\beta}} = \left[\sum_{t=1}^{T} \boldsymbol{x}_t\boldsymbol{x}_t'\right]^{-1} \sum_{t=1}^{T} \boldsymbol{x}_t y_t, \quad \text{Cov}(\hat{\boldsymbol{\beta}}) = \sigma_e^2 \left[\sum_{t=1}^{T} \boldsymbol{x}_t\boldsymbol{x}_t'\right]^{-1},$$

where σ_e^2 is the variance of e_t and is estimated by the variance of the residuals of the regression. In the presence of serial correlations or conditional heteroscedasticity, the prior covariance matrix estimator is inconsistent, often resulting in inflating the t-ratios of $\hat{\boldsymbol{\beta}}$.

The estimator of White (1980) is

$$\text{Cov}(\hat{\boldsymbol{\beta}})_{\text{HC}} = \left[\sum_{t=1}^{T} \boldsymbol{x}_t\boldsymbol{x}_t'\right]^{-1} \left[\frac{T}{T-k}\sum_{t=1}^{T} \hat{e}_t^2 \boldsymbol{x}_t\boldsymbol{x}_t'\right]\left[\sum_{t=1}^{T} \boldsymbol{x}_t\boldsymbol{x}_t'\right]^{-1}, \tag{2.49}$$

where $\hat{e}_t = y_t - \boldsymbol{x}_t'\hat{\boldsymbol{\beta}}$ is the residual at time t. The estimator of Newey and West (1987) is

$$\text{Cov}(\hat{\boldsymbol{\beta}})_{\text{HAC}} = \left[\sum_{t=1}^{T} \boldsymbol{x}_t\boldsymbol{x}_t'\right]^{-1} \hat{\boldsymbol{C}}_{\text{HAC}}\left[\sum_{t=1}^{T} \boldsymbol{x}_t\boldsymbol{x}_t'\right]^{-1}, \tag{2.50}$$

where

$$\hat{\boldsymbol{C}}_{\text{HAC}} = \sum_{t=1}^{T} \hat{e}_t^2\boldsymbol{x}_t\boldsymbol{x}_t' + \sum_{j=1}^{\ell} w_j \sum_{t=j+1}^{T} (\boldsymbol{x}_t\hat{e}_t\hat{e}_{t-j}\boldsymbol{x}_{t-j}' + \boldsymbol{x}_{t-j}\hat{e}_{t-j}\hat{e}_t\boldsymbol{x}_t'),$$

where ℓ is a truncation parameter and w_j is a weight function such as the Bartlett weight function defined by

$$w_j = 1 - \frac{j}{\ell+1}.$$

Other weight functions can also be used. Newey and West suggest choosing ℓ to be the integer part of $4(T/100)^{2/9}$. This estimator essentially uses a nonparametric method to estimate the covariance matrix of $\left\{\sum_{t=1}^{T} \hat{e}_t\boldsymbol{x}_t\right\}$.

For illustration, we employ the first differenced interest rate series in Eq. (2.45). The t-ratio of the coefficient of c_{1t} is 104.63 if both serial correlation and heteroscedasticity in residuals are ignored; it becomes 46.73 when the HC estimator is used, and it reduces to 40.08 when the HAC estimator is used. The S-Plus demonstration below also uses a regression that includes lagged values $c_{1,t-1}$ and $c_{3,t-1}$ as regressors to take care of serial correlations in the residuals.

S-Plus Demonstration

% denotes explanation.

```
> x=matrix(scan(file='w-gs1n36299.txt'),3)  % Load data
> gs1=x[1,]     % 1-year interest rate
> gs3=x[2,]     %  3-year interest rate
> dgs3=diff(gs3)
> dgs1=diff(gs1)
```

```
> reg.fit=OLS(dgs3~dgs1)  % Fit a simple linear regression
> summary(reg.fit)

Call:
OLS(formula = dgs3 ~ dgs1)

Residuals:
     Min       1Q  Median      3Q     Max
 -0.3806 -0.0334 -0.0005  0.0344  0.4742

Coefficients:
               Value Std. Error  t value Pr(>|t|)
(Intercept)   0.0002   0.0015     0.1609   0.8722
       dgs1   0.7811   0.0075   104.6283   0.0000

Regression Diagnostics:

         R-Squared 0.8479
Adjusted R-Squared 0.8478
Durbin-Watson Stat 1.6158

> summary(reg.fit,correction="white")  % Use HC estimator

Coefficients:
              Value Std. Error t value Pr(>|t|)
(Intercept)  0.0002  0.0015     0.1609  0.8722
       dgs1  0.7811  0.0167    46.7260  0.0000

> summary(reg.fit,correction="nw")  % Use HAC estimator

Coefficients:
              Value Std. Error t value Pr(>|t|)
(Intercept)  0.0002  0.0017     0.1436  0.8858
       dgs1  0.7811  0.0195    40.0841  0.0000

  % Below, fit a regression model with time series error
> reg.ts=OLS(dgs3~dgs1+tslag(dgs3,1)+tslag(dgs1,1),na.rm=T)
> summary(reg.ts)

Call:
OLS(formula = dgs3~dgs1+tslag(dgs3,1)+tslag(dgs1,1), na.rm = T)

Residuals:
     Min       1Q  Median      3Q     Max
 -0.3652 -0.0329 -0.0005  0.0333  0.4506

Coefficients:
                     Value Std. Error   t value  Pr(>|t|)
   (Intercept)      0.0002     0.0015    0.1426    0.8866
```

```
           dgs1    0.7851   0.0078  100.4694   0.0000
tslag(dgs3, 1)    0.1920   0.0221    8.6685   0.0000
tslag(dgs1, 1)   -0.1634   0.0190   -8.6219   0.0000

Regression Diagnostics:

         R-Squared 0.8537
Adjusted R-Squared 0.8535
Durbin-Watson Stat 1.9740
```

2.11 LONG-MEMORY MODELS

We have discussed that for a stationary time series the ACF decays exponentially to zero as lag increases. Yet for a unit-root nonstationary time series, it can be shown that the sample ACF converges to 1 for all fixed lags as the sample size increases; see Chan and Wei (1988) and Tiao and Tsay (1983). There exist some time series whose ACF decays slowly to zero at a polynomial rate as the lag increases. These processes are referred to as long-memory time series. One such example is the fractionally differenced process defined by

$$(1-B)^d x_t = a_t, \quad -0.5 < d < 0.5, \tag{2.51}$$

where $\{a_t\}$ is a white noise series. Properties of model (2.51) have been widely studied in the literature (e.g., Hosking, 1981). We summarize some of these properties below.

1. If $d < 0.5$, then x_t is a weakly stationary process and has the infinite MA representation

$$x_t = a_t + \sum_{i=1}^{\infty} \psi_i a_{t-i}, \quad \text{with} \quad \psi_k = \frac{d(1+d)\cdots(k-1+d)}{k!}$$
$$= \frac{(k+d-1)!}{k!(d-1)!}.$$

2. If $d > -0.5$, then x_t is invertible and has the infinite AR representation

$$x_t = \sum_{i=1}^{\infty} \pi_i x_{t-i} + a_t, \quad \text{with} \quad \pi_k = \frac{-d(1-d)\cdots(k-1-d)}{k!}$$
$$= \frac{(k-d-1)!}{k!(-d-1)!}.$$

3. For $-0.5 < d < 0.5$, the ACF of x_t is

$$\rho_k = \frac{d(1+d)\cdots(k-1+d)}{(1-d)(2-d)\cdots(k-d)}, \quad k = 1, 2, \ldots.$$

In particular, $\rho_1 = d/(1-d)$ and

$$\rho_k \approx \frac{(-d)!}{(d-1)!} k^{2d-1}, \quad \text{as} \quad k \to \infty.$$

4. For $-0.5 < d < 0.5$, the PACF of x_t is $\phi_{k,k} = d/(k-d)$ for $k = 1, 2, \ldots$.
5. For $-0.5 < d < 0.5$, the spectral density function $f(\omega)$ of x_t, which is the Fourier transform of the ACF of x_t, satisfies

$$f(\omega) \sim \omega^{-2d}, \quad \text{as} \quad \omega \to 0, \tag{2.52}$$

where $\omega \in [0, 2\pi]$ denotes the frequency.

Of particular interest here is the behavior of the ACF of x_t when $d < 0.5$. The property says that $\rho_k \sim k^{2d-1}$, which decays at a polynomial, instead of exponential, rate. For this reason, such an x_t process is called a long-memory time series. A special characteristic of the spectral density function in Eq. (2.52) is that the spectrum diverges to infinity as $\omega \to 0$. However, the spectral density function of a stationary ARMA process is bounded for all $\omega \in [0, 2\pi]$.

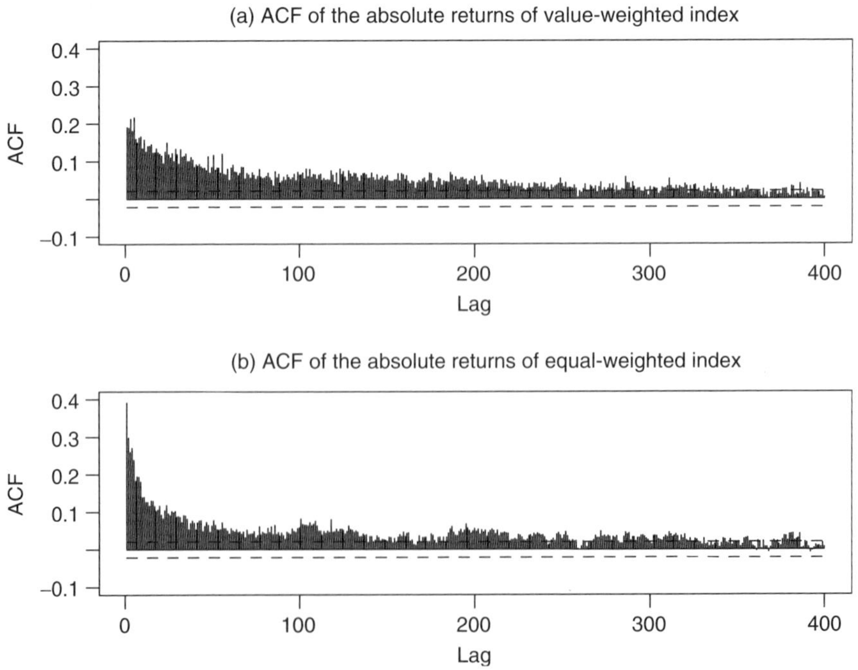

Figure 2.22. Sample autocorrelation function of the absolute series of daily simple returns for the CRSP value- and equal-weighted indexes: (a) the value-weighted index return and (b) the equal-weighted index return. The sample period is from July 3, 1962 to December 31, 1997.

Earlier we used the binomial theorem for noninteger powers

$$(1-B)^d = \sum_{k=0}^{\infty}(-1)^k \binom{d}{k} B^k, \quad \binom{d}{k} = \frac{d(d-1)\cdots(d-k+1)}{k!}.$$

If the fractionally differenced series $(1-B)^d x_t$ follows an ARMA(p, q) model, then x_t is called an ARFIMA(p, d, q) process, which is a generalized ARIMA model by allowing for noninteger d.

In practice, if the sample ACF of a time series is not large in magnitude, but decays slowly, then the series may have long memory. As an illustration, Figure 2.22 shows the sample ACFs of the absolute series of daily simple returns for the CRSP value- and equal-weighted indexes from July 3, 1962 to December 31, 1997. The ACFs are relatively small in magnitude but decay very slowly; they appear to be significant at the 5% level even after 300 lags. For more information about the behavior of sample ACFs of absolute return series, see Ding, Granger, and Engle (1993). For the pure fractionally differenced model in Eq. (2.51), one can estimate d using either a maximum likelihood method or a regression method with logged periodogram at the lower frequencies. Finally, long-memory models have attracted some attention in the finance literature in part because of the work on fractional Brownian motion in the continuous-time models.

APPENDIX: SOME SCA COMMANDS

Commands Used in Section 2.4

The data file is '`m-vw.txt`' and comments start with '–'. These comments explain the function of each command.

```
-- load data into SCA and denote the series by vw.
input vw. file 'm-vw.txt'
-- compute 10 lags of PACF.
pacf vw. maxl 10.
-- compute AIC for AR(1) to AR(10).
miden vw. no ccm. arfits 1 to 10.
-- specify an AR(3) model and denote the model by m1.
tsm m1. model (1,2,3)vw=c0+noise.
-- estimate the model and store the residuals in r1.
estim m1. hold resi(r1)
-- compute ACF of the residuals, including Q statistics.
acf r1.
-- refine the model to an AR(5).
tsm m1. model (1,2,3,4,5)vw=c0+noise.
-- estimate the model and store the residuals in r1.
estim m1. hold resi(r1)
-- compute ACF of the residuals.
acf r1. maxl 10.
```

```
-- compute p-value of the Q(5) statistic.
p=1.0-cdfc(11.2,5)
-- print p-value.
print p
-- re-estimate the model using the first 858 observations.
estim m1. span 1,858.
-- compute 1-step to 6-step ahead forecasts at origin 858.
ufore m1. orig 858. nofs 6.
-- quit SCA.
stop
```

Commands Used in Section 2.9

The 1-year maturity interest rates are in the file '`wgs1yr.txt`' and the 3-year rates are in the file '`wgs3yr.txt`'.

```
-- load data into SCA, denote the data by rate1 and rate3.
input date, rate1. file 'wgs1yr.txt'
--
input date,rate3. file 'wgs3yr.txt'
-- specify a simple linear regression model.
tsm m1. model rate3=b0+(b1)rate1+noise.
-- estimate the specified model and store residual in r1.
estim m1. hold resi(r1).
-- compute 10 lags of residual acf.
acf r1. maxl 10.
--difference the series & denote the new ones by c1t and c3t
diff old rate1,rate3. new c1t, c3t. compress.
--specify a linear regression model for the differenced data
tsm m2. model c3t=h0+(h1)c1t+noise.
-- estimation
estim m2. hold resi(r2).
-- compute residual acf.
acf r2. maxl 10.
-- specify a regression model with time series errors.
tsm m3. model c3t=g0+(g1)c1t+(1)noise.
-- estimate the model using the exact likelihood method.
estim m3. method exact. hold resi(r3).
-- compute residual acf.
acf r3. maxl 10.
-- refine the model to include more MA lags.
tsm m4. model c3t=g0+(g1)c1t+(1,4,6)noise.
-- estimation
estim m4. method exact. hold resi(r4).
-- compute residual acf.
acf r4. maxl 10.
-- exit SCA
stop
```

EXERCISES

If not specifically specified, use 5% significance level to draw conclusions in the exercises.

2.1. Suppose that the simple return of a monthly bond index follows the MA(1) model

$$R_t = a_t + 0.2a_{t-1}, \quad \sigma_a = 0.025.$$

Assume that $a_{100} = 0.01$. Compute the 1-step and 2-step ahead forecasts of the return at the forecast origin $t = 100$. What are the standard deviations of the associated forecast errors? Also compute the lag-1 and lag-2 autocorrelations of the return series.

2.2. Suppose that the daily log return of a security follows the model

$$r_t = 0.01 + 0.2r_{t-2} + a_t,$$

where $\{a_t\}$ is a Gaussian white noise series with mean zero and variance 0.02. What are the mean and variance of the return series r_t? Compute the lag-1 and lag-2 autocorrelations of r_t. Assume that $r_{100} = -0.01$, and $r_{99} = 0.02$. Compute the 1-step and 2-step ahead forecasts of the return series at the forecast origin $t = 100$. What are the associated standard deviations of the forecast errors?

2.3. Consider the monthly U.S. unemployment rate from January 1951 to February 2004 in the file `m-unemhelp.txt`. The data are seasonally adjusted and obtained from the Federal Reserve Bank in St. Louis. Build a time series model for the series and use the model to forecast the unemployment rate for March, April, and May of 2004. In addition, compute the average period of business cycles if they exist. (Note that more than one model fit the data well. You only need an adequate model.)

2.4. Consider the monthly simple returns of the Decile 1, Decile 5, and Decile 10 of NYSE/AMEX/NASDAQ based on market capitalization. The data span is from January 1960 to December 2003, and the data are obtained from CRSP.

(a) For each return series, test the null hypothesis that the first 12 lags of autocorrelations are zero at the 5% level. Draw your conclusion.

(b) Build an AR and an MA model for the series of Decile 5.

(c) Use the AR and MA models built to produce 1-step to 3-step ahead forecasts of the series.

2.5. Consider the daily simple returns of IBM stock from 1962 to 2002 in the file `d-ibmvwew6202.txt`. Compute the first 100 lags of the ACF of the absolute daily simple returns of IBM stock. Is there evidence of long-range dependence? Why?

2.6. Consider the demand for electricity of a manufacturing sector in the United States. The data are logged, denote the demand of a fixed day of each month, and are in `power6.txt`. Build a time series model for the series and use the fitted model to produce 1-step to 24-step ahead forecasts.

2.7. Consider the daily simple return of CRSP equal-weighted index, including distributions, from January 1980 to December 1999 in file `d-ew8099.txt` (date, ew). Indicator variables for Mondays, Tuesdays, Wednesdays, and Thursdays are in the first four columns of `wkdays8099.txt`. Use a regression model to study the effects of trading days on the index return. What is the fitted model? Are the weekday effects significant in the returns at the 5% level? Use the HAC estimator of the covariance matrix to obtain the t-ratio of regression estimates. Does it change the conclusion of weekday effect? Are there serial correlations in the regression residuals? If yes, build a regression model with time series error to study weekday effects.

2.8. As demonstrated by the prior exercise, daily returns of equal-weighted index have some weekday effects. How about daily returns of S&P composite index? To answer this question, consider the daily returns of S&P composite index from January 3, 2000 to December 31, 2003. The data are in the file `d-dell3dx0003.txt`, which has 12 columns. The first four columns are daily simple returns of Dell, vw, ew, and sp. Columns 5–9 are indicators for Monday to Friday, respectively. Columns 10–12 are year, month, and day. There are 1004 data points. Perform all tests using the 5% significance level, and answer the following questions:

(a) Is there a Friday effect on the daily simple returns of S&P composite index? You may employ a simple linear regression model to answer this question. Estimate the model and test the hypothesis that there is no Friday effect. Draw your conclusion.

(b) Check the residual serial correlations using $Q(12)$ statistic. Are there any significant serial correlations in the residuals?

2.9. Now consider similar questions of the previous exercise for individual stock returns. We use the daily simple returns of Dell stock in this exercise.

(a) Is there a Friday effect on the daily simple returns of Dell stock? Estimate your model and test the hypothesis that there is no Friday effect. Draw your conclusion.

(b) Are there serial correlations in the residuals? Use $Q(12)$ to perform the test. Draw your conclusion.

(c) Refine the above model by using the technique of a regression model with time series errors. In there a significant Friday effect based on the refined model?

2.10. Consider the monthly yields of Moody's AAA &BAA seasoned bonds from January 1919 to March 2004. The data are obtained from the Federal Reserve Bank in St. Louis. Monthly yields are averages of daily yields. Obtain the summary statistics (sample mean, standard deviation, skewness, excess kurtosis, minimum, and maximum) of the two yield series. Are the bond yields skewed? Do they have heavy tails? Answer the questions using 5% significance level.

2.11. Consider the monthly AAA bond yields of the prior exercise. Build a time series model for the series.

2.12. Again, consider the two bond yield series, that is, AAA and BAA. What is the relationship between the two series? To answer this question, build a time series model using yields of AAA bond as the dependent variable and yields of BAA bond as independent variable.

2.13. Consider the monthly log returns of CRSP equal-weighted index from January 1962 to December 1999 for 456 observations. You may obtain the data from CRSP directly or from the file `m-ew6299.txt` on the Web.

(a) Build an AR model for the series and check the fitted model.

(b) Build an MA model for the series and check the fitted model.

(c) Compute 1-step and 2-step ahead forecasts of the AR and MA models built in the previous two questions.

(d) Compare the fitted AR and MA models.

2.14. This problem is concerned with the dynamic relationship between the spot and futures prices of the S&P 500 index. The data file `sp5may.dat` has three columns: log(futures price), log(spot price), and cost-of-carry ($\times 100$). The data were obtained from the Chicago Mercantile Exchange for the S&P 500 stock index in May 1993 and its June futures contract. The time interval is 1 minute (intraday). Several authors used the data to study index futures arbitrage. Here we focus on the first two columns. Let f_t and s_t be the log prices of futures and spot, respectively. Consider $y_t = f_t - f_{t-1}$ and $x_t = s_t - s_{t-1}$. Build a regression model with time series errors between $\{y_t\}$ and $\{x_t\}$, with y_t being the dependent variable.

2.15. The quarterly gross domestic product implicit price deflator is often used as a measure of inflation. The file `q-gdpdef.dat` contains the data for the United States from the first quarter of 1947 to the first quarter of 2004. Data format is year, month, and deflator. The data are seasonally adjusted and equal to 100 for year 2000. Build an ARIMA model for the series and check the validity of the fitted model. The data are obtained from the Federal Reserve Bank of St. Louis.

REFERENCES

Akaike, H. (1973). Information theory and an extension of the maximum likelihood principle. In B.N. Petrov and F. Csaki (eds.), *2nd International Symposium on Information Theory*, pp. 267–281. Akademia Kiado, Budapest.

Box, G. E. P., Jenkins, G. M., and Reinsel, G. C. (1994). *Time Series Analysis: Forecasting and Control*, 3rd edition. Prentice Hall, Englewood Cliffs, NJ.

Box, G. E. P. and Pierce, D. (1970). Distribution of residual autocorrelations in autoregressive-integrated moving average time series models. *Journal of the American Statistical Association* **65**: 1509–1526.

Brockwell, P. J. and Davis, R. A. (1991). *Time Series: Theory and Methods*, 2nd edition. Springer-Verlag, New York.

Brockwell, P. J. and Davis, R. A. (1996). *Introduction to Time Series and Forecasting*. Springer, New York.

Chan, N. H. and Wei, C. Z. (1988). Limiting distributions of least squares estimates of unstable autoregressive processes. *Annals of Statistics* **16**: 367–401.

Dickey, D. A. and Fuller, W. A. (1979). Distribution of the estimates for autoregressive time series with a unit root. *Journal of the American Statistical Association*, **74:** 427–431.

Ding, Z., Granger, C. W. J., and Engle, R. F. (1993). A long memory property of stock returns and a new model. *Journal of Empirical Finance* **1**: 83–106.

Eicker, F. (1967). Limit theorems for regression with unequal and dependent Errors. In L. LeCam and J. Neyman (eds.), *Proceedings of the 5th Berkeley Symposium on Mathematical Statistics and Probability*. University of California Press, Berkeley.

Fuller, W. A. (1976). *Introduction to Statistical Time Series*. Wiley, New York.

Greene, W. H. (2000). *Econometric Analysis*, 4th edition. Prentice-Hall, Upper Saddle River, NJ.

Hosking, J. R. M. (1981). Fractional differencing. *Biometrika* **68**: 165–176.

Ljung, G. and Box, G. E. P. (1978). On a measure of lack of fit in time series models. *Biometrika* **66**: 67–72.

Newey, W. and West, K. (1987). A simple positive semidefinite, heteroscedasticity and autocorrelation consistent covariance matrix. *Econometrica* **55**: 863–898.

Phillips, P. C. B. (1987). Time series regression with a unit root. *Econometrica* **55**: 277–301.

Shumway, R. H. and Stoffer, D. S. (2000). *Time Series Analysis and Its Applications*. Springer-Velag, New York.

Tiao, G. C. and Tsay, R. S. (1983). Consistency properties of least squares estimates of autoregressive parameters in ARMA models. *Annals of Statistics* **11**: 856–871.

Tsay, R. S. and Tiao, G. C. (1984). Consistent estimates of autoregressive parameters and extended sample autocorrelation function for stationary and nonstationary ARMA models. *Journal of the American Statistical Association* **79**: 84–96.

White, H. (1980). A heteroscedasticity consistent covariance matrix estimator and a direct test for heteroscedasticity. *Econometrica* **48**: 827–838.

CHAPTER 3

Conditional Heteroscedastic Models

The objective of this chapter is to study some statistical methods and econometric models available in the literature for modeling the volatility of an asset return. The models are referred to as conditional heteroscedastic models.

Volatility is an important factor in options trading. Here volatility means the conditional standard deviation of the underlying asset return. Consider, for example, the price of a European *call option*, which is a contract giving its holder the right, but not the obligation, to buy a fixed number of shares of a specified common stock at a fixed price on a given date. The fixed price is called the *strike price* and is commonly denoted by K. The given date is called the expiration date. The important time span here is the time to expiration, and we denote it by ℓ. The well-known Black–Scholes option pricing formula states that the price of such a call option is

$$c_t = P_t\Phi(x) - Kr^{-\ell}\Phi(x - \sigma_t\sqrt{\ell}), \quad \text{and} \quad x = \frac{\ln(P_t/Kr^{-\ell})}{\sigma_t\sqrt{\ell}} + \tfrac{1}{2}\sigma_t\sqrt{\ell}, \quad (3.1)$$

where P_t is the current price of the underlying stock, r is the risk-free interest rate, σ_t is the conditional standard deviation of the log return of the specified stock, and $\Phi(x)$ is the cumulative distribution function of the standard normal random variable evaluated at x. A derivation of the formula is given later in Chapter 6. The formula has several nice interpretations, but it suffices to say here that the conditional standard deviation σ_t of the log return of the underlying stock plays an important role. This volatility evolves over time and is the main topic of the chapter. If the option holder can exercise her right any time on or before the expiration date, then the option is called an *American call option*.

Volatility has many other financial applications. As discussed in Chapter 7, volatility modeling provides a simple approach to calculating value at risk of a financial position in risk management. It also plays an important role in asset allocation under the mean-variance framework. Furthermore, modeling the volatility of a time series can improve the efficiency in parameter estimation and the accuracy

Analysis of Financial Time Series, Second Edition By Ruey S. Tsay

in interval forecast. Finally, the volatility index of a market has recently become a financial instrument. The VIX volatility index compiled by the Chicago Board of Option Exchange (CBOE) started to trade in futures on March 26, 2004.

The univariate volatility models discussed in this chapter include the autoregressive conditional heteroscedastic (ARCH) model of Engle (1982), the generalized ARCH (GARCH) model of Bollerslev (1986), the exponential GARCH (EGARCH) model of Nelson (1991), the conditional heteroscedastic autoregressive moving-average (CHARMA) model of Tsay (1987), the random coefficient autoregressive (RCA) model of Nicholls and Quinn (1982), and the stochastic volatility (SV) models of Melino and Turnbull (1990), Taylor (1994), Harvey, Ruiz, and Shephard (1994), and Jacquier, Polson, and Rossi (1994). We also discuss advantages and weaknesses of each volatility model and show some applications of the models. Multivariate volatility models, including those with time-varying correlations, are discussed in Chapter 10. The chapter also discusses some alternative approaches to volatility modeling in Section 3.15, including use of daily high and low prices of an asset.

3.1 CHARACTERISTICS OF VOLATILITY

A special feature of stock volatility is that it is not directly observable. For example, consider the daily log returns of IBM stock. The daily volatility is not directly observable from the return data because there is only one observation in a trading day. If intraday data of the stock, such as 10-minute returns, are available, then one can estimate the daily volatility. See Section 3.15. The accuracy of such an estimate deserves a careful study, however. For example, stock volatility consists of intraday volatility and overnight volatility with the latter denoting variation between trading days. The high-frequency intraday returns contain only very limited information about the overnight volatility. The unobservability of volatility makes it difficult to evaluate the forecasting performance of conditional heteroscedastic models. We discuss this issue later.

In options markets, if one accepts the idea that the prices are governed by an econometric model such as the Blac–Scholes formula, then one can use the price to obtain the "implied" volatility. Yet this approach is often criticized for using a specific model, which is based on some assumptions that might not hold in practice. For instance, from the observed prices of a European call option, one can use the Black–Scholes formula in Eq. (3.1) to deduce the conditional standard deviation σ_t. The resulting value of σ_t is called the *implied volatility* of the underlying stock. However, this implied volatility is derived under the assumption that the price of the underlying asset follows a geometric Brownian motion. It might be different from the actual volatility. Experience shows that implied volatility of an asset return tends to be larger than that obtained by using a GARCH type of volatility model. This might be due to the risk premium for volatility or to the way daily returns are calculated. The VIX of CBOE is an implied volatility.

Although volatility is not directly observable, it has some characteristics that are commonly seen in asset returns. First, there exist volatility clusters (i.e., volatility may be high for certain time periods and low for other periods). Second, volatility evolves over time in a continuous manner—that is, volatility jumps are rare. Third, volatility does not diverge to infinity—that is, volatility varies within some fixed range. Statistically speaking, this means that volatility is often stationary. Fourth, volatility seems to react differently to a big price increase or a big price drop, referred to as the *leverage* effect. These properties play an important role in the development of volatility models. Some volatility models were proposed specifically to correct the weaknesses of the existing ones for their inability to capture the characteristics mentioned earlier. For example, the EGARCH model was developed to capture the asymmetry in volatility induced by big "positive" and "negative" asset returns.

3.2 STRUCTURE OF A MODEL

Let r_t be the log return of an asset at time index t. The basic idea behind volatility study is that the series $\{r_t\}$ is either serially uncorrelated or with minor lower order serial correlations, but it is a dependent series. For illustration, Figure 3.1 shows the ACF and PACF of some functions of the monthly log stock returns

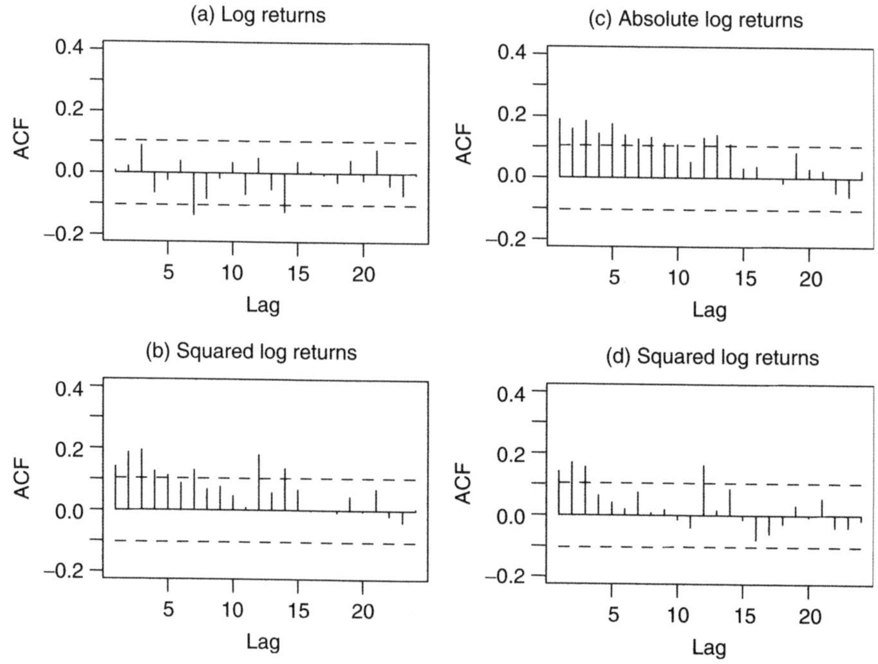

Figure 3.1. Sample ACF and PACF of various functions of monthly log stock returns of Intel Corporation from January 1973 to December 2003: (a) ACF of the log returns, (b) ACF of the squared returns, (c) ACF of the absolute returns, and (d) PACF of the squared returns.

of Intel Corporation from January 1973 to December 2003. Figure 3.1a shows the sample ACF of the return, which suggests no significant serial correlations except for a minor one at lag 7. Figure 3.1c shows the sample ACF of the absolute log returns (i.e., $|r_t|$), whereas Figure 3.1b shows the sample ACF of the squared returns r_t^2. These two plots clearly suggest that the monthly returns are not serially independent. Combining the three plots, it seems that the returns are indeed serially uncorrelated, but dependent. Volatility models attempt to capture such dependence in the return series.

To put the volatility models in proper perspective, it is informative to consider the conditional mean and variance of r_t given F_{t-1}; that is,

$$\mu_t = E(r_t|F_{t-1}), \qquad \sigma_t^2 = \text{Var}(r_t|F_{t-1}) = E[(r_t - \mu_t)^2|F_{t-1}], \tag{3.2}$$

where F_{t-1} denotes the information set available at time $t-1$. Typically, F_{t-1} consists of all linear functions of the past returns. As shown by the empirical examples of Chapter 2 and Figure 3.1, serial dependence of a stock return series r_t is weak if it exists at all. Therefore, the equation for μ_t in (3.2) should be simple, and we assume that r_t follows a simple time series model such as a stationary ARMA(p, q) model with some explanatory variables. In other words, we entertain the model

$$r_t = \mu_t + a_t, \qquad \mu_t = \phi_0 + \sum_{i=1}^{k} \beta_i x_{it} + \sum_{i=1}^{p} \phi_i r_{t-i} - \sum_{i=1}^{q} \theta_i a_{t-i}, \tag{3.3}$$

for r_t, where k, p, and q are non-negative integers, and x_{it} are explanatory variables.

Model (3.3) illustrates a possible financial application of the linear time series models of Chapter 2. The order (p, q) of an ARMA model may depend on the frequency of the return series. For example, daily returns of a market index often show some minor serial correlations, but monthly returns of the index may not contain any significant serial correlation. The explanatory variables x_t in Eq. (3.3) are flexible. For example, a dummy variable can be used for the Mondays to study the effect of weekend on daily stock returns. In the capital asset pricing model (CAPM), the mean equation of r_t can be written as $r_t = \phi_0 + \beta r_{m,t} + a_t$, where $r_{m,t}$ denotes the market return.

Combining Eqs. (3.2) and (3.3), we have

$$\sigma_t^2 = \text{Var}(r_t|F_{t-1}) = \text{Var}(a_t|F_{t-1}). \tag{3.4}$$

The conditional heteroscedastic models of this chapter are concerned with the evolution of σ_t^2. The manner under which σ_t^2 evolves over time distinguishes one volatility model from another.

Conditional heteroscedastic models can be classified into two general categories. Those in the first category use an exact function to govern the evolution of σ_t^2, whereas those in the second category use a stochastic equation to describe σ_t^2. The GARCH model belongs to the first category whereas the stochastic volatility model is in the second category.

Throughout the book, a_t is referred to as the *shock* or *innovation* of an asset return at time t and σ_t is the positive square root of σ_t^2. The model for μ_t in Eq. (3.3) is referred to as the *mean* equation for r_t and the model for σ_t^2 is the *volatility* equation for r_t. Therefore, modeling conditional heteroscedasticity amounts to augmenting a dynamic equation, which governs the time evolution of the conditional variance of the asset return, to a time series model.

3.3 MODEL BUILDING

Building a volatility model for an asset return series consists of four steps:

1. Specify a mean equation by testing for serial dependence in the data and, if necessary, building an econometric model (e.g., an ARMA model) for the return series to remove any linear dependence.
2. Use the residuals of the mean equation to test for ARCH effects.
3. Specify a volatility model if ARCH effects are statistically significant and perform a joint estimation of the mean and volatility equations.
4. Check the fitted model carefully and refine it if necessary.

For most asset return series, the serial correlations are weak, if any. Thus, building a mean equation amounts to removing the sample mean from the data if the sample mean is significantly different from zero. For some daily return series, a simple AR model might be needed. In some cases, the mean equation may employ some explanatory variables such as an indicator variable for weekend or January effects.

In what follows, we use S-Plus in empirical illustrations. Other software packages (e.g., Eviews, SCA, R, and RATS) can also be used.

3.3.1 Testing for ARCH Effect

For ease in notation, let $a_t = r_t - \mu_t$ be the residuals of the mean equation. The squared series a_t^2 is then used to check for conditional heteroscedasticity, which is also known as the *ARCH* effects. Two tests are available. The first test is to apply the usual Ljung–Box statistics $Q(m)$ to the $\{a_t^2\}$ series; see McLeod and Li (1983). The null hypothesis is that the first m lags of ACF of the a_t^2 series are zero. The second test for conditional heteroscedasticity is the Lagrange multiplier test of Engle (1982). This test is equivalent to the usual F statistic for testing $\alpha_i = 0$ $(i = 1, \ldots, m)$ in the linear regression

$$a_t^2 = \alpha_0 + \alpha_1 a_{t-1}^2 + \cdots + \alpha_m a_{t-m}^2 + e_t, \quad t = m + 1, \ldots, T,$$

where e_t denotes the error term, m is a prespecified positive integer, and T is the sample size. Specifically, the null hypothesis is $H_o\colon \alpha_1 = \cdots = \alpha_m = 0$. Let $SSR_0 = \sum_{t=m+1}^{T}(a_t^2 - \overline{\omega})^2$, where $\overline{\omega} = (1/T)\sum_{t=1}^{T} a_t^2$ is the sample mean of a_t^2, and $SSR_1 = \sum_{t=m+1}^{T} \hat{e}_t^2$, where $\hat{e}_t$ is the least squares residual of the prior linear regression. Then we have

$$F = \frac{(SSR_0 - SSR_1)/m}{SSR_1/(T - 2m - 1)},$$

which is asymptotically distributed as a chi-squared distribution with m degrees of freedom under the null hypothesis. The decision rule is to reject the null hypothesis if $F > \chi_m^2(\alpha)$, where $\chi_m^2(\alpha)$ is the upper $100(1-\alpha)$th percentile of χ_m^2, or the p-value of F is less than α.

To demonstrate, we consider the monthly log stock returns of Intel Corporation from 1973 to 2003; see Example 3.1 below. The series does not have significant serial correlations so that it can be directly used to test for the ARCH effect. Indeed, the $Q(m)$ statistics of the return series give $Q(12) = 18.57$ with p-value 0.10, confirming no serial correlations in the data. On the other hand, the Lagrange multiplier test shows strong ARCH effects with test statistic $F \approx 43.5$, the p-value of which is close to zero.

S-Plus Demonstration

Denote the return series by `intc`. Note that the command `archTest` applies directly to the a_t series, not to a_t^2.

```
> autocorTest(intc,lag=12)
Test for Autocorrelation: Ljung-Box
Null Hypothesis: no autocorrelation

Test Statistics:
Test Stat 18.5664  p.value  0.0995

Dist. under Null: chi-square with 12 degrees of freedom
Total Observ.: 372

> archTest(intc, lag=12)
Test for ARCH Effects: LM Test
Null Hypothesis: no ARCH effects

Test Statistics:
Test Stat 43.5041  p.value  0.0000

Dist. under Null: chi-square with 12 degrees of freedom
```

3.4 THE ARCH MODEL

The first model that provides a systematic framework for volatility modeling is the ARCH model of Engle (1982). The basic idea of ARCH models is that (a) the shock a_t of an asset return is serially uncorrelated, but dependent, and (b) the dependence of a_t can be described by a simple quadratic function of its lagged values. Specifically, an ARCH(m) model assumes that

$$a_t = \sigma_t \epsilon_t, \quad \sigma_t^2 = \alpha_0 + \alpha_1 a_{t-1}^2 + \cdots + \alpha_m a_{t-m}^2, \tag{3.5}$$

where $\{\epsilon_t\}$ is a sequence of independent and identically distributed (iid) random variables with mean zero and variance 1, $\alpha_0 > 0$, and $\alpha_i \geq 0$ for $i > 0$. The coefficients α_i must satisfy some regularity conditions to ensure that the unconditional variance of a_t is finite. In practice, ϵ_t is often assumed to follow the standard normal or a standardized Student-t distribution or a generalized error distribution.

From the structure of the model, it is seen that large past squared shocks $\{a_{t-i}^2\}_{i=1}^m$ imply a large conditional variance σ_t^2 for the innovation a_t. Consequently, a_t tends to assume a large value (in modulus). This means that, under the ARCH framework, large shocks tend to be followed by another large shock. Here I use the word *tend* because a large variance does not necessarily produce a large realization. It only says that the probability of obtaining a large variate is greater than that of a smaller variance. This feature is similar to the volatility clusterings observed in asset returns.

The ARCH effect also occurs in other financial time series. Figure 3.2 shows the time plots of (a) the percentage changes in Deutsche mark/U.S. dollar exchange rate measured in 10-minute intervals from June 5, 1989 to June 19, 1989 for 2488

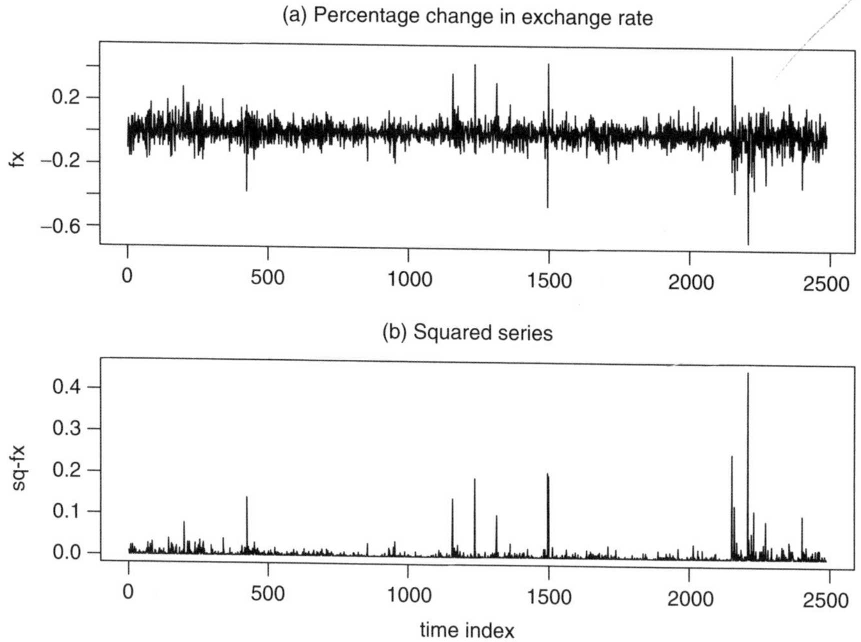

Figure 3.2. (a) Time plot of 10-minute returns of the exchange rate between Deutsche mark and U.S. dollar and (b) the squared returns.

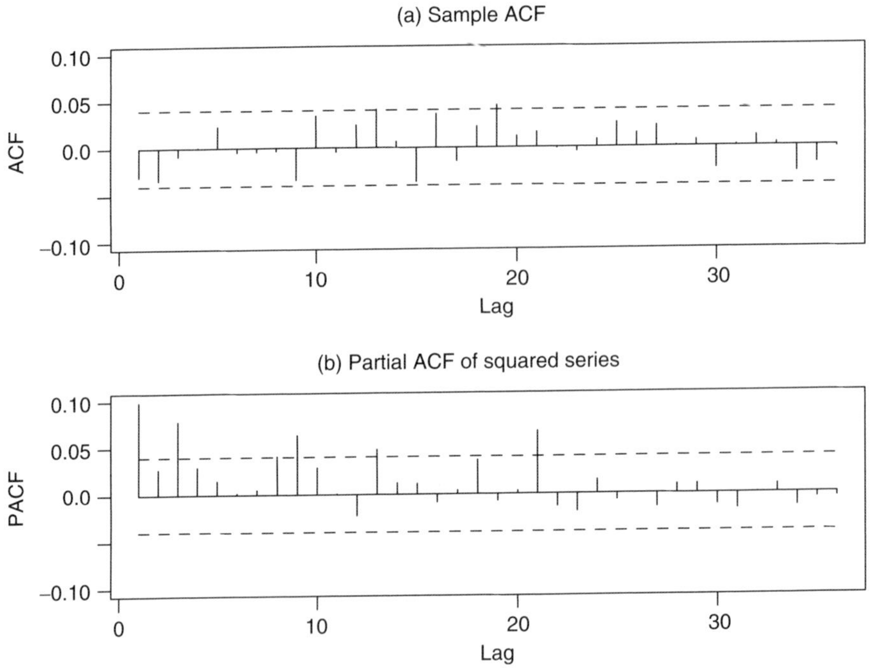

Figure 3.3. (a) Sample autocorrelation function of the return series of mark/dollar exchange rate and (b) sample partial autocorrelation function of the squared returns.

observations, and (b) the squared series of the percentage changes. Big percentage changes occurred occasionally, but there were certain stable periods. Figure 3.3a shows the sample ACF of the percentage change series. Clearly, the series has no serial correlation. Figure 3.3b shows the sample PACF of the squared series of percentage change. It is seen that there are some big spikes in the PACF. Such spikes suggest that the percentage changes are not serially independent and have some ARCH effects.

Remark. Some authors use h_t to denote the conditional variance in Eq. (3.5). In this case, the shock becomes $a_t = \sqrt{h_t}\epsilon_t$. □

3.4.1 Properties of ARCH Models

To understand the ARCH models, it pays to carefully study the ARCH(1) model

$$a_t = \sigma_t \epsilon_t, \quad \sigma_t^2 = \alpha_0 + \alpha_1 a_{t-1}^2,$$

where $\alpha_0 > 0$ and $\alpha_1 \geq 0$. First, the unconditional mean of a_t remains zero because

$$E(a_t) = E[E(a_t|F_{t-1})] = E[\sigma_t E(\epsilon_t)] = 0.$$

Second, the unconditional variance of a_t can be obtained as

$$\begin{aligned}\mathrm{Var}(a_t) &= E(a_t^2) = E[E(a_t^2|F_{t-1})]\\ &= E(\alpha_0 + \alpha_1 a_{t-1}^2) = \alpha_0 + \alpha_1 E(a_{t-1}^2).\end{aligned}$$

Because a_t is a stationary process with $E(a_t) = 0$, $\mathrm{Var}(a_t) = \mathrm{Var}(a_{t-1}) = E(a_{t-1}^2)$. Therefore, we have $\mathrm{Var}(a_t) = \alpha_0 + \alpha_1 \mathrm{Var}(a_t)$ and $\mathrm{Var}(a_t) = \alpha_0/(1-\alpha_1)$. Since the variance of a_t must be positive, we require $0 \le \alpha_1 < 1$. Third, in some applications, we need higher order moments of a_t to exist and, hence, α_1 must also satisfy some additional constraints. For instance, to study its tail behavior, we require that the fourth moment of a_t is finite. Under the normality assumption of ϵ_t in Eq. (3.5), we have

$$E(a_t^4|F_{t-1}) = 3[E(a_t^2|F_{t-1})]^2 = 3(\alpha_0 + \alpha_1 a_{t-1}^2)^2.$$

Therefore,

$$E(a_t^4) = E[E(a_t^4|F_{t-1})] = 3E(\alpha_0 + \alpha_1 a_{t-1}^2)^2 = 3E(\alpha_0^2 + 2\alpha_0\alpha_1 a_{t-1}^2 + \alpha_1^2 a_{t-1}^4).$$

If a_t is fourth-order stationary with $m_4 = E(a_t^4)$, then we have

$$\begin{aligned}m_4 &= 3[\alpha_0^2 + 2\alpha_0\alpha_1 \mathrm{Var}(a_t) + \alpha_1^2 m_4]\\ &= 3\alpha_0^2\left(1 + 2\frac{\alpha_1}{1-\alpha_1}\right) + 3\alpha_1^2 m_4.\end{aligned}$$

Consequently,

$$m_4 = \frac{3\alpha_0^2(1+\alpha_1)}{(1-\alpha_1)(1-3\alpha_1^2)}.$$

This result has two important implications: (a) since the fourth moment of a_t is positive, we see that α_1 must also satisfy the condition $1 - 3\alpha_1^2 > 0$; that is, $0 \le \alpha_1^2 < \frac{1}{3}$; and (b) the unconditional kurtosis of a_t is

$$\frac{E(a_t^4)}{[\mathrm{Var}(a_t)]^2} = 3\frac{\alpha_0^2(1+\alpha_1)}{(1-\alpha_1)(1-3\alpha_1^2)} \times \frac{(1-\alpha_1)^2}{\alpha_0^2} = 3\frac{1-\alpha_1^2}{1-3\alpha_1^2} > 3.$$

Thus, the excess kurtosis of a_t is positive and the tail distribution of a_t is heavier than that of a normal distribution. In other words, the shock a_t of a conditional Gaussian ARCH(1) model is more likely than a Gaussian white noise series to produce "outliers." This is in agreement with the empirical finding that "outliers" appear more often in asset returns than that implied by an iid sequence of normal random variates.

These properties continue to hold for general ARCH models, but the formulas become more complicated for higher order ARCH models. The condition $\alpha_i \ge 0$ in Eq. (3.5) can be relaxed. It is a condition to ensure that the conditional variance σ_t^2

is positive for all t. In fact, a natural way to achieve positiveness of the conditional variance is to rewrite an ARCH(m) model as

$$a_t = \sigma_t \epsilon_t, \quad \sigma_t^2 = \alpha_0 + A'_{m,t-1} \Omega A_{m,t-1}, \tag{3.6}$$

where $A_{m,t-1} = (a_{t-1}, \ldots, a_{t-m})'$ and Ω is an $m \times m$ non-negative definite matrix. The ARCH(m) model in Eq. (3.5) requires Ω to be diagonal. Thus, Engle's model uses a parsimonious approach to approximate a quadratic function. A simple way to achieve Eq. (3.6) is to employ a random-coefficient model for a_t; see the CHARMA and RCA models discussed later.

3.4.2 Weaknesses of ARCH Models

The advantages of ARCH models include properties discussed in the previous subsection. The model also has some weaknesses:

1. The model assumes that positive and negative shocks have the same effects on volatility because it depends on the square of the previous shocks. In practice, it is well known that price of a financial asset responds differently to positive and negative shocks.
2. The ARCH model is rather restrictive. For instance, α_1^2 of an ARCH(1) model must be in the interval $[0, \frac{1}{3}]$ if the series has a finite fourth moment. The constraint becomes complicated for higher order ARCH models. In practice, it limits the ability of ARCH models with Gaussian innovations to capture excess kurtosis.
3. The ARCH model does not provide any new insight for understanding the source of variations of a financial time series. It merely provides a mechanical way to describe the behavior of the conditional variance. It gives no indication about what causes such behavior to occur.
4. ARCH models are likely to overpredict the volatility because they respond slowly to large isolated shocks to the return series.

3.4.3 Building an ARCH Model

Among volatility models, specifying an ARCH model is relatively easy. Details are given below.

Order Determination

If an ARCH effect is found to be significant, one can use the PACF of a_t^2 to determine the ARCH order. Using PACF of a_t^2 to select the ARCH order can be justified as follows. From the model in Eq. (3.5), we have

$$\sigma_t^2 = \alpha_0 + \alpha_1 a_{t-1}^2 + \cdots + \alpha_m a_{t-m}^2.$$

For a given sample, a_t^2 is an unbiased estimate of σ_t^2. Therefore, we expect that a_t^2 is linearly related to $a_{t-1}^2, \ldots, a_{t-m}^2$ in a manner similar to that of an autoregressive model of order m. Note that a single a_t^2 is generally not an efficient estimate of σ_t^2, but it can serve as an approximation that could be informative in specifying the order m.

Alternatively, define $\eta_t = a_t^2 - \sigma_t^2$. It can be shown that $\{\eta_t\}$ is an un-correlated series with mean 0. The ARCH model then becomes

$$a_t^2 = \alpha_0 + \alpha_1 a_{t-1}^2 + \cdots + \alpha_m a_{t-m}^2 + \eta_t,$$

which is in the form of an AR(m) model for a_t^2, except that $\{\eta_t\}$ is not an iid series. From Chapter 2, PACF of a_t^2 is a useful tool to determine the order m. Because $\{\eta_t\}$ are not identically distributed, the least squares estimates of the prior model are consistent, but not efficient. The PACF of a_t^2 may not be effective when the sample size is small.

Estimation

Three likelihood functions are commonly used in ARCH estimation. Under the normality assumption, the likelihood function of an ARCH(m) model is

$$\begin{aligned} f(a_1, \ldots, a_T|\boldsymbol{\alpha}) &= f(a_T|F_{T-1}) f(a_{T-1}|F_{T-2}) \cdots f(a_{m+1}|F_m) f(a_1, \ldots, a_m|\boldsymbol{\alpha}) \\ &= \prod_{t=m+1}^{T} \frac{1}{\sqrt{2\pi\sigma_t^2}} \exp\left(-\frac{a_t^2}{2\sigma_t^2}\right) \times f(a_1, \ldots, a_m|\boldsymbol{\alpha}), \end{aligned}$$

where $\boldsymbol{\alpha} = (\alpha_0, \alpha_1, \ldots, \alpha_m)'$ and $f(a_1, \ldots, a_m|\boldsymbol{\alpha})$ is the joint probability density function of $a_1, \ldots, a_m$. Since the exact form of $f(a_1, \ldots, a_m|\boldsymbol{\alpha})$ is complicated, it is commonly dropped from the prior likelihood function, especially when the sample size is sufficiently large. This results in using the conditional likelihood function

$$f(a_{m+1}, \ldots, a_T|\boldsymbol{\alpha}, a_1, \ldots, a_m) = \prod_{t=m+1}^{T} \frac{1}{\sqrt{2\pi\sigma_t^2}} \exp\left(-\frac{a_t^2}{2\sigma_t^2}\right),$$

where σ_t^2 can be evaluated recursively. We refer to estimates obtained by maximizing the prior likelihood function as the conditional maximum likelihood estimates (MLEs) under normality.

Maximizing the conditional likelihood function is equivalent to maximizing its logarithm, which is easier to handle. The conditional log likelihood function is

$$\ell(a_{m+1}, \ldots, a_T|\boldsymbol{\alpha}, a_1, \ldots, a_m) = \sum_{t=m+1}^{T} \left(-\frac{1}{2}\ln(2\pi) - \frac{1}{2}\ln(\sigma_t^2) - \frac{1}{2}\frac{a_t^2}{\sigma_t^2}\right).$$

Since the first term $\ln(2\pi)$ does not involve any parameters, the log likelihood function becomes

$$\ell(a_{m+1}, \ldots, a_T|\boldsymbol{\alpha}, a_1, \ldots, a_m) = -\sum_{t=m+1}^{T} \left(\frac{1}{2}\ln(\sigma_t^2) + \frac{1}{2}\frac{a_t^2}{\sigma_t^2}\right),$$

where $\sigma_t^2 = \alpha_0 + \alpha_1 a_{t-1}^2 + \cdots + \alpha_m a_{t-m}^2$ can be evaluated recursively.

In some applications, it is more appropriate to assume that ϵ_t follows a heavy-tailed distribution such as a standardized Student-t distribution. Let x_v be a Student-t distribution with v degrees of freedom. Then $\text{Var}(x_v) = v/(v-2)$ for $v > 2$, and we use $\epsilon_t = x_v/\sqrt{v/(v-2)}$. The probability density function of ϵ_t is

$$f(\epsilon_t|v) = \frac{\Gamma((v+1)/2)}{\Gamma(v/2)\sqrt{(v-2)\pi}}\left(1+\frac{\epsilon_t^2}{v-2}\right)^{-(v+1)/2}, \quad v > 2, \tag{3.7}$$

where $\Gamma(x)$ is the usual gamma function (i.e., $\Gamma(x) = \int_0^\infty y^{x-1}e^{-y}\,dy$). Using $a_t = \sigma_t\epsilon_t$, we obtain the conditional likelihood function of a_t as

$$f(a_{m+1},\ldots,a_T|\boldsymbol{\alpha}, A_m) = \prod_{t=m+1}^{T}\frac{\Gamma((v+1)/2)}{\Gamma(v/2)\sqrt{(v-2)\pi}}\frac{1}{\sigma_t}\left(1+\frac{a_t^2}{(v-2)\sigma_t^2}\right)^{-(v+1)/2},$$

where $v > 2$ and $A_m = (a_1, a_2, \ldots, a_m)$. We refer to the estimates that maximize the prior likelihood function as the conditional MLEs under t-distribution. The degrees of freedom of the t-distribution can be specified a priori or estimated jointly with other parameters. A value between 3 and 6 is often used if it is prespecified.

If the degrees of freedom v of the Student-t distribution is prespecified, then the conditional log likelihood function is

$$\ell(a_{m+1},\ldots,a_T|\boldsymbol{\alpha}, A_m) = -\sum_{t=m+1}^{T}\left[\frac{v+1}{2}\ln\left(1+\frac{a_t^2}{(v-2)\sigma_t^2}\right)+\frac{1}{2}\ln(\sigma_t^2)\right]. \tag{3.8}$$

If one wishes to estimate v jointly with other parameters, then the log likelihood function becomes

$$\begin{aligned}
&\ell(a_{m+1},\ldots,a_T|\boldsymbol{\alpha}, v, A_m)\\
&\quad = (T-m)[\ln(\Gamma((v+1)/2)) - \ln(\Gamma(v/2)) - 0.5\ln((v-2)\pi)]\\
&\qquad + \ell(a_{m+1},\ldots,a_T|\boldsymbol{\alpha}, A_m),
\end{aligned}$$

where the second term is given in Eq. (3.8).

Finally, ϵ_t may assume a generalized error distribution (GED) with probability density function

$$f(x) = \frac{v\exp\left(-\frac{1}{2}|x/\lambda|^v\right)}{\lambda 2^{(1+1/v)}\Gamma(1/v)}, \qquad -\infty < x < \infty, \quad 0 < v \le \infty, \tag{3.9}$$

where $\Gamma(.)$ is the gamma function and

$$\lambda = [2^{(-2/v)}\Gamma(1/v)/\Gamma(3/v)]^{1/2}.$$

This distribution reduces to a Gaussian distribution if $v = 2$ and it has heavy tails when $v < 2$. The conditional log likelihood function $\ell(a_{m+1},\ldots,a_T|\boldsymbol{\alpha}, \mathbf{A}_m)$ can easily be obtained.

Model Checking

For a properly specified ARCH model, the standardized residuals

$$\tilde{a}_t = \frac{a_t}{\sigma_t}$$

form a sequence of iid random variables. Therefore, one can check the adequacy of a fitted ARCH model by examining the series $\{\tilde{a}_t\}$. In particular, the Ljung–Box statistics of $\tilde{a}_t$ can be used to check the adequacy of the mean equation and that of $\tilde{a}_t^2$ can be used to test the validity of the volatility equation. The skewness, kurtosis, and quantile-to-quantile plot (i.e., QQ-plot) of $\{\tilde{a}_t\}$ can be used to check the validity of the distribution assumption. Many residual plots are available in S-Plus for model checking.

Forecasting

Forecasts of the ARCH model in Eq. (3.5) can be obtained recursively as those of an AR model. Consider an ARCH(m) model. At the forecast origin h, the 1-step ahead forecast of σ_{h+1}^2 is

$$\sigma_h^2(1) = \alpha_0 + \alpha_1 a_h^2 + \cdots + \alpha_m a_{h+1-m}^2.$$

The 2-step ahead forecast is

$$\sigma_h^2(2) = \alpha_0 + \alpha_1 \sigma_h^2(1) + \alpha_2 a_h^2 + \cdots + \alpha_m a_{h+2-m}^2,$$

and the ℓ-step ahead forecast for $\sigma_{h+\ell}^2$ is

$$\sigma_h^2(\ell) = \alpha_0 + \sum_{i=1}^{m} \alpha_i \sigma_h^2(\ell - i), \tag{3.10}$$

where $\sigma_h^2(\ell - i) = a_{h+\ell-i}^2$ if $\ell - i \le 0$.

3.4.4 Some Examples

In this subsection, we illustrate ARCH modeling by considering two examples.

Example 3.1. We first apply the modeling procedure to build a simple ARCH model for the monthly log returns of Intel stock. The sample ACF and PACF of the squared returns in Figure 3.1 clearly show the existence of conditional heteroscedasticity. This is confirmed by the ARCH effect test shown in Section 3.3.1, and we proceed to identify the order of an ARCH model. The sample PACF in Figure 3.1d indicates that an ARCH(3) model might be appropriate. Consequently, we specify the model

$$r_t = \mu + a_t, \quad a_t = \sigma_t \epsilon_t, \quad \sigma_t^2 = \alpha_0 + \alpha_1 a_{t-1}^2 + \alpha_2 a_{t-2}^2 + \alpha_3 a_{t-3}^2$$

for the monthly log returns of Intel stock. Assuming that ϵ_t are iid standard normal, we obtain the fitted model

$$r_t = 0.0171 + a_t, \quad \sigma_t^2 = 0.0120 + 0.1787a_{t-1}^2 + 0.0772a_{t-2}^2 + 0.0572a_{t-3}^2,$$

where the standard errors of the parameters are 0.0066, 0.0011, 0.0803, 0.0506, and 0.0769, respectively; see the output below. While the estimates meet the general requirement of an ARCH(3) model, the estimates of α_2 and α_3 appear to be statistically nonsignificant at the 5% level. Therefore, the model can be simplified.

S-Plus Demonstration

Output edited and % marks explanation.

```
> arch3.fit=garch(intc~1,~garch(3,0))
> summary(arch3.fit)
Call:
garch(formula.mean = intc ~ 1, formula.var = ~ garch(3, 0))

Mean Equation: intc ~ 1
Conditional Variance Equation:  ~ garch(3, 0)
Conditional Distribution:  gaussian
-------------------------------------------------------------
Estimated Coefficients:
-------------------------------------------------------------
          Value Std.Error t value Pr(>|t|)
      C 0.01713  0.006626  2.5860 0.005047  % one-sided
      A 0.01199  0.001107 10.8325 0.000000  % p-value
ARCH(1) 0.17874  0.080294  2.2260 0.013309
ARCH(2) 0.07720  0.050552  1.5271 0.063800
ARCH(3) 0.05722  0.076928  0.7438 0.228747
-------------------------------------------------------------
> arch1=garch(intc~1,~garch(1,0)) % A simplified model
> summary(arch1)
Call:
garch(formula.mean = intc ~ 1, formula.var = ~ garch(1,0))

Mean Equation: intc ~ 1
Conditional Variance Equation:  ~ garch(1, 0)
Conditional Distribution:  gaussian
-------------------------------------------------------------
Estimated Coefficients:
-------------------------------------------------------------
          Value Std.Error t value  Pr(>|t|)
      C 0.01741  0.006231   2.794 2.737e-03
      A 0.01258  0.001246  10.091 0.000e+00
ARCH(1) 0.35258  0.088515   3.983 4.094e-05
-------------------------------------------------------------
> stdresi=arch1$residuals/arch1$sigma.t   % Standardized
> autocorTest(stdresi,lag=10)             % residuals
```

```
Null Hypothesis: no autocorrelation
Test Statistics:
Test Stat 13.7820  p.value  0.1832

Dist. under Null: chi-square with 10 degrees of freedom
> archTest(stdresi,lag=10)  % ARCH test for residuals

Null Hypothesis: no ARCH effects
Test Statistics:
Test Stat 11.3793  p.value  0.3287

Dist. under Null: chi-square with 10 degrees of freedom
> arch1$asymp.sd  % Obtain unconditional variance
[1] 0.1393796

> plot(arch1)  % Obtain various plots, including the
               % fitted volatility series.
```

Dropping the two nonsignificant parameters, we obtain the model

$$r_t = 0.0174 + a_t, \quad \sigma_t^2 = 0.0126 + 0.3526a_{t-1}^2, \tag{3.11}$$

where the standard errors of the parameters are 0.0062, 0.0012, and 0.0885, respectively. All the estimates are highly significant. Figure 3.4 shows the standardized residuals $\{\tilde{a}_t\}$ and the sample ACF of some functions of $\{\tilde{a}_t\}$. The Ljung–Box statistics of standardized residuals give $Q(10) = 13.78$ with p-value 0.18 and those of $\{\tilde{a}_t^2\}$ give $Q(10) = 11.38$ with p-value 0.33. See the output. Consequently, the ARCH(1) model in Eq. (3.11) is adequate for describing the conditional heteroscedasticity of the data at the 5% significance level.

The ARCH(1) model in Eq. (3.11) has some interesting properties. First, the expected monthly log return for Intel stock is about 1.74%, which is remarkable, especially since the sample includes the period after the Internet bubble. Second, $\hat{\alpha}_1^2 = 0.353^2 < \frac{1}{3}$ so that the unconditional fourth moment of the monthly log return of Intel stock exists. Third, the unconditional standard deviation of r_t is $\sqrt{0.0126/(1 - 0.352)} = 0.1394$. Finally, the ARCH(1) model can be used to predict the monthly volatility of Intel stock returns.

***t* Innovation**

For comparison, we also fit an ARCH(1) model with Student-t innovations to the series. The resulting model is

$$r_t = 0.0221 + a_t, \quad \sigma_t^2 = 0.0134 + 0.2492a_{t-1}^2, \tag{3.12}$$

where standard errors of the parameters are 0.0060, 0.0020, and 0.1156, respectively. The estimated degrees of freedom is 6.16 with standard error 1.65. All the estimates are significant at the 5% level, but the t-ratio of $\hat{\alpha}_1$ is only 2.16. The unconditional standard deviation of a_t is $\sqrt{0.0134/(1 - 0.2492)} = 0.1336$, which

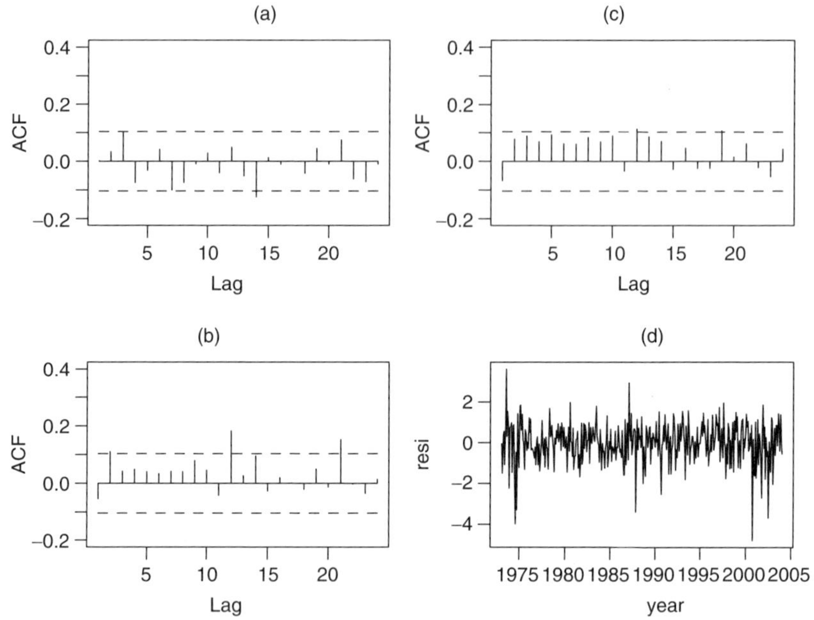

Figure 3.4. Model checking statistics of the Gaussian ARCH(1) model in Eq. (3.11) for the monthly log returns of Intel stock from January 1973 to December 2003: parts (a), (b), and (c) show the sample ACF of the standardized residuals, their squared series, and absolute series, respectively; part (d) is the time plot of standardized residuals.

is close to that obtained under normality. The Ljung–Box statistics of the standardized residuals give $Q(12) = 16.1$ with p-value 0.19, confirming that the mean equation is adequate. However, the Ljung–Box statistics for the squared standardized residuals show $Q(12) = 29.91$ with p-value 0.0029. The volatility equation is inadequate at the 5% level. Further analysis shows that the Lagrange multiplier test gives $Q(10) = 13.07$ with p-value 0.22. The inadequacy in the volatility equation is due to some higher order serial dependence in the squared standardized residuals.

Comparing models (3.11) and (3.12), we see that (a) using a heavy-tailed distribution for ϵ_t reduces the ARCH effect, and (b) the difference between the two models is small for this particular instance. Finally, a more appropriate conditional heteroscedastic model for this data set is a GARCH(1,1) model, which is discussed in the next section.

S-Plus Demonstration

With t innovations.

```
> arch1t=garch(intc~1,~garch(1,0),cond.dist='t')
> summary(arch1t)
Call:
garch(formula.mean = intc ~ 1, formula.var = ~ garch(1, 0),
      cond.dist = "t")
```

```
Mean Equation: intc ~ 1
Conditional Variance Equation:  ~ garch(1, 0)
Conditional Distribution:  t
 with estimated parameter 6.159751 and standard error 1.647094
Estimated Coefficients:
--------------------------------------------------
          Value Std.Error t value  Pr(>|t|)
      C 0.02213  0.006010   3.681 1.333e-04
      A 0.01338  0.001965   6.809 2.001e-11
ARCH(1) 0.24916  0.115574   2.156 1.587e-02
--------------------------------------------------
AIC(4) = -477.9073, BIC(4) = -462.2317

Ljung-Box test for standardized residuals:
--------------------------------------------------
 Statistic P-value Chi^2-d.f.
      16.1  0.1868          12

Ljung-Box test for squared standardized residuals:
--------------------------------------------------
 Statistic  P-value Chi^2-d.f.
     29.91 0.002882          12
```

Remark. In S-Plus, the command `garch` allows for several conditional distributions. They are specified by `cond.dist = ''t''` or `''ged''`. The default is Gaussian. □

Example 3.2. Consider the percentage changes of the exchange rate between mark and dollar in 10-minute intervals. The data are shown in Figure 3.2a. As shown in Figure 3.3a, the series has no serial correlations. However, the sample PACF of the squared series a_t^2 shows some big spikes, especially at lags 1 and 3. There are some large PACF at higher lags, but the lower order lags tend to be more important. Following the procedure discussed in the previous subsection, we specify an ARCH(3) model for the series. Using the conditional Gaussian likelihood function, we obtain the fitted model $r_t = 0.0018 + \sigma_t \epsilon_t$ and

$$\sigma_t^2 = 0.22 \times 10^{-2} + 0.322 a_{t-1}^2 + 0.074 a_{t-2}^2 + 0.093 a_{t-3}^2,$$

where all the estimates in the volatility equation are statistically significant at the 5% significance level. The standard errors of the volatility parameters are 0.47×10^{-6}, 0.017, 0.016, and 0.014, respectively. Model checking, using the standardized residual $\tilde{a}_t$, indicates that the model is adequate.

3.5 THE GARCH MODEL

Although the ARCH model is simple, it often requires many parameters to adequately describe the volatility process of an asset return. For instance, consider the monthly excess returns of the S&P 500 index of Example 3.3 below. An ARCH(9) model is needed for the volatility process. Some alternative models must be sought. Bollerslev (1986) proposes a useful extension known as the generalized ARCH (GARCH) model. For a log return series r_t, let $a_t = r_t - \mu_t$ be the innovation at time t. Then a_t follows a GARCH(m, s) model if

$$a_t = \sigma_t \epsilon_t, \qquad \sigma_t^2 = \alpha_0 + \sum_{i=1}^{m} \alpha_i a_{t-i}^2 + \sum_{j=1}^{s} \beta_j \sigma_{t-j}^2, \tag{3.13}$$

where again $\{\epsilon_t\}$ is a sequence of iid random variables with mean 0 and variance 1.0, $\alpha_0 > 0$, $\alpha_i \geq 0$, $\beta_j \geq 0$, and $\sum_{i=1}^{\max(m,s)}(\alpha_i + \beta_i) < 1$. Here it is understood that $\alpha_i = 0$ for $i > m$ and $\beta_j = 0$ for $j > s$. The latter constraint on $\alpha_i + \beta_i$ implies that the unconditional variance of a_t is finite, whereas its conditional variance σ_t^2 evolves over time. As before, ϵ_t is often assumed to be a standard normal or standardized Student-t distribution or generalized error distribution. Equation (3.13) reduces to a pure ARCH(m) model if $s = 0$. The α_i and β_j are referred to as ARCH and GARCH parameters, respectively.

To understand properties of GARCH models, it is informative to use the following representation. Let $\eta_t = a_t^2 - \sigma_t^2$ so that $\sigma_t^2 = a_t^2 - \eta_t$. By plugging $\sigma_{t-i}^2 = a_{t-i}^2 - \eta_{t-i}$ $(i = 0, \ldots, s)$ into Eq. (3.13), we can rewrite the GARCH model as

$$a_t^2 = \alpha_0 + \sum_{i=1}^{\max(m,s)} (\alpha_i + \beta_i) a_{t-i}^2 + \eta_t - \sum_{j=1}^{s} \beta_j \eta_{t-j}. \tag{3.14}$$

It is easy to check that $\{\eta_t\}$ is a martingale difference series (i.e., $E(\eta_t) = 0$ and $\text{cov}(\eta_t, \eta_{t-j}) = 0$ for $j \geq 1$). However, $\{\eta_t\}$ in general is not an iid sequence. Equation (3.14) is an ARMA form for the squared series a_t^2. Thus, a GARCH model can be regarded as an application of the ARMA idea to the squared series a_t^2. Using the unconditional mean of an ARMA model, we have

$$E(a_t^2) = \frac{\alpha_0}{1 - \sum_{i=1}^{\max(m,s)}(\alpha_i + \beta_i)}$$

provided that the denominator of the prior fraction is positive.

The strengths and weaknesses of GARCH models can easily be seen by focusing on the simplest GARCH(1,1) model with

$$\sigma_t^2 = \alpha_0 + \alpha_1 a_{t-1}^2 + \beta_1 \sigma_{t-1}^2, \quad 0 \leq \alpha_1, \beta_1 \leq 1, (\alpha_1 + \beta_1) < 1. \tag{3.15}$$

First, a large a_{t-1}^2 or σ_{t-1}^2 gives rise to a large σ_t^2. This means that a large a_{t-1}^2 tends to be followed by another large a_t^2, generating, again, the well-known behavior of volatility clustering in financial time series. Second, it can be shown that if $1 - 2\alpha_1^2 - (\alpha_1 + \beta_1)^2 > 0$, then

$$\frac{E(a_t^4)}{[E(a_t^2)]^2} = \frac{3[1 - (\alpha_1 + \beta_1)^2]}{1 - (\alpha_1 + \beta_1)^2 - 2\alpha_1^2} > 3.$$

Consequently, similar to ARCH models, the tail distribution of a GARCH(1,1) process is heavier than that of a normal distribution. Third, the model provides a simple parametric function that can be used to describe the volatility evolution.

Forecasts of a GARCH model can be obtained using methods similar to those of an ARMA model. Consider the GARCH(1,1) model in Eq. (3.15) and assume that the forecast origin is h. For 1-step ahead forecast, we have

$$\sigma_{h+1}^2 = \alpha_0 + \alpha_1 a_h^2 + \beta_1 \sigma_h^2,$$

where a_h and σ_h^2 are known at the time index h. Therefore, the 1-step ahead forecast is

$$\sigma_h^2(1) = \alpha_0 + \alpha_1 a_h^2 + \beta_1 \sigma_h^2.$$

For multistep ahead forecasts, we use $a_t^2 = \sigma_t^2 \epsilon_t^2$ and rewrite the volatility equation in Eq. (3.15) as

$$\sigma_{t+1}^2 = \alpha_0 + (\alpha_1 + \beta_1)\sigma_t^2 + \alpha_1 \sigma_t^2(\epsilon_t^2 - 1).$$

When $t = h + 1$, the equation becomes

$$\sigma_{h+2}^2 = \alpha_0 + (\alpha_1 + \beta_1)\sigma_{h+1}^2 + \alpha_1 \sigma_{h+1}^2(\epsilon_{h+1}^2 - 1).$$

Since $E(\epsilon_{h+1}^2 - 1|F_h) = 0$, the 2-step ahead volatility forecast at the forecast origin h satisfies the equation

$$\sigma_h^2(2) = \alpha_0 + (\alpha_1 + \beta_1)\sigma_h^2(1).$$

In general, we have

$$\sigma_h^2(\ell) = \alpha_0 + (\alpha_1 + \beta_1)\sigma_h^2(\ell - 1), \quad \ell > 1. \tag{3.16}$$

This result is exactly the same as that of an ARMA(1,1) model with AR polynomial $1 - (\alpha_1 + \beta_1)B$. By repeated substitutions in Eq. (3.16), we obtain that the ℓ-step ahead forecast can be written as

$$\sigma_h^2(\ell) = \frac{\alpha_0[1 - (\alpha_1 + \beta_1)^{\ell-1}]}{1 - \alpha_1 - \beta_1} + (\alpha_1 + \beta_1)^{\ell-1}\sigma_h^2(1).$$

Therefore,

$$\sigma_h^2(\ell) \to \frac{\alpha_0}{1 - \alpha_1 - \beta_1}, \quad \text{as} \quad \ell \to \infty$$

provided that $\alpha_1 + \beta_1 < 1$. Consequently, the multistep ahead volatility forecasts of a GARCH(1,1) model converge to the unconditional variance of a_t as the forecast horizon increases to infinity provided that $\text{Var}(a_t)$ exists.

The literature on GARCH models is enormous; see Bollerslev, Chou, and Kroner (1992), Bollerslev, Engle, and Nelson (1994), and the references therein. The model encounters the same weaknesses as the ARCH model. For instance, it responds equally to positive and negative shocks. In addition, recent empirical studies of high-frequency financial time series indicate that the tail behavior of GARCH models remains too short even with standardized Student-t innovations. For further information about kurtosis of GARCH models, see Section 3.16.

3.5.1 An Illustrative Example

The modeling procedure of ARCH models can also be used to build a GARCH model. However, specifying the order of a GARCH model is not easy. Only lower order GARCH models are used in most applications, say, GARCH(1,1), GARCH(2,1), and GARCH(1,2) models. The conditional maximum likelihood method continues to apply provided that the starting values of the volatility $\{\sigma_t^2\}$ are assumed to be known. Consider, for instance, a GARCH(1,1) model. If σ_1^2 is treated as fixed, then σ_t^2 can be computed recursively for a GARCH(1,1) model. In some applications, the sample variance of a_t serves as a good starting value of σ_1^2. The fitted model can be checked by using the standardized residual $\tilde{a}_t = a_t/\sigma_t$ and its squared process.

Example 3.3. In this example, we consider the monthly excess returns of the S&P 500 index starting from 1926 for 792 observations. The series is shown in Figure 3.5. Denote the excess return series by r_t. Figure 3.6 shows the sample ACF of r_t and the sample PACF of r_t^2. The r_t series has some serial correlations at lags 1 and 3, but the key feature is that the PACF of r_t^2 shows strong linear dependence. If an MA(3) model is entertained, we obtain

$$r_t = 0.0062 + a_t + 0.0944a_{t-1} - 0.1407a_{t-3}, \quad \hat{\sigma}_a = 0.0576$$

for the series, where all of the coefficients are significant at the 5% level. However, for simplicity, we use instead an AR(3) model

$$r_t = \phi_1 r_{t-1} + \phi_2 r_{t-2} + \phi_3 r_{t-3} + \beta_0 + a_t.$$

The fitted AR(3) model, under the normality assumption, is

$$r_t = 0.088r_{t-1} - 0.023r_{t-2} - 0.123r_{t-3} + 0.0066 + a_t, \quad \hat{\sigma}_a^2 = 0.00333. \quad (3.17)$$

For the GARCH effects, we use the GARCH(1,1) model

$$a_t = \sigma_t \epsilon_t, \quad \sigma_t^2 = \alpha_0 + \beta_1 \sigma_{t-1}^2 + \alpha_1 a_{t-1}^2.$$

A joint estimation of the AR(3)–GARCH(1,1) model gives

$$r_t = 0.0078 + 0.032r_{t-1} - 0.029r_{t-2} - 0.008r_{t-3} + a_t,$$
$$\sigma_t^2 = 0.000084 + 0.1213a_{t-1}^2 + 0.8523\sigma_{t-1}^2.$$

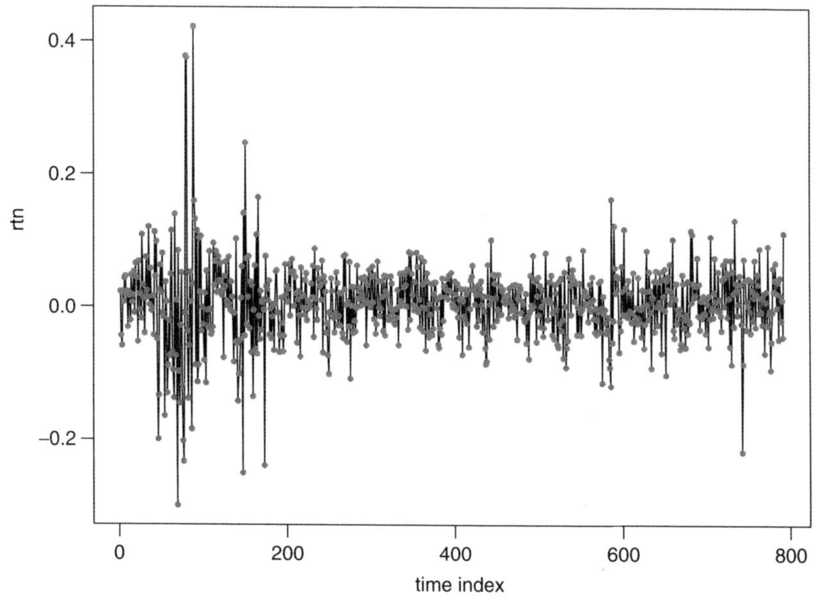

Figure 3.5. Time series plot of the monthly excess returns of the S&P 500 index.

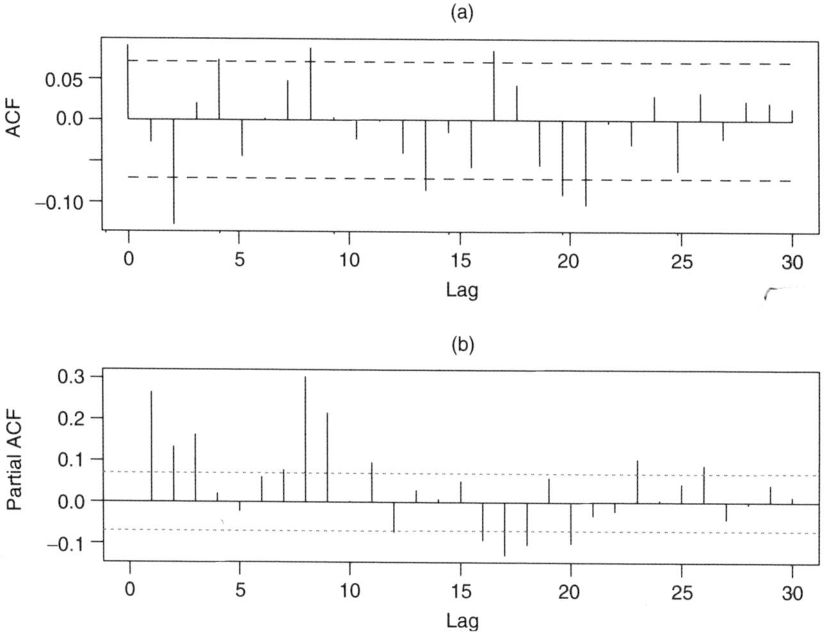

Figure 3.6. (a) Sample ACF of the monthly excess returns of the S&P 500 index and (b) sample PACF of the squared monthly excess returns.

From the volatility equation, the implied unconditional variance of a_t is

$$\frac{0.000084}{1 - 0.8523 - 0.1213} = 0.00317,$$

which is close to that of Eq. (3.17). However, t-ratios of the parameters in the mean equation suggest that all three AR coefficients are insignificant at the 5% level. Therefore, we refine the model by dropping all AR parameters. The refined model is

$$r_t = 0.0076 + a_t, \quad \sigma_t^2 = 0.000086 + 0.1216a_{t-1}^2 + 0.8511\sigma_{t-1}^2. \qquad (3.18)$$

The standard error of the constant in the mean equation is 0.0015, whereas those of the parameters in the volatility equation are 0.000024, 0.0197, and 0.0190, respectively. The unconditional variance of a_t is $0.000086/(1 - 0.8511 - 0.1216) = 0.00314$. This is a simple stationary GARCH(1,1) model. Figure 3.7 shows the estimated volatility process, σ_t, and the standardized shocks $\tilde{a}_t = a_t/\sigma_t$ for the GARCH(1,1) model in Eq. (3.18). The $\tilde{a}_t$ series appears to be a white noise process. Figure 3.8 provides the sample ACF of the standardized residuals $\tilde{a}_t$ and

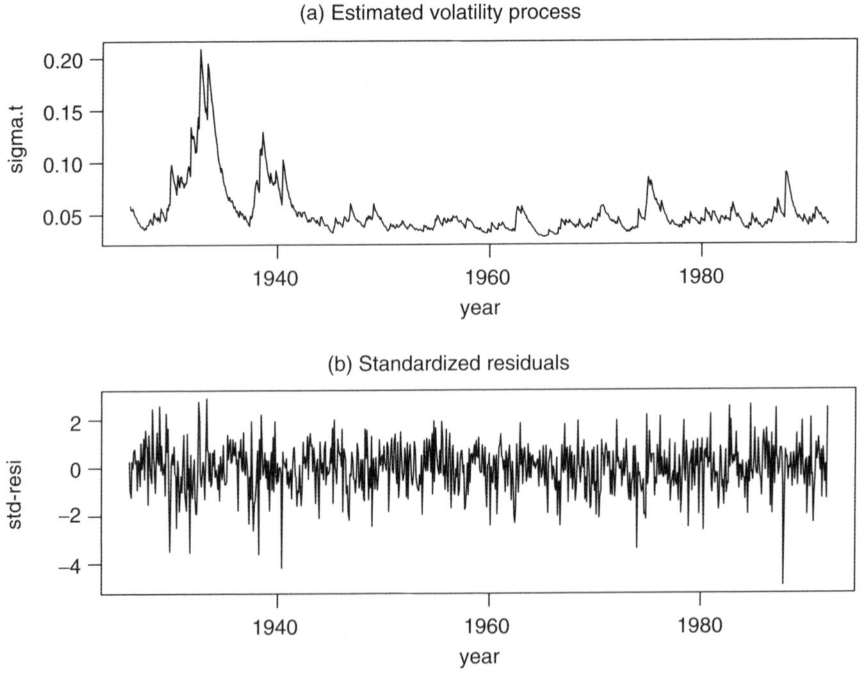

Figure 3.7. (a) Time series plot of estimated volatility (σ_t) for the monthly excess returns of the S&P 500 index and (b) the standardized shocks of the monthly excess returns of the S&P 500 index. Both plots are based on the GARCH(1,1) model in Eq. (3.18).

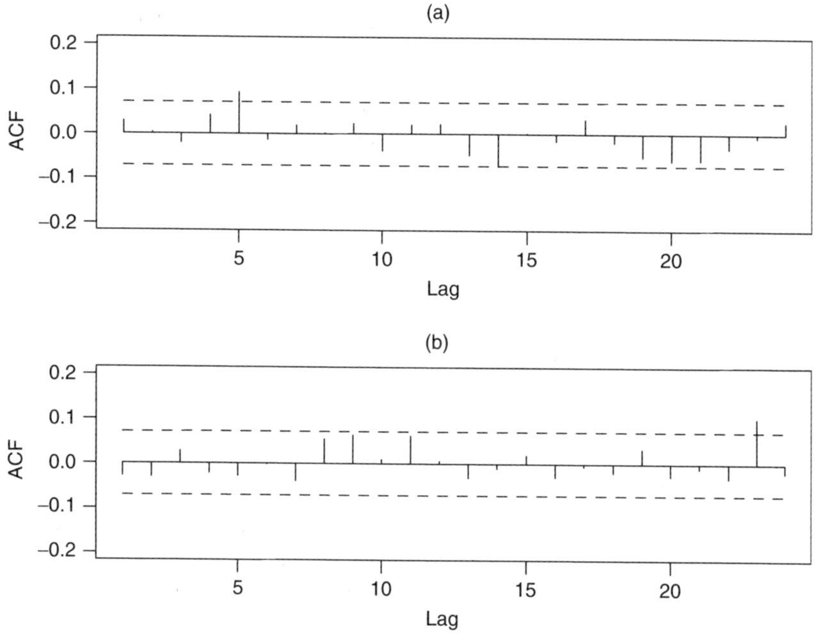

Figure 3.8. Model checking of the GARCH(1,1) model in Eq. (3.18) for monthly excess returns of the S&P 500 index: (a) sample ACF of standardized residuals and (b) sample ACF of the squared standardized residuals.

the squared process $\tilde{a}_t^2$. These ACFs fail to suggest any significant serial correlations or conditional heteroscedasticity in the standardized residual series. More specifically, we have $Q(12) = 11.99(0.45)$ and $Q(24) = 28.52(0.24)$ for $\tilde{a}_t$, and $Q(12) = 13.11(0.36)$ and $Q(24) = 26.45(0.33)$ for $\tilde{a}_t^2$, where the number in parentheses is the p-value of the test statistic. Thus, the model appears to be adequate in describing the linear dependence in the return and volatility series. Note that the fitted model shows $\hat{\alpha}_1 + \hat{\beta}_1 = 0.9772$, which is close to 1. This phenomenon is commonly observed in practice and it leads to imposing the constraint $\alpha_1 + \beta_1 = 1$ in a GARCH(1,1) model, resulting in an integrated GARCH (or IGARCH) model; see Section 3.6.

Finally, to forecast the volatility of monthly excess returns of the S&P 500 index, we can use the volatility equation in Eq. (3.18). For instance, at the forecast origin h, we have $\sigma_{h+1}^2 = 0.000086 + 0.1216a_h^2 + 0.8511\sigma_h^2$. The 1-step ahead forecast is then

$$\sigma_h^2(1) = 0.000086 + 0.1216a_h^2 + 0.8511\sigma_h^2,$$

where a_h is the residual of the mean equation at time h and σ_h is obtained from the volatility equation. The starting value σ_0^2 is fixed at either zero or the unconditional variance of a_t. For multistep ahead forecasts, we use the recursive formula in Eq. (3.16). Table 3.1 shows some mean and volatility forecasts for the monthly

Table 3.1. Volatility Forecasts for the Monthly Excess Returns of the S&P 500 Index[a]

Horizon	1	2	3	4	5	∞
Return	0.0076	0.0076	0.0076	0.0076	0.0076	0.0076
Volatility	0.0536	0.0537	0.0537	0.0538	0.0538	0.0560

[a]The forecast origin is $h = 792$, which corresponds to December 1991. Here volatility denotes conditional standard deviation.

excess return of the S&P 500 index with forecast origin $h = 792$ based on the GARCH(1,1) model in Eq. (3.18).

Some S-Plus Commands Used in Example 3.3

```
> fit=garch(sp~ar(3),~garch(1,1))
> summary(fit)
> fit=garch(sp~1,~garch(1,1))
> summary(fit)
> names(fit)
 [1] "residuals" "sigma.t"     "df.residual" "coef" "model"
 [6] "cond.dist" "likelihood" "opt.index"    "cov"
[10] "prediction" "call"       "asymp.sd"    "series"
> % Next, compute the standardized residuals
> stdresi=fit$residuals/fit$sigma.t
> autocorTest(stdresi,lag=24)
> autocorTest(stdresi^2,lag=24)
> predict(fit,5) % Compute predictions
```

Note that in the prior commands the volatility series σ_t is stored in `fit$sigma.t` and the residual series of the returns in `fit$residuals`.

t Innovation

Assuming that ϵ_t follows a standardized Student-t distribution with 5 degrees of freedom, we reestimate the GARCH(1,1) model and obtain

$$r_t = 0.0085 + a_t, \quad \sigma_t^2 = 0.00012 + 0.1121 a_{t-1}^2 + 0.8432 \sigma_{t-1}^2, \tag{3.19}$$

where the standard errors of the parameters are 0.0015, 0.51×10^{-4}, 0.0296, and 0.0371, respectively. This model is essentially an IGARCH(1,1) model as $\hat{\alpha}_1 + \hat{\beta}_1 \approx 0.95$, which is close to 1. The Ljung–Box statistics of the standardized residuals give $Q(10) = 11.38$ with p-value 0.33 and those of the $\{\tilde{a}_t^2\}$ series give $Q(10) = 10.48$ with p-value 0.40. Thus, the fitted GARCH(1,1) model with Student-t distribution is adequate.

S-Plus Commands Used

```
> fit1 = garch(sp~1,~garch(1,1),cond.dist='t',cond.par=5,
+ cond.est=F)
> summary(fit1)
> stresi=fit1$residuals/fit1$sigma.t
> autocorTest(stresi,lag=10)
> autocorTest(stresi^2,lag=10)
```

Estimation of Degrees of Freedom

If we further extend the GARCH(1,1) model by estimating the degrees of freedom of the Student-t distribution used, we obtain the model

$$r_t = 0.0085 + a_t, \quad \sigma_t^2 = 0.00012 + 0.1121 a_{t-1}^2 + 0.8432 \sigma_{t-1}^2, \tag{3.20}$$

where the estimated degrees of freedom is 7.02. Standard errors of the estimates in Eq. (3.20) are close to those in Eq. (3.19). The standard error of the estimated degrees of freedom is 1.78. Consequently, we cannot reject the hypothesis of using a standardized Student-t distribution with 5 degrees of freedom at the 5% significance level.

S-Plus Commands Used

```
> fit2 = garch(sp~1,~garch(1,1),cond.dist='t')
> summary(fit2)
```

3.5.2 Forecasting Evaluation

Since the volatility of an asset return is not directly observable, comparing the forecasting performance of different volatility models is a challenge to data analysts. In the literature, some researchers use out-of-sample forecasts and compare the volatility forecasts $\sigma_h^2(\ell)$ with the shock $a_{h+\ell}^2$ in the forecasting sample to assess the forecasting performance of a volatility model. This approach often finds a low correlation coefficient between $a_{h+\ell}^2$ and $\sigma_h^2(\ell)$, that is, low R^2. However, such a finding is not surprising because $a_{h+\ell}^2$ alone is not an adequate measure of the volatility at time index $h + \ell$. Consider the 1-step ahead forecasts. From a statistical point of view, $E(a_{h+1}^2|F_h) = \sigma_{h+1}^2$ so that a_{h+1}^2 is a consistent estimate of σ_{h+1}^2. But it is not an accurate estimate of σ_{h+1}^2 because a single observation of a random variable with a known mean value cannot provide an accurate estimate of its variance. Consequently, such an approach to evaluate forecasting performance of volatility models is strictly speaking not proper. For more information concerning forecasting evaluation of GARCH models, readers are referred to Andersen and Bollerslev (1998).

3.5.3 A Two-Pass Estimation Method

Based on Eq. (3.14), a two-pass estimation method can be used to estimate GARCH models. First, ignoring any ARCH effects, one estimates the mean equation of a return series using the methods discussed in Chapter 2 (e.g., maximum likelihood method). Denote the residual series by a_t. Second, treating $\{a_t^2\}$ as an observed time series, one applies the maximum likelihood method to estimate parameters of Eq. (3.14). Denote the AR and MA coefficient estimates by $\hat{\phi}_i$ and $\hat{\theta}_i$. The GARCH estimates are obtained as $\hat{\beta}_i = \hat{\theta}_i$ and $\hat{\alpha}_i = \hat{\phi}_i - \hat{\theta}_i$. Obviously, such estimates are approximations to the true parameters and their statistical properties have not been rigorously investigated. However, limited experience shows that this simple approach often provides good approximations, especially when the sample size is moderate or large. For instance, consider the monthly excess return series of the S&P 500 index of Example 3.3. Using the conditional MLE method in SCA, we obtain the model

$$r_t = 0.0061 + a_t, \quad a_t^2 = 0.00014 + 0.9583a_{t-1}^2 + \eta_t - 0.8456\eta_{t-1},$$

where all estimates are significantly different from zero at the 5% level. From the estimates, we have $\hat{\beta}_1 = 0.8456$ and $\hat{\alpha}_1 = 0.9583 - 0.8456 = 0.1127$. These approximate estimates are very close to those in Eq. (3.18) or (3.20). Furthermore, the fitted volatility series of the two-pass method is very close to that of Figure 3.7a.

3.6 THE INTEGRATED GARCH MODEL

If the AR polynomial of the GARCH representation in Eq. (3.14) has a unit root, then we have an IGARCH model. Thus, IGARCH models are unit-root GARCH models. Similar to ARIMA models, a key feature of IGARCH models is that the impact of past squared shocks $\eta_{t-i} = a_{t-i}^2 - \sigma_{t-i}^2$ for $i > 0$ on a_t^2 is persistent.

An IGARCH(1,1) model can be written as

$$a_t = \sigma_t \epsilon_t, \quad \sigma_t^2 = \alpha_0 + \beta_1 \sigma_{t-1}^2 + (1 - \beta_1) a_{t-1}^2,$$

where $\{\epsilon_t\}$ is defined as before and $1 > \beta_1 > 0$. For the monthly excess returns of the S&P 500 index, an estimated IGARCH(1,1) model is

$$r_t = 0.0067 + a_t, \quad a_t = \sigma_t \epsilon_t,$$
$$\sigma_t^2 = 0.000119 + 0.8059\sigma_{t-1}^2 + 0.1941a_{t-1}^2,$$

where the standard errors of the estimates in the volatility equation are 0.0017, 0.000013, and 0.0144, respectively. The parameter estimates are close to those of the GARCH(1,1) model shown before, but there is a major difference between the two models. The unconditional variance of a_t, hence that of r_t, is not defined under the above IGARCH(1,1) model. This seems hard to justify for an excess return series. From a theoretical point of view, the IGARCH phenomenon might be caused by occasional level shifts in volatility. The actual cause of persistence in volatility deserves a careful investigation.

When $\alpha_1 + \beta_1 = 1$, repeated substitutions in Eq. (3.16) give

$$\sigma_h^2(\ell) = \sigma_h^2(1) + (\ell - 1)\alpha_0, \quad \ell \geq 1, \tag{3.21}$$

where h is the forecast origin. Consequently, the effect of $\sigma_h^2(1)$ on future volatilities is also persistent, and the volatility forecasts form a straight line with slope α_0. Nelson (1990) studies some probability properties of the volatility process σ_t^2 under an IGARCH model. The process σ_t^2 is a martingale for which some nice results are available in the literature. Under certain conditions, the volatility process is strictly stationary, but not weakly stationary because it does not have the first two moments.

The case of $\alpha_0 = 0$ is of particular interest in studying the IGARCH(1,1) model. In this case, the volatility forecasts are simply $\sigma_h^2(1)$ for all forecast horizons; see Eq. (3.21). This special IGARCH(1,1) model is the volatility model used in RiskMetrics, which is an approach for calculating value at risk; see Chapter 7. The model is also an exponential smoothing model for the $\{a_t^2\}$ series. To see this, rewrite the model as

$$\begin{aligned}\sigma_t^2 &= (1-\beta_1)a_{t-1}^2 + \beta_1\sigma_{t-1}^2 \\ &= (1-\beta_1)a_{t-1}^2 + \beta_1[(1-\beta)a_{t-2}^2 + \beta_1\sigma_{t-2}^2] \\ &= (1-\beta_1)a_{t-1}^2 + (1-\beta_1)\beta_1 a_{t-2}^2 + \beta_1^2\sigma_{t-2}^2\end{aligned}$$

By repeated substitutions, we have

$$\sigma_t^2 = (1-\beta_1)(a_{t-1}^2 + \beta_1 a_{t-2}^2 + \beta_1^2 a_{t-3}^3 + \cdots),$$

which is the well-known exponential smoothing formation with β_1 being the discounting factor. Exponential smoothing methods can thus be used to estimate such an IGARCH(1,1) model.

3.7 THE GARCH-M MODEL

In finance, the return of a security may depend on its volatility. To model such a phenomenon, one may consider the GARCH-M model, where "M" stands for GARCH *in the mean*. A simple GARCH(1,1)-M model can be written as

$$\begin{aligned}r_t &= \mu + c\sigma_t^2 + a_t, \quad a_t = \sigma_t\epsilon_t, \\ \sigma_t^2 &= \alpha_0 + \alpha_1 a_{t-1}^2 + \beta_1\sigma_{t-1}^2,\end{aligned} \tag{3.22}$$

where μ and c are constants. The parameter c is called the risk premium parameter. A positive c indicates that the return is positively related to its volatility. Other specifications of risk premium have also been used in the literature, including $r_t = \mu + c\sigma_t + a_t$ and $r_t = \mu + c\ln(\sigma_t^2) + a_t$.

The formulation of the GARCH-M model in Eq. (3.22) implies that there are serial correlations in the return series r_t. These serial correlations are introduced by those in the volatility process $\{\sigma_t^2\}$. The existence of risk premium is, therefore, another reason that some historical stock returns have serial correlations.

For illustration, we consider a GARCH(1,1)-M model with Gaussian innovations for the monthly excess returns of the S&P 500 index from January 1926 to December 1991. The fitted model is

$$r_t = 0.0055 + 1.09\sigma_t^2 + a_t, \quad \sigma_t^2 = 8.76\times 10^{-5} + 0.123a_{t-1}^2 + 0.849\sigma_{t-1}^2,$$

where the standard errors for the two parameters in the mean equation are 0.0023 and 0.818, respectively, and those for the parameters in the volatility equation are 2.51×10^{-5}, 0.0205, and 0.0196, respectively. The estimated risk premium for the index return is positive but is not statistically significant at the 5% level. Here the result is obtained using S-Plus. Other forms of GARCH-M specification in S-Plus are given in Table 3.2. The idea of risk premium applies to other GARCH models.

Table 3.2. GARCH-M Models Allowed in S-Plus[a]

$g(\sigma_t)$	Command
σ_t^2	var.in.mean
σ_t	sd.in.mean
$\ln(\sigma_t^2)$	logvar.in.mean

[a] The mean equation is $r_t = \mu + cg(\sigma_t) + a_t$.

S-Plus Demonstration

```
> sp.fit = garch(sp~1+var.in.mean,~garch(1,1))
> summary(sp.fit)
```

3.8 THE EXPONENTIAL GARCH MODEL

To overcome some weaknesses of the GARCH model in handling financial time series, Nelson (1991) proposes the exponential GARCH (EGARCH) model. In particular, to allow for asymmetric effects between positive and negative asset returns, he considers the weighted innovation

$$g(\epsilon_t) = \theta\epsilon_t + \gamma[|\epsilon_t| - E(|\epsilon_t|)], \tag{3.23}$$

where θ and γ are real constants. Both ϵ_t and $|\epsilon_t| - E(|\epsilon_t|)$ are zero-mean iid sequences with continuous distributions. Therefore, $E[g(\epsilon_t)] = 0$. The asymmetry of $g(\epsilon_t)$ can easily be seen by rewriting it as

$$g(\epsilon_t) = \begin{cases} (\theta + \gamma)\epsilon_t - \gamma E(|\epsilon_t|) & \text{if } \epsilon_t \geq 0, \\ (\theta - \gamma)\epsilon_t - \gamma E(|\epsilon_t|) & \text{if } \epsilon_t < 0. \end{cases}$$

Remark. For the standard Gaussian random variable ϵ_t, $E(|\epsilon_t|) = \sqrt{2/\pi}$. For the standardized Student-t distribution in Eq. (3.7), we have

$$E(|\epsilon_t|) = \frac{2\sqrt{v-2}\,\Gamma((v+1)/2)}{(v-1)\Gamma(v/2)\sqrt{\pi}}. \qquad \square$$

An EGARCH(m, s) model can be written as

$$a_t = \sigma_t\epsilon_t, \quad \ln(\sigma_t^2) = \alpha_0 + \frac{1 + \beta_1 B + \cdots + \beta_{s-1}B^{s-1}}{1 - \alpha_1 B - \cdots - \alpha_m B^m} g(\epsilon_{t-1}), \tag{3.24}$$

where α_0 is a constant, B is the back-shift (or lag) operator such that $Bg(\epsilon_t) = g(\epsilon_{t-1})$, and $1 + \beta_1 B + \cdots + \beta_{s-1}B^{s-1}$ and $1 - \alpha_1 B - \cdots - \alpha_m B^m$ are polynomials with zeros outside the unit circle and have no common factors. By outside the unit circle, we mean that absolute values of the zeros are greater than 1. Again, Eq. (3.24) uses the usual ARMA parameterization to describe the evolution of the conditional variance of a_t. Based on this representation, some properties of the EGARCH model can be obtained in a similar manner as those of the GARCH model. For instance, the unconditional mean of $\ln(\sigma_t^2)$ is α_0. However, the model differs from the GARCH model in several ways. First, it uses logged conditional variance to relax the positiveness constraint of model coefficients. Second, the use of $g(\epsilon_t)$ enables the model to respond asymmetrically to positive and negative lagged values of a_t. Some additional properties of the EGARCH model can be found in Nelson (1991).

To better understand the EGARCH model, let us consider the simple model with order (1,1):

$$a_t = \sigma_t \epsilon_t, \qquad (1 - \alpha B)\ln(\sigma_t^2) = (1-\alpha)\alpha_0 + g(\epsilon_{t-1}), \tag{3.25}$$

where the ϵ_t are iid standard normal and the subscript of α_1 is omitted. In this case, $E(|\epsilon_t|) = \sqrt{2/\pi}$ and the model for $\ln(\sigma_t^2)$ becomes

$$(1-\alpha B)\ln(\sigma_t^2) = \begin{cases} \alpha_* + (\gamma+\theta)\epsilon_{t-1} & \text{if } \epsilon_{t-1} \geq 0, \\ \alpha_* + (\gamma-\theta)(-\epsilon_{t-1}) & \text{if } \epsilon_{t-1} < 0, \end{cases} \tag{3.26}$$

where $\alpha_* = (1-\alpha)\alpha_0 - \sqrt{2/\pi}\gamma$. This is a nonlinear function similar to that of the threshold autoregressive (TAR) model of Tong (1978, 1990). It suffices to say that for this simple EGARCH model the conditional variance evolves in a nonlinear manner depending on the sign of a_{t-1}. Specifically, we have

$$\sigma_t^2 = \sigma_{t-1}^{2\alpha}\exp(\alpha_*)\begin{cases} \exp\left((\gamma+\theta)\dfrac{a_{t-1}}{\sigma_{t-1}}\right) & \text{if } a_{t-1} \geq 0, \\ \exp\left((\gamma-\theta)\dfrac{|a_{t-1}|}{\sigma_{t-1}}\right) & \text{if } a_{t-1} < 0. \end{cases}$$

The coefficients $(\gamma+\theta)$ and $(\gamma-\theta)$ show the asymmetry in response to positive and negative a_{t-1}. The model is, therefore, nonlinear if $\theta \neq 0$. Since negative shocks tend to have larger impacts, we expect θ to be negative. For higher order EGARCH models, the nonlinearity becomes much more complicated. Cao and Tsay (1992) use nonlinear models, including EGARCH models, to obtain multi-step ahead volatility forecasts. We discuss nonlinearity in financial time series in Chapter 4.

3.8.1 An Alternative Model Form

An alternative form for the EGARCH(m, s) model is

$$\ln(\sigma_t^2) = \alpha_0 + \sum_{i=1}^{s}\alpha_i \frac{|a_{t-i}| + \gamma_i a_{t-i}}{\sigma_{t-i}} + \sum_{j=1}^{m}\beta_j \ln(\sigma_{t-j}^2). \tag{3.27}$$

Here a positive a_{t-i} contributes $\alpha_i(1+\gamma_i)|\epsilon_{t-i}|$ to the log volatility, whereas a negative a_{t-i} gives $\alpha_i(1-\gamma_i)|\epsilon_{t-i}|$, where $\epsilon_{t-i} = a_{t-i}/\sigma_{t-i}$. The γ_i parameter thus signifies the leverage effect of a_{t-i}. Again, we expect γ_i to be negative in real applications. This is the model form used in S-Plus.

3.8.2 An Illustrative Example

Nelson (1991) applies an EGARCH model to the daily excess returns of the value-weighted market index from the Center for Research in Security Prices from July 1962 to December 1987. The excess returns are obtained by removing monthly Treasury bill returns from the value-weighted index returns, assuming that the Treasury bill return was constant for each calendar day within a given month. There are 6408 observations. Denote the excess return by r_t. The model used is as follows:

$$\begin{aligned} r_t &= \phi_0 + \phi_1 r_{t-1} + c\sigma_t^2 + a_t, \\ \ln(\sigma_t^2) &= \alpha_0 + \ln(1 + wN_t) + \frac{1 + \beta B}{1 - \alpha_1 B - \alpha_2 B^2} g(\epsilon_{t-1}), \end{aligned} \tag{3.28}$$

where σ_t^2 is the conditional variance of a_t given F_{t-1}, N_t is the number of nontrading days between trading days $t-1$ and t, α_0 and w are real parameters, $g(\epsilon_t)$ is defined in Eq. (3.23), and ϵ_t follows a generalized error distribution in Eq. (3.9). Similar to a GARCH-M model, the parameter c in Eq. (3.28) is the risk premium parameter. Table 3.3 gives the parameter estimates and their standard errors of the model. The mean equation of model (3.28) has two features that are of interest. First, it uses an AR(1) model to take care of possible serial correlation in the excess returns. Second, it uses the volatility σ_t^2 as a regressor to account for risk premium. The estimated risk premium is negative, but statistically insignificant.

3.8.3 Second Example

As another illustration, we consider the monthly log returns of IBM stock from January 1926 to December 1997 for 864 observations. An AR(1)–EGARCH(1,1) model is entertained and the fitted model is

$$r_t = 0.0105 + 0.092 r_{t-1} + a_t, \quad a_t = \sigma_t \epsilon_t, \tag{3.29}$$

$$\begin{aligned} \ln(\sigma_t^2) &= -5.496 + \frac{g(\epsilon_{t-1})}{1 - 0.856B}, \\ g(\epsilon_{t-1}) &= -0.0795\epsilon_{t-1} + 0.2647\left[|\epsilon_{t-1}| - \sqrt{2/\pi}\right], \end{aligned} \tag{3.30}$$

Table 3.3. Estimated AR(1)–EGARCH(2,2) Model for the Daily Excess Returns of the Value-Weighted CRSP Market Index: July 1962 to December 1987

Parameter	α_0	w	γ	α_1	α_2	β
Estimate	−10.06	0.183	0.156	1.929	−0.929	−0.978
Error	0.346	0.028	0.013	0.015	0.015	0.006
Parameter	θ	ϕ_0	ϕ_1	c	v	
Estimate	−0.118	$3.5 \cdot 10^{-4}$	0.205	−3.361	1.576	
Error	0.009	$9.9 \cdot 10^{-5}$	0.012	2.026	0.032	

where $\{\epsilon_t\}$ is a sequence of independent standard Gaussian random variates. All parameter estimates are statistically significant at the 5% level. For model checking, the Ljung–Box statistics give $Q(10) = 6.31(0.71)$ and $Q(20) = 21.4(0.32)$ for the standardized residual process $\tilde{a}_t = a_t/\sigma_t$ and $Q(10) = 4.13(0.90)$ and $Q(20) = 15.93(0.66)$ for the squared process $\tilde{a}_t^2$, where again the number in parentheses denotes p-value. Therefore, there is no serial correlation or conditional heteroscedasticity in the standardized residuals of the fitted model. The prior AR(1)–EGARCH(1,1) model is adequate.

From the estimated volatility equation in (3.30) and using $\sqrt{2/\pi} \approx 0.7979$, we obtain the volatility equation as

$$\ln(\sigma_t^2) = -1.001 + 0.856\ln(\sigma_{t-1}^2) + \begin{cases} 0.1852\epsilon_{t-1} & \text{if } \epsilon_{t-1} \geq 0, \\ -0.3442\epsilon_{t-1} & \text{if } \epsilon_{t-1} < 0. \end{cases}$$

Taking antilog transformation, we have

$$\sigma_t^2 = \sigma_{t-1}^{2\times 0.856} e^{-1.001} \times \begin{cases} e^{0.1852\epsilon_{t-1}} & \text{if } \epsilon_{t-1} \geq 0, \\ e^{-0.3442\epsilon_{t-1}} & \text{if } \epsilon_{t-1} < 0. \end{cases}$$

This equation highlights the asymmetric responses in volatility to the past positive and negative shocks under an EGARCH model. For example, for a standardized shock with magnitude 2 (i.e., two standard deviations), we have

$$\frac{\sigma_t^2(\epsilon_{t-1} = -2)}{\sigma_t^2(\epsilon_{t-1} = 2)} = \frac{\exp[-0.3442 \times (-2)]}{\exp(0.1852 \times 2)} = e^{0.318} = 1.374.$$

Therefore, the impact of a negative shock of size two standard deviations is about 37.4% higher than that of a positive shock of the same size. This example clearly demonstrates the asymmetric feature of EGARCH models. In general, the bigger the shock, the larger the difference in volatility impact.

Finally, we extend the sample period to include the log returns from 1998 to 2003 so that there are 936 observations and use S-Plus to fit an EGARCH(1,1) model. The results are given below.

S-Plus Demonstration

Output edited.

```
> ibm.egarch=garch(ibmln~1,~egarch(1,1),leverage=T,
+ cond.dist='ged')

> summary(ibm.egarch)
Call:
garch(formula.mean = ibmln ~ 1, formula.var =  ~ egarch(1,1),
      leverage = T,cond.dist = "ged")

Mean Equation: ibmln ~ 1
```

```
Conditional Variance Equation:  ~ egarch(1, 1)
Conditional Distribution:  ged
with estimated parameter 1.5003 and standard error 0.09912
-------------------------------------------------------------
Estimated Coefficients:
-------------------------------------------------------------
            Value Std.Error t value  Pr(>|t|)
       C  0.01181  0.002012   5.870 3.033e-09
       A -0.55680  0.171602  -3.245 6.088e-04
 ARCH(1)  0.22025  0.052824   4.169 1.669e-05
GARCH(1)  0.92910  0.026743  34.742 0.000e+00
  LEV(1) -0.26400  0.126096  -2.094 1.828e-02
-------------------------------------------------------------
Ljung-Box test for standardized residuals:
-------------------------------------------------------------
 Statistic P-value Chi^2-d.f.
     17.87  0.1195         12

Ljung-Box test for squared standardized residuals:
-------------------------------------------------------------
 Statistic P-value Chi^2-d.f.
     6.723  0.8754         12
```

The fitted GARCH(1,1) model is

$$\begin{aligned} r_t &= 0.0118 + a_t, \quad a_t = \sigma_t \epsilon_t, \\ \ln(\sigma_t^2) &= -0.557 + 0.220 \frac{|a_{t-1}| - 0.264 a_{t-1}}{\sigma_{t-1}} + 0.929 \ln(\sigma_{t-1}^2), \end{aligned} \tag{3.31}$$

where ϵ_t follows a GED distribution with parameter 1.5. This model is adequate based on the Ljung–Box statistics of the standardized residual series and its squared process. As expected, the output shows that the estimated leverage effect is negative and is statistically significant at the 5% level with t-ratio -2.094.

3.8.4 Forecasting Using an EGARCH Model

We use the EGARCH(1,1) model to illustrate multistep ahead forecasts of EGARCH models, assuming that the model parameters are known and the innovations are standard Gaussian. For such a model, we have

$$\begin{aligned} \ln(\sigma_t^2) &= (1 - \alpha_1)\alpha_0 + \alpha_1 \ln(\sigma_{t-1}^2) + g(\epsilon_{t-1}), \\ g(\epsilon_{t-1}) &= \theta \epsilon_{t-1} + \gamma(|\epsilon_{t-1}| - \sqrt{2/\pi}). \end{aligned}$$

Taking exponentials, the model becomes

$$\begin{aligned} \sigma_t^2 &= \sigma_{t-1}^{2\alpha_1} \exp[(1 - \alpha_1)\alpha_0] \exp[g(\epsilon_{t-1})], \\ g(\epsilon_{t-1}) &= \theta \epsilon_{t-1} + \gamma(|\epsilon_{t-1}| - \sqrt{2/\pi}). \end{aligned} \tag{3.32}$$

Let h be the forecast origin. For the 1-step ahead forecast, we have

$$\sigma_{h+1}^2 = \sigma_h^{2\alpha_1} \exp[(1-\alpha_1)\alpha_0] \exp[g(\epsilon_h)],$$

where all of the quantities on the right-hand side are known. Thus, the 1-step ahead volatility forecast at the forecast origin h is simply $\hat{\sigma}_h^2(1) = \sigma_{h+1}^2$ given earlier. For the 2-step ahead forecast, Eq. (3.32) gives

$$\sigma_{h+2}^2 = \sigma_{h+1}^{2\alpha_1} \exp[(1-\alpha_1)\alpha_0] \exp[g(\epsilon_{h+1})].$$

Taking conditional expectation at time h, we have

$$\hat{\sigma}_h^2(2) = \hat{\sigma}_h^{2\alpha_1}(1) \exp[(1-\alpha_1)\alpha_0] E_h\{\exp[g(\epsilon_{h+1})]\},$$

where E_h denotes a conditional expectation taken at the time origin h. The prior expectation can be obtained as follows:

$$\begin{aligned} E\{\exp[g(\epsilon)]\} &= \int_{-\infty}^{\infty} \exp[\theta\epsilon + \gamma(|\epsilon| - \sqrt{2/\pi})] f(\epsilon) d\epsilon \\ &= \exp\left(-\gamma\sqrt{2/\pi}\right) \left[\int_0^{\infty} e^{(\theta+\gamma)\epsilon} \frac{1}{\sqrt{2\pi}} e^{-\epsilon^2/2} d\epsilon \right. \\ &\qquad \left. + \int_{-\infty}^{0} e^{(\theta-\gamma)\epsilon} \frac{1}{\sqrt{2\pi}} e^{-\epsilon^2/2} d\epsilon \right] \\ &= \exp\left(-\gamma\sqrt{2/\pi}\right) \left[e^{(\theta+\gamma)^2/2} \Phi(\theta+\gamma) + e^{(\theta-\gamma)^2/2} \Phi(\gamma-\theta) \right], \end{aligned}$$

where $f(\epsilon)$ and $\Phi(x)$ are the probability density function and CDF of the standard normal distribution, respectively. Consequently, the 2-step ahead volatility forecast is

$$\begin{aligned} \hat{\sigma}_h^2(2) &= \hat{\sigma}_h^{2\alpha_1}(1) \exp\left[(1-\alpha_1)\alpha_0 - \gamma\sqrt{2/\pi}\right] \\ &\quad \times \{\exp[(\theta+\gamma)^2/2]\Phi(\theta+\gamma) + \exp[(\theta-\gamma)^2/2]\Phi(\gamma-\theta)\}. \end{aligned}$$

Repeating the previous procedure, we obtain a recursive formula for a j-step ahead forecast:

$$\begin{aligned} \hat{\sigma}_h^2(j) &= \hat{\sigma}_h^{2\alpha_1}(j-1) \exp(\omega) \\ &\quad \times \{\exp[(\theta+\gamma)^2/2]\Phi(\theta+\gamma) + \exp[(\theta-\gamma)^2/2]\Phi(\gamma-\theta)\}, \end{aligned}$$

where $\omega = (1-\alpha_1)\alpha_0 - \gamma\sqrt{2/\pi}$. The values of $\Phi(\theta+\gamma)$ and $\Phi(\theta-\gamma)$ can be obtained from most statistical packages. Alternatively, accurate approximations to these values can be obtained by using the method in Appendix B of Chapter 6.

For illustration, consider the AR(1)–EGARCH(1,1) model of the previous subsection for the monthly log returns of IBM stock, ending December 1997. Using the fitted EGARCH(1,1) model, we can compute the volatility forecasts for the series. At the forecast origin $t = 864$, the forecasts are $\hat{\sigma}^2_{864}(1) = 6.05 \times 10^{-3}$, $\hat{\sigma}^2_{864}(2) = 5.82 \times 10^{-3}$, $\hat{\sigma}^2_{864}(3) = 5.63 \times 10^{-3}$, and $\hat{\sigma}^2_{864}(10) = 4.94 \times 10^{-3}$. These forecasts converge gradually to the sample variance 4.37×10^{-3} of the shock process a_t of Eq. (3.29).

3.9 THE THRESHOLD GARCH MODEL

Another volatility model commonly used to handle leverage effects is the threshold GARCH (or TGARCH) model; see Glosten, Jagannathan, and Runkle (1993) and Zakoian (1994). A TGARCH(m, s) model assumes the form

$$\sigma_t^2 = \alpha_0 + \sum_{i=1}^{s}(\alpha_i + \gamma_i N_{t-i})a_{t-i}^2 + \sum_{j=1}^{m}\beta_j\sigma_{t-j}^2, \tag{3.33}$$

where N_{t-i} is an indicator for *negative* a_{t-i}, that is,

$$N_{t-i} = \begin{cases} 1 & \text{if } a_{t-i} < 0, \\ 0 & \text{if } a_{t-i} \geq 0, \end{cases}$$

and α_i, γ_i, and β_j are non-negative parameters satisfying conditions similar to those of GARCH models. From the model, it is seen that a positive a_{t-i} contributes $\alpha_i a_{t-i}^2$ to σ_t^2, whereas a negative a_{t-i} has a larger impact $(\alpha_i + \gamma_i)a_{t-i}^2$ with $\gamma_i > 0$. The model uses zero as its *threshold* to separate the impacts of past shocks. Other threshold values can also be used; see Chapter 4 for the general concept of threshold models. Model (3.33) is also called the GJR model because Glosten et al. (1993) proposed essentially the same model.

For illustration, consider the monthly log returns of IBM stock from 1926 to 2003. The fitted TGARCH(1,1) model with conditional GED innovations is

$$\begin{aligned} r_t &= 0.0121 + a_t, \qquad a_t = \sigma_t\epsilon_t, \\ \sigma_t^2 &= 3.45 \times 10^{-4} + (0.0658 + 0.0843N_{t-1})a_{t-1}^2 + 0.8182\sigma_{t-1}^2, \end{aligned} \tag{3.34}$$

where the estimated parameter of the GED is 1.51 with standard error 0.099. The standard error of the parameter for the mean equation is 0.002 and the standard errors of the parameters in the volatility equation are $1.26 \times {}^{-4}$, 0.0314, 0.0395, and 0.049, respectively. To check the fitted model, we have $Q(12) = 18.34(0.106)$ for the standardized residual $\tilde{a}_t$ and $Q(12) = 5.36(0.95)$ for $\tilde{a}_t^2$. The model is adequate in modeling the first two conditional moments of the log return series. Based on the fitted model, the leverage effect is significant at the 5% level.

S-Plus Commands Used

```
> ibm.tgarch = garch(ibmln~1,~tgarch(1,1),leverage=T,
+ cond.dist='ged')
> summary(ibm.tgarch)
> plot(ibm.tgarch)
```

It is interesting to compare the two models in Eqs. (3.31) and (3.34) for the monthly log returns of IBM stock. Assume that $a_{t-1} = \pm 2\sigma_{t-1}$ so that $\epsilon_{t-1} = \pm 2$. The EGARCH(1,1) model gives

$$\frac{\sigma_t^2(\epsilon_{t-1} = -2)}{\sigma_t^2(\epsilon_{t-1} = 2)} = e^{0.22\times 2\times 0.632} \approx 1.264.$$

On the other hand, ignoring the constant term 0.000345, the TGARCH(1,1) model gives

$$\frac{\sigma_t^2(\epsilon_{t-1} = -2)}{\sigma_t^2(\epsilon_{t-1} = 2)} \approx \frac{[(0.0658 + 0.0843)4 + 0.8182]\sigma_{t-1}^2}{(0.0658 \times 4 + 0.8182)\sigma_{t-1}^2} = 1.312.$$

The two models provide similar leverage effects.

3.10 THE CHARMA MODEL

Many other econometric models have been proposed in the literature to describe the evolution of the conditional variance σ_t^2 in Eq. (3.2). We mention the conditional heteroscedastic ARMA (CHARMA) model that uses random coefficients to produce conditional heteroscedasticity; see Tsay (1987). The CHARMA model is not the same as the ARCH model, but the two models have similar second-order conditional properties. A CHARMA model is defined as

$$r_t = \mu_t + a_t, \quad a_t = \delta_{1t}a_{t-1} + \delta_{2t}a_{t-2} + \cdots + \delta_{mt}a_{t-m} + \eta_t, \tag{3.35}$$

where $\{\eta_t\}$ is a Gaussian white noise series with mean zero and variance σ_η^2, $\{\boldsymbol{\delta}_t\} = \{(\delta_{1t}, \ldots, \delta_{mt})'\}$ is a sequence of iid random vectors with mean zero and non-negative definite covariance matrix $\boldsymbol{\Omega}$, and $\{\boldsymbol{\delta}_t\}$ is independent of $\{\eta_t\}$. In this section, we use some basic properties of vector and matrix operations to simplify the presentation. Readers may consult Appendix A of Chapter 8 for a brief review of these properties. For $m > 0$, the model can be written as

$$a_t = \boldsymbol{a}_{t-1}'\boldsymbol{\delta}_t + \eta_t,$$

where $\boldsymbol{a}_{t-1} = (a_{t-1}, \ldots, a_{t-m})'$ is a vector of lagged values of a_t and is available at time $t-1$. The conditional variance of a_t of the CHARMA model in Eq. (3.35) is then

$$\begin{aligned}\sigma_t^2 &= \sigma_\eta^2 + \boldsymbol{a}_{t-1}'\text{Cov}(\boldsymbol{\delta}_t)\boldsymbol{a}_{t-1} \\ &= \sigma_\eta^2 + (a_{t-1}, \ldots, a_{t-m})\boldsymbol{\Omega}(a_{t-1}, \ldots, a_{t-m})'. \end{aligned} \tag{3.36}$$

Denote the (i, j)th element of $\boldsymbol{\Omega}$ by ω_{ij}. Because the matrix is symmetric, we have $\omega_{ij} = \omega_{ji}$. If $m = 1$, then Eq. (3.36) reduces to $\sigma_t^2 = \sigma_\eta^2 + \omega_{11}a_{t-1}^2$, which is an ARCH(1) model. If $m = 2$, then Eq. (3.36) reduces to

$$\sigma_t^2 = \sigma_\eta^2 + \omega_{11}a_{t-1}^2 + 2\omega_{12}a_{t-1}a_{t-2} + \omega_{22}a_{t-2}^2,$$

which differs from an ARCH(2) model by the cross-product term $a_{t-1}a_{t-2}$. In general, the conditional variance of a CHARMA(m) model is equivalent to that of an ARCH(m) model if $\boldsymbol{\Omega}$ is a diagonal matrix. Because $\boldsymbol{\Omega}$ is a covariance matrix, which is non-negative definite, and σ_η^2 is a variance, which is positive, we have $\sigma_t^2 \geq \sigma_\eta^2 > 0$ for all t. In other words, the positiveness of σ_t^2 is automatically satisfied under a CHARMA model.

An obvious difference between ARCH and CHARMA models is that the latter use cross-products of the lagged values of a_t in the volatility equation. The cross-product terms might be useful in some applications. For example, in modeling an asset return series, cross-product terms denote interactions between previous returns. It is conceivable that stock volatility may depend on such interactions. However, the number of cross-product terms increases rapidly with the order m, and some constraints are needed to keep the model simple. A possible constraint is to use a small number of cross-product terms in a CHARMA model. Another difference between the two models is that higher order properties of CHARMA models are harder to obtain than those of ARCH models because it is in general harder to handle multiple random variables.

For illustration, we employ the CHARMA model

$$r_t = \phi_0 + a_t, \qquad a_t = \delta_{1t}a_{t-1} + \delta_{2t}a_{t-2} + \eta_t$$

for the monthly excess returns of the S&P 500 index used before in GARCH modeling. The fitted model is

$$r_t = 0.00635 + a_t, \quad \sigma_t^2 = 0.00179 + (a_{t-1}, a_{t-2})\widehat{\boldsymbol{\Omega}}(a_{t-1}, a_{t-2})',$$

where

$$\widehat{\boldsymbol{\Omega}} = \begin{bmatrix} 0.1417(0.0333) & -0.0594(0.0365) \\ -0.0594(0.0365) & 0.3081(0.0340) \end{bmatrix},$$

where the numbers in parentheses are standard errors. The cross-product term of $\widehat{\boldsymbol{\Omega}}$ has a t-ratio of -1.63, which is marginally significant at the 10% level. If we refine the model to

$$r_t = \phi_0 + a_t, \qquad a_t = \delta_{1t}a_{t-1} + \delta_{2t}a_{t-2} + \delta_{3t}a_{t-3} + \eta_t,$$

but assume that δ_{3t} is uncorrelated with $(\delta_{1t}, \delta_{2t})$, then we obtain the fitted model

$$r_t = 0.0068 + a_t, \quad \sigma_t^2 = 0.00136 + (a_{t-1}, a_{t-2}, a_{t-3})\widehat{\boldsymbol{\Omega}}(a_{t-1}, a_{t-2}, a_{t-3})',$$

where the elements of $\widehat{\boldsymbol{\Omega}}$ and their standard errors, shown in parentheses, are

$$\widehat{\boldsymbol{\Omega}} = \begin{bmatrix} 0.1212(0.0355) & -0.0622(0.0283) & 0 \\ -0.0622(0.0283) & 0.1913(0.0254) & 0 \\ 0 & 0 & 0.2988(0.0420) \end{bmatrix}.$$

All of the estimates are now statistically significant at the 5% level. From the model, $a_t = r_t - 0.0068$ is the deviation of the monthly excess return from its average. The fitted CHARMA model shows that there is some interaction effect between the first two lagged deviations. Indeed, the volatility equation can be written approximately as

$$\sigma_t^2 = 0.00136 + 0.12a_{t-1}^2 - 0.12a_{t-1}a_{t-2} + 0.19a_{t-2}^2 + 0.30a_{t-3}^2.$$

The conditional variance is slightly larger when $a_{t-1}a_{t-2}$ is negative.

3.10.1 Effects of Explanatory Variables

The CHARMA model can easily be generalized so that the volatility of r_t may depend on some explanatory variables. Let $\{x_{it}\}_{i=1}^m$ be m explanatory variables available at time t. Consider the model

$$r_t = \mu_t + a_t, \qquad a_t = \sum_{i=1}^m \delta_{it}x_{i,t-1} + \eta_t, \tag{3.37}$$

where $\boldsymbol{\delta}_t = (\delta_{1t}, \ldots, \delta_{mt})'$ and η_t are random vector and variable defined in Eq. (3.35). Then the conditional variance of a_t is

$$\sigma_t^2 = \sigma_\eta^2 + (x_{1,t-1}, \ldots, x_{m,t-1})\boldsymbol{\Omega}(x_{1,t-1}, \ldots, x_{m,t-1})'.$$

In application, the explanatory variables may include some lagged values of a_t.

3.11 RANDOM COEFFICIENT AUTOREGRESSIVE MODELS

In the literature, the random coefficient autoregressive (RCA) model is introduced to account for variability among different subjects under study, similar to the panel data analysis in econometrics and the hierarchical model in statistics. We classify the RCA model as a conditional heteroscedastic model, but historically it is used to obtain a better description of the conditional mean equation of the process by allowing for the parameters to evolve over time. A time series r_t is said to follow an RCA(p) model if it satisfies

$$r_t = \phi_0 + \sum_{i=1}^p (\phi_i + \delta_{it})r_{t-i} + a_t, \tag{3.38}$$

where p is a positive integer, $\{\boldsymbol{\delta}_t\} = \{(\delta_{1t}, \ldots, \delta_{pt})'\}$ is a sequence of independent random vectors with mean zero and covariance matrix $\boldsymbol{\Omega}_\delta$, and $\{\boldsymbol{\delta}_t\}$ is independent of $\{a_t\}$; see Nicholls and Quinn (1982) for further discussions of the model. The conditional mean and variance of the RCA model in Eq. (3.38) are

$$\mu_t = E(r_t|F_{t-1}) = \phi_0 + \sum_{i=1}^p \phi_i r_{t-i},$$

$$\sigma_t^2 = \sigma_a^2 + (r_{t-1}, \ldots, r_{t-p})\boldsymbol{\Omega}_\delta(r_{t-1}, \ldots, r_{t-p})',$$

which is in the same form as that of a CHARMA model. However, there is a subtle difference between RCA and CHARMA models. For the RCA model, the volatility is a quadratic function of the observed lagged values r_{t-i}. Yet the volatility is a quadratic function of the lagged innovations a_{t-i} in a CHARMA model.

3.12 THE STOCHASTIC VOLATILITY MODEL

An alternative approach to describe the volatility evolution of a financial time series is to introduce an innovation to the conditional variance equation of a_t; see Melino and Turnbull (1990), Taylor (1994), Harvey, Ruiz, and Shephard (1994), and Jacquier, Polson, and Rossi (1994). The resulting model is referred to as a stochastic volatility (SV) model. Similar to EGARCH models, to ensure positiveness of the conditional variance, SV models use $\ln(\sigma_t^2)$ instead of σ_t^2. A SV model is defined as

$$a_t = \sigma_t \epsilon_t, \qquad (1 - \alpha_1 B - \cdots - \alpha_m B^m)\ln(\sigma_t^2) = \alpha_0 + v_t, \tag{3.39}$$

where the ϵ_t are iid $N(0, 1)$, the v_t are iid $N(0, \sigma_v^2)$, $\{\epsilon_t\}$ and $\{v_t\}$ are independent, α_0 is a constant, and all zeros of the polynomial $1 - \sum_{i=1}^{m} \alpha_i B^i$ are greater than 1 in modulus. Adding the innovation v_t substantially increases the flexibility of the model in describing the evolution of σ_t^2, but it also increases the difficulty in parameter estimation. To estimate a SV model, we need a quasi-likelihood method via Kalman filtering or a Monte Carlo method. Jacquier, Polson, and Rossi (1994) provide some comparison of estimation results between quasi-likelihood and Markov chain Monte Carlo (MCMC) methods. The difficulty in estimating a SV model is understandable because for each shock a_t the model uses two innovations ϵ_t and v_t. We discuss a MCMC method to estimate SV models in Chapter 12. For more discussions on stochastic volatility models, see Taylor (1994).

The appendixes of Jacquier, Polson, and Rossi (1994) provide some properties of the SV model when $m = 1$. For instance, with $m = 1$, we have

$$\ln(\sigma_t^2) \sim N\left(\frac{\alpha_0}{1 - \alpha_1}, \frac{\sigma_v^2}{1 - \alpha_1^2}\right) \equiv N(\mu_h, \sigma_h^2),$$

and $E(a_t^2) = \exp(\mu_h + \sigma_h^2/2)$, $E(a_t^4) = 3\exp(2\mu_h^2 + 2\sigma_h^2)$, and $\text{corr}(a_t^2, a_{t-i}^2) = [\exp(\sigma_h^2 \alpha_1^i) - 1]/[3\exp(\sigma_h^2) - 1]$. Limited experience shows that SV models often provided improvements in model fitting, but their contributions to out-of-sample volatility forecasts received mixed results.

3.13 THE LONG-MEMORY STOCHASTIC VOLATILITY MODEL

More recently, the SV model is further extended to allow for long memory in volatility, using the idea of fractional difference. As stated in Chapter 2, a time series is a long-memory process if its autocorrelation function decays at a hyperbolic, instead

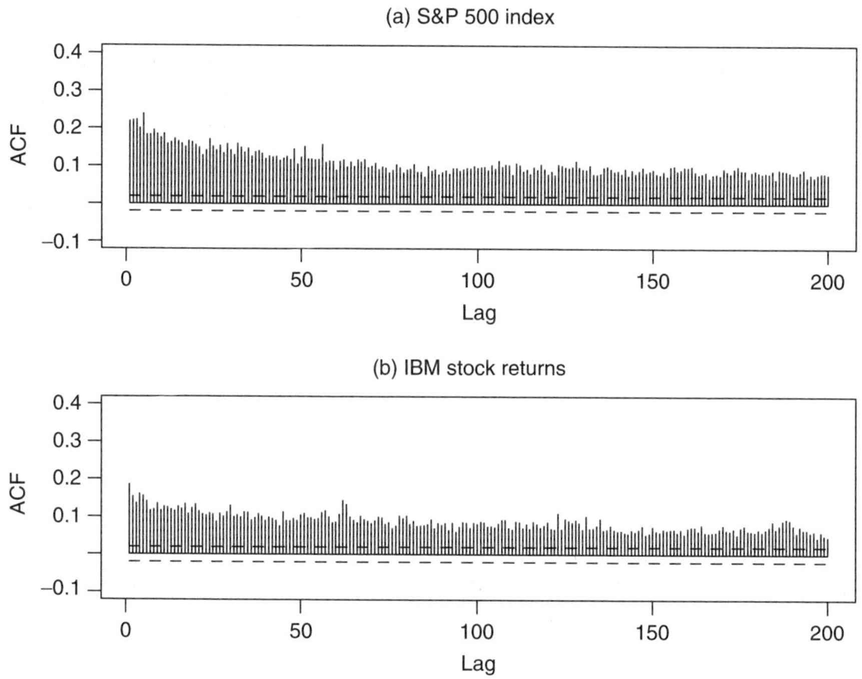

Figure 3.9. The sample ACF of daily absolute log returns for (a) the S&P 500 index and (b) IBM stock for the period from July 3, 1962 to December 31, 2003. The two horizontal lines denote the asymptotic 5% limits.

of an exponential, rate as the lag increases. The extension to long-memory models in volatility study is motivated by the fact that the autocorrelation function of the squared or absolute-valued series of an asset return often decays slowly, even though the return series has no serial correlation; see Ding, Granger, and Engle (1993). Figure 3.9 shows the sample ACF of the daily absolute returns for IBM stock and the S&P 500 index from July 3, 1962 to December 31, 2003. These sample ACFs are positive with moderate magnitude, but decay slowly.

A simple long-memory stochastic volatility (LMSV) model can be written as

$$a_t = \sigma_t \epsilon_t, \qquad \sigma_t = \sigma \exp(u_t/2), \qquad (1-B)^d u_t = \eta_t, \tag{3.40}$$

where $\sigma > 0$, the ϵ_t are iid $N(0,1)$, the η_t are iid $N(0, \sigma_\eta^2)$ and independent of ϵ_t, and $0 < d < 0.5$. The feature of long memory stems from the fractional difference $(1-B)^d$, which implies that the ACF of u_t decays slowly at a hyperbolic, instead of an exponential, rate as the lag increases. For model (3.40), we have

$$\begin{aligned}
\ln(a_t^2) &= \ln(\sigma^2) + u_t + \ln(\epsilon_t^2) \\
&= [\ln(\sigma^2) + E(\ln \epsilon_t^2)] + u_t + [\ln(\epsilon_t^2) - E(\ln \epsilon_t^2)] \\
&\equiv \mu + u_t + e_t.
\end{aligned}$$

Thus, the $\ln(a_t^2)$ series is a Gaussian long-memory signal plus a non-Gaussian white noise; see Breidt, Crato, and de Lima (1998). Estimation of the long-memory stochastic volatility model is complicated, but the fractional difference parameter d can be estimated by using either a quasi-maximum likelihood method or a regression method. Using the log series of squared daily returns for companies in the S&P 500 index, Bollerslev and Jubinski (1999) and Ray and Tsay (2000) found that the median estimate of d is about 0.38. For applications, Ray and Tsay (2000) studied common long-memory components in daily stock volatilities of groups of companies classified by various characteristics. They found that companies in the same industrial or business sector tend to have more common long-memory components (e.g., big U.S. national banks and financial institutions).

3.14 APPLICATION

In this section, we apply the volatility models discussed in this chapter to investigate some problems of practical importance. The data used are the monthly log returns of IBM stock and the S&P 500 index from January 1926 to December 1999. There are 888 observations, and the returns are in percentages and include dividends. Figure 3.10 shows the time plots of the two return series. Note that the result of this section was obtained by the RATS program.

Example 3.4. The questions we address here are whether the daily volatility of a stock is lower in the summer and, if so, by how much. Affirmative answers to these two questions have practical implications in stock option pricing. We use the monthly log returns of IBM stock shown in Figure 3.10a as an illustrative example.

Denote the monthly log return series by r_t. If Gaussian GARCH models are entertained, we obtain the GARCH(1,1) model

$$\begin{aligned} r_t &= 1.23 + 0.099 r_{t-1} + a_t, \qquad a_t = \sigma_t \epsilon_t, \\ \sigma_t^2 &= 3.206 + 0.103 a_{t-1}^2 + 0.825 \sigma_{t-1}^2, \end{aligned} \tag{3.41}$$

for the series. The standard errors of the two parameters in the mean equation are 0.222 and 0.037, respectively, whereas those of the parameters in the volatility equation are 0.947, 0.021, and 0.037, respectively. Using the standardized residuals $\tilde{a}_t = a_t/\sigma_t$, we obtain $Q(10) = 7.82(0.553)$ and $Q(20) = 21.22(0.325)$, where p-value is in parentheses. Therefore, there are no serial correlations in the residuals of the mean equation. The Ljung–Box statistics of the $\tilde{a}_t^2$ series show $Q(10) = 2.89(0.98)$ and $Q(20) = 7.26(0.99)$, indicating that the standardized residuals have no conditional heteroscedasticity. The fitted model seems adequate. This model serves as a starting point for further study.

To study the summer effect on stock volatility of an asset, we define an indicator variable

$$u_t = \begin{cases} 1 & \text{if } t \text{ is June, July, or August} \\ 0 & \text{otherwise} \end{cases} \tag{3.42}$$

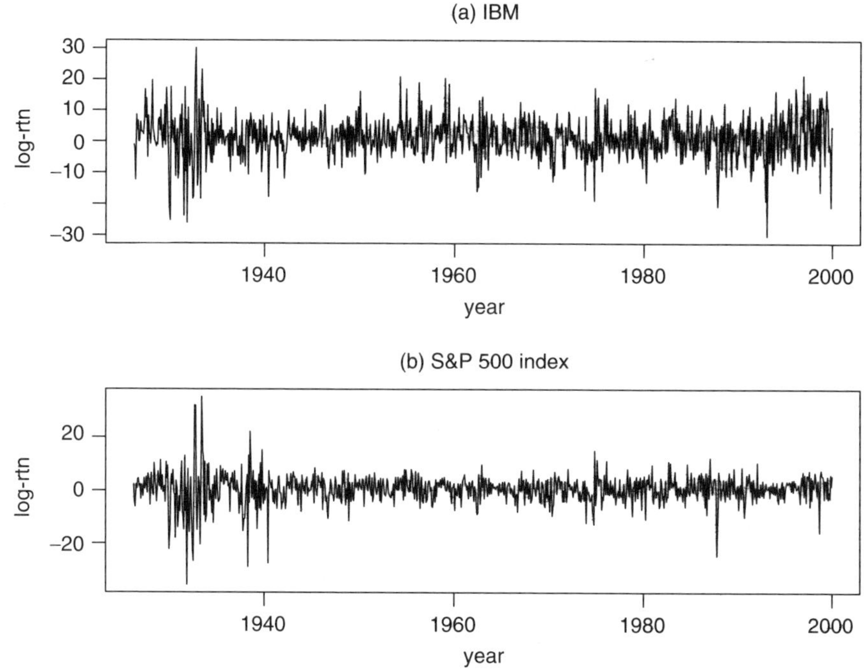

Figure 3.10. Time plots of monthly log returns for (a) IBM stock and (b) the S&P 500 index. The sample period is from January 1926 to December 1999. The returns are in percentages and include dividends.

and modify the volatility equation to

$$\sigma_t^2 = \alpha_0 + \alpha_1 a_{t-1}^2 + \beta_1 \sigma_{t-1}^2 + u_t(\alpha_{00} + \alpha_{10} a_{t-1}^2 + \beta_{10} \sigma_{t-1}^2).$$

This equation uses two GARCH(1,1) models to describe the volatility of a stock return; one model for the summer months and the other for the remaining months. For the monthly log returns of IBM stock, estimation results show that the estimates of α_{10} and β_{10} are statistically nonsignificant at the 10% level. Therefore, we refine the equation and obtain the model

$$\begin{aligned} r_t &= 1.21 + 0.099 r_{t-1} + a_t, \quad a_t = \sigma_t \epsilon_t, \\ \sigma_t^2 &= 4.539 + 0.113 a_{t-1}^2 + 0.816 \sigma_{t-1}^2 - 5.154 u_t. \end{aligned} \tag{3.43}$$

The standard errors of the parameters in the mean equation are 0.218 and 0.037, respectively, and those of the parameters in the volatility equation are 1.071, 0.022, 0.037, and 1.900, respectively. The Ljung–Box statistics for the standardized residuals $\tilde{a}_t = a_t/\sigma_t$ show $Q(10) = 7.66(0.569)$ and $Q(20) = 21.64(0.302)$. Therefore, there are no serial correlations in the standardized residuals. The Ljung–Box statistics for $\tilde{a}_t^2$ give $Q(10) = 3.38(0.97)$ and $Q(20) = 6.82(0.99)$, indicating no conditional heteroscedasticity in the standardized residuals, either. The refined model seems adequate.

Comparing the volatility models in Eqs. (3.41) and (3.43), we obtain the following conclusions. First, because the coefficient −5.514 is significantly different from zero with p-value 0.0067, the summer effect on stock volatility is statistically significant at the 1% level. Furthermore, the negative sign of the estimate confirms that the volatility of IBM monthly log stock returns is indeed lower during the summer. Second, rewrite the volatility model in Eq. (3.43) as

$$\sigma_t^2 = \begin{cases} -0.615 + 0.113a_{t-1}^2 + 0.816\sigma_{t-1}^2 & \text{if } t \text{ is June, July, or August,} \\ 4.539 + 0.113a_{t-1}^2 + 0.816\sigma_{t-1}^2, & \text{otherwise.} \end{cases}$$

The negative constant term $-0.615 = 4.539 - 5.514$ is counterintuitive. However, since the standard errors of 4.539 and 5.514 are relatively large, the estimated difference −0.615 might not be significantly different from zero. To verify the assertion, we refit the model by imposing the constraint that the constant term of the volatility equation is zero for the summer months. This can easily be done by using the equation

$$\sigma_t^2 = \alpha_1 a_{t-1}^2 + \beta_1 \sigma_{t-1}^2 + \gamma(1 - u_t).$$

The fitted model is

$$\begin{aligned} r_t &= 1.21 + 0.099 r_{t-1} + a_t, \quad a_t = \sigma_t \epsilon_t, \\ \sigma_t^2 &= 0.114 a_{t-1}^2 + 0.811 \sigma_{t-1}^2 + 4.552(1 - u_t). \end{aligned} \tag{3.44}$$

The standard errors of the parameters in the mean equation are 0.219 and 0.038, respectively, and those of the parameters in the volatility equation are 0.022, 0.034, and 1.094, respectively. The Ljung–Box statistics of the standardized residuals show $Q(10) = 7.68$ and $Q(20) = 21.67$ and those of the $\tilde{a}_t^2$ series give $Q(10) = 3.17$ and $Q(20) = 6.85$. These test statistics are close to what we had before and are not significant at the 5% level.

The volatility Eq. (3.44) can readily be used to assess the summer effect on the IBM stock volatility. For illustration, based on the model in Eq. (3.44), the medians of a_t^2 and σ_t^2 are 29.4 and 75.1, respectively, for the IBM monthly log returns in 1999. Using these values, we have $\sigma_t^2 = 0.114 \times 29.4 + 0.811 \times 75.1 = 64.3$ for the summer months and $\sigma_t^2 = 68.8$ for the other months. The ratio of the two volatilities is $64.3/68.8 \approx 93\%$. Thus, there is a 7% reduction in the volatility of the monthly log return of IBM stock in the summer months.

Example 3.5. The S&P 500 index is widely used in the derivative markets. As such, modeling its volatility is a subject of intensive study. The question we ask in this example is whether the past returns of individual components of the index contribute to the modeling of the S&P 500 index volatility in the presence of its own returns. A thorough investigation on this topic is beyond the scope of this chapter, but we use the past returns of IBM stock as explanatory variables to address the question.

The data used are shown in Figure 3.10. Denote by r_t the monthly log return series of the S&P 500 index. Using the r_t series and Gaussian GARCH models, we obtain the following special GARCH(2,1) model:

$$r_t = 0.609 + a_t, \quad a_t = \sigma_t \epsilon_t, \quad \sigma_t^2 = 0.717 + 0.147 a_{t-2}^2 + 0.839 \sigma_{t-1}^2. \tag{3.45}$$

The standard error of the constant term in the mean equation is 0.138 and those of the parameters in the volatility equation are 0.214, 0.021, and 0.017, respectively. Based on the standardized residuals $\tilde{a}_t = a_t/\sigma_t$, we have $Q(10) = 11.51(0.32)$ and $Q(20) = 23.71(0.26)$, where the number in parentheses denotes p-value. For the $\tilde{a}_t^2$ series, we have $Q(10) = 9.42(0.49)$ and $Q(20) = 13.01(0.88)$. Therefore, the model seems adequate at the 5% significance level.

Next, we evaluate the contributions, if any, of using the past returns of IBM stock, which is a component of the S&P 500 index, in modeling the index volatility. As a simple illustration, we modify the volatility equation as

$$\sigma_t^2 = \alpha_0 + \alpha_2 a_{t-2}^2 + \beta_1 \sigma_{t-1}^2 + \gamma (x_{t-1} - 1.24)^2,$$

where x_t is the monthly log return of IBM stock and 1.24 is the sample mean of x_t. The fitted model for r_t becomes

$$\begin{aligned} r_t &= 0.616 + a_t, \quad a_t = \sigma_t \epsilon_t, \\ \sigma_t^2 &= 1.069 + 0.148 a_{t-2}^2 + 0.834 \sigma_{t-1}^2 - 0.007 (x_{t-1} - 1.24)^2. \end{aligned} \tag{3.46}$$

The standard error of the parameter in the mean equation is 0.139 and the standard errors of the parameters in the volatility equation are 0.271, 0.020, 0.018, and 0.002, respectively. For model checking, we have $Q(10) = 11.39(0.33)$ and $Q(20) = 23.63(0.26)$ for the standardized residuals $\tilde{a}_t = a_t/\sigma_t$ and $Q(10) = 9.35(0.50)$ and $Q(20) = 13.51(0.85)$ for the $\tilde{a}_t^2$ series. Therefore, the model is adequate.

Since the p-value for testing $\gamma = 0$ is 0.0039, the contribution of the lag-1 IBM stock return to the S&P 500 index volatility is statistically significant at the 1% level. The negative sign is understandable because it implies that using the lag-1 past return of IBM stock reduces the volatility of the S&P 500 index return. Table 3.4 gives the fitted volatility of the S&P 500 index from July to December

Table 3.4. Fitted Volatilities for the Monthly Log Returns of the S&P 500 Index from July to December 1999 Using Models with and Without the Past Log Return of IBM Stock

Month	7/99	8/99	9/99	10/99	11/99	12/99
Model (3.45)	26.30	26.01	24.73	21.69	20.71	22.46
Model (3.46)	23.32	23.13	22.46	20.00	19.45	18.27

of 1999 using models (3.45) and (3.46). From the table, the past value of IBM log stock return indeed contributes to the modeling of the S&P 500 index volatility.

3.15 ALTERNATIVE APPROACHES

In this section, we discuss two alternative methods to volatility modeling.

3.15.1 Use of High-Frequency Data

French, Schwert, and Stambaugh (1987) consider an alternative approach for volatility estimation that uses high-frequency data to calculate volatility of low-frequency returns. In recent years, this approach has attracted substantial interest due to the availability of high-frequency financial data; see Andersen, Bollerslev, Diebold, and Labys (2001a, b).

Suppose that we are interested in the monthly volatility of an asset for which daily returns are available. Let r_t^m be the monthly log return of the asset at month t. Assume that there are n trading days in month t and the daily log returns of the asset in the month are $\{r_{t,i}\}_{i=1}^n$. Using properties of log returns, we have

$$r_t^m = \sum_{i=1}^n r_{t,i}.$$

Assuming that the conditional variance and covariance exist, we have

$$\text{Var}(r_t^m|F_{t-1}) = \sum_{i=1}^n \text{Var}(r_{t,i}|F_{t-1}) + 2\sum_{i<j} \text{Cov}[(r_{t,i}, r_{t,j})|F_{t-1}], \tag{3.47}$$

where F_{t-1} denotes the information available at month $t-1$ (inclusive). The prior equation can be simplified if additional assumptions are made. For example, if we assume that $\{r_{t,i}\}$ is a white noise series, then

$$\text{Var}(r_t^m|F_{t-1}) = n\text{Var}(r_{t,1}),$$

where $\text{Var}(r_{t,1})$ can be estimated from the daily returns $\{r_{t,i}\}_{i=1}^n$ by

$$\hat{\sigma}^2 = \frac{\sum_{i=1}^n (r_{t,i} - \bar{r}_t)^n}{n-1},$$

where $\bar{r}_t$ is the sample mean of the daily log returns in month t (i.e., $\bar{r}_t = \left(\sum_{i=1}^n r_{t,i}\right)/n$). The estimated monthly volatility is then

$$\hat{\sigma}_m^2 = \frac{n}{n-1}\sum_{i=1}^n (r_{t,i} - \bar{r}_t)^2. \tag{3.48}$$

If $\{r_{t,i}\}$ follows an MA(1) model, then

$$\text{Var}(r_t^m|F_{t-1}) = n\text{Var}(r_{t,1}) + 2(n-1)\text{Cov}(r_{t,1}, r_{t,2}),$$

which can be estimated by

$$\hat{\sigma}_m^2 = \frac{n}{n-1}\sum_{i=1}^{n}(r_{t,i} - \bar{r}_t)^2 + 2\sum_{i=1}^{n-1}(r_{t,i} - \bar{r}_t)(r_{t,i+1} - \bar{r}_t). \tag{3.49}$$

The previous approach for volatility estimation is simple, but it encounters several difficulties in practice. First, the model for daily returns $\{r_{t,i}\}$ is unknown. This complicates the estimation of covariances in Eq. (3.47). Second, there are roughly 21 trading days in a month, resulting in a small sample size. The accuracy of the estimates of variance and covariance in Eq. (3.47) might be questionable. The accuracy depends on the dynamic structure of $\{r_{t,i}\}$ and their distribution. If the daily log returns have high excess kurtosis and serial correlations, then the sample estimates $\hat{\sigma}_m^2$ in Eqs. (3.48) and (3.49) may not even be consistent; see Bai, Russell, and Tiao (2004). Further research is needed to make this approach valuable.

Example 3.6. Consider the monthly volatility of the log returns of the S&P 500 index from January 1980 to December 1999. We calculate the volatility by three methods. In the first method, we use daily log returns and Eq. (3.48) (i.e., assuming that the daily log returns form a white noise series). The second method also uses daily returns but assumes an MA(1) model (i.e., using Eq. (3.49)). The third method applies a GARCH(1,1) model to the monthly returns from January 1962 to December 1999. We use a longer data span to obtain a more accurate estimate of the monthly volatility. The GARCH(1,1) model used is

$$r_t^m = 0.658 + a_t, \quad a_t = \sigma_t \epsilon_t, \quad \sigma_t^2 = 3.349 + 0.086 a_{t-1}^2 + 0.735 \sigma_{t-1}^2,$$

where ϵ_t is a standard Gaussian white noise series. Figure 3.11 shows the time plots of the estimated monthly volatility. Clearly the estimated volatilities based on daily returns are much higher than those based on monthly returns and a GARCH(1,1) model. In particular, the estimated volatility for October 1987 was about 680 when daily returns are used. The plots shown were truncated to have the same scale.

In Eq. (3.48), if we further assume that the sample mean $\bar{r}_t$ is zero, then we have $\hat{\sigma}_m^2 \approx \sum_{i=1}^{n} r_{t,i}^2$. In this case, the cumulative sum of squares of daily log returns in a month is used as an estimate of monthly volatility. This concept has been generalized to estimate daily volatility of an asset by using intradaily log returns. Let r_t be the daily log return of an asset. Suppose that there are n equally spaced intradaily log returns available such that $r_t = \sum_{i=1}^{n} r_{t,i}$. The quantity

$$\text{RV}_t = \sum_{i=1}^{n} r_{t,i}^2,$$

is called the *realized* volatility of r_t; see Andersen et al. (2001a, b). Mathematically, realized volatility is a quadratic variation of r_t and it assumes that $\{r_{t,i}\}_{i=1}^{n}$ forms an iid sequence with mean zero and finite variance. Limited experience indicates that $\ln(\text{RV}_t)$ often follows approximately a Gaussian ARIMA(0,1,q) model, which

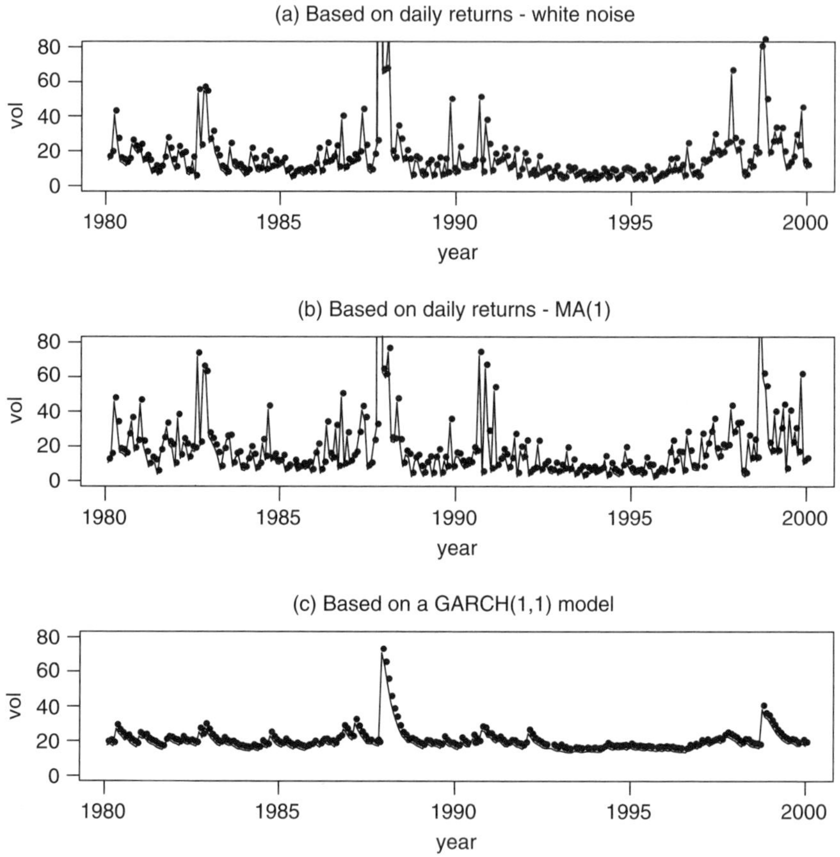

Figure 3.11. Time plots of estimated monthly volatility for the log returns of the S&P 500 index from January 1980 to December 1999: (a) assumes that the daily log returns form a white noise series, (b) assumes that the daily log returns follow an MA(1) model, and (c) uses monthly returns from January 1962 to December 1999 and a GARCH(1,1) model.

can be used to produce forecasts. See demonstration in Section 11.1 for further information.

Advantages of realized volatility include simplicity and making use of intradaily returns. Intuitively, one would like to use as much information as possible by choosing a large n. However, when the time interval between $r_{t,i}$ is small, the returns are subject to the effects of market microstructure, for example, bid–ask bounce, which often result in a biased estimate of the volatility. The problem of choosing an optimal time interval for constructing realized volatility has attracted much research lately. For heavily traded assets in the United States, a time interval of 3–15 minutes is often used. Another problem of using realized volatility for stock returns is that the overnight return, which is the return from the closing price of day $t-1$ to the opening price of t, tends to be substantial. Ignoring overnight returns can seriously underestimate the volatility. On the other hand, our limited experience shows that overnight returns appear to be small for index returns or foreign exchange returns.

In a series of recent articles, Barndorff-Nielsen and Shephard (2004) have used high-frequency returns to study bi-power variations of an asset return and developed some methods to detect jumps in volatility.

3.15.2 Use of Daily Open, High, Low, and Close Prices

For many assets, daily opening, high, low, and closing prices are available. Parkinson (1980), Garman and Klass (1980), Rogers and Satchell (1991), and Yang and Zhang (2000) showed that one can use such information to improve volatility estimation. Figure 3.12 shows a time plot of price versus time for the tth trading day, assuming that time is continuous. For an asset, define the following variables:

- C_t = the closing price of the tth trading day.
- O_t = the opening price of the tth trading day.
- f = fraction of the day (in interval [0,1]) that trading is closed.
- H_t = the highest price of the tth trading period.
- L_t = the lowest price of the tth trading period.
- F_{t-1} = public information available at time $t-1$.

The conventional variance (or volatility) is $\sigma_t^2 = E[(C_t - C_{t-1})^2|F_{t-1}]$. Garman and Klass (1980) considered several estimates of σ_t^2 assuming that the price follows

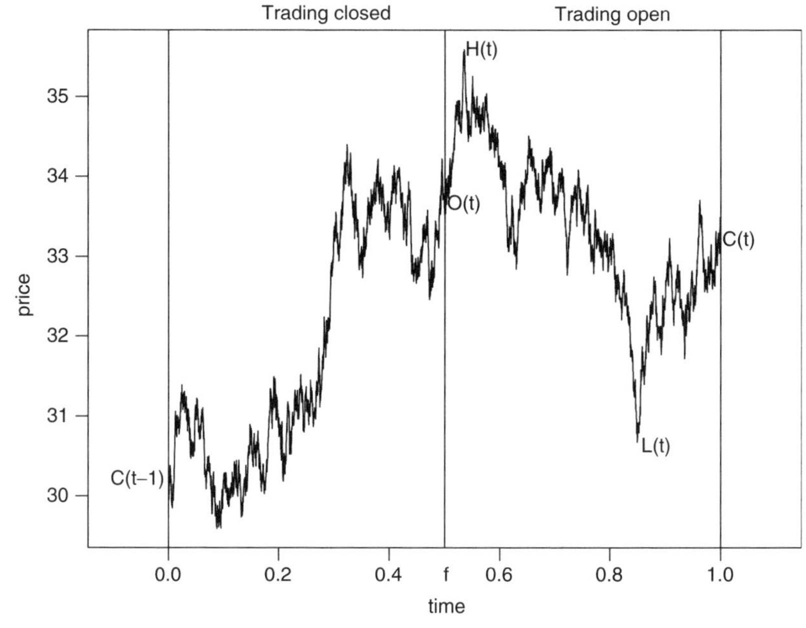

Figure 3.12. Time plot of price over time: scale for price is arbitrary.

a simple diffusion model without drift; see Chapter 6 for more information about stochastic diffusion models. The estimators considered include:

- $\hat{\sigma}^2_{0,t} = (C_t - C_{t-1})^2$.
- $\hat{\sigma}^2_{1,t} = \dfrac{(O_t - C_{t-1})^2}{2f} + \dfrac{(C_t - O_t)^2}{2(1-f)}, \quad 0 < f < 1.$
- $\hat{\sigma}^2_{2,t} = \dfrac{(H_t - L_t)^2}{4\ln(2)} \approx 0.3607(H_t - L_t)^2$.
- $\hat{\sigma}^2_{3,t} = 0.17\dfrac{(O_t - C_{t-1})^2}{f} + 0.83\dfrac{(H_t - L_t)^2}{(1-f)4\ln(2)}, \quad 0 < f < 1.$
- $\hat{\sigma}^2_{5,t} = 0.5(H_t - L_t)^2 - [2\ln(2) - 1](C_t - O_t)^2$, which is $\approx 0.5(H_t - L_t)^2 - 0.386(C_t - O_t)^2$.
- $\hat{\sigma}^2_{6,t} = 0.12\dfrac{(O_t - C_{t-1})^2}{f} + 0.88\dfrac{\hat{\sigma}^2_{5,t}}{1-f}, \quad 0 < f < 1.$

A more precise, but complicated, estimator $\hat{\sigma}^2_{4,t}$ was also considered. However, it is close to $\hat{\sigma}^2_{5,t}$. Defining the efficiency factor of a volatility estimator as

$$\text{Eff}(\hat{\sigma}^2_{i,t}) = \frac{\text{Var}(\hat{\sigma}^2_{0,t})}{\text{Var}(\hat{\sigma}^2_{i,t})},$$

Garman and Klass (1980) found that $\text{Eff}(\hat{\sigma}^2_{i,t})$ is approximately 2, 5.2, 6.2, 7.4, and 8.4 for $i = 1, 2, 3, 5$, and 6, respectively, for the simple diffusion model entertained. Note that $\hat{\sigma}^2_{2,t}$ was derived by Parkinson (1980) with $f = 0$.

Define the following:

- $o_t = \ln(O_t) - \ln(C_{t-1})$, the normalized open.
- $u_t = \ln(H_t) - \ln(O_t)$, the normalized high.
- $d_t = \ln(L_t) - \ln(O_t)$, the normalized low.
- $c_t = \ln(C_t) - \ln(O_t)$, the normalized close.

Suppose that there are n days of data available and the volatility is constant over the period. Yang and Zhang (2000) recommend the estimate

$$\hat{\sigma}^2_{yz} = \hat{\sigma}^2_o + k\hat{\sigma}^2_c + (1-k)\hat{\sigma}^2_{rs}$$

as a robust estimator of the volatility, where

$$\hat{\sigma}^2_o = \frac{1}{n-1}\sum_{t=1}^{n}(o_t - \bar{o})^2 \quad \text{with} \quad \bar{o} = \frac{1}{n}\sum_{t=1}^{n} o_t,$$

$$\hat{\sigma}^2_c = \frac{1}{n-1}\sum_{t=1}^{n}(c_t - \bar{c})^2 \quad \text{with} \quad \bar{c} = \frac{1}{n}\sum_{t=1}^{n} c_t,$$

$$\hat{\sigma}^2_{rs} = \frac{1}{n}\sum_{t=1}^{n}[u_t(u_t - c_t) + d_t(d_t - c_t)],$$

$$k = \frac{0.34}{1.34 + (n+1)/(n-1)}.$$

The estimate $\hat{\sigma}^2_{rs}$ was proposed by Rogers and Satchell (1991), and the quantity k is chosen to minimize the variance of the estimator of $\hat{\sigma}^2_{yz}$, which is a linear combination of three estimates.

The quantity $H_t - L_t$ is called the *range* of the price in the tth day. This estimator has led to the use of range-based volatility estimates; see, for instance, Alizadeh, Brandt, and Diebold (2002). In practice, stock prices are only observed at discrete time points. As such, the observed daily high is likely lower than H_t and the observed daily low is likely higher than L_t. Consequently, the observed daily price range tends to underestimate the actual range and, hence, may lead to underestimation of volatility. This bias in volatility estimation depends on the trading frequency and tick size of the stocks. For intensively traded stocks, the bias should be negligible. For other stocks, further study is needed to better understand the performance of range-based volatility estimation.

3.16 KURTOSIS OF GARCH MODELS

Uncertainty in volatility estimation is an important issue, but it is often overlooked. To assess the variability of an estimated volatility, one must consider the kurtosis of a volatility model. In this section, we derive the excess kurtosis of a GARCH(1,1) model. The same idea applies to other GARCH models, however. The model considered is

$$a_t = \sigma_t \epsilon_t, \quad \sigma_t^2 = \alpha_0 + \alpha_1 a_{t-1}^2 + \beta_1 \sigma_{t-1}^2,$$

where $\alpha_0 > 0$, $\alpha_1 \geq 0$, $\beta_1 \geq 0$, $\alpha_1 + \beta_1 < 1$, and $\{\epsilon_t\}$ is an iid sequence satisfying

$$E(\epsilon_t) = 0, \quad \text{Var}(\epsilon_t) = 1, \quad E(\epsilon_t^4) = K_\epsilon + 3,$$

where K_ϵ is the excess kurtosis of the innovation ϵ_t. Based on the assumption, we have the following:

- $\text{Var}(a_t) = E(\sigma_t^2) = \alpha_0/[1 - (\alpha_1 + \beta_1)]$.
- $E(a_t^4) = (K_\epsilon + 3)E(\sigma_t^4)$ provided that $E(\sigma_t^4)$ exists.

Taking the square of the volatility model, we have

$$\sigma_t^4 = \alpha_0^2 + \alpha_1^2 a_{t-1}^4 + \beta_1^2 \sigma_{t-1}^4 + 2\alpha_0\alpha_1 a_{t-1}^2 + 2\alpha_0\beta_1\sigma_{t-1}^2 + 2\alpha_1\beta_1\sigma_{t-1}^2 a_{t-1}^2.$$

Taking expectation of the equation and using the two properties mentioned earlier, we obtain

$$E(\sigma_t^4) = \frac{\alpha_0^2(1 + \alpha_1 + \beta_1)}{[1 - (\alpha_1 + \beta_1)][1 - \alpha_1^2(K_\epsilon + 2) - (\alpha_1 + \beta_1)^2]},$$

provided that $1 > \alpha_1 + \beta_1 \geq 0$ and $1 - \alpha_1^2(K_\epsilon + 2) - (\alpha_1 + \beta_1)^2 > 0$. The excess kurtosis of a_t, if it exists, is then

$$K_a = \frac{E(a_t^4)}{[E(a_t^2)]^2} - 3$$
$$= \frac{(K_\epsilon + 3)[1 - (\alpha_1 + \beta_1)^2]}{1 - 2\alpha_1^2 - (\alpha_1 + \beta_1)^2 - K_\epsilon \alpha_1^2} - 3.$$

This excess kurtosis can be written in an informative expression. First, consider the case that ϵ_t is normally distributed. In this case, $K_\epsilon = 0$, and some algebra shows that

$$K_a^{(g)} = \frac{6\alpha_1^2}{1 - 2\alpha_1^2 - (\alpha_1 + \beta_1)^2},$$

where the superscript (g) is used to denote Gaussian distribution. This result has two important implications: (a) the kurtosis of a_t exists if $1 - 2\alpha_1^2 - (\alpha_1 + \beta_1)^2 > 0$, and (b) if $\alpha_1 = 0$, then $K_a^{(g)} = 0$, meaning that the corresponding GARCH(1,1) model does not have heavy tails.

Second, consider the case that ϵ_t is not Gaussian. Using the prior result, we have

$$K_a = \frac{K_\epsilon - K_\epsilon(\alpha_1 + \beta_1) + 6\alpha_1^2 + 3K_\epsilon \alpha_1^2}{1 - 2\alpha_1^2 - (\alpha_1 + \beta_1)^2 - K_\epsilon \alpha_1^2}$$
$$= \frac{K_\epsilon[1 - 2\alpha_1^2 - (\alpha_1 + \beta_1)^2] + 6\alpha_1^2 + 5K_\epsilon \alpha_1^2}{1 - 2\alpha_1^2 - (\alpha_1 + \beta_1)^2 - K_\epsilon \alpha_1^2}$$
$$= \frac{K_\epsilon + K_a^{(g)} + \frac{5}{6}K_\epsilon K_a^{(g)}}{1 - \frac{1}{6}K_\epsilon K_a^{(g)}}.$$

This result was obtained originally by George C. Tiao; see Bai, Russell, and Tiao (2003). It holds for all GARCH models provided that the kurtosis exists. For instance, if $\beta_1 = 0$, then the model reduces to an ARCH(1) model. In this case, it is easy to verify that $K_a^{(g)} = 6\alpha_1^2/(1 - 3\alpha_1^2)$ provided that $1 > 3\alpha_1^2$ and the excess kurtosis of a_t is

$$K_a = \frac{(K_\epsilon + 3)(1 - \alpha_1^2)}{1 - (K_\epsilon + 3)\alpha_1^2} - 3 = \frac{K_\epsilon + 2K_\epsilon \alpha_1^2 + 6\alpha_1^2}{1 - 3\alpha_1^2 - K_\epsilon \alpha_1^2}$$
$$= \frac{K_\epsilon(1 - 3\alpha_1^2) + 6\alpha_1^2 + 5K_\epsilon \alpha_1^2}{1 - 3\alpha_1^2 - K_\epsilon \alpha_1^2}$$
$$= \frac{K_\epsilon + K_a^{(g)} + \frac{5}{6}K_\epsilon K_a^{(g)}}{1 - \frac{1}{6}K_\epsilon K_a^{(g)}}.$$

The prior result shows that for a GARCH(1,1) model the coefficient α_1 plays a critical role in determining the tail behavior of a_t. If $\alpha_1 = 0$, then $K_a^{(g)} = 0$ and

$K_a = K_\epsilon$. In this case, the tail behavior of a_t is similar to that of the standardized noise ϵ_t. Yet if $\alpha_1 > 0$, then $K_a^{(g)} > 0$ and the a_t process has heavy tails.

For a (standardized) Student-t distribution with v degrees of freedom, we have $E(\epsilon_t^4) = 6/(v-4) + 3$ if $v > 4$. Therefore, the excess kurtosis of ϵ_t is $K_\epsilon = 6/(v-4)$ for $v > 4$. This is part of the reason that we used t_5 in the chapter when the degrees of freedom of a t-distribution are prespecified. The excess kurtosis of a_t becomes $K_a = [6 + (v+1)K_a^{(g)}]/[v - 4 - K_a^{(g)}]$ provided that $1 - 2\alpha_1^2(v-1)/(v-4) - (\alpha_1 + \beta_1)^2 > 0$.

APPENDIX: SOME RATS PROGRAMS FOR ESTIMATING VOLATILITY MODELS

The data file used in the illustration is `sp500.txt`, which contains the monthly excess returns of the S&P 500 index with 792 observations. Comments in a RATS program start with *.

A Gaussian GARCH(1,1) Model with a Constant Mean Equation

```
all 0  792:1
open data sp500.txt
data(org=obs) / rt
*** initialize the conditional variance function
set h = 0.0
*** specify the parameters of the model
nonlin mu a0 a1 b1
*** specify the mean equation
frml at = rt(t)-mu
*** specify the volatility equation
frml gvar = a0+a1*at(t-1)**2+b1*h(t-1)
*** specify the log likelihood function
frml garchln = -0.5*log(h(t)=gvar(t))-0.5*at(t)**2/h(t)
*** sample period used in estimation
smpl 2 792
*** initial estimates
compute a0 = 0.01, a1 = 0.1, b1 = 0.5, mu = 0.1
maximize(method=bhhh,recursive,iterations=150) garchln
set fv = gvar(t)
set resid = at(t)/sqrt(fv(t))
set residsq = resid(t)*resid(t)
*** Checking standardized residuals
cor(qstats,number=20,span=10) resid
*** Checking squared standardized residuals
cor(qstats,number=20,span=10) residsq
```

A GARCH(1,1) Model with Student-t Innovation

```
all 0  792:1
open data sp500.txt
data(org=obs) / rt
set h = 0.0
```

```
nonlin mu a0 a1 b1 v
frml at = rt(t)-mu
frml gvar = a0+a1*at(t-1)**2+b1*h(t-1)
frml tt = at(t)**2/(h(t)=gvar(t))
frml tln = %LNGAMMA((v+1)/2.)-%LNGAMMA(v/2.)-0.5*log(v-2.)
frml gln = tln-((v+1)/2.)*log(1.0+tt(t)/(v-2.0))-0.5*log(h(t))
smpl  2 792
compute a0 = 0.01, a1 = 0.1, b1 = 0.5, mu = 0.1, v = 10
maximize(method=bhhh,recursive,iterations=150) gln
set fv = gvar(t)
set resid = at(t)/sqrt(fv(t))
set residsq = resid(t)*resid(t)
cor(qstats,number=20,span=10) resid
cor(qstats,number=20,span=10) residsq
```

An AR(1)–EGARCH(1,1) Model for Monthly Log Returns of IBM Stock

```
all 0  864:1
open data m-ibm.txt
data(org=obs) / rt
set h = 0.0
nonlin c0 p1 th ga a0 a1
frml at = rt(t)-c0-p1*rt(t-1)
frml epsi = at(t)/(sqrt(exp(h(t))))
frml g = th*epsi(t)+ga*(abs(epsi(t))-sqrt(2./%PI))
frml gvar = a1*h(t-1)+(1-a1)*a0+g(t-1)
frml garchln = -0.5*(h(t)=gvar(t))-0.5*epsi(t)**2
smpl 3  864
compute c0 = 0.01, p1 = 0.01, th = 0.1, ga = 0.1
compute a0 = 0.01, a1 = 0.5
maximize(method=bhhh,recursive,iterations=150) garchln
set fv = gvar(t)
set resid = epsi(t)
set residsq = resid(t)*resid(t)
cor(qstats,number=20,span=10) resid
cor(qstats,number=20,span=10) residsq
```

EXERCISES

3.1. Derive multistep ahead forecasts for a GARCH(1,2) model at the forecast origin h.

3.2. Derive multistep ahead forecasts for a GARCH(2,1) model at the forecast origin h.

3.3. Suppose that $r_1, \ldots, r_n$ are observations of a return series that follows the AR(1)–GARCH(1,1) model

$$r_t = \mu + \phi_1 r_{t-1} + a_t, \quad a_t = \sigma_t \epsilon_t, \quad \sigma_t^2 = \alpha_0 + \alpha_1 a_{t-1}^2 + \beta_1 \sigma_{t-1}^2,$$

where ϵ_t is a standard Gaussian white noise series. Derive the conditional log likelihood function of the data.

3.4. In the previous equation, assume that ϵ_t follows a standardized Student-t distribution with v degrees of freedom. Derive the conditional log likelihood function of the data.

3.5. Consider the monthly simple returns of Intel stock from 1973 to 2003 in `m-intc7303.txt`. Transform the returns into log returns. Build a GARCH model for the transformed series and compute 1-step to 5-step ahead volatility forecasts at the forecast origin December 2003.

3.6. The file `m-mrk4603.txt` contains monthly simple returns of Merck stock from June 1946 to December 2003. The file has two columns denoting date and simple return. Transform the simple returns to log returns.

(a) Is there any evidence of serial correlations in the log returns? Use autocorrelations and 5% significance level to answer the question. If yes, remove the serial correlations.

(b) Is there any evidence of ARCH effects in the log returns? Use the residual series if there is serial correlation in part (a). Use Ljung–Box statistics for the squared returns (or residuals) with 6 and 12 lags of autocorrelation and 5% significance level to answer the question.

(c) Identify an ARCH model for the data and fit the identified model. Write down the fitted model.

3.7. The file `m-3m4603.txt` contains two columns. They are date and the monthly simple return for 3M stock. Transform the returns to log returns.

(a) Is there any evidence of ARCH effects in the log returns? Use Ljung–Box statistics with 6 and 12 lags of autocorrelations and 5% significance level to answer the question.

(b) Use the PACF of the squared returns to identify an ARCH model. What is the fitted model?

(c) There are 695 data points. Refit the model using the first 690 observations and use the fitted model to predict the volatilities for t from 691 to 695 (the forecast origin is 690).

(d) Build an ARCH-M model for the log return series of 3M stock. Test the hypothesis that the risk premium is zero at the 5% significance level. Draw your conclusion.

(e) Build an EGARCH model for the log return series of 3M stock using the first 690 observations. Use the fitted model to compute 1-step to 5-step ahead volatility forecasts at the forecast origin $h = 690$.

3.8. The file `m-gmsp5003.txt` contains the dates and monthly simple returns of General Motors stock and the S&P 500 index from 1950 to 2003.

(a) Build a GARCH model with Gaussian innovations for the log returns of GM stock. Check the model and write down the fitted model.

(b) Build a GARCH-M model with Gaussian innovations for the log returns of GM stock. What is the fitted model?

(c) Build a GARCH model with Student-t distribution for the log returns of GM stock, including estimation of the degrees of freedom. Write down the fitted model. Let v be the degrees of freedom of the Student-t distribution. Test the hypothesis $H_o: v = 6$ versus $H_a: v \neq 6$, using the 5% significance level.

(d) Build an EGARCH model for the log returns of GM stock. What is the fitted model?

(e) Obtain 1-step to 6-step ahead volatility forecasts for all the models obtained. Compare the forecasts.

3.9. Consider the monthly log returns of GM stock in `m-gmsp5003.txt`. Build an adequate TGARCH model for the series. Write down the fitted model and test for the significance of the leverage effect. Obtain 1-step to 6-step ahead volatility forecasts.

3.10. Again, consider the returns in `m-gmsp5003.txt`.

(a) Build a Gaussian GARCH model for the monthly log returns of the S&P 500 index. Check the model carefully.

(b) Is there a summer effect on the volatility of the index return? Use the GARCH model built in part (a) to answer this question.

(c) Are lagged returns of GM stock useful in modeling the index volatility? Again, use the GARCH model of part (a) as a baseline model for comparison.

3.11. The file `d-gmsp9303.txt` contains the daily simple returns of GM stock and the S&P composite index from 1993 to 2003. It has three columns denoting date, GM return, and SP return.

(a) Compute the daily log returns of GM stock. Is there any evidence of ARCH effects in the log returns? You may use 10 lags of the squared returns and 5% significance level to perform the test.

(b) Compute the PACF of the squared log returns (10 lags).

(c) Specify a GARCH model for the GM log return using a normal distribution for the innovations. Perform model checking and write down the fitted model.

(d) Find an adequate GARCH model for the series but using the generalized error distribution for the innovations. Write down the fitted model.

3.12. Consider the daily simple returns of the S&P composite index in the file `d-gmsp9303.txt`.

(a) Is there any ARCH effect in the simple return series? Use 10 lags of the squared returns and 5% significance level to perform the test.

(b) Build an adequate GARCH model for the simple return series.

(c) Compute 1-step to 4-step ahead forecasts of the simple return and its volatility based on the fitted model.

3.13. Again, consider the daily simple returns of GM stock in the file `d-gmsp9303.txt`.

(a) Find an adequate GARCH-M model for the series. Write down the fitted model.

(b) Find an adequate EGARCH model for the series. Is the "leverage" effect significant at the 5% level?

3.14. Revisit the file `d-gmsp9303.txt`. However, we shall investigate the value of using market volatility in modeling volatility of individual stocks. Convert the two simple return series into *percentage* log return series.

(a) Build an AR(5)–GARCH(1,1) model with generalized error distribution for the log S&P returns. The AR(5) contains only lags 3 and 5. Denote the fitted volatility series by "spvol."

(b) Estimate a GARCH(1,1) model with `spvol` as an exogenous variable to the log GM return series. Check the adequacy of the model, and write down the fitted model. In S-Plus, the command is

```
fit = garch(gm ~ 1, ~garch(1,1)+spvol, cond.dist='ged')
```

(c) Discuss the implication of the fitted model.

3.15. Again, consider the percentage daily log returns of GM stock and the S&P 500 index from 1993 to 2003 as before, but we shall investigate whether the volatility of GM stock has any contribution in modeling the S&P 500 index volatility. Follow the steps below to perform the analysis.

(a) Fit a GARCH(1,1) model with generalized error distribution to the percentage log returns of GM stock. Denote the fitted volatility by `gmvol`. Build an adequate GARCH model plus `gmvol` as the exogenous variable for the log S&P return series. Write down the fitted model.

(b) Is the volatility of GM stock returns helpful in modeling the volatility of the S&P index returns? Why?

REFERENCES

Alizadeh, S., Brandt, M., and Diebold, F. X. (2002). Range-based estimation of stochastic volatility models. *Journal of Finance* **57**: 1047–1092.

Andersen, T. G. and Bollerslev, T. (1998). Answering the skeptics: Yes, standard volatility models do provide accurate forecasts. *International Economic Review* **39**: 885–905.

Andersen, T. G., Bollerslev, T., Diebold, F. X., and Labys, P. (2001a). The distribution of realized exchange rate volatility. *Journal of the American Statistical Association* **96**: 42–55.

Andersen, T. G., Bollerslev, T., Diebold, F. X., and Labys, P. (2001b). The distribution of realized stock return volatility. *Journal of Financial Economics* **61**: 43–76.

Bai, X., Russell, J. R., and Tiao, G. C. (2003). Kurtosis of GARCH and stochastic volatility models with non-normal innovations. *Journal of Econometrics* **114**: 349–360.

Bai, X., Russell, J. R., and Tiao, G. C. (2004). Effects of non-normality and dependence on the precision of variance estimates using high-frequency financial data. Revised working paper, Graduate School of Business, University of Chicago.

Barndorff-Nielsen, O. E. and Shephard, N. (2004). Power and bi-power variations with stochastic volatility and jumps (with discussion). *Journal of Financial Econometrics* **2**: 1–48.

Bollerslev, T. (1986). Generalized autoregressive conditional heteroskedasticity. *Journal of Econometrics* **31**: 307–327.

Bollerslev, T. (1990). Modeling the coherence in short-run nominal exchange rates: a multivariate generalized ARCH approach. *Review of Economics and Statistics* **72**: 498–505.

Bollerslev, T., Chou, R. Y., and Kroner, K. F. (1992). ARCH modeling in finance. *Journal of Econometrics* **52**: 5–59.

Bollerslev, T., Engle, R. F., and Nelson, D. B. (1994). ARCH model. In R. F. Engle and D. C. McFadden (eds.), *Handbook of Econometrics IV*, pp. 2959–3038. Elsevier Science, Amsterdam.

Bollerslev, T. and Jubinski, D. (1999). Equality trading volume and volatility: latent information arrivals and common long-run dependencies. *Journal of Business & Economic Statistics* **17**: 9–21.

Breidt, F. J., Crato, N., and de Lima, P. (1998). On the detection and estimation of long memory in stochastic volatility. *Journal of Econometrics* **83**: 325–348.

Cao, C. and Tsay, R. S. (1992). Nonlinear time series analysis of stock volatilities. *Journal of Applied Econometrics* **7**: s165–s185.

Ding, Z., Granger, C. W. J., and Engle, R. F. (1993). A long memory property of stock returns and a new model. *Journal of Empirical Finance* **1**: 83–106.

Engle, R. F. (1982). Autoregressive conditional heteroscedasticity with estimates of the variance of United Kingdom inflations. *Econometrica* **50**: 987–1007.

French, K. R., Schwert, G. W., and Stambaugh, R. F. (1987). Expected stock returns and volatility. *Journal of Financial Economics* **19**: 3–29.

Garman, M. B. and Klass, M. J. (1980). On the estimation of security price volatilities from historical data. *Journal of Business* **53**: 67–78.

Glosten, L. R., Jagannathan, R., and Runkle, D. E. (1993). On the relation between the expected value and the volatility of nominal excess return on stocks. *Journal of Finance* **48**: 1779–1801.

Harvey, A. C., Ruiz, E., and Shephard, N. (1994). Multivariate stochastic variance models. *Review of Economic Studies* **61**: 247–264.

Jacquier, E., Polson, N. G., and Rossi, P. (1994). Bayesian analysis of stochastic volatility models (with discussion). *Journal of Business & Economic Statistics* **12**: 371–417.

McLeod, A. I. and Li, W. K. (1983). Diagnostic checking ARMA time series models using squared-residual autocorrelations. *Journal of Time Series Analysis* **4**: 269–273.

Melino, A. and Turnbull, S. M. (1990). Pricing foreign currency options with stochastic volatility. *Journal of Econometrics* **45**: 239–265.

Nelson, D. B. (1990). Stationarity and persistence in the GARCH(1,1) model. *Econometric Theory* **6**: 318–334.

Nelson, D. B. (1991). Conditional heteroskedasticity in asset returns: A new approach. *Econometrica* **59**: 347–370.

Nicholls, D. F. and Quinn, B. G. (1982). *Random Coefficient Autoregressive Models: An Introduction*, Lecture Notes in Statistics, 11. Springer-Verlag, New York.

Parkinson, M. (1980). The extreme value method for estimating the variance of the rate of return. *Journal of Business* **53**: 61–65.

Ray, B. K. and Tsay, R. S. (2000). Long-range dependence in daily stock volatilities. *Journal of Business & Economic Statistics* **18**: 254–262.

Rogers, L. C. G. and Satchell, S. E. (1991). Estimating variance from high, low and closing prices. *Annals of Applied Probability* **1**: 504–512.

Taylor, S. J. (1994). Modeling stochastic volatility: A review and comparative study. *Mathematical Finance* **4**: 183–204.

Tong, H. (1978). On a threshold model. In C. H. Chen (ed.), *Pattern Recognition and Signal Processing*. Sijhoff & Noordhoff, Amsterdam.

Tong, H. (1990). *Non-Linear Time Series: A Dynamical System Approach*. Oxford University Press, Oxford, UK.

Tsay, R. S. (1987). Conditional heteroscedastic time series models. *Journal of the American Statistical Association* **82**: 590–604.

Yang, D. and Zhang, Q. (2000). Drift-independent volatility estimation based on high, low, open, and close prices. *Journal of Business* **73**: 477–491.

Zakoian, J. M. (1994). Threshold heteroscedastic models. *Journal of Economic Dynamics and Control* **18**: 931–955.

CHAPTER 4

Nonlinear Models and Their Applications

This chapter focuses on nonlinearity in financial data and nonlinear econometric models useful in analysis of financial time series. Consider a univariate time series x_t, which, for simplicity, is observed at equally spaced time points. We denote the observations by $\{x_t|t = 1, \ldots, T\}$, where T is the sample size. As stated in Chapter 2, a purely stochastic time series x_t is said to be linear if it can be written as

$$x_t = \mu + \sum_{i=0}^{\infty} \psi_i a_{t-i}, \tag{4.1}$$

where μ is a constant, ψ_i are real numbers with $\psi_0 = 1$, and $\{a_t\}$ is a sequence of independent and identically distributed (iid) random variables with a well-defined distribution function. We assume that the distribution of a_t is continuous and $E(a_t) = 0$. In many cases, we further assume that $\text{Var}(a_t) = \sigma_a^2$ or, even stronger, that a_t is Gaussian. If $\sigma_a^2 \sum_{i=1}^{\infty} \psi_i^2 < \infty$, then x_t is weakly stationary (i.e., the first two moments of x_t are time-invariant). The ARMA process of Chapter 2 is linear because it has an MA representation in Eq. (4.1). Any stochastic process that does not satisfy the condition of Eq. (4.1) is said to be nonlinear. The prior definition of nonlinearity is for purely stochastic time series. One may extend the definition by allowing the mean of x_t to be a linear function of some exogenous variables, including the time index and some periodic functions. But such a mean function can be handled easily by the methods discussed in Chapter 2, and we do not discuss it here. Mathematically, a purely stochastic time series model for x_t is a function of an iid sequence consisting of the current and past shocks—that is,

$$x_t = f(a_t, a_{t-1}, \ldots). \tag{4.2}$$

The linear model in Eq. (4.1) says that $f(.)$ is a linear function of its arguments. Any nonlinearity in $f(.)$ results in a nonlinear model. The general nonlinear model in Eq. (4.2) is not directly applicable because it contains too many parameters.

Analysis of Financial Time Series, Second Edition By Ruey S. Tsay

To put nonlinear models available in the literature in a proper perspective, we write the model of x_t in terms of its conditional moments. Let F_{t-1} be the σ-field generated by available information at time $t-1$ (inclusive). Typically, F_{t-1} denotes the collection of linear combinations of elements in $\{x_{t-1}, x_{t-2}, \ldots\}$ and $\{a_{t-1}, a_{t-2}, \ldots\}$. The conditional mean and variance of x_t given F_{t-1} are

$$\mu_t = E(x_t|F_{t-1}) \equiv g(F_{t-1}), \quad \sigma_t^2 = \text{Var}(x_t|F_{t-1}) \equiv h(F_{t-1}), \tag{4.3}$$

where $g(.)$ and $h(.)$ are well-defined functions with $h(.) > 0$. Thus, we restrict the model to

$$x_t = g(F_{t-1}) + \sqrt{h(F_{t-1})}\epsilon_t,$$

where $\epsilon_t = a_t/\sigma_t$ is a standardized shock (or innovation). For the linear series x_t in Eq. (4.1), $g(.)$ is a linear function of elements of F_{t-1} and $h(.) = \sigma_a^2$. The development of nonlinear models involves making extensions of the two equations in Eq. (4.3). If $g(.)$ is nonlinear, x_t is said to be *nonlinear in mean*. If $h(.)$ is time-variant, then x_t is *nonlinear in variance*. The conditional heteroscedastic models of Chapter 3 are nonlinear in variance because their conditional variances σ_t^2 evolve over time. In fact, except for the GARCH-M models, in which μ_t depends on σ_t^2 and hence also evolves over time, all of the volatility models of Chapter 3 focus on modifications or extensions of the conditional variance equation in Eq. (4.3). Based on the well-known Wold decomposition, a weakly stationary and purely stochastic time series can be expressed as a linear function of uncorrelated shocks. For stationary volatility series, these shocks are uncorrelated, but dependent. The models discussed in this chapter represent another extension to nonlinearity derived from modifying the conditional mean equation in Eq. (4.3).

Many nonlinear time series models have been proposed in the statistical literature, such as the bilinear models of Granger and Andersen (1978), the threshold autoregressive (TAR) model of Tong (1978), the state-dependent model of Priestley (1980), and the Markov switching model of Hamilton (1989). The basic idea underlying these nonlinear models is to let the conditional mean μ_t evolve over time according to some simple parametric nonlinear function. Recently, a number of nonlinear models have been proposed by making use of advances in computing facilities and computational methods. Examples of such extensions include the nonlinear state-space modeling of Carlin, Polson, and Stoffer (1992), the functional-coefficient autoregressive model of Chen and Tsay (1993a), the nonlinear additive autoregressive model of Chen and Tsay (1993b), and the multivariate adaptive regression spline of Lewis and Stevens (1991). The basic idea of these extensions is either using simulation methods to describe the evolution of the conditional distribution of x_t or using data-driven methods to explore the nonlinear characteristics of a series. Finally, nonparametric and semiparametric methods such as kernel regression and artificial neural networks have also been applied to explore the nonlinearity in a time series. We discuss some nonlinear models in Section 4.3 that are applicable to financial time series. The discussion includes some nonparametric and semiparametric methods.

Apart from the development of various nonlinear models, there is substantial interest in studying test statistics that can discriminate linear series from nonlinear ones. Both parametric and nonparametric tests are available. Most parametric tests employ either the Lagrange multiplier or likelihood ratio statistics. Nonparametric tests depend on either higher order spectra of x_t or the concept of dimension correlation developed for chaotic time series. We review some nonlinearity tests in Section 4.2. Sections 4.3 and 4.4 discuss modeling and forecasting of nonlinear models. Finally, an application of nonlinear models is given in Section 4.5.

4.1 NONLINEAR MODELS

Most nonlinear models developed in the statistical literature focus on the conditional mean equation in Eq. (4.3); see Priestley (1988) and Tong (1990) for summaries of nonlinear models. Our goal here is to introduce some nonlinear models that are applicable to financial time series.

4.1.1 Bilinear Model

The linear model in Eq. (4.1) is simply the first-order Taylor series expansion of the $f(.)$ function in Eq. (4.2). As such, a natural extension to nonlinearity is to employ the second-order terms in the expansion to improve the approximation. This is the basic idea of bilinear models, which can be defined as

$$x_t = c + \sum_{i=1}^{p} \phi_i x_{t-i} - \sum_{j=1}^{q} \theta_j a_{t-j} + \sum_{i=1}^{m} \sum_{j=1}^{s} \beta_{ij} x_{t-i} a_{t-j} + a_t, \tag{4.4}$$

where p, q, m, and s are non-negative integers. This model was introduced by Granger and Andersen (1978) and has been widely investigated. Subba Rao and Gabr (1984) discuss some properties and applications of the model, and Liu and Brockwell (1988) study general bilinear models. Properties of bilinear models such as stationarity conditions are often derived by (a) putting the model in a state-space form (see Chapter 11) and (b) using the state transition equation to express the state as a product of past innovations and random coefficient vectors. A special generalization of the bilinear model in Eq. (4.4) has conditional heteroscedasticity. For example, consider the model

$$x_t = \mu + \sum_{i=1}^{s} \beta_i a_{t-i} a_t + a_t, \tag{4.5}$$

where $\{a_t\}$ is a white noise series. The first two conditional moments of x_t are

$$E(x_t|F_{t-1}) = \mu, \quad \text{Var}(x_t|F_{t-1}) = \left(1 + \sum_{i=1}^{s} \beta_i a_{t-i}\right)^2 \sigma_a^2,$$

which are similar to that of the RCA or CHARMA model of Chapter 3.

Example 4.1. Consider the monthly simple returns of the CRSP equal-weighted index from January 1926 to December 1997 for 864 observations. Denote the series by R_t. The sample PACF of R_t shows significant partial autocorrelations at lags 1 and 3, whereas that of R_t^2 suggests that the conditional heteroscedasticity might depend on the past three innovations. Therefore, we employ the special bilinear model

$$R_t = \mu + \phi_1 R_{t-1} + \phi_3 R_{t-3} + (1 + \beta_1 a_{t-1} + \beta_2 a_{t-2} + \beta_3 a_{t-3}) a_t$$

for the series. Assuming that the conditional distribution of a_t is normal, we use the conditional maximum likelihood method and obtain the fitted model

$$\begin{aligned} R_t &= 0.014 + 0.160 R_{t-1} - 0.104 R_{t-3} \\ &\quad + (1 + 0.337 a_{t-1} - 0.022 a_{t-2} - 0.601 a_{t-3}) a_t, \end{aligned} \tag{4.6}$$

where $\hat{\sigma}_a^2 = 0.0052$ and the standard errors of the parameters are, in the order of appearance, 0.003, 0.026, 0.018, 0.083, 0.084, and 0.079. The only insignificant estimate is the coefficient of a_{t-2}. Define

$$\hat{a}_t = \frac{R_t - 0.014 - 0.160 R_{t-1} + 0.014 R_{t-3}}{1 + 0.337 \hat{a}_{t-1} - 0.022 \hat{a}_{t-2} - 0.601 \hat{a}_{t-3}},$$

where $\hat{a}_t = 0$ for $t \leq 3$ as the residual series of the model. The sample ACF of $\hat{a}_t$ shows no significant serial correlations, but the series is not independent because the squared series $\hat{a}_t^2$ has significant serial correlations. The validity of model (4.6) deserves further investigation. For comparison, we also consider an ARCH(3) model for the series and obtain

$$\begin{aligned} R_t &= 0.013 + 0.222 R_{t-1} - 0.140 R_{t-3} + a_t, \\ \sigma_t^2 &= 0.002 + 0.168 a_{t-1}^2 + 0.00001 a_{t-2}^2 + 0.274 a_{t-3}^2, \end{aligned} \tag{4.7}$$

where all estimates but the coefficient of a_{t-2}^2 are highly significant. The standardized residual series and its squared series show no serial correlations, indicating that the ARCH(3) model is adequate for the data. Models (4.6) and (4.7) appear to be similar, but the latter seems to fit the data better.

4.1.2 Threshold Autoregressive (TAR) Model

This model is motivated by several nonlinear characteristics commonly observed in practice such as asymmetry in declining and rising patterns of a process. It uses piecewise linear models to obtain a better approximation of the conditional mean equation. However, in contrast to the traditional piecewise linear model that allows for model changes to occur in the "time" space, the TAR model uses threshold space to improve linear approximation. Let us start with a simple 2-regime AR(1) model

$$x_t = \begin{cases} -1.5 x_{t-1} + a_t & \text{if } x_{t-1} < 0, \\ 0.5 x_{t-1} + a_t & \text{if } x_{t-1} \geq 0, \end{cases} \tag{4.8}$$

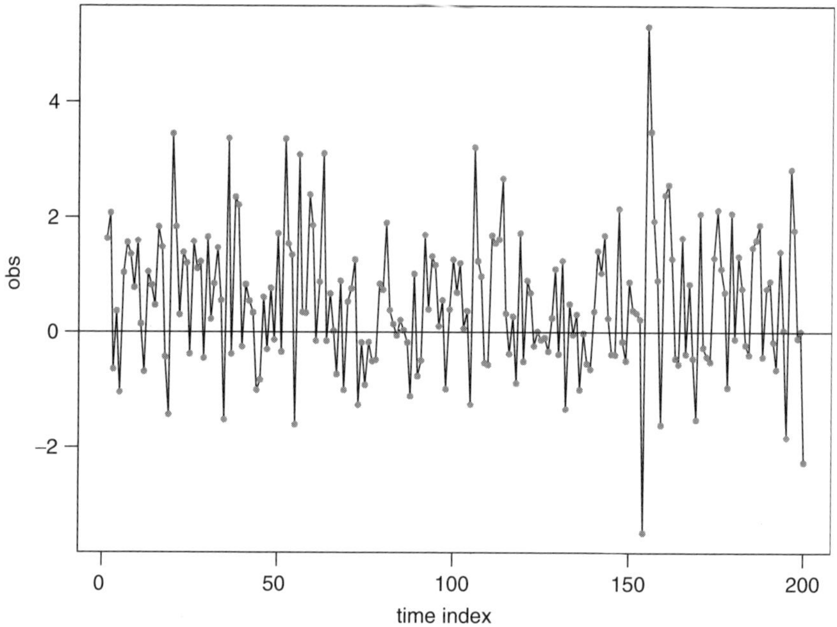

Figure 4.1. Time plot of a simulated 2-regime TAR(1) series.

where the a_t are iid $N(0, 1)$. Here the threshold variable is x_{t-1} so that the delay is 1, and the threshold is 0. Figure 4.1 shows the time plot of a simulated series of x_t with 200 observations. A horizontal line of zero is added to the plot, which illustrates several characteristics of TAR models. First, despite the coefficient -1.5 in the first regime, the process x_t is geometrically ergodic and stationary. In fact, the necessary and sufficient condition for model (4.8) to be geometrically ergodic is $\phi_1^{(1)} < 1$, $\phi_1^{(2)} < 1$, and $\phi_1^{(1)}\phi_1^{(2)} < 1$, where $\phi_1^{(i)}$ is the AR coefficient of regime i; see Petruccelli and Woolford (1984) and Chen and Tsay (1991). Ergodicity is an important concept in time series analysis. For example, the statistical theory showing that the sample mean $\bar{x} = \left(\sum_{t=1}^{T} x_t\right)/T$ of x_t converges to the mean of x_t is referred to as the *ergodic theorem*, which can be regarded as the counterpart of the central limit theory for the iid case. Second, the series exhibits an asymmetric increasing and decreasing pattern. If x_{t-1} is negative, then x_t tends to switch to a positive value due to the negative and explosive coefficient -1.5. Yet when x_{t-1} is positive, it tends to take multiple time indexes for x_t to reduce to a negative value. Consequently, the time plot of x_t shows that regime 2 has more observations than regime 1, and the series contains large upward jumps when it becomes negative. The series is therefore not time-reversible. Third, the model contains no constant terms, but $E(x_t)$ is not zero. The sample mean of the particular realization is 0.61 with a standard deviation of 0.07. In general, $E(x_t)$ is a weighted average of the conditional means of the two regimes, which are nonzero. The weight for each regime is simply the probability that x_t is in that regime under its stationary distribution. It is also clear from the discussion that, for a TAR model to have zero mean, nonzero constant terms in some of the regimes are needed. This is very different from a stationary linear model for which a nonzero constant implies that the mean of x_t is not zero.

A time series x_t is said to follow a k-regime self-exciting TAR (SETAR) model with threshold variable x_{t-d} if it satisfies

$$x_t = \phi_0^{(j)} + \phi_1^{(j)} x_{t-1} - \cdots - \phi_p^{(j)} x_{t-p} + a_t^{(j)}, \qquad \text{if} \quad \gamma_{j-1} \le x_{t-d} < \gamma_j, \tag{4.9}$$

where k and d are positive integers, $j = 1, \ldots, k$, γ_i are real numbers such that $-\infty = \gamma_0 < \gamma_1 < \cdots < \gamma_{k-1} < \gamma_k = \infty$, the superscript (j) is used to signify the regime, and $\{a_t^{(j)}\}$ are iid sequences with mean 0 and variance σ_j^2 and are mutually independent for different j. The parameter d is referred to as the *delay parameter* and γ_j are the *thresholds*. Here it is understood that the AR models are different for different regimes; otherwise, the number of regimes can be reduced. Equation (4.9) says that a SETAR model is a piecewise linear AR model in the threshold space. It is similar in spirit to the usual piecewise linear models in regression analysis, where model changes occur in the order in which observations are taken. The SETAR model is nonlinear provided that $k > 1$.

Properties of general SETAR models are hard to obtain, but some of them can be found in Tong (1990), Chan (1993), Chan and Tsay (1998), and the references therein. In recent years, there is increasing interest in TAR models and their applications; see, for instance, Hansen (1997), Tsay (1998), and Montgomery et al. (1998). Tsay (1989) proposed a testing and modeling procedure for univariate SETAR models. The model in Eq. (4.9) can be generalized by using a threshold variable z_t that is measurable with respect to F_{t-1} (i.e., a function of elements of F_{t-1}). The main requirements are that z_t is stationary with a continuous distribution function over a compact subset of the real line and that z_{t-d} is known at time t. Such a generalized model is referred to as an *open-loop TAR model.*

Example 4.2. To demonstrate the application of TAR models, consider the U.S. monthly civilian unemployment rate, seasonally adjusted and measured in percentage, from January 1948 to March 2004 for 675 observations. The data are obtained from the Bureau of Labor Statistics, Department of Labor, and are shown in Figure 4.2. The plot shows two main characteristics of the data. First, there appears to be a slow, but upward trend in the overall unemployment rate. Second, the unemployment rate tends to increase rapidly and decrease slowly. Thus, the series is not time-reversible and may not be unit-root stationary, either.

Because the sample autocorrelation function decays slowly, we employ the first differenced series $y_t = (1 - B)u_t$ in the analysis, where u_t is the monthly unemployment rate. Using univariate ARIMA models, we obtain the model

$$(1 - 1.18B + 0.33B^2)(1 - 0.51B^{12})y_t = (1 - 1.17B + 0.48B^2)(1 - 0.82B^{12})a_t, \tag{4.10}$$

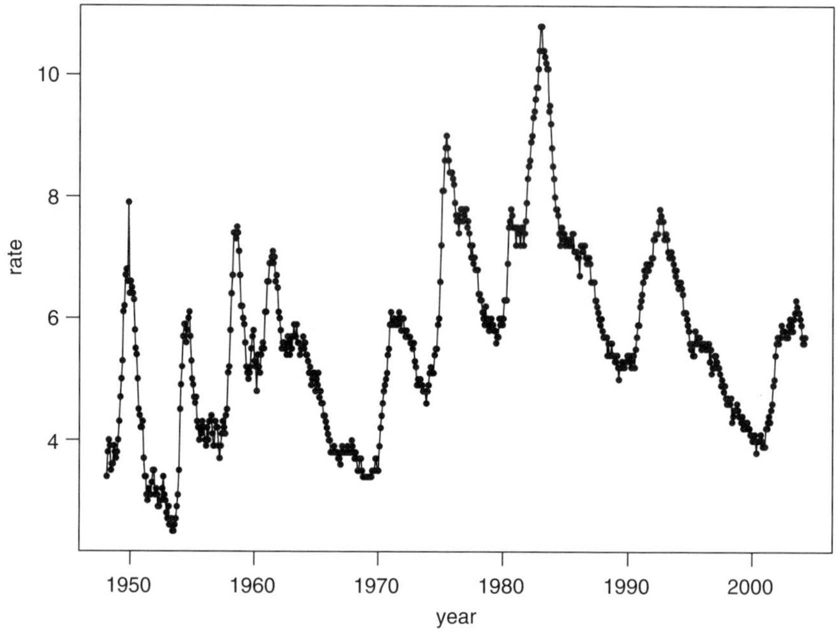

Figure 4.2. Time plot of monthly U.S. civilian unemployment rate, seasonally adjusted, from January 1948 to March 2004.

where $\hat{\sigma}_a = 0.190$ and all estimates are statistically significant at the 5% level with minimum t-ratio of -2.01 for the AR(2) coefficient. The residuals of model (4.10) give $Q(12) = 9.9$ and $Q(24) = 22.4$, indicating that the fitted model adequately describes the serial dependence of the data. Note that the seasonal AR and MA coefficients are highly significant with standard error 0.05 and 0.045, respectively, even though the data were seasonally adjusted. The adequacy of seasonal adjustment deserves further study.

To model nonlinearity in the data, we employ TAR models and obtain the model

$$y_t = \begin{cases} 0.069y_{t-2} + 0.153y_{t-3} + 0.106y_{t-4} - 0.181y_{t-12} + a_{1t} & \text{if } y_{t-1} \le 0.1, \\ 0.401y_{t-2} + 0.208y_{t-3} - 0.139y_{t-12} + a_{2t} & \text{if } y_{t-1} > 0.1, \end{cases} \tag{4.11}$$

where the standard errors of a_{it} are 0.183 and 0.223, respectively, the standard errors of the AR parameters in regime 1 are 0.048, 0.044, 0.043, and 0.038 whereas those of the AR parameters in regime 2 are 0.057, 0.060, and 0.079, respectively. The number of data points in regimes 1 and 2 are 422 and 240, respectively. The residuals of model (4.11) also fail to show any significant serial correlation. Based on the fitted TAR model, the dynamic dependence in the data appears to be stronger when the change in monthly unemployment rate is greater than 0.1%. This is understandable because a substantial increase in the unemployment rate is indicative of weakening in the U.S. economy, and policy makers might be more inclined to take action to help the economy, which in turn may affect the dynamics of the unemployment rate series. Consequently, model (4.11) is capable of describing the time-varying dynamics of the U.S. unemployment rate.

The MA representation of model (4.10) is

$$\psi(B) \approx 1 + 0.01B + 0.15B^2 + 0.18B^3 + 0.16B^4 + \cdots.$$

It is then not surprising to see that no y_{t-1} term appears in model (4.11).

As mentioned in Chapter 3, threshold models can be used in finance to handle the asymmetric responses in volatility between positive and negative returns. The models can also be used to study arbitrage tradings in index futures and cash prices; see Chapter 8 on multivariate time series analysis. Here we focus on volatility modeling and introduce an alternative approach to parameterization of TGARCH models. In some applications, this new general TGARCH model fares better than the GJR model of Chapter 3.

Example 4.3. Consider the daily log returns, in percentage and including dividends, of IBM stock from July 3, 1962 to December 31, 2003 for 10,446 observations. Figure 4.3 shows the time plot of the series, which is one of the longer return series analyzed in the book. The volatility seems to be larger in the latter years of the data. Because general TGARCH models are used in the analysis, we use the SCA package to perform estimation in this example.

If GARCH models of Chapter 3 are entertained, we obtain the following AR(2)–GARCH(1,1) model for the series:

$$\begin{aligned} r_t &= 0.062 - 0.024 r_{t-2} + a_t, \quad a_t = \sigma_t \epsilon_t, \\ \sigma_t^2 &= 0.037 + 0.077 a_{t-1}^2 + 0.913 \sigma_{t-1}^2, \end{aligned} \tag{4.12}$$

where r_t is the log return, $\{\epsilon_t\}$ is a Gaussian white noise sequence with mean zero and variance 1.0, the standard errors of the parameters in the mean equation are 0.015 and 0.010, and those of the volatility equation are 0.004, 0.003, and 0.003, respectively. All estimates are statistically significant at the 5% level. The Ljung–Box statistics of the standardized residuals give $Q(10) = 5.19(0.88)$ and $Q(20) = 24.38(0.23)$, where the number in parentheses denotes p-value. For the squared standardized residuals, we obtain $Q(10) = 11.67(0.31)$ and $Q(20) = 18.25(0.57)$. The model is adequate in modeling the serial dependence and conditional heteroscedasticity of the data. But the unconditional mean for r_t of model (4.12) is 0.060, which is substantially larger than the sample mean 0.039, indicating that the model might be misspecified.

Next, we employ the TGARCH model of Chapter 3 and obtain

$$\begin{aligned} r_t &= 0.014 - 0.028 r_{t-2} + a_t, \quad a_t = \sigma_t \epsilon_t, \\ \sigma_t^2 &= 0.075 + 0.081 P_{t-1} a_{t-1}^2 + 0.157 N_{t-1} a_{t-1}^2 + 0.863 \sigma_{t-1}^2, \end{aligned} \tag{4.13}$$

where $P_{t-1} = 1 - N_{t-1}$, N_{t-1} is the indicator for negative a_{t-1} such that $N_{t-1} = 1$ if $a_{t-1} < 0$ and $= 0$ otherwise, the standard errors of the parameters in the mean

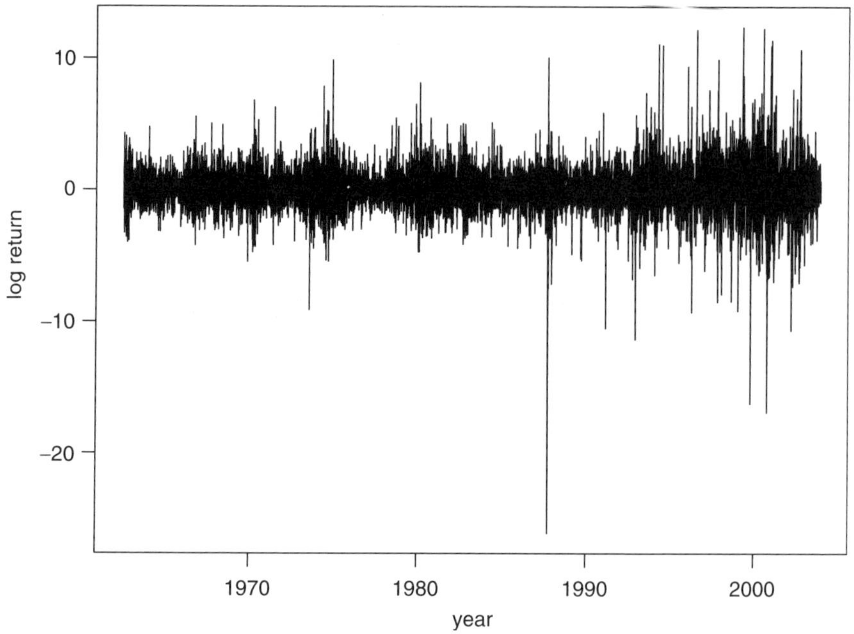

Figure 4.3. Time plot of the daily log returns for IBM stock from July 3, 1962 to December 31, 2003.

equation are 0.013 and 0.009, and those of the volatility equation are 0.007, 0.008, 0.010, and 0.010, respectively. All estimates except the constant term of the mean equation are significant. Let $\tilde{a}_t$ be the standardized residuals of model (4.13). We have $Q(10) = 2.47(0.99)$ and $Q(20) = 25.90(0.17)$ for the $\{\tilde{a}_t\}$ series and $Q(10) = 97.07(0.00)$ and $Q(20) = 170.3(0.00)$ for $\{\tilde{a}_t^2\}$. The model fails to describe the conditional heteroscedasticity of the data.

The idea of TAR models can be used to refine the prior TGARCH model by allowing for increased flexibility in modeling the asymmetric response in volatility. More specifically, we consider an AR(2)–TAR–GARCH(1,1) model for the series and obtain

$$\begin{aligned} r_t &= 0.033 - 0.023 r_{t-2} + a_t, \quad a_t = \sigma_t \epsilon_t, \\ \sigma_t^2 &= 0.075 + 0.041 a_{t-1}^2 + 0.903 \sigma_{t-1}^2 \\ &\quad + (0.030 a_{t-1}^2 + 0.062 \sigma_{t-1}^2) N_{t-1}, \end{aligned} \tag{4.14}$$

where N_{t-1} is defined in Eq. (4.13). All estimates in model (4.14) are significantly different from zero at the usual 1% level. Let $\hat{a}_t$ be the standardized residuals of model (4.14). We obtain $Q(10) = 6.09(0.81)$ and $Q(20) = 25.29(0.19)$ for $\{\hat{a}_t\}$ and $Q(10) = 13.54(0.20)$ and $Q(20) = 19.56(0.49)$ for $\{\hat{a}_t^2\}$. Thus, model (4.14) is adequate in modeling the serial correlation and conditional heteroscedasticity of the daily log returns of IBM stock considered. The unconditional mean return of model (4.14) is 0.033, which is much closer to the sample mean 0.039 than those implied by models (4.12) and (4.13). Comparing the two fitted TGARCH models, we see that the asymmetric behavior in daily IBM stock volatility is much stronger than what is allowed in a GJR model. Specifically, the coefficient of σ_{t-1}^2 also depends on the sign of a_{t-1}. Note that model (4.14) can be further refined by imposing the constraint that the sum of the coefficients of a_{t-1}^2 and σ_{t-1}^2 is one when $a_{t-1} < 0$.

Remark. A RATS program to estimate the AR(2)–TAR–GARCH(1,1) model used is given in Appendix A. The results might be slightly different from those of SCA given in the text. □

4.1.3 Smooth Transition AR (STAR) Model

A criticism of the SETAR model is that its conditional mean equation is not continuous. The thresholds $\{\gamma_j\}$ are the discontinuity points of the conditional mean function μ_t. In response to this criticism, smooth TAR models have been proposed; see Chan and Tong (1986) and Teräsvirta (1994) and the references therein. A time series x_t is said to follow a 2-regime STAR(p) model if it satisfies

$$x_t = c_0 + \sum_{i=1}^{p} \phi_{0,i} x_{t-i} + F\left(\frac{x_{t-d} - \Delta}{s}\right)\left(c_1 + \sum_{i=1}^{p} \phi_{1,i} x_{t-i}\right) + a_t, \qquad (4.15)$$

where d is the delay parameter, Δ and s are parameters representing the location and scale of model transition, and $F(.)$ is a smooth transition function. In practice, $F(.)$ often assumes one of three forms—namely, logistic, exponential, or a cumulative distribution function. From Eq. (4.15), the conditional mean of a STAR model is a weighted linear combination between the following two equations:

$$\mu_{1t} = c_0 + \sum_{i=1}^{p} \phi_{0,i} x_{t-i},$$

$$\mu_{2t} = (c_0 + c_1) + \sum_{i=1}^{p} (\phi_{0,i} + \phi_{1,i}) x_{t-i}.$$

The weights are determined in a continuous manner by $F((x_{t-d} - \Delta)/s)$. The prior two equations also determine properties of a STAR model. For instance, a prerequisite for the stationarity of a STAR model is that all zeros of both AR polynomials are outside the unit circle. An advantage of the STAR model over the TAR model is that the conditional mean function is differentiable. However, experience shows that the transition parameters Δ and s of a STAR model are hard to estimate. In particular, most empirical studies show that standard errors of the estimates of Δ and s are often quite large, resulting in t-ratios about 1.0; see Teräsvirta (1994). This uncertainty leads to various complications in interpreting an estimated STAR model.

Example 4.4. To illustrate the application of STAR models in financial time series analysis, we consider the monthly simple stock returns for Minnesota Mining and Manufacturing (3M) Company from February 1946 to December 1997. If ARCH models are entertained, we obtain the following ARCH(2) model:

$$R_t = 0.014 + a_t, \quad a_t = \sigma_t \epsilon_t, \quad \sigma_t^2 = 0.003 + 0.108 a_{t-1}^2 + 0.151 a_{t-2}^2, \tag{4.16}$$

where standard errors of the estimates are 0.002, 0.0003, 0.045, and 0.058, respectively. As discussed before, such an ARCH model fails to show the asymmetric responses of stock volatility to positive and negative prior shocks. The STAR model provides a simple alternative that may overcome this difficulty. Applying STAR models to the monthly returns of 3M stock, we obtain the model

$$\begin{aligned} R_t &= 0.017 + a_t, \quad a_t = \sigma_t \epsilon_t, \\ \sigma_t^2 &= (0.002 + 0.256 a_{t-1}^2 + 0.141 a_{t-2}^2) + \frac{0.002 - 0.314 a_{t-1}^2}{1 + \exp(-1000 a_{t-1})}, \end{aligned} \tag{4.17}$$

where the standard error of the constant term in the mean equation is 0.002 and the standard errors of the estimates in the volatility equation are 0.0003, 0.092, 0.056, 0.001, and 0.102, respectively. The scale parameter 1000 of the logistic transition function is fixed a priori to simplify the estimation. This STAR model provides some support for asymmetric responses to positive and negative prior shocks. For a large negative a_{t-1}, the volatility model approaches the ARCH(2) model

$$\sigma_t^2 = 0.002 + 0.256 a_{t-1}^2 + 0.141 a_{t-2}^2.$$

Yet for a large positive a_{t-1}, the volatility process behaves like the ARCH(2) model

$$\sigma_t^2 = 0.005 - 0.058 a_{t-1}^2 + 0.141 a_{t-2}^2.$$

The negative coefficient of a_{t-1}^2 in the prior model is counterintuitive, but the magnitude is small. As a matter of fact, for a large positive shock a_{t-1}, the ARCH effects appear to be weak even though the parameter estimates remain statistically significant. The RATS program used is given in Appendix A.

4.1.4 Markov Switching Model

The idea of using probability switching in nonlinear time series analysis is discussed in Tong (1983). Using a similar idea, but emphasizing aperiodic transition between various states of an economy, Hamilton (1989) considers the Markov switching autoregressive (MSA) model. Here the transition is driven by a hidden two-state Markov chain. A time series x_t follows an MSA model if it satisfies

$$x_t = \begin{cases} c_1 + \sum_{i=1}^{p} \phi_{1,i} x_{t-i} + a_{1t} & \text{if } s_t = 1, \\ c_2 + \sum_{i=1}^{p} \phi_{2,i} x_{t-i} + a_{2t} & \text{if } s_t = 2, \end{cases} \tag{4.18}$$

where s_t assumes values in {1,2} and is a first-order Markov chain with transition probabilities

$$P(s_t = 2|s_{t-1} = 1) = w_1, \quad P(s_t = 1|s_{t-1} = 2) = w_2.$$

The innovational series $\{a_{1t}\}$ and $\{a_{2t}\}$ are sequences of iid random variables with mean zero and finite variance and are independent of each other. A small w_i means that the model tends to stay longer in state i. In fact, $1/w_i$ is the expected duration of the process to stay in state i. From the definition, an MSA model uses a hidden Markov chain to govern the transition from one conditional mean function to another. This is different from that of a SETAR model for which the transition is determined by a particular lagged variable. Consequently, a SETAR model uses a deterministic scheme to govern the model transition whereas an MSA model uses a stochastic scheme. In practice, the stochastic nature of the states implies that one is never certain about which state x_t belongs to in an MSA model. When the sample size is large, one can use some filtering techniques to draw inference on the state of x_t. Yet as long as x_{t-d} is observed, the regime of x_t is known in a SETAR model. This difference has important practical implications in forecasting. For instance, forecasts of an MSA model are always a linear combination of forecasts produced by submodels of individual states. But those of a SETAR model only come from a single regime provided that x_{t-d} is observed. Forecasts of a SETAR model also become a linear combination of those produced by models of individual regimes when the forecast horizon exceeds the delay d. It is much harder to estimate an MSA model than other models because the states are not directly observable. Hamilton (1990) uses the EM algorithm, which is a statistical method iterating between taking expectation and maximization. McCulloch and Tsay (1994) consider a Markov chain Monte Carlo (MCMC) method to estimate a general MSA model. We discuss MCMC methods in Chapter 12.

McCulloch and Tsay (1993) generalize the MSA model in Eq. (4.18) by letting the transition probabilities w_1 and w_2 be logistic, or probit, functions of some explanatory variables available at time $t - 1$. Chen, McCulloch, and Tsay (1997) use the idea of Markov switching as a tool to perform model comparison and selection between non-nested nonlinear time series models (e.g., comparing bilinear and SETAR models). Each competing model is represented by a state. This approach to select a model is a generalization of the odds ratio commonly used in Bayesian analysis. Finally, the MSA model can easily be generalized to the case of more than two states. The computational intensity involved increases rapidly, however. For more discussions of Markov switching models in econometrics, see Hamilton (1994, Chapter 22).

Example 4.5. Consider the growth rate, in percentages, of the U.S. quarterly real gross national product (GNP) from the second quarter of 1947 to the first quarter of 1991. The data are seasonally adjusted and shown in Figure 4.4, where a horizontal line of zero growth is also given. It is reassuring to see that a majority of the growth rates are positive. This series has been widely used in nonlinear

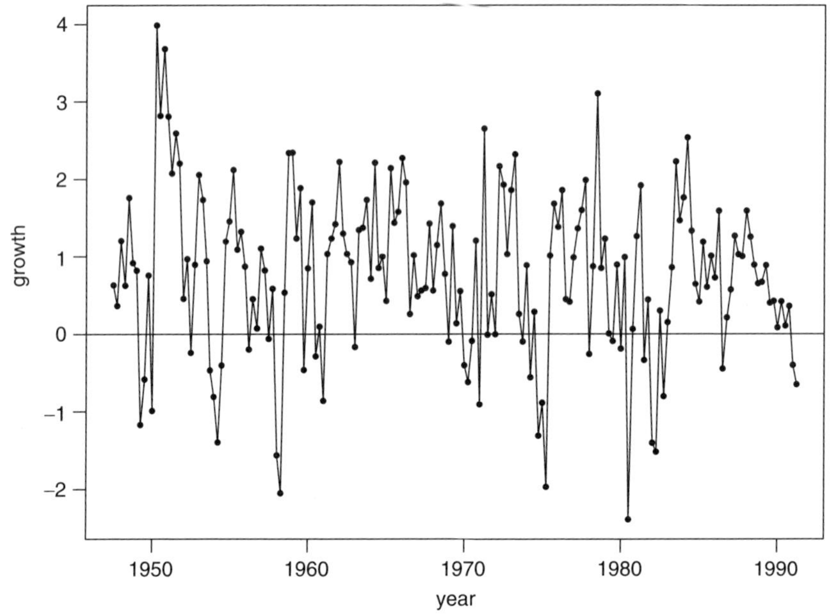

Figure 4.4. Time plot of the growth rate of the U.S. quarterly real GNP from 1947.II to 1991.I. The data are seasonally adjusted and in percentages.

analysis of economic time series. Tiao and Tsay (1994) and Potter (1995) use TAR models, whereas Hamilton (1989) and McCulloch and Tsay (1994) employ Markov switching models.

Employing the MSA model in Eq. (4.18) with $p = 4$ and using a Markov chain Monte Carlo method, which is discussed in Chapter 12, McCulloch and Tsay (1994) obtain the estimates shown in Table 4.1. The results have several interesting findings. First, the mean growth rate of the marginal model for state 1 is $0.909/(1 - 0.265 - 0.029 + 0.126 + 0.11) = 0.965$ and that of state 2 is $-0.42/(1 - 0.216 - 0.628 + 0.073 + 0.097) = -1.288$. Thus, state 1 corresponds to quarters with positive growth, or expansion periods, whereas state 2 consists of quarters with negative growth, or a contraction period. Second, the relatively large posterior standard deviations of the parameters in state 2 reflect that there are few observations in that state. This is expected as Figure 4.4 shows few quarters with negative growth. Third, the transition probabilities appear to be different for different states. The estimates indicate that it is more likely for the U.S. GNP to get out of a contraction period than to jump into one—0.286 versus 0.118. Fourth, treating $1/w_i$ as the expected duration for the process to stay in state i, we see that the expected durations for a contraction period and an expansion period are approximately 3.69 and 11.31 quarters. Thus, on average, a contraction in the U.S. economy lasts about a year, whereas an expansion can last for 3 years. Finally, the estimated AR coefficients of x_{t-2} differ substantially between the two states, indicating that the dynamics of the U.S. economy are different between expansion and contraction periods.

Table 4.1. Estimation Results of a Markov Switching Model with $p = 4$ for the Growth Rate of U.S. Quarterly Real GNP, Seasonally Adjusted[a]

Parameter	c_i	ϕ_1	ϕ_2	ϕ_3	ϕ_4	σ_i	w_i
			State 1				
Estimate	0.909	0.265	0.029	−0.126	−0.110	0.816	0.118
Standard error	0.202	0.113	0.126	0.103	0.109	0.125	0.053
			State 2				
Estimate	−0.420	0.216	0.628	−0.073	−0.097	1.017	0.286
Standard error	0.324	0.347	0.377	0.364	0.404	0.293	0.064

[a]The estimates and their standard errors are posterior means and standard errors of a Gibbs sampling with 5000 iterations.

4.1.5 Nonparametric Methods

In some financial applications, we may not have sufficient knowledge to prespecify the nonlinear structure between two variables Y and X. In other applications, we may wish to take advantage of the advances in computing facilities and computational methods to explore the functional relationship between Y and X. These considerations lead to the use of nonparametric methods and techniques. Nonparametric methods, however, are not without cost. They are highly data dependent and can easily result in overfitting. Our goal here is to introduce some nonparametric methods for financial applications and some nonlinear models that make use of nonparametric methods and techniques. The nonparametric methods discussed include kernel regression, local least squares estimation, and neural network.

The essence of nonparametric methods is *smoothing*. Consider two financial variables Y and X, which are related by

$$Y_t = m(X_t) + a_t, \tag{4.19}$$

where $m(.)$ is an arbitrary, smooth, but unknown function and $\{a_t\}$ is a white noise sequence. We wish to estimate the nonlinear function $m(.)$ from the data. For simplicity, consider the problem of estimating $m(.)$ at a particular date for which $X = x$. That is, we are interested in estimating $m(x)$. Suppose that at $X = x$ we have repeated independent observations $y_1, \ldots, y_T$. Then the data become

$$y_t = m(x) + a_t, \quad t = 1, \ldots, T.$$

Taking the average of the data, we have

$$\frac{\sum_{t=1}^{T} y_t}{T} = m(x) + \frac{\sum_{t=1}^{T} a_t}{T}.$$

By the law of large numbers, the average of the shocks converges to zero as T increases. Therefore, the average $\overline{y} = \left(\sum_{t=1}^{T} y_t\right)/T$ is a consistent estimate of

$m(x)$. That the average $\overline{y}$ provides a consistent estimate of $m(x)$ or, alternatively, that the average of shocks converges to zero shows the power of smoothing.

In financial time series, we do not have repeated observations available at $X = x$. What we observed are $\{(y_t, x_t)\}$ for $t = 1, \ldots, T$. But if the function $m(.)$ is sufficiently smooth, then the value of Y_t for which $X_t \approx x$ continues to provide accurate approximation of $m(x)$. The value of Y_t for which X_t is far away from x provides less accurate approximation for $m(x)$. As a compromise, one can use a weighted average of y_t instead of the simple average to estimate $m(x)$. The weight should be larger for those Y_t with X_t close to x and smaller for those Y_t with X_t far away from x. Mathematically, the estimate of $m(x)$ for a given x can be written as

$$\hat{m}(x) = \frac{1}{T}\sum_{t=1}^{T} w_t(x) y_t, \tag{4.20}$$

where the weights $w_t(x)$ are larger for those y_t with x_t close to x and smaller for those y_t with x_t far away from x. In Eq. (4.20), we assume that the weights sum to T. One can treat $1/T$ as part of the weights and make the weights sum to one.

From Eq. (4.20), the estimate $\hat{m}(x)$ is simply a *local weighted average* with weights determined by two factors. The first factor is the distance measure (i.e., the distance between x_t and x). The second factor is the assignment of weight for a given distance. Different ways to determine the distance between x_t and x and to assign the weight using the distance give rise to different nonparametric methods. In what follows, we discuss the commonly used kernel regression and local linear regression methods.

Kernel Regression

Kernel regression is perhaps the most commonly used nonparametric method in smoothing. The weights here are determined by a *kernel*, which is typically a probability density function, is denoted by $K(x)$, and satisfies

$$K(x) \geq 0, \qquad \int K(z)\,dz = 1.$$

However, to increase the flexibility in distance measure, one often rescales the kernel using a variable $h > 0$, which is referred to as the *bandwidth*. The rescaled kernel becomes

$$K_h(x) = \frac{1}{h}K(x/h), \qquad \int K_h(z)\,dz = 1. \tag{4.21}$$

The weight function can now be defined as

$$w_t(x) = \frac{K_h(x - x_t)}{\sum_{t=1}^{T} K_h(x - x_t)}, \tag{4.22}$$

where the denominator is a normalization constant that makes the smoother adaptive to the local intensity of the X variable and ensures the weights sum to one.

Plugging Eq. (4.22) into the smoothing formula (4.20), we have the well-known Nadaraya–Watson kernel estimator

$$\hat{m}(x) = \sum_{t=1}^{T} w_t(x)y_t = \frac{\sum_{t=1}^{T} K_h(x - x_t)y_t}{\sum_{t=1}^{T} K_h(x - x_t)}; \tag{4.23}$$

see Nadaraya (1964) and Watson (1964). In practice, many choices are available for the kernel $K(x)$. However, theoretical and practical considerations lead to a few choices, including the Gaussian kernel

$$K_h(x) = \frac{1}{h\sqrt{2\pi}} \exp(-\frac{x^2}{2h^2})$$

and the *Epanechnikov* kernel (Epanechnikov, 1969)

$$K_h(x) = \frac{0.75}{h}\left(1 - \frac{x^2}{h^2}\right) I\left(\left|\frac{x}{h}\right| \le 1\right),$$

where $I(A)$ is an indicator such that $I(A) = 1$ if A holds and $I(A) = 0$ otherwise. Figure 4.5 shows the Gaussian and Epanechnikov kernels for $h = 1$.

To understand the role played by the bandwidth h, we evaluate the Nadaraya–Watson estimator with the Epanechnikov kernel at the observed values

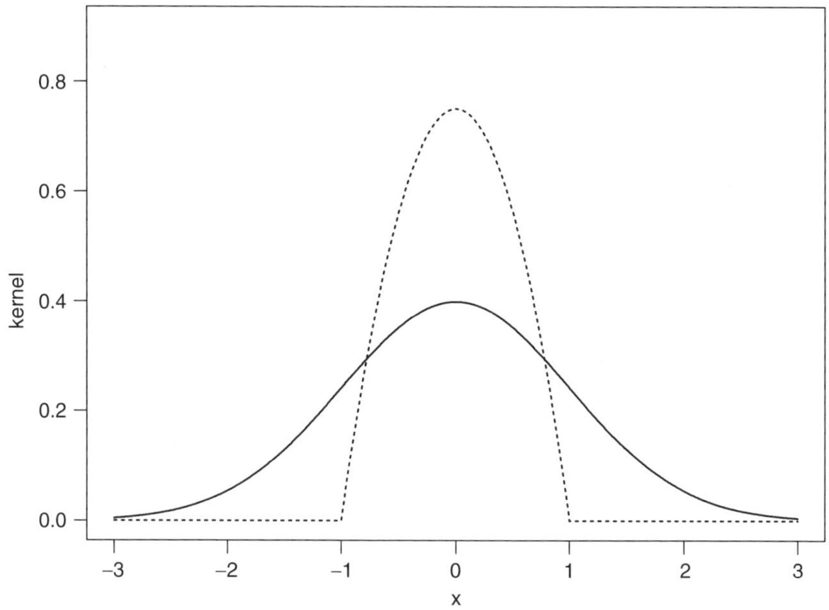

Figure 4.5. Standard normal kernel (solid line) and Epanechnikov kernel (dashed line) with bandwidth $h = 1$.

$\{x_t\}$ and consider two extremes. First, if $h \to 0$, then

$$\hat{m}(x_t) \to \frac{K_h(0)y_t}{K_h(0)} = y_t,$$

indicating that small bandwidths reproduce the data. Second, if $h \to \infty$, then

$$\hat{m}(x_t) \to \frac{\sum_{t=1}^{T} K_h(0)y_t}{\sum_{t=1}^{T} K_h(0)} = \frac{1}{T}\sum_{t=1}^{T} y_t = \overline{y},$$

suggesting that large bandwidths lead to an oversmoothed curve—the sample mean. In general, the bandwidth function h acts as follows. If h is very small, then the weights focus on a few observations that are in the neighborhood around each x_t. If h is very large, then the weights will spread over a larger neighborhood of x_t. Consequently, the choice of h plays an important role in kernel regression. This is the well-known problem of bandwidth selection in kernel regression.

Bandwidth Selection

There are several approaches for bandwidth selection; see Härdle (1990) and Fan and Yao (2003). The first approach is the plug-in method, which is based on the asymptotic expansion of the mean integrated squared error (MISE) for kernel smoothers

$$\text{MISE} = E\int_{-\infty}^{\infty} [\hat{m}(x) - m(x)]^2 dx,$$

where $m(.)$ is the true function. The quantity $E[\hat{m}(x) - m(x)]^2$ of the MISE is a pointwise measure of the mean squared error (MSE) of $\hat{m}(x)$ evaluated at x. Under some regularity conditions, one can derive the *optimal bandwidth* that minimizes the MISE. The optimal bandwidth typically depends on several unknown quantities that must be estimated from the data with some preliminary smoothing. Several iterations are often needed to obtain a reasonable estimate of the optimal bandwidth. In practice, the choice of preliminary smoothing can become a problem. Fan and Yao (2003) give a normal reference bandwidth selector as

$$\hat{h}_{\text{opt}} = \begin{cases} 1.06sT^{-1/5} & \text{for the Gaussian kernel,} \\ 2.34sT^{-1/5} & \text{for the Epanechnikov kernel,} \end{cases}$$

where s is the sample standard error of the independent variable, which is assumed to be stationary.

The second approach to bandwidth selection is the leave-one-out *cross-validation*. First, one observation (x_j, y_j) is left out. The remaining $T - 1$ data points are used to obtain the following smoother at x_j:

$$\hat{m}_{h,j}(x_j) = \frac{1}{T-1}\sum_{t \neq j} w_t(x_j)y_t,$$

which is an estimate of y_j, where the weights $w_t(x_j)$ sum to $T-1$. Second, perform step 1 for $j = 1, \ldots, T$ and define the function

$$CV(h) = \frac{1}{T}\sum_{j=1}^{T}[y_j - \hat{m}_{h,j}(x_j)]^2 W(x_j),$$

where $W(.)$ is a non-negative weight function satisfying $\sum_{j=1}^{n} W(x_j) = T$, that can be used to down-weight the boundary points if necessary. Decreasing the weights assigned to data points close to the boundary is needed because those points often have fewer neighboring observations. The function $CV(h)$ is called the cross-validation function because it validates the ability of the smoother to predict $\{y_t\}_{t=1}^{T}$. One chooses the bandwidth h that minimizes the $CV(.)$ function.

Local Linear Regression Method

Assume that the second derivative of $m(.)$ in model (4.19) exists and is continuous at x, where x is a given point in the support of $m(.)$. Denote the data available by $\{(y_t, x_t)\}_{t=1}^{T}$. The local linear regression method to nonparametric regression is to find a and b that minimize

$$L(a,b) = \sum_{t=1}^{T}[y_t - a - b(x - x_t)]^2 K_h(x - x_t), \tag{4.24}$$

where $K_h(.)$ is a kernel function defined in Eq. (4.21) and h is a bandwidth. Denote the resulting value of a by $\hat{a}$. The estimate of $m(x)$ is then defined as $\hat{a}$. In practice, x assumes an observed value of the independent variable. The estimate $\hat{b}$ can be used as an estimate of the first derivative of $m(.)$ evaluated at x.

Under the least squares theory, Eq. (4.24) is a weighted least squares problem and one can derive a closed-form solution for a. Specifically, taking the partial derivatives of $L(a,b)$ with respect to both a and b and equating the derivatives to zero, we have a system of two equations with two unknowns:

$$\sum_{t=1}^{T} K_h(x - x_t)y_t = a\sum_{t=1}^{T} K_h(x - x_t) + b\sum_{t=1}^{T}(x - x_t)K_h(x - x_t),$$

$$\sum_{t=1}^{T} y_t(x - x_t)K_h(x - x_t) = a\sum_{t=1}^{T}(x - x_t)K_h(x - x_t) + b\sum_{t=1}^{T}(x - x_t)^2 K_h(x - x_t).$$

Define

$$s_{T,\ell} = \sum_{t=1}^{T} K_h(x - x_t)(x - x_t)^{\ell}, \quad \ell = 0, 1, 2.$$

The prior system of equations becomes

$$\begin{bmatrix} s_{T,0} & s_{T,1} \\ s_{T,1} & s_{T,2} \end{bmatrix}\begin{bmatrix} a \\ b \end{bmatrix} = \begin{bmatrix} \sum_{t=1}^{T} K_h(x - x_t)y_t \\ \sum_{t=1}^{T}(x - x_t)K_h(x - x_t)y_t \end{bmatrix}.$$

Consequently, we have

$$\hat{a} = \frac{s_{T,2}\sum_{t=1}^{T} K_h(x - x_t)y_t - s_{T,1}\sum_{t=1}^{T}(x - x_t)K_h(x - x_t)y_t}{s_{T,0}s_{T,2} - s_{T,1}^2}.$$

The numerator and denominator of the prior fraction can be further simplified as

$$\begin{aligned} s_{T,2}\sum_{t=1}^{T} K_h(x - x_t)y_t - s_{T,1}\sum_{t=1}^{T}(x - x_t)K_h(x - x_t)y_t \\ = \sum_{t=1}^{T}[K_h(x - x_t)(s_{T,2} - (x - x_t)s_{T,1})]y_t. \end{aligned}$$

$$\begin{aligned} s_{T,0}s_{T,2} - s_{T,1}^2 &= \sum_{t=1}^{T} K_h(x - x_t)s_{T,2} - \sum_{t=1}^{T}(x - x_t)K_h(x - x_t)s_{T,1} \\ &= \sum_{t=1}^{T} K_h(x - x_t)[s_{T,2} - (x - x_t)s_{T,1}]. \end{aligned}$$

In summary, we have

$$\hat{a} = \frac{\sum_{t=1}^{T} w_t y_t}{\sum_{t=1}^{T} w_t}, \tag{4.25}$$

where w_t is defined as

$$w_t = K_h(x - x_t)[s_{T,2} - (x - x_t)s_{T,1}].$$

In practice, to avoid possible zero in the denominator, we use $\hat{m}(x)$ next to estimate $m(x)$:

$$\hat{m}(x) = \frac{\sum_{t=1}^{T} w_t y_t}{\sum_{t=1}^{T} w_t + 1/T^2}. \tag{4.26}$$

Notice that a nice feature of Eq. (4.26) is that the weight w_t satisfies

$$\sum_{t=1}^{T}(x - x_t)w_t = 0.$$

Also, if one assumes that $m(.)$ of Eq. (4.19) has the first derivative and finds the minimizer of

$$\sum_{t=1}^{T}(y_t - a)^2 K_h(x - x_t),$$

then the resulting estimator is the Nadaraya–Watson estimator mentioned earlier. In general, if one assumes that $m(x)$ has a bounded kth derivative, then one can replace the linear polynomial in Eq. (4.24) by a $(k-1)$-order polynomial. We refer to the estimator in Eq. (4.26) as the local linear regression smoother. Fan (1993) shows that, under some regularity conditions, the local linear regression estimator has some important sampling properties. The selection of bandwidth can be carried out via the same methods as before.

Time Series Application

In time series analysis, the explanatory variables are often the lagged values of the series. Consider the simple case of a single explanatory variable. Here model (4.19) becomes

$$x_t = m(x_{t-1}) + a_t,$$

and the kernel regression and local linear regression method discussed before are directly applicable. When multiple explanatory variables exist, some modifications are needed to implement the nonparametric methods. For the kernel regression, one can use a multivariate kernel such as a multivariate normal density function with a prespecified covariance matrix:

$$K_h(\boldsymbol{x}) = \frac{1}{(h\sqrt{2\pi})^p|\boldsymbol{\Sigma}|^{1/2}} \exp\left(-\frac{1}{2h^2}\boldsymbol{x}'\boldsymbol{\Sigma}^{-1}\boldsymbol{x}\right),$$

where p is the number of explanatory variables and $\boldsymbol{\Sigma}$ is a prespecified positive-definite matrix. Alternatively, one can use the product of univariate kernel functions as a multivariate kernel—for example,

$$K_h(\boldsymbol{x}) = \prod_{i=1}^{p} \frac{0.75}{h_i}\left(1 - \frac{x_i^2}{h_i^2}\right) I\left(\left|\frac{x_i}{h_i}\right| < 1\right).$$

This latter approach is simple, but it overlooks the relationship between the explanatory variables.

Example 4.6. To illustrate the application of nonparametric methods in finance, consider the weekly 3-month Treasury bill secondary market rate from 1970 to 1997 for 1460 observations. The data are obtained from the Federal Reserve Bank of St. Louis and are shown in Figure 4.6. This series has been used in the literature as an example of estimating stochastic diffusion equations using discretely observed data. See references in Chapter 6. Here we consider a simple model

$$y_t = \mu(x_{t-1})dt + \sigma(x_{t-1})dw_t,$$

where x_t is the 3-month Treasury bill rate, $y_t = x_t - x_{t-1}$, w_t is a standard Brownian motion, and $\mu(.)$ and $\sigma(.)$ are smooth functions of x_{t-1}, and apply the local smoothing function `lowess` of S-Plus to obtain nonparametric estimates of $\mu(.)$ and $\sigma(.)$; see Cleveland (1979). For simplicity, we use $|y_t|$ as a proxy of the volatility of x_t.

For the simple model considered, $\mu(x_{t-1})$ is the conditional mean of y_t given x_{t-1}; that is, $\mu(x_{t-1}) = E(y_t|x_{t-1})$. Figure 4.7a shows the scatterplot of $y(t)$ versus

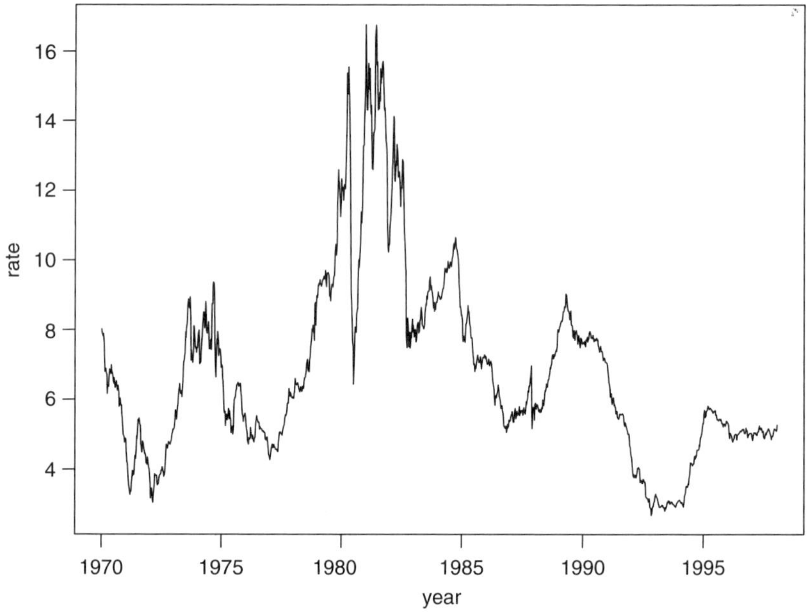

Figure 4.6. Time plot of U.S. weekly 3-month Treasury bill rate in the secondary market from 1970 to 1997.

x_{t-1}. The plot also contains the local smooth estimate of $\mu(x_{t-1})$ obtained by `lowess` of S-Plus. The estimate is essentially zero. However, to better understand the estimate, Figure 4.7b shows the estimate $\hat{\mu}(x_{t-1})$ on a finer scale. It is interesting to see that $\hat{\mu}(x_{t-1})$ is positive when x_{t-1} is small, but becomes negative when x_{t-1} is large. This is in agreement with the common sense that when the interest rate is high, it is expected to come down, and when the rate is low, it is expected to increase. Figure 4.7c shows the scatterplot of $|y(t)|$ versus x_{t-1} and the estimate of $\hat{\sigma}(x_{t-1})$ via `lowess`. The plot confirms that the higher the interest rate, the larger the volatility. Figure 4.7d shows the estimate $\hat{\sigma}(x_{t-1})$ on a finer scale. Clearly, the volatility is an increasing function of x_{t-1} and the slope seems to accelerate when x_{t-1} is approaching 10%. This example demonstrates that simple nonparametric methods can be helpful in understanding the dynamic structure of a financial time series.

S-Plus Commands

Used in Example 4.6

```
> z1=matrix(scan(file='w-3mtbs7097.txt'),4)
> x=z1[4,1:1460]/100
> y=(z1[4,2:1461]-z1[4,1:1460])/100
> par(mfcol=c(2,2))
> plot(x,y,pch='*',xlab='x(t-1)',ylab='y(t)')
```

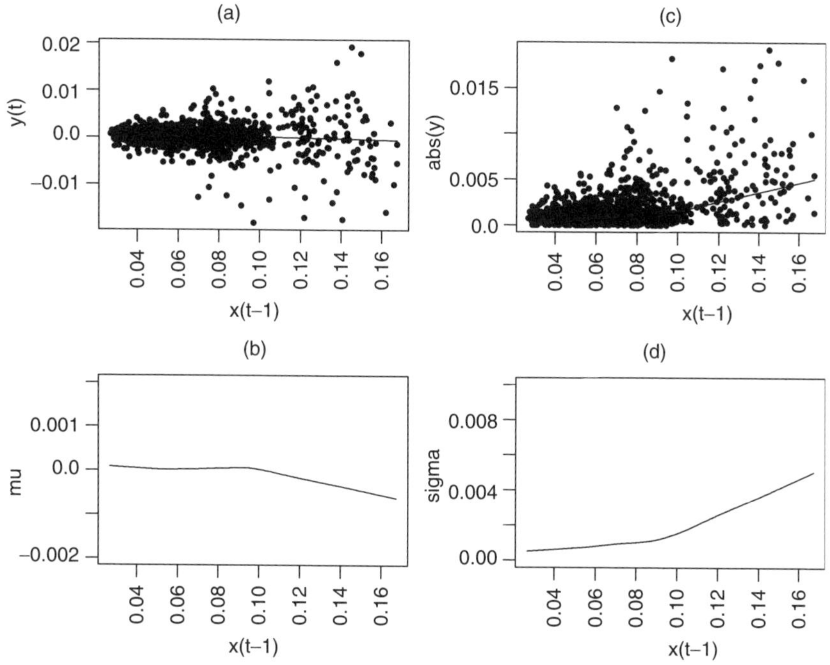

Figure 4.7. Estimation of conditional mean and volatility of weekly 3-month Treasury bill rate via a local smoothing method: (a) y_t versus x_{t-1}, where $y_t = x_t - x_{t-1}$ and x_t is the interest rate; (b) estimate of $\mu(x_{t-1})$; (c) $|y_t|$ versus x_{t-1}; and (d) estimate of $\sigma(x_{t-1})$.

```
> lines(lowess(x,y))
> title(main='(a) y(t) vs x(t-1)')
> fit=lowess(x,y)
> plot(fit$x,fit$y,xlab='x(t-1)',ylab='mu',type='l',
+ ylim= c(-.002,.002))
> title(main='(b) Estimate of mu(.)')
> plot(x,abs(y),pch='*',xlab='x(t-1)',ylab='abs(y)')
> lines(lowess(x,abs(y)))
> title(main='(c) abs(y) vs x(t-1)')
> fit2=lowess(x,abs(y))
> plot(fit2$x,fit2$y,type='l',xlab='x(t-1)',ylab='sigma',
+ ylim= c(0,.01))
> title(main='(d) Estimate of sigma(.)')
```

The following nonlinear models are derived with the help of nonparametric methods.

4.1.6 Functional Coefficient AR Model

Recent advances in nonparametric techniques enable researchers to relax parametric constraints in proposing nonlinear models. In some cases, nonparametric methods are used in a preliminary study to help select a parametric nonlinear model. This is the approach taken by Chen and Tsay (1993a) in proposing the functional-coefficient autoregressive (FAR) model that can be written as

$$x_t = f_1(X_{t-1})x_{t-1} + \cdots + f_p(X_{t-1})x_{t-p} + a_t, \tag{4.27}$$

where $X_{t-1} = (x_{t-1}, \ldots, x_{t-k})'$ is a vector of lagged values of x_t. If necessary, X_{t-1} may also include other explanatory variables available at time $t-1$. The functions $f_i(.)$ of Eq. (4.27) are assumed to be continuous, even twice differentiable, almost surely with respect to their arguments. Most of the nonlinear models discussed before are special cases of the FAR model. In application, one can use nonparametric methods such as kernel regression or local linear regression to estimate the functional coefficients $f_i(.)$, especially when the dimension of X_{t-1} is low (e.g., X_{t-1} is a scalar). Recently, Cai, Fan, and Yao (2000) applied the local linear regression method to estimate $f_i(.)$ and showed that substantial improvements in 1-step ahead forecasts can be achieved by using FAR models.

4.1.7 Nonlinear Additive AR Model

A major difficulty in applying nonparametric methods to nonlinear time series analysis is the "curse of dimensionality." Consider a general nonlinear AR(p) process $x_t = f(x_{t-1}, \ldots, x_{t-p}) + a_t$. A direct application of nonparametric methods to estimate $f(.)$ would require p-dimensional smoothing, which is hard to do when p is large, especially if the number of data points is not large. A simple, yet effective way to overcome this difficulty is to entertain an additive model that only requires lower dimensional smoothing. A time series x_t follows a nonlinear additive AR (NAAR) model if

$$x_t = f_0(t) + \sum_{i=1}^{p} f_i(x_{t-i}) + a_t, \tag{4.28}$$

where the $f_i(.)$ are continuous functions almost surely. Because each function $f_i(.)$ has a single argument, it can be estimated nonparametrically using one-dimensional smoothing techniques and hence avoids the curse of dimensionality. In application, an iterative estimation method that estimates $f_i(.)$ nonparametrically conditioned on estimates of $f_j(.)$ for all $j \neq i$ is used to estimate a NAAR model; see Chen and Tsay (1993b) for further details and examples of NAAR models.

The additivity assumption is rather restrictive and needs to be examined carefully in application. Chen, Liu, and Tsay (1995) consider test statistics for checking the additivity assumption.

4.1.8 Nonlinear State-Space Model

Making use of recent advances in MCMC methods (Gelfand and Smith, 1990), Carlin, Polson, and Stoffer (1992) propose a Monte Carlo approach for nonlinear state-space modeling. The model considered is

$$S_t = f_t(S_{t-1}) + u_t, \quad x_t = g_t(S_t) + v_t, \tag{4.29}$$

where S_t is the state vector, $f_t(.)$ and $g_t(.)$ are known functions depending on some unknown parameters, $\{u_t\}$ is a sequence of iid multivariate random vectors with zero mean and non-negative definite covariance matrix $\mathbf{\Sigma}_u$, $\{v_t\}$ is a sequence of iid random variables with mean zero and variance σ_v^2, and $\{u_t\}$ is independent of $\{v_t\}$. Monte Carlo techniques are employed to handle the nonlinear evolution of the state transition equation because the whole conditional distribution function of S_t given S_{t-1} is needed for a nonlinear system. Other numerical smoothing methods for nonlinear time series analysis have been considered by Kitagawa (1998) and the references therein. MCMC methods (or computing-intensive numerical methods) are powerful tools for nonlinear time series analysis. Their potential has not been fully explored. However, the assumption of knowing $f_t(.)$ and $g_t(.)$ in model (4.29) may hinder practical use of the proposed method. A possible solution to overcome this limitation is to use nonparametric methods such as the analyses considered in FAR and NAAR models to specify $f_t(.)$ and $g_t(.)$ before using nonlinear state-space models.

4.1.9 Neural Networks

A popular topic in modern data analysis is neural network, which can be classified as a semiparametric method. The literature on neural network is enormous, and its application spreads over many scientific areas with varying degrees of success; see Section 2 of Ripley (1993) for a list of applications and Section 10 for remarks concerning its application in finance. Cheng and Titterington (1994) provide information on neural networks from a statistical viewpoint. In this subsection, we focus solely on the *feed-forward* neural networks in which inputs are connected to one or more *neurons*, or *nodes*, in the input layer, and these nodes are connected forward to further layers until they reach the output layer. Figure 4.8 shows an example of a simple feed-forward network for univariate time series analysis with one hidden layer. The input layer has two nodes, and the hidden layer has three. The input nodes are connected forward to each and every node in the hidden layer, and these hidden nodes are connected to the single node in the output layer. We call the network a 2-3-1 feed-forward network. More complicated neural networks, including those with feedback connections, have been proposed in the literature, but the feed-forward networks are most relevant to our study.

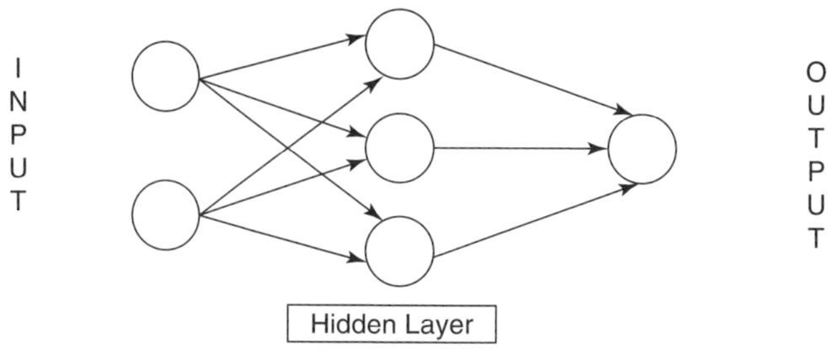

Figure 4.8. A feed-forward neural network with one hidden layer for univariate time series analysis.

Feed-Forward Neural Networks

A neural network processes information from one layer to the next by an "activation function." Consider a feed-forward network with one hidden layer. The jth node in the hidden layer is defined as

$$h_j = f_j\left(\alpha_{0j} + \sum_{i\to j} w_{ij}x_i\right), \tag{4.30}$$

where x_i is the value of the ith input node, $f_j(.)$ is an activation function typically taken to be the logistic function

$$f_j(z) = \frac{\exp(z)}{1+\exp(z)},$$

α_{0j} is called the bias, the summation $i \to j$ means summing over all input nodes feeding to j, and w_{ij} are the weights. For illustration, the jth node of the hidden layer of the 2-3-1 feed-forward network in Figure 4.8 is

$$h_j = \frac{\exp(\alpha_{0j} + w_{1j}x_1 + w_{2j}x_2)}{1+\exp(\alpha_{0j} + w_{1j}x_1 + w_{2j}x_2)}, \quad j = 1, 2, 3. \tag{4.31}$$

For the output layer, the node is defined as

$$o = f_o\left(\alpha_{0o} + \sum_{j\to o} w_{jo}h_j\right), \tag{4.32}$$

where the activation function $f_o(.)$ is either linear or a Heaviside function. If $f_o(.)$ is linear, then

$$o = \alpha_{0o} + \sum_{j=1}^{k} w_{jo}h_j,$$

where k is the number of nodes in the hidden layer. By a Heaviside function, we mean $f_o(z) = 1$ if $z > 0$ and $f_o(z) = 0$ otherwise. A neuron with a Heaviside function is called a *threshold neuron*, with "1" denoting that the neuron fires its message. For example, the output of the 2-3-1 network in Figure 4.8 is

$$o = \alpha_{0o} + w_{1o}h_1 + w_{2o}h_2 + w_{3o}h_3,$$

if the activation function is linear; it is

$$o = \begin{cases} 1 & \text{if } \alpha_{0o} + w_{1o}h_1 + w_{2o}h_2 + w_{3o}h_3 > 0, \\ 0 & \text{if } \alpha_{0o} + w_{1o}h_1 + w_{2o}h_2 + w_{3o}h_3 \le 0, \end{cases}$$

if $f_o(.)$ is a Heaviside function.

Combining the layers, the output of a feed-forward neural network can be written as

$$o = f_o \left[\alpha_{0o} + \sum_{j \to o} w_{jo} f_j \left(\alpha_{0j} + \sum_{i \to j} w_{ij} x_i \right) \right]. \tag{4.33}$$

If one also allows for direct connections from the input layer to the output layer, then the network becomes

$$o = f_o \left[\alpha_{0o} + \sum_{i \to o} \alpha_{io} x_i + \sum_{j \to o} w_{jo} f_j \left(\alpha_{0j} + \sum_{i \to j} w_{ij} x_i \right) \right], \tag{4.34}$$

where the first summation is summing over the input nodes. When the activation function of the output layer is linear, the direct connections from the input nodes to the output node represent a linear function between the inputs and output. Consequently, in this particular case model (4.34) is a generalization of linear models. For the 2-3-1 network in Figure 4.8, if the output activation function is linear, then Eq. (4.33) becomes

$$o = \alpha_{0o} + \sum_{j=1}^{3} w_{jo} h_j,$$

where h_j is given in Eq. (4.31). The network thus has 13 parameters. If Eq. (4.34) is used, then the network becomes

$$o = \alpha_{0o} + \sum_{i=1}^{2} \alpha_{io} x_i + \sum_{j=1}^{3} w_{jo} h_j,$$

where again h_j is given in Eq. (4.31). The number of parameters of the network increases to 15.

We refer to the function in Eq. (4.33) or (4.34) as a semiparametric function because its functional form is known, but the number of nodes and their biases and weights are unknown. The direct connections from the input layer to the output layer in Eq. (4.34) mean that the network can skip the hidden layer. We refer to such a network as a *skip-layer* feed-forward network.

Feed-forward networks are known as *multilayer percetrons* in the neural network literature. They can approximate any continuous function uniformly on compact sets by increasing the number of nodes in the hidden layer; see Hornik, Stinchcombe, and White (1989), Hornik (1993), and Chen and Chen (1995). This property of neural networks is the universal approximation property of the multilayer percetrons. In short, feed-forward neural networks with a hidden layer can be seen as a way to parameterize a general continuous nonlinear function.

Training and Forecasting

Application of neural networks involves two steps. The first step is to *train* the network (i.e., to build a network, including determining the number of nodes and estimating their biases and weights). The second step is inference, especially forecasting. The data are often divided into two nonoverlapping subsamples in the training stage. The first subsample is used to estimate the parameters of a given feed-forward neural network. The network so built is then used in the second subsample to perform forecasting and compute its forecasting accuracy. By comparing the forecasting performance, one selects the network that outperforms the others as the "best" network for making inference. This is the idea of cross-validation widely used in statistical model selection. Other model selection methods are also available.

In a time series application, let $\{(r_t, \boldsymbol{x}_t)|t = 1, \ldots, T\}$ be the available data for network training, where $\boldsymbol{x}_t$ denotes the vector of inputs and r_t is the series of interest (e.g., log returns of an asset). For a given network, let o_t be the output of the network with input $\boldsymbol{x}_t$; see Eq. (4.34). Training a neural network amounts to choosing its biases and weights to minimize some fitting criterion—for example, the least squares

$$S^2 = \sum_{t=1}^{T} (r_t - o_t)^2.$$

This is a nonlinear estimation problem that can be solved by several iterative methods. To ensure the smoothness of the fitted function, some additional constraints can be added to the prior minimization problem. In the neural network literature, the *back propagation* (BP) learning algorithm is a popular method for network training. The BP method, introduced by Bryson and Ho (1969), works backward starting with the output layer and uses a gradient rule to modify the biases and weights iteratively. Appendix 2A of Ripley (1993) provides a derivation of back propagation. Once a feed-forward neural network is built, it can be used to compute forecasts in the forecasting subsample.

Example 4.7. To illustrate applications of the neural network in finance, we consider the monthly log returns, in percentages and including dividends, for IBM stock from January 1926 to December 1999. We divide the data into two subsamples. The first subsample consisting of returns from January 1926 to December 1997 for 864 observations is used for modeling. Using model (4.34) with three inputs and two nodes in the hidden layer, we obtain a 3-2-1 network for the series. The three inputs are r_{t-1}, r_{t-2}, and r_{t-3} and the biases and weights are given next:

$$\hat{r}_t = 3.22 - 1.81 f_1(\boldsymbol{r}_{t-1}) - 2.28 f_2(\boldsymbol{r}_{t-1}) - 0.09 r_{t-1} - 0.05 r_{t-2} - 0.12 r_{t-3}, \tag{4.35}$$

where $\boldsymbol{r}_{t-1} = (r_{t-1}, r_{t-2}, r_{t-3})$ and the two logistic functions are

$$f_1(\boldsymbol{r}_{t-1}) = \frac{\exp(-8.34 - 18.97 r_{t-1} + 2.17 r_{t-2} - 19.17 r_{t-3})}{1 + \exp(-8.34 - 18.97 r_{t-1} + 2.17 r_{t-2} - 19.17 r_{t-3})},$$

$$f_2(\boldsymbol{r}_{t-1}) = \frac{\exp(39.25 - 22.17 r_{t-1} - 17.34 r_{t-2} - 5.98 r_{t-3})}{1 + \exp(39.25 - 22.17 r_{t-1} - 17.34 r_{t-2} - 5.98 r_{t-3})}.$$

The standard error of the residuals for the prior model is 6.56. For comparison, we also built an AR model for the data and obtained

$$r_t = 1.101 + 0.077r_{t-1} + a_t, \quad \sigma_a = 6.61. \tag{4.36}$$

The residual standard error is slightly greater than that of the feed-forward model in Eq. (4.35).

Forecast Comparison

The monthly returns of IBM stock in 1998 and 1999 form the second subsample and are used to evaluate the out-of-sample forecasting performance of neural networks. As a benchmark for comparison, we use the sample mean of r_t in the first subsample as the 1-step ahead forecast for all the monthly returns in the second subsample. This corresponds to assuming that the log monthly price of IBM stock follows a random walk with drift. The mean squared forecast error (MSFE) of this benchmark model is 91.85. For the AR(1) model in Eq. (4.36), the MSFE of 1-step ahead forecasts is 91.70. Thus, the AR(1) model slightly outperforms the benchmark. For the 3-2-1 feed-forward network in Eq. (4.35), the MSFE is 91.74, which is essentially the same as that of the AR(1) model.

Remark. The estimation of feed-forward networks is done by using the S-Plus program with default starting weights; see Venables and Ripley (1999) for more information. Our limited experience shows that the estimation results vary. For the IBM stock returns used in Example 4.7, the out-of-sample MSFE for a 3-2-1 network can be as low as 89.46 and as high as 93.65. If we change the number of nodes in the hidden layer, the range for the MSFE becomes even wider. The S-Plus commands used in Example 4.7 are given in Appendix B. □

Example 4.8. Nice features of the feed-forward network include its flexibility and wide applicability. For illustration, we use the network with a Heaviside activation function for the output layer to forecast the direction of price movement for IBM stock considered in Example 4.7. Define a direction variable as

$$d_t = \begin{cases} 1 & \text{if } r_t \geq 0, \\ 0 & \text{if } r_t < 0. \end{cases}$$

We use eight input nodes consisting of the first four lagged values of both r_t and d_t and four nodes in the hidden layer to build an 8-4-1 feed-forward network for d_t in the first subsample. The resulting network is then used to compute the 1-step ahead probability of an "upward movement" (i.e., a positive return) for the following month in the second subsample. Figure 4.9 shows a typical output of probability forecasts and the actual directions in the second subsample with the latter denoted by circles. A horizontal line of 0.5 is added to the plot. If we take a rigid approach by letting $\hat{d}_t = 1$ if the probability forecast is greater than or equal to 0.5 and $\hat{d}_t = 0$ otherwise, then the neural network has a successful rate of 0.58. The success rate of the network varies substantially from one estimation to another, and the network uses

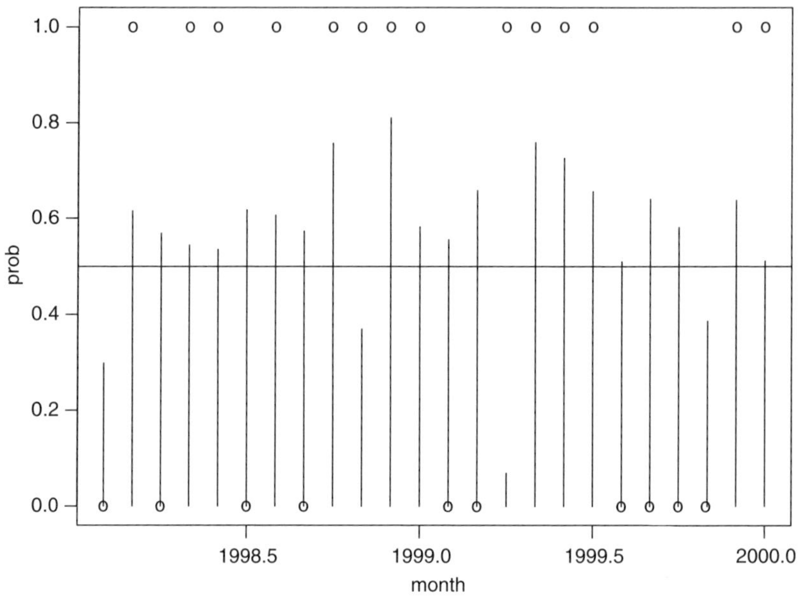

Figure 4.9. One-step ahead probability forecasts for a positive monthly return for IBM stock using an 8-4-1 feed-forward neural network. The forecasting period is from January 1998 to December 1999.

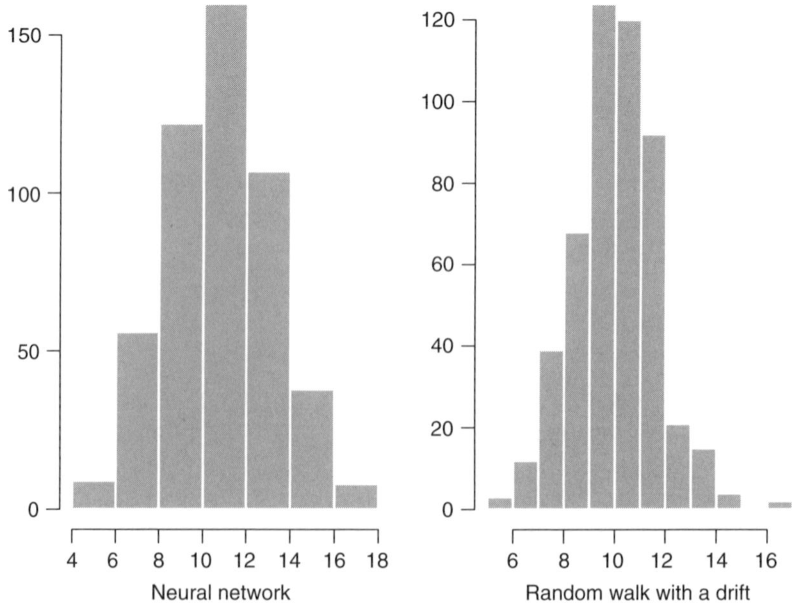

Figure 4.10. Histograms of the number of forecasting errors for the directional movements of monthly log returns of IBM stock. The forecasting period is from January 1998 to December 1999.

49 parameters. To gain more insight, we did a simulation study of running the 8-4-1 feed-forward network 500 times and computed the number of errors in predicting the upward and downward movement using the same method as before. The mean and median of errors over the 500 runs are 11.28 and 11, respectively, whereas the maximum and minimum number of errors are 18 and 4. For comparison, we also did a simulation with 500 runs using a random walk with drift—that is,

$$\hat{d}_t = \begin{cases} 1 & \text{if } \hat{r}_t = 1.19 + \epsilon_t \geq 0, \\ 0 & \text{otherwise,} \end{cases}$$

where 1.19 is the average monthly log return for IBM stock from January 1926 to December 1997 and $\{\epsilon_t\}$ is a sequence of iid $N(0, 1)$ random variables. The mean and median of the number of forecast errors become 10.53 and 11, whereas the maximum and minimum number of errors are 17 and 5, respectively. Figure 4.10 shows the histograms of the number of forecast errors for the two simulations. The results show that the 8-4-1 feed-forward neural network does not outperform the simple model that assumes a random walk with drift for the monthly log price of IBM stock.

4.2 NONLINEARITY TESTS

In this section, we discuss some nonlinearity tests available in the literature that have decent power against the nonlinear models considered in Section 4.3. The tests discussed include both parametric and nonparametric statistics. The Ljung–Box statistics of squared residuals, the bispectral test, and the Brock, Dechert, and Scheinkman (BDS) test are nonparametric methods. The RESET test (Ramsey, 1969), the F tests of Tsay (1986, 1989), and other Lagrange multiplier and likelihood ratio tests depend on specific parametric functions. Because nonlinearity may occur in many ways, there exists no single test that dominates the others in detecting nonlinearity.

4.2.1 Nonparametric Tests

Under the null hypothesis of linearity, residuals of a properly specified linear model should be independent. Any violation of independence in the residuals indicates inadequacy of the entertained model, including the linearity assumption. This is the basic idea behind various nonlinearity tests. In particular, some of the nonlinearity tests are designed to check for possible violation in quadratic forms of the underlying time series.

Q-Statistic of Squared Residuals

McLeod and Li (1983) apply the Ljung–Box statistics to the squared residuals of an ARMA(p, q) model to check for model inadequacy. The test statistic is

$$Q(m) = T(T+2)\sum_{i=1}^{m} \frac{\hat{\rho}_i^2(a_t^2)}{T-i},$$

where T is the sample size, m is a properly chosen number of autocorrelations used in the test, a_t denotes the residual series, and $\hat{\rho}_i(a_t^2)$ is the lag-i ACF of a_t^2. If the entertained linear model is adequate, $Q(m)$ is asymptotically a chi-squared random variable with $m-p-q$ degrees of freedom. As mentioned in Chapter 3, the prior Q-statistic is useful in detecting conditional heteroscedasticity of a_t and is asymptotically equivalent to the Lagrange multiplier test statistic of Engle (1982) for ARCH models; see Section 3.4.3. The null hypothesis of the statistics is $H_o: \beta_1 = \cdots = \beta_m = 0$, where β_i is the coefficient of a_{t-i}^2 in the linear regression

$$a_t^2 = \beta_0 + \beta_1 a_{t-1}^2 + \cdots + \beta_m a_{t-m}^2 + e_t$$

for $t = m+1, \ldots, T$. Because the statistic is computed from residuals (not directly from the observed returns), the number of degrees of freedom is $m-p-q$.

Bispectral Test

This test can be used to test for linearity and Gaussianity. It depends on the result that a properly normalized bispectrum of a linear time series is constant over all frequencies and that the constant is zero under normality. The bispectrum of a time series is the Fourier transform of its third-order moments. For a stationary time series x_t in Eq. (4.1), the third-order moment is defined as

$$c(u, v) = g \sum_{k=-\infty}^{\infty} \psi_k \psi_{k+u} \psi_{k+v}, \tag{4.37}$$

where u and v are integers, $g = E(a_t^3)$, $\psi_0 = 1$, and $\psi_k = 0$ for $k < 0$. Taking Fourier transforms of Eq. (4.37), we have

$$b_3(w_1, w_2) = \frac{g}{4\pi^2} \Gamma[-(w_1 + w_2)] \Gamma(w_1) \Gamma(w_2), \tag{4.38}$$

where $\Gamma(w) = \sum_{u=0}^{\infty} \psi_u \exp(-iwu)$ with $i = \sqrt{-1}$, and w_i are frequencies. Yet the spectral density function of x_t is given by

$$p(w) = \frac{\sigma_a^2}{2\pi} |\Gamma(w)|^2,$$

where w denotes the frequency. Consequently, the function

$$b(w_1, w_2) = \frac{|b_3(w_1, w_2)|^2}{p(w_1)p(w_2)p(w_1 + w_2)} = \text{constant for all } (w_1, w_2). \tag{4.39}$$

The bispectrum test makes use of the property in Eq. (4.39). Basically, it estimates the function $b(w_1, w_2)$ in Eq. (4.39) over a suitably chosen grid of points and applies a test statistic similar to Hotelling's T^2 statistic to check the constancy of $b(w_1, w_2)$. For a linear Gaussian series, $E(a_t^3) = g = 0$ so that the bispectrum is zero for all frequencies (w_1, w_2). For further details of the bispectral test, see Priestley (1988), Subba Rao and Gabr (1984), and Hinich (1982). Limited experience shows that the test has decent power when the sample size is large.

BDS Statistic

Brock, Dechert, and Scheinkman (1987) propose a test statistic, commonly referred to as the *BDS test*, to detect the iid assumption of a time series. The statistic is, therefore, different from other test statistics discussed because the latter mainly focus on either the second- or third-order properties of x_t. The basic idea of the BDS test is to make use of a "correlation integral" popular in chaotic time series analysis. Given a k-dimensional time series X_t and observations $\{X_t\}_{t=1}^{T_k}$, define the correlation integral as

$$C_k(\delta) = \lim_{T_k \to \infty} \frac{2}{T_k(T_k - 1)} \sum_{i<j} I_\delta(X_i, X_j), \tag{4.40}$$

where $I_\delta(u, v)$ is an indicator variable that equals one if $\|u - v\| < \delta$, and zero otherwise, where $\|.\|$ is the supnorm. The correlation integral measures the fraction of data pairs of $\{X_t\}$ that are within a distance of δ from each other. Consider next a time series x_t. Construct k-dimensional vectors $X_t^k = (x_t, x_{t+1}, \ldots, x_{t+k-1})'$, which are called *k-histories*. The idea of the BDS test is as follows. Treat a k-history as a point in the k-dimensional space. If $\{x_t\}_{t=1}^{T}$ are indeed iid random variables, then the k-histories $\{X_t\}_{t=1}^{T_k}$ should show no pattern in the k-dimensional space. Consequently, the correlation integrals should satisfy the relation $C_k(\delta) = [C_1(\delta)]^k$. Any departure from the prior relation suggests that x_t are not iid. As a simple, but informative example, consider a sequence of iid random variables from the uniform distribution over [0, 1]. Let $[a, b]$ be a subinterval of [0, 1] and consider the "2-history" (x_t, x_{t+1}), which represents a point in the two-dimensional space. Under the iid assumption, the expected number of 2-histories in the subspace $[a, b] \times [a, b]$ should equal the square of the expected number of x_t in $[a, b]$. This idea can be formally examined by using sample counterparts of correlation integrals. Define

$$C_\ell(\delta, T) = \frac{2}{T_k(T_k - 1)} \sum_{i<j} I_\delta(X_i^*, X_j^*), \quad \ell = 1, k,$$

where $T_\ell = T - \ell + 1$ and $X_i^* = x_i$ if $\ell = 1$ and $X_i^* = X_i^k$ if $\ell = k$. Under the null hypothesis that $\{x_t\}$ are iid with a nondegenerated distribution function $F(.)$, Brock, Dechert, and Scheinkman (1987) show that

$$C_k(\delta, T) \to [C_1(\delta)]^k \quad \text{with probability 1,} \quad \text{as} \quad T \to \infty$$

for any fixed k and δ. Furthermore, the statistic $\sqrt{T}\{C_k(\delta, T) - [C_1(\delta, T)]^k\}$ is asymptotically distributed as normal with mean zero and variance

$$\sigma_k^2(\delta) = 4 \left(N^k + 2 \sum_{j=1}^{k-1} N^{k-j} C^{2j} + (k-1)^2 C^{2k} - k^2 N C^{2k-2} \right),$$

where $C = \int[F(z+\delta) - F(z-\delta)]dF(z)$ and $N = \int[F(z+\delta) - F(z-\delta)]^2 dF(z)$. Note that $C_1(\delta, T)$ is a consistent estimate of C, and N can be consistently estimated by

$$N(\delta, T) = \frac{6}{T_k(T_k-1)(T_k-2)} \sum_{t<s<u} I_\delta(x_t, x_s) I_\delta(x_s, x_u).$$

The BDS test statistic is then defined as

$$D_k(\delta, T) = \sqrt{T}\{C_k(\delta, T) - [C_1(\delta, T)]^k\}/\sigma_k(\delta, T), \tag{4.41}$$

where $\sigma_k(\delta, T)$ is obtained from $\sigma_k(\delta)$ when C and N are replaced by $C_1(\delta, T)$ and $N(\delta, T)$, respectively. This test statistic has a standard normal limiting distribution. For further discussion and examples of applying the BDS test, see Hsieh (1989) and Brock, Hsieh, and LeBaron (1991). In application, one should remove linear dependence, if any, from the data before applying the BDS test. The test may be sensitive to the choices of δ and k, especially when k is large.

4.2.2 Parametric Tests

Turning to parametric tests, we consider the RESET test of Ramsey (1969) and its generalizations. We also discuss some test statistics for detecting threshold nonlinearity. To simplify the notation, we use vectors and matrices in the discussion. If necessary, readers may consult Appendix A of Chapter 8 for a brief review on vectors and matrices.

The RESET Test

Ramsey (1969) proposes a specification test for linear least squares regression analysis. The test is referred to as a RESET test and is readily applicable to linear AR models. Consider the linear AR(p) model

$$x_t = \boldsymbol{X}'_{t-1}\boldsymbol{\phi} + a_t, \tag{4.42}$$

where $\boldsymbol{X}_{t-1} = (1, x_{t-1}, \ldots, x_{t-p})'$ and $\boldsymbol{\phi} = (\phi_0, \phi_1, \ldots, \phi_p)'$. The first step of the RESET test is to obtain the least squares estimate $\widehat{\boldsymbol{\phi}}$ of Eq. (4.42) and compute the fit $\hat{x}_t = \boldsymbol{X}'_{t-1}\widehat{\boldsymbol{\phi}}$, the residual $\hat{a}_t = x_t - \hat{x}_t$, and the sum of squared residuals $SSR_0 = \sum_{t=p+1}^{T} \hat{a}_t^2$, where T is the sample size. In the second step, consider the linear regression

$$\hat{a}_t = \boldsymbol{X}'_{t-1}\boldsymbol{\alpha}_1 + \boldsymbol{M}'_{t-1}\boldsymbol{\alpha}_2 + v_t, \tag{4.43}$$

where $\boldsymbol{M}_{t-1} = (\hat{x}_t^2, \ldots, \hat{x}_t^{s+1})'$ for some $s \geq 1$, and compute the least squares residuals

$$\hat{v}_t = \hat{a}_t - \boldsymbol{X}'_{t-1}\widehat{\boldsymbol{\alpha}}_1 - \boldsymbol{M}'_{t-1}\widehat{\boldsymbol{\alpha}}_2$$

and the sum of squared residuals $SSR_1 = \sum_{t=p+1}^{T} \hat{v}_t^2$ of the regression. The basic idea of the RESET test is that if the linear AR(p) model in Eq. (4.42) is adequate, then $\boldsymbol{\alpha}_1$ and $\boldsymbol{\alpha}_2$ of Eq. (4.43) should be zero. This can be tested by the usual F statistic of Eq. (4.43) given by

$$F = \frac{(SSR_0 - SSR_1)/g}{SSR_1/(T - p - g)} \quad \text{with} \quad g = s + p + 1, \tag{4.44}$$

which, under the linearity and normality assumption, has an F distribution with degrees of freedom g and $T - p - g$.

Remark. Because $\hat{x}_t^k$ for $k = 2, \ldots, s+1$ tend to be highly correlated with $\boldsymbol{X}_{t-1}$ and among themselves, principal components of $\boldsymbol{M}_{t-1}$ that are not co-linear with $\boldsymbol{X}_{t-1}$ are often used in fitting Eq. (4.43). Principal component analysis is a statistical tool for dimension reduction; see Chapter 8 for more information. □

Keenan (1985) proposes a nonlinearity test for time series that uses $\hat{x}_t^2$ only and modifies the second step of the RESET test to avoid multicollinearity between $\hat{x}_t^2$ and $\boldsymbol{X}_{t-1}$. Specifically, the linear regression (4.43) is divided into two steps. In step 2(a), one removes linear dependence of $\hat{x}_t^2$ on $\boldsymbol{X}_{t-1}$ by fitting the regression

$$\hat{x}_t^2 = \boldsymbol{X}_{t-1}'\boldsymbol{\beta} + u_t$$

and obtaining the residual $\hat{u}_t = \hat{x}_t^2 - \boldsymbol{X}_{t-1}\widehat{\boldsymbol{\beta}}$. In step 2(b), consider the linear regression

$$\hat{a}_t = \hat{u}_t\alpha + v_t,$$

and obtain the sum of squared residuals $SSR_1 = \sum_{t=p+1}^{T}(\hat{a}_t - \hat{u}_t\hat{\alpha})^2 = \sum_{t=p+1}^{T} \hat{v}_t^2$ to test the null hypothesis $\alpha = 0$.

The F Test

To improve the power of Keenan's test and the RESET test, Tsay (1986) uses a different choice of the regressor $\boldsymbol{M}_{t-1}$. Specifically, he suggests using $\boldsymbol{M}_{t-1} = vech(\boldsymbol{X}_{t-1}\boldsymbol{X}_{t-1}')$, where $vech(\boldsymbol{A})$ denotes the half-stacking vector of the matrix $\boldsymbol{A}$ using elements on and below the diagonal only; see Appendix B of Chapter 8 for more information about the operator. For example, if $p = 2$, then $\boldsymbol{M}_{t-1} = (x_{t-1}^2, x_{t-1}x_{t-2}, x_{t-2}^2)'$. The dimension of $\boldsymbol{M}_{t-1}$ is $p(p+1)/2$ for an AR(p) model. In practice, the test is simply the usual partial F statistic for testing $\boldsymbol{\alpha} = 0$ in the linear least squares regression

$$x_t = \boldsymbol{X}_{t-1}'\boldsymbol{\phi} + \boldsymbol{M}_{t-1}'\boldsymbol{\alpha} + e_t,$$

where e_t denotes the error term. Under the assumption that x_t is a linear AR(p) process, the partial F statistic follows an F distribution with degrees of freedom

g and $T - p - g - 1$, where $g = p(p+1)/2$. We refer to this F test as the *Ori-F test*. Luukkonen, Saikkonen, and Teräsvirta (1988) further extend the test by augmenting $\boldsymbol{M}_{t-1}$ with cubic terms x_{t-i}^3 for $i = 1, \ldots, p$.

Threshold Test

When the alternative model under study is a SETAR model, one can derive specific test statistics to increase the power of the test. One of the specific tests is the likelihood ratio statistic. This test, however, encounters the difficulty of undefined parameters under the null hypothesis of linearity because the threshold is undefined for a linear AR process. Another specific test seeks to transform testing threshold nonlinearity into detecting model changes. It is then interesting to discuss the differences between these two specific tests for threshold nonlinearity.

To simplify the discussion, let us consider the simple case that the alternative model is a 2-regime SETAR model with threshold variable x_{t-d}. The null hypothesis H_o: x_t follows the linear AR(p) model

$$x_t = \phi_0 + \sum_{i=1}^{p} \phi_i x_{t-i} + a_t, \tag{4.45}$$

whereas the alternative hypothesis H_a: x_t follows the SETAR model

$$x_t = \begin{cases} \phi_0^{(1)} + \sum_{i=1}^{p} \phi_i^{(1)} x_{t-i} + a_{1t} & \text{if } x_{t-d} < r_1, \\ \phi_0^{(2)} + \sum_{i=1}^{p} \phi_i^{(2)} x_{t-i} + a_{2t} & \text{if } x_{t-d} \ge r_1, \end{cases} \tag{4.46}$$

where r_1 is the threshold. For a given realization $\{x_t\}_{t=1}^T$ and assuming normality, let $l_0(\hat{\boldsymbol{\phi}}, \hat{\sigma}_a^2)$ be the log likelihood function evaluated at the maximum likelihood estimates of $\boldsymbol{\phi} = (\phi_0, \ldots, \phi_p)'$ and σ_a^2. This is easy to compute. The likelihood function under the alternative is also easy to compute if the threshold r_1 is given. Let $l_1(r_1; \hat{\boldsymbol{\phi}}_1, \hat{\sigma}_1^2; \hat{\boldsymbol{\phi}}_2, \hat{\sigma}_2^2)$ be the log likelihood function evaluated at the maximum likelihood estimates of $\boldsymbol{\phi}_i = (\phi_0^{(i)}, \ldots, \phi_p^{(i)})'$ and σ_i^2 conditioned on knowing the threshold r_1. The log likelihood ratio $l(r_1)$ defined as

$$l(r_1) = l_1(r_1; \hat{\boldsymbol{\phi}}_1, \hat{\sigma}_1^2; \hat{\boldsymbol{\phi}}_2, \hat{\sigma}_2^2) - l_0(\hat{\boldsymbol{\phi}}, \hat{\sigma}_a^2)$$

is then a function of the threshold r_1, which is unknown. Yet under the null hypothesis, there is no threshold and r_1 is not defined. The parameter r_1 is referred to as a *nuisance parameter* under the null hypothesis. Consequently, the asymptotic distribution of the likelihood ratio is very different from that of the conventional likelihood ratio statistics. See Chan (1991) for further details and critical values of the test. A common approach is to use $l_{\max} = \sup_{v<r_1<u} l(r_1)$ as the test statistic, where v and u are prespecified lower and upper bounds of the threshold. Davis (1987) and Andrews and Ploberger (1994) provide further discussion on hypothesis testing involving nuisance parameters under the null hypothesis. Simulation is often used to obtain empirical critical values of the test statistic $l_{\max}$, which depends on

the choices of v and u. The average of $l(r_1)$ over $r_1 \in [v, u]$ is also considered by Andrews and Ploberger as a test statistic.

Tsay (1989) makes use of arranged autoregression and recursive estimation to derive an alternative test for threshold nonlinearity. The arranged autoregression seeks to transfer the SETAR model under the alternative hypothesis H_a into a model change problem with the threshold r_1 serving as the change point. To see this, the SETAR model in Eq. (4.46) says that x_t follows essentially two linear models depending on whether $x_{t-d} < r_1$ or $x_{t-d} \geq r_1$. For a realization $\{x_t\}_{t=1}^{T}$, x_{t-d} can assume values $\{x_1, \ldots, x_{T-d}\}$. Let $x_{(1)} \leq x_{(2)} \leq \cdots \leq x_{(T-d)}$ be the ordered statistics of $\{x_t\}_{t=1}^{T-d}$ (i.e., arranging the observations in increasing order). The SETAR model can then be written as

$$x_{(j)+d} = \beta_0 + \sum_{i=1}^{p} \beta_i x_{(j)+d-i} + a_{(j)+d}, \quad j = 1, \ldots, T-d, \tag{4.47}$$

where $\beta_i = \phi_i^{(1)}$ if $x_{(j)} < r_1$ and $\beta_i = \phi_i^{(2)}$ if $x_{(j)} \geq r_1$. Consequently, the threshold r_1 is a change point for the linear regression in Eq. (4.47), and we refer to Eq. (4.47) as an arranged autoregression (in increasing order of the threshold x_{t-d}). Note that the arranged autoregression in (4.47) does not alter the dynamic dependence of x_t on x_{t-i} for $i = 1, \ldots, p$ because $x_{(j)+d}$ still depends on $x_{(j)+d-i}$ for $i = 1, \ldots, p$. What is done is simply to present the SETAR model in the threshold space instead of in the time space. That is, the equation with a smaller x_{t-d} appears before that with a larger x_{t-d}. The threshold test of Tsay (1989) is obtained as follows.

Step 1. Fit Eq. (4.47) using $j = 1, \ldots, m$, where m is a prespecified positive integer (e.g., 30). Denote the least squares estimates of β_i by $\hat{\beta}_{i,m}$, where m denotes the number of data points used in estimation.

Step 2. Compute the predictive residual

$$\hat{a}_{(m+1)+d} = x_{(m+1)+d} - \hat{\beta}_{0,m} - \sum_{i=1}^{p} \hat{\beta}_{i,m} x_{(m+1)+d-i}$$

and its standard error. Let $\hat{e}_{(m+1)+d}$ be the standardized predictive residual.

Step 3. Use the recursive least squares method to update the least squares estimates to $\hat{\beta}_{i,m+1}$ by incorporating the new data point $x_{(m+1)+d}$.

Step 4. Repeat steps 2 and 3 until all data points are processed.

Step 5. Consider the linear regression of the standardized predictive residual

$$\hat{e}_{(m+j)+d} = \alpha_0 + \sum_{i=1}^{p} \alpha_i x_{(m+j)+d-i} + v_t, \quad j = 1, \ldots, T-d-m \tag{4.48}$$

and compute the usual F statistic for testing $\alpha_i = 0$ in Eq. (4.48) for $i = 0, \ldots, p$. Under the null hypothesis that x_t follows a linear AR(p) model, the F ratio has a limiting F distribution with degrees of freedom $p + 1$ and $T - d - m - p$.

We refer to the earlier F test as a *TAR-F test*. The idea behind the test is that under the null hypothesis there is no model change in the arranged autoregression in Eq. (4.47) so that the standardized predictive residuals should be close to iid with mean zero and variance 1. In this case, they should have no correlations with the regressors $x_{(m+j)+d-i}$. For further details including formulas for a recursive least squares method and some simulation study on performance of the TAR-F test, see Tsay (1989). The TAR-F test avoids the problem of nuisance parameters encountered by the likelihood ratio test. It does not require knowing the threshold r_1. It simply tests that the predictive residuals have no correlations with regressors if the null hypothesis holds. Therefore, the test does not depend on knowing the number of regimes in the alternative model. Yet the TAR-F test is not as powerful as the likelihood ratio test if the true model is indeed a 2-regime SETAR model with a known innovational distribution.

4.2.3 Applications

In this subsection, we apply some of the nonlinearity tests discussed previously to five time series. For a real financial time series, an AR model is used to remove any serial correlation in the data, and the tests apply to the residual series of the model. The five series employed are as follows:

1. r_{1t}: A simulated series of iid $N(0, 1)$ with 500 observations.
2. r_{2t}: A simulated series of iid Student-t distribution with 6 degrees of freedom. The sample size is 500.
3. a_{3t}: The residual series of monthly log returns of CRSP equal-weighted index from 1926 to 1997 with 864 observations. The linear AR model used is

$$(1 - 0.180B + 0.099B^3 - 0.105B^9)r_{3t} = 0.0086 + a_{3t}.$$

4. a_{4t}: The residual series of monthly log returns of CRSP value-weighted index from 1926 to 1997 with 864 observations. The linear AR model used is

$$(1 - 0.098B + 0.111B^3 - 0.088B^5)r_{4t} = 0.0078 + a_{4t}.$$

5. a_{5t}: The residual series of monthly log returns of IBM stock from 1926 to 1997 with 864 observations. The linear AR model used is

$$(1 - 0.077B)r_{5t} = 0.011 + a_{5t}.$$

Table 4.2 shows the results of the nonlinearity test. For the simulated series and IBM returns, the F tests are based on an AR(6) model. For the index returns, the AR order is the same as the model given earlier. For the BDS test, we chose $\delta = \hat{\sigma}_a$ and $\delta = 1.5\hat{\sigma}_a$ with $k = 2, \ldots, 5$. Also given in the table are the Ljung–Box statistics that confirm no serial correlation in the residual series before applying nonlinearity tests. Compared with their asymptotic critical values, the BDS test and

Table 4.2. Nonlinearity Tests for Simulated Series and Some Log Stock Returns[a]

Data	Q (5)	Q (10)	BDS($\delta = 1.5\hat{\sigma}_a$) 2	3	4	5
$N(0, 1)$	3.2	6.5	−0.32	−0.14	−0.15	−0.33
t_6	0.9	1.7	−0.87	−1.18	−1.56	−1.71
ln(ew)	2.9	4.9	9.94	11.72	12.83	13.65
ln(vw)	1.0	9.8	8.61	9.88	10.70	11.29
ln(ibm)	0.6	7.1	4.96	6.09	6.68	6.82
Data	**Ori-F**	**$d = 1$ TAR-F**	**BDS($\delta = \hat{\sigma}_a$) 2**	**3**	**4**	**5**
$N(0, 1)$	1.13	0.87	−0.77	−0.71	−1.04	−1.27
t_6	0.69	0.81	−0.35	−0.76	−1.25	−1.49
ln(ew)	5.05	6.77	10.01	11.85	13.14	14.45
ln(vw)	4.95	6.85	7.01	7.83	8.64	9.53
ln(ibm)	1.32	1.51	3.82	4.70	5.45	5.72

[a]The sample size of simulated series is 500 and that of stock returns is 864. The BDS test uses $k = 2, \ldots, 5$.

F tests are insignificant at the 5% level for the simulated series. However, the BDS tests are highly significant for the real financial time series. The F tests also show significant results for the index returns, but they fail to suggest nonlinearity in the IBM log returns. In summary, the tests confirm that the simulated series are linear and suggest that the stock returns are nonlinear.

4.3 MODELING

Nonlinear time series modeling necessarily involves subjective judgment. However, there are some general guidelines to follow. It starts with building an adequate linear model on which nonlinearity tests are based. For financial time series, the Ljung–Box statistics and Engle's test are commonly used to detect conditional heteroscedasticity. For general series, other tests of Section 4.2 apply. If nonlinearity is statistically significant, then one chooses a class of nonlinear models to entertain. The selection here may depend on the experience of the analyst and the substantive matter of the problem under study. For volatility models, the order of an ARCH process can often be determined by checking the partial autocorrelation function of the squared series. For GARCH and EGARCH models, only lower orders such as (1,1), (1,2), and (2,1) are considered in most applications. Higher order models are hard to estimate and understand. For TAR models, one may use the procedures given in Tong (1990) and Tsay (1989, 1998) to build an adequate model. When the sample size is sufficiently large, one may apply nonparametric techniques to explore the nonlinear feature of the data and choose a proper nonlinear model accordingly; see Chen and Tsay (1993a) and Cai, Fan, and Yao (2000). The MARS procedure of Lewis and Stevens (1991) can also be used to explore the dynamic structure of the data. Finally, information criteria such as the Akaike information criterion (Akaike, 1974) and the generalized odd ratios in Chen, McCulloch, and Tsay (1997) can be used to discriminate between competing nonlinear models. The chosen model should be carefully checked before it is used for prediction.

4.4 FORECASTING

Unlike the linear model, there exist no closed-form formulas to compute forecasts of most nonlinear models when the forecast horizon is greater than 1. We use parametric bootstraps to compute nonlinear forecasts. It is understood that the model used in forecasting has been rigorously checked and is judged to be adequate for the series under study. By a model, we mean the dynamic structure and innovational distributions. In some cases, we may treat the estimated parameters as given.

4.4.1 Parametric Bootstrap

Let T be the forecast origin and ℓ be the forecast horizon ($\ell > 0$). That is, we are at time index T and interested in forecasting $x_{T+\ell}$. The parametric bootstrap considered computes realizations $x_{T+1}, \ldots, X_{T+\ell}$ sequentially by (a) drawing a new innovation from the specified innovational distribution of the model, and (b) computing x_{T+i} using the model, data, and previous forecasts $x_{T+1}, \ldots, x_{T+i-1}$. This results in a realization for $x_{T+\ell}$. The procedure is repeated M times to obtain M realizations of $x_{T+\ell}$ denoted by $\{x_{T+\ell}^{(j)}\}_{j=1}^{M}$. The point forecast of $x_{T+\ell}$ is then the sample average of $x_{T+\ell}^{(j)}$. Let the forecast be $x_T(\ell)$. We used $M = 3000$ in some applications and the results seem fine. The realizations $\{x_{T+\ell}^{(j)}\}_{j=1}^{M}$ can also be used to obtain an empirical distribution of $x_{T+\ell}$. We make use of this empirical distribution later to evaluate forecasting performance.

4.4.2 Forecasting Evaluation

There are many ways to evaluate the forecasting performance of a model, ranging from directional measures to magnitude measures to distributional measures. A directional measure considers the future direction (up or down) implied by the model. Predicting that tomorrow's S&P 500 index will go up or down is an example of directional forecasts that are of practical interest. Predicting the year-end value of the daily S&P 500 index belongs to the case of magnitude measure. Finally, assessing the likelihood that the daily S&P 500 index will go up 10% or more between now and the year end requires knowing the future conditional probability distribution of the index. Evaluating the accuracy of such an assessment needs a distributional measure.

In practice, the available data set is divided into two subsamples. The first subsample of the data is used to build a nonlinear model, and the second subsample is used to evaluate the forecasting performance of the model. We refer to the two subsamples of data as *estimation* and *forecasting subsamples*. In some studies, a rolling forecasting procedure is used in which a new data point is moved from the forecasting subsample into the estimation subsample as the forecast origin advances. In what follows, we briefly discuss some measures of forecasting performance that are commonly used in the literature. Keep in mind, however, that there exists no widely accepted single measure to compare models. A utility function based on the objective of the forecast might be needed to better understand the comparison.

Directional Measure

A typical measure here is to use a 2×2 contingency table that summarizes the number of "hits" and "misses" of the model in predicting ups and downs of $x_{T+\ell}$ in the forecasting subsample. Specifically, the contingency table is given as

Actual	Predicted		
	up	down	
up	m_{11}	m_{12}	m_{10}
down	m_{21}	m_{22}	m_{20}
	m_{01}	m_{02}	m

where m is the total number of ℓ-step ahead forecasts in the forecasting subsample, m_{11} is the number of "hits" in predicting upward movements, m_{21} is the number of "misses" in predicting downward movements of the market, and so on. Larger values in m_{11} and m_{22} indicate better forecasts. The test statistic

$$\chi^2 = \sum_{i=1}^{2}\sum_{j=1}^{2} \frac{(m_{ij} - m_{i0}m_{0j}/m)^2}{m_{i0}m_{0j}/m}$$

can then be used to evaluate the performance of the model. A large χ^2 signifies that the model outperforms the chance of random choice. Under some mild conditions, χ^2 has an asymptotic chi-squared distribution with 1 degree of freedom. For further discussion of this measure, see Dahl and Hylleberg (1999).

For illustration of the directional measure, consider the 1-step ahead probability forecasts of the 8-4-1 feed-forward neural network shown in Figure 4.9. The 2×2 table of "hits" and "misses" of the network is

Actual	Predicted		
	up	down	
up	12	2	14
down	8	2	10
	20	4	24

The table shows that the network predicts the upward movement well, but fares poorly in forecasting the downward movement of the stock. The chi-squared statistic of the table is 0.137 with p-value 0.71. Consequently, the network does not significantly outperform a random-walk model with equal probabilities for "upward" and "downward" movements.

Magnitude Measure

Three statistics are commonly used to measure performance of point forecasts. They are the mean squared error (MSE), mean absolute deviation (MAD), and mean absolute percentage error (MAPE). For ℓ-step ahead forecasts, these measures are defined as

$$MSE(\ell) = \frac{1}{m}\sum_{j=0}^{m-1}[x_{T+\ell+j} - x_{T+j}(\ell)]^2, \tag{4.49}$$

$$MAD(\ell) = \frac{1}{m}\sum_{j=0}^{m-1}|x_{T+\ell+j} - x_{T+j}(\ell)|, \tag{4.50}$$

$$MAPE(\ell) = \frac{1}{m}\sum_{j=0}^{m-1}\left|\frac{x_{T+j}(\ell)}{x_{T+j+\ell}} - 1\right|, \tag{4.51}$$

where m is the number of ℓ-step ahead forecasts available in the forecasting subsample. In application, one often chooses one of the above three measures, and the model with the smallest magnitude on that measure is regarded as the best ℓ-step ahead forecasting model. It is possible that different ℓ may result in selecting different models. The measures also have other limitations in model comparison; see, for instance, Clements and Hendry (1993).

Distributional Measure

Practitioners recently began to assess forecasting performance of a model using its predictive distributions. Strictly speaking, a predictive distribution incorporates parameter uncertainty in forecasts. We call it *conditional predictive distribution* if the parameters are treated as fixed. The empirical distribution of $x_{T+\ell}$ obtained by the parametric bootstrap is a conditional predictive distribution. This empirical distribution is often used to compute a distributional measure. Let $u_T(\ell)$ be the percentile of the observed $x_{T+\ell}$ in the prior empirical distribution. We then have a set of m percentiles $\{u_{T+j}(\ell)\}_{j=0}^{m-1}$, where again m is the number of ℓ-step ahead forecasts in the forecasting subsample. If the model entertained is adequate, $\{u_{T+j}(\ell)\}$ should be a random sample from the uniform distribution on [0, 1]. For a sufficiently large m, one can compute the Kolmogorov–Smirnov statistic of $\{u_{T+j}(\ell)\}$ with respect to uniform [0, 1]. The statistic can be used for both model checking and forecasting comparison.

4.5 APPLICATION

In this section, we illustrate nonlinear time series models by analyzing the quarterly U.S. civilian unemployment rate, seasonally adjusted, from 1948 to 1993. This

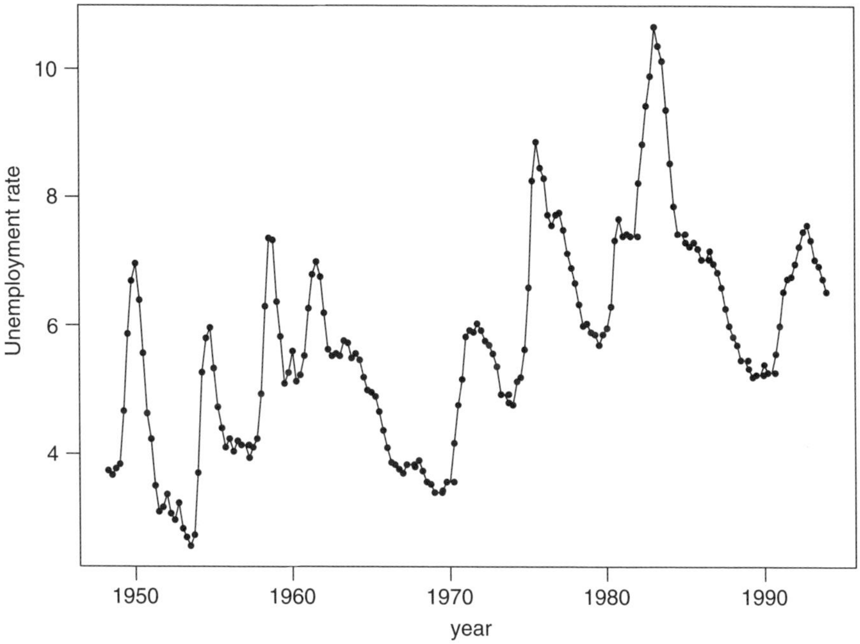

Figure 4.11. Time plot of the U.S. quarterly unemployment rate, seasonally adjusted, from 1948 to 1993.

series was analyzed in detail by Montgomery, Zarnowitz, Tsay, and Tiao (1998). We repeat some of the analyses here using nonlinear models. Figure 4.11 shows the time plot of the data. Well-known characteristics of the series include that (a) it tends to move countercyclically with U.S. business cycles, and (b) the rate rises quickly but decays slowly. The latter characteristic suggests that the dynamic structure of the series is nonlinear.

Denote the series by x_t and let $\Delta x_t = x_t - x_{t-1}$ be the change in unemployment rate. The linear model

$$(1 - 0.31B^4)(1 - 0.65B)\Delta x_t = (1 - 0.78B^4)a_t, \quad \hat{\sigma}_a^2 = 0.090 \qquad (4.52)$$

was built by Montgomery et al. (1998), where the standard errors of the three coefficients are 0.11, 0.06, and 0.07, respectively. This is a seasonal model even though the data were seasonally adjusted. It indicates that the seasonal adjustment procedure used did not successfully remove the seasonality. This model is used as a benchmark model for forecasting comparison.

To test for nonlinearity, we apply some of the nonlinearity tests of Section 4.2 with an AR(5) model for the differenced series Δx_t. The results are given in Table 4.3. All of the tests reject the linearity assumption. In fact, the linearity assumption is rejected for all AR(p) models we applied, where $p = 2, \ldots, 10$.

Table 4.3. Nonlinearity Test for Changes in the U.S. Quarterly Unemployment Rate: 1948.II–1993.IV[a]

Type	Ori-F	LST	TAR(1)	TAR(2)	TAR(3)	TAR(4)
Test	2.80	2.83	2.41	2.16	2.84	2.98
p-Value	0.0007	0.0002	0.0298	0.0500	0.0121	0.0088

[a]An AR(5) model was used in the tests, where LST denotes the test of Luukkonen et al. (1988) and TAR(d) means threshold test with delay d.

Using a modeling procedure similar to that of Tsay (1989), Montgomery et al. (1998) build the following TAR model for the Δx_t series:

$$\Delta x_t = \begin{cases} 0.01 + 0.73\Delta x_{t-1} + 0.10\Delta x_{t-2} + a_{1t} & \text{if } \Delta x_{t-2} \le 0.1, \\ 0.18 + 0.80\Delta x_{t-1} - 0.56\Delta x_{t-2} + a_{2t} & \text{otherwise.} \end{cases} \tag{4.53}$$

The sample variances of a_{1t} and a_{2t} are 0.76 and 0.165, respectively, the standard errors of the three coefficients of regime 1 are 0.03, 0.10, and 0.12, respectively, and those of regime 2 are 0.09, 0.1, and 0.16. This model says that the change in the U.S. quarterly unemployment rate, Δx_t, behaves like a piecewise linear model in the reference space of $x_{t-2} - x_{t-3}$ with threshold 0.1. Intuitively, the model implies that the dynamics of unemployment act differently depending on the recent change in the unemployment rate. In the first regime, the unemployment rate has had either a decrease or a minor increase. Here the economy should be stable, and essentially the change in the rate follows a simple AR(1) model because the lag-2 coefficient is insignificant. In the second regime, there is a substantial jump in the unemployment rate (0.1 or larger). This typically corresponds to the contraction phase in the business cycle. It is also the period during which government interventions and industrial restructuring are likely to occur. Here Δx_t follows an AR(2) model with a positive constant, indicating an upward trend in x_t. The AR(2) polynomial contains two complex characteristic roots, which indicate possible cyclical behavior in Δx_t. Consequently, the chance of having a turning point in x_t increases, suggesting that the period of large increases in x_t should be short. This implies that the contraction phases in the U.S. economy tend to be shorter than the expansion phases.

Applying a Markov chain Monte Carlo method, Montgomery et al. (1998) obtain the following Markov switching model for Δx_t:

$$\Delta x_t = \begin{cases} -0.07 + 0.38\Delta x_{t-1} - 0.05\Delta x_{t-2} + \epsilon_{1t} & \text{if } s_t = 1, \\ 0.16 + 0.86\Delta x_{t-1} - 0.38\Delta x_{t-2} + \epsilon_{2t} & \text{if } s_t = 2. \end{cases} \tag{4.54}$$

The conditional means of Δx_t are -0.10 for $s_t = 1$ and 0.31 for $s_t = 2$. Thus, the first state represents the expansionary periods in the economy, and the second state represents the contractions. The sample variances of ϵ_{1t} and ϵ_{2t} are 0.031 and 0.192, respectively. The standard errors of the three parameters in state $s_t = 1$ are 0.03,

0.14, and 0.11, and those of state $s_t = 2$ are 0.04, 0.13, and 0.14, respectively. The state transition probabilities are $P(s_t = 2|s_{t-1} = 1) = 0.084(0.060)$ and $P(s_t = 1|s_{t-1} = 2) = 0.126(0.053)$, where the number in parentheses is the corresponding standard error. This model implies that in the second state the unemployment rate x_t has an upward trend with an AR(2) polynomial possessing complex characteristic roots. This feature of the model is similar to the second regime of the TAR model in Eq. (4.53). In the first state, the unemployment rate x_t has a slightly decreasing trend with a much weaker autoregressive structure.

Forecasting Performance

A rolling procedure was used by Montgomery et al. (1998) to forecast the unemployment rate x_t. The procedure works as follows:

1. Begin with forecast origin $T = 83$, corresponding to 1968.II, which was used in the literature to monitor the performance of various econometric models in forecasting unemployment rate. Estimate the linear, TAR, and MSA models using the data from 1948.I to the forecast origin (inclusive).
2. Perform 1-quarter to 5-quarter ahead forecasts and compute the forecast errors of each model. Forecasts of nonlinear models used are computed by using the parametric bootstrap method of Section 4.4.
3. Advance the forecast origin by 1 and repeat the estimation and forecasting processes until all data are employed.
4. Use MSE and mean forecast error to compare performance of the models.

Table 4.4 shows the relative MSE of forecasts and mean forecast errors for the linear model in Eq. (4.52), the TAR model in Eq. (4.53), and the MSA model in Eq. (4.54), using the linear model as a benchmark. The comparisons are based on overall performance as well as the status of the U.S. economy at the forecast origin. From the table, we make the following observations:

1. For the overall comparison, the TAR model and the linear model are very close in MSE, but the TAR model has smaller biases. Yet the MSA model has the highest MSE and smallest biases.
2. For forecast origins in economic contractions, the TAR model shows improvements over the linear model both in MSE and bias. The MSA model also shows some improvement over the linear model, but the improvement is not as large as that of the TAR model.
3. For forecast origins in economic expansions, the linear model outperforms both nonlinear models.

The results suggest that the contributions of nonlinear models over linear ones in forecasting the U.S. quarterly unemployment rate are mainly in the periods when the U.S. economy is in contraction. This is not surprising because, as mentioned before, it is during the economic contractions that government interventions and

Table 4.4. Out-of-Sample Forecast Comparison Among Linear, TAR, and MSA Models for the U.S. Quarterly Unemployment Rate[a]

	Relative MSE of Forecast				
Model	1-step	2-step	3-step	4-step	5-step
			Overall Comparison		
Linear	1.00	1.00	1.00	1.00	1.00
TAR	1.00	1.04	0.99	0.98	1.03
MSA	1.19	1.39	1.40	1.45	1.61
MSE	0.08	0.31	0.67	1.13	1.54
			Forecast Origins in Economic Contractions		
Linear	1.00	1.00	1.00	1.00	1.00
TAR	0.85	0.91	0.83	0.72	0.72
MSA	0.97	1.03	0.96	0.86	1.02
MSE	0.22	0.97	2.14	3.38	3.46
			Forecast Origins in Economic Expansions		
Linear	1.00	1.00	1.00	1.00	1.00
TAR	1.06	1.13	1.10	1.15	1.17
MSA	1.31	1.64	1.73	1.84	1.87
MSE	0.06	0.21	0.45	0.78	1.24
	Mean of Forecast Errors				
Model	1-step	2-step	3-step	4-step	5-step
			Overall Comparison		
Linear	0.03	0.09	0.17	0.25	0.33
TAR	−0.10	−0.02	−0.03	−0.03	−0.01
MSA	0.00	−0.02	−0.04	−0.07	−0.12
			Forecast Origins in Economic Contractions		
Linear	0.31	0.68	1.08	1.41	1.38
TAR	0.24	0.56	0.87	1.01	0.86
MSA	0.20	0.41	0.57	0.52	0.14
			Forecast Origins in Economic Expansions		
Linear	−0.01	0.00	0.03	0.08	0.17
TAR	−0.05	−0.11	−0.17	−0.19	−0.14
MSA	−0.03	−0.08	−0.13	−0.17	−0.16

[a]The starting forecast origin is 1968.II, where the row marked by MSE shows the MSE of the benchmark linear model.

industrial restructuring are most likely to occur. These external events could introduce nonlinearity in the U.S. unemployment rate. Intuitively, such improvements are important because it is during the contractions that people pay more attention to economic forecasts.

APPENDIX A: SOME RATS PROGRAMS FOR NONLINEAR VOLATILITY MODELS

Program Used to Estimate an AR(2)–TAR–GARCH(1,1) Model for Daily Log Returns of IBM Stock

Assume that the data file is `d-ibmln03.txt`.

```
all 0 10446:1
open data d-ibmln03.txt
data(org=obs) / rt
set h = 0.0
nonlin mu p2 a0 a1 b1 a2 b2
frml at = rt(t)-mu-p2*rt(t-2)
frml gvar = a0 + a1*at(t-1)**2+b1*h(t-1) $
            + %if(at(t-1) < 0,a2*at(t-1)**2+b2*h(t-1),0)
frml garchln = -0.5*log(h(t)=gvar(t))-0.5*at(t)**2/h(t)
smpl 4 10446
compute mu = 0.03, p2 = -0.03
compute a0 = 0.07, a1 = 0.05, a2 = 0.05, b1 = 0.85, b2 = 0.05
maximize(method=simplex,iterations=10) garchln
smpl 4  10446
maximize(method=bhhh,recursive,iterations=150) garchln
set fv = gvar(t)
set resid = at(t)/sqrt(fv(t))
set residsq = resid(t)*resid(t)
cor(qstats,number=20,span=10) resid
cor(qstats,number=20,span=10) residsq
```

Program Used to Estimate a Smooth TAR Model for the Monthly Simple Returns of 3M Stock

The data file is `'m-mmm.txt'`.

```
all 0 623:1
open data m-mmm.txt
data(org=obs) / mmm
set h = 0.0
nonlin a0 a1 a2  a00 a11 mu
frml at = mmm(t) - mu
frml var1 =  a0+a1*at(t-1)**2+a2*at(t-2)**2
frml var2 = a00+a11*at(t-1)**2
frml gvar = var1(t)+var2(t)/(1.0+exp(-at(t-1)*1000.0))
frml garchlog = -0.5*log(h(t)=gvar(t))-0.5*at(t)**2/h(t)
```

```
smpl 3 623
compute a0 = .01, a1 = 0.2, a2 = 0.1
compute a00 = .01, a11 = -.2, mu = 0.02
maximize(method=bhhh,recursive,iterations=150) garchlog
set fv = gvar(t)
set resid = at(t)/sqrt(fv(t))
set residsq = resid(t)*resid(t)
cor(qstats,number=20,span=10) resid
cor(qstats,number=20,span=10) residsq
```

APPENDIX B: S-PLUS COMMANDS FOR NEURAL NETWORK

The following commands are used in S-Plus to build the 3-2-1 skip-layer feed-forward network of Example 4.7. A line starting with # denotes a comment. The data file is `'m-ibmln.txt'`.

```
# load the data into S-Plus workspace.
x_scan(file='m-ibmln.txt')
# select the output: r(t)
y_x[4:864]
# obtain the input variables: r(t-1), r(t-2), and r(t-3)
ibm.x_cbind(x[3:863],x[2:862],x[1:861])
# build a 3-2-1 network with skip layer connections
# and linear output.
ibm.nn_nnet(ibm.x,y,size=2,linout=T,skip=T,maxit=10000,
decay=1e-2,reltol=1e-7,abstol=1e-7,range=1.0)
# print the summary results of the network
summary(ibm.nn)
# compute \& print the residual sum of squares.
sse_sum((y-predict(ibm.nn,ibm.x))^2)
print(sse)
#eigen(nnet.Hess(ibm.nn,ibm.x,y),T)$values
# setup the input variables in the forecasting subsample
ibm.p_cbind(x[864:887],x[863:886],x[862:885])
# compute the forecasts
yh_predict(ibm.nn,ibm.p)
# The observed returns in the forecasting subsample
yo_x[865:888]
# compute \& print the sum of squares of forecast errors
ssfe_sum((yo-yh)^2)
print(ssfe)
# quit S-Plus
q()
```

EXERCISES

4.1. Consider the daily simple returns of Johnson and Johnson stock from January 1990 to December 2003. The data are in the file `d-jnj9003.txt` or can be obtained from CRSP. Convert the returns into log returns in percentage.

(a) Build a GJR model for the log return series. Write down the fitted model. Is the leverage effect significant at the 1% level?

(b) Build a general threshold volatility model for the log return series.

(c) Compare the two TGARCH models.

4.2. Consider the monthly simple returns of General Electric (GE) stock from January 1926 to December 2003. You may download the data from CRSP or use the file `m-ge2603.txt` on the Web. Convert the returns into log returns in percentages. Build a TGARCH model with GED innovations for the series using a_{t-1} as the threshold variable with zero threshold, where a_{t-1} is the shock at time $t-1$. Write down the fitted model. Is the leverage effect significant at the 5% level?

4.3. Suppose that the monthly log returns of GE stock, measured in percentages, follow a smooth threshold GARCH(1,1) model. For the sampling period from January 1926 to December 1999, the fitted model is

$$r_t = 1.06 + a_t, \quad a_t = \sigma_t \epsilon_t$$

$$\sigma_t^2 = 0.103a_{t-1}^2 + 0.952\sigma_{t-1}^2 + \frac{1}{1+\exp(-10a_{t-1})}(4.490 - 0.193\sigma_{t-1}^2),$$

where all of the estimates are highly significant, the coefficient 10 in the exponent is fixed a priori to simplify the estimation, and $\{\epsilon_t\}$ are iid $N(0, 1)$. Assume that $a_{888} = 16.0$ and $\sigma_{888}^2 = 50.2$. What is the 1-step ahead volatility forecast $\widehat{\sigma}_{888}^2(1)$? Suppose instead that $a_{888} = -16.0$. What is the 1-step ahead volatility forecast $\widehat{\sigma}_{888}^2(1)$?

4.4. Suppose that the monthly log returns, in percentages, of a stock follow the following Markov switching model:

$$r_t = 1.25 + a_t, \quad a_t = \sigma_t \epsilon_t,$$

$$\sigma_t^2 = \begin{cases} 0.10a_{t-1}^2 + 0.93\sigma_{t-1}^2 & \text{if } s_t = 1, \\ 4.24 + 0.10a_{t-1}^2 + 0.78\sigma_{t-1}^2 & \text{if } s_t = 2, \end{cases}$$

where the transition probabilities are

$$P(s_t = 2|s_{t-1} = 1) = 0.15, \qquad P(s_t = 1|s_{t-1} = 2) = 0.05.$$

Suppose that $a_{100} = 6.0$, $\sigma_{100}^2 = 50.0$, and $s_{100} = 2$ with probability 1.0. What is the 1-step ahead volatility forecast at the forecast origin $t = 100$? Also, if the probability of $s_{100} = 2$ is reduced to 0.8, what is the 1-step ahead volatility forecast at the forecast origin $t = 100$?

4.5. Consider the monthly simple returns of GE stock from January 1926 to December 2003. Use the last three years of data for forecasting evaluation.

(a) Using lagged returns $r_{t-1}, r_{t-2}, r_{t-3}$ as input, build a 3-2-1 feed-forward network to forecast 1-step ahead returns. Calculate the mean squared error of forecasts.

(b) Again, use lagged returns $r_{t-1}, r_{t-2}, r_{t-3}$ and their signs (directions) to build a 6-5-1 feed-forward network to forecast the 1-step ahead direction of GE stock price movement with 1 denoting upward movement. Calculate the mean squared error of forecasts.

Note: Let `rtn` denote a time series in S-Plus. To create a direction variable for `rtn`, use the command

```
drtn = ifelse(rtn > 0, 1, 0)
```

4.6. Because of the existence of inverted yield curves in the term structure of interest rates, the spread of interest rates should be nonlinear. To verify this, consider the weekly U.S. interest rates of (a) Treasury 1-year constant maturity rate, and (b) Treasury 3-year constant maturity rate. As in Chapter 2, denote the two interest rates by r_{1t} and r_{3t}, respectively, and the data span is from January 5, 1962 to September 10, 1999. The data are in files `w-gs3yr.txt` and `w-gs1yr.txt` on the Web and can be obtained from the Federal Reserve Bank of St. Louis.

(a) Let $s_t = r_{3t} - r_{1t}$ be the spread in log interest rates. Is $\{s_t\}$ linear? Perform some nonlinearity tests and draw the conclusion using the 5% significance level.

(b) Let $s_t^* = (r_{3t} - r_{3,t-1}) - (r_{1t} - r_{1,t-1}) = s_t - s_{t-1}$ be the change in interest rate spread. Is $\{s_t^*\}$ linear? Perform some nonlinearity tests and draw the conclusion using the 5% significance level.

(c) Build a threshold model for the s_t series and check the fitted model.

(d) Build a threshold model for the s_t^* series and check the fitted model.

REFERENCES

Akaike, H. (1974). A new look at the statistical model identification. *IEEE Transactions on Automatic Control* **AC-19**: 716–723.

Andrews, D. W. K. and Ploberger, W. (1994). Optimal tests when a nuisance parameter is present only under the alternative. *Econometrica* **62**: 1383–1414.

Brock, W., Dechert, W. D., and Scheinkman, J. (1987). A test for independence based on the correlation dimension. Working paper, Department of Economics, University of Wisconsin, Madison.

Brock, W., Hsieh, D. A., and LeBaron, B. (1991). *Nonlinear Dynamics, Chaos and Instability: Statistical Theory and Economic Evidence*. MIT Press, Cambridge, MA.

Bryson, A. E. and Ho, Y. C. (1969). *Applied Optimal Control*. Blaisdell, New York.

Cai, Z., Fan, J., and Yao, Q. (2000). Functional-coefficient regression models for nonlinear time series. *Journal of the American Statistical Association* **95**: 941–956.

Carlin, B. P., Polson, N. G., and Stoffer, D. S. (1992). A Monte Carlo approach to nonnormal and nonlinear state space modeling. *Journal of the American Statistical Association* **87**: 493–500.

Chan, K. S. (1991). Percentage points of likelihood ratio tests for threshold autoregression. *Journal of the Royal Statistical Society Series B* **53**: 691–696.

Chan, K. S. (1993). Consistency and limiting distribution of the least squares estimator of a continuous autoregressive model. *The Annals of Statistics* **21**: 520–533.

Chan, K. S. and Tong, H. (1986). On estimating thresholds in autoregressive models. *Journal of Time Series Analysis* **7**: 179–190.

Chan, K. S. and Tsay, R. S. (1998). Limiting properties of the conditional least squares estimator of a continuous TAR model. *Biometrika* **85**: 413–426.

Chen, C., McCulloch, R. E., and Tsay, R. S. (1997). A unified approach to estimating and modeling univariate linear and nonlinear time series. *Statistica Sinica* **7**: 451–472.

Chen, R. and Tsay, R. S. (1991). On the ergodicity of TAR(1) processes. *Annals of Applied Probability* **1**: 613–634.

Chen, R. and Tsay, R. S. (1993a). Functional-coefficient autoregressive models. *Journal of the American Statistical Association* **88**: 298–308.

Chen, R. and Tsay, R. S. (1993b). Nonlinear additive ARX models. *Journal of the American Statistical Association* **88**: 955–967.

Chen, R., Liu, J., and Tsay, R. S. (1995). Additivity tests for nonlinear autoregressive models. *Biometrika* **82**: 369–383.

Chen, T. and Chen, H. (1995). Universal approximation to nonlinear operators by neural networks with arbitrary activation functions and its application to dynamical systems. *IEEE Transactions on Neural Networks* **6**: 911–917.

Cheng, B. and Titterington, D. M. (1994). Neural networks: A review from a statistical perspective. *Statistical Science* **9**: 2–54.

Clements, M. P. and Hendry, D. F. (1993). On the limitations of comparing mean square forecast errors. *Journal of Forecasting* **12**: 617–637.

Cleveland, W. S. (1979). Robust locally weighted regression and smoothing scatterplots. *Journal of the American Statistical Association* **74**: 829–836.

Dahl, C. M. and Hylleberg, S. (1999). Specifying nonlinear econometric models by flexible regression models and relative forecast performance. Working paper, Department of Economics, University of Aarhus, Denmark.

Davis, R. B. (1987). Hypothesis testing when a nuisance parameter is present only under the alternative. *Biometrika* **74**: 33–43.

Engle, R. F. (1982). Autoregressive conditional heteroscedasticity with estimates of the variance of United Kingdom inflations. *Econometrica* **50**: 987–1007.

Epanechnikov, V. (1969). Nonparametric estimates of a multivariate probability density. *Theory of Probability and Its Applications* **14**: 153–158.

Fan, J. (1993). Local linear regression smoothers and their minimax efficiencies. *The Annals of Statistics* **21**: 196–216.

Fan, J. and Yao, Q. (2003), *Nonlinear Time Series: Nonparametric and Parametric Methods*. Springer-Verlag, New York.

Gelfand, A. E. and Smith, A. F. M. (1990). Sampling-based approaches to calculating marginal densities. *Journal of the American Statistical Association* **85**: 398–409.

Granger, C. W. J. and Andersen, A. P. (1978). *An Introduction to Bilinear Time Series Models*. Vandenhoek and Ruprecht, Gottingen.

Hamilton, J. D. (1989). A new approach to the economic analysis of nonstationary time series and the business cycle. *Econometrica* **57**: 357–384.

Hamilton, J. D. (1990). Analysis of time series subject to changes in regime. *Journal of Econometrics* **45**: 39–70.

Hamilton, J. D. (1994). *Time Series Analysis*. Princeton University Press, Princeton, NJ.

Härdle, W. (1990). *Applied Nonparametric Regression*. Cambridge University Press, New York.

Hansen, B. E. (1997). Inference in TAR models. *Studies in Nonlinear Dynamics and Econometrics* **1**: 119–131.

Hinich, M. (1982). Testing for Gaussianity and linearity of a stationary time series. *Journal of Time Series Analysis* **3**: 169–176.

Hornik, K. (1993). Some new results on neural network approximation. *Neural Networks* **6**: 1069–1072.

Hornik, K., Stinchcombe, M., and White, H. (1989). Multilayer feedforward networks are universal approximators. *Neural Networks* **2**: 359–366.

Hsieh, D. A. (1989). Testing for nonlinear dependence in daily foreign exchange rates. *Journal of Business* **62**: 339–368.

Keenan, D. M. (1985). A Tukey non-additivity-type test for time series nonlinearity. *Biometrika* **72**: 39–44.

Kitagawa, G. (1998). A self-organizing state space model. *Journal of the American Statistical Association* **93**: 1203–1215.

Lewis, P. A. W. and Stevens, J. G. (1991). Nonlinear modeling of time series using multivariate adaptive regression spline (MARS). *Journal of the American Statistical Association* **86**: 864–877.

Liu, J. and Brockwell, P. J. (1988). On the general bilinear time-series model. *Journal of Applied Probability* **25**: 553–564.

Luukkonen, R., Saikkonen, P., and Teräsvirta, T. (1988). Testing linearity against smooth transition autoregressive models. *Biometrika* **75**: 491–499.

McCulloch, R. E. and Tsay, R. S. (1993). Bayesian inference and prediction for mean and variance shifts in autoregressive time series. *Journal of the American Statistical Association* **88**: 968–978.

McCulloch, R. E. and Tsay, R. S. (1994). Statistical inference of macroeconomic time series via Markov switching models. *Journal of Time Series Analysis* **15**: 523–539.

McLeod, A. I. and Li, W. K. (1983). Diagnostic checking ARMA time series models using squared-residual autocorrelations. *Journal of Time Series Analysis* **4**: 269–273.

Montgomery, A. L., Zarnowitz, V., Tsay, R. S., and Tiao, G. C. (1998). Forecasting the U.S. unemployment rate. *Journal of the American Statistical Association* **93**: 478–493.

Nadaraya, E. A. (1964). On estimating regression. *Theory and Probability Application* **10**: 186–190.

Petruccelli, J. and Woolford, S. W. (1984). A threshold AR(1) model. *Journal of Applied Probability* **21**: 270–286.

Potter, S. M. (1995). A nonlinear approach to U.S. GNP. *Journal of Applied Econometrics* **10**: 109–125.

Priestley, M. B. (1980). State-dependent models: a general approach to nonlinear time series analysis. *Journal of Time Series Analysis* **1**: 47–71.

Priestley, M. B. (1988). *Non-linear and Non-stationary Time Series Analysis*. Academic Press, London.

Ramsey, J. B. (1969). Tests for specification errors in classical linear least squares regression analysis. *Journal of the Royal Statistical Society Series B* **31**: 350–371.

Ripley, B. D. (1993). Statistical aspects of neural networks. In O. E. Barndorff-Nielsen, J. L. Jensen, and W. S. Kendall, (eds.), *Networks and Chaos—Statistical and Probabilistic Aspects*, pp. 40–123. Chapman and Hall, London.

Subba Rao, T. and Gabr, M. M. (1984). *An Introduction to Bispectral Analysis and Bilinear Time Series Models*, Lecture Notes in Statistics, 24. Springer-Verlag, New York.

Teräsvirta, T. (1994). Specification, estimation, and evaluation of smooth transition autoregressive models. *Journal of the American Statistical Association* **89**: 208–218.

Tiao, G. C. and Tsay, R. S. (1994). Some advances in nonlinear and adaptive modeling in time series. *Journal of Forecasting* **13**: 109–131.

Tong, H. (1978). On a threshold model. In C. H. Chen (ed.), *Pattern Recognition and Signal Processing*. Sijhoff & Noordhoff, Amsterdam.

Tong, H. (1983). *Threshold Models in Nonlinear Time Series Analysis*, Lecture Notes in Statistics. Springer-Verlag, New York.

Tong, H. (1990). *Non-Linear Time Series: A Dynamical System Approach*. Oxford University Press, Oxford, UK.

Tsay, R. S. (1986). Nonlinearity tests for time series. *Biometrika* **73**: 461–466.

Tsay, R. S. (1989). Testing and modeling threshold autoregressive processes. *Journal of the American Statistical Association* **84**: 231–240.

Tsay, R. S. (1998). Testing and modeling multivariate threshold models. *Journal of the American Statistical Association* **93**: 1188–1202.

Venables, W. N. and Ripley, B. D. (1999). *Modern Applied Statistics with S-Plus*, 3rd edition. Springer-Verlag, New York.

Watson, G. S. (1964). Smooth regression analysis. *Sankhya Series A* **26**: 359–372.

CHAPTER 5

High-Frequency Data Analysis and Market Microstructure

High-frequency data are observations taken at fine time intervals. In finance, they often mean observations taken daily or at a finer time scale. These data have become available primarily due to advances in data acquisition and processing techniques, and they have attracted much attention because they are important in empirical study of market microstructure. The ultimate high-frequency data in finance are the transaction-by-transaction or trade-by-trade data in security markets. Here time is often measured in seconds. The Trades and Quotes (TAQ) database of the New York Stock Exchange (NYSE) contains all equity transactions reported on the *Consolidated Tape* from 1992 to the present, which includes transactions on the NYSE, AMEX, NASDAQ, and the regional exchanges. The Berkeley Options Data Base provides similar data for options transactions from August 1976 to December 1996. Transactions data for many other securities and markets, both domestic and foreign, are continuously collected and processed. Wood (2000) provides some historical perspective of high-frequency financial study.

High-frequency financial data are important in studying a variety of issues related to the trading process and market microstructure. They can be used to compare the efficiency of different trading systems in price discovery (e.g., the open out-cry system of the NYSE and the computer trading system of NASDAQ). They can also be used to study the dynamics of bid and ask quotes of a particular stock (e.g., Hasbrouck, 1999; Zhang, Russell, and Tsay, 2001b). In an order-driven stock market (e.g., the Taiwan Stock Exchange), high-frequency data can be used to study the order dynamics and, more interesting, to investigate the question of "who provides the market liquidity." Cho, Russell, Tiao, and Tsay (2003) use intraday 5-minute returns of more than 340 stocks traded on the Taiwan Stock Exchange to study the impact of daily stock price limits and find significant evidence of magnet effects toward the price ceiling.

However, high-frequency data have some unique characteristics that do not appear in lower frequencies. Analysis of these data thus introduces new challenges

Analysis of Financial Time Series, Second Edition By Ruey S. Tsay

to financial economists and statisticians. In this chapter, we study these special characteristics, consider methods for analyzing high-frequency data, and discuss implications of the results obtained. In particular, we discuss nonsynchronous trading, bid–ask spread, duration models, price movements that are in multiples of tick size, and bivariate models for price changes and time durations between transactions associated with price changes. The models discussed are also applicable to other scientific areas such as telecommunications and environmental studies.

5.1 NONSYNCHRONOUS TRADING

We begin with nonsynchronous trading. Stock tradings such as those on the NYSE do not occur in a synchronous manner; different stocks have different trading frequencies, and even for a single stock the trading intensity varies from hour to hour and from day to day. Yet we often analyze a return series in a fixed time interval such as daily, weekly, or monthly. For daily series, price of a stock is its *closing* price, which is the last transaction price of the stock in a trading day. The actual time of the last transaction of the stock varies from day to day. As such we incorrectly assume daily returns as an equally spaced time series with a 24-hour interval. It turns out that such an assumption can lead to erroneous conclusions about the predictability of stock returns even if the true return series are serially independent.

For daily stock returns, nonsynchronous trading can introduce (a) lag-1 cross-correlation between stock returns, (b) lag-1 serial correlation in a portfolio return, and (c) in some situations negative serial correlations of the return series of a single stock. Consider stocks A and B. Assume that the two stocks are independent and stock A is traded more frequently than stock B. For special news affecting the market that arrives near the closing hour on one day, stock A is more likely than B to show the effect of the news on the same day simply because A is traded more frequently. The effect of the news on B will eventually appear, but it may be delayed until the following trading day. If this situation indeed happens, return of stock A appears to lead that of stock B. Consequently, the return series may show a significant lag-1 cross-correlation from A to B even though the two stocks are independent. For a portfolio that holds stocks A and B, the prior cross-correlation would become a significant lag-1 serial correlation.

In a more complicated manner, nonsynchronous trading can also induce erroneous negative serial correlations for a single stock. There are several models available in the literature to study this phenomenon; see Campbell, Lo, and MacKinlay (1997) and the references therein. Here we adopt a simplified version of the model proposed in Lo and MacKinlay (1990). Let r_t be the continuously compounded return of a security at the time index t. For simplicity, assume that $\{r_t\}$ is a sequence of independent and identically distributed random variables with mean $E(r_t) = \mu$ and variance $\text{Var}(r_t) = \sigma^2$. For each time period, the probability that the security is not traded is π, which is time-invariant and independent of r_t. Let r_t^o be the observed return. When there is no trade at time index t, we have $r_t^o = 0$ because there is no information available. Yet when there is a trade at time index t, we define r_t^o as the cumulative return from the previous trade (i.e., $r_t^o = r_t + r_{t-1} + \cdots + r_{t-k_t}$, where k_t is the largest non-negative integer such that no trade occurred in the periods $t - k_t, t - k_t + 1, \ldots, t - 1$). Mathematically, the relationship between r_t and r_t^o is

$$r_t^o = \begin{cases} 0 & \text{with probability } \pi \\ r_t & \text{with probability } (1-\pi)^2 \\ r_t + r_{t-1} & \text{with probability } (1-\pi)^2\pi \\ r_t + r_{t-1} + r_{t-2} & \text{with probability } (1-\pi)^2\pi^2 \\ \vdots & \vdots \\ \sum_{i=0}^{k} r_{t-i} & \text{with probability } (1-\pi)^2\pi^k \\ \vdots & \vdots \end{cases} \tag{5.1}$$

These probabilities are easy to understand. For example, $r_t^o = r_t$ if and only if there are trades at both t and $t-1$, $r_t^o = r_t + r_{t-1}$ if and only if there are trades at t and $t-2$, but no trade at $t-1$, and $r_t^o = r_t + r_{t-1} + r_{t-2}$ if and only if there are trades at t and $t-3$, but no trades at $t-1$ and $t-2$, and so on. As expected, the total probability is 1 given by

$$\pi + (1-\pi)^2[1 + \pi + \pi^2 + \cdots] = \pi + (1-\pi)^2\frac{1}{1-\pi} = \pi + 1 - \pi = 1.$$

We are ready to consider the moment equations of the observed return series $\{r_t^o\}$. First, the expectation of r_t^o is

$$\begin{aligned} E(r_t^o) &= (1-\pi)^2 E(r_t) + (1-\pi)^2\pi E(r_t + r_{t-1}) + \cdots \\ &= (1-\pi)^2\mu + (1-\pi)^2\pi 2\mu + (1-\pi)^2\pi^2 3\mu + \cdots \\ &= (1-\pi)^2\mu[1 + 2\pi + 3\pi^2 + 4\pi^3 + \cdots] \\ &= (1-\pi)^2\mu\frac{1}{(1-\pi)^2} = \mu. \end{aligned} \tag{5.2}$$

In the prior derivation, we use the result $1 + 2\pi + 3\pi^2 + 4\pi^3 + \cdots = 1/(1-\pi)^2$. Next, for the variance of r_t^o, we use $\text{Var}(r_t^o) = E[(r_t^o)^2] - [E(r_t^o)]^2$ and

$$E(r_t^o)^2 = (1-\pi)^2 E[(r_t)^2] + (1-\pi)^2\pi E[(r_t + r_{t-1})^2] + \cdots$$

$$= (1-\pi)^2[(\sigma^2 + \mu^2) + \pi(2\sigma^2 + 4\mu^2) + \pi^2(3\sigma^2 + 9\mu^2) + \cdots] \tag{5.3}$$

$$= (1-\pi)^2\{\sigma^2[1 + 2\pi + 3\pi^2 + \cdots] + \mu^2[1 + 4\pi + 9\pi^2 + \cdots]\} \tag{5.4}$$

$$= \sigma^2 + \mu^2\left[\frac{2}{1-\pi} - 1\right]. \tag{5.5}$$

In Eq. (5.3), we use

$$E\left(\sum_{i=0}^{k} r_{t-i}\right)^2 = \text{Var}\left(\sum_{i=0}^{k} r_{t-i}\right) + \left[E\left(\sum_{i=0}^{k} r_{t-i}\right)\right]^2 = (k+1)\sigma^2 + [(k+1)\mu]^2$$

under the serial independence assumption of r_t. Using techniques similar to that of Eq. (5.2), we can show that the first term of Eq. (5.4) reduces to σ^2. For the second term of Eq. (5.4), we use the identity

$$1 + 4\pi + 9\pi^2 + 16\pi^3 + \cdots = \frac{2}{(1-\pi)^3} - \frac{1}{(1-\pi)^2},$$

which can be obtained as follows. Let

$$H = 1 + 4\pi + 9\pi^2 + 16\pi^3 + \cdots \quad \text{and} \quad G = 1 + 3\pi + 5\pi^2 + 7\pi^3 + \cdots.$$

Then $(1-\pi)H = G$ and

$$\begin{aligned}(1-\pi)G &= 1 + 2\pi + 2\pi^2 + 2\pi^3 + \cdots \\ &= 2(1 + \pi + \pi^2 + \cdots) - 1 = \frac{2}{(1-\pi)} - 1.\end{aligned}$$

Consequently, from Eqs. (5.2) and (5.5), we have

$$\text{Var}(r_t^o) = \sigma^2 + \mu^2\left[\frac{2}{1-\pi} - 1\right] - \mu^2 = \sigma^2 + \frac{2\pi\mu^2}{1-\pi}. \tag{5.6}$$

Consider next the lag-1 autocovariance of $\{r_t^o\}$. Here we use $\text{Cov}(r_t^o, r_{t-1}^o) = E(r_t^o r_{t-1}^o) - E(r_t^0)E(r_{t-1}^o) = E(r_t^o r_{t-1}^o) - \mu^2$. The question then reduces to finding $E(r_t^o r_{t-1}^o)$. Notice that $r_t^o r_{t-1}^o$ is zero if there is no trade at t, no trade at $t-1$, or no trade at both t and $t-1$. Therefore, we have

$$r_t^o r_{t-1}^o = \begin{cases} 0 & \text{with probability } 2\pi - \pi^2 \\ r_t r_{t-1} & \text{with probability } (1-\pi)^3 \\ r_t(r_{t-1} + r_{t-2}) & \text{with probability } (1-\pi)^3\pi \\ r_t(r_{t-1} + r_{t-2} + r_{t-3}) & \text{with probability } (1-\pi)^3\pi^2 \\ \vdots & \vdots \\ r_t(\sum_{i=1}^{k} r_{t-i}) & \text{with probability } (1-\pi)^3\pi^{k-1} \\ \vdots & \vdots \end{cases} \tag{5.7}$$

Again the total probability is unity. To understand the prior result, notice that $r_t^o r_{t-1}^o = r_t r_{t-1}$ if and only if there are three consecutive trades at $t-2$, $t-1$, and t. Using Eq. (5.7) and the fact that $E(r_t r_{t-j}) = E(r_t)E(r_{t-j}) = \mu^2$ for $j > 0$, we have

$$\begin{aligned} E(r_t^o r_{t-1}^o) &= (1-\pi)^3 \left\{ E(r_t r_{t-1}) + \pi E[r_t(r_{t-1} + r_{t-2})] \right. \\ &\quad \left. + \pi^2 E\left[r_t \left(\sum_{i=1}^{3} r_{t-i} \right) \right] + \cdots \right\} \\ &= (1-\pi)^3 \mu^2 [1 + 2\pi + 3\pi^2 + \cdots] = (1-\pi)\mu^2. \end{aligned}$$

The lag-1 autocovariance of $\{r_t^o\}$ is then

$$\text{Cov}(r_t^o, r_{t-1}^o) = -\pi\mu^2. \tag{5.8}$$

Provided that μ is not zero, the nonsynchronous trading induces a *negative* lag-1 autocorrelation in r_t^o given by

$$\rho_1(r_t^o) = \frac{-(1-\pi)\pi\mu^2}{(1-\pi)\sigma^2 + 2\pi\mu^2}.$$

In general, we can extend the prior result and show that

$$\text{Cov}(r_t^o, r_{t-j}^o) = -\mu^2\pi^j, \quad j \geq 1.$$

The magnitude of the lag-1 ACF depends on the choices of μ, π, and σ and can be substantial. Thus, when $\mu \neq 0$, the nonsynchronous trading induces negative autocorrelations in an observed security return series.

The previous discussion can be generalized to the return series of a portfolio that consists of N securities; see Campbell, Lo, and MacKinlay (1997, Chapter 3). In the time series literature, effects of nonsynchronous trading on the return of a single security are equivalent to that of random temporal aggregation on a time series, with the trading probability π governing the mechanism of aggregation.

5.2 BID–ASK SPREAD

In some stock exchanges (e.g., NYSE), market makers play an important role in facilitating trades. They provide market liquidity by standing ready to buy or sell whenever the public wishes to buy or sell. By market liquidity, we mean the ability to buy or sell significant quantities of a security quickly, anonymously, and with little price impact. In return for providing liquidity, market makers are granted monopoly rights by the exchange to post different prices for purchases and sales of a security. They buy at the *bid* price P_b and sell at a higher ask price P_a. (For the public, P_b is the sale price and P_a is the purchase price.) The difference $P_a - P_b$

is call the *bid–ask spread*, which is the primary source of compensation for market makers. Typically, the bid–ask spread is small—namely, one or two ticks.

The existence of a bid–ask spread, although small in magnitude, has several important consequences in time series properties of asset returns. We briefly discuss the bid–ask bounce—namely, the bid–ask spread introduces *negative* lag-1 serial correlation in an asset return. Consider the simple model of Roll (1984). The observed market price P_t of an asset is assumed to satisfy

$$P_t = P_t^* + I_t \frac{S}{2}, \tag{5.9}$$

where $S = P_a - P_b$ is the bid–ask spread, P_t^* is the time-t fundamental value of the asset in a frictionless market, and $\{I_t\}$ is a sequence of independent binary random variables with equal probabilities (i.e., $I_t = 1$ with probability 0.5 and $= -1$ with probability 0.5). The I_t can be interpreted as an order-type indicator, with 1 signifying buyer-initiated transaction and -1 seller-initiated transaction. Alternatively, the model can be written as

$$P_t = P_t^* + \begin{cases} +S/2 & \text{with probability 0.5,} \\ -S/2 & \text{with probability 0.5.} \end{cases}$$

If there is no change in P_t^*, then the observed process of price changes is

$$\Delta P_t = (I_t - I_{t-1})\frac{S}{2}. \tag{5.10}$$

Under the assumption of I_t in Eq. (5.9), $E(I_t) = 0$ and $\text{Var}(I_t) = 1$, and we have $E(\Delta P_t) = 0$ and

$$\text{Var}(\Delta P_t) = S^2/2, \tag{5.11}$$

$$\text{Cov}(\Delta P_t, \Delta P_{t-1}) = -S^2/4, \tag{5.12}$$

$$\text{Cov}(\Delta P_t, \Delta P_{t-j}) = 0, \quad j > 1. \tag{5.13}$$

Therefore, the autocorrelation function of ΔP_t is

$$\rho_j(\Delta P_t) = \begin{cases} -0.5 & \text{if } j = 1, \\ 0 & \text{if } j > 1. \end{cases} \tag{5.14}$$

The bid–ask spread thus introduces a negative lag-1 serial correlation in the series of observed price changes. This is referred to as the *bid–ask bounce* in the finance literature. Intuitively, the bounce can be seen as follows. Assume that the fundamental price P_t^* is equal to $(P_a + P_b)/2$. Then P_t assumes the value P_a or P_b. If the previously observed price is P_a (the higher value), then the current observed price is either unchanged or lower at P_b. Thus, ΔP_t is either 0 or $-S$. However, if the previous observed price is P_b (the lower value), then ΔP_t is either 0 or S. The negative lag-1 correlation in ΔP_t becomes apparent. The bid–ask spread does not introduce any serial correlation beyond lag 1, however.

A more realistic formulation is to assume that P_t^* follows a random walk so that $\Delta P_t^* = P_t^* - P_{t-1}^* = \epsilon_t$, which forms a sequence of independent and identically distributed random variables with mean zero and variance σ^2. In addition, $\{\epsilon_t\}$ is independent of $\{I_t\}$. In this case, $\text{Var}(\Delta P_t) = \sigma^2 + S^2/2$, but $\text{Cov}(\Delta P_t, \Delta P_{t-j})$ remains unchanged. Therefore,

$$\rho_1(\Delta P_t) = \frac{-S^2/4}{S^2/2 + \sigma^2} \leq 0.$$

The magnitude of the lag-1 autocorrelation of ΔP_t is reduced, but the negative effect remains when $S = P_a - P_b > 0$. In finance, it might be of interest to study the components of the bid–ask spread. Interested readers are referred to Campbell, Lo, and MacKinlay (1997) and the references therein.

The effect of bid–ask spread continues to exist in portfolio returns and in multivariate financial time series. Consider the bivariate case. Denote the bivariate order-type indicator by $I_t = (I_{1t}, I_{2t})'$, where I_{1t} is for the first security and I_{2t} for the second security. If I_{1t} and I_{2t} are contemporaneously positively correlated, then the bid–ask spreads can introduce negative lag-1 cross-correlations.

5.3 EMPIRICAL CHARACTERISTICS OF TRANSACTIONS DATA

Let t_i be the calendar time, measured in seconds from midnight, at which the ith transaction of an asset takes place. Associated with the transaction are several variables such as the transaction price, the transaction volume, the prevailing bid and ask quotes, and so on. The collection of t_i and the associated measurements are referred to as the *transactions data*. These data have several important characteristics that do not exist when the observations are aggregated over time. Some of the characteristics are given next.

1. *Unequally Spaced Time Intervals*. Transactions such as stock tradings on an exchange do not occur at equally spaced time intervals. As such, the observed transaction prices of an asset do not form an equally spaced time series. The time duration between trades becomes important and might contain useful information about market microstructure (e.g., trading intensity).
2. *Discrete-Valued Prices*. The price change of an asset from one transaction to the next only occurs in multiples of tick size. On the NYSE, the tick size was one-eighth of a dollar before June 24, 1997 and was one-sixteenth of a dollar before January 29, 2001. All NYSE and AMEX stocks started to trade in decimals on January 29, 2001. Therefore, the price is a discrete-valued variable in transactions data. In some markets, price change may also be subject to limit constraints set by regulators.
3. *Existence of a Daily Periodic or Diurnal Pattern*. Under the normal trading conditions, transaction activity can exhibit a periodic pattern. For instance, on the NYSE, transactions are "heavier" at the beginning and closing of the trading hours and "thinner" during lunch hour, resulting in a U-shape

transaction intensity. Consequently, time durations between transactions also exhibit a daily cyclical pattern.

4. *Multiple Transactions Within a Single Second*. It is possible that multiple transactions, even with different prices, occur at the same time. This is partly due to the fact that time is measured in seconds that may be too long a time scale in periods of heavy trading.

To demonstrate these characteristics, we consider first the IBM transactions data from November 1, 1990 to January 31, 1991. These data are from the Trades, Orders Reports, and Quotes (TORQ) dataset; see Hasbrouck (1992). There are 63 trading days and 60,328 transactions. To simplify the discussion, we ignore the price changes between trading days and focus on the transactions that occurred in the normal trading hours from 9:30 am to 4:00 pm Eastern time. It is well known that overnight stock returns differ substantially from intraday returns; see Stoll and Whaley (1990) and the references therein. Table 5.1 gives the frequencies in percentages of price change measured in the tick size of \$1/8 = \$0.125. From the table, we make the following observations:

1. About two-thirds of the intraday transactions were without price change.
2. The price changed in one tick approximately 29% of the intraday transactions.
3. Only 2.6% of the transactions were associated with two-tick price changes.
4. Only about 1.3% of the transactions resulted in price changes of three ticks or more.
5. The distribution of positive and negative price changes was approximately symmetric.

Consider next the number of transactions in a 5-minute time interval. Denote the series by x_t. That is, x_1 is the number of IBM transactions from 9:30 am to 9:35 am on November 1, 1990 Eastern time, x_2 is the number of transactions from 9:35 am to 9:40 am, and so on. The time gaps between trading days are ignored. Figure 5.1a shows the time plot of x_t, and Figure 5.1b the sample ACF of x_t for lags 1 to 260. Of particular interest is the cyclical pattern of the ACF with a periodicity of 78, which is the number of 5-minute intervals in a trading day. The number of transactions thus exhibits a daily pattern. To further illustrate the daily trading pattern, Figure 5.2 shows the average number of transactions within 5-minute time intervals over the 63 days. There are 78 such averages. The plot exhibits a "smiling" or U shape, indicating heavier trading at the opening and closing of the market and thinner trading during the lunch hours.

Table 5.1. Frequencies of Price Change in Multiples of Tick Size for IBM Stock from November 1, 1990 to January 31, 1991

Number (tick)	≤ -3	-2	-1	0	1	2	≥ 3
Percentage	0.66	1.33	14.53	67.06	14.53	1.27	0.63

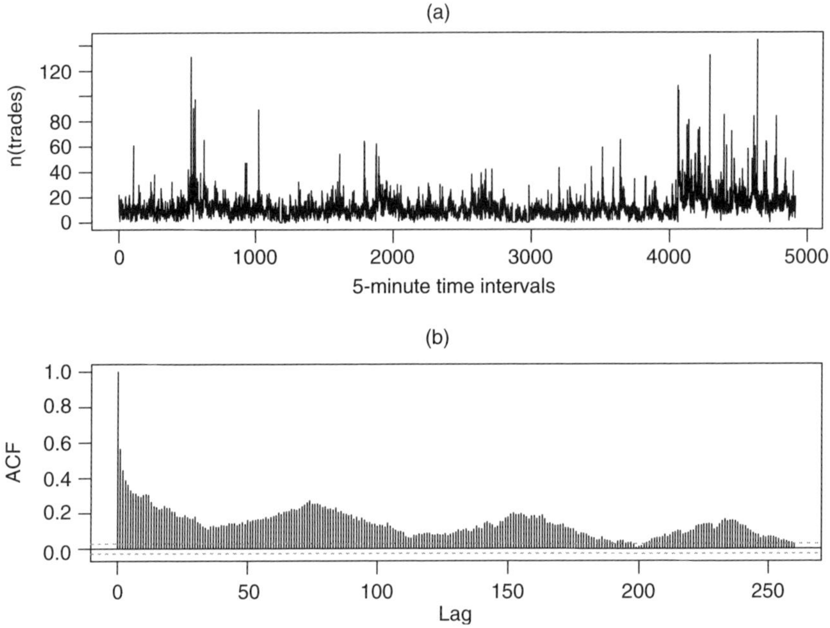

Figure 5.1. IBM intraday transactions data from 11/01/90 to 1/31/91: (a) the number of transactions in 5-minute time intervals and (b) the sample ACF of the series in part(a).

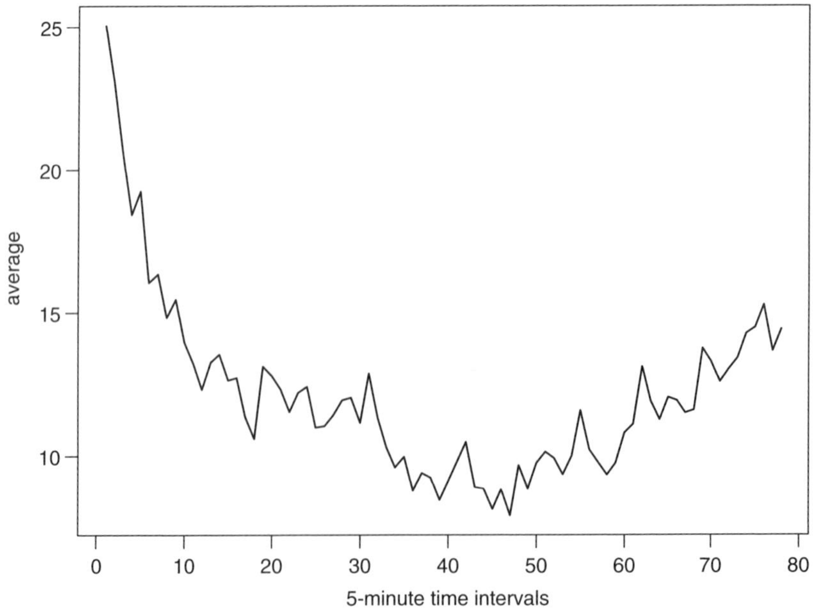

Figure 5.2. Time plot of the average number of transactions in 5-minute time intervals. There are 78 observations, averaging over the 63 trading days from 11/01/90 to 1/31/91 for IBM stock.

Since we focus on transactions that occurred during normal trading hours of a trading day, there are 59,838 time intervals in the data. These intervals are called the intraday *durations* between trades. For IBM stock, there were 6531 zero time intervals. That is, during the normal trading hours of the 63 trading days from November 1, 1990 to January 31, 1991, multiple transactions in a second occurred 6531 times, which is about 10.91%. Among these multiple transactions, 1002 of them had different prices, which is about 1.67% of the total number of intraday transactions. Therefore, multiple transactions (i.e., zero durations) may become an issue in statistical modeling of the time durations between trades.

Table 5.2 provides a two-way classification of price movements. Here price movements are classified into "up," "unchanged," and "down." We denote them by "+," "0," and "−," respectively. The table shows the price movements between two consecutive trades (i.e., from the $(i-1)$th to the ith transaction) in the sample. From the table, trade-by-trade data show that:

1. Consecutive price increases or decreases are relatively rare, which are about 441/59837 = 0.74% and 410/59837 = 0.69%, respectively.
2. There is a slight edge to move from "up" to "unchanged" rather than to "down"; see row 1 of the table.
3. There is a high tendency for the price to remain "unchanged."
4. The probabilities of moving from "down" to "up" or "unchanged" are about the same; see row 3.

The first observation mentioned before is a clear demonstration of bid–ask bounce, showing *price reversals* in intraday transactions data. To confirm this phenomenon, we consider a directional series D_i for price movements, where D_i assumes the value +1, 0, and −1 for up, unchanged, and down price movement, respectively, for the ith transaction. The ACF of $\{D_i\}$ has a single spike at lag 1 with value −0.389, which is highly significant for a sample size of 59,837 and confirms the price reversal in consecutive trades.

As a second illustration, we consider the transactions data of IBM stock in December 1999 obtained from the TAQ database. The normal trading hours are

Table 5.2. Two-Way Classification of Price Movements in Consecutive Intraday Trades for IBM Stock[a]

	ith Trade			
$(i-1)$th Trade	+	0	−	Margin
+	441	5498	3948	9887
0	4867	29779	5473	40119
−	4580	4841	410	9831
Margin	9888	40118	9831	59837

[a] The price movements are classified into "up," "unchanged," and "down." The data span is from 11/01/90 to 1/31/91.

from 9:30 am to 4:00 pm Eastern time, except for December 31 when the market closed at 1:00 pm. Comparing with the 1990–1991 data, two important changes have occurred. First, the number of intraday tradings has increased sixfold. There were 134,120 intraday tradings in December 1999 alone. The increased trading intensity also increased the chance of multiple transactions within a second. The percentage of trades with zero time duration doubled to 22.98%. At the extreme, there were 42 transactions within a given second that happened twice on December 3, 1999. Second, the tick size of price movement was \$1/16 = \$0.0625 instead of \$1/8. The change in tick size should reduce the bid–ask spread. Figure 5.3 shows the daily number of transactions in the new sample. Figure 5.4a shows the time plot of time durations between trades, measured in seconds, and Figure 5.4b is the time plot of price changes in consecutive intraday trades, measured in multiples of the tick size of \$1/16. As expected, Figures 5.3 and 5.4a show clearly the inverse relationship between the daily number of transactions and the time interval between trades. Figure 5.4b shows two unusual price movements for IBM stock on December 3, 1999. They were a drop of 63 ticks followed by an immediate jump of 64 ticks and a drop of 68 ticks followed immediately by a jump of 68 ticks. Unusual price movements like these occurred infrequently in intraday transactions.

Focusing on trades recorded within regular trading hours, we have 61,149 trades out of 133,475 with no price change. This is about 45.8% and substantially lower than that between November 1990 and January 1991. It seems that reducing the tick size increased the chance of a price change. Table 5.3 gives the percentages of trades associated with a price change. The price movements remain approximately symmetric with respect to zero. Large price movements in intraday tradings are still relatively rare.

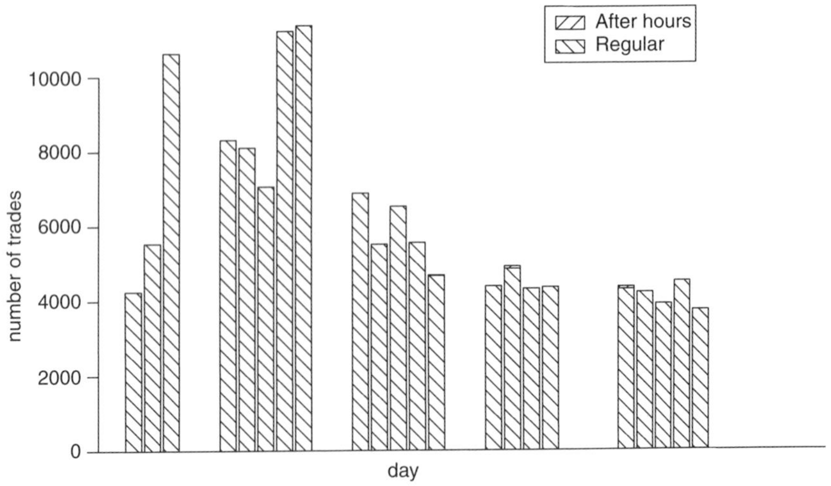

Figure 5.3. IBM transactions data for December 1999. The plot shows the number of transactions in each trading day with the after-hours portion denoting the number of trades with time stamp after 4:00 pm.

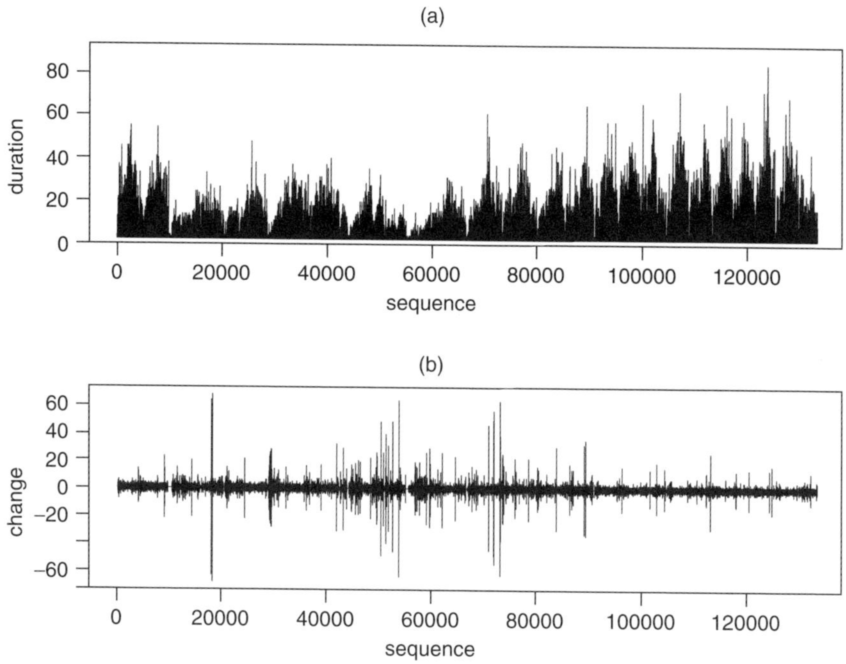

Figure 5.4. IBM transactions data for December 1999. (a) The time plot of time durations between trades. (b) The time plot of price changes in consecutive trades measured in multiples of the tick size of \$1/16. Only data during normal trading hours are included.

Table 5.3. Percentages of Intraday Transactions Associated with a Price Change for IBM Stock Traded in December 1999[a]

Size	1	2	3	4	5	6	7	>7
				Upward Movements				
Percentage	18.03	5.80	1.79	0.66	0.25	0.15	0.09	0.32
				Downward Movements				
Percentage	18.24	5.57	1.79	0.71	0.24	0.17	0.10	0.31

[a]The percentage of transactions without price change is 45.8% and the total number of transactions recorded within regular trading hours is 133,475. The size is measured in multiples of tick size \$1/16.

Remark. The recordkeeping of high-frequency data is often not as good as that of observations taken at lower frequencies. Data cleaning becomes a necessity in high-frequency data analysis. For transactions data, missing observations may happen in many ways, and the accuracy of the exact transaction time might be questionable for some trades. For example, recorded trading times may be beyond 4:00 pm Eastern time even before the opening of after-hours tradings. How to handle these observations deserves a careful study. A proper method of data cleaning requires a deep understanding of the way in which the market operates. As such, it is important to specify clearly and precisely the methods used in data cleaning. These methods must be taken into consideration in making inference. □

Again, let t_i be the calendar time, measured in seconds from midnight, when the ith transaction took place. Let P_{t_i} be the transaction price. The price change from the $(i-1)$th to the ith trade is $y_i \equiv \Delta P_{t_i} = P_{t_i} - P_{t_{i-1}}$ and the time duration is $\Delta t_i = t_i - t_{i-1}$. Here it is understood that the subscript i in Δt_i and y_i denotes the time sequence of transactions, not the calendar time. In what follows, we consider models for y_i and Δt_i both individually and jointly.

5.4 MODELS FOR PRICE CHANGES

The discreteness and concentration on "no change" make it difficult to model the intraday price changes. Campbell, Lo, and MacKinlay (1997) discuss several econometric models that have been proposed in the literature. Here we mention two models that have the advantage of employing explanatory variables to study the intraday price movements. The first model is the ordered probit model used by Hauseman, Lo, and MacKinlay (1992) to study the price movements in transactions data. The second model has been considered recently by McCulloch and Tsay (2000) and is a simplified version of the model proposed by Rydberg and Shephard (2003); see also Ghysels (2000).

5.4.1 Ordered Probit Model

Let y_i^* be the unobservable price change of the asset under study (i.e., $y_i^* = P_{t_i}^* - P_{t_{i-1}}^*$), where P_t^* is the *virtual* price of the asset at time t. The ordered probit model assumes that y_i^* is a continuous random variable and follows the model

$$y_i^* = \boldsymbol{x}_i \boldsymbol{\beta} + \epsilon_i, \tag{5.15}$$

where $\boldsymbol{x}_i$ is a p-dimensional row vector of explanatory variables available at time t_{i-1}, $\boldsymbol{\beta}$ is a $p \times 1$ parameter vector, $E(\epsilon_i|\boldsymbol{x}_i) = 0$, $\text{Var}(\epsilon_i|\boldsymbol{x}_i) = \sigma_i^2$, and $\text{Cov}(\epsilon_i, \epsilon_j) = 0$ for $i \neq j$. The conditional variance σ_i^2 is assumed to be a positive function of the explanatory variable $\boldsymbol{w}_i$—that is,

$$\sigma_i^2 = g(\boldsymbol{w}_i), \tag{5.16}$$

where $g(.)$ is a positive function. For financial transactions data, $\boldsymbol{w}_i$ may contain the time interval $t_i - t_{i-1}$ and some conditional heteroscedastic variables. Typically, one also assumes that the conditional distribution of ϵ_i given $\boldsymbol{x}_i$ and $\boldsymbol{w}_i$ is Gaussian.

Suppose that the observed price change y_i may assume k possible values. In theory, k can be infinity, but countable. In practice, k is finite and may involve combining several categories into a single value. For example, we have $k = 7$ in Table 5.1, where the first value "−3 ticks" means that the price change is −3 ticks or lower. We denote the k possible values as $\{s_1, \ldots, s_k\}$. The ordered probit model postulates the relationship between y_i and y_i^* as

$$y_i = s_j \quad \text{if} \quad \alpha_{j-1} < y_i^* \le \alpha_j, \qquad j = 1, \ldots, k, \tag{5.17}$$

where α_j are real numbers satisfying $-\infty = \alpha_0 < \alpha_1 < \cdots < \alpha_{k-1} < \alpha_k = \infty$. Under the assumption of conditional Gaussian distribution, we have

$$\begin{aligned}
P(y_i = s_j|\boldsymbol{x}_i, \boldsymbol{w}_i) &= P(\alpha_{j-1} < \boldsymbol{x}_i\boldsymbol{\beta} + \epsilon_i \le \alpha_j|\boldsymbol{x}_i, \boldsymbol{w}_i) \\
&= \begin{cases} P(\boldsymbol{x}_i\boldsymbol{\beta} + \epsilon_i \le \alpha_1|\boldsymbol{x}_i, \boldsymbol{w}_i) & \text{if } j = 1, \\ P(\alpha_{j-1} < \boldsymbol{x}_i\boldsymbol{\beta} + \epsilon_i \le \alpha_j|\boldsymbol{x}_i, \boldsymbol{w}_i) & \text{if } j = 2, \ldots, k-1, \\ P(\alpha_{k-1} < \boldsymbol{x}_i\boldsymbol{\beta} + \epsilon_i|\boldsymbol{x}_i, \boldsymbol{w}_i) & \text{if } j = k, \end{cases} \\
&= \begin{cases} \Phi\left[\dfrac{\alpha_1 - \boldsymbol{x}_i\boldsymbol{\beta}}{\sigma_i(\boldsymbol{w}_i)}\right] & \text{if } j = 1, \\ \Phi\left[\dfrac{\alpha_j - \boldsymbol{x}_i\boldsymbol{\beta}}{\sigma_i(\boldsymbol{w}_i)}\right] - \Phi\left[\dfrac{\alpha_{j-1} - \boldsymbol{x}_i\boldsymbol{\beta}}{\sigma_i(\boldsymbol{w}_i)}\right] & \text{if } j = 2, \ldots, k-1, \\ 1 - \Phi\left[\dfrac{\alpha_{k-1} - \boldsymbol{x}_i\boldsymbol{\beta}}{\sigma_i(\boldsymbol{w}_i)}\right] & \text{if } j = k, \end{cases}
\end{aligned} \tag{5.18}$$

where $\Phi(x)$ is the cumulative distribution function of the standard normal random variable evaluated at x, and we write $\sigma_i(\boldsymbol{w}_i)$ to denote that σ_i^2 is a positive function of $\boldsymbol{w}_i$. From the definition, an ordered probit model is driven by an unobservable continuous random variable. The observed values, which have a natural ordering, can be regarded as categories representing the underlying process.

The ordered probit model contains parameters $\boldsymbol{\beta}$, $\alpha_i (i = 1, \ldots, k-1)$, and those in the conditional variance function $\sigma_i(\boldsymbol{w}_i)$ in Eq. (5.16). These parameters can be estimated by the maximum likelihood or Markov chain Monte Carlo methods.

Example 5.1. Hauseman, Lo, and MacKinlay (1992) apply the ordered probit model to the 1988 transactions data of more than 100 stocks. Here we only report their result for IBM. There are 206,794 trades. The sample mean (standard deviation) of price change y_i, time duration Δt_i, and bid–ask spread are −0.0010(0.753), 27.21(34.13), and 1.9470(1.4625), respectively. The bid–ask spread is measured in ticks. The model used has nine categories for price movement, and the functional specifications are

$$\begin{aligned}
\boldsymbol{x}_i\boldsymbol{\beta} = \beta_1 \Delta t_i^* &+ \sum_{v=1}^{3} \beta_{v+1} y_{i-v} + \sum_{v=1}^{3} \beta_{v+4} \text{SP5}_{i-v} + \sum_{v=1}^{3} \beta_{v+7} \text{IBS}_{i-v} \\
&+ \sum_{v=1}^{3} \beta_{v+10}[T_\lambda(V_{i-v}) \times \text{IBS}_{i-v}],
\end{aligned} \tag{5.19}$$

$$\sigma_i^2(\boldsymbol{w}_i) = 1.0 + \gamma_1^2 \Delta t_i^* + \gamma_2^2 \text{AB}_{i-1}, \tag{5.20}$$

where $T_\lambda(V) = (V^\lambda - 1)/\lambda$ is the Box–Cox (1964) transformation of V with $\lambda \in [0, 1]$ and the explanatory variables are defined by the following:

- $\Delta t_i^* = (t_i - t_{i-1})/100$ is a rescaled time duration between the $(i-1)$th and ith trades with time measured in seconds.
- AB_{i-1} is the bid–ask spread prevailing at time t_{i-1} in ticks.
- y_{i-v} $(v = 1, 2, 3)$ is the lagged value of price change at t_{i-v} in ticks. With $k = 9$, the possible values of price changes are $\{-4, -3, -2, -1, 0, 1, 2, 3, 4\}$ in ticks.
- V_{i-v} $(v = 1, 2, 3)$ is the lagged value of dollar volume at the $(i-v)$th transaction, defined as the price of the $(i-v)$th transaction in dollars times the number of shares traded (denominated in hundreds of shares). That is, the dollar volume is in hundreds of dollars.
- SP5_{i-v} $(v = 1, 2, 3)$ is the 5-minute continuously compounded returns of the Standard and Poor's 500 index futures price for the contract maturing in the closest month beyond the month in which transaction $(i-v)$ occurred, where the return is computed with the futures price recorded 1 minute before the nearest round minute *prior* to t_{i-v} and the price recorded 5 minutes before this.
- IBS_{i-v} $(v = 1, 2, 3)$ is an indicator variable defined by

$$\text{IBS}_{i-v} = \begin{cases} 1 & \text{if } P_{i-v} > (P_{i-v}^a + P_{i-v}^b)/2, \\ 0 & \text{if } P_{i-v} = (P_{i-v}^a + P_{i-v}^b)/2, \\ -1 & \text{if } P_{i-v} < (P_{i-v}^a + P_{i-v}^b)/2, \end{cases}$$

where P_j^a and P_j^b are the ask and bid price at time t_j.

The parameter estimates and their t-ratios are given in Table 5.4. All the t-ratios are large except one, indicating that the estimates are highly significant. Such high t-ratios are not surprising as the sample size is large. For the heavily traded IBM stock, the estimation results suggest the following conclusions:

1. The boundary partitions are not equally spaced, but are almost symmetric with respect to zero.
2. The transaction duration Δt_i affects both the conditional mean and conditional variance of y_i in Eqs. (5.19) and (5.20).
3. The coefficients of lagged price changes are negative and highly significant, indicating *price reversals*.
4. As expected, the bid–ask spread at time t_{i-1} significantly affects the conditional variance.

Table 5.4. Parameter Estimates of the Ordered Probit Model in Eqs. (5.19) and (5.20) for the 1988 Transaction Data of IBM, Where t Denotes the t-Ratio[a]

Boundary Partitions of the Probit Model								
Parameter	α_1	α_2	α_3	α_4	α_5	α_6	α_7	α_8
Estimate	−4.67	−4.16	−3.11	−1.34	1.33	3.13	4.21	4.73
t	−145.7	−157.8	−171.6	−155.5	154.9	167.8	152.2	138.9
Equation Parameters of the Probit Model								
Parameter	γ_1	γ_2	β_1: Δt_i^*	β_2: y_{-1}	β_3	β_4	β_5	β_6
Estimate	0.40	0.52	−0.12	−1.01	−0.53	−0.21	1.12	−0.26
t	15.6	71.1	−11.4	−135.6	−85.0	−47.2	54.2	−12.1
Parameter	β_7	β_8	β_9:	β_{10}	β_{11}	β_{12}	β_{13}	
Estimate	0.01	−1.14	−0.37	−0.17	0.12	0.05	0.02	
t	0.26	−63.6	−21.6	−10.3	47.4	18.6	7.7	

[a]Reprinted with permission from Elsevier.

5.4.2 A Decomposition Model

An alternative approach to modeling price change is to decompose it into three components and use conditional specifications for the components; see Rydberg and Shephard (2003). The three components are an indicator for price change, the direction of price movement if there is a change, and the size of price change if a change occurs. Specifically, the price change at the ith transaction can be written as

$$y_i \equiv P_{t_i} - P_{t_{i-1}} = A_i D_i S_i, \tag{5.21}$$

where A_i is a binary variable defined as

$$A_i = \begin{cases} 1 & \text{if there is a price change at the } i\text{th trade,} \\ 0 & \text{if price remains the same at the } i\text{th trade,} \end{cases} \tag{5.22}$$

D_i is also a discrete variable signifying the *direction* of the price change if a change occurs—that is,

$$D_i|(A_i = 1) = \begin{cases} 1 & \text{if price increases at the } i\text{th trade,} \\ -1 & \text{if price drops at the } i\text{th trade,} \end{cases} \tag{5.23}$$

where $D_i|(A_i = 1)$ means that D_i is defined under the condition of $A_i = 1$, and S_i is the size of the price change in ticks if there is a change at the ith trade and $S_i = 0$ if there is no price change at the ith trade. When there is a price change, S_i is a positive integer-valued random variable.

Note that D_i is not needed when $A_i = 0$, and there is a natural ordering in the decomposition. D_i is well defined only when $A_i = 1$ and S_i is meaningful when $A_i = 1$ and D_i is given. Model specification under the decomposition makes use of the ordering.

Let F_i be the information set available at the ith transaction. Examples of elements in F_i are Δt_{i-j}, A_{i-j}, D_{i-j}, and S_{i-j} for $j \geq 0$. The evolution of price change under model (5.21) can then be partitioned as

$$P(y_i|F_{i-1}) = P(A_i D_i S_i|F_{i-1}) = P(S_i|D_i, A_i, F_{i-1})P(D_i|A_i, F_{i-1})P(A_i|F_{i-1}). \tag{5.24}$$

Since A_i is a binary variable, it suffices to consider the evolution of the probability $p_i = P(A_i = 1)$ over time. We assume that

$$\ln\left(\frac{p_i}{1-p_i}\right) = \boldsymbol{x}_i\boldsymbol{\beta} \quad \text{or} \quad p_i = \frac{e^{\boldsymbol{x}_i\boldsymbol{\beta}}}{1+e^{\boldsymbol{x}_i\boldsymbol{\beta}}}, \tag{5.25}$$

where $\boldsymbol{x}_i$ is a finite-dimensional vector consisting of elements of F_{i-1} and $\boldsymbol{\beta}$ is a parameter vector. Conditioned on $A_i = 1$, D_i is also a binary variable, and we use the following model for $\delta_i = P(D_i = 1|A_i = 1)$:

$$\ln\left(\frac{\delta_i}{1-\delta_i}\right) = \boldsymbol{z}_i\boldsymbol{\gamma} \quad \text{or} \quad \delta_i = \frac{e^{\boldsymbol{z}_i\boldsymbol{\gamma}}}{1+e^{\boldsymbol{z}_i\boldsymbol{\gamma}}}, \tag{5.26}$$

where $\boldsymbol{z}_i$ is a finite-dimensional vector consisting of elements of F_{i-1} and $\boldsymbol{\gamma}$ is a parameter vector. To allow for asymmetry between positive and negative price changes, we assume that

$$S_i|(D_i, A_i = 1) \sim 1 + \begin{cases} g(\lambda_{u,i}) & \text{if } D_i = 1, A_i = 1, \\ g(\lambda_{d,i}) & \text{if } D_i = -1, A_i = 1, \end{cases} \tag{5.27}$$

where $g(\lambda)$ is a geometric distribution with parameter λ and the parameters $\lambda_{j,i}$ evolve over time as

$$\ln\left(\frac{\lambda_{j,i}}{1-\lambda_{j,i}}\right) = \boldsymbol{w}_i\boldsymbol{\theta}_j \quad \text{or} \quad \lambda_{j,i} = \frac{e^{\boldsymbol{w}_i\boldsymbol{\theta}_j}}{1+e^{\boldsymbol{w}_i\boldsymbol{\theta}_j}}, \qquad j = u, d, \tag{5.28}$$

where $\boldsymbol{w}_i$ is again a finite-dimensional explanatory variable in F_{i-1} and $\boldsymbol{\theta}_j$ is a parameter vector.

In Eq. (5.27), the probability mass function of a random variable x, which follows the geometric distribution $g(\lambda)$, is

$$p(x = m) = \lambda(1-\lambda)^m, \quad m = 0, 1, 2, \ldots.$$

We added 1 to the geometric distribution so that the price change, if it occurs, is at least 1 tick. In Eq. (5.28), we take the logistic transformation to ensure that $\lambda_{j,i} \in [0, 1]$.

The previous specification classifies the ith trade, or transaction, into one of three categories:

1. *No price change*: $A_i = 0$ and the associated probability is $(1 - p_i)$.
2. *A price increase*: $A_i = 1$, $D_i = 1$, and the associated probability is $p_i\delta_i$. The size of the price increase is governed by $1 + g(\lambda_{u,i})$.

3. *A price drop*: $A_i = 1$, $D_i = -1$, and the associated probability is $p_i(1-\delta_i)$. The size of the price drop is governed by $1 + g(\lambda_{d,i})$.

Let $I_i(j)$ for $j = 1, 2, 3$ be the indicator variables of the prior three categories. That is, $I_i(j) = 1$ if the jth category occurs and $I_i(j) = 0$ otherwise. The log likelihood function of Eq. (5.24) becomes

$$\begin{aligned}
&\ln[P(y_i|F_{i-1})] \\
&\quad = I_i(1)\ln[(1-p_i)] + I_i(2)[\ln(p_i) + \ln(\delta_i) + \ln(\lambda_{u,i}) + (S_i - 1)\ln(1-\lambda_{u,i})] \\
&\qquad + I_i(3)[\ln(p_i) + \ln(1-\delta_i) + \ln(\lambda_{d,i}) + (S_i - 1)\ln(1-\lambda_{d,i})],
\end{aligned}$$

and the overall log likelihood function is

$$\ln[P(y_1, \ldots, y_n|F_0)] = \sum_{i=1}^{n} \ln[P(y_i|F_{i-1})], \tag{5.29}$$

which is a function of parameters $\boldsymbol{\beta}$, $\boldsymbol{\gamma}$, $\boldsymbol{\theta}_u$, and $\boldsymbol{\theta}_d$.

Example 5.2. We illustrate the decomposition model by analyzing the intraday transactions of IBM stock from November 1, 1990 to January 31, 1991. There were 63 trading days and 59,838 intraday transactions in the normal trading hours. The explanatory variables used are:

1. A_{i-1}: the action indicator of the previous trade (i.e., the $(i-1)$th trade within a trading day).
2. D_{i-1}: the direction indicator of the previous trade.
3. S_{i-1}: the size of the previous trade.
4. V_{i-1}: the volume of the previous trade, divided by 1000.
5. Δt_{i-1}: time duration from the $(i-2)$th to $(i-1)$th trade.
6. BA_i: The bid–ask spread prevailing at the time of transaction.

Because we use lag-1 explanatory variables, the actual sample size is 59,775. It turns out that V_{i-1}, Δt_{i-1}, and BA_i are not statistically significant for the model entertained. Thus, only the first three explanatory variables are used. The model employed is

$$\begin{aligned}
\ln\left(\frac{p_i}{1-p_i}\right) &= \beta_0 + \beta_1 A_{i-1}, \\
\ln\left(\frac{\delta_i}{1-\delta_i}\right) &= \gamma_0 + \gamma_1 D_{i-1}, \\
\ln\left(\frac{\lambda_{u,i}}{1-\lambda_{u,i}}\right) &= \theta_{u,0} + \theta_{u,1} S_{i-1}, \\
\ln\left(\frac{\lambda_{d,i}}{1-\lambda_{d,i}}\right) &= \theta_{d,0} + \theta_{d,1} S_{i-1}.
\end{aligned} \tag{5.30}$$

Table 5.5. Parameter Estimates of the ADS Model in Eq. (5.30) for IBM Intraday Transactions from 11/01/90 to 1/31/91

Parameter	β_0	β_1	γ_0	γ_1
Estimate	−1.057	0.962	−0.067	−2.307
Standard error	0.104	0.044	0.023	0.056
Parameter	$\theta_{u,0}$	$\theta_{u,1}$	$\theta_{d,0}$	$\theta_{d,1}$
Estimate	2.235	−0.670	2.085	−0.509
Standard error	0.029	0.050	0.187	0.139

The parameter estimates, using the log likelihood function in Eq. (5.29), are given in Table 5.5. The estimated simple model shows some dynamic dependence in the price change. In particular, the trade-by-trade price changes of IBM stock exhibit some appealing features:

1. The probability of a price change depends on the previous price change. Specifically, we have

$$P(A_i = 1|A_{i-1} = 0) = 0.258, \quad P(A_i = 1|A_{i-1} = 1) = 0.476.$$

The result indicates that a price change may occur in clusters and, as expected, most transactions are without price change. When no price change occurred at the $(i-1)$th trade, then only about one out of four trades in the subsequent transaction has a price change. When there is a price change at the $(i-1)$th transaction, the probability of a price change in the ith trade increases to about 0.5.

2. The direction of price change is governed by

$$P(D_i = 1|F_{i-1}, A_i) = \begin{cases} 0.483 & \text{if } D_{i-1} = 0 \text{ (i.e., } A_{i-1} = 0), \\ 0.085 & \text{if } D_{i-1} = 1,\ A_i = 1, \\ 0.904 & \text{if } D_{i-1} = -1,\ A_i = 1. \end{cases}$$

This result says that (a) if no price change occurred at the $(i-1)$th trade, then the chances for a price increase or decrease at the ith trade are about even; and (b) the probabilities of consecutive price increases or decreases are very low. The probability of a price increase at the ith trade given that a price change occurs at the ith trade and there was a price increase at the $(i-1)$th trade is only 8.6%. However, the probability of a price increase is about 90% given that a price change occurs at the ith trade and there was a price decrease at the $(i-1)$th trade. Consequently, this result shows the effect of bid–ask bounce and supports price reversals in high-frequency trading.

3. There is weak evidence suggesting that big price changes have a higher probability to be followed by another big price change. Consider the size of a price

increase. We have

$$S_i|(D_i = 1) \sim 1 + g(\lambda_{u,i}), \quad \lambda_{u,i} = 2.235 - 0.670S_{i-1}.$$

Using the probability mass function of a geometric distribution, we obtain that the probability of a price increase by one tick is 0.827 at the ith trade if the transaction results in a price increase and $S_{i-1} = 1$. The probability reduces to 0.709 if $S_{i-1} = 2$ and to 0.556 if $S_{i-1} = 3$. Consequently, the probability of a large S_i is proportional to S_{i-1} given that there is a price increase at the ith trade.

A difference between the ADS and ordered probit models is that the former does not require any truncation or grouping in the size of a price change.

5.5 DURATION MODELS

Duration models are concerned with time intervals between trades. Longer durations indicate lack of trading activities, which in turn signify a period of no new information. The dynamic behavior of durations thus contains useful information about intraday market activities. Using concepts similar to the ARCH models for volatility, Engle and Russell (1998) propose an autoregressive conditional duration (ACD) model to describe the evolution of time durations for (heavily traded) stocks. Zhang, Russell, and Tsay (2001a) extend the ACD model to account for nonlinearity and structural breaks in the data. In this section, we introduce some simple duration models. As mentioned before, intraday transactions exhibit some diurnal pattern. Therefore, we focus on the adjusted time duration

$$\Delta t_i^* = \Delta t_i / f(t_i), \tag{5.31}$$

where $f(t_i)$ is a deterministic function consisting of the cyclical component of Δt_i. Obviously, $f(t_i)$ depends on the underlying asset and the systematic behavior of the market. In practice, there are many ways to estimate $f(t_i)$, but no single method dominates the others in terms of statistical properties. A common approach is to use smoothing spline. Here we use simple quadratic functions and indicator variables to take care of the deterministic component of daily trading activities.

For the IBM data employed in the illustration of ADS models, we assume

$$f(t_i) = \exp[d(t_i)], \quad d(t_i) = \beta_0 + \sum_{j=1}^{7} \beta_j f_j(t_i), \tag{5.32}$$

where

$$f_1(t_i) = -\left(\frac{t_i - 43200}{14400}\right)^2, \quad f_3(t_i) = \begin{cases} -\left(\dfrac{t_i - 38700}{7500}\right)^2 & \text{if } t_i < 43200 \\ 0 & \text{otherwise,} \end{cases}$$

$$f_2(t_i) = -\left(\frac{t_i - 48300}{9300}\right)^2, \quad f_4(t_i) = \begin{cases} -\left(\dfrac{t_i - 48600}{9000}\right)^2 & \text{if } t_i \geq 43200 \\ 0 & \text{otherwise,} \end{cases}$$

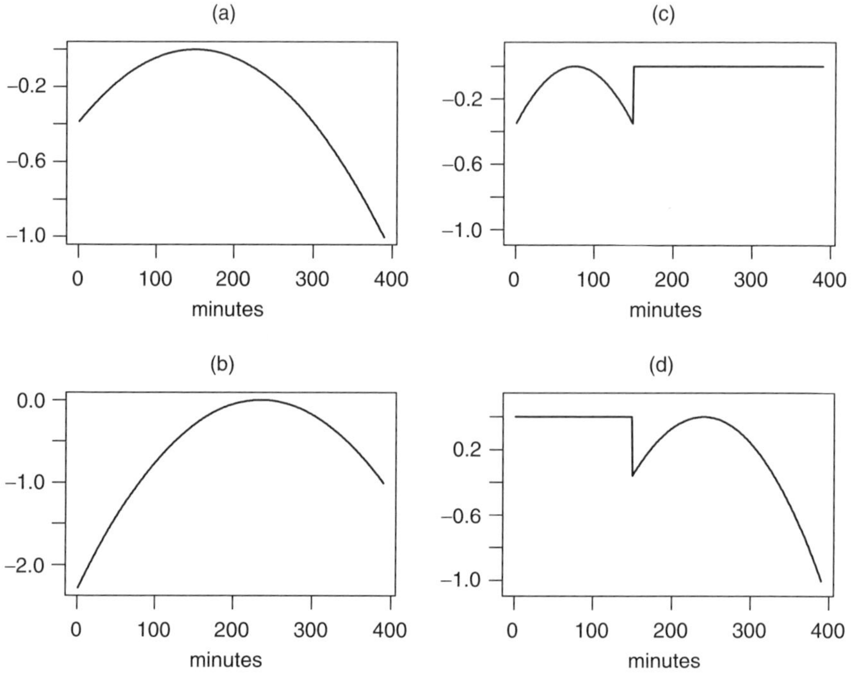

Figure 5.5. Quadratic functions used to remove the deterministic component of IBM intraday trading durations: (a)–(d) are the functions $f_1(.)$ to $f_4(.)$ of Eq. (5.32), respectively.

$f_5(t_i)$ and $f_6(t_i)$ are indicator variables for the first and second 5 minutes of market opening (i.e., $f_5(.) = 1$ if and only if t_i is between 9:30 am and 9:35 am Eastern time), and $f_7(t_i)$ is the indicator for the last 30 minutes of daily trading (i.e., $f_7(t_i) = 1$ if and only if the trade occurred between 3:30 pm and 4:00 pm Eastern time). Figure 5.5 shows the plot of $f_i(.)$ for $i = 1, \ldots, 4$, where the time scale on the x-axis is in minutes. Note that $f_3(43200) = f_4(43200)$, where 43,200 corresponds to 12:00 noon.

The coefficients β_j of Eq. (5.32) are obtained by the least squares method of the linear regression

$$\ln(\Delta t_i) = \beta_0 + \sum_{j=1}^{7} \beta_j f_j(t_i) + \epsilon_i.$$

The fitted model is

$$\begin{aligned}\ln(\widehat{\Delta t_i}) &= 2.555 + 0.159 f_1(t_i) + 0.270 f_2(t_i) + 0.384 f_3(t_i) \\ &\quad + 0.061 f_4(t_i) - 0.611 f_5(t_i) - 0.157 f_6(t_i) + 0.073 f_7(t_i).\end{aligned}$$

Figure 5.6 shows the time plot of average durations in 5-minute time intervals over the 63 trading days before and after adjusting for the deterministic component. Figure 5.6a shows the average durations of Δt_i and, as expected, exhibits a diurnal

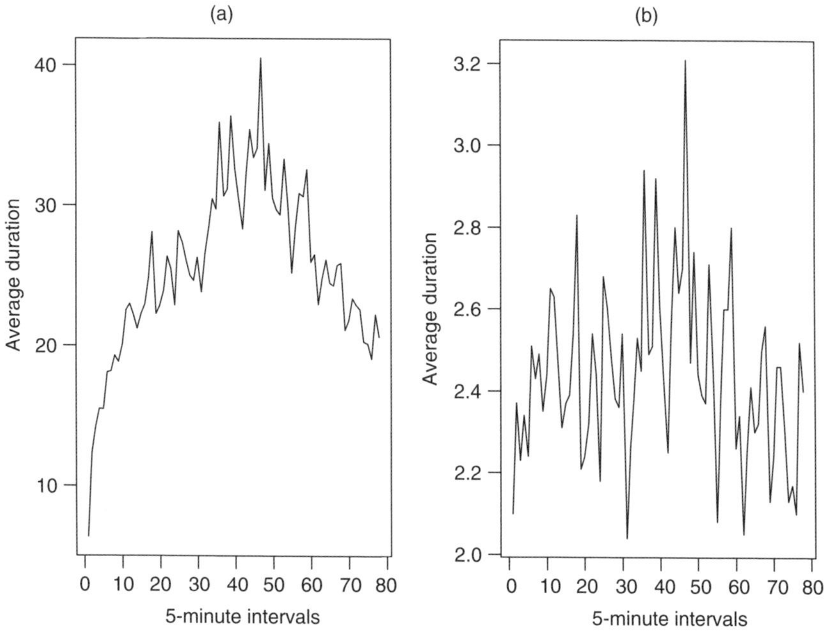

Figure 5.6. IBM transactions data from 11/01/90 to 1/31/91: (a) the average durations in 5-minute time intervals and (b) the average durations in 5-minute time intervals after adjusting for the deterministic component.

pattern. Figure 5.6b shows the average durations of Δt_i^* (i.e., after the adjustment), and the diurnal pattern is largely removed.

5.5.1 The ACD Model

The autoregressive conditional duration (ACD) model uses the idea of GARCH models to study the dynamic structure of the adjusted duration Δt_i^* of Eq. (5.31). For ease in notation, we define $x_i = \Delta t_i^*$.

Let $\psi_i = E(x_i|F_{i-1})$ be the conditional expectation of the adjusted duration between the $(i-1)$th and ith trades, where F_{i-1} is the information set available at the $(i-1)$th trade. In other words, ψ_i is the expected adjusted duration given F_{i-1}. The basic ACD model is defined as

$$x_i = \psi_i \epsilon_i, \tag{5.33}$$

where $\{\epsilon_i\}$ is a sequence of independent and identically distributed non-negative random variables such that $E(\epsilon_i) = 1$. In Engle and Russell (1998), ϵ_i follows a standard exponential or a standardized Weibull distribution, and ψ_i assumes the form

$$\psi_i = \omega + \sum_{j=1}^{r} \gamma_j x_{i-j} + \sum_{j=1}^{s} \omega_j \psi_{i-j}. \tag{5.34}$$

Such a model is referred to as an ACD(r, s) model. When the distribution of ϵ_i is exponential, the resulting model is called an EACD(r, s) model. Similarly, if ϵ_i follows a Weibull distribution, the model is a WACD(r, s) model. If necessary, readers are referred to Appendix A for a quick review of exponential and Weibull distributions.

Similar to GARCH models, the process $\eta_i = x_i - \psi_i$ is a martingale difference sequence (i.e., $E(\eta_i|F_{i-1}) = 0$), and the ACD(r, s) model can be written as

$$x_i = \omega + \sum_{j=1}^{\max(r,s)} (\gamma_j + \omega_j)x_{i-j} - \sum_{j=1}^{s} \omega_j \eta_{i-j} + \eta_j, \tag{5.35}$$

which is in the form of an ARMA process with non-Gaussian innovations. It is understood here that $\gamma_j = 0$ for $j > r$ and $\omega_j = 0$ for $j > s$. Such a representation can be used to obtain the basic conditions for weak stationarity of the ACD model. For instance, taking expectation on both sides of Eq. (5.35) and assuming weak stationarity, we have

$$E(x_i) = \frac{\omega}{1 - \sum_{j=1}^{\max(r,s)} (\gamma_j + \omega_j)}.$$

Therefore, we assume $\omega > 0$ and $1 > \sum_j (\gamma_j + \omega_j)$ because the expected duration is positive. As another application of Eq. (5.35), we study properties of the EACD(1,1) model.

EACD(1,1) Model

An EACD(1,1) model can be written as

$$x_i = \psi_i \epsilon_i, \quad \psi_i = \omega + \gamma_1 x_{i-1} + \omega_1 \psi_{i-1}, \tag{5.36}$$

where ϵ_i follows the standard exponential distribution. Using the moments of a standard exponential distribution in Appendix A, we have $E(\epsilon_i) = 1$, $\text{Var}(\epsilon_i) = 1$, and $E(\epsilon_i^2) = \text{Var}(x_i) + [E(x_i)]^2 = 2$. Assuming that x_i is weakly stationary (i.e., the first two moments of x_i are time-invariant), we derive the variance of x_i. First, taking the expectation of Eq. (5.36), we have

$$E(x_i) = E[E(\psi_i \epsilon_i|F_{i-1})] = E(\psi_i), \quad E(\psi_i) = \omega + \gamma_1 E(x_{i-1}) + \omega_1 E(\psi_{i-1}). \tag{5.37}$$

Under weak stationarity, $E(\psi_i) = E(\psi_{i-1})$ so that Eq. (5.37) gives

$$\mu_x \equiv E(x_i) = E(\psi_i) = \frac{\omega}{1 - \gamma_1 - \omega_1}. \tag{5.38}$$

Next, because $E(\epsilon_i^2) = 2$, we have $E(x_i^2) = E[E(\psi_i^2 \epsilon_i^2|F_{i-1})] = 2E(\psi_i^2)$.

Taking the square of ψ_i in Eq. (5.36) and the expectation and using weak stationarity of ψ_i and x_i, we have, after some algebra, that

$$E(\psi_i^2) = \mu_x^2 \times \frac{1-(\gamma_1+\omega_1)^2}{1-2\gamma_1^2-\omega_1^2-2\gamma_1\omega_1}. \tag{5.39}$$

Finally, using $\mathrm{Var}(x_i) = E(x_i^2) - [E(x_i)]^2$ and $E(x_i^2) = 2E(\psi_i^2)$, we have

$$\mathrm{Var}(x_i) = 2E(\psi_i^2) - \mu_x^2 = \mu_x^2 \times \frac{1-\omega_1^2-2\gamma_1\omega_1}{1-\omega_1^2-2\gamma_1\omega_1-2\gamma_1^2},$$

where μ_x is defined in Eq. (5.38). This result shows that, to have time-invariant unconditional variance, the EACD(1,1) model in Eq. (5.36) must satisfy $1 > 2\gamma_1^2 + \omega_1^2 + 2\gamma_1\omega_1$. The variance of a WACD(1,1) model can be obtained by using the same techniques and the first two moments of a standardized Weibull distribution.

ACD Models with a Generalized Gamma Distribution

In the statistical literature, intensity function is often expressed in terms of hazard function. As shown in Appendix B, the hazard function of an EACD model is constant over time and that of a WACD model is a monotonous function. These hazard functions are rather restrictive in application as the intensity function of stock transactions might not be constant or monotone over time. To increase the flexibility of the associated hazard function, Zhang, Russell, and Tsay (2001a) employ a (standardized) generalized gamma distribution for ϵ_i. See Appendix A for some basic properties of a generalized gamma distribution. The resulting hazard function may assume various patterns, including U shape or inverted U shape. We refer to an ACD model with innovations that follow a generalized gamma distribution as a GACD(r, s) model.

5.5.2 Simulation

To illustrate ACD processes, we generated 500 observations from the ACD(1,1) model

$$x_i = \psi_i\epsilon_i, \qquad \psi_i = 0.3 + 0.2x_{i-1} + 0.7\psi_{i-1} \tag{5.40}$$

using two different innovational distributions for ϵ_i. In case 1, ϵ_i is assumed to follow a standardized Weibull distribution with parameter $\alpha = 1.5$. In case 2, ϵ_i follows a (standardized) generalized gamma distribution with parameters $\kappa = 1.5$ and $\alpha = 0.5$.

Figure 5.7a shows the time plot of the WACD(1,1) series, whereas Figure 5.8a is the GACD(1,1) series. Figure 5.9 plots the histograms of both simulated series. The difference between the two models is evident. Finally, the sample ACFs of the two simulated series are shown in Figure 5.10a and Figure 5.11b, respectively. The serial dependence of the data is clearly seen.

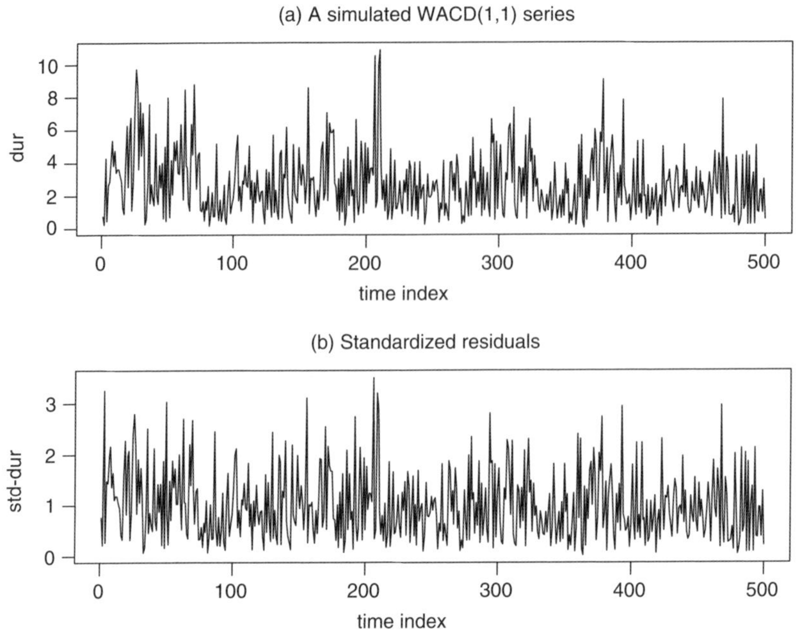

Figure 5.7. A simulated WACD(1,1) series in Eq. (5.40): (a) the original series and (b) the standardized series after estimation. There are 500 observations.

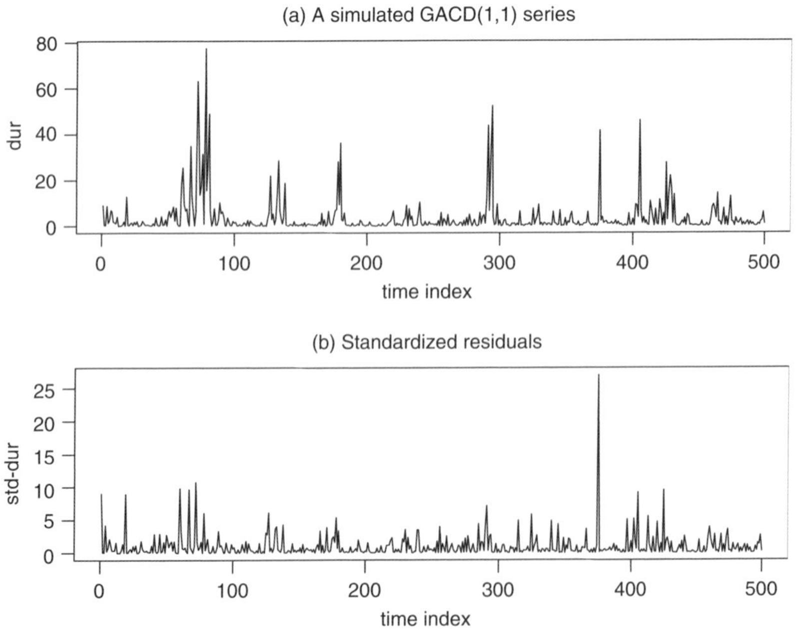

Figure 5.8. A simulated GACD(1,1) series in Eq. (5.40): (a) the original series and (b) the standardized series after estimation. There are 500 observations.

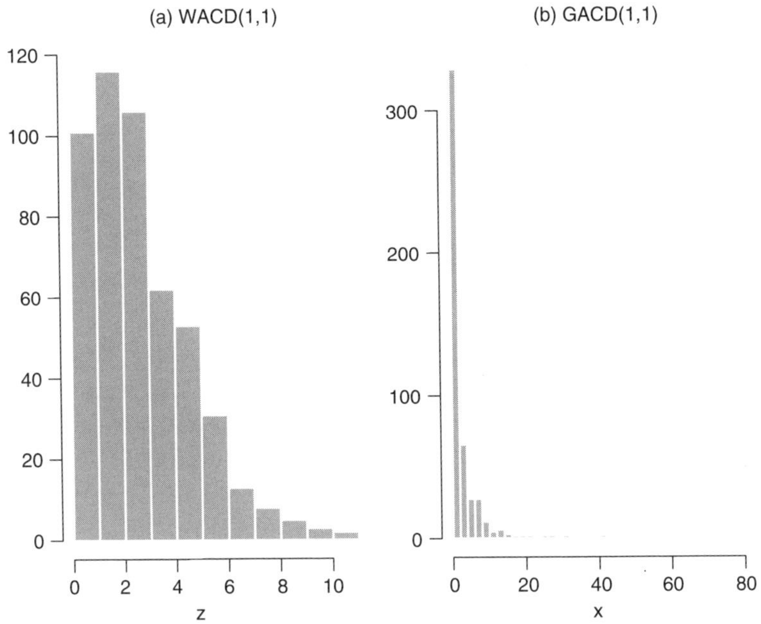

Figure 5.9. Histograms of simulated duration processes with 500 observations: (a) WACD(1,1) model and (b) GACD(1,1) model.

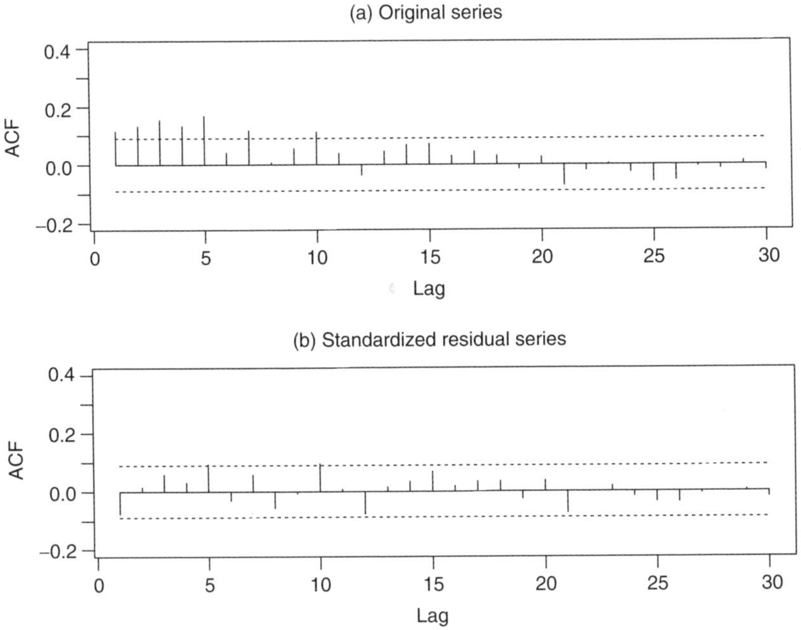

Figure 5.10. The sample autocorrelation function of a simulated WACD(1,1) series with 500 observations: (a) the original series and (b) the standardized residual series.

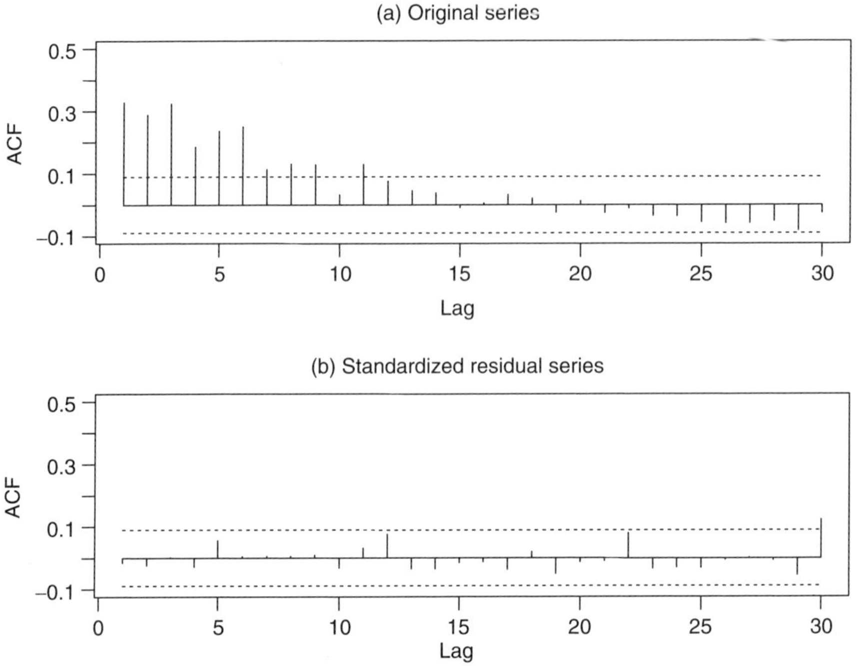

Figure 5.11. The sample autocorrelation function of a simulated GACD(1,1) series with 500 observations: (a) the original series and (b) the standardized residual series.

5.5.3 Estimation

For an ACD(r, s) model, let $i_o = \max(r, s)$ and $\boldsymbol{x}_t = (x_1, \ldots, x_t)'$. The likelihood function of the durations $x_1, \ldots, x_T$ is

$$f(\boldsymbol{x}_T|\boldsymbol{\theta}) = \left[\prod_{i=i_o+1}^{T} f(x_i|F_{i-1}, \boldsymbol{\theta})\right] \times f(\boldsymbol{x}_{i_o}|\boldsymbol{\theta}),$$

where $\boldsymbol{\theta}$ denotes the vector of model parameters, and T is the sample size. The marginal probability density function $f(\boldsymbol{x}_{i_o}|\boldsymbol{\theta})$ of the previous equation is rather complicated for a general ACD model. Because its impact on the likelihood function is diminishing as the sample size T increases, this marginal density is often ignored, resulting in use of the conditional likelihood method. For a WACD model, we use the probability density function (pdf) of Eq. (5.55) and obtain the conditional log likelihood function

$$\ell(\boldsymbol{x}|\boldsymbol{\theta}, \boldsymbol{x}_{i_o}) = \sum_{i=i_0+1}^{T} \alpha \ln\left[\Gamma\left(1 + \frac{1}{\alpha}\right)\right] + \ln\left(\frac{\alpha}{x_i}\right) + \alpha \ln\left(\frac{x_i}{\psi_i}\right) - \left(\frac{\Gamma(1 + 1/\alpha)x_i}{\psi_i}\right)^{\alpha}, \tag{5.41}$$

where $\psi_i = \omega + \sum_{j=1}^{r} \gamma_j x_{i-j} + \sum_{j=1}^{s} \omega_j \psi_{i-j}, \boldsymbol{\theta} = (\omega, \gamma_1, \ldots, \gamma_r, \omega_1, \ldots, \omega_s, \alpha)'$ and $\boldsymbol{x} = (x_{i_o+1}, \ldots, x_T)'$. When $\alpha = 1$, the (conditional) log likelihood function reduces to that of an EACD(r, s) model.

For a GACD(r, s) model, the conditional log likelihood function is

$$\ell(\boldsymbol{x}|\boldsymbol{\theta}, \boldsymbol{x}_{i_o}) = \sum_{i=i_o+1}^{T} \ln\left(\frac{\alpha}{\Gamma(\kappa)}\right) + (\kappa\alpha - 1)\ln(x_i) - \kappa\alpha\ln(\lambda\psi_i) - \left(\frac{x_i}{\lambda\psi_i}\right)^{\alpha}, \tag{5.42}$$

where $\lambda = \Gamma(\kappa)/\Gamma(\kappa + 1/\alpha)$ and the parameter vector $\boldsymbol{\theta}$ now also includes κ. As expected, when $\kappa = 1$, $\lambda = 1/\Gamma(1 + 1/\alpha)$ and the log likelihood function in Eq. (5.42) reduces to that of a WACD(r, s) model in Eq. (5.41). This log likelihood function can be rewritten in many ways to simplify the estimation.

Under some regularity conditions, the conditional maximum likelihood estimates are asymptotically normal; see Engle and Russell (1998) and the references therein. In practice, simulation can be used to obtain finite-sample reference distributions for the problem of interest once a duration model is specified.

Example 5.3. (Simulated ACD(1,1) series continued). Consider the simulated WACD(1,1) and GACD(1,1) series of Eq. (5.40). We apply the conditional likelihood method and obtain the results in Table 5.6. The estimates appear to be reasonable. Let $\hat{\psi}_i$ be the 1-step ahead prediction of ψ_i and $\hat{\epsilon}_i = x_i/\hat{\psi}_i$ be the standardized series, which can be regarded as standardized residuals of the series. If the model is adequately specified, $\{\hat{\epsilon}_i\}$ should behave as a sequence of independent and identically distributed random variables. Figure 5.7b and Figure 5.8b show the time plot of $\hat{\epsilon}_i$ for both models. The sample ACF of $\hat{\epsilon}_i$ for both fitted models are shown in Figure 5.10b and Figure 5.11b, respectively. It is evident that no significant serial correlations are found in the $\hat{\epsilon}_i$ series.

Table 5.6. Estimation Results for Simulated ACD(1,1) Series with 500 Observations for WACD(1,1) Series and GACD(1,1) Series

WACD(1,1) Model					
Parameter	ω	γ_1	ω_1	α	
True	0.3	0.2	0.7	1.5	
Estimate	0.364	0.100	0.767	1.477	
Standard error	(0.139)	(0.025)	(0.060)	(0.052)	
GACD(1,1) Model					
Parameter	ω	γ_1	ω_1	α	κ
True	0.3	0.2	0.7	0.5	1.5
Estimate	0.401	0.343	0.561	0.436	2.077
Standard error	(0.117)	(0.074)	(0.065)	(0.078)	(0.653)

Example 5.4. As an illustration of duration models, we consider the transaction durations of IBM stock on five consecutive trading days from November 1 to November 7, 1990. Focusing on positive transaction durations, we have 3534 observations. In addition, the data have been adjusted by removing the deterministic component in Eq. (5.32). That is, we employ 3534 positive adjusted durations as defined in Eq. (5.31).

Figure 5.12a shows the time plot of the adjusted (positive) durations for the first five trading days of November 1990, and Figure 5.13a gives the sample ACF of the series. There exist some serial correlations in the adjusted durations. We fit a WACD(1,1) model to the data and obtain the model

$$x_i = \psi_i \epsilon_i, \quad \psi_i = 0.169 + 0.064 x_{i-1} + 0.885 \psi_{i-1}, \tag{5.43}$$

where $\{\epsilon_i\}$ is a sequence of independent and identically distributed random variates that follow the standardized Weibull distribution with parameter $\hat{\alpha} = 0.879(0.012)$, where 0.012 is the estimated standard error. Standard errors of the estimates in Eq. (5.43) are 0.039, 0.010, and 0.018, respectively. All t-ratios of the estimates are greater than 4.2, indicating that the estimates are significant at the 1% level. Figure 5.12b shows the time plot of $\hat{\epsilon}_i = x_i/\hat{\psi}_i$, and Figure 5.13b provides the sample ACF of $\hat{\epsilon}_i$. The Ljung–Box statistics show $Q(10) = 4.96$ and $Q(20) =$

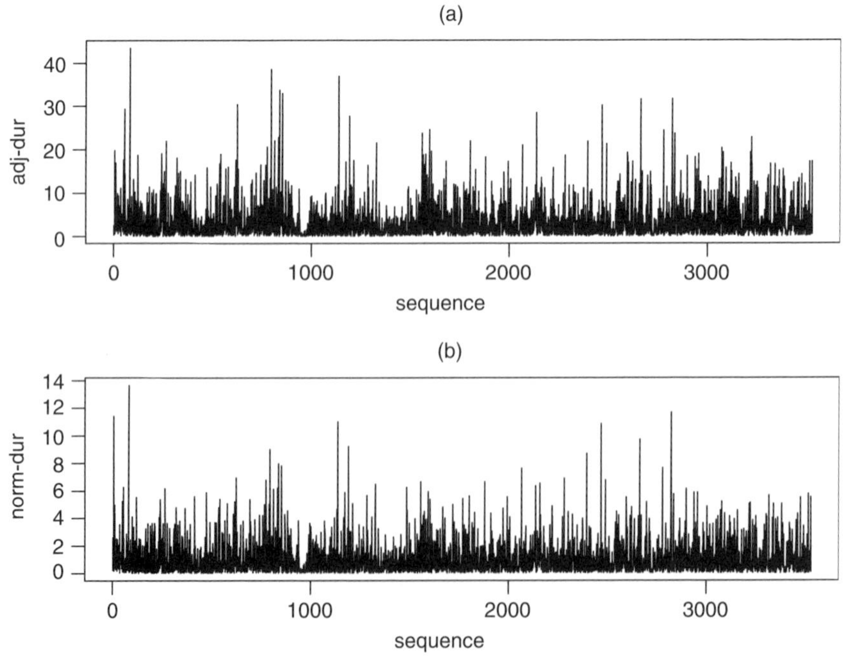

Figure 5.12. Time plots of durations for IBM stock traded in the first five trading days of November 1990: (a) the adjusted series and (b) the normalized innovations of an WACD(1,1) model. There are 3534 nonzero durations.

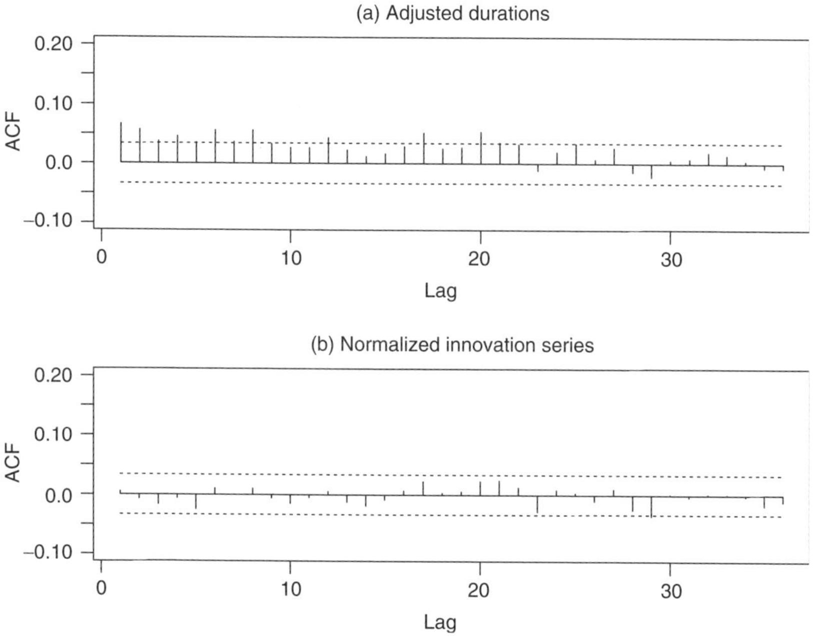

Figure 5.13. The sample autocorrelation function of adjusted durations for IBM stock traded in the first five trading days of November 1990: (a) the adjusted series and (b) the normalized innovations for a WACD(1,1) model.

10.75 for the $\hat{\epsilon}_i$ series. Clearly, the standardized innovations have no significant serial correlations. In fact, the sample autocorrelations of the squared series $\{\hat{\epsilon}_i^2\}$ are also small with $Q(10) = 6.20$ and $Q(20) = 11.16$, further confirming lack of serial dependence in the normalized innovations. In addition, the mean and standard deviation of a standardized Weibull distribution with $\alpha = 0.879$ are 1.00 and 1.14, respectively. These numbers are close to the sample mean and standard deviation of $\{\hat{\epsilon}_i\}$, which are 1.01 and 1.22, respectively. The fitted model seems adequate.

In model (5.43), the estimated coefficients show $\hat{\gamma}_1 + \hat{\omega}_1 \approx 0.949$, indicating certain persistence in the adjusted durations. The expected adjusted duration is $0.169/(1 - 0.064 - 0.885) = 3.31$ seconds, which is close to the sample mean 3.29 of the adjusted durations. The estimated α of the standardized Weibull distribution is 0.879, which is less than but close to 1. Thus, the conditional hazard function is monotonously decreasing at a slow rate.

If a generalized gamma distribution function is used for the innovations, then the fitted GACD(1,1) model is

$$x_i = \psi_i \epsilon_i, \quad \psi_i = 0.141 + 0.063x_{i-1} + 0.897\psi_{i-1}, \qquad (5.44)$$

where $\{\epsilon_i\}$ follows a standardized, generalized gamma distribution in Eq. (5.56) with parameters $\kappa = 4.248(1.046)$ and $\alpha = 0.395(0.053)$, where the number in parentheses denotes estimated standard error. Standard errors of the three parameters in Eq. (5.44) are 0.041, 0.010, and 0.019, respectively. All of the estimates are statistically significant at the 1% level. Again, the normalized innovational process $\{\hat{\epsilon}_i\}$ and its squared series have no significant serial correlation, where $\hat{\epsilon}_i = x_i/\hat{\psi}_i$ based on model (5.44). Specifically, for the $\hat{\epsilon}_i$ process, we have $Q(10) = 4.95$ and $Q(20) = 10.28$. For the $\hat{\epsilon}_i^2$ series, we have $Q(10) = 6.36$ and $Q(20) = 10.89$.

The expected duration of model (5.44) is 3.52, which is slightly greater than that of the WACD(1,1) model in Eq. (5.43). Similarly, the persistence parameter $\hat{\gamma}_1 + \hat{\omega}_1$ of model (5.44) is also slightly higher at 0.96.

Remark. Estimation of EACD models can be carried out by using programs for ARCH models with some minor modification; see Engle and Russell (1998). In this book, we use either the RATS program or some Fortran programs developed by the author to estimate the duration models. Limited experience indicates that it is harder to estimate a GACD model than an EACD or a WACD model. RATS programs used to estimate WACD and GACD models are given in Appendix C. □

5.6 NONLINEAR DURATION MODELS

Nonlinear features are also commonly found in high-frequency data. As an illustration, we apply some nonlinearity tests discussed in Chapter 4 to the normalized innovations $\hat{\epsilon}_i$ of the WACD(1,1) model for the IBM transaction durations in Example 5.4; see Eq. (5.43). Based on an AR(4) model, the test results are given in part (a) of Table 5.7. As expected from the model diagnostics of Example 5.4, the Ori-F test indicates no quadratic nonlinearity in the normalized innovations. However, the TAR-F test statistics suggest strong nonlinearity.

Based on the test results in Table 5.7, we entertain a threshold duration model with two regimes for the IBM intraday durations. The threshold variable is x_{t-1} (i.e., lag-1 adjusted duration). The estimated threshold value is 3.79. The fitted

Table 5.7. Nonlinearity Tests for IBM Transaction Durations from November 1 to November 7, 1990[a]

Type	Ori-F	TAR-F(1)	TAR-F(2)	TAR-F(3)	TAR-F(4)
	(a) Normalized Innovations of a WACD(1,1) Model				
Test	0.343	3.288	3.142	3.128	0.297
p-Value	0.969	0.006	0.008	0.008	0.915
	(b) Normalized Innovations of a Threshold WACD(1,1) Model				
Test	0.163	0.746	1.899	1.752	0.270
p-Value	0.998	0.589	0.091	0.119	0.929

[a]Only intraday durations are used. The number in parentheses of TAR-F tests denotes time delay.

threshold WACD(1,1) model is $x_i = \psi_i \epsilon_i$, where

$$\psi_i = \begin{cases} 0.020 + 0.257x_{i-1} + 0.847\psi_{i-1}, & \epsilon_i \sim w(0.901) \text{ if } x_{i-1} \le 3.79, \\ 1.808 + 0.027x_{i-1} + 0.501\psi_{i-1}, & \epsilon_i \sim w(0.845) \text{ if } x_{i-1} > 3.79, \end{cases} \tag{5.45}$$

where $w(\alpha)$ denotes a standardized Weibull distribution with parameter α. The number of observations in the two regimes are 2503 and 1030, respectively. In Eq. (5.45), the standard errors of the parameters for the first regime are 0.043, 0.041, 0.024, and 0.014, whereas those for the second regime are 0.526, 0.020, 0.147, and 0.020, respectively.

Consider the normalized innovations $\hat{\epsilon}_i = x_i/\hat{\psi}_i$ of the threshold WACD(1,1) model in Eq. (5.45). We obtain $Q(12) = 9.8$ and $Q(24) = 23.9$ for $\hat{\epsilon}_i$ and $Q(12) = 8.0$ and $Q(24) = 16.7$ for $\hat{\epsilon}_i^2$. Thus, there are no significant serial correlations in the $\hat{\epsilon}_i$ and $\hat{\epsilon}_i^2$ series. Furthermore, applying the same nonlinearity tests as before to this newly normalized innovational series $\hat{\epsilon}_i$, we detect no nonlinearity; see part (b) of Table 5.7. Consequently, the two-regime threshold WACD(1,1) model in Eq. (5.45) is adequate.

If we classify the two regimes as heavy and thin trading periods, then the threshold model suggests that the trading dynamics measured by intraday transaction durations are different between heavy and thin trading periods for IBM stock even after the adjustment of diurnal pattern. This is not surprising as market activities are often driven by the arrival of news and other information.

The estimated threshold WACD(1,1) model in Eq. (5.45) contains some insignificant parameters. We refine the model and obtain the result:

$$\psi_i = \begin{cases} 0.225x_{i-1} + 0.867\psi_{i-1}, & \epsilon_i \sim w(0.902) \text{ if } x_{i-1} \le 3.79, \\ 1.618 + 0.614\psi_{i-1}, & \epsilon_i \sim w(0.846) \quad \text{ if } x_{i-1} > 3.79. \end{cases}$$

All of the estimates of the refined model are highly significant. The Ljung–Box statistics of the standardized innovations $\hat{\epsilon}_i = x_i/\hat{\psi}_i$ show $Q(10) = 5.91(0.82)$ and $Q(20) = 16.04(0.71)$ and those of $\hat{\epsilon}_i^2$ give $Q(10) = 5.35(0.87)$ and $Q(20) = 15.20(0.76)$, where the number in parentheses is the p-value. Therefore, the refined model is adequate. The RATS program used to estimate the prior model is given in Appendix C.

5.7 BIVARIATE MODELS FOR PRICE CHANGE AND DURATION

In this section, we introduce a model that considers jointly the process of price change and the associated duration. As mentioned before, many intraday transactions of a stock result in no price change. Those transactions are highly relevant to trading intensity, but they do not contain direct information on price movement. Therefore, to simplify the complexity involved in modeling price change, we focus on transactions that result in a price change and consider a price change and duration (PCD) model to describe the multivariate dynamics of price change and the associated time duration.

We continue to use the same notation as before, but the definition is changed to transactions with a price change. Let t_i be the calendar time of the ith price change of an asset. As before, t_i is measured in seconds from midnight of a trading day. Let P_{t_i} be the transaction price when the ith price change occurred and $\Delta t_i = t_i - t_{i-1}$ be the time duration between price changes. In addition, let N_i be the number of trades in the time interval (t_{i-1}, t_i) that result in no price change. This new variable is used to represent trading intensity during a period of no price change. Finally, let D_i be the direction of the ith price change with $D_i = 1$ when price goes up and $D_i = -1$ when the price comes down, and let S_i be the size of the ith price change measured in ticks. Under the new definitions, the price of a stock evolves over time by

$$P_{t_i} = P_{t_{i-1}} + D_i S_i, \tag{5.46}$$

and the transactions data consist of $\{\Delta t_i, N_i, D_i, S_i\}$ for the ith price change. The PCD model is concerned with the joint analysis of $(\Delta t_i, N_i, D_i, S_i)$.

Remark. Focusing on transactions associated with a price change can reduce the sample size dramatically. For example, consider the intraday data of IBM stock from November 1, 1990 to January 31, 1991. There were 60,265 intraday trades, but only 19,022 of them resulted in a price change. In addition, there is no diurnal pattern in time durations between price changes. □

To illustrate the relationship among the price movements of all transactions and those of transactions associated with a price change, we consider the intraday tradings of IBM stock on November 21, 1990. There were 726 transactions on that day during normal trading hours, but only 195 trades resulted in a price change. Figure 5.14 shows the time plot of the price series for both cases. As expected, the price series are the same.

The PCD model decomposes the joint distribution of $(\Delta t_i, N_i, D_i, S_i)$ given F_{i-1} as

$$\begin{aligned} f(\Delta t_i, N_i, D_i, S_i|F_{i-1}) \\ = f(S_i|D_i, N_i, \Delta t_i, F_{i-1}) f(D_i|N_i, \Delta t_i, F_{i-1}) f(N_i|\Delta t_i, F_{i-1}) f(\Delta t_i|F_{i-1}). \end{aligned} \tag{5.47}$$

This partition enables us to specify suitable econometric models for the conditional distributions and, hence, to simplify the modeling task. There are many ways to specify models for the conditional distributions. A proper specification might depend on the asset under study. Here we employ the specifications used by McCulloch and Tsay (2000), who use generalized linear models for the discrete-valued variables and a time series model for the continuous variable $\ln(\Delta t_i)$.

For the time duration between price changes, we use the model

$$\ln(\Delta t_i) = \beta_0 + \beta_1 \ln(\Delta t_{i-1}) + \beta_2 S_{i-1} + \sigma \epsilon_i, \tag{5.48}$$

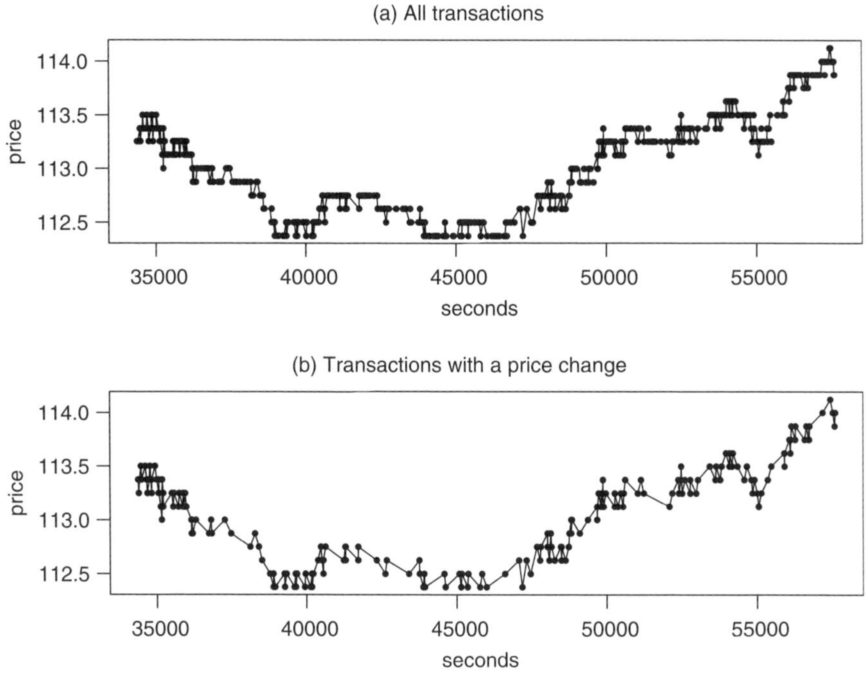

Figure 5.14. Time plots of the intraday transaction prices of IBM stock on November 21, 1990: (a) all transactions and (b) transactions that resulted in a price change.

where σ is a positive number and $\{\epsilon_i\}$ is a sequence of iid $N(0, 1)$ random variables. This is a multiple linear regression model with lagged variables. Other explanatory variables can be added if necessary. The log transformation is used to ensure the positiveness of time duration.

The conditional model for N_i is further partitioned into two parts because empirical data suggest a concentration of N_i at 0. The first part of the model for N_i is the logit model

$$p(N_i = 0|\Delta t_i, F_{i-1}) = \text{logit}[\alpha_0 + \alpha_1 \ln(\Delta t_i)], \tag{5.49}$$

where $\text{logit}(x) = \exp(x)/[1 + \exp(x)]$, whereas the second part of the model is

$$N_i|(N_i > 0, \Delta t_i, F_{i-1}) \sim 1 + g(\lambda_i), \quad \lambda_i = \frac{\exp[\gamma_0 + \gamma_1 \ln(\Delta t_i)]}{1 + \exp[\gamma_0 + \gamma_1 \ln(\Delta t_i)]}, \tag{5.50}$$

where $\sim$ means "is distributed as," and $g(\lambda)$ denotes a geometric distribution with parameter λ, which is in the interval (0, 1).

The model for direction D_i is

$$D_i|(N_i, \Delta t_i, F_{i-1}) = \text{sign}(\mu_i + \sigma_i \epsilon), \tag{5.51}$$

where ϵ is a $N(0, 1)$ random variable, and

$$\mu_i = \omega_0 + \omega_1 D_{i-1} + \omega_2 \ln(\Delta t_i),$$

$$\ln(\sigma_i) = \beta \left| \sum_{j=1}^{4} D_{i-j} \right| = \beta |D_{i-1} + D_{i-2} + D_{i-3} + D_{i-4}|.$$

In other words, D_i is governed by the sign of a normal random variable with mean μ_i and variance σ_i^2. A special characteristic of the prior model is the function for $\ln(\sigma_i)$. For intraday transactions, a key feature is the *price reversal* between consecutive price changes. This feature is modeled by the dependence of D_i on D_{i-1} in the mean equation with a negative ω_1 parameter. However, there exists an occasional local trend in the price movement. The previous variance equation allows for such a local trend by increasing the uncertainty in the direction of price movement when the past data showed evidence of a local trend. For a normal distribution with a fixed mean, increasing its variance makes a random draw have the same chance to be positive and negative. This in turn increases the chance for a sequence of all positive or all negative draws. Such a sequence produces a local trend in price movement.

To allow for different dynamics between positive and negative price movements, we use different models for the size of a price change. Specifically, we have

$$S_i|(D_i = -1, N_i, \Delta t_i, F_{i-1}) \sim p(\lambda_{d,i}) + 1, \quad \text{with}$$
$$\ln(\lambda_{d,i}) = \eta_{d,0} + \eta_{d,1} N_i + \eta_{d,2} \ln(\Delta t_i) + \eta_{d,3} S_{i-1} \tag{5.52}$$
$$S_i|(D_i = 1, N_i, \Delta t_i, F_{i-1}) \sim p(\lambda_{u,i}) + 1, \quad \text{with}$$
$$\ln(\lambda_{u,i}) = \eta_{u,0} + \eta_{u,1} N_i + \eta_{u,2} \ln(\Delta t_i) + \eta_{u,3} S_{i-1}, \tag{5.53}$$

where $p(\lambda)$ denotes a Poisson distribution with parameter λ, and 1 is added to the size because the minimum size is 1 tick when there is a price change.

The specified models in Eqs. (5.48)–(5.53) can be estimated jointly by either the maximum likelihood method or the Markov chain Monte Carlo methods. Based on Eq. (5.47), the models consist of six conditional models that can be estimated separately.

Example 5.5. Consider the intraday transactions of IBM stock on November 21, 1990. There are 194 price changes within normal trading hours. Figure 5.15 shows the histograms of $\ln(\Delta t_i)$, N_i, D_i, and S_i. The data for D_i are about equally distributed between "upward" and "downward" movements. Only a few transactions resulted in a price change of more than 1 tick; as a matter of fact, there were seven changes with two ticks and one change with three ticks. Using Markov chain Monte Carlo (MCMC) methods (see Chapter 12), we obtained the following models for the data. The reported estimates and their standard deviations are the posterior means and standard deviations of MCMC draws with 9500 iterations. The model for the time duration between price changes is

$$\ln(\Delta t_i) = 4.023 + 0.032 \ln(\Delta t_{i-1}) - 0.025 S_{i-1} + 1.403 \epsilon_i,$$

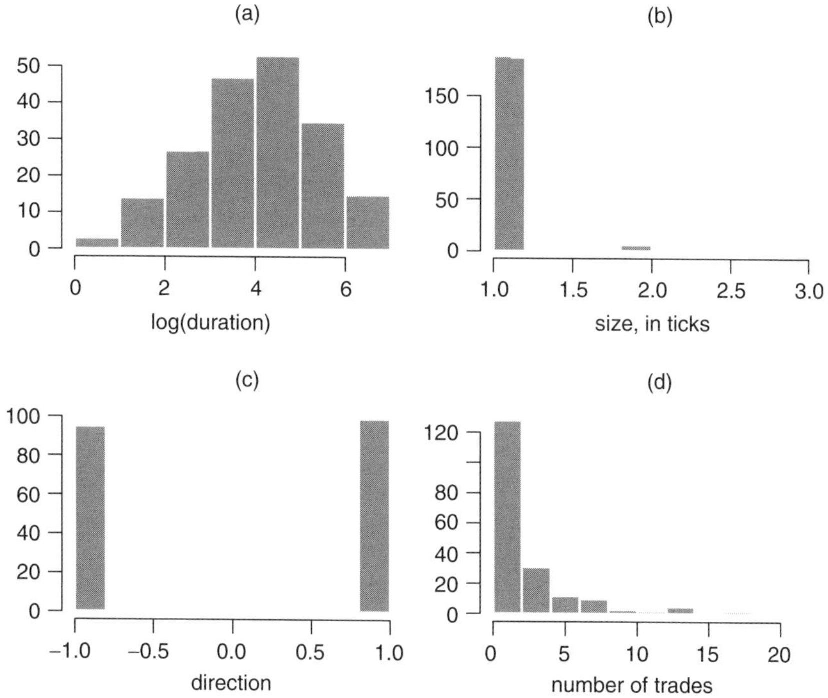

Figure 5.15. Histograms of intraday transactions data for IBM stock on November 21, 1990: (a) log durations between price changes, (b) direction of price movement, (c) size of price change measured in ticks, and (d) number of trades without a price change.

where standard deviations of the coefficients are 0.415, 0.073, 0.384, and 0.073, respectively. The fitted model indicates that there was no dynamic dependence in the time duration. For the N_i variable, we have

$$\Pr(N_i > 0 | \Delta t_i, F_{i-1}) = \text{logit}[-0.637 + 1.740 \ln(\Delta t_i)],$$

where standard deviations of the estimates are 0.238 and 0.248, respectively. Thus, as expected, the number of trades with no price change in the time interval (t_{i-1}, t_i) depends positively on the length of the interval. The magnitude of N_i when it is positive is

$$N_i | (N_i > 0, \Delta t_i, F_{i-1}) \sim 1 + g(\lambda_i), \quad \lambda_i = \frac{\exp[0.178 - 0.910 \ln(\Delta t_i)]}{1 + \exp[0.178 - 0.910 \ln(\Delta t_i)]},$$

where standard deviations of the estimates are 0.246 and 0.138, respectively. The negative and significant coefficient of $\ln(\Delta t_i)$ means that N_i is positively related to the length of the duration Δt_i because a large $\ln(\Delta t_i)$ implies a small λ_i, which in turn implies higher probabilities for larger N_i; see the geometric distribution in Eq. (5.27).

The fitted model for D_i is

$$\mu_i = 0.049 - 0.840 D_{i-1} - 0.004 \ln(\Delta t_i),$$
$$\ln(\sigma_i) = 0.244 |D_{i-1} + D_{i-2} + D_{i-3} + D_{i-4}|,$$

where standard deviations of the parameters in the mean equation are 0.129, 0.132, and 0.082, respectively, whereas the standard deviation for the parameter in the variance equation is 0.182. The price reversal is clearly shown by the highly significant negative coefficient of D_{i-1}. The marginally significant parameter in the variance equation is exactly as expected. Finally, the fitted models for the size of a price change are

$$\ln(\lambda_{d,i}) = 1.024 - 0.327 N_i + 0.412 \ln(\Delta t_i) - 4.474 S_{i-1},$$
$$\ln(\lambda_{u,i}) = -3.683 - 1.542 N_i + 0.419 \ln(\Delta t_i) + 0.921 S_{i-1},$$

where standard deviations of the parameters for the "down size" are 3.350, 0.319, 0.599, and 3.188, respectively, whereas those for the "up size" are 1.734, 0.976, 0.453, and 1.459. The interesting estimates of the prior two equations are the negative estimates of the coefficient of N_i. A large N_i means there were more transactions in the time interval (t_{i-1}, t_i) with no price change. This can be taken as evidence of no new information available in the time interval (t_{i-1}, t_i). Consequently, the size for the price change at t_i should be small. A small $\lambda_{u,i}$ or $\lambda_{d,i}$ for a Poisson distribution gives precisely that.

In summary, granted that a sample of 194 observations in a given day may not contain sufficient information about the trading dynamics of IBM stock, but the fitted models appear to provide some sensible results. McCulloch and Tsay (2000) extend the PCD model to a hierarchical framework to handle all the data of the 63 trading days between November 1, 1990 and January 31, 1991. Many of the parameter estimates become significant in this extended sample, which has more than 19,000 observations. For example, the overall estimate of the coefficient of $\ln(\Delta t_{i-1})$ in the model for time duration ranges from 0.04 to 0.1, which is small, but significant.

Finally, using transactions data to test microstructure theory often requires a careful specification of the variables used. It also requires a deep understanding of the way by which the market operates and the data are collected. However, ideas of the econometric models discussed in this chapter are useful and widely applicable in analysis of high-frequency data.

APPENDIX A: REVIEW OF SOME PROBABILITY DISTRIBUTIONS

Exponential Distribution

A random variable X has an exponential distribution with parameter $\beta > 0$ if its probability density function (pdf) is given by

$$f(x|\beta) = \begin{cases} \dfrac{1}{\beta} e^{-x/\beta} & \text{if } x \geq 0, \\ 0 & \text{otherwise.} \end{cases}$$

Denoting such a distribution by $X \sim \exp(\beta)$, we have $E(X) = \beta$ and $\mathrm{Var}(X) = \beta^2$. The cumulative distribution function (CDF) of X is

$$F(x|\beta) = \begin{cases} 0 & \text{if } x < 0, \\ 1 - e^{-x/\beta} & \text{if } x \geq 0. \end{cases}$$

When $\beta = 1$, X is said to have a standard exponential distribution.

Gamma Function

For $\kappa > 0$, the gamma function $\Gamma(\kappa)$ is defined by

$$\Gamma(\kappa) = \int_0^\infty x^{\kappa-1} e^{-x} dx.$$

The most important properties of the gamma function are:

1. For any $\kappa > 1$, $\Gamma(\kappa) = (\kappa - 1)\Gamma(\kappa - 1)$.
2. For any positive integer m, $\Gamma(m) = (m - 1)!$.
3. $\Gamma(\frac{1}{2}) = \sqrt{\pi}$.

The integration

$$\Gamma(y|\kappa) = \int_0^y x^{\kappa-1} e^{-x} dx, \quad y > 0$$

is an *incomplete* gamma function. Its values have been tabulated in the literature. Computer programs are now available to evaluate the incomplete gamma function.

Gamma Distribution

A random variable X has a gamma distribution with parameter κ and β ($\kappa > 0$, $\beta > 0$) if its pdf is given by

$$f(x|\kappa, \beta) = \begin{cases} \dfrac{1}{\beta^\kappa \Gamma(\kappa)} x^{\kappa-1} e^{-x/\beta} & \text{if } x \geq 0, \\ 0 & \text{otherwise.} \end{cases}$$

By changing variable $y = x/\beta$, one can easily obtain the moments of X:

$$\begin{aligned} E(X^m) &= \int_0^\infty x^m f(x|\kappa, \beta) dx = \frac{1}{\beta^\kappa \Gamma(\kappa)} \int_0^\infty x^{\kappa+m-1} e^{-x/\beta} dx \\ &= \frac{\beta^m}{\Gamma(\kappa)} \int_0^\infty y^{\kappa+m-1} e^{-y} dy = \frac{\beta^m \Gamma(\kappa + m)}{\Gamma(\kappa)}. \end{aligned}$$

In particular, the mean and variance of X are $E(X) = \kappa\beta$ and $\mathrm{Var}(X) = \kappa\beta^2$. When $\beta = 1$, the distribution is called a standard gamma distribution with parameter κ.

We use the notation $G \sim \text{gamma}(\kappa)$ to denote that G follows a standard gamma distribution with parameter κ. The moments of G are

$$E(G^m) = \frac{\Gamma(\kappa + m)}{\Gamma(\kappa)}, \quad m > 0. \tag{5.54}$$

Weibull Distribution

A random variable X has a Weibull distribution with parameters α and β ($\alpha > 0$, $\beta > 0$) if its pdf is given by

$$f(x|\alpha, \beta) = \begin{cases} \dfrac{\alpha}{\beta^\alpha} x^{\alpha-1} e^{-(x/\beta)^\alpha} & \text{if } x \geq 0, \\ 0 & \text{if } x < 0, \end{cases}$$

where β and α are the scale and shape parameters of the distribution. The mean and variance of X are

$$E(X) = \beta\Gamma\left(1 + \frac{1}{\alpha}\right), \quad \text{Var}(X) = \beta^2 \left\{\Gamma\left(1 + \frac{2}{\alpha}\right) - \left[\Gamma\left(1 + \frac{1}{\alpha}\right)\right]^2\right\},$$

and the CDF of X is

$$F(x|\alpha, \beta) = \begin{cases} 0 & \text{if } x < 0, \\ 1 - e^{-(x/\beta)^\alpha} & \text{if } x \geq 0. \end{cases}$$

When $\alpha = 1$, the Weibull distribution reduces to an exponential distribution.

Define $Y = X/[\beta\Gamma(1 + 1/\alpha)]$. We have $E(Y) = 1$ and the pdf of Y is

$$f(y|\alpha) = \begin{cases} \alpha\left[\Gamma\left(1 + \dfrac{1}{\alpha}\right)\right]^\alpha y^{\alpha-1} \exp\left\{-\left[\Gamma\left(1 + \dfrac{1}{\alpha}\right)y\right]^\alpha\right\} & \text{if } y \geq 0, \\ 0 & \text{otherwise}, \end{cases} \tag{5.55}$$

where the scale parameter β disappears due to standardization. The CDF of the standardized Weibull distribution is

$$F(y|\alpha) = \begin{cases} 0 & \text{if } y < 0, \\ 1 - \exp\left\{-\left[\Gamma\left(1 + \dfrac{1}{\alpha}\right)y\right]^\alpha\right\} & \text{if } y > 0, \end{cases}$$

and we have $E(Y) = 1$ and $\text{Var}(Y) = \Gamma(1 + 2/\alpha)/[\Gamma(1 + 1/\alpha)]^2 - 1$. For a duration model with Weibull innovations, the pdf in Eq. (5.55) is used in the maximum likelihood estimation.

Generalized Gamma Distribution

A random variable X has a generalized gamma distribution with parameter α, β, κ ($\alpha > 0$, $\beta > 0$, and $\kappa > 0$) if its pdf is given by

$$f(x|\alpha, \beta, \kappa) = \begin{cases} \dfrac{\alpha x^{\kappa\alpha-1}}{\beta^{\kappa\alpha}\Gamma(\kappa)} \exp\left[-\left(\dfrac{x}{\beta}\right)^{\alpha}\right] & \text{if } x \geq 0, \\ 0 & \text{otherwise,} \end{cases}$$

where β is a scale parameter, and α and κ are shape parameters. This distribution can be written as

$$G = \left(\frac{X}{\beta}\right)^{\alpha},$$

where G is a standard gamma random variable with parameter κ. The pdf of X can be obtained from that of G by the technique of changing variables. Similarly, the moments of X can be obtained from that of G in Eq. (5.54) by

$$E(X^m) = E[(\beta G^{1/\alpha})^m] = \beta^m E(G^{m/\alpha}) = \beta^m \frac{\Gamma(\kappa + m/\alpha)}{\Gamma(\kappa)} = \frac{\beta^m \Gamma(\kappa + m/\alpha)}{\Gamma(\kappa)}.$$

When $\kappa = 1$, the generalized gamma distribution reduces to that of a Weibull distribution. Thus, the exponential and Weibull distributions are special cases of the generalized gamma distribution.

The expectation of a generalized gamma distribution is $E(X) = \beta\Gamma(\kappa + 1/\alpha)/\Gamma(\kappa)$. In duration models, we need a distribution with unit expectation. Therefore, defining a random variable $Y = \lambda X/\beta$, where $\lambda = \Gamma(\kappa)/\Gamma(\kappa + 1/\alpha)$, we have $E(Y) = 1$ and the pdf of Y is

$$f(y|\alpha, \kappa) = \begin{cases} \dfrac{\alpha y^{\kappa\alpha-1}}{\lambda^{\kappa\alpha}\Gamma(\kappa)} \exp\left[-\left(\dfrac{y}{\lambda}\right)^{\alpha}\right] & \text{if } y > 0, \\ 0 & \text{otherwise,} \end{cases} \tag{5.56}$$

where again the scale parameter β disappears and $\lambda = \Gamma(\kappa)/\Gamma(\kappa + 1/\alpha)$.

APPENDIX B: HAZARD FUNCTION

A useful concept in modeling duration is the *hazard function* implied by a distribution function. For a random variable X, the *survival function* is defined as

$$S(x) \equiv P(X > x) = 1 - P(X \leq x) = 1 - \text{CDF}(x), \quad x > 0,$$

which gives the probability that a subject, which follows the distribution of X, survives at the time x. The hazard function (or intensity function) of X is then defined by

$$h(x) = \frac{f(x)}{S(x)}, \tag{5.57}$$

where $f(.)$ and $S(.)$ are the pdf and survival function of X, respectively.

Example 5.6. For the Weibull distribution with parameters α and β, the survival function and hazard function are

$$S(x|\alpha, \beta) = \exp\left[-\left(\frac{x}{\beta}\right)^{\alpha}\right], \quad h(x|\alpha, \beta) = \frac{\alpha}{\beta^{\alpha}}x^{\alpha-1}, \quad x > 0.$$

In particular, when $\alpha = 1$, we have $h(x|\beta) = 1/\beta$. Therefore, for an exponential distribution, the hazard function is constant. For a Weibull distribution, the hazard is a monotone function. If $\alpha > 1$, then the hazard function is monotonously increasing. If $\alpha < 1$, the hazard function is monotonously decreasing. For the generalized gamma distribution, the survival function and, hence, the hazard function involve the incomplete gamma function. Yet the hazard function may exhibit various patterns, including U shape or inverted U shape. Thus, the generalized gamma distribution provides a flexible approach to modeling the duration of stock transactions.

For the standardized Weibull distribution, the survival and hazard functions are

$$S(y|\alpha) = \exp\left\{-\left[\Gamma\left(1+\frac{1}{\alpha}\right)y\right]^{\alpha}\right\}, \quad h(y|\alpha) = \alpha\left[\Gamma\left(1+\frac{1}{\alpha}\right)\right]^{\alpha} y^{\alpha-1}, \quad y > 0.$$

APPENDIX C: SOME RATS PROGRAMS FOR DURATION MODELS

The data used are adjusted time durations of intraday transactions of IBM stock from November 1 to November 9, 1990. The file name is `ibm1to5.txt` and it has 3534 observations.

Program for Estimating a WACD(1,1) Model

```
all 0  3534:1
open data ibm1to5.txt
data(org=obs) / x r1
set psi = 1.0
nonlin a0 a1 b1 al
frml gvar = a0+a1*x(t-1)+b1*psi(t-1)
frml gma = %LNGAMMA(1.0+1.0/al)
frml gln =al*gma(t)+log(al)-log(x(t)) $
  +al*log(x(t)/(psi(t)=gvar(t)))-(exp(gma(t))*x(t)/psi(t))**al
smpl 2 3534
compute a0 = 0.2, a1 = 0.1, b1 = 0.1, al = 0.8
maximize(method=bhhh,recursive,iterations=150) gln
set fv = gvar(t)
set resid = x(t)/fv(t)
set residsq = resid(t)*resid(t)
cor(qstats,number=20,span=10) resid
cor(qstats,number=20,span=10) residsq
```

Program for Estimating a GACD(1,1) Model

```
all 0  3534:1
open data ibm1to5.txt
data(org=obs) / x r1
set psi = 1.0
nonlin a0 a1 b1 al ka
frml cv = a0+a1*x(t-1)+b1*psi(t-1)
frml gma = %LNGAMMA(ka)
frml lam = exp(gma(t))/exp(%LNGAMMA(ka+(1.0/al)))
frml xlam = x(t)/(lam(t)*(psi(t)=cv(t)))
frml gln =-gma(t)+log(al/x(t))+ka*al*log(xlam(t))-(xlam(t))**al
smpl 2 3534
compute a0 = 0.238, a1 = 0.075, b1 = 0.857, al = 0.5, ka = 4.0
nlpar(criterion=value,cvcrit=0.00001)
maximize(method=bhhh,recursive,iterations=150) gln
set fv = cv(t)
set resid = x(t)/fv(t)
set residsq = resid(t)*resid(t)
cor(qstats,number=20,span=10) resid
cor(qstats,number=20,span=10) residsq
```

Program for Estimating a TAR-WACD(1,1) Model

The threshold 3.79 is prespecified.

```
all 0 3534:1
open data ibm1to5.txt
data(org=obs) / x rt
set psi = 1.0
nonlin a1 a2 al b0 b2 bl
frml u = ((x(t-1)-3.79)/abs(x(t-1)-3.79)+1.0)/2.0
frml cp1 = a1*x(t-1)+a2*psi(t-1)
frml gma1 = %LNGAMMA(1.0+1.0/al)
frml cp2 = b0+b2*psi(t-1)
frml gma2 = %LNGAMMA(1.0+1.0/bl)
frml cp = cp1(t)*(1-u(t))+cp2(t)*u(t)
frml gln1 =al*gma1(t)+log(al)-log(x(t)) $
 +al*log(x(t)/(psi(t)=cp(t)))-(exp(gma1(t))*x(t)/psi(t))**al
frml gln2 =bl*gma2(t)+log(bl)-log(x(t)) $
 +bl*log(x(t)/(psi(t)=cp(t)))-(exp(gma2(t))*x(t)/psi(t))**bl
frml gln = gln1(t)*(1-u(t))+gln2(t)*u(t)
smpl 2 3534
compute a1 = 0.2, a2 = 0.85, al = 0.9
compute b0 = 1.8, b2 = 0.5, bl = 0.8
maximize(method=bhhh,recursive,iterations=150) gln
set fv = cp(t)
set resid = x(t)/fv(t)
set residsq = resid(t)*resid(t)
cor(qstats,number=20,span=10) resid
cor(qstats,number=20,span=10) residsq
```

EXERCISES

5.1. Let r_t be the log return of an asset at time t. Assume that $\{r_t\}$ is a Gaussian white noise series with mean 0.05 and variance 1.5. Suppose that the probability of a trade at each time point is 40% and is independent of r_t. Denote the observed return by r_t^o. Is r_t^o serially correlated? If yes, calculate the first three lags of autocorrelations of r_t^o.

5.2. Let P_t be the observed market price of an asset, which is related to the fundamental value of the asset P_t^* via Eq. (5.9). Assume that $\Delta P_t^* = P_t^* - P_{t-1}^*$ forms a Gaussian white noise series with mean zero and variance 1.0. Suppose that the bid–ask spread is two ticks. What is the lag-1 autocorrelation of the price change series $\Delta P_t = P_t - P_{t-1}$ when the tick size is \$1/8? What is the lag-1 autocorrelation of the price change when the tick size is \$1/16?

5.3. The file `ibm-d2-dur.txt` contains the adjusted durations between trades of IBM stock on November 2, 1990. The file has three columns consisting of day, time of trade measured in seconds from midnight, and adjusted durations.

(a) Build an EACD model for the adjusted duration and check the fitted model.

(b) Build a WACD model for the adjusted duration and check the fitted model.

(c) Build a GACD model for the adjusted duration and check the fitted model.

(d) Compare the prior three duration models.

5.4. The file `mmm9912-dtp.txt` contains the transactions data of the stock of 3M Company in December 1999. There are three columns: day of the month, time of transaction in seconds from midnight, and transaction price. Transactions that occurred after 4:00 pm Eastern time are excluded.

(a) Is there a diurnal pattern in 3M stock trading? You may construct a time series n_t, which denotes the number of trades in a 5-minute time interval to answer this question.

(b) Use the price series to confirm the existence of a bid–ask bounce in intraday trading of 3M stock.

(c) Tabulate the frequencies of price change in multiples of tick size \$1/16. You may combine changes with 5 ticks or more into a category and those with −5 ticks or beyond into another category.

5.5. Consider again the transactions data of 3M stock in December 1999.

(a) Use the data to construct an intraday 5-minute log return series. Use the simple average of all transaction prices within a 5-minute interval as the stock price for the interval. Is the series serially correlated? You may use Ljung–Box statistics to test the hypothesis with the first 10 lags of the sample autocorrelation function.

(b) There are seventy-seven 5-minute returns in a normal trading day. Some researchers suggest that the sum of squares of the intraday 5-minute returns can be used as a measure of daily volatility. Apply this approach and calculate the daily volatility of the log return of 3M stock in December 1999. Discuss the validity of such a procedure to estimate daily volatility.

5.6. The file `mmm9912-adur.txt` contains an adjusted intraday trading duration of 3M stock in December 1999. There are thirty-nine 10-minute time intervals in a trading day. Let d_i be the average of all log durations for the ith 10-minute interval across all trading days in December 1999. Define an adjusted duration as $t_j/\exp(d_i)$, where j is in the ith 10-minute interval. Note that more sophisticated methods can be used to adjust the diurnal pattern of trading duration. Here we simply use a local average.

(a) Is there a diurnal pattern in the adjusted duration series? Why?

(b) Build a duration model for the adjusted series using exponential innovations. Check the fitted model.

(c) Build a duration model for the adjusted series using Weibull innovations. Check the fitted model.

(d) Build a duration model for the adjusted series using generalized gamma innovations. Check the fitted model.

(e) Compare and comment on the three duration models built before.

5.7. To gain experience in analyzing high-frequency financial data, consider the trade data of GE stock from December 1 to December 5, 2003 in the file `taq-t-ge-dec5.txt`. The file has four major columns; day, time (hour, minute, second), price, and volume. Ignore all transactions outside normal trading hours (9:30 am to 4:00 pm Eastern time). Construct a time series of the number of trades in an intraday 5-minute time interval. Is there any diurnal pattern in the constructed series? You can simply compute the sample ACF of the series to answer this question. The number of trades is in the file `taq-ge-dec5-nt.txt`.

5.8. Again, consider the high-frequency data of GE stock from December 1 to December 5, 2003 and ignore the transactions outside normal trading hours. Construct an intraday 5-minute return series. Note that the price of the stock in a 5-minute interval (e.g., 9:30 and 9:35 am) is the last transaction price within the time interval. For simplicity, ignore overnight returns. Are there serial correlations in the 5-minute return series? Use 10 lags of the ACF and 5% level to perform the test. See file `taq-ge-dec5-5m.txt`.

5.9. Consider the same problem as in Exercise 5.8, but use 10-minute time intervals. See file `taq-ge-dec5-10m.txt`.

5.10. Again, consider the high-frequency data of GE stock and ignore transactions outside normal trading hours. Compute the percentage of consecutive transactions without price change in the sample.

REFERENCES

Box, G. E. P. and Cox, D. R. (1964). An analysis of transformations. *Journal of the Royal Statistical Society Series B* **26**: 211–243.

Campbell, J. Y., Lo, A. W., and MacKinlay, A. C. (1997). *The Econometrics of Financial Markets*. Princeton University Press, Princeton, NJ.

Cho, D., Russell, J. R., Tiao, G. C., and Tsay, R. S. (2003). The magnet effect of price limits: Evidence from high frequency data on Taiwan stock exchange. *Journal of Empirical Finance* **10**: 133–168.

Engle, R. F. and Russell, J. R. (1998). Autoregressive conditional duration: a new model for irregularly spaced transaction data. *Econometrica* **66**: 1127–1162.

Ghysels, E. (2000). Some econometric recipes for high-frequency data cooking. *Journal of Business and Economic Statistics* **18**: 154–163.

Hasbrouck, J. (1992). *Using the TORQ Database*. Stern School of Business, New York University, New York.

Hasbrouck, J. (1999). The dynamics of discrete bid and ask quotes. *Journal of Finance* **54**: 2109–2142.

Hauseman, J., Lo, A., and MacKinlay, C. (1992). An ordered probit analysis of transaction stock prices. *Journal of Financial Economics* **31**: 319–379.

Lo, A. and MacKinlay, A. C. (1990). An econometric analysis of nonsynchronous trading. *Journal of Econometrics* **45**: 181–212.

McCulloch, R. E. and Tsay, R. S. (2000). Nonlinearity in high frequency data and hierarchical models. *Studies in Nonlinear Dynamics and Econometrics* **5**: 1–17.

Roll, R. (1984). A simple implicit measure of the effective bid–ask spread in an efficient market. *Journal of Finance* **39**: 1127–1140.

Rydberg, T. H. and Shephard, N. (2003). Dynamics of trade-by-trade price movements: Decomposition and models. *Journal of Financial Econometrics* **1**: 2–25.

Stoll, H. and Whaley, R. (1990). Stock market structure and volatility. *Review of Financial Studies* **3**: 37–71.

Wood, R. A. (2000). Market microstructure research databases: History and projections. *Journal of Business & Economic Statistics* **18**: 140–145.

Zhang, M. Y., Russell, J. R., and Tsay, R. S. (2001a). A nonlinear autoregressive conditional duration model with applications to financial transaction data. *Journal of Econometrics* **104**: 179–207.

Zhang, M. Y., Russell, J. R., and Tsay, R. S. (2001b). Determinants of bid and ask quotes and implications for the cost of trading. Working paper, Graduate School of Business, University of Chicago.

CHAPTER 6

Continuous-Time Models and Their Applications

The price of a financial asset evolves over time and forms a *stochastic process*, which is a statistical term used to describe the evolution of a random variable over time. The observed prices are a realization of the underlying stochastic process. The theory of stochastic process is the basis on which the observed prices are analyzed and statistical inference is made.

There are two types of stochastic process for modeling the price of an asset. The first type is called the *discrete-time stochastic process*, in which the price changes at discrete time points. All the processes discussed in the previous chapters belong to this category. For example, the daily closing price of IBM stock on the New York Stock Exchange forms a discrete-time stochastic process. Here the price changes only at the closing of a trading day. Price movements within a trading day are not necessarily relevant to the observed daily price. The second type of stochastic process is the *continuous-time process*, in which the price changes continuously, even though the price is only observed at discrete time points. One can think of the price as the "true value" of the stock that always exists and is time varying.

For both types of process, the price can be continuous or discrete. A continuous price can assume any positive real number, whereas a discrete price can only assume a countable number of possible values. Assume that the price of an asset is a continuous-time stochastic process. If the price is a continuous random variable, then we have a continuous-time continuous process. If the price itself is discrete, then we have a continuous-time discrete process. Similar classifications apply to discrete-time processes. The series of price change in Chapter 5 is an example of a discrete-time discrete process.

In this chapter, we treat the price of an asset as a continuous-time continuous stochastic process. Our goal is to introduce the statistical theory and tools needed to model financial assets and to price options. We begin the chapter with some terminologies of stock options used in the chapter. In Section 6.2, we provide a brief

Analysis of Financial Time Series, Second Edition By Ruey S. Tsay

introduction of Brownian motion, which is also known as a Wiener process. We then discuss some diffusion equations and stochastic calculus, including the well-known Ito's lemma. Most option pricing formulas are derived under the assumption that the price of an asset follows a diffusion equation. We use the Black–Scholes formula to demonstrate the derivation. Finally, to handle the price variations caused by rare events (e.g., a profit warning), we also study some simple diffusion models with jumps.

If the price of an asset follows a diffusion equation, then the price of an option contingent to the asset can be derived by using hedging methods. However, with jumps the market becomes incomplete and there is no perfect hedging of options. The price of an option is then valued either by using diversifiability of jump risk or defining a notion of risk and choosing a price and a hedge that minimize this risk. For basic applications of stochastic processes in derivative pricing, see Cox and Rubinstein (1985) and Hull (2002).

6.1 OPTIONS

A stock option is a financial contract that gives the holder the right to trade a certain number of shares of a specified common stock by a certain date for a specified price. There are two types of options. A *call option* gives the holder the right to buy the underlying stock; see Chapter 3 for a formal definition. A *put option* gives the holder the right to sell the underlying stock. The specified price in the contract is called the *strike price* or *exercise price*. The date in the contract is known as the *expiration date* or *maturity*. *American options* can be exercised at any time up to the expiration date. *European options* can be exercised only on the expiration date.

The value of a stock option depends on the value of the underlying stock. Let K be the strike price and P be the stock price. A call option is *in-the-money* when $P > K$, *at-the-money* when $P = K$, and *out-of-the-money* when $P < K$. A put option is in-the-money when $P < K$, at-the-money when $P = K$, and out-of-the-money when $P > K$. In general, an option is in-the-money when it would lead to a positive cash flow to the holder if it were exercised immediately. An option is out-of-the-money when it would lead to a negative cash flow to the holder if it were exercised immediately. Finally, an option is at-the-money when it would lead to zero cash flow if it were exercised immediately. Obviously, only in-the-money options are exercised in practice. For more information on options, see Hull (2002).

6.2 SOME CONTINUOUS-TIME STOCHASTIC PROCESSES

In mathematical statistics, a continuous-time continuous stochastic process is defined on a probability space $(\Omega, F, \mathbf{P})$, where Ω is a nonempty space, F is a σ-field consisting of subsets of Ω, and $\mathbf{P}$ is a probability measure; see Chapter 1 of Billingsley (1986). The process can be written as $\{x(\eta, t)\}$, where t denotes time and is continuous in $[0, \infty)$. For a given t, $x(\eta, t)$ is a real-valued continuous random variable (i.e., a mapping from Ω to the real line), and η is an element of Ω.

For the price of an asset at time t, the range of $x(\eta, t)$ is the set of non-negative real numbers. For a given η, $\{x(\eta, t)\}$ is a time series with values depending on the time t. For simplicity, we write a continuous-time stochastic process as $\{x_t\}$ with the understanding that, for a given t, x_t is a random variable. In the literature, some authors use $x(t)$ instead of x_t to emphasize that t is continuous. However, we use the same notation x_t, but call it a continuous-time stochastic process.

6.2.1 The Wiener Process

In a discrete-time econometric model, we assume that the shocks form a white noise process, which is not predictable. What is the counterpart of shocks in a continuous-time model? The answer is the increments of a *Wiener process*, which is also known as a *standard Brownian motion*. There are many ways to define a Wiener process $\{w_t\}$. We use a simple approach that focuses on the small change $\Delta w_t = w_{t+\Delta t} - w_t$ associated with a small increment Δt in time. A continuous-time stochastic process $\{w_t\}$ is a Wiener process if it satisfies

1. $\Delta w_t = \epsilon\sqrt{\Delta t}$, where ϵ is a standard normal random variable; and
2. Δw_t is independent of w_j for all $j \le t$.

The second condition is a Markov property saying that conditional on the present value w_t, any past information of the process, w_j with $j < t$, is irrelevant to the future $w_{t+\ell}$ with $\ell > 0$. From this property, it is easily seen that for any two nonoverlapping time intervals Δ_1 and Δ_2, the increments $w_{t_1+\Delta_1} - w_{t_1}$ and $w_{t_2+\Delta_2} - w_{t_2}$ are independent. In finance, this Markov property is related to a weak form of efficient market.

From the first condition, Δw_t is normally distributed with mean zero and variance Δt. That is, $\Delta w_t \sim N(0, \Delta t)$, where $\sim$ denotes probability distribution. Consider next the process w_t. We assume that the process starts at $t = 0$ with initial value w_0, which is fixed and often set to zero. Then $w_t - w_0$ can be treated as a sum of many small increments. More specifically, define $T = t/\Delta t$, where Δt is a small positive increment. Then

$$w_t - w_0 = w_{T\Delta t} - w_0 = \sum_{i=1}^{T} \Delta w_i = \sum_{i=1}^{T} \epsilon_i \sqrt{\Delta t},$$

where $\Delta w_i = w_{i\Delta t} - w_{(i-1)\Delta t}$. Because the ϵ_i are independent, we have

$$E(w_t - w_0) = 0, \quad \text{Var}(w_t - w_0) = \sum_{i=1}^{T} \Delta t = T\Delta t = t.$$

Thus, the increment in w_t from time 0 to time t is normally distributed with mean zero and variance t. To put it formally, for a Wiener process w_t, we have

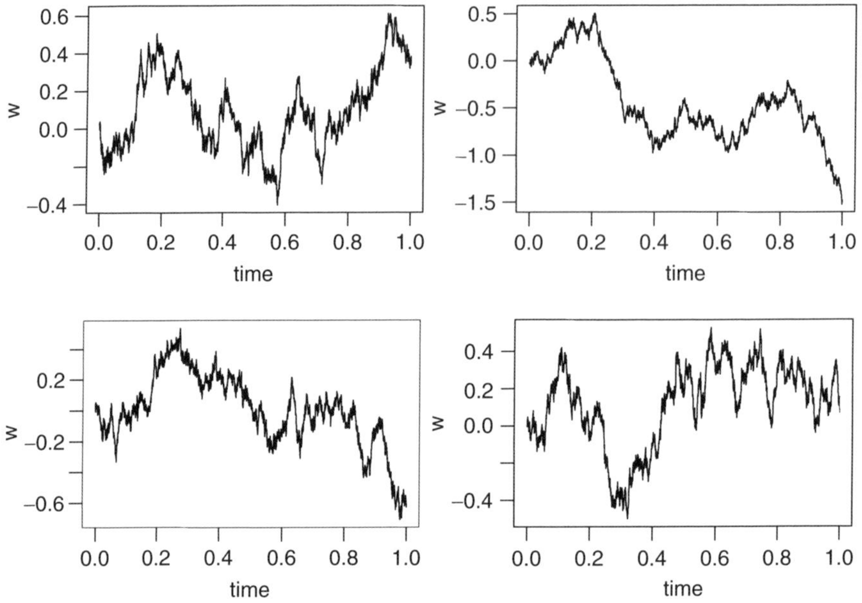

Figure 6.1. Four simulated Wiener processes.

that $w_t - w_0 \sim N(0, t)$. This says that the variance of a Wiener process increases linearly with the length of time interval.

Figure 6.1 shows four simulated Wiener processes on the unit time interval [0, 1]. They are obtained by using a simple version of Donsker's theorem in the statistical literature with $n = 3000$; see Donsker (1951) or Billingsley (1968). The four plots start with $w_0 = 0$ but drift apart as time increases, illustrating that the variance of a Wiener process increases with time. A simple time transformation from [0, 1) to $[0, \infty)$ can be used to obtain simulated Wiener processes for $t \in [0, \infty)$.

Donsker's Theorem

Assume that $\{z_i\}_{i=1}^n$ is a sequence of independent standard normal random variates. For any $t \in [0, 1]$, let $[nt]$ be the integer part of nt. Define $w_{n,t} = (1/\sqrt{n}) \sum_{i=1}^{[nt]} z_i$. Then $w_{n,t}$ converges in distribution to a Wiener process w_t on [0, 1] as n goes to infinity.

S-Plus Commands for Generating a Wiener Process

```
n = 3000
epsi = rnorm(n,0,1)
w=cumsum(epsi)/sqrt(n)
plot(w,type='l')
```

Remark. A formal definition of a Brownian motion w_t on a probability space $(\Omega, F, \mathbf{P})$ is that it is a real-valued, continuous stochastic process for $t \geq 0$ with independent and stationary increments. In other words, w_t satisfies

1. *Continuity*: the map from t to w_t is continuous almost surely with respect to the probability measure $\mathbf{P}$;
2. *Independent increments*: if $s \leq t$, $w_t - w_s$ is independent of w_v for all $v \leq s$; and
3. *Stationary increments*: if $s \leq t$, $w_t - w_s$ and $w_{t-s} - w_0$ have the same probability distribution.

It can be shown that the probability distribution of the increment $w_t - w_s$ is normal with mean $\mu(t-s)$ and variance $\sigma^2(t-s)$. Furthermore, for any given time indexes $0 \leq t_1 < t_2 < \cdots < t_k$, the random vector $(w_{t_1}, w_{t_2}, \ldots, w_{t_k})$ follows a multivariate normal distribution. Finally, a Brownian motion is *standard* if $w_0 = 0$ almost surely, $\mu = 0$, and $\sigma^2 = 1$. □

Remark. An important property of Brownian motions is that their paths are not differentiable almost surely. In other words, for a standard Brownian motion w_t, it can be shown that dw_t/dt does not exist for all elements of Ω except for elements in a subset $\Omega_1 \subset \Omega$ such that $\mathbf{P}(\Omega_1) = 0$. As a result, we cannot use the usual integration in calculus to handle integrals involving a standard Brownian motion when we consider the value of an asset over time. Another approach must be sought. This is the purpose of discussing Ito's calculus in the next section. □

6.2.2 Generalized Wiener Processes

The Wiener process is a special stochastic process with zero drift and variance proportional to the length of the time interval. This means that the rate of change in expectation is zero and the rate of change in variance is 1. In practice, the mean and variance of a stochastic process can evolve over time in a more complicated manner. Hence, further generalization of a stochastic process is needed. To this end, we consider the *generalized Wiener process* in which the expectation has a drift rate μ and the rate of variance change is σ^2. Denote such a process by x_t and use the notation dy for a small change in the variable y. Then the model for x_t is

$$dx_t = \mu\, dt + \sigma\, dw_t, \tag{6.1}$$

where w_t is a Wiener process. If we consider a discretized version of Eq. (6.1), then

$$x_t - x_0 = \mu t + \sigma \epsilon \sqrt{t}$$

for increment from 0 to t. Consequently,

$$E(x_t - x_0) = \mu t, \quad \text{Var}(x_t - x_0) = \sigma^2 t.$$

The results say that the increment in x_t has a growth rate of μ for the expectation and a growth rate of σ^2 for the variance. In the literature, μ and σ of Eq. (6.1) are referred to as the drift and volatility parameters of the generalized Wiener process x_t.

6.2.3 Ito Processes

The drift and volatility parameters of a generalized Wiener process are time-invariant. If one further extends the model by allowing μ and σ to be functions of the stochastic process x_t, then we have an Ito process. Specifically, a process x_t is an Ito process if it satisfies

$$dx_t = \mu(x_t, t)\, dt + \sigma(x_t, t)\, dw_t, \tag{6.2}$$

where w_t is a Wiener process. This process plays an important role in mathematical finance and can be written as

$$x_t = x_0 + \int_0^t \mu(x_s, s)\, ds + \int_0^t \sigma(x_s, s)\, dw_s,$$

where x_0 denotes the starting value of the process at time 0 and the last term on the right-hand side is a stochastic integral. Equation (6.2) is referred to as a stochastic diffusion equation with $\mu(x_t, t)$ and $\sigma(x_t, t)$ being the drift and diffusion functions, respectively.

The Wiener process is a special Ito process because it satisfies Eq. (6.2) with $\mu(x_t, t) = 0$ and $\sigma(x_t, t) = 1$.

6.3 ITO'S LEMMA

In finance, when using continuous-time models, it is common to assume that the price of an asset is an Ito process. Therefore, to derive the price of a financial derivative, one needs to use Ito's calculus. In this section, we briefly review Ito's lemma by treating it as a natural extension of the differentiation in calculus. Ito's lemma is the basis of stochastic calculus.

6.3.1 Review of Differentiation

Let $G(x)$ be a differentiable function of x. Using Taylor expansion, we have

$$\Delta G \equiv G(x + \Delta x) - G(x) = \frac{\partial G}{\partial x}\Delta x + \frac{1}{2}\frac{\partial^2 G}{\partial x^2}(\Delta x)^2 + \frac{1}{6}\frac{\partial^3 G}{\partial x^3}(\Delta x)^3 + \cdots.$$

Taking the limit as $\Delta x \to 0$ and ignoring the higher order terms of Δx, we have

$$dG = \frac{\partial G}{\partial x}\, dx.$$

When G is a function of x and y, we have

$$\Delta G = \frac{\partial G}{\partial x}\Delta x + \frac{\partial G}{\partial y}\Delta y + \frac{1}{2}\frac{\partial^2 G}{\partial x^2}(\Delta x)^2 + \frac{\partial^2 G}{\partial x\,\partial y}\Delta x \Delta y + \frac{1}{2}\frac{\partial^2 G}{\partial y^2}(\Delta y)^2 + \cdots.$$

Taking the limit as $\Delta x \to 0$ and $\Delta y \to 0$, we have

$$dG = \frac{\partial G}{\partial x}dx + \frac{\partial G}{\partial y}dy.$$

6.3.2 Stochastic Differentiation

Turn next to the case in which G is a differentiable function of x_t and t, and x_t is an Ito process. The Taylor expansion becomes

$$\Delta G = \frac{\partial G}{\partial x}\Delta x + \frac{\partial G}{\partial t}\Delta t + \frac{1}{2}\frac{\partial^2 G}{\partial x^2}(\Delta x)^2 + \frac{\partial^2 G}{\partial x\,\partial t}\Delta x\ \Delta t + \frac{1}{2}\frac{\partial^2 G}{\partial t^2}(\Delta t)^2 + \cdots. \quad (6.3)$$

A discretized version of Ito process is

$$\Delta x = \mu\ \Delta t + \sigma\epsilon\sqrt{\Delta t}, \quad (6.4)$$

where, for simplicity, we omit the arguments of μ and σ, and $\Delta x = x_{t+\Delta t} - x_t$. From Eq. (6.4), we have

$$(\Delta x)^2 = \mu^2(\Delta t)^2 + \sigma^2\epsilon^2\Delta t + 2\mu\sigma\epsilon(\Delta t)^{3/2} = \sigma^2\epsilon^2\Delta t + H(\Delta t), \quad (6.5)$$

where $H(\Delta t)$ denotes higher order terms of Δt. This result shows that $(\Delta x)^2$ contains a term of order Δt, which cannot be ignored when we take the limit as $\Delta t \to 0$. However, the first term on the right-hand side of Eq. (6.5) has some nice properties:

$$E(\sigma^2\epsilon^2\Delta t) = \sigma^2\Delta t,$$
$$\text{Var}(\sigma^2\epsilon^2\Delta t) = E[\sigma^4\epsilon^4(\Delta t)^2] - [E(\sigma^2\epsilon^2\Delta t)]^2 = 2\sigma^4(\Delta t)^2,$$

where we use $E(\epsilon^4) = 3$ for a standard normal random variable. These two properties show that $\sigma^2\epsilon^2\Delta t$ converges to a nonstochastic quantity $\sigma^2\Delta t$ as $\Delta t \to 0$. Consequently, from Eq. (6.5), we have

$$(\Delta x)^2 \to \sigma^2\,dt \quad \text{as} \quad \Delta t \to 0.$$

Plugging the prior result into Eq. (6.3) and using Ito's equation of x_t in Eq. (6.2), we obtain

$$\begin{aligned} dG &= \frac{\partial G}{\partial x}dx + \frac{\partial G}{\partial t}dt + \frac{1}{2}\frac{\partial^2 G}{\partial x^2}\sigma^2\,dt \\ &= \left(\frac{\partial G}{\partial x}\mu + \frac{\partial G}{\partial t} + \frac{1}{2}\frac{\partial^2 G}{\partial x^2}\sigma^2\right)dt + \frac{\partial G}{\partial x}\sigma\,dw_t, \end{aligned}$$

which is the well-known Ito's lemma in stochastic calculus.

Recall that we suppressed the argument (x_t, t) from the drift and volatility terms μ and σ in the derivation of Ito's lemma. To avoid any possible confusion in the future, we restate the lemma as follows.

Ito's Lemma

Assume that x_t is a continuous-time stochastic process satisfying

$$dx_t = \mu(x_t, t)\, dt + \sigma(x_t, t)\, dw_t,$$

where w_t is a Wiener process. Furthermore, $G(x_t, t)$ is a differentiable function of x_t and t. Then,

$$dG = \left[\frac{\partial G}{\partial x}\mu(x_t, t) + \frac{\partial G}{\partial t} + \frac{1}{2}\frac{\partial^2 G}{\partial x^2}\sigma^2(x_t, t)\right] dt + \frac{\partial G}{\partial x}\sigma(x_t, t)\, dw_t. \qquad (6.6)$$

Example 6.1. As a simple illustration, consider the square function $G(w_t, t) = w_t^2$ of the Wiener process. Here we have $\mu(w_t, t) = 0$, $\sigma(w_t, t) = 1$ and

$$\frac{\partial G}{\partial w_t} = 2w_t, \quad \frac{\partial G}{\partial t} = 0, \quad \frac{\partial^2 G}{\partial w_t^2} = 2.$$

Therefore,

$$dw_t^2 = (2w_t \times 0 + 0 + \tfrac{1}{2} \times 2 \times 1)\, dt + 2w_t\, dw_t = dt + 2w_t\, dw_t. \qquad (6.7)$$

6.3.3 An Application

Let P_t be the price of a stock at time t, which is continuous in $[0, \infty)$. In the literature, it is common to assume that P_t follows the special Ito process

$$dP_t = \mu P_t\, dt + \sigma P_t\, dw_t, \qquad (6.8)$$

where μ and σ are constant. Using the notation of the general Ito process in Eq. (6.2), we have $\mu(x_t, t) = \mu x_t$ and $\sigma(x_t, t) = \sigma x_t$, where $x_t = P_t$. Such a special process is referred to as a *geometric Brownian motion*. We now apply Ito's lemma to obtain a continuous-time model for the logarithm of the stock price P_t. Let $G(P_t, t) = \ln(P_t)$ be the log price of the underlying stock. Then we have

$$\frac{\partial G}{\partial P_t} = \frac{1}{P_t}, \quad \frac{\partial G}{\partial t} = 0, \quad \frac{1}{2}\frac{\partial^2 G}{\partial P_t^2} = \frac{1}{2}\frac{(-1)}{P_t^2}.$$

Consequently, via Ito's lemma, we obtain

$$\begin{aligned} d\ln(P_t) &= \left(\frac{1}{P_t}\mu P_t + \frac{1}{2}\frac{(-1)}{P_t^2}\sigma^2 P_t^2\right) dt + \frac{1}{P_t}\sigma P_t\, dw_t \\ &= \left(\mu - \frac{\sigma^2}{2}\right) dt + \sigma\, dw_t. \end{aligned}$$

This result shows that the logarithm of a price follows a generalized Wiener process with drift rate $\mu - \sigma^2/2$ and variance rate σ^2 if the price is a geometric Brownian motion. Consequently, the change in logarithm of price (i.e., log return) between current time t and some future time T is normally distributed with mean $(\mu - \sigma^2/2)(T - t)$ and variance $\sigma^2(T - t)$. If the time interval $T - t = \Delta$ is fixed and we are interested in equally spaced increments in log price, then the increment series is a Gaussian process with mean $(\mu - \sigma^2/2)\Delta$ and variance $\sigma^2\Delta$.

6.3.4 Estimation of μ and σ

The two unknown parameters μ and σ of the geometric Brownian motion in Eq. (6.8) can be estimated empirically. Assume that we have $n + 1$ observations of stock price P_t at equally spaced time interval Δ (e.g., daily, weekly, or monthly). We measure Δ in years. Denote the observed prices as $\{P_0, P_1, \ldots, P_n\}$ and let $r_t = \ln(P_t) - \ln(P_{t-1})$ for $t = 1, \ldots, n$.

Since $P_t = P_{t-1}\exp(r_t)$, r_t is the continuously compounded return in the tth time interval. Using the result of the previous subsection and assuming that the stock price P_t follows a geometric Brownian motion, we obtain that r_t is normally distributed with mean $(\mu - \sigma^2/2)\Delta$ and variance $\sigma^2\Delta$. In addition, the r_t are not serially correlated.

For simplicity, define $\mu_r = E(r_t) = (\mu - \sigma^2/2)\Delta$ and $\sigma_r^2 = \text{var}(r_t) = \sigma^2\Delta$. Let $\bar{r}$ and s_r be the sample mean and standard deviation of the data—that is,

$$\bar{r} = \frac{\sum_{t=1}^{n} r_t}{n}, \qquad s_r = \sqrt{\frac{1}{n-1}\sum_{t=1}^{n}(r_t - \bar{r})^2}.$$

As mentioned in Chapter 1, $\bar{r}$ and s_r are consistent estimates of the mean and standard deviation of r_i, respectively. That is, $\bar{r} \to \mu_r$ and $s_r \to \sigma_r$ as $n \to \infty$. Therefore, we may estimate σ by

$$\hat{\sigma} = \frac{s_r}{\sqrt{\Delta}}.$$

Furthermore, it can be shown that the standard error of this estimate is approximately $\hat{\sigma}/\sqrt{2n}$. From $\hat{\mu}_r = \bar{r}$, we can estimate μ by

$$\hat{\mu} = \frac{\bar{r}}{\Delta} + \frac{\hat{\sigma}^2}{2} = \frac{\bar{r}}{\Delta} + \frac{s_r^2}{2\Delta}.$$

When the series r_t is serially correlated or when the price of the asset does not follow the geometric Brownian motion in Eq. (6.8), then other estimation methods must be used to estimate the drift and volatility parameters of the diffusion equation. We return to this issue later.

Example 6.2. Consider the daily log returns of IBM stock in 1998. Figure 6.2a shows the time plot of the data, which have 252 observations. Figure 6.2b shows the sample autocorrelations of the series. It is seen that the log returns are indeed serially uncorrelated. The Ljung–Box statistic gives $Q(10) = 4.9$, which is highly insignificant compared with a chi-squared distribution with 10 degrees of freedom.

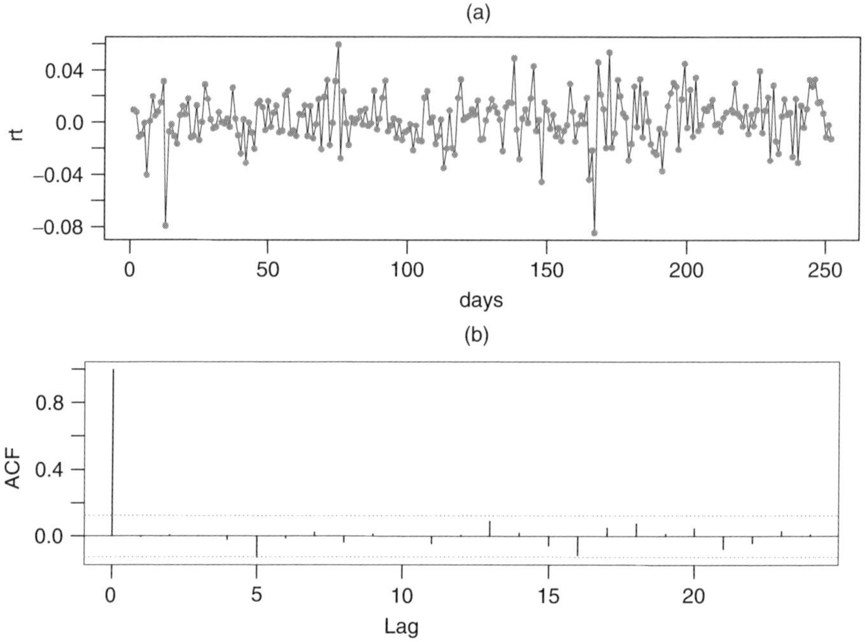

Figure 6.2. Daily returns of IBM stock in 1998: (a) log returns and (b) sample autocorrelations.

If we assume that the price of IBM stock in 1998 follows the geometric Brownian motion in Eq. (6.8), then we can use the daily log returns to estimate the parameters μ and σ. From the data, we have $\overline{r} = 0.002276$ and $s_r = 0.01915$. Since 1 trading day is equivalent to $\Delta = 1/252$ year, we obtain that

$$\hat{\sigma} = \frac{s_r}{\sqrt{\Delta}} = 0.3040, \quad \hat{\mu} = \frac{\overline{r}}{\Delta} + \frac{\hat{\sigma}^2}{2} = 0.6198.$$

Thus, the estimated expected return was 61.98% and the standard deviation was 30.4% per annum for IBM stock in 1998.

The normality assumption of the daily log returns may not hold, however. In this particular instance, the skewness −0.464(0.153) and excess kurtosis 2.396(0.306) raise some concern, where the number in parentheses denotes asymptotic standard error.

Example 6.3. Consider the daily log return of the stock of Cisco Systems, Inc. in 1999. There are 252 observations, and the sample mean and standard deviation are 0.00332 and 0.026303, respectively. The log return series also shows no serial correlation with $Q(12) = 10.8$, which is not significant even at the 10% level. Therefore, we have

$$\hat{\sigma} = \frac{s_r}{\sqrt{\Delta}} = \frac{0.026303}{\sqrt{1.0/252.0}} = 0.418, \quad \hat{\mu} = \frac{\overline{r}}{\Delta} + \frac{\hat{\sigma}^2}{2} = 0.924.$$

Consequently, the estimated expected return for Cisco Systems' stock was 92.4% per annum, and the estimated standard deviation was 41.8% per annum in 1999.

6.4 DISTRIBUTIONS OF STOCK PRICES AND LOG RETURNS

The result of the previous section shows that if one assumes that price of a stock follows the geometric Brownian motion

$$dP_t = \mu P_t\, dt + \sigma P_t\, dw_t,$$

then the logarithm of the price follows a generalized Wiener process

$$d\ln(P_t) = \left(\mu - \frac{\sigma^2}{2}\right) dt + \sigma\, dw_t,$$

where P_t is the price of the stock at time t and w_t is a Wiener process. Therefore, the change in log price from time t to T is normally distributed as

$$\ln(P_T) - \ln(P_t) \sim N\left[\left(\mu - \frac{\sigma^2}{2}\right)(T-t), \sigma^2(T-t)\right]. \quad (6.9)$$

Consequently, conditional on the price P_t at time t, the log price at time $T > t$ is normally distributed as

$$\ln(P_T) \sim N\left[\ln(P_t) + \left(\mu - \frac{\sigma^2}{2}\right)(T-t), \sigma^2(T-t)\right]. \quad (6.10)$$

Using the result of lognormal distribution discussed in Chapter 1, we obtain the (conditional) mean and variance of P_T as

$$E(P_T) = P_t \exp[\mu(T-t)],$$
$$\text{Var}(P_T) = P_t^2 \exp[2\mu(T-t)]\{\exp[\sigma^2(T-t)] - 1\}.$$

Note that the expectation confirms that μ is the expected rate of return of the stock.

The prior distribution of stock price can be used to make inference. For example, suppose that the current price of stock A is \$50, the expected return of the stock is 15% per annum, and the volatility is 40% per annum. Then the expected price of stock A in 6 months (0.5 year) and the associated variance are given by

$$E(P_T) = 50\exp(0.15 \times 0.5) = 53.89,$$
$$\text{Var}(P_T) = 2500\exp(0.3 \times 0.5)[\exp(0.16 \times 0.5) - 1] = 241.92.$$

The standard deviation of the price 6 months from now is $\sqrt{241.92} = 15.55$.

Next, let r be the continuously compounded rate of return per annum from time t to T. Then we have

$$P_T = P_t \exp[r(T-t)],$$

where T and t are measured in years. Therefore,

$$r = \frac{1}{T-t} \ln\left(\frac{P_T}{P_t}\right).$$

By Eq. (6.9), we have

$$\ln\left(\frac{P_T}{P_t}\right) \sim N\left[\left(\mu - \frac{\sigma^2}{2}\right)(T-t), \sigma^2(T-t)\right].$$

Consequently, the distribution of the continuously compounded rate of return per annum is

$$r \sim N\left(\mu - \frac{\sigma^2}{2}, \frac{\sigma^2}{T-t}\right).$$

The continuously compounded rate of return is, therefore, normally distributed with mean $\mu - \sigma^2/2$ and standard deviation $\sigma/\sqrt{T-t}$.

Consider a stock with an expected rate of return of 15% per annum and a volatility of 10% per annum. The distribution of the continuously compounded rate of return of the stock over 2 years is normal with mean $0.15 - 0.01/2 = 0.145$ or 14.5% per annum and standard deviation $0.1/\sqrt{2} = 0.071$ or 7.1% per annum. These results allow us to construct confidence intervals (C.I.) for r. For instance, a 95% C.I. for r is $0.145 \pm 1.96 \times 0.071$ per annum (i.e., 0.6%, 28.4%).

6.5 DERIVATION OF BLACK–SCHOLES DIFFERENTIAL EQUATION

In this section, we use Ito's lemma and assume no arbitrage to derive the Black–Scholes differential equation for the price of a derivative contingent to a stock valued at P_t. Assume that the price P_t follows the geometric Brownian motion in Eq. (6.8) and $G_t = G(P_t, t)$ is the price of a derivative (e.g., a call option) contingent on P_t. By Ito's lemma,

$$dG_t = \left(\frac{\partial G_t}{\partial P_t}\mu P_t + \frac{\partial G_t}{\partial t} + \frac{1}{2}\frac{\partial^2 G_t}{\partial P_t^2}\sigma^2 P_t^2\right) dt + \frac{\partial G_t}{\partial P_t}\sigma P_t \, dw_t.$$

The discretized versions of the process and previous result are

$$\Delta P_t = \mu P_t \, \Delta t + \sigma P_t \, \Delta w_t, \tag{6.11}$$

$$\Delta G_t = \left(\frac{\partial G_t}{\partial P_t}\mu P_t + \frac{\partial G_t}{\partial t} + \frac{1}{2}\frac{\partial^2 G_t}{\partial P_t^2}\sigma^2 P_t^2\right) \Delta t + \frac{\partial G_t}{\partial P_t}\sigma P_t \, \Delta w_t, \tag{6.12}$$

where ΔP_t and ΔG_t are changes in P_t and G_t in a small time interval Δt. Because $\Delta w_t = \epsilon\sqrt{\Delta t}$ for both Eqs. (6.11) and (6.12), one can construct a portfolio of the stock and the derivative that does not involve the Wiener process. The appropriate portfolio is short on derivative and long $\partial G_t/\partial P_t$ shares of the stock. Denote the value of the portfolio by V_t. By construction,

$$V_t = -G_t + \frac{\partial G_t}{\partial P_t} P_t. \tag{6.13}$$

The change in V_t is then

$$\Delta V_t = -\Delta G_t + \frac{\partial G_t}{\partial P_t} \Delta P_t. \tag{6.14}$$

Substituting Eqs. (6.11) and (6.12) into Eq. (6.14), we have

$$\Delta V_t = \left(-\frac{\partial G_t}{\partial t} - \frac{1}{2} \frac{\partial^2 G_t}{\partial P_t^2} \sigma^2 P_t^2 \right) \Delta t. \tag{6.15}$$

This equation does not involve the stochastic component Δw_t. Therefore, under the no arbitrage assumption, the portfolio V_t must be riskless during the small time interval Δt. In other words, the assumptions used imply that the portfolio must instantaneously earn the same rate of return as other short-term, risk-free securities. Otherwise there exists an arbitrage opportunity between the portfolio and the short-term, risk-free securities. Consequently, we have

$$\Delta V_t = r V_t \, \Delta t = (r \Delta t) V_t, \tag{6.16}$$

where r is the risk-free interest rate. By Eqs. (6.13)–(6.16), we have

$$\left(\frac{\partial G_t}{\partial t} + \frac{1}{2} \frac{\partial^2 G_t}{\partial P_t^2} \sigma^2 P_t^2 \right) \Delta t = r \left(G_t - \frac{\partial G_t}{\partial P_t} P_t \right) \Delta t.$$

Therefore,

$$\frac{\partial G_t}{\partial t} + r P_t \frac{\partial G_t}{\partial P_t} + \frac{1}{2} \sigma^2 P_t^2 \frac{\partial^2 G_t}{\partial P_t^2} = r G_t. \tag{6.17}$$

This is the Black–Scholes differential equation for derivative pricing. It can be solved to obtain the price of a derivative with P_t as the underlying variable.

The solution so obtained depends on the boundary conditions of the derivative. For a European call option, the boundary condition is

$$G_T = \max(P_T - K, 0),$$

where T is the expiration time and K is the strike price. For a European put option, the boundary condition becomes

$$G_T = \max(K - P_T, 0).$$

Example 6.4. As a simple example, consider a forward contract on a stock that pays no dividend. In this case, the value of the contract is given by

$$G_t = P_t - K \exp[-r(T - t)],$$

where K is the delivery price, r is the risk-free interest rate, and T is the expiration time. For such a function, we have

$$\frac{\partial G_t}{\partial t} = -rK \exp[-r(T-t)], \quad \frac{\partial G_t}{\partial P_t} = 1, \quad \frac{\partial^2 G_t}{\partial P_t^2} = 0.$$

Substituting these quantities into the left-hand side of Eq. (6.17) yields

$$-rK \exp[-r(T-t)] + rP_t = r\{P_t - K \exp[-r(T-t)]\},$$

which equals the right-hand side of Eq. (6.17). Thus, the Black–Scholes differential equation is indeed satisfied.

6.6 BLACK–SCHOLES PRICING FORMULAS

Black and Scholes (1973) successfully solve their differential equation in Eq. (6.17) to obtain exact formulas for the price of European call and put options. In what follows, we derive these formulas using what is called *risk-neutral valuation* in finance.

6.6.1 Risk-Neutral World

The drift parameter μ drops out from the Black–Scholes differential equation. In finance, this means the equation is independent of risk preferences. In other words, risk preferences cannot affect the solution of the equation. A nice consequence of this property is that one can assume that investors are risk-neutral. In a risk-neutral world, we have the following results:

- The expected return on all securities is the risk-free interest rate r.
- The present value of any cash flow can be obtained by discounting its expected value at the risk-free rate.

6.6.2 Formulas

The expected value of a European call option at maturity in a risk-neutral world is

$$E_*[\max(P_T - K, 0)],$$

where E_* denotes expected value in a risk-neutral world. The price of the call option at time t is

$$c_t = \exp[-r(T-t)]E_*[\max(P_T - K, 0)]. \tag{6.18}$$

Yet in a risk-neutral world, we have $\mu = r$, and by Eq. (6.10), $\ln(P_T)$ is normally distributed as

$$\ln(P_T) \sim N\left[\ln(P_t) + \left(r - \frac{\sigma^2}{2}\right)(T-t), \sigma^2(T-t)\right].$$

Let $g(P_T)$ be the probability density function of P_T. Then the price of the call option in Eq. (6.18) is

$$c_t = \exp[-r(T-t)] \int_K^\infty (P_T - K) g(P_T)\, dP_T.$$

By changing the variable in the integration and some algebraic calculations (details are given in Appendix A), we have

$$c_t = P_t \Phi(h_+) - K \exp[-r(T-t)] \Phi(h_-), \tag{6.19}$$

where $\Phi(x)$ is the cumulative distribution function (CDF) of the standard normal random variable evaluated at x,

$$h_+ = \frac{\ln(P_t/K) + (r + \sigma^2/2)(T-t)}{\sigma\sqrt{T-t}},$$

$$h_- = \frac{\ln(P_t/K) + (r - \sigma^2/2)(T-t)}{\sigma\sqrt{T-t}} = h_+ - \sigma\sqrt{T-t}.$$

In practice, $\Phi(x)$ can easily be obtained from most statistical packages. Alternatively, one can use an approximation given in Appendix B.

The Black–Scholes call formula in Eq. (6.19) has some nice interpretations. First, if we exercise the call option on the expiration date, we receive the stock, but we have to pay the strike price. This exchange will take place only when the call finishes in-the-money (i.e., $P_T > K$). The first term $P_t\Phi(h_+)$ is the present value of receiving the stock if and only if $P_T > K$ and the second term $-K\exp[-r(T-t)]\Phi(h_-)$ is the present value of paying the strike price if and only if $P_T > K$. A second interpretation is particularly useful. As shown in the derivation of the Black–Scholes differential equation in Section 6.5, $\Phi(h_+) = \partial G_t/\partial P_t$ is the number of shares in the portfolio that does not involve uncertainty, the Wiener process. This quantity is known as the *delta* in hedging. We know that $c_t = P_t\Phi(h_+) + B_t$, where B_t is the dollar amount invested in risk-free bonds in the portfolio (or short on the derivative). We can then see that $B_t = -K\exp[-r(T-t)]\Phi(h_-)$ directly from inspection of the Black–Scholes formula. The first term of the formula, $P_t\Phi(h_+)$, is the amount invested in the stock, whereas the second term, $K\exp[-r(T-t)]\Phi(h_-)$, is the amount borrowed.

Similarly, we can obtain the price of a European put option as

$$p_t = K\exp[-r(T-t)]\Phi(-h_-) - P_t\Phi(-h_+). \tag{6.20}$$

Since the standard normal distribution is symmetric with respect to its mean 0.0, we have $\Phi(x) = 1 - \Phi(-x)$ for all x. Using this property, we have $\Phi(-h_i) = 1 - \Phi(h_i)$. Thus, the information needed to compute the price of a put option is the same as that of a call option. Alternatively, using the symmetry of normal distribution, it is easy to verify that

$$p_t - c_t = K\exp[-r(T-t)] - P_t,$$

which is referred to as the *put–call parity* and can be used to obtain p_t from c_t. The put–call parity can also be obtained by considering the following two portfolios:

1. *Portfolio A*. One European call option plus an amount of cash equal to $K\exp[-r(T-t)]$.
2. *Portfolio B*. One European put option plus one share of the underlying stock.

The payoff of these two portfolios is

$$\max(P_T, K)$$

at the expiration of the options. Since the options can only be exercised at the expiration date, the portfolios must have identical value today. This means

$$c_t + K\exp[-r(T-t)] = p_t + P_t,$$

which is the put–call parity given earlier.

Example 6.5. Suppose that the current price of Intel stock is \$80 per share with volatility $\sigma = 20\%$ per annum. Suppose further that the risk-free interest rate is 8% per annum. What is the price of a European call option on Intel with a strike price of \$90 that will expire in 3 months?

From the assumptions, we have $P_t = 80$, $K = 90$, $T - t = 0.25$, $\sigma = 0.2$, and $r = 0.08$. Therefore,

$$h_+ = \frac{\ln(80/90) + (0.08 + 0.04/2) \times 0.25}{0.2\sqrt{0.25}} = -0.9278,$$

$$h_- = h_+ - 0.2\sqrt{0.25} = -1.0278.$$

Using any statistical software (e.g., Minitab or SCA) or the approximation in Appendix B, we have

$$\Phi(-0.9278) = 0.1767, \quad \Phi(-1.0278) = 0.1520.$$

Consequently, the price of a European call option is

$$c_t = \$80\Phi(-0.9278) - \$90\Phi(-1.0278)\exp(-0.02) = \$0.73.$$

The stock price has to rise by \$10.73 for the purchaser of the call option to break even.

Under the same assumptions, the price of a European put option is

$$p_t = \$90\exp(-0.08 \times 0.25)\Phi(1.0278) - \$80\Phi(0.9278) = \$8.95.$$

Thus, the stock price can rise an additional \$1.05 for the purchaser of the put option to break even.

Example 6.6. The strike price of the previous example is well beyond the current stock price. A more realistic strike price is \$81. Assume that the other conditions of the previous example continue to hold. We now have $P_t = 80$, $K = 81$, $r = 0.08$, and $T - t = 0.25$, and the h_i become

$$h_+ = \frac{\ln(80/81) + (0.08 + 0.04/2) \times 0.25}{0.2\sqrt{0.25}} = 0.125775,$$

$$h_- = h_+ - 0.2\sqrt{0.25} = 0.025775.$$

Using the approximation in Appendix B, we have $\Phi(0.125775) = 0.5500$ and $\Phi(0.025775) = 0.5103$. The price of a European call option is then

$$c_t = \$80\Phi(0.125775) - \$81\exp(-0.02)\Phi(0.025775) = \$3.49.$$

The price of the stock has to rise by \$4.49 for the purchaser of the call option to break even. On the other hand, under the same assumptions, the price of a European put option is

$$\begin{aligned} p_t &= \$81\exp(-0.02)\Phi(-0.025775) - \$80\Phi(-0.125775) \\ &= \$81\exp(-0.02) \times 0.48972 - \$80 \times 0.44996 = \$2.89. \end{aligned}$$

The stock price must fall \$1.89 for the purchaser of the put option to break even.

6.6.3 Lower Bounds of European Options

Consider the call option of a nondividend-paying stock. It can be shown that the price of a European call option satisfies

$$c_t \geq P_t - K\exp[-r(T - t)];$$

that is, the lower bound for a European call price is $P_t - K\exp[-r(T - t)]$. This result can be verified by considering two portfolios:

1. *Portfolio A*. One European call option plus an amount of cash equal to $K\exp[-r(T - t)]$.
2. *Portfolio B*. One share of the stock.

For portfolio A, if the cash is invested at the risk-free interest rate, it will result in K at time T. If $P_T > K$, the call option is exercised at time T and the portfolio is worth P_T. If $P_T < K$, the call option expires worthless and the portfolio is worth K. Therefore, the value of portfolio is

$$\max(P_T, K).$$

The value of portfolio B is P_T at time T. Hence, portfolio A is always worth more than (or, at least, equal to) portfolio B. It follows that portfolio A must be worth more than portfolio B today; that is,

$$c_t + K \exp[-r(T-t)] \geq P_t, \quad \text{or} \quad c_t \geq P_t - K \exp[-r(T-t)].$$

Furthermore, since $c_t \geq 0$, we have

$$c_t \geq \max(P_t - K \exp[-r(T-t)], 0).$$

A similar approach can be used to show that the price of a corresponding European put option satisfies

$$p_t \geq \max(K \exp[-r(T-t)] - P_t, 0).$$

Example 6.7. Suppose that $P_t = \$30$, $K = \$28$, $r = 6\%$ per annum, and $T - t = 0.5$. In this case,

$$P_t - K \exp[-r(T-t)] = \$[30 - 28 \exp(-0.06 \times 0.5)] \approx \$2.83.$$

Assume that the European call price of the stock is \$2.50, which is less than the theoretical minimum of \$2.83. An arbitrageur can buy the call option and short the stock. This provides a new cash flow of \$(30 − 2.50) = \$27.50. If invested for 6 months at the risk-free interest rate, the \$27.50 grows to \$27.50 exp(0.06 × 0.5) = \$28.34. At the expiration time, if $P_T > \$28$, the arbitrageur exercises the option, closes out the short position, and makes a profit of \$(28.34 − 28) = \$0.34. On the other hand, if $P_T < \$28$, the stock is bought in the market to close the short position. The arbitrageur then makes an even greater profit. For illustration, suppose that $P_T = \$27.00$, then the profit is \$(28.34 − 27.00) = \$1.34.

6.6.4 Discussion

From the formulas, the price of a call or put option depends on five variables—namely, the current stock price P_t, the strike price K, the time to expiration $T - t$ measured in years, the volatility σ per annum, and the interest rate r per annum. It pays to study the effects of these five variables on the price of an option.

Marginal Effects

Consider first the marginal effects of the five variables on the price of a call option c_t. By marginal effects we mean that changing one variable while holding the others fixed. The effects on a call option can be summarized as follows:

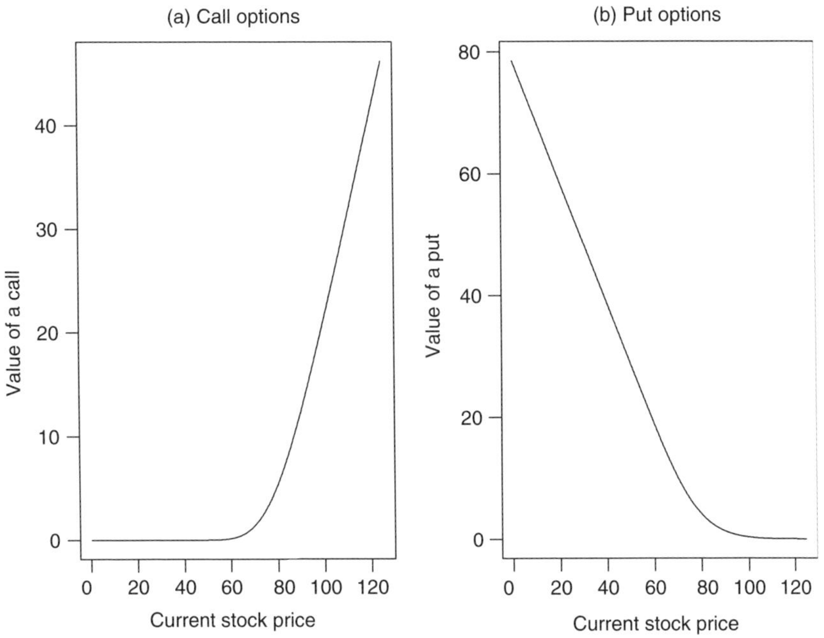

Figure 6.3. Marginal effects of the current stock price on the price of an option with $K = 80$, $T - t = 0.25$, $\sigma = 0.3$, and $r = 0.06$: (a) call option and (b) put option.

1. *Current Stock Price* P_t. c_t is positively related to $\ln(P_t)$. In particular, $c_t \to 0$ as $P_t \to 0$ and $c_t \to \infty$ as $P_t \to \infty$. Figure 6.3a illustrates the effects with $K = 80$, $r = 6\%$ per annum, $T - t = 0.25$ year, and $\sigma = 30\%$ per annum.
2. *Strike Price* K. c_t is negatively related to $\ln(K)$. In particular, $c_t \to P_t$ as $K \to 0$ and $c_t \to 0$ as $K \to \infty$.
3. *Time to Expiration*. c_t is related to $T - t$ in a complicated manner, but we can obtain the limiting results by writing h_+ and h_- as

$$h_+ = \frac{\ln(P_t/K)}{\sigma\sqrt{T-t}} + \frac{(r + \sigma^2/2)\sqrt{T-t}}{\sigma},$$

$$h_- = \frac{\ln(P_t/K)}{\sigma\sqrt{T-t}} + \frac{(r - \sigma^2/2)\sqrt{T-t}}{\sigma}.$$

If $P_t < K$, then $c_t \to 0$ as $(T - t) \to 0$. If $P_t > K$, then $c_t \to P_t - K$ as $(T - t) \to 0$ and $c_t \to P_t$ as $(T - t) \to \infty$. Figure 6.4a shows the marginal effects of $T - t$ on c_t for three different current stock prices. The fixed variables are $K = 80$, $r = 6\%$, and $\sigma = 30\%$. The solid, dotted, and dashed lines of the plot are for $P_t = 70$, 80, and 90, respectively.

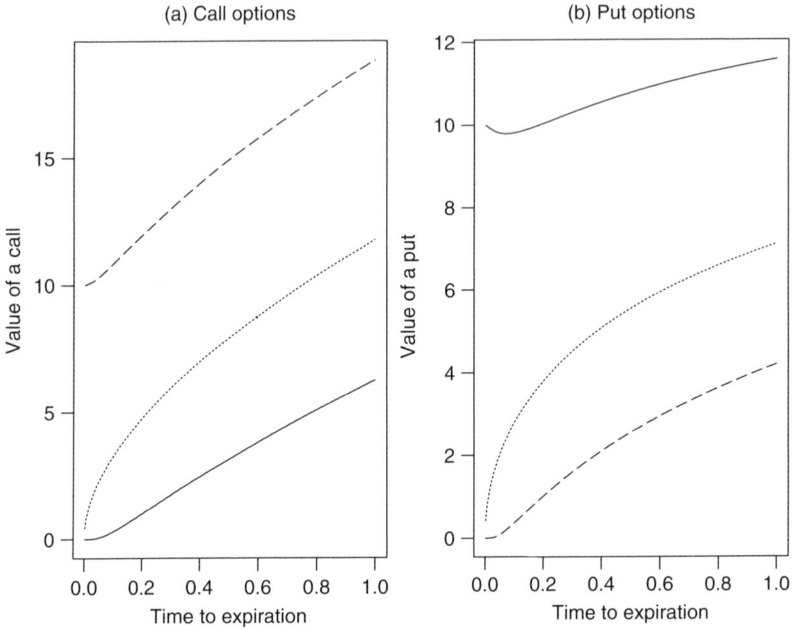

Figure 6.4. Marginal effects of the time to expiration on the price of an option with $K = 80$, $\sigma = 0.3$, and $r = 0.06$: (a) call option and (b) put option. The solid, dotted, and dashed lines are for the current stock price $P_t = 70$, 80, and 90, respectively.

4. *Volatility* σ. Rewriting h_+ and h_- as

$$h_+ = \frac{\ln(P_t/K) + r(T-t)}{\sigma\sqrt{T-t}} + \frac{\sigma}{2}\sqrt{T-t},$$

$$h_- = \frac{\ln(P_t/K) + r(T-t)}{\sigma\sqrt{T-t}} - \frac{\sigma}{2}\sqrt{T-t},$$

we obtain that (a) if $\ln(P_t/K) + r(T-t) < 0$, then $c_t \to 0$ as $\sigma \to 0$, and (b) if $\ln(P_t/K) + r(T-t) \geq 0$, then $c_t \to P_t - Ke^{-r(T-t)}$ as $\sigma \to 0$ and $c_t \to P_t$ as $\sigma \to \infty$. Figure 6.5a shows the effects of σ on c_t for $K = 80$, $T - t = 0.25$, $r = 0.06$, and three different values of P_t. The solid, dotted, and dashed lines are for $P_t = 70$, 80, and 90, respectively.

5. *Interest Rate*. c_t is positively related to r such that $c_t \to P_t$ as $r \to \infty$.

The marginal effects of the five variables on a put option can be obtained similarly. Figures 6.3b, 6.4b, and 6.5b illustrate the effects for some selected cases.

Some Joint Effects

Figure 6.6 shows the joint effects of volatility and strike price on a call option, where the other variables are fixed at $P_t = 80$, $r = 0.06$, and $T - t = 0.25$. As

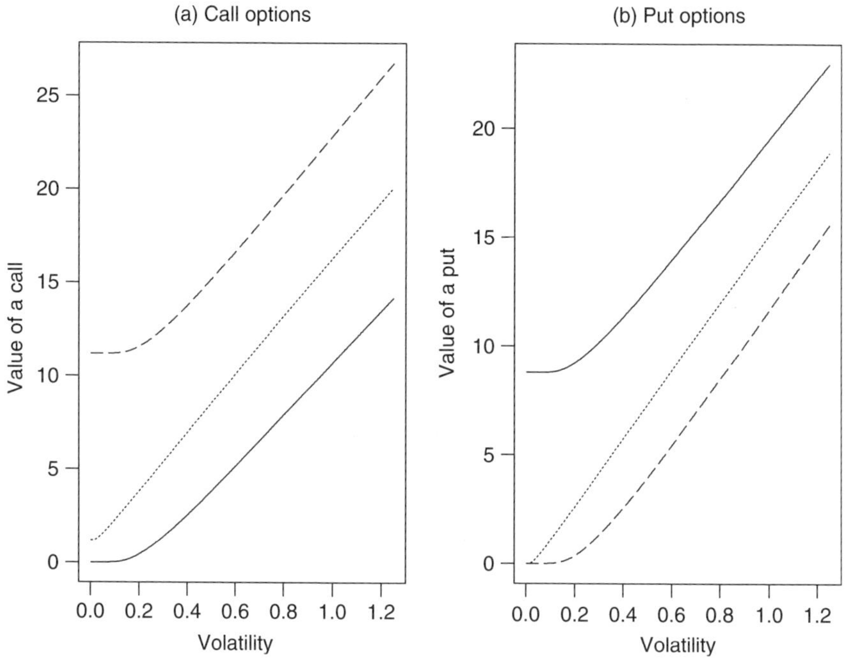

Figure 6.5. Marginal effects of stock volatility on the price of an option with $K = 80$, $T - t = 0.25$, and $r = 0.06$: (a) call option and (b) put option. The solid, dotted, and dashed lines are for the current stock price $P_t = 70$, 80, and 90, respectively.

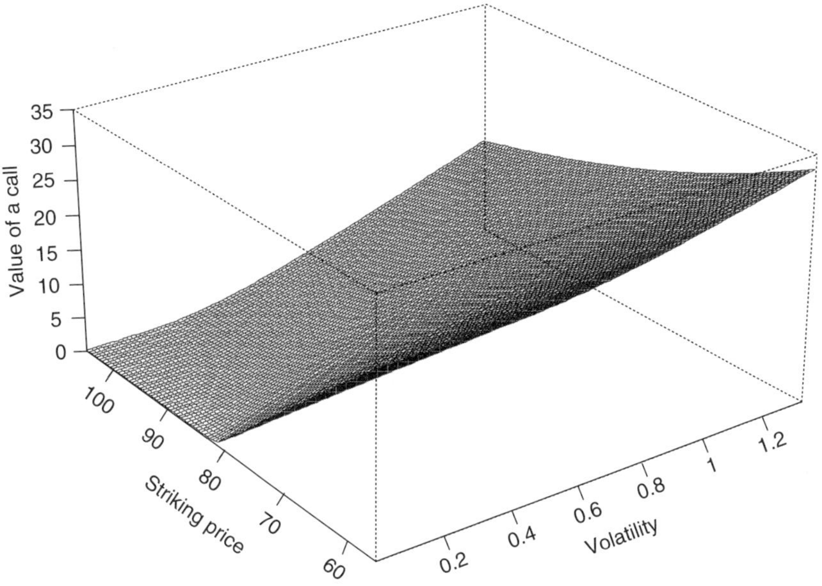

Figure 6.6. Joint effects of stock volatility and the strike price on a call option with $P_t = 80$, $r = 0.06$, and $T - t = 0.25$.

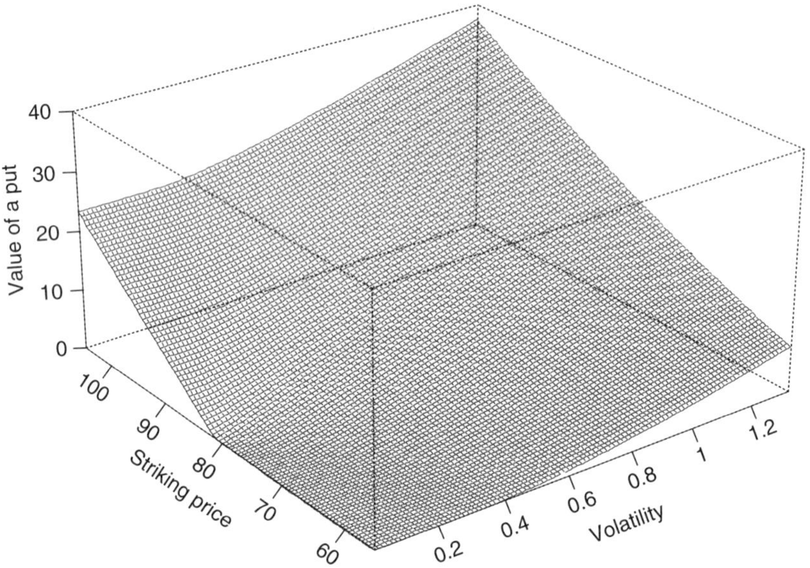

Figure 6.7. Joint effects of stock volatility and the strike price on a put option with $K = 80$, $T - t = 0.25$, and $r = 0.06$.

expected, the price of a call option is higher when the volatility is high and the strike price is well below the current stock price. Figure 6.7 shows the effects on a put option under the same conditions. The price of a put option is higher when the volatility is high and the strike price is well above the current stock price. Furthermore, the plot also shows that the effects of a strike price on the price of a put option becomes more linear as the volatility increases.

6.7 AN EXTENSION OF ITO'S LEMMA

In derivative pricing, a derivative may be contingent on multiple securities. When the prices of these securities are driven by multiple factors, the price of the derivative is a function of several stochastic processes. The two-factor model for the term structure of interest rate is an example of two stochastic processes. In this section, we briefly discuss the extension of Ito's lemma to the case of several stochastic processes.

Consider a k-dimensional continuous-time process $\boldsymbol{x}_t = (x_{1t}, \ldots, x_{kt})'$, where k is a positive integer and x_{it} is a continuous-time stochastic process satisfying

$$dx_{it} = \mu_i(\boldsymbol{x}_t)\, dt + \sigma_i(\boldsymbol{x}_t)\, dw_{it}, \quad i = 1, \ldots, k, \tag{6.21}$$

where w_{it} is a Wiener process. It is understood that the drift and volatility functions $\mu_i(x_{it})$ and $\sigma_i(x_{it})$ are functions of time index t as well. We omit t from their arguments to simplify the notation. For $i \neq j$, the Wiener processes w_{it} and w_{jt} are different. We assume that the correlation between dw_{it} and dw_{jt} is ρ_{ij}. This means that ρ_{ij} is the correlation between the two standard normal random variables ϵ_i and ϵ_j defined by $\Delta w_{it} = \epsilon_i \Delta t$ and $\Delta w_{jt} = \epsilon_j \Delta t$. Assume that $G_t = G(\boldsymbol{x}_t, t)$ is a function of the stochastic processes x_{it} and time t. The Taylor expansion gives

$$\begin{aligned}\Delta G_t &= \sum_{i=1}^{k} \frac{\partial G_t}{\partial x_{it}} \Delta x_{it} + \frac{\partial G_t}{\partial t} \Delta t + \frac{1}{2} \sum_{i=1}^{k} \sum_{j=1}^{k} \frac{\partial^2 G_t}{\partial x_{it} \partial x_{jt}} \Delta x_{it} \Delta x_{jt} \\ &\quad + \frac{1}{2} \sum_{i=1}^{k} \frac{\partial^2 G_t}{\partial x_{it} \partial t} \Delta x_{it} \Delta t + \cdots .\end{aligned}$$

The discretized version of Eq. (6.21) is

$$\Delta w_{it} = \mu_i(\boldsymbol{x}_t) \Delta t + \sigma_i(\boldsymbol{x}_t) \Delta w_{it}, \quad i = 1, \ldots, k.$$

Using a similar argument as that of Eq. (6.5) in Section 6.3, we can obtain that

$$\lim_{\Delta t \to 0} (\Delta x_{it})^2 \to \sigma_i^2(\boldsymbol{x}_t)\, dt, \tag{6.22}$$

$$\lim_{\Delta t \to 0} (\Delta x_{it} \Delta x_{jt}) \to \sigma_i(\boldsymbol{x}_t) \sigma_j(\boldsymbol{x}_t) \rho_{ij}\, dt. \tag{6.23}$$

Using Eqs. (6.21)–(6.23), taking the limit as $\Delta t \to 0$, and ignoring higher order terms of Δt, we have

$$\begin{aligned}dG_t &= \left[\sum_{i=1}^{k} \frac{\partial G_t}{\partial x_{it}} \mu_i(\boldsymbol{x}_t) + \frac{\partial G_t}{\partial t} + \frac{1}{2} \sum_{i=1}^{k} \sum_{j=1}^{k} \frac{\partial^2 G_t}{\partial x_{it} \partial x_{jt}} \sigma_i(\boldsymbol{x}_t) \sigma_j(\boldsymbol{x}_t) \rho_{ij} \right] dt \\ &\quad + \sum_{i=1}^{k} \frac{\partial G_t}{\partial x_{it}} \sigma_i(\boldsymbol{x}_t)\, dw_{it}.\end{aligned} \tag{6.24}$$

This is a generalization of Ito's lemma to the case of multiple stochastic processes.

6.8 STOCHASTIC INTEGRAL

We briefly discuss stochastic integration so that the price of an asset can be obtained under the assumption that it follows an Ito process. We deduce the integration result using Ito's formula. For a rigorous treatment on the topic, readers may consult textbooks on stochastic calculus. First, like the usual integration of a deterministic function, integration is the opposite of differentiation so that

$$\int_0^t dx_s = x_t - x_0$$

continues to hold for a stochastic process x_t. In particular, for the Wiener process w_t, we have $\int_0^t dw_s = w_t$ because $w_0 = 0$. Next, consider the integration $\int_0^t w_s\, dw_s$. Using the prior result and taking integration of Eq. (6.7), we have

$$w_t^2 = t + 2\int_0^t w_s\, dw_s.$$

Therefore,

$$\int_0^t w_s\, dw_s = \tfrac{1}{2}(w_t^2 - t).$$

This is different from the usual deterministic integration for which $\int_0^t y\, dy = (y_t^2 - y_0^2)/2$.

Turn to the case that x_t is a geometric Brownian motion—that is, x_t satisfies

$$dx_t = \mu x_t\, dt + \sigma x_t\, dw_t,$$

where μ and σ are constant with $\sigma > 0$; see Eq. (6.8). Applying Ito's lemma to $G(x_t, t) = \ln(x_t)$, we obtain

$$d\ln(x_t) = \left(\mu - \frac{\sigma^2}{2}\right) dt + \sigma\, dw_t.$$

Performing the integration and using the results obtained before, we have

$$\int_0^t d\ln(x_s) = \left(\mu - \frac{\sigma^2}{2}\right)\int_0^t ds + \sigma\int_0^t dw_s.$$

Consequently,

$$\ln(x_t) = \ln(x_0) + (\mu - \sigma^2/2)t + \sigma w_t$$

and

$$x_t = x_0 \exp[(\mu - \sigma^2/2)t + \sigma w_t].$$

Changing the notation x_t to P_t for the price of an asset, we have a solution for the price under the assumption that it is a geometric Brownian motion. The price is

$$P_t = P_0 \exp[(\mu - \sigma^2/2)t + \sigma w_t]. \tag{6.25}$$

6.9 JUMP DIFFUSION MODELS

Empirical studies have found that the stochastic diffusion model based on Brownian motion fails to explain some characteristics of asset returns and the prices of their derivatives (e.g., the "volatility smile" of implied volatilities; see Bakshi, Cao, and Chen, 1997, and the references therein). Volatility smile is referred to as the convex function between the implied volatility and strike price of an option. Both out-of-the-money and in-the-money options tend to have higher implied volatilities than at-the-money options especially in the foreign exchange markets. Volatility smile is less pronounced for equity options. The inadequacy of the standard stochastic diffusion model has led to the developments of alternative continuous-time models. For example, jump diffusion and stochastic volatility models have been proposed in the literature to overcome the inadequacy; see Merton (1976) and Duffie (1995).

Jumps in stock prices are often assumed to follow a probability law. For example, the jumps may follow a Poisson process, which is a continuous-time discrete process. For a given time t, let X_t be the number of times a special event occurs during the time period $[0, t]$. Then X_t is a Poisson process if

$$\Pr(X_t = m) = \frac{\lambda^m t^m}{m!} \exp(-\lambda t), \quad \lambda > 0.$$

That is, X_t follows a Poisson distribution with parameter λt. The parameter λ governs the occurrence of the special event and is referred to as the *rate* or *intensity* of the process. A formal definition also requires that X_t be a right-continuous homogeneous Markov process with left-hand limit.

In this section, we discuss a simple jump diffusion model proposed by Kou (2002). This simple model enjoys several nice properties. The returns implied by the model are leptokurtic and asymmetric with respect to zero. In addition, the model can reproduce volatility smile and provide analytical formulas for the prices of many options. The model consists of two parts, with the first part being continuous and following a geometric Brownian motion and the second part being a jump process. The occurrences of jump are governed by a Poisson process, and the jump size follows a double exponential distribution. Let P_t be the price of an asset at time t. The simple jump diffusion model postulates that the price follows the stochastic differential equation

$$\frac{dP_t}{P_t} = \mu\, dt + \sigma\, dw_t + d\left(\sum_{i=1}^{n_t} (J_i - 1)\right), \tag{6.26}$$

where w_t is a Wiener process, n_t is a Poisson process with rate λ, and $\{J_i\}$ is a sequence of independent and identically distributed non-negative random variables such that $X = \ln(J)$ has a double exponential distribution with probability density function

$$f_X(x) = \frac{1}{2\eta} e^{-|x-\kappa|/\eta}, \quad 0 < \eta < 1. \tag{6.27}$$

The double exponential distribution is also referred to as the *Laplacian distribution*. In model (6.26), n_t, w_t, and J_i are independent so that there is no relation between the randomness of the model. Notice that n_t is the number of jumps in the time interval $[0, t]$ and follows a Poisson distribution with parameter λt, where λ is a constant. At the ith jump, the proportion of price jump is $J_i - 1$.

The double exponential distribution can be written as

$$X - \kappa = \begin{cases} \xi & \text{with probability } 0.5, \\ -\xi & \text{with probability } 0.5, \end{cases} \tag{6.28}$$

where ξ is an exponential random variable with mean η and variance η^2. The probability density function of ξ is

$$f(x) = \frac{1}{\eta} e^{-x/\eta}, \quad 0 < x < \infty.$$

Some useful properties of the double exponential distribution are

$$E(X) = \kappa, \quad \text{Var}(X) = 2\eta^2, \quad E(e^X) = \frac{e^\kappa}{1 - \eta^2}.$$

For finite samples, it is hard to distinguish a double exponential distribution from a Student-t distribution. However, a double exponential distribution is more tractable analytically and can generate a higher probability concentration (e.g., higher peak) around its mean value. As stated in Chapter 1, histograms of observed asset returns tend to have a higher peak than the normal density. Figure 6.8 shows the probability density function of a double exponential random variable in the solid line and that of a normal random variable in the dotted line. Both variables have mean zero and variance 0.0008. The high peak of the double exponential density is clearly seen.

Solving the stochastic differential equation in Eq. (6.26), we obtain the dynamics of the asset price as

$$P_t = P_0 \exp[(\mu - \sigma^2/2)t + \sigma w_t] \prod_{i=1}^{n_t} J_i, \tag{6.29}$$

where it is understood that $\prod_{i=1}^{0} = 1$. This result is a generalization of Eq. (6.25) by including the stochastic jumps. It can be obtained as follows. Let t_i be the time of the ith jump. For $t \in [0, t_1)$, there is no jump and the price is given in Eq. (6.25). Consequently, the left-hand price limit at time t_1 is

$$P_{t_1^-} = P_0 \exp[(\mu - \sigma^2/2)t_1 + \sigma w_{t_1}].$$

At time t_1, the proportion of price jump is $J_1 - 1$ so that the price becomes

$$P_{t_1} = (1 + J_1 - 1)P_{t_1^-} = J_1 P_{t_1^-} = P_0 \exp[(\mu - \sigma^2/2)t_1 + \sigma w_{t_1}]J_1.$$

For $t \in (t_1, t_2)$, there is no jump in the interval $(t_1, t]$ so that

$$P_t = P_{t_1} \exp[(\mu - \sigma^2/2)(t - t_1) + \sigma(w_t - w_{t_1})].$$

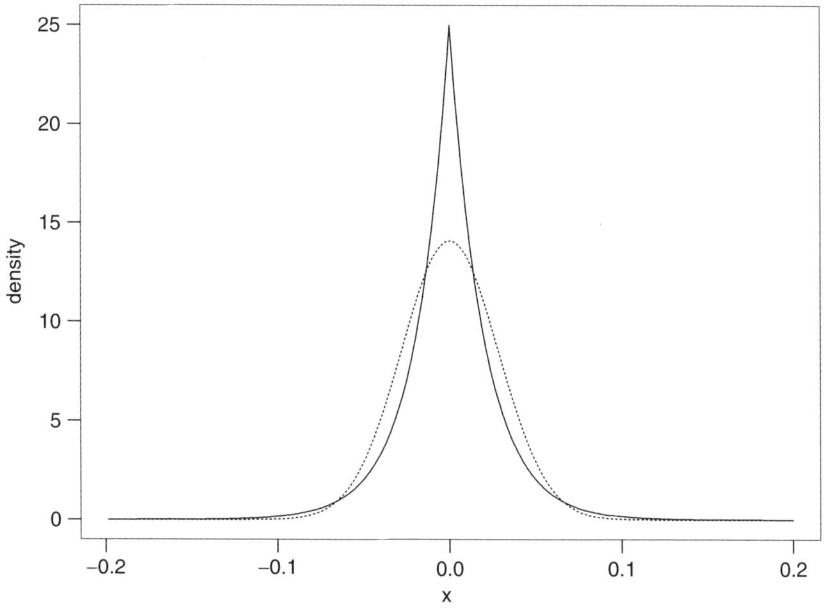

Figure 6.8. Probability density functions of a double exponential and a normal random variable with mean zero and variance 0.0008. The solid line denotes the double exponential distribution.

Plugging in P_{t_1}, we have

$$P_t = P_0 \exp[(\mu - \sigma^2/2)t + \sigma w_t] J_1.$$

Repeating the scheme, we obtain Eq. (6.29).

From Eq. (6.29), the simple return of the underlying asset in a small time increment Δt becomes

$$\frac{P_{t+\Delta t} - P_t}{P_t} = \exp\left((\mu - \tfrac{1}{2}\sigma^2)\Delta t + \sigma(w_{t+\Delta t} - w_t) + \sum_{i=n_t+1}^{n_{t+\Delta t}} X_i \right) - 1,$$

where it is understood that a summation over an empty set is zero and $X_i = \ln(J_i)$. For a small Δt, we may use the approximation $e^x \approx 1 + x + x^2/2$ and the result $(\Delta w_t)^2 \approx \Delta t$ discussed in Section 6.3 to obtain

$$\begin{aligned}\frac{P_{t+\Delta t} - P_t}{P_t} &\approx (\mu - \tfrac{1}{2}\sigma^2)\Delta t + \sigma \ \Delta w_t + \sum_{i=n_t+1}^{n_{t+\Delta t}} X_i + \tfrac{1}{2}\sigma^2(\Delta w_t)^2 \\ &\approx \mu \ \Delta t + \sigma\epsilon\sqrt{\Delta t} + \sum_{i=n_t+1}^{n_{t+\Delta t}} X_i,\end{aligned}$$

where $\Delta w_t = w_{t+\Delta t} - w_t$ and ϵ is a standard normal random variable.

Under the assumption of a Poisson process, the probability of having one jump in the time interval $(t, t + \Delta t]$ is $\lambda\ \Delta t$ and that of having more than one jump is $o(\Delta t)$, where the symbol $o(\Delta t)$ means that if we divide this term by Δt then its value tends to zero as Δt tends to zero. Therefore, for a small Δt, by ignoring multiple jumps, we have

$$\sum_{i=n_t+1}^{n_{t+\Delta t}} X_i \approx \begin{cases} X_{n_t+1} & \text{with probability } \lambda\ \Delta t, \\ 0 & \text{with probability } 1 - \lambda\ \Delta t. \end{cases}$$

Combining the prior results, we see that the simple return of the underlying asset is approximately distributed as

$$\frac{P_{t+\Delta t} - P_t}{P_t} \approx \mu\ \Delta t + \sigma\epsilon\sqrt{\Delta t} + I \times X, \tag{6.30}$$

where I is a Bernoulli random variable with $\Pr(I = 1) = \lambda\ \Delta t$ and $\Pr(I = 0) = 1 - \lambda\ \Delta t$, and X is a double exponential random variable defined in Eq. (6.28). Equation (6.30) reduces to that of a geometric Brownian motion without jumps.

Let $G = \mu\ \Delta t + \sigma\epsilon\sqrt{\Delta t} + I \times X$ be the random variable on the right-hand side of Eq. (6.30). Using the independence between the exponential and normal distributions used in the model, Kou (2002) obtains the probability density function of G as

$$\begin{aligned} g(x) = {} & \frac{\lambda\ \Delta t}{2\eta} e^{\sigma^2 \Delta t/(2\eta^2)} \left[e^{-\omega/\eta} \Phi\left(\frac{\omega\eta - \sigma^2 \Delta t}{\sigma\eta\sqrt{\Delta t}} \right) + e^{\omega/\eta} \Phi\left(\frac{\omega\eta + \sigma^2 \Delta t}{\sigma\eta\sqrt{\Delta t}} \right) \right] \\ & + (1 - \lambda\ \Delta t) \frac{1}{\sigma\sqrt{\Delta t}} f\left(\frac{x - \mu\ \Delta t}{\sigma\sqrt{\Delta t}} \right), \end{aligned} \tag{6.31}$$

where $\omega = x - \mu\ \Delta t - \kappa$, and $f(.)$ and $\Phi(.)$ are, respectively, the probability density and cumulative distribution functions of the standard normal random variable. Furthermore,

$$E(G) = \mu\ \Delta t + \kappa\lambda\ \Delta t, \quad \text{Var}(G) = \sigma^2 \Delta t + \lambda\ \Delta t[2\eta^2 + \kappa^2(1 - \lambda\ \Delta t)].$$

Figure 6.9 shows some comparisons between probability density functions of a normal distribution and the distribution of Eq. (6.31). Both distributions have mean zero and variance 2.0572×10^{-4}. The mean and variance are obtained by assuming that the return of the underlying asset satisfies $\mu = 20\%$ per annum, $\sigma = 20\%$ per annum, $\Delta t = 1$ day $= 1/252$ year, $\lambda = 10$, $\kappa = -0.02$, and $\eta = 0.02$. In other words, we assume that there are about 10 daily jumps per year with average jump size -2%, and the jump size standard error is 2%. These values are reasonable for a U.S. stock. From the plots, the leptokurtic feature of the distribution derived from the jump diffusion process in Eq. (6.26) is clearly shown. The distribution has a higher peak and fatter tails than the corresponding normal distribution.

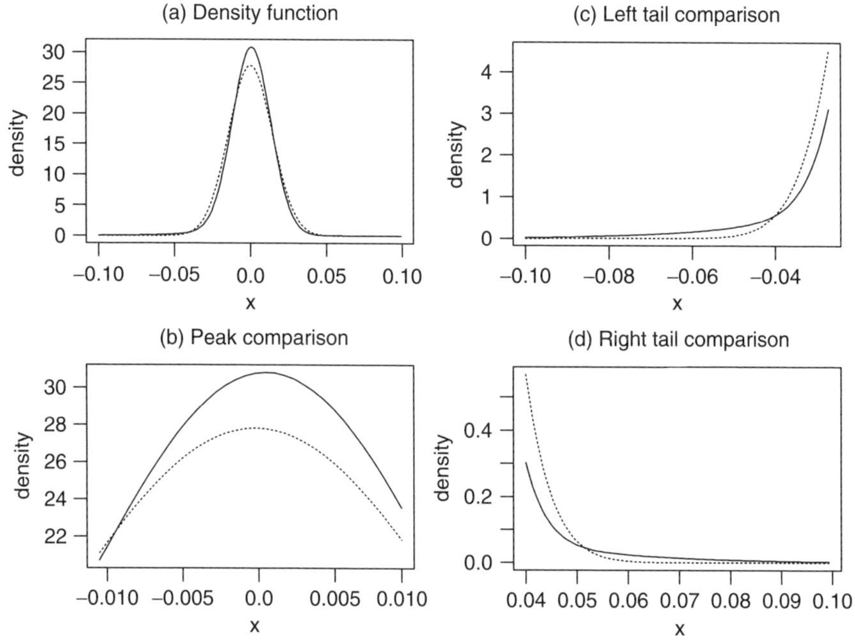

Figure 6.9. Density comparisons between a normal distribution and the distribution of Eq. (6.31). The dotted line denotes the normal distribution. Both distributions have mean zero and variance 2.0572×10^{-4}. (a) Overall comparison, (b) comparison of the peaks, (c) left tails, and (d) right tails.

6.9.1 Option Pricing Under Jump Diffusion

In the presence of random jumps, the market becomes incomplete. In this case, the standard hedging arguments are not applicable to price an option. But we can still derive an option pricing formula that does not depend on attitudes toward risk by assuming that the number of securities available is very large so that the risk of the sudden jumps is diversifiable and the market will therefore pay no risk premium over the risk-free rate for bearing this risk. Alternatively, for a given set of risk premiums, one can consider a risk-neutral measure P^* such that

$$\begin{aligned}\frac{dP_t}{P_t} &= [r - \lambda E(J-1)]\,dt + \sigma\,dw_t + d\left(\sum_{i=1}^{n_t}(J_i - 1)\right)\\ &= (r - \lambda\psi)\,dt + \sigma\,dw_t + d\left(\sum_{i=1}^{n_t}(J_i - 1)\right),\end{aligned}$$

where r is the risk-free interest rate, $J = \exp(X)$ such that X follows the double exponential distribution of Eq. (6.27), $\psi = e^{\kappa}/(1-\eta^2) - 1$, $0 < \eta < 1$, and the parameters κ, η, ψ, and σ become risk-neutral parameters taking consideration of the risk premiums; see Kou (2002) for more details. The unique solution of the prior equation is given by

$$P_t = P_0 \exp\left[\left(r - \frac{\sigma^2}{2} - \lambda\psi\right)t + \sigma w_t\right]\prod_{i=1}^{n_t} J_i.$$

To price a European option in the jump diffusion model, it remains to compute the expectation, under the measure P^*, of the discounted final payoff of the option. In particular, the price of a European call option at time t is given by

$$\begin{aligned} c_t &= E_*[e^{-r(T-t)}(P_T - K)_+] \\ &= E_*\left[e^{-r(T-t)}\left(P_t \exp[(r - \sigma^2/2 - \lambda\psi)(T-t) + \sigma\sqrt{T-t}\epsilon]\prod_{i=1}^{n_T} J_i - K\right)_+\right], \end{aligned} \tag{6.32}$$

where T is the expiration time, $(T-t)$ is the time to expiration measured in years, K is the strike price, $(y)_+ = \max(0, y)$, and ϵ is a standard normal random variable. Kou (2002) shows that c_t is analytically tractable as

$$\begin{aligned} c_t &= \sum_{n=1}^{\infty}\sum_{j=1}^{n} e^{-\lambda(T-t)}\frac{\lambda^n(T-t)^n}{n!}\frac{2^j}{2^{2n-1}}\binom{2n-j-1}{n-1}(A_{1,n,j} + A_{2,n,j} + A_{3,n,j}) \\ &\quad + e^{-\lambda(T-t)}\left[P_t e^{-\lambda\psi(T-t)}\Phi(h_+) - Ke^{-r(T-t)}\Phi(h_-)\right], \end{aligned} \tag{6.33}$$

where $\Phi(.)$ is the CDF of the standard normal random variable,

$$\begin{aligned} A_{1,n,j} &= P_t\, e^{-\lambda\psi(T-t)+n\kappa}\frac{1}{2}\left(\frac{1}{(1-\eta)^j} + \frac{1}{(1+\eta)^j}\right)\Phi(b_+) - e^{-r(T-t)}K\Phi(b_-), \\ A_{2,n,j} &= \tfrac{1}{2}e^{-r(T-t)-\omega/\eta+\sigma^2(T-t)/(2\eta^2)}K \\ &\quad \times \sum_{i=0}^{j-1}\left(\frac{1}{(1-\eta)^{j-i}} - 1\right)\left(\frac{\sigma\sqrt{T-t}}{\eta}\right)^i \frac{1}{\sqrt{2\pi}} Hh_i(c_-), \\ A_{3,n,j} &= \tfrac{1}{2}e^{-r(T-t)+\omega/\eta+\sigma^2(T-t)/(2\eta^2)}K \\ &\quad \times \sum_{i=0}^{j-1}\left(1 - \frac{1}{(1+\eta)^{j-i}}\right)\left(\frac{\sigma\sqrt{T-t}}{\eta}\right)^i \frac{1}{\sqrt{2\pi}} Hh_i(c_+), \\ b_\pm &= \frac{\ln(P_t/K) + (r \pm \sigma^2/2 - \lambda\psi)(T-t) + n\kappa}{\sigma\sqrt{T-t}}, \\ h_\pm &= \frac{\ln(P_t/K) + (r \pm \sigma^2/2 - \lambda\psi)(T-t)}{\sigma\sqrt{T-t}}, \end{aligned}$$

$$c_{\pm} = \frac{\sigma\sqrt{T-t}}{\eta} \pm \frac{\omega}{\sigma\sqrt{T-t}},$$
$$\omega = \ln(K/P_t) + \lambda\psi(T-t) - (r-\sigma^2/2)(T-t) - n\kappa,$$
$$\psi = \frac{e^{\kappa}}{1-\eta^2} - 1,$$

and the $Hh_i(.)$ functions are defined as

$$Hh_n(x) = \frac{1}{n!}\int_x^{\infty} (s-x)^n e^{-s^2/2}\, ds, \quad n = 0, 1, \ldots, \tag{6.34}$$

and $Hh_{-1}(x) = \exp(-x^2/2)$, which is $\sqrt{2\pi} f(x)$ with $f(x)$ being the probability density function of a standard normal random variable; see Abramowitz and Stegun (1972). The $Hh_n(x)$ functions satisfy the recursion

$$nHh_n(x) = Hh_{n-2}(x) - xHh_{n-1}(x), \quad n \geq 1, \tag{6.35}$$

with starting values $Hh_{-1}(x) = e^{-x^2/2}$ and $Hh_0(x) = \sqrt{2\pi}\Phi(-x)$.

The pricing formula involves an infinite series, but its numerical value can be approximated quickly and accurately through truncation (e.g., the first 10 terms). Also, if $\lambda = 0$ (i.e., there are no jumps), then it is easily seen that c_t reduces to the Black–Scholes formula for a call option discussed before.

Finally, the price of a European put option under the jump diffusion model considered can be obtained by using the put–call parity; that is,

$$p_t = c_t + Ke^{-r(T-t)} - P_t.$$

Pricing formulas for other options under the jump diffusion model in Eq. (6.26) can be found in Kou (2002).

Example 6.8. Consider the stock of Example 6.6, which has a current price of \$80. As before, assume that the strike price of a European option is $K = \$85$ and other parameters are $r = 0.08$ and $T - t = 0.25$. In addition, assume that the price of the stock follows the jump diffusion model in Eq. (6.26) with parameters $\lambda = 10$, $\kappa = -0.02$, and $\eta = 0.02$. In other words, there are about 10 jumps per year with average jump size -2% and jump size standard error 2%. Using the formula in Eq. (6.33), we obtain $c_t = \$3.92$, which is higher than the \$3.49 of Example 6.6 when there are no jumps. The corresponding put option assumes the value $p_t = \$3.31$, which is also higher than what we had before. As expected, adding the jumps while keeping the other parameters fixed increases the prices of both European options. Keep in mind, however, that adding the jump process to the stock price in a real application often leads to different estimates for the stock volatility σ.

6.10 ESTIMATION OF CONTINUOUS-TIME MODELS

Next, we consider the problem of estimating directly the diffusion equation (i.e., Ito process) from discretely sampled data. Here the drift and volatility functions $\mu(x_t, t)$ and $\sigma(x_t, t)$ are time-varying and may not follow a specific parametric form. This is a topic of considerable interest in recent years. Details of the available methods are beyond the scope of this chapter. Hence, we only outline the approaches proposed in the literature. Interested readers can consult the corresponding references and Lo (1988).

There are several approaches available for estimating a diffusion equation. The first approach is the quasi-maximum likelihood approach, which makes use of the fact that for a small time interval dw_t is normally distributed; see Kessler (1997) and the references therein. The second approach uses methods of moments; see Conley, Hansen, Luttmer, and Scheinkman (1997) and the references therein. The third approach uses nonparametric methods; see Ait-Sahalia (1996, 2002). The fourth approach uses semiparametric and reprojection methods; see Gallant and Long (1997) and Gallant and Tauchen (1997). Recently, many researchers have applied Markov chain Monte Carlo methods to estimate the diffusion equation; see Eraker (2001) and Elerian, Chib, and Shephard (2001).

APPENDIX A: INTEGRATION OF BLACK–SCHOLES FORMULA

In this appendix, we derive the price of a European call option given in Eq. (6.19). Let $x = \ln(P_T)$. By changing variable and using $g(P_T)\,dP_T = f(x)\,dx$, where $f(x)$ is the probability density function of x, we have

$$\begin{aligned} c_t &= \exp[-r(T-t)] \int_K^\infty (P_T - K) g(P_T)\,dP_t \\ &= e^{-r(T-t)} \int_{\ln(K)}^\infty (e^x - K) f(x)\,dx \\ &= e^{-r(T-t)} \left(\int_{\ln(K)}^\infty e^x f(x)\,dx - K \int_{\ln(K)}^\infty f(x)\,dx \right). \end{aligned} \tag{6.36}$$

Because $x = \ln(P_T) \sim N[\ln(P_t) + (r - \sigma^2/2)(T-t), \sigma^2(T-t)]$, the integration of the second term of Eq. (6.36) reduces to

$$\begin{aligned} \int_{\ln(K)}^\infty f(x)\,dx &= 1 - \int_{-\infty}^{\ln(K)} f(x)\,dx \\ &= 1 - \text{CDF}(\ln(K)) \\ &= 1 - \Phi(-h_-) = \Phi(h_-), \end{aligned}$$

where CDF(ln(K)) is the cumulative distribution function (CDF) of $x = \ln(P_T)$ evaluated at ln(K), $\Phi(.)$ is the CDF of the standard normal random variable, and

$$-h_- = \frac{\ln(K) - \ln(P_t) - (r - \sigma^2/2)(T-t)}{\sigma\sqrt{T-t}}$$
$$= \frac{-\ln(P_t/K) - (r - \sigma^2/2)(T-t)}{\sigma\sqrt{T-t}}.$$

The integration of the first term of Eq. (6.36) can be written as

$$\int_{\ln(K)}^{\infty} \frac{1}{\sqrt{2\pi}\sqrt{\sigma^2(T-t)}} \exp\left(x - \frac{[x - \ln(P_t) - (r-\sigma^2/2)(T-t)]^2}{2\sigma^2(T-t)}\right) dx,$$

where the exponent can be simplified to

$$x - \frac{\{x - [\ln(P_t) + (r-\sigma^2/2)(T-t)]\}^2}{2\sigma^2(T-t)}$$
$$= -\frac{\{x - [\ln(P_t) + (r+\sigma^2/2)(T-t)]\}^2}{2\sigma^2(T-t)} + \ln(P_t) + r(T-t).$$

Consequently, the first integration becomes

$$\int_{\ln(K)}^{\infty} e^x f(x)\, dx = P_t e^{r(T-t)} \int_{\ln(K)}^{\infty} \frac{1}{\sqrt{2\pi}\sqrt{\sigma^2(T-t)}}$$
$$\times \exp\left(-\frac{\{x - [\ln(P_t) + (r+\sigma^2/2)(T-t)]\}^2}{2\sigma^2(T-t)}\right) dx,$$

which involves the CDF of a normal distribution with mean $\ln(P_t) + (r + \sigma^2/2)(T-t)$ and variance $\sigma^2(T-t)$. By using the same techniques as those of the second integration shown before, we have

$$\int_{\ln(K)}^{\infty} e^x f(x)\, dx = P_t e^{r(T-t)} \Phi(h_+),$$

where h_+ is given by

$$h_+ = \frac{\ln(P_t/K) + (r+\sigma^2/2)(T-t)}{\sigma\sqrt{T-t}}.$$

Putting the two integration results together, we have

$$c_t = e^{-r(T-t)}[P_t e^{r(T-t)}\Phi(h_+) - K\Phi(h_-)] = P_t\Phi(h_+) - Ke^{-r(T-t)}\Phi(h_-).$$

APPENDIX B: APPROXIMATION TO STANDARD NORMAL PROBABILITY

The CDF $\Phi(x)$ of a standard normal random variable can be approximated by

$$\Phi(x) = \begin{cases} 1 - f(x)[c_1 k + c_2 k^2 + c_3 k^3 + c_4 k^4 + c_5 k^5] & \text{if } x \geq 0, \\ 1 - \Phi(-x) & \text{if } x < 0, \end{cases}$$

where $f(x) = \exp(-x^2/2)/\sqrt{2\pi}$, $k = 1/(1 + 0.2316419x)$, $c_1 = 0.319381530$, $c_2 = -0.356563782$, $c_3 = 1.781477937$, $c_4 = -1.821255978$, and $c_5 = 1.330274429$.

For illustration, using the earlier approximation, we obtain $\Phi(1.96) = 0.975002$, $\Phi(0.82) = 0.793892$, and $\Phi(-0.61) = 0.270931$. These probabilities are very close to that obtained from a typical normal probability table.

EXERCISES

6.1. Assume that the log price $p_t = \ln(P_t)$ follows a stochastic differential equation

$$dp_t = \gamma\, dt + \sigma\, dw_t,$$

where w_t is a Wiener process. Derive the stochastic equation for the price P_t.

6.2. Considering the forward price F of a nondividend-paying stock, we have

$$F_{t,T} = P_t\, e^{r(T-t)},$$

where r is the risk-free interest rate, which is constant, and P_t is the current stock price. Suppose P_t follows the geometric Brownian motion $dP_t = \mu P_t\, dt + \sigma P_t\, dw_t$. Derive a stochastic diffusion equation for $F_{t,T}$.

6.3. Assume that the price of IBM stock follows Ito process

$$dP_t = \mu P_t\, dt + \sigma P_t\, dw_t,$$

where μ and σ are constant and w_t is a standard Brownian motion. Consider the daily log returns of IBM stock in 1997. The average return and the sample standard deviation are 0.00131 and 0.02215, respectively. Use the data to estimate the parameters μ and σ assuming that there were 252 trading days in 1997.

6.4. Suppose that the current price of a stock is \$120 per share with volatility $\sigma = 50\%$ per annum. Suppose further that the risk-free interest rate is 7% per annum and the stock pays no dividend. (a) What is the price of a European call option contingent on the stock with a strike price of \$125 that will expire in 3 months? (b) What is the price of a European put option on the same stock with a strike price of \$118 that will expire in 3 months? If the volatility σ is increased to 80% per annum, then what are the prices of the two options?

6.5. Derive the limiting marginal effects of the five variables K, P_t, $T-t$, σ, and r on a European put option contingent on a stock.

6.6. A stock price is currently \$60 per share and follows the geometric Brownian motion $dP_t = \mu P_t\,dt + \sigma P_t\,dt$. Assume that the expected return μ from the stock is 20% per annum and its volatility is 40% per annum. What is the probability distribution for the stock price in 2 years? Obtain the mean and standard deviation of the distribution and construct a 95% confidence interval for the stock price.

6.7. A stock price is currently \$60 per share and follows the geometric Brownian motion $dP_t = \mu P_t\,dt + \sigma P_t\,dt$. Assume that the expected return μ from the stock is 20% per annum and its volatility is 40% per annum. What is the probability distribution for the continuously compounded rate of return of the stock over 2 years? Obtain the mean and standard deviation of the distribution.

6.8. Suppose that the current price of stock A is \$70 per share and the price follows the jump diffusion model in Eq. (6.26). Assume that the risk-free interest rate is 8% per annum, the stock pays no dividend, and its volatility (σ) is 30% per annum. In addition, the price on average has about 15 jumps per year with average jump size −2% and jump volatility 3%. What is the price of a European call option with strike price \$75 that will expire in 3 months? What is the price of the corresponding European put option?

6.9. Consider the European call option of a nondividend-paying stock. Suppose that $P_t = \$20$, $K = \$18$, $r = 6\%$ per annum, and $T - t = 0.5$ year. If the price of a European call option of the stock is \$2.10, what opportunities are there for an arbitrageur?

6.10. Consider the put option of a nondividend-paying stock. Suppose that $P_t = \$44$, $K = \$47$, $r = 6\%$ per annum, and $T - t = 0.5$ year. If the European put option of the stock is selling at \$1.00, what opportunities are there for an arbitrageur?

REFERENCES

Abramowitz, M. and Stegun, I. A. (1972). *Handbook of Mathematical Functions*, 10th edition. U.S. National Bureau of Standards, Washington, DC.

Ait-Sahalia, Y. (1996). Testing continuous-time models for the spot interest rate. *Review of Financial Studies* **9**: 385–426.

Ait-Sahalia, Y. (2002). Maximum likelihood estimation of discretely sampled diffusions: A closed-form approach. *Econometrica* **70**: 223–262.

Bakshi, G., Cao, C., and Chen, Z. (1997). Empirical performance of alternative option pricing models. *Journal of Finance* **52**: 2003–2049.

Billingsley, P. (1968). *Convergence of Probability Measures*. Wiley, Hoboken, NJ.

Billingsley, P. (1986). *Probability and Measure*, 2nd edition. Wiley, Hoboken, NJ.

Black, F. and Scholes, M. (1973). The pricing of options and corporate liabilities. *Journal of Political Economy* **81**: 637–654.

Conley, T. G., Hansen, L. P., Luttmer, E. G. J., and Scheinkman, J. A. (1997). Short-term interest rates as subordinated diffusions. *Review of Financial Studies* **10**: 525–577.

Cox, J. C. and Rubinstein, M. (1985). *Options Markets*. Prentice Hall, Englewood Cliffs, NJ.

Donsker, M. (1951). An invariance principle for certain probability limit theorems. *Memoirs American Mathematical Society*, No. 6.

Duffie, D. (1995). *Dynamic Asset Pricing Theory*, 2nd edition. Princeton University Press, Princeton, NJ.

Elerian, O., Chib, S., and Shephard, N. (2001). Likelihood inference for discretely observed non-linear diffusions. *Econometrica* **69**: 959–993.

Eraker, B. (2001). MCMC analysis of diffusion models with application to finance. *Journal of Business & Economic Statistics* **19**: 177–191.

Gallant, A. R. and Long, J. R. (1997). Estimating stochastic diffusion equations efficiently by minimum chi-squared. *Biometrika* **84**: 125–141.

Gallant, A. R. and Tauchen, G. (1997). The relative efficiency of method of moments estimators. Working paper, Economics Department, University of North Carolina.

Hull, J. C. (2002). *Options, Futures, and Other Derivatives*, 5th edition. Prentice Hall, Upper Saddle River, NJ.

Kessler, M. (1997). Estimation of an ergodic diffusion from discrete observations. *Scandinavian Journal of Statistics* **24**: 1–19.

Kou, S. (2002). A jump diffusion model for option pricing. *Management Science* **48**: 1086–1101.

Lo, A. W. (1988). Maximum likelihood estimation of generalized Ito's processes with discretely sampled data. *Econometric Theory* **4**: 231–247.

Merton, R. C. (1976). Option pricing when the underlying stock returns are discontinuous. *Journal of Financial Economics* **5**: 125–144.

CHAPTER 7

Extreme Values, Quantile Estimation, and Value at Risk

Extreme price movements in the financial markets are rare, but important. The stock market crash on Wall Street in October 1987 and other big financial crises such as the Long Term Capital Management have attracted a great deal of attention among practitioners and researchers, and some people even called for government regulations on the derivative markets. In recent years, the seemingly large daily price movements in high-tech stocks have further generated discussions on market risk and margin setting for financial institutions. As a result, value at risk (VaR) has become a widely used measure of market risk in risk management.

In this chapter, we discuss various methods for calculating VaR and the statistical theories behind these methods. In particular, we consider the extreme value theory developed in the statistical literature for studying rare (or extraordinary) events and its application to VaR. Both unconditional and conditional concepts of extreme values are discussed. The unconditional approach to VaR calculation for a financial position uses the historical returns of the instruments involved to compute VaR. However, a conditional approach uses the historical data and explanatory variables to calculate VaR.

Other approaches to VaR calculation discussed in the chapter are RiskMetrics, econometric modeling using volatility models, and empirical quantile. We use daily log returns of IBM stock to illustrate the actual calculation of all the methods discussed. The results obtained can therefore be used to compare the performance of different methods. Figure 7.1 shows the time plot of daily log returns of IBM stock from July 3, 1962 to December 31, 1998 for 9190 observations.

7.1 VALUE AT RISK

There are several types of risk in financial markets. Credit risk, operational risk, and market risk are the three main categories of financial risk. Value at risk (VaR)

Analysis of Financial Time Series, Second Edition By Ruey S. Tsay

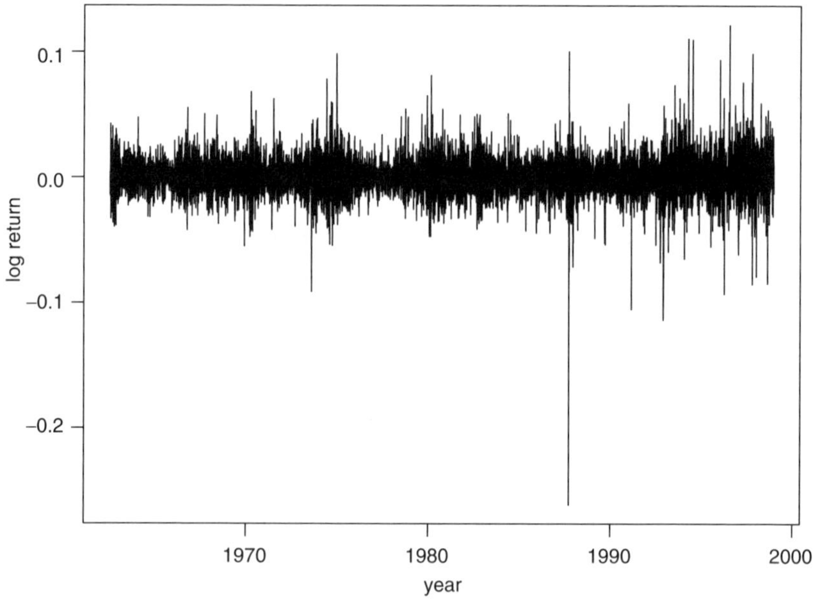

Figure 7.1. Time plot of daily log returns of IBM stock from July 3, 1962 to December 31, 1998.

is mainly concerned with market risk, but the concept is also applicable to other types of risk. VaR is a single estimate of the amount by which an institution's position in a risk category could decline due to general market movements during a given holding period; see Duffie and Pan (1997) and Jorion (1997) for a general exposition of VaR. The measure can be used by financial institutions to assess their risks or by a regulatory committee to set margin requirements. In either case, VaR is used to ensure that the financial institutions can still be in business after a catastrophic event. From the viewpoint of a financial institution, VaR can be defined as the maximal loss of a financial position during a given time period for a given probability. In this view, one treats VaR as a measure of loss associated with a rare (or extraordinary) event under normal market conditions. Alternatively, from the viewpoint of a regulatory committee, VaR can be defined as the minimal loss under extraordinary market circumstances. Both definitions will lead to the same VaR measure, even though the concepts appear to be different.

In what follows, we define VaR under a probabilistic framework. Suppose that at the time index t we are interested in the risk of a financial position for the next ℓ periods. Let $\Delta V(\ell)$ be the change in value of the assets in the financial position from time t to $t+\ell$. This quantity is measured in dollars and is a random variable at the time index t. Denote the cumulative distribution function (CDF) of $\Delta V(\ell)$ by $F_\ell(x)$. We define the VaR of a long position over the time horizon ℓ with probability p as

$$p = \Pr[\Delta V(\ell) \le \text{VaR}] = F_\ell(\text{VaR}). \tag{7.1}$$

Since the holder of a long financial position suffers a loss when $\Delta V(\ell) < 0$, the VaR defined in Eq. (7.1) typically assumes a negative value when p is small. The negative sign signifies a loss. From the definition, the probability that the holder would encounter a loss greater than or equal to VaR over the time horizon ℓ is p. Alternatively, VaR can be interpreted as follows. With probability $(1 - p)$, the potential loss encountered by the holder of the financial position over the time horizon ℓ is less than or equal to VaR.

The holder of a short position suffers a loss when the value of the asset increases [i.e., $\Delta V(\ell) > 0$]. The VaR is then defined as

$$p = \Pr[\Delta V(\ell) \geq \text{VaR}] = 1 - \Pr[\Delta V(\ell) \leq \text{VaR}] = 1 - F_\ell(\text{VaR}).$$

For a small p, the VaR of a short position typically assumes a positive value. The positive sign signifies a loss.

The previous definitions show that VaR is concerned with tail behavior of the CDF $F_\ell(x)$. For a long position, the left tail of $F_\ell(x)$ is important. Yet a short position focuses on the right tail of $F_\ell(x)$. Notice that the definition of VaR in Eq. (7.1) continues to apply to a short position if one uses the distribution of $-\Delta V(\ell)$. Therefore, it suffices to discuss methods of VaR calculation using a long position.

For any univariate CDF $F_\ell(x)$ and probability p, such that $0 < p < 1$, the quantity

$$x_p = \inf\{x | F_\ell(x) \geq p\}$$

is called the pth quantile of $F_\ell(x)$, where inf denotes the smallest real number satisfying $F_\ell(x) \geq p$. If the CDF $F_\ell(x)$ of Eq. (7.1) is known, then VaR is simply its pth quantile (i.e., VaR $= x_p$). The CDF is unknown in practice, however. Studies of VaR are essentially concerned with estimation of the CDF and/or its quantile, especially the tail behavior of the CDF.

In practical applications, calculation of VaR involves several factors:

1. The probability of interest p, such as $p = 0.01$ or $p = 0.05$.
2. The time horizon ℓ. It might be set by a regulatory committee, such as 1 day or 10 days.
3. The frequency of the data, which might not be the same as the time horizon ℓ. Daily observations are often used.
4. The CDF $F_\ell(x)$ or its quantiles.
5. The amount of the financial position or the mark-to-market value of the portfolio.

Among these factors, the CDF $F_\ell(x)$ is the focus of econometric modeling. Different methods for estimating the CDF give rise to different approaches to VaR calculation.

Remark. The definition of VaR in Eq. (7.1) is in dollar amount. Since log returns correspond approximately to percentage changes in value of a financial position, we use log returns r_t in data analysis. The VaR calculated from the quantile of the distribution of r_{t+1} given information available at time t is therefore in percentage. The dollar amount of VaR is then the cash value of the financial position times the VaR of the log return series. That is, VaR = Value × VaR(of log returns). If necessary, one can also use the approximation VaR = Value × [exp(VaR of log returns) − 1]. □

Remark. VaR is a prediction concerning possible loss of a portfolio in a given time horizon. It should be computed using the *predictive distribution* of future returns of the financial position. For example, the VaR for a 1-day horizon of a portfolio using daily returns r_t should be calculated using the predictive distribution of r_{t+1} given information available at time t. From a statistical viewpoint, predictive distribution takes into account the parameter uncertainty in a properly specified model. However, predictive distribution is hard to obtain, and most of the available methods for VaR calculation ignore the effects of parameter uncertainty. □

7.2 RiskMetrics

J. P. Morgan developed the RiskMetrics™ methodology to VaR calculation; see Longerstaey and More (1995). In its simple form, RiskMetrics assumes that the continuously compounded daily return of a portfolio follows a conditional normal distribution. Denote the daily log return by r_t and the information set available at time $t-1$ by F_{t-1}. RiskMetrics assumes that $r_t|F_{t-1} \sim N(\mu_t, \sigma_t^2)$, where μ_t is the conditional mean and σ_t^2 is the conditional variance of r_t. In addition, the method assumes that the two quantities evolve over time according to the simple model:

$$\mu_t = 0, \quad \sigma_t^2 = \alpha\sigma_{t-1}^2 + (1-\alpha)r_{t-1}^2, \quad 1 > \alpha > 0. \tag{7.2}$$

Therefore, the method assumes that the logarithm of the daily price, $p_t = \ln(P_t)$, of the portfolio satisfies the difference equation $p_t - p_{t-1} = a_t$, where $a_t = \sigma_t\epsilon_t$ is an IGARCH(1,1) process without drift. The value of α is often in the interval (0.9, 1) with a typical value of 0.94.

A nice property of such a special random-walk IGARCH model is that the conditional distribution of a multiperiod return is easily available. Specifically, for a k-period horizon, the log return from time $t+1$ to time $t+k$ (inclusive) is $r_t[k] = r_{t+1} + \cdots + r_{t+k-1} + r_{t+k}$. We use the square bracket $[k]$ to denote a k-horizon return. Under the special IGARCH(1,1) model in Eq. (7.2), the conditional distribution $r_t[k]|F_t$ is normal with mean zero and variance $\sigma_t^2[k]$, where $\sigma_t^2[k]$ can be computed using the forecasting method discussed in Chapter 3. Using the independence assumption of ϵ_t and model (7.2), we have

$$\sigma_t^2[k] = \mathrm{Var}(r_t[k]|F_t) = \sum_{i=1}^{k} \mathrm{Var}(a_{t+i}|F_t),$$

where $\text{Var}(a_{t+i}|F_t) = E(\sigma^2_{t+i}|F_t)$ can be obtained recursively. Using $r_{t-1} = a_{t-1} = \sigma_{t-1}\epsilon_{t-1}$, we can rewrite the volatility equation of the IGARCH(1,1) model in Eq. (7.2) as

$$\sigma_t^2 = \sigma_{t-1}^2 + (1-\alpha)\sigma_{t-1}^2(\epsilon_{t-1}^2 - 1) \quad \text{for all } t.$$

In particular, we have

$$\sigma_{t+i}^2 = \sigma_{t+i-1}^2 + (1-\alpha)\sigma_{t+i-1}^2(\epsilon_{t+i-1}^2 - 1) \quad \text{for} \quad i = 2, \ldots, k.$$

Since $E(\epsilon_{t+i-1}^2 - 1|F_t) = 0$ for $i \geq 2$, the prior equation shows that

$$E(\sigma_{t+i}^2|F_t) = E(\sigma_{t+i-1}^2|F_t) \quad \text{for} \quad i = 2, \ldots, k. \tag{7.3}$$

For the 1-step ahead volatility forecast, Eq. (7.2) shows that $\sigma_{t+1}^2 = \alpha\sigma_t^2 + (1-\alpha)r_t^2$. Therefore, Eq. (7.3) shows that $\text{Var}(r_{t+i}|F_t) = \sigma_{t+1}^2$ for $i \geq 1$ and, hence, $\sigma_t^2[k] = k\sigma_{t+1}^2$. The results show that $r_t[k]|F_t \sim N(0, k\sigma_{t+1}^2)$. Consequently, under the special IGARCH(1,1) model in Eq. (7.2) the conditional variance of $r_t[k]$ is proportional to the time horizon k. The conditional standard deviation of a k-period horizon log return is then $\sqrt{k}\sigma_{t+1}$.

Suppose that the financial position is a long position so that loss occurs when there is a big price drop (i.e., a large negative return). If the probability is set to 5%, then RiskMetrics uses $1.65\sigma_{t+1}$ to measure the risk of the portfolio; that is, it uses the one-sided 5% quantile of a normal distribution with mean zero and standard deviation σ_{t+1}. The actual 5% quantile is $-1.65\sigma_{t+1}$, but the negative sign is ignored with the understanding that it signifies a loss. Consequently, if the standard deviation is measured in percentage, then the daily VaR of the portfolio under RiskMetrics is

$$\text{VaR} = \text{Amount of position} \times 1.65\sigma_{t+1},$$

and that of a k-day horizon is

$$\text{VaR}(k) = \text{Amount of position} \times 1.65\sqrt{k}\sigma_{t+1},$$

where the argument (k) of VaR is used to denote the time horizon. Consequently, under RiskMetrics, we have

$$\text{VaR}(k) = \sqrt{k} \times \text{VaR}.$$

This is referred to as the *square root of time rule* in VaR calculation under RiskMetrics.

Example 7.1. The sample standard deviation of the continuously compounded daily return of the German mark/U.S. dollar exchange rate was about 0.53% in June 1997. Suppose that an investor was long in \$10 million worth of mark/dollar exchange rate contract. Then the 5% VaR for a 1-day horizon of the investor is

$$\$10{,}000{,}000 \times (1.65 \times 0.0053) = \$87{,}450.$$

The corresponding VaR for a 1-month horizon (30 days) is

$$\$10{,}000{,}000 \times (\sqrt{30} \times 1.65 \times 0.0053) \approx \$478{,}983.$$

Example 7.2. Consider the daily IBM log returns of Figure 7.1. As mentioned in Chapter 1, the sample mean of the returns is significantly different from zero. However, for demonstration of VaR calculation using RiskMetrics, we assume in this example that the conditional mean is zero and the volatility of the returns follows an IGARCH(1,1) model without drift. The fitted model is

$$r_t = a_t, \quad a_t = \sigma_t \epsilon_t, \quad \sigma_t^2 = 0.9396\sigma_{t-1}^2 + (1 - 0.9396)a_{t-1}^2, \tag{7.4}$$

where $\{\epsilon_t\}$ is a standard Gaussian white noise series. As expected, this model is rejected by the Q-statistics. For instance, we have a highly significant statistic $Q(10) = 56.19$ for the squared standardized residuals.

From the data and the fitted model, we have $r_{9190} = -0.0128$ and $\hat{\sigma}_{9190}^2 = 0.0003472$. Therefore, the 1-step ahead volatility forecast is $\hat{\sigma}_{9190}^2(1) = 0.000336$. The 5% quantile of the conditional distribution $r_{9191}|F_{9190}$ is $-1.65 \times \sqrt{0.000336} = -0.03025$, where it is understood that the negative sign signifies a loss. Consequently, the 1-day horizon 5% VaR of a long position of \$10 million is

$$\text{VaR} = \$10{,}000{,}000 \times 0.03025 = \$302{,}500.$$

The 1% quantile is $-2.3262 \times \sqrt{0.000336} = -0.04265$, and the corresponding 1% VaR for the same long position is \$426,500.

Remark. To implement RiskMetrics in S-Plus, one can use `ewma1` (exponentially weighted moving-average of order 1) under the `mgarch` (multivariate GARCH) command to obtain the estimate of $1 - \alpha$. Then, use the command `predict` to obtain volatility forecasts. For the IBM data used, the estimate of α is $1 - 0.036 = 0.964$ and the 1-step ahead volatility forecast is $\hat{\sigma}_{9190}(1) = 0.01888$. Please see the demonstration below. This leads to VaR $= \$10{,}000{,}000 \times (1.65 \times 0.01888) = \$311{,}520$ and VaR $= \$439{,}187$ for $p = 0.05$ and 0.01, respectively. These two values are slightly higher than those of Example 7.2, which are based on estimates of the RATS package. □

S-Plus Demonstration

Output simplified.

```
> ibm.risk=mgarch(ibm~-1, ~ewma1)
> ibm.risk
ALPHA 0.036
> predict(ibm.risk,2)
$sigma.pred 0.01888
```

7.2.1 Discussion

An advantage of RiskMetrics is simplicity. It is easy to understand and apply. Another advantage is that it makes risk more transparent in the financial markets. However, as security returns tend to have heavy tails (or fat tails), the normality assumption used often results in underestimation of VaR. Other approaches to VaR calculation avoid making such an assumption.

The square root of time rule is a consequence of the special model used by RiskMetrics. If either the zero mean assumption or the special IGARCH(1,1) model assumption of the log returns fails, then the rule is invalid. Consider the simple model

$$r_t = \mu + a_t, \quad a_t = \sigma_t \epsilon_t, \quad \mu \neq 0,$$
$$\sigma_t^2 = \alpha \sigma_{t-1}^2 + (1-\alpha) a_{t-1}^2,$$

where $\{\epsilon_t\}$ is a standard Gaussian white noise series. The assumption that $\mu \neq 0$ holds for returns of many heavily traded stocks on the NYSE; see Chapter 1. For this simple model, the distribution of r_{t+1} given F_t is $N(\mu, \sigma_{t+1}^2)$. The 5% quantile used to calculate the 1-period horizon VaR becomes $\mu - 1.65\sigma_{t+1}$. For a k-period horizon, the distribution of $r_t[k]$ given F_t is $N(k\mu, k\sigma_{t+1}^2)$, where as before $r_t[k] = r_{t+1} + \cdots + r_{t+k}$. The 5% quantile used in the k-period horizon VaR calculation is $k\mu - 1.65\sqrt{k}\sigma_{t+1} = \sqrt{k}(\sqrt{k}\mu - 1.65\sigma_{t+1})$. Consequently, $\text{VaR}(k) \neq \sqrt{k} \times \text{VaR}$ when the mean return is not zero. It is also easy to show that the rule fails when the volatility model of the return is not an IGARCH(1,1) model without drift.

7.2.2 Multiple Positions

In some applications, an investor may hold multiple positions and needs to compute the overall VaR of the positions. RiskMetrics adopts a simple approach for doing such a calculation under the assumption that daily log returns of each position follow a random-walk IGARCH(1,1) model. The additional quantities needed are the cross-correlation coefficients between the returns. Consider the case of two positions. Let VaR_1 and VaR_2 be the VaR for the two positions and ρ_{12} be the cross-correlation coefficient between the two returns—that is, $\rho_{12} = \text{Cov}(r_{1t}, r_{2t})/[\text{Var}(r_{1t})\text{Var}(r_{2t})]^{0.5}$. Then the overall VaR of the investor is

$$\text{VaR} = \sqrt{\text{VaR}_1^2 + \text{VaR}_2^2 + 2\rho_{12}\text{VaR}_1\text{VaR}_2}.$$

The generalization of VaR to a position consisting of m instruments is straightforward as

$$\text{VaR} = \sqrt{\sum_{i=1}^{m} \text{VaR}_i^2 + 2\sum_{i<j}^{m} \rho_{ij}\text{VaR}_i\text{VaR}_j},$$

where ρ_{ij} is the cross-correlation coefficient between returns of the ith and jth instruments and VaR_i is the VaR of the ith instrument.

7.3 AN ECONOMETRIC APPROACH TO VaR CALCULATION

A general approach to VaR calculation is to use the time series econometric models of Chapters 2–4. For a log return series, the time series models of Chapter 2 can be used to model the mean equation, and the conditional heteroscedastic models of Chapter 3 or 4 are used to handle the volatility. For simplicity, we use GARCH models in our discussion and refer to the approach as an *econometric approach* to VaR calculation. Other volatility models, including the nonlinear ones in Chapter 4, can also be used.

Consider the log return r_t of an asset. A general time series model for r_t can be written as

$$r_t = \phi_0 + \sum_{i=1}^{p} \phi_i r_{t-i} + a_t - \sum_{j=1}^{q} \theta_j a_{t-j}, \tag{7.5}$$

$$a_t = \sigma_t \epsilon_t,$$

$$\sigma_t^2 = \alpha_0 + \sum_{i=1}^{u} \alpha_i a_{t-i}^2 + \sum_{j=1}^{v} \beta_j \sigma_{t-j}^2. \tag{7.6}$$

Equations (7.5) and (7.6) are the mean and volatility equations for r_t. These two equations can be used to obtain 1-step ahead forecasts of the conditional mean and conditional variance of r_t assuming that the parameters are known. Specifically, we have

$$\hat{r}_t(1) = \phi_0 + \sum_{i=1}^{p} \phi_i r_{t+1-i} - \sum_{j=1}^{q} \theta_j a_{t+1-j},$$

$$\hat{\sigma}_t^2(1) = \alpha_0 + \sum_{i=1}^{u} \alpha_i a_{t+1-i}^2 + \sum_{j=1}^{v} \beta_j \sigma_{t+1-j}^2.$$

If one further assumes that ϵ_t is Gaussian, then the conditional distribution of r_{t+1} given the information available at time t is $N[\hat{r}_t(1), \hat{\sigma}_t^2(1)]$. Quantiles of this conditional distribution can easily be obtained for VaR calculation. For example, the 5% quantile is $\hat{r}_t(1) - 1.65\hat{\sigma}_t(1)$. If one assumes that ϵ_t is a standardized Student-t distribution with v degrees of freedom, then the quantile is $\hat{r}_t(1) - t_v^*(p)\hat{\sigma}_t(1)$, where $t_v^*(p)$ is the pth quantile of a standardized Student-t distribution with v degrees of freedom.

The relationship between quantiles of a Student-t distribution with v degrees of freedom, denoted by t_v, and those of its standardized distribution, denoted by t_v^*, is

$$p = \Pr(t_v \le q) = \Pr\left(\frac{t_v}{\sqrt{v/(v-2)}} \le \frac{q}{\sqrt{v/(v-2)}}\right) = \Pr\left(t_v^* \le \frac{q}{\sqrt{v/(v-2)}}\right),$$

where $v > 2$. That is, if q is the pth quantile of a Student-t distribution with v degrees of freedom, then $q/\sqrt{v/(v-2)}$ is the pth quantile of a standardized

Student-t distribution with v degrees of freedom. Therefore, if ϵ_t of the GARCH model in Eq. (7.6) is a standardized Student-t distribution with v degrees of freedom and the probability is p, then the quantile used to calculate the 1-period horizon VaR at time index t is

$$\hat{r}_t(1) + \frac{t_v(p)\hat{\sigma}_t(1)}{\sqrt{v/(v-2)}},$$

where $t_v(p)$ is the pth quantile of a Student-t distribution with v degrees of freedom and assumes a negative value for a small p.

Example 7.3. Consider again the daily IBM log returns of Example 7.2. We use two volatility models to calculate VaR of 1-day horizon at $t = 9190$ for a long position of \$10 million. These econometric models are reasonable based on the modeling techniques of Chapters 2 and 3.

CASE 1. Assume that ϵ_t is standard normal. The fitted model is

$$r_t = 0.00066 - 0.0247r_{t-2} + a_t, \quad a_t = \sigma_t\epsilon_t,$$
$$\sigma_t^2 = 0.00000389 + 0.0799a_{t-1}^2 + 0.9073\sigma_t^2.$$

From the data, we have $r_{9189} = -0.00201$, $r_{9190} = -0.0128$, and $\sigma_{9190}^2 = 0.00033455$. Consequently, the prior AR(2)–GARCH(1,1) model produces 1-step ahead forecasts as

$$\hat{r}_{9190}(1) = 0.00071 \quad \text{and} \quad \hat{\sigma}_{9190}^2(1) = 0.0003211.$$

The 5% quantile is then

$$0.00071 - 1.6449 \times \sqrt{0.0003211} = -0.02877,$$

where it is understood that the negative sign denotes the left tail of the conditional normal distribution. The VaR for a long position of \$10 million with probability 0.05 is VaR = \$10,000,000 × 0.02877 = \$287,700. The result shows that, with probability 95%, the potential loss of holding that position next day is \$287,200 or less assuming that the AR(2)–GARCH(1,1) model holds. If the probability is 0.01, then the 1% quantile is

$$0.00071 - 2.3262 \times \sqrt{0.0003211} = -0.0409738.$$

The VaR for the position becomes \$409,738.

CASE 2. Assume that ϵ_t is a standardized Student-t distribution with 5 degrees of freedom. The fitted model is

$$r_t = 0.0003 - 0.0335r_{t-2} + a_t, \quad a_t = \sigma_t\epsilon_t,$$
$$\sigma_t^2 = 0.000003 + 0.0559a_{t-1}^2 + 0.9350\sigma_{t-1}^2.$$

From the data, we have $r_{9189} = -0.00201$, $r_{9190} = -0.0128$, and $\sigma^2_{9190} = 0.000349$. Consequently, the prior Student-t AR(2)–GARCH(1,1) model produces 1-step ahead forecasts

$$\hat{r}_{9190}(1) = 0.000367 \quad \text{and} \quad \hat{\sigma}^2_{9190}(1) = 0.0003386.$$

The 5% quantile of a Student-t distribution with 5 degrees of freedom is -2.015 and that of its standardized distribution is $-2.015/\sqrt{5/3} = -1.5608$. Therefore, the 5% quantile of the conditional distribution of r_{9191} given F_{9190} is

$$0.000367 - 1.5608\sqrt{0.0003386} = -0.028354.$$

The VaR for a long position of \$10 million is

$$\text{VaR} = \$10{,}000{,}000 \times 0.028352 = \$283{,}520,$$

which is essentially the same as that obtained under the normality assumption. The 1% quantile of the conditional distribution is

$$0.000367 - (3.3649/\sqrt{5/3})\sqrt{0.0003386} = -0.0475943.$$

The corresponding VaR is \$475,943. Comparing with that of Case 1, we see the heavy-tail effect of using a Student-t distribution with 5 degrees of freedom; it increases the VaR when the tail probability becomes smaller. In S-Plus, the quantile of a Student-t distribution with m degrees of freedom can be obtained by `xp = qt(p,m)`, for example, `xp = qt(0.01,5.23)`.

7.3.1 Multiple Periods

Suppose that at time h we want to compute the k-horizon VaR of an asset whose log return is r_t. The variable of interest is the k-period log return at the forecast origin h (i.e., $r_h[k] = r_{h+1} + \cdots + r_{h+k}$). If the return r_t follows the time series model in Eqs. (7.5) and (7.6), then the conditional mean and variance of $r_h[k]$ given the information set F_h can be obtained by the forecasting methods discussed in Chapters 2 and 3.

Expected Return and Forecast Error

The conditional mean $E(r_h[k]|F_h)$ can be obtained by the forecasting method of ARMA models in Chapter 2. Specifically, we have

$$\hat{r}_h[k] = r_h(1) + \cdots + r_h(k),$$

where $r_h(\ell)$ is the ℓ-step ahead forecast of the return at the forecast origin h. These forecasts can be computed recursively as discussed in Section 2.6.4. Using the MA representation

$$r_t = \mu + a_t + \psi_1 a_{t-1} + \psi_2 a_{t-2} + \cdots$$

of the ARMA model in Eq. (7.5), we can write the ℓ-step ahead forecast error at the forecast origin h as

$$e_h(\ell) = r_{h+\ell} - r_h(\ell) = a_{h+\ell} + \psi_1 a_{h+\ell-1} + \cdots + \psi_{\ell-1} a_{h+1};$$

see Eq. (2.33) and the associated forecast error. The forecast error of the expected k-period return $\hat{r}_h[k]$ is the sum of 1-step to k-step forecast errors of r_t at the forecast origin h and can be written as

$$\begin{aligned} e_h[k] &= e_h(1) + e_h(2) + \cdots + e_h(k) \\ &= a_{h+1} + (a_{h+2} + \psi_1 a_{h+1}) + \cdots + \sum_{i=0}^{k-1} \psi_i a_{h+k-i} \\ &= a_{h+k} + (1 + \psi_1) a_{h+k-1} + \cdots + \left(\sum_{i=0}^{k-1} \psi_i \right) a_{h+1}, \end{aligned} \tag{7.7}$$

where $\psi_0 = 1$.

Expected Volatility

The volatility forecast of the k-period return at the forecast origin h is the conditional variance of $e_h[k]$ given F_h. Using the independent assumption of ϵ_{t+i} for $i = 1, \ldots, k$, where $a_{t+i} = \sigma_{t+i}\epsilon_{t+i}$, we have

$$\begin{aligned} \mathrm{V}_h(e_h[k]) &= \mathrm{V}_h(a_{h+k}) + (1 + \psi_1)^2 \mathrm{V}_h(a_{h+k-1}) + \cdots + \left(\sum_{i=0}^{k-1} \psi_i \right)^2 \mathrm{V}_h(a_{h+1}) \\ &= \sigma_h^2(k) + (1 + \psi_1)^2 \sigma_h^2(k-1) + \cdots + \left(\sum_{i=0}^{k-1} \psi_i \right)^2 \sigma_h^2(1), \end{aligned} \tag{7.8}$$

where $\mathrm{V}_h(z)$ denotes the conditional variance of z given F_h and $\sigma_h^2(\ell)$ is the ℓ-step ahead volatility forecast at the forecast origin h. If the volatility model is the GARCH model in Eq. (7.6), then these volatility forecasts can be obtained recursively by the methods discussed in Chapter 3.

As an illustration, consider the special time series model

$$\begin{aligned} r_t &= \mu + a_t, \quad a_t = \sigma_t \epsilon_t, \\ \sigma_t^2 &= \alpha_0 + \alpha_1 a_{t-1}^2 + \beta_1 \sigma_{t-1}^2. \end{aligned}$$

Then we have $\psi_i = 0$ for all $i > 0$. The point forecast of the k-period return at the forecast origin h is $\hat{r}_h[k] = k\mu$ and the associated forecast error is

$$e_h[k] = a_{h+k} + a_{h+k-1} + \cdots + a_{h+1}.$$

Consequently, the volatility forecast for the k-period return at the forecast origin h is

$$\text{Var}(e_h[k]|F_h) = \sum_{\ell=1}^{k} \sigma_h^2(\ell).$$

Using the forecasting method of GARCH(1,1) models in Section 3.5, we have

$$\begin{aligned}\sigma_h^2(1) &= \alpha_0 + \alpha_1 a_h^2 + \beta_1 \sigma_h^2,\\ \sigma_h^2(\ell) &= \alpha_0 + (\alpha_1 + \beta_1)\sigma_h^2(\ell - 1), \quad \ell = 2, \ldots, k.\end{aligned} \tag{7.9}$$

Using Eq. (7.9), we obtain that for the case of $\psi_i = 0$ for $i > 0$,

$$\text{Var}(e_h[k]|F_h) = \frac{\alpha_0}{1-\phi}\left[k - \frac{1-\phi^k}{1-\phi}\right] + \frac{1-\phi^k}{1-\phi}\sigma_h^2(1), \tag{7.10}$$

where $\phi = \alpha_1 + \beta_1 < 1$. If $\psi_i \neq 0$ for some $i > 0$, then one should use the general formula of $\text{Var}(e_h[k]|F_h)$ in Eq. (7.8). If ϵ_t is Gaussian, then the conditional distribution of $r_h[k]$ given F_h is normal with mean $k\mu$ and variance $\text{Var}(e_h[k]|F_h)$. The quantiles needed in VaR calculation are readily available. If the conditional distribution of a_t is not Gaussian (e.g., a Student-t or generalized error distribution), simulation can be used to obtain the multiperiod VaR.

Example 7.3 (Continued). Consider the Gaussian AR(2)–GARCH(1,1) model of Example 7.3 for the daily log returns of IBM stock. Suppose that we are interested in the VaR of a 15-day horizon starting at the forecast origin 9190 (i.e., December 31, 1998). We can use the fitted model to compute the conditional mean and variance for the 15-day log return via $r_{9190}[15] = \sum_{i=1}^{15} r_{9190+i}$ given F_{9190}. The conditional mean is 0.00998 and the conditional variance is 0.0047948, which is obtained by the recursion in Eq. (7.9). The 5% quantile of the conditional distribution is then $0.00998 - 1.6449\sqrt{0.0047948} = -0.1039191$. Consequently, the 15-day horizon VaR for a long position of \$10 million is VaR = \$10,000,000 × 0.1039191 = \$1,039,191. This amount is smaller than \$287,700 × $\sqrt{15}$ = \$1,114,257. This example further demonstrates that the square root of time rule used by RiskMetrics holds only for the special white noise IGARCH(1,1) model used. When the conditional mean is not zero, proper steps must be taken to compute the k-horizon VaR.

7.4 QUANTILE ESTIMATION

Quantile estimation provides a nonparametric approach to VaR calculation. It makes no specific distributional assumption on the return of a portfolio except that the distribution continues to hold within the prediction period. There are two types of quantile methods. The first method is to use empirical quantile directly, and the second method uses quantile regression.

7.4.1 Quantile and Order Statistics

Assuming that the distribution of return in the prediction period is the same as that in the sample period, one can use the empirical quantile of the return r_t to calculate VaR. Let $r_1, \ldots, r_n$ be the returns of a portfolio in the sample period. The *order statistics* of the sample are these values arranged in increasing order. We use the notation

$$r_{(1)} \le r_{(2)} \le \cdots \le r_{(n)}$$

to denote the arrangement and refer to $r_{(i)}$ as the ith order statistic of the sample. In particular, $r_{(1)}$ is the sample minimum and $r_{(n)}$ the sample maximum.

Assume that the returns are independent and identically distributed random variables that have a continuous distribution with probability density function (pdf) $f(x)$ and CDF $F(x)$. Then we have the following asymptotic result from the statistical literature (e.g., Cox and Hinkley, 1974, Appendix 2), for the order statistic $r_{(\ell)}$, where $\ell = np$ with $0 < p < 1$.

RESULT. Let x_p be the pth quantile of $F(x)$, that is, $x_p = F^{-1}(p)$. Assume that the pdf $f(x)$ is not zero at x_p (i.e., $f(x_p) \neq 0$). Then the order statistic $r_{(\ell)}$ is asymptotically normal with mean x_p and variance $p(1-p)/[nf^2(x_p)]$. That is,

$$r_{(\ell)} \sim N\left[x_p, \frac{p(1-p)}{n[f(x_p)]^2}\right], \quad \ell = np. \tag{7.11}$$

Based on the prior result, one can use $r_{(\ell)}$ to estimate the quantile x_p, where $\ell = np$. In practice, the probability of interest p may not satisfy that np is a positive integer. In this case, one can use simple interpolation to obtain quantile estimates. More specifically, for noninteger np, let ℓ_1 and ℓ_2 be the two neighboring positive integers such that $\ell_1 < np < \ell_2$. Define $p_i = \ell_i/n$. The previous result shows that $r_{(\ell_i)}$ is a consistent estimate of the quantile x_{p_i}. From the definition, $p_1 < p < p_2$. Therefore, the quantile x_p can be estimated by

$$\hat{x}_p = \frac{p_2 - p}{p_2 - p_1} r_{(\ell_1)} + \frac{p - p_1}{p_2 - p_1} r_{(\ell_2)}. \tag{7.12}$$

Example 7.4. Consider the daily log returns of Intel stock from December 15, 1972 to December 31, 1997. There are 6329 observations. The empirical 5% quantile of the data can be obtained as

$$\hat{x}_{0.05} = 0.55 r_{(316)} + 0.45 r_{(317)} = -4.229\%,$$

where $np = 6329 \times 0.05 = 316.45$ and $r_{(i)}$ is the ith order statistic of the sample. In this particular instance, $r_{(316)} = -4.237\%$ and $r_{(317)} = -4.220\%$. Here we use the lower tail of the empirical distribution because it is relevant to holding a long position in VaR calculation.

Example 7.5. Consider again the daily log returns of IBM stock from July 3, 1962 to December 31, 1998. Using all 9190 observations, the empirical 5% quantile can be obtained as $(r_{(459)} + r_{(460)})/2 = -0.021603$, where $r_{(i)}$ is the ith order statistic and $np = 9190 \times 0.05 = 459.5$. The VaR of a long position of \$10 million is \$216,030, which is much smaller than those obtained by the econometric approach discussed before. Because the sample size is 9190, we have $91 < 9190 \times 0.01 < 92$. Let $p_1 = 91/9190 = 0.0099$ and $p_2 = 92/9190 = 0.01001$. The empirical 1% quantile can be obtained as

$$\begin{aligned}\hat{x}_{0.01} &= \frac{p_2 - 0.01}{p_2 - p_1} r_{(91)} + \frac{0.01 - p_1}{p_2 - p_1} r_{(92)} \\ &= \frac{0.00001}{0.00011}(-3.658) + \frac{0.0001}{0.00011}(-3.657) \\ &\approx -3.657.\end{aligned}$$

The 1% 1-day horizon VaR of the long position is \$365,709. Again this amount is lower than those obtained before by other methods.

Discussion. Advantages of using the prior quantile method to VaR calculation include (a) simplicity and (b) using no specific distributional assumption. However, the approach has several drawbacks. First, it assumes that the distribution of the return r_t remains unchanged from the sample period to the prediction period. Given that VaR is concerned mainly with tail probability, this assumption implies that the predicted loss cannot be greater than that of the historical loss. It is definitely not so in practice. Second, for extreme quantiles (i.e., when p is close to zero or unity), the empirical quantiles are not efficient estimates of the theoretical quantiles. Third, the direct quantile estimation fails to take into account the effect of explanatory variables that are relevant to the portfolio under study. In real application, VaR obtained by the empirical quantile can serve as a lower bound for the actual VaR. □

7.4.2 Quantile Regression

In real application, one often has explanatory variables available that are important to the problem under study. For example, the action taken by Federal Reserve Banks on interest rates could have important impacts on the returns of U.S. stocks. It is then more appropriate to consider the distribution function $r_{t+1}|F_t$, where F_t includes the explanatory variables. In other words, we are interested in the quantiles of the distribution function of r_{t+1} given F_t. Such a quantile is referred to as a *regression quantile* in the literature; see Koenker and Bassett (1978).

To understand regression quantile, it is helpful to cast the empirical quantile of the previous subsection as an estimation problem. For a given probability p, the pth quantile of $\{r_t\}$ is obtained by

$$\hat{x}_p = \text{argmin}_\beta \sum_{i=1}^{n} w_p(r_i - \beta),$$

where $w_p(z)$ is defined by

$$w_p(z) = \begin{cases} pz & \text{if } z \geq 0, \\ (p-1)z & \text{if } z < 0. \end{cases}$$

Regression quantile is a generalization of such an estimate.

To see the generalization, suppose that we have the linear regression

$$r_t = \boldsymbol{\beta}' \boldsymbol{x}_t + a_t, \tag{7.13}$$

where $\boldsymbol{\beta}$ is a k-dimensional vector of parameters and $\boldsymbol{x}_t$ is a vector of predictors that are elements of F_{t-1}. The conditional distribution of r_t given F_{t-1} is a translation of the distribution of a_t because $\boldsymbol{\beta}' \boldsymbol{x}_t$ is known. Viewing the problem this way, Koenker and Bassett (1978) suggest estimating the conditional quantile $x_p | F_{t-1}$ of r_t given F_{t-1} as

$$\hat{x}_p | F_{t-1} \equiv \inf\{\boldsymbol{\beta}_o' \boldsymbol{x} | R_p(\boldsymbol{\beta}_o) = \min\}, \tag{7.14}$$

where "$R_p(\boldsymbol{\beta}_o) = \min$" means that $\boldsymbol{\beta}_o$ is obtained by

$$\boldsymbol{\beta}_o = \text{argmin}_{\boldsymbol{\beta}} \sum_{t=1}^{n} w_p(r_t - \boldsymbol{\beta}' \boldsymbol{x}_t),$$

where $w_p(.)$ is defined as before. A computer program to obtain such an estimated quantile can be found in Koenker and D'Orey (1987).

7.5 EXTREME VALUE THEORY

In this section, we review some extreme value theory in the statistical literature. Denote the return of an asset, measured in a fixed time interval such as daily, by r_t. Consider the collection of n returns, $\{r_1, \ldots, r_n\}$. The minimum return of the collection is $r_{(1)}$, that is, the smallest order statistic, whereas the maximum return is $r_{(n)}$, the maximum order statistic. Specifically, $r_{(1)} = \min_{1 \leq j \leq n}\{r_j\}$ and $r_{(n)} = \max_{1 \leq j \leq n}\{r_j\}$. We focus on properties of the minimum return $r_{(1)}$ because this minimum is highly relevant to VaR calculation for a long position. However, the theory discussed also applies to the maximum return of an asset over a given time period because properties of the maximum return can be obtained from those of the minimum by a simple sign change. Specifically, we have $r_{(n)} = -\min_{1 \leq j \leq n}\{-r_j\} = -r^c_{(1)}$, where $r^c_t = -r_t$ with the superscript c denoting sign change. The maximum return is relevant to holding a short financial position.

7.5.1 Review of Extreme Value Theory

Assume that the returns r_t are serially independent with a common cumulative distribution function $F(x)$ and that the range of the return r_t is $[l, u]$. For log returns, we have $l = -\infty$ and $u = \infty$. Then the CDF of $r_{(1)}$, denoted by $F_{n,1}(x)$, is given by

$$\begin{aligned}
F_{n,1}(x) &= \Pr[r_{(1)} \le x] = 1 - \Pr[r_{(1)} > x] \\
&= 1 - \Pr(r_1 > x, r_2 > x, \ldots, r_n > x) \\
&= 1 - \prod_{j=1}^{n} \Pr(r_j > x) \quad \text{(by independence)} \\
&= 1 - \prod_{j=1}^{n} [1 - \Pr(r_j \le x)] \\
&= 1 - \prod_{j=1}^{n} [1 - F(x)] \quad \text{(by common distribution)} \\
&= 1 - [1 - F(x)]^n. \qquad (7.15)
\end{aligned}$$

In practice, the CDF $F(x)$ of r_t is unknown and, hence, $F_{n,1}(x)$ of $r_{(1)}$ is unknown. However, as n increases to infinity, $F_{n,1}(x)$ becomes degenerated—namely, $F_{n,1}(x) \to 0$ if $x \le l$ and $F_{n,1}(x) \to 1$ if $x > l$ as n goes to infinity. This degenerated CDF has no practical value. Therefore, the extreme value theory is concerned with finding two sequences $\{\beta_n\}$ and $\{\alpha_n\}$, where $\alpha_n > 0$, such that the distribution of $r_{(1*)} \equiv (r_{(1)} - \beta_n)/\alpha_n$ converges to a nondegenerated distribution as n goes to infinity. The sequence $\{\beta_n\}$ is a location series and $\{\alpha_n\}$ is a series of scaling factors. Under the independent assumption, the limiting distribution of the normalized minimum $r_{(1*)}$ is given by

$$F_*(x) = \begin{cases} 1 - \exp[-(1 + kx)^{1/k}] & \text{if } k \neq 0, \\ 1 - \exp[-\exp(x)] & \text{if } k = 0, \end{cases} \qquad (7.16)$$

for $x < -1/k$ if $k < 0$ and for $x > -1/k$ if $k > 0$, where the subscript $*$ signifies the minimum. The case of $k = 0$ is taken as the limit when $k \to 0$. The parameter k is referred to as the *shape parameter* that governs the tail behavior of the limiting distribution. The parameter $\alpha = -1/k$ is called the *tail index* of the distribution.

The limiting distribution in Eq. (7.16) is the *generalized extreme value* (GEV) *distribution* of Jenkinson (1955) for the minimum. It encompasses the three types of limiting distribution of Gnedenko (1943):

- Type I: $k = 0$, the Gumbel family. The CDF is

$$F_*(x) = 1 - \exp[-\exp(x)], \quad -\infty < x < \infty. \qquad (7.17)$$

- Type II: $k < 0$, the Fréchet family. The CDF is

$$F_*(x) = \begin{cases} 1 - \exp[-(1 + kx)^{1/k}] & \text{if } x < -1/k, \\ 1 & \text{otherwise.} \end{cases} \qquad (7.18)$$

- Type III: $k > 0$, the Weibull family. The CDF here is

$$F_*(x) = \begin{cases} 1 - \exp[-(1+kx)^{1/k}] & \text{if } x > -1/k, \\ 0 & \text{otherwise.} \end{cases}$$

Gnedenko (1943) gave necessary and sufficient conditions for the CDF $F(x)$ of r_t to be associated with one of the three types of limiting distribution. Briefly speaking, the tail behavior of $F(x)$ determines the limiting distribution $F_*(x)$ of the minimum. The (left) tail of the distribution declines exponentially for the Gumbel family, by a power function for the Fréchet family, and is finite for the Weibull family (Figure 7.2). Readers are referred to Embrechts, Kuppelberg, and Mikosch (1997) for a comprehensive treatment of the extreme value theory. For risk management, we are mainly interested in the Fréchet family that includes stable and Student-t distributions. The Gumbel family consists of thin-tailed distributions such as normal and lognormal distributions. The probability density function (pdf) of the generalized limiting distribution in Eq. (7.16) can be obtained easily by differentiation:

$$f_*(x) = \begin{cases} (1+kx)^{1/k-1}\exp[-(1+kx)^{1/k}] & \text{if } k \neq 0, \\ \exp[x - \exp(x)] & \text{if } k = 0, \end{cases} \tag{7.19}$$

where $-\infty < x < \infty$ for $k = 0$, $x < -1/k$ for $k < 0$, and $x > -1/k$ for $k > 0$.

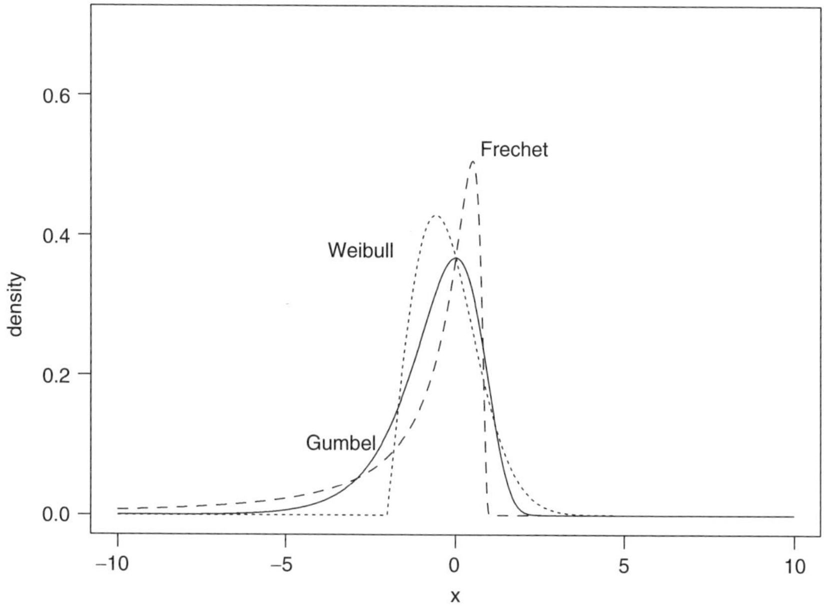

Figure 7.2. Probability density functions of extreme value distributions for minimum. The solid line is for a Gumbel distribution, the dotted line is for the Weibull distribution with $k = 0.5$, and the dashed line is for the Fréchet distribution with $k = -0.9$.

The aforementioned extreme value theory has two important implications. First, the tail behavior of the CDF $F(x)$ of r_t, not the specific distribution, determines the limiting distribution $F_*(x)$ of the (normalized) minimum. Thus, the theory is generally applicable to a wide range of distributions for the return r_t. The sequences $\{\beta_n\}$ and $\{\alpha_n\}$, however, may depend on the CDF $F(x)$. Second, Feller (1971, p. 279) shows that the tail index k does not depend on the time interval of r_t. That is, the tail index (or equivalently the shape parameter) is invariant under time aggregation. This second feature of the limiting distribution becomes handy in the VaR calculation.

The extreme value theory has been extended to serially dependent observations $\{r_t\}_{t=1}^n$ provided that the dependence is weak. Berman (1964) shows that the same form of the limiting extreme value distribution holds for stationary normal sequences provided that the autocorrelation function of r_t is squared summable (i.e., $\sum_{i=1}^{\infty} \rho_i^2 < \infty$), where ρ_i is the lag-i autocorrelation function of r_t. For further results concerning the effect of serial dependence on the extreme value theory, readers are referred to Leadbetter, Lindgren, and Rootzén (1983, Chapter 3).

7.5.2 Empirical Estimation

The extreme value distribution contains three parameters—k, β_n, and α_n. These parameters are referred to as the *shape*, *location*, and *scale parameters*, respectively. They can be estimated by using either parametric or nonparametric methods. We review some of the estimation methods.

For a given sample, there is only a single minimum or maximum, and we cannot estimate the three parameters with only an extreme observation. Alternative ideas must be used. One of the ideas used in the literature is to divide the sample into subsamples and apply the extreme value theory to the subsamples. Assume that there are T returns $\{r_j\}_{j=1}^T$ available. We divide the sample into g non-overlapping subsamples each with n observations, assuming for simplicity that $T = ng$. In other words, we divide the data as

$$\{r_1, \ldots, r_n | r_{n+1}, \ldots, r_{2n} | r_{2n+1}, \ldots, r_{3n} | \cdots | r_{(g-1)n+1}, \ldots, r_{ng}\}$$

and write the observed returns as r_{in+j}, where $1 \le j \le n$ and $i = 0, \ldots, g-1$. Note that each subsample corresponds to a subperiod of the data span. When n is sufficiently large, we hope that the extreme value theory applies to each subsample. In application, the choice of n can be guided by practical considerations. For example, for daily returns, $n = 21$ corresponds approximately to the number of trading days in a month and $n = 63$ denotes the number of trading days in a quarter.

Let $r_{n,i}$ be the minimum of the ith subsample (i.e., $r_{n,i}$ is the smallest return of the ith subsample), where the subscript n is used to denote the size of the subsample. When n is sufficiently large, $x_{n,i} = (r_{n,i} - \beta_n)/\alpha_n$ should follow an extreme value distribution, and the collection of subsample minima $\{r_{n,i} | i = 1, \ldots, g\}$ can then be regarded as a sample of g observations from that extreme value distribution. Specifically, we define

$$r_{n,i} = \min_{1\le j\le n} \{r_{(i-1)n+j}\}, \quad i = 1, \ldots, g. \tag{7.20}$$

The collection of subsample minima $\{r_{n,i}\}$ are the data we use to estimate the unknown parameters of the extreme value distribution. Clearly, the estimates obtained may depend on the choice of subperiod length n.

The Parametric Approach

Two parametric approaches are available. They are the maximum likelihood and regression methods.

Maximum Likelihood Method

Assuming that the subperiod minima $\{r_{n,i}\}$ follow a generalized extreme value distribution such that the pdf of $x_i = (r_{n,i} - \beta_n)/\alpha_n$ is given in Eq. (7.19), we can obtain the pdf of $r_{n,i}$ by a simple transformation as

$$f(r_{n,i}) = \begin{cases} \dfrac{1}{\alpha_n}\left(1 + \dfrac{k_n(r_{n,i} - \beta_n)}{\alpha_n}\right)^{1/k_n - 1} \exp\left[-\left(1 + \dfrac{k_n(r_{n,i} - \beta_n)}{\alpha_n}\right)^{1/k_n}\right] & \text{if } k_n \neq 0, \\ \dfrac{1}{\alpha_n}\exp\left[\dfrac{r_{n,i} - \beta_n}{\alpha_n} - \exp\left(\dfrac{r_{n,i} - \beta_n}{\alpha_n}\right)\right] & \text{if } k_n = 0, \end{cases}$$

where it is understood that $1 + k_n(r_{n,i} - \beta_n)/\alpha_n > 0$ if $k_n \neq 0$. The subscript n is added to the shape parameter k to signify that its estimate depends on the choice of n. Under the independence assumption, the likelihood function of the subperiod minima is

$$\ell(r_{n,1}, \ldots, r_{n,g}|k_n, \alpha_n, \beta_n) = \prod_{i=1}^{g} f(r_{n,i}).$$

Nonlinear estimation procedures can then be used to obtain maximum likelihood estimates of k_n, β_n, and α_n. These estimates are unbiased, asymptotically normal, and of minimum variance under proper assumptions. See Embrechts et al. (1997) and Coles (2001) for details. We apply this approach to some stock return series later.

Regression Method

This method assumes that $\{r_{n,i}\}_{i=1}^{g}$ is a random sample from the generalized extreme value distribution in Eq. (7.16) and makes use of properties of order statistics; see Gumbel (1958). Denote the order statistics of the subperiod minima $\{r_{n,i}\}_{i=1}^{g}$ as

$$r_{n(1)} \le r_{n(2)} \le \cdots \le r_{n(g)}.$$

Using properties of order statistics (e.g., Cox and Hinkley, 1974, p. 467), we have

$$E\{F_*[r_{n(i)}]\} = \frac{i}{g+1}, \quad i = 1, \ldots, g. \tag{7.21}$$

For simplicity, we separate the discussion into two cases depending on the value of k. First, consider the case of $k \neq 0$. From Eq. (7.16), we have

$$F_*[r_{n(i)}] = 1 - \exp\left[-\left(1 + k_n \frac{r_{n(i)} - \beta_n}{\alpha_n}\right)^{1/k_n}\right]. \tag{7.22}$$

Consequently, using Eqs. (7.21) and (7.22) and approximating expectation by an observed value, we have

$$\frac{i}{g+1} = 1 - \exp\left[-\left(1 + k_n \frac{r_{n(i)} - \beta_n}{\alpha_n}\right)^{1/k_n}\right].$$

Therefore,

$$\exp\left[-\left(1 + k_n \frac{r_{n(i)} - \beta_n}{\alpha_n}\right)^{1/k_n}\right] = 1 - \frac{i}{g+1} = \frac{g+1-i}{g+1}, \quad i = 1, \ldots, g.$$

Taking the natural logarithm twice, the prior equation gives

$$\ln\left[-\ln\left(\frac{g+1-i}{g+1}\right)\right] = \frac{1}{k_n} \ln\left(1 + k_n \frac{r_{n(i)} - \beta_n}{\alpha_n}\right), \quad i = 1, \ldots, g.$$

In practice, letting e_i be the deviation between the previous two quantities and assuming that the series $\{e_t\}$ is not serially correlated, we have a regression setup

$$\ln\left[-\ln\left(\frac{g+1-i}{g+1}\right)\right] = \frac{1}{k_n} \ln\left(1 + k_n \frac{r_{n(i)} - \beta_n}{\alpha_n}\right) + e_i, \quad i = 1, \ldots, g. \tag{7.23}$$

The least squares estimates of k_n, β_n, and α_n can be obtained by minimizing the sum of squares of e_i.

When $k_n = 0$, the regression setup reduces to

$$\ln\left[-\ln\left(\frac{g+1-i}{g+1}\right)\right] = \frac{1}{\alpha_n} r_{n(i)} - \frac{\beta_n}{\alpha_n} + e_i, \quad i = 1, \ldots, g.$$

The least squares estimates are consistent but less efficient than the likelihood estimates. We use the likelihood estimates in this chapter.

The Nonparametric Approach

The shape parameter k can be estimated using some nonparametric methods. We mention two such methods here. These two methods are proposed by Hill (1975) and Pickands (1975) and are referred to as the Hill estimator and Pickands estimator, respectively. Both estimators apply directly to the returns $\{r_t\}_{t=1}^{T}$. Thus, there is no need to consider subsamples. Denote the order statistics of the sample as

$$r_{(1)} \le r_{(2)} \le \cdots \le r_{(T)}.$$

Let q be a positive integer. The two estimators of k are defined as

$$k_p(q) = -\frac{1}{\ln(2)} \ln\left(\frac{-r_{(q)} + r_{(2q)}}{-r_{(2q)} + r_{(4q)}}\right), \tag{7.24}$$

$$k_h(q) = \frac{-1}{q} \sum_{i=1}^{q} \left[\ln(-r_{(i)}) - \ln(-r_{(q+1)})\right], \tag{7.25}$$

where the argument (q) is used to emphasize that the estimators depend on q. The choice of q differs between Hill and Pickands estimators. It has been investigated by several researchers, but there is no general consensus on the best choice available. Dekkers and De Haan (1989) show that $k_p(q)$ is consistent if q increases at a properly chosen pace with the sample size T. In addition, $\sqrt{q}[k_p(q) - k]$ is asymptotically normal with mean zero and variance $k^2(2^{-2k+1} + 1)/[2(2^{-k} - 1)\ln(2)]^2$. The Hill estimator is applicable to the Fréchet distribution only, but it is more efficient than the Pickands estimator when applicable. Goldie and Smith (1987) show that $\sqrt{q}[k_h(q) - k]$ is asymptotically normal with mean zero and variance k^2. In practice, one may plot the Hill estimator $k_h(q)$ against q and find a proper q such that the estimate appears to be stable. The estimated tail index $\alpha = -1/k_h(q)$ can then be used to obtain extreme quantiles of the return series; see Zivot and Wang (2003).

7.5.3 Application to Stock Returns

We apply the extreme value theory to the daily log returns of IBM stock from July 3, 1962 to December 31, 1998. The returns are measured in percentages, and the sample size is 9190 (i.e., $T = 9190$). Figure 7.3 shows the time plots of extreme daily log returns when the length of the subperiod is 21 days, which corresponds approximately to a month. The October 1987 crash is clearly seen from the plot. Excluding the 1987 crash, the range of extreme daily log returns is between 0.5% and 13%.

Table 7.1 summarizes some estimation results of the shape parameter k via the Hill estimator. Three choices of q are reported in the table, and the results are stable. To provide an overall picture of the performance of the Hill estimator, Figure 7.4 shows the scatterplots of the Hill estimator $k_h(q)$ against q. For both positive and negative extreme daily log returns, the estimator is stable except for cases when q is small. The estimated shape parameters are about -0.30 and are significantly different from zero at the asymptotic 5% level. The plots also indicate that the shape parameter k appears to be smaller for the negative extremes, indicating that the daily log return may have a heavier left tail. Overall, the result indicates that

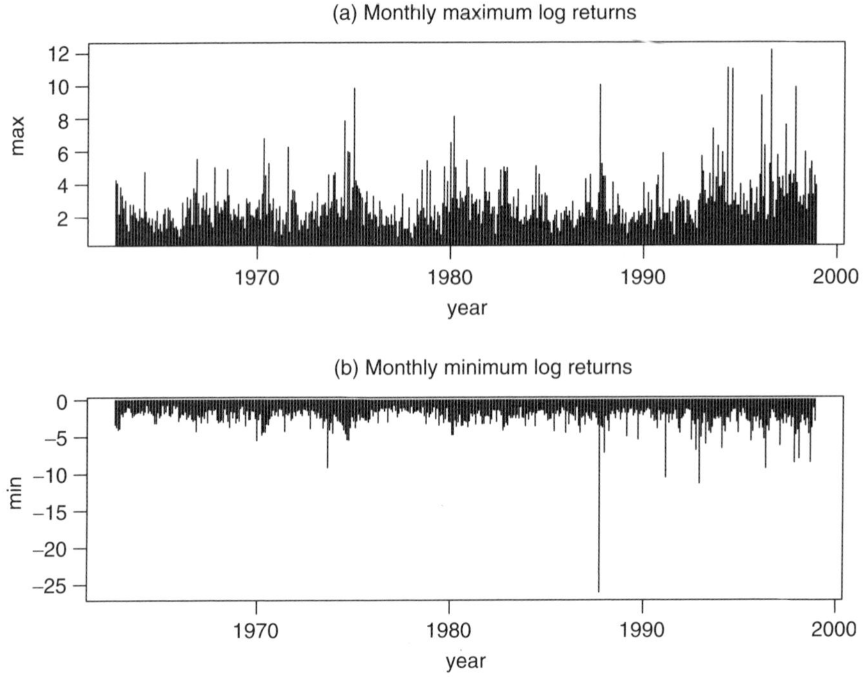

Figure 7.3. Maximum and minimum daily log returns of IBM stock when the subperiod is 21 trading days. The data span is from July 3, 1962 to December 31, 1998: (a) positive returns and (b) negative returns.

Table 7.1. Results of the Hill Estimator[a] for Daily Log Returns of IBM Stock from July 3, 1962 to December 31, 1998

q	190	200	210
Maximum	−0.300(0.022)	−0.297(0.021)	−0.303(0.021)
Minimum	−0.290(0.021)	−0.292(0.021)	−0.289(0.020)

[a] Standard errors are in parentheses.

the distribution of daily log returns of IBM stock belongs to the Fréchet family. The analysis thus rejects the normality assumption commonly used in practice. Such a conclusion is in agreement with that of Longin (1996), who used a U.S. stock market index series. In S-Plus, the Hill estimator can be obtained using the command `hill`, for example,

```
ibm.hill = hill(ibm,option='xi',end=500).
```

Next, we apply the maximum likelihood method to estimate parameters of the generalized extreme value distribution for IBM daily log returns. Table 7.2 summarizes the estimation results for different choices of the length of subperiods ranging

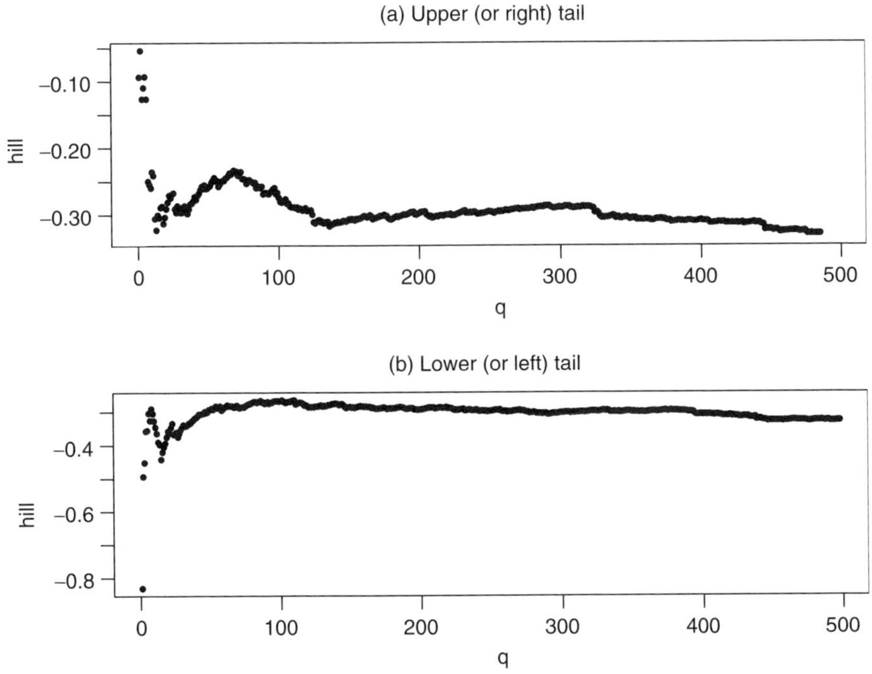

Figure 7.4. Scatterplots of the Hill estimator for the daily log returns of IBM stock. The sample period is from July 3, 1962 to December 31, 1998: (a) positive returns and (b) negative returns.

from 1 month ($n = 21$) to 1 year ($n = 252$). From the table, we make the following observations:

- Estimates of the location and scale parameters β_n and α_n increase in modulus as n increases. This is expected as magnitudes of the subperiod minimum and maximum are nondecreasing functions of n.
- Estimates of the shape parameter (or equivalently the tail index) are stable for the negative extremes when $n \geq 63$ and are approximately -0.33.
- Estimates of the shape parameter are less stable for the positive extremes. The estimates are smaller in magnitude but remain significantly different from zero.
- The results for $n = 252$ have higher variabilities as the number of subperiods g is relatively small.

Again the conclusion obtained is similar to that of Longin (1996), who provided a good illustration of applying the extreme value theory to stock market returns.

The results of Table 7.2 were obtained using a Fortran program developed by Professor Richard Smith and modified by the author. S-Plus can also be used to perform the estimation. I demonstrate below the commands used in analyzing the minimal returns of subperiods of 21 trading days. Note that the returns are multiplied by -100 because (a) S-Plus focuses on the right-hand tail of a distribution

Table 7.2. Maximum Likelihood Estimates[a] of the Extreme Value Distribution for Daily Log Returns of IBM Stock from July 3, 1962 to December 31, 1998

Length of Subperiod	Scale α_n	Location β_n	Shape k_n
	Minimal Returns		
1 month ($n = 21$, $g = 437$)	0.823(0.035)	−1.902(0.044)	−0.197(0.036)
1 quarter ($n = 63$, $g = 145$)	0.945(0.077)	−2.583(0.090)	−0.335(0.076)
6 months ($n = 126$, $g = 72$)	1.147(0.131)	−3.141(0.153)	−0.330(0.101)
1 year ($n = 252$, $g = 36$)	1.542(0.242)	−3.761(0.285)	−0.322(0.127)
	Maximal Returns		
1 month ($n = 21$, $g = 437$)	0.931(0.039)	2.184(0.050)	−0.168(0.036)
1 quarter ($n = 63$, $g = 145$)	1.157(0.087)	3.012(0.108)	−0.217(0.066)
6 months ($n = 126$, $g = 72$)	1.292(0.158)	3.471(0.181)	−0.349(0.130)
1 year ($n = 252$, $g = 36$)	1.624(0.271)	4.475(0.325)	−0.264(0.186)

[a]Standard errors are in parentheses.

and (b) the returns used are in percentages. Furthermore, `(xi, sigma, mu)` in S-Plus corresponds to $(-k_n, \alpha_n, \beta_n)$ of the table. The estimates obtained by S-Plus are close to those in Table 7.2.

S-Plus Demonstration of GEV Estimation

Return series is `ibm`.

```
> length(ibm)
[1] 9190
> grp=floor(9190/21)
> grp
[1] 437
> for (i in 1:grp){
+ jend=9190-(i-1)*21
+ jst=jend-21+1
+ xmin[i]=min(ibm[jst:jend])
+ }
> y=xmin*(-100)
> nibm.gev.21=gev(y)
> names(nibm.gev.21)
[1] "n.all"    "n"        "call"      "block"    "data"
[6] "par.ests" "par.ses" "varcov" "converged" "nllh.final"
> nibm.gev.21$par.ests
       xi     sigma       mu
 0.1953325 0.8187631 1.921797
> nibm.gev.21$par.ses
        xi      sigma          mu
 0.03539358 0.03456347 0.04387343
```

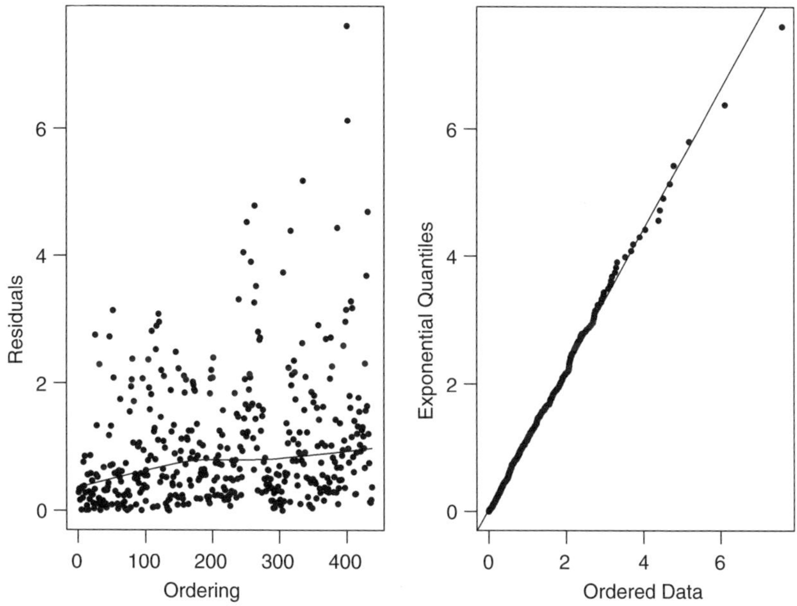

Figure 7.5. Residual plots from fitting a GEV distribution to daily negative IBM log returns, in percentage, for data from July 3, 1962 to December 31, 1998 with a subperiod length of 21 days.

```
> plot(nibm.gev.21)
Make a plot selection (or 0 to exit):
1: plot: Scatterplot of Residuals
2: plot: QQplot of Residuals
Selection:
```

Define the residuals of a GEV distribution fit as

$$w_i = \left(1 + k_n \frac{r_{n,i} - \beta_n}{\alpha_n}\right)^{1/k_n}.$$

Using the pdf of the GEV distribution and transformation of variables, one can easily show that $\{w_i\}$ should form an iid random sample of exponentially distributed random variables if the fitted model is correctly specified. Figure 7.5 shows the residual plots of the GEV distribution fit to the daily negative IBM log returns with subperiod length of 21 days. The left panel gives the residuals and the right panel shows a quantile-to-quantile (QQ) plot against an exponential distribution. The plots indicate that the fit is reasonable.

7.6 EXTREME VALUE APPROACH TO VaR

In this section, we discuss an approach to VaR calculation using the extreme value theory. The approach is similar to that of Longin (1999a,b), who proposed an eight-step procedure for the same purpose. We divide the discussion into two parts. The first part is concerned with parameter estimation using the method discussed in the previous subsections. The second part focuses on VaR calculation by relating the probabilities of interest associated with different time intervals.

Part I

Assume that there are T observations of an asset return available in the sample period. We partition the sample period into g nonoverlapping subperiods of length n such that $T = ng$. If $T = ng + m$ with $1 \leq m < n$, then we delete the first m observations from the sample. The extreme value theory discussed in the previous section enables us to obtain estimates of the location, scale, and shape parameters β_n, α_n, and k_n for the subperiod minima $\{r_{n,i}\}$. Plugging the maximum likelihood estimates into the CDF in Eq. (7.16) with $x = (r - \beta_n)/\alpha_n$, we can obtain the quantile of a given probability of the generalized extreme value distribution. Because we focus on holding a long financial position, the lower probability (or left) quantiles are of interest. Let p^* be a small probability that indicates the potential loss of a long position and r_n^* be the p^*th quantile of the subperiod minimum under the limiting generalized extreme value distribution. Then we have

$$p^* = \begin{cases} 1 - \exp\left[-\left(1 + \dfrac{k_n(r_n^* - \beta_n)}{\alpha_n}\right)^{1/k_n}\right] & \text{if } k_n \neq 0, \\[2ex] 1 - \exp\left[-\exp\left(\dfrac{r_n^* - \beta_n}{\alpha_n}\right)\right] & \text{if } k_n = 0, \end{cases}$$

where it is understood that $1 + k_n(r_n^* - \beta_n)/\alpha_n > 0$ for $k_n \neq 0$. Rewriting this equation as

$$\ln(1 - p^*) = \begin{cases} -\left(1 + \dfrac{k_n(r_n^* - \beta_n)}{\alpha_n}\right)^{1/k_n} & \text{if } k_n \neq 0, \\[2ex] -\exp\left(\dfrac{r_n^* - \beta_n}{\alpha_n}\right) & \text{if } k_n = 0, \end{cases}$$

we obtain the quantile as

$$r_n^* = \begin{cases} \beta_n - \dfrac{\alpha_n}{k_n}\{1 - [-\ln(1 - p^*)]^{k_n}\} & \text{if } k_n \neq 0, \\[2ex] \beta_n + \alpha_n \ln[-\ln(1 - p^*)] & \text{if } k_n = 0. \end{cases} \tag{7.26}$$

In financial applications, the case of $k_n \neq 0$ is of major interest.

Part II

For a given lower (or left tail) probability p^*, the quantile r_n^* of Eq. (7.26) is the VaR based on the extreme value theory for the subperiod minima. The next step is to make explicit the relationship between subperiod minima and the observed return r_t series.

Because most asset returns are either serially uncorrelated or have weak serial correlations, we may use the relationship in Eq. (7.15) and obtain

$$p^* = P(r_{n,i} \le r_n^*) = 1 - [1 - P(r_t \le r_n^*)]^n$$

or, equivalently,

$$1 - p^* = [1 - P(r_t \le r_n^*)]^n. \tag{7.27}$$

This relationship between probabilities allows us to obtain VaR for the original asset return series r_t. More precisely, for a specified small lower probability p, the pth quantile of r_t is r_n^* if the probability p^* is chosen based on Eq. (7.27), where $p = P(r_t \le r_n^*)$. Consequently, for a given small probability p, the VaR of holding a long position in the asset underlying the log return r_t is

$$\text{VaR} = \begin{cases} \beta_n - \dfrac{\alpha_n}{k_n}\{1 - [-n\ln(1-p)]^{k_n}\} & \text{if } k_n \ne 0, \\ \beta_n + \alpha_n \ln[-n\ln(1-p)] & \text{if } k_n = 0, \end{cases} \tag{7.28}$$

where n is the length of subperiod.

Summary

We summarize the approach of applying the traditional extreme value theory to VaR calculation as follows:

1. Select the length of the subperiod n and obtain subperiod minima $\{r_{n,i}\}$, $i = 1, \ldots, g$, where $g = [T/n]$.
2. Obtain the maximum likelihood estimates of β_n, α_n, and k_n.
3. Check the adequacy of the fitted extreme value model; see the next section for some methods of model checking.
4. If the extreme value model is adequate, apply Eq. (7.28) to calculate VaR.

Remark. Since we focus on holding a long financial position and, hence, on the quantile in the left tail of a return distribution, the quantile is negative. Yet it is customary in practice to use a positive number for VaR calculation. Thus, in using Eq. (7.28), one should be aware that the negative sign signifies a loss. □

Example 7.6. Consider the daily log return, in percentage, of IBM stock from July 7, 1962 to December 31, 1998. From Table 7.2, we have $\hat{\alpha}_n = 0.945$, $\hat{\beta}_n = -2.583$, and $\hat{k}_n = -0.335$ for $n = 63$. Therefore, for the left-tail probability $p = 0.01$, the corresponding VaR is

$$\begin{aligned} \text{VaR} &= -2.583 - \frac{0.945}{-0.335}\left\{1 - [-63\ln(1-0.01)]^{-0.335}\right\} \\ &= -3.04969. \end{aligned}$$

Thus, for daily log returns of the stock, the 1% quantile is -3.04969. If one holds a long position on the stock worth \$10 million, then the estimated VaR with probability 1% is $10,000,000 $\times$ 0.0304969 = $304,969. If the probability is 0.05, then the corresponding VaR is $166,641.

If we chose $n = 21$ (i.e., approximately 1 month), then $\hat{\alpha}_n = 0.823$, $\hat{\beta}_n = -1.902$, and $\hat{k}_n = -0.197$. The 1% quantile of the extreme value distribution is

$$\text{VaR} = -1.902 - \frac{0.823}{-0.197}\{1 - [-21\ln(1 - 0.01)]^{-0.197}\} = -3.40013.$$

Therefore, for a long position of $10,000,000, the corresponding 1-day horizon VaR is $340,013 at the 1% risk level. If the probability is 0.05, then the corresponding VaR is $184,127. In this particular case, the choice of $n = 21$ gives higher VaR values.

It is somewhat surprising to see that the VaR values obtained in Example 7.6 using the extreme value theory are smaller than those of Example 7.3 that uses a GARCH(1,1) model. In fact, the VaR values of Example 7.6 are even smaller than those based on the empirical quantile in Example 7.5. This is due in part to the choice of probability 0.05. If one chooses probability 0.001 = 0.1% and considers the same financial position, then we have VaR = $546,641 for the Gaussian AR(2)–GARCH(1,1) model and VaR = $666,590 for the extreme value theory with $n = 21$. Furthermore, the VaR obtained here via the traditional extreme value theory may not be adequate because the independent assumption of daily log returns is often rejected by statistical testings. Finally, the use of subperiod minima overlooks the fact of volatility clustering in the daily log returns. The new approach of extreme value theory discussed in the next section overcomes these weaknesses.

Remark. As shown by the results of Example 7.6, the VaR calculation based on the traditional extreme value theory depends on the choice of n, which is the length of subperiods. For the limiting extreme value distribution to hold, one would prefer a large n. But a larger n means a smaller g when the sample size T is fixed, where g is the effective sample size used in estimating the three parameters α_n, β_n, and k_n. Therefore, some compromise between the choices of n and g is needed. A proper choice may depend on the returns of the asset under study. We recommend that one should check the stability of the resulting VaR in applying the traditional extreme value theory. □

7.6.1 Discussion

We have applied various methods of VaR calculation to the daily log returns of IBM stock for a long position of $10 million. Consider the VaR of the position for the next trading day. If the probability is 5%, which means that with probability 0.95 the loss will be less than or equal to the VaR for the next trading day, then the results obtained are

1. $302,500 for the RiskMetrics,
2. $287,200 for a Gaussian AR(2)–GARCH(1,1) model,

3. \$283,520 for an AR(2)–GARCH(1,1) model with a standardized Student-t distribution with 5 degrees of freedom,
4. \$216,030 for using the empirical quantile, and
5. \$184,127 for applying the traditional extreme value theory using monthly minima (i.e., subperiod length $n = 21$).

If the probability is 1%, then the VaR is

1. \$426,500 for the RiskMetrics,
2. \$409,738 for a Gaussian AR(2)–GARCH(1,1) model,
3. \$475,943 for an AR(2)–GARCH(1,1) model with a standardized Student-t distribution with 5 degrees of freedom,
4. \$365,709 for using the empirical quantile, and
5. \$340,013 for applying the traditional extreme value theory using monthly minima (i.e., subperiod length $n = 21$).

If the probability is 0.1%, then the VaR becomes

1. \$566,443 for the RiskMetrics,
2. \$546,641 for a Gaussian AR(2)–GARCH(1,1) model,
3. \$836,341 for an AR(2)–GARCH(1,1) model with a standardized Student-t distribution with 5 degrees of freedom,
4. \$780,712 for using the empirical quantile, and
5. \$666,590 for applying the traditional extreme value theory using monthly minima (i.e., subperiod length $n = 21$).

There are substantial differences among different approaches. This is not surprising because there exists substantial uncertainty in estimating tail behavior of a statistical distribution. Since there is no true VaR available to compare the accuracy of different approaches, we recommend that one applies several methods to gain insight into the range of VaR.

The choice of tail probability also plays an important role in VaR calculation. For the daily IBM stock returns, the sample size is 9190 so that the empirical quantiles of 5% and 1% are decent estimates of the quantiles of the return distribution. In this case, we can treat the results based on empirical quantiles as conservative estimates of the true VaR (i.e., lower bounds). In this view, the approach based on the traditional extreme value theory seems to underestimate the VaR for the daily log returns of IBM stock. The conditional approach of extreme value theory discussed in the next section overcomes this weakness.

When the tail probability is small (e.g., 0.1%), the empirical quantile is a less reliable estimate of the true quantile. The VaR based on empirical quantiles can no longer serve as a lower bound of the true VaR. Finally, the earlier results show clearly the effects of using a heavy-tail distribution in VaR calculation when the tail probability is small. The VaR based on either a Student-t distribution with 5 degrees of freedom or the extreme value distribution is greater than that based on the normal assumption when the probability is 0.1%.

7.6.2 Multiperiod VaR

The square root of time rule of the RiskMetrics methodology becomes a special case under the extreme value theory. The proper relationship between ℓ-day and 1-day horizons is

$$\text{VaR}(\ell) = \ell^{1/\alpha}\text{VaR} = \ell^{-k}\text{VaR},$$

where α is the tail index and k is the shape parameter of the extreme value distribution; see Danielsson and de Vries (1997a). This relationship is referred to as the α-root of time rule. Here $\alpha = -1/k$, not the scale parameter α_n.

For illustration, consider the daily log returns of IBM stock in Example 7.6. If we use $p = 0.05$ and the results of $n = 21$, then for a 30-day horizon we have

$$\text{VaR}(30) = (30)^{0.335}\text{VaR} = 3.125 \times \$184,127 = \$575,397.$$

Because $\ell^{0.335} < \ell^{0.5}$, the α-root of time rule produces lower ℓ-day horizon VaR than the square root of time rule does.

7.6.3 VaR for a Short Position

In this subsection, we give the formulas of VaR calculation for holding short positions. Here the quantity of interest is the subperiod maximum and the limiting extreme value distribution becomes

$$F_*(r) = \begin{cases} \exp\left[-\left(1 - \dfrac{k_n(r-\beta_n)}{\alpha_n}\right)^{1/k_n}\right] & \text{if } k_n \neq 0, \\ \exp\left[-\exp\left(\dfrac{r-\beta_n}{\alpha_n}\right)\right] & \text{if } k_n = 0, \end{cases} \tag{7.29}$$

where r denotes a value of the subperiod maximum and it is understood that $1 - k_n(r-\beta_n)/\alpha_n > 0$ for $k_n \neq 0$.

Following similar procedures as those of long positions, we obtain the $(1-p)$th quantile of the return r_t as

$$\text{VaR} = \begin{cases} \beta_n + \dfrac{\alpha_n}{k_n}\left\{1 - \left[-n\ln(1-p)\right]^{k_n}\right\} & \text{if } k_n \neq 0, \\ \beta_n + \alpha_n \ln[-n\ln(1-p)] & \text{if } k_n = 0, \end{cases} \tag{7.30}$$

where p is a small probability denoting the chance of loss for holding a short position and n is the length of subperiod.

7.6.4 Return Level

Another risk measure based on the extreme values of subperiods is the *return level*. The g n-subperiod return level, $L_{n,g}$, is defined as the level that is exceeded in one out of every g subperiods of length n. That is,

$$P(r_{n,i} < L_{n,g}) = \frac{1}{g},$$

where $r_{n,i}$ denotes subperiod minimum. The subperiod in which the return level is exceeded is called a *stress period*. If the subperiod length n is sufficiently large so that normalized $r_{n,i}$ follows the GEV distribution, then the return level is

$$L_{n,g} = \beta_n + \frac{\alpha_n}{k_n}\{[-\ln(1-1/g)]^{k_n} - 1\},$$

provided that $k_n \neq 0$. Note that this is precisely the quantile of extreme value distribution given in Eq. (7.26) with tail probability $p^* = 1/g$, even though we write it in a slightly different way. Thus, return level applies to the subperiod minimum (or maximum), not to the underlying returns. This marks the difference between VaR and return level.

For the daily negative IBM log returns with subperiod length of 21 days, we can use the fitted model to obtain the return level for 12 such subperiods (i.e., $g = 12$). The return level is −4.4835%.

S-Plus Commands for Obtaining Return Level

```
> rl.21.12=rlevel.gev(nibm.gev.21, k.blocks=12,
+ type='profile')
> class(rl.21.12)
[1] "list"
> names(rl.21.12)
[1] "Range"  "rlevel"
> rl.21.12$rlevel
[1] 4.483506
```

In S-Plus, the number of subperiods is denoted by `k.blocks` and the subcommand, `type='profile'`, produces a plot of the profile log-likelihood confidence interval for the return level. The plot is not shown here. Another subcommand for type is `type='RetLevel'`.

If the subperiod maximum is used, the return level is defined as $P(r_{n,i} > L_{n,g}) = 1/g$, where $r_{n,i}$ denotes the subperiod maximum. Again, using the GEV distribution for maximum, we have

$$L_{n,g} = \beta_n + \frac{\alpha_n}{k_n}\{1 - [-\ln(1-1/g)]^{k_n}\},$$

where g is the number of subperiods.

7.7 A NEW APPROACH BASED ON THE EXTREME VALUE THEORY

The aforementioned approach to VaR calculation using the extreme value theory encounters some difficulties. First, the choice of subperiod length n is not clearly defined. Second, the approach is unconditional and, hence, does not take into consideration effects of other explanatory variables. To overcome these difficulties, a modern approach to extreme value theory has been proposed in the statistical literature; see Davison and Smith (1990) and Smith (1989). Instead of focusing on the extremes (maximum or minimum), the new approach focuses on exceedances of the measurement over some high threshold and the times at which the exceedances occur. Thus, this new approach is also referred to as *peaks over thresholds* (POT). For illustration, consider the daily log returns r_t of IBM stock used in this chapter and a long position on the stock. Let η be a prespecified high threshold. We may choose $\eta = -2.5\%$. Suppose that the ith exceedance occurs at day t_i (i.e., $r_{t_i} \leq \eta$). Then the new approach focuses on the data $(t_i, r_{t_i} - \eta)$. Here $r_{t_i} - \eta$ is the exceedance over the threshold η and t_i is the time at which the ith exceedance occurs. Similarly, for a short position, we may choose $\eta = 2\%$ and focus on the data $(t_i, r_{t_i} - \eta)$ for which $r_{t_i} \geq \eta$.

In practice, the occurrence times $\{t_i\}$ provide useful information about the intensity of the occurrence of important "rare events" (e.g., less than the threshold η for a long position). A cluster of t_i indicates a period of large market declines. The exceeding amount (or exceedance) $r_{t_i} - \eta$ is also of importance as it provides the actual quantity of interest.

Based on the prior introduction, the new approach does not require the choice of a subperiod length n, but it requires the specification of threshold η. Different choices of the threshold η lead to different estimates of the shape parameter k (and hence the tail index $-1/k$). In the literature, some researchers believe that the choice of η is a statistical problem as well as a financial one, and it cannot be determined based purely on statistical theory. For example, different financial institutions (or investors) have different risk tolerances. As such, they may select different thresholds even for an identical financial position. For the daily log returns of IBM stock considered in this chapter, the calculated VaR is not sensitive to the choice of η.

The choice of threshold η also depends on the observed log returns. For a stable return series, $\eta = -2.5\%$ may fare well for a long position. For a volatile return series (e.g., daily returns of a dot-com stock), η may be as low as -10%. Limited experience shows that η can be chosen so that the number of exceedances is sufficiently large (e.g., about 5% of the sample). For a more formal study on the choice of η, see Danielsson and de Vries (1997b).

7.7.1 Statistical Theory

Again consider the log return r_t of an asset. Suppose that the ith exceedance occurs at t_i. Focusing on the exceedance $r_t - \eta$ and exceeding time t_i results in a fundamental change in statistical thinking. Instead of using the marginal distribution (e.g., the limiting distribution of the minimum or maximum), the new approach employs a conditional distribution to handle the magnitude of exceedance given that the measurement exceeds a threshold. The chance of exceeding the threshold is governed by a probability law. In other words, the new approach considers the conditional distribution of $x = r_t - \eta$ given $r_t \le \eta$ for a long position. Occurrence of the event $\{r_t \le \eta\}$ follows a point process (e.g., a Poisson process). See Section 6.9 for the definition of a Poisson process. In particular, if the intensity parameter λ of the process is time-invariant, then the Poisson process is homogeneous. If λ is time-variant, then the process is nonhomogeneous. The concept of Poisson process can be generalized to the multivariate case.

For ease in presentation, in what follows we use a positive threshold and the right-hand side of a return distribution to discuss the statistical theory behind the new approach of extreme value theory. This corresponds to holding a short financial position. However, the theory applies equally well to holding a long position if it is applied to the r_t^c series, where $r_t^c = -r_t$. This is easily seen because $r_t^c \ge \eta$ for a positive threshold is equivalent to $r_t \le -\eta$, where $-\eta$ becomes a negative threshold.

The basic theory of the new approach is to consider the conditional distribution of $r = x + \eta$ given $r > \eta$ for the limiting distribution of the maximum given in Eq. (7.29). Since there is no need to choose the subperiod length n, we do not use it as a subscript of the parameters. Then the conditional distribution of $r \le x + \eta$ given $r > \eta$ is

$$\Pr(r \le x + \eta | r > \eta) = \frac{\Pr(\eta \le r \le x + \eta)}{\Pr(r > \eta)} = \frac{\Pr(r \le x + \eta) - \Pr(r \le \eta)}{1 - \Pr(r \le \eta)}. \tag{7.31}$$

Using the CDF $F_*(.)$ of Eq. (7.29) and the approximation $e^{-y} \approx 1 - y$ and after some algebra, we obtain that

$$\begin{aligned}
&\Pr(r \le x + \eta | r > \eta) \\
&= \frac{F_*(x+\eta) - F_*(\eta)}{1 - F_*(\eta)} \\
&= \frac{\exp\left[-\left(1 - \dfrac{k(x+\eta-\beta)}{\alpha}\right)^{1/k}\right] - \exp\left[-\left(1 - \dfrac{k(\eta-\beta)}{\alpha}\right)^{1/k}\right]}{1 - \exp\left[-\left(1 - \dfrac{k(\eta-\beta)}{\alpha}\right)^{1/k}\right]} \\
&\approx 1 - \left(1 - \frac{kx}{\alpha - k(\eta - \beta)}\right)^{1/k},
\end{aligned} \tag{7.32}$$

where $x > 0$ and $1 - k(\eta - \beta)/\alpha > 0$. As is seen later, this approximation makes explicit the connection of the new approach to the traditional extreme value theory.

The case of $k = 0$ is taken as the limit of $k \to 0$ so that

$$\Pr(r \le x + \eta | r > \eta) \approx 1 - \exp(-x/\alpha).$$

The distribution with cumulative distribution function

$$G_{k,\psi(\eta)}(x) = \begin{cases} 1 - \left[1 - \dfrac{kx}{\psi(\eta)}\right]^{1/k} & \text{for } k \ne 0, \\ 1 - \exp[-x/\psi(\eta)] & \text{for } k = 0, \end{cases} \quad (7.33)$$

where $\psi(\eta) > 0$, $x \ge 0$ when $k \le 0$, and $0 \le x \le \psi(\eta)/k$ when $k > 0$, is called the *generalized Pareto distribution* (GPD). Thus, the result of Eq. (7.32) shows that the conditional distribution of r given $r > \eta$ is well approximated by a GPD with parameters k and $\psi(\eta) = \alpha - k(\eta - \beta)$. See Embrechts et al. (1997) for further information. An important property of the GPD is as follows. Suppose that the excess distribution of r given a threshold η_o is a GPD with shape parameter k and scale parameter $\psi(\eta_o)$. Then, for an arbitrary threshold $\eta > \eta_o$, the excess distribution over the threshold η is also a GPD with shape parameter k and scale parameter $\psi(\eta) = \psi(\eta_o) - k(\eta - \eta_o)$.

When $k = 0$, the GPD in Eq. (7.33) reduces to an exponential distribution. This result motivates the use of a QQ-plot of excess returns over a threshold against exponential distribution to infer the tail behavior of the returns. If $k = 0$, then the QQ-plot should be linear. Figure 7.6a shows the QQ-plot of daily negative IBM log returns used in this chapter with threshold 0.025. The nonlinear feature of the plot clearly shows that the left-tail of the daily IBM log returns is heavier than that of a normal distribution, that is, $k \ne 0$.

S-Plus Commands Used to Produce Figure 7.6

```
> par(mfcol=c(2,1))
> qplot(-ibm,threshold=0.025,
+ main='Negative daily IBM log returns')
> meplot(-ibm)
> title(main='Mean excess plot')
```

7.7.2 Mean Excess Function

Given a high threshold η_o, suppose that the excess $r - \eta_o$ follows a GPD with parameter k and $\psi(\eta_o)$, where $0 > k > -1$. Then the *mean excess* over the threshold η_o is

$$E(r - \eta_o | r > \eta_o) = \frac{\psi(\eta_o)}{1 + k}.$$

For any $\eta > \eta_o$, define the *mean excess function* $e(\eta)$ as

$$e(\eta) = E(r - \eta | r > \eta) = \frac{\psi(\eta_o) - k(\eta - \eta_o)}{1 + k}.$$

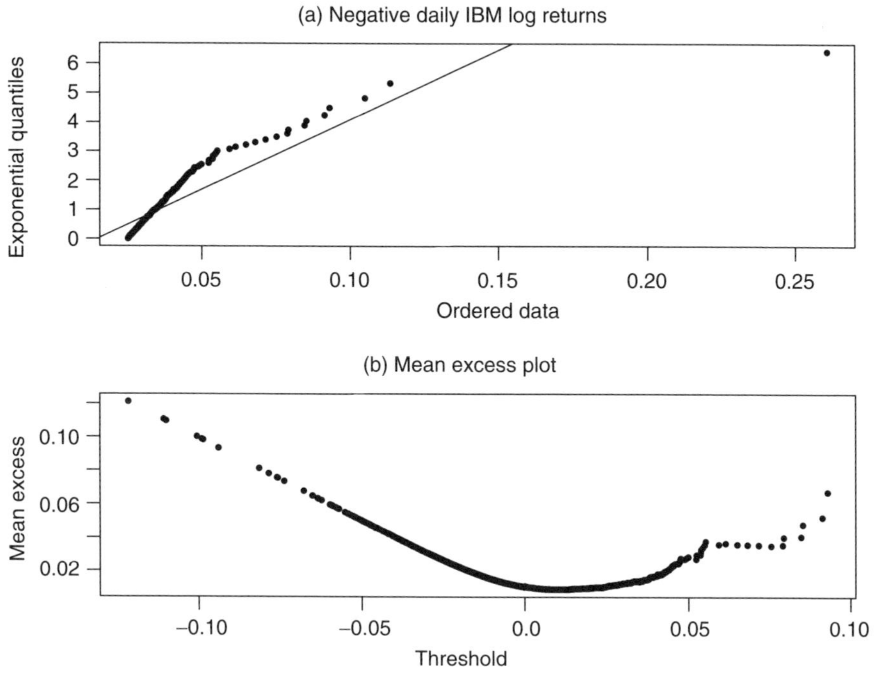

Figure 7.6. Plots for daily negative IBM log returns from July 3, 1962 to December 31, 1998. (a) QQ-plot of excess returns over the threshold 2.5% and (b) the mean excess plot.

In other words, for any $y > 0$,

$$e(\eta_o + y) = E[r - (\eta_o + y)|r > \eta_o + y] = \frac{\psi(\eta_o) - ky}{1 + k}.$$

Thus, for a fixed k, the mean excess function is a linear function of $y = \eta - \eta_o$. This result leads to a simple graphical method to infer the appropriate threshold value η_o for the GPD. Define the *empirical mean excess function* as

$$e_T(\eta) = \frac{1}{N_\eta} \sum_{i=1}^{N_\eta} (r_{t_i} - \eta), \tag{7.34}$$

where N_η is the number of returns that exceed η and r_{t_i} are the values of the corresponding returns. See the next subsection for more information on the notation. The scatterplot of $e_T(\eta)$ against η is called the *mean excess plot*, which should be linear in η for $\eta > \eta_o$. Figure 7.6b shows the mean excess plot of the daily negative IBM log returns. It shows that, among others, a threshold of about 3% is reasonable for the negative return series. In S-Plus, the command for mean excess plot is `meplot`.

7.7.3 A New Approach to Modeling Extreme Values

Using the statistical result in Eq. (7.32) and considering jointly the exceedances and exceeding times, Smith (1989) proposes a two-dimensional Poisson process to model (t_i, r_{t_i}). This approach was used by Tsay (1999) to study VaR in risk management. We follow the same approach.

Assume that the baseline time interval is D, which is typically a year. In the United States, $D = 252$ is used as there are typically 252 trading days in a year. Let t be the time interval of the data points (e.g., daily) and denote the data span by $t = 1, 2, \ldots, T$, where T is the total number of data points. For a given threshold η, the exceeding times over the threshold are denoted by $\{t_i,\ i = 1, \ldots, N_\eta\}$ and the observed log return at t_i is r_{t_i}. Consequently, we focus on modeling $\{(t_i, r_{t_i})\}$ for $i = 1, \ldots, N_\eta$, where N_η depends on the threshold η.

The new approach to applying the extreme value theory is to postulate that the exceeding times and the associated returns (i.e., (t_i, r_{t_i})) jointly form a two-dimensional Poisson process with intensity measure given by

$$\Lambda[(D_2, D_1) \times (r, \infty)] = \frac{D_2 - D_1}{D} S(r; k, \alpha, \beta), \tag{7.35}$$

where

$$S(r; k, \alpha, \beta) = \left[1 - \frac{k(r - \beta)}{\alpha}\right]_+^{1/k},$$

$0 \le D_1 \le D_2 \le T$, $r > \eta$, $\alpha > 0$, β, and k are parameters, and the notation $[x]_+$ is defined as $[x]_+ = \max(x, 0)$. This intensity measure says that the occurrence of exceeding the threshold is proportional to the length of the time interval $[D_1, D_2]$ and the probability is governed by a survival function similar to the exponent of the CDF $F_*(r)$ in Eq. (7.29). A survival function of a random variable X is defined as $S(x) = \Pr(X > x) = 1 - \Pr(X \le x) = 1 - CDF(x)$. When $k = 0$, the intensity measure is taken as the limit of $k \to 0$; that is,

$$\Lambda[(D_2, D_1) \times (r, \infty)] = \frac{D_2 - D_1}{D} \exp\left[\frac{-(r - \beta)}{\alpha}\right].$$

In Eq. (7.35), the length of time interval is measured with respect to the baseline interval D.

The idea of using the intensity measure in Eq. (7.35) becomes clear when one considers its implied conditional probability of $r = x + \eta$ given $r > \eta$ over the time interval $[0, D]$, where $x > 0$,

$$\frac{\Lambda[(0, D) \times (x + \eta, \infty)]}{\Lambda[(0, D) \times (\eta, \infty)]} = \left[\frac{1 - k(x + \eta - \beta)/\alpha}{1 - k(\eta - \beta)/\alpha}\right]^{1/k} = \left[1 - \frac{kx}{\alpha - k(\eta - \beta)}\right]^{1/k},$$

which is precisely the survival function of the conditional distribution given in Eq. (7.32). This survival function is obtained from the extreme limiting distribution for maximum in Eq. (7.29). We use survival function here because it denotes the probability of exceedance.

The relationship between the limiting extreme value distribution in Eq. (7.29) and the intensity measure in Eq. (7.35) directly connects the new approach of extreme value theory to the traditional one.

Mathematically, the intensity measure in Eq. (7.35) can be written as an integral of an intensity function:

$$\Lambda[(D_2, D_1) \times (r, \infty)] = \int_{D_1}^{D_2} \int_{r}^{\infty} \lambda(t, z; k, \alpha, \beta)\, dt\, dz,$$

where the intensity function $\lambda(t, z; k, \alpha, \beta)$ is defined as

$$\lambda(t, z; k, \alpha, \beta) = \frac{1}{D} g(z; k, \alpha, \beta), \tag{7.36}$$

where

$$g(z; k, \alpha, \beta) = \begin{cases} \dfrac{1}{\alpha}\left[1 - \dfrac{k(z-\beta)}{\alpha}\right]^{1/k-1} & \text{if } k \neq 0, \\ \dfrac{1}{\alpha}\exp\left[\dfrac{-(z-\beta)}{\alpha}\right] & \text{if } k = 0. \end{cases}$$

Using the results of a Poisson process, we can write down the likelihood function for the observed exceeding times and their corresponding returns $\{(t_i, r_{t_i})\}$ over the two-dimensional space $[0, N] \times (\eta, \infty)$ as

$$L(k, \alpha, \beta) = \left(\prod_{i=1}^{N_\eta} \frac{1}{D} g(r_{t_i}; k, \alpha, \beta)\right) \times \exp\left[-\frac{T}{D} S(\eta; k, \alpha, \beta)\right]. \tag{7.37}$$

The parameters k, α, and β can then be estimated by maximizing the logarithm of this likelihood function. Since the scale parameter α is non-negative, we use $\ln(\alpha)$ in the estimation.

Example 7.7. Consider again the daily log returns of IBM stock from July 3, 1962 to December 31, 1998. There are 9190 daily returns. Table 7.3 gives some estimation results of the parameters k, α, and β for three choices of the threshold when the negative series $\{-r_t\}$ is used. We use the negative series $\{-r_t\}$, instead of $\{r_t\}$, because we focus on holding a long financial position. The table also shows the number of exceeding times for a given threshold. It is seen that the chance of dropping 2.5% or more in a day for IBM stock occurred with probability $310/9190 \approx 3.4\%$. Because the sample mean of IBM stock returns is not zero, we also consider the case when the sample mean is removed from the original daily log returns. From the table, removing the sample mean has little impact on the parameter estimates. These parameter estimates are used next to calculate

Table 7.3. Estimation Results[a] of a Two-Dimensional Homogeneous Poisson Model for the Daily Negative Log Returns of IBM Stock from July 3, 1962 to December 31, 1998

Thr.	Exc.	Shape Parameter k	Log(Scale) $\ln(\alpha)$	Location β
		Original Log Returns		
3.0%	175	−0.30697(0.09015)	0.30699(0.12380)	4.69204(0.19058)
2.5%	310	−0.26418(0.06501)	0.31529(0.11277)	4.74062(0.18041)
2.0%	554	−0.18751(0.04394)	0.27655(0.09867)	4.81003(0.17209)
		Removing the Sample Mean		
3.0%	184	−0.30516(0.08824)	0.30807(0.12395)	4.73804(0.19151)
2.5%	334	−0.28179(0.06737)	0.31968(0.12065)	4.76808(0.18533)
2.0%	590	−0.19260(0.04357)	0.27917(0.09913)	4.84859(0.17255)

[a]The baseline time interval is 252 (i.e., 1 year). The numbers in parentheses are standard errors, where "Thr." and "Exc." stand for threshold and the number of exceedings.

VaR, keeping in mind that in a real application one needs to check carefully the adequacy of a fitted Poisson model. We discuss methods of model checking in the next subsection.

7.7.4 VaR Calculation Based on the New Approach

As shown in Eq. (7.32), the two-dimensional Poisson process model used, which employs the intensity measure in Eq. (7.35), has the same parameters as those of the extreme value distribution in Eq. (7.29). Therefore, one can use the same formula as that of Eq. (7.30) to calculate VaR of the new approach. More specifically, for a given upper tail probability p, the $(1-p)$th quantile of the log return r_t is

$$\text{VaR} = \begin{cases} \beta + \dfrac{\alpha}{k}\left\{1 - \left[-D\ln(1-p)\right]^{k}\right\} & \text{if } k \neq 0, \\ \beta + \alpha \ln[-D\ln(1-p)] & \text{if } k = 0, \end{cases} \tag{7.38}$$

where D is the baseline time interval used in estimation. In the United States, one typically uses $D = 252$, which is approximately the number of trading days in a year.

Example 7.8. Consider again the case of holding a long position of IBM stock valued at \$10 million. We use the estimation results of Table 7.3 to calculate 1-day horizon VaR for the tail probabilities of 0.05 and 0.01.

- Case I: Use the original daily log returns. The three choices of threshold η result in the following VaR values:

1. $\eta = 3.0\%$: VaR(5%) = \$228,239, VaR(1%) = \$359.303.
2. $\eta = 2.5\%$: VaR(5%) = \$219,106, VaR(1%) = \$361,119.
3. $\eta = 2.0\%$: VaR(5%) = \$212,981, VaR(1%) = \$368.552.

- Case II: The sample mean of the daily log returns is removed. The three choices of threshold η result in the following VaR values:
  1. $\eta = 3.0\%$: VaR(5%) = \$232,094, VaR(1%) = \$363,697.
  2. $\eta = 2.5\%$: VaR(5%) = \$225,782, VaR(1%) = \$364,254.
  3. $\eta = 2.0\%$: VaR(5%) = \$217,740, VaR(1%) = \$372,372.

As expected, removing the sample mean, which is positive, slightly increases the VaR. However, the VaR is rather stable among the three threshold values used. In practice, we recommend that one removes the sample mean first before applying this new approach to VaR calculation.

Discussion. Compared with the VaR of Example 7.6 that uses the traditional extreme value theory, the new approach provides a more stable VaR calculation. The traditional approach is rather sensitive to the choice of the subperiod length n. □

7.7.5 An Alternative Parameterization

As mentioned before, for a given threshold η, the GPD can also be parameterized by the shape parameter k and the scale parameter $\psi(\eta) = \alpha - k(\eta - \beta)$. This is the parameterization used in S-Plus. In fact, `(xi,beta)` of S-Plus corresponds to $(-k, \psi(\eta))$ of this chapter. The command for estimating a GPD model in S-Plus is `gpd`. For illustration, consider the daily negative IBM log return series from 1962 to 1998. The results are given below:

```
> nibm.gpd = gpd(-ibm,threshold=0.025)
> names(nibm.gpd)
 [1] "n"                    "data"
 [3] "upper.exceed"         "lower.exceed"
 [5] "upper.thresh"         "lower.thresh"
 [7] "p.less.upper.thresh" "p.larger.lower.thresh"
 [9] "n.upper.exceed"       "n.lower.exceed"
[11] "upper.method"         "lower.method"
[13] "upper.par.ests"       "lower.par.ests"
[15] "upper.par.ses"        "lower.par.ses"
[17] "upper.varcov"         "lower.varcov"
[19] "upper.info"           "lower.info"
[21] "upper.converged"      "lower.converged"
[23] "upper.nllh.final"     "lower.nllh.final"
> nibm.gpd$upper.thresh
[1] 0.025
> nibm.gpd$n.upper.exceed  % number of exceedances
[1] 310
```

```
> nibm.gpd$p.less.upper.thresh % 1-prob(exceedance)
[1] 0.9662677
> nibm.gpd$upper.par.ests
       xi        beta
 0.2641418 0.00778777
> nibm.gpd$upper.par.ses
         xi          beta
 0.06659759 0.0006715558
> par(mfcol=c(2,2))
> plot(nibm.gpd)

Make a plot selection (or 0 to exit):
1: plot: Excess Distribution
2: plot: Tail of Underlying Distribution
3: plot: Scatterplot of Residuals
4: plot: QQplot of Residuals
Selection:
```

Note that the results are very close to those in Table 7.3, where percentage log returns are used. The estimates of k and $\psi(\eta)$ are -0.26418 and $\alpha - k(\eta - \beta) = \exp(0.31529) - (-0.26418)(2.5 - 4.7406) = 0.77873$, respectively, in Table 7.3. In terms of log returns, the estimate of $\psi(\eta)$ is 0.007787, which is the same as the S-Plus estimate.

Figure 7.7 shows the diagnostic plots for the GPD fit to the daily negative log returns of IBM stock. The QQ-plot (lower-right panel) and the tail probability estimate (in log scale and in the lower-left panel) show some minor deviation from a straight line, indicating further improvement is possible.

From the conditional distributions in Eqs. (7.31) and (7.32) and the GPD in Eq. (7.33), we have

$$\frac{F(y) - F(\eta)}{1 - F(\eta)} \approx G_{\eta,\psi(\eta)}(x),$$

where $y = x + \eta$ with $x > 0$. If we estimate the CDF $F(\eta)$ of the returns by the empirical CDF, then

$$\hat{F}(\eta) = \frac{T - N_\eta}{T},$$

where N_η is the number of exceedances of the threshold η and T is the sample size. Consequently,

$$\begin{aligned} F(y) &= F(\eta) + G(x)[1 - F(\eta)] \\ &\approx 1 - \frac{N_\eta}{T}\left[1 - \frac{k(y-\eta)}{\psi(\eta)}\right]^{1/k}. \end{aligned}$$

This leads to an alternative estimate of the quantile of $F(y)$ for use in VaR calculation. Specifically, for an upper tail probability p, where $0 < p < 0.05$, let

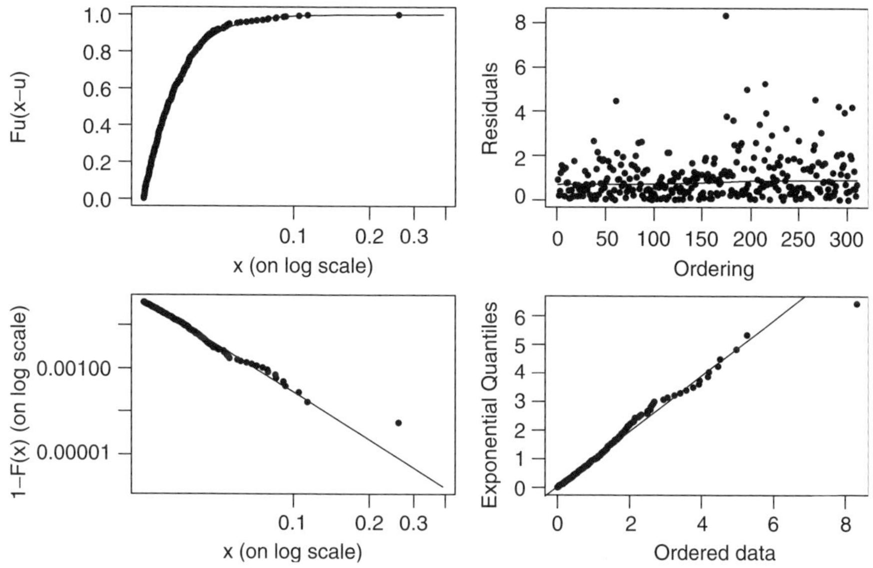

Figure 7.7. Diagnostic plots for GPD fit to the daily negative log returns of IBM stock from July 3, 1962 to December 31, 1998.

$q = 1 - p$. Then, the qth quantile of $F(y)$, denoted by VaR_q, can be estimated by

$$\text{VaR}_q = \eta + \frac{\psi(\eta)}{k}\left\{1 - \left[\frac{T}{N_\eta}(1-q)\right]^k\right\}, \tag{7.39}$$

where, as before, η is the threshold, T is the sample size, N_η is the number of exceedances, and $\psi(\eta)$ and k are the scale and shape parameters of the GPD distribution. This method to VaR calculation is used in S-Plus.

Another commonly used risk measure associated with VaR is the *expected shortfall* (ES), which is defined as the expected loss given that the VaR is exceeded. Specifically, for a given probability q (typically $0.95 \le q \le 1$), the expected shortfall is defined by

$$\text{ES}_q = E(r|r > \text{VaR}_q) = \text{VaR}_q + E(r - \text{VaR}_q|r > \text{VaR}_q). \tag{7.40}$$

Using properties of the GPD, it can be shown that

$$E(r - \text{VaR}_q|r > \text{VaR}_q) = \frac{\psi(\eta) - k(\text{VaR}_q - \eta)}{1+k},$$

provided that $0 > k > -1$. Consequently, we have

$$\text{ES}_q = \frac{\text{VaR}_q}{1+k} + \frac{\psi(\eta) + k\eta}{1+k}.$$

To illustrate the new method to VaR and ES calculations, we again use the daily negative log returns of IBM stock with threshold 2.5%. The S-Plus command is `riskmeasures`:

```
> riskmeasures(nibm.gpd, c(0.95,0.99))
        p   quantile      sfall
[1,] 0.95 0.02208893 0.03162723
[2,] 0.99 0.03616619 0.05075763
```

From the output, the VaR values for the financial position are \$220,889 and \$361,661, respectively, for tail probability of 0.05 and 0.01. These two values are rather close to those given in Example 7.8 that are based on the method of the previous subsection. The expected shortfalls for the financial position are \$316,272 and \$507,576, respectively, for tail probability of 0.05 and 0.01.

7.7.6 Use of Explanatory Variables

The two-dimensional Poisson process model discussed earlier is *homogeneous* because the three parameters k, α, and β are constant over time. In practice, such a model may not be adequate. Furthermore, some explanatory variables are often available that may influence the behavior of the log returns r_t. A nice feature of the new extreme value theory approach to VaR calculation is that it can easily take explanatory variables into consideration. We discuss such a framework in this subsection. In addition, we also discuss methods that can be used to check the adequacy of a fitted two-dimensional Poisson process model.

Suppose that $\boldsymbol{x}_t = (x_{1t}, \ldots, x_{vt})'$ is a vector of v explanatory variables that are available *prior to* time t. For asset returns, the volatility σ_t^2 of r_t discussed in Chapter 3 is an example of explanatory variables. Another example of explanatory variables in the U.S. equity markets is an indicator variable denoting the meetings of the Federal Open Market Committee. A simple way to make use of explanatory variables is to postulate that the three parameters k, α, and β are time-varying and are linear functions of the explanatory variables. Specifically, when explanatory variables $\boldsymbol{x}_t$ are available, we assume that

$$\begin{aligned} k_t &= \gamma_0 + \gamma_1 x_{1t} + \cdots + \gamma_v x_{vt} \equiv \gamma_0 + \boldsymbol{\gamma}'\boldsymbol{x}_t, \\ \ln(\alpha_t) &= \delta_0 + \delta_1 x_{1t} + \cdots + \delta_v x_{vt} \equiv \delta_0 + \boldsymbol{\delta}'\boldsymbol{x}_t, \\ \beta_t &= \theta_0 + \theta_1 x_{1t} + \cdots + \theta_v x_{vt} \equiv \theta_0 + \boldsymbol{\theta}'\boldsymbol{x}_t. \end{aligned} \tag{7.41}$$

If $\boldsymbol{\gamma} = \boldsymbol{0}$, then the shape parameter $k_t = \gamma_0$, which is time-invariant. Thus, testing the significance of $\boldsymbol{\gamma}$ can provide information about the contribution of the explanatory variables to the shape parameter. Similar methods apply to the scale and location parameters. In Eq. (7.41), we use the same explanatory variables for all three parameters k_t, $\ln(\alpha_t)$, and β_t. In an application, different explanatory variables may be used for different parameters.

When the three parameters of the extreme value distribution are time-varying, we have an *inhomogeneous* Poisson process. The intensity measure becomes

$$\Lambda[(D_1, D_2) \times (r, \infty)] = \frac{D_2 - D_1}{D} \left[1 - \frac{k_t(r - \beta_t)}{\alpha_t}\right]_+^{1/k_t}, \quad r > \eta. \tag{7.42}$$

The likelihood function of the exceeding times and returns $\{(t_i, r_{t_i})\}$ becomes

$$L = \left(\prod_{i=1}^{N_\eta} \frac{1}{D} g(r_{t_i}; k_{t_i}, \alpha_{t_i}, \beta_{t_i})\right) \times \exp\left[-\frac{1}{D}\int_0^T S(\eta; k_t, \alpha_t, \beta_t)\, dt\right],$$

which reduces to

$$L = \left(\prod_{i=1}^{N_\eta} \frac{1}{D} g(r_{t_i}; k_{t_i}, \alpha_{t_i}, \beta_{t_i})\right) \times \exp\left[-\frac{1}{D}\sum_{t=1}^{T} S(\eta; k_t, \alpha_t, \beta_t)\right] \tag{7.43}$$

if one assumes that the parameters k_t, α_t, and β_t are constant within each trading day, where $g(z; k_t, \alpha_t, \beta_t)$ and $S(\eta; k_t, \alpha_t, \beta_t)$ are given in Eqs. (7.36) and (7.35), respectively. For given observations $\{r_t, \boldsymbol{x}_t | t = 1, \ldots, T\}$, the baseline time interval D, and the threshold η, the parameters in Eq. (7.41) can be estimated by maximizing the logarithm of the likelihood function in Eq. (7.43). Again we use $\ln(\alpha_t)$ to satisfy the positive constraint of α_t.

Remark. The parameterization in Eq. (7.41) is similar to that of the volatility models of Chapter 3 in the sense that the three parameters are exact functions of the available information at time t. Other functions can be used if necessary. □

7.7.7 Model Checking

Checking an entertained two-dimensional Poisson process model for exceedance times and excesses involves examining three key features of the model. The first feature is to verify the adequacy of the exceedance rate, the second feature is to examine the distribution of exceedances, and the final feature is to check the independence assumption of the model. We discuss briefly some statistics that are useful for checking these three features. These statistics are based on some basic statistical theory concerning distributions and stochastic processes.

Exceedance Rate

A fundamental property of univariate Poisson processes is that the time durations between two consecutive events are independent and exponentially distributed. To exploit a similar property for checking a two-dimensional process model, Smith and Shively (1995) propose examining the time durations between consecutive exceedances. If the two-dimensional Poisson process model is appropriate for the exceedance times and excesses, the time duration between the ith and $(i-1)$th exceedances should follow an exponential distribution. More specifically, letting $t_0 = 0$, we expect that

$$z_{t_i} = \int_{t_{i-1}}^{t_i} \frac{1}{D} g(\eta; k_s, \alpha_s, \beta_s)\, ds, \quad i = 1, 2, \ldots$$

are independent and identically distributed (iid) as a standard exponential distribution. Because daily returns are discrete-time observations, we employ the time durations

$$z_{t_i} = \frac{1}{D} \sum_{t=t_{i-1}+1}^{t_i} S(\eta; k_t, \alpha_t, \beta_t) \quad (7.44)$$

and use the QQ-plot to check the validity of the iid standard exponential distribution. If the model is adequate, the QQ-plot should show a straight line through the origin with unit slope.

Distribution of Excesses

Under the two-dimensional Poisson process model considered, the conditional distribution of the excess $x_t = r_t - \eta$ over the threshold η is a GPD with shape parameter k_t and scale parameter $\psi_t = \alpha_t - k_t(\eta - \beta_t)$. Therefore, we can make use of the relationship between a standard exponential distribution and GPD, and define

$$w_{t_i} = \begin{cases} -\dfrac{1}{k_{t_i}} \ln\left(1 - k_{t_i} \dfrac{r_{t_i} - \eta}{\psi_{t_i}}\right)_+ & \text{if } k_{t_i} \neq 0, \\ \dfrac{r_{t_i} - \eta}{\psi_{t_i}} & \text{if } k_{t_i} = 0. \end{cases} \quad (7.45)$$

If the model is adequate, $\{w_{t_i}\}$ are independent and exponentially distributed with mean 1; see also Smith (1999). We can then apply the QQ-plot to check the validity of the GPD assumption for excesses.

Independence

A simple way to check the independence assumption, after adjusting for the effects of explanatory variables, is to examine the sample autocorrelation functions of z_{t_i} and w_{t_i}. Under the independence assumption, we expect that both z_{t_i} and w_{t_i} have no serial correlations.

7.7.8 An Illustration

In this subsection, we apply a two-dimensional inhomogeneous Poisson process model to the daily log returns, in percentages, of IBM stock from July 3, 1962 to December 31, 1998. We focus on holding a long position of \$10 million. The analysis enables us to compare the results with those obtained before by using other approaches to calculating VaR.

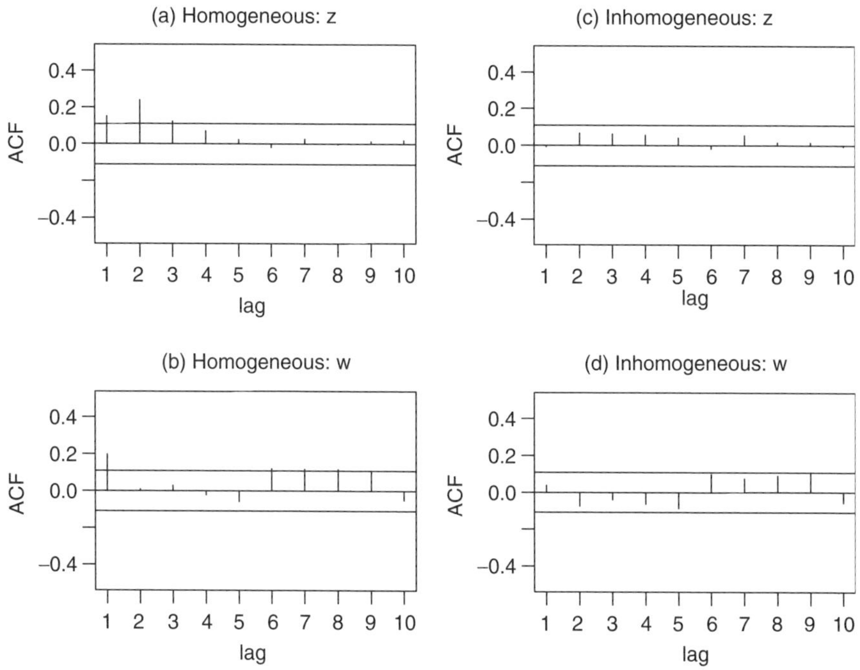

Figure 7.8. Sample autocorrelation functions of the z and w measures for two-dimensional Poisson models. Parts (a) and (b) are for the homogeneous model and parts (c) and (d) are for the inhomogeneous model. The data are daily mean-corrected log returns, in percentages, of IBM stock from July 3, 1962 to December 31, 1998, and the threshold is 2.5%. A long financial position is used.

We begin by pointing out that the two-dimensional homogeneous model of Example 7.7 needs further refinements because the fitted model fails to pass the model checking statistics of the previous subsection. Figures 7.8a and 7.8b show the autocorrelation functions of the statistics z_{t_i} and w_{t_i}, defined in Eqs. (7.44) and (7.45), of the homogeneous model when the threshold is $\eta = 2.5\%$. The horizontal lines in the plots denote asymptotic limits of two standard errors. It is seen that both z_{t_i} and w_{t_i} series have some significant serial correlations. Figures 7.9a and 7.9b show the QQ-plots of z_{t_i} and w_{t_i} series. The straight line in each plot is the theoretical line, which passes through the origin and has a unit slope under the assumption of a standard exponential distribution. The QQ-plot of z_{t_i} shows some discrepancy.

To refine the model, we use the mean-corrected log return series

$$r_t^o = r_t - \bar{r}, \quad \bar{r} = \frac{1}{9190} \sum_{t=1}^{9190} r_t,$$

where r_t is the daily log return in percentages, and employ the following explanatory variables:

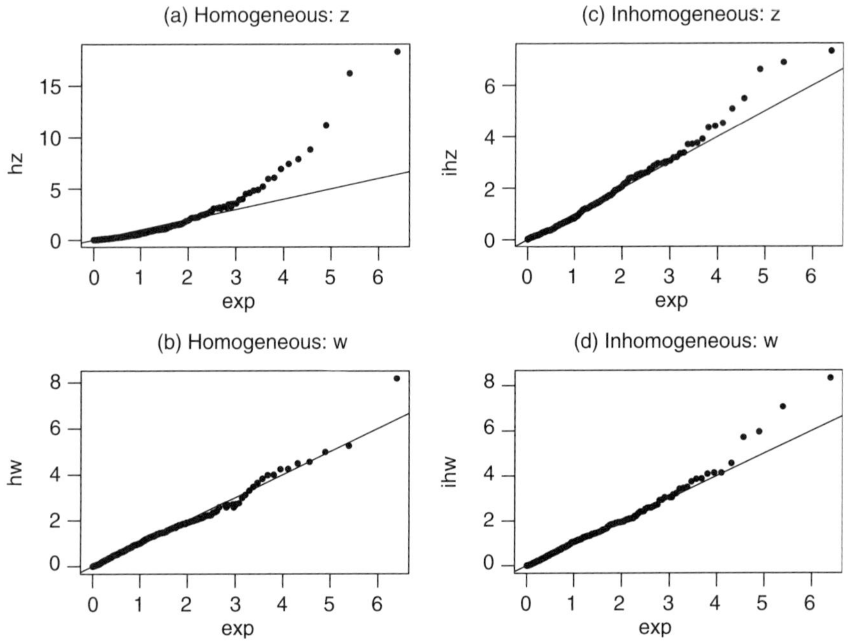

Figure 7.9. Quantile-to-quantile plot of the z and w measures for two-dimensional Poisson models. Parts (a) and (b) are for the homogeneous model and parts (c) and (d) are for the inhomogeneous model. The data are daily mean-corrected log returns, in percentages, of IBM stock from July 3, 1962 to December 31, 1998, and the threshold is 2.5%. A long financial position is used.

1. x_{1t}: an indicator variable for October, November, and December. That is, $x_{1t} = 1$ if t is in October, November, or December. This variable is chosen to take care of the fourth-quarter effect (or year-end effect), if any, on the daily IBM stock returns.
2. x_{2t}: an indicator variable for the behavior of the previous trading day. Specifically, $x_{2t} = 1$ if and only if the log return $r_{t-1}^o \leq -2.5\%$. Since we focus on holding a long position with threshold 2.5%, an exceedance occurs when the daily price drops over 2.5%. Therefore, x_{2t} is used to capture the possibility of panic selling when the price of IBM stock dropped 2.5% or more on the previous trading day.
3. x_{3t}: a qualitative measurement of volatility, which is the number of days between $t-1$ and $t-5$ (inclusive) that has a log return with magnitude exceeding the threshold. In our case, x_{3t} is the number of r_{t-i}^o satisfying $|r_{t-i}^o| \geq 2.5\%$ for $i = 1, \ldots, 5$.
4. x_{4t}: an annual trend defined as $x_{4t} =$ (year of time $t - 1961)/38$. This variable is used to detect any trend in the behavior of extreme returns of IBM stock.
5. x_{5t}: a volatility series based on a Gaussian GARCH(1,1) model for the mean-corrected series r_t^o. Specifically, $x_{5t} = \sigma_t$, where σ_t^2 is the conditional

variance of the GARCH(1,1) model

$$r_t^o = a_t, \quad a_t = \sigma_t \epsilon_t, \quad \epsilon_t \sim N(0, 1),$$
$$\sigma_t^2 = 0.04565 + 0.0807 a_{t-1}^2 + 0.9031 \sigma_{t-1}^2.$$

These five explanatory variables are all available at time $t - 1$. We use two volatility measures (x_{3t} and x_{5t}) to study the effect of market volatility on VaR. As shown in Example 7.3 by the fitted AR(2)–GARCH(1,1) model, the serial correlations in r_t are weak so that we do not entertain any ARMA model for the mean equation.

Using the prior five explanatory variables and deleting insignificant parameters, we obtain the estimation results shown in Table 7.4. Figures 7.8c and 7.8d and Figures 7.9c and 7.9d show the model checking statistics for the fitted two-dimensional inhomogeneous Poisson process model when the threshold is $\eta =$ 2.5%. All autocorrelation functions of z_{t_i} and w_{t_i} are within the asymptotic two standard-error limits. The QQ-plots also show marked improvements as they indicate no model inadequacy. Based on these checking results, the inhomogeneous model seems adequate.

Consider the case of threshold 2.5%. The estimation results show the following:

1. All three parameters of the intensity function depend significantly on the annual time trend. In particular, the shape parameter has a negative annual

Table 7.4. Estimation Results[a] of a Two-Dimensional Inhomogeneous Poisson Process Model for Daily Log Returns, in Percentages, of IBM Stock from July 3, 1962 to December 31, 1998

Parameter	Constant	Coefficient of x_{3t}	Coefficient of x_{4t}	Coefficient of x_{5t}
		Threshold 2.5% with 334 Exceedances		
β_t	0.3202		1.4772	2.1991
(Std. error)	(0.3387)		(0.3222)	(0.2450)
$\ln(\alpha_t)$	−0.8119	0.3305	1.0324	
(Std. error)	(0.1798)	(0.0826)	(0.2619)	
k_t	−0.1805	−0.2118	−0.3551	0.2602
(Std. error)	(0.1290)	(0.0580)	(0.1503)	(0.0461)
		Threshold 3.0% with 184 Exceedances		
β_t	1.1569			2.1918
(Std. error)	(0.4082)			(0.2909)
$\ln(\alpha_t)$	−0.0316	0.3336		
(Std. error)	(0.1201)	(0.0861)		
k_t	−0.6008	−0.2480		0.3175
(Std. error)	(0.1454)	(0.0731)		(0.0685)

[a]Four explanatory variables defined in the text are used. The model is for holding a long position on IBM stock. The sample mean of the log returns is removed from the data.

trend, indicating that the log returns of IBM stock are moving farther away from normality as time passes. Both the location and scale parameters increase over time.

2. Indicators for the fourth quarter, x_{1t}, and for panic selling, x_{2t}, are not significant for all three parameters.
3. The location and shape parameters are positively affected by the volatility of the GARCH(1,1) model; see the coefficients of x_{5t}. This is understandable because the variability of log returns increases when the volatility is high. Consequently, the dependence of log returns on the tail index is reduced.
4. The scale and shape parameters depend significantly on the qualitative measure of volatility. Signs of the estimates are also plausible.

The explanatory variables for December 31, 1998 assumed the values $x_{3,9190} = 0$, $x_{4,9190} = 0.9737$, and $x_{5,9190} = 1.9766$. Using these values and the fitted model in Table 7.4, we obtain

$$k_{9190} = -0.01195, \quad \ln(\alpha_{9190}) = 0.19331, \quad \beta_{9190} = 6.105.$$

Assume that the tail probability is 0.05. The VaR quantile shown in Eq. (7.38) gives VaR = 3.03756%. Consequently, for a long position of \$10 million, we have

$$\text{VaR} = \$10{,}000{,}000 \times 0.0303756 = \$303{,}756.$$

If the tail probability is 0.01, the VaR is \$497,425. The 5% VaR is slightly larger than that of Example 7.3, which uses a Gaussian AR(2)–GARCH(1,1) model. The 1% VaR is larger than that of Case 1 of Example 7.3. Again, as expected, the effect of extreme values (i.e., heavy tails) on VaR is more pronounced when the tail probability used is small.

An advantage of using explanatory variables is that the parameters are adaptive to the change in market conditions. For example, the explanatory variables for December 30, 1998 assumed the values $x_{3,9189} = 1$, $x_{4,9189} = 0.9737$, and $x_{5,9189} = 1.8757$. In this case, we have

$$k_{9189} = -0.2500, \quad \ln(\alpha_{9189}) = 0.52385, \quad \beta_{9189} = 5.8834.$$

The 95% quantile (i.e., the tail probability is 5%) then becomes 2.69139%. Consequently, the VaR is

$$\text{VaR} = \$10{,}000{,}000 \times 0.0269139 = \$269{,}139.$$

If the tail probability is 0.01, then VaR becomes \$448,323. Based on this example, the homogeneous Poisson model shown in Example 7.8 seems to underestimate the VaR.

EXERCISES

7.1. Consider the daily returns of GE stock from July 3, 1962 to December 31, 1999. The data can be obtained from CRSP or the file `d-ge6299.txt` Convert the simple returns into log returns. Suppose that you hold a long position on the stock valued at \$1 million. Use the tail probability 0.05. Compute the value at risk of your position for 1-day horizon and 15-day horizon using the following methods:

(a) The RiskMetrics method.

(b) A Gaussian ARMA–GARCH model.

(c) An ARMA–GARCH model with a Student-t distribution. You should also estimate the degrees of freedom.

(d) The traditional extreme value theory with subperiod length $n = 21$.

7.2. The file `d-csco9199.txt` contains the daily simple returns of Cisco Systems stock from 1991 to 1999 with 2275 observations. Transform the simple returns to log returns. Suppose that you hold a long position of Cisco stock valued at \$1 million. Compute the value at risk of your position for the next trading day using probability $p = 0.01$.

(a) Use the RiskMetrics method.

(b) Use a GARCH model with a conditional Gaussian distribution.

(c) Use a GARCH model with a Student-t distribution. You may also estimate the degrees of freedom.

(d) Use the unconditional sample quantile.

(e) Use a two-dimensional homogeneous Poisson process with threshold 2%; that is, focusing on the exceeding times and exceedances that the daily stock price drops 2% or more. Check the fitted model.

(f) Use a two-dimensional nonhomogeneous Poisson process with threshold 2%. The explanatory variables are (1) an annual time trend, (2) a dummy variable for October, November, and December, and (3) a fitted volatility based on a Gaussian GARCH(1,1) model. Perform a diagnostic check on the fitted model.

(g) Repeat the prior two-dimensional nonhomogeneous Poisson process with threshold 2.5% or 3%. Comment on the selection of threshold.

7.3. Use Hill's estimator and the data `d-csco9199.txt` to estimate the tail index for daily log returns of Cisco stock.

7.4. The file `d-hwp3dx8099.txt` contains dates and the daily simple returns of Hewlett-Packard, the CRSP value-weighted index, equal-weighted index, and the S&P 500 index from 1980 to 1999. The returns include dividend distributions. Transform the simple returns to log returns. Assume that the tail probability of interest is 0.01. Calculate value at risk for the following financial positions for the first trading day of year 2000.

(a) Long on Hewlett-Packard stock of \$1 million dollars and the S&P 500 index of \$1 million using RiskMetrics. The α coefficient of the IGARCH(1,1) model for each series should be estimated.

(b) The same position as part (a), but using a univariate ARMA–GARCH model for each return series.

(c) A long position on Hewlett-Packard stock of \$1 million using a two-dimensional nonhomogeneous Poisson model with the following explanatory variables: (1) an annual time trend, (2) a fitted volatility based on a Gaussian GARCH model for Hewlett-Packard stock, (3) a fitted volatility based on a Gaussian GARCH model for the S&P 500 index returns, and (4) a fitted volatility based on a Gaussian GARCH model for the value-weighted index return. Perform a diagnostic check for the fitted models. Are the market volatility as measured by the S&P 500 index and value-weighted index returns helpful in determining the tail behavior of stock returns of Hewlett-Packard? You may choose several thresholds.

7.5. Consider the daily returns of Alcoa (AA) stock and the S&P 500 composite index (SPX) from 1980 to 2003. The simple returns and dates are in the file `d-aaspx8003.txt`. Transform the simple returns to log returns and focus on the daily negative log returns of AA stock.

(a) Fit the generalized extreme value distribution to the negative AA log returns, in percentages, with subperiods of 21 trading days. Write down the parameter estimates and their standard errors. Obtain a scatterplot and a QQ-plot of the residuals.

(b) What is the return level of the prior fitted model when 24 subperiods of 21 days are used?

(c) Obtain a QQ-plot (against exponential distribution) of the negative log returns with threshold 2.5% and a mean excess plot of the returns.

(d) Fit a generalize Pareto distribution to the negative log returns with threshold 3.5%. Write down the parameter estimates and their standard errors.

(e) Obtain (i) a plot of excess distribution, (ii) a plot of the tail of the underlying distribution, (iii) a scatterplot of residuals, and (iv) a QQ-plot of the residuals for the fitted GPD.

(f) Based on the fitted GPD model, compute the VaR and expected shortfall for probabilities $q = 0.95$, 0.99, and 0.999.

7.6. Consider, again, the daily log returns of Alcoa (AA) stock in Exercise 7.5. Focus now on the daily positive log returns. Answer the same questions as in Exercise 7.5. However, use threshold 3% in fitting the GPD model.

7.7. Consider the daily returns of SPX in `d-aaspx8003.txt`. Transform the returns into log returns and focus on the daily negative log returns.

(a) Fit the generalized extreme value distribution to the negative SPX log returns, in percentages, with subperiods of 21 trading days. Write down the parameter estimates and their standard errors. Obtain a scatterplot and a QQ-plot of the residuals.

(b) What is the return level of the prior fitted model when 24 subperiods of 21 days are used?

(c) Obtain a QQ-plot (against exponential distribution) of the negative log returns with threshold 2.5% and a mean excess plot of the returns.

(d) Fit a generalize Pareto distribution to the negative log returns with threshold 2.5%. Write down the parameter estimates and their standard errors.

(e) Obtain (i) a plot of excess distribution, (ii) a plot of the tail of the underlying distribution, (iii) a scatterplot of residuals, and (iv) a QQ-plot of the residuals for the fitted GPD.

(f) Based on the fitted GPD model, compute the VaR and expected shortfall for probabilities $q = 0.95$, 0.99, and 0.999.

REFERENCES

Berman, S. M. (1964). Limiting theorems for the maximum term in stationary sequences. *Annals of Mathematical Statistics* **35**: 502–516.

Coles, S. (2001). *An Introduction to Statistical Modeling of Extreme Values*. Springer-Verlag, New York.

Cox, D. R. and Hinkley, D. V. (1974). *Theoretical Statistics*. Chapman and Hall, London.

Danielsson, J. and de Vries, C. G. (1997a). Value at risk and extreme returns. Working paper, London School of Economics, London, U.K.

Danielsson, J. and de Vries, C. G. (1997b). Tail index and quantile estimation with very high frequency data. *Journal of Empirical Finance* **4**: 241–257.

Davison, A. C. and Smith, R. L. (1990). Models for exceedances over high thresholds (with discussion). *Journal of the Royal Statistical Society Series B* **52**: 393–442.

Dekkers, A. L. M. and De Haan, L. (1989). On the estimation of extreme value index and large quantile estimation. *Annals of Statistics* **17**: 1795–1832.

Duffie, D. and Pan, J. (1997). An overview of value at risk. *Journal of Derivatives* **Spring**: 7–48.

Embrechts, P., Kuppelberg, C., and Mikosch, T. (1997). *Modelling Extremal Events*. Springer Verlag, Berlin.

Feller, W. (1971). *An Introduction to Probability Theory and Its Applications*, Volume 2. Wiley, Hoboken, NJ.

Goldie, C. M., and Smith, R. L. (1987). Slow variation with remainder: Theory and applications. *Quarterly Journal of Mathematics* **38**: 45–71.

Gnedenko, B. V. (1943). Sur la distribution limite du terme maximum of d'une série Aléatorie. *Annals of Mathematics* **44**: 423–453.

Gumbel, E. J. (1958). *Statistics of Extremes*. Columbia University Press, New York.

Hill, B. M. (1975). A simple general approach to inference about the tail of a distribution. *Annals of Statistics* **3**: 1163–1173.

Jenkinson, A. F. (1955). The frequency distribution of the annual maximum (or minimum) of meteorological elements. *Quarterly Journal of the Royal Meteorological Society* **81**: 158–171.

Jorion, P. (1997). *Value at Risk: The New Benchmark for Controlling Market Risk*. McGraw-Hill, Chicago.

Koenker, R. W. and Bassett, G. W. (1978). Regression quantiles. *Econometrica* **46**: 33–50.

Koenker, R. W. and D'Orey, V. (1987). Computing regression quantiles. *Applied Statistics* **36**: 383–393.

Leadbetter, M. R., Lindgren, G., and Rootzén, H. (1983). *Extremes and Related Properties of Random Sequences and Processes*. Springer-Verlag, New York.

Longerstaey, J. and More, L. (1995). *Introduction to RiskMetrics*™, 4th edition. Morgan Guaranty Trust Company, New York.

Longin, F. M. (1996). The asymptotic distribution of extreme stock market returns. *Journal of Business* **69**: 383–408.

Longin, F. M. (1999a). Optimal margin level in futures markets: Extreme price movements. *The Journal of Futures Markets* **19**: 127–152.

Longin, F. M. (1999b). From value at risk to stress testing: the extreme value approach. Working paper, Centre for Economic Policy Research, London, UK.

Pickands, J. (1975). Statistical inference using extreme order statistics. *Annals of Statistics* **3**: 119–131.

Smith, R. L. (1989). Extreme value analysis of environmental time series: An application to trend detection in ground-level ozone (with discussion). *Statistical Science* **4**: 367–393.

Smith, R. L. (1999). Measuring risk with extreme value theory. Working paper, Department of Statistics, University of North Carolina at Chapel Hill.

Smith, R. L. and Shively, T. S. (1995). A point process approach to modeling trends in tropospheric ozone. *Atmospheric Environment* **29**: 3489–3499.

Tsay, R. S. (1999). Extreme value analysis of financial data. Working paper, Graduate School of Business, University of Chicago.

Zivot, E. and Wang, J. (2003). *Modeling Financial Time Series with S-Plus*. Springer-Verlag, New York.

CHAPTER 8

Multivariate Time Series Analysis and Its Applications

Economic globalization and internet communication have accelerated the integration of world financial markets in recent years. Price movements in one market can spread easily and instantly to another market. For this reason, financial markets are more dependent on each other than ever before, and one must consider them jointly to better understand the dynamic structure of global finance. One market may lead the other market under some circumstances, yet the relationship may be reversed under other circumstances. Consequently, knowing how the markets are interrelated is of great importance in finance. Similarly, for an investor or a financial institution holding multiple assets, the dynamic relationships between returns of the assets play an important role in decision making. In this and the next two chapters, we introduce econometric models and methods useful for studying jointly multiple return series. In the statistical literature, these models and methods belong to vector or multivariate time series analysis.

A multivariate time series consists of multiple single series referred to as *components*. As such, concepts of vector and matrix are important in multivariate time series analysis. We use boldface notation to indicate vectors and matrices. If necessary, readers may consult Appendix A of this chapter for some basic operations and properties of vectors and matrices. Appendix B provides some results of multivariate normal distribution, which is widely used in multivariate statistical analysis (e.g., Johnson and Wichern, 1998).

Let $\boldsymbol{r}_t = (r_{1t}, r_{2t}, \ldots, r_{kt})'$ be the log returns of k assets at time t, where $\boldsymbol{a}'$ denotes the transpose of $\boldsymbol{a}$. For example, an investor holding stocks of IBM, Microsoft, Exxon Mobil, General Motors, and Wal-Mart Stores may consider the five-dimensional daily log returns of these companies. Here r_{1t} denotes the daily log return of IBM stock, r_{2t} is that of Microsoft, and so on. As a second example, an investor who is interested in global investment may consider the return series of the S&P 500 index of the United States, the FTSE 100 index of the United

Kingdom, and the Nikkei 225 index of Japan. Here the series is three-dimensional, with r_{1t} denoting the return of the S&P 500 index, r_{2t} the return of the FTSE 100 index, and r_{3t} the return of the Nikkei 225. The goal of this chapter is to study econometric models for analyzing the multivariate process $\boldsymbol{r}_t$.

Many of the models and methods discussed in previous chapters can be generalized directly to the multivariate case. But there are situations in which the generalization requires some attention. In some situations, one needs new models and methods to handle the complicated relationships between multiple series. In this chapter, we discuss these issues with emphasis on intuition and applications. For statistical theory of multivariate time series analysis, readers are referred to Lütkepohl (1991) and Reinsel (1993).

8.1 WEAK STATIONARITY AND CROSS-CORRELATION MATRICES

Consider a k-dimensional time series $\boldsymbol{r}_t = (r_{1t}, \ldots, r_{kt})'$. The series $\boldsymbol{r}_t$ is *weakly stationary* if its first and second moments are time-invariant. In particular, the mean vector and covariance matrix of a weakly stationary series are constant over time. Unless stated explicitly to the contrary, we assume that the return series of financial assets are weakly stationary.

For a weakly stationary time series $\boldsymbol{r}_t$, we define its mean vector and covariance matrix as

$$\boldsymbol{\mu} = E(\boldsymbol{r}_t), \quad \boldsymbol{\Gamma}_0 = E[(\boldsymbol{r}_t - \boldsymbol{\mu})(\boldsymbol{r}_t - \boldsymbol{\mu})'], \tag{8.1}$$

where the expectation is taken element by element over the joint distribution of $\boldsymbol{r}_t$. The mean $\boldsymbol{\mu}$ is a k-dimensional vector consisting of the unconditional expectations of the components of $\boldsymbol{r}_t$. The covariance matrix $\boldsymbol{\Gamma}_0$ is a $k \times k$ matrix. The ith diagonal element of $\boldsymbol{\Gamma}_0$ is the variance of r_{it}, whereas the (i, j)th element of $\boldsymbol{\Gamma}_0$ is the covariance between r_{it} and r_{jt}. We write $\boldsymbol{\mu} = (\mu_1, \ldots, \mu_k)'$ and $\boldsymbol{\Gamma}_0 = [\Gamma_{ij}(0)]$ when the elements are needed.

8.1.1 Cross-Correlation Matrices

Let $\boldsymbol{D}$ be a $k \times k$ diagonal matrix consisting of the standard deviations of r_{it} for $i = 1, \ldots, k$. In other words, $\boldsymbol{D} = \text{diag}\{\sqrt{\Gamma_{11}(0)}, \ldots, \sqrt{\Gamma_{kk}(0)}\}$. The concurrent, or lag-zero, cross-correlation matrix of $\boldsymbol{r}_t$ is defined as

$$\boldsymbol{\rho}_0 \equiv [\rho_{ij}(0)] = \boldsymbol{D}^{-1}\boldsymbol{\Gamma}_0\boldsymbol{D}^{-1}.$$

More specifically, the (i, j)th element of $\boldsymbol{\rho}_0$ is

$$\rho_{ij}(0) = \frac{\Gamma_{ij}(0)}{\sqrt{\Gamma_{ii}(0)\Gamma_{jj}(0)}} = \frac{\text{Cov}(r_{it}, r_{jt})}{\text{std}(r_{it})\text{std}(r_{jt})},$$

which is the correlation coefficient between r_{it} and r_{jt}. In time series analysis, such a correlation coefficient is referred to as a concurrent, or contemporaneous, correlation coefficient because it is the correlation of the two series at time t. It is easy to see that $\rho_{ij}(0) = \rho_{ji}(0)$, $-1 \le \rho_{ij}(0) \le 1$, and $\rho_{ii}(0) = 1$ for $1 \le i, j \le k$. Thus, $\boldsymbol{\rho}(0)$ is a symmetric matrix with unit diagonal elements.

An important topic in multivariate time series analysis is the lead–lag relationships between component series. To this end, the cross-correlation matrices are used to measure the strength of linear dependence between time series. The lag-ℓ cross-covariance matrix of $\boldsymbol{r}_t$ is defined as

$$\boldsymbol{\Gamma}_\ell \equiv [\Gamma_{ij}(\ell)] = E[(\boldsymbol{r}_t - \boldsymbol{\mu})(\boldsymbol{r}_{t-\ell} - \boldsymbol{\mu})'], \tag{8.2}$$

where $\boldsymbol{\mu}$ is the mean vector of $\boldsymbol{r}_t$. Therefore, the (i, j)th element of $\boldsymbol{\Gamma}_\ell$ is the covariance between r_{it} and $r_{j,t-\ell}$. For a weakly stationary series, the cross-covariance matrix $\boldsymbol{\Gamma}_\ell$ is a function of ℓ, not the time index t.

The lag-ℓ cross-correlation matrix (CCM) of $\boldsymbol{r}_t$ is defined as

$$\boldsymbol{\rho}_\ell \equiv [\rho_{ij}(\ell)] = \boldsymbol{D}^{-1}\boldsymbol{\Gamma}_\ell \boldsymbol{D}^{-1}, \tag{8.3}$$

where, as before, $\boldsymbol{D}$ is the diagonal matrix of standard deviations of the individual series r_{it}. From the definition,

$$\rho_{ij}(\ell) = \frac{\Gamma_{ij}(\ell)}{\sqrt{\Gamma_{ii}(0)\Gamma_{jj}(0)}} = \frac{\text{Cov}(r_{it}, r_{j,t-\ell})}{\text{std}(r_{it})\text{std}(r_{jt})}, \tag{8.4}$$

which is the correlation coefficient between r_{it} and $r_{j,t-\ell}$. When $\ell > 0$, this correlation coefficient measures the linear dependence of r_{it} on $r_{j,t-\ell}$, which occurred prior to time t. Consequently, if $\rho_{ij}(\ell) \neq 0$ and $\ell > 0$, we say that the series r_{jt} *leads* the series r_{it} at lag ℓ. Similarly, $\rho_{ji}(\ell)$ measures the linear dependence of r_{jt} and $r_{i,t-\ell}$, and we say that the series r_{it} *leads* the series r_{jt} at lag ℓ if $\rho_{ji}(\ell) \neq 0$ and $\ell > 0$. Equation (8.4) also shows that the diagonal element $\rho_{ii}(\ell)$ is simply the lag-ℓ autocorrelation coefficient of r_{it}.

Based on this discussion, we obtain some important properties of the cross-correlations when $\ell > 0$. First, in general, $\rho_{ij}(\ell) \neq \rho_{ji}(\ell)$ for $i \neq j$ because the two correlation coefficients measure different linear relationships between $\{r_{it}\}$ and $\{r_{jt}\}$. Therefore, $\boldsymbol{\Gamma}_\ell$ and $\boldsymbol{\rho}_\ell$ are in general not symmetric. Second, using $\text{Cov}(x, y) = \text{Cov}(y, x)$ and the weak stationarity assumption, we have

$$\text{Cov}(r_{it}, r_{j,t-\ell}) = \text{Cov}(r_{j,t-\ell}, r_{it}) = \text{Cov}(r_{jt}, r_{i,t+\ell}) = \text{Cov}(r_{jt}, r_{i,t-(-\ell)}),$$

so that $\Gamma_{ij}(\ell) = \Gamma_{ji}(-\ell)$. Because $\Gamma_{ji}(-\ell)$ is the (j, i)th element of the matrix $\boldsymbol{\Gamma}_{-\ell}$ and the equality holds for $1 \le i, j \le k$, we have $\boldsymbol{\Gamma}_\ell = \boldsymbol{\Gamma}'_{-\ell}$ and $\boldsymbol{\rho}_\ell = \boldsymbol{\rho}'_{-\ell}$. Consequently, unlike the univariate case, $\boldsymbol{\rho}_\ell \neq \boldsymbol{\rho}_{-\ell}$ for a general vector time series when $\ell > 0$. Because $\boldsymbol{\rho}_\ell = \boldsymbol{\rho}'_{-\ell}$, it suffices in practice to consider the cross-correlation matrices $\boldsymbol{\rho}_\ell$ for $\ell \ge 0$.

8.1.2 Linear Dependence

Considered jointly, the cross-correlation matrices $\{\boldsymbol{\rho}_\ell | \ell = 0, 1, \ldots\}$ of a weakly stationary vector time series contain the following information:

1. The diagonal elements $\{\rho_{ii}(\ell) | \ell = 0, 1, \ldots\}$ are the autocorrelation function of r_{it}.

2. The off-diagonal element $\rho_{ij}(0)$ measures the concurrent linear relationship between r_{it} and r_{jt}.
3. For $\ell > 0$, the off-diagonal element $\rho_{ij}(\ell)$ measures the linear dependence of r_{it} on the past value $r_{j,t-\ell}$.

Therefore, if $\rho_{ij}(\ell) = 0$ for all $\ell > 0$, then r_{it} does not depend linearly on any past value $r_{j,t-\ell}$ of the r_{jt} series.

In general, the linear relationship between two time series $\{r_{it}\}$ and $\{r_{jt}\}$ can be summarized as follows:

1. r_{it} and r_{jt} have no linear relationship if $\rho_{ij}(\ell) = \rho_{ji}(\ell) = 0$ for all $\ell \geq 0$.
2. r_{it} and r_{jt} are concurrently correlated if $\rho_{ij}(0) \neq 0$.
3. r_{it} and r_{jt} have no lead–lag relationship if $\rho_{ij}(\ell) = 0$ and $\rho_{ji}(\ell) = 0$ for all $\ell > 0$. In this case, we say the two series are uncoupled.
4. There is a *unidirectional relationship* from r_{it} to r_{jt} if $\rho_{ij}(\ell) = 0$ for all $\ell > 0$, but $\rho_{ji}(v) \neq 0$ for some $v > 0$. In this case, r_{it} does not depend on any past value of r_{jt}, but r_{jt} depends on some past values of r_{it}.
5. There is a *feedback relationship* between r_{it} and r_{jt} if $\rho_{ij}(\ell) \neq 0$ for some $\ell > 0$ and $\rho_{ji}(v) \neq 0$ for some $v > 0$.

The conditions stated earlier are sufficient conditions. A more informative approach to study the relationship between time series is to build a multivariate model for the series because a properly specified model considers simultaneously the serial and cross-correlations among the series.

8.1.3 Sample Cross-Correlation Matrices

Given the data $\{\boldsymbol{r}_t | t = 1, \ldots, T\}$, the cross-covariance matrix $\boldsymbol{\Gamma}_\ell$ can be estimated by

$$\widehat{\boldsymbol{\Gamma}}_\ell = \frac{1}{T} \sum_{t=\ell+1}^{T} (\boldsymbol{r}_t - \bar{\boldsymbol{r}})(\boldsymbol{r}_{t-\ell} - \bar{\boldsymbol{r}})', \quad \ell \geq 0, \tag{8.5}$$

where $\bar{\boldsymbol{r}} = \left(\sum_{t=1}^{T} \boldsymbol{r}_t\right)/T$ is the vector of sample means. The cross-correlation matrix $\boldsymbol{\rho}_\ell$ is estimated by

$$\widehat{\boldsymbol{\rho}}_\ell = \widehat{\boldsymbol{D}}^{-1} \widehat{\boldsymbol{\Gamma}}_\ell \widehat{\boldsymbol{D}}^{-1}, \quad \ell \geq 0, \tag{8.6}$$

where $\widehat{\boldsymbol{D}}$ is the $k \times k$ diagonal matrix of the sample standard deviations of the component series.

Similar to the univariate case, asymptotic properties of the sample cross-correlation matrix $\widehat{\boldsymbol{\rho}}_\ell$ have been investigated under various assumptions; see, for instance, Fuller (1976, Chapter 6). The estimate is consistent but is biased in a finite sample. For asset return series, the finite sample distribution of $\widehat{\boldsymbol{\rho}}_\ell$ is rather complicated partly because of the presence of conditional heteroscedasticity and high kurtosis. If the finite-sample distribution of cross-correlations is needed, we recommend that proper bootstrap resampling methods be used to obtain an approximate estimate of the distribution. For many applications, a crude approximation of the variance of $\hat{\rho}_{ij}(\ell)$ is sufficient.

Example 8.1. Consider the monthly log returns of IBM stock and the S&P 500 index from January 1926 to December 1999 with 888 observations. The returns include dividend payments and are in percentages. Denote the returns of IBM stock and the S&P 500 index by r_{1t} and r_{2t}, respectively. These two returns form a bivariate time series $\boldsymbol{r}_t = (r_{1t}, r_{2t})'$. Figure 8.1 shows the time plots of $\boldsymbol{r}_t$ using the same scale. Figure 8.2 shows some scatterplots of the two series. The plots show that the two return series are concurrently correlated. Indeed, the sample concurrent correlation coefficient between the two returns is 0.64, which is statistically significant at the 5% level. However, the cross-correlations at lag 1 are weak if any.

Table 8.1 provides some summary statistics and cross-correlation matrices of the two series. For a bivariate series, each CCM is a 2×2 matrix with four correlations. Empirical experience indicates that it is rather hard to absorb simultaneously many cross-correlation matrices, especially when the dimension k is greater than 3. To overcome this difficulty, we use the simplifying notation of Tiao and Box (1981)

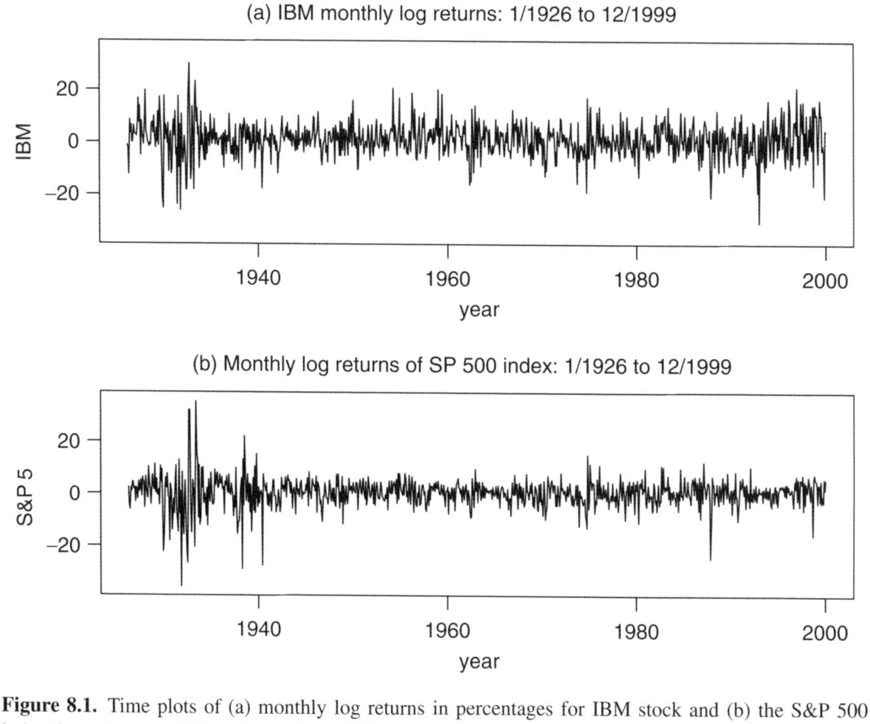

Figure 8.1. Time plots of (a) monthly log returns in percentages for IBM stock and (b) the S&P 500 index from January 1926 to December 1999.

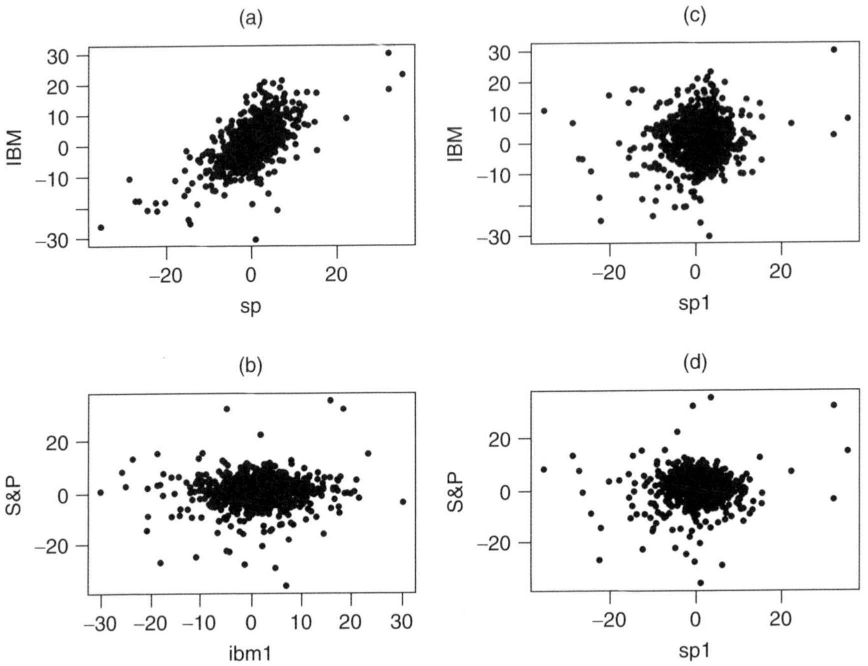

Figure 8.2. Some scatterplots for monthly log returns of IBM stock and the S&P 500 index: (a) concurrent plot of IBM versus S&P 500 (b) S&P 500 versus lag-1 IBM, (c) IBM versus lag-1 S&P 500, and (d) S&P 500 versus lag-1 S&P 500.

and define a simplified cross-correlation matrix consisting of three symbols "+," "−," and "." where

1. "+" means that the corresponding correlation coefficient is greater than or equal to $2/\sqrt{T}$,
2. "−" means that the corresponding correlation coefficient is less than or equal to $-2/\sqrt{T}$, and
3. "." means that the corresponding correlation coefficient is between $-2/\sqrt{T}$ and $2/\sqrt{T}$,

where $1/\sqrt{T}$ is the asymptotic 5% critical value of the sample correlation under the assumption that $\boldsymbol{r}_t$ is a white noise series.

Table 8.1c shows the simplified CCM for the monthly log returns of IBM stock and the S&P 500 index. It is easily seen that significant cross-correlations at the approximate 5% level appear mainly at lags 1 and 3. An examination of the sample CCMs at these two lags indicates that (a) S&P 500 index returns have some marginal autocorrelations at lags 1 and 3, and (b) IBM stock returns depend weakly on the previous returns of the S&P 500 index. The latter observation is based on the significance of cross-correlations at the (1, 2)th element of lag-1 and lag-3 CCMs.

Table 8.1. Summary Statistics and Cross-Correlation Matrices of Monthly Log Returns of IBM Stock and the S&P 500 Index: January 1926 to December 1999

(a) Summary Statistics

Ticker	Mean	Standard Error	Skewness	Excess Kurtosis	Minimum	Maximum
IBM	1.240	6.729	−0.237	1.917	−30.37	30.10
S&P 500	0.537	5.645	−0.521	8.117	−35.58	35.22

(b) Cross-Correlation Matrices

Lag 1		Lag 2		Lag 3		Lag 4		Lag 5	
0.08	0.10	0.02	−0.06	−0.02	−0.07	−0.02	−0.03	0.00	0.07
0.04	0.08	0.02	−0.02	−0.07	−0.11	0.04	0.02	0.00	0.08

(c) Simplified Notation

$$\begin{bmatrix} + & + \\ \bullet & + \end{bmatrix} \quad \begin{bmatrix} \bullet & \bullet \\ \bullet & \bullet \end{bmatrix} \quad \begin{bmatrix} \bullet & - \\ - & - \end{bmatrix} \quad \begin{bmatrix} \bullet & \bullet \\ \bullet & \bullet \end{bmatrix} \quad \begin{bmatrix} \bullet & \bullet \\ \bullet & + \end{bmatrix}$$

Figure 8.3 shows the sample autocorrelations and cross-correlations of the two series. Since the ACF is symmetric with respect to lag 0, only those of positive lags are shown. Because lagged values of the S&P 500 index return are used to compute the cross-correlations, the plot associated with positive lags in Figure 8.3c shows the dependence of IBM stock return on the past S&P 500 index returns, and the plot associated with negative lags shows the linear dependence of the index return on the past IBM stock returns. The horizontal lines in the plots are the asymptotic two standard-error limits of the sample auto- and cross-correlation coefficients. From the plots, the dynamic relationship is weak between the two return series, but their contemporaneous correlation is statistically significant.

Example 8.2. Consider the simple returns of monthly indexes of U.S. government bonds with maturities in 30 years, 20 years, 10 years, 5 years, and 1 year. The data obtained from the CRSP database have 696 observations starting from January 1942 to December 1999. Let $\boldsymbol{r}_t = (r_{1t}, \ldots, r_{5t})'$ be the return series with decreasing time to maturity. Figure 8.4 shows the time plots of $\boldsymbol{r}_t$ on the same scale. The variability of the 1-year bond returns is much smaller than that of returns with longer maturities. The sample means and standard deviations of the data are $\widehat{\boldsymbol{\mu}} = 10^{-2}(0.43, 0.45, 0.45, 0.46, 0.44)'$ and $\widehat{\boldsymbol{\sigma}} = 10^{-2}(2.53, 2.43, 1.97, 1.39, 0.53)'$. The concurrent correlation matrix of the series is

$$\widehat{\boldsymbol{\rho}}_0 = \begin{bmatrix} 1.00 & 0.98 & 0.92 & 0.85 & 0.63 \\ 0.98 & 1.00 & 0.91 & 0.86 & 0.64 \\ 0.92 & 0.91 & 1.00 & 0.90 & 0.68 \\ 0.85 & 0.86 & 0.90 & 1.00 & 0.82 \\ 0.63 & 0.64 & 0.68 & 0.82 & 1.00 \end{bmatrix}.$$

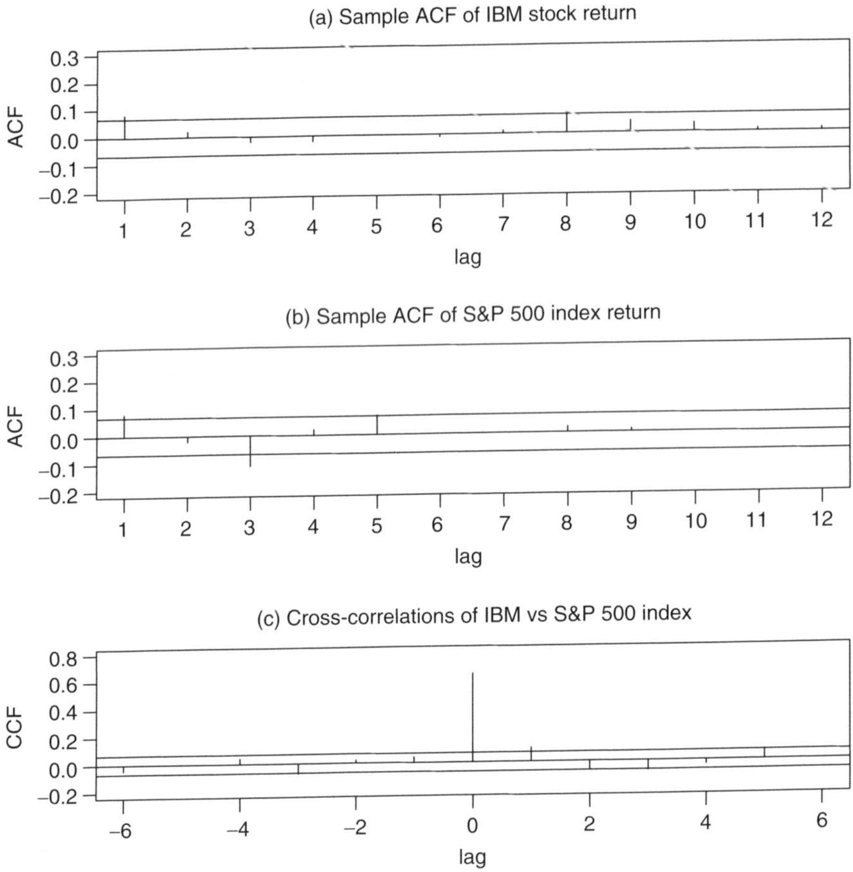

Figure 8.3. Sample auto- and cross-correlation functions of two monthly log returns: (a) sample ACF of IBM stock returns, (b) sample ACF of S&P 500 index returns, and (c) cross-correlations between IBM stock return and lagged S&P 500 index returns.

It is not surprising that (a) the series have high concurrent correlations, and (b) the correlations between long-term bonds are higher than those between short-term bonds.

Table 8.2 gives the lag-1 and lag-2 cross-correlation matrices of $\boldsymbol{r}_t$ and the corresponding simplified matrices. Most of the significant cross-correlations are at lag 1, and the five return series appear to be intercorrelated. In addition, lag-1 and lag-2 sample ACFs of the 1-year bond returns are substantially higher than those of other series with longer maturities.

8.1.4 Multivariate Portmanteau Tests

The univariate Ljung–Box statistic $Q(m)$ has been generalized to the multivariate case by Hosking (1980, 1981) and Li and McLeod (1981). For a multivariate series, the null hypothesis of the test statistic is $H_0 : \boldsymbol{\rho}_1 = \cdots = \boldsymbol{\rho}_m = \mathbf{0}$, and the

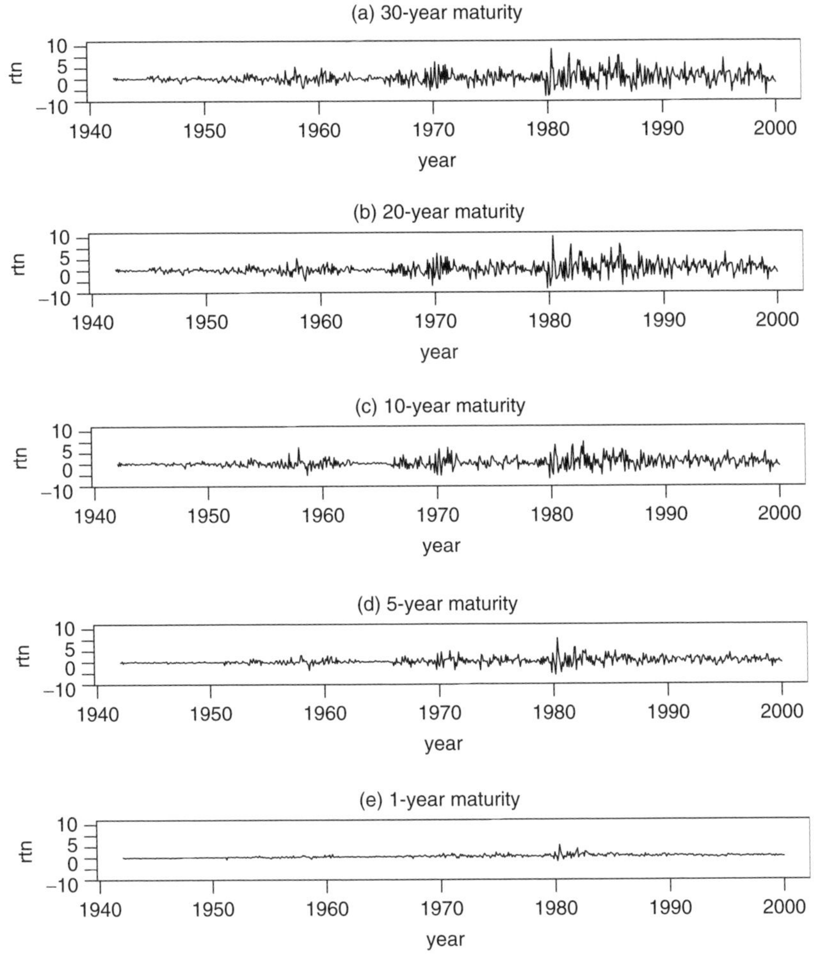

Figure 8.4. Time plots of monthly simple returns of five indexes of U.S. government bonds with maturities in (a) 30 years, (b) 20 years, (c) 10 years, (d) 5 years, and (e) 1 year. The sample period is from January 1942 to December 1999.

alternative hypothesis $H_a : \boldsymbol{\rho}_i \neq \mathbf{0}$ for some $i \in \{1, \ldots, m\}$. Thus, the statistic is used to test that there are no auto- and cross-correlations in the vector series $\boldsymbol{r}_t$. The test statistic assumes the form

$$Q_k(m) = T^2 \sum_{\ell=1}^{m} \frac{1}{T-\ell} tr(\widehat{\boldsymbol{\Gamma}}_\ell' \widehat{\boldsymbol{\Gamma}}_0^{-1} \widehat{\boldsymbol{\Gamma}}_\ell \widehat{\boldsymbol{\Gamma}}_0^{-1}), \tag{8.7}$$

where T is the sample size, k is the dimension of $\boldsymbol{r}_t$, and $tr(\boldsymbol{A})$ is the trace of the matrix $\boldsymbol{A}$, which is the sum of the diagonal elements of $\boldsymbol{A}$. Under the null hypothesis and some regularity conditions, $Q_k(m)$ follows asymptotically a chi-squared distribution with k^2m degrees of freedom.

Table 8.2. Sample Cross-Correlation Matrices of Monthly Simple Returns of Five Indexes of U.S. Government Bonds: January 1942 to December 1999

Lag 1					Lag 2				
Cross-Correlations									
0.10	0.08	0.11	0.12	0.16	−0.01	0.00	0.00	−0.03	0.03
0.10	0.08	0.12	0.14	0.17	−0.01	0.00	0.00	−0.04	0.02
0.09	0.08	0.09	0.13	0.18	0.01	0.01	0.01	−0.02	0.07
0.14	0.12	0.15	0.14	0.22	−0.02	−0.01	0.00	−0.04	0.07
0.17	0.15	0.21	0.22	0.40	−0.02	0.00	0.02	0.02	0.22
Simplified Cross-Correlation Matrices									
$\begin{bmatrix} + & + & + & + & + \\ + & + & + & + & + \\ + & + & + & + & + \\ + & + & + & + & + \\ + & + & + & + & + \end{bmatrix}$					$\begin{bmatrix} \cdot & \cdot & \cdot & \cdot & \cdot \\ \cdot & \cdot & \cdot & \cdot & \cdot \\ \cdot & \cdot & \cdot & \cdot & \cdot \\ \cdot & \cdot & \cdot & \cdot & \cdot \\ \cdot & \cdot & \cdot & \cdot & + \end{bmatrix}$				

Remark. The $Q_k(m)$ statistics can be rewritten in terms of the sample cross-correlation matrixes $\widehat{\boldsymbol{\rho}}_\ell$. Using the Kronecker product $\otimes$ and vectorization of matrices discussed in Appendix A of this chapter, we have

$$Q_k(m) = T^2 \sum_{\ell=1}^{m} \frac{1}{T-\ell} \boldsymbol{b}'_\ell (\widehat{\boldsymbol{\rho}}_0^{-1} \otimes \widehat{\boldsymbol{\rho}}_0^{-1}) \boldsymbol{b}_\ell,$$

where $\boldsymbol{b}_\ell = \text{vec}(\widehat{\boldsymbol{\rho}}'_\ell)$. The test statistic proposed by Li and McLeod (1981) is

$$Q_k^*(m) = T \sum_{\ell=1}^{m} \boldsymbol{b}'_\ell (\widehat{\boldsymbol{\rho}}_0^{-1} \otimes \widehat{\boldsymbol{\rho}}_0^{-1}) \boldsymbol{b}_\ell + \frac{k^2 m(m+1)}{2T},$$

which is asymptotically equivalent to $Q_k(m)$. □

Applying the $Q_k(m)$ statistics to the bivariate monthly log returns of IBM stock and the S&P 500 index of Example 8.1, we have $Q_2(1) = 9.81$, $Q_2(5) = 47.06$, and $Q_2(10) = 71.65$. Based on asymptotic chi-squared distributions with degrees of freedom 4, 20, and 40, the p-values of these $Q_2(m)$ statistics are 0.044, 0.001, and 0.002, respectively. The portmanteau tests thus confirm the existence of serial dependence in the bivariate return series at the 5% significance level. For the five-dimensional monthly simple returns of bond indexes in Example 8.2, we have $Q_5(5) = 1065.63$, which is highly significant compared with a chi-squared distribution with 125 degrees of freedom.

The $Q_k(m)$ statistic is a joint test for checking the first m cross-correlation matrices of $\boldsymbol{r}_t$. If it rejects the null hypothesis, then we build a multivariate model for the series to study the lead–lag relationships between the component series. In what follows, we discuss some simple vector models useful for modeling the linear dynamic structure of a multivariate financial time series.

8.2 VECTOR AUTOREGRESSIVE MODELS

A simple vector model useful in modeling asset returns is the vector autoregressive (VAR) model. A multivariate time series $\boldsymbol{r}_t$ is a VAR process of order 1, or VAR(1) for short, if it follows the model

$$\boldsymbol{r}_t = \boldsymbol{\phi}_0 + \boldsymbol{\Phi}\boldsymbol{r}_{t-1} + \boldsymbol{a}_t, \tag{8.8}$$

where $\boldsymbol{\phi}_0$ is a k-dimensional vector, $\boldsymbol{\Phi}$ is a $k \times k$ matrix, and $\{\boldsymbol{a}_t\}$ is a sequence of serially uncorrelated random vectors with mean zero and covariance matrix $\boldsymbol{\Sigma}$. In application, the covariance matrix $\boldsymbol{\Sigma}$ is required to be positive definite; otherwise, the dimension of $\boldsymbol{r}_t$ can be reduced. In the literature, it is often assumed that $\boldsymbol{a}_t$ is multivariate normal.

Consider the bivariate case (i.e., $k = 2$, $\boldsymbol{r}_t = (r_{1t}, r_{2t})'$, and $\boldsymbol{a}_t = (a_{1t}, a_{2t})'$). The VAR(1) model consists of the following two equations:

$$r_{1t} = \phi_{10} + \Phi_{11} r_{1,t-1} + \Phi_{12} r_{2,t-1} + a_{1t},$$
$$r_{2t} = \phi_{20} + \Phi_{21} r_{1,t-1} + \Phi_{22} r_{2,t-1} + a_{2t},$$

where Φ_{ij} is the (i, j)th element of $\boldsymbol{\Phi}$ and ϕ_{i0} is the ith element of $\boldsymbol{\phi}_0$. Based on the first equation, Φ_{12} denotes the linear dependence of r_{1t} on $r_{2,t-1}$ in the presence of $r_{1,t-1}$. Therefore, Φ_{12} is the conditional effect of $r_{2,t-1}$ on r_{1t} given $r_{1,t-1}$. If $\Phi_{12} = 0$, then r_{1t} does not depend on $r_{2,t-1}$, and the model shows that r_{1t} only depends on its own past. Similarly, if $\Phi_{21} = 0$, then the second equation shows that r_{2t} does not depend on $r_{1,t-1}$ when $r_{2,t-1}$ is given.

Consider the two equations jointly. If $\Phi_{12} = 0$ and $\Phi_{21} \neq 0$, then there is a unidirectional relationship from r_{1t} to r_{2t}. If $\Phi_{12} = \Phi_{21} = 0$, then r_{1t} and r_{2t} are uncoupled. If $\Phi_{12} \neq 0$ and $\Phi_{21} \neq 0$, then there is a feedback relationship between the two series.

8.2.1 Reduced and Structural Forms

In general, the coefficient matrix $\boldsymbol{\Phi}$ of Eq. (8.8) measures the dynamic dependence of $\boldsymbol{r}_t$. The concurrent relationship between r_{1t} and r_{2t} is shown by the off-diagonal element σ_{12} of the covariance matrix $\boldsymbol{\Sigma}$ of $\boldsymbol{a}_t$. If $\sigma_{12} = 0$, then there is no concurrent linear relationship between the two component series. In the econometric literature, the VAR(1) model in Eq. (8.8) is called a *reduced-form* model because it does not show explicitly the concurrent dependence between the component series. If necessary, an explicit expression involving the concurrent relationship can be deduced from the reduced-form model by a simple linear transformation. Because $\boldsymbol{\Sigma}$ is positive definite, there exists a lower triangular matrix $\boldsymbol{L}$ with unit diagonal elements and a diagonal matrix $\boldsymbol{G}$ such that $\boldsymbol{\Sigma} = \boldsymbol{LGL}'$; see Appendix A on Cholesky decomposition. Therefore, $\boldsymbol{L}^{-1}\boldsymbol{\Sigma}(\boldsymbol{L}')^{-1} = \boldsymbol{G}$.

Define $\boldsymbol{b}_t = (b_{1t}, \ldots, b_{kt})' = \boldsymbol{L}^{-1}\boldsymbol{a}_t$. Then

$$E(\boldsymbol{b}_t) = \boldsymbol{L}^{-1}E(\boldsymbol{a}_t) = \boldsymbol{0}, \quad \mathrm{Cov}(\boldsymbol{b}_t) = \boldsymbol{L}^{-1}\boldsymbol{\Sigma}(\boldsymbol{L}^{-1})' = \boldsymbol{L}^{-1}\boldsymbol{\Sigma}(\boldsymbol{L}')^{-1} = \boldsymbol{G}.$$

Since $\boldsymbol{G}$ is a diagonal matrix, the components of $\boldsymbol{b}_t$ are uncorrelated. Multiplying $\boldsymbol{L}^{-1}$ from the left to model (8.8), we obtain

$$\boldsymbol{L}^{-1}\boldsymbol{r}_t = \boldsymbol{L}^{-1}\boldsymbol{\phi}_0 + \boldsymbol{L}^{-1}\boldsymbol{\Phi}\boldsymbol{r}_{t-1} + \boldsymbol{L}^{-1}\boldsymbol{a}_t = \boldsymbol{\phi}_0^* + \boldsymbol{\Phi}^*\boldsymbol{r}_{t-1} + \boldsymbol{b}_t, \tag{8.9}$$

where $\boldsymbol{\phi}_0^* = \boldsymbol{L}^{-1}\boldsymbol{\phi}_0$ is a k-dimensional vector and $\boldsymbol{\Phi}^* = \boldsymbol{L}^{-1}\boldsymbol{\Phi}$ is a $k \times k$ matrix. Because of the special matrix structure, the kth row of $\boldsymbol{L}^{-1}$ is in the form $(w_{k1}, w_{k2}, \ldots, w_{k,k-1}, 1)$. Consequently, the kth equation of model (8.9) is

$$r_{kt} + \sum_{i=1}^{k-1} w_{ki} r_{it} = \phi_{k,0}^* + \sum_{i=1}^{k} \Phi_{ki}^* r_{i,t-1} + b_{kt}, \tag{8.10}$$

where $\phi_{k,0}^*$ is the kth element of $\boldsymbol{\phi}_0^*$ and Φ_{ki}^* is the (k, i)th element of $\boldsymbol{\Phi}^*$. Because b_{kt} is uncorrelated with b_{it} for $1 \le i < k$, Eq. (8.10) shows explicitly the concurrent linear dependence of r_{kt} on r_{it}, where $1 \le i \le k-1$. This equation is referred to as a *structural equation* for r_{kt} in the econometric literature.

For any other component r_{it} of $\boldsymbol{r}_t$, we can rearrange the VAR(1) model so that r_{it} becomes the last component of $\boldsymbol{r}_t$. The prior transformation method can then be applied to obtain a structural equation for r_{it}. Therefore, the reduced-form model (8.8) is equivalent to the structural form used in the econometric literature. In time series analysis, the reduced-form model is commonly used for two reasons. The first reason is ease in estimation. The second and main reason is that the concurrent correlations cannot be used in forecasting.

Example 8.3. To illustrate the transformation from a reduced-form model to structural equations, consider the bivariate AR(1) model

$$\begin{bmatrix} r_{1t} \\ r_{2t} \end{bmatrix} = \begin{bmatrix} 0.2 \\ 0.4 \end{bmatrix} + \begin{bmatrix} 0.2 & 0.3 \\ -0.6 & 1.1 \end{bmatrix} \begin{bmatrix} r_{1,t-1} \\ r_{2,t-1} \end{bmatrix} + \begin{bmatrix} a_{1t} \\ a_{2t} \end{bmatrix}, \quad \boldsymbol{\Sigma} = \begin{bmatrix} 2 & 1 \\ 1 & 1 \end{bmatrix}.$$

For this particular covariance matrix $\boldsymbol{\Sigma}$, the lower triangular matrix

$$\boldsymbol{L}^{-1} = \begin{bmatrix} 1.0 & 0.0 \\ -0.5 & 1.0 \end{bmatrix}$$

provides a Cholesky decomposition (i.e., $\boldsymbol{L}^{-1}\boldsymbol{\Sigma}(\boldsymbol{L}')^{-1}$ is a diagonal matrix). Premultiplying $\boldsymbol{L}^{-1}$ to the previous bivariate AR(1) model, we obtain

$$\begin{bmatrix} 1.0 & 0.0 \\ -0.5 & 1.0 \end{bmatrix} \begin{bmatrix} r_{1t} \\ r_{2t} \end{bmatrix} = \begin{bmatrix} 0.2 \\ 0.3 \end{bmatrix} + \begin{bmatrix} 0.2 & 0.3 \\ -0.7 & 0.95 \end{bmatrix} \begin{bmatrix} r_{1,t-1} \\ r_{2,t-1} \end{bmatrix} + \begin{bmatrix} b_{1t} \\ b_{2t} \end{bmatrix},$$

$$\boldsymbol{G} = \begin{bmatrix} 2 & 0 \\ 0 & 0.5 \end{bmatrix},$$

where $\boldsymbol{G} = \mathrm{Cov}(\boldsymbol{b}_t)$. The second equation of this transformed model gives

$$r_{2t} = 0.3 + 0.5r_{1t} - 0.7r_{1,t-1} + 0.95r_{2,t-1} + b_{2t},$$

which shows explicitly the linear dependence of r_{2t} on r_{1t}.

Rearranging the order of elements in $\boldsymbol{r}_t$, the bivariate AR(1) model becomes

$$\begin{bmatrix} r_{2t} \\ r_{1t} \end{bmatrix} = \begin{bmatrix} 0.4 \\ 0.2 \end{bmatrix} + \begin{bmatrix} 1.1 & -0.6 \\ 0.3 & 0.2 \end{bmatrix} \begin{bmatrix} r_{2,t-1} \\ r_{1,t-1} \end{bmatrix} + \begin{bmatrix} a_{2t} \\ a_{1t} \end{bmatrix}, \quad \boldsymbol{\Sigma} = \begin{bmatrix} 1 & 1 \\ 1 & 2 \end{bmatrix}.$$

The lower triangular matrix needed in the Cholesky decomposition of $\boldsymbol{\Sigma}$ becomes

$$\boldsymbol{L}^{-1} = \begin{bmatrix} 1.0 & 0.0 \\ -1.0 & 1.0 \end{bmatrix}.$$

Premultiplying $\boldsymbol{L}^{-1}$ to the earlier rearranged VAR(1) model, we obtain

$$\begin{bmatrix} 1.0 & 0.0 \\ -1.0 & 1.0 \end{bmatrix} \begin{bmatrix} r_{2t} \\ r_{1t} \end{bmatrix} = \begin{bmatrix} 0.4 \\ -0.2 \end{bmatrix} + \begin{bmatrix} 1.1 & -0.6 \\ -0.8 & 0.8 \end{bmatrix} \begin{bmatrix} r_{2,t-1} \\ r_{1,t-1} \end{bmatrix} + \begin{bmatrix} c_{1t} \\ c_{2t} \end{bmatrix},$$

$$\boldsymbol{G} = \begin{bmatrix} 1 & 0 \\ 0 & 1 \end{bmatrix},$$

where $\boldsymbol{G} = \mathrm{Cov}(\boldsymbol{c}_t)$. The second equation now gives

$$r_{1t} = -0.2 + 1.0r_{2t} - 0.8r_{2,t-1} + 0.8r_{1,t-1} + c_{2t}.$$

Again this equation shows explicitly the concurrent linear dependence of r_{1t} on r_{2t}.

8.2.2 Stationarity Condition and Moments of a VAR(1) Model

Assume that the VAR(1) model in Eq. (8.8) is weakly stationary. Taking expectation of the model and using $E(\boldsymbol{a}_t) = \boldsymbol{0}$, we obtain

$$E(\boldsymbol{r}_t) = \boldsymbol{\phi}_0 + \boldsymbol{\Phi} E(\boldsymbol{r}_{t-1}).$$

Since $E(\boldsymbol{r}_t)$ is time-invariant, we have

$$\boldsymbol{\mu} \equiv E(\boldsymbol{r}_t) = (\boldsymbol{I} - \boldsymbol{\Phi})^{-1}\boldsymbol{\phi}_0$$

provided that the matrix $\boldsymbol{I} - \boldsymbol{\Phi}$ is nonsingular, where $\boldsymbol{I}$ is the $k \times k$ identity matrix.

Using $\boldsymbol{\phi}_0 = (\boldsymbol{I} - \boldsymbol{\Phi})\boldsymbol{\mu}$, the VAR(1) model in Eq. (8.8) can be written as

$$(\boldsymbol{r}_t - \boldsymbol{\mu}) = \boldsymbol{\Phi}(\boldsymbol{r}_{t-1} - \boldsymbol{\mu}) + \boldsymbol{a}_t.$$

Let $\tilde{\boldsymbol{r}}_t = \boldsymbol{r}_t - \boldsymbol{\mu}$ be the mean-corrected time series. Then the VAR(1) model becomes

$$\tilde{\boldsymbol{r}}_t = \boldsymbol{\Phi}\tilde{\boldsymbol{r}}_{t-1} + \boldsymbol{a}_t. \tag{8.11}$$

This model can be used to derive properties of a VAR(1) model. By repeated substitutions, we can rewrite Eq. (8.11) as

$$\tilde{\boldsymbol{r}}_t = \boldsymbol{a}_t + \boldsymbol{\Phi}\boldsymbol{a}_{t-1} + \boldsymbol{\Phi}^2\boldsymbol{a}_{t-2} + \boldsymbol{\Phi}^3\boldsymbol{a}_{t-3} + \cdots.$$

This expression shows several characteristics of a VAR(1) process. First, since $\boldsymbol{a}_t$ is serially uncorrelated, it follows that $\text{Cov}(\boldsymbol{a}_t, \boldsymbol{r}_{t-1}) = \boldsymbol{0}$. In fact, $\boldsymbol{a}_t$ is not correlated with $\boldsymbol{r}_{t-\ell}$ for all $\ell > 0$. For this reason, $\boldsymbol{a}_t$ is referred to as the *shock* or *innovation* of the series at time t. It turns out that, similar to the univariate case, $\boldsymbol{a}_t$ is uncorrelated with the past value $\boldsymbol{r}_{t-j}$ $(j > 0)$ for all time series models. Second, postmultiplying the expression by $\boldsymbol{a}_t'$, taking expectation, and using the fact of no serial correlations in the $\boldsymbol{a}_t$ process, we obtain $\text{Cov}(\boldsymbol{r}_t, \boldsymbol{a}_t) = \boldsymbol{\Sigma}$. Third, for a VAR(1) model, $\boldsymbol{r}_t$ depends on the past innovation $\boldsymbol{a}_{t-j}$ with coefficient matrix $\boldsymbol{\Phi}^j$. For such dependence to be meaningful, $\boldsymbol{\Phi}^j$ must converge to zero as $j \to \infty$. This means that the k eigenvalues of $\boldsymbol{\Phi}$ must be less than 1 in modulus; otherwise, $\boldsymbol{\Phi}^j$ will either explode or converge to a nonzero matrix as $j \to \infty$. As a matter of fact, the requirement that all eigenvalues of $\boldsymbol{\Phi}$ are less than 1 in modulus is the necessary and sufficient condition for weak stationarity of $\boldsymbol{r}_t$ provided that the covariance matrix of $\boldsymbol{a}_t$ exists. Notice that this stationarity condition reduces to that of the univariate AR(1) case in which the condition is $|\phi| < 1$. Furthermore, because

$$|\lambda \boldsymbol{I} - \boldsymbol{\Phi}| = \lambda^k \left| \boldsymbol{I} - \boldsymbol{\Phi}\frac{1}{\lambda} \right|,$$

the eigenvalues of $\boldsymbol{\Phi}$ are the inverses of the zeros of the determinant $|\boldsymbol{I} - \boldsymbol{\Phi}B|$. Thus, an equivalent sufficient and necessary condition for stationarity of $\boldsymbol{r}_t$ is that all zeros of the determinant $|\boldsymbol{\Phi}(B)|$ are greater than one in modulus; that is, all zeros are outside the unit circle in the complex plane. Fourth, using the expression, we have

$$\text{Cov}(\boldsymbol{r}_t) = \boldsymbol{\Gamma}_0 = \boldsymbol{\Sigma} + \boldsymbol{\Phi}\boldsymbol{\Sigma}\boldsymbol{\Phi}' + \boldsymbol{\Phi}^2\boldsymbol{\Sigma}(\boldsymbol{\Phi}^2)' + \cdots = \sum_{i=0}^{\infty} \boldsymbol{\Phi}^i\boldsymbol{\Sigma}(\boldsymbol{\Phi}^i)',$$

where it is understood that $\boldsymbol{\Phi}^0 = \boldsymbol{I}$, the $k \times k$ identity matrix.

Postmultiplying $\tilde{\boldsymbol{r}}_{t-\ell}'$ to Eq. (8.11), taking expectation, and using the result $\text{Cov}(\boldsymbol{a}_t, \boldsymbol{r}_{t-j}) = E(\boldsymbol{a}_t\tilde{\boldsymbol{r}}_{t-j}') = \boldsymbol{0}$ for $j > 0$, we obtain

$$E(\tilde{\boldsymbol{r}}_t\tilde{\boldsymbol{r}}_{t-\ell}') = \boldsymbol{\Phi}E(\tilde{\boldsymbol{r}}_{t-1}\tilde{\boldsymbol{r}}_{t-\ell})', \quad \ell > 0.$$

Therefore,

$$\boldsymbol{\Gamma}_\ell = \boldsymbol{\Phi}\boldsymbol{\Gamma}_{\ell-1}, \quad \ell > 0, \tag{8.12}$$

where $\boldsymbol{\Gamma}_j$ is the lag-j cross-covariance matrix of $\boldsymbol{r}_t$. Again this result is a generalization of that of a univariate AR(1) process. By repeated substitutions, Eq. (8.12) shows that

$$\boldsymbol{\Gamma}_\ell = \boldsymbol{\Phi}^\ell \boldsymbol{\Gamma}_0, \quad \text{for} \quad \ell > 0.$$

Pre- and postmultiplying Eq. (8.12) by $\boldsymbol{D}^{-1/2}$, we obtain

$$\boldsymbol{\rho}_\ell = \boldsymbol{D}^{-1/2}\boldsymbol{\Phi}\boldsymbol{\Gamma}_{\ell-1}\boldsymbol{D}^{-1/2} = \boldsymbol{D}^{-1/2}\boldsymbol{\Phi}\boldsymbol{D}^{1/2}\boldsymbol{D}^{-1/2}\boldsymbol{\Gamma}_{\ell-1}\boldsymbol{D}^{-1/2} = \boldsymbol{\Upsilon}\boldsymbol{\rho}_{\ell-1},$$

where $\boldsymbol{\Upsilon} = \boldsymbol{D}^{-1/2}\boldsymbol{\Phi}\boldsymbol{D}^{1/2}$. Consequently, the CCM of a VAR(1) model satisfies

$$\boldsymbol{\rho}_\ell = \boldsymbol{\Upsilon}^\ell \boldsymbol{\rho}_0, \quad \text{for} \quad \ell > 0.$$

8.2.3 Vector AR(p) Models

The generalization of VAR(1) to VAR(p) models is straightforward. The time series $\boldsymbol{r}_t$ follows a VAR(p) model if it satisfies

$$\boldsymbol{r}_t = \boldsymbol{\phi}_0 + \boldsymbol{\Phi}_1\boldsymbol{r}_{t-1} + \cdots + \boldsymbol{\Phi}_p\boldsymbol{r}_{t-p} + \boldsymbol{a}_t, \quad p > 0, \tag{8.13}$$

where $\boldsymbol{\phi}_0$ and $\boldsymbol{a}_t$ are defined as before, and $\boldsymbol{\Phi}_j$ are $k \times k$ matrices. Using the back-shift operator B, the VAR(p) model can be written as

$$(\boldsymbol{I} - \boldsymbol{\Phi}_1 B - \cdots - \boldsymbol{\Phi}_p B^p)\boldsymbol{r}_t = \boldsymbol{\phi}_0 + \boldsymbol{a}_t,$$

where $\boldsymbol{I}$ is the $k \times k$ identity matrix. This representation can be written in a compact form as

$$\boldsymbol{\Phi}(B)\boldsymbol{r}_t = \boldsymbol{\phi}_0 + \boldsymbol{a}_t,$$

where $\boldsymbol{\Phi}(B) = \boldsymbol{I} - \boldsymbol{\Phi}_1 B - \cdots - \boldsymbol{\Phi}_p B^p$ is a matrix polynomial. If $\boldsymbol{r}_t$ is weakly stationary, then we have

$$\boldsymbol{\mu} = E(\boldsymbol{r}_t) = (\boldsymbol{I} - \boldsymbol{\Phi}_1 - \cdots - \boldsymbol{\Phi}_p)^{-1}\boldsymbol{\phi}_0 = [\boldsymbol{\Phi}(1)]^{-1}\boldsymbol{\phi}_0$$

provided that the inverse exists. Let $\tilde{\boldsymbol{r}}_t = \boldsymbol{r}_t - \boldsymbol{\mu}$. The VAR($p$) model becomes

$$\tilde{\boldsymbol{r}}_t = \boldsymbol{\Phi}_1\tilde{\boldsymbol{r}}_{t-1} + \cdots + \boldsymbol{\Phi}_p\tilde{\boldsymbol{r}}_{t-p} + \boldsymbol{a}_t. \tag{8.14}$$

Using this equation and the same techniques as those for VAR(1) models, we obtain that:

- $\text{Cov}(\boldsymbol{r}_t, \boldsymbol{a}_t) = \boldsymbol{\Sigma}$, the covariance matrix of $\boldsymbol{a}_t$;
- $\text{Cov}(\boldsymbol{r}_{t-\ell}, \boldsymbol{a}_t) = \boldsymbol{0}$ for $\ell > 0$;
- $\boldsymbol{\Gamma}_\ell = \boldsymbol{\Phi}_1\boldsymbol{\Gamma}_{\ell-1} + \cdots + \boldsymbol{\Phi}_p\boldsymbol{\Gamma}_{\ell-p}$ for $\ell > 0$.

The last property is called the moment equations of a VAR(p) model. It is a multivariate version of the Yule–Walker equation of a univariate AR(p) model. In terms of CCM, the moment equations become

$$\boldsymbol{\rho}_\ell = \boldsymbol{\Upsilon}_1 \boldsymbol{\rho}_{\ell-1} + \cdots + \boldsymbol{\Upsilon}_p \boldsymbol{\rho}_{\ell-p} \quad \text{for} \quad \ell > 0,$$

where $\boldsymbol{\Upsilon}_i = \boldsymbol{D}^{-1/2}\boldsymbol{\Phi}_i \boldsymbol{D}^{1/2}$.

A simple approach to understanding properties of the VAR(p) model in Eq. (8.13) is to make use of the results of the VAR(1) model in Eq. (8.8). This can be achieved by transforming the VAR(p) model of $\boldsymbol{r}_t$ into a kp-dimensional VAR(1) model. Specifically, let $\boldsymbol{x}_t = (\tilde{\boldsymbol{r}}'_{t-p+1}, \tilde{\boldsymbol{r}}'_{t-p+2}, \ldots, \tilde{\boldsymbol{r}}'_t)'$ and $\boldsymbol{b}_t = (0, \ldots, 0, \boldsymbol{a}'_t)'$ be two kp-dimensional processes. The mean of $\boldsymbol{b}_t$ is zero and the covariance matrix of $\boldsymbol{b}_t$ is a $kp \times kp$ matrix with zero everywhere except for the lower right corner, which is $\boldsymbol{\Sigma}$. The VAR(p) model for $\boldsymbol{r}_t$ can then be written in the form

$$\boldsymbol{x}_t = \boldsymbol{\Phi}^* \boldsymbol{x}_{t-1} + \boldsymbol{b}_t, \tag{8.15}$$

where $\boldsymbol{\Phi}^*$ is a $kp \times kp$ matrix given by

$$\boldsymbol{\Phi}^* = \begin{bmatrix} \mathbf{0} & \boldsymbol{I} & \mathbf{0} & \mathbf{0} & \cdots & \mathbf{0} \\ \mathbf{0} & \mathbf{0} & \boldsymbol{I} & \mathbf{0} & \cdots & \mathbf{0} \\ \vdots & \vdots & \vdots & & & \vdots \\ \mathbf{0} & \mathbf{0} & \mathbf{0} & \mathbf{0} & \cdots & \boldsymbol{I} \\ \boldsymbol{\Phi}_p & \boldsymbol{\Phi}_{p-1} & \boldsymbol{\Phi}_{p-2} & \boldsymbol{\Phi}_{p-3} & \cdots & \boldsymbol{\Phi}_1 \end{bmatrix},$$

where $\mathbf{0}$ and $\boldsymbol{I}$ are the $k \times k$ zero matrix and identity matrix, respectively. In the literature, $\boldsymbol{\Phi}^*$ is called the *companion* matrix of the matrix polynomial $\boldsymbol{\Phi}(B)$.

Equation (8.15) is a VAR(1) model for $\boldsymbol{x}_t$, which contains $\boldsymbol{r}_t$ as its last k components. The results of a VAR(1) model shown in the previous subsection can now be used to derive properties of the VAR(p) model via Eq. (8.15). For example, from the definition, $\boldsymbol{x}_t$ is weakly stationary if and only if $\boldsymbol{r}_t$ is weakly stationary. Therefore, the necessary and sufficient condition of weak stationarity for the VAR(p) model in Eq. (8.13) is that all eigenvalues of $\boldsymbol{\Phi}^*$ in Eq. (8.15) are less than 1 in modulus. Similar to the VAR(1) case, it can be shown that the condition is equivalent to all zeros of the determinant $|\boldsymbol{\Phi}(B)|$ being outside the unit circle.

Of particular relevance to financial time series analysis is the structure of the coefficient matrices $\boldsymbol{\Phi}_\ell$ of a VAR(p) model. For instance, if the (i, j)th element $\Phi_{ij}(\ell)$ of $\boldsymbol{\Phi}_\ell$ is zero for all ℓ, then r_{it} does not depend on the past values of r_{jt}. The structure of the coefficient matrices $\boldsymbol{\Phi}_\ell$ thus provides information on the lead–lag relationship between the components of $\boldsymbol{r}_t$.

8.2.4 Building a VAR(p) Model

We continue to use the iterative procedure of order specification, estimation, and model checking to build a vector AR model for a given time series. The concept of partial autocorrelation function of a univariate series can be generalized to specify the order p of a vector series. Consider the following consecutive VAR models:

$$
\begin{aligned}
\boldsymbol{r}_t &= \boldsymbol{\phi}_0 + \boldsymbol{\Phi}_1 \boldsymbol{r}_{t-1} + \boldsymbol{a}_t \\
\boldsymbol{r}_t &= \boldsymbol{\phi}_0 + \boldsymbol{\Phi}_1 \boldsymbol{r}_{t-1} + \boldsymbol{\Phi}_2 \boldsymbol{r}_{t-2} + \boldsymbol{a}_t \\
\vdots &= \vdots \\
\boldsymbol{r}_t &= \boldsymbol{\phi}_0 + \boldsymbol{\Phi}_1 \boldsymbol{r}_{t-1} + \cdots + \boldsymbol{\Phi}_i \boldsymbol{r}_{t-i} + \boldsymbol{a}_t \\
\vdots &= \vdots
\end{aligned}
\tag{8.16}
$$

Parameters of these models can be estimated by the ordinary least squares (OLS) method. This is called the multivariate linear regression estimation in multivariate statistical analysis; see Johnson and Wichern (1998).

For the ith equation in Eq. (8.16), let $\widehat{\boldsymbol{\Phi}}_j^{(i)}$ be the OLS estimate of $\boldsymbol{\Phi}_j$ and let $\widehat{\boldsymbol{\phi}}_0^{(i)}$ be the estimate of $\boldsymbol{\phi}_0$, where the superscript (i) is used to denote that the estimates are for a VAR(i) model. Then the residual is

$$\widehat{\boldsymbol{a}}_t^{(i)} = \boldsymbol{r}_t - \widehat{\boldsymbol{\phi}}_0^{(i)} - \widehat{\boldsymbol{\Phi}}_1^{(i)} \boldsymbol{r}_{t-1} - \cdots - \widehat{\boldsymbol{\Phi}}_i^{(i)} \boldsymbol{r}_{t-i}.$$

For $i = 0$, the residual is defined as $\widehat{\boldsymbol{r}}_t^{(0)} = \boldsymbol{r}_t - \overline{\boldsymbol{r}}$, where $\overline{\boldsymbol{r}}$ is the sample mean of $\boldsymbol{r}_t$. The residual covariance matrix is defined as

$$\widehat{\boldsymbol{\Sigma}}_i = \frac{1}{T - 2i - 1} \sum_{t=i+1}^{T} \widehat{\boldsymbol{a}}_t^{(i)} (\widehat{\boldsymbol{a}}_t^{(i)})', \quad i \geq 0. \tag{8.17}$$

To specify the order p, one can test the hypothesis $H_o : \boldsymbol{\Phi}_\ell = \boldsymbol{0}$ versus the alternative hypothesis $H_a : \boldsymbol{\Phi}_\ell \neq \boldsymbol{0}$ sequentially for $\ell = 1, 2, \ldots$. For example, using the first equation in Eq. (8.16), we can test the hypothesis $H_o : \boldsymbol{\Phi}_1 = \boldsymbol{0}$ versus the alternative hypothesis $H_a : \boldsymbol{\Phi}_1 \neq \boldsymbol{0}$. The test statistic is

$$M(1) = -(T - k - \tfrac{5}{2}) \ln \left(\frac{|\widehat{\boldsymbol{\Sigma}}_1|}{|\widehat{\boldsymbol{\Sigma}}_0|} \right),$$

where $\widehat{\boldsymbol{\Sigma}}_i$ is defined in Eq. (8.17) and $|\boldsymbol{A}|$ denotes the determinant of the matrix $\boldsymbol{A}$. Under some regularity conditions, the test statistic $M(1)$ is asymptotically a chi-squared distribution with k^2 degrees of freedom; see Tiao and Box (1981).

In general, we use the ith and $(i-1)$th equations in Eq. (8.16) to test $H_o : \boldsymbol{\Phi}_i = \boldsymbol{0}$ versus $H_a : \boldsymbol{\Phi}_i \neq \boldsymbol{0}$; that is, testing a VAR(i) model versus a VAR($i-1$) model. The test statistic is

$$M(i) = -(T - k - i - \tfrac{3}{2}) \ln \left(\frac{|\widehat{\boldsymbol{\Sigma}}_i|}{|\widehat{\boldsymbol{\Sigma}}_{i-1}|} \right). \tag{8.18}$$

Asymptotically, $M(i)$ is distributed as a chi-squared distribution with k^2 degrees of freedom.

Alternatively, one can use the Akaike information criterion (AIC) or its variants to select the order p. Assume that $\boldsymbol{a}_t$ is multivariate normal and consider the ith equation in Eq. (8.16). One can estimate the model by the maximum likelihood (ML) method. For AR models, the OLS estimates $\widehat{\boldsymbol{\phi}}_0$ and $\widehat{\boldsymbol{\Phi}}_j$ are equivalent to the (conditional) ML estimates. However, there are differences between the estimates of $\boldsymbol{\Sigma}$. The ML estimate of $\boldsymbol{\Sigma}$ is

$$\tilde{\boldsymbol{\Sigma}}_i = \frac{1}{T} \sum_{t=i+1}^{T} \widehat{\boldsymbol{a}}_t^{(i)} [\widehat{\boldsymbol{a}}_t^{(i)}]'. \tag{8.19}$$

The AIC of a VAR(i) model under the normality assumption is defined as

$$\text{AIC}(i) = \ln(|\tilde{\boldsymbol{\Sigma}}_i|) + \frac{2k^2 i}{T}.$$

For a given vector time series, one selects the AR order p such that $\text{AIC}(p) = \min_{0 \le i \le p_0} \text{AIC}(i)$, where p_0 is a prespecified positive integer.

Other information criteria available for VAR(i) models are

$$\text{BIC}(i) = \ln(|\tilde{\boldsymbol{\Sigma}}_i|) + \frac{k^2 i \ln(T)}{T},$$

$$\text{HQ}(i) = \ln(|\tilde{\boldsymbol{\Sigma}}_i|) + \frac{2k^2 i \ln(\ln(T))}{T}.$$

The HQ criterion is proposed by Hannan and Quinn (1979).

Example 8.4. Assuming that the bivariate series of monthly log returns of IBM stock and the S&P 500 index discussed in Example 8.1 follows a VAR model, we apply the $M(i)$ statistics and AIC to the data. Table 8.3 shows the results of these statistics. Both statistics indicate that a VAR(3) model might be adequate for the data. The $M(i)$ statistics are marginally significant at lags 1, 3, and 5 at the 5% level. The minimum of AIC occurs at order 3. For this particular instance, the $M(i)$ statistics are nonsignificant at the 1% level, confirming the previous observation that the dynamic linear dependence between the two return series is weak.

Table 8.3. Order-Specification Statistics[a] for the Monthly Log Returns of IBM Stock and the S&P 500 Index from January 1926 to December 1999

Order	1	2	3	4	5	6
$M(i)$	9.81	8.93	12.57	6.08	9.56	2.80
AIC	6.757	6.756	6.750	6.753	6.751	6.756

[a]The 5% and 1% critical values of a chi-squared distribution with 4 degrees of freedom are 9.5 and 13.3.

Estimation and Model Checking

For a specified VAR model, one can estimate the parameters using either the ordinary least squares method or the maximum likelihood method. The two methods are asymptotically equivalent. Under some regularity conditions, the estimates are asymptotically normal; see Reinsel (1993). A fitted model should then be checked carefully for any possible inadequacy. The $Q_k(m)$ statistic can be applied to the residual series to check the assumption that there are no serial or cross-correlations in the residuals. For a fitted VAR(p) model, the $Q_k(m)$ statistic of the residuals is asymptotically a chi-squared distribution with $k^2m - g$ degrees of freedom, where g is the number of estimated parameters in the AR coefficient matrices.

Example 8.4 (Continued). Table 8.4a shows the estimation results of a VAR(3) model for the bivariate series of monthly log returns of IBM stock and the S&P 500 index. The specified model is in the form

$$\boldsymbol{r}_t = \boldsymbol{\phi}_0 + \boldsymbol{\Phi}_1 \boldsymbol{r}_{t-1} + \boldsymbol{\Phi}_3 \boldsymbol{r}_{t-3} + \boldsymbol{a}_t, \tag{8.20}$$

where the first component of $\boldsymbol{r}_t$ denotes IBM stock returns. For this particular instance, we only use AR coefficient matrices at lags 1 and 3 because of the weak serial dependence of the data. In general, when the $M(i)$ statistics and the AIC criterion specify a VAR(3) model, all three AR lags should be used. Table 8.4b shows the estimation results after some statistically insignificant parameters are set to zero. The $Q_k(m)$ statistics of the residual series for the fitted model in Table 8.4b give $Q_2(4) = 18.17$ and $Q_2(8) = 41.26$. Since the fitted VAR(3) model has four parameters in the AR coefficient matrices, these two $Q_k(m)$ statistics are distributed asymptotically as a chi-squared distribution with degrees of freedom 12 and 28, respectively. The p-values of the test statistics are 0.111 and 0.051, and hence the fitted model is adequate at the 5% significance level. As shown by the univariate analysis, the return series are likely to have conditional heteroscedasticity. We discuss multivariate volatility in Chapter 10.

From the fitted model in Table 8.4b, we make the following observations. (a) The concurrent correlation coefficient between the two innovational series is $23.51/\sqrt{44.48 \times 31.29} = 0.63$, which, as expected, is close to the sample correlation coefficient between r_{1t} and r_{2t}. (b) The two log return series have positive and significant means, implying that the log prices of the two series had an upward trend over the data span. (c) The model shows that

$$\text{IBM}_t = 1.24 + 0.117\text{SP5}_{t-1} - 0.083\text{SP5}_{t-3} + a_{1t},$$

$$\text{SP5}_t = 0.57 + 0.073\text{SP5}_{t-1} - 0.109\text{SP5}_{t-3} + a_{2t}.$$

Consequently, at the 5% significance level, there is a unidirectional dynamic relationship from the monthly S&P 500 index return to the IBM return. If the S&P 500 index represents the U.S. stock market, then IBM return is affected by the past movements of the market. However, past movements of IBM stock returns do not

Table 8.4. Estimation Results of a VAR(3) Model for the Monthly Log Returns, in Percentages, of IBM Stock and the S&P 500 Index from January 1926 to December 1999

Parameter	ϕ_0	$\boldsymbol{\Phi}_1$		$\boldsymbol{\Phi}_3$		$\boldsymbol{\Sigma}$	
(a) Full Model							
Estimate	1.20	0.011	0.108	0.039	−0.112	44.44	23.51
	0.58	−0.013	0.084	−0.007	−0.105	23.51	31.29
Standard error	0.23	0.043	0.051	0.044	0.052		
	0.19	0.036	0.043	0.037	0.044		
(b) Simplified Model							
Estimate	1.24	0	0.117	0	−0.083	44.48	23.51
	0.57	0	0.073	0	−0.109	23.51	31.29
Standard error	0.23	—	0.040	—	0.040		
	0.19	—	0.033	—	0.033		

significantly affect the U.S. market, even though the two returns have substantial concurrent correlation. Finally, the fitted model can be written as

$$\begin{bmatrix} \text{IBM}_t \\ \text{SP5}_t \end{bmatrix} = \begin{bmatrix} 1.24 \\ 0.57 \end{bmatrix} + \begin{bmatrix} 0.117 \\ 0.073 \end{bmatrix} \text{SP5}_{t-1} - \begin{bmatrix} 0.083 \\ 0.109 \end{bmatrix} \text{SP5}_{t-3} + \begin{bmatrix} a_{1t} \\ a_{2t} \end{bmatrix},$$

indicating that SP5_t is the driving factor of the bivariate series.

Forecasting

Treating a properly built model as the true model, one can apply the same techniques as those in the univariate analysis to produce forecasts and standard deviations of the associated forecast errors. For a VAR(p) model, the 1-step ahead forecast at the time origin h is $\boldsymbol{r}_h(1) = \boldsymbol{\phi}_0 + \sum_{i=1}^{p} \boldsymbol{\Phi}_i \boldsymbol{r}_{h+1-i}$, and the associated forecast error is $\boldsymbol{e}_h(1) = \boldsymbol{a}_{h+1}$. The covariance matrix of the forecast error is $\boldsymbol{\Sigma}$. For 2-step ahead forecasts, we substitute $\boldsymbol{r}_{h+1}$ by its forecast to obtain

$$\boldsymbol{r}_h(2) = \boldsymbol{\phi}_0 + \boldsymbol{\Phi}_1 \boldsymbol{r}_h(1) + \sum_{i=2}^{p} \boldsymbol{\Phi}_i \boldsymbol{r}_{h+2-i},$$

and the associated forecast error is

$$\boldsymbol{e}_h(2) = \boldsymbol{a}_{h+2} + \boldsymbol{\Phi}_1[\boldsymbol{r}_t - \boldsymbol{r}_h(1)] = \boldsymbol{a}_{h+2} + \boldsymbol{\Phi}_1 \boldsymbol{a}_{h+1}.$$

The covariance matrix of the forecast error is $\boldsymbol{\Sigma} + \boldsymbol{\Phi}_1 \boldsymbol{\Sigma} \boldsymbol{\Phi}_1'$. If $\boldsymbol{r}_t$ is weakly stationary, then the ℓ-step ahead forecast $\boldsymbol{r}_h(\ell)$ converges to its mean vector $\boldsymbol{\mu}$ as

Table 8.5. Forecasts of a VAR(3) Model for the Monthly Log Returns, in Percentages, of IBM Stock and the S&P 500 Index: Forecast Origin December 1999

Step	1	2	3	4	5	6
IBM forecast	1.40	1.12	0.82	1.21	1.27	1.31
Standard error	6.67	6.70	6.70	6.72	6.72	6.72
S&P forecast	0.32	0.38	−0.02	0.53	0.56	0.61
Standard error	5.59	5.61	5.61	5.64	5.64	5.64

the forecast horizon ℓ increases and the covariance matrix of its forecast error converges to the covariance matrix of $\boldsymbol{r}_t$.

Table 8.5 provides 1-step to 6-step ahead forecasts of the monthly log returns, in percentages, of IBM stock and the S&P 500 index at the forecast origin $h = 888$. These forecasts are obtained by the refined VAR(3) model in Table 8.4.

In summary, building a VAR model involves three steps: (a) use the test statistic $M(i)$ or some information criterion to identify the order, (b) estimate the specified model by using the least squares method and, if necessary, reestimate the model by removing statistically insignificant parameters, and (c) use the $Q_k(m)$ statistic of the residuals to check the adequacy of a fitted model. Other characteristics of the residual series, such as conditional heteroscedasticity and outliers, can also be checked. If the fitted model is adequate, then it can be used to obtain forecasts and make inference concerning the dynamic relationship between the variables.

We used SCA to perform the analysis in this subsection. The commands used include `miden`, `mtsm`, `mest`, and `mfore`, where the prefix `m` stands for multivariate. Details of the commands and output are shown below.

SCA Demonstration

Output edited and % denotes explanation.

```
input ibm,sp5. file 'm-ibmspln.txt'
 -- % Order selection
miden ibm,sp5. no ccm. arfits 1 to 6.

 TIME PERIOD ANALYZED . . . . . . . . . . . . .  1  TO   888

 SERIES    NAME              MEAN        STD. ERROR
    1     IBM               1.2402        6.7249
    2     SP5               0.5372        5.6415
=========  STEPWISE AUTOREGRESSION SUMMARY  ======
 -------------------------------------------------------
     I RESIDUAL I EIGENVAL.I CHI-SQ  I           I SIGN.
 LAG I VARIANCESI OF SIGMA I  TEST   I   AIC     I
 ----+----------+----------+---------+----------+------
   1 I .447E+02 I .135E+02 I    9.81 I    6.757 I . +
```

```
     I .318E+02 I .629E+02 I          I           I . .
----+----------+----------+---------+----------+------
   2 I .443E+02 I .135E+02 I     8.93 I     6.756 I + -
     I .317E+02 I .625E+02 I          I           I . .
----+----------+----------+---------+----------+------
   3 I .441E+02 I .134E+02 I    12.57 I     6.750 I . -
     I .313E+02 I .619E+02 I          I           I . -
----+----------+----------+---------+----------+------
   4 I .441E+02 I .133E+02 I     6.08 I     6.753 I . .
     I .312E+02 I .619E+02 I          I           I . .
----+----------+----------+---------+----------+------
   5 I .437E+02 I .133E+02 I     9.56 I     6.751 I . +
     I .309E+02 I .613E+02 I          I           I - +
----+----------+----------+---------+----------+------
   6 I .437E+02 I .133E+02 I     2.80 I     6.756 I . .
     I .308E+02 I .613E+02 I          I           I . .
------------------------------------------------------
CHI-SQUARED CRITICAL VALUES WITH 4 DEGREES OF FREEDOM ARE
              5 PERCENT:   9.5     1 PERCENT:  13.3
   -- % Specify a VAR(3) model with lags 1 & 3 only.
mtsm fit1. series ibm, sp5. @
model (i-p1*b-p3*b**3)series=c+noise.

 SUMMARY FOR MULTIVARIATE ARMA MODEL --   FIT1

  PARAMETER     FACTOR     ORDER    CONSTRAINT
  1        C   CONSTANT      0         CC
  2       P1    REG AR       1         CP1
  3       P3    REG AR       3         CP3
 -- % Perform multivariate estimation
mestim fit1. hold resi(r1,r2)
 ----- CONSTANT VECTOR (STD ERROR) -----
     1.201  (     0.232  )
     0.583  (     0.194  )
  ----- PHI MATRICES -----
 ESTIMATES OF  PHI(1) MATRIX AND SIGNIFICANCE
      .011      .108       . +
     -.013      .084       . .
  STANDARD ERRORS
      .043      .051
      .036      .043
 ESTIMATES OF  PHI(3) MATRIX AND SIGNIFICANCE
      .039    -.112       . -
     -.007    -.105       . -
  STANDARD ERRORS
      .044      .052
      .037      .044
 ----------------------
 ERROR COVARIANCE MATRIX
```

```
 -----------------------
                1           2
   1    44.438125
   2    23.518578   31.287280
 -- % Set parameter to 0
p1(1,1)=0
 --
p1(2,1)=0
 -- % Set constraint to fix the parameter
cp1(1,1)=1
 --
cp1(2,1)=1
 --
p3(1,1)=0
 --
p3(2,1)=0
 --
cp3(1,1)=1
 --
cp3(2,1)=1
 --
mestim fit1. hold resi(r1,r2).
 ----- CONSTANT VECTOR (STD ERROR) -----
     1.243  (    0.226  )
     0.566  (    0.190  )
 ----- PHI MATRICES -----
 ESTIMATES OF  PHI(1) MATRIX AND SIGNIFICANCE
      .000     .117       . +
      .000     .073       . +
 STANDARD ERRORS
      --      .040
      --      .033
 ESTIMATES OF  PHI(3) MATRIX AND SIGNIFICANCE
     .000    -.083       . -
     .000    -.109       . -
 STANDARD ERRORS
      --      .040
      --      .033
 -----------------------
 ERROR COVARIANCE MATRIX
 -----------------------
                1           2
   1    44.482888
   2    23.506951   31.293592
 -- % Compute residual CCM
miden r1,r2. maxl 12.
 -- % Produce 1 to 6-step ahead forecasts
mfore fit1. nofs 6.
```

8.2.5 Impulse Response Function

Similar to the univariate case, a VAR(p) model can be written as a linear function of the past innovations, that is,

$$\boldsymbol{r}_t = \boldsymbol{\mu} + \boldsymbol{a}_t + \boldsymbol{\Psi}_1 \boldsymbol{a}_{t-1} + \boldsymbol{\Psi}_2 \boldsymbol{a}_{t-2} + \cdots, \qquad (8.21)$$

where $\boldsymbol{\mu} = [\boldsymbol{\Phi}(1)]^{-1}\boldsymbol{\phi}_0$ provided that the inverse exists, and the coefficient matrices $\boldsymbol{\psi}_i$ can be obtained by equating the coefficients of B^i in the equation

$$(\boldsymbol{I} - \boldsymbol{\Phi}_1 B - \cdots - \boldsymbol{\Phi}_p B^p)(\boldsymbol{I} + \boldsymbol{\Psi}_1 B + \boldsymbol{\Psi}_2 B^2 + \cdots) = \boldsymbol{I},$$

where $\boldsymbol{I}$ is the identity matrix. This is a moving-average representation of $\boldsymbol{r}_t$ with the coefficient matrix $\boldsymbol{\Psi}_i$ being the impact of the past innovation $\boldsymbol{a}_{t-i}$ on $\boldsymbol{r}_t$. Equivalently, $\boldsymbol{\Psi}_i$ is the effect of $\boldsymbol{a}_t$ on the future observation $\boldsymbol{r}_{t+i}$. Therefore, $\boldsymbol{\Psi}_i$ is often referred to as the *impulse response function* of $\boldsymbol{r}_t$. However, since the components of $\boldsymbol{a}_t$ are often correlated, the interpretation of elements in $\boldsymbol{\Psi}_i$ of Eq. (8.21) is not straightforward. To aid interpretation, one can use the Cholesky decomposition mentioned earlier to transform the innovations so that the resulting components are uncorrelated. Specifically, there exists a lower triangular matrix $\boldsymbol{L}$ such that $\boldsymbol{\Sigma} = \boldsymbol{L}\boldsymbol{G}\boldsymbol{L}'$, where $\boldsymbol{G}$ is a diagonal matrix and the diagonal elements of $\boldsymbol{L}$ are unity. See Eq. (8.9). Let $\boldsymbol{b}_t = \boldsymbol{L}^{-1}\boldsymbol{a}_t$. Then, $\text{Cov}(\boldsymbol{b}_t) = \boldsymbol{G}$ so that the elements b_{jt} are uncorrelated. Rewrite Eq. (8.21) as

$$\begin{aligned}\boldsymbol{r}_t &= \boldsymbol{\mu} + \boldsymbol{a}_t + \boldsymbol{\Psi}_1 \boldsymbol{a}_{t-1} + \boldsymbol{\Psi}_2 \boldsymbol{a}_{t-2} + \cdots \\ &= \boldsymbol{\mu} + \boldsymbol{L}\boldsymbol{L}^{-1}\boldsymbol{a}_t + \boldsymbol{\Psi}_1 \boldsymbol{L}\boldsymbol{L}^{-1}\boldsymbol{a}_{t-1} + \boldsymbol{\Psi}_2 \boldsymbol{L}\boldsymbol{L}^{-1}\boldsymbol{a}_{t-2} + \cdots \\ &= \boldsymbol{\mu} + \boldsymbol{\Psi}_0^* \boldsymbol{b}_t + \boldsymbol{\Psi}_1^* \boldsymbol{b}_{t-1} + \boldsymbol{\Psi}_2^* \boldsymbol{b}_{t-2} + \cdots, \end{aligned} \qquad (8.22)$$

where $\boldsymbol{\Psi}_0^* = \boldsymbol{L}$ and $\boldsymbol{\Psi}_i^* = \boldsymbol{\Psi}_i \boldsymbol{L}$. The coefficient matrices $\boldsymbol{\Psi}_i^*$ are called the *impulse response function* of $\boldsymbol{r}_t$ with the orthogonal innovations $\boldsymbol{b}_t$. Specifically, the (i, j)th element of $\boldsymbol{\Psi}_\ell^*$, that is, $\Psi_{ij}^*(\ell)$, is the impact of $b_{j,t}$ on the future observation $r_{i,t+\ell}$. In practice, one can further normalize the orthogonal innovation $\boldsymbol{b}_t$ such that the variance of b_{it} is one. A weakness of the above orthogonalization is that the result depends on the ordering of the components of $\boldsymbol{r}_t$. In particular, $b_{1t} = a_{1t}$ so that a_{1t} is not transformed. Different orderings of the components of $\boldsymbol{r}_t$ may lead to different impulse response functions.

Both SCA and S-Plus enable one to obtain the impulse response function of a fitted VAR model. To demonstrate analysis of VAR models in S-Plus, we again use the monthly log return series of IBM stock and the S&P 500 index of Example 8.1. For details of S-Plus commands, see Zivot and Wang (2003).

S-Plus Demonstration

Output edited.

```
> x=matrix(scan(file='m-ibmspln.txt'),2) % Load data
> ibm=x[1,]
> sp5=x[2,]
```

```
> y=cbind(ibm,sp5)    % Create a vector series
> y1=data.frame(y)    % create a data frame
> ord.choice=VAR(y1,max.ar=6) % order selection
> ord.choice$info
       ar(1)    ar(2)    ar(3)    ar(4)    ar(5)    ar(6)
BIC 10998.47 11016.61 11031.07 11052.05 11069.49 11093.78
> ord.choice=VAR(y1,max.ar=6,criterion='AIC')
> ord.choice$info
       ar(1)    ar(2)    ar(3)    ar(4)    ar(5)    ar(6)
AIC 10969.78 10968.79 10964.11 10965.97 10964.28 10969.44
```

The AIC selects a VAR(3) model as before, but BIC selects a VAR(1) model. For simplicity, we shall use VAR(1) specification in the demonstration. Note that different normalizations are used between the two packages so that the values of information criteria appear to be different; see the AIC in Table 8.3. This is not important because normalization does not affect order selection. Turn to estimation.

```
> var1.fit=VAR(y~ar(1))  % Estimation
> summary(var1.fit)
Call:
VAR(formula = y ~ ar(1))
Coefficients:
                ibm     sp5
(Intercept)  1.1627  0.4993
  (std.err)  0.2290  0.1925
   (t.stat)  5.0777  2.5935

   ibm.lag1  0.0192 -0.0054
  (std.err)  0.0433  0.0364
   (t.stat)  0.4429 -0.1487

   sp5.lag1  0.1062  0.0802
  (std.err)  0.0517  0.0435
   (t.stat)  2.0544  1.8454
Regression Diagnostics:
                  ibm    sp5
     R-squared 0.0105 0.0058
Adj. R-squared 0.0082 0.0036
  Resid. Scale 6.7043 5.6376

> plot(var1.fit)
Make a plot selection (or 0 to exit):
1: plot: All
2: plot: Response and Fitted Values
3: plot: Residuals
...
8: plot: PACF of Squared Residuals
Selection: 3
```

The fitted model is

$$\begin{aligned}\text{IBM}_t &= 1.16 + 0.02\text{IBM}_{t-1} + 0.11\text{SP5}_{t-1} + a_{1t},\\ \text{SP5}_t &= 0.50 - 0.01\text{IBM}_{t-1} + 0.08\text{SP5}_{t-1} + a_{2t}.\end{aligned}$$

Based on t-statistics of the estimates in the output, only the lagged variable SP5_{t-1} is informative in both equations. Figure 8.5 shows the time plots of the two residual series, where the two horizontal lines indicate the two standard-error limits. As expected, there exist clusters of outlying observations.

Next, we compute 1-step to 6-step ahead forecasts and the impulse response function of the fitted VAR(1) model when the IBM stock return is the first component of $\boldsymbol{r}_t$. Compared with those of a VAR(3) model in Table 8.5, the forecasts of the VAR(1) model converge faster to the sample mean of the series.

```
> var1.pred=predict(var1.fit,n.predict=6) % Compute prediction
> summary(var1.pred)
Predicted Values with Standard Errors:
                ibm    sp5
1-step-ahead 1.8472 0.9255
   (std.err) 6.7043 5.6376
2-step-ahead 1.2964 0.5636
   (std.err) 6.7394 5.6539
3-step-ahead 1.2474 0.5375
   (std.err) 6.7397 5.6540
...
6-step-ahead 1.2434 0.5356
   (std.err) 6.7397 5.6540
```

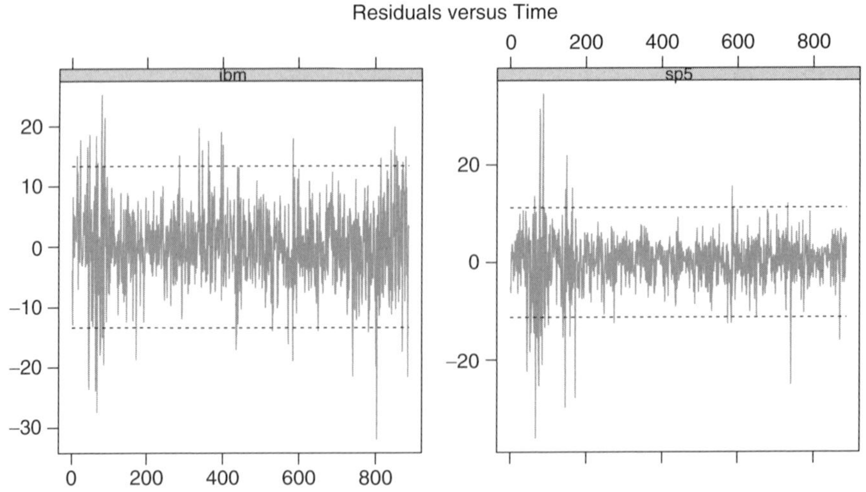

Figure 8.5. Residual plots of fitting a VAR(1) model to the monthly log returns, in percentages, of IBM stock and the S&P 500 index. The sample period is from January 1926 to December 1999.

```
> plot(var1.pred,y, n.old=12)  % Plot forecasts
> var1.irf=impRes(var1.fit,period=6,std.err='asymptotic')
> summary(var1.irf)
Impulse Response Function:

(with responses in rows, and innovations in columns)
, , lag.0
              ibm    sp5
       ibm 6.6929 0.0000
(std.err) 0.1589 0.0000
       sp5 3.5645 4.3553
(std.err) 0.1690 0.1034
, , lag.1
              ibm    sp5
       ibm 0.5069 0.4624
(std.err) 0.2244 0.2249
       sp5 0.2496 0.3492
(std.err) 0.1885 0.1891
....
> plot(var1.irf)
```

Figure 8.6 shows the forecasts and their pointwise 95% confidence intervals along with the last 12 data points of the series. Figure 8.7 shows the impulse response functions of the fitted VAR(1) model where the IBM stock return is the first component of $\boldsymbol{r}_t$. Since the dynamic dependence of the returns is weak, the impulse response functions exhibit simple patterns and decay quickly.

8.3 VECTOR MOVING-AVERAGE MODELS

A vector moving-average model of order q, or VMA(q), is in the form

$$\boldsymbol{r}_t = \boldsymbol{\theta}_0 + \boldsymbol{a}_t - \boldsymbol{\Theta}_1 \boldsymbol{a}_{t-1} - \cdots - \boldsymbol{\Theta}_q \boldsymbol{a}_{t-q} \quad \text{or} \quad \boldsymbol{r}_t = \boldsymbol{\theta}_0 + \boldsymbol{\Theta}(B)\boldsymbol{a}_t, \qquad (8.23)$$

where $\boldsymbol{\theta}_0$ is a k-dimensional vector, $\boldsymbol{\Theta}_i$ are $k \times k$ matrices, and $\boldsymbol{\Theta}(B) = \boldsymbol{I} - \boldsymbol{\Theta}_1 B - \cdots - \boldsymbol{\Theta}_q B^q$ is the MA matrix polynomial in the back-shift operator B. Similar to the univariate case, VMA(q) processes are weakly stationary provided that the covariance matrix $\boldsymbol{\Sigma}$ of $\boldsymbol{a}_t$ exists. Taking expectation of Eq. (8.23), we obtain that $\boldsymbol{\mu} = E(\boldsymbol{r}_t) = \boldsymbol{\theta}_0$. Thus, the constant vector $\boldsymbol{\theta}_0$ is the mean vector of $\boldsymbol{r}_t$ for a VMA model.

Let $\tilde{\boldsymbol{r}}_t = \boldsymbol{r}_t - \boldsymbol{\theta}_0$ be the mean-corrected VAR(q) process. Then using Eq. (8.23) and the fact that $\{\boldsymbol{a}_t\}$ has no serial correlations, we have

1. $\text{Cov}(\boldsymbol{r}_t, \boldsymbol{a}_t) = \boldsymbol{\Sigma}$,
2. $\boldsymbol{\Gamma}_0 = \boldsymbol{\Sigma} + \boldsymbol{\Theta}_1 \boldsymbol{\Sigma} \boldsymbol{\Theta}_1' + \cdots + \boldsymbol{\Theta}_q \boldsymbol{\Sigma} \boldsymbol{\Theta}_q'$,
3. $\boldsymbol{\Gamma}_\ell = \boldsymbol{0}$ if $\ell > q$, and
4. $\boldsymbol{\Gamma}_\ell = \sum_{j=\ell}^{q} \boldsymbol{\Theta}_j \boldsymbol{\Sigma} \boldsymbol{\Theta}_{j-\ell}' \quad$ if $1 \le \ell \le q$, where $\boldsymbol{\Theta}_0 = -\boldsymbol{I}$.

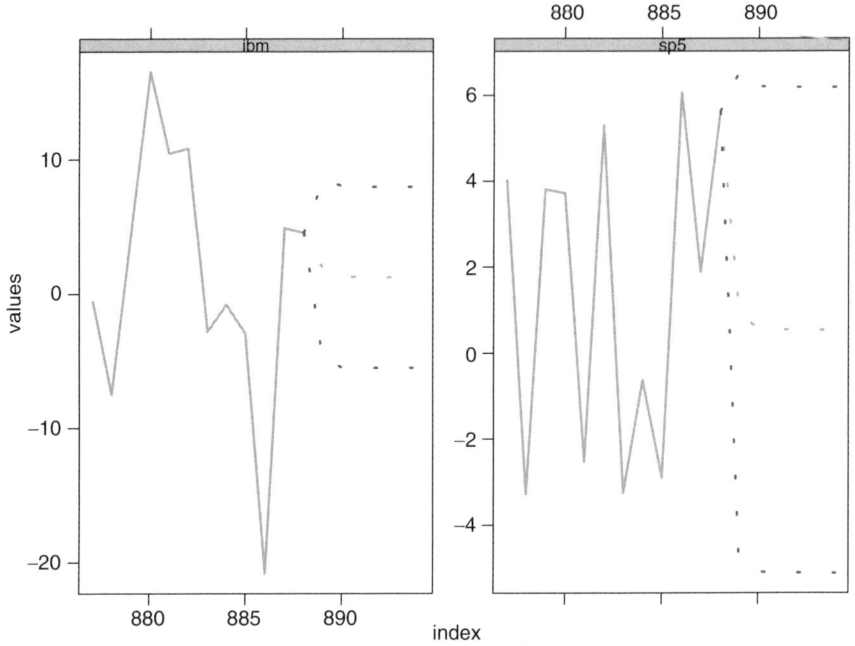

Figure 8.6. Forecasting plots of a fitted VAR(1) model to the monthly log returns, in percentages, of IBM stock and the S&P 500 index. The sample period is from January 1926 to December 1999.

Since $\mathbf{\Gamma}_\ell = \mathbf{0}$ for $\ell > q$, the cross-correlation matrices (CCMs) of a VMA(q) process $\boldsymbol{r}_t$ satisfy

$$\boldsymbol{\rho}_\ell = \mathbf{0}, \quad \ell > q. \tag{8.24}$$

Therefore, similar to the univariate case, the sample CCMs can be used to identify the order of a VMA process.

To better understand the VMA processes, let us consider the bivariate MA(1) model

$$\boldsymbol{r}_t = \boldsymbol{\theta}_0 + \boldsymbol{a}_t - \mathbf{\Theta}\boldsymbol{a}_{t-1} = \boldsymbol{\mu} + \boldsymbol{a}_t - \mathbf{\Theta}\boldsymbol{a}_{t-1}, \tag{8.25}$$

where, for simplicity, the subscript of $\mathbf{\Theta}_1$ is removed. This model can be written explicitly as

$$\begin{bmatrix} r_{1t} \\ r_{2t} \end{bmatrix} = \begin{bmatrix} \mu_1 \\ \mu_2 \end{bmatrix} + \begin{bmatrix} a_{1t} \\ a_{2t} \end{bmatrix} - \begin{bmatrix} \Theta_{11} & \Theta_{12} \\ \Theta_{21} & \Theta_{22} \end{bmatrix} \begin{bmatrix} a_{1,t-1} \\ a_{2,t-1} \end{bmatrix}. \tag{8.26}$$

It says that the current return series $\boldsymbol{r}_t$ only depends on the current and past shocks. Therefore, the model is a finite-memory model.

Consider the equation for r_{1t} in Eq. (8.26). The parameter Θ_{12} denotes the linear dependence of r_{1t} on $a_{2,t-1}$ in the presence of $a_{1,t-1}$. If $\Theta_{12} = 0$, then r_{1t} does not depend on the lagged values of a_{2t} and, hence, the lagged values of r_{2t}. Similarly,

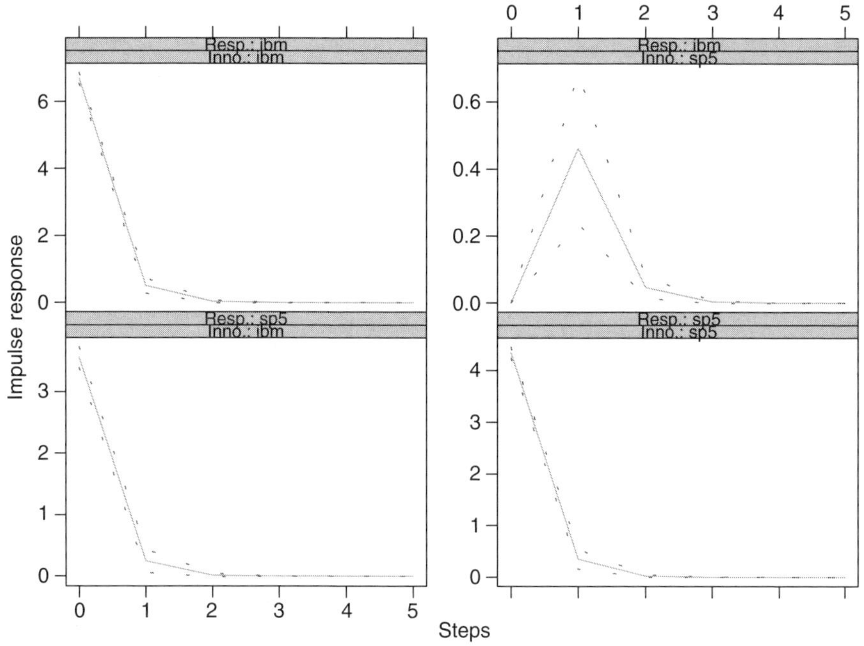

Figure 8.7. Plots of impulse response functions of orthogonal innovations for a fitted VAR(1) model to the monthly log returns, in percentages, of IBM stock and the S&P 500 index. The sample period is from January 1926 to December 1999.

if $\Theta_{21} = 0$, then r_{2t} does not depend on the past values of r_{1t}. The off-diagonal elements of $\mathbf{\Theta}$ thus show the dynamic dependence between the component series. For this simple VMA(1) model, we can classify the relationships between r_{1t} and r_{2t} as follows:

1. They are uncoupled series if $\Theta_{12} = \Theta_{21} = 0$.
2. There is a unidirectional dynamic relationship from r_{1t} to r_{2t} if $\Theta_{12} = 0$, but $\Theta_{21} \neq 0$. The opposite unidirectional relationship holds if $\Theta_{21} = 0$, but $\Theta_{12} \neq 0$.
3. There is a feedback relationship between r_{1t} and r_{2t} if $\Theta_{12} \neq 0$ and $\Theta_{21} \neq 0$.

Finally, the concurrent correlation between r_{it} is the same as that between a_{it}. The previous classification can be generalized to a VMA(q) model.

Estimation

Unlike the VAR models, estimation of VMA models is much more involved; see Hillmer and Tiao (1979), Lütkepohl (1991), and the references therein. For the likelihood approach, there are two methods available. The first is the conditional likelihood method that assumes that $\boldsymbol{a}_t = \mathbf{0}$ for $t \leq 0$. The second is the exact likelihood method that treats $\boldsymbol{a}_t$ with $t \leq 0$ as additional parameters of the model. To gain some insight into the problem of estimation, we consider the VMA(1) model in Eq. (8.25). Suppose that the data are $\{\boldsymbol{r}_t|t = 1, \ldots, T\}$ and $\boldsymbol{a}_t$ is multivariate normal. For a VMA(1) model, the data depend on $\boldsymbol{a}_0$.

Conditional MLE

The conditional likelihood method assumes that $\boldsymbol{a}_0 = \boldsymbol{0}$. Under such an assumption and rewriting the model as $\boldsymbol{a}_t = \boldsymbol{r}_t - \boldsymbol{\theta}_0 + \boldsymbol{\Theta}\boldsymbol{a}_{t-1}$, we can compute the shock $\boldsymbol{a}_t$ recursively as

$$\boldsymbol{a}_1 = \boldsymbol{r}_1 - \boldsymbol{\theta}_0, \quad \boldsymbol{a}_2 = \boldsymbol{r}_2 - \boldsymbol{\theta}_0 + \boldsymbol{\Theta}_1\boldsymbol{a}_1, \quad \cdots.$$

Consequently, the likelihood function of the data becomes

$$f(\boldsymbol{r}_1, \ldots, \boldsymbol{r}_T|\boldsymbol{\theta}_0, \boldsymbol{\Theta}_1, \boldsymbol{\Sigma}) = \prod_{t=1}^{T} \frac{1}{(2\pi)^{k/2}|\boldsymbol{\Sigma}|^{1/2}} \exp\left(-\tfrac{1}{2}\boldsymbol{a}_t'\boldsymbol{\Sigma}^{-1}\boldsymbol{a}_t\right),$$

which can be evaluated to obtain the parameter estimates.

Exact MLE

For the exact likelihood method, $\boldsymbol{a}_0$ is an unknown vector that must be estimated from the data to evaluate the likelihood function. For simplicity, let $\tilde{\boldsymbol{r}}_t = \boldsymbol{r}_t - \boldsymbol{\theta}_0$ be the mean-corrected series. Using $\tilde{\boldsymbol{r}}_t$ and Eq. (8.25), we have

$$\boldsymbol{a}_t = \tilde{\boldsymbol{r}}_t + \boldsymbol{\Theta}\boldsymbol{a}_{t-1}. \tag{8.27}$$

By repeated substitutions, $\boldsymbol{a}_0$ is related to all $\tilde{\boldsymbol{r}}_t$ as

$$\begin{aligned}
\boldsymbol{a}_1 &= \tilde{\boldsymbol{r}}_1 + \boldsymbol{\Theta}\boldsymbol{a}_0,\\
\boldsymbol{a}_2 &= \tilde{\boldsymbol{r}}_2 + \boldsymbol{\Theta}\boldsymbol{a}_1 = \tilde{\boldsymbol{r}}_2 + \boldsymbol{\Theta}\tilde{\boldsymbol{r}}_1 + \boldsymbol{\Theta}^2\boldsymbol{a}_0,\\
\vdots &= \vdots \\
\boldsymbol{a}_T &= \tilde{\boldsymbol{r}}_T + \boldsymbol{\Theta}\tilde{\boldsymbol{r}}_{T-1} + \cdots + \boldsymbol{\Theta}^{T-1}\tilde{\boldsymbol{r}}_1 + \boldsymbol{\Theta}^T\boldsymbol{a}_0.
\end{aligned} \tag{8.28}$$

Thus, $\boldsymbol{a}_0$ is a linear function of the data if $\boldsymbol{\theta}_0$ and $\boldsymbol{\Theta}$ are given. This result enables us to estimate $\boldsymbol{a}_0$ using the data and initial estimates of $\boldsymbol{\theta}_0$ and $\boldsymbol{\Theta}$. More specifically, given $\boldsymbol{\theta}_0$, $\boldsymbol{\Theta}$, and the data, we can define

$$\boldsymbol{r}_t^* = \tilde{\boldsymbol{r}}_t + \boldsymbol{\Theta}\tilde{\boldsymbol{r}}_{t-1} + \cdots + \boldsymbol{\Theta}^{t-1}\tilde{\boldsymbol{r}}_1, \quad \text{for} \quad t = 1, 2, \ldots, T.$$

Equation (8.28) can then be rewritten as

$$\begin{aligned}
\boldsymbol{r}_1^* &= -\boldsymbol{\Theta}\boldsymbol{a}_0 + \boldsymbol{a}_1,\\
\boldsymbol{r}_2^* &= -\boldsymbol{\Theta}^2\boldsymbol{a}_0 + \boldsymbol{a}_2,\\
\vdots &= \vdots\\
\boldsymbol{r}_T^* &= -\boldsymbol{\Theta}^T\boldsymbol{a}_0 + \boldsymbol{a}_T.
\end{aligned}$$

This is in the form of a multiple linear regression with parameter vector $\boldsymbol{a}_0$, even though the covariance matrix $\boldsymbol{\Sigma}$ of $\boldsymbol{a}_t$ may not be a diagonal matrix. If initial estimate of $\boldsymbol{\Sigma}$ is also available, one can premultiply each equation of the prior system by $\boldsymbol{\Sigma}^{-1/2}$, which is the square-root matrix of $\boldsymbol{\Sigma}$. The resulting system is indeed a multiple linear regression, and the ordinary least squares method can be used to obtain an estimate of $\boldsymbol{a}_0$. Denote the estimate by $\widehat{\boldsymbol{a}}_0$.

Using the estimate $\widehat{a}_0$, we can compute the shocks $\boldsymbol{a}_t$ recursively as

$$\boldsymbol{a}_1 = \boldsymbol{r}_1 - \boldsymbol{\theta}_0 + \boldsymbol{\Theta}\widehat{a}_0, \quad \boldsymbol{a}_2 = \boldsymbol{r}_2 - \boldsymbol{\theta}_0 + \boldsymbol{\Theta}\boldsymbol{a}_1, \quad \ldots.$$

This recursion is a linear transformation from $(\boldsymbol{a}_0, \boldsymbol{r}_1, \ldots, \boldsymbol{r}_T)$ to $(\boldsymbol{a}_0, \boldsymbol{a}_1, \ldots, \boldsymbol{a}_T)$, from which we can (a) obtain the joint distribution of $\boldsymbol{a}_0$ and the data, and (2) integrate out $\boldsymbol{a}_0$ to derive the exact likelihood function of the data. The resulting likelihood function can then be evaluated to obtain the exact ML estimates. For details, see Hillmer and Tiao (1979).

In summary, the exact likelihood method works as follows. Given initial estimates of $\boldsymbol{\theta}_0$, $\boldsymbol{\Theta}$, and $\boldsymbol{\Sigma}$, one uses Eq. (8.28) to derive an estimate of $\boldsymbol{a}_0$. This estimate is in turn used to compute $\boldsymbol{a}_t$ recursively using Eq. (8.27) and starting with $\boldsymbol{a}_1 = \tilde{\boldsymbol{r}}_1 + \boldsymbol{\Theta}\widehat{\boldsymbol{a}}_0$. The resulting $\{\boldsymbol{a}_t\}_{t=1}^{T}$ are then used to evaluate the exact likelihood function of the data to update the estimates of $\boldsymbol{\theta}_0$, $\boldsymbol{\Theta}$, and $\boldsymbol{\Sigma}$. The whole process is then repeated until the estimates converge. This iterative method to evaluate the exact likelihood function applies to the general VMA(q) models.

From the previous discussion, the exact likelihood method requires more intensive computation than the conditional likelihood approach does. But it provides more accurate parameter estimates, especially when some eigenvalues of $\boldsymbol{\Theta}$ are close to 1 in modulus. Hillmer and Tiao (1979) provide some comparison between the conditional and exact likelihood estimations of VMA models. In multivariate time series analysis, the exact maximum likelihood method becomes important if one suspects that the data might have been overdifferenced. Overdifferencing may occur in many situations (e.g., differencing individual components of a cointegrated system; see discussion later on cointegration).

In summary, building a VMA model involves three steps: (a) use the sample cross-correlation matrices to specify the order q—for a VMA(q) model, $\boldsymbol{\rho}_\ell = \boldsymbol{0}$ for $\ell > q$; (b) estimate the specified model by using either the conditional or exact likelihood method—the exact method is preferred when the sample size is not large; and (c) the fitted model should be checked for adequacy (e.g., applying the $Q_k(m)$ statistics to the residual series). Finally, forecasts of a VMA model can be obtained by using the same procedure as a univariate MA model.

Example 8.5. Consider again the bivariate series of monthly log returns in percentages of IBM stock and the S&P 500 index from January 1926 to December 1999. Since significant cross-correlations occur mainly at lags 1 and 3, we employ

Table 8.6. Estimation Results for Monthly Log Returns of IBM Stock and the S&P 500 Index Using the Vector Moving-Average Model in Eq. (8.29): January 1926 to December 1999

Parameter	$\boldsymbol{\theta}_0$	$\boldsymbol{\Theta}_1$		$\boldsymbol{\Theta}_3$		$\boldsymbol{\Sigma}$	
(a) Full Model with Conditional Likelihood Method							
Estimate	1.24	−0.013	−0.121	−0.038	0.108	44.48	23.52
	0.54	0.020	−0.101	0.014	0.105	23.52	31.20
Standard error	0.24	0.043	0.051	0.044	0.052		
	0.18	0.036	0.043	0.036	0.043		
(b) Full Model with Exact Likelihood Method							
Estimate	1.24	−0.013	−0.121	−0.038	0.108	44.48	23.52
	0.54	0.020	−0.101	0.013	0.105	23.52	31.20
Standard error	0.24	0.043	0.051	0.044	0.052		
	0.18	0.036	0.043	0.036	0.043		
(c) Simplified Model with Exact Likelihood Method							
Estimate	1.24	0.000	−0.126	0.000	0.082	44.54	23.51
	0.54	0.000	−0.084	0.000	0.114	23.51	31.21
Standard error	0.23	—	0.040	—	0.040		
	0.18	—	0.033	—	0.033		

the VMA(3) model

$$\boldsymbol{r}_t = \boldsymbol{\theta}_0 + \boldsymbol{a}_t - \boldsymbol{\Theta}_1\boldsymbol{a}_{t-1} - \boldsymbol{\Theta}_3\boldsymbol{a}_{t-3} \tag{8.29}$$

for the data. Table 8.6 shows the estimation results of the model. The $Q_k(m)$ statistics for the residuals of the simplified model give $Q_2(4) = 17.25$ and $Q_2(8) = 39.30$. Compared with chi-squared distributions with 12 and 28 degrees of freedom, the p-values of these statistics are 0.1404 and 0.0762, respectively. Thus, the model is adequate at the 5% significance level.

From Table 8.6, we make the following observations:

1. The difference between conditional and exact likelihood estimates is small for this particular example. This is not surprising because the sample size is not small and, more important, the dynamic structure of the data is weak.
2. The VMA(3) model provides essentially the same dynamic relationship for the series as that of the VAR(3) model in Example 8.4. The monthly log return of IBM stock depends on the previous returns of the S&P 500 index. The market return, in contrast, does not depend on lagged returns of IBM stock. In other words, the dynamic structure of the data is driven by the market return, not by IBM return. The concurrent correlation between the two returns remains strong, however.

8.4 VECTOR ARMA MODELS

Univariate ARMA models can also be generalized to handle vector time series. The resulting models are called VARMA models. The generalization, however, encounters some new issues that do not occur in developing VAR and VMA models. One of the issues is the *identifiability* problem. Unlike the univariate ARMA models, VARMA models may not be uniquely defined. For example, the VMA(1) model

$$\begin{bmatrix} r_{1t} \\ r_{2t} \end{bmatrix} = \begin{bmatrix} a_{1t} \\ a_{2t} \end{bmatrix} - \begin{bmatrix} 0 & 2 \\ 0 & 0 \end{bmatrix} \begin{bmatrix} a_{1,t-1} \\ a_{2,t-1} \end{bmatrix}$$

is *identical* to the VAR(1) model

$$\begin{bmatrix} r_{1t} \\ r_{2t} \end{bmatrix} - \begin{bmatrix} 0 & -2 \\ 0 & 0 \end{bmatrix} \begin{bmatrix} r_{1,t-1} \\ r_{2,t-1} \end{bmatrix} = \begin{bmatrix} a_{1t} \\ a_{2t} \end{bmatrix}.$$

The equivalence of the two models can easily be seen by examining their component models. For the VMA(1) model, we have

$$r_{1t} = a_{1t} - 2a_{2,t-1}, \quad r_{2t} = a_{2t}.$$

For the VAR(1) model, the equations are

$$r_{1t} + 2r_{2,t-1} = a_{1t}, \quad r_{2t} = a_{2t}.$$

From the model for r_{2t}, we have $r_{2,t-1} = a_{2,t-1}$. Therefore, the models for r_{1t} are identical. This type of identifiability problem is harmless because either model can be used in a real application.

Another type of identifiability problem is more troublesome. Consider the VARMA(1,1) model

$$\begin{bmatrix} r_{1t} \\ r_{2t} \end{bmatrix} - \begin{bmatrix} 0.8 & -2 \\ 0 & 0 \end{bmatrix} \begin{bmatrix} r_{1,t-1} \\ r_{2,t-1} \end{bmatrix} = \begin{bmatrix} a_{1t} \\ a_{2t} \end{bmatrix} - \begin{bmatrix} -0.5 & 0 \\ 0 & 0 \end{bmatrix} \begin{bmatrix} a_{1,t-1} \\ a_{2,t-1} \end{bmatrix}.$$

This model is identical to the VARMA(1,1) model

$$\begin{bmatrix} r_{1t} \\ r_{2t} \end{bmatrix} - \begin{bmatrix} 0.8 & -2+\eta \\ 0 & \omega \end{bmatrix} \begin{bmatrix} r_{1,t-1} \\ r_{2,t-1} \end{bmatrix} = \begin{bmatrix} a_{1t} \\ a_{2t} \end{bmatrix} - \begin{bmatrix} -0.5 & \eta \\ 0 & \omega \end{bmatrix} \begin{bmatrix} a_{1,t-1} \\ a_{2,t-1} \end{bmatrix},$$

for any nonzero ω and η. In this particular instance, the equivalence occurs because we have $r_{2t} = a_{2t}$ in both models. The effects of the parameters ω and η on the system cancel out between AR and MA parts of the second model. Such an identifiability problem is serious because, without proper constraints, the likelihood function of a vector ARMA(1,1) model for the data is not uniquely defined, resulting in a situation similar to the exact multicollinearity in a regression analysis.

This type of identifiability problem can occur in a vector model even if none of the components is a white noise series.

These two simple examples highlight the new issues involved in the generalization to VARMA models. Building a VARMA model for a given data set thus requires some attention. In the time series literature, methods of *structural specification* have been proposed to overcome the identifiability problem; see Tiao and Tsay (1989), Tsay (1991), and the references therein. We do not discuss the detail of structural specification here because VAR and VMA models are sufficient in most financial applications. When VARMA models are used, only lower order models are entertained (e.g., a VARMA(1,1) or VARMA(2,1) model) especially when the time series involved are not seasonal.

A VARMA(p, q) model can be written as

$$\boldsymbol{\Phi}(B)\boldsymbol{r}_t = \boldsymbol{\phi}_0 + \boldsymbol{\Theta}(B)\boldsymbol{a}_t,$$

where $\boldsymbol{\Phi}(B) = \boldsymbol{I} - \boldsymbol{\Phi}_1 B - \cdots - \boldsymbol{\Phi}_p B^p$ and $\boldsymbol{\Theta}(B) = \boldsymbol{I} - \boldsymbol{\Theta}_1 B - \cdots - \boldsymbol{\Theta}_q B^q$ are two $k \times k$ matrix polynomials. We assume that the two matrix polynomials have no left common factors; otherwise, the model can be simplified. The necessary and sufficient condition of weak stationarity for $\boldsymbol{r}_t$ is the same as that for the VAR(p) model with matrix polynomial $\boldsymbol{\Phi}(B)$. For $v > 0$, the (i, j)th elements of the coefficient matrices $\boldsymbol{\Phi}_v$ and $\boldsymbol{\Theta}_v$ measure the linear dependence of r_{1t} on $r_{j,t-v}$ and $a_{j,t-v}$, respectively. If the (i, j)th element is zero for all AR and MA coefficient matrices, then r_{it} does not depend on the lagged values of r_{jt}. However, the converse proposition does not hold in a VARMA model. In other words, nonzero coefficients at the (i, j)th position of AR and MA matrices may exist even when r_{it} does not depend on any lagged value of r_{jt}.

To illustrate, consider the following bivariate model:

$$\begin{bmatrix} \Phi_{11}(B) & \Phi_{12}(B) \\ \Phi_{21}(B) & \Phi_{22}(B) \end{bmatrix} \begin{bmatrix} r_{1t} \\ r_{2t} \end{bmatrix} = \begin{bmatrix} \Theta_{11}(B) & \Theta_{12}(B) \\ \Theta_{21}(B) & \Theta_{22}(B) \end{bmatrix} \begin{bmatrix} a_{1t} \\ a_{2t} \end{bmatrix}.$$

Here the necessary and sufficient conditions for the existence of a unidirectional dynamic relationship from r_{1t} to r_{2t} are

$$\Phi_{22}(B)\Theta_{12}(B) - \Phi_{12}(B)\Theta_{22}(B) = 0,$$

but

$$\Phi_{11}(B)\Theta_{21}(B) - \Phi_{21}(B)\Theta_{11}(B) \neq 0. \tag{8.30}$$

These conditions can be obtained as follows. Letting

$$\Omega(B) = |\boldsymbol{\Phi}(B)| = \Phi_{11}(B)\Phi_{22}(B) - \Phi_{12}(B)\Phi_{21}(B)$$

be the determinant of the AR matrix polynomial and premultiplying the model by the matrix

$$\begin{bmatrix} \Phi_{22}(B) & -\Phi_{12}(B) \\ -\Phi_{21}(B) & \Phi_{11}(B) \end{bmatrix},$$

we can rewrite the bivariate model as

$$\Omega(B)\begin{bmatrix} r_{1t} \\ r_{2t} \end{bmatrix} =$$

$$\begin{bmatrix} \Phi_{22}(B)\Theta_{11}(B) - \Phi_{12}(B)\Theta_{21}(B) & \Phi_{22}(B)\Theta_{12}(B) - \Phi_{12}(B)\Theta_{22}(B) \\ \Phi_{11}(B)\Theta_{21}(B) - \Phi_{21}(B)\Theta_{11}(B) & \Phi_{11}(B)\Theta_{22}(B) - \Phi_{21}(B)\Theta_{12}(B) \end{bmatrix}\begin{bmatrix} a_{1t} \\ a_{2t} \end{bmatrix}.$$

Consider the equation for r_{1t}. The first condition in Eq. (8.30) shows that r_{1t} does not depend on any past value of a_{2t} or r_{2t}. From the equation for r_{2t}, the second condition in Eq. (8.30) implies that r_{2t} indeed depends on some past values of a_{1t}. Based on Eq. (8.30), $\Theta_{12}(B) = \Phi_{12}(B) = 0$ is a sufficient, but not necessary, condition for the unidirectional relationship from r_{1t} to r_{2t}.

Estimation of a VARMA model can be carried out by either the conditional or exact maximum likelihood method. The $Q_k(m)$ statistic continues to apply to the residual series of a fitted model, but the degrees of freedom of its asymptotic chi-squared distribution are $k^2m - g$, where g is the number of estimated parameters in both the AR and MA coefficient matrices.

Example 8.6. To demonstrate VARMA modeling, we consider two U.S. monthly interest-rate series. The first series is the 1-year Treasury constant maturity rate, and the second series is the 3-year Treasury constant maturity rate. The data are obtained from the Federal Reserve Bank of St. Louis, and the sampling period is from April 1953 to January 2001. There are 574 observations. To ensure the positiveness of U.S. interest rates, we analyze the log series. Figure 8.8 shows the time plots of the two log interest-rate series. The solid line denotes the 1-year maturity rate. The two series moved closely in the sampling period.

The $M(i)$ statistics and AIC criterion specify a VAR(4) model for the data. However, we employ a VARMA(2,1) model because the two models provide similar fits. Table 8.7 shows the parameter estimates of the VARMA(2,1) model obtained by the exact likelihood method. We removed the insignificant parameters and reestimated the simplified model. The residual series of the fitted model has some minor serial and cross-correlations at lags 7 and 11. Figure 8.9 shows the residual plots and indicates the existence of some outlying data points. The model can be further improved, but it seems to capture the dynamic structure of the data reasonably well.

The final VARMA(2,1) model shows some interesting characteristics of the data. First, the interest-rate series are highly contemporaneously correlated. The concurrent correlation coefficient is $2.5/\sqrt{3.58 \times 2.19} = 0.893$. Second, there is a unidirectional linear relationship from the 3-year rate to the 1-year rate because the $(2, 1)$th elements of all AR and MA matrices are zero, but some $(1, 2)$th element is not zero. As a matter of fact, the model in Table 8.7 shows that

$$\begin{aligned} r_{3t} &= 0.025 + 0.99r_{3,t-1} + a_{3t} + 0.47a_{3,t-1}, \\ r_{1t} &= 0.028 + 1.82r_{1,t-1} - 0.84r_{1,t-2} - 0.97r_{3,t-1} + 0.98r_{3,t-2} \\ &\quad + a_{1t} - 0.90a_{1,t-1} + 1.66a_{3,t-1}, \end{aligned}$$

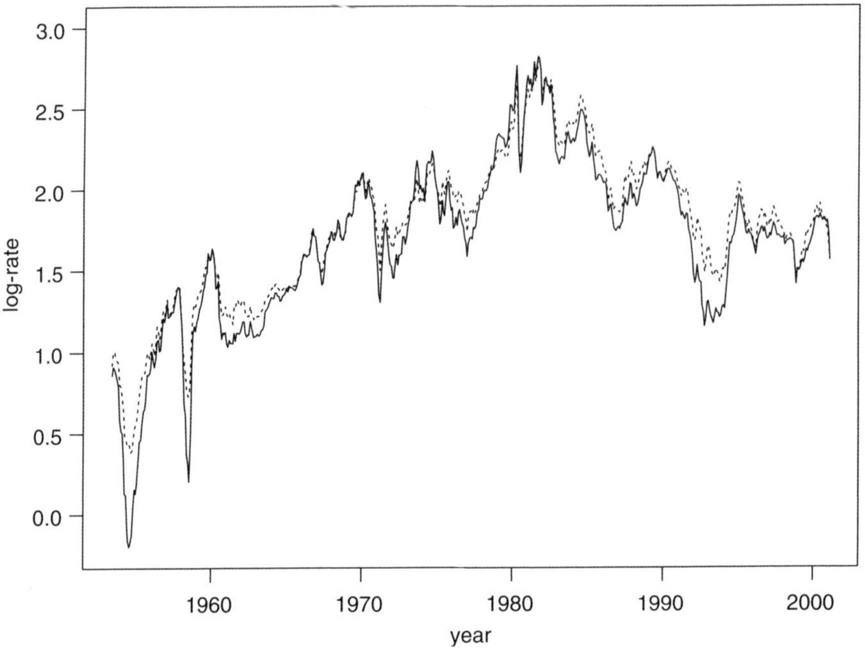

Figure 8.8. Time plots of log U.S. monthly interest rates from April 1953 to January 2001. The solid line denotes the 1-year Treasury constant maturity rate, and the dashed line denotes the 3-year rate.

Table 8.7. Parameter Estimates of a VARMA(2,1) Model for Two Monthly U.S. Interest-Rate Series Based on the Exact Likelihood Method

Parameter	$\boldsymbol{\Phi}_1$		$\boldsymbol{\Phi}_2$		$\boldsymbol{\phi}_0$	$\boldsymbol{\Theta}_1$		$\boldsymbol{\Sigma} \times 10^3$	
Estimate	1.82	−0.97	−0.84	0.98	0.028	0.90	−1.66	3.58	2.50
		0.99			0.025		−0.47	2.50	2.19
Standard error	0.03	0.08	0.03	0.08	0.014	0.03	0.10		
		0.01			0.011		0.04		

where r_{it} is the log series of i-year interest rate and a_{it} is the corresponding shock series. Therefore, the 3-year interest rate does not depend on the past values of the 1-year rate, but the 1-year rate depends on the past values of the 3-year rate. Third, the two interest-rate series appear to be unit-root nonstationary. Using the back-shift operator B, the model can be rewritten approximately as

$$(1 - B)r_{3t} = 0.03 + (1 + 0.47B)a_{3t},$$

$$(1 - B)(1 - 0.82B)r_{1t} = 0.03 - 0.97B(1 - B)r_{3,t} + (1 - 0.9B)a_{1t} + 1.66Ba_{3,t}.$$

Finally, the SCA commands used in the analysis are given in Appendix C.

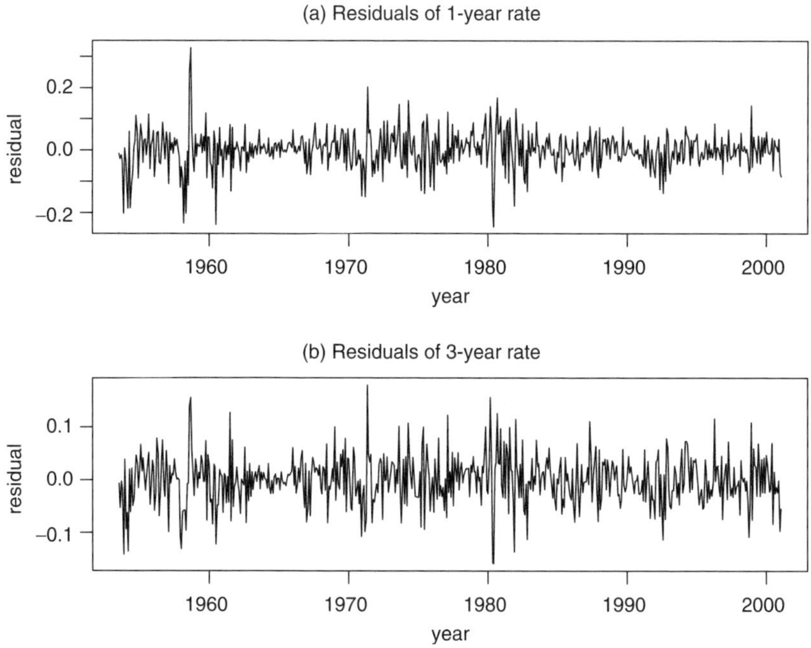

Figure 8.9. Residual plots for log U.S. monthly interest-rate series of Example 8.6. The fitted model is a VARMA(2,1).

8.4.1 Marginal Models of Components

Given a vector model for $\boldsymbol{r}_t$, the implied univariate models for the components r_{it} are the *marginal* models. For a k-dimensional ARMA(p, q) model, the marginal models are ARMA$[kp, (k-1)p+q]$. This result can be obtained in two steps. First, the marginal model of a VMA(q) model is univariate MA(q). Assume that $\boldsymbol{r}_t$ is a VMA(q) process. Because the cross-correlation matrix of $\boldsymbol{r}_t$ vanishes after lag q (i.e., $\boldsymbol{\rho}_\ell = \mathbf{0}$ for $\ell > q$), the ACF of r_{it} is zero beyond lag q. Therefore, r_{it} is an MA process and its univariate model is in the form $r_{it} = \theta_{i,0} + \sum_{j=1}^{q} \theta_{i,j} b_{i,t-j}$, where $\{b_{it}\}$ is a sequence of uncorrelated random variables with mean zero and variance σ_{ib}^2. The parameters $\theta_{i,j}$ and σ_{ib} are functions of the parameters of the VMA model for $\boldsymbol{r}_t$.

The second step to obtain the result is to diagonalize the AR matrix polynomial of a VARMA(p, q) model. For illustration, consider the bivariate AR(1) model

$$\begin{bmatrix} 1-\Phi_{11}B & -\Phi_{12}B \\ -\Phi_{21}B & 1-\Phi_{22}B \end{bmatrix} \begin{bmatrix} r_{1t} \\ r_{2t} \end{bmatrix} = \begin{bmatrix} a_{1t} \\ a_{2t} \end{bmatrix}.$$

Premultiplying the model by the matrix polynomial

$$\begin{bmatrix} 1-\Phi_{22}B & \Phi_{12}B \\ \Phi_{21}B & 1-\Phi_{11}B \end{bmatrix},$$

we obtain

$$[(1-\Phi_{11}B)(1-\Phi_{22}B)-\Phi_{12}\Phi_{22}B^2]\begin{bmatrix} r_{1t} \\ r_{2t} \end{bmatrix}=\begin{bmatrix} 1-\Phi_{22}B & -\Phi_{12}B \\ -\Phi_{21}B & 1-\Phi_{11}B \end{bmatrix}\begin{bmatrix} a_{1t} \\ a_{2t} \end{bmatrix}.$$

The left-hand side of the prior equation shows that the univariate AR polynomials for r_{it} are of order 2. In contrast, the right-hand side of the equation is in a VMA(1) form. Using the result of VMA models in step 1, we show that the univariate model for r_{it} is ARMA(2,1). The technique generalizes easily to the k-dimensional VAR(1) model, and the marginal models are ARMA$(k, k-1)$. More generally, for a k-dimensional VAR(p) model, the marginal models are ARMA$[kp, (k-1)p]$. The result for VARMA models follows directly from those of VMA and VAR models.

The order $[kp, (k-1)p+q]$ is the maximum order (i.e., the upper bound) for the marginal models. The actual marginal order of r_{it} can be much lower.

8.5 UNIT-ROOT NONSTATIONARITY AND COINTEGRATION

When modeling several unit-root nonstationary time series jointly, one may encounter the case of *cointegration*. Consider the bivariate ARMA(1,1) model

$$\begin{bmatrix} x_{1t} \\ x_{2t} \end{bmatrix}-\begin{bmatrix} 0.5 & -1.0 \\ -0.25 & 0.5 \end{bmatrix}\begin{bmatrix} x_{1,t-1} \\ x_{2,t-1} \end{bmatrix}=\begin{bmatrix} a_{1t} \\ a_{2t} \end{bmatrix}-\begin{bmatrix} 0.2 & -0.4 \\ -0.1 & 0.2 \end{bmatrix}\begin{bmatrix} a_{1,t-1} \\ a_{2,t-1} \end{bmatrix}, \tag{8.31}$$

where the covariance matrix $\boldsymbol{\Sigma}$ of the shock $\boldsymbol{a}_t$ is positive definite. This is not a weakly stationary model because the two eigenvalues of the AR coefficient matrix are 0 and 1. Figure 8.10 shows the time plots of a simulated series of the model with 200 data points and $\boldsymbol{\Sigma}=\boldsymbol{I}$, whereas Figure 8.11 shows the sample autocorrelations of the two component series x_{it}. It is easy to see that the two series have high autocorrelations and exhibit features of unit-root nonstationarity. The two marginal models of $\boldsymbol{x}_t$ are indeed unit-root nonstationary. Rewrite the model as

$$\begin{bmatrix} 1-0.5B & B \\ 0.25B & 1-0.5B \end{bmatrix}\begin{bmatrix} x_{1t} \\ x_{2t} \end{bmatrix}=\begin{bmatrix} 1-0.2B & 0.4B \\ 0.1B & 1-0.2B \end{bmatrix}\begin{bmatrix} a_{1t} \\ a_{2t} \end{bmatrix}.$$

Premultiplying the above equation by

$$\begin{bmatrix} 1-0.5B & -B \\ -0.25B & 1-0.5B \end{bmatrix},$$

we obtain the result

$$\begin{bmatrix} 1-B & 0 \\ 0 & 1-B \end{bmatrix}\begin{bmatrix} x_{1t} \\ x_{2t} \end{bmatrix}=\begin{bmatrix} 1-0.7B & -0.6B \\ -0.15B & 1-0.7B \end{bmatrix}\begin{bmatrix} a_{1t} \\ a_{2t} \end{bmatrix}.$$

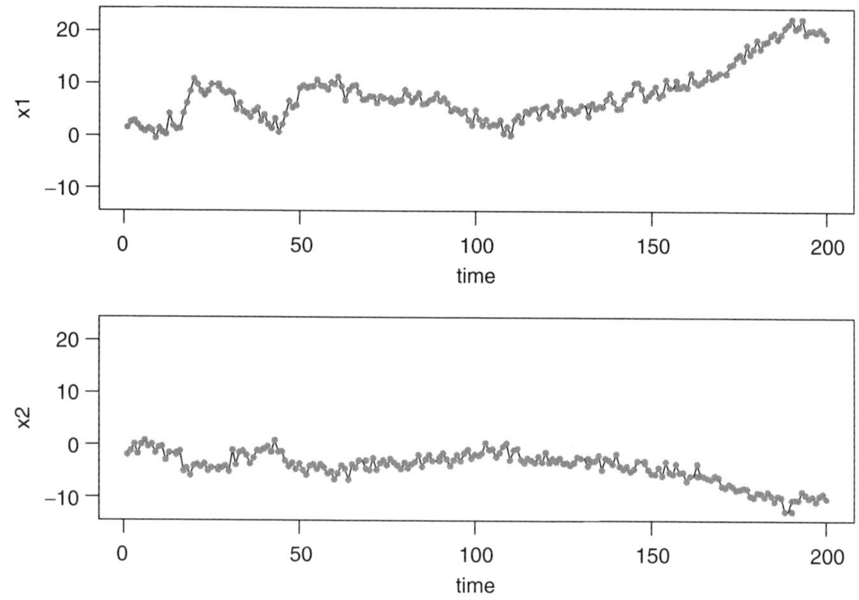

Figure 8.10. Time plots of a simulated series based on model (8.31) with identity covariance matrix for the shocks.

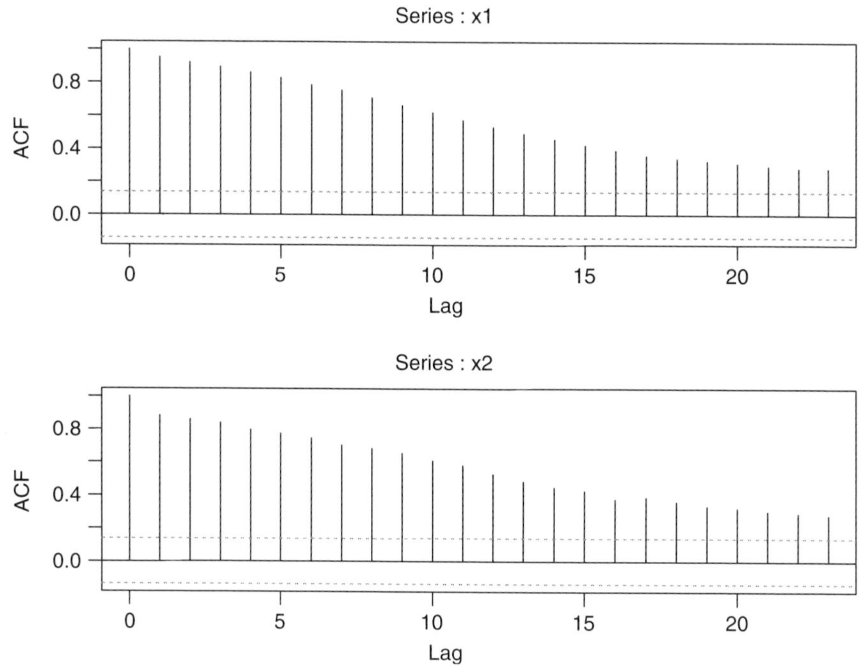

Figure 8.11. Sample autocorrelation functions of two simulated component series. There are 200 observations, and the model is given by Eq. (8.31) with identity covariance matrix for the shocks.

Therefore, each component x_{it} of the model is unit-root nonstationary and follows an ARIMA(0,1,1) model.

However, we can consider a linear transformation by defining

$$\begin{bmatrix} y_{1t} \\ y_{2t} \end{bmatrix} = \begin{bmatrix} 1.0 & -2.0 \\ 0.5 & 1.0 \end{bmatrix} \begin{bmatrix} x_{1t} \\ x_{2t} \end{bmatrix} \equiv \boldsymbol{L}\boldsymbol{x}_t,$$

$$\begin{bmatrix} b_{1t} \\ b_{2t} \end{bmatrix} = \begin{bmatrix} 1.0 & -2.0 \\ 0.5 & 1.0 \end{bmatrix} \begin{bmatrix} a_{1t} \\ a_{2t} \end{bmatrix} \equiv \boldsymbol{L}\boldsymbol{a}_t.$$

The VARMA model of the transformed series $\boldsymbol{y}_t$ can be obtained as follows:

$$\begin{aligned} \boldsymbol{L}\boldsymbol{x}_t &= \boldsymbol{L\Phi x}_{t-1} + \boldsymbol{L}\boldsymbol{a}_t - \boldsymbol{L\Theta a}_{t-1} \\ &= \boldsymbol{L\Phi L}^{-1}\boldsymbol{L}\boldsymbol{x}_{t-1} + \boldsymbol{L}\boldsymbol{a}_t - \boldsymbol{L\Theta L}^{-1}\boldsymbol{L}\boldsymbol{a}_{t-1} \\ &= \boldsymbol{L\Phi L}^{-1}(\boldsymbol{L}\boldsymbol{x}_{t-1}) + \boldsymbol{b}_t - \boldsymbol{L\Theta L}^{-1}\boldsymbol{b}_{t-1}. \end{aligned}$$

Thus, the model for $\boldsymbol{y}_t$ is

$$\begin{bmatrix} y_{1t} \\ y_{2t} \end{bmatrix} - \begin{bmatrix} 1.0 & 0 \\ 0 & 0 \end{bmatrix} \begin{bmatrix} y_{1,t-1} \\ y_{2,t-1} \end{bmatrix} = \begin{bmatrix} b_{1t} \\ b_{2t} \end{bmatrix} - \begin{bmatrix} 0.4 & 0 \\ 0 & 0 \end{bmatrix} \begin{bmatrix} b_{1,t-1} \\ b_{2,t-1} \end{bmatrix}. \qquad (8.32)$$

From the prior model, we see that (a) y_{1t} and y_{2t} are uncoupled series with concurrent correlation equal to that between the shocks b_{1t} and b_{2t}, (b) y_{1t} follows a univariate ARIMA(0,1,1) model, and (c) y_{2t} is a white noise series (i.e., $y_{2t} = b_{2t}$). In particular, the model in Eq. (8.32) shows that there is *only* a single unit root in the system. Consequently, the unit roots of x_{1t} and x_{2t} are introduced by the unit root of y_{1t}. In the literature, y_{1t} is referred to as the *common trend* of x_{1t} and x_{2t}.

The phenomenon that both x_{1t} and x_{2t} are unit-root nonstationary, but there is only a single unit root in the vector series, is referred to as *cointegration* in the econometric and time series literature. Another way to define cointegration is to focus on linear transformations of unit-root nonstationary series. For the simulated example of model (8.31), the transformation shows that the linear combination $y_{2t} = 0.5x_{1t} + x_{2t}$ does not have a unit root. Consequently, x_{1t} and x_{2t} are cointegrated if (a) both of them are unit-root nonstationary, and (b) they have a linear combination that is unit-root stationary.

Generally speaking, for a k-dimensional unit-root nonstationary time series, cointegration exists if there are less than k unit roots in the system. Let h be the number of unit roots in the k-dimensional series $\boldsymbol{x}_t$. Cointegration exists if $0 < h < k$, and the quantity $k - h$ is called the number of cointegrating factors. Alternatively, the number of cointegrating factors is the number of different linear combinations that are unit-root stationary. The linear combinations are called the cointegrating vectors. For the prior simulated example, $y_{2t} = (0.5, 1)\boldsymbol{x}_t$ so that $(0.5, 1)'$ is a cointegrating vector for the system. For more discussions on cointegration and cointegration tests, see Box and Tiao (1977), Engle and Granger (1987), Stock and Watson (1988), and Johansen (1988). We discuss cointegrated VAR models in Section 8.6.

The concept of cointegration is interesting and has attracted a lot of attention in the literature. However, there are difficulties in testing for cointegration in a real application. The main source of difficulties is that cointegration tests overlook the scaling effects of the component series. Interested readers are referred to Cochrane (1988) and Tiao, Tsay, and Wang (1993) for further discussion.

While I have some misgivings on the practical value of cointegration tests, the idea of cointegration is highly relevant in financial study. For example, consider the stock of Finnish Nokia Corporation. Its price on the Helsinki Stock Market must move in unison with the price of its American Depositary Receipts on the New York Stock Exchange; otherwise there exists some arbitrage opportunity for investors. If the stock price has a unit root, then the two price series must be cointegrated. In practice, such a cointegration can exist after adjusting for transaction costs and exchange-rate risk. We discuss issues like this later in Section 8.7.

8.5.1 An Error-Correction Form

Because there are more unit-root nonstationary components than the number of unit roots in a cointegrated system, differencing individual components to achieve stationarity results in overdifferencing. Overdifferencing leads to the problem of unit roots in the MA matrix polynomial, which in turn may encounter difficulties in parameter estimation. If the MA matrix polynomial contains unit roots, the vector time series is said to be noninvertible.

Engle and Granger (1987) discuss an error-correction representation for a cointegrated system that overcomes the difficulty of estimating noninvertible VARMA models. Consider the cointegrated system in Eq. (8.31). Let $\Delta \boldsymbol{x}_t = \boldsymbol{x}_t - \boldsymbol{x}_{t-1}$ be the differenced series. Subtracting $\boldsymbol{x}_{t-1}$ from both sides of the equation, we obtain a model for $\Delta \boldsymbol{x}_t$ as

$$\begin{bmatrix} \Delta x_{1t} \\ \Delta x_{2t} \end{bmatrix} = \begin{bmatrix} -0.5 & -1.0 \\ -0.25 & -0.5 \end{bmatrix} \begin{bmatrix} x_{1,t-1} \\ x_{2,t-1} \end{bmatrix} + \begin{bmatrix} a_{1t} \\ a_{2t} \end{bmatrix} - \begin{bmatrix} 0.2 & -0.4 \\ -0.1 & 0.2 \end{bmatrix} \begin{bmatrix} a_{1,t-1} \\ a_{2,t-1} \end{bmatrix}$$

$$= \begin{bmatrix} -1 \\ -0.5 \end{bmatrix} [0.5, 1.0] \begin{bmatrix} x_{1,t-1} \\ x_{2,t-1} \end{bmatrix} + \begin{bmatrix} a_{1t} \\ a_{2t} \end{bmatrix} - \begin{bmatrix} 0.2 & -0.4 \\ -0.1 & 0.2 \end{bmatrix} \begin{bmatrix} a_{1,t-1} \\ a_{2,t-1} \end{bmatrix}.$$

This is a stationary model because both $\Delta \boldsymbol{x}_t$ and $[0.5, 1.0]\boldsymbol{x}_t = y_{2t}$ are unit-root stationary. Because $\boldsymbol{x}_{t-1}$ is used on the right-hand side of the previous equation, the MA matrix polynomial is the same as before and, hence, the model does not encounter the problem of noninvertibility. Such a formulation is referred to as an error-correction model for $\Delta \boldsymbol{x}_t$, and it can be extended to the general cointegrated VARMA model. For a cointegrated VARMA(p, q) model with m cointegrating factors ($m < k$), an error-correction representation is

$$\Delta \boldsymbol{x}_t = \boldsymbol{\alpha}\boldsymbol{\beta}'\boldsymbol{x}_{t-1} + \sum_{i=1}^{p-1} \boldsymbol{\Phi}_i^* \Delta \boldsymbol{x}_{t-i} + \boldsymbol{a}_t - \sum_{j=1}^{q} \boldsymbol{\Theta}_j \boldsymbol{a}_{t-j}, \tag{8.33}$$

where $\boldsymbol{\alpha}$ and $\boldsymbol{\beta}$ are $k \times m$ full-rank matrices. The AR coefficient matrices $\boldsymbol{\Phi}_i^*$ are functions of the original coefficient matrices $\boldsymbol{\Phi}_j$. Specifically, we have

$$\boldsymbol{\Phi}_j^* = -\sum_{i=j+1}^{p} \boldsymbol{\Phi}_i, \quad j = 1, \ldots, p-1,$$

$$\boldsymbol{\alpha}\boldsymbol{\beta}' = \boldsymbol{\Phi}_p + \boldsymbol{\Phi}_{p-1} + \cdots + \boldsymbol{\Phi}_1 - \boldsymbol{I} = -\boldsymbol{\Phi}(1). \tag{8.34}$$

These results can be obtained by equating coefficient matrices of the AR matrix polynomials. The time series $\boldsymbol{\beta}'\boldsymbol{x}_t$ is unit-root stationary, and the columns of $\boldsymbol{\beta}$ are the cointegrating vectors of $\boldsymbol{x}_t$.

Existence of the stationary series $\boldsymbol{\beta}'\boldsymbol{x}_{t-1}$ in the error-correction representation (8.33) is natural. It can be regarded as a "compensation" term for the overdifferenced system $\Delta\boldsymbol{x}_t$. The stationarity of $\boldsymbol{\beta}'\boldsymbol{x}_{t-1}$ can be justified as follows. The theory of unit-root time series shows that the sample correlation coefficient between a unit-root nonstationary series and a stationary series converges to zero as the sample size goes to infinity; see Tsay and Tiao (1990) and the references therein. In an error-correction representation, $\boldsymbol{x}_{t-1}$ is unit-root nonstationary, but $\Delta\boldsymbol{x}_t$ is stationary. Therefore, the only way that $\Delta\boldsymbol{x}_t$ can relate meaningfully to $\boldsymbol{x}_{t-1}$ is through a stationary series $\boldsymbol{\beta}'\boldsymbol{x}_{t-1}$.

Remark. Our discussion of cointegration assumes that all unit roots are of multiplicity 1, but the concept can be extended to cases in which the unit roots have different multiplicities. Also, if the number of cointegrating factors m is given, then the error-correction model in Eq. (8.33) can be estimated by likelihood methods. We discuss the simple case of cointegrated VAR models in the next section. Finally, there are many ways to construct an error-correction representation. In fact, one can use any $\boldsymbol{\alpha}\boldsymbol{\beta}'\boldsymbol{x}_{t-v}$ for $1 \le v \le p$ in Eq. (8.33) with some modifications to the AR coefficient matrices $\boldsymbol{\Phi}_i^*$. □

8.6 COINTEGRATED VAR MODELS

To better understand cointegration, we focus on VAR models for their simplicity in estimation. Consider a k-dimensional VAR(p) time series $\boldsymbol{x}_t$ with possible time trend so that the model is

$$\boldsymbol{x}_t = \boldsymbol{\mu}_t + \boldsymbol{\Phi}_1\boldsymbol{x}_{t-1} + \cdots + \boldsymbol{\Phi}_p\boldsymbol{x}_{t-p} + \boldsymbol{a}_t, \tag{8.35}$$

where the innovation $\boldsymbol{a}_t$ is assumed to be Gaussian and $\boldsymbol{\mu}_t = \boldsymbol{\mu}_0 + \boldsymbol{\mu}_1 t$, where $\boldsymbol{\mu}_0$ and $\boldsymbol{\mu}_1$ are k-dimensional constant vectors. Write $\boldsymbol{\Phi}(B) = \boldsymbol{I} - \boldsymbol{\Phi}_1 B - \cdots - \boldsymbol{\Phi}_p B^p$. Recall that if all zeros of the determinant $|\boldsymbol{\Phi}(B)|$ are outside the unit circle, then

$\boldsymbol{x}_t$ is unit-root stationary. In the literature, a unit-root stationary series is said to be an $I(0)$ process; that is, it is not integrated. If $|\boldsymbol{\Phi}(1)| = 0$, then $\boldsymbol{x}_t$ is unit-root nonstationary. For simplicity, we assume that $\boldsymbol{x}_t$ is at most an integrated process of order 1, that is, an $I(1)$ process. This means that $(1 - B)x_{it}$ is unit-root stationary if x_{it} itself is not.

An error-correction model (ECM) for the VAR(p) process $\boldsymbol{x}_t$ is

$$\Delta \boldsymbol{x}_t = \boldsymbol{\mu}_t + \boldsymbol{\Pi} \boldsymbol{x}_{t-1} + \boldsymbol{\Phi}_1^* \Delta \boldsymbol{x}_{t-1} + \cdots + \boldsymbol{\Phi}_{p-1}^* \Delta \boldsymbol{x}_{t-p+1} + \boldsymbol{a}_t, \tag{8.36}$$

where $\boldsymbol{\Phi}_j^*$ are defined in Eq. (8.34) and $\boldsymbol{\Pi} = \boldsymbol{\alpha}\boldsymbol{\beta}' = -\boldsymbol{\Phi}(1)$. We refer to the term $\boldsymbol{\Pi}\boldsymbol{x}_{t-1}$ of Eq. (8.36) as the *error-correction term*, which plays a key role in cointegration study. Notice that $\boldsymbol{\Phi}_i$ can be recovered from the ECM representation via

$$\boldsymbol{\Phi}_1 = \boldsymbol{I} + \boldsymbol{\Pi} + \boldsymbol{\Phi}_1^*,$$
$$\boldsymbol{\Phi}_i = \boldsymbol{\Phi}_i^* - \boldsymbol{\Phi}_{i-1}^*, \quad i = 2, \ldots, p,$$

where $\boldsymbol{\Phi}_p^* = \boldsymbol{0}$, the zero matrix. Based on the assumption that $\boldsymbol{x}_t$ is at most $I(1)$, $\Delta \boldsymbol{x}_t$ of Eq. (8.36) is an $I(0)$ process.

If $\boldsymbol{x}_t$ contains unit roots, then $|\boldsymbol{\Phi}(1)| = 0$ so that $\boldsymbol{\Pi} = -\boldsymbol{\Phi}(1)$ is singular. Therefore, three cases are of interest in considering the ECM in Eq. (8.36):

1. Rank($\boldsymbol{\Pi}$) $= 0$. This implies $\boldsymbol{\Pi} = \boldsymbol{0}$ and $\boldsymbol{x}_t$ is not cointegrated. The ECM of Eq. (8.36) reduces to

$$\Delta \boldsymbol{x}_t = \boldsymbol{\mu}_t + \boldsymbol{\Phi}_1^* \Delta \boldsymbol{x}_{t-1} + \cdots + \boldsymbol{\Phi}_{p-1}^* \Delta \boldsymbol{x}_{t-p+1} + \boldsymbol{a}_t,$$

so that $\Delta \boldsymbol{x}_t$ follows a VAR($p - 1$) model with deterministic trend $\boldsymbol{\mu}_t$.

2. Rank($\boldsymbol{\Pi}$) $= k$. This implies that $|\boldsymbol{\Phi}(1)| \neq 0$ and $\boldsymbol{x}_t$ contains no unit roots; that is, $\boldsymbol{x}_t$ is $I(0)$. The ECM model is not informative and one studies $\boldsymbol{x}_t$ directly.

3. $0 <$ Rank($\boldsymbol{\Pi}$) $= m < k$. In this case, one can write $\boldsymbol{\Pi}$ as

$$\boldsymbol{\Pi} = \boldsymbol{\alpha}\boldsymbol{\beta}', \tag{8.37}$$

where $\boldsymbol{\alpha}$ and $\boldsymbol{\beta}$ are $k \times m$ matrices with Rank($\boldsymbol{\alpha}$) = Rank($\boldsymbol{\beta}$) $= m$. The ECM of Eq. (8.36) becomes

$$\Delta \boldsymbol{x}_t = \boldsymbol{\mu}_t + \boldsymbol{\alpha}\boldsymbol{\beta}' \boldsymbol{x}_{t-1} + \boldsymbol{\Phi}_1^* \Delta \boldsymbol{x}_{t-1} + \cdots + \boldsymbol{\Phi}_{p-1}^* \Delta \boldsymbol{x}_{t-p+1} + \boldsymbol{a}_t. \tag{8.38}$$

This means that $\boldsymbol{x}_t$ is cointegrated with m linearly independent cointegrating vectors, $\boldsymbol{w}_t = \boldsymbol{\beta}' \boldsymbol{x}_t$, and has $k - m$ unit roots that give $k - m$ common stochastic trends of $\boldsymbol{x}_t$.

If $\boldsymbol{x}_t$ is cointegrated with Rank($\boldsymbol{\Pi}$) $= m$, then a simple way to obtain a presentation of the $k - m$ common trends is to obtain an orthogonal complement matrix $\boldsymbol{\alpha}_\perp$ of $\boldsymbol{\alpha}$; that is, $\boldsymbol{\alpha}_\perp$ is a $k \times (k - m)$ matrix such that $\boldsymbol{\alpha}'_\perp \boldsymbol{\alpha} = \boldsymbol{0}$, a $(k - m) \times m$ zero matrix, and use $\boldsymbol{y}_t = \boldsymbol{\alpha}'_\perp \boldsymbol{x}_t$. To see this, one can premultiply the ECM by $\boldsymbol{\alpha}'_\perp$ and use $\boldsymbol{\Pi} = \boldsymbol{\alpha}\boldsymbol{\beta}'$ to see that there would be no error-correction term in the resulting equation. Consequently, the $(k-m)$-dimensional series $\boldsymbol{y}_t$ should have $k-m$ unit roots. For illustration, consider the bivariate example of Section 8.5.1. For this special series, $\boldsymbol{\alpha} = (-1, -0.5)'$ and $\boldsymbol{\alpha}_\perp = (1, -2)'$. Therefore, $y_t = (1, -2)\boldsymbol{x}_t = x_{1t} - 2x_{2t}$, which is precisely the unit-root nonstationary series y_{1t} in Eq. (8.32).

Note that the factorization in Eq. (8.37) is not unique, because for any $m \times m$ orthogonal matrix $\boldsymbol{\Omega}$ satisfying $\boldsymbol{\Omega}\boldsymbol{\Omega}' = \boldsymbol{I}$, we have

$$\boldsymbol{\alpha}\boldsymbol{\beta}' = \boldsymbol{\alpha}\boldsymbol{\Omega}\boldsymbol{\Omega}'\boldsymbol{\beta}' = (\boldsymbol{\alpha}\boldsymbol{\Omega})(\boldsymbol{\beta}\boldsymbol{\Omega})' \equiv \boldsymbol{\alpha}_*\boldsymbol{\beta}_*',$$

where both $\boldsymbol{\alpha}_*$ and $\boldsymbol{\beta}_*$ are also of rank m. Additional constraints are needed to uniquely identify $\boldsymbol{\alpha}$ and $\boldsymbol{\beta}$. It is common to require that $\boldsymbol{\beta}' = [\boldsymbol{I}_m, \boldsymbol{\beta}_1']$, where $\boldsymbol{I}_m$ is the $m \times m$ identity matrix and $\boldsymbol{\beta}_1$ is a $(k-m) \times m$ matrix. In practice, this may require reordering of the elements of $\boldsymbol{x}_t$ such that the first m components all have a unit root. The elements of $\boldsymbol{\alpha}$ and $\boldsymbol{\beta}$ must also satisfy other constraints for the process $\boldsymbol{w}_t = \boldsymbol{\beta}'\boldsymbol{x}_t$ to be unit-root stationary. For example, consider the case of a bivariate VAR(1) model with one cointegrating vector. Here $k = 2$, $m = 1$, and the ECM is

$$\Delta \boldsymbol{x}_t = \boldsymbol{\mu}_t + \begin{bmatrix} \alpha_1 \\ \alpha_2 \end{bmatrix} [1, \beta_1]\boldsymbol{x}_{t-1} + \boldsymbol{a}_t.$$

Premultiplying the prior equation by $\boldsymbol{\beta}'$, using $w_{t-i} = \boldsymbol{\beta}'\boldsymbol{x}_{t-i}$, and moving w_{t-1} to the right-hand side of the equation, we obtain

$$w_t = \boldsymbol{\beta}'\boldsymbol{\mu}_t + (1 + \alpha_1 + \alpha_2\beta_1)w_{t-1} + b_t,$$

where $b_t = \boldsymbol{\beta}'\boldsymbol{a}_t$. This implies that w_t is a stationary AR(1) process. Consequently, α_i and β_1 must satisfy the stationarity constraint $|1 + \alpha_1 + \alpha_2\beta_1| < 1$.

The prior discussion shows that the rank of $\boldsymbol{\Pi}$ in the ECM of Eq. (8.36) is the number of cointegrating vectors. Thus, to test for cointegration, one can examine the rank of $\boldsymbol{\Pi}$. This is the approach taken by Johansen (1988, 1995) and Reinsel and Ahn (1992).

8.6.1 Specification of the Deterministic Function

Similar to the univariate case, the limiting distributions of cointegration tests depend on the deterministic function $\boldsymbol{\mu}_t$. In this subsection, we discuss some specifications of $\boldsymbol{\mu}_t$ that have been proposed in the literature. To understand some of the statements made below, keep in mind that $\boldsymbol{\alpha}_\perp'\boldsymbol{x}_t$ provides a presentation for the common stochastic trends of $\boldsymbol{x}_t$ if it is cointegrated.

1. $\boldsymbol{\mu}_t = \boldsymbol{0}$: In this case, all the component series of $\boldsymbol{x}_t$ are $I(1)$ without drift and the stationary series $\boldsymbol{w}_t = \boldsymbol{\beta}'\boldsymbol{x}_t$ has mean zero.
2. $\boldsymbol{\mu}_t = \boldsymbol{\mu}_0 = \boldsymbol{\alpha}\boldsymbol{c}_0$, where $\boldsymbol{c}_0$ is an m-dimensional nonzero constant vector. The ECM becomes

$$\Delta \boldsymbol{x}_t = \boldsymbol{\alpha}(\boldsymbol{\beta}'\boldsymbol{x}_{t-1} + \boldsymbol{c}_0) + \boldsymbol{\Phi}_1^*\Delta \boldsymbol{x}_{t-1} + \cdots + \boldsymbol{\Phi}_{p-1}^*\Delta \boldsymbol{x}_{t-p+1} + \boldsymbol{a}_t,$$

so that the components of $\boldsymbol{x}_t$ are $I(1)$ without drift, but $\boldsymbol{w}_t$ have a nonzero mean $-\boldsymbol{c}_0$. This is referred to as the case of restricted constant.

3. $\boldsymbol{\mu}_t = \boldsymbol{\mu}_0$, which is nonzero. Here the component series of $\boldsymbol{x}_t$ are $I(1)$ with drift $\boldsymbol{\mu}_0$ and $\boldsymbol{w}_t$ may have a nonzero mean.
4. $\boldsymbol{\mu}_t = \boldsymbol{\mu}_0 + \boldsymbol{\alpha}\boldsymbol{c}_1 t$, where $\boldsymbol{c}_1$ is a nonzero vector. The ECM becomes

$$\Delta \boldsymbol{x}_t = \boldsymbol{\mu}_0 + \boldsymbol{\alpha}(\boldsymbol{\beta}'\boldsymbol{x}_{t-1} + \boldsymbol{c}_1 t) + \boldsymbol{\Phi}_1^* \Delta \boldsymbol{x}_{t-1} + \cdots + \boldsymbol{\Phi}_{p-1}^* \Delta \boldsymbol{x}_{t-p+1} + \boldsymbol{a}_t,$$

so that the components of $\boldsymbol{x}_t$ are $I(1)$ with drift $\boldsymbol{\mu}_0$ and $\boldsymbol{w}_t$ has a linear time trend related to $\boldsymbol{c}_1 t$. This is the case of restricted trend.

5. $\boldsymbol{\mu}_t = \boldsymbol{\mu}_0 + \boldsymbol{\mu}_1 t$, where $\boldsymbol{\mu}_i$ are nonzero. Here both the constant and trend are unrestricted. The components of $\boldsymbol{x}_t$ are $I(1)$ and have a quadratic time trend and $\boldsymbol{w}_t$ have a linear trend.

Obviously, the last case is not common in empirical work. The first case is not common for economic time series but may represent the log price series of some assets. The third case is also useful in modeling asset prices.

8.6.2 Maximum Likelihood Estimation

In this subsection, we briefly outline the maximum likelihood estimation of a cointegrated VAR(p) model. Suppose that the data are $\{\boldsymbol{x}_t | t = 1, \ldots, T\}$. Without loss of generality, we write $\boldsymbol{\mu}_t = \boldsymbol{\mu}\boldsymbol{d}_t$, where $\boldsymbol{d}_t = [1, t]'$, and it is understood that $\boldsymbol{\mu}_t$ depends on the specification of the previous subsection. For a given m, which is the rank of $\boldsymbol{\Pi}$, the ECM model becomes

$$\Delta \boldsymbol{x}_t = \boldsymbol{\mu}\boldsymbol{d}_t + \boldsymbol{\alpha}\boldsymbol{\beta}'\boldsymbol{x}_{t-1} + \boldsymbol{\Phi}_1^* \Delta \boldsymbol{x}_{t-1} + \cdots + \boldsymbol{\Phi}_{p-1}^* \Delta \boldsymbol{x}_{t-p+1} + \boldsymbol{a}_t, \qquad (8.39)$$

where $t = p+1, \ldots, T$. A key step in the estimation is to concentrate the likelihood function with respect to the deterministic term and the stationary effects. This is done by considering the following two multivariate linear regressions:

$$\Delta \boldsymbol{x}_t = \boldsymbol{\gamma}_0 \boldsymbol{d}_t + \boldsymbol{\Omega}_1 \Delta \boldsymbol{x}_{t-1} + \cdots + \boldsymbol{\Omega}_{p-1} \Delta \boldsymbol{x}_{t-p+1} + \boldsymbol{u}_t, \qquad (8.40)$$

$$\boldsymbol{x}_{t-1} = \boldsymbol{\gamma}_1 \boldsymbol{d}_t + \boldsymbol{\Xi}_1 \Delta \boldsymbol{x}_{t-1} + \cdots + \boldsymbol{\Xi}_{p-1} \Delta \boldsymbol{x}_{t-p+1} + \boldsymbol{v}_t. \qquad (8.41)$$

Let $\hat{\boldsymbol{u}}_t$ and $\hat{\boldsymbol{v}}_t$ be the residuals of Eqs. (8.40) and (8.41), respectively. Define the sample covariance matrices

$$\boldsymbol{S}_{00} = \frac{1}{T-p} \sum_{t=p+1}^{T} \hat{\boldsymbol{u}}_t \hat{\boldsymbol{u}}_t', \quad \boldsymbol{S}_{01} = \frac{1}{T-p} \sum_{t=p+1}^{T} \hat{\boldsymbol{u}}_t \hat{\boldsymbol{v}}_t', \quad \boldsymbol{S}_{11} = \frac{1}{T-p} \sum_{t=p+1}^{T} \hat{\boldsymbol{v}}_t \hat{\boldsymbol{v}}_t'.$$

Next, compute the eigenvalues and eigenvectors of $\boldsymbol{S}_{10}\boldsymbol{S}_{00}^{-1}\boldsymbol{S}_{01}$ with respect to $\boldsymbol{S}_{11}$. This amounts to solving the eigenvalue problem

$$|\lambda \boldsymbol{S}_{11} - \boldsymbol{S}_{10}\boldsymbol{S}_{00}^{-1}\boldsymbol{S}_{01}| = 0.$$

Denote the eigenvalue and eigenvector pairs by $(\hat{\lambda}_i, \boldsymbol{e}_i)$, where $\hat{\lambda}_1 > \hat{\lambda}_2 > \cdots > \hat{\lambda}_k$. Here the eigenvectors are normalized so that $\boldsymbol{e}'\boldsymbol{S}_{11}\boldsymbol{e} = \boldsymbol{I}$, where $\boldsymbol{e} = [\boldsymbol{e}_1, \ldots, \boldsymbol{e}_k]$ is the matrix of eigenvectors.

The unnormalized maximum likelihood estimate (MLE) of the cointegrating vector $\boldsymbol{\beta}$ is $\hat{\boldsymbol{\beta}} = [\boldsymbol{e}_1, \ldots, \boldsymbol{e}_m]$, from which we can obtain a MLE for $\boldsymbol{\beta}$ that satisfies the identifying constraint and normalization condition. Denote the resulting estimate by $\hat{\boldsymbol{\beta}}_c$ with the subscript c signifying constraints. The MLE of other parameters can then be obtained by the multivariate linear regression

$$\Delta \boldsymbol{x}_t = \boldsymbol{\mu} \boldsymbol{d}_t + \boldsymbol{\alpha} \hat{\boldsymbol{\beta}}_c' \boldsymbol{x}_{t-1} + \boldsymbol{\Phi}_1^* \Delta \boldsymbol{x}_{t-1} + \cdots + \boldsymbol{\Phi}_{p-1}^* \Delta \boldsymbol{x}_{t-p+1} + \boldsymbol{a}_t.$$

The maximized value of the likelihood function based on m cointegrating vectors is

$$L_{\max}^{-2/T} \propto |\boldsymbol{S}_{00}| \prod_{i=1}^{m} (1 - \hat{\lambda}_i).$$

This value is used in the maximum likelihood ratio test for testing $\text{Rank}(\boldsymbol{\Pi}) = m$. Finally, estimates of the orthogonal complements of $\boldsymbol{\alpha}$ and $\boldsymbol{\beta}$ can be obtained using

$$\hat{\boldsymbol{\alpha}}_{\perp} = \boldsymbol{S}_{00}^{-1} \boldsymbol{S}_{11} [\boldsymbol{e}_{m+1}, \ldots, \boldsymbol{e}_k], \quad \hat{\boldsymbol{\beta}}_{\perp} = \boldsymbol{S}_{11} [\boldsymbol{e}_{m+1}, \ldots, \boldsymbol{e}_k].$$

8.6.3 A Cointegration Test

For a specified deterministic term $\boldsymbol{\mu}_t$, we now discuss the maximum likelihood test for testing the rank of the $\boldsymbol{\Pi}$ matrix in Eq. (8.36). Let $H(m)$ be the null hypothesis that the rank of $\boldsymbol{\Pi}$ is m. For example, under $H(0)$, $\text{Rank}(\boldsymbol{\Pi}) = 0$ so that $\boldsymbol{\Pi} = \boldsymbol{0}$ and there is no cointegration. The hypotheses of interest are

$$H(0) \subset \cdots \subset H(m) \subset \cdots \subset H(k).$$

For testing purpose, the ECM in Eq. (8.39) becomes

$$\Delta \boldsymbol{x}_t = \boldsymbol{\mu} \boldsymbol{d}_t + \boldsymbol{\Pi} \boldsymbol{x}_{t-1} + \boldsymbol{\Phi}_1^* \Delta \boldsymbol{x}_{t-1} + \cdots + \boldsymbol{\Phi}_{p-1}^* \Delta \boldsymbol{x}_{t-p+1} + \boldsymbol{a}_t,$$

where $t = p+1, \ldots, T$. Our goal is to test the rank of $\boldsymbol{\Pi}$. Mathematically, the rank of $\boldsymbol{\Pi}$ is the number of nonzero eigenvalues of $\boldsymbol{\Pi}$, which can be obtained if a consistent estimate of $\boldsymbol{\Pi}$ is available. Based on the prior equation, which is in the form of a multivariate linear regression, we see that $\boldsymbol{\Pi}$ is related to the covariance matrix between $\boldsymbol{x}_{t-1}$ and $\Delta \boldsymbol{x}_t$ after adjusting for the effects of $\boldsymbol{d}_t$ and $\Delta \boldsymbol{x}_{t-i}$ for $i = 1, \ldots, p-1$. The necessary adjustments can be achieved by the techniques of multivariate linear regression shown in the previous subsection. Indeed, the adjusted series of $\boldsymbol{x}_{t-1}$ and $\Delta \boldsymbol{x}_t$ are $\hat{\boldsymbol{v}}_t$ and $\hat{\boldsymbol{u}}_t$, respectively. The equation of interest for the cointegration test then becomes

$$\hat{\boldsymbol{u}}_t = \boldsymbol{\Pi} \hat{\boldsymbol{v}}_t + \boldsymbol{a}_t.$$

Under the normality assumption, the likelihood ratio test for testing the rank of $\boldsymbol{\Pi}$ in the prior equation can be done by using the canonical correlation analysis between $\hat{\boldsymbol{u}}_t$ and $\hat{\boldsymbol{v}}_t$. See Johnson and Wichern (1998) for information on canonical correlation analysis. The associated canonical correlations are the *partial canonical correlations* between $\Delta \boldsymbol{x}_{t-1}$ and $\boldsymbol{x}_{t-1}$ because the effects of $\boldsymbol{d}_t$ and $\Delta \boldsymbol{x}_{t-i}$ have been adjusted. The quantities $\{\hat{\lambda}_i\}$ are the squared canonical correlations between $\hat{\boldsymbol{u}}_t$ and $\hat{\boldsymbol{v}}_t$.

Consider the hypotheses

$$H_o : \text{Rank}(\boldsymbol{\Pi}) = m \quad \text{versus} \quad H_a : \text{Rank}(\boldsymbol{\Pi}) > m.$$

Johansen (1988) proposes the likelihood ratio (LR) statistic

$$LK_{\text{tr}}(m) = -(T - p) \sum_{i=m+1}^{k} \ln(1 - \hat{\lambda}_i) \tag{8.42}$$

to perform the test. If $\text{Rank}(\boldsymbol{\Pi}) = m$, then $\hat{\lambda}_i$ should be small for $i > m$ and hence $LK_{\text{tr}}(m)$ should be small. This test is referred to as the *trace* cointegration test. Due the presence of unit roots, the asymptotic distribution of $LK_{\text{tr}}(m)$ is not chi-squared, but a function of standard Brownian motions. Thus, critical values of $LK_{\text{tr}}(m)$ must be obtained via simulation.

Johansen (1988) also considers a sequential procedure to determine the number of cointegrating vectors. Specifically, the hypotheses of interest are

$$H_o : \text{Rank}(\boldsymbol{\Pi}) = m \quad \text{versus} \quad H_a : \text{Rank}(\boldsymbol{\Pi}) = m + 1.$$

The LK ratio test statistic, called the maximum eigenvalue statistic, is

$$LK_{\text{max}}(m) = -(T - p) \ln(1 - \hat{\lambda}_{m+1}).$$

Again, critical values of the test statistics are nonstandard and must be evaluated via simulation.

8.6.4 Forecasting of Cointegrated VAR Models

The fitted ECM model can be used to produce forecasts. First, conditioned on the estimated parameters, the ECM equation can be used to produce forecasts of the differenced series $\Delta \boldsymbol{x}_t$. Such forecasts can in turn be used to obtain forecasts of $\boldsymbol{x}_t$. A difference between ECM forecasts and the traditional VAR forecasts is that the ECM approach imposes the cointegration relationships in producing the forecasts.

8.6.5 An Example

To demonstrate the analysis of cointegrated VAR models, we consider two weekly U.S. short-term interest rates. The series are the 3-month Treasury bill (TB) rate and 6-month Treasury bill rate from December 12, 1958 to August 6, 2004 for 2383 observations. The TB rates are from the secondary market and obtained from the Federal Reserve Bank of St. Loius. Figure 8.12 shows the time plots of the interest rates. As expected, the two series move closely together.

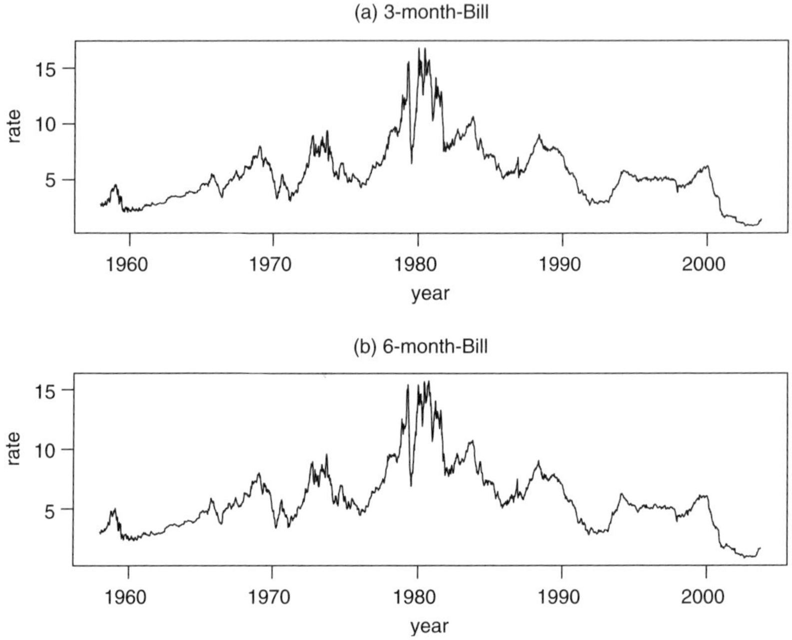

Figure 8.12. Time plots of weekly U.S. interest rate from December 12, 1958 to August 6, 2004. (a) The 3-month Treasury bill rate and (b) the 6-month Treasury bill rate. The rates are from the secondary market.

Our analysis uses the S-Plus software with commands `VAR` for VAR analysis, `coint` for cointegration test, and `VECM` for vector error-correction estimation. Denote the two series by `tb3m` and `tb6m` and define the vector series $\boldsymbol{x}_t = (\text{tb3m}_t, \text{tb6m}_t)'$. The augmented Dickey–Fuller unit-root tests fail to reject the hypothesis of a unit root in the individual series; see Chapter 2. Indeed, the test statistics are -2.34 and -2.33 with p-value about 0.16 for the 3-month and 6-month interest rate when an AR(3) model is used. Thus, we proceed to VAR modeling.

For the bivariate series $\boldsymbol{x}_t$, the BIC criterion selects a VAR(3) model.

```
> x=cbind(tb3m,tb6m)
> y=data.frame(x)
> ord.choice$ar.order
[1] 3
```

To perform a cointegration test, we choose a restricted constant for $\boldsymbol{\mu}_t$ because there is no reason a priori to believe the existence of a drift in the U.S. interest rate. Both Johansen's tests confirm that the two series are cointegrated with one cointegrating vector when a VAR(3) model is entertained.

```
> cointst.rc=coint(x,trend='rc', lags=2)  % lags = p-1.
```

```
> cointst.rc
Call:
coint(Y = x, lags = 2, trend = "rc")

Trend Specification:
H1*(r): Restricted constant

Trace tests sign. at the 5% level are flagged by ' +'.
Trace tests sign. at the 1% level are flagged by '++'.
Max Eig. tests sign. at the 5% level are flagged by ' *'.
Max Eig. tests sign. at the 1% level are flagged by '**'.

Tests for Cointegration Rank:
         Eigenvalue Trace Stat  95% CV  99% CV
H(0)++**  0.0322    83.2712     19.96   24.60
H(1)      0.0023     5.4936      9.24   12.97

         Max Stat  95% CV  99% CV
H(0)++**  77.7776  15.67   20.20
H(1)       5.4936   9.24   12.97
```

Next, we perform the maximum likelihood estimation of the specified cointegrated VAR(3) model using an ECM presentation. The results are given below:

```
> vecm.fit=VECM(cointst.rc)
> summary(vecm.fit)
Call:
VECM(test = cointst.rc)

Cointegrating Vectors:
             coint.1
              1.0000

      tb6m   -1.0124
 (std.err)    0.0086
  (t.stat) -118.2799

Intercept*    0.2254
 (std.err)    0.0545
  (t.stat)    4.1382

VECM Coefficients:
             tb3m    tb6m
  coint.1 -0.0949 -0.0211
(std.err)  0.0199  0.0179
 (t.stat) -4.7590 -1.1775

tb3m.lag1  0.0466 -0.0419
(std.err)  0.0480  0.0432
```

```
 (t.stat)  0.9696 -0.9699

tb6m.lag1  0.2650  0.3164
(std.err)  0.0538  0.0484
 (t.stat)  4.9263  6.5385

tb3m.lag2 -0.2067 -0.0346
(std.err)  0.0481  0.0433
 (t.stat) -4.2984 -0.8005

tb6m.lag2  0.2547  0.0994
(std.err)  0.0543  0.0488
 (t.stat)  4.6936  2.0356

Regression Diagnostics:
                  tb3m   tb6m
     R-squared 0.1081 0.0913
Adj. R-squared 0.1066 0.0898
  Resid. Scale 0.2009 0.1807

> plot(vecm.fit)
Make a plot selection (or 0 to exit):

1: plot: All
2: plot: Response and Fitted Values
3: plot: Residuals
...
13: plot: PACF of Squared Cointegrating Residuals
Selection:
```

As expected, the output shows that the stationary series is $w_t \approx \text{tb3m}_t - \text{tb6m}_t$ and the mean of w_t is about -0.225. The fitted ECM model is

$$\Delta \boldsymbol{x}_t = \begin{bmatrix} -0.09 \\ -0.02 \end{bmatrix} (w_{t-1} + 0.23) + \begin{bmatrix} 0.05 & 0.27 \\ -0.04 & 0.32 \end{bmatrix} \Delta \boldsymbol{x}_{t-1} + \begin{bmatrix} -0.21 & 0.25 \\ -0.03 & 0.10 \end{bmatrix} \Delta \boldsymbol{x}_{t-2} + \boldsymbol{a}_t,$$

and the estimated standard errors of a_{it} are 0.20 and 0.18, respectively. Adequacy of the fitted ECM model can be examined via various plots. For illustration, Figure 8.13 shows the cointegrating residuals. Some large residuals are shown in the plot, which occurred in the early 1980s when the interest rates were high and volatile.

Finally, we use the fitted ECM model to produce 1-step to 10-step ahead forecasts for both $\Delta \boldsymbol{x}_t$ and $\boldsymbol{x}_t$. The forecast origin is August 6, 2004.

```
> vecm.fst=predict(vecm.fit, n.predict=10)
> summary(vecm.fst)
```

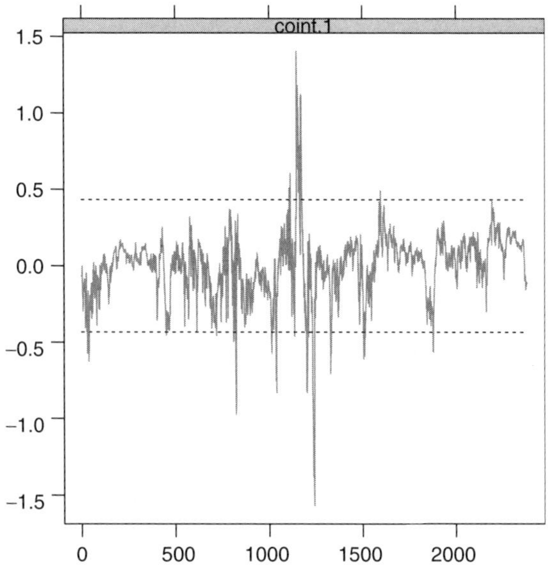

Figure 8.13. Time plot of cointegrating residuals for an ECM fit to the weekly U.S. interest rate series. The data span is from December 12, 1958 to August 6, 2004.

```
Predicted Values with Standard Errors:

                  tb3m    tb6m
 1-step-ahead -0.0378 -0.0642
    (std.err)  0.2009  0.1807
 2-step-ahead -0.0870 -0.0864
    (std.err)  0.3222  0.2927
 ...
10-step-ahead -0.2276 -0.1314
    (std.err)  0.8460  0.8157
> plot(vecm.fst,xold=diff(x),n.old=12)

> vecm.fit.level=VECM(cointst.rc,levels=T)
> vecm.fst.level=predict(vecm.fit.level, n.predict=10)
> summary(vecm.fst.level)

Predicted Values with Standard Errors:
                 tb3m   tb6m
 1-step-ahead 1.4501 1.7057
    (std.err) 0.2009 0.1807
 2-step-ahead 1.4420 1.7017
    (std.err) 0.3222 0.2927
 ...
10-step-ahead 1.4722 1.7078
    (std.err) 0.8460 0.8157
> plot(vecm.fst.level, xold=x, n.old=50)
```

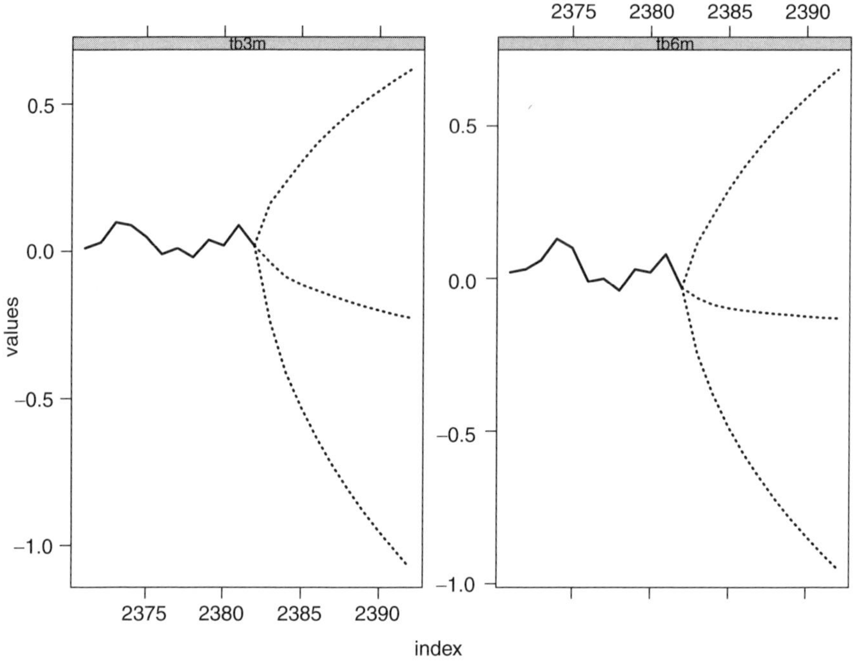

Figure 8.14. Forecasting plots of a fitted ECM model for the weekly U.S. interest rate series. The forecasts are for the differenced series and the forecast origin is August 6, 2004.

The forecasts are shown in Figures 8.14 and 8.15 for the differenced data and the original series, respectively, along with some observed data points. The dashed lines in the plots are pointwise 95% confidence intervals. Because of unit-root nonstationarity, the intervals are wide and not informative.

8.7 THRESHOLD COINTEGRATION AND ARBITRAGE

In this section, we focus on detecting arbitrage opportunities in index trading by using multivariate time series methods. We also demonstrate that simple univariate nonlinear models of Chapter 4 can be extended naturally to the multivariate case in conjunction with the idea of cointegration.

Our study considers the relationship between the price of the S&P 500 index futures and the price of the shares underlying the index on the cash market. Let $f_{t,\ell}$ be the log price of the index futures at time t with maturity ℓ, and let s_t be the log price of the shares underlying the index on the cash market at time t. A version of the *cost-of-carry model* in the finance literature states

$$f_{t,\ell} - s_t = (r_{t,\ell} - q_{t,\ell})(\ell - t) + z_t^*, \tag{8.43}$$

where $r_{t,\ell}$ is the risk-free interest rate, $q_{t,\ell}$ is the dividend yield with respect to the cash price at time t, and $(\ell - t)$ is the time to maturity of the futures contract;

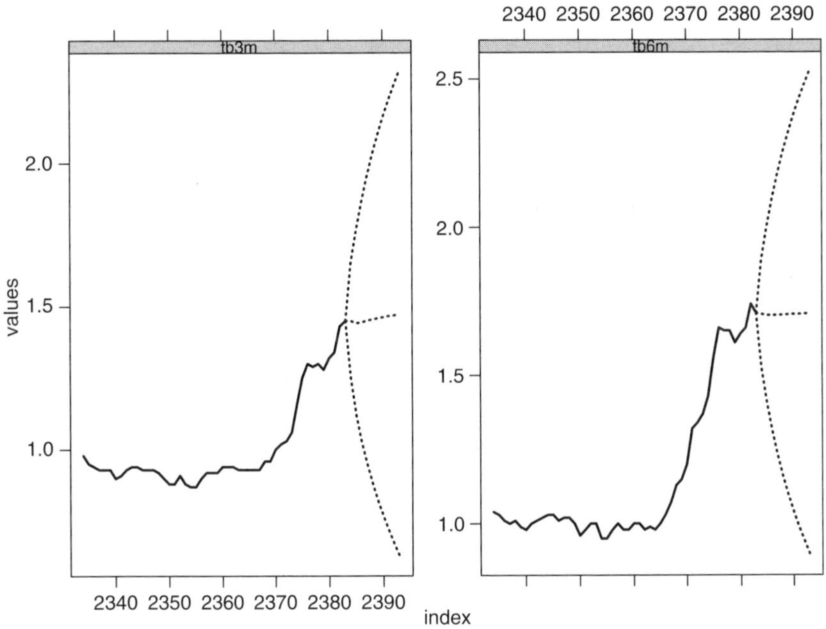

Figure 8.15. Forecasting plots of a fitted ECM model for the weekly U.S. interest rate series. The forecasts are for the interest rates and the forecast origin is August 6, 2004.

see Brenner and Kroner (1995), Dwyer, Locke, and Yu (1996), and the references therein.

The z_t^* process of model (8.43) must be unit-root stationary; otherwise there exist *persistent* arbitrage opportunities. Here an arbitrage trading consists of simultaneously buying (short-selling) the security index and selling (buying) the index futures whenever the log prices diverge by more than the cost of carrying the index over time until maturity of the futures contract. Under the weak stationarity of z_t^*, for arbitrage to be profitable, z_t^* must exceed a certain value in modulus determined by transaction costs and other economic and risk factors.

It is commonly believed that the $f_{t,\ell}$ and s_t series of the S&P 500 index contain a unit root, but Eq. (8.43) indicates that they are cointegrated after adjusting for the effect of interest rate and dividend yield. The cointegrating vector is $(1, -1)$ after the adjustment, and the cointegrated series is z_t^*. Therefore, one should use an error-correction form to model the return series $\boldsymbol{r}_t = (\Delta f_t, \Delta s_t)'$, where $\Delta f_t = f_{t,\ell} - f_{t-1,\ell}$ and $\Delta s_t = s_t - s_{t-1}$, where for ease in notation we drop the maturity time ℓ from the subscript of Δf_t.

8.7.1 Multivariate Threshold Model

In practice, arbitrage tradings affect the dynamics of the market, and hence the model for $\boldsymbol{r}_t$ may vary over time depending on the presence or absence of arbitrage tradings. Consequently, the prior discussions lead naturally to the model

$$\boldsymbol{r}_t = \begin{cases} \boldsymbol{c}_1 + \sum_{i=1}^{p} \boldsymbol{\Phi}_i^{(1)} \boldsymbol{r}_{t-i} + \boldsymbol{\beta}_1 z_{t-1} + \boldsymbol{a}_t^{(1)} & \text{if } z_{t-1} \le \gamma_1, \\ \boldsymbol{c}_2 + \sum_{i=1}^{p} \boldsymbol{\Phi}_i^{(2)} \boldsymbol{r}_{t-i} + \boldsymbol{\beta}_2 z_{t-1} + \boldsymbol{a}_t^{(2)} & \text{if } \gamma_1 < z_{t-1} \le \gamma_2, \\ \boldsymbol{c}_3 + \sum_{i=1}^{p} \boldsymbol{\Phi}_i^{(3)} \boldsymbol{r}_{t-i} + \boldsymbol{\beta}_3 z_{t-1} + \boldsymbol{a}_t^{(3)} & \text{if } \gamma_2 < z_{t-1}, \end{cases} \tag{8.44}$$

where $z_t = 100z_t^*$, $\gamma_1 < 0 < \gamma_2$ are two real numbers, and $\{\boldsymbol{a}_t^{(i)}\}$ are sequences of two-dimensional white noises and are independent of each other. Here we use $z_t = 100z_t^*$ because the actual value of z_t^* is relatively small.

The model in Eq. (8.44) is referred to as a multivariate threshold model with three regimes. The two real numbers γ_1 and γ_2 are the thresholds and z_{t-1} is the threshold variable. The threshold variable z_{t-1} is supported by the data; see Tsay (1998). In general, one can select z_{t-d} as a threshold variable by considering $d \in \{1, \ldots, d_0\}$, where d_0 is a prespecified positive integer.

Model (8.44) is a generalization of the threshold autoregressive model of Chapter 4. It is also a generalization of the error-correlation model of Eq. (8.33). As mentioned earlier, an arbitrage trading is profitable only when z_t^* or, equivalently, z_t is large in modulus. Therefore, arbitrage tradings only occurred in regimes 1 and 3 of model (8.44). As such, the dynamic relationship between $f_{t,\ell}$ and s_t in regime 2 is determined mainly by the normal market force, and hence the two series behave more or less like a random walk. In other words, the two log prices in the middle regime should be free from arbitrage effects and, hence, free from the cointegration constraint. From an econometric viewpoint, this means that the estimate of $\boldsymbol{\beta}_2$ in the middle regime should be insignificant.

In summary, we expect that the cointegration effects between the log price of the futures and the log price of security index on the cash market are significant in regimes 1 and 3, but insignificant in regime 2. This phenomenon is referred to as a *threshold cointegration*; see Balke and Fomby (1997).

8.7.2 The Data

The data used in this case study are the intraday transaction data of the S&P 500 index in May 1993 and its June futures contract traded at the Chicago Mercantile Exchange; see Forbes, Kalb, and Kofman (1999), who used the data to construct a minute-by-minute bivariate price series with 7060 observations. To avoid the undue influence of unusual returns, I replaced 10 extreme values (5 on each side) by the simple average of their two nearest neighbors. This step does not affect the qualitative conclusion of the analysis but may affect the conditional heteroscedasticity in the data. For simplicity, we do not consider conditional heteroscedasticity in the study. Figure 8.16 shows the time plots of the log returns of the index futures and cash prices and the associated threshold variable $z_t = 100z_t^*$ of model (8.43).

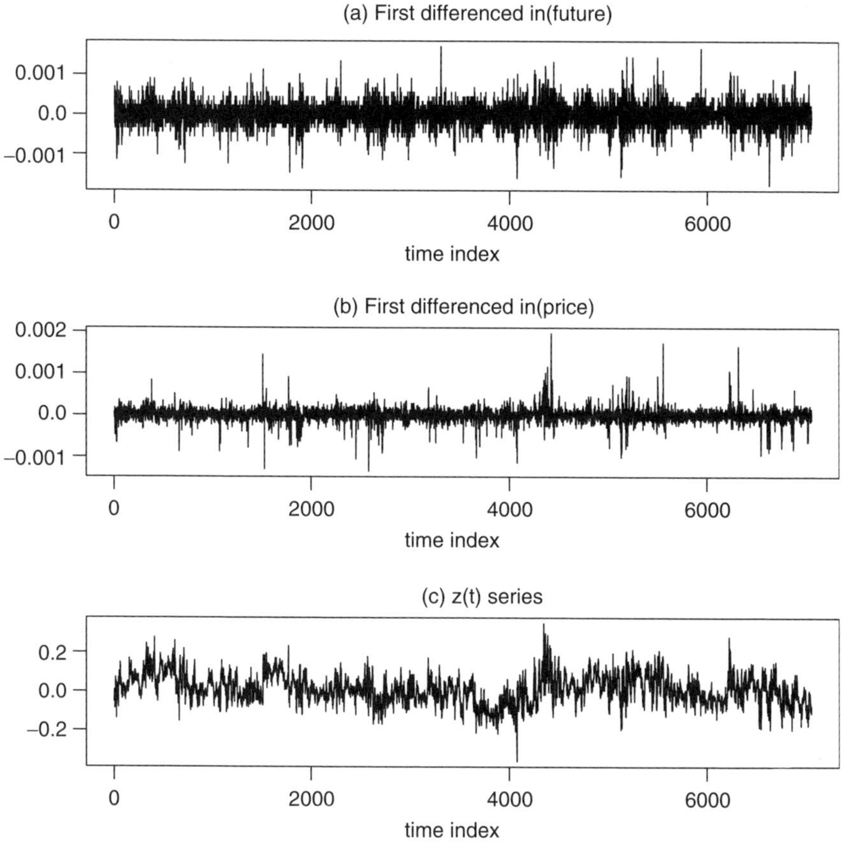

Figure 8.16. Time plots of 1-minute log returns of the S&P 500 index futures and cash prices and the associated threshold variable in May 1993: (a) log returns of the index futures, (b) log returns of the index cash prices, and (c) the z_t series.

8.7.3 Estimation

A formal specification of the multivariate threshold model in Eq. (8.44) includes selecting the threshold variable, determining the number of regimes, and choosing the order p for each regime. Interested readers are referred to Tsay (1998) and Forbes, Kalb, and Kofman (1999). The thresholds γ_1 and γ_2 can be estimated by using some information criteria (e.g., the Akaike information criterion [AIC] or the sum of squares of residuals). Assuming $p = 8$, $d \in \{1, 2, 3, 4\}$, $\gamma_1 \in [-0.15, -0.02]$, and $\gamma_2 \in [0.025, 0.145]$, and using a grid search method with 300 points on each of the two intervals, the AIC selects z_{t-1} as the threshold variable with thresholds $\hat{\gamma}_1 = -0.0226$ and $\hat{\gamma}_2 = 0.0377$. Details of the parameter estimates are given in Table 8.8.

From Table 8.8, we make the following observations. First, the t-ratios of $\widehat{\boldsymbol{\beta}}_2$ in the middle regime show that, as expected, the estimates are insignificant at the 5% level, confirming that there is no cointegration between the two log prices in

Table 8.8. Least Squares Estimates and Their t-Ratios of the Multivariate Threshold Model in Eq. (8.44) for the S&P 500 Index Data in May 1993[a]

	Regime 1		Regime 2		Regime 3	
	Δf_t	Δs_t	Δf_t	Δs_t	Δf_t	Δs_t
ϕ_0	0.00002	0.00005	0.00000	0.00000	−0.00001	−0.00005
t	(1.47)	(7.64)	(−0.07)	(0.53)	(−0.74)	(−6.37)
Δf_{t-1}	−0.08468	0.07098	−0.03861	0.04037	−0.04102	0.02305
t	(−3.83)	(6.15)	(−1.53)	(3.98)	(−1.72)	(1.96)
Δf_{t-2}	−0.00450	0.15899	0.04478	0.08621	−0.02069	0.09898
t	(−0.20)	(13.36)	(1.85)	(8.88)	(−0.87)	(8.45)
Δf_{t-3}	0.02274	0.11911	0.07251	0.09752	0.00365	0.08455
t	(0.95)	(9.53)	(3.08)	(10.32)	(0.15)	(7.02)
Δf_{t-4}	0.02429	0.08141	0.01418	0.06827	−0.02759	0.07699
t	(0.99)	(6.35)	(0.60)	(7.24)	(−1.13)	(6.37)
Δf_{t-5}	0.00340	0.08936	0.01185	0.04831	−0.00638	0.05004
t	(0.14)	(7.10)	(0.51)	(5.13)	(−0.26)	(4.07)
Δf_{t-6}	0.00098	0.07291	0.01251	0.03580	−0.03941	0.02615
t	(0.04)	(5.64)	(0.54)	(3.84)	(−1.62)	(2.18)
Δf_{t-7}	−0.00372	0.05201	0.02989	0.04837	−0.02031	0.02293
t	(−0.15)	(4.01)	(1.34)	(5.42)	(−0.85)	(1.95)
Δf_{t-8}	0.00043	0.00954	0.01812	0.02196	−0.04422	0.00462
t	(0.02)	(0.76)	(0.85)	(2.57)	(−1.90)	(0.40)
Δs_{t-1}	−0.08419	0.00264	−0.07618	−0.05633	0.06664	0.11143
t	(−2.01)	(0.12)	(−1.70)	(−3.14)	(1.49)	(5.05)
Δs_{t-2}	−0.05103	0.00256	−0.10920	−0.01521	0.04099	−0.01179
t	(−1.18)	(0.11)	(−2.59)	(−0.90)	(0.92)	(−0.53)
Δs_{t-3}	0.07275	−0.03631	−0.00504	0.01174	−0.01948	−0.01829
t	(1.65)	(−1.58)	(−0.12)	(0.71)	(−0.44)	(−0.84)
Δs_{t-4}	0.04706	0.01438	0.02751	0.01490	0.01646	0.00367
t	(1.03)	(0.60)	(0.71)	(0.96)	(0.37)	(0.17)
Δs_{t-5}	0.08118	0.02111	0.03943	0.02330	−0.03430	−0.00462
t	(1.77)	(0.88)	(0.97)	(1.43)	(−0.83)	(−0.23)
Δs_{t-6}	0.04390	0.04569	0.01690	0.01919	0.06084	−0.00392
t	(0.96)	(1.92)	(0.44)	(1.25)	(1.45)	(−0.19)
Δs_{t-7}	−0.03033	0.02051	−0.08647	0.00270	−0.00491	0.03597
t	(−0.70)	(0.91)	(−2.09)	(0.16)	(−0.13)	(1.90)
Δs_{t-8}	−0.02920	0.03018	0.01887	−0.00213	0.00030	0.02171
t	(−0.68)	(1.34)	(0.49)	(−0.14)	(0.01)	(1.14)
z_{t-1}	0.00024	0.00097	−0.00010	0.00012	0.00025	0.00086
t	(1.34)	(10.47)	(−0.30)	(0.86)	(1.41)	(9.75)

[a]The number of data points for the three regimes are 2234, 2410, and 2408, respectively.

the absence of arbitrage opportunities. Second, Δf_t depends negatively on Δf_{t-1} in all three regimes. This is in agreement with the bid–ask bounce discussed in Chapter 5. Third, past log returns of the index futures seem to be more informative than the past log returns of the cash prices because there are more significant t-ratios in Δf_{t-i} than in Δs_{t-i}. This is reasonable because futures series are in general more liquid. For more information on index arbitrage, see Dwyer, Locke, and Yu (1996).

APPENDIX A: REVIEW OF VECTORS AND MATRICES

In this appendix, we briefly review some algebra and properties of vectors and matrices. No proofs are given as they can be found in standard textbooks on matrices (e.g., Graybill, 1969).

An $m \times n$ real-valued matrix is an m by n array of real numbers. For example,

$$\boldsymbol{A} = \begin{bmatrix} 2 & 5 & 8 \\ -1 & 3 & 4 \end{bmatrix}$$

is a 2×3 matrix. This matrix has two rows and three columns. In general, an $m \times n$ matrix is written as

$$\boldsymbol{A} \equiv [a_{ij}] = \begin{bmatrix} a_{11} & a_{12} & \cdots & a_{1,n-1} & a_{1n} \\ a_{21} & a_{22} & \cdots & a_{2,n-1} & a_{2n} \\ \vdots & \vdots & & \vdots & \vdots \\ a_{m1} & a_{m2} & \cdots & a_{m,n-1} & a_{mn} \end{bmatrix}. \tag{8.45}$$

The positive integers m and n are the *row dimension* and *column dimension* of $\boldsymbol{A}$. The real number a_{ij} is referred to as the (i, j)th element of $\boldsymbol{A}$. In particular, the elements a_{ii} are the *diagonal elements* of the matrix.

An $m \times 1$ matrix forms an m-dimensional column vector, and a $1 \times n$ matrix is an n-dimensional row vector. In the literature, a vector is often meant to be a column vector. If $m = n$, then the matrix is a square matrix. If $a_{ij} = 0$ for $i \neq j$ and $m = n$, then the matrix $\boldsymbol{A}$ is a *diagonal matrix*. If $a_{ij} = 0$ for $i \neq j$ and $a_{ii} = 1$ for all i, then $\boldsymbol{A}$ is the $m \times m$ *identity matrix*, which is commonly denoted by $\boldsymbol{I}_m$ or simply $\boldsymbol{I}$ if the dimension is clear.

The $n \times m$ matrix

$$\boldsymbol{A}' = \begin{bmatrix} a_{11} & a_{21} & \cdots & a_{m-1,1} & a_{m1} \\ a_{12} & a_{22} & \cdots & a_{m-1,2} & a_{m2} \\ \vdots & \vdots & & \vdots & \vdots \\ a_{1n} & a_{2n} & \cdots & a_{m-1,n} & a_{mn} \end{bmatrix}$$

is the *transpose* of the matrix $\boldsymbol{A}$. For example,

$$\begin{bmatrix} 2 & -1 \\ 5 & 3 \\ 8 & 4 \end{bmatrix} \quad \text{is the transpose of} \quad \begin{bmatrix} 2 & 5 & 8 \\ -1 & 3 & 4 \end{bmatrix}.$$

We use the notation $\boldsymbol{A}' = [a'_{ij}]$ to denote the transpose of $\boldsymbol{A}$. From the definition, $a'_{ij} = a_{ji}$ and $(\boldsymbol{A}')' = \boldsymbol{A}$. If $\boldsymbol{A}' = \boldsymbol{A}$, then $\boldsymbol{A}$ is a *symmetric matrix*.

Basic Operations

Suppose that $\boldsymbol{A} = [a_{ij}]_{m\times n}$ and $\boldsymbol{C} = [c_{ij}]_{p\times q}$ are two matrices with dimensions given in the subscript. Let b be a real number. Some basic matrix operations are defined next:

- Addition: $\boldsymbol{A} + \boldsymbol{C} = [a_{ij} + c_{ij}]_{m\times n}$ if $m = p$ and $n = q$.
- Subtraction: $\boldsymbol{A} - \boldsymbol{C} = [a_{ij} - c_{ij}]_{m\times n}$ if $m = p$ and $n = q$.
- Scalar multiplication: $b\boldsymbol{A} = [ba_{ij}]_{m\times n}$.
- Multiplication: $\boldsymbol{AC} = [\sum_{v=1}^{n} a_{iv}c_{vj}]_{m\times q}$ provided that $n = p$.

When the dimensions of matrices satisfy the condition for multiplication to take place, the two matrices are said to be *conformable*. An example of matrix multiplication is

$$\begin{bmatrix} 2 & 1 \\ 1 & 1 \end{bmatrix}\begin{bmatrix} 1 & 2 & 3 \\ -1 & 2 & -4 \end{bmatrix} = \begin{bmatrix} 2\cdot 1 - 1\cdot 1 & 2\cdot 2 + 1\cdot 2 & 2\cdot 3 - 1\cdot 4 \\ 1\cdot 1 - 1\cdot 1 & 1\cdot 2 + 1\cdot 2 & 1\cdot 3 - 1\cdot 4 \end{bmatrix}$$
$$= \begin{bmatrix} 1 & 6 & 2 \\ 0 & 4 & -1 \end{bmatrix}.$$

Important rules of matrix operations include (a) $(\boldsymbol{AC})' = \boldsymbol{C}'\boldsymbol{A}'$ and (b) $\boldsymbol{AC} \neq \boldsymbol{CA}$ in general.

Inverse, Trace, Eigenvalue, and Eigenvector

A square matrix $\boldsymbol{A}_{m\times m}$ is *nonsingular* or *invertible* if there exists a unique matrix $\boldsymbol{C}_{m\times m}$ such that $\boldsymbol{AC} = \boldsymbol{CA} = \boldsymbol{I}_m$, the $m \times m$ identity matrix. In this case, $\boldsymbol{C}$ is called the *inverse* matrix of $\boldsymbol{A}$ and is denoted by $\boldsymbol{C} = \boldsymbol{A}^{-1}$.

The trace of $\boldsymbol{A}_{m\times m}$ is the sum of its diagonal elements (i.e., $tr(\boldsymbol{A}) = \sum_{i=1}^{m} a_{ii}$). It is easy to see that (a) $tr(\boldsymbol{A} + \boldsymbol{C}) = tr(\boldsymbol{A}) + tr(\boldsymbol{C})$, (b) $tr(\boldsymbol{A}) = tr(\boldsymbol{A}')$, and (c) $tr(\boldsymbol{AC}) = tr(\boldsymbol{CA})$ provided that the two matrices are conformable.

A number λ and an $m \times 1$ vector $\boldsymbol{b}$, possibly complex-valued, are a right *eigenvalue* and *eigenvector* pair of the matrix $\boldsymbol{A}$ if $\boldsymbol{Ab} = \lambda\boldsymbol{b}$. There are m possible eigenvalues for the matrix $\boldsymbol{A}$. For a real-valued matrix $\boldsymbol{A}$, complex eigenvalues occur in conjugated pairs. The matrix $\boldsymbol{A}$ is nonsingular if and only if all of its eigenvalues are nonzero. Denote the eigenvalues by $\{\lambda_i | i = 1, \ldots, m\}$: we have $tr(\boldsymbol{A}) = \sum_{i=1}^{m} \lambda_i$. In addition, the *determinant* of the matrix $\boldsymbol{A}$ can be defined as $|\boldsymbol{A}| = \prod_{i=1}^{m} \lambda_i$. For a general definition of determinant of a matrix, see a standard textbook on matrices (e.g., Graybill, 1969).

Finally, the rank of the matrix $\boldsymbol{A}_{m\times n}$ is the number of nonzero eigenvalues of the symmetric matrix $\boldsymbol{AA}'$. Also, for a nonsingular matrix $\boldsymbol{A}$, $(\boldsymbol{A}^{-1})' = (\boldsymbol{A}')^{-1}$.

Positive-Definite Matrix

A square matrix $\boldsymbol{A}$ ($m \times m$) is a *positive-definite* matrix if (a) $\boldsymbol{A}$ is symmetric, and (b) all eigenvalues of $\boldsymbol{A}$ are positive. Alternatively, $\boldsymbol{A}$ is a positive-definite matrix if for any nonzero m-dimensional vector $\boldsymbol{b}$, we have $\boldsymbol{b}'\boldsymbol{Ab} > 0$.

Useful properties of a positive-definite matrix $\boldsymbol{A}$ include (a) all eigenvalues of $\boldsymbol{A}$ are real and positive, and (b) the matrix can be decomposed as

$$\boldsymbol{A} = \boldsymbol{P\Lambda P}',$$

where $\boldsymbol{\Lambda}$ is a diagonal matrix consisting of all eigenvalues of $\boldsymbol{A}$ and $\boldsymbol{P}$ is an $m \times m$ matrix consisting of the m right eigenvectors of $\boldsymbol{A}$. It is common to write the eigenvalues as $\lambda_1 \geq \lambda_2 \geq \cdots \geq \lambda_m$ and the eigenvectors as $\boldsymbol{e}_1, \ldots, \boldsymbol{e}_m$ such that $\boldsymbol{A}\boldsymbol{e}_i = \lambda_i \boldsymbol{e}_i$ and $\boldsymbol{e}_i'\boldsymbol{e}_i = 1$. In addition, these eigenvectors are orthogonal to each other—namely, $\boldsymbol{e}_i'\boldsymbol{e}_j = 0$ if $i \neq j$—if the eigenvalues are distinct. The matrix $\boldsymbol{P}$ is an *orthogonal* matrix and the decomposition is referred to as the *spectral decomposition* of the matrix $\boldsymbol{A}$. Consider, for example, the simple 2×2 matrix

$$\boldsymbol{\Sigma} = \begin{bmatrix} 2 & 1 \\ 1 & 2 \end{bmatrix},$$

which is positive definite. Simple calculations show that

$$\begin{bmatrix} 2 & 1 \\ 1 & 2 \end{bmatrix}\begin{bmatrix} 1 \\ 1 \end{bmatrix} = 3\begin{bmatrix} 1 \\ 1 \end{bmatrix}, \quad \begin{bmatrix} 2 & 1 \\ 1 & 2 \end{bmatrix}\begin{bmatrix} 1 \\ -1 \end{bmatrix} = \begin{bmatrix} 1 \\ -1 \end{bmatrix}.$$

Therefore, 3 and 1 are eigenvalues of $\boldsymbol{\Sigma}$ with normalized eigenvectors $(1/\sqrt{2}, 1/\sqrt{2})'$ and $(1/\sqrt{2}, -1/\sqrt{2})'$, respectively. It is easy to verify that the spectral decomposition holds—that is,

$$\begin{bmatrix} \frac{1}{\sqrt{2}} & \frac{1}{\sqrt{2}} \\ \frac{1}{\sqrt{2}} & \frac{-1}{\sqrt{2}} \end{bmatrix}\begin{bmatrix} 2 & 1 \\ 1 & 2 \end{bmatrix}\begin{bmatrix} \frac{1}{\sqrt{2}} & \frac{1}{\sqrt{2}} \\ \frac{1}{\sqrt{2}} & \frac{-1}{\sqrt{2}} \end{bmatrix} = \begin{bmatrix} 3 & 0 \\ 0 & 1 \end{bmatrix}.$$

For a symmetric matrix $\boldsymbol{A}$, there exists a lower triangular matrix $\boldsymbol{L}$ with diagonal elements being 1 and a diagonal matrix $\boldsymbol{G}$ such that $\boldsymbol{A} = \boldsymbol{L}\boldsymbol{G}\boldsymbol{L}'$; see Chapter 1 of Strang (1980). If $\boldsymbol{A}$ is positive definite, then the diagonal elements of $\boldsymbol{G}$ are positive. In this case, we have

$$\boldsymbol{A} = \boldsymbol{L}\sqrt{\boldsymbol{G}}\sqrt{\boldsymbol{G}}\boldsymbol{L}' = (\boldsymbol{L}\sqrt{\boldsymbol{G}})(\boldsymbol{L}\sqrt{\boldsymbol{G}})',$$

where $\boldsymbol{L}\sqrt{\boldsymbol{G}}$ is again a lower triangular matrix and the square root is taken element by element. Such a decomposition is called the *Cholesky decomposition* of $\boldsymbol{A}$. This decomposition shows that a positive-definite matrix $\boldsymbol{A}$ can be diagonalized as

$$\boldsymbol{L}^{-1}\boldsymbol{A}(\boldsymbol{L}')^{-1} = \boldsymbol{L}^{-1}\boldsymbol{A}(\boldsymbol{L}^{-1})' = \boldsymbol{G}.$$

Since $\boldsymbol{L}$ is a lower triangular matrix with unit diagonal elements, $\boldsymbol{L}^{-1}$ is also a lower triangular matrix with unit diagonal elements. Consider again the prior 2×2 matrix $\boldsymbol{\Sigma}$. It is easy to verify that

$$\boldsymbol{L} = \begin{bmatrix} 1.0 & 0.0 \\ 0.5 & 1.0 \end{bmatrix} \quad \text{and} \quad \boldsymbol{G} = \begin{bmatrix} 2.0 & 0.0 \\ 0.0 & 1.5 \end{bmatrix}$$

satisfy $\boldsymbol{\Sigma} = \boldsymbol{L}\boldsymbol{G}\boldsymbol{L}'$. In addition,

$$\boldsymbol{L}^{-1} = \begin{bmatrix} 1.0 & 0.0 \\ -0.5 & 1.0 \end{bmatrix} \quad \text{and} \quad \boldsymbol{L}^{-1}\boldsymbol{\Sigma}(\boldsymbol{L}^{-1})' = \boldsymbol{G}.$$

Vectorization and Kronecker Product

Writing an $m \times n$ matrix $\boldsymbol{A}$ in its columns as $\boldsymbol{A} = [\boldsymbol{a}_1, \ldots, \boldsymbol{a}_n]$, we define the stacking operation as $\text{vec}(\boldsymbol{A}) = (\boldsymbol{a}_1', \boldsymbol{a}_2', \ldots, \boldsymbol{a}_m')'$, which is an $mn \times 1$ vector. For two matrices $\boldsymbol{A}_{m\times n}$ and $\boldsymbol{C}_{p\times q}$, the Kronecker product between $\boldsymbol{A}$ and $\boldsymbol{C}$ is

$$\boldsymbol{A} \otimes \boldsymbol{C} = \begin{bmatrix} a_{11}\boldsymbol{C} & a_{12}\boldsymbol{C} & \cdots & a_{1n}\boldsymbol{C} \\ a_{21}\boldsymbol{C} & a_{22}\boldsymbol{C} & \cdots & a_{2n}\boldsymbol{C} \\ \vdots & \vdots & & \vdots \\ a_{m1}\boldsymbol{C} & a_{m2}\boldsymbol{C} & \cdots & a_{mn}\boldsymbol{C} \end{bmatrix}_{mp\times nq}.$$

For example, assume that

$$\boldsymbol{A} = \begin{bmatrix} 2 & 1 \\ -1 & 3 \end{bmatrix}, \quad \boldsymbol{C} = \begin{bmatrix} 4 & -1 & 3 \\ -2 & 5 & 2 \end{bmatrix}.$$

Then $\text{vec}(\boldsymbol{A}) = (2, -1, 1, 3)'$, $\text{vec}(\boldsymbol{C}) = (4, -2, -1, 5, 3, 2)'$, and

$$\boldsymbol{A} \otimes \boldsymbol{C} = \begin{bmatrix} 8 & -2 & 6 & 4 & -1 & 3 \\ -4 & 10 & 4 & -2 & 5 & 2 \\ -4 & 1 & -3 & 12 & -3 & 9 \\ 2 & -5 & -2 & -6 & 15 & 6 \end{bmatrix}.$$

Assuming that the dimensions are appropriate, we have the following useful properties for the two operators:

1. $\boldsymbol{A} \otimes \boldsymbol{C} \neq \boldsymbol{C} \otimes \boldsymbol{A}$ in general.
2. $(\boldsymbol{A} \otimes \boldsymbol{C})' = \boldsymbol{A}' \otimes \boldsymbol{C}'$.
3. $\boldsymbol{A} \otimes (\boldsymbol{C} + \boldsymbol{D}) = \boldsymbol{A} \otimes \boldsymbol{C} + \boldsymbol{A} \otimes \boldsymbol{D}$.
4. $(\boldsymbol{A} \otimes \boldsymbol{C})(\boldsymbol{F} \otimes \boldsymbol{G}) = (\boldsymbol{AF}) \otimes (\boldsymbol{CG})$.
5. If $\boldsymbol{A}$ and $\boldsymbol{C}$ are invertible, then $(\boldsymbol{A} \otimes \boldsymbol{C})^{-1} = \boldsymbol{A}^{-1} \otimes \boldsymbol{C}^{-1}$.
6. For square matrices $\boldsymbol{A}$ and $\boldsymbol{C}$, $tr(\boldsymbol{A} \otimes \boldsymbol{C}) = tr(\boldsymbol{A})tr(\boldsymbol{C})$.
7. $\text{vec}(\boldsymbol{A} + \boldsymbol{C}) = \text{vec}(\boldsymbol{A}) + \text{vec}(\boldsymbol{C})$.
8. $\text{vec}(\boldsymbol{ABC}) = (\boldsymbol{C}' \otimes \boldsymbol{A})\text{vec}(\boldsymbol{B})$.
9. $tr(\boldsymbol{AC}) = \text{vec}(\boldsymbol{C}')'\text{vec}(\boldsymbol{A}) = \text{vec}(\boldsymbol{A}')'\text{vec}(\boldsymbol{C})$.
10. $$\begin{aligned} tr(\boldsymbol{ABC}) &= \text{vec}(\boldsymbol{A}')'(\boldsymbol{C}' \otimes \boldsymbol{I})\text{vec}(\boldsymbol{B}) = \text{vec}(\boldsymbol{A}')'(\boldsymbol{I} \otimes \boldsymbol{B})\text{vec}(\boldsymbol{C}) \\ &= \text{vec}(\boldsymbol{B}')'(\boldsymbol{A}' \otimes \boldsymbol{I})\text{vec}(\boldsymbol{C}) = \text{vec}(\boldsymbol{B}')'(\boldsymbol{I} \otimes \boldsymbol{C})\text{vec}(\boldsymbol{A}) \\ &= \text{vec}(\boldsymbol{C}')'(\boldsymbol{B}' \otimes \boldsymbol{I})\text{vec}(\boldsymbol{A}) = \text{vec}(\boldsymbol{C}')'(\boldsymbol{I} \otimes \boldsymbol{A})\text{vec}(\boldsymbol{B}). \end{aligned}$$

In multivariate statistical analysis, we often deal with symmetric matrices. It is therefore convenient to generalize the stacking operation to the *half-stacking* operation, which consists of elements on or below the main diagonal. Specifically, for a symmetric square matrix $\boldsymbol{A} = [a_{ij}]_{k\times k}$, define

$$\text{vech}(\boldsymbol{A}) = (\boldsymbol{a}_{1.}', \boldsymbol{a}_{2*}', \ldots, \boldsymbol{a}_{k*}')',$$

where $\boldsymbol{a}_{1.}$ is the first column of $\boldsymbol{A}$, and $\boldsymbol{a}_{i*} = (a_{ii}, a_{i+1,i}, \ldots, a_{ki})'$ is a $(k-i+1)$-dimensional vector. The dimension of vech($\boldsymbol{A}$) is $k(k+1)/2$. For example, suppose that $k=3$. Then we have $\text{vech}(\boldsymbol{A}) = (a_{11}, a_{21}, a_{31}, a_{22}, a_{32}, a_{33})'$, which is a six-dimensional vector.

APPENDIX B: MULTIVARIATE NORMAL DISTRIBUTIONS

A k-dimensional random vector $\boldsymbol{x} = (x_1, \ldots, x_k)'$ follows a multivariate normal distribution with mean $\boldsymbol{\mu} = (\mu_1, \ldots, \mu_k)'$ and positive-definite covariance matrix $\boldsymbol{\Sigma} = [\sigma_{ij}]$ if its probability density function (pdf) is

$$f(\boldsymbol{x}|\boldsymbol{\mu}, \boldsymbol{\Sigma}) = \frac{1}{(2\pi)^{k/2}|\boldsymbol{\Sigma}|^{1/2}} \exp[-\tfrac{1}{2}(\boldsymbol{x}-\boldsymbol{\mu})'\boldsymbol{\Sigma}^{-1}(\boldsymbol{x}-\boldsymbol{\mu})]. \tag{8.46}$$

We use the notation $\boldsymbol{x} \sim N_k(\boldsymbol{\mu}, \boldsymbol{\Sigma})$ to denote that $\boldsymbol{x}$ follows such a distribution. This normal distribution plays an important role in multivariate statistical analysis and it has several nice properties. Here we consider only those properties that are relevant to our study. Interested readers are referred to Johnson and Wichern (1998) for details.

To gain insight into multivariate normal distributions, consider the bivariate case (i.e., $k=2$). In this case, we have

$$\boldsymbol{\Sigma} = \begin{bmatrix} \sigma_{11} & \sigma_{12} \\ \sigma_{12} & \sigma_{22} \end{bmatrix}, \quad \boldsymbol{\Sigma}^{-1} = \frac{1}{\sigma_{11}\sigma_{22} - \sigma_{12}^2} \begin{bmatrix} \sigma_{22} & -\sigma_{12} \\ -\sigma_{12} & \sigma_{11} \end{bmatrix}.$$

Using the correlation coefficient $\rho = \sigma_{12}/(\sigma_1\sigma_2)$, where $\sigma_i = \sqrt{\sigma_{ii}}$ is the standard deviation of x_i, we have $\sigma_{12} = \rho\sqrt{\sigma_{11}\sigma_{22}}$ and $|\boldsymbol{\Sigma}| = \sigma_{11}\sigma_{22}(1-\rho^2)$. The pdf of $\boldsymbol{x}$ then becomes

$$f(x_1, x_2|\boldsymbol{\mu}, \boldsymbol{\Sigma}) = \frac{1}{2\pi\sigma_1\sigma_2\sqrt{1-\rho^2}} \exp\left(-\frac{1}{2(1-\rho^2)}[Q(\boldsymbol{x}, \boldsymbol{\mu}, \boldsymbol{\Sigma})]\right),$$

where

$$Q(\boldsymbol{x}, \boldsymbol{\mu}, \boldsymbol{\Sigma}) = \left(\frac{x_1-\mu_1}{\sigma_1}\right)^2 + \left(\frac{x_2-\mu_2}{\sigma_2}\right)^2 - 2\rho\left(\frac{x_1-\mu_1}{\sigma_1}\right)\left(\frac{x_2-\mu_2}{\sigma_2}\right).$$

Chapter 4 of Johnson and Wichern (1998) contains some plots of this pdf function.

Let $\boldsymbol{c} = (c_1, \ldots, c_k)'$ be a nonzero k-dimensional vector. Partition the random vector as $\boldsymbol{x} = (\boldsymbol{x}_1', \boldsymbol{x}_2')'$, where $\boldsymbol{x}_1 = (x_1, \ldots, x_p)'$ and $\boldsymbol{x}_2 = (x_{p+1}, \ldots, x_k)'$ with $1 \le p < k$. Also partition $\boldsymbol{\mu}$ and $\boldsymbol{\Sigma}$ accordingly as

$$\begin{bmatrix} \boldsymbol{x}_1 \\ \boldsymbol{x}_2 \end{bmatrix} \sim N\left(\begin{bmatrix} \boldsymbol{\mu}_1 \\ \boldsymbol{\mu}_2 \end{bmatrix}, \begin{bmatrix} \boldsymbol{\Sigma}_{11} & \boldsymbol{\Sigma}_{12} \\ \boldsymbol{\Sigma}_{21} & \boldsymbol{\Sigma}_{22} \end{bmatrix}\right).$$

Some properties of $\boldsymbol{x}$ are as follows:

1. $\boldsymbol{c}'\boldsymbol{x} \sim N(\boldsymbol{c}'\boldsymbol{\mu}, \boldsymbol{c}'\boldsymbol{\Sigma}\boldsymbol{c})$. That is, any nonzero linear combination of $\boldsymbol{x}$ is univariate normal. The inverse of this property also holds. Specifically, if $\boldsymbol{c}'\boldsymbol{x}$ is univariate normal for any nonzero vector $\boldsymbol{c}$, then $\boldsymbol{x}$ is multivariate normal.

2. The marginal distribution of $\boldsymbol{x}_i$ is normal. In fact, $\boldsymbol{x}_i \sim N_{k_i}(\boldsymbol{\mu}_i, \boldsymbol{\Sigma}_{ii})$ for $i = 1$ and 2, where $k_1 = p$ and $k_2 = k - p$.
3. $\boldsymbol{\Sigma}_{12} = \boldsymbol{0}$ if and only if $\boldsymbol{x}_1$ and $\boldsymbol{x}_2$ are independent.
4. The random variable $y = (\boldsymbol{x} - \boldsymbol{\mu})'\boldsymbol{\Sigma}^{-1}(\boldsymbol{x} - \boldsymbol{\mu})$ follows a chi-squared distribution with m degrees of freedom.
5. The conditional distribution of $\boldsymbol{x}_1$ given $\boldsymbol{x}_2 = \boldsymbol{b}$ is also normally distributed as

$$(\boldsymbol{x}_1|\boldsymbol{x}_2 = \boldsymbol{b}) \sim N_p[\boldsymbol{\mu}_1 + \boldsymbol{\Sigma}_{12}\boldsymbol{\Sigma}_{22}^{-1}(\boldsymbol{b} - \boldsymbol{\mu}_2), \boldsymbol{\Sigma}_{11} - \boldsymbol{\Sigma}_{12}\boldsymbol{\Sigma}_{22}^{-1}\boldsymbol{\Sigma}_{21}].$$

The last property is useful in many scientific areas. For instance, it forms the basis for time series forecasting under the normality assumption and for recursive least squares estimation.

APPENDIX C: SOME SCA COMMANDS

The following SCA commands are used in the analysis of Example 8.6.

```
input x1,x2. file 'm-gs1n3-5301.txt'  % Load data
 --
r1=ln(x1)  % Take log transformation
 --
r2=ln(x2)
 --
miden r1,r2. no ccm. arfits 1 to 8.
 --  % Denote the model by v21.
mtsm v21. series r1,r2.  @
model (i-p1*b-p2*b**2)series=c+(i-t1*b)noise.
 --
mestim v21.   % Initial estimation
 --
p1(2,1)=0     % Set zero constraints
 --
cp1(2,1)=1
 --
p2(2,1)=0
 --
cp2(2,1)=1
 --
p2(2,2)=0
 --
cp2(2,2)=1
 --
t1(2,1)=0
 --
ct1(2,1)=1
 -- % Refine estimation and store residuals
mestim v21. method exact. hold resi(res1,res2)
 --
miden res1,res2.
```

EXERCISES

8.1. Consider the monthly log stock returns, in percentages and including dividends, of Merck & Company, Johnson & Johnson, General Electric, General Motors, Ford Motor Company, and value-weighted index from January 1960 to December 1999; see the file `m-mrk2vw.txt`, which has six columns in the order listed before.

(a) Compute the sample mean, covariance matrix, and correlation matrix of the data.

(b) Test the hypothesis $H_o: \boldsymbol{\rho}_1 = \cdots = \boldsymbol{\rho}_6 = \mathbf{0}$, where $\boldsymbol{\rho}_i$ is the lag-i cross-correlation matrix of the data. Draw conclusions based on the 5% significance level.

(c) Is there any lead–lag relationship among the six return series?

8.2. The Federal Reserve Bank of St. Louis publishes selected interest rates and U.S. financial data on its Web site: `http://research.stlouisfed.org/fred2/`. Consider the monthly 1-year and 10-year Treasury constant maturity rates from April 1953 to October 2000 for 571 observations; see the file `m-gs1n10.txt`. The rates are in percentages.

(a) Let $c_t = r_t - r_{t-1}$ be the change series of the monthly interest rate r_t. Build a bivariate autoregressive model for the two change series. Discuss the implications of the model. Transform the model into a structural form.

(b) Build a bivariate moving-average model for the two change series. Discuss the implications of the model and compare it with the bivariate AR model built earlier.

8.3. Again consider the monthly 1-year and 10-year Treasury constant maturity rates from April 1953 to October 2000. Consider the log series of the data and build a VARMA model for the series. Discuss the implications of the model obtained.

8.4. Again consider the monthly 1-year and 10-year Treasury constant maturity rates from April 1953 to October 2000. Are the two interest rate series threshold-cointegrated? Use the interest spread $s_t = r_{10,t} - r_{1,t}$ as the threshold variable, where r_{it} is the i-year Treasury constant maturity rate. If they are threshold-cointegrated, build a multivariate threshold model for the two series.

8.5. The bivariate AR(4) model $\boldsymbol{x}_t - \boldsymbol{\Phi}_4 \boldsymbol{x}_{t-4} = \boldsymbol{\phi}_0 + \boldsymbol{a}_t$ is a special seasonal model with periodicity 4, where $\{\boldsymbol{a}_t\}$ is a sequence of independent and identically distributed normal random vectors with mean zero and covariance matrix $\boldsymbol{\Sigma}$. Such a seasonal model may be useful in studying quarterly earnings of a company. (a) Assume that $\boldsymbol{x}_t$ is weakly stationary. Derive the mean vector and covariance matrix of $\boldsymbol{x}_t$. (b) Derive the necessary and sufficient condition of weak stationarity for $\boldsymbol{x}_t$. (c) Show that $\boldsymbol{\Gamma}_\ell = \boldsymbol{\Phi}_4 \boldsymbol{\Gamma}_{\ell-4}$ for $\ell > 0$, where $\boldsymbol{\Gamma}_\ell$ is the lag-ℓ autocovariance matrix of $\boldsymbol{x}_t$.

8.6. The bivariate MA(4) model $\boldsymbol{x}_t = \boldsymbol{a}_t - \boldsymbol{\Theta}_4 \boldsymbol{a}_{t-4}$ is another seasonal model with periodicity 4, where $\{\boldsymbol{a}_t\}$ is a sequence of independent and identically distributed normal random vectors with mean zero and covariance matrix $\boldsymbol{\Sigma}$. Derive the covariance matrices $\boldsymbol{\Gamma}_\ell$ of $\boldsymbol{x}_t$ for $\ell = 0, \ldots, 5$.

8.7. Consider the monthly U.S. 1-year and 3-year Treasury constant maturity rates from April 1953 to March 2004. The data can be obtained from the Federal Reserve Bank of St. Louis or from the file `m-gs1n3-5304.txt` (1-year, 3-year, dates). See also Example 8.6 that uses a shorter data span. Here we use the interest rates directly without the log transformation and define $\boldsymbol{x}_t = (x_{1t}, x_{2t})'$, where x_{1t} is the 1-year maturity rate and x_{2t} is the 3-year maturity rate.

(a) Identify a VAR model for the bivariate interest rate series. Write down the fitted model.

(b) Compute the impulse response functions of the fitted VAR model. It suffices to use the first 6 lags.

(c) Use the fitted VAR model to produce 1-step to 12-step ahead forecasts of the interest rates, assuming that the forecast origin is March 2004.

(d) Are the two interest rate series cointegrated, when a restricted constant term is used? Use 5% significance level to perform the test.

(e) If the series are cointegrated, build an ECM for the series. Write down the fitted model.

(f) Use the fitted ECM to produce 1-step to 12-step ahead forecasts of the interest rates, assuming that the forecast origin is March 2004.

(g) Compare the forecasts produced by the VAR model and the ECM.

REFERENCES

Balke, N. S. and Fomby, T. B. (1997). Threshold cointegration. *International Economic Review* **38**: 627–645.

Box, G. E. P. and Tiao, G. C. (1977). A canonical analysis of multiple time series. *Biometrika* **64**: 355–366.

Brenner, R. J. and Kroner, K. F. (1995). Arbitrage, cointegration, and testing the unbiasedness hypothesis in financial markets. *Journal of Financial and Quantitative Analysis* **30**: 23–42.

Cochrane, J. H. (1988). How big is the random walk in the GNP? *Journal of Political Economy* **96**: 893–920.

Dwyer, G. P. Jr., Locke, P., and Yu, W. (1996). Index arbitrage and nonlinear dynamics between the S&P 500 futures and cash. *Review of Financial Studies* **9**: 301–332.

Engle, R. F. and Granger, C. W. J. (1987). Co-integration and error correction representation, estimation and testing. *Econometrica* **55**: 251–276.

Forbes, C. S., Kalb, G. R. J., and Kofman, P. (1999). Bayesian arbitrage threshold analysis. *Journal of Business & Economic Statistics* **17**: 364–372.

Fuller, W. A. (1976). *Introduction to Statistical Time Series*. Wiley, Hoboken, NJ.

Graybill, F. A. (1969). *Introduction to Matrices with Applications in Statistics*. Wadsworth, Belmont, CA.

Hannan, E. J. and Quinn, B. G. (1979). The determination of the order of an autoregression. *Journal of the Royal Statistical Society Series B* **41**: 190–195.

Hillmer, S. C. and Tiao, G. C. (1979). Likelihood function of stationary multiple autoregressive moving average models. *Journal of the American Statistical Association* **74**: 652–660.

Hosking, J. R. M. (1980). The multivariate portmanteau statistic. *Journal of the American Statistical Association* **75**: 602–608.

Hosking, J. R. M. (1981). Lagrange-multiplier tests of multivariate time series models. *Journal of the Royal Statistical Society Series B* **43**: 219–230.

Johansen, S. (1988). Statistical analysis of co-integration vectors. *Journal of Economic Dynamics and Control* **12**: 231–254.

Johansen, S. (1995). *Likelihood Based Inference in Cointegrated Vector Error Correction Models*. Oxford University Press, Oxford, UK.

Johnson, R. A. and Wichern, D. W. (1998). *Applied Multivariate Statistical Analysis*, 4th edition. Prentice Hall, Upper Saddle River, NJ.

Li, W. K. and McLeod, A. I. (1981). Distribution of the residual autocorrelations in multivariate ARMA time series models. *Journal of the Royal Statistical Society Series B* **43**: 231–239.

Lütkepohl, H. (1991). *Introduction to Multiple Time Series Analysis*. Springer-Verlag, New York.

Reinsel, G. C. (1993). *Elements of Multivariate Time Series Analysis*. Springer-Verlag, New York.

Reinsel, G. C. and Ahn, S. K. (1992). Vector autoregressive models with unit roots and reduced rank structure: estimation, likelihood ratio test, and forecasting. *Journal of Time Series Analysis* **13**: 353–375.

Stock, J. H. and Watson, M.W. (1988). Testing for common trends. *Journal of the American Statistical Association* **83**: 1097–1107.

Strang, G. (1980). *Linear Algebra and Its Applications*, 2nd edition. Harcourt Brace Jovanovich, Chicago.

Tiao, G. C. and Box, G. E. P. (1981). Modeling multiple time series with applications. *Journal of the American Statistical Association* **76**: 802–816.

Tiao, G. C. and Tsay, R. S. (1989). Model specification in multivariate time series (with discussions). *Journal of the Royal Statistical Society Series B* **51**: 157–213.

Tiao, G. C., Tsay, R. S., and Wang, T. (1993). Usefulness of linear transformations in multivariate time series analysis. *Empirical Economics* **18**: 567–593.

Tsay, R. S. (1991). Two canonical forms for vector ARMA processes. *Statistica Sinica* **1**: 247–269.

Tsay, R. S. (1998). Testing and modeling multivariate threshold models. *Journal of the American Statistical Association* **93**: 1188–1202.

Tsay, R. S., and Tiao, G. C. (1990). Asymptotic properties of multivariate nonstationary processes with applications to autoregressions. *Annals of Statistics* **18**: 220–250.

Zivot, E. and Wang, J. (2003). *Modeling Financial Time Series with S-Plus*. Springer-Verlag, New York.

CHAPTER 9

Principal Component Analysis and Factor Models

Most financial portfolios consist of multiple assets, and their returns depend concurrently and dynamically on many economic and financial variables. Therefore, it is important to use proper multivariate statistical analyses to study the behavior and properties of portfolio returns. However, as demonstrated in the previous chapter, analysis of multiple asset returns often requires high-dimensional statistical models that are complicated and hard to apply. To simplify the task of modeling multiple returns, we discuss in this chapter some dimension reduction methods to search for the underlying structure of the assets. *Principal component analysis* (PCA) is perhaps the most commonly used statistical method in dimension reduction, and we start our discussion with the method. In practice, observed return series often exhibit similar characteristics leading to the belief that they might be driven by some common sources, often referred to as common factors. To study the common pattern in asset returns and to simplify portfolio analysis, various factor models have been proposed in the literature to analyze multiple asset returns. The second goal of this chapter is to introduce some useful factor models and demonstrate their applications in finance.

Three types of factor models are available for studying asset returns; see Connor (1995) and Campbell, Lo, and MacKinlay (1997). The first type is the *macroeconomic factor models* that use macroeconomic variables such as growth rate of GDP, interest rates, inflation rate, and unemployment numbers to describe the common behavior of asset returns. Here the factors are observable and the model can be estimated via linear regression methods. The second type is the *fundamental factor models* that use firm or asset specific attributes such as firm size, book and market values, and industrial classification to construct common factors. The third type is the *statistical factor models* that treat the common factors as unobservable or latent variables to be estimated from the returns series. In this chapter, we discuss all three types of factor models and their applications in finance. Principal component

Analysis of Financial Time Series, Second Edition By Ruey S. Tsay

analysis and factor models for asset returns are also discussed in Alexander (2001) and Zivot and Wang (2003).

The chapter is organized as follows. Section 9.1 introduces a general factor model for asset returns, and Section 9.2 discusses macroeconomic factor models with some simple examples. The fundamental factor model and its applications are given in Section 9.3. Section 9.4 introduces principal component analysis that serves as the basic method for statistical factor analysis. The PCA can also be used to reduce the dimension in multivariate analysis. Section 9.5 discusses the orthogonal factor models, including factor rotation and its estimation, and provides several examples. Finally, Section 9.6 introduces asymptotic principal component analysis.

9.1 A FACTOR MODEL

Suppose that there are k assets and T time periods. Let r_{it} be the return of asset i in the time period t. A general form for the factor model is

$$r_{it} = \alpha_i + \beta_{i1} f_{1t} + \cdots + \beta_{im} f_{mt} + \epsilon_{it}, \quad t = 1, \ldots, T; \quad i = 1, \ldots, k, \tag{9.1}$$

where α_i is a constant representing the intercept, $\{f_{jt} | j = 1, \ldots, m\}$ are m common factors, β_{ij} is the *factor loading* for asset i on the jth factor, and ϵ_{it} is the *specific factor* of asset i.

For asset returns, the factor $\boldsymbol{f}_t = (f_{1t}, \ldots, f_{mt})'$ is assumed to be an m-dimensional stationary process such that

$$E(\boldsymbol{f}_t) = \boldsymbol{\mu}_f,$$
$$\text{Cov}(\boldsymbol{f}_t) = \boldsymbol{\Sigma}_f, \quad \text{an } m \times m \text{ matrix},$$

and the asset specific factor ϵ_{it} is a white noise series and uncorrelated with the common factors f_{jt} and other specific factors. Specifically, we assume that

$$E(\epsilon_{it}) = 0 \quad \text{for all } i \text{ and } t,$$
$$\text{Cov}(f_{jt}, \epsilon_{is}) = 0 \quad \text{for all } j, i, t \text{ and } s,$$
$$\text{Cov}(\epsilon_{it}, \epsilon_{js}) = \begin{cases} \sigma_i^2, & \text{if } i = j \text{ and } t = s, \\ 0, & \text{otherwise.} \end{cases}$$

Thus, the common factors are uncorrelated with the specific factors, and the specific factors are uncorrelated among each other. The common factors, however, need not be uncorrelated with each other in some factor models.

In some applications, the number of assets k may be larger than the number of time periods T. We discuss an approach to analyze such data in Section 9.6. It is also common to assume that the factors, hence $\boldsymbol{r}_t$, are serially uncorrelated in factor analysis. In applications, if the observed returns are serially dependent, then the models in Chapter 8 can be used to remove the serial dependence.

In matrix form, the factor model in Eq. (9.1) can be written as

$$r_{it} = \alpha_i + \boldsymbol{\beta}_i' \boldsymbol{f}_t + \epsilon_{it},$$

where $\boldsymbol{\beta}_i = (\beta_{i1}, \ldots, \beta_{im})'$, and the joint model for the k assets at time t is

$$\boldsymbol{r}_t = \boldsymbol{\alpha} + \boldsymbol{\beta} \boldsymbol{f}_t + \boldsymbol{\epsilon}_t, \quad t = 1, \ldots, T \tag{9.2}$$

where $\boldsymbol{r}_t = (r_{1t}, \ldots, r_{kt})'$, $\boldsymbol{\beta} = [\beta_{ij}]$ is a $k \times m$ factor-loading matrix, and $\boldsymbol{\epsilon}_t = (\epsilon_{1t}, \ldots, \epsilon_{kt})'$ is the error vector with $\mathrm{Cov}(\boldsymbol{\epsilon}_t) = \boldsymbol{D} = \mathrm{diag}\{\sigma_1^2, \ldots, \sigma_k^2\}$, a $k \times k$ diagonal matrix. The covariance matrix of the return $\boldsymbol{r}_t$ is then

$$\mathrm{Cov}(\boldsymbol{r}_t) = \boldsymbol{\beta} \boldsymbol{\Sigma}_f \boldsymbol{\beta}' + \boldsymbol{D}.$$

The model presentation in Eq. (9.2) is in a *cross-sectional* regression form if the factors f_{jt} are observed.

Treating the factor model in Eq. (9.1) as a time series, we have

$$\boldsymbol{R}_i = \alpha_i \boldsymbol{1}_T + \boldsymbol{F} \boldsymbol{\beta}_i + \boldsymbol{E}_i, \tag{9.3}$$

for the ith asset ($i = 1, \ldots, k$), where $\boldsymbol{R}_i = (r_{i1}, \ldots, r_{iT})'$, $\boldsymbol{1}_T$ is a T-dimensional vector of ones, $\boldsymbol{F}$ is a $T \times m$ matrix whose tth row is $\boldsymbol{f}_t'$, and $\boldsymbol{E}_i = (\epsilon_{i1}, \ldots, \epsilon_{iT})'$. The covariance matrix of $\boldsymbol{E}_i$ is $\mathrm{Cov}(\boldsymbol{E}_i) = \sigma_i^2 \boldsymbol{I}$, a diagonal $T \times T$ matrix.

Finally, we can rewrite Eq. (9.2) as

$$\boldsymbol{r}_t = \boldsymbol{\xi} \boldsymbol{g}_t + \boldsymbol{\epsilon}_t,$$

where $\boldsymbol{g}_t = (1, \boldsymbol{f}_t')'$ and $\boldsymbol{\xi} = [\boldsymbol{\alpha}, \boldsymbol{\beta}]$, which is a $k \times (m+1)$ matrix. Taking the transpose of the prior equation and stacking all data together, we have

$$\boldsymbol{R} = \boldsymbol{G} \boldsymbol{\xi}' + \boldsymbol{E}, \tag{9.4}$$

where $\boldsymbol{R}$ is a $T \times k$ matrix of returns whose tth row is $\boldsymbol{r}_t'$ or, equivalently, whose ith column is $\boldsymbol{R}_i$ of Eq. (9.3), $\boldsymbol{G}$ is a $T \times (m+1)$ matrix whose tth row is $\boldsymbol{g}_t'$, and $\boldsymbol{E}$ is a $T \times k$ matrix of specific factors whose tth row is $\boldsymbol{\epsilon}_t'$. If the common factors $\boldsymbol{f}_t$ are observed, then Eq. (9.4) is a special form of the *multivariate linear regression* (MLR) model; see Johnson and Wichern (2002). For a general MLR model, the covariance matrix of $\boldsymbol{\epsilon}_t$ need not be diagonal.

9.2 MACROECONOMETRIC FACTOR MODELS

For macroeconomic factor models, the factors are observed and we can apply the least squares method to the MLR model in Eq. (9.4) to perform estimation. The estimate is

$$\widehat{\boldsymbol{\xi}}' = \begin{bmatrix} \widehat{\boldsymbol{\alpha}}' \\ \widehat{\boldsymbol{\beta}}' \end{bmatrix} = (\boldsymbol{G}'\boldsymbol{G})^{-1}(\boldsymbol{G}'\boldsymbol{R}),$$

from which the estimates of $\boldsymbol{\alpha}$ and $\boldsymbol{\beta}$ are readily available. The residuals of Eq. (9.4) are

$$\widehat{\boldsymbol{E}} = \boldsymbol{R} - \boldsymbol{G}\widehat{\boldsymbol{\xi}}'.$$

Based on the model assumption, the covariance matrix of $\boldsymbol{\epsilon}_t$ is estimated by

$$\widehat{\boldsymbol{D}} = \text{diag}(\widehat{\boldsymbol{E}}'\widehat{\boldsymbol{E}}/(T - m - 1)),$$

where diag($\boldsymbol{A}$) means a diagonal matrix consisting of the diagonal elements of the matrix $\boldsymbol{A}$. Furthermore, the R-square of the ith asset of Eq. (9.3) is

$$\text{R-square}_i = 1 - \frac{[\widehat{\boldsymbol{E}}'\widehat{\boldsymbol{E}}]_{i,i}}{[\boldsymbol{R}'\boldsymbol{R}]_{i,i}}, \quad i = 1, \ldots, k,$$

where $\boldsymbol{A}_{i,i}$ denotes the (i, i)th element of the matrix $\boldsymbol{A}$.

Note that the prior estimation does not impose the constraint that the specific factors $\boldsymbol{\epsilon}_{it}$ are uncorrelated with each other. Consequently, the estimates obtained are not efficient in general. However, imposing the orthogonalization constraint requires nontrivial computation and is often ignored. One can check the off-diagonal elements of the matrix $\widehat{\boldsymbol{E}}'\widehat{\boldsymbol{E}}/(T - m - 1)$ to verify the adequacy of the fitted model.

9.2.1 A Single-Factor Model

The best known macroeconomic factor model in finance is the *market model*; see Sharpe (1970). This is a single-factor model and can be written as

$$r_{it} = \alpha_i + \beta_i r_{Mt} + \epsilon_{it}, \quad i = 1, \ldots, k; \quad t = 1, \ldots, T, \tag{9.5}$$

where r_{it} is the excess return of the ith asset and r_{mt} is the excess return of the market. To illustrate, we consider monthly returns of 13 stocks and use the return of the S&P 500 index as the market return. The stocks used and their tick symbols are given in Table 9.1, and the sample period is from January 1990 to December 2003 so that $k = 13$ and $T = 168$. We use the monthly series of three-month Treasury bill rates of the secondary market as the risk-free interest rate to obtain simple excess returns of the stock and market index. The returns are in percentages.

We use S-Plus to implement the estimation method discussed in the previous subsection. Most of the commands used apply to the free software R.

```
> da=matrix(scan(file='m-fac9003.txt'),14)
> x=t(da)
> xmtx=cbind(rep(1,168),x[,14])
> rtn=x[,1:13]
> xit.hat=solve(xmtx,rtn)
> beta.hat=t(xit.hat[2,])
> E.hat=rtn-xmtx%*%xit.hat
> D.hat=diag(crossprod(E.hat)/(168-2))
> r.square=1-(168-2)*D.hat/diag(var(rtn,SumSquares=T))
```

Table 9.1. Stocks Used and Their Tick Symbols in the Analysis of a Single-Factor Model[a]

Tick	Company	$\bar{r}(\sigma_r)$	Tick	Company	$\bar{r}(\sigma_r)$
AA	Alcoa	1.09(9.49)	KMB	Kimberly-Clark	0.78(6.50)
AGE	A.G. Edwards	1.36(10.2)	MEL	Mellon Financial	1.36(7.80)
CAT	Caterpillar	1.23(8.71)	NYT	New York Times	0.81(7.37)
F	Ford Motor	0.97(9.77)	PG	Procter & Gamble	1.08(6.75)
FDX	FedEx	1.14(9.49)	TRB	Chicago Tribune	0.95(7.84)
GM	General Motors	0.64(9.28)	TXN	Texas Instrument	2.19(13.8)
HPQ	Hewlett-Packard	1.37(0.42)	SP5	S&P 500 index	0.42(4.33)

[a]Sample means (standard errors) of excess returns are also given. The sample period is from January 1990 to December 2003.

The estimates of β_i, σ_i^2, and R^2 for the ith asset return are given below:

```
> t(rbind(beta.hat,sqrt(D.hat),r.square))
        beta.hat  sigma(i)  r.square
   AA     1.292     7.694     0.347
  AGE     1.514     7.808     0.415
  CAT     0.941     7.725     0.219
    F     1.219     8.241     0.292
  FDX     0.805     8.854     0.135
   GM     1.046     8.130     0.238
  HPQ     1.628     9.469     0.358
  KMB     0.550     6.070     0.134
  MEL     1.123     6.120     0.388
  NYT     0.771     6.590     0.205
   PG     0.469     6.459     0.090
  TRB     0.718     7.215     0.157
  TXN     1.796    11.474     0.316
```

Figure 9.1 shows the bar plots of $\hat{\beta}_i$ and R^2 of the 13 stocks. The financial stocks, AGE and MEL, and the high-tech stocks, HPQ and TXN, seem to have higher β and R^2. On the other hand, KMB and PG have lower β and R^2. The R^2 ranges from 0.09 to 0.41, indicating that the market return explains less than 50% of the variabilities of the individual stocks used.

The covariance and correlation matrices of $\boldsymbol{r}_t$ under the market model can be estimated using the following:

```
> cov.r=var(x[,14])*(t(beta.hat)%*%beta.hat)+diag(D.hat)
> sd.r=sqrt(diag(cov.r))
> corr.r=cov.r/outer(sd.r,sd.r)
> print(corr.r,digits=1,width=2)
    AA  AGE CAT  F  FDX  GM HPQ KMB MEL NYT  PG TRB TXN
 AA 1.0 0.4 0.3 0.3 0.2 0.3 0.4 0.2 0.4 0.3 0.2 0.2 0.3
```

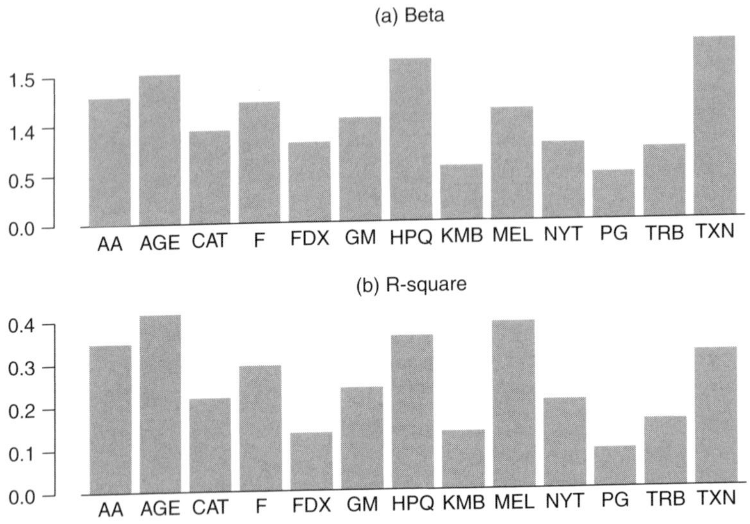

Figure 9.1. Bar plots of the (a) beta and (b) R-square for fitting a single-factor market model to the monthly excess returns of 13 stocks. The S&P 500 index excess return is used as the market index. The sample period is from January 1990 to December 2003.

```
AGE 0.4 1.0 0.3 0.3 0.2 0.3 0.4 0.2 0.4 0.3 0.2 0.3 0.4
CAT 0.3 0.3 1.0 0.3 0.2 0.2 0.3 0.2 0.3 0.2 0.1 0.2 0.3
  F 0.3 0.3 0.3 1.0 0.2 0.3 0.3 0.2 0.3 0.2 0.2 0.2 0.3
FDX 0.2 0.2 0.2 0.2 1.0 0.2 0.2 0.1 0.2 0.2 0.1 0.1 0.2
 GM 0.3 0.3 0.2 0.3 0.2 1.0 0.3 0.2 0.3 0.2 0.1 0.2 0.3
HPQ 0.4 0.4 0.3 0.3 0.2 0.3 1.0 0.2 0.4 0.3 0.2 0.2 0.3
KMB 0.2 0.2 0.2 0.2 0.1 0.2 0.2 1.0 0.2 0.2 0.1 0.1 0.2
MEL 0.4 0.4 0.3 0.3 0.2 0.3 0.4 0.2 1.0 0.3 0.2 0.2 0.3
NYT 0.3 0.3 0.2 0.2 0.2 0.2 0.3 0.2 0.3 1.0 0.1 0.2 0.3
 PG 0.2 0.2 0.1 0.2 0.1 0.1 0.2 0.1 0.2 0.1 1.0 0.1 0.2
TRB 0.2 0.3 0.2 0.2 0.1 0.2 0.2 0.1 0.2 0.2 0.1 1.0 0.2
TXN 0.3 0.4 0.3 0.3 0.2 0.3 0.3 0.2 0.3 0.3 0.2 0.2 1.0
```

We can compare these estimated correlations with the sample correlations of the excess returns.

```
> print(cor(rtn),digits=1,width=2)
     AA AGE CAT   F FDX  GM HPQ KMB MEL NYT  PG TRB TXN
 AA 1.0 0.3 0.6 0.5 0.2 0.4 0.5 0.3 0.4 0.4 0.1 0.3 0.5
AGE 0.3 1.0 0.3 0.3 0.3 0.3 0.3 0.3 0.4 0.4 0.2 0.2 0.3
CAT 0.6 0.3 1.0 0.4 0.2 0.3 0.2 0.3 0.4 0.3 0.1 0.4 0.3
  F 0.5 0.3 0.4 1.0 0.3 0.6 0.3 0.3 0.4 0.4 0.1 0.3 0.3
FDX 0.2 0.3 0.2 0.3 1.0 0.2 0.3 0.3 0.2 0.2 0.1 0.3 0.2
 GM 0.4 0.3 0.3 0.6 0.2 1.0 0.3 0.3 0.4 0.2 0.1 0.3 0.3
HPQ 0.5 0.3 0.2 0.3 0.3 0.3 1.0 0.1 0.3 0.3 0.1 0.2 0.6
KMB 0.3 0.3 0.3 0.2 0.3 0.3 0.1 1.0 0.3 0.2 0.3 0.3 0.1
```

```
MEL 0.4 0.4 0.4 0.4 0.2 0.4 0.3 0.4 1.0 0.3 0.4 0.3 0.3
NYT 0.4 0.4 0.3 0.4 0.3 0.2 0.3 0.2 0.3 1.0 0.2 0.5 0.2
 PG 0.1 0.2 0.1 0.1 0.1 0.1 0.1 0.3 0.4 0.2 1.0 0.3 0.1
TRB 0.3 0.2 0.4 0.3 0.3 0.3 0.2 0.3 0.3 0.5 0.3 1.0 0.2
TXN 0.5 0.3 0.3 0.3 0.2 0.3 0.6 0.1 0.3 0.2 0.1 0.2 1.0
```

In finance, one can use the concept of *the global minimum variance portfolio* (GMVP) to compare the covariance matrix implied by a fitted factor model with the sample covariance matrix of the returns. For a given covariance matrix $\mathbf{\Sigma}$, the global minimum variance portfolio is the portfolio $\boldsymbol{\omega}$ that solves

$$\min_{\boldsymbol{\omega}} \sigma^2_{p,\boldsymbol{\omega}} = \boldsymbol{\omega}'\mathbf{\Sigma}\boldsymbol{\omega} \quad \text{such that} \quad \boldsymbol{\omega}'\mathbf{1} = 1$$

and is given by

$$\boldsymbol{\omega} = \frac{\mathbf{\Sigma}^{-1}\mathbf{1}}{\mathbf{1}'\mathbf{\Sigma}^{-1}\mathbf{1}},$$

where $\mathbf{1}$ is the k-dimensional vector of ones.

For the market model considered, the GMVP for the fitted model and the data are as follows:

```
> w.gmin.model=solve(cov.r)%*%rep(1,nrow(cov.r))
> w.gmin.model=w.gmin.model/sum(w.gmin.model)
> t(w.gmin.model)
          AA       AGE      CAT       F      FDX     GM
[1,] 0.0117 -0.0306 0.0792 0.0225 0.0802 0.0533
         HPQ      KMB      MEL      NYT      PG      TRB      TXN
[1,] -0.0354 0.2503 0.0703 0.1539 0.2434 0.1400 -0.0388
> w.gmin.data=solve(var(rtn))%*%rep(1,nrow(cov.r))
> w.gmin.data=w.gmin.data/sum(w.gmin.data)
> t(w.gmin.data)
          AA       AGE      CAT       F       FDX     GM
[1,] -0.0073 -0.0085 0.0866 -0.0232 0.0943 0.0916
         HPQ      KMB      MEL      NYT      PG      TRB      TXN
[1,] 0.0345 0.2296 0.0495 0.1790 0.2651 0.0168  -0.0080
```

Comparing the two GMVPs, the weights assigned to TRB stock differ markedly. The two portfolios, however, have larger weights for KMB, NYT, and PG stocks.

Finally, we examine the residual covariance and correlation matrices to verify the assumption that the special factors are not correlated among the 13 stocks. The first four columns of the residual correlation matrix are given below and there exist some large values in the residual cross-correlations, for example, Cor(CAT,AA) = 0.45 and Cor(GM,F) = 0.48.

```
> resi.cov=t(E.hat)%*%E.hat/(168-2)
> resi.sd=sqrt(diag(resi.cov))
```

```
> resi.cor=resi.cov/outer(resi.sd,resi.sd)
> print(resi.cor,digits=1,width=2)
       AA   AGE   CAT     F
 AA  1.00 -0.13  0.45  0.22
AGE -0.13  1.00 -0.03 -0.01
CAT  0.45 -0.03  1.00  0.23
  F  0.22 -0.01  0.23  1.00
FDX  0.00  0.14  0.05  0.07
 GM  0.14 -0.09  0.15  0.48
HPQ  0.24 -0.13 -0.07 -0.00
KMB  0.16  0.06  0.18  0.05
MEL -0.02  0.06  0.09  0.10
NYT  0.13  0.10  0.07  0.19
 PG -0.15 -0.02 -0.01 -0.07
TRB  0.12 -0.02  0.25  0.16
TXN  0.19 -0.17  0.09 -0.02
```

9.2.2 Multifactor Models

Chen, Roll, and Ross (1986) consider a multifactor model for stock returns. The factors used consist of *unexpected changes* or *surprises* of macroeconomic variables. Here unexpected changes denote the residuals of the macroeconomic variables after removing their dynamic dependence. A simple way to obtain unexpected changes is to fit a VAR model of Chapter 8 to the macroeconomic variables. For illustration, we consider the following two monthly macroeconomic variables:

1. Consumer price index (CPI) for all urban consumers: all items and with index 1982–1984 = 100.
2. Civilian employment numbers 16 years and over (CE16): measured in thousands.

Both CPI and CE16 series are seasonally adjusted, and the data span is from January 1975 to December 2003. We use a longer period to obtain the surprise series of the variables. For both series, we construct the growth rate series by taking the first difference of the logged data. The growth rates are in percentages.

To obtain the surprise series, we use the BIC criterion to identify a VAR(3) model. Thus, the two macroeconomic factors used in the factor model are the residuals of a VAR(3) model from 1990 to 2003. For the excess returns, we use the same 13 stocks as before. Details of the analysis are given below:

```
> da=matrix(scan(file='m-cpice16-dp7503.txt'),2)
> cpi=da[1,]
> cen=da[2,]
> x1=cbind(cpi,cen)
> y1=data.frame(x1)
> ord.choice=VAR(y1,max.ar=13)
> ord.choice$info
```

```
       ar(1)    ar(2)    ar(3)    ar(4)    ar(5)    ar(6)
BIC   36.992   38.093   28.234   46.241   60.677   75.810

       ar(7)   ar(8)    ar(9)  ar(10)   ar(11)   ar(12)   ar(13)
BIC   86.23   99.294   111.27  125.46   138.01   146.71   166.92
> var3.fit=VAR(x1~ar(3))
> res=var3.fit$residuals[166:333,1:2]
> da=matrix(scan(file='m-fac9003.txt'),14)
> xmtx = cbind(rep(1,168),res)
> da=t(da)
> rtn=da[,1:13]
> xit.hat=solve(xmtx,rtn)
> beta.hat=t(xit.hat[2:3,])
> E.hat=rtn - xmtx%*%xit.hat
> D.hat=diag(crossprod(E.hat)/(168-3))
> r.square=1-(168-3)*D.hat/diag(var(rtn,SumSquares=T))
```

Figure 9.2 shows the bar plots of the beta estimates and R^2 for the 13 stocks. It is interesting to see that all excess returns are negatively related to the unexpected changes of CPI growth rate. This seems reasonable. However, the R^2 of all excess

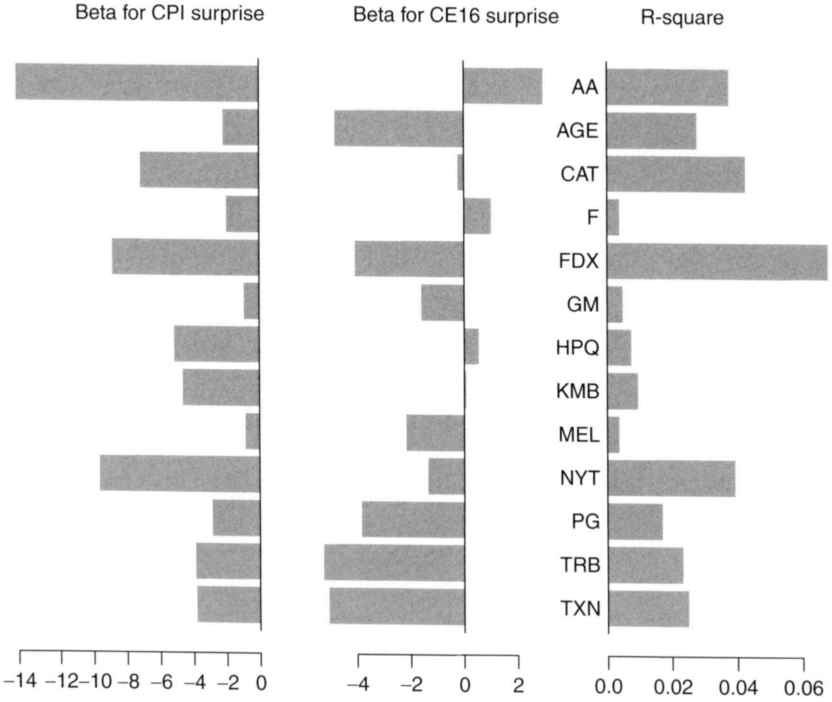

Figure 9.2. Bar plots of the betas and R-square for fitting a two-factor model to the monthly excess returns of 13 stocks. The sample period is from January 1990 to December 2003.

returns are low, indicating that the two macroeconomic variables used have very little explanatory power in understanding the excess returns of the 13 stocks.

The estimated covariance and correlation matrices of the two-factor model can be obtained using the following:

```
> cov.rtn=beta.hat%*%var(res)%*%t(beta.hat)+diag(D.hat)
> sd.rtn=sqrt(diag(cov.rtn))
> cor.rtn = cov.rtn/outer(sd.rtn,sd.rtn)
> print(cor.rtn,diits=1,width=2)
```

The correlation matrix is very close to the identity matrix, indicating that the two-factor model used does not fit the excess returns well. Finally, the correlation matrix of the residuals of the two-factor model is given by the following:

```
> cov.resi=t(E.hat)%*%E.hat/(168-3)
> sd.resi=sqrt(diag(cov.resi))
> cor.resi=cov.resi/outer(sd.resi,sd.resi)
> print(cor.resi,digits=1,width=2)
```

As expected, this correlation matrix is close to that of the original excess returns given before and is omitted.

9.3 FUNDAMENTAL FACTOR MODELS

Fundamental factor models use observable asset specific fundamentals such as industrial classification, market capitalization, book value, and style classification (growth or value) to construct common factors that explain the excess returns. There are two approaches to fundamental factor models available in the literature. The first approach is proposed by Bar Rosenberg, founder of BARRA Inc., and is referred to as the BARRA approach; see Grinold and Kahn (2000). In contrast to the macroeconomic factor models, this approach treats the observed asset specific fundamentals as the factor betas, $\boldsymbol{\beta}_i$, and estimates the factors $\boldsymbol{f}_t$ at each time index t via regression methods. The betas are time-invariant, but the realizations $\boldsymbol{f}_t$ evolve over time. The second approach is the Fama–French approach proposed by Fama and French (1992). In this approach, the factor realization f_{jt} for a given specific fundamental is obtained by constructing some hedge portfolio based on the observed fundamental. We briefly discuss the two approaches in the next two subsections.

9.3.1 BARRA Factor Model

Assume that the excess returns and, hence, the factor realizations are mean-corrected. At each time index t, the factor model in Eq. (9.2) reduces to

$$\tilde{\boldsymbol{r}}_t = \boldsymbol{\beta}\boldsymbol{f}_t + \boldsymbol{\epsilon}_t, \tag{9.6}$$

where $\tilde{\boldsymbol{r}}_t$ denotes the (sample) mean-corrected excess returns and, for simplicity in notation, we continue to use $\boldsymbol{f}_t$ as factor realizations. Since $\boldsymbol{\beta}$ is given, the model in Eq. (9.6) is a multiple linear regression with k observations and m unknowns. Because the number of common factors m should be less than the number of assets k, the regression is estimable. However, the regression is not homogeneous because the covariance matrix of $\boldsymbol{\epsilon}_t$ is $\boldsymbol{D} = \text{diag}\{\sigma_1^2, \ldots, \sigma_k^2\}$ with $\sigma_i^2 = \text{Var}(\epsilon_{it})$, which depends on the ith asset. Consequently, the factor realization at time index t can be estimated by the *weighted least squares* (WLS) method using the standard errors of the specific factors as the weights. The resulting estimate is

$$\widehat{\boldsymbol{f}}_t = \left(\boldsymbol{\beta}\boldsymbol{D}^{-1}\boldsymbol{\beta}'\right)^{-1}\left(\boldsymbol{\beta}\boldsymbol{D}^{-1}\boldsymbol{\beta}'\tilde{\boldsymbol{r}}_t\right). \tag{9.7}$$

In practice, the covariance matrix $\boldsymbol{D}$ is unknown so that we use a two-step procedure to perform the estimation.

In step one, the ordinary least squares (OLS) method is used at each time index t to obtain a preliminary estimate of $\boldsymbol{f}_t$ as

$$\widehat{\boldsymbol{f}}_{t,o} = (\boldsymbol{\beta}'\boldsymbol{\beta})^{-1}(\boldsymbol{\beta}'\tilde{\boldsymbol{r}}_t),$$

where the second subscript o is used to denote the OLS estimate. This estimate of factor realization is consistent, but not efficient. The residual of the OLS regression is

$$\boldsymbol{\epsilon}_{t,o} = \tilde{\boldsymbol{r}}_t - \boldsymbol{\beta}\widehat{\boldsymbol{f}}_{t,o}.$$

Since the residual covariance matrix is time-invariant, we can pool the residuals together (for $t = 1, \ldots, T$) to obtain an estimate of $\boldsymbol{D}$ as

$$\widehat{\boldsymbol{D}}_o = \text{diag}\left\{\frac{1}{T-1}\sum_{t=1}^{T}(\boldsymbol{\epsilon}_{t,o}\boldsymbol{\epsilon}_{t,o}')\right\}.$$

In step two, we plug in the estimate $\widehat{\boldsymbol{D}}_o$ to obtain a refined estimate of the factor realization

$$\widehat{\boldsymbol{f}}_{t,g} = \left(\boldsymbol{\beta}'\widehat{\boldsymbol{D}}_o^{-1}\boldsymbol{\beta}\right)^{-1}\left(\boldsymbol{\beta}'\widehat{\boldsymbol{D}}_o^{-1}\boldsymbol{\beta}\tilde{\boldsymbol{r}}_t\right), \tag{9.8}$$

where the second subscript g denotes the *generalized least squares* (GLS) estimate, which is a sample version of the WLS estimate. The residual of the refined regression is

$$\boldsymbol{\epsilon}_{t,g} = \tilde{\boldsymbol{r}}_t - \boldsymbol{\beta}\widehat{\boldsymbol{f}}_{t,g},$$

from which we estimate the residual variance matrix as

$$\widehat{\boldsymbol{D}}_g = \text{diag}\left\{\frac{1}{T-1}\sum_{t=1}^{T}(\boldsymbol{\epsilon}_{t,g}\boldsymbol{\epsilon}_{t,g}')\right\}.$$

Finally, the covariance matrix of the estimated factor realizations is

$$\widehat{\boldsymbol{\Sigma}}_f = \frac{1}{T-1}\sum_{t=1}^{T}(\widehat{\boldsymbol{f}}_{t,g} - \overline{\boldsymbol{f}}_g)(\widehat{\boldsymbol{f}}_{t,g} - \overline{\boldsymbol{f}}_g)',$$

where

$$\overline{\boldsymbol{f}}_g = \frac{1}{T}\sum_{t=1}^{T}\widehat{\boldsymbol{f}}_{t,g}.$$

From Eq. (9.6), the covariance matrix of the excess returns under the BARRA approach is

$$\text{Cov}(\boldsymbol{r}_t) = \boldsymbol{\beta}\widehat{\boldsymbol{\Sigma}}_f\boldsymbol{\beta}' + \widehat{\boldsymbol{D}}_g.$$

Industry Factor Model

For illustration, we consider monthly excess returns of ten stocks and use industrial classification as the specific asset fundamental. The stocks used are given in Table 9.2 and can be classified into three industrial sectors—namely, financial services, computer and high-tech industry, and other. The sample period is again from January 1990 to December 2003. Under the BARRA framework, there are three common factors representing the three industrial sectors and the betas are indicators for the three industrial sectors; that is,

$$\tilde{r}_{it} = \beta_{i1}f_{1t} + \beta_{i2}f_{2t} + \beta_{i3}f_{3t} + \epsilon_{it}, \quad i = 1, \ldots, 10, \tag{9.9}$$

with the betas being

$$\beta_{ij} = \begin{cases} 1 & \text{if asset } i \text{ belongs to the } j \text{ industrial sector,} \\ 0 & \text{otherwise,} \end{cases} \tag{9.10}$$

Table 9.2. Stocks Used and Their Tick Symbols in the Analysis of Industrial Factor Model[a]

Tick	Company	$\overline{r}(\sigma_r)$	Tick	Company	$\overline{r}(\sigma_r)$
AGE	A.G. Edwards	1.36(10.2)	IBM	International Business Machines	1.06(9.47)
C	Citigroup	2.08(9.60)			
MWD	Morgan Stanley	1.87(11.2)	AA	Alcoa	1.09(9.49)
MER	Merrill Lynch	2.08(10.4)	CAT	Caterpillar	1.23(8.71)
DELL	Dell Inc.	4.82(16.4)	PG	Procter & Gamble	1.08(6.75)
HPQ	Hewlett-Packard	1.37(11.8)			

[a] Sample mean and standard deviation of the excess returns are also given. The sample span is from January 1990 to December 2003.

where $j = 1, 2, 3$ representing the financial, high-tech, and other sector, respectively. For instance, the beta vector for the IBM stock return is $\boldsymbol{\beta}_i = (0, 1, 0)'$ and that for Alcoa stock return is $\boldsymbol{\beta}_i = (0, 0, 1)'$.

In Eq. (9.9), f_{1t} is the factor realization of the *financial services* sector, f_{2t} is that of the *computer and high-tech* sector, and f_{3t} is for the other sector. Because the β_{ij} are indicator variables, the OLS estimate of $\boldsymbol{f}_t$ is extremely simple. Indeed, $\boldsymbol{f}_t$ is the vector consisting of the averages of sector excess returns at time t. Specifically,

$$\widehat{\boldsymbol{f}}_{t,o} = \begin{bmatrix} \dfrac{\text{AGE}_t + \text{C}_t + \text{MDW}_t + \text{MER}_t}{4} \\[2ex] \dfrac{\text{DELL}_t + \text{HPQ}_t + \text{IBM}_t}{3} \\[2ex] \dfrac{\text{AA}_t + \text{CAT}_t + \text{PG}_t}{3} \end{bmatrix}.$$

The specific factor of the ith asset is simply the deviation of its excess return from its industrial sample average. One can then obtain an estimate of the residual variance matrix $\boldsymbol{D}$ to perform the generalized least squares estimation. We use S-Plus to perform the analysis. First, load the returns into S-Plus, remove the sample means, create the industrial dummies, and compute the sample correlation matrix of the returns.

```
> da=matrix(scan(file='m-barra-9003.txt'),10)
> rm = matrix(rowMeans(da),1)
> rtn.rm = da - t(rm)%*%rep(1,168)
> fin = c(rep(1,4),rep(0,6))
> tech = c(rep(0,4),rep(1,3),rep(0,3)
> oth = c(rep(0,7),rep(1,3))
> ind.dum = cbind(fin,tech,oth)
> ind.dum
      fin tech oth
 [1,]   1    0   0
 [2,]   1    0   0
 [3,]   1    0   0
 [4,]   1    0   0
 [5,]   0    1   0
 [6,]   0    1   0
 [7,]   0    1   0
 [8,]   0    0   1
 [9,]   0    0   1
[10,]   0    0   1
> rtn=t(rtn.rm)
> cov.rtn=var(rtn)
> sd.rtn=sqrt(diag(cov.rtn))
> corr.rtn=cov.rtn/outer(sd.rtn,sd.rtn)
> print(corr.rtn,digits=1,width=2)
```

```
     AGE  C   MWD MER DELL HPQ IBM AA  CAT PG
AGE  1.0 0.6 0.6 0.6 0.3  0.3 0.3 0.3 0.3 0.2
C    0.6 1.0 0.7 0.7 0.2  0.4 0.4 0.4 0.4 0.3
MWD  0.6 0.7 1.0 0.8 0.3  0.5 0.4 0.4 0.3 0.3
MER  0.6 0.7 0.8 1.0 0.2  0.5 0.3 0.4 0.3 0.3
DELL 0.3 0.2 0.3 0.2 1.0  0.5 0.4 0.3 0.1 0.1
HPQ  0.3 0.4 0.5 0.5 0.4  1.0 0.5 0.5 0.2 0.1
IBM  0.3 0.4 0.4 0.3 0.4  0.5 1.0 0.4 0.3-0.0
AA   0.3 0.4 0.4 0.4 0.3  0.5 0.4 1.0 0.6 0.1
CAT  0.3 0.4 0.3 0.3 0.1  0.2 0.3 0.6 1.0 0.1
PG   0.2 0.3 0.3 0.3 0.1  0.1-0.0 0.1 0.1 1.0
```

The OLS estimates, their residuals, and residual variances are estimated as below:

```
> F.hat.o = solve(crossprod(ind.dum))%*%t(ind.dum)%*%rtn.rm
>  E.hat.o = rtn.rm - ind.dum%*%F.hat.o
> diagD.hat.o=rowVars(E.hat.o)
```

One can then obtain the generalized least squares estimates.

```
> Dinv.hat = diag(diagD.hat.o^(-1))
> H1 = t(ind.dum)%*%Dinv.hat%*%ind.dum
> Hmtx=solve(H1)%*%t(ind.dum)%*%Dinv.hat
> F.hat.g = Hmtx%*%rtn.rm
> F.hat.gt=t(F.hat.g)
> E.hat.g = rtn.rm - ind.dum%*%F.hat.g
> diagD.hat.g = rowVars(E.hat.g)
> t(Hmtx)
           fin     tech      oth
 [1,]   0.1870   0.0000   0.0000
 [2,]   0.2548   0.0000   0.0000
 [3,]   0.2586   0.0000   0.0000
 [4,]   0.2995   0.0000   0.0000
 [5,]   0.0000   0.2272   0.0000
 [6,]   0.0000   0.4015   0.0000
 [7,]   0.0000   0.3713   0.0000
 [8,]   0.0000   0.0000   0.3319
 [9,]   0.0000   0.0000   0.4321
[10,]   0.0000   0.0000   0.2360
> cov.ind=ind.dum%*%var(F.hat.gt)%*%t(ind.dum) +
+ diag(diagD.hat.g)
> sd.ind=sqrt(diag(cov.ind))
> corr.ind=cov.ind/outer(sd.ind,sd.ind)
> print(corr.ind,digits=1,width=2)
     AGE C   MWD MER DELL HPQ IBM AA  CAT PG
AGE  1.0 0.7 0.7 0.7 0.3  0.3 0.3 0.3 0.3 0.3
C    0.7 1.0 0.8 0.8 0.3  0.4 0.4 0.3 0.3 0.3
MWD  0.7 0.8 1.0 0.8 0.3  0.4 0.4 0.3 0.4 0.3
```

```
MER  0.7 0.8 0.8 1.0 0.3  0.4 0.4 0.3 0.4 0.3
DELL 0.3 0.3 0.3 0.3 1.0  0.5 0.5 0.2 0.2 0.2
HPQ  0.3 0.4 0.4 0.4 0.5  1.0 0.7 0.3 0.3 0.2
IBM  0.3 0.4 0.4 0.4 0.5  0.7 1.0 0.3 0.3 0.2
AA   0.3 0.3 0.3 0.3 0.2  0.3 0.3 1.0 0.7 0.5
CAT  0.3 0.3 0.4 0.4 0.2  0.3 0.3 0.7 1.0 0.6
PG   0.3 0.3 0.3 0.3 0.2  0.2 0.2 0.5 0.6 1.0
```

The model-based correlations of stocks within an industrial sector are larger than their sample counterparts. For instance, the sample correlation between CAT and PG stock returns is only 0.1, but the correlation based on the fitted model is 0.6. Finally, Figure 9.3 shows the time plots of the factor realizations based on the generalized least squares estimation.

Factor Mimicking Portfolio

Consider the special case of BARRA factor models with a single factor. Here the WLS estimate of f_t in Eq. (9.7) has a nice interpretation. Consider a portfolio

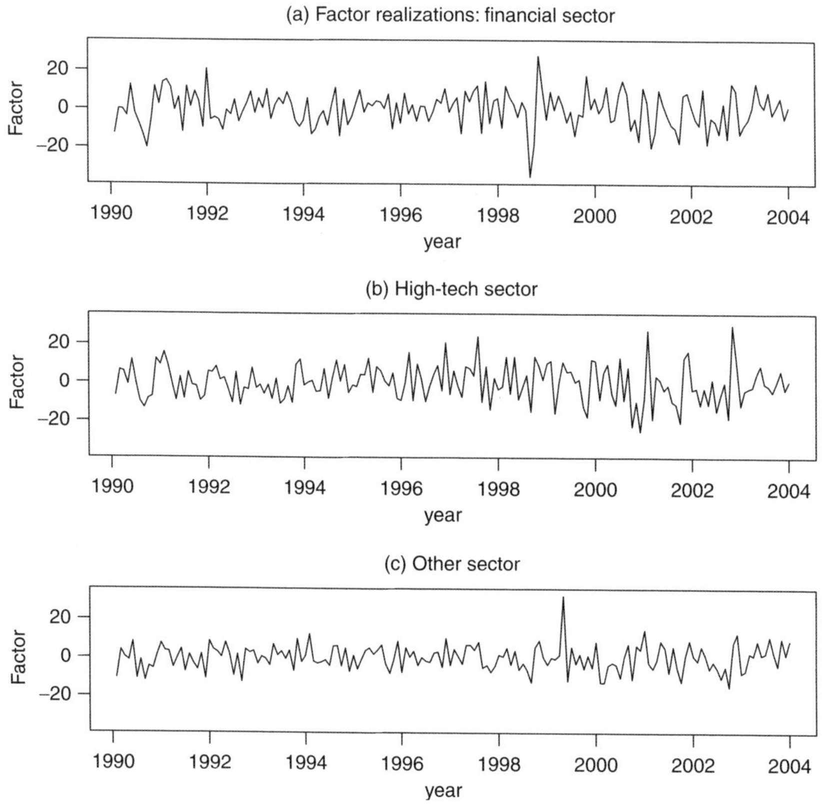

Figure 9.3. Estimated factor realizations of a BARRA industrial factor model for 10 monthly stock returns in three industrial sectors.

$\boldsymbol{\omega} = (\omega_1, \ldots, \omega_k)'$ of the k assets that solves

$$\min_{\boldsymbol{\omega}} \left(\tfrac{1}{2}\boldsymbol{\omega}'\boldsymbol{D}\boldsymbol{\omega}\right) \quad \text{such that} \quad \boldsymbol{\omega}'\boldsymbol{\beta} = 1.$$

It turns out that the solution to this portfolio problem is given by

$$\boldsymbol{\omega}' = (\boldsymbol{\beta}'\boldsymbol{D}^{-1}\boldsymbol{\beta})^{-1}(\boldsymbol{\beta}'\boldsymbol{D}^{-1}).$$

Thus, the estimated factor realization is the portfolio return

$$\hat{f}_t = \boldsymbol{\omega}'\boldsymbol{r}_t.$$

If the portfolio $\boldsymbol{\omega}$ is normalized such that $\sum_{i=1}^{k} \omega_i = 1$, it is referred to as a *factor mimicking portfolio*. For multiple factors, one can apply the idea to each factor individually.

Remark. In practice, the sample mean of an excess return is often not significantly different from zero. Thus, one may not need to remove the sample mean before fitting a BARRA factor model. □

9.3.2 Fama–French Approach

For a given asset fundamental (e.g., ratio of book-to-market value), Fama and French (1992) determined factor realizations using a two-step procedure. First, they sorted the assets based on the values of the observed fundamental. Then they formed a hedge portfolio which is long in the top quintile (1/3) of the sorted assets and short in the bottom quintile of the sorted assets. The observed return on this hedge portfolio at time t is the observed factor realization for the given asset fundamental. The procedure is repeated for each asset fundamental under consideration. Finally, given the observed factor realizations $\{\boldsymbol{f}_t | t = 1, \ldots, T\}$, the betas for each asset are estimated using a time series regression method. These authors identify three observed fundamentals that explain high percentages of variability in excess returns. The three fundamentals used by Fama and French are (a) the overall market return (market excess return), (b) the performance of small stocks relative to large stocks (SMB, small minus big), and (c) the performance of value stocks relative to growth stocks (HML, high minus low). The size sorted by market equity and the ratio of book equity to market equity is used to define value and growth stocks with value stocks having high book equity to market equity ratio.

Remark. The concepts of *factor* may differ between factor models. The *three factors* used in the Fama–French approach are three financial fundamentals. One can combine the fundamentals to create a new *attribute* of the stocks and refer to the resulting model as a single-factor model. This is particularly so because the model used is a linear statistical model. Thus, care needs to be exercised when one refers to the number of factors in a factor model. On the other hand, the number of factors is more well defined in statistical factor models, which we discuss next. □

9.4 PRINCIPAL COMPONENT ANALYSIS

An important topic in multivariate time series analysis is the study of the covariance (or correlation) structure of the series. For example, the covariance structure of a vector return series plays an important role in portfolio selection. In what follows, we discuss some statistical methods useful in studying the covariance structure of a vector time series.

Given a k-dimensional random variable $\boldsymbol{r} = (r_1, \ldots, r_k)'$ with covariance matrix $\boldsymbol{\Sigma}_r$, a *principal component analysis* (PCA) is concerned with using a few linear combinations of r_i to explain the structure of $\boldsymbol{\Sigma}_r$. If $\boldsymbol{r}$ denotes the monthly log returns of k assets, then PCA can be used to study the source of variations of these k asset returns. Here the keyword is *few* so that simplification can be achieved in multivariate analysis.

9.4.1 Theory of PCA

PCA applies to either the covariance matrix $\boldsymbol{\Sigma}_r$ or the correlation matrix $\boldsymbol{\rho}_r$ of $\boldsymbol{r}$. Since the correlation matrix is the covariance matrix of the standardized random vector $\boldsymbol{r}^* = \boldsymbol{S}^{-1}\boldsymbol{r}$, where $\boldsymbol{S}$ is the diagonal matrix of standard deviations of the components of $\boldsymbol{r}$, we use covariance matrix in our theoretical discussion. Let $\boldsymbol{w}_i = (w_{i1}, \ldots, w_{ik})'$ be a k-dimensional vector, where $i = 1, \ldots, k$. Then

$$y_i = \boldsymbol{w}_i'\boldsymbol{r} = \sum_{j=1}^{k} w_{ij} r_j$$

is a linear combination of the random vector $\boldsymbol{r}$. If $\boldsymbol{r}$ consists of the simple returns of k stocks, then y_i is the return of a portfolio that assigns weight w_{ij} to the jth stock. Since multiplying a constant to $\boldsymbol{w}_i$ does not affect the proportion of allocation assigned to the jth stock, we standardize the vector $\boldsymbol{w}_i$ so that $\boldsymbol{w}_i'\boldsymbol{w}_i = \sum_{j=1}^{k} w_{ij}^2 = 1$.

Using properties of a linear combination of random variables, we have

$$\text{Var}(y_i) = \boldsymbol{w}_i'\boldsymbol{\Sigma}_r\boldsymbol{w}_i, \quad i = 1, \ldots, k, \tag{9.11}$$

$$\text{Cov}(y_i, y_j) = \boldsymbol{w}_i'\boldsymbol{\Sigma}_r\boldsymbol{w}_j, \quad i, j = 1, \ldots, k. \tag{9.12}$$

The idea of PCA is to find linear combinations $\boldsymbol{w}_i$ such that y_i and y_j are uncorrelated for $i \neq j$ and the variances of y_i are as large as possible. More specifically:

1. The first principal component of $\boldsymbol{r}$ is the linear combination $y_1 = \boldsymbol{w}_1'\boldsymbol{r}$ that maximizes $\text{Var}(y_1)$ subject to the constraint $\boldsymbol{w}_1'\boldsymbol{w}_1 = 1$.
2. The second principal component of $\boldsymbol{r}$ is the linear combination $y_2 = \boldsymbol{w}_2'\boldsymbol{r}$ that maximizes $\text{Var}(y_2)$ subject to the constraints $\boldsymbol{w}_2'\boldsymbol{w}_2 = 1$ and $\text{Cov}(y_2, y_1) = 0$.

3. The ith principal component of $\boldsymbol{r}$ is the linear combination $y_i = \boldsymbol{w}_i'\boldsymbol{r}$ that maximizes $\text{Var}(y_i)$ subject to the constraints $\boldsymbol{w}_i'\boldsymbol{w}_i = 1$ and $\text{Cov}(y_i, y_j) = 0$ for $j = 1, \ldots, i-1$.

Since the covariance matrix $\boldsymbol{\Sigma}_r$ is non-negative definite, it has a spectral decomposition; see Appendix A of Chapter 8. Let $(\lambda_1, \boldsymbol{e}_1), \ldots, (\lambda_k, \boldsymbol{e}_k)$ be the eigenvalue–eigenvector pairs of $\boldsymbol{\Sigma}_r$, where $\lambda_1 \geq \lambda_2 \geq \cdots \geq \lambda_k \geq 0$. We have the following statistical result.

Result 9.1. The ith principal component of $\boldsymbol{r}$ is $y_i = \boldsymbol{e}_i'\boldsymbol{r} = \sum_{j=1}^{k} e_{ij} r_j$ for $i = 1, \ldots, k$. Moreover,

$$\text{Var}(y_i) = \boldsymbol{e}_i'\boldsymbol{\Sigma}_r\boldsymbol{e}_i = \lambda_i, \quad i = 1, \ldots, k,$$

$$\text{Cov}(y_i, y_j) = \boldsymbol{e}_i'\boldsymbol{\Sigma}_r\boldsymbol{e}_j = 0, \quad i \neq j.$$

If some eigenvalues λ_i are equal, the choices of the corresponding eigenvectors $\boldsymbol{e}_i$ and hence y_i are not unique. In addition, we have

$$\sum_{i=1}^{k} \text{Var}(r_i) = tr(\boldsymbol{\Sigma}_r) = \sum_{i=1}^{k} \lambda_i = \sum_{i=1}^{k} \text{Var}(y_i). \tag{9.13}$$

The result of Eq. (9.13) says that

$$\frac{\text{Var}(y_i)}{\sum_{i=1}^{k} \text{Var}(r_i)} = \frac{\lambda_i}{\lambda_1 + \cdots + \lambda_k}.$$

Consequently, the proportion of total variance in $\boldsymbol{r}$ explained by the ith principal component is simply the ratio between the ith eigenvalue and the sum of all eigenvalues of $\boldsymbol{\Sigma}_r$. One can also compute the cumulative proportion of total variance explained by the first i principal components (i.e., $(\sum_{j=1}^{i} \lambda_j)/(\sum_{j=1}^{k} \lambda_j)$). In practice, one selects a small i such that the prior cumulative proportion is large.

Since $tr(\boldsymbol{\rho}_r) = k$, the proportion of variance explained by the ith principal component becomes λ_i/k when the correlation matrix is used to perform the PCA.

A by-product of the PCA is that a zero eigenvalue of $\boldsymbol{\Sigma}_r$, or $\boldsymbol{\rho}_r$, indicates the existence of an *exact* linear relationship between the components of $\boldsymbol{r}$. For instance, if the smallest eigenvalue $\lambda_k = 0$, then by Result 9.1 $\text{Var}(y_k) = 0$. Therefore, $y_k = \sum_{j=1}^{k} e_{kj} r_j$ is a constant and there are only $k - 1$ random quantities in $\boldsymbol{r}$. In this case, the dimension of $\boldsymbol{r}$ can be reduced. For this reason, PCA has been used in the literature as a tool for dimension reduction.

9.4.2 Empirical PCA

In application, the covariance matrix $\boldsymbol{\Sigma}_r$ and the correlation matrix $\boldsymbol{\rho}_r$ of the return vector $\boldsymbol{r}$ are unknown, but they can be estimated consistently by the sample covariance and correlation matrices under some regularity conditions. Assuming that the returns are weakly stationary and the data consist of $\{\boldsymbol{r}_t | t = 1, \ldots, T\}$, we have the following estimates:

$$\widehat{\boldsymbol{\Sigma}}_r \equiv [\hat{\sigma}_{ij,r}] = \frac{1}{T-1}\sum_{t=1}^{T}(\boldsymbol{r}_t - \overline{\boldsymbol{r}})(\boldsymbol{r}_t - \overline{\boldsymbol{r}})', \quad \overline{\boldsymbol{r}} = \frac{1}{T}\sum_{t=1}^{T}\boldsymbol{r}_t, \tag{9.14}$$

$$\widehat{\boldsymbol{\rho}}_r = \widehat{\boldsymbol{S}}^{-1}\widehat{\boldsymbol{\Sigma}}_r\widehat{\boldsymbol{S}}^{-1}, \tag{9.15}$$

where $\widehat{\boldsymbol{S}} = \text{diag}\{\sqrt{\hat{\sigma}_{11,r}}, \ldots, \sqrt{\hat{\sigma}_{kk,r}}\}$ is the diagonal matrix of sample standard errors of $\boldsymbol{r}_t$. Methods to compute eigenvalues and eigenvectors of a symmetric matrix can then be used to perform the PCA. Most statistical packages now have the capability to perform principal component analysis. In S-Plus, the basic command of PCA is `princomp`, and in FinMetrics the command is `mfactor`.

Example 9.1. Consider the monthly log returns of International Business Machines, Hewlett-Packard, Intel Corporation, Merrill Lynch, and Morgan Stanley Dean Witter from January 1990 to December 1999. The returns are in percentages and include dividends. The data set has 120 observations. Figure 9.4 shows the time plots of these five monthly return series. As expected, returns of companies in the same industrial sector tend to exhibit similar patterns.

Denote the returns by $\boldsymbol{r}' = $ (IBM, HPQ, INTC, MER, MWD). The sample mean vector of the returns is (1.47, 1.97, 3.05, 2.30, 2.36)$'$ and the sample covariance and correlation matrices are

$$\widehat{\boldsymbol{\Sigma}}_r = \begin{bmatrix} 73.10 & & & & \\ 36.48 & 103.60 & & & \\ 27.08 & 48.86 & 113.96 & & \\ 16.06 & 37.59 & 27.96 & 105.56 & \\ 16.33 & 40.72 & 26.86 & 85.47 & 109.91 \end{bmatrix},$$

$$\widehat{\boldsymbol{\rho}}_r = \begin{bmatrix} 1.00 & & & & \\ 0.42 & 1.00 & & & \\ 0.30 & 0.45 & 1.00 & & \\ 0.18 & 0.36 & 0.26 & 1.00 & \\ 0.18 & 0.38 & 0.24 & 0.79 & 1.00 \end{bmatrix}.$$

Table 9.3 gives the results of PCA using both the covariance and correlation matrices. Also given are eigenvalues, eigenvectors, and proportions of variabilities explained by the principal components. Consider the correlation matrix and denote the sample eigenvalues and eigenvectors by $\hat{\lambda}_i$ and $\widehat{\boldsymbol{e}}_i$. We have

$$\hat{\lambda}_1 = 2.456, \quad \widehat{\boldsymbol{e}}_1 = (0.342, 0.474, 0.387, 0.503, 0.505)',$$

$$\hat{\lambda}_2 = 1.145, \quad \widehat{\boldsymbol{e}}_2 = (0.525, 0.314, 0.405, -0.481, -0.481)'$$

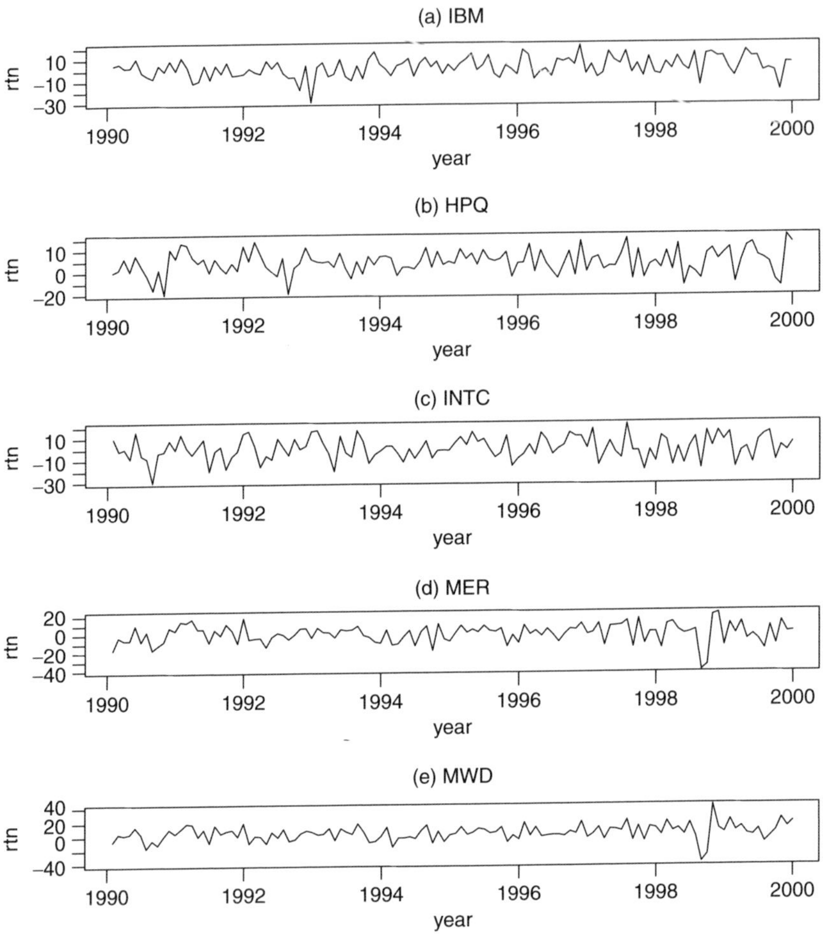

Figure 9.4. Time plots of monthly log returns in percentages and including dividends for (a) International Business Machines, (b) Hewlett-Packard, (c) Intel, (d) Merrill Lynch, and (e) Morgan Stanley Dean Witter from January 1990 to December 1999.

for the first two principal components. These two components explain about 72% of the total variability of the data, and they have interesting interpretations. The first component is a roughly equally weighted linear combination of the stock returns. This component might represent the general movement of the stock market and hence is a *market component*. The second component represents the difference between the two industrial sectors—namely, technologies versus financial services. It might be an *industrial component*. Similar interpretations of principal components can also be found by using the covariance matrix of $\boldsymbol{r}$.

An informal but useful procedure to determine the number of principal components needed in an application is to examine the *scree plot*, which is the time plot of

Table 9.3. Results of Principal Component Analysis[a] for the Monthly Log Returns, Including Dividends, of Stocks of IBM, Hewlett-Packard, Intel, Merrill Lynch, and Morgan Stanley Dean Witter from January 1990 to December 1999

Using Sample Covariance Matrix					
Eigenvalue	256.16	116.14	64.91	46.82	22.11
Proportion	0.506	0.229	0.128	0.093	0.044
Cumulative	0.506	0.736	0.864	0.956	1.000
Eigenvector	0.246	0.327	0.586	−0.700	0.018
	0.461	0.360	0.428	0.687	−0.050
	0.409	0.585	−0.683	−0.153	0.033
	0.522	−0.452	−0.082	−0.115	−0.710
	0.536	−0.467	−0.036	−0.042	0.701
Using Sample Correlation Matrix					
Eigenvalue	2.456	1.145	0.699	0.495	0.205
Proportion	0.491	0.229	0.140	0.099	0.041
Cumulative	0.491	0.720	0.860	0.959	1.000
Eigenvector	0.342	0.525	0.691	−0.362	−0.012
	0.474	0.314	−0.043	0.820	0.050
	0.387	0.405	−0.717	−0.414	−0.034
	0.503	−0.481	0.052	−0.147	0.701
	0.505	−0.481	0.071	−0.062	−0.711

[a]The eigenvectors are in columns.

the eigenvalues $\hat{\lambda}_i$ ordered from the largest to the smallest (i.e., a plot of $\hat{\lambda}_i$ versus i). Figure 9.5a shows the scree plot for the five stock returns of Example 9.1. By looking for an elbow in the scree plot, indicating that the remaining eigenvalues are relatively small and all about the same size, one can determine the appropriate number of components. For both plots in Figure 9.5, two components appear to be appropriate. Finally, except for the case in which $\lambda_j = 0$ for $j > i$, selecting the first i principal components only provides an approximation to the total variance of the data. If a small i can provide a good approximation, then the simplification becomes valuable.

Remark. I have extended the data of Example 9.1 to December 2003. The PCA results of the extended data provide essentially the same information as that shown in the text and, hence, are omitted. The S-Plus commands used to perform the PCA are given below. The S-Plus gives the square root of the eigenvalue and denotes it as standard deviation.

```
> da=matrix(scan(file='m-pca5c-9003.txt'),6)
> rtn = t(da[1:5,])
> pca.cov = princomp(rtn)
> names(pca.cov)
```

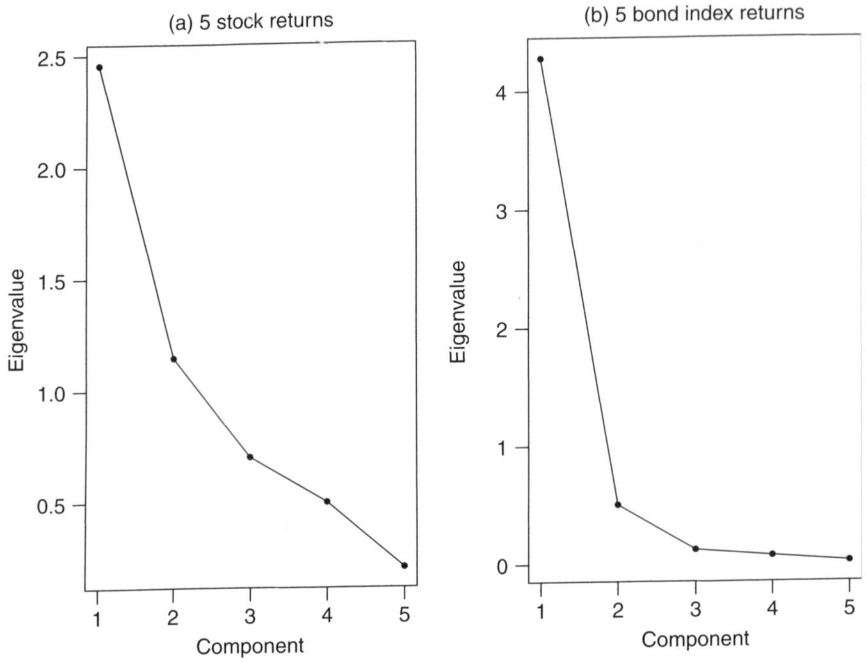

Figure 9.5. Scree plots for two 5-dimensional asset returns: (a) series of Example 9.1 and (b) bond index returns of Example 9.3.

```
> summary(pca.cov)
> pca.cov$loadings
> screeplot(pca.cov)
```

□

9.5 STATISTICAL FACTOR ANALYSIS

We now turn to statistical factor analysis. One of the main difficulties in multivariate statistical analysis is the "curse of dimensionality." In particular, the number of parameters of a parametric model often increase dramatically when the order of the model or the dimension of the time series is increased. Simplifying methods are often sought to overcome the curse of dimensionality. From an empirical viewpoint, multivariate data often exhibit similar patterns indicating the existence of common structure hidden in the data. Statistical factor analysis is one of those simplifying methods available in the literature. The aim of statistical factor analysis is to identify, from the observed data, a few factors that can account for most of the variations in the covariance or correlation matrix of the data.

Traditional statistical factor analysis assumes that the data have no serial correlations. This assumption is often violated by financial data taken with frequency less than or equal to a week. However, the assumption appears to be reasonable for asset returns with lower frequencies (e.g., monthly returns of stocks or market indexes). If the assumption is violated, then one can use the parametric models discussed in this book to remove the linear dynamic dependence of the data and apply factor analysis to the residual series.

In what follows, we discuss statistical factor analysis based on the *orthogonal factor model*. Consider the return $\boldsymbol{r}_t = (r_{1t}, \ldots, r_{kt})'$ of k assets at time period t and assume that the return series $\boldsymbol{r}_t$ is weakly stationary with mean $\boldsymbol{\mu}$ and covariance matrix $\boldsymbol{\Sigma}_r$. The statistical factor model postulates that $\boldsymbol{r}_t$ is linearly dependent on a few *unobservable* random variables $\boldsymbol{f}_t = (f_{1t}, \ldots, f_{mt})'$ and k additional noises $\boldsymbol{\epsilon}_t = (\epsilon_{1t}, \ldots, \epsilon_{kt})'$. Here $m < k$, f_{it} are the common factors, and ϵ_{it} are the errors. Mathematically, the statistical factor model is also in the form of Eq. (9.1) except that the intercept $\boldsymbol{\alpha}$ is replaced by the mean return $\boldsymbol{\mu}$. Thus, a statistical factor model is in the form

$$\boldsymbol{r}_t - \boldsymbol{\mu} = \boldsymbol{\beta} \boldsymbol{f}_t + \boldsymbol{\epsilon}_t, \tag{9.16}$$

where $\boldsymbol{\beta} = [\beta_{ij}]_{k\times m}$ is the *matrix of factor loadings*, β_{ij} is the loading of the ith variable on the jth factor, and ϵ_{it} is the *specific error* of r_{it}. A key feature of the statistical factor model is that the m factors f_{it} and the factor-loadings β_{ij} are *unobservable*. As such, Eq. (9.16) is not a multivariate linear regression model, even though it has a similar appearance. This special feature also distinguishes a statistical factor model from other factor models discussed earlier.

The factor model in Eq. (9.16) is an orthogonal factor model if it satisfies the following assumptions:

1. $E(\boldsymbol{f}_t) = \boldsymbol{0}$ and $\text{Cov}(\boldsymbol{f}_t) = \boldsymbol{I}_m$, the $m \times m$ identity matrix;
2. $E(\boldsymbol{\epsilon}_t) = \boldsymbol{0}$ and $\text{Cov}(\boldsymbol{\epsilon}_t) = \boldsymbol{D} = \text{diag}\{\sigma_1^2, \ldots, \sigma_k^2\}$ (i.e., $\boldsymbol{D}$ is a $k \times k$ diagonal matrix); and
3. $\boldsymbol{f}_t$ and $\boldsymbol{\epsilon}_t$ are independent so that $\text{Cov}(\boldsymbol{f}_t, \boldsymbol{\epsilon}_t) = E(\boldsymbol{f}_t\boldsymbol{\epsilon}_t') = \boldsymbol{0}_{m\times k}$.

Under the previous assumptions, it is easy to see that

$$\begin{aligned} \boldsymbol{\Sigma}_r = \text{Cov}(\boldsymbol{r}_t) &= E[(\boldsymbol{r}_t - \boldsymbol{\mu})(\boldsymbol{r}_t - \boldsymbol{\mu})'] \\ &= E[(\boldsymbol{\beta}\boldsymbol{f}_t + \boldsymbol{\epsilon}_t)(\boldsymbol{\beta}\boldsymbol{f}_t + \boldsymbol{\epsilon}_t)'] \\ &= \boldsymbol{\beta}\boldsymbol{\beta}' + \boldsymbol{D} \end{aligned} \tag{9.17}$$

and

$$\text{Cov}(\boldsymbol{r}_t, \boldsymbol{f}_t) = E[(\boldsymbol{r}_t - \boldsymbol{\mu})\boldsymbol{f}_t'] = \boldsymbol{\beta} E(\boldsymbol{f}_t\boldsymbol{f}_t') + E(\boldsymbol{\epsilon}_t\boldsymbol{f}_t') = \boldsymbol{\beta}. \tag{9.18}$$

Using Eqs. (9.17) and (9.18), we see that for the orthogonal factor model in Eq. (9.16)

$$\begin{aligned} \text{Var}(r_{it}) &= \beta_{i1}^2 + \cdots + \beta_{im}^2 + \sigma_i^2, \\ \text{Cov}(r_{it}, r_{jt}) &= \beta_{i1}\beta_{j1} + \cdots + \beta_{im}\beta_{jm}, \\ \text{Cov}(r_{it}, f_{jt}) &= \beta_{ij}. \end{aligned}$$

The quantity $\beta_{i1}^2 + \cdots + \beta_{im}^2$, which is the portion of the variance of r_{it} contributed by the m common factors, is called the *communality*. The remaining portion σ_i^2 of the variance of r_{it} is called the *uniqueness* or *specific variance*. Let $c_i^2 = \beta_{i1}^2 + \cdots + \beta_{im}^2$ be the communality, which is the sum of squares of the loadings of the ith variable on the m common factors. The variance of component r_{it} becomes $\text{Var}(r_{it}) = c_i^2 + \sigma_i^2$.

In practice, not every covariance matrix has an orthogonal factor representation. In other words, there exists a random variable $\boldsymbol{r}_t$ that does not have any orthogonal factor representation. Furthermore, the orthogonal factor representation of a random variable is not unique. In fact, for any $m \times m$ orthogonal matrix $\boldsymbol{P}$ satisfying $\boldsymbol{P}\boldsymbol{P}' = \boldsymbol{P}'\boldsymbol{P} = \boldsymbol{I}$, let $\boldsymbol{\beta}^* = \boldsymbol{\beta}\boldsymbol{P}$ and $\boldsymbol{f}_t^* = \boldsymbol{P}'\boldsymbol{f}_t$. Then

$$\boldsymbol{r}_t - \boldsymbol{\mu} = \boldsymbol{\beta}\boldsymbol{f}_t + \boldsymbol{\epsilon}_t = \boldsymbol{\beta}\boldsymbol{P}\boldsymbol{P}'\boldsymbol{f}_t + \boldsymbol{\epsilon}_t = \boldsymbol{\beta}^*\boldsymbol{f}_t^* + \boldsymbol{\epsilon}_t.$$

In addition, $E(\boldsymbol{f}_t^*) = \boldsymbol{0}$ and $\text{Cov}(\boldsymbol{f}_t^*) = \boldsymbol{P}'\text{Cov}(\boldsymbol{f}_t)\boldsymbol{P} = \boldsymbol{P}'\boldsymbol{P} = \boldsymbol{I}$. Thus, $\boldsymbol{\beta}^*$ and $\boldsymbol{f}_t^*$ form another orthogonal factor model for $\boldsymbol{r}_t$. This nonuniqueness of orthogonal factor representation is a weakness as well as an advantage for factor analysis. It is a weakness because it makes the meaning of factor loading arbitrary. It is an advantage because it allows us to perform rotations to find common factors that have nice interpretations. Because $\boldsymbol{P}$ is an orthogonal matrix, the transformation $\boldsymbol{f}_t^* = \boldsymbol{P}'\boldsymbol{f}_t$ is a rotation in the m-dimensional space.

9.5.1 Estimation

The orthogonal factor model in Eq. (9.16) can be estimated by two methods. The first estimation method uses the principal component analysis of the previous section. This method does not require the normality assumption of the data nor the prespecification of the number of common factors. It applies to both the covariance and correlation matrices. But as mentioned in PCA, the solution is often an approximation. The second estimation method is the maximum likelihood method that uses normal density and requires a prespecification for the number of common factors.

Principal Component Method

Again let $(\hat{\lambda}_1, \widehat{\boldsymbol{e}}_1), \ldots, (\hat{\lambda}_k, \widehat{\boldsymbol{e}}_k)$ be pairs of the eigenvalues and eigenvectors of the sample covariance matrix $\widehat{\boldsymbol{\Sigma}}_r$, where $\hat{\lambda}_1 \geq \hat{\lambda}_2 \geq \cdots \geq \hat{\lambda}_k$. Let $m < k$ be the number of common factors. Then the matrix of factor loadings is given by

$$\widehat{\boldsymbol{\beta}} \equiv [\hat{\beta}_{ij}] = \left[\sqrt{\hat{\lambda}_1}\widehat{\boldsymbol{e}}_1 \middle| \sqrt{\hat{\lambda}_2}\widehat{\boldsymbol{e}}_2 \middle| \cdots \middle| \sqrt{\hat{\lambda}_m}\widehat{\boldsymbol{e}}_m\right]. \tag{9.19}$$

The estimated specific variances are the diagonal elements of the matrix $\widehat{\boldsymbol{\Sigma}}_r - \widehat{\boldsymbol{\beta}}\widehat{\boldsymbol{\beta}}'$. That is, $\widehat{\boldsymbol{D}} = \text{diag}\{\hat{\sigma}_1^2, \ldots, \hat{\sigma}_k^2\}$, where $\hat{\sigma}_i^2 = \hat{\sigma}_{ii,r} - \sum_{j=1}^m \hat{\beta}_{ij}^2$, where $\hat{\sigma}_{ii,r}$ is the (i, i)th element of $\widehat{\boldsymbol{\Sigma}}_r$. The communalities are estimated by

$$\hat{c}_i^2 = \hat{\beta}_{i1}^2 + \cdots + \hat{\beta}_{im}^2.$$

The error matrix caused by approximation is

$$\widehat{\boldsymbol{\Sigma}}_r - (\widehat{\boldsymbol{\beta}}\widehat{\boldsymbol{\beta}}' + \widehat{\boldsymbol{D}}).$$

Ideally, we would like this matrix to be close to zero. It can be shown that the sum of squared elements of $\widehat{\boldsymbol{\Sigma}}_r - (\widehat{\boldsymbol{\beta}}\widehat{\boldsymbol{\beta}}' + \widehat{\boldsymbol{D}})$ is less than or equal to $\hat{\lambda}_{m+1}^2 + \cdots + \hat{\lambda}_k^2$. Therefore, the approximation error is bounded by the sum of squares of the neglected eigenvalues.

From the solution in Eq. (9.19), the estimated factor loadings based on the principal component method do not change as the number of common factors m is increased.

Maximum Likelihood Method

If the common factors $\boldsymbol{f}_t$ and the specific factors $\boldsymbol{\epsilon}_t$ are jointly normal, then $\boldsymbol{r}_t$ is multivariate normal with mean $\boldsymbol{\mu}$ and covariance matrix $\boldsymbol{\Sigma}_r = \boldsymbol{\beta}\boldsymbol{\beta}' + \boldsymbol{D}$. The maximum likelihood method can then be used to obtain estimates of $\boldsymbol{\beta}$ and $\boldsymbol{D}$ under the constraint $\boldsymbol{\beta}'\boldsymbol{D}^{-1}\boldsymbol{\beta} = \boldsymbol{\Delta}$, which is a diagonal matrix. Here $\boldsymbol{\mu}$ is estimated by the sample mean. For more details of this method, readers are referred to Johnson and Wichern (2002).

In using the maximum likelihood method, the number of common factors must be given a priori. In practice, one can use a modified likelihood ratio test to check the adequacy of a fitted m-factor model. The test statistic is

$$\text{LR}(m) = -[T - 1 - \tfrac{1}{6}(2k+5) - \tfrac{2}{3}m](\ln|\widehat{\boldsymbol{\Sigma}}_r| - \ln|\widehat{\boldsymbol{\beta}}\widehat{\boldsymbol{\beta}}' + \widehat{\boldsymbol{D}}|), \tag{9.20}$$

which, under the null hypothesis of m factors, is asymptotically distributed as a chi-squared distribution with $\frac{1}{2}[(k-m)^2 - k - m]$ degrees of freedom. We discuss some methods for selecting m in Section 9.6.1.

9.5.2 Factor Rotation

As mentioned before, for any $m \times m$ orthogonal matrix $\boldsymbol{P}$,

$$\boldsymbol{r}_t - \boldsymbol{\mu} = \boldsymbol{\beta}\boldsymbol{f}_t + \boldsymbol{\epsilon}_t = \boldsymbol{\beta}^*\boldsymbol{f}_t^* + \boldsymbol{\epsilon}_t,$$

where $\boldsymbol{\beta}^* = \boldsymbol{\beta}\ \boldsymbol{P}$ and $\boldsymbol{f}_t^* = \boldsymbol{P}'\boldsymbol{f}_t$. In addition,

$$\boldsymbol{\beta}\boldsymbol{\beta}' + \boldsymbol{D} = \boldsymbol{\beta}\boldsymbol{P}\ \boldsymbol{P}'\boldsymbol{\beta}' + \boldsymbol{D} = \boldsymbol{\beta}^*(\boldsymbol{\beta}^*)' + \boldsymbol{D}.$$

This result indicates that the communalities and the specific variances remain unchanged under an orthogonal transformation. It is then reasonable to find an orthogonal matrix $\boldsymbol{P}$ to transform the factor model so that the common factors have nice interpretations. Such a transformation is equivalent to rotating the common factors in the m-dimensional space. In fact, there are infinite possible factor rotations available. Kaiser (1958) proposes a *varimax* criterion to select the rotation that works well in many applications. Denote the rotated matrix of factor loadings by $\boldsymbol{\beta}^* = [\beta^*_{ij}]$ and the ith communality by c_i^2. Define $\tilde{\beta}^*_{ij} = \beta^*_{ij}/c_i$ to be the rotated coefficients scaled by the (positive) square root of communalities. The varimax procedure selects the orthogonal matrix $\boldsymbol{P}$ that maximizes the quantity

$$V = \frac{1}{k}\sum_{j=1}^{m}\left[\sum_{i=1}^{k}(\tilde{\beta}^*_{ij})^4 - \frac{1}{k}\left(\sum_{i=1}^{k}\tilde{\beta}^{*2}_{ij}\right)^2\right].$$

This complicated expression has a simple interpretation. Maximizing V corresponds to spreading out the squares of the loadings on each factor as much as possible. Consequently, the procedure is to find groups of large and negligible coefficients in any column of the rotated matrix of factor loadings. In a real application, factor rotation is used to aid the interpretations of common factors. It may be helpful in some applications, but not informative in others. There are many criteria available for factor rotation.

9.5.3 Applications

Given the data $\{\boldsymbol{r}_t\}$ of asset returns, the statistical factor analysis enables us to search for common factors that explain the variabilities of the returns. Since factor analysis assumes no serial correlations in the data, one should check the validity of this assumption before using factor analysis. The multivariate portmanteau statistics can be used for this purpose. If serial correlations are found, one can build a VARMA model to remove the dynamic dependence in the data and apply the factor analysis to the residual series. For many returns series, the correlation matrix of the residuals of a linear model is often very close to the correlation matrix of the original data. In this case, the effect of dynamic dependence on factor analysis is negligible.

We consider three examples in this subsection. The first two examples use the Minitab software to perform the analysis and the third example uses S-Plus. Other packages can also be used.

Example 9.2. Consider again the monthly log stock returns of IBM, Hewlett-Packard, Intel, Merrill Lynch, and Morgan Stanley Dean Witter used in Example 9.1. To check the assumption of no serial correlations, we compute the portmanteau statistics and obtain $Q_5(1) = 34.28$, $Q_5(4) = 114.30$, and $Q_5(8) = 216.78$. Compared with chi-squared distributions with 25, 100, and 200 degrees of freedom, the p-values of these test statistics are 0.102, 0.156, and 0.198, respectively. Therefore, the assumption of no serial correlations cannot be rejected even at the 10% level.

Table 9.4 shows the results of factor analysis based on the correlation matrix using both the principal component and maximum likelihood methods. We assume that the number of common factors is 2, which is reasonable according to the principal component analysis of Example 9.1. From the table, the factor analysis reveals several interesting findings:

- The two factors identified by the principal component method explain more variability than those identified by the maximum likelihood method.

Table 9.4. Factor Analysis of the Monthly Log Stock Returns[a] of IBM, Hewlett-Packard, Intel, Merrill Lynch, and Morgan Stanley Dean Witter

Variable	Estimates of Factor Loadings		Rotated Factor Loadings		Communalities
	f_1	f_2	f_1^*	f_2^*	$1-\sigma_i^2$
		Principal Component Method			
IBM	0.536	0.561	0.011	0.776	0.602
HPQ	0.744	0.335	0.317	0.752	0.665
INTC	0.607	0.433	0.151	0.730	0.556
MER	0.788	−0.515	0.928	0.158	0.887
MWD	0.791	−0.514	0.930	0.161	0.891
Variance	2.456	1.145	1.850	1.751	3.601
Proportion	0.491	0.229	0.370	0.350	0.720
		Maximum Likelihood Method			
IBM	0.191	0.496	0.087	0.524	0.282
HPQ	0.394	0.689	0.247	0.755	0.630
INTC	0.250	0.511	0.141	0.551	0.323
MER	0.800	0.072	0.769	0.232	0.645
MWD	0.994	−0.015	0.976	0.186	0.988
Variance	1.881	0.987	1.632	1.236	2.868
Proportion	0.376	0.197	0.326	0.247	0.574

[a]The returns include dividends and are from January 1990 to December 1999. The analysis is based on the sample cross-correlation matrix and assumes two common factors.

- Based on the rotated factor loadings, the two estimation methods identify essentially the same two common factors for the data. The financial stocks (Merrill Lynch and Morgan Stanley Dean Witter) load heavily on the first factor, whereas the technology stocks (IBM, Hewlett-Packard, and Intel) load highly on the second factor. These two rotated factors jointly differentiate the industrial sectors.
- In this particular instance, the varimax rotation does not change much the two factors identified by the maximum likelihood method. Yet the first unrotated factor identified by the principal component method was destroyed by the rotation. This is not surprising in view of the idea behind the varimax criterion.
- The specific variances of IBM and Intel stock returns are relatively large based on the maximum likelihood method, indicating that these two stocks have their own features that are worth further investigation.

Example 9.3. In this example, we consider the monthly log returns of U.S. bond indexes with maturities in 30 years, 20 years, 10 years, 5 years, and 1 year.

The data are described in Example 9.2 but have been transformed into log returns. There are 696 observations. As shown in Example 9.2, there is serial dependence in the data. However, removing serial dependence by fitting a VARMA(2,1) model has hardly any effects on the concurrent correlation matrix. As a matter of fact, the correlation matrices before and after fitting a VARMA(2,1) model are

$$\widehat{\boldsymbol{\rho}}_o = \begin{bmatrix} 1.0 & & & & \\ 0.98 & 1.0 & & & \\ 0.92 & 0.91 & 1.0 & & \\ 0.85 & 0.86 & 0.90 & 1.0 & \\ 0.63 & 0.64 & 0.67 & 0.81 & 1.0 \end{bmatrix}, \quad \widehat{\boldsymbol{\rho}} = \begin{bmatrix} 1.0 & & & & \\ 0.98 & 1.0 & & & \\ 0.92 & 0.92 & 1.0 & & \\ 0.85 & 0.86 & 0.90 & 1.0 & \\ 0.66 & 0.67 & 0.71 & 0.84 & 1.0 \end{bmatrix},$$

where $\widehat{\boldsymbol{\rho}}_o$ is the correlation matrix of the original log returns. Therefore, we apply factor analysis directly to the return series.

Table 9.5 shows the results of statistical factor analysis of the data. For both estimation methods, the first two common factors explain more than 90% of the total variability of the data. Indeed, the high communalities indicate that the specific

Table 9.5. Factor Analysis of the Monthly Log Returns of U.S. Bond Indexes with Maturities in 30 Years, 20 Years, 10 Years, 5 Years, and 1 Year[a]

	Estimates of Factor Loadings		Rotated Factor Loadings		Communalities
Variable	f_1	f_2	f_1^*	f_2^*	$1-\sigma_i^2$
	Principal Component Method				
30 years	0.952	0.253	0.927	0.333	0.970
20 years	0.954	0.240	0.922	0.345	0.968
10 years	0.956	0.140	0.866	0.429	0.934
5 years	0.955	−0.142	0.704	0.660	0.931
1 year	0.800	−0.585	0.325	0.936	0.982
Variance	4.281	0.504	3.059	1.726	4.785
Proportion	0.856	0.101	0.612	0.345	0.957
	Maximum Likelihood Method				
30 years	0.849	−0.513	0.895	0.430	0.985
20 years	0.857	−0.486	0.876	0.451	0.970
10 years	0.896	−0.303	0.744	0.584	0.895
5 years	1.000	0.000	0.547	0.837	1.000
1 year	0.813	0.123	0.342	0.747	0.675
Variance	3.918	0.607	2.538	1.987	4.525
Proportion	0.784	0.121	0.508	0.397	0.905

[a]The data are from January 1942 to December 1999. The analysis is based on the sample cross-correlation matrix and assumes two common factors.

variances are very small for the five bond index returns. Because the results of the two methods are close, we only discuss that of the principal component method. The unrotated factor loadings indicate that (a) all five return series load roughly equally on the first factor, and (b) the loadings on the second factor are positively correlated with the time to maturity. Therefore, the first common factor represents the general U.S. bond returns, and the second factor shows the "time-to-maturity" effect. Furthermore, the loadings of the second factor sum approximately to zero. Therefore, this common factor can also be interpreted as the contrast between long-term and short-term bonds. Here a long-term bond means one with maturity 10 years or longer. For the rotated factors, the loadings are also interesting. The loadings for the first rotated factor are proportional to the time to maturity, whereas the loadings of the second factor are inversely proportional to the time to maturity.

Example 9.4. Again, consider the monthly excess returns of the ten stocks in Table 9.2. The sample span is from January 1990 to December 2003 and the returns are in percentages. Our goal here is to demonstrate the use of statistical factor models using the S-Plus command `factanal`. We started with a two-factor model, but it is rejected by the likelihood ratio test of Eq. (9.20). The test statistic is $\text{LR}(2) = 72.96$. Based on the asymptotic χ^2_{26} distribution, p-value of the test statistic is close to zero.

```
> da=matrix(scan(file='m-barra-9003.txt'),10)
> rtn=t(da)
> stat.fac=factanal(rtn,factors=2,method='mle')
> stat.fac
Sums of squares of loadings:
  Factor1 Factor2
 2.696479 2.19149

Component names:
 "loadings" "uniquenesses" "correlation" "criteria"
 "factors" "dof" "method"  "center" "scale" "n.obs"
 "scores" "call"
```

We then applied a three-factor model that appears to be reasonable at the 5% significance level. The p-value of the LR(3) statistic is 0.0892.

```
> stat.fac=factanal(rtn,factor=3,method='mle')
> stat.fac
Test of the hypothesis that 3 factors are sufficient
versus the alternative that more are required:
The chi square statistic is 26.48 on 18 degrees of freedom.
The p-value is 0.0892

> summary(stat.fac)
Importance of factors:
```

```
                   Factor1   Factor2   Factor3
   SS loadings      2.635     1.825     1.326
Proportion Var      0.264     0.183     0.133
Cumulative Var      0.264     0.446     0.579

Uniquenesses:
   AGE     C     MWD   MER  DELL   HPQ   IBM
 0.479 0.341 0.201 0.216 0.690 0.346 0.638
   AA    CAT    PG
 0.417 0.000 0.885

Loadings:
     Factor1 Factor2 Factor3
AGE   0.678   0.217   0.121
C     0.739   0.259   0.213
MWD   0.817   0.356
MER   0.819   0.329
DELL  0.102   0.547
HPQ   0.230   0.771
IBM   0.200   0.515   0.238
AA    0.194   0.546   0.497
CAT   0.198   0.138   0.970
PG    0.331
```

The factor loadings can also be shown graphically using

```
> plot(loadings(stat.fac))
```

and the plots are in Figure 9.6. From the plots, factor 1 represents essentially the financial service sector, and factor 2 mainly consists of the excess returns from the high-tech stocks and the Alcoa stock. Factor 3 depends heavily on excess returns of CAT and AA stocks and, hence, represents the remaining industrial sector.

Factor rotation can be obtained using the command `rotate`, which allows for many rotation methods, and factor realizations are available from the command `predict`.

```
> stat.fac2 = rotate(stat.fac,rotation='quartimax')
> loadings(stat.fac2)
     Factor1 Factor2 Factor3
AGE   0.700   0.171
C     0.772   0.216   0.124
MWD   0.844   0.291
MER   0.844   0.264
DELL  0.144   0.536
HPQ   0.294   0.753
IBM   0.258   0.518   0.164
AA    0.278   0.575   0.418
CAT   0.293   0.219   0.931
```

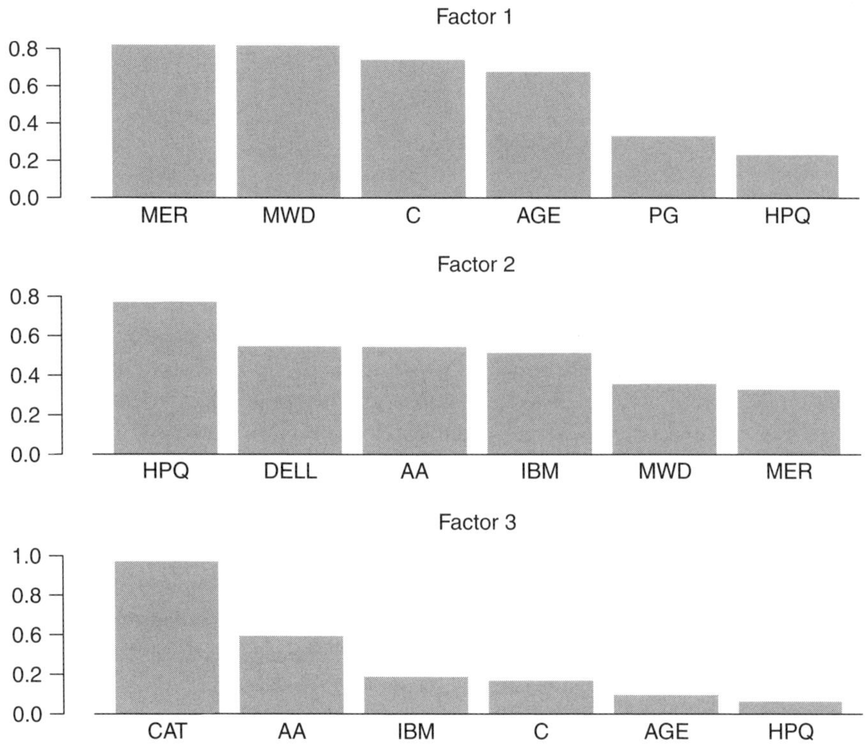

Figure 9.6. Plots of factor loadings when a three-factor statistical factor model is fitted to the ten monthly excess stock returns in Table 9.2.

```
PG    0.334
> factor.real=predict(stat.fac,type='weighted.ls')
```

Finally, we obtained the correlation matrix of the ten excess returns based on the fitted three-factor statistical factor model. As expected, the correlations are closer to their sample counterparts than those of the industrial factor model in Section 9.3.1. One can also use GMVP to compare the covariance matrices of the returns and the statistical factor model.

```
> corr.fit=fitted(stat.fac)
> print(corr.fit,digits=1,width=2)
     AGE  C   MWD MER DELL HPQ IBM AA  CAT PG
AGE  1.0 0.6 0.6 0.6 0.19 0.3 0.3 0.3 0.3 0.2
C    0.6 1.0 0.7 0.7 0.22 0.4 0.3 0.4 0.4 0.3
MWD  0.6 0.7 1.0 0.8 0.28 0.5 0.4 0.4 0.3 0.3
MER  0.6 0.7 0.8 1.0 0.26 0.5 0.4 0.4 0.3 0.3
DELL 0.2 0.2 0.3 0.3 1.00 0.5 0.3 0.3 0.1 0.0
HPQ  0.3 0.4 0.5 0.4 0.45 1.0 0.5 0.5 0.2 0.1
```

```
IBM  0.3 0.3 0.4 0.3 0.31 0.5 1.0 0.4 0.3 0.1
AA   0.3 0.4 0.4 0.4 0.33 0.5 0.4 1.0 0.6 0.1
CAT  0.3 0.4 0.3 0.3 0.11 0.2 0.3 0.6 1.0 0.1
PG   0.2 0.3 0.3 0.3 0.03 0.1 0.1 0.1 0.1 1.0
```

9.6 ASYMPTOTIC PRINCIPAL COMPONENT ANALYSIS

So far, our discussion of PCA assumes that the number of assets is smaller than the number of time periods, that is, $k < T$. To deal with situations of a small T and large k, Conner and Korajczyk (1986, 1988) developed the concept of *asymptotic principal component analysis* (APCA), which is similar to the traditional PCA but relies on the asymptotic results as the number of assets k increases to infinity. Thus, the APCA is based on eigenvalue–eigenvector analysis of the $T \times T$ matrix

$$\widehat{\mathbf{\Omega}}_T = \frac{1}{k-1}\sum_{i=1}^{k}(\boldsymbol{R}_i - \overline{\boldsymbol{R}})(\boldsymbol{R}_i - \overline{\boldsymbol{R}})',$$

where $\boldsymbol{R}_i$ is the time series of ith asset as defined in Eq. (9.3), and $\overline{\boldsymbol{R}} = (1/k) \times \sum_{i=1}^{k} \boldsymbol{R}_i$. In other words, $\overline{\boldsymbol{R}}$ is the time series of the average returns of all stocks used. Alternatively, using the notation in Eq. (9.4), we have

$$\widehat{\mathbf{\Omega}}_T = \frac{1}{k-1}(\boldsymbol{R} - \overline{\boldsymbol{R}} \otimes \mathbf{1}_k')(\boldsymbol{R} - \overline{\boldsymbol{R}} \otimes \mathbf{1}_k')',$$

where $\mathbf{1}_k$ is the k-dimensional vector of ones. Conner and Korajczyk showed that as $k \to \infty$ eigenvalue–eigenvector analysis of $\widehat{\mathbf{\Omega}}_T$ is equivalent to the traditional statistical factor analysis. In other words, the APCA estimates of the factors $\boldsymbol{f}_t$ are the first m eigenvectors of $\widehat{\mathbf{\Omega}}_T$. Let $\widehat{\boldsymbol{F}}_t$ be the $m \times T$ matrix consisting of the first m eigenvectors of $\widehat{\mathbf{\Omega}}_T$. Then $\widehat{\boldsymbol{f}}_t$ is the tth column of $\widehat{\boldsymbol{F}}_t$. Using an idea similar to the estimation of BARRA factor models, Connor and Korajczyk (1988) propose refining the estimation of $\widehat{\boldsymbol{f}}_t$ as follows:

1. Use the sample covariance matrix $\widehat{\mathbf{\Omega}}_T$ to obtain an initial estimate of $\widehat{\boldsymbol{f}}_t$ for $t = 1, \ldots, T$.
2. For each asset, perform the OLS estimation of the model

$$r_{it} = \alpha_i + \boldsymbol{\beta}_i'\widehat{\boldsymbol{f}}_t + \epsilon_{it}, \quad t = 1, \ldots, T,$$

   and compute the residual variance $\hat{\sigma}_i^2$.
3. Form the diagonal matrix $\widehat{\boldsymbol{D}} = \text{diag}\{\hat{\sigma}_1^2, \ldots, \hat{\sigma}_k^2\}$ and rescale the returns as

$$\boldsymbol{R}_* = \boldsymbol{R}\widehat{\boldsymbol{D}}^{-1/2}.$$

4. Compute the $T \times T$ covariance matrix using $\boldsymbol{R}_*$ as

$$\widehat{\boldsymbol{\Omega}}_* = \frac{1}{k-1}(\boldsymbol{R}_* - \overline{\boldsymbol{R}}_* \otimes \boldsymbol{1}_k')(\boldsymbol{R}_* - \overline{\boldsymbol{R}}_* \otimes \boldsymbol{1}_k')',$$

where $\overline{\boldsymbol{R}}_*$ is the vector of row averages of $\boldsymbol{R}_*$, and perform eigenvalue–eigenvector analysis of $\widehat{\boldsymbol{\Omega}}_*$ to obtain a refined estimate of $\boldsymbol{f}_t$.

9.6.1 Selecting the Number of Factors

Two methods are available in the literature to help select the number of factors in factor analysis. The first method proposed by Connor and Korajczyk (1993) makes use of the idea that if m is the proper number of common factors, then there should be no significant decrease in the cross-sectional variance of the asset specific error ϵ_{it} when the number of factors moves from m to $m+1$. The second method proposed by Bai and Ng (2002) adopts some information criteria to select the number of factors. This latter method is based on the observation that the eigenvalue–eigenvector analysis of $\widehat{\boldsymbol{\Omega}}_T$ solves the least squares problem

$$\min_{\alpha,\boldsymbol{\beta},\boldsymbol{f}_t} \frac{1}{kT}\sum_{i=1}^{k}\sum_{t=1}^{T}(r_{it} - \alpha_i - \boldsymbol{\beta}_i'\boldsymbol{f}_t)^2.$$

Assume that there are m factors so that $\boldsymbol{f}_t$ is m-dimensional. Let $\hat{\sigma}_i^2(m)$ be the residual variance of the inner regression of the prior least squares problem for asset i. This is done by using $\widehat{\boldsymbol{f}}_t$ obtained from the APCA analysis. Define the cross-sectional average of the residual variances as

$$\hat{\sigma}^2(m) = \frac{1}{k}\sum_{i=1}^{k}\hat{\sigma}_i^2(m).$$

The criteria proposed by Bai and Ng (2002) are

$$C_{p1}(m) = \hat{\sigma}^2(m) + m\hat{\sigma}^2(M)\left(\frac{k+T}{kT}\right)\ln\left(\frac{kT}{k+T}\right),$$

$$C_{p2}(m) = \hat{\sigma}^2(m) + m\hat{\sigma}^2(M)\left(\frac{k+T}{kT}\right)\ln(P_{kT}^2),$$

where M is a prespecified positive integer denoting the maximum number of factors and $P_{kT} = \min(\sqrt{k}, \sqrt{T})$. One selects m that minimizes either $C_{p1}(m)$ or $C_{p2}(m)$ for $0 \le m \le M$. In practice, the two criteria may select different numbers of factors.

9.6.2 An Example

To demonstrate asymptotic principal component analysis, we consider monthly simple returns of 40 stocks from January 2001 to December 2003 for 36 observations.

Table 9.6. Tick Symbols of Stocks Used in Asymptotic Principal Component Analysis for Sample Period from January 2001 to December 2003

Market	Tick Symbol				
NASDAQ	INTC	MSFT	SUNW	CSCO	AMAT
	ORCL	SIRI	COCO	CORV	SUPG
	YHOO	JDSU	QCOM	CIEN	DELL
	ERTS	EBAY	ADCT	AAPL	JNPR
NYSE	LU	PFE	NT	BAC	BSX
	GE	TXN	XOM	FRX	Q
	F	TWX	C	MOT	JPM
	TYC	HPQ	NOK	WMT	AMD

Thus, we have $k = 40$ and $T = 36$. The tick symbols of stocks used are given in Table 9.6. These stocks are among those heavily traded on NASDAQ and the NYSE on a particular day of September 2004. The main S-Plus command used is `mfactor`.

To select the number of factors, we used the two methods discussed earlier. The Connor–Korajczyk method selects $m = 1$ whereas the Bai–Ng method uses $m = 6$. For the latter method, the two criteria provide different results.

```
> dim(rtn)  % rtn is the return data.
[1] 36 40
> nf.ck=mfactor(rtn,k='ck',max.k=10,sig=0.05)
> nf.ck
Call:
mfactor(x = rtn, k = "ck", max.k = 10, sig = 0.05)

Factor Model:
 Factors Variables Periods
       1        40      36
Factor Loadings:
       Min. 1st Qu. Median   Mean 3rd Qu.  Max.
F.1  0.069  0.432   0.629   0.688  1.071  1.612

Regression R-squared:
   Min. 1st Qu. Median   Mean 3rd Qu.   Max.
 0.090  0.287   0.487   0.456  0.574   0.831
> nf.bn=mfactor(rtn,k='bn',max.k=10,sig=0.05)
Warning messages:
Cp1 & Cp2 did not yield same result.The smaller one is used.
> nf.bn$k
[1] 6
```

Using $m = 6$, we apply APCA to the returns. The scree plot and estimated factor returns can also be obtained.

```
> apca = mfactor(rtn,k=6)
> apca
Call:
mfactor(x = rtn, k = 6)
Factor Model:
 Factors Variables Periods
       6        40      36
Factor Loadings:
           Min  1st Qu. Median    Mean  3rd Qu.  Max.
F.1      0.048   0.349   0.561   0.643   0.952  2.222
F.2     -1.737   0.084   0.216   0.214   0.323  1.046
F.3     -1.512   0.002   0.076   0.102   0.255  1.093
F.4     -0.965  -0.035   0.078   0.048   0.202  0.585
F.5     -0.722  -0.008   0.056   0.066   0.214  0.729
F.6     -0.840  -0.088   0.003   0.003   0.071  0.635
Regression R-squared:
   Min. 1st Qu. Median  Mean 3rd Qu.  Max.
 0.219  0.480   0.695  0.651  0.801  0.999

> screeplot.mfactor(apca)
> fplot(factors(apca))
```

Figure 9.7 shows the scree plot of the APCA for the 40 stock returns. The six common factors used explain about 89.4% of the variability. Figure 9.8 gives the time plots of the returns of the six estimated factors.

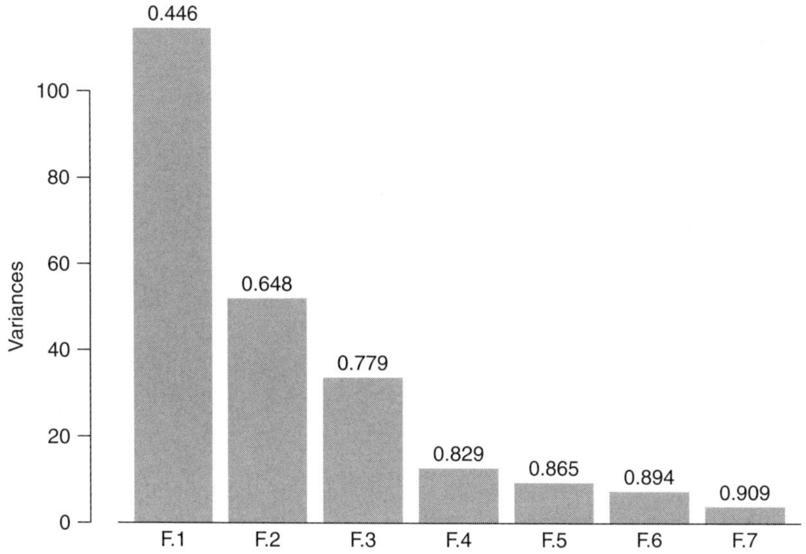

Figure 9.7. Scree plot of asymptotic principal component analysis applied to monthly simple returns of 40 stocks. The sample period is from January 2001 to December 2003.

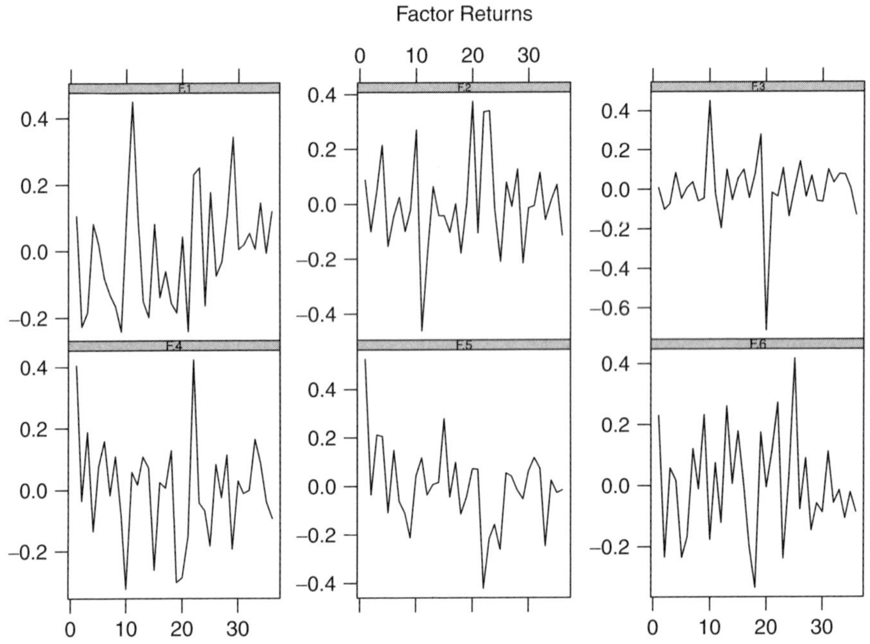

Figure 9.8. Time plots of factor returns derived from applying the asymptotic principal component analysis to monthly simple returns of 40 stocks. The sample period is from January 2001 to December 2003.

EXERCISES

9.1. Consider the monthly log stock returns, in percentages and including dividends, of Merck & Company, Johnson & Johnson, General Electric, General Motors, Ford Motor Company, and value-weighted index from January 1960 to December 1999; see the file `m-mrk2vw.txt`, which has six columns in the order listed before.

(**a**) Perform a principal component analysis of the data using the sample covariance matrix.

(**b**) Perform a principal component analysis of the data using the sample correlation matrix.

(**c**) Perform a statistical factor analysis on the data. Identify the number of common factors. Obtain estimates of factor loadings using both the principal component and maximum likelihood methods.

9.2. The file `m-excess-c10sp-9003.txt` contains the monthly simple excess returns of ten stocks and the S&P 500 index. The three-month Treasury bill rate on the secondary market is used to compute the excess returns. The sample period is from January 1990 to December 2003 for 168 observations. The 11 columns in the file contain the returns for ABT, LLY, MRK, PFE, F, GM, BP,

CVX, RD, XOM, and SP5, respectively. Analyze the ten stock excess returns using the single-factor market model. Plot the beta estimate and R-square for each stock, and use the global minimum variance portfolio to compare the covariance matrices of the fitted model and the data.

9.3. Again, consider the ten stock returns in `m-excess-c10sp-9003.txt`. The stocks are from companies in three industrial sectors. ABT, LLY, MRK, and PFE are major drug companies, F and GM are automobile companies, and the rest are big oil companies. Analyze the excess returns using the BARRA industrial factor model. Plot the three-factor realizations and comment on the adequacy of the fitted model.

9.4. Again, consider the ten excess stock returns in the file `m-excess-c10sp-9003.txt`. Perform a principal component analysis on the returns and obtain the scree plot. How many common factors are there? Why? Interpret the common factors.

9.5. Again, consider the ten excess stock returns in the file `m-excess-c10sp-9003.txt`. Perform a statistical factor analysis. How many common factors are there if the 5% significance level is used? Plot the estimated factor loadings of the fitted model. Are the common factors meaningful?

9.6. The file `m-fedip.txt` contains year, month, effective federal funds rate, and the industrial production index from July 1954 to December 2003. The industrial production index is seasonally adjusted. Use the federal funds rate and the industrial production index as the macroeconomic variables. Fit a macroeconomic factor model to the ten excess returns in `m-excess-c10sp-9003.txt`. You can use a VAR model to obtain the surprise series of the macroeconomic variables. Comment on the fitted factor model.

REFERENCES

Alexander, C. (2001). *Market Models: A Guide to Financial Data Analysis.* Wiley, Hoboken, NJ.

Bai, J. and Ng, S. (2002). Determining the number of factors in approximate factor models. *Econometrica* **70**: 191–221.

Campbell, J. Y., Lo, A. W., and MacKinlay, A. C. (1997). *The Econometrics of Financial Markets.* Princeton University Press, Princeton, NJ.

Chen, N. F., Roll, R., and Ross, S. A. (1986). Economic forces and the stock market. *The Journal of Business* **59**: 383–404.

Connor, G. (1995). The three types of factor models: A comparison of their explanatory power. *Financial Analysts Journal* **51**: 42–46.

Connor, G. and Korajczyk, R. A. (1986). Performance measurement with the arbitrage pricing theory: A new framework for analysis. *Journal of Financial Econometrics* **15**: 373–394.

Connor, G. and Korajczyk, R. A. (1988). Risk and return in an equilibrium APT: Application of a new test methodology. *Journal of Financial Econometrics* **21**: 255–289.

Connor, G. and Korajczyk, R. A. (1993). A test for the number of factors in an approximate factor model. *Journal of Finance* **48**: 1263–1292.

Fama, E. and French, K. R. (1992). The cross-section of expected stock returns. *Journal of Finance* **47**: 427–465.

Grinold, R. C. and Kahn, R. N. (2000). *Active Portfolio Management: A Quantitative Approach for Producing Superior Returns and Controlling Risk*, 2nd edition. McGraw-Hill, New York.

Johnson, R. A. and Wichern, D. W. (2002). *Applied Multivariate Statistical Analysis*, 5th edition. Prentice Hall, Upper Saddle River, NJ.

Kaiser, H. F. (1958). The varimax criterion for analytic rotation in factor analysis. *Psychometrika* **23**: 187–200.

Sharpe, W. (1970). *Portfolio Theory and Capital Markets*. McGraw-Hill, New York.

Zivot, E. and Wang, J. (2003). *Modeling Financial Time Series with S-Plus*. Springer-Verlag, New York.

CHAPTER 10

Multivariate Volatility Models and Their Applications

In this chapter, we generalize the univariate volatility models of Chapter 3 to the multivariate case and discuss some methods for simplifying the dynamic relationships between volatility processes of multiple asset returns. Multivariate volatilities have many important financial applications. They play an important role in portfolio selection and asset allocation, and they can be used to compute the value at risk of a financial position consisting of multiple assets.

Consider a multivariate return series $\{\boldsymbol{r}_t\}$. We adopt the same approach as the univariate case by rewriting the series as

$$\boldsymbol{r}_t = \boldsymbol{\mu}_t + \boldsymbol{a}_t,$$

where $\boldsymbol{\mu}_t = E(\boldsymbol{r}_t|\boldsymbol{F}_{t-1})$ is the conditional expectation of $\boldsymbol{r}_t$ given the past information $\boldsymbol{F}_{t-1}$, and $\boldsymbol{a}_t = (a_{1t}, \ldots, a_{kt})'$ is the shock, or innovation, of the series at time t. The $\boldsymbol{\mu}_t$ process is assumed to follow the conditional expectation of a multivariate time series model of Chapter 8. For most return series, it suffices to employ a simple vector ARMA structure with exogenous variables for $\boldsymbol{\mu}_t$—that is,

$$\boldsymbol{\mu}_t = \boldsymbol{\Upsilon}\boldsymbol{x}_t + \sum_{i=1}^{p} \boldsymbol{\Phi}_i \boldsymbol{r}_{t-i} - \sum_{i=1}^{q} \boldsymbol{\Theta}_i \boldsymbol{a}_{t-i}, \qquad (10.1)$$

where $\boldsymbol{x}_t$ denotes an m-dimensional vector of exogenous (or explanatory) variables with $x_{1t} = 1$, $\boldsymbol{\Upsilon}$ is a $k \times m$ matrix, and p and q are non-negative integers. We refer to Eq. (10.1) as the mean equation of $\boldsymbol{r}_t$.

The conditional covariance matrix of $\boldsymbol{a}_t$ given $\boldsymbol{F}_{t-1}$ is a $k \times k$ positive-definite matrix $\boldsymbol{\Sigma}_t$ defined by $\boldsymbol{\Sigma}_t = \text{Cov}(\boldsymbol{a}_t|\boldsymbol{F}_{t-1})$. Multivariate volatility modeling is concerned with the time evolution of $\boldsymbol{\Sigma}_t$. We refer to a model for the $\{\boldsymbol{\Sigma}_t\}$ process as a volatility model for the return series $\boldsymbol{r}_t$.

Analysis of Financial Time Series, Second Edition By Ruey S. Tsay

There are many ways to generalize univariate volatility models to the multivariate case, but the curse of dimensionality quickly becomes a major obstacle in applications because there are $k(k+1)/2$ quantities in $\boldsymbol{\Sigma}_t$ for a k-dimensional return series. To illustrate, there are 15 conditional variances and covariances in $\boldsymbol{\Sigma}_t$ for a five-dimensional return series. The goal of this chapter is to introduce some relatively simple multivariate volatility models that are useful, yet remain manageable in real application. In particular, we discuss some models that allow for time-varying correlation coefficients between asset returns. Time-varying correlations are useful in finance. For example, they can be used to estimate the time-varying beta of the market model for a return series.

We begin by using an exponentially weighted approach to estimate the covariance matrix in Section 10.1. This estimated covariance matrix can serve as a benchmark for multivariate volatility estimation. Section 10.2 discusses some generalizations of univariate GARCH models that are available in the literature. We then introduce two methods to reparameterize $\boldsymbol{\Sigma}_t$ for volatility modeling in Section 10.3. The reparameterization based on the Cholesky decomposition is found to be useful. We study some volatility models for bivariate returns in Section 10.4, using the GARCH model as an example. In this particular case, the volatility model can be bivariate or three-dimensional. Section 10.5 is concerned with volatility models for higher dimensional returns and Section 10.6 addresses the issue of dimension reduction. We demonstrate some applications of multivariate volatility models in Section 10.7. Finally, Section 10.8 gives a multivariate Student-t distribution useful for volatility modeling.

10.1 EXPONENTIALLY WEIGHTED ESTIMATE

Given the innovations $F_{t-1} = \{\boldsymbol{a}_1, \ldots, \boldsymbol{a}_{t-1}\}$, the (unconditional) covariance matrix of the innovation can be estimated by

$$\widehat{\boldsymbol{\Sigma}} = \frac{1}{t-1}\sum_{j=1}^{t-1} \boldsymbol{a}_j \boldsymbol{a}'_j,$$

where it is understood that the mean of $\boldsymbol{a}_j$ is zero. This estimate assigns equal weight $1/(t-1)$ to each term in the summation. To allow for a time-varying covariance matrix and to emphasize that recent innovations are more relevant, one can use the idea of exponential smoothing and estimate the covariance matrix of $\boldsymbol{a}_t$ by

$$\widehat{\boldsymbol{\Sigma}}_t = \frac{1-\lambda}{1-\lambda^{t-1}}\sum_{j=1}^{t-1} \lambda^{j-1} \boldsymbol{a}_{t-j} \boldsymbol{a}'_{t-j}, \tag{10.2}$$

where $0 < \lambda < 1$ and the weights $(1-\lambda)\lambda^{j-1}/(1-\lambda^{t-1})$ sum to one. For a sufficiently large t such that $\lambda^{t-1} \approx 0$, the prior equation can be rewritten as

$$\widehat{\boldsymbol{\Sigma}}_t = (1-\lambda)\boldsymbol{a}_{t-1}\boldsymbol{a}'_{t-1} + \lambda\widehat{\boldsymbol{\Sigma}}_{t-1}.$$

Therefore, the covariance estimate in Eq. (10.2) is referred to as the exponentially weighted moving-average (EWMA) estimate of the covariance matrix.

Suppose that the return data are $\{\boldsymbol{r}_1, \ldots, \boldsymbol{r}_T\}$. For a given λ and initial estimate $\widehat{\boldsymbol{\Sigma}}_1$, $\widehat{\boldsymbol{\Sigma}}_t$ can be computed recursively. If one assumes that $\boldsymbol{a}_t = \boldsymbol{r}_t - \boldsymbol{\mu}_t$ follows a multivariate normal distribution with mean zero and covariance matrix $\boldsymbol{\Sigma}_t$, where $\boldsymbol{\mu}_t$ is a function of parameter $\boldsymbol{\Theta}$, then λ and $\boldsymbol{\Theta}$ can be estimated jointly by the maximum likelihood method, because the log likelihood function of the data is

$$\ln L(\boldsymbol{\Theta}, \lambda) \propto -\frac{1}{2}\sum_{t=1}^{T} \ln(|\boldsymbol{\Sigma}_t|) - \frac{1}{2}\sum_{t=1}^{T}(\boldsymbol{r}_t - \boldsymbol{\mu}_t)\boldsymbol{\Sigma}_t^{-1}(\boldsymbol{r}_t - \boldsymbol{\mu}_t)',$$

which can be evaluated recursively by substituting $\widehat{\boldsymbol{\Sigma}}_t$ for $\boldsymbol{\Sigma}_t$.

Example 10.1. To illustrate, consider the daily log returns of the stock market indexes for Hong Kong and Japan from January 1, 1996 to October 16, 1997 for 469 observations. The indexes are dollar denominated and the returns are in percentages. We select the sample period to avoid the effect of an Asian financial crisis, which hit the Hong Kong market on October 17, 1997. The data are obtained from Datastream. Figure 10.1 shows the time plots of the two index

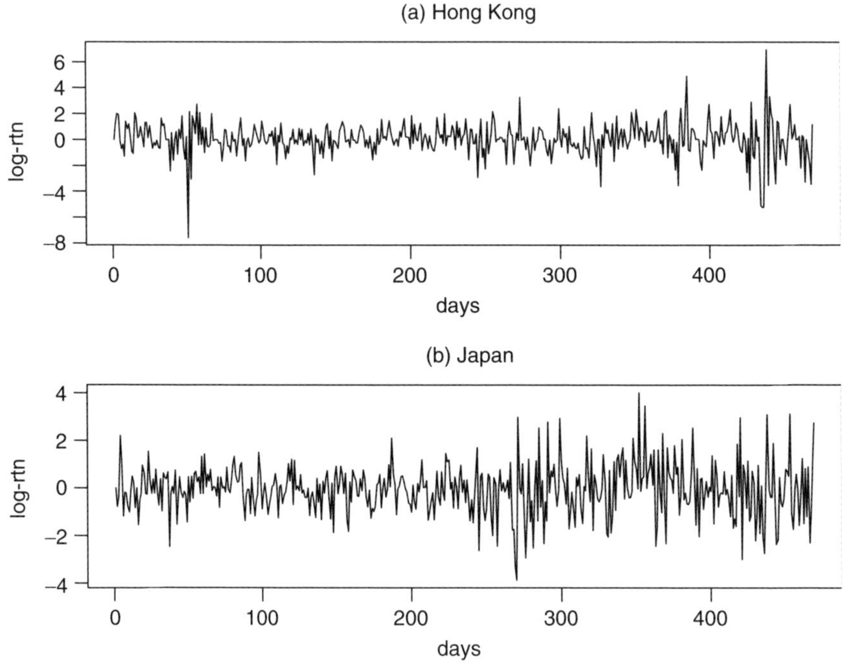

Figure 10.1. Time plots of daily log returns in percentages of stock market indexes for Hong Kong and Japan from January 1, 1996 to October 16, 1997: (a) the Hong Kong market and (b) the Japanese market.

returns. Let r_{1t} and r_{2t} be the log returns of the Hong Kong and Japanese markets, respectively. If univariate GARCH models are entertained, we obtain the models

$$\begin{aligned} r_{1t} &= 0.090 - 0.094 r_{1,t-6} + a_{1t}, \quad a_{1t} = \sigma_{1t}\epsilon_{1t}, \\ \sigma_{1t}^2 &= 0.126 + 0.103 a_{1,t-1}^2 + 0.818\sigma_{1,t-1}^2 \end{aligned} \tag{10.3}$$

and

$$\begin{aligned} r_{2t} &= -0.046 + a_{2t}, \quad a_{2t} = \sigma_{2t}\epsilon_{2t}, \\ \sigma_{2t}^2 &= 0.007 + 0.054 a_{2,t-1}^2 + 0.942\sigma_{2,t-1}^2, \end{aligned} \tag{10.4}$$

where all of the parameter estimates are significant at the 5% level except for the constant terms of the returns and α_0 of the Japanese market returns. The Ljung–Box statistics of the standardized residuals and their squared series of the two univariate models fail to indicate any model inadequacy. Figure 10.2 shows the estimated volatilities of the two univariate GARCH(1,1) models. The Hong Kong stock market appears to be more volatile than the Japanese stock market, but the Japanese market shows increased volatilities in the second half of the sample. The model-based asymptotic standard errors of the index returns are 1.259 and 1.393, respectively, for the Hong Kong and Japanese markets. The sample

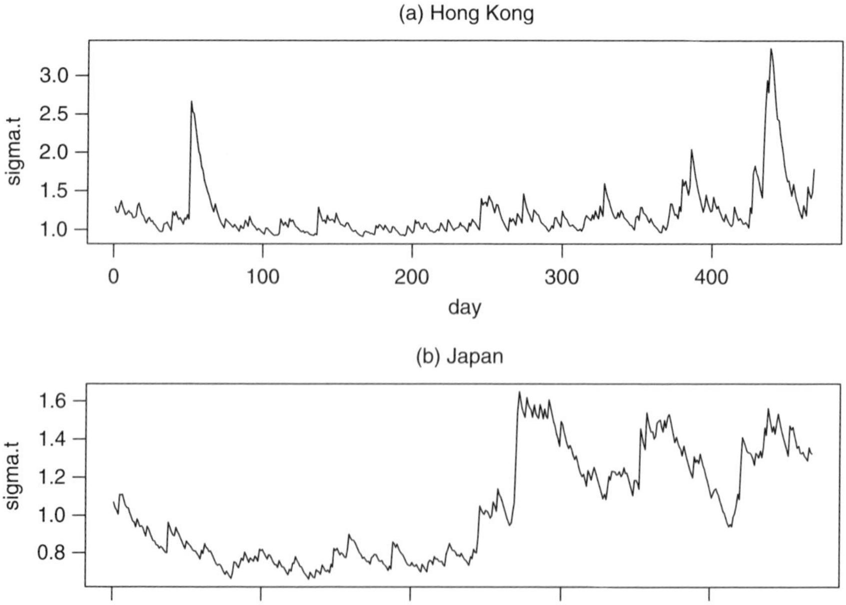

Figure 10.2. Estimated volatilities (standard error) for daily log returns in percentages of stock market indexes for Hong Kong and Japan from January 1, 1996 to October 16, 1997: (a) the Hong Kong market and (b) the Japanese market. Univariate models are used.

standard errors of the data are 1.296 and 1.067. Thus, the univariate model for the Japanese market index returns overestimates its unconditional volatility. This might be caused by the IGARCH feature of Eq. (10.4), which in turn may be caused by the observed jump in volatility in the second half of the data.

Turn to bivariate modeling. For simplicity, we ignore the minor lag-6 serial correlation of the Hong Kong returns and apply the EWMA approach to obtain volatility estimates, using the command `mgarch` in S-Plus FinMetrics:

```
> hkja.ewma=mgarch 1, formula.var = ~ ewma1, trace = F)
Mean Equation: rtn ~ 1

Conditional Variance Equation:  ~ ewma1
Coefficients:
 C(1)   0.06394  % Expected perc. return of Hong Kong market
 C(2)  -0.05478  % Expected perc. return of Japanese market
ALPHA   0.03711
```

The estimate of λ is $1 - \hat{\alpha} = 1 - 0.03711 \approx 0.963$, which is in the typical range commonly seen in practice. Figure 10.3 shows the estimated volatility series by the EWMA approach. Compared with those in Figure 10.2, the EWMA approach produces smoother volatility series, even though the two plots show similar volatility patterns.

10.2 SOME MULTIVARIATE GARCH MODELS

Many authors have generalized univariate volatility models to the multivariate case. In this section, we discuss some of the generalizations. For more details, readers are referred to a recent survey article by Bauwens, Laurent, and Rombouts (2004).

10.2.1 Diagonal VEC Model

Bollerslev, Engle, and Wooldridge (1988) generalize the exponentially weighted moving-average approach to propose the model

$$\boldsymbol{\Sigma}_t = \boldsymbol{A}_0 + \sum_{i=1}^{m} \boldsymbol{A}_i \odot (\boldsymbol{a}_{t-i}\boldsymbol{a}'_{t-i}) + \sum_{j=1}^{s} \boldsymbol{B}_j \odot \boldsymbol{\Sigma}_{t-j}, \tag{10.5}$$

where m and s are non-negative integers, $\boldsymbol{A}_i$ and $\boldsymbol{B}_j$ are symmetric matrices, and $\odot$ denotes Hadamard product; that is, element-by-element multiplication. This is referred to as the diagonal VEC(m, s) model or DVEC(m, s) model. To appreciate

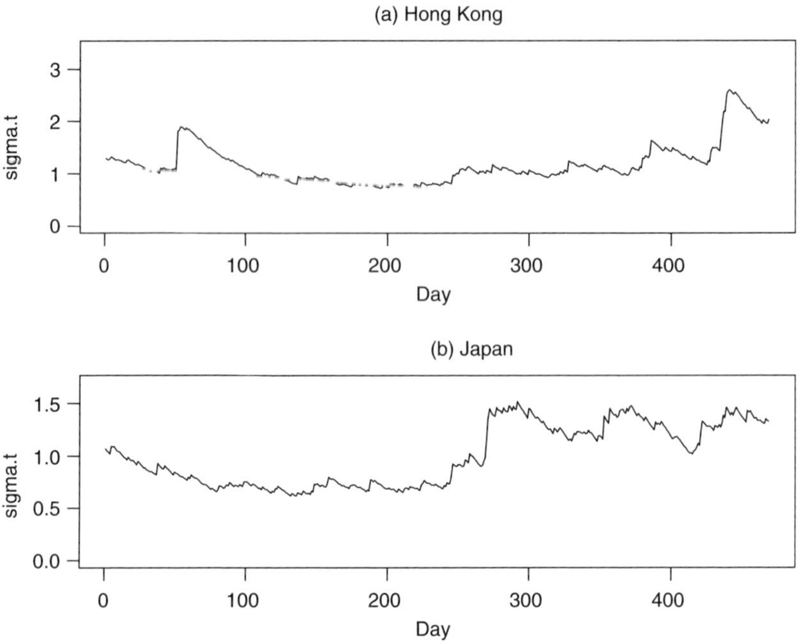

Figure 10.3. Estimated volatilities (standard error) for daily log returns in percentages of stock market indices for Hong Kong and Japan from January 1, 1996 to October 16, 1997: (a) the Hong Kong market and (b) the Japanese market. The exponentially weighted moving-average approach is used.

the model, consider the bivariate DVEC(1,1) case satisfying

$$\begin{bmatrix} \sigma_{11,t} & \\ \sigma_{21,t} & \sigma_{22,t} \end{bmatrix} = \begin{bmatrix} A_{11,0} & \\ A_{21,0} & A_{22,0} \end{bmatrix} + \begin{bmatrix} A_{11,1} & \\ A_{21,1} & A_{22,1} \end{bmatrix} \odot \begin{bmatrix} a_{1,t-1}^2 & \\ a_{1,t-1}a_{2,t-1} & a_{2,t-1}^2 \end{bmatrix} + \begin{bmatrix} B_{11,1} & \\ B_{21,1} & B_{22,1} \end{bmatrix} \odot \begin{bmatrix} \sigma_{11,t-1} & \\ \sigma_{21,t-1} & \sigma_{22,t-1} \end{bmatrix},$$

where only the lower triangular part of the model is given. Specifically, the model is

$$\begin{aligned} \sigma_{11,t} &= A_{11,0} + A_{11,1}a_{1,t-1}^2 + B_{11,1}\sigma_{11,t-1}, \\ \sigma_{21,t} &= A_{21,0} + A_{21,1}a_{1,t-1}a_{2,t-1} + B_{21,1}\sigma_{21,t-1}, \\ \sigma_{22,t} &= A_{22,0} + A_{22,1}a_{2,t-1}^2 + B_{22,1}\sigma_{22,t-1}, \end{aligned}$$

where each element of $\boldsymbol{\Sigma}_t$ depends only on its own past value and the corresponding product term in $\boldsymbol{a}_{t-1}\boldsymbol{a}'_{t-1}$. That is, each element of a DVEC model follows a GARCH(1,1) type model. The model is, therefore, simple. However, it may not

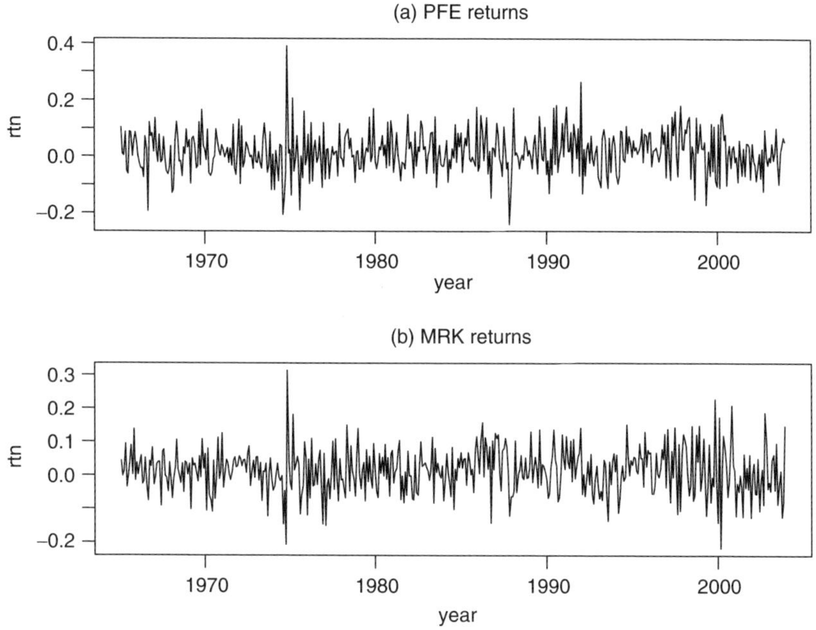

Figure 10.4. Time plot of monthly simple returns, including dividends, for Pfizer and Merck stocks from January 1965 to December 2003: (a) Pfizer stock and (b) Merck stock.

produce a positive-definite covariance matrix. Furthermore, the model does not allow for dynamic dependence between volatility series.

Example 10.2. For illustration, consider the monthly simple returns, including dividends, of two major drug companies from January 1965 to December 2003 for 468 observations. Let r_{1t} be the return series of Pfizer stock and r_{2t} the return of Merck stock. The bivariate return series $\boldsymbol{r}_t = (r_{1t}, r_{2t})'$, shown in Figure 10.4, has no significant serial correlations. Therefore, the mean equation of $\boldsymbol{r}_t$ consists of a constant term only. We fit a DVEC(1,1) model to the series using the command `mgarch` in FinMetrics of S-Plus:

```
> rtn=cbind(pfe,mrk)  % Output edited.
> drug.dvec=mgarch(rtn~1,~dvec(1,1))
> summary(drug.dvec)
Call:
mgarch(formula.mean = rtn ~ 1, formula.var =  ~ dvec(1, 1))
Mean Equation: rtn ~ 1
Conditional Variance Equation:  ~ dvec(1, 1)
Conditional Distribution:  gaussian

Estimated Coefficients:
                   Value Std.Error t value  Pr(>|t|)
```

```
           C(1) 0.0164424 3.422e-03    4.805 1.047e-06
           C(2) 0.0150987 3.139e-03    4.810 1.025e-06
        A(1, 1) 0.0008181 4.348e-04    1.881 3.027e-02
        A(2, 1) 0.0001021 4.979e-05    2.050 2.048e-02
        A(2, 2) 0.0001408 7.067e-05    1.992 2.348e-02
  ARCH(1; 1, 1) 0.0727734 2.973e-02    2.448 7.363e-03
  ARCH(1; 2, 1) 0.0259816 9.537e-03    2.724 3.343e-03
  ARCH(1; 2, 2) 0.0518917 1.753e-02    2.961 1.614e-03
 GARCH(1; 1, 1) 0.7777585 9.525e-02    8.165 1.554e-15
 GARCH(1; 2, 1) 0.9407037 2.191e-02   42.928 0.000e+00
 GARCH(1; 2, 2) 0.9203388 2.684e-02   34.296 0.000e+00

Ljung-Box test for standardized residuals:
    Statistic P-value Chi^2-d.f.
pfe     10.07  0.6096         12
mrk     14.91  0.2461         12

Ljung-Box test for squared standardized residuals:
    Statistic P-value Chi^2-d.f.
pfe     18.30  0.1068         12
mrk      5.04  0.9566         12
> names(drug.dvec)
 [1] "residuals"    "sigma.t"        "df.residual" "coef"
 [5] "model"        "cond.dist"      "likelihood"  "opt.index"
 [9] "cov"          "std.residuals"  "R.t"         "S.t"
[13] "prediction"   "call"           "series"
```

From the output, all parameter estimates are significant at the 5% level, and the fitted volatility model is

$$\begin{aligned}
\sigma_{11,t} &= 0.00082 + 0.073a_{1,t-1}^2 + 0.778\sigma_{11,t-1},\\
\sigma_{21,t} &= 0.00010 + 0.026a_{1,t-1}a_{2,t-1} + 0.941\sigma_{21,t-1},\\
\sigma_{22,t} &= 0.00014 + 0.052a_{2,t-1}^2 + 0.920\sigma_{22,t-1}.
\end{aligned}$$

The output also provides some model checking statistics for individual stock returns. For instance, the Ljung–Box statistics for the standardized residual series and its squared series of Pfizer stock returns give $Q(12) = 10.07(0.61)$ and $Q(12) = 18.30(0.11)$, respectively, where the number in parentheses denotes p-value. Thus, checking the fitted model individually, one cannot reject the DVEC(1,1) model. A more informative model checking approach is to apply the multivariate Q-statistics to the bivariate standardized residual series and its squared process. For this particular DVEC(1,1) model, we have $Q_2(10) = 42.04(0.38)$ and $Q_2^*(10) = 67.33(0.004)$, respectively, where Q_2^* denotes the Q-statistics for the bivariate squared residual series. Based on bivariate statistics, the mean equation is adequate at the 5% significance level, but the DVEC(1,1) model is rejected for the volatility at the 1% level. Figure 10.5 shows the fitted volatility and correlation series. These series are stored

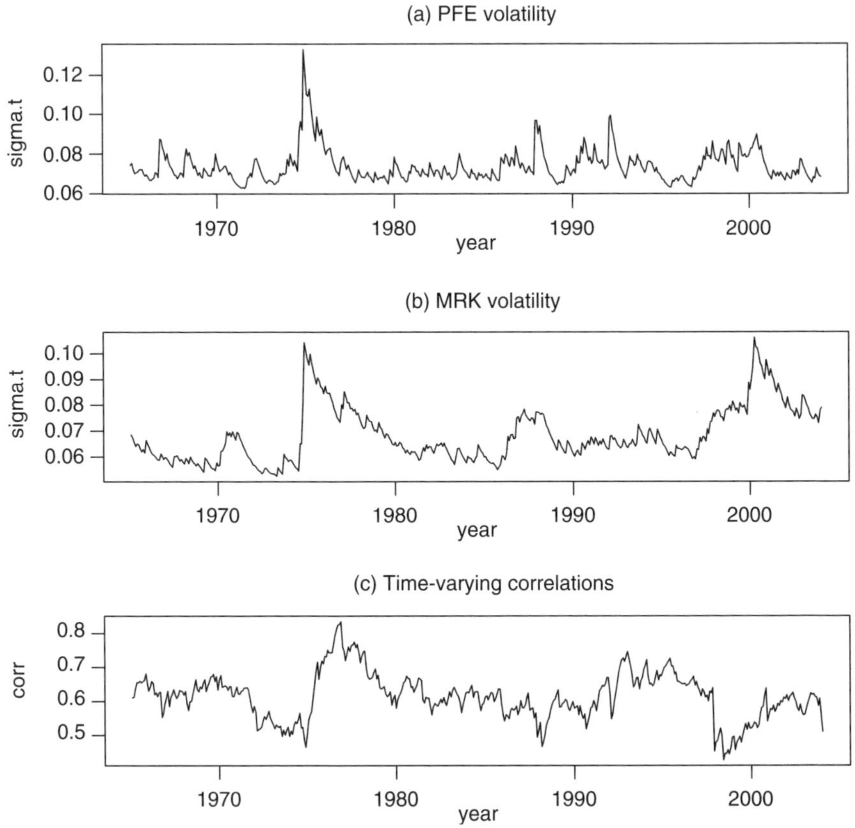

Figure 10.5. Estimated volatilities (standard error) and time-varying correlations of a DVEC(1,1) model for monthly simple returns of two major drug companies from January 1965 to December 2003: (a) Pfizer stock volatility, (b) Merck stock volatility, and (c) time-varying correlations.

in ``sigma.t'' and ``R.t'', respectively. The correlations range from 0.42 to 0.84.

10.2.2 BEKK Model

To guarantee the positive-definite constraint, Engle and Kroner (1995) propose the BEKK model,

$$\boldsymbol{\Sigma}_t = \boldsymbol{A}\boldsymbol{A}' + \sum_{i=1}^{m} \boldsymbol{A}_i(\boldsymbol{a}_{t-i}\boldsymbol{a}'_{t-i})\boldsymbol{A}'_i + \sum_{j=1}^{s} \boldsymbol{B}_j \boldsymbol{\Sigma}_{t-j} \boldsymbol{B}'_j, \tag{10.6}$$

where $\boldsymbol{A}$ is a lower triangular matrix and $\boldsymbol{A}_i$ and $\boldsymbol{B}_j$ are $k \times k$ matrices. Based on the symmetric parameterization of the model, $\boldsymbol{\Sigma}_t$ is almost surely positive definite provided that $\boldsymbol{A}\boldsymbol{A}'$ is positive definite. This model also allows for dynamic dependence between the volatility series. On the other hand, the model has several disadvantages. First, the parameters in $\boldsymbol{A}_i$ and $\boldsymbol{B}_j$ do not have direct interpretations concerning lagged values of volatilities or shocks. Second, the number of parameters employed is $k^2(m+s)+k(k+1)/2$, which increases rapidly with m and s. Limited experience shows that many of the estimated parameters are statistically insignificant, introducing additional complications in modeling.

Example 10.3. To illustrate, we consider the monthly simple returns of Pfizer and Merck stocks of Example 10.2 and employ a BEKK(1,1) model. Again, S-Plus is used to perform the estimation:

```
> drug.bekk=mgarch(rtn~1,~bekk(1,1))
> summary(drug.bekk)
Call:
mgarch(formula.mean = rtn ~ 1, formula.var =  ~ bekk(1, 1))
Mean Equation: rtn ~ 1
Conditional Variance Equation:  ~ bekk(1, 1)
Conditional Distribution:  gaussian

Estimated Coefficients:
                     Value Std.Error    t value  Pr(>|t|)
            C(1)  0.0164770  0.003470  4.749e+00 1.369e-06
            C(2)  0.0142816  0.003172  4.503e+00 4.255e-06
         A(1, 1)  0.0245803  0.008837  2.782e+00 2.815e-03
         A(2, 1)  0.0116134  0.005953  1.951e+00 2.584e-02
         A(2, 2)  0.0002018  0.267625  7.541e-04 4.997e-01
   ARCH(1; 1, 1)  0.2994052  0.093304  3.209e+00 7.125e-04
   ARCH(1; 2, 1)  0.1952856  0.075092  2.601e+00 4.802e-03
   ARCH(1; 1, 2) -0.0818745  0.097810 -8.371e-01 2.015e-01
   ARCH(1; 2, 2)  0.0929540  0.082626  1.125e+00 1.306e-01
  GARCH(1; 1, 1)  0.8987843  0.074407  1.208e+01 0.000e+00
  GARCH(1; 2, 1) -0.0674587  0.059595 -1.132e+00 1.291e-01
  GARCH(1; 1, 2)  0.0163848  0.046402  3.531e-01 3.621e-01
  GARCH(1; 2, 2)  0.9889547  0.040158  2.463e+01 0.000e+00

Ljung-Box test for standardized residuals:
    Statistic P-value Chi^2-d.f.
pfe     10.13  0.6044         12
mrk     15.25  0.2278         12

Ljung-Box test for squared standardized residuals:
    Statistic P-value Chi^2-d.f.
pfe    18.314  0.1065         12
mrk     7.174  0.8459         12
```

Model checking statistics based on the individual residual series and provided by S-Plus fail to suggest any model inadequacy of the fitted BEKK(1,1) model. Using the bivariate standardized residuals, we have $Q_2(10) = 41.57(0.40)$ and

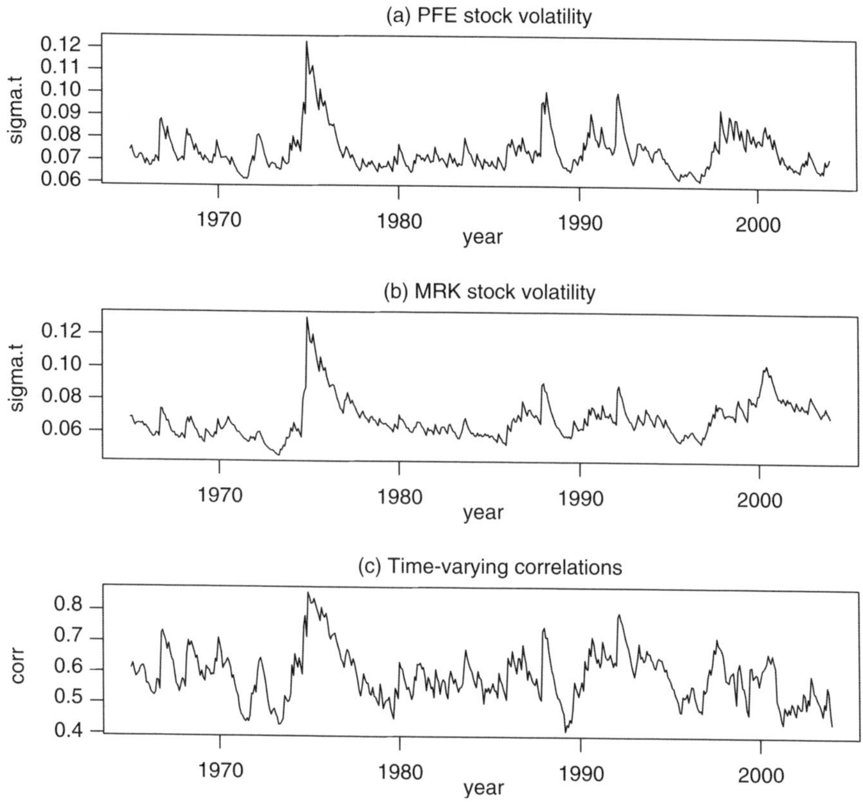

Figure 10.6. Estimated volatilities (standard error) and time-varying correlations of a BEKK(1,1) model for monthly simple returns of two major drug companies from January 1965 to December 2003: (a) Pfizer stock volatility, (b) Merck stock volatility, and (c) time-varying correlations.

$Q_2^*(10) = 65.71(0.006)$. Thus, similar to the DVEC(1,1) case, the Ljung–Box statistics also reject the volatility model at the 1% significance level. Figure 10.6 shows the fitted volatilities and the time-varying correlations of the BEKK(1,1) model. Compared with Figure 10.5, there are some differences between the two fitted volatility models. For instance, the time-varying correlations of the BEKK(1,1) model appear to be more volatile.

The volatility equation of the fitted BEKK(1,1) model is

$$\begin{bmatrix} \sigma_{11,t} & \sigma_{12,t} \\ \sigma_{21,t} & \sigma_{22,t} \end{bmatrix} = \begin{bmatrix} 0.025 & 0 \\ 0.012 & 0.0002 \end{bmatrix} \begin{bmatrix} 0.025 & 0.012 \\ 0 & 0.0002 \end{bmatrix}$$
$$+ \begin{bmatrix} 0.299 & -0.082 \\ 0.195 & 0.093 \end{bmatrix} \begin{bmatrix} a_{1,t-1}^2 & a_{1,t-1}a_{2,t-1} \\ a_{2,t-1}a_{1,t-1} & a_{2,t-1}^2 \end{bmatrix} \begin{bmatrix} 0.299 & 0.195 \\ -0.082 & 0.093 \end{bmatrix}$$
$$+ \begin{bmatrix} 0.899 & 0.016 \\ -0.067 & 0.989 \end{bmatrix} \begin{bmatrix} \sigma_{11,t-1} & \sigma_{12,t-1} \\ \sigma_{21,t-1} & \sigma_{22,t-1} \end{bmatrix} \begin{bmatrix} 0.899 & -0.067 \\ 0.016 & 0.989 \end{bmatrix},$$

where six estimates are insignificant at the 5% level. In particular, the constant matrix $\boldsymbol{A}$ contains only a single significant parameter. Furthermore, one needs to perform matrix multiplication to decipher the fitted model.

10.3 REPARAMETERIZATION

A useful step in multivariate volatility modeling is to reparameterize $\boldsymbol{\Sigma}_t$ by making use of its symmetric property. We consider two reparameterizations.

10.3.1 Use of Correlations

The first reparameterization of $\boldsymbol{\Sigma}_t$ is to use the conditional correlation coefficients and variances of $\boldsymbol{a}_t$. Specifically, we write $\boldsymbol{\Sigma}_t$ as

$$\boldsymbol{\Sigma}_t \equiv [\sigma_{ij,t}] = \boldsymbol{D}_t \boldsymbol{\rho}_t \boldsymbol{D}_t, \tag{10.7}$$

where $\boldsymbol{\rho}_t$ is the conditional correlation matrix of $\boldsymbol{a}_t$, and $\boldsymbol{D}_t$ is a $k \times k$ diagonal matrix consisting of the conditional standard deviations of elements of $\boldsymbol{a}_t$ (i.e., $\boldsymbol{D}_t = \text{diag}\{\sqrt{\sigma_{11,t}}, \ldots, \sqrt{\sigma_{kk,t}}\}$).

Because $\boldsymbol{\rho}_t$ is symmetric with unit diagonal elements, the time evolution of $\boldsymbol{\Sigma}_t$ is governed by that of the conditional variances $\sigma_{ii,t}$ and the elements $\rho_{ij,t}$ of $\boldsymbol{\rho}_t$, where $j < i$ and $1 \le i \le k$. Therefore, to model the volatility of $\boldsymbol{a}_t$, it suffices to consider the conditional variances and correlation coefficients of a_{it}. Define the $k(k+1)/2$-dimensional vector

$$\boldsymbol{\Xi}_t = (\sigma_{11,t}, \ldots, \sigma_{kk,t}, \boldsymbol{\varrho}_t')', \tag{10.8}$$

where $\boldsymbol{\varrho}_t$ is a $k(k-1)/2$-dimensional vector obtained by stacking columns of the correlation matrix $\boldsymbol{\rho}_t$, but using only elements below the main diagonal. Specifically, for a k-dimensional return series,

$$\boldsymbol{\varrho}_t = (\rho_{21,t}, \ldots, \rho_{k1,t} | \rho_{32,t}, \ldots, \rho_{k2,t} | \cdots | \rho_{k,k-1,t})'.$$

To illustrate, for $k = 2$, we have $\boldsymbol{\varrho}_t = \rho_{21,t}$ and

$$\boldsymbol{\Xi}_t = (\sigma_{11,t}, \sigma_{22,t}, \rho_{21,t})', \tag{10.9}$$

which is a three-dimensional vector, and for $k = 3$, we have $\boldsymbol{\varrho}_t = (\rho_{21,t}, \rho_{31,t}, \rho_{32,t})'$ and

$$\boldsymbol{\Xi}_t = (\sigma_{11,t}, \sigma_{22,t}, \sigma_{33,t}, \rho_{21,t}, \rho_{31,t}, \rho_{32,t})', \tag{10.10}$$

which is a six-dimensional random vector.

If $\boldsymbol{a}_t$ is a bivariate normal random variable, then Ξ_t is given in Eq. (10.9) and the conditional density function of $\boldsymbol{a}_t$ given $\boldsymbol{F}_{t-1}$ is

$$f(a_{1t}, a_{2t}|\Xi_t) = \frac{1}{2\pi\sqrt{\sigma_{11,t}\sigma_{22,t}(1-\rho_{21,t}^2)}} \exp\left(-\frac{Q(a_{1t}, a_{2t}, \Xi_t)}{2(1-\rho_{21,t}^2)}\right),$$

where

$$Q(a_{1t}, a_{2t}, \Xi_t) = \frac{a_{1t}^2}{\sigma_{11,t}} + \frac{a_{2t}^2}{\sigma_{22,t}} - \frac{2\rho_{21,t}a_{1t}a_{2t}}{\sqrt{\sigma_{11,t}\sigma_{22,t}}}.$$

The log probability density function of $\boldsymbol{a}_t$ relevant to the maximum likelihood estimation is

$$\ell(a_{1t}, a_{2t}, \Xi_t)$$
$$= -\frac{1}{2}\left\{\ln[\sigma_{11,t}\sigma_{22,t}(1-\rho_{21,t}^2)] + \frac{1}{1-\rho_{21,t}^2}\left(\frac{a_{1t}^2}{\sigma_{11,t}} + \frac{a_{2t}^2}{\sigma_{22,t}} - \frac{2\rho_{21,t}a_{1t}a_{2t}}{\sqrt{\sigma_{11,t}\sigma_{22,t}}}\right)\right\}. \quad (10.11)$$

This reparameterization is useful because it models covariances and correlations directly. Yet the approach has several weaknesses. First, the likelihood function becomes complicated when $k \geq 3$. Second, the approach requires a constrained maximization in estimation to ensure the positive definiteness of $\boldsymbol{\Sigma}_t$. The constraint becomes complicated when k is large.

10.3.2 Cholesky Decomposition

The second reparameterization of $\boldsymbol{\Sigma}_t$ is to use the Cholesky decomposition; see Appendix A of Chapter 8. This approach has some advantages in estimation as it requires no parameter constraints for the positive definiteness of $\boldsymbol{\Sigma}_t$; see Pourahmadi (1999). In addition, the reparameterization is an orthogonal transformation so that the resulting likelihood function is extremely simple. Details of the transformation are given next.

Because $\boldsymbol{\Sigma}_t$ is positive definite, there exist a lower triangular matrix $\boldsymbol{L}_t$ with unit diagonal elements and a diagonal matrix $\boldsymbol{G}_t$ with positive diagonal elements such that

$$\boldsymbol{\Sigma}_t = \boldsymbol{L}_t\boldsymbol{G}_t\boldsymbol{L}_t'. \quad (10.12)$$

This is the well-known Cholesky decomposition of $\boldsymbol{\Sigma}_t$. A feature of the decomposition is that the lower off-diagonal elements of $\boldsymbol{L}_t$ and the diagonal elements of $\boldsymbol{G}_t$ have nice interpretations. We demonstrate the decomposition by studying carefully the bivariate and three-dimensional cases. For the bivariate case, we have

$$\boldsymbol{\Sigma}_t = \begin{bmatrix} \sigma_{11,t} & \sigma_{21,t} \\ \sigma_{21,t} & \sigma_{22,t} \end{bmatrix}, \quad \boldsymbol{L}_t = \begin{bmatrix} 1 & 0 \\ q_{21,t} & 1 \end{bmatrix}, \quad \boldsymbol{G}_t = \begin{bmatrix} g_{11,t} & 0 \\ 0 & g_{22,t} \end{bmatrix},$$

where $g_{ii,t} > 0$ for $i = 1$ and 2. Using Eq. (10.12), we have

$$\boldsymbol{\Sigma}_t = \begin{bmatrix} \sigma_{11,t} & \sigma_{12,t} \\ \sigma_{12,t} & \sigma_{22,t} \end{bmatrix} = \begin{bmatrix} g_{11,t} & q_{21,t}g_{11,t} \\ q_{21,t}g_{11,t} & g_{22,t} + q_{21,t}^2 g_{11,t} \end{bmatrix}.$$

Equating elements of the prior matrix equation, we obtain

$$\sigma_{11,t} = g_{11,t}, \quad \sigma_{21,t} = q_{21,t}g_{11,t}, \quad \sigma_{22,t} = g_{22,t} + q_{21,t}^2 g_{11,t}. \tag{10.13}$$

Solving the prior equations, we have

$$g_{11,t} = \sigma_{11,t}, \quad q_{21,t} = \frac{\sigma_{21,t}}{\sigma_{11,t}}, \quad g_{22,t} = \sigma_{22,t} - \frac{\sigma_{21,t}^2}{\sigma_{11,t}}. \tag{10.14}$$

However, consider the simple linear regression

$$a_{2t} = \beta a_{1t} + b_{2t}, \tag{10.15}$$

where b_{2t} denotes the error term. From the well-known least squares theory, we have

$$\beta = \frac{\text{Cov}(a_{1t}, a_{2t})}{\text{Var}(a_{1t})} = \frac{\sigma_{21,t}}{\sigma_{11,t}},$$

$$\text{Var}(b_{2t}) = \text{Var}(a_{2t}) - \beta^2\text{Var}(a_{1t}) = \sigma_{22,t} - \frac{\sigma_{21,t}^2}{\sigma_{11,t}}.$$

Furthermore, the error term b_{2t} is uncorrelated with the regressor a_{1t}. Consequently, using Eq. (10.14), we obtain

$$g_{11,t} = \sigma_{11,t}, \quad q_{21,t} = \beta, \quad g_{22,t} = \text{Var}(b_{2t}), \quad b_{2t} \perp a_{1t},$$

where $\perp$ denotes no correlation. In summary, the Cholesky decomposition of the 2×2 matrix $\boldsymbol{\Sigma}_t$ amounts to performing an orthogonal transformation from $\boldsymbol{a}_t$ to $\boldsymbol{b}_t = (b_{1t}, b_{2t})'$ such that

$$b_{1t} = a_{1t} \quad \text{and} \quad b_{2t} = a_{2t} - q_{21,t}a_{1t},$$

where $q_{21,t} = \beta$ is obtained by the linear regression (10.15) and $\text{Cov}(\boldsymbol{b}_t)$ is a diagonal matrix with diagonal elements $g_{ii,t}$. The transformed quantities $q_{21,t}$ and $g_{ii,t}$ can be interpreted as follows:

1. The first diagonal element of $\boldsymbol{G}_t$ is simply the variance of a_{1t}.
2. The second diagonal element of $\boldsymbol{G}_t$ is the residual variance of the simple linear regression in Eq. (10.15).

3. The element $q_{21,t}$ of the lower triangular matrix $\boldsymbol{L}_t$ is the coefficient β of the regression in Eq. (10.15).

The prior properties continue to hold for the higher dimensional case. For example, consider the three-dimensional case in which

$$\boldsymbol{L}_t = \begin{bmatrix} 1 & 0 & 0 \\ q_{21,t} & 1 & 0 \\ q_{31,t} & q_{32,t} & 1 \end{bmatrix}, \quad \boldsymbol{G}_t = \begin{bmatrix} g_{11,t} & 0 & 0 \\ 0 & g_{22,t} & 0 \\ 0 & 0 & g_{3,t} \end{bmatrix}.$$

From the decomposition in Eq. (10.12), we have

$$\begin{bmatrix} \sigma_{11,t} & \sigma_{21,t} & \sigma_{31,t} \\ \sigma_{21,t} & \sigma_{22,t} & \sigma_{32,t} \\ \sigma_{31,t} & \sigma_{32,t} & \sigma_{33,t} \end{bmatrix} =$$

$$\begin{bmatrix} g_{11,t} & q_{21,t}g_{11,t} & q_{31,t}g_{11,t} \\ q_{21,t}g_{11,t} & q_{21,t}^2 g_{11,t} + g_{22,t} & q_{31,t}q_{21,t}g_{11,t} + q_{32,t}g_{22,t} \\ q_{31,t}g_{11,t} & q_{31,t}q_{21,t}g_{11,t} + q_{32,t}g_{22,t} & q_{31,t}^2 g_{11,t} + q_{32,t}^2 g_{22,t} + g_{33,t} \end{bmatrix}.$$

Equating elements of the prior matrix equation, we obtain

$$\sigma_{11,t} = g_{11,t}, \quad \sigma_{21,t} = q_{21,t}g_{11,t}, \quad \sigma_{22,t} = q_{21,t}^2 g_{11,t} + g_{22,t}, \quad \sigma_{31,t} = q_{31,t}g_{11,t},$$
$$\sigma_{32,t} = q_{31,t}q_{21,t}g_{11,t} + q_{32,t}g_{22,t}, \quad \sigma_{33,t} = q_{31,t}^2 g_{11,t} + q_{32,t}^2 g_{22,t} + g_{33,t}$$

or, equivalently,

$$g_{11,t} = \sigma_{11,t}, \quad q_{21,t} = \frac{\sigma_{21,t}}{\sigma_{11,t}}, \quad g_{22,t} = \sigma_{22,t} - q_{21,t}^2 g_{11,t},$$
$$q_{31,t} = \frac{\sigma_{31,t}}{\sigma_{11,t}}, \quad q_{32,t} = \frac{1}{g_{22,t}}\left(\sigma_{32,t} - \frac{\sigma_{31,t}\sigma_{21,t}}{\sigma_{11,t}}\right),$$
$$g_{33,t} = \sigma_{33,t} - q_{31,t}^2 g_{11,t} - q_{32,t}^2 g_{22,t}.$$

These quantities look complicated, but they are simply the coefficients and residual variances of the orthogonal transformation

$$b_{1t} = a_{1t},$$
$$b_{2t} = a_{2t} - \beta_{21}b_{1t},$$
$$b_{3t} = a_{3t} - \beta_{31}b_{1t} - \beta_{32}b_{2t},$$

where β_{ij} are the coefficients of least squares regressions

$$a_{2t} = \beta_{21}b_{1t} + b_{2t},$$
$$a_{3t} = \beta_{31}b_{1t} + \beta_{32}b_{2t} + b_{3t}.$$

In other words, we have $q_{ij,t} = \beta_{ij}$, $g_{ii,t} = \mathrm{Var}(b_{it})$ and $b_{it} \perp b_{jt}$ for $i \neq j$.

Based on the prior discussion, using Cholesky decomposition amounts to doing an orthogonal transformation from $\boldsymbol{a}_t$ to $\boldsymbol{b}_t$, where $b_{1t} = a_{1t}$, and b_{it}, for $1 < i \le k$, is defined recursively by the least squares regression

$$a_{it} = q_{i1,t}b_{1t} + q_{i2,t}b_{2t} + \cdots + q_{i(i-1),t}b_{(i-1)t} + b_{it}, \tag{10.16}$$

where $q_{ij,t}$ is the (i, j)th element of the lower triangular matrix $\boldsymbol{L}_t$ for $1 \le j < i$. We can write this transformation as

$$\boldsymbol{b}_t = \boldsymbol{L}_t^{-1}\boldsymbol{a}_t, \quad \text{or} \quad \boldsymbol{a}_t = \boldsymbol{L}_t\boldsymbol{b}_t, \tag{10.17}$$

where, as mentioned before, $\boldsymbol{L}_t^{-1}$ is also a lower triangular matrix with unit diagonal elements. The covariance matrix of $\boldsymbol{b}_t$ is the diagonal matrix $\boldsymbol{G}_t$ of the Cholesky decomposition because

$$\text{Cov}(\boldsymbol{b}_t) = \boldsymbol{L}_t^{-1}\boldsymbol{\Sigma}_t(\boldsymbol{L}_t^{-1})' = \boldsymbol{G}_t.$$

The parameter vector relevant to volatility modeling under such a transformation becomes

$$\boldsymbol{\Xi}_t = (g_{11,t}, \ldots, g_{kk,t}, q_{21,t}, q_{31,t}, q_{32,t}, \ldots, q_{k1,t}, \ldots, q_{k(k-1),t})', \tag{10.18}$$

which is also a $k(k+1)/2$-dimensional vector.

The previous orthogonal transformation also dramatically simplifies the likelihood function of the data. Using the fact that $|\boldsymbol{L}_t| = 1$, we have

$$|\boldsymbol{\Sigma}_t| = |\boldsymbol{L}_t\boldsymbol{G}_t\boldsymbol{L}_t'| = |\boldsymbol{G}_t| = \prod_{i=1}^{k} g_{ii,t}. \tag{10.19}$$

If the conditional distribution of $\boldsymbol{a}_t$ given the past information is multivariate normal $N(\boldsymbol{0}, \boldsymbol{\Sigma}_t)$, then the conditional distribution of the transformed series $\boldsymbol{b}_t$ is multivariate normal $N(\boldsymbol{0}, \boldsymbol{G}_t)$, and the log likelihood function of the data becomes extremely simple. Indeed, we have the log probability density of $\boldsymbol{a}_t$ as

$$\ell(\boldsymbol{a}_t, \boldsymbol{\Sigma}_t) = \ell(\boldsymbol{b}_t, \boldsymbol{\Xi}_t) = -\frac{1}{2}\sum_{i=1}^{k}\left(\ln(g_{ii,t}) + \frac{b_{it}^2}{g_{ii,t}}\right), \tag{10.20}$$

where for simplicity the constant term is omitted and $g_{ii,t}$ is the variance of b_{it}.

Using the Cholesky decomposition to reparameterize $\boldsymbol{\Sigma}_t$ has several advantages. First, from Eq. (10.19), $\boldsymbol{\Sigma}_t$ is positive-definite if $g_{ii,t} > 0$ for all i. Consequently, the positive-definite constraint of $\boldsymbol{\Sigma}_t$ can easily be achieved by modeling $\ln(g_{ii,t})$ instead of $g_{ii,t}$. Second, elements of the parameter vector $\boldsymbol{\Xi}_t$ in Eq. (10.18) have nice interpretations. They are the coefficients and residual variances of multiple linear regressions that orthogonalize the shocks to the returns. Third, the correlation coefficient between a_{1t} and a_{2t} is

$$\rho_{21,t} = \frac{\sigma_{21,t}}{\sqrt{\sigma_{11,t}\sigma_{22,t}}} = q_{21,t} \times \frac{\sqrt{\sigma_{11,t}}}{\sqrt{\sigma_{22,t}}},$$

which is time-varying if $q_{21,t} \neq 0$. In particular, if $q_{21,t} = c \neq 0$, then $\rho_{21,t} = c\sqrt{\sigma_{11,t}}/\sqrt{\sigma_{22,t}}$, which continues to be time-varying provided that the variance ratio $\sigma_{11,t}/\sigma_{22,t}$ is not a constant. This time-varying property applies to other correlation coefficients when the dimension of $\boldsymbol{r}_t$ is greater than 2 and is a major difference between the two approaches for reparameterizing $\boldsymbol{\Sigma}_t$.

Using Eq. (10.16) and the orthogonality among the transformed shocks b_{it}, we obtain

$$\sigma_{ii,t} = \text{Var}(a_{it}|F_{t-1}) = \sum_{v=1}^{i} q_{iv,t}^2 g_{vv,t}, \quad i = 1, \ldots, k,$$

$$\sigma_{ij,t} = \text{Cov}(a_{it}, a_{jt}|F_{t-1}) = \sum_{v=1}^{j} q_{iv,t} q_{jv,t} g_{vv,t}, \quad j < i, \quad i = 2, \ldots, k,$$

where $q_{vv,t} = 1$ for $v = 1, \ldots, k$. These equations show the parameterization of $\boldsymbol{\Sigma}_t$ under the Cholesky decomposition.

10.4 GARCH MODELS FOR BIVARIATE RETURNS

Since the same techniques can be used to generalize many univariate volatility models to the multivariate case, we focus our discussion on the multivariate GARCH model. Other multivariate volatility models can also be used.

For a k-dimensional return series $\boldsymbol{r}_t$, a multivariate GARCH model uses "exact equations" to describe the evolution of the $k(k+1)/2$-dimensional vector Ξ_t over time. By exact equation, we mean that the equation does not contain any stochastic shock. However, the exact equation may become complicated even in the simplest case of $k = 2$ for which Ξ_t is three-dimensional. To keep the model simple, some restrictions are often imposed on the equations.

10.4.1 Constant-Correlation Models

To keep the number of volatility equations low, Bollerslev (1990) considers the special case in which the correlation coefficient $\rho_{21,t} = \rho_{21}$ is time-invariant, where $|\rho_{21}| < 1$. Under such an assumption, ρ_{21} is a constant parameter and the volatility model consists of two equations for Ξ_t^*, which is defined as $\Xi_t^* = (\sigma_{11,t}, \sigma_{22,t})'$. A GARCH(1,1) model for Ξ_t^* becomes

$$\Xi_t^* = \boldsymbol{\alpha}_0 + \boldsymbol{\alpha}_1 \boldsymbol{a}_{t-1}^2 + \boldsymbol{\beta}_1 \Xi_{t-1}^*, \tag{10.21}$$

where $\boldsymbol{a}_{t-1}^2 = (a_{1,t-1}^2, a_{2,t-1}^2)'$, $\boldsymbol{\alpha}_0$ is a two-dimensional positive vector, and $\boldsymbol{\alpha}_1$ and $\boldsymbol{\beta}_1$ are 2×2 non-negative definite matrices. More specifically, the model can be expressed in detail as

$$\begin{bmatrix} \sigma_{11,t} \\ \sigma_{22,t} \end{bmatrix} = \begin{bmatrix} \alpha_{10} \\ \alpha_{20} \end{bmatrix} + \begin{bmatrix} \alpha_{11} & \alpha_{12} \\ \alpha_{21} & \alpha_{22} \end{bmatrix} \begin{bmatrix} a_{1,t-1}^2 \\ a_{2,t-1}^2 \end{bmatrix} + \begin{bmatrix} \beta_{11} & \beta_{12} \\ \beta_{21} & \beta_{22} \end{bmatrix} \begin{bmatrix} \sigma_{11,t-1} \\ \sigma_{22,t-1} \end{bmatrix}, \tag{10.22}$$

where $\alpha_{i0} > 0$ for $i = 1$ and 2. Defining $\boldsymbol{\eta}_t = \boldsymbol{a}_t^2 - \Xi_t^*$, we can rewrite the prior model as

$$\boldsymbol{a}_t^2 = \boldsymbol{\alpha}_0 + (\boldsymbol{\alpha}_1 + \boldsymbol{\beta}_1)\boldsymbol{a}_{t-1}^2 + \boldsymbol{\eta}_t - \boldsymbol{\beta}_1\boldsymbol{\eta}_{t-1},$$

which is a bivariate ARMA(1,1) model for the $\boldsymbol{a}_t^2$ process. This result is a direct generalization of the univariate GARCH(1,1) model of Chapter 3. Consequently, some properties of model (10.22) are readily available from those of the bivariate ARMA(1,1) model of Chapter 8. In particular, we have the following results:

1. If all of the eigenvalues of $\boldsymbol{\alpha}_1 + \boldsymbol{\beta}_1$ are positive, but less than 1, then the bivariate ARMA(1,1) model for $\boldsymbol{a}_t^2$ is weakly stationary and, hence, $E(\boldsymbol{a}_t^2)$ exists. This implies that the shock process $\boldsymbol{a}_t$ of the returns has a positive-definite unconditional covariance matrix. The unconditional variances of the elements of $\boldsymbol{a}_t$ are $(\sigma_1^2, \sigma_2^2)' = (\boldsymbol{I} - \boldsymbol{\alpha}_1 - \boldsymbol{\beta}_1)^{-1}\boldsymbol{\phi}_0$, and the unconditional covariance between a_{1t} and a_{2t} is $\rho_{21}\sigma_1\sigma_2$.
2. If $\alpha_{12} = \beta_{12} = 0$, then the volatility of a_{1t} does not depend on the past volatility of a_{2t}. Similarly, if $\alpha_{21} = \beta_{21} = 0$, then the volatility of a_{2t} does not depend on the past volatility of a_{1t}.
3. If both $\boldsymbol{\alpha}_1$ and $\boldsymbol{\beta}_1$ are diagonal, then the model reduces to two univariate GARCH(1,1) models. In this case, the two volatility processes are not dynamically related.
4. Volatility forecasts of the model can be obtained by using forecasting methods similar to those of a vector ARMA(1,1) model; see the univariate case in Chapter 3. The 1-step ahead volatility forecast at the forecast origin h is

$$\Xi_h^*(1) = \boldsymbol{\alpha}_0 + \boldsymbol{\alpha}_1\boldsymbol{a}_h^2 + \boldsymbol{\beta}_1\Xi_h^*.$$

For the ℓ-step ahead forecast, we have

$$\Xi_h^*(\ell) = \boldsymbol{\alpha}_0 + (\boldsymbol{\alpha}_1 + \boldsymbol{\beta}_1)\Xi_h^*(\ell - 1), \quad \ell > 1.$$

These forecasts are for the marginal volatilities of a_{it}. The ℓ-step ahead forecast of the covariance between a_{1t} and a_{2t} is $\hat{\rho}_{21}[\sigma_{11,h}(\ell)\sigma_{22,h}(\ell)]^{0.5}$, where $\hat{\rho}_{21}$ is the estimate of ρ_{21} and $\sigma_{ii,h}(\ell)$ are the elements of $\Xi_h^*(\ell)$.

Example 10.4. Again, consider the daily log returns of Hong Kong and Japanese markets of Example 10.1. Using bivariate GARCH models, we obtain two models that fit the data well. The mean equations of the first bivariate model are

$$r_{1t} = -0.118 r_{1,t-6} + a_{1t},$$
$$r_{2t} = a_{2t},$$

where the standard error of the AR(6) coefficient is 0.044. The volatility equations of the first model are

$$\begin{bmatrix} \sigma_{11,t} \\ \sigma_{22,t} \end{bmatrix} = \begin{bmatrix} 0.275 \\ (0.079) \\ 0.051 \\ (0.014) \end{bmatrix} + \begin{bmatrix} \begin{matrix} 0.112 \\ (0.032) \end{matrix} & \cdot \\ \cdot & \begin{matrix} 0.091 \\ (0.026) \end{matrix} \end{bmatrix} \begin{bmatrix} a_{1,t-1}^2 \\ a_{2,t-1}^2 \end{bmatrix}$$
$$+ \begin{bmatrix} \begin{matrix} 0.711 \\ (0.068) \end{matrix} & \cdot \\ \cdot & \begin{matrix} 0.869 \\ (0.028) \end{matrix} \end{bmatrix} \begin{bmatrix} \sigma_{11,t-1} \\ \sigma_{22,t-1} \end{bmatrix}, \qquad (10.23)$$

where the numbers in parentheses are standard errors. The estimated correlation coefficient between a_{1t} and a_{2t} is 0.226 with standard error 0.047.

Let $\tilde{\boldsymbol{a}}_t = (\tilde{a}_{1t}, \tilde{a}_{2t})'$ be the standardized residuals, where $\tilde{a}_{it} = a_{it}/\sqrt{\sigma_{ii,t}}$. The Ljung–Box statistics of $\tilde{\boldsymbol{a}}_t$ give $Q_2(4) = 22.29(0.10)$ and $Q_2(8) = 34.83(0.29)$, where the number in parentheses denotes p-value. Here the p-values are based on chi-squared distributions with 15 and 31 degrees of freedom, respectively, because an AR(6) coefficient is used in the mean equation. The Ljung–Box statistics for the $\tilde{\boldsymbol{a}}_t^2$ process give $Q_2^*(4) = 9.54(0.85)$ and $Q_2^*(8) = 18.58(0.96)$. Consequently, there are no serial correlations or conditional heteroscedasticities in the bivariate standardized residuals of model (10.23). The unconditional innovational variances of the two residuals are 1.55 and 1.28, respectively, for the Hong Kong and Japanese markets.

The model in Eq. (10.23) shows two uncoupled volatility equations, indicating that the volatilities of the two markets are not dynamically related, but they are contemporaneously correlated. We refer to the model as a bivariate *diagonal constant-correlation* model. If the minor lag-6 serial correlation of Hong Kong market returns is omitted, then the constant-correlation models can easily be estimated using S-Plus:

```
> hkja.ccc = mgarch(rtn~1,~ccc(1,1),trace=F)
> summary(hkja.ccc)
```

The mean equations of the second bivariate GARCH model are

$$r_{1t} = -0.143 r_{1,t-6} + a_{1t},$$
$$r_{2t} = a_{2t},$$

where the standard error of the AR(6) coefficient is 0.042, and the volatility equations of the second model are

$$\begin{bmatrix} \sigma_{11,t} \\ \sigma_{22,t} \end{bmatrix} = \begin{bmatrix} 0.378 \\ (0.103) \\ \cdot \\ \end{bmatrix} + \begin{bmatrix} 0.108 & \cdot \\ (0.030) & \\ \cdot & 0.172 \\ & (0.035) \end{bmatrix} \begin{bmatrix} a^2_{1,t-1} \\ a^2_{2,t-1} \end{bmatrix}$$

$$+ \begin{bmatrix} \cdot & 0.865 \\ & (0.109) \\ 0.321 & 0.869 \\ (0.135) & (0.028) \end{bmatrix} \begin{bmatrix} \sigma_{11,t-1} \\ \sigma_{22,t-1} \end{bmatrix}, \qquad (10.24)$$

where the numbers in parentheses are standard errors. The estimated correlation coefficient between a_{1t} and a_{2t} is 0.236 with standard error 0.045. Defining the standardized residuals as before, we obtain $Q_2(4) = 24.22(0.06)$ and $Q_2(8) = 35.52(0.26)$ for the standardized residuals of the prior model and $Q_2^*(4) = 17.45(0.29)$ and $Q_2^*(8) = 24.55(0.79)$ for the squared standardized residuals. These Ljung–Box statistics are not significant at the 5% level, and hence the model in Eq. (10.24) is also adequate. The unconditional innovational variances of the prior model are 1.71 and 1.32, respectively, for the Hong Kong and Japanese markets.

In contrast with model (10.23), this second bivariate GARCH(1,1) model shows a feedback relationship between the two markets. It is then interesting to compare the two volatility models. First, the unconditional innovational variances of model (10.24) are closer to those of the univariate models in Eqs. (10.3) and (10.4). Second, Figure 10.7 shows the fitted volatility processes of model (10.23), whereas Figure 10.8 shows those of model (10.24). Because model (10.23) implies no dynamic volatility dependence between the two markets, Figure 10.7 is similar to that of Figure 10.2. In contrast, Figure 10.8 shows evidence of mutual impacts between the two markets. Third, the maximized log likelihood function for model (10.23) is -535.13 for $t = 8, \ldots, 469$, whereas that of model (10.24) is -540.32; see the log probability density function in Eq. (10.11). Therefore, model (10.23) is preferred if one uses the likelihood principle. Finally, because practical implications of the two bivariate volatility models differ dramatically, further investigation is needed to separate them. Such an investigation may use a longer sample period or include more variables (e.g., using some U.S. market returns).

Example 10.5. As a second illustration, consider the monthly log returns, in percentages, of IBM stock and the S&P 500 index from January 1926 to December 1999 used in Chapter 8. Let r_{1t} and r_{2t} be the monthly log returns for IBM stock and the S&P 500 index, respectively. If a constant-correlation GARCH(1,1) model is entertained, we obtain the mean equations

$$r_{1t} = 1.351 + 0.072r_{1,t-1} + 0.055r_{1,t-2} - 0.119r_{2,t-2} + a_{1t},$$

$$r_{2t} = 0.703 + a_{2t},$$

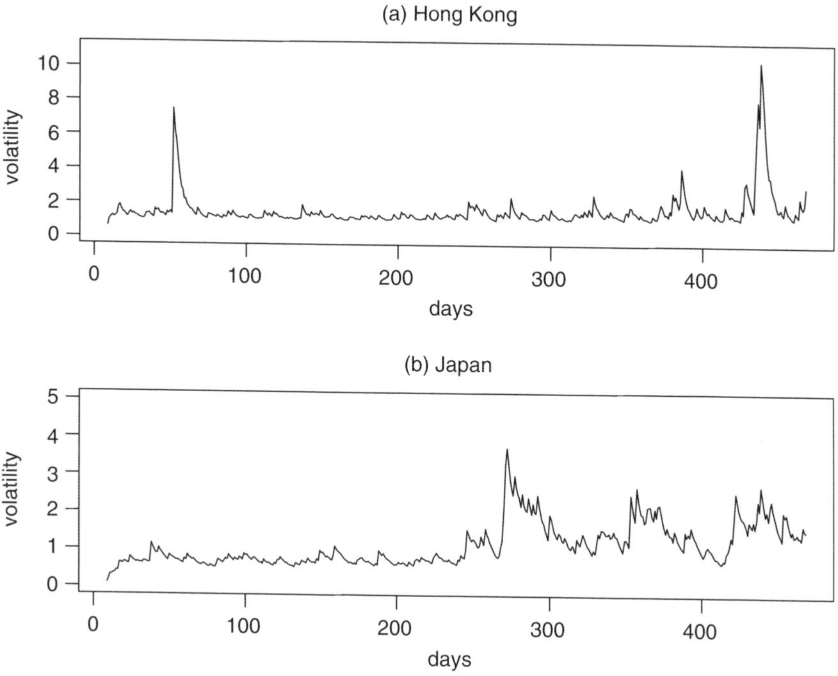

Figure 10.7. Estimated volatilities for daily log returns in percentages of stock market indexes for Hong Kong and Japan from January 1, 1996 to October 16, 1997: (a) the Hong Kong market and (b) the Japanese market. The model used is Eq. (10.23).

where standard errors of the parameters in the first equation are 0.225, 0.029, 0.034, and 0.044, respectively, and standard error of the parameter in the second equation is 0.155. The volatility equations are

$$\begin{bmatrix} \sigma_{11,t} \\ \sigma_{22,t} \end{bmatrix} = \begin{bmatrix} 2.98 \\ (0.59) \\ 2.09 \\ (0.47) \end{bmatrix} + \begin{bmatrix} 0.079 & \cdot \\ (0.013) & \\ 0.042 & 0.045 \\ (0.009) & (0.010) \end{bmatrix} \begin{bmatrix} a^2_{1,t-1} \\ a^2_{2,t-1} \end{bmatrix}$$
$$+ \begin{bmatrix} 0.873 & -0.031 \\ (0.020) & (0.009) \\ -0.066 & 0.913 \\ (0.015) & (0.014) \end{bmatrix} \begin{bmatrix} \sigma_{11,t-1} \\ \sigma_{22,t-1} \end{bmatrix}, \qquad (10.25)$$

where the numbers in parentheses are standard errors. The constant correlation coefficient is 0.614 with standard error 0.020. Using the standardized residuals, we obtain the Ljung–Box statistics $Q_2(4) = 16.77(0.21)$ and $Q_2(8) = 32.40(0.30)$, where the p-values shown in parentheses are obtained from chi-squared distributions with 13 and 29 degrees of freedom, respectively. Here the degrees of

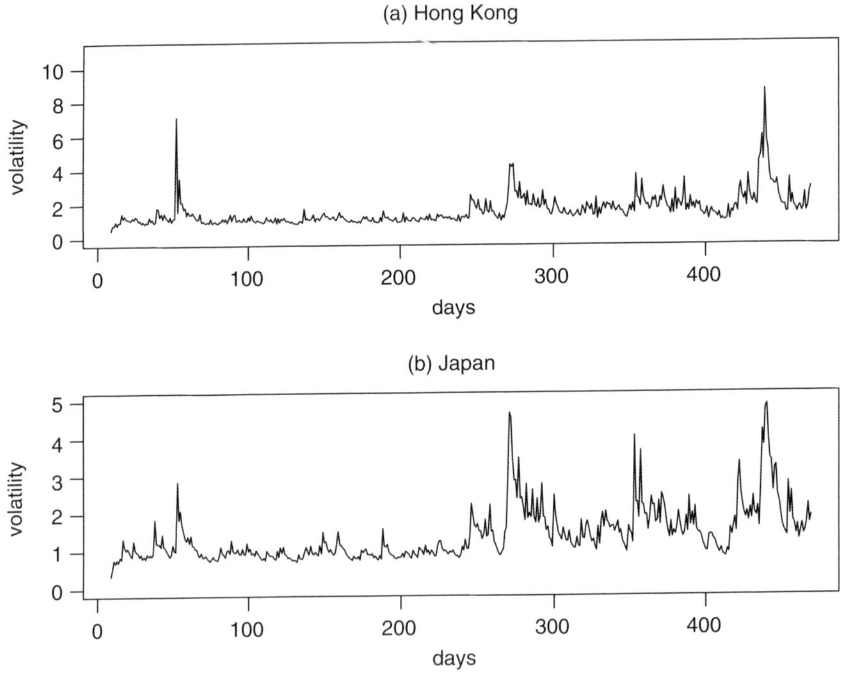

Figure 10.8. Estimated volatilities for daily log returns in percentages of stock market indices for Hong Kong and Japan from January 1, 1996 to October 16, 1997: (a) the Hong Kong market and (b) the Japanese market. The model used is Eq. (10.24).

freedom have been adjusted because the mean equations contain three lagged predictors. For the squared standardized residuals, we have $Q_2^*(4) = 18.00(0.16)$ and $Q_2^*(8) = 39.09(0.10)$. Therefore, at the 5% significance level, the standardized residuals $\tilde{\boldsymbol{a}}_t$ have no serial correlations or conditional heteroscedasticities. This bivariate GARCH(1,1) model shows a feedback relationship between the volatilities of the two monthly log returns.

10.4.2 Time-Varying Correlation Models

A major drawback of the constant-correlation volatility models is that the correlation coefficient tends to change over time in a real application. Consider the monthly log returns of IBM stock and the S&P 500 index used in Example 10.5. It is hard to justify that the S&P 500 index return, which is a weighted average, can maintain a constant-correlation coefficient with IBM return over the past 70 years. Figure 10.9 shows the sample correlation coefficient between the two monthly log return series using a moving window of 120 observations (i.e., 10 years). The correlation changes over time and appears to be decreasing in recent years. The decreasing trend in correlation is not surprising because the ranking of

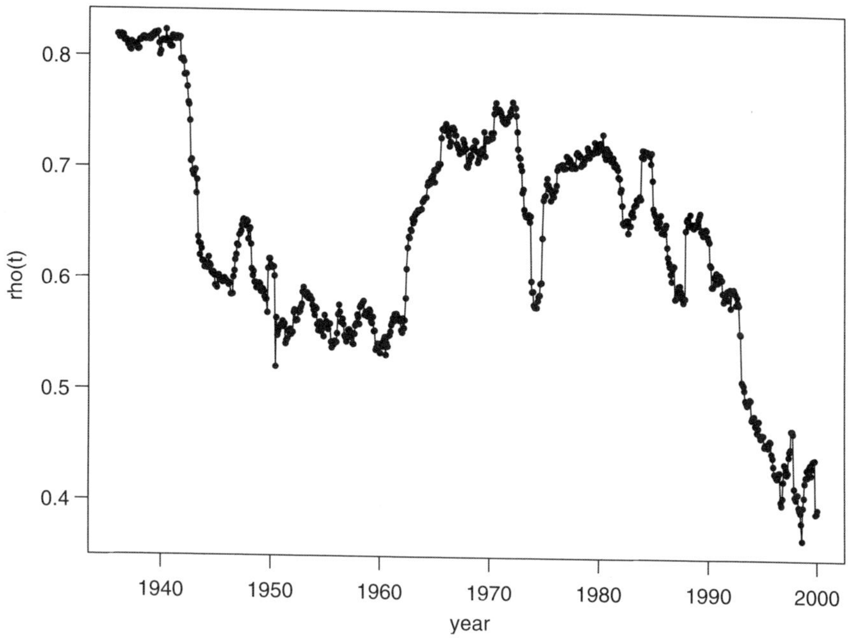

Figure 10.9. The sample correlation coefficient between monthly log returns of IBM stock and the S&P 500 index. The correlation is computed by a moving window of 120 observations. The sample period is from January 1926 to December 1999.

IBM market capitalization among large U.S. industrial companies has changed in recent years. A Lagrange multiplier statistic was proposed recently by Tse (2000) to test constant-correlation coefficients in a multivariate GARCH model.

A simple way to relax the constant-correlation constraint within the GARCH framework is to specify an exact equation for the conditional correlation coefficient. This can be done by two methods using the two reparameterizations of $\boldsymbol{\Sigma}_t$ discussed in Section 10.3. First, we use the correlation coefficient directly. Because the correlation coefficient between the returns of IBM stock and S&P 500 index is positive and must be in the interval [0, 1], we employ the equation

$$\rho_{21,t} = \frac{\exp(q_t)}{1 + \exp(q_t)}, \tag{10.26}$$

where

$$q_t = \varpi_0 + \varpi_1 \rho_{21,t-1} + \varpi_2 \frac{a_{1,t-1} a_{2,t-1}}{\sqrt{\sigma_{11,t-1}\sigma_{22,t-1}}},$$

where $\sigma_{ii,t-1}$ is the conditional variance of the shock $a_{i,t-1}$. We refer to this equation as a GARCH(1,1) model for the correlation coefficient because it uses the lag-1 cross-correlation and the lag-1 cross-product of the two shocks. If $\varpi_1 = \varpi_2 = 0$, then model (10.26) reduces to the case of constant correlation.

In summary, a time-varying correlation bivariate GARCH(1,1) model consists of two sets of equations. The first set of equations consists of a bivariate GARCH(1,1) model for the conditional variances and the second set of equation is a GARCH(1,1) model for the correlation in Eq. (10.26). In practice, a negative sign can be added to Eq. (10.26) if the correlation coefficient is negative. In general, when the sign of correlation is unknown, we can use the Fisher transformation for correlation

$$q_t = \ln\left(\frac{1+\rho_{21,t}}{1-\rho_{21,t}}\right) \quad \text{or} \quad \rho_{21,t} = \frac{\exp(q_t)-1}{\exp(q_t)+1}$$

and employ a GARCH model for q_t to model the time-varying correlation between two returns.

Example 10.5 (Continued). Augmenting Eq. (10.26) to the GARCH(1,1) model in Eq. (10.25) for the monthly log returns of IBM stock and the S&P 500 index and performing a joint estimation, we obtain the following model for the two series:

$$\begin{aligned} r_{1t} &= 1.318 + 0.076 r_{1,t-1} - 0.068 r_{2,t-2} + a_{1t}, \\ r_{2t} &= 0.673 + a_{2t}, \end{aligned}$$

where standard errors of the three parameters in the first equation are 0.215, 0.026, and 0.034, respectively, and standard error of the parameter in the second equation is 0.151. The volatility equations are

$$\begin{aligned} \begin{bmatrix} \sigma_{11,t} \\ \sigma_{22,t} \end{bmatrix} &= \begin{bmatrix} 2.80 \\ (0.58) \\ 1.71 \\ (0.40) \end{bmatrix} + \begin{bmatrix} 0.084 & \cdot \\ (0.013) & \\ 0.037 & 0.054 \\ (0.009) & (0.010) \end{bmatrix} \begin{bmatrix} a^2_{1,t-1} \\ a^2_{2,t-1} \end{bmatrix} \\ &+ \begin{bmatrix} 0.864 & -0.020 \\ (0.021) & (0.009) \\ -0.058 & 0.914 \\ (0.014) & (0.013) \end{bmatrix} \begin{bmatrix} \sigma_{11,t-1} \\ \sigma_{22,t-1} \end{bmatrix}, \end{aligned} \tag{10.27}$$

where, as before, standard errors are in parentheses. The conditional correlation equation is

$$\rho_t = \frac{\exp(q_t)}{1+\exp(q_t)}, \quad q_t = -2.024 + 3.983\rho_{t-1} + 0.088\frac{a_{1,t-1}a_{2,t-1}}{\sqrt{\sigma_{11,t-1}\sigma_{22,t-1}}}, \tag{10.28}$$

where standard errors of the estimates are 0.050, 0.090, and 0.019, respectively. The parameters of the prior correlation equation are highly significant. Applying the Ljung–Box statistics to the standardized residuals $\tilde{\boldsymbol{a}}_t$, we have $Q_2(4) = 20.57(0.11)$ and $Q_2(8) = 36.08(0.21)$. For the squared standardized residuals, we have $Q_2^*(4) = 16.69(0.27)$ and $Q_2^*(8) = 36.71(0.19)$. Therefore, the standardized residuals of the model have no significant serial correlations or conditional heteroscedasticities.

It is interesting to compare this time-varying correlation GARCH(1,1) model with the constant-correlation GARCH(1,1) model in Eq. (10.25). First, the mean and volatility equations of the two models are close. Second, Figure 10.10 shows the fitted conditional-correlation coefficient between the monthly log returns of IBM stock and the S&P 500 index based on model (10.28). The plot shows that the correlation coefficient fluctuated over time and became smaller in recent years. This latter characteristic is in agreement with that of Figure 10.9. Third, the average of the fitted correlation coefficients is 0.612, which is essentially the estimate 0.614 of the constant-correlation model in Eq. (10.25). Fourth, using the sample variances of r_{it} as the starting values for the conditional variances and the observations from $t = 4$ to $t = 888$, the maximized log likelihood function is -3691.21 for the constant-correlation GARCH(1,1) model and -3679.64 for the time-varying correlation GARCH(1,1) model. Thus, the time-varying correlation model shows some significant improvement over the constant-correlation model. Finally, consider the 1-step ahead volatility forecasts of the two models at the forecast origin $h = 888$. For the constant-correlation model in Eq. (10.25), we have $a_{1,888} = 3.075$, $a_{2,888} = 4.931$, $\sigma_{11,888} = 77.91$, and $\sigma_{22,888} = 21.19$. Therefore, the 1-step ahead forecast for the conditional covariance matrix is

$$\widehat{\boldsymbol{\Sigma}}_{888}(1) = \begin{bmatrix} 71.09 & 21.83 \\ 21.83 & 17.79 \end{bmatrix},$$

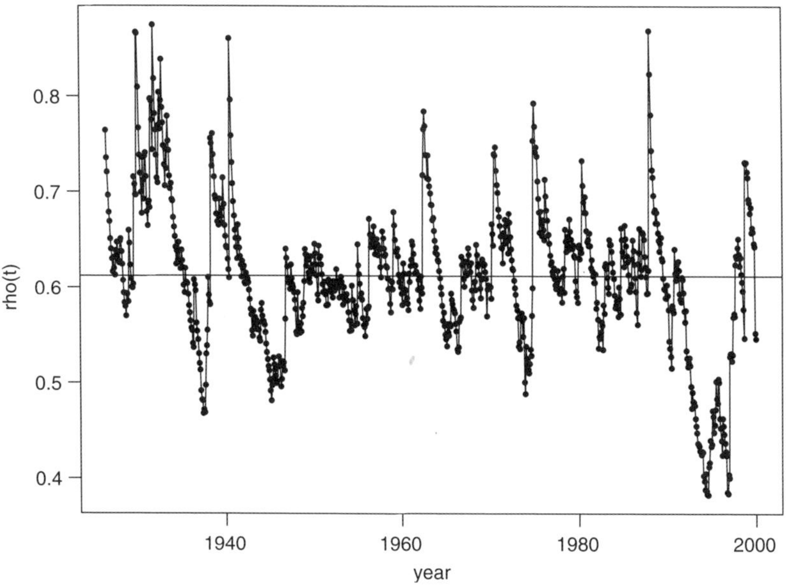

Figure 10.10. The fitted conditional correlation coefficient between monthly log returns of IBM stock and the S&P 500 index using the time-varying correlation GARCH(1,1) model of Example 10.5. The horizontal line denotes the average 0.612 of the correlation coefficients.

where the covariance is obtained by using the constant-correlation coefficient 0.614. For the time-varying correlation model in Eqs. (10.27) and (10.28), we have $a_{1,888} = 3.287$, $a_{2,888} = 4.950$, $\sigma_{11,888} = 83.35$, $\sigma_{22,888} = 28.56$, and $\rho_{888} = 0.546$. The 1-step ahead forecast for the covariance matrix is

$$\widehat{\boldsymbol{\Sigma}}_{888}(1) = \begin{bmatrix} 75.15 & 23.48 \\ 23.48 & 24.70 \end{bmatrix},$$

where the forecast of the correlation coefficient is 0.545.

In the second method, we use the Cholesky decomposition of $\boldsymbol{\Sigma}_t$ to model time-varying correlations. For the bivariate case, the parameter vector is $\boldsymbol{\Xi}_t = (g_{11,t}, g_{22,t}, q_{21,t})'$; see Eq. (10.18). A simple GARCH(1,1) type model for $\boldsymbol{a}_t$ is

$$\begin{aligned} g_{11,t} &= \alpha_{10} + \alpha_{11} b_{1,t-1}^2 + \beta_{11} g_{11,t-1}, \\ q_{21,t} &= \gamma_0 + \gamma_1 q_{21,t-1} + \gamma_2 a_{2,t-1}, \\ g_{22,t} &= \alpha_{20} + \alpha_{21} b_{1,t-1}^2 + \alpha_{22} b_{2,t-1}^2 + \beta_{21} g_{11,t-1} + \beta_{22} g_{22,t-1}, \end{aligned} \tag{10.29}$$

where $b_{1t} = a_{1t}$ and $b_{2t} = a_{2t} - q_{21,t} a_{1t}$. Thus, b_{1t} assumes a univariate GARCH(1,1) model, b_{2t} uses a bivariate GARCH(1,1) model, and $q_{21,t}$ is autocorrelated and uses $a_{2,t-1}$ as an additional explanatory variable. The probability density function relevant to maximum likelihood estimation is given in Eq. (10.20) with $k = 2$.

Example 10.5 (Continued). Again we use the monthly log returns of IBM stock and the S&P 500 index to demonstrate the volatility model in Eq. (10.29). Using the same specification as before, we obtain the fitted mean equations as

$$\begin{aligned} r_{1t} &= 1.364 + 0.075 r_{1,t-1} - 0.058 r_{2,t-2} + a_{1t}, \\ r_{2t} &= 0.643 + a_{2t}, \end{aligned}$$

where standard errors of the parameters in the first equation are 0.219, 0.027, and 0.032, respectively, and the standard error of the parameter in the second equation is 0.154. These two mean equations are close to what we obtained before. The fitted volatility model is

$$\begin{aligned} g_{11,t} &= 3.714 + 0.113 b_{1,t-1}^2 + 0.804 g_{11,t-1}, \\ q_{21,t} &= 0.0029 + 0.9915 q_{21,t-1} - 0.0041 a_{2,t-1}, \\ g_{22,t} &= 1.023 + 0.021 b_{1,t-1}^2 + 0.052 b_{2,t-1}^2 - 0.040 g_{11,t-1} + 0.937 g_{22,t-1}, \end{aligned} \tag{10.30}$$

where $b_{1t} = a_{1t}$ and $b_{2t} = a_{2t} - q_{21,t} b_{1t}$. Standard errors of the parameters in the equation of $g_{11,t}$ are 1.033, 0.022, and 0.037, respectively; those of the parameters in the equation of $q_{21,t}$ are 0.001, 0.002, and 0.0004; and those of the parameters in the equation of $g_{22,t}$ are 0.344, 0.007, 0.013, and 0.015, respectively. All estimates are statistically significant at the 1% level.

The conditional covariance matrix $\boldsymbol{\Sigma}_t$ can be obtained from model (10.30) by using the Cholesky decomposition in Eq. (10.12). For the bivariate case, the relationship is given specifically in Eq. (10.13). Consequently, we obtain the time-varying correlation coefficient as

$$\rho_t = \frac{\sigma_{21,t}}{\sqrt{\sigma_{11,t}\sigma_{22,t}}} = \frac{q_{21,t}\sqrt{g_{11,t}}}{\sqrt{g_{22,t} + q_{21,t}^2 g_{11,t}}}. \tag{10.31}$$

Using the fitted values of $\sigma_{11,t}$ and $\sigma_{22,t}$, we can compute the standardized residuals to perform model checking. The Ljung–Box statistics for the standardized residuals of model (10.30) give $Q_2(4) = 19.77(0.14)$ and $Q_2(8) = 34.22(0.27)$. For the squared standardized residuals, we have $Q_2^*(4) = 15.34(0.36)$ and $Q_2^*(8) = 31.87(0.37)$. Thus, the fitted model is adequate in describing the conditional mean and volatility. The model shows a strong dynamic dependence in the correlation; see the coefficient 0.9915 in Eq. (10.30).

Figure 10.11 shows the fitted time-varying correlation coefficient in Eq. (10.31). It shows a smoother correlation pattern than that of Figure 10.10 and confirms the decreasing trend of the correlation coefficient. In particular, the fitted correlation coefficients in recent years are smaller than those of the other models. The two time-varying correlation models for the monthly log returns of IBM stock and the S&P 500 index have comparable maximized likelihood functions of about −3672, indicating the fits are similar. However, the approach based on the Cholesky decomposition may have some advantages. First, it does not require any parameter constraint in estimation to ensure the positive definiteness of $\boldsymbol{\Sigma}_t$. If one also uses log transformation for $g_{ii,t}$, then no constraints are needed for the entire volatility model. Second, the log likelihood function becomes simple under the transformation. Third, the time-varying parameters $q_{ij,t}$ and $g_{ii,t}$ have nice interpretations. However, the transformation makes inference a bit more complicated because the fitted model may depend on the ordering of elements in $\boldsymbol{a}_t$; recall that a_{1t} is not transformed. In theory, the ordering of elements in $\boldsymbol{a}_t$ should have no impact on volatility.

Finally, the 1-step ahead forecast of the conditional covariance matrix at the forecast origin $t = 888$ for the new time-varying correlation model is

$$\widehat{\boldsymbol{\Sigma}}_{888}(1) = \begin{bmatrix} 73.45 & 7.34 \\ 7.34 & 17.87 \end{bmatrix}.$$

The correlation coefficient of the prior forecast is 0.203, which is substantially smaller than those of the previous two models. However, forecasts of the conditional variances are similar as before.

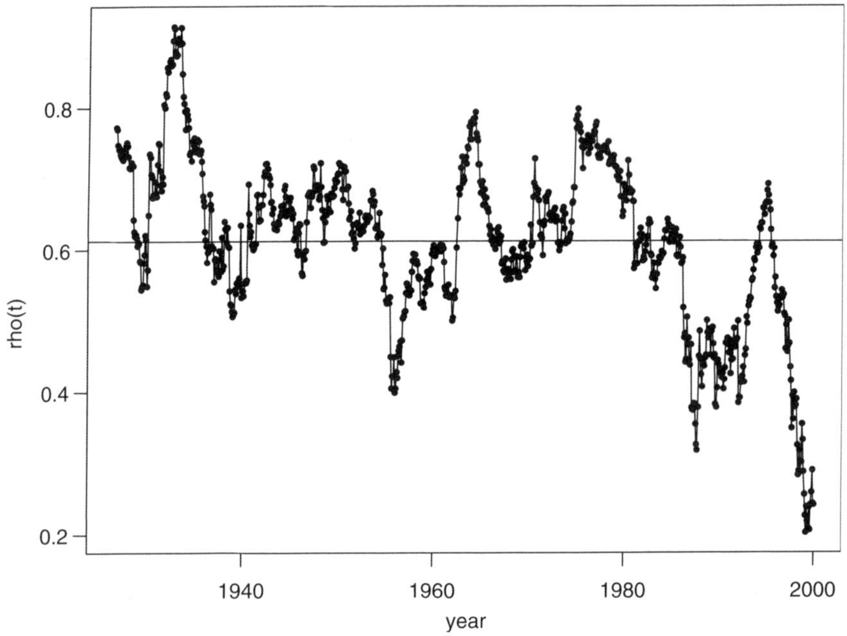

Figure 10.11. The fitted conditional correlation coefficient between monthly log returns of IBM stock and the S&P 500 index using the time-varying correlation GARCH(1,1) model of Example 10.5 with Cholesky decomposition. The horizontal line denotes the average 0.612 of the estimated coefficients.

10.4.3 Some Recent Developments

Using the parameterization in Eq. (10.7), several authors have proposed parsimonious models for $\boldsymbol{\rho}_t$ to describe the time-varying correlations. We discuss two such developments.

For k-dimensional returns, Tse and Tsui (2002) assume that the conditional correlation matrix $\boldsymbol{\rho}_t$ follows the model

$$\boldsymbol{\rho}_t = (1 - \theta_1 - \theta_2)\boldsymbol{\rho} + \theta_1 \boldsymbol{\rho}_{t-1} + \theta_2 \boldsymbol{\psi}_{t-1},$$

where θ_1 and θ_2 are scalar parameters, $\boldsymbol{\rho}$ is a $k \times k$ positive-definite matrix with unit diagonal elements, and $\boldsymbol{\psi}_{t-1}$ is the $k \times k$ sample correlation matrix using shocks from $t - m, \ldots, t - 1$ for a prespecified m. Estimation of the two scalar parameters θ_1 and θ_2 requires special constraints to ensure positive definiteness of the correlation matrix. This is a parsimonious model, but it might be hard to implement in real application. The choice of $\boldsymbol{\rho}$ and m deserves a careful investigation.

Engle (2002) proposes the model

$$\boldsymbol{\rho}_t = \boldsymbol{J}_t \boldsymbol{Q}_t \boldsymbol{J}_t,$$

where $\boldsymbol{Q}_t = (q_{ij,t})_{k\times k}$ is a positive-definite matrix, $\boldsymbol{J}_t = \text{diag}\{q_{11,t}^{-1/2}, \ldots, q_{kk,t}^{-1/2}\}$, and $\boldsymbol{Q}_t$ satisfies

$$\boldsymbol{Q}_t = (1 - \theta_1 - \theta_2)\overline{\boldsymbol{Q}} + \theta_1 \boldsymbol{\epsilon}_{t-1}\boldsymbol{\epsilon}'_{t-1} + \theta_2 \boldsymbol{Q}_{t-1},$$

where $\boldsymbol{\epsilon}_t$ is the standardized innovation vector with elements $\epsilon_{it} = a_{it}/\sqrt{\sigma_{ii,t}}$, $\overline{\boldsymbol{Q}}$ is the unconditional covariance matrix of $\boldsymbol{\epsilon}_t$, and θ_1 and θ_2 are non-negative scalar parameters satisfying $0 < \theta_1 + \theta_2 < 1$. The $\boldsymbol{J}_t$ matrix is a normalization matrix to guarantee that $\boldsymbol{R}_t$ is a correlation matrix.

An obvious drawback of the prior two models is that θ_1 and θ_2 are scalar so that all the conditional correlations have the same dynamics. This might be hard to justify in real applications, especially when the dimension k is large.

10.5 HIGHER DIMENSIONAL VOLATILITY MODELS

In this section, we make use of the sequential nature of Cholesky decomposition to suggest a strategy for building a high-dimensional volatility model. Again write the vector return series as $\boldsymbol{r}_t = \boldsymbol{\mu}_t + \boldsymbol{a}_t$. The mean equations for $\boldsymbol{r}_t$ can be specified by using the methods of Chapter 8. A simple vector AR model is often sufficient. Here we focus on building a volatility model using the shock process $\boldsymbol{a}_t$.

Based on the discussion of Cholesky decomposition in Section 10.3, the orthogonal transformation from a_{it} to b_{it} only involves b_{jt} for $j < i$. In addition, the time-varying volatility models built in Section 10.4 appear to be nested in the sense that the model for $g_{ii,t}$ depends only on quantities related to b_{jt} for $j < i$. Consequently, we consider the following sequential procedure to build a multivariate volatility model:

1. Select a market index or a stock return that is of major interest. Build a univariate volatility model for the selected return series.
2. Augment a second return series to the system, perform the orthogonal transformation on the shock process of this new return series, and build a bivariate volatility model for the system. The parameter estimates of the univariate model in step 1 can be used as the starting values in bivariate estimation.
3. Augment a third return series to the system, perform the orthogonal transformation on this newly added shock process, and build a three-dimensional volatility model. Again parameter estimates of the bivariate model can be used as the starting values in the three-dimensional estimation.
4. Continue the augmentation until a joint volatility model is built for all the return series of interest.

Finally, model checking should be performed in each step to ensure the adequacy of the fitted model. Experience shows that this sequential procedure can simplify substantially the complexity involved in building a high-dimensional volatility model. In particular, it can markedly reduce the computing time in estimation.

Example 10.6. We demonstrate the proposed sequential procedure by building a volatility model for the daily log returns of the S&P 500 index and the stocks of Cisco Systems and Intel Corporation. The data span is from January 2, 1991 to December 31, 1999 with 2275 observations. The log returns are in percentages and shown in Figure 10.12. Components of the return series are ordered as $\boldsymbol{r}_t = (\text{SP5}_t, \text{CSCO}_t, \text{INTC}_t)'$. The sample means, standard errors, and correlation matrix of the data are

$$\widehat{\boldsymbol{\mu}} = \begin{bmatrix} 0.066 \\ 0.257 \\ 0.156 \end{bmatrix}, \quad \begin{bmatrix} \hat{\sigma}_1 \\ \hat{\sigma}_2 \\ \hat{\sigma}_3 \end{bmatrix} = \begin{bmatrix} 0.875 \\ 2.853 \\ 2.464 \end{bmatrix}, \quad \widehat{\boldsymbol{\rho}} = \begin{bmatrix} 1.00 & 0.52 & 0.50 \\ 0.52 & 1.00 & 0.47 \\ 0.50 & 0.47 & 1.00 \end{bmatrix}.$$

Using the Ljung–Box statistics to detect any serial dependence in the return series, we obtain $Q_3(1) = 26.20$, $Q_3(4) = 79.73$, and $Q_3(8) = 123.68$. These test

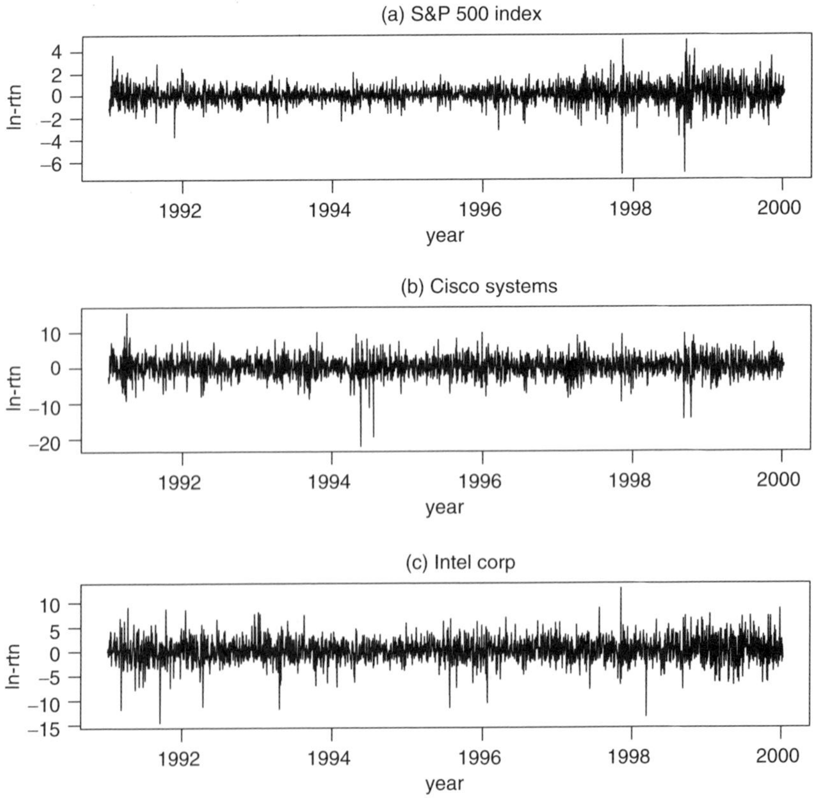

Figure 10.12. Time plots of daily log returns in percentages of (a) the S&P 500 index and stocks of (b) Cisco Systems and (c) Intel Corporation from January 2, 1991 to December 31, 1999.

Table 10.1. Sample Cross-Correlation Matrices of Daily Log Returns of the S&P 500 Index and the Stocks of Cisco Systems and Intel Corporation from January 2, 1991 to December 31, 1999

Lag					
1	2	3	4	5	6
. . .	. . .	− . .	. . .	− . .	. . .
. . .	. − .	. . .	. . .	− . .	. − .
− . .	. . .	. . .	. . .	− . .	. . .

statistics are highly significant with p-values close to zero as compared with chi-squared distributions with degrees of freedom 9, 36, and 72, respectively. There is indeed some serial dependence in the data. Table 10.1 gives the first five lags of sample cross-correlation matrices shown in the simplified notation of Chapter 8. An examination of the table shows that (a) the daily log returns of the S&P 500 index does not depend on the past returns of Cisco or Intel, (b) the log return of Cisco stock has some serial correlations and depends on the past returns of the S&P 500 index (see lags 2 and 5), and (c) the log return of Intel stock depends on the past returns of the S&P 500 index (see lags 1 and 5). These observations are similar to those between the returns of IBM stock and the S&P 500 index analyzed in Chapter 8. They suggest that returns of individual large-cap companies tend to be affected by the past behavior of the market. However, the market return is not significantly affected by the past returns of individual companies.

Turning to volatility modeling and following the suggested procedure, we start with the log returns of the S&P 500 index and obtain the model

$$
\begin{aligned}
r_{1t} &= 0.078 + 0.042 r_{1,t-1} - 0.062 r_{1,t-3} - 0.048 r_{1,t-4} - 0.052 r_{1,t-5} + a_{1t}, \\
\sigma_{11,t} &= 0.013 + 0.092 a_{1,t-1}^2 + 0.894 \sigma_{11,t-1},
\end{aligned}
\tag{10.32}
$$

where standard errors of the parameters in the mean equation are 0.016, 0.023, 0.020, 0.022, and 0.020, respectively, and those of the parameters in the volatility equation are 0.002, 0.006, and 0.007, respectively. Univariate Ljung–Box statistics of the standardized residuals and their squared series fail to detect any remaining serial correlation or conditional heteroscedasticity in the data. Indeed, we have $Q(10) = 7.38(0.69)$ for the standardized residuals and $Q(10) = 3.14(0.98)$ for the squared series.

Augmenting the daily log returns of Cisco stock to the system, we build a bivariate model with mean equations given by

$$
\begin{aligned}
r_{1t} &= 0.065 - 0.046 r_{1,t-3} + a_{1t}, \\
r_{2t} &= 0.325 + 0.195 r_{1,t-2} - 0.091 r_{2,t-2} + a_{2t},
\end{aligned}
\tag{10.33}
$$

where all of the estimates are statistically significant at the 1% level. Using the notation of Cholesky decomposition, we obtain the volatility equations as

$$\begin{aligned} g_{11,t} &= 0.006 + 0.051b_{1,t-1}^2 + 0.943g_{11,t-1}, \\ q_{21,t} &= 0.331 + 0.790q_{21,t-1} - 0.041a_{2,t-1}, \\ g_{22,t} &= 0.177 + 0.082b_{2,t-1}^2 + 0.890g_{22,t-1}, \end{aligned} \tag{10.34}$$

where $b_{1t} = a_{1t}$, $b_{2t} = a_{2t} - q_{21,t}b_{1t}$, standard errors of the parameters in the equation of $g_{11,t}$ are 0.001, 0.005, and 0.006, those of the parameters in the equation of $q_{21,t}$ are 0.156, 0.099, and 0.011, and those of the parameters in the equation of $g_{22,t}$ are 0.029, 0.008, and 0.011, respectively. The bivariate Ljung–Box statistics of the standardized residuals fail to detect any remaining serial dependence or conditional heteroscedasticity. The bivariate model is adequate. Comparing with Eq. (10.32), we see that the difference between the marginal and univariate models of r_{1t} is small.

The next and final step is to augment the daily log returns of Intel stock to the system. The mean equations become

$$\begin{aligned} r_{1t} &= 0.065 - 0.043r_{1,t-3} + a_{1t}, \\ r_{2t} &= 0.326 + 0.201r_{1,t-2} - 0.089r_{2,t-1} + a_{2t}, \\ r_{3t} &= 0.192 - 0.264r_{1,t-1} + 0.059r_{3,t-1} + a_{3t}, \end{aligned} \tag{10.35}$$

where standard errors of the parameters in the first equation are 0.016 and 0.017, those of the parameters in the second equation are 0.052, 0.059, and 0.021, and those of the parameters in the third equation are 0.050, 0.057, and 0.022, respectively. All estimates are statistically significant at about the 1% level. As expected, the mean equations for r_{1t} and r_{2t} are essentially the same as those in the bivariate case.

The three-dimensional time-varying volatility model becomes a bit more complicated, but it remains manageable as

$$\begin{aligned} g_{11,t} &= 0.006 + 0.050b_{1,t-1}^2 + 0.943g_{11,t-1}, \\ q_{21,t} &= 0.277 + 0.824q_{21,t-1} - 0.035a_{2,t-1}, \\ g_{22,t} &= 0.178 + 0.082b_{2,t-1}^2 + 0.889g_{22,t-1}, \\ q_{31,t} &= 0.039 + 0.973q_{31,t-1} + 0.010a_{3,t-1}, \\ q_{32,t} &= 0.006 + 0.981q_{32,t-1} + 0.004a_{2,t-1}, \\ g_{33,t} &= 1.188 + 0.053b_{3,t-1}^2 + 0.687g_{33,t-1} - 0.019g_{22,t-1}, \end{aligned} \tag{10.36}$$

where $b_{1t} = a_{1t}$, $b_{2t} = a_{2t} - q_{21,t}b_{1t}$, $b_{3t} = a_{3t} - q_{31,t}b_{1t} - q_{32,t}b_{2t}$, and standard errors of the parameters are given in Table 10.2. Except for the constant term of the $q_{32,t}$ equation, all estimates are significant at the 5% level. Let $\tilde{\boldsymbol{a}}_t =$

Table 10.2. Standard Errors of Parameter[a] Estimates of a Three-Dimensional Volatility Model for the Daily Log Returns in Percentages of the S&P 500 Index and Stocks of Cisco Systems and Intel Corporation from January 2, 1991 to December 31, 1999

Equation	Standard Error				Equation	Standard Error		
$g_{11,t}$	0.001	0.005	0.006		$q_{21,t}$	0.135	0.086	0.010
$g_{22,t}$	0.029	0.009	0.011		$q_{31,t}$	0.017	0.012	0.004
$g_{33,t}$	0.407	0.015	0.100	0.008	$q_{32,t}$	0.004	0.013	0.001

[a]The ordering of the parameter is the same as appears in Eq. (10.36).

$(a_{1t}/\hat{\sigma}_{1t}, a_{2t}/\hat{\sigma}_{2t}, a_{3t}/\hat{\sigma}_{3t})'$ be the standardized residual series, where $\hat{\sigma}_{it} = \sqrt{\hat{\sigma}_{ii,t}}$ is the fitted conditional standard error of the ith return. The Ljung–Box statistics of $\tilde{\boldsymbol{a}}_t$ give $Q_3(4) = 34.48(0.31)$ and $Q_3(8) = 60.42(0.70)$, where the degrees of freedom of the chi-squared distributions are 31 and 67, respectively, after adjusting for the number of parameters used in the mean equations. For the squared standardized residual series $\tilde{\boldsymbol{a}}_t^2$, we have $Q_3^*(4) = 28.71(0.58)$ and $Q_3^*(8) = 52.00(0.91)$. Therefore, the fitted model appears to be adequate in modeling the conditional means and volatilities.

The three-dimensional volatility model in Eq. (10.36) shows some interesting features. First, it is essentially a time-varying correlation GARCH(1,1) model because only lag-1 variables are used in the equations. Second, the volatility of the daily log returns of the S&P 500 index does not depend on the past volatilities of Cisco or Intel stock returns. Third, by taking the inverse transformation of the Cholesky decomposition, the volatilities of daily log returns of Cisco and Intel stocks depend on the past volatility of the market return; see the relationships between elements of $\boldsymbol{\Sigma}_t$, $\boldsymbol{L}_t$, and $\boldsymbol{G}_t$ given in Section 10.3. Fourth, the correlation quantities $q_{ij,t}$ have high persistence with large AR(1) coefficients.

Figure 10.13 shows the fitted volatility processes of the model (i.e., $\hat{\sigma}_{ii,t}$) for the data. The volatility of the index return is much smaller than those of the two individual stock returns. The plots also show that the volatility of the index return has increased in recent years, but this is not the case for the return of Cisco Systems. Figure 10.14 shows the time-varying correlation coefficients between the three return series. Of particular interest is to compare Figures 10.13 and 10.14. They show that the correlation coefficient between two return series increases when the returns are volatile. This is in agreement with the empirical study of relationships between international stock market indexes for which the correlation between two markets tends to increase during a financial crisis.

The volatility model in Eq. (10.36) consists of two sets of equations. The first set of equations describes the time evolution of conditional variances (i.e., $g_{ii,t}$), and the second set of equations deals with correlation coefficients (i.e., $q_{ij,t}$ with $i > j$). For this particular data set, an AR(1) model might be sufficient for the correlation equations. Similarly, a simple AR model might also be sufficient for the conditional variances. Define $\boldsymbol{v}_t = (v_{11,t}, v_{22,t}, v_{33,t})'$, where $v_{ii,t} = \ln(g_{ii,t})$,

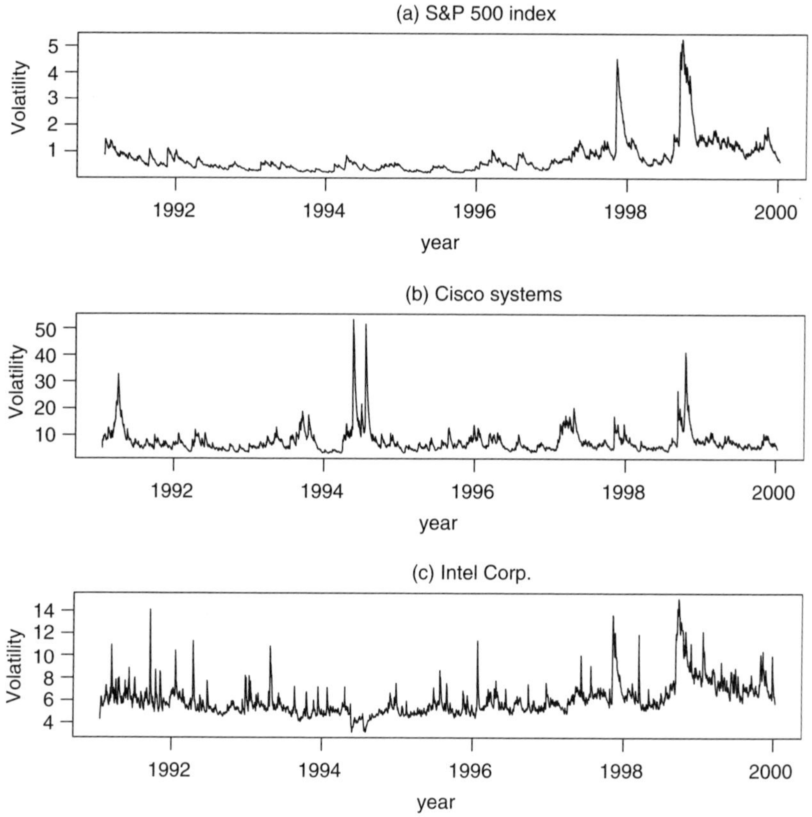

Figure 10.13. Time plots of fitted volatilities for daily log returns, in percentages, of (a) the S&P 500 index and stocks of (b) Cisco Systems and (c) Intel Corporation from January 2, 1991 to December 31, 1999.

and $\boldsymbol{q}_t = (q_{21,t}, q_{31,t}, q_{32,t})'$. The previous discussion suggests that we can use the simple lag-1 models

$$\boldsymbol{v}_t = \boldsymbol{c}_1 + \boldsymbol{\beta}_1 \boldsymbol{v}_{t-1}, \quad \boldsymbol{q}_t = \boldsymbol{c}_2 + \boldsymbol{\beta}_2 \boldsymbol{q}_{t-1}$$

as exact functions to model the volatility of asset returns, where $\boldsymbol{c}_i$ are constant vectors and $\boldsymbol{\beta}_i$ are 3×3 real-valued matrices. If a noise term is also included in the above equations, then the models become

$$\boldsymbol{v}_t = \boldsymbol{c}_1 + \boldsymbol{\beta}_1 \boldsymbol{v}_{t-1} + \boldsymbol{e}_{1t}, \quad \boldsymbol{q}_t = \boldsymbol{c}_2 + \boldsymbol{\beta}_2 \boldsymbol{q}_{t-1} + \boldsymbol{e}_{2t},$$

where $\boldsymbol{e}_{it}$ are random shocks with mean zero and a positive-definite covariance matrix, and we have a simple multivariate stochastic volatility model. In a recent manuscript, Chib, Nardari, and Shephard (1999) use Markov chain Monte Carlo (MCMC) methods to study high-dimensional stochastic volatility models. The

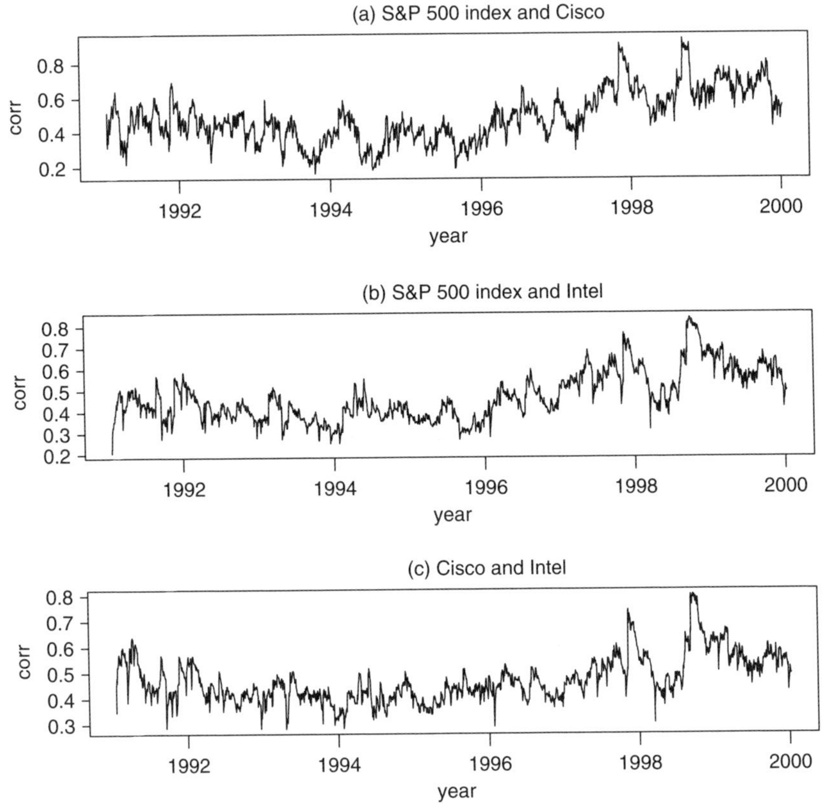

Figure 10.14. Time plots of fitted time-varying correlation coefficients between daily log returns of the S&P 500 index and stocks of Cisco Systems and Intel Corporation from January 2, 1991 to December 31, 1999.

model considered there allows for time-varying correlations, but in a relatively restrictive manner. Additional references of multivariate volatility model include Harvey, Ruiz, and Shephard (1995). We discuss MCMC methods in volatility modeling in Chapter 12.

10.6 FACTOR–VOLATILITY MODELS

Another approach to simplifying the dynamic structure of a multivariate volatility process is to use factor models. In practice, the "common factors" can be determined a priori by substantive matter or empirical methods. As an illustration, we use the factor analysis of Chapter 8 to discuss factor–volatility models. Because volatility models are concerned with the evolution over time of the conditional covariance matrix of $\boldsymbol{a}_t$, where $\boldsymbol{a}_t = \boldsymbol{r}_t - \boldsymbol{\mu}_t$, a simple way to identify the "common factors" in volatility is to perform a principal component analysis (PCA) on $\boldsymbol{a}_t$; see the

PCA of Chapter 8. Building a factor–volatility model thus involves a three-step procedure:

- Select the first few principal components that explain a high percentage of variability in $\boldsymbol{a}_t$.
- Build a volatility model for the selected principal components.
- Relate the volatility of each a_{it} series to the volatilities of the selected principal components.

The objective of such a procedure is to reduce the dimension but maintain an accurate approximation of the multivariate volatility.

Example 10.7. Consider again the monthly log returns, in percentages, of IBM stock and the S&P 500 index of Example 10.5. Using the bivariate AR(3) model of Example 8.4, we obtain an innovational series $\boldsymbol{a}_t$. Performing a PCA on $\boldsymbol{a}_t$ based on its covariance matrix, we obtained eigenvalues 63.373 and 13.489. The first eigenvalue explains 82.2% of the generalized variance of $\boldsymbol{a}_t$. Therefore, we may choose the first principal component $x_t = 0.797a_{1t} + 0.604a_{2t}$ as the common factor. Alternatively, as shown by the model in Example 8.4, the serial dependence in $\boldsymbol{r}_t$ is weak and, hence, one can perform the PCA on $\boldsymbol{r}_t$ directly. For this particular instance, the two eigenvalues of the sample covariance matrix of $\boldsymbol{r}_t$ are 63.625 and 13.513, which are essentially the same as those based on $\boldsymbol{a}_t$. The first principal component explains approximately 82.5% of the generalized variance of $\boldsymbol{r}_t$, and the corresponding common factor is $x_t = 0.796r_{1t} + 0.605r_{2t}$. Consequently, for the two monthly log return series considered, the effect of the conditional mean equations on PCA is negligible.

Based on the prior discussion and for simplicity, we use $x_t = 0.796r_{1t} + 0.605r_{2t}$ as a common factor for the two monthly return series. Figure 10.15a shows the time plot of this common factor. If univariate Gaussian GARCH models are entertained, we obtain the following model for x_t:

$$\begin{aligned} x_t &= 1.317 + 0.096x_{t-1} + a_t, \quad a_t = \sigma_t\epsilon_t, \\ \sigma_t^2 &= 3.834 + 0.110a_{t-1}^2 + 0.825\sigma_{t-1}^2. \end{aligned} \tag{10.37}$$

All parameter estimates of the previous model are highly significant at the 1% level, and the Ljung–Box statistics of the standardized residuals and their squared series fail to detect any model inadequacy. Figure 10.15b shows the fitted volatility of x_t (i.e., the sample σ_t^2 series in Eq. (10.37)).

Using σ_t^2 of model (10.37) as a common volatility factor, we obtain the following model for the original monthly log returns. The mean equations are

$$\begin{aligned} r_{1t} &= 1.140 + 0.079r_{1,t-1} + 0.067r_{1,t-2} - 0.122r_{2,t-2} + a_{1t}, \\ r_{2t} &= 0.537 + a_{2t}, \end{aligned}$$

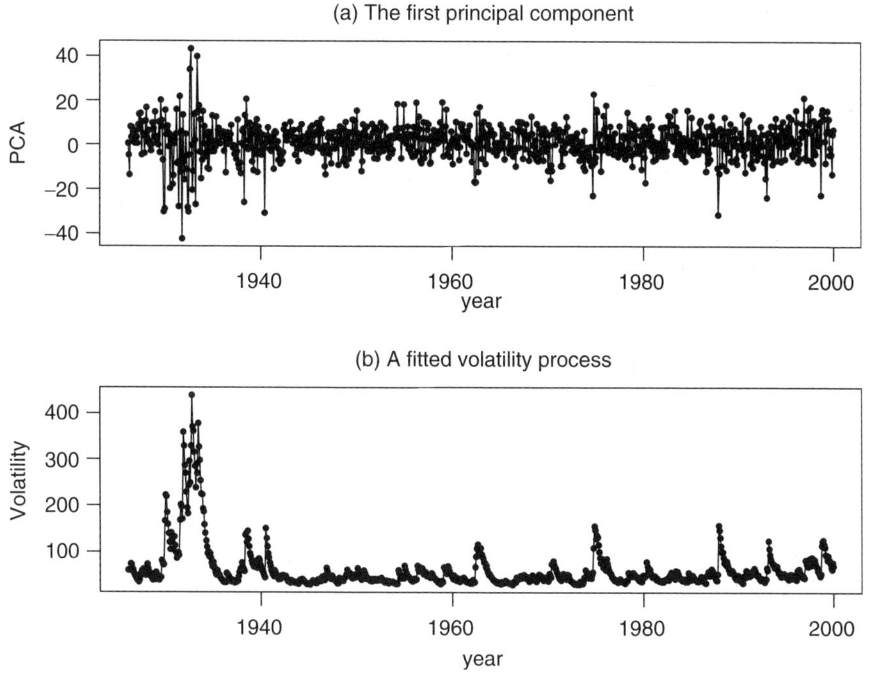

Figure 10.15. (a) Time plot of the first principal component of the monthly log returns of IBM stock and the S&P 500 index. (b) The fitted volatility process based on a GARCH(1,1) model.

where standard errors of the parameters in the first equation are 0.211, 0.030, 0.031, and 0.043, respectively, and standard error of the parameter in the second equation is 0.165. The conditional variance equation is

$$\begin{bmatrix} \sigma_{11,t} \\ \sigma_{22,t} \end{bmatrix} = \begin{bmatrix} 19.08 \\ (3.70) \\ -5.62 \\ (2.36) \end{bmatrix} + \begin{bmatrix} 0.098 & \cdot \\ (0.044) & \\ \cdot & \cdot \end{bmatrix} \begin{bmatrix} a^2_{1,t-1} \\ a^2_{2,t-1} \end{bmatrix} + \begin{bmatrix} 0.333 \\ (0.076) \\ 0.596 \\ (0.050) \end{bmatrix} \sigma^2_t, \quad (10.38)$$

where, as before, standard errors are in parentheses, and σ_t^2 is obtained from model (10.37). The conditional correlation equation is

$$\rho_t = \frac{\exp(q_t)}{1+\exp(q_t)}, \quad q_t = -2.098 + 4.120\rho_{t-1} + 0.078\frac{a_{1,t-1}a_{2,t-1}}{\sqrt{\sigma_{11,t-1}\sigma_{22,t-1}}}, \quad (10.39)$$

where standard errors of the three parameters are 0.025, 0.038, and 0.015, respectively. Defining the standardized residuals as before, we obtain $Q_2(4) = 15.37(0.29)$ and $Q_2(8) = 34.24(0.23)$, where the number in parentheses denotes p-value. Therefore, the standardized residuals have no serial correlations. Yet we have $Q_2^*(4) = 20.25(0.09)$ and $Q_2^*(8) = 61.95(0.0004)$ for the squared standardized residuals.

The volatility model in Eq. (10.38) does not adequately handle the conditional heteroscedasticity of the data especially at higher lags. This is not surprising as the single common factor only explains about 82.5% of the generalized variance of the data.

Comparing the factor model in Eqs. (10.38) and (10.39) with the time-varying correlation model in Eqs. (10.27) and (10.28), we see that (a) the correlation equations of the two models are essentially the same, (b) as expected the factor model uses fewer parameters in the volatility equation, and (c) the common-factor model provides a reasonable approximation to the volatility process of the data.

Remark. In Example 10.7, we used a two-step estimation procedure. In the first step, a volatility model is built for the common factor. The estimated volatility is treated as given in the second step to estimate the multivariate volatility model. Such an estimation procedure is simple but may not be efficient. A more efficient estimation procedure is to perform a joint estimation. This can be done relatively easily provided that the common factors are known. For example, for the monthly log returns of Example 10.7, a joint estimation of Eqs. (10.37)–(10.39) can be performed if the common factor $x_t = 0.769r_{1t} + 0.605r_{2t}$ is treated as given. □

10.7 APPLICATION

We illustrate the application of multivariate volatility models by considering the value at risk (VaR) of a financial position with multiple assets. Suppose that an investor holds a long position in the stocks of Cisco Systems and Intel Corporation each worth \$1 million. We use the daily log returns for the two stocks from January 2, 1991 to December 31, 1999 to build volatility models. The VaR is computed using the 1-step ahead forecasts at the end of data span and 5% critical values.

Let VaR_1 be the value at risk for holding the position on Cisco Systems stock and VaR_2 for holding Intel stock. Results of Chapter 7 show that the overall daily VaR for the investor is

$$\text{VaR} = \sqrt{\text{VaR}_1^2 + \text{VaR}_2^2 + 2\rho \text{VaR}_1 \text{VaR}_2}.$$

In this illustration, we consider three approaches to volatility modeling for calculating VaR. For simplicity, we do not report standard errors for the parameters involved or model checking statistics. Yet all of the estimates are statistically significant at the 5% level and the models are adequate based on the Ljung–Box statistics of the standardized residual series and their squared series. The log returns are in percentages so that the quantiles are divided by 100 in VaR calculation. Let r_{1t} be the return of Cisco stock and r_{2t} the return of Intel stock.

Univariate Models
This approach uses a univariate volatility model for each stock return and uses the sample correlation coefficient of the stock returns to estimate ρ. The univariate volatility models for the two stock returns are

$$\begin{aligned} r_{1t} &= 0.380 + 0.034 r_{1,t-1} - 0.061 r_{1,t-2} - 0.055 r_{1,t-3} + a_{1t}, \\ \sigma_{1t}^2 &= 0.599 + 0.117 a_{1,t-1}^2 + 0.814 \sigma_{1,t-1}^2 \end{aligned}$$

and

$$\begin{aligned} r_{2t} &= 0.187 + a_{2t}, \\ \sigma_{2t}^2 &= 0.310 + 0.032 a_{2,t-1}^2 + 0.918 \sigma_{2,t-1}^2. \end{aligned}$$

The sample correlation coefficient is 0.473. The 1-step ahead forecasts needed in VaR calculation at the forecast origin $t = 2275$ are

$$\hat{r}_1 = 0.626, \quad \hat{\sigma}_1^2 = 4.152, \quad \hat{r}_2 = 0.187, \quad \hat{\sigma}_2^2 = 6.087, \quad \hat{\rho} = 0.473.$$

The 5% quantiles for both daily returns are

$$q_1 = 0.626 - 1.65\sqrt{4.152} = -2.736, \quad q_2 = 0.187 - 1.65\sqrt{6.087} = -3.884,$$

where the negative sign denotes loss. For the individual stocks, $\text{VaR}_1 = \$1000000 q_1/100 = \$27{,}360$ and $\text{VaR}_2 = \$1000000 q_2/100 = \$38{,}840$. Consequently, the overall VaR for the investor is $\text{VaR} = \$57{,}117$.

Constant-Correlation Bivariate Model
This approach employs a bivariate GARCH(1,1) model for the stock returns. The correlation coefficient is assumed to be constant over time, but it is estimated jointly with other parameters. The model is

$$\begin{aligned} r_{1t} &= 0.385 + 0.038 r_{1,t-1} - 0.060 r_{1,t-2} - 0.047 r_{1,t-3} + a_{1t}, \\ r_{2t} &= 0.222 + a_{2t}, \\ \sigma_{11,t} &= 0.624 + 0.110 a_{1,t-1}^2 + 0.816 \sigma_{11,t-1}, \\ \sigma_{22,t} &= 0.664 + 0.038 a_{2,t-1}^2 + 0.853 \sigma_{22,t-1}, \end{aligned}$$

and $\hat{\rho} = 0.475$. This is a diagonal bivariate GARCH(1,1) model. The 1-step ahead forecasts for VaR calculation at the forecast origin $t = 2275$ are

$$\hat{r}_1 = 0.373, \quad \hat{\sigma}_1^2 = 4.287, \quad \hat{r}_2 = 0.222, \quad \hat{\sigma}_2^2 = 5.706, \quad \hat{\rho} = 0.475.$$

Consequently, we have $\text{VaR}_1 = \$30{,}432$ and $\text{VaR}_2 = \$37{,}195$. The overall 5% VaR for the investor is $\text{VaR} = \$58{,}180$.

Time-Varying Correlation Model

Finally, we allow the correlation coefficient to evolve over time by using the Cholesky decomposition. The fitted model is

$$
\begin{aligned}
r_{1t} &= 0.355 + 0.039r_{1,t-1} - 0.057r_{1,t-2} - 0.038r_{1,t-3} + a_{1t}, \\
r_{2t} &= 0.206 + a_{2t}, \\
g_{11,t} &= 0.420 + 0.091b_{1,t-1}^2 + 0.858g_{11,t-1}, \\
q_{21,t} &= 0.123 + 0.689q_{21,t-1} - 0.014a_{2,t-1}, \\
g_{22,t} &= 0.080 + 0.013b_{2,t-1}^2 + 0.971g_{22,t-1},
\end{aligned}
$$

where $b_{1t} = a_{1t}$ and $b_{2t} = a_{2t} - q_{21,t}a_{1t}$. The 1-step ahead forecasts for VaR calculation at the forecast origin $t = 2275$ are

$$\hat{r}_1 = 0.352, \quad \hat{r}_2 = 0.206, \quad \hat{g}_{11} = 4.252, \quad \hat{q}_{21} = 0.421, \quad \hat{g}_{22} = 5.594.$$

Therefore, we have $\hat{\sigma}_1^2 = 4.252$, $\hat{\sigma}_{21} = 1.791$, and $\hat{\sigma}_2^2 = 6.348$. The correlation coefficient is $\hat{\rho} = 0.345$. Using these forecasts, we have $\text{VaR}_1 = \$30{,}504$, $\text{VaR}_2 = \$39{,}512$, and the overall value at risk VaR = \$57,648.

The estimated VaR values of the three approaches are similar. The univariate models give the lowest VaR, whereas the constant-correlation model produces the highest VaR. The range of the difference is about \$1100. The time-varying volatility model seems to produce a compromise between the two extreme models.

10.8 MULTIVARIATE *t* DISTRIBUTION

Empirical analysis indicates that the multivariate Gaussian innovations used in the previous sections may fail to capture the kurtosis of asset returns. In this situation, a multivariate Student-t distribution might be useful. There are many versions of the multivariate Student-t distribution. We give a simple version here for volatility modeling.

A k-dimensional random vector $\boldsymbol{x} = (x_1, \ldots, x_k)'$ has a multivariate Student-t distribution with v degrees of freedom and parameters $\boldsymbol{\mu} = \boldsymbol{0}$ and $\boldsymbol{\Sigma} = \boldsymbol{I}$ (the identity matrix) if its probability density function (pdf) is

$$f(\boldsymbol{x}|v) = \frac{\Gamma((v+k)/2)}{(\pi v)^{k/2}\Gamma(v/2)}(1 + v^{-1}\boldsymbol{x}'\boldsymbol{x})^{-(v+k)/2}, \tag{10.40}$$

where $\Gamma(y)$ is the gamma function; see Mardia, Kent, and Bibby (1979, p. 57). The variance of each component x_i in Eq. (10.40) is $v/(v-2)$ and hence we define $\boldsymbol{\epsilon}_t = \sqrt{(v-2)/v}\boldsymbol{x}$ as the standardized multivariate Student-t distribution with v degrees of freedom. By transformation, the pdf of $\boldsymbol{\epsilon}_t$ is

$$f(\boldsymbol{\epsilon}_t|v) = \frac{\Gamma((v+k)/2)}{[\pi(v-2)]^{k/2}\Gamma(v/2)}[1 + (v-2)^{-1}\boldsymbol{\epsilon}_t'\boldsymbol{\epsilon}_t]^{-(v+k)/2}. \tag{10.41}$$

For volatility modeling, we write $\boldsymbol{a}_t = \boldsymbol{\Sigma}_t^{1/2}\boldsymbol{\epsilon}_t$ and assume that $\boldsymbol{\epsilon}_t$ follows the multivariate Student-t distribution in Eq. (10.41). By transformation, the pdf of $\boldsymbol{a}_t$ is

$$f(\boldsymbol{a}_t|v, \boldsymbol{\Sigma}_t) = \frac{\Gamma((v+k)/2)}{[\pi(v-2)]^{k/2}\Gamma(v/2)|\boldsymbol{\Sigma}_t|^{1/2}}\left(1+(v-2)^{-1}\boldsymbol{a}_t'\boldsymbol{\Sigma}_t^{-1}\boldsymbol{a}_t\right)^{-(v+k)/2}.$$

Furthermore, if we use the Cholesky decomposition of $\boldsymbol{\Sigma}_t$, then the pdf of the transformed shock $\boldsymbol{b}_t$ becomes

$$f(\boldsymbol{b}_t|v, \boldsymbol{L}_t, \boldsymbol{G}_t) = \frac{\Gamma((v+k)/2)}{[\pi(v-2)]^{k/2}\Gamma(v/2)\prod_{j=1}^k g_{jj,t}^{1/2}}\left(1+(v-2)^{-1}\sum_{j=1}^k \frac{b_{jt}^2}{g_{jj,t}}\right)^{(v+k)/2},$$

where $\boldsymbol{a}_t = \boldsymbol{L}_t\boldsymbol{b}_t$ and $g_{jj,t}$ is the conditional variance of b_{jt}. Because this pdf does not involve any matrix inversion, the conditional likelihood function of the data is easy to evaluate.

APPENDIX: SOME REMARKS ON ESTIMATION

The estimation of multivariate ARMA models in this chapter is done by using the time series program SCA of Scientific Computing Associates. The estimation of multivariate volatility models is done by using either the S-Plus package with FinMetrics or the Regression Analysis for Time Series (RATS) program. Below are some run streams for estimating multivariate volatility models using the RATS program. A line starting with * means "comment" only.

Estimation of the Diagonal Constant-Correlation AR(2)–GARCH(1,1) Model for Example 10.5

The program includes some Ljung–Box statistics for each component and some fitted values for the last few observations. The data file is `m-ibmspln.txt`, which has two columns, and there are 888 observations.

```
all 0 888:1
open data m-ibmspln.txt
data(org=obs) / r1 r2
set h1 = 0.0
set h2 = 0.0
nonlin  a0 a1 b1 a00 a11 b11 rho c1 c2 p1
frml a1t = r1(t)-c1-p1*r2(t-1)
frml a2t = r2(t)-c2
frml gvar1 = a0+a1*a1t(t-1)**2+b1*h1(t-1)
frml gvar2 = a00+a11*a2t(t-1)**2+b11*h2(t-1)
frml gdet = -0.5*(log(h1(t)=gvar1(t))+log(h2(t)=gvar2(t)) $
          +log(1.0-rho**2))
```

```
frml gln = gdet(t)-0.5/(1.0-rho**2)*((a1t(t)**2/h1(t)) $
    +(a2t(t)**2/h2(t))-2*rho*a1t(t)*a2t(t)/sqrt(h1(t)*h2(t)))
smpl 3 888
compute c1 = 1.22, c2 = 0.57, p1 = 0.1, rho = 0.1
compute a0 = 3.27, a1 = 0.1, b1 = 0.6
compute  a00 = 1.17, a11 = 0.13, b11 = 0.8
maximize(method=bhhh,recursive,iterations=150) gln
set fv1 = gvar1(t)
set resi1 = a1t(t)/sqrt(fv1(t))
set residsq = resi1(t)*resi1(t)
* Checking standardized residuals *
cor(qstats,number=12,span=4) resi1
* Checking squared standardized residuals *
cor(qstats,number=12,span=4) residsq
set fv2 = gvar2(t)
set resi2 = a2t(t)/sqrt(fv2(t))
set residsq = resi2(t)*resi2(t)
* Checking standardized residuals *
cor(qstats,number=12,span=4) resi2
* Checking squared standardized residuals *
cor(qstats,number=12,span=4) residsq
* Last few observations needed for computing forecasts *
set shock1 = a1t(t)
set shock2 = a2t(t)
print 885  888 shock1 shock2 fv1 fv2
```

Estimation of the Time-Varying Coefficient Model in Example 10.5

```
all 0 888:1
open data m-ibmspln.txt
data(org=obs) / r1 r2
set h1 = 45.0
set h2 = 31.0
set rho = 0.8
nonlin  a0 a1 b1 f1 a00 a11 b11 d11 f11 c1 c2 p1 p3 q0 q1 q2
frml a1t = r1(t)-c1-p1*r1(t-1)-p3*r2(t-2)
frml a2t = r2(t)-c2
frml gvar1 = a0+a1*a1t(t-1)**2+b1*h1(t-1)+f1*h2(t-1)
frml gvar2 = a00+a11*a2t(t-1)**2+b11*h2(t-1)+f11*h1(t-1) $
             +d11*a1t(t-1)**2
frml rh1 = q0 + q1*rho(t-1) $
              + q2*a1t(t-1)*a2t(t-1)/sqrt(h1(t-1)*h2(t-1))
frml rh = exp(rh1(t))/(1+exp(rh1(t)))
frml gdet = -0.5*(log(h1(t)=gvar1(t))+log(h2(t)=gvar2(t)) $
     +log(1.0-(rho(t)=rh(t))**2))
frml gln = gdet(t)-0.5/(1.0-rho(t)**2)*((a1t(t)**2/h1(t)) $
  +(a2t(t)**2/h2(t))-2*rho(t)*a1t(t)*a2t(t)/sqrt(h1(t)*h2(t)))
smpl 4 888
compute c1 = 1.4, c2 = 0.7, p1 = 0.1,  p3 = -0.1
```

```
compute a0 = 2.95, a1 = 0.08, b1 = 0.87, f1 = -.03
compute a00 = 2.05, a11 = 0.05
compute  b11 = 0.92, f11=-.06, d11=.04, q0 = -2.0
compute  q1 = 3.0, q2 = 0.1
nlpar(criterion=value,cvcrit=0.00001)
maximize(method=bhhh,recursive,iterations=150) gln
set fv1 = gvar1(t)
set resi1 = a1t(t)/sqrt(fv1(t))
set residsq = resi1(t)*resi1(t)
* Checking standardized residuals *
cor(qstats,number=16,span=4) resi1
* Checking squared standardized residuals *
cor(qstats,number=16,span=4) residsq
set fv2 = gvar2(t)
set resi2 = a2t(t)/sqrt(fv2(t))
set residsq = resi2(t)*resi2(t)
* Checking standardized residuals *
cor(qstats,number=16,span=4) resi2
* Checking squared standardized residuals *
cor(qstats,number=16,span=4) residsq
* Last few observations needed for computing forecasts *
set rhohat = rho(t)
set shock1 = a1t(t)
set shock2 = a2t(t)
print 885  888 shock1 shock2 fv1 fv2 rhohat
```

Estimation of the Time-Varying Coefficient Model in Example 10.5 Using Cholesky Decomposition

```
all 0 888:1
open data m-ibmspln.txt
data(org=obs) / r1 r2
set h1 = 45.0
set h2 = 20.0
set q = 0.8
nonlin  a0 a1 b1 a00 a11 b11 d11 f11 c1 c2 p1 p3 t0 t1 t2
frml a1t = r1(t)-c1-p1*r1(t-1)-p3*r2(t-2)
frml a2t = r2(t)-c2
frml v1 = a0+a1*a1t(t-1)**2+b1*h1(t-1)
frml qt = t0 + t1*q(t-1) + t2*a2t(t-1)
frml bt = a2t(t) - (q(t)=qt(t))*a1t(t)
frml v2 = a00+a11*bt(t-1)**2+b11*h2(t-1)+f11*h1(t-1) $
          +d11*a1t(t-1)**2
frml gdet = -0.5*(log(h1(t) = v1(t))+ log(h2(t)=v2(t)))
frml garchln = gdet-0.5*(a1t(t)**2/h1(t)+bt(t)**2/h2(t))
smpl 5 888
compute c1 = 1.4, c2 = 0.7, p1 = 0.1, p3 = -0.1
compute a0 = 1.0, a1 = 0.08, b1 = 0.87
compute a00 = 2.0, a11 = 0.05, b11 = 0.8
compute  d11=.04, f11=-.06, t0 =0.2, t1 = 0.1, t2 = 0.1
```

```
nlpar(criterion=value,cvcrit=0.00001)
maximize(method=bhhh,recursive,iterations=150) garchln
set fv1 = v1(t)
set resi1 = a1t(t)/sqrt(fv1(t))
set residsq = resi1(t)*resi1(t)
* Checking standardized residuals *
cor(qstats,number=16,span=4) resi1
* Checking squared standardized residuals *
cor(qstats,number=16,span=4) residsq
set fv2 = v2(t)+qt(t)**2*v1(t)
set resi2 = a2t(t)/sqrt(fv2(t))
set residsq = resi2(t)*resi2(t)
* Checking standardized residuals *
cor(qstats,number=16,span=4) resi2
* Checking squared standardized residuals *
cor(qstats,number=16,span=4) residsq
* Last few observations needed for forecasts *
set rhohat = qt(t)*sqrt(v1(t)/fv2(t))
set shock1 = a1t(t)
set shock2 = a2t(t)
set g22 = v2(t)
set q21 = qt(t)
set b2t = bt(t)
print 885  888 shock1 shock2 fv1 fv2 rhohat g22 q21 b2t
```

Estimation of the Three-Dimensional Time-Varying Correlation Volatility Model in Example 10.6 Using Cholesky Decomposition

Initial estimates are obtained by a sequential modeling procedure.

```
all 0 2275:1
open data d-cscointc.txt
data(org=obs) / r1 r2 r3
set h1 = 1.0
set h2 = 4.0
set h3 = 3.0
set q21 = 0.8
set q31 = 0.3
set q32 = 0.3
nonlin  c1 c2 c3 p3 p21 p22 p31 p33 a0 a1 a2 t0 t1 t2 b0 b1 $
        b2 u0 u1 u2 w0 w1 w2 d0 d1 d2 d5
frml a1t = r1(t)-c1-p3*r1(t-3)
frml a2t = r2(t)-c2-p21*r1(t-2)-p22*r2(t-2)
frml a3t = r3(t)-c3-p31*r1(t-1)-p33*r3(t-1)
frml v1 = a0+a1*a1t(t-1)**2+a2*h1(t-1)
frml q1t = t0 + t1*q21(t-1) + t2*a2t(t-1)
frml bt = a2t(t) - (q21(t)=q1t(t))*a1t(t)
frml v2 = b0+b1*bt(t-1)**2+b2*h2(t-1)
```

```
frml q2t = u0 + u1*q31(t-1) + u2*a3t(t-1)
frml q3t = w0 + w1*q32(t-1) + w2*a2t(t-1)
frml b1t = a3t(t)-(q31(t)=q2t(t))*a1t(t)-(q32(t)=q3t(t))*bt(t)
frml v3 = d0+d1*b1t(t-1)**2+d2*h3(t-1)+d5*h2(t-1)
frml gdet = -0.5*(log(h1(t) = v1(t))+ log(h2(t)=v2(t)) $
            +log(h3(t)=v3(t)))
frml garchln = gdet-0.5*(a1t(t)**2/h1(t)+bt(t)**2/h2(t) $
            +b1t(t)**2/h3(t))
smpl 8 2275
compute c1 = 0.07, c2 = 0.33, c3 = 0.19, p1 = 0.1, p3 = -0.04
compute p21 =0.2, p22 = -0.1, p31 = -0.26, p33 = 0.06
compute a0 = .01, a1 = 0.05, a2 = 0.94
compute t0 = 0.28, t1 =0.82, t2 = -0.035
compute b0 = .17, b1 = 0.08, b2 = 0.89
compute u0= 0.04, u1 = 0.97, u2 = 0.01
compute  w0 =0.006, w1=0.98, w2=0.004
compute d0 =1.38, d1 = 0.06, d2 = 0.64, d5 = -0.027
nlpar(criterion=value,cvcrit=0.00001)
maximize(method=bhhh,recursive,iterations=250) garchln
set fv1 = v1(t)
set resi1 = a1t(t)/sqrt(fv1(t))
set residsq = resi1(t)*resi1(t)
* Checking standardized residuals *
cor(qstats,number=12,span=4) resi1
* Checking squared standardized residuals *
cor(qstats,number=12,span=4) residsq
set fv2 = v2(t)+q1t(t)**2*v1(t)
set resi2 = a2t(t)/sqrt(fv2(t))
set residsq = resi2(t)*resi2(t)
* Checking standardized residuals *
cor(qstats,number=12,span=4) resi2
* Checking squared standardized residuals *
cor(qstats,number=12,span=4) residsq
set fv3 = v3(t)+q2t(t)**2*v1(t)+q3t(t)**2*v2(t)
set resi3 = a3t(t)/sqrt(fv3(t))
set residsq = resi3(t)*resi3(t)
* Checking standardized residuals *
cor(qstats,number=12,span=4) resi3
* Checking squared standardized residuals *
cor(qstats,number=12,span=4) residsq
* print standardized residuals and correlation-coefficients
set rho21 = q1t(t)*sqrt(v1(t)/fv2(t))
set rho31 = q2t(t)*sqrt(v1(t)/fv3(t))
set rho32 = (q2t(t)*q1t(t)*v1(t) $
            +q3t(t)*v2(t))/sqrt(fv2(t)*fv3(t))
print 10  2275 resi1 resi2 resi3
print 10 2275 rho21 rho31 rho32
print 10 2275 fv1 fv2 fv3
```

EXERCISES

10.1. Consider the monthly log returns of the S&P composite index, IBM stock, and Hewlett-Packard (HPQ) stock from January 1962 to December 2003 for 504 observations. The log returns are in the file `m-spibmhpq6203.txt`. Use the exponentially weighted moving-average method to obtain a multivariate volatility series for the three return series. What is the estimated λ? Plot the three volatility series.

10.2. Focus on the monthly log returns of IBM and HPQ stocks from January 1962 to December 2003. Fit a DVEC(1,1) model to the bivariate return series. Is the model adequate? Plot the fitted volatility series and the time-varying correlations.

10.3. Focus on the monthly log returns of the S&P composite index and HPQ stock. Build a BEKK model for the bivariate series. What is the fitted model? Plot the fitted volatility series and the time-varying correlations.

10.4. Build a constant-correlation volatility model for the three monthly log returns of the S&P composite index, IBM stock, and HPQ stock. Write down the fitted model. Is the model adequate? Why?

10.5. The file `m-spibmge.txt` contains the monthly log returns in percentages of the S&P 500 index, IBM stock, and General Electric stock from January 1926 to December 1999. The returns include dividends. Focus on the monthly log returns in percentages of GE stock and the S&P 500 index. Build a constant-correlation GARCH model for the bivariate series. Check the adequacy of the fitted model, and obtain the 1-step ahead forecast of the covariance matrix at the forecast origin December 1999.

10.6. Focus on the monthly log returns in percentages of GE stock and the S&P 500 index. Build a time-varying correlation GARCH model for the bivariate series using a logistic function for the correlation coefficient. Check the adequacy of the fitted model, and obtain the 1-step ahead forecast of the covariance matrix at the forecast origin December 1999.

10.7. Focus on the monthly log returns in percentages of GE stock and the S&P 500 index. Build a time-varying correlation GARCH model for the bivariate series using the Cholesky decomposition. Check the adequacy of the fitted model, and obtain the 1-step ahead forecast of the covariance matrix at the forecast origin December 1999. Compare the model with the other two models built in the previous exercises.

10.8. Consider the three-dimensional return series jointly. Build a multivariate time-varying volatility model for the data, using the Cholesky decomposition. Discuss the implications of the model and compute the 1-step ahead volatility forecast at the forecast origin $t = 888$.

10.9. An investor is interested in daily value at risk of his position on holding long \$0.5 million of Dell stock and \$1 million of Cisco Systems stock. Use 5% critical values and the daily log returns from February 20, 1990 to December 31, 1999 to do the calculation. The data are in the file `d-dellcsco9099.txt`. Apply the three approaches to volatility modeling in Section 10.7 and compare the results.

REFERENCES

Bauwens, L., Laurent, S. and Rombouts, J. V. K. (2004). Multivariate GARCH models: a survey. *Journal of Applied Econometrics* (to appear).

Bollerslev, T. (1990). Modeling the coherence in short-term nominal exchange rates: A multivariate generalized ARCH approach. *Review of Economics and Statistics* **72**: 498–505.

Bollerslev, T., Engle, R. F., and Wooldridge, J. M. (1988). A capital-asset pricing model with time-varying covariances. *Journal of Political Economy* **96**: 116–131.

Chib, S., Nardari, F. and Shephard, N. (1999). Analysis of high dimensional multivariate stochastic volatility models. Working paper, Washington University, St. Louis.

Engle, R. F. (2002). Dynamic conditional correlation: a simple class of multivariate GARCH models. *Journal of Business and Economic Statistics* **20**: 339–350.

Engle, R. F. and Kroner, K. F. (1995). Multivariate simultaneous generalized ARCH. *Econometric Theory* **11**: 122–150.

McCulloch, R.E., Polson, N., and Tsay, R. S. (2000), "Multivariate volatility models," Working paper, Graduate School of Business, University of Chicago.

Mardia, K. V., Kent, J. T., and Bibby, J. M. (1979). *Multivariate Analysis*. Academic Press, New York.

Pourahmadi, M. (1999). Joint mean-covariance models with applications to longitudinal data: Unconstrained parameterization. *Biometrika* **86**: 677–690.

Tse, Y. K. (2000). A test for constant correlations in a multivariate GARCH model. *Journal of Econometrics* **98**: 107–127.

Tse, Y. K. and Tsui, A. K. C. (2002). A multivariate GARCH model with time-varying correlations. *Journal of Business & Economic Statistics* **20**: 351–362.

CHAPTER 11

State-Space Models and Kalman Filter

The state-space model provides a flexible approach to time series analysis, especially for simplifying maximum likelihood estimation and handling missing values. In this chapter, we discuss the relationship between the state-space model and the ARIMA model, the Kalman filter algorithm, various smoothing methods, and some applications. We begin with a simple model that shows the basic ideas of the state-space approach to time series analysis before introducing the general state-space model. For demonstrations, we use the model to analyze realized volatility series of asset returns, the time-varying coefficient market models, and the quarterly earnings per share of a company.

There are many books on statistical analysis using the state-space model. Durbin and Koopman (2001) provide a recent treatment of the approach, Kim and Nelson (1999) focus on economic applications and regime switching, and Anderson and Moore (1979) give a nice summary of theory and applications of the approach for engineering and optimal control. Many time series textbooks include the Kalman filter and state-space model. For example, Chan (2002), Shumway and Stoffer (2000), Hamilton (1994), and Harvey (1993) all have chapters on the topic. West and Harrison (1997) provide a Bayesian treatment with emphasis on forecasting, and Kitagawa and Gersch (1996) use a smoothing prior approach.

The derivation of Kalman filter and smoothing algorithms necessarily involves heavy notation. Therefore, Section 11.4 could be dry for readers who are interested mainly in the concept and applications of state-space models and can be skipped on the first read.

11.1 LOCAL TREND MODEL

Consider the univariate time series y_t satisfying

$$y_t = \mu_t + e_t, \quad e_t \sim N(0, \sigma_e^2), \tag{11.1}$$

Analysis of Financial Time Series, Second Edition By Ruey S. Tsay

$$\mu_{t+1} = \mu_t + \eta_t, \quad \eta_t \sim N(0, \sigma_\eta^2), \tag{11.2}$$

where $\{e_t\}$ and $\{\eta_t\}$ are two independent Gaussian white noise series and $t = 1, \ldots, T$. The initial value μ_1 is either given or follows a known distribution, and it is independent of $\{e_t\}$ and $\{\eta_t\}$ for $t > 0$. Here μ_t is a pure *random walk* of Chapter 2 with initial value μ_1 and y_t is an observed version of μ_t with added noise a_t. In the literature, μ_t is referred to as the *trend* of the series, which is not directly observable, and y_t is the observed data with observational noise e_t. The dynamic dependence of y_t is governed by that of μ_t because $\{e_t\}$ is not serially correlated.

The model in Eqs. (11.1) and (11.2) can readily be used to analyze realized volatility of an asset price; see Example 11.1 below. Here μ_t represents the underlying log volatility of the asset price and y_t is the logarithm of realized volatility. The true log volatility is not directly observed but evolves over time according to a random-walk model. On the other hand, y_t is constructed from high-frequency transactions data and subjected to the influence of market microstructure. The standard deviation of e_t denotes the scale used to measure the impact of market microstructure.

The model in Eqs. (11.1) and (11.2) is a special *linear Gaussian state-space model*. The variable μ_t is called the *state* of the system at time t and is not directly observed. Equation (11.1) provides the link between the data y_t and the state μ_t and is called the *observation equation* with *measurement error* e_t. Equation (11.2) governs the time evolution of the state variable and is the *state equation* (or *state transition equation*) with innovation η_t. The model is also called a *local level model* in Durbin and Koopman (2001, Chapter 2), which is a simple case of the *structural time series model* of Harvey (1993).

Relationship to ARIMA Model

If there is no measurement error in Eq. (11.1), that is, $\sigma_e = 0$, then $y_t = \mu_t$, which is an ARIMA(0,1,0) model. If $\sigma_e > 0$, that is, there exist measurement errors, then y_t is an ARIMA(0,1,1) model satisfying

$$(1 - B)y_t = (1 - \theta B)a_t, \tag{11.3}$$

where $\{a_t\}$ is a Gaussian white noise with mean zero and variance σ_a^2. The values of θ and σ_a^2 are determined by σ_e and σ_η. This result can be derived as follows.

From Eq. (11.2), we have

$$(1 - B)\mu_{t+1} = \eta_t, \quad \text{or} \quad \mu_{t+1} = \frac{1}{1 - B}\eta_t.$$

Using this result, Eq. (11.1) can be written as

$$y_t = \frac{1}{1 - B}\eta_{t-1} + e_t.$$

Multiplying by $(1 - B)$, we have

$$(1 - B)y_t = \eta_{t-1} + e_t - e_{t-1}.$$

Let $(1 - B)y_t = w_t$. We have $w_t = \eta_{t-1} + e_t - e_{t-1}$. Under the assumptions, it is easy to see that (a) w_t is Gaussian, (b) $\text{Var}(w_t) = 2\sigma_e^2 + \sigma_\eta^2$, (c) $\text{Cov}(w_t, w_{t-1}) = -\sigma_e^2$, and (d) $\text{Cov}(w_t, w_{t-j}) = 0$ for $j > 1$. Consequently, w_t follows an MA(1) model and can be written as $w_t = (1 - \theta B)a_t$. By equating the variance and lag-1 autocovariance of $w_t = (1 - \theta B)a_t = \eta_{t-1} + e_t - e_{t-1}$, we have

$$(1 + \theta^2)\sigma_a^2 = 2\sigma_e^2 + \sigma_\eta^2,$$

$$\theta\sigma_a^2 = \sigma_e^2.$$

For given σ_e^2 and σ_η^2, one considers the ratio of the prior two equations to form a quadratic function of θ. This quadratic form has two solutions so one should select the one that satisfies $|\theta| < 1$. The value of σ_a^2 can then be easily obtained. Thus, the state-space model in Eqs. (11.1) and (11.2) is also an ARIMA(0,1,1) model, which is the simple exponential smoothing model of Chapter 2.

On the other hand, for an ARIMA(0,1,1) model with positive θ, one can use the prior two identities to solve for σ_e^2 and σ_η^2, and obtain a local trend model. If θ is negative, then the model can still be put in a state-space form without the observational error, that is, $\sigma_e = 0$. In fact, as will be seen later, an ARIMA model can be transformed into state-space models in many ways. Thus, the linear state-space model is closely related to the ARIMA model.

In practice, what one observes is the y_t series. Thus, based on the data alone, the decision of using ARIMA models or linear state-space models is not critical. Both model representations have pros and cons. The objective of data analysis, substantive issues, and experience all play a role in choosing a statistical model.

Example 11.1. To illustrate the ideas of the state-space model and Kalman filter, we consider the intradaily realized volatility of Alcoa stock from January 2, 2003 to May 7, 2004 for 340 observations. The daily realized volatility used is the sum of squares of intraday 10-minute log returns measured in percentage. No overnight returns or the first 10-minute intraday returns are used. See Chapter 3 for more information about realized volatility. The series used in the demonstration is the logarithm of the daily realized volatility.

Figure 11.1 shows the time plot of the logarithms of the realized volatility of Alcoa stock from January 2, 2003 to May 7, 2004. The transactions data are obtained from the TAQ database of the NYSE. If ARIMA models are entertained, we obtain an ARIMA(0,1,1) model

$$(1 - B)y_t = (1 - 0.855B)a_t, \quad \hat{\sigma}_a = 0.5184, \tag{11.4}$$

where y_t is the log realized volatility, and the standard error of $\hat{\theta}$ is 0.029. The residuals show $Q(12) = 12.4$ with p-value 0.33, indicating that there is no significant

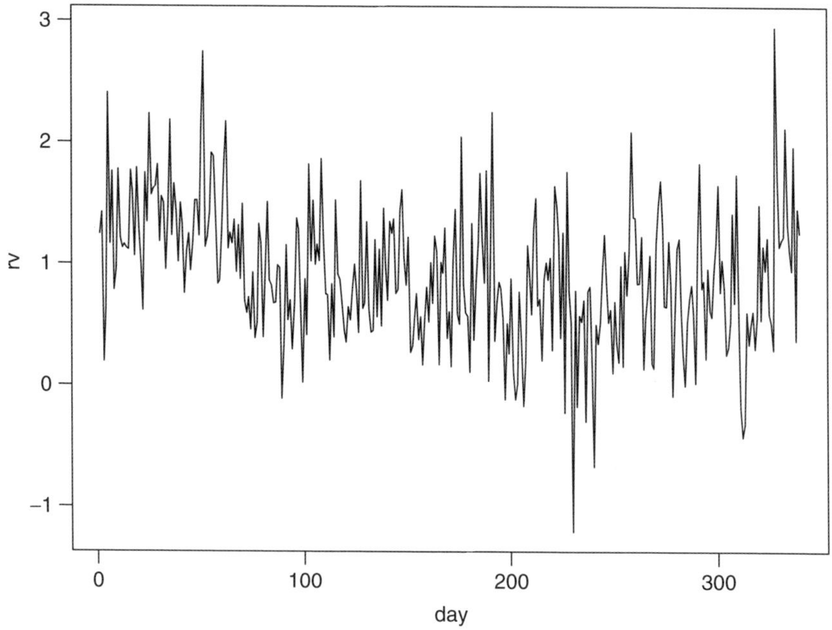

Figure 11.1. Time plot of the logarithms of intradaily realized volatility of Alcoa stock from January 2, 2003 to May 7, 2004. The realized volatility is computed from the intraday 10-minute log returns measured in percentage.

serial correlation in the residuals. Similarly, the squared residuals give $Q(12) = 8.2$ with p-value 0.77, suggesting no ARCH effects in the series.

Since $\hat{\theta}$ is positive, we can transform the ARIMA(0,1,1) model into a local trend model in Eqs. (11.1) and (11.2). The maximum likelihood estimates of the two parameters are $\hat{\sigma}_\eta = 0.0735$ and $\hat{\sigma}_e = 0.4803$. The measurement errors have a larger variance than the state innovations, confirming that intraday high-frequency returns are subject to measurement errors. Details of estimation will be discussed in Section 11.1.7. Here we treat the two estimates as given and use the model to demonstrate application of the Kalman filter.

11.1.1 Statistical Inference

Return to the state-space model in Eqs. (11.1) and (11.2). The aim of the analysis is to infer properties of the state μ_t from the data $\{y_t | t = 1, \ldots, T\}$ and the model. Three types of inference are commonly discussed in the literature. They are *filtering*, *prediction*, and *smoothing*. Let $F_t = \{y_1, \ldots, y_t\}$ be the information available at time t (inclusive) and assume that the model is known, including all parameters. The three types of inference can briefly be described as follows:

- *Filtering*. Filtering means to recover the state variable μ_t given F_t, that is, to remove the measurement errors from the data.

- *Prediction*. Prediction means to forecast μ_{t+h} or y_{t+h} for $h > 0$ given F_t, where t is the forecast origin.
- *Smoothing*. Smoothing is to estimate μ_t given F_T, where $T > t$.

A simple analogy of the three types of inference is reading a handwritten note. Filtering is figuring out the word you are reading based on knowledge accumulated from the beginning of the note, predicting is to guess the next word, and smoothing is deciphering a particular word once you have read through the note.

To describe the inference more precisely, we introduce some notation. Let $\mu_{t|j} = E(\mu_t|F_j)$ and $\Sigma_{t|j} = \text{Var}(\mu_t|F_j)$ be, respectively, the conditional mean and variance of μ_t given F_j. Similarly, $y_{t|j}$ denotes the conditional mean of y_t given F_j. Furthermore, let $v_t = y_t - y_{t|t-1}$ and $V_t = \text{Var}(v_t|F_{t-1})$ be the 1-step ahead forecast error and its variance of y_t given F_{t-1}. Note that the forecast error v_t is independent of F_{t-1} so that the conditional variance is the same as the unconditional variance; that is, $\text{Var}(v_t|F_{t-1}) = \text{Var}(v_t)$. From Eq. (11.1),

$$y_{t|t-1} = E(y_t|F_{t-1}) = E(\mu_t + e_t|F_{t-1}) = E(\mu_t|F_{t-1}) = \mu_{t|t-1}.$$

Consequently,

$$v_t = y_t - y_{t|t-1} = y_t - \mu_{t|t-1} \tag{11.5}$$

and

$$\begin{aligned} V_t &= \text{Var}(y_t - \mu_{t|t-1}|F_{t-1}) = \text{Var}(\mu_t + e_t - \mu_{t|t-1}|F_{t-1}) \\ &= \text{Var}(\mu_t - \mu_{t|t-1}|F_{t-1}) + \text{Var}(e_t|F_{t-1}) = \Sigma_{t|t-1} + \sigma_e^2. \end{aligned} \tag{11.6}$$

It is also easy to see that

$$\begin{aligned} E(v_t) &= E[E(v_t|F_{t-1})] = E[E(y_t - y_{t|t-1}|F_{t-1})] = E[y_{t|t-1} - y_{t|t-1}] = 0, \\ \text{Cov}(v_t, y_j) &= E(v_t y_j) = E[E(v_t y_j|F_{t-1})] = E[y_j E(v_t|F_{t-1})] = 0, \quad j < t. \end{aligned}$$

Thus, as expected, the 1-step ahead forecast error is uncorrelated (hence, independent) with y_j for $j < t$. Furthermore, for the linear model in Eqs. (11.1) and (11.2), $\mu_{t|t} = E(\mu_t|F_t) = E(\mu_t|F_{t-1}, v_t)$ and $\Sigma_{t|t} = \text{Var}(\mu_t|F_t) = \text{Var}(\mu_t|F_{t-1}, v_t)$. In other words, the information set F_t can be written as $F_t = \{F_{t-1}, y_t\} = \{F_{t-1}, v_t\}$.

The following properties of multivariate normal distribution are useful in studying the Kalman filter under normality. They can be shown via the multivariate linear regression method or factorization of the joint density. See, also, Appendix B of Chapter 8. For random vectors $\boldsymbol{w}$ and $\boldsymbol{m}$, denote the mean vectors and covariance matrix as $E(\boldsymbol{w}) = \boldsymbol{\mu}_w$, $E(\boldsymbol{m}) = \boldsymbol{\mu}_m$, and $\text{Cov}(\boldsymbol{m}, \boldsymbol{w}) = \boldsymbol{\Sigma}_{mw}$, respectively.

Theorem 11.1. *Suppose that $\boldsymbol{x}$, $\boldsymbol{y}$, and $\boldsymbol{z}$ are three random vectors such that their joint distribution is multivariate normal. In addition, assume that the diagonal block covariance matrix $\boldsymbol{\Sigma}_{ww}$ is nonsingular for $w = x, y, z$, and $\boldsymbol{\Sigma}_{yz} = \boldsymbol{0}$. Then,*

1. $E(\boldsymbol{x}|\boldsymbol{y}) = \boldsymbol{\mu}_x + \boldsymbol{\Sigma}_{xy}\boldsymbol{\Sigma}_{yy}^{-1}(\boldsymbol{y} - \boldsymbol{\mu}_y)$.
2. $\text{Var}(\boldsymbol{x}|\boldsymbol{y}) = \boldsymbol{\Sigma}_{xx} - \boldsymbol{\Sigma}_{xx}\boldsymbol{\Sigma}_{yy}^{-1}\boldsymbol{\Sigma}_{yx}$.

3. $E(\boldsymbol{x}|\boldsymbol{y}, z) = E(\boldsymbol{x}|\boldsymbol{y}) + \boldsymbol{\Sigma}_{xz}\boldsymbol{\Sigma}_{zz}^{-1}(z - \boldsymbol{\mu}_z)$.

4. $\text{Var}(\boldsymbol{x}|\boldsymbol{y}, z) = \text{Var}(\boldsymbol{x}|\boldsymbol{y}) - \boldsymbol{\Sigma}_{xz}\boldsymbol{\Sigma}_{zz}^{-1}\boldsymbol{\Sigma}_{zx}$.

11.1.2 Kalman Filter

The goal of the *Kalman filter* is to update knowledge of the state variable recursively when a new data point becomes available. That is, knowing the conditional distribution of μ_t given F_{t-1} and the new data y_t, we would like to obtain the conditional distribution of μ_t given F_t, where, as before, $F_j = \{y_1, \ldots, y_j\}$. Since $F_t = \{F_{t-1}, v_t\}$, giving y_t and F_{t-1} is equivalent to giving v_t and F_{t-1}. Consequently, to derive the Kalman filter, it suffices to consider the joint conditional distribution of $(\mu_t, v_t)'$ given F_{t-1} before applying Theorem 11.1.

The conditional distribution of v_t given F_{t-1} is normal with mean zero and variance given in Eq. (11.6), and that of μ_t given F_{t-1} is also normal with mean $\mu_{t|t-1}$ and variance $\Sigma_{t|t-1}$. Furthermore, the joint distribution of $(\mu_t, v_t)'$ given F_{t-1} is also normal. Thus, what remains to be solved is the conditional covariance between μ_t and v_t given F_{t-1}. From the definition,

$$\begin{aligned}
\text{Cov}(\mu_t, v_t|F_{t-1}) &= E(\mu_t v_t|F_{t-1}) = E[\mu_t(y_t - \mu_{t|t-1})|F_{t-1}] \quad \text{(by Eq.(11.5))} \\
&= E[\mu_t(\mu_t + e_t - \mu_{t|t-1})|F_{t-1}] \\
&= E[\mu_t(\mu_t - \mu_{t|t-1})|F_{t-1}] + E(\mu_t e_t|F_{t-1}) \\
&= E[(\mu_t - \mu_{t|t-1})^2|F_{t-1}] = \text{Var}(\mu_t|F_{t-1}) = \Sigma_{t|t-1}, \qquad (11.7)
\end{aligned}$$

where we have used the fact that $E[\mu_{t|t-1}(\mu_t - \mu_{t|t-1})|F_{t-1}] = 0$. Putting the results together, we have

$$\begin{bmatrix} \mu_t \\ v_t \end{bmatrix}_{F_{t-1}} \sim N\left(\begin{bmatrix} \mu_{t|t-1} \\ 0 \end{bmatrix}, \begin{bmatrix} \Sigma_{t|t-1} & \Sigma_{t|t-1} \\ \Sigma_{t|t-1} & V_t \end{bmatrix}\right).$$

By Theorem 11.1, the conditional distribution of μ_t given F_t is normal with mean and variance

$$\mu_{t|t} = \mu_{t|t-1} + \frac{\Sigma_{t|t-1} v_t}{V_t} = \mu_{t|t-1} + K_t v_t, \qquad (11.8)$$

$$\Sigma_{t|t} = \Sigma_{t|t-1} - \frac{\Sigma_{t|t-1}^2}{V_t} = \Sigma_{t|t-1}(1 - K_t), \qquad (11.9)$$

where $K_t = \Sigma_{t|t-1}/V_t$ is commonly referred to as the *Kalman gain*, which is the regression coefficient of μ_t on v_t. From Eq. (11.8), Kalman gain is the factor that governs the contribution of the new shock v_t to the state variable μ_t.

Next, one can make use of the knowledge of μ_t given F_t to predict μ_{t+1} via Eq. (11.2). Specifically, we have

$$\mu_{t+1|t} = E(\mu_t + \eta_t|F_t) = E(\mu_t|F_t) = \mu_{t|t}, \qquad (11.10)$$

$$\Sigma_{t+1|t} = \text{Var}(\mu_{t+1}|F_t) = \text{Var}(\mu_t|F_t) + \text{Var}(\eta_t) = \Sigma_{t|t} + \sigma_\eta^2. \qquad (11.11)$$

Once the new data y_{t+1} is observed, one can repeat the above procedure to update knowledge of μ_{t+1}. This is the famous *Kalman filter* algorithm proposed by Kalman (1960).

In summary, putting Eqs. (11.5)–(11.11) together and conditioning on the initial assumption that μ_1 is distributed as $N(\mu_{1|0}, \Sigma_{1|0})$, the Kalman filter for the local trend model is as follows:

$$\begin{aligned} v_t &= y_t - \mu_{t|t-1}, \\ V_t &= \Sigma_{t|t-1} + \sigma_e^2, \\ K_t &= \Sigma_{t|t-1}/V_t, \\ \mu_{t+1|t} &= \mu_{t|t-1} + K_t v_t, \\ \Sigma_{t+1|t} &= \Sigma_{t|t-1}(1 - K_t) + \sigma_\eta^2, \quad t = 1, \ldots, T. \end{aligned} \tag{11.12}$$

There are many ways to derive the Kalman filter. We use Theorem 11.1, which describes some properties of multivariate normal distribution, for its simplicity. In practice, the choice of initial values $\Sigma_{1|0}$ and $\mu_{1|0}$ requires some attention and we shall discuss it later in Section 11.1.6. For the local trend model in Eqs. (11.1) and (11.2), the two parameters σ_e and σ_η can be estimated via the maximum likelihood method. Again, the Kalman filter is useful in evaluating the likelihood function of the data in estimation. We shall discuss estimation in Section 11.1.7.

Example 11.1 (Continued). To illustrate application of the Kalman filter, we use the fitted state-space model for daily realized volatility of Alcoa stock returns and apply the Kalman filter algorithm to the data with $\Sigma_{1|0} = \infty$ and $\mu_{1|0} = 0$. The choice of these initial values will be discussed in Section 11.1.6. Figure 11.2a shows the time plot of the filtered state variable $\mu_{t|t}$ and Figure 11.2b is the time plot of the 1-step ahead forecast error v_t. Compared with Figure 11.1, the filtered states are smoother. The forecast errors appear to be stable and center around zero. These forecast errors are out-of-sample 1-step ahead prediction errors.

11.1.3 Properties of Forecast Error

The one-step ahead forecast errors $\{v_t\}$ are useful in many applications, hence it pays to study carefully their properties. Given the initial values $\Sigma_{1|0}$ and $\mu_{1|0}$, which are independent of y_t, the Kalman filter enables us to compute v_t recursively as a linear function of $\{y_1, \ldots, y_t\}$. Specifically, by repeated substitutions,

$$\begin{aligned} v_1 &= y_1 - \mu_{1|0}, \\ v_2 &= y_2 - \mu_{2|1} = y_2 - \mu_{1|0} - K_1(y_1 - \mu_{1|0}), \\ v_3 &= y_3 - \mu_{3|2} = y_3 - \mu_{1|0} - K_2(y_2 - \mu_{1|0}) - K_1(1 - K_2)(y_1 - \mu_{1|0}), \end{aligned}$$

and so on. This transformation can be written in matrix form as

$$\boldsymbol{v} = \boldsymbol{K}(\boldsymbol{y} - \mu_{1|0}\mathbf{1}_T), \tag{11.13}$$

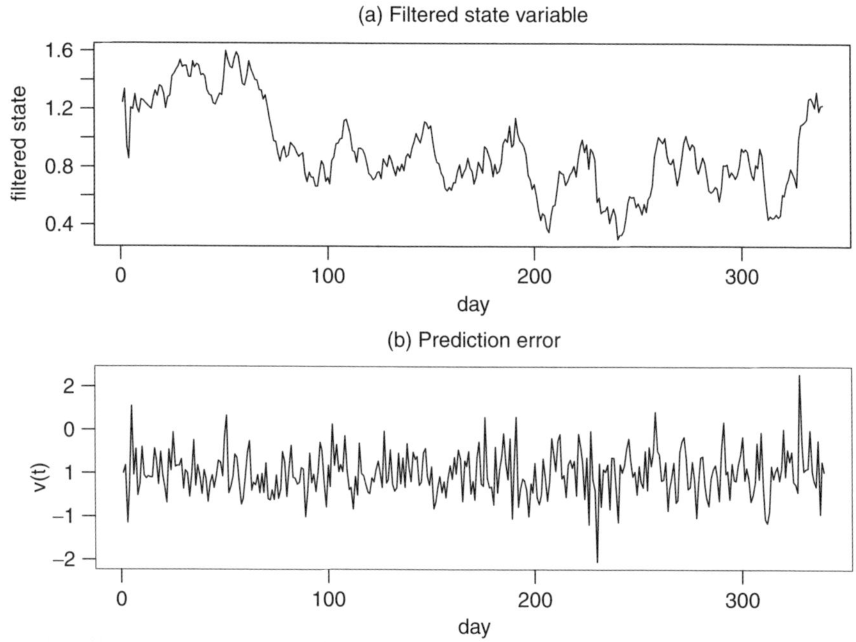

Figure 11.2. Time plots of output of the Kalman filter applied to the daily realized log volatility of Alcoa stock based on the local trend state-space model: (a) the filtered state $\mu_{t|t}$ and (b) the one-step ahead forecast error v_t.

where $\boldsymbol{v} = (v_1, \ldots, v_T)'$, $\boldsymbol{y} = (y_1, \ldots, y_T)'$, $\mathbf{1}_T$ is the T-dimensional vector of ones, and $\boldsymbol{K}$ is a lower triangular matrix defined as

$$\boldsymbol{K} = \begin{bmatrix} 1 & 0 & 0 & \cdots & 0 \\ k_{21} & 1 & 0 & \cdots & 0 \\ k_{31} & k_{32} & 1 & & 0 \\ \vdots & \vdots & & & \vdots \\ k_{T1} & k_{T2} & k_{T3} & \cdots & 1 \end{bmatrix},$$

where $k_{i,i-1} = -K_{i-1}$ and $k_{ij} = -(1 - K_{i-1})(1 - K_{i-2}) \cdots (1 - K_{j+1})K_j$ for $i = 2, \ldots, T$ and $j = 1, \ldots, i-2$. It should be noted that, from the definition, the Kalman gain K_t does not depend on $\mu_{1|0}$ or the data $\{y_1, \ldots, y_t\}$; it depends on $\Sigma_{1|0}$ and σ_e^2 and σ_η^2.

The transformation in Eq. (11.13) has several important implications. First, $\{v_t\}$ are mutually independent under the normality assumption. To show this, consider the joint probability density function of the data

$$p(y_1, \ldots, y_T) = p(y_1) \prod_{j=2}^{T} p(y_j | F_{j-1}).$$

Equation (11.13) indicates that the transformation from y_t to v_t has a unit Jacobian so that $p(\boldsymbol{v}) = p(\boldsymbol{y})$. Furthermore, since $\mu_{1|0}$ is given, $p(v_1) = p(y_1)$. Consequently, the joint probability density function of $\boldsymbol{v}$ is

$$p(\boldsymbol{v}) = p(\boldsymbol{y}) = p(y_1)\prod_{j=2}^{T} p(y_j|F_{j-1}) = p(v_1)\prod_{j}^{T} p(v_j) = \prod_{j=1}^{T} p(v_j).$$

This shows that $\{v_t\}$ are mutually independent.

Second, the Kalman filter provides a Cholesky decomposition of the covariance matrix of $\boldsymbol{y}$. To see this, let $\boldsymbol{\Omega} = \text{Cov}(\boldsymbol{y})$. Equation (11.13) shows that $\text{Cov}(\boldsymbol{v}) = \boldsymbol{K\Omega K}'$. On the other hand, $\{v_t\}$ are mutually independent with $\text{Var}(v_t) = V_t$. Therefore, $\boldsymbol{K\Omega K}' = \text{diag}\{V_1, \ldots, V_T\}$, which is precisely a Cholesky decomposition of $\boldsymbol{\Omega}$. The elements k_{ij} of the matrix $\boldsymbol{K}$ thus have some nice interpretations; see Chapter 10.

State Error Recursion

Turn to the estimation error of the state variable μ_t. Define

$$x_t = \mu_t - \mu_{t|t-1}$$

as the forecast error of the state variable μ_t given data F_{t-1}. From Section 11.1.1, $\text{Var}(x_t|F_{t-1}) = \Sigma_{t|t-1}$. From the Kalman filter in Eq. (11.12),

$$v_t = y_t - \mu_{t|t-1} = \mu_t + e_t - \mu_{t|t-1} = x_t + e_t,$$

and

$$\begin{aligned} x_{t+1} &= \mu_{t+1} - \mu_{t+1|t} = \mu_t + \eta_t - (\mu_{t|t-1} + K_t v_t) \\ &= x_t + \eta_t - K_t v_t = x_t + \eta_t - K_t(x_t + e_t) = L_t x_t + \eta_t - K_t e_t, \end{aligned}$$

where $L_t = 1 - K_t = 1 - \Sigma_{t|t-1}/V_t = (V_t - \Sigma_{t|t-1})/V_t = \sigma_e^2/V_t$. Consequently, for the state errors, we have

$$v_t = x_t + e_t, \quad x_{t+1} = L_t x_t + \eta_t - K_t e_t, \quad t = 1, \ldots, T, \tag{11.14}$$

where $x_1 = \mu_1 - \mu_{1|0}$. Equation (11.14) is in the form of a time-varying state-space model with x_t being the state variable and v_t the observation.

11.1.4 State Smoothing

Next we consider the estimation of the state variables $\{\mu_1, \ldots, \mu_T\}$ given the data F_T and the model. That is, given the state-space model in Eqs. (11.1) and (11.2), we wish to obtain the conditional distribution $\mu_t|F_T$ for all t. To this end, we first recall some facts available about the model:

- All distributions involved are normal so that we can write the conditional distribution of μ_t given F_T as $N(\mu_{t|T}, \Sigma_{t|T})$, where $t \le T$. We refer to $\mu_{t|T}$ as the *smoothed state* at time t and $\Sigma_{t|T}$ as the *smoothed state variance*.

- Based on the properties of $\{v_t\}$ shown in Section 11.1.3, $\{v_1, \ldots, v_T\}$ are mutually independent and are linear functions of $\{y_1, \ldots, y_T\}$.
- If $y_1, \ldots, y_T$ are fixed, then F_{t-1} and $\{v_t, \ldots, v_T\}$ are fixed, and vice versa.
- $\{v_t, \ldots, v_T\}$ are independent of F_{t-1} with mean zero and variance $\text{Var}(v_j) = V_j$ for $j \geq t$.

Applying Theorem 11.1(3) to the conditional joint distribution of $(\mu_t, v_t, \ldots, v_T)$ given F_{t-1}, we have

$$
\begin{aligned}
\mu_{t|T} &= E(\mu_t|F_T) = E(\mu_t|F_{t-1}, v_t, \ldots, v_T) \\
&= E(\mu_t|F_{t-1}) + \text{Cov}[\mu_t, (v_t, \ldots, v_T)']\text{Cov}[(v_t, \ldots, v_T)']^{-1}(v_t, \ldots, v_T)' \\
&= \mu_{t|t-1} + \begin{bmatrix} \text{Cov}(\mu_t, v_t) \\ \text{Cov}(\mu_t, v_{t+1}) \\ \vdots \\ \text{Cov}(\mu_t, v_T) \end{bmatrix}' \begin{bmatrix} V_t & 0 & \cdots & 0 \\ 0 & V_{t+1} & \cdots & 0 \\ \vdots & \vdots & & \vdots \\ 0 & 0 & \cdots & V_T \end{bmatrix}^{-1} \begin{bmatrix} v_t \\ v_{t+1} \\ \vdots \\ v_T \end{bmatrix} \\
&= \mu_{t|t-1} + \sum_{j=t}^{T} \text{Cov}(\mu_t, v_j) V_j^{-1} v_j. \qquad (11.15)
\end{aligned}
$$

From the definition and independence of $\{v_t\}$, $\text{Cov}(\mu_t, v_j) = \text{Cov}(x_t, v_j)$ for $j = t, \ldots, T$, and

$$
\begin{aligned}
\text{Cov}(x_t, v_t) &= E[x_t(x_t + e_t)] = \text{Var}(x_t) = \Sigma_{t|t-1}, \\
\text{Cov}(x_t, v_{t+1}) &= E[x_t(x_{t+1} + e_{t+1})] = E[x_t(L_t x_t + \eta_t - K_t e_t)] = \Sigma_{t|t-1} L_t.
\end{aligned}
$$

Similarly, we have

$$
\begin{aligned}
\text{Cov}(x_t, v_{t+2}) &= E[x_t(x_{t+2} + e_{t+2})] = \cdots = \Sigma_{t|t-1} L_t L_{t+1}, \\
\vdots &= \vdots \\
\text{Cov}(x_t, v_T) &= E[x_t(x_T + e_T)] = \cdots = \Sigma_{t|t-1} \prod_{j=t}^{T-1} L_j.
\end{aligned}
$$

Consequently, Eq. (11.15) becomes

$$
\begin{aligned}
\mu_{t|T} &= \mu_{t|t-1} + \Sigma_{t|t-1} \frac{v_t}{V_t} + \Sigma_{t|t-1} L_t \frac{v_{t+1}}{V_{t+1}} + \Sigma_{t|t-1} L_t L_{t+1} \frac{v_{t+2}}{V_{t+2}} + \cdots \\
&\equiv \mu_{t|t-1} + \Sigma_{t|t-1} q_{t-1},
\end{aligned}
$$

where

$$
q_{t-1} = \frac{v_t}{V_t} + L_t \frac{v_{t+1}}{V_{t+1}} + L_t L_{t+1} \frac{v_{t+2}}{V_{t+2}} + \cdots + \left(\prod_{j=t}^{T-1} L_j \right) \frac{v_T}{V_T} \qquad (11.16)
$$

is a weighted linear combination of the innovations $\{v_t, \ldots, v_T\}$. This weighted sum satisfies

$$q_{t-1} = \frac{v_t}{V_t} + L_t \left[\frac{v_{t+1}}{V_{t+1}} + L_{t+1} \frac{v_{t+2}}{V_{t+2}} + \cdots + \left(\prod_{j=t+1}^{T-1} L_j \right) \frac{v_T}{V_T} \right]$$
$$= \frac{v_t}{V_t} + L_t q_t.$$

Therefore, using the initial value $q_T = 0$, we have the backward recursion

$$q_{t-1} = \frac{v_t}{V_t} + L_t q_t, \quad t = T, T-1, \ldots, 1. \tag{11.17}$$

Putting Eqs. (11.15)–(11.17) together, we have a backward recursive algorithm to compute the smoothed state variables:

$$q_{t-1} = V_t^{-1} v_t + L_t q_t, \quad \mu_{t|T} = \mu_{t|t-1} + \Sigma_{t|t-1} q_{t-1}, \quad t = T, \ldots, 1, \tag{11.18}$$

where $q_T = 0$, and $\mu_{t|t-1}$, $\Sigma_{t|t-1}$ and L_t are available from the Kalman filter in Eq. (11.12).

Smoothed State Variance

The variance of the smoothed state variable $\mu_{t|T}$ can be derived in a similar manner via Theorem 11.1(4). Specifically, letting $\boldsymbol{v}_t^T = (v_t, \ldots, v_T)'$, we have

$$\Sigma_{t|T} = \text{Var}(\mu_t | F_T) = \text{Var}(\mu_t | F_{t-1}, v_t, \ldots, v_T)$$
$$= \text{Var}(\mu_t | F_{t-1}) - \text{Cov}[\mu_t, (\boldsymbol{v}_t^T)'] \text{Cov}[(\boldsymbol{v}_t^T)]^{-1} \text{Cov}[\mu_t, (\boldsymbol{v}_t^T)]$$
$$= \Sigma_{t|t-1} - \sum_{j=t}^{T} [\text{Cov}(\mu_t, v_j)]^2 V_j^{-1}, \tag{11.19}$$

where $\text{Cov}(\mu_t, v_j) = \text{Cov}(x_t, v_j)$ are given earlier after Eq. (11.15). Thus,

$$\Sigma_{t|T} = \Sigma_{t|t-1} - \Sigma_{t|t-1}^2 \frac{1}{V_t} - \Sigma_{t|t-1}^2 L_t^2 \frac{1}{V_{t+1}} - \cdots - \Sigma_{t|t-1}^2 \left(\prod_{j=t}^{T-1} L_j^2 \right) \frac{1}{V_T}$$
$$\equiv \Sigma_{t|t-1} - \Sigma_{t|t-1}^2 M_{t-1}, \tag{11.20}$$

where

$$M_{t-1} = \frac{1}{V_t} + L_t^2 \frac{1}{V_{t+1}} + L_t^2 L_{t+1}^2 \frac{1}{V_{t+2}} + \cdots + \left(\prod_{j=t}^{T-1} L_j^2 \right) \frac{1}{V_T}$$

is a weighted linear combination of the inverses of variances of the 1-step ahead forecast errors after time $t-1$. Let $M_T = 0$ because no 1-step ahead forecast error is available after time index T. The statistic M_{t-1} can be written as

$$M_{t-1} = \frac{1}{V_t} + L_t^2 \left[\frac{1}{V_{t+1}} + L_{t+1}^2 \frac{1}{V_{t+2}} + \cdots + \left(\prod_{j=t+1}^{T-1} L_j^2 \right) \frac{1}{V_T} \right]$$

$$= \frac{1}{V_t} + L_t^2 M_t, \quad t = T, T-1, \ldots, 1.$$

Note that from the independence of $\{v_t\}$ and Eq. (11.16), we have

$$\text{Var}(q_{t-1}) = \frac{1}{V_t} + L_t^2 \frac{1}{V_{t+1}} + \cdots + \left(\prod_{j=t}^{T-1} L_j^2 \right) \frac{1}{V_T} = M_{t-1}.$$

Combining the results, variances of the smoothed state variables can be computed efficiently via the backward recursion

$$M_{t-1} = V_t^{-1} + L_t^2 M_t, \quad \Sigma_{t|T} = \Sigma_{t|t-1} - \Sigma_{t|t-1}^2 M_{t-1}, \quad t = T, \ldots, 1, \quad (11.21)$$

where $M_T = 0$.

Example 11.1 (Continued). Applying the Kalman filter and state-smoothing algorithms in Eqs. (11.18) and (11.21) to the daily realized volatility of Alcoa stock using the fitted state-space model, we can easily compute the filtered state $\mu_{t|t}$ and the smoothed state $\mu_{t|T}$ and their variances. Figure 11.3 shows the filtered state variable and its 95% pointwise confidence interval, whereas Figure 11.4 provides the time plot of smoothed state variable and its 95% pointwise confidence interval. As expected, the smoothed state variables are smoother than the filtered state variables. The confidence intervals for the smoothed state variables are also narrower than those of the filtered state variables. Note that the width of the 95% confidence interval of $\mu_{1|1}$ depends on the initial value $\Sigma_{1|0}$.

11.1.5 Missing Values

An advantage of the state-space model is in handling missing values. Suppose that the observations $\{y_t\}_{t=\ell+1}^{\ell+h}$ are missing, where $h \geq 1$ and $1 \leq \ell < T$. There are several ways to handle missing values in state-space formulation. Here we discuss a method that keeps the original time scale and model form. For $t \in \{\ell + 1, \ldots, \ell + h\}$, we can use Eq. (11.2) to express μ_t as a linear combination of $\mu_{\ell+1}$ and $\{\eta_j\}_{j=\ell+1}^{t-1}$. Specifically,

$$\mu_t = \mu_{t-1} + \eta_{t-1} = \cdots = \mu_{\ell+1} + \sum_{j=\ell+1}^{t-1} \eta_j,$$

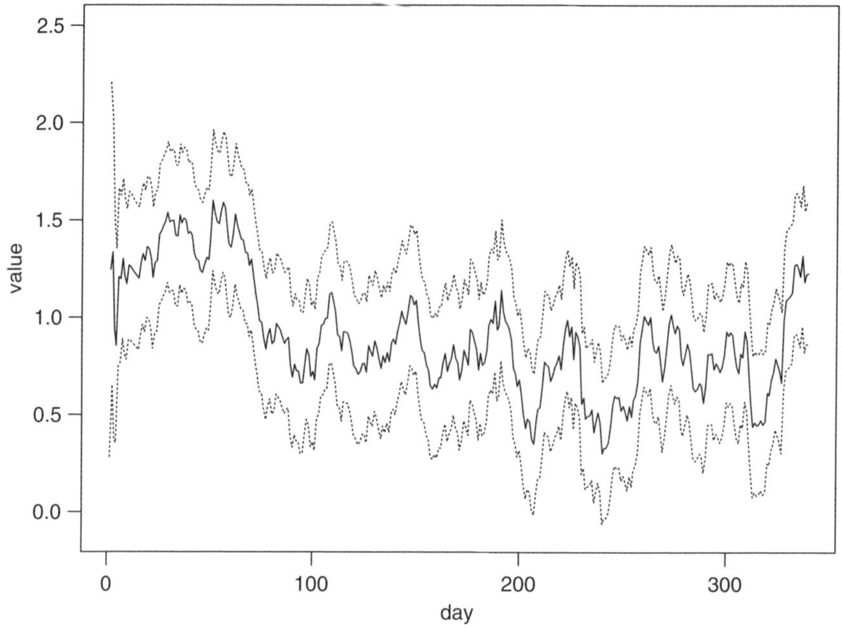

Figure 11.3. Filtered state variable $\mu_{t|t}$ and its 95% pointwise confidence interval for the daily log realized volatility of Alcoa stock returns based on the fitted local trend state-space model.

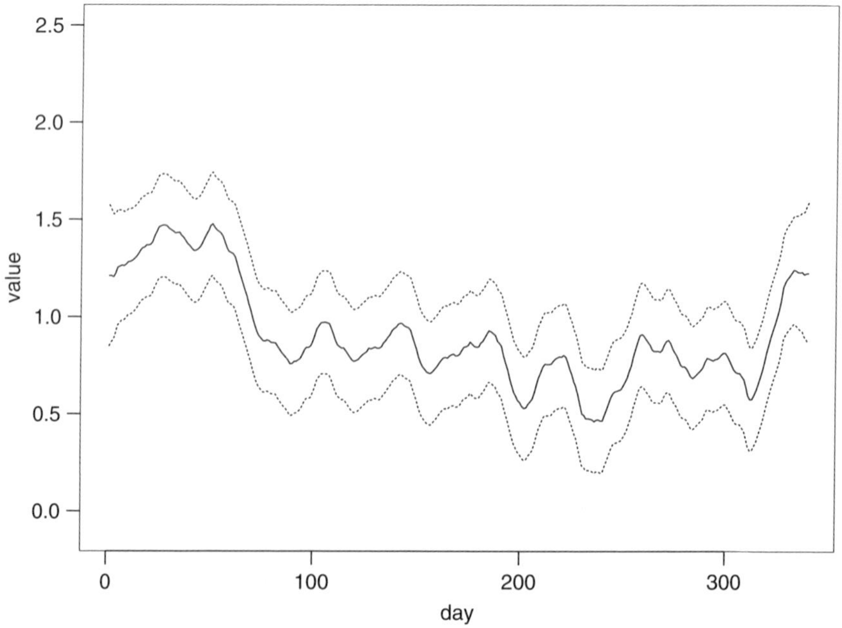

Figure 11.4. Smoothed state variable $\mu_{t|T}$ and its 95% pointwise confidence interval for the daily log realized volatility of Alcoa stock returns based on the fitted local trend state-space model.

where it is understood that the summation term is zero if its lower limit is greater than its upper limit. Therefore, for $t \in \{\ell+1, \ldots, \ell+h\}$,

$$E(\mu_t|F_{t-1}) = E(\mu_t|F_\ell) = \mu_{\ell+1|\ell},$$
$$\mathrm{Var}(\mu_t|F_{t-1}) = \mathrm{Var}(\mu_t|F_\ell) = \Sigma_{\ell+1|\ell} + (t-\ell-1)\sigma_\eta^2.$$

Consequently, we have

$$\mu_{t|t-1} = \mu_{t-1|t-2}, \quad \Sigma_{t|t-1} = \Sigma_{t-1|t-2} + \sigma_\eta^2, \tag{11.22}$$

for $t = \ell+2, \ldots, \ell+h$. These results show that we can continue to apply the Kalman filter algorithm in Eq. (11.12) by taking $v_t = 0$ and $K_t = 0$ for $t = \ell + 1, \ldots, \ell+h$. This is rather natural because when y_t is missing, there is no new innovation or new Kalman gain so that $v_t = 0$ and $K_t = 0$.

11.1.6 Effect of Initialization

In this subsection, we consider the effects of initial condition $\mu_1 \sim N(\mu_{1|0}, \Sigma_{1|0})$ on the Kalman filter and state smoothing. From the Kalman filter in Eq. (11.12),

$$v_1 = y_1 - \mu_{1|0}, \quad V_1 = \Sigma_{1|0} + \sigma_e^2,$$

and, by Eqs. (11.8)–(11.11),

$$\mu_{2|1} = \mu_{1|0} + \frac{\Sigma_{1|0}}{V_1} v_1 = \mu_{1|0} + \frac{\Sigma_{1|0}}{\Sigma_{1|0}+\sigma_e^2}(y_1 - \mu_{1|0}),$$
$$\Sigma_{2|1} = \Sigma_{1|0}\left(1 - \frac{\Sigma_{1|0}}{\Sigma_{1|0}+\sigma_e^2}\right) + \sigma_\eta^2 = \frac{\Sigma_{1|0}}{\Sigma_{1|0}+\sigma_e^2}\sigma_e^2 + \sigma_\eta^2.$$

Therefore, letting $\Sigma_{1|0}$ increase to infinity, we have $\mu_{2|1} = y_1$ and $\Sigma_{2|1} = \sigma_e^2 + \sigma_\eta^2$. This is equivalent to treating y_1 as fixed and assuming $\mu_1 \sim N(y_1, \sigma_e^2)$. In the literature, this approach to initializing the Kalman filter is called *diffuse initialization* because a very large $\Sigma_{1|0}$ means one is uncertain about the initial condition.

Next, turn to the effect of diffuse initialization on state smoothing. It is obvious that based on the results of Kalman filtering, state smoothing is not affected by the diffuse initialization for $t = T, \ldots, 2$. Thus, we focus on μ_1 given F_T. From Eq. (11.18) and the definition of $L_1 = 1 - K_1 = V_1^{-1}\sigma_e^2$,

$$\begin{aligned}\mu_{1|T} &= \mu_{1|0} + \Sigma_{1|0} q_0 \\ &= \mu_{1|0} + \Sigma_{1|0}\left[\frac{1}{\Sigma_{1|0}+\sigma_e^2} v_1 + \left(1 - \frac{\Sigma_{1|0}}{\Sigma_{1|0}+\sigma_e^2}\right) q_1\right] \\ &= \mu_{1|0} + \frac{\Sigma_{1|0}}{\Sigma_{1|0}+\sigma_e^2}(v_1 + \sigma_e^2 q_1).\end{aligned}$$

Letting $\Sigma_{1|0} \to \infty$, we have $\mu_{1|T} = \mu_{1|0} + v_1 + \sigma_e^2 q_1 = y_1 + \sigma_e^2 q_1$. Furthermore, from Eq. (11.21) and using $V_1 = \Sigma_{1|0} + \sigma_e^2$, we have

$$\begin{aligned}
\Sigma_{1|T} &= \Sigma_{1|0} - \Sigma_{1|0}^2 \left[\frac{1}{\Sigma_{1|0} + \sigma_e^2} + \left(1 - \frac{\Sigma_{1|0}}{\Sigma_{1|0} + \sigma_e^2}\right)^2 M_1 \right] \\
&= \Sigma_{1|0} \left(1 - \frac{\Sigma_{1|0}}{\Sigma_{1|0} + \sigma_e^2}\right) - \left(1 - \frac{\Sigma_{1|0}}{\Sigma_{1|0} + \sigma_e^2}\right)^2 \Sigma_{1|0}^2 M_1 \\
&= \left(\frac{\Sigma_{1|0}}{\Sigma_{1|0} + \sigma_e^2}\right) \sigma_e^2 - \left(\frac{\Sigma_{1|0}}{\Sigma_{1|0} + \sigma_e^2}\right)^2 \sigma_e^4 M_1.
\end{aligned}$$

Thus, letting $\Sigma_{1|0} \to \infty$, we obtain $\Sigma_{1|T} = \sigma_e^2 - \sigma_e^4 M_1$.

Based on the prior discussion, we suggest using diffuse initialization when little is known about the initial value μ_1. However, it might be hard to justify the use of a random variable with infinite variance in real applications. If necessary, one can treat μ_1 as an additional parameter of the state-space model and estimate it jointly with other parameters. This latter approach is closely related to the exact maximum likelihood estimation of Chapters 2 and 8.

11.1.7 Estimation

In this subsection, we consider the estimation of σ_e and σ_η of the local trend model in Eqs. (11.1) and (11.2). Based on properties of forecast errors discussed in Section 11.1.3, the Kalman filter provides an efficient way to evaluate the likelihood function of the data for estimation. Specifically, the likelihood function under normality is

$$\begin{aligned}
p(y_1, \ldots, y_T | \sigma_e, \sigma_\eta) &= p(y_1 | \sigma_e, \sigma_\eta) \prod_{t=2}^{T} (y_t | F_{t-1}, \sigma_e, \sigma_\eta) \\
&= p(y_1 | \sigma_e, \sigma_\eta) \prod_{t=2}^{T} (v_t | F_{t-1}, \sigma_e, \sigma_\eta),
\end{aligned}$$

where $y_1 \sim N(\mu_{1|0}, V_1)$ and $v_t = (y_t - \mu_{t|t-1}) \sim N(0, V_t)$. Consequently, assuming $\mu_{1|0}$ and $\Sigma_{1|0}$ are known, and taking the logarithms, we have

$$\ln[L(\sigma_e, \sigma_\eta)] = -\frac{T}{2} \ln(2\pi) - \frac{1}{2} \sum_{t=1}^{T} \left(\ln(V_t) + \frac{v_t^2}{V_t} \right), \qquad (11.23)$$

which involves v_t and V_t. Therefore, the log likelihood function, including cases with missing values, can be evaluated recursively via the Kalman filter. Many software packages perform state-space model estimation via a Kalman filter algorithm such as Matlab, RATS, and S-Plus. In this chapter, we use the *SsfPack* program developed by Koopman, Shephard, and Doornik (1999) and available in S-Plus and OX. Both *SsfPack* and OX are free and can be downloaded from their Web sites.

Table 11.1. State-Space Form and Notation in S-Plus

State-Space Parameter	S-Plus Name
$\boldsymbol{\delta}$	`mDelta`
$\boldsymbol{\Phi}$	`mPhi`
$\boldsymbol{\Omega}$	`mOmega`
$\boldsymbol{\Sigma}$	`mSigma`

Table 11.2. Some Commands of *SsfPack* Package

Command	Function
`SsfFit`	Maximum likelihood estimation
`CheckSsf`	Create ``Ssf'' object in S-Plus
`KalmanFil`	Perform Kalman filtering
`KalmanSmo`	Perform state smoothing
`SsfMomentEst` with task ``STFIL''	Compute filtered state and variance
`SsfMomentEst` with task ``STSMO''	Compute smoothed state and variance
`SsfCondDens` with task ``STSMO''	Compute smoothed state without variance

11.1.8 S-Plus Commands Used

We provide here the *SsfPack* commands used to perform analysis of the daily realized volatility of Alcoa stock returns. Only brief explanations are given. For further details of the commands used, see Durbin and Koopman (2001, Section 6.6). S-Plus uses specific notation to specify a state-space model; see Table 11.1. The notation must be followed closely. In Table 11.2, we give some commands and their functions.

In our analysis, we first perform maximum likelihood estimation of the state-space model in Eqs. (11.1) and (11.2) to obtain estimates of σ_e and σ_η. The initial values used are $\Sigma_{1|0} = -1$ and $\mu_{1|0} = 0$, where "-1" signifies diffuse initialization, that is, $\Sigma_{1|0}$ is very large. We then treat the fitted model as given to perform Kalman filtering and state smoothing.

SsfPack and S-Plus Commands for State-Space Model

```
> da = matrix(scan(file='aa-rv-0304.txt'),2) % load data
> y = log(da[1,]) % log(RV)

> ltm.start=c(3,1)  % Initial parameter values
> P1 = -1   % Initialization of Kalman filter
> a1 = 0

> ltm.m=function(parm){   % Specify a function for the
+ sigma.eta=parm[1]       % local trend model.
+ sigma.e=parm[2]
```

```
+ ssf.m=list(mPhi=as.matrix(c(1,1)),
+ mOmega=diag(c(sigma.eta^2,sigma.e^2)),
+ mSigma=as.matrix(c(P1,a1)))
+ CheckSsf(ssf.m)
+ }
% perform estimation
> ltm.mle=SsfFit(ltm.start,y,"ltm.m",lower=c(0,0),
+ upper=c(100,100))
> ltm.mle$parameters
[1] 0.07350827 0.48026284
> sigma.eta=ltm.mle$parameter[1]
> sigma.eta
[1] 0.07350827
> sigma.e=ltm.mle$parameters[2]
> sigma.e
[1] 0.4802628
% Specify a state-space model in S-Plus.
> ssf.ltm.list=list(mPhi=as.matrix(c(1,1)),
+ mOmega=diag(c(sigma.eta^2,sigma.e^2)),
+ mSigma=as.matrix(c(P1,a1)))
% check validity of the specified model.
> ssf.ltm=CheckSsf(ssf.ltm.list)
> ssf.ltm
$mPhi:
     [,1]
[1,]    1
[2,]    1
$mOmega:
          [,1]      [,2]
[1,] 0.0054035 0.0000000
[2,] 0.0000000 0.2306524
$mSigma:
     [,1]
[1,]   -1
[2,]    0
$mDelta:
     [,1]
[1,]    0
[2,]    0
$mJPhi:
[1] 0
$mJOmega:
[1] 0
$mJDelta:
[1] 0
$mX:
[1] 0
$cT:
[1] 0
```

```
$cX:
[1] 0
$cY:
[1] 1
$cSt:
[1] 1
attr(, "class"):
[1] "ssf"
% Apply Kalman filter
> KalmanFil.ltm=KalmanFil(y,ssf.ltm,task="STFIL")
> names(KalmanFil.ltm)
 [1] "mOut"         "innov" "std.innov" "mGain" "loglike"
 [6] "loglike.conc" "dVar"  "mEst"      "mOffP" "task"
[11] "err"          "call"
> par(mfcol=c(2,1))   % Obtain plot
> plot(1:340,KalmanFil.ltm$mEst[,1],xlab='day',
+ ylab='filtered state',type='l')
> title(main='(a) Filtered state variable')
> plot(1:340,KalmanFil.ltm$mOut[,1],xlab='day',
+ ylab='v(t)',type='l')
> title(main='(b) Prediction error')
% Obtain residuals and their variances
> KalmanSmo.ltm=KalmanSmo(KalmanFil.ltm,ssf.ltm)
> names(KalmanSmo.ltm)
[1] "state.residuals"   "response.residuals" "state.variance"
[4] "response.variance" "aux.residuals"      "scores"
[7] "call"
% Next, filtered states
> FiledEst.ltm=SsfMomentEst(y,ssf.ltm,task="STFIL")
> names(FiledEst.ltm)
[1] "state.moment"      "state.variance"  "response.moment"
[4] "response.variance" "task"
% Smoothed states
> SmoedEst.ltm=SsfMomentEst(y,ssf.ltm,task="STSMO")
> names(SmoedEst.ltm)
[1] "state.moment"      "state.variance"  "response.moment"
[4] "response.variance" "task"
% Obtain plots of filtered and smoothed states with 95% C.I.
> up=FiledEst.ltm$state.moment +
+  2*sqrt(FiledEst.ltm$state.variance)
> lw=FiledEst.ltm$state.moment -
+  2*sqrt(FiledEst.ltm$state.variance)
> par(mfcol=c(1,1))
> plot(1:340,FiledEst.ltm$state.moment,type='l',xlab='day',
+ ylab='value',ylim=c(-0.1,2.5))
> lines(1:340,up,lty=2)
> lines(1:340,lw,lty=2)
> title(main='Filed state variable')
> up=SmoedEst.ltm$state.moment +
```

```
+  2*sqrt(SmoedEst.ltm$state.variance)
> lw=SmoedEst.ltm$state.moment -
+  2*sqrt(SmoedEst.ltm$state.variance)
> plot(1:340,SmoedEst.ltm$state.moment,type='l',xlab='day',
+  ylab='value',ylim=c(-0.1,2.5))
> lines(1:340,up,lty=2)
> lines(1:340,lw,lty=2)
> title(main='Smoothed state variable')
% Model checking
> resi=KalmanFil.ltm$mOut[,1]*sqrt(KalmanFil.ltm$mOut[,3])
> archTest(resi)
> autocorTest(resi)
```

For the daily realized volatility of Alcoa stock returns, the fitted local trend model is adequate based on residual analysis. Specifically, given the parameter estimates, we use the Kalman filter to obtain the 1-step ahead forecast error v_t and its variance V_t. We then compute the standardized forecast error $\tilde{v}_t = v_t/\sqrt{V_t}$ and check the serial correlations and ARCH effects of $\{\tilde{v}_t\}$. We found that $Q(25) = 23.37(0.56)$ for the standardized forecast errors and the LM test statistic for ARCH effect is 18.48(0.82) for 25 lags, where the number in parentheses denotes p-value.

11.2 LINEAR STATE-SPACE MODELS

We now consider the general state-space model. Many dynamic time series models in economics and finance can be represented in state-space form. Examples include the ARIMA models, dynamic linear models with unobserved components, time-varying regression models, and stochastic volatility models. A general Gaussian linear state-space model assumes the form

$$\boldsymbol{s}_{t+1} = \boldsymbol{d}_t + \boldsymbol{T}_t\boldsymbol{s}_t + \boldsymbol{R}_t\boldsymbol{\eta}_t, \tag{11.24}$$

$$\boldsymbol{y}_t = \boldsymbol{c}_t + \boldsymbol{Z}_t\boldsymbol{s}_t + \boldsymbol{e}_t, \tag{11.25}$$

where $\boldsymbol{s}_t = (s_{1t}, \ldots, s_{mt})'$ is an m-dimensional state vector, $\boldsymbol{y}_t = (y_{1t}, \ldots, y_{kt})'$ is a k-dimensional observation vector, $\boldsymbol{d}_t$ and $\boldsymbol{c}_t$ are m- and k-dimensional deterministic vectors, $\boldsymbol{T}_t$ and $\boldsymbol{Z}_t$ are $m \times m$ and $k \times m$ coefficient matrices, $\boldsymbol{R}_t$ is an $m \times n$ matrix often consisting of a subset of columns of the $m \times m$ identity matrix, and $\{\boldsymbol{\eta}_t\}$ and $\{\boldsymbol{e}_t\}$ are n- and k-dimensional Gaussian white noise series such that

$$\boldsymbol{\eta}_t \sim N(\boldsymbol{0}, \boldsymbol{Q}_t), \quad \boldsymbol{e}_t \sim N(\boldsymbol{0}, \boldsymbol{H}_t),$$

where $\boldsymbol{Q}_t$ and $\boldsymbol{H}_t$ are positive-definite matrices. We assume that $\{\boldsymbol{e}_t\}$ and $\{\boldsymbol{\eta}_t\}$ are independent, but this condition can be relaxed if necessary. The initial state $\boldsymbol{s}_1$ is

$N(\boldsymbol{\mu}_{1|0}, \boldsymbol{\Sigma}_{1|0})$, where $\boldsymbol{\mu}_{1|0}$ and $\boldsymbol{\Sigma}_{1|0}$ are given, and is independent of $\boldsymbol{e}_t$ and $\boldsymbol{\eta}_t$ for $t > 0$.

Equation (11.25) is the *measurement* or *observation* equation that relates the vector of observations $\boldsymbol{y}_t$ to the state vector $\boldsymbol{s}_t$, the explanatory variable $\boldsymbol{c}_t$, and the measurement error $\boldsymbol{e}_t$. Equation (11.24) is the *state* or *transition* equation that describes a first-order Markov chain to govern the state transition with innovation $\boldsymbol{\eta}_t$. The matrices $\boldsymbol{T}_t$, $\boldsymbol{R}_t$, $\boldsymbol{Q}_t$, $\boldsymbol{Z}_t$, and $\boldsymbol{H}_t$ are known and referred to as *system matrices*. These matrices are often sparse, and they can be functions of some parameters $\boldsymbol{\theta}$, which can be estimated by the maximum likelihood method.

The state-space model in Eqs. (11.24) and (11.25) can be rewritten in a compact form as

$$\begin{bmatrix} \boldsymbol{s}_{t+1} \\ \boldsymbol{y}_t \end{bmatrix} = \boldsymbol{\delta}_t + \boldsymbol{\Phi}_t \boldsymbol{s}_t + \boldsymbol{u}_t, \tag{11.26}$$

where

$$\boldsymbol{\delta}_t = \begin{bmatrix} \boldsymbol{d}_t \\ \boldsymbol{c}_t \end{bmatrix}, \quad \boldsymbol{\Phi}_t = \begin{bmatrix} \boldsymbol{T}_t \\ \boldsymbol{Z}_t \end{bmatrix}, \quad \boldsymbol{u}_t = \begin{bmatrix} \boldsymbol{R}_t \boldsymbol{\eta}_t \\ \boldsymbol{e}_t \end{bmatrix},$$

and $\{\boldsymbol{u}_t\}$ is a sequence of Gaussian white noises with mean zero and covariance matrix

$$\boldsymbol{\Omega}_t = \mathrm{Cov}(\boldsymbol{u}_t) = \begin{bmatrix} \boldsymbol{R}_t \boldsymbol{Q}_t \boldsymbol{R}_t' & \boldsymbol{0} \\ \boldsymbol{0} & \boldsymbol{H}_t \end{bmatrix}.$$

The case of diffuse initialization is achieved by using

$$\boldsymbol{\Sigma}_{1|0} = \boldsymbol{\Sigma}_* + \lambda \boldsymbol{\Sigma}_\infty,$$

where $\boldsymbol{\Sigma}_*$ and $\boldsymbol{\Sigma}_\infty$ are $m \times m$ symmetric positive-definite matrices and λ is a large real number, which can approach infinity. In S-Plus and *SsfPack*, the notation

$$\boldsymbol{\Sigma} = \begin{bmatrix} \boldsymbol{\Sigma}_{1|0} \\ \boldsymbol{\mu}_{1|0}' \end{bmatrix}_{(m+1)\times m}$$

is used; see the notation in Table 11.1.

In many applications, the system matrices are time-invariant. However, these matrices can be time-varying, making the state-space model flexible.

11.3 MODEL TRANSFORMATION

To appreciate the flexibility of the state-space model, we rewrite some well-known econometric and financial models in state-space form.

11.3.1 CAPM with Time-Varying Coefficients

First, consider the capital asset pricing model (CAPM) with time-varying intercept and slope. The model is

$$
\begin{aligned}
r_t &= \alpha_t + \beta_t r_{M,t} + e_t, \quad e_t \sim N(0, \sigma_e^2), \\
\alpha_{t+1} &= \alpha_t + \eta_t, \quad \eta_t \sim N(0, \sigma_\eta^2), \\
\beta_{t+1} &= \beta_t + \epsilon_t, \quad \epsilon_t \sim N(0, \sigma_\epsilon^2),
\end{aligned}
\tag{11.27}
$$

where r_t is the excess return of an asset, $r_{M,t}$ is the excess return of the market, and the innovations $\{e_t, \eta_t, \epsilon_t\}$ are mutually independent. This CAPM allows for time-varying α and β that evolve as a random walk over time. We can easily rewrite the model as

$$
\begin{bmatrix} \alpha_{t+1} \\ \beta_{t+1} \end{bmatrix} = \begin{bmatrix} 1 & 0 \\ 0 & 1 \end{bmatrix} \begin{bmatrix} \alpha_t \\ \beta_t \end{bmatrix} + \begin{bmatrix} \eta_t \\ \epsilon_t \end{bmatrix},
$$

$$
r_t = [1, r_{M,t}] \begin{bmatrix} \alpha_t \\ \beta_t \end{bmatrix} + e_t.
$$

Thus, the time-varying CAPM is a special case of the state-space model with $\boldsymbol{s}_t = (\alpha_t, \beta_t)'$, $\boldsymbol{T}_t = \boldsymbol{R}_t = \boldsymbol{I}_2$, the 2×2 identity matrix, $\boldsymbol{d}_t = \boldsymbol{0}$, $c_t = 0$, $\boldsymbol{Z}_t = (1, r_{M,t})$, $\boldsymbol{H}_t = \sigma_e^2$, and $\boldsymbol{Q}_t = \text{diag}\{\sigma_\eta^2, \sigma_\epsilon^2\}$. Furthermore, in the form of Eq. (11.26), we have $\boldsymbol{\delta}_t = \boldsymbol{0}$, $\boldsymbol{u}_t = (\eta_t, \epsilon_t, e_t)'$,

$$
\boldsymbol{\Phi}_t = \begin{bmatrix} 1 & 0 \\ 0 & 1 \\ 1 & r_{M,t} \end{bmatrix}, \quad \boldsymbol{\Omega}_t = \begin{bmatrix} \sigma_\eta^2 & 0 & 0 \\ 0 & \sigma_\epsilon^2 & 0 \\ 0 & 0 & \sigma_e^2 \end{bmatrix}.
$$

If diffuse initialization is used, then

$$
\boldsymbol{\Sigma} = \begin{bmatrix} -1 & 0 \\ 0 & -1 \\ 0 & 0 \end{bmatrix}.
$$

SsfPack/S-Plus Specification of Time-Varying Models

For the CAPM in Eq. (11.27), $\boldsymbol{\Phi}_t$ contains $r_{M,t}$, which is time-varying. Some special input is required to specify such a model in *SsfPack*. Basically, it requires two additional variables: (a) a data matrix $\boldsymbol{X}$ that stores $\boldsymbol{Z}_t$ and (b) an index matrix for $\boldsymbol{\Phi}_t$ that identifies $\boldsymbol{Z}_t$ from the data matrix. The notation for index matrices of the state-space model in Eq. (11.26) is given in Table 11.3. Note that the matrix $\boldsymbol{J}_\Phi$ must have the same dimension as $\boldsymbol{\Phi}_t$. The elements of $\boldsymbol{J}_\Phi$ are all set to "-1" except the elements for which the corresponding elements of $\boldsymbol{\Phi}_t$ are time-varying. The non-negative index value of $\boldsymbol{J}_\Phi$ indicates the column of the data matrix $\boldsymbol{X}$, which contains the time-varying values.

Table 11.3. Notation and Name Used in *SsfPack*/S-Plus for Time-Varying State-Space Model

Index Matrix	Name Used in *SsfPack*/S-Plus
$\boldsymbol{J}_\delta$	`mJDelta`
$\boldsymbol{J}_\Phi$	`mJPhi`
$\boldsymbol{J}_\Omega$	`mJOmega`
Time-Varying Data Matrix	**Name Used in *SsfPack*/S-Plus**
$\boldsymbol{X}$	`mX`

To illustrate, consider the monthly simple excess returns of General Motors stock from January 1990 to December 2003 used in Chapter 9. The monthly simple excess return of the S&P 500 composite index is used as the market return. The specification of a time-varying CAPM requires values of the variances σ_η^2, σ_ϵ^2, and σ_e^2. Suppose that $(\sigma_\eta, \sigma_\epsilon, \sigma_e) = (0.02, 0.04, 0.1)$. The state-space specification for the CAPM under *SsfPack*/S-Plus is given below:

```
> X.mtx=cbind(1,sp) % Here 'sp' is the market excess returns.
> Phi.t = rbind(diag(2),rep(0,2))
> Sigma=-Phi.t
> sigma.eta=.02
> sigma.ep=.04
> sigma.e=.1
> Omega=diag(c(sigma.eta^2,sigma.ep^2,sigma.e^2))
> JPhi = matrix(-1,3,2) % Create a 3-by-2 matrix of -1.
> JPhi[3,1]=1
> JPhi[3,2]=2
> ssf.tv.capm=list(mPhi=Phi.t,
+ mOmega=Omega,
+ mJPhi=JPhi,
+ mSigma=Sigma,
+ mX=X.mtx)
> ssf.tv.capm
$mPhi:
     [,1] [,2]
[1,]    1    0
[2,]    0    1
[3,]    0    0
 $mOmega:
       [,1]   [,2] [,3]
[1,] 4e-04 0.0000 0.00
[2,] 0e+00 0.0016 0.00
[3,] 0e+00 0.0000 0.01
 $mJPhi:
     [,1] [,2]
```

```
[1,]   -1   -1
[2,]   -1   -1
[3,]    1    2
 $mSigma:
      [,1] [,2]
[1,]   -1    0
[2,]    0   -1
[3,]    0    0
 $mX:
numeric matrix: 168 rows, 2 columns.
                  sp
 [1,] 1 -0.075187
  ...
[168,] 1  0.05002
```

11.3.2 ARMA Models

Consider a zero-mean ARMA(p, q) process y_t of Chapter 2,

$$\phi(B)y_t = \theta(B)a_t, \quad a_t \sim N(0, \sigma_a^2), \tag{11.28}$$

where $\phi(B) = 1 - \sum_{i=1}^{p} \phi_i B^i$ and $\theta(B) = 1 - \sum_{j=1}^{q} \theta_j B^j$, and p and q are nonnegative integers. There are many ways to transform such an ARMA model into a state-space form. We discuss three methods available in the literature. Let $m = \max(p, q + 1)$ and rewrite the ARMA model in Eq. (11.28) as

$$y_t = \sum_{i=1}^{m} \phi_i y_{t-i} + a_t - \sum_{j=1}^{m-1} \theta_j a_{t-j}, \tag{11.29}$$

where $\phi_i = 0$ for $i > p$ and $\theta_j = 0$ for $j > q$. In particular, $\theta_m = 0$ because $m > q$.

Akaike's Approach

Akaike (1975) defines the state vector $\boldsymbol{s}_t$ as the minimum collection of variables that contains all the information needed to produce forecasts at the forecast origin t. It turns out that, for the ARMA process in Eq. (11.28) with $m = \max(p, q + 1)$, $\boldsymbol{s}_t = (y_{t|t}, y_{t+1|t}, \ldots, y_{t+m-1|t})'$, where $y_{t+j|t} = E(y_{t+j}|F_t)$ is the conditional expectation of y_{t+j} given $F_t = \{y_1, \ldots, y_t\}$. Since $y_{t|t} = y_t$, the first element of $\boldsymbol{s}_t$ is y_t. Thus, the observation equation is

$$y_t = \boldsymbol{Z}\boldsymbol{s}_t, \tag{11.30}$$

where $\boldsymbol{Z} = (1, 0, \ldots, 0)_{1\times m}$. We derive the transition equation in several steps. First, from the definition,

$$s_{1,t+1} = y_{t+1} = y_{t+1|t} + (y_{t+1} - y_{t+1|t}) = s_{2t} + a_{t+1}, \tag{11.31}$$

where s_{it} is the ith element of $\boldsymbol{s}_t$. Next, consider the MA representation of ARMA models given in Chapter 2. That is,

$$y_t = a_t + \psi_1 a_{t-1} + \psi_2 a_{t-2} + \cdots = \sum_{i=0}^{\infty} \psi_i a_{t-i},$$

where $\psi_0 = 1$ and other ψ-weights can be obtained by equating coefficients of B^i in $1 + \sum_{i=1}^{\infty} \psi_i B^i = \theta(B)/\phi(B)$. In particular, we have

$$\begin{aligned}
\psi_1 &= \phi_1 - \theta_1, \\
\psi_2 &= \phi_1\psi_1 + \phi_2 - \theta_2, \\
\vdots &= \vdots \\
\psi_{m-1} &= \phi_1\psi_{m-2} + \phi_2\psi_{m-3} + \cdots + \phi_{m-2}\psi_1 + \phi_{m-1} - \theta_{m-1} \\
&= \sum_{i=1}^{m-1} \phi_i \psi_{m-1-i} - \theta_{m-1}.
\end{aligned} \tag{11.32}$$

Using the MA representation, we have, for $j > 0$,

$$\begin{aligned}
y_{t+j|t} = E(y_{t+j}|F_t) &= E\left(\sum_{i=0}^{\infty} \psi_i a_{t+j-i}|F_t\right) \\
&= \psi_j a_t + \psi_{j+1} a_{t-1} + \psi_{j+2} a_{t-2} + \cdots
\end{aligned}$$

and

$$\begin{aligned}
y_{t+j|t+1} = E(y_{t+j}|F_{t+1}) &= \psi_{j-1} a_{t+1} + \psi_j a_t + \psi_{j+1} a_{t-1} + \cdots \\
&= \psi_{j-1} a_{t+1} + y_{t+j|t}.
\end{aligned}$$

Thus, for $j > 0$, we have

$$y_{t+j|t+1} = y_{t+j|t} + \psi_{j-1} a_{t+1}. \tag{11.33}$$

This result is referred to as the forecast updating formula of ARMA models. It provides a simple way to update the forecast from origin t to origin $t + 1$ when y_{t+1} becomes available. The new information of y_{t+1} is contained in the innovation a_{t+1}, and the time-t forecast is revised based on this new information with weight ψ_{j-1} to compute the time-$(t + 1)$ forecast.

Finally, from Eq. (11.29) and using $E(a_{t+j}|F_{t+1}) = 0$ for $j > 1$, we have

$$y_{t+m|t+1} = \sum_{i=1}^{m} \phi_i y_{t+m-i|t+1} - \theta_{m-1} a_{t+1}.$$

Taking Eq. (11.33), the prior equation becomes

$$\begin{aligned} y_{t+m|t+1} &= \sum_{i=1}^{m-1} \phi_i (y_{t+m-i|t} + \psi_{m-i-1} a_{t+1}) + \psi_m y_{t|t} - \theta_{m-1} a_{t+1} \\ &= \sum_{i=1}^{m} \phi_i y_{t+m-i|t} + \left(\sum_{i=1}^{m-1} \phi_i \psi_{m-1-i} - \theta_{m-1} \right) a_{t+1} \\ &= \sum_{i=1}^{m} \phi_i y_{t+m-i|t} + \psi_{m-1} a_{t+1}, \end{aligned} \tag{11.34}$$

where the last equality uses Eq. (11.32). Combining Eqs. (11.31), (11.33) for $j = 2, \ldots, m-1$, and (11.34) together, we have

$$\begin{bmatrix} y_{t+1} \\ y_{t+2|t+1} \\ \vdots \\ y_{t+m-1|t+1} \\ y_{t+m|t+1} \end{bmatrix} = \begin{bmatrix} 0 & 1 & 0 & \cdot & 0 \\ 0 & 0 & 1 & & 0 \\ \vdots & & & & \vdots \\ 0 & 0 & 0 & \cdot & 1 \\ \phi_m & \phi_{m-1} & \phi_{m-2} & \cdot & \phi_1 \end{bmatrix} \begin{bmatrix} y_t \\ y_{t+1|t} \\ \vdots \\ y_{t+m-2|t} \\ y_{t+m-1|t} \end{bmatrix} + \begin{bmatrix} 1 \\ \psi_1 \\ \vdots \\ \psi_{m-2} \\ \psi_{m-1} \end{bmatrix} a_{t+1}. \tag{11.35}$$

Thus, the transition equation of Akaike's approach is

$$\boldsymbol{s}_{t+1} = \boldsymbol{T} \boldsymbol{s}_t + \boldsymbol{R} \eta_t, \quad \eta_t \sim N(0, \sigma_a^2), \tag{11.36}$$

where $\eta_t = a_{t+1}$, and $\boldsymbol{T}$ and $\boldsymbol{R}$ are the coefficient matrices in Eq. (11.35).

Harvey's Approach

Harvey (1993, Section 4.4) provides a state-space form with an m-dimensional state vector $\boldsymbol{s}_t$, the first element of which is y_t, that is, $s_{1t} = y_t$. The other elements of $\boldsymbol{s}_t$ are obtained recursively. From the ARMA$(m, m-1)$ model, we have

$$\begin{aligned} y_{t+1} &= \phi_1 y_t + \sum_{i=2}^{m} \phi_i y_{t+1-i} - \sum_{j=1}^{m-1} \theta_j a_{t+1-j} + a_{t+1} \\ &\equiv \phi_1 s_{1t} + s_{2t} + \eta_t, \end{aligned}$$

where $s_{2t} = \sum_{i=2}^{m} \phi_i y_{t+1-i} - \sum_{j=1}^{m-1} \theta_j a_{t+1-j}$, $\eta_t = a_{t+1}$, and as defined earlier $s_{1t} = y_t$. Focusing on $s_{2,t+1}$, we have

$$\begin{aligned} s_{2,t+1} &= \sum_{i=2}^{m} \phi_i y_{t+2-i} - \sum_{j=1}^{m-1} \theta_j a_{t+2-j} \\ &= \phi_2 y_t + \sum_{i=3}^{m} \phi_i y_{t+2-i} - \sum_{j=2}^{m-1} \theta_j a_{t+2-j} - \theta_1 a_{t+1} \\ &\equiv \phi_2 s_{1t} + s_{3t} + (-\theta_1) \eta_t, \end{aligned}$$

where $s_{3t} = \sum_{i=3}^{m} \phi_i y_{t+2-i} - \sum_{j=2}^{m-1} \theta_j a_{t+2-j}$. Next, considering $s_{3,t+1}$, we have

$$
\begin{aligned}
s_{3,t+1} &= \sum_{i=3}^{m} \phi_i y_{t+3-i} - \sum_{j=2}^{m-1} \theta_j a_{t+3-j} \\
&= \phi_3 y_t + \sum_{i=4}^{m} \phi_i y_{t+3-i} - \sum_{j=3}^{m-1} \theta_j a_{t+3-j} + (-\theta_2) a_{t+1} \\
&\equiv \phi_3 s_{1t} + s_{4t} + (-\theta_2)\eta_t,
\end{aligned}
$$

where $s_{4t} = \sum_{i=4}^{m} \phi_i y_{t+3-i} - \sum_{j=3}^{m-1} \theta_j a_{t+3-j}$. Repeating the procedure, we have $s_{mt} = \sum_{i=m}^{m} \phi_i y_{t+m-1-i} - \sum_{j=m-1}^{m-1} \theta_j a_{t+m-1-j} = \phi_m y_{t-1} - \theta_{m-1} a_t$. Finally,

$$
\begin{aligned}
s_{m,t+1} &= \phi_m y_t - \theta_{m-1} a_{t+1} \\
&= \phi_m s_{1t} + (-\theta_{m-1})\eta_t.
\end{aligned}
$$

Putting the prior equations together, we have a state-space form

$$
\boldsymbol{s}_{t+1} = \boldsymbol{T}\boldsymbol{s}_t + \boldsymbol{R}\eta_t, \quad \eta_t \sim N(0, \sigma_a^2), \tag{11.37}
$$

$$
y_t = \boldsymbol{Z}\boldsymbol{s}_t, \tag{11.38}
$$

where the system matrices are time-invariant defined as $\boldsymbol{Z} = (1, 0, \ldots, 0)_{1\times m}$,

$$
\boldsymbol{T} = \begin{bmatrix} \phi_1 & 1 & 0 & \cdots & 0 \\ \phi_2 & 0 & 1 & & 0 \\ \vdots & & & & \vdots \\ \phi_{m-1} & 0 & 0 & \cdots & 1 \\ \phi_m & 0 & 0 & \cdots & 0 \end{bmatrix}, \quad \boldsymbol{R} = \begin{bmatrix} 1 \\ -\theta_1 \\ \vdots \\ -\theta_{m-1} \end{bmatrix},
$$

and $\boldsymbol{d}_t$, $\boldsymbol{c}_t$, and $\boldsymbol{H}_t$ are all zero. The model in Eqs. (11.37) and (11.38) has no measurement errors. It has an advantage that the AR and MA coefficients are directly used in the system matrices.

Aoki's Approach

Aoki (1987, Chapter 4) discusses several ways to convert an ARMA model into a state-space form. First, consider the MA model, that is, $y_t = \theta(B)a_t$. In this case, we can simply define $\boldsymbol{s}_t = (a_{t-q}, a_{t-q+2}, \ldots, a_{t-1})'$ and obtain the state-space form

$$
\begin{bmatrix} a_{t-q+1} \\ a_{t-q+2} \\ \vdots \\ a_{t-1} \\ a_t \end{bmatrix} = \begin{bmatrix} 0 & 1 & 0 & \cdots & 0 \\ 0 & 0 & 1 & & 0 \\ \vdots & & & & \vdots \\ 0 & 0 & 0 & & 1 \\ 0 & 0 & 0 & \cdots & 0 \end{bmatrix} \begin{bmatrix} a_{t-q} \\ a_{t-q+1} \\ \vdots \\ a_{t-2} \\ a_{t-1} \end{bmatrix} + \begin{bmatrix} 0 \\ 0 \\ \vdots \\ 0 \\ 1 \end{bmatrix} a_t,
$$

$$
y_t = (-\theta_q, -\theta_{q-1}, \ldots, -\theta_1)\boldsymbol{s}_t + a_t, \tag{11.39}
$$

Note that, in this particular case, a_t appears in both state and measurement equations.

Next, consider the AR model, that is, $\phi(B)z_t = a_t$. Aoki (1987) introduces two methods. The first method is a straightforward one by defining $\boldsymbol{s}_t = (z_{t-p+1}, \ldots, z_t)'$ to obtain

$$\begin{bmatrix} z_{t-p+2} \\ z_{t-p+3} \\ \vdots \\ z_{t+2} \\ z_{t+1} \end{bmatrix} = \begin{bmatrix} 0 & 1 & 0 & \cdots & 0 \\ 0 & 0 & 1 & & 0 \\ \vdots & & & & \vdots \\ 0 & 0 & 0 & & 1 \\ \phi_p & \phi_{p-1} & \phi_{p-2} & \cdots & \phi_1 \end{bmatrix} \begin{bmatrix} z_{t-p+1} \\ z_{t-p+2} \\ \vdots \\ z_{t+1} \\ z_t \end{bmatrix} + \begin{bmatrix} 0 \\ 0 \\ \vdots \\ 0 \\ 1 \end{bmatrix} a_{t+1},$$

$$z_t = (0, 0, \cdots, 0, 1)\boldsymbol{s}_t. \tag{11.40}$$

The second method defines the state vector in the same way as the first method except that a_t is removed from the last element; that is, $\boldsymbol{s}_t = z_t - a_t$ if $p = 1$ and $\boldsymbol{s}_t = (z_{t-p+1}, \ldots, z_{t-1}, z_t - a_t)'$ if $p > 1$. Simple algebra shows that

$$\begin{bmatrix} z_{t-p+2} \\ z_{t-p+3} \\ \vdots \\ z_t \\ z_{t+1} - a_{t+1} \end{bmatrix} = \begin{bmatrix} 0 & 1 & 0 & \cdot & 0 \\ 0 & 0 & 1 & & 0 \\ \vdots & & & & \vdots \\ 0 & 0 & 0 & & 1 \\ \phi_p & \phi_{p-1} & \phi_{p-2} & \cdot & \phi_1 \end{bmatrix} \begin{bmatrix} z_{t-p+1} \\ z_{t-p+2} \\ \vdots \\ z_{t-1} \\ z_t - a_t \end{bmatrix} + \begin{bmatrix} 0 \\ 0 \\ \vdots \\ 1 \\ \phi_1 \end{bmatrix} a_t,$$

$$z_t = (0, 0, \ldots, 0, 1)\boldsymbol{s}_t + a_t. \tag{11.41}$$

Again, a_t appears in both transition and measurement equations.

Turn to the ARMA(p, q) model $\phi(B)y_t = \theta(B)a_t$. For simplicity, we assume $q < p$ and introduce an auxiliary variable $z_t = [1/\phi(B)]a_t$. Then, we have

$$\phi(B)z_t = a_t, \quad y_t = \theta(B)z_t.$$

Since z_t is an AR(p) model, we can use the transition equation in Eq. (11.40) or Eq. (11.41). If Eq. (11.40) is used, we can use $y_t = \theta(B)z_t$ to construct the measurement equation as

$$y_t = (-\theta_{p-1}, -\theta_{p-2}, \ldots, -\theta_1, 1)\boldsymbol{s}_t, \tag{11.42}$$

where it is understood that $p > q$ and $\theta_j = 0$ for $j > q$. On the other hand, if Eq. (11.41) is used as the transition equation, we construct the measurement equation as

$$y_t = (-\theta_{p-1}, -\theta_{p-2}, \ldots, -\theta_1, 1)\boldsymbol{s}_t + a_t. \tag{11.43}$$

In summary, there are many state-space representations for an ARMA model. Each representation has its pros and cons. For estimation and forecasting purposes, one can choose any one of those representations. On the other hand, for a time-invariant coefficient state-space model in Eqs. (11.24) and (11.25), one can use the Cayley–Hamilton theorem to show that the observation y_t follows an ARMA(m, m) model, where m is the dimension of the state vector.

SsfPack Command

In *SsfPack*/S-Plus, a command `GetSsfArma` can be used to transform an ARMA model into a state-space form. Harvey's approach is used. To illustrate, consider the AR(1) model

$$y_t = 0.6y_{t-1} + a_t, \quad a_t \sim N(0, 0.4^2).$$

The state-space form of the model is

```
> ssf.ar1 = GetSsfArma(ar=0.6,sigma=0.4)
> ssf.ar1
$mPhi:
      [,1]
[1,]   0.6
[2,]   1.0
$mOmega:
      [,1] [,2]
[1,] 0.16    0
[2,] 0.00    0
$mSigma:
      [,1]
[1,] 0.25
[2,] 0.00
```

Since the AR(1) model is stationary, the program uses $\boldsymbol{\Sigma}_{1|0} = \text{Var}(y_t) = (0.4)^2/(1 - 0.6^2) = 0.25$ and $\boldsymbol{\mu}_{1|0} = 0$. These values appear in the matrix `mSigma`.

As a second example, consider the ARMA(2,1) model

$$y_t = 1.2y_{t-1} - 0.35y_{t-2} + a_t - 0.25a_{t-1}, \quad a_t \sim N(0, 1.1^2).$$

The state-space form of the model is

```
> arma21.m = list(ar=c(1.2,-0.35),ma=c(-0.25),sigma=1.1)
> ssf.arma21= GetSsfArma(model=arma21.m)
> ssf.arma21
$mPhi:
      [,1] [,2]
[1,]  1.20    1
[2,] -0.35    0
[3,]  1.00    0
$mOmega:
        [,1]      [,2] [,3]
[1,]  1.2100 -0.302500    0
[2,] -0.3025  0.075625    0
[3,]  0.0000  0.000000    0
$mSigma:
           [,1]       [,2]
```

```
[1,]  4.060709 -1.4874057
[2,] -1.487406  0.5730618
[3,]  0.000000  0.0000000
```

As expected, the output shows that

$$T = \begin{bmatrix} 1.2 & 1 \\ -0.35 & 0 \end{bmatrix}, \qquad Z = (1, 0),$$

and mPhi and mOmega follow the format of Eq. (11.26), and the covariance matrix of $(y_t, y_{t-1})'$ is used in mSigma. Note that in *SsfPack*, the MA polynomial of an ARMA model assumes the form $\theta(B) = 1 + \theta_1 B + \cdots + \theta_q B^q$, not the form $\theta(B) = 1 - \theta_1 B - \cdots - \theta_q B^q$ commonly used in the literature.

11.3.3 Linear Regression Model

Multiple linear regression models can also be represented in state-space form. Consider the model

$$y_t = \boldsymbol{x}_t' \boldsymbol{\beta} + e_t, \qquad e_t \sim N(0, \sigma_e^2),$$

where $\boldsymbol{x}_t$ is a p-dimensional explanatory variable and $\boldsymbol{\beta}$ is a p-dimensional parameter vector. Let $\boldsymbol{s}_t = \boldsymbol{\beta}$ for all t. Then the model can be written as

$$\begin{bmatrix} \boldsymbol{s}_{t+1} \\ y_t \end{bmatrix} = \begin{bmatrix} \boldsymbol{I}_p \\ \boldsymbol{x}_t' \end{bmatrix} \boldsymbol{s}_t + \begin{bmatrix} \boldsymbol{0}_p \\ e_t \end{bmatrix}. \tag{11.44}$$

Thus, the system matrices are $\boldsymbol{T}_t = \boldsymbol{I}_p$, $\boldsymbol{Z}_t = \boldsymbol{x}_t'$, $\boldsymbol{d}_t = \boldsymbol{0}$, $c_t = 0$, $\boldsymbol{H}_t = \boldsymbol{0}$, and $\boldsymbol{Q}_t = \sigma_e^2$. Since the state vector is fixed, a diffuse initialization should be used.

One can extend the regression model so that $\boldsymbol{\beta}_t$ is random, say,

$$\boldsymbol{\beta}_{t+1} = \boldsymbol{\beta}_t + \boldsymbol{R}_t \eta_t, \qquad \eta_t \sim N(0, 1),$$

and $\boldsymbol{R}_t = (\sigma_1, \ldots, \sigma_p)'$ with $\sigma_i \geq 0$. If $\sigma_i = 0$, then β_i is time-invariant.

SsfPack Command

In *SsfPack*, the command GetSsfReg creates a state-space form for the multiple linear regression model. The command has an input argument that contains the data matrix of explanatory variables. To illustrate, consider the simple market model

$$r_t = \beta_0 + \beta_1 r_{M,t} + e_t, \qquad t = 1, \ldots, 168,$$

where r_t is the return of an asset and $r_{M,t}$ is the market return, for example, the S&P 500 composite index return. The state-space form can be obtained as

```
> ssf.reg=GetSsfReg(cbind(1,sp))  % 'sp' is market return.
> ssf.reg
$mPhi:
     [,1] [,2]
[1,]    1    0
[2,]    0    1
[3,]    0    0
$mOmega:
     [,1] [,2] [,3]
[1,]    0    0    0
[2,]    0    0    0
[3,]    0    0    1
$mSigma:
     [,1] [,2]
[1,]   -1    0
[2,]    0   -1
[3,]    0    0
$mJPhi:
     [,1] [,2]
[1,]   -1   -1
[2,]   -1   -1
[3,]    1    2
$mX:
numeric matrix: 168 rows, 2 columns.
                 sp
 [1,] 1 -0.075187
...
[168,] 1  0.05002
```

11.3.4 Linear Regression Models with ARMA Errors

Consider the regression model with ARMA(p, q) errors,

$$y_t = \boldsymbol{x}_t'\boldsymbol{\beta} + z_t, \quad \phi(B)z_t = \theta(B)a_t, \tag{11.45}$$

where $a_t \sim N(0, \sigma_a^2)$ and $\boldsymbol{x}_t$ is a k-dimensional vector of explanatory variables. A special case of this model is the nonzero mean ARMA(p, q) model in which $\boldsymbol{x}_t = 1$ for all t and $\boldsymbol{\beta}$ becomes a scalar parameter. Let $\boldsymbol{s}_t$ be a state vector for the z_t series, for example, that defined in Eq. (11.37). We can define a state vector $\boldsymbol{s}_t^*$ for y_t as

$$\boldsymbol{s}_t^* = \begin{bmatrix} \boldsymbol{s}_t \\ \boldsymbol{\beta}_t \end{bmatrix}, \tag{11.46}$$

where $\boldsymbol{\beta}_t = \boldsymbol{\beta}$ for all t. Then, a state-space form for y_t is

$$\boldsymbol{s}_{t+1}^* = \boldsymbol{T}^*\boldsymbol{s}_t^* + \boldsymbol{R}^*\eta_t, \tag{11.47}$$

$$y_t = \boldsymbol{Z}_t^*\boldsymbol{s}_t^*, \tag{11.48}$$

where $\boldsymbol{Z}_t^* = (1, 0, \ldots, 0, \boldsymbol{x}_t')_{1\times(m+k)}$, $m = \max(p, q+1)$, and

$$\boldsymbol{T}^* = \begin{bmatrix} \boldsymbol{T} & \boldsymbol{0} \\ \boldsymbol{0} & \boldsymbol{I}_k \end{bmatrix}, \quad \boldsymbol{R}^* = \begin{bmatrix} \boldsymbol{R} \\ \boldsymbol{0} \end{bmatrix},$$

where $\boldsymbol{T}$ and $\boldsymbol{R}$ are defined in Eq. (11.37). In a compact form, we have the state-space model

$$\begin{bmatrix} \boldsymbol{s}_{t+1}^* \\ y_t \end{bmatrix} = \begin{bmatrix} \boldsymbol{T}^* \\ \boldsymbol{Z}_t^* \end{bmatrix} \boldsymbol{s}_t^* + \begin{bmatrix} \boldsymbol{R}^*\eta_t \\ 0 \end{bmatrix}.$$

SsfPack Command

SsfPack uses the command `GetSsfRegArma` to construct a state-space form for linear regression models with ARMA errors. The arguments of the command can be found using the command `args(GetSsfRegArma)`. They consist of a data matrix for the explanatory variables and ARMA model specification. To illustrate, consider the model

$$y_t = \beta_0 + \beta_1 x_t + z_t, \quad t = 1, \ldots, 168,$$

$$z_t = 1.2z_{t-1} - 0.35z_{t-2} + a_t - 0.25a_{t-1}, \quad a_t \sim N(0, \sigma_a^2).$$

We use the notation `X` to denote the $T \times 2$ matrix of regressors $(1, x_t)$. A state-space form for the prior model can be obtained as

```
> ssf.reg.arma21=GetSsfRegArma(X,ar=c(1.2,-0.35),
+ ma=c(-0.25))
> ssf.reg.arma21
$mPhi:
      [,1] [,2] [,3] [,4]
[1,]  1.20    1    0    0
[2,] -0.35    0    0    0
[3,]  0.00    0    1    0
[4,]  0.00    0    0    1
[5,]  1.00    0    0    0
$mOmega:
      [,1]    [,2] [,3] [,4] [,5]
[1,]  1.00 -0.2500    0    0    0
[2,] -0.25  0.0625    0    0    0
[3,]  0.00  0.0000    0    0    0
[4,]  0.00  0.0000    0    0    0
[5,]  0.00  0.0000    0    0    0
$mSigma:
         [,1]      [,2] [,3] [,4]
[1,]  3.35595 -1.229260    0    0
[2,] -1.22926  0.473604    0    0
[3,]  0.00000  0.000000   -1    0
[4,]  0.00000  0.000000    0   -1
```

```
[5,]  0.00000  0.000000    0    0
$mJPhi:
      [,1] [,2] [,3] [,4]
[1,]    -1   -1   -1   -1
[2,]    -1   -1   -1   -1
[3,]    -1   -1   -1   -1
[4,]    -1   -1   -1   -1
[5,]    -1   -1    1    2
$mX:
numeric matrix: 168 rows, 2 columns.
             xt
  [1,] 1 0.4993
...
[168,] 1 0.7561
```

11.3.5 Scalar Unobserved Component Model

The basic univariate unobserved component model, or the *structural time series model* (STSM), assumes the form

$$y_t = \mu_t + \gamma_t + \varpi_t + e_t, \tag{11.49}$$

where μ_t, γ_t, and ϖ_t represent the unobserved *trend, seasonal*, and *cycle* components, respectively, and e_t is the unobserved *irregular* component. In the literature, a nonstationary (possibly double-unit-root) model is commonly used for the trend component:

$$\begin{aligned} \mu_{t+1} &= \mu_t + \beta_t + \eta_t, \quad \eta_t \sim N(0, \sigma_\eta^2), \\ \beta_t &= \beta_{t-1} + \varsigma_t, \quad \varsigma_t \sim N(0, \sigma_\varsigma^2), \end{aligned} \tag{11.50}$$

where $\mu_1 \sim N(0, \xi)$ and $\beta_1 \sim N(0, \xi)$ with ξ a large real number, for example, $\xi = 10^8$. See, for instance, Kitagawa and Gersch (1996). If $\sigma_\varsigma = 0$, then μ_t follows a random walk with drift β_1. If $\sigma_\varsigma = \sigma_\eta = 0$, then μ_t represents a linear deterministic trend.

The seasonal component γ_t assumes the form

$$(1 + B + \cdots + B^{s-1})\gamma_t = \omega_t, \quad \omega_t \sim N(0, \sigma_\omega^2), \tag{11.51}$$

where s is the number of seasons in a year, that is, the period of the seasonality. If $\sigma_\omega = 0$, then the seasonal pattern is deterministic. The cycle component is postulated as

$$\begin{bmatrix} \varpi_{t+1} \\ \varpi_{t+1}^* \end{bmatrix} = \delta \begin{bmatrix} \cos(\lambda_c) & \sin(\lambda_c) \\ -\sin(\lambda_c) & \cos(\lambda_c) \end{bmatrix} \begin{bmatrix} \varpi_t \\ \varpi_t^* \end{bmatrix} + \begin{bmatrix} \varepsilon_t \\ \varepsilon_t^* \end{bmatrix}, \tag{11.52}$$

Table 11.4. Arguments of the Command `GetSsfStsm` in *SsfPack*/S-Plus

Argument	STSM Parameter
`irregular`	σ_e
`level`	σ_η
`slope`	σ_ς
`seasonalDummy`	σ_ω, s
`seasonalTrig`	σ_ω, s
`seasonalHS`	σ_ω, s
`Cycle0`	σ_ε, λ_c, δ
⋮	⋮
`Cycle9`	σ_ε, λ_c, δ

where

$$\begin{bmatrix} \varepsilon_t \\ \varepsilon_t^* \end{bmatrix} \sim N\left(\begin{bmatrix} 0 \\ 0 \end{bmatrix}, \sigma_\varepsilon^2(1-\delta^2)\boldsymbol{I}_2\right),$$

$\varpi_0 \sim N(0, \sigma_\varepsilon^2)$, $\varpi_0^* \sim N(0, \sigma_\varepsilon^2)$, and $\mathrm{Cov}(\varpi_0, \varpi_0^*) = 0$, $\delta \in (0, 1]$ is called a *damping* factor, and the frequency of the cycle is $\lambda_c = 2\pi/q$ with q being the period. If $\delta = 1$, then the cycle becomes a deterministic sine–cosine wave.

SsfPack/S-Plus Command

The command `GetSsfStsm` constructs a state-space form for the structural time series model. It allows for 10 cycle components; see the output of the command `args(GetSsfStsm)`. Table 11.4 provides a summary of the arguments and their corresponding symbols of the model. To illustrate, consider the local trend model in Eqs. (11.1) and (11.2) with $\sigma_e = 0.4$ and $\sigma_\eta = 0.2$. This is a special case of the scalar unobserved component model. One can obtain a state-space form as

```
> ssf.stsm=GetSsfStsm(irregular=0.4,level=0.2)
> ssf.stsm
$mPhi:
     [,1]
[1,]    1
[2,]    1
$mOmega:
     [,1] [,2]
[1,] 0.04 0.00
[2,] 0.00 0.16
$mSigma:
     [,1]
[1,]   -1
[2,]    0
```

11.4 KALMAN FILTER AND SMOOTHING

In this section, we study the Kalman filter and various smoothing methods for the general state-space model in Eqs. (11.24) and (11.25). The derivation follows closely the steps taken in Section 11.1. For readers interested in applications, this section can be skipped at the first read. A good reference for this section is Durbin and Koopman (2001, Chapter 4).

11.4.1 Kalman Filter

Recall that the aim of the Kalman filter is to obtain recursively the conditional distribution of $\boldsymbol{s}_{t+1}$ given the data $F_t = \{\boldsymbol{y}_1, \ldots, \boldsymbol{y}_t\}$ and the model. Since the conditional distribution involved is normal, it suffices to study the conditional mean and covariance matrix. Let $\boldsymbol{s}_{j|i}$ and $\boldsymbol{\Sigma}_{j|i}$ be the conditional mean and covariance matrix of $\boldsymbol{s}_j$ given F_i, that is, $\boldsymbol{s}_j|F_i \sim N(\boldsymbol{s}_{j|i}, \boldsymbol{\Sigma}_{j|i})$. From Eq. (11.24),

$$\boldsymbol{s}_{t+1|t} = E(\boldsymbol{d}_t + \boldsymbol{T}_t\boldsymbol{s}_t + \boldsymbol{R}_t\boldsymbol{\eta}_t|F_t) = \boldsymbol{d}_t + \boldsymbol{T}_t\boldsymbol{s}_{t|t}, \tag{11.53}$$

$$\boldsymbol{\Sigma}_{t+1|t} = \text{Var}(\boldsymbol{T}_t\boldsymbol{s}_t + \boldsymbol{R}_t\boldsymbol{\eta}_t|F_t) = \boldsymbol{T}_t\boldsymbol{\Sigma}_{t|t}\boldsymbol{T}_t' + \boldsymbol{R}_t\boldsymbol{Q}_t\boldsymbol{R}_t'. \tag{11.54}$$

Similarly to that of Section 11.1, let $\boldsymbol{y}_{t|t-1}$ be the conditional mean of y_t given F_{t-1}. From Eq. (11.25),

$$\boldsymbol{y}_{t|t-1} = \boldsymbol{c}_t + \boldsymbol{Z}_t\boldsymbol{s}_{t|t-1}.$$

Let

$$\boldsymbol{v}_t = \boldsymbol{y}_t - \boldsymbol{y}_{t|t-1} = \boldsymbol{y}_t - (\boldsymbol{c}_t + \boldsymbol{Z}_t\boldsymbol{s}_{t|t-1}) = \boldsymbol{Z}_t(\boldsymbol{s}_t - \boldsymbol{s}_{t|t-1}) + \boldsymbol{e}_t, \tag{11.55}$$

be the 1-step ahead forecast error of $\boldsymbol{y}_t$ given F_{t-1}. It is easy to see that (a) $E(\boldsymbol{v}_t|F_{t-1}) = \boldsymbol{0}$; (b) $\boldsymbol{v}_t$ is independent of F_{t-1}, that is, $\text{Cov}(\boldsymbol{v}_t, \boldsymbol{y}_j) = \boldsymbol{0}$ for $1 \le j < t$; and (c) $\{\boldsymbol{v}_t\}$ is a sequence of independent normal random vectors. Also, let $\boldsymbol{V}_t = \text{Var}(\boldsymbol{v}_t|F_{t-1}) = \text{Var}(\boldsymbol{v}_t)$ be the covariance matrix of the 1-step ahead forecast error. From Eq. (11.55), we have

$$\boldsymbol{V}_t = \text{Var}[\boldsymbol{Z}_t(\boldsymbol{s}_t - \boldsymbol{s}_{t|t-1}) + \boldsymbol{e}_t] = \boldsymbol{Z}_t\boldsymbol{\Sigma}_{t|t-1}\boldsymbol{Z}_t' + \boldsymbol{H}_t. \tag{11.56}$$

Since $F_t = \{F_{t-1}, \boldsymbol{y}_t\} = \{F_{t-1}, \boldsymbol{v}_t\}$, we can apply Theorem 11.1 to obtain

$$\begin{aligned}
\boldsymbol{s}_{t|t} &= E(\boldsymbol{s}_t|F_t) = E(\boldsymbol{s}_t|F_{t-1}, \boldsymbol{v}_t) \\
&= E(\boldsymbol{s}_t|F_{t-1}) + \text{Cov}(\boldsymbol{s}_t, \boldsymbol{v}_t)[\text{Var}(\boldsymbol{v}_t)]^{-1}\boldsymbol{v}_t \\
&= \boldsymbol{s}_{t|t-1} + \boldsymbol{C}_t\boldsymbol{V}_t^{-1}\boldsymbol{v}_t,
\end{aligned} \tag{11.57}$$

where $\boldsymbol{C}_t = \text{Cov}(\boldsymbol{s}_t, \boldsymbol{v}_t|F_{t-1})$ given by

$$\begin{aligned}
\boldsymbol{C}_t &= \text{Cov}(\boldsymbol{s}_t, \boldsymbol{v}_t|F_{t-1}) = \text{Cov}[\boldsymbol{s}_t, \boldsymbol{Z}_t(\boldsymbol{s}_t - \boldsymbol{s}_{t|t-1}) + \boldsymbol{e}_t|F_{t-1}] \\
&= \text{Cov}[\boldsymbol{s}_t, \boldsymbol{Z}_t(\boldsymbol{s}_t - \boldsymbol{s}_{t|t-1})|F_{t-1}] = \boldsymbol{\Sigma}_{t|t-1}\boldsymbol{Z}_t'.
\end{aligned}$$

Here we assume that $\boldsymbol{V}_t$ is invertible, because $\boldsymbol{H}_t$ is. Using Eqs. (11.53) and (11.57), we obtain

$$\boldsymbol{s}_{t+1|t} = \boldsymbol{d}_t + \boldsymbol{T}_t\boldsymbol{s}_{t|t-1} + \boldsymbol{T}_t\boldsymbol{C}_t\boldsymbol{V}_t^{-1}\boldsymbol{v}_t = \boldsymbol{d}_t + \boldsymbol{T}_t\boldsymbol{s}_{t|t-1} + \boldsymbol{K}_t\boldsymbol{v}_t, \tag{11.58}$$

where

$$\boldsymbol{K}_t = \boldsymbol{T}_t\boldsymbol{C}_t\boldsymbol{V}_t^{-1} = \boldsymbol{T}_t\boldsymbol{\Sigma}_{t|t-1}\boldsymbol{Z}_t'\boldsymbol{V}_t^{-1}, \tag{11.59}$$

which is the *Kalman gain* at time t. Applying Theorem 11.1(2), we have

$$\begin{aligned}\boldsymbol{\Sigma}_{t|t} &= \text{Var}(\boldsymbol{s}_t|F_{t-1})\\ &= \text{Var}(\boldsymbol{s}_t|F_{t-1}) - \text{Cov}(\boldsymbol{s}_t, \boldsymbol{v}_t)[\text{Var}(\boldsymbol{v}_t)]^{-1}\text{Cov}(\boldsymbol{s}_t, \boldsymbol{v}_t)'\\ &= \boldsymbol{\Sigma}_{t|t-1} - \boldsymbol{C}_t\boldsymbol{V}_t^{-1}\boldsymbol{C}_t'\\ &= \boldsymbol{\Sigma}_{t|t-1} - \boldsymbol{\Sigma}_{t|t-1}\boldsymbol{Z}_t'\boldsymbol{V}_t^{-1}\boldsymbol{Z}_t\boldsymbol{\Sigma}_{t|t-1}.\end{aligned} \tag{11.60}$$

Plugging Eq. (11.60) into Eq. (11.54) and using Eq. (11.59), we obtain

$$\boldsymbol{\Sigma}_{t+1|t} = \boldsymbol{T}_t\boldsymbol{\Sigma}_{t|t-1}\boldsymbol{L}_t' + \boldsymbol{R}_t\boldsymbol{Q}_t\boldsymbol{R}_t', \tag{11.61}$$

where

$$\boldsymbol{L}_t = \boldsymbol{T}_t - \boldsymbol{K}_t\boldsymbol{Z}_t.$$

Putting the prior equations together, we obtain the celebrated Kalman filter for the state-space model in Eqs. (11.24) and (11.25). Given the starting values $\boldsymbol{s}_{1|0}$ and $\boldsymbol{\Sigma}_{1|0}$, the Kalman filter algorithm is

$$\begin{aligned}\boldsymbol{v}_t &= \boldsymbol{y}_t - \boldsymbol{c}_t - \boldsymbol{Z}_t\boldsymbol{s}_{t|t-1},\\ \boldsymbol{V}_t &= \boldsymbol{Z}_t\boldsymbol{\Sigma}_{t|t-1}\boldsymbol{Z}_t' + \boldsymbol{H}_t,\\ \boldsymbol{K}_t &= \boldsymbol{T}_t\boldsymbol{\Sigma}_{t|t-1}\boldsymbol{Z}_t'\boldsymbol{V}_t^{-1},\\ \boldsymbol{L}_t &= \boldsymbol{T}_t - \boldsymbol{K}_t\boldsymbol{Z}_t,\\ \boldsymbol{s}_{t+1|t} &= \boldsymbol{d}_t + \boldsymbol{T}_t\boldsymbol{s}_{t|t-1} + \boldsymbol{K}_t\boldsymbol{v}_t,\\ \boldsymbol{\Sigma}_{t+1|t} &= \boldsymbol{T}_t\boldsymbol{\Sigma}_{t|t-1}\boldsymbol{L}_t' + \boldsymbol{R}_t\boldsymbol{Q}_t\boldsymbol{R}_t', \quad t = 1, \ldots, T.\end{aligned} \tag{11.62}$$

If the filtered quantities $\boldsymbol{s}_{t|t}$ and $\boldsymbol{\Sigma}_{t|t}$ are also of interest, then we modify the filter to include the contemporaneous filtering equations in Eqs. (11.57) and (11.60). The resulting algorithm is

$$\begin{aligned}\boldsymbol{v}_t &= \boldsymbol{y}_t - \boldsymbol{c}_t - \boldsymbol{Z}_t\boldsymbol{s}_{t|t-1},\\ \boldsymbol{C}_t &= \boldsymbol{\Sigma}_{t|t-1}\boldsymbol{Z}_t',\end{aligned}$$

$$\begin{aligned}
\boldsymbol{V}_t &= \boldsymbol{Z}_t \boldsymbol{\Sigma}_{t|t-1} \boldsymbol{Z}_t' + \boldsymbol{H}_t = \boldsymbol{Z}_t \boldsymbol{C}_t + \boldsymbol{H}_t, \\
\boldsymbol{s}_{t|t} &= \boldsymbol{s}_{t|t-1} + \boldsymbol{C}_t \boldsymbol{V}_t^{-1} \boldsymbol{v}_t, \\
\boldsymbol{\Sigma}_{t|t} &= \boldsymbol{\Sigma}_{t|t-1} - \boldsymbol{C}_t \boldsymbol{V}_t^{-1} \boldsymbol{C}_t', \\
\boldsymbol{s}_{t+1|t} &= \boldsymbol{d}_t + \boldsymbol{T}_t \boldsymbol{s}_{t|t}, \\
\boldsymbol{\Sigma}_{t+1|t} &= \boldsymbol{T}_t \boldsymbol{\Sigma}_{t|t} \boldsymbol{T}_t' + \boldsymbol{R}_t \boldsymbol{Q}_t \boldsymbol{R}_t'.
\end{aligned}$$

Steady State

If the state-space model is time-invariant, that is, all system matrices are time-invariant, then the matrices $\boldsymbol{\Sigma}_{t|t-1}$ converge to a constant matrix $\boldsymbol{\Sigma}_*$, which is a solution of the matrix equation

$$\boldsymbol{\Sigma}_* = \boldsymbol{T}\boldsymbol{\Sigma}_*\boldsymbol{T}' - \boldsymbol{T}\boldsymbol{\Sigma}_*\boldsymbol{Z}\boldsymbol{V}^{-1}\boldsymbol{Z}\boldsymbol{\Sigma}_*\boldsymbol{T}' + \boldsymbol{R}\boldsymbol{Q}\boldsymbol{R}',$$

where $\boldsymbol{V} = \boldsymbol{Z}\boldsymbol{\Sigma}_*\boldsymbol{Z}' + \boldsymbol{H}$. The solution that is reached after convergence to $\boldsymbol{\Sigma}_*$ is referred to as the *steady-state solution* of the Kalman filter. Once the steady state is reached, $\boldsymbol{V}_t$, $\boldsymbol{K}_t$, and $\boldsymbol{\Sigma}_{t+1|t}$ are all constant. This can lead to considerable saving in computing time.

11.4.2 State Estimation Error and Forecast Error

Define the state prediction error as

$$\boldsymbol{x}_t = \boldsymbol{s}_t - \boldsymbol{s}_{t|t-1}.$$

From the definition, the covariance matrix of $\boldsymbol{x}_t$ is $\text{Var}(\boldsymbol{x}_t|F_{t-1}) = \text{Var}(\boldsymbol{s}_t|F_{t-1}) = \boldsymbol{\Sigma}_{t|t-1}$. Following Section 11.1, we investigate properties of $\boldsymbol{x}_t$. First, from Eq. (11.55),

$$\boldsymbol{v}_t = \boldsymbol{Z}_t(\boldsymbol{s}_t - \boldsymbol{s}_{t|t-1}) + \boldsymbol{e}_t = \boldsymbol{Z}_t\boldsymbol{x}_t + \boldsymbol{e}_t.$$

Second, from Eqs. (11.62) and (11.24), and the prior equation, we have

$$\begin{aligned}
\boldsymbol{x}_{t+1} &= \boldsymbol{s}_{t+1} - \boldsymbol{s}_{t+1|t} \\
&= \boldsymbol{T}_t(\boldsymbol{s}_t - \boldsymbol{s}_{t|t-1}) + \boldsymbol{R}_t\boldsymbol{\eta}_t - \boldsymbol{K}_t\boldsymbol{v}_t \\
&= \boldsymbol{T}_t\boldsymbol{x}_t + \boldsymbol{R}_t\boldsymbol{\eta}_t - \boldsymbol{K}_t(\boldsymbol{Z}_t\boldsymbol{x}_t + \boldsymbol{e}_t) \\
&= \boldsymbol{L}_t\boldsymbol{x}_t + \boldsymbol{R}_t\boldsymbol{\eta}_t - \boldsymbol{K}_t\boldsymbol{e}_t,
\end{aligned}$$

where, as before, $\boldsymbol{L}_t = \boldsymbol{T}_t - \boldsymbol{K}_t\boldsymbol{Z}_t$. Consequently, we obtain a state-space form for $\boldsymbol{v}_t$ as

$$\boldsymbol{v}_t = \boldsymbol{Z}_t\boldsymbol{x}_t + \boldsymbol{e}_t, \quad \boldsymbol{x}_{t+1} = \boldsymbol{L}_t\boldsymbol{x}_t + \boldsymbol{R}_t\boldsymbol{\eta}_t - \boldsymbol{K}_t\boldsymbol{e}_t, \tag{11.63}$$

with $\boldsymbol{x}_1 = \boldsymbol{s}_1 - \boldsymbol{s}_{1|0}$ for $t = 1, \ldots, T$.

Finally, similar to the local trend model in Section 11.1, we can show that the 1-step ahead forecast errors $\{\boldsymbol{v}_t\}$ are independent of each other and $\{\boldsymbol{v}_t, \ldots, \boldsymbol{v}_T\}$ is independent of F_{t-1}.

11.4.3 State Smoothing

State smoothing focuses on the conditional distribution of $\boldsymbol{s}_t$ given F_T. Notice that (a) F_{t-1} and $\{\boldsymbol{v}_t, \ldots, \boldsymbol{v}_T\}$ are independent and (b) $\boldsymbol{v}_t$ are serially independent. We can apply Theorem 11.1 to the joint distribution of $\boldsymbol{s}_t$ and $\{\boldsymbol{v}_t, \ldots, \boldsymbol{v}_T\}$ given F_{t-1} and obtain

$$\begin{aligned} \boldsymbol{s}_{t|T} &= E(\boldsymbol{s}_t|F_T) = E(\boldsymbol{s}_t|F_{t-1}, \boldsymbol{v}_t, \ldots, \boldsymbol{v}_T) \\ &= E(\boldsymbol{s}_t|F_{t-1}) + \sum_{j=t}^{T} \mathrm{Cov}(\boldsymbol{s}_t, \boldsymbol{v}_j)[\mathrm{Var}(\boldsymbol{v}_t)]^{-1}\boldsymbol{v}_t \\ &= \boldsymbol{s}_{t|t-1} + \sum_{j=t}^{T} \mathrm{Cov}(\boldsymbol{s}_t, \boldsymbol{v}_j)\boldsymbol{V}_t^{-1}\boldsymbol{v}_t, \end{aligned} \tag{11.64}$$

where the covariance matrices are conditional on F_{t-1}. The covariance matrices $\mathrm{Cov}(\boldsymbol{s}_t, \boldsymbol{v}_j)$ for $j = t, \ldots, T$ can by derived as follows. By Eq. (11.63),

$$\begin{aligned} \mathrm{Cov}(\boldsymbol{s}_t, \boldsymbol{v}_j) &= E(\boldsymbol{s}_t\boldsymbol{v}_j') \\ &= E[\boldsymbol{s}_t(\boldsymbol{Z}_j\boldsymbol{x}_j + \boldsymbol{e}_j)'] = E(\boldsymbol{s}_t\boldsymbol{x}_j')\boldsymbol{Z}_j', \quad j = t, \ldots, T. \end{aligned} \tag{11.65}$$

Furthermore,

$$\begin{aligned} E(\boldsymbol{s}_t\boldsymbol{x}_t') &= E[\boldsymbol{s}_t(\boldsymbol{s}_t - \boldsymbol{s}_{t|t-1})'] = \mathrm{Var}(\boldsymbol{s}_t) = \boldsymbol{\Sigma}_{t|t-1}, \\ E(\boldsymbol{s}_t\boldsymbol{x}_{t+1}') &= E[\boldsymbol{s}_t(\boldsymbol{L}_t\boldsymbol{x}_t + \boldsymbol{R}_t\boldsymbol{\eta}_t - \boldsymbol{K}_t\boldsymbol{e}_t)'] = \boldsymbol{\Sigma}_{t|t-1}\boldsymbol{L}_t', \\ E(\boldsymbol{s}_t\boldsymbol{x}_{t+2}') &= \boldsymbol{\Sigma}_{t|t-1}\boldsymbol{L}_t'\boldsymbol{L}_{t+1}', \\ \vdots &= \vdots \\ E(\boldsymbol{s}_t\boldsymbol{x}_T') &= \boldsymbol{\Sigma}_{t|t-1}\boldsymbol{L}_t' \cdots \boldsymbol{L}_{T-1}'. \end{aligned} \tag{11.66}$$

Plugging the prior two equations into Eq. (11.64), we have

$$\begin{aligned} \boldsymbol{s}_{T|T} &= \boldsymbol{s}_{T|T-1} + \boldsymbol{\Sigma}_{T|T-1}\boldsymbol{Z}_T'\boldsymbol{V}_T^{-1}\boldsymbol{v}_T, \\ \boldsymbol{s}_{T-1|T} &= \boldsymbol{s}_{T-1|T-2} + \boldsymbol{\Sigma}_{T|T-1}\boldsymbol{Z}_{T-1}'\boldsymbol{V}_{T-1}^{-1}\boldsymbol{v}_{T-1} + \boldsymbol{\Sigma}_{T|T-1}\boldsymbol{L}_{T-1}'\boldsymbol{Z}_T'\boldsymbol{V}_T^{-1}\boldsymbol{v}_T, \\ \boldsymbol{s}_{t|T} &= \boldsymbol{s}_{t|t-1} + \boldsymbol{\Sigma}_{t|t-1}\boldsymbol{Z}_t'\boldsymbol{V}_t^{-1}\boldsymbol{v}_t + \boldsymbol{\Sigma}_{t|t-1}\boldsymbol{L}_t'\boldsymbol{Z}_{t+1}'\boldsymbol{V}_{t+1}^{-1}\boldsymbol{v}_{t+1} \\ &\quad + \cdots + \boldsymbol{\Sigma}_{t|t-1}\boldsymbol{L}_t'\boldsymbol{L}_{t+1}' \cdots \boldsymbol{L}_{T-1}'\boldsymbol{Z}_T'\boldsymbol{V}_T^{-1}\boldsymbol{v}_T, \end{aligned}$$

for $t = T-2, T-3, \ldots, 1$, where it is understood that $\boldsymbol{L}_t' \cdots \boldsymbol{L}_{T-1}' = \boldsymbol{I}_m$ when $t = T$. These smoothed state vectors can be expressed as

$$\boldsymbol{s}_{t|T} = \boldsymbol{s}_{t|t-1} + \boldsymbol{\Sigma}_{t|t-1}\boldsymbol{q}_{t-1}, \tag{11.67}$$

where $\boldsymbol{q}_{T-1} = \boldsymbol{Z}_T'\boldsymbol{V}_T^{-1}\boldsymbol{v}_T$, $\boldsymbol{q}_{T-2} = \boldsymbol{Z}_{T-1}'\boldsymbol{V}_{T-1}^{-1}\boldsymbol{v}_{T-1} + \boldsymbol{L}_{T-1}'\boldsymbol{Z}_T'\boldsymbol{V}_T^{-1}\boldsymbol{v}_T$, and

$$\boldsymbol{q}_{t-1} = \boldsymbol{Z}_t'\boldsymbol{V}_t^{-1}\boldsymbol{v}_t + \boldsymbol{L}_t'\boldsymbol{Z}_{t+1}'\boldsymbol{V}_{t+1}^{-1}\boldsymbol{v}_{t+1} + \cdots + \boldsymbol{L}_t'\boldsymbol{L}_{t+1}'\cdots\boldsymbol{L}_{T-1}'\boldsymbol{Z}_T'\boldsymbol{V}_T^{-1}\boldsymbol{v}_T,$$

for $t = T-2, T-3, \ldots, 1$. The quantity $\boldsymbol{q}_{t-1}$ is a weighted sum of the 1-step ahead forecast errors $\boldsymbol{v}_j$ occurring after time $t-1$. From the definition in the prior equation, $\boldsymbol{q}_t$ can be computed recursively backward as

$$\boldsymbol{q}_{t-1} = \boldsymbol{Z}_t'\boldsymbol{V}_t^{-1}\boldsymbol{v}_t + \boldsymbol{L}_t'\boldsymbol{q}_t, \quad t = T, \ldots, 1, \tag{11.68}$$

with $\boldsymbol{q}_T = \boldsymbol{0}$. Putting the equations together, we have a backward recursion for the smoothed state vectors as

$$\boldsymbol{q}_{t-1} = \boldsymbol{Z}_t'\boldsymbol{V}_t^{-1}\boldsymbol{v}_t + \boldsymbol{L}_t'\boldsymbol{q}_t, \quad \boldsymbol{s}_{t|T} = \boldsymbol{s}_{t|t-1} + \boldsymbol{\Sigma}_{t|t-1}\boldsymbol{q}_{t-1}, \quad t = T, \ldots, 1, \tag{11.69}$$

starting with $\boldsymbol{q}_T = \boldsymbol{0}$, where $\boldsymbol{s}_{t|t-1}$, $\boldsymbol{\Sigma}_{t|t-1}$, $\boldsymbol{L}_t$, and $\boldsymbol{V}_t$ are available from the Kalman filter. This algorithm is referred to as the *fixed interval smoother* in the literature; see de Jong (1989) and the references therein.

Covariance Matrix of Smoothed State Vector

Next, we derive the covariance matrices of the smoothed state vectors. Applying Theorem 11.1(4) to the conditional joint distribution of $\boldsymbol{s}_t$ and $\{\boldsymbol{v}_t, \ldots, \boldsymbol{v}_T\}$ given F_{t-1}, we have

$$\boldsymbol{\Sigma}_{t|T} = \boldsymbol{\Sigma}_{t|t-1} - \sum_{j=t}^{T} \mathrm{Cov}(\boldsymbol{s}_t, \boldsymbol{v}_j)[\mathrm{Var}(\boldsymbol{v}_j)]^{-1}[\mathrm{Cov}(\boldsymbol{s}_t, \boldsymbol{v}_j)]'.$$

Using the covariance matrices in Eqs. (11.65) and (11.66), we further obtain

$$\begin{aligned}\boldsymbol{\Sigma}_{t|T} &= \boldsymbol{\Sigma}_{t|t-1} - \boldsymbol{\Sigma}_{t|t-1}\boldsymbol{Z}_t'\boldsymbol{V}_t^{-1}\boldsymbol{Z}_t\boldsymbol{\Sigma}_{t|t-1} - \boldsymbol{\Sigma}_{t|t-1}\boldsymbol{L}_t'\boldsymbol{Z}_{t+1}'\boldsymbol{V}_{t+1}^{-1}\boldsymbol{Z}_{t+1}\boldsymbol{L}_t\boldsymbol{\Sigma}_{t|t-1}\\ &\quad - \cdots - \boldsymbol{\Sigma}_{t|t-1}\boldsymbol{L}_t'\cdots\boldsymbol{L}_{T-1}'\boldsymbol{Z}_T'\boldsymbol{V}_T^{-1}\boldsymbol{Z}_T\boldsymbol{L}_{T-1}\cdots\boldsymbol{L}_t\boldsymbol{\Sigma}_{t|t-1}\\ &= \boldsymbol{\Sigma}_{t|t-1} - \boldsymbol{\Sigma}_{t|t-1}\boldsymbol{M}_{t-1}\boldsymbol{\Sigma}_{t|t-1},\end{aligned}$$

where

$$\begin{aligned}\boldsymbol{M}_{t-1} &= \boldsymbol{Z}_t'\boldsymbol{V}_t^{-1}\boldsymbol{Z}_t + \boldsymbol{L}_t'\boldsymbol{Z}_{t+1}'\boldsymbol{V}_{t+1}^{-1}\boldsymbol{Z}_{t+1}\boldsymbol{L}_t\\ &\quad + \cdots + \boldsymbol{L}_t'\cdots\boldsymbol{L}_{T-1}'\boldsymbol{Z}_T'\boldsymbol{V}_T^{-1}\boldsymbol{Z}_T\boldsymbol{L}_{T-1}\cdots\boldsymbol{L}_t.\end{aligned}$$

Again, $\boldsymbol{L}_t'\cdots\boldsymbol{L}_{T-1} = \boldsymbol{I}_m$ when $t = T$. From its definition, the $\boldsymbol{M}_{t-1}$ matrix satisfies

$$\boldsymbol{M}_{t-1} = \boldsymbol{Z}_t'\boldsymbol{V}_t^{-1}\boldsymbol{Z}_t + \boldsymbol{L}_t'\boldsymbol{M}_t\boldsymbol{L}_t, \quad t = T, \ldots, 1, \tag{11.70}$$

with the starting value $\boldsymbol{M}_T = \boldsymbol{0}$. Collecting the results, we obtain a backward recursion to compute $\boldsymbol{\Sigma}_{t|T}$ as

$$\boldsymbol{M}_{t-1} = \boldsymbol{Z}_t'\boldsymbol{V}_t^{-1}\boldsymbol{Z}_t, +\boldsymbol{L}_t'\boldsymbol{M}_t\boldsymbol{L}_t, \quad \boldsymbol{\Sigma}_{t|T} = \boldsymbol{\Sigma}_{t|t-1} - \boldsymbol{\Sigma}_{t|t-1}\boldsymbol{M}_{t-1}\boldsymbol{\Sigma}_{t|t-1}, \quad (11.71)$$

for $t = T, \ldots, 1$ with $\boldsymbol{M}_T = \boldsymbol{0}$. Note that, like that of the local trend model in Section 11.1, $\boldsymbol{M}_t = \text{Var}(\boldsymbol{q}_t)$.

Combining the two backward recursions of smoothed state vectors, we have

$$\begin{aligned} \boldsymbol{q}_{t-1} &= \boldsymbol{Z}_t'\boldsymbol{V}_t^{-1}\boldsymbol{v}_t + \boldsymbol{L}_t'\boldsymbol{q}_t, \\ \boldsymbol{s}_{t|T} &= \boldsymbol{s}_{t|t-1} + \boldsymbol{\Sigma}_{t|t-1}\boldsymbol{q}_{t-1}, \\ \boldsymbol{M}_{t-1} &= \boldsymbol{Z}_t'\boldsymbol{V}_t^{-1}\boldsymbol{Z}_t + \boldsymbol{L}_t'\boldsymbol{M}_t\boldsymbol{L}_t, \\ \boldsymbol{\Sigma}_{t|T} &= \boldsymbol{\Sigma}_{t|t-1} - \boldsymbol{\Sigma}_{t|t-1}\boldsymbol{M}_{t-1}\boldsymbol{\Sigma}_{t|t-1}, \quad t = T, \ldots, 1, \end{aligned} \quad (11.72)$$

with $\boldsymbol{q}_T = \boldsymbol{0}$ and $\boldsymbol{M}_T = \boldsymbol{0}$.

Suppose that the state-space model in Eqs. (11.24) and (11.25) is known. Application of the Kalman filter and state smoothing can proceed in two steps. First, the Kalman filter in Eq. (11.62) is used for $t = 1, \ldots, T$ and the quantities $\boldsymbol{v}_t, \boldsymbol{V}_t$, $\boldsymbol{K}_t$, $\boldsymbol{s}_{t|t-1}$, and $\boldsymbol{\Sigma}_{t|t-1}$ are stored. Second, the state smoothing algorithm in Eq. (11.72) is applied for $t = T, T-1, \ldots, 1$ to obtain $\boldsymbol{s}_{t|T}$ and $\boldsymbol{\Sigma}_{t|T}$.

11.4.4 Disturbance Smoothing

Let $\boldsymbol{e}_{t|T} = E(\boldsymbol{e}_t|F_T)$ and $\boldsymbol{\eta}_{t|T} = E(\boldsymbol{\eta}_t|F_T)$ be the smoothed disturbances of the observation and transition equation, respectively. These *smoothed disturbances* are useful in many applications, for example, in model checking. In this subsection, we study recursive algorithms to compute smoothed disturbances and their covariance matrices. Again, applying Theorem 11.1 to the conditional joint distribution of $\boldsymbol{e}_t$ and $\{\boldsymbol{v}_t, \ldots, \boldsymbol{v}_T\}$ given F_{t-1}, we obtain

$$\boldsymbol{e}_{t|T} = E(\boldsymbol{e}_t|F_{t-1}, \boldsymbol{v}_t, \ldots, \boldsymbol{v}_T) = \sum_{j=t}^{T} E(\boldsymbol{e}_t\boldsymbol{v}_j')\boldsymbol{V}_j^{-1}\boldsymbol{v}_j, \quad (11.73)$$

where $E(\boldsymbol{e}_t|F_{t-1}) = \boldsymbol{0}$ is used. Using Eq. (11.63),

$$E(\boldsymbol{e}_t\boldsymbol{v}_j') = E(\boldsymbol{e}_t\boldsymbol{x}_j')\boldsymbol{Z}_j' + E(\boldsymbol{e}_t\boldsymbol{e}_j').$$

Since $E(\boldsymbol{e}_t\boldsymbol{x}_t') = \boldsymbol{0}$, we have

$$E(\boldsymbol{e}_t\boldsymbol{v}_j') = \begin{cases} \boldsymbol{H}_t, & \text{if } j = t, \\ E(\boldsymbol{e}_t\boldsymbol{x}_j')\boldsymbol{Z}_j', & \text{for } j = t+1, \ldots, T. \end{cases} \quad (11.74)$$

Using Eq. (11.63) repeatedly and the independence between $\{\boldsymbol{e}_t\}$ and $\{\boldsymbol{\eta}_t\}$, we obtain

$$\begin{aligned} E(\boldsymbol{e}_t\boldsymbol{x}'_{t+1}) &= -\boldsymbol{H}_t\boldsymbol{K}'_t, \\ E(\boldsymbol{e}_t\boldsymbol{x}'_{t+2}) &= -\boldsymbol{H}_t\boldsymbol{K}'_t\boldsymbol{L}'_{t+1}, \\ \vdots &= \vdots \\ E(\boldsymbol{e}_t\boldsymbol{x}'_{T}) &= -\boldsymbol{H}_t\boldsymbol{K}'_t\boldsymbol{L}'_{t+1}\cdots\boldsymbol{L}'_{T-1}, \end{aligned} \tag{11.75}$$

where it is understood that $\boldsymbol{L}'_{t+1}\cdots\boldsymbol{L}'_{T-1} = \boldsymbol{I}_m$ if $t = T-1$. Based on Eqs. (11.74) and (11.75),

$$\begin{aligned} \boldsymbol{e}_{t|T} &= \boldsymbol{H}_t(\boldsymbol{V}_t^{-1}\boldsymbol{v}_t - \boldsymbol{K}'_t\boldsymbol{Z}'_{t+1}\boldsymbol{V}_{t+1}^{-1}\boldsymbol{v}_{t+1} - \cdots - \boldsymbol{K}'_t\boldsymbol{L}'_{t+1}\cdots\boldsymbol{L}'_{T-1}\boldsymbol{Z}'_T\boldsymbol{V}_T^{-1}\boldsymbol{v}_T) \\ &= \boldsymbol{H}_t(\boldsymbol{V}_t^{-1}\boldsymbol{v}_t - \boldsymbol{K}'_t\boldsymbol{q}_t) \\ &= \boldsymbol{H}_t\boldsymbol{o}_t, \quad t = T, \ldots, 1, \end{aligned} \tag{11.76}$$

where $\boldsymbol{q}_t$ is defined in Eq. (11.67) and $\boldsymbol{o}_t = \boldsymbol{V}_t^{-1}\boldsymbol{v}_t - \boldsymbol{K}'_t\boldsymbol{q}_t$. We refer to $\boldsymbol{o}_t$ as the *smoothing measurement error*.

The smoothed disturbance $\boldsymbol{\eta}_{t|T}$ can be derived analogously and we have

$$\boldsymbol{\eta}_{t|T} = \sum_{j=t}^{T} E(\boldsymbol{\eta}_t\boldsymbol{v}'_j)\boldsymbol{V}_j^{-1}\boldsymbol{v}_j. \tag{11.77}$$

The state-space form in Eq. (11.67) gives

$$E(\boldsymbol{\eta}_t\boldsymbol{v}'_j) = \begin{cases} \boldsymbol{Q}_t\boldsymbol{R}'_t\boldsymbol{Z}'_{t+1}, & \text{if } j = t+1, \\ E(\boldsymbol{\eta}_t\boldsymbol{x}'_j)\boldsymbol{Z}'_j, & \text{if } j = t+2, \ldots, T, \end{cases}$$

where

$$\begin{aligned} E(\boldsymbol{\eta}_t\boldsymbol{x}'_{t+2}) &= \boldsymbol{Q}_t\boldsymbol{R}'_t\boldsymbol{L}'_{t+1}, \\ E(\boldsymbol{\eta}_t\boldsymbol{x}'_{t+3}) &= \boldsymbol{Q}_t\boldsymbol{R}'_t\boldsymbol{L}'_{t+1}\boldsymbol{L}'_{t+2}, \\ \vdots &= \vdots \\ E(\boldsymbol{\eta}_t\boldsymbol{x}'_{T}) &= \boldsymbol{Q}_t\boldsymbol{R}'_t\boldsymbol{L}'_{t+1}\cdots\boldsymbol{L}'_{T-1}, \end{aligned}$$

for $t = 1, \ldots, T$. Consequently, Eq. (11.77) implies

$$\begin{aligned} \boldsymbol{\eta}_{t|T} &= \boldsymbol{Q}_t\boldsymbol{R}'_t(\boldsymbol{Z}'_{t+1}\boldsymbol{V}_{t+1}^{-1}\boldsymbol{v}_{t+1} + \boldsymbol{L}'_{t+1}\boldsymbol{Z}'_{t+2}\boldsymbol{V}_{t+2}^{-1}\boldsymbol{v}_{t+2} \\ &\quad + \cdots + \boldsymbol{L}'_{t+1}\cdots\boldsymbol{L}'_{T-1}\boldsymbol{Z}_T\boldsymbol{V}_T^{-1}\boldsymbol{v}_T) \\ &= \boldsymbol{Q}_t\boldsymbol{R}'_t\boldsymbol{q}_t, \quad t = T, \ldots, 1, \end{aligned} \tag{11.78}$$

where $\boldsymbol{q}_t$ is defined earlier in Eq. (11.68).

Koopman (1993) uses the smoothed disturbance $\boldsymbol{\eta}_{t|T}$ to derive a new recursion for computing $\boldsymbol{s}_{t|T}$. From the transition equation in Eq. (11.24),

$$\boldsymbol{s}_{t+1|T} = \boldsymbol{d}_t + \boldsymbol{T}_t \boldsymbol{s}_{t|T} + \boldsymbol{R}_t \boldsymbol{\eta}_{t|T}.$$

Using Eq. (11.78), we have

$$\boldsymbol{s}_{t+1|T} = \boldsymbol{d}_t + \boldsymbol{T}_t \boldsymbol{s}_{t|T} + \boldsymbol{R}_t \boldsymbol{Q}_t \boldsymbol{R}_t' \boldsymbol{q}_t, \quad t = 1, \ldots, T, \tag{11.79}$$

where the initial value is $\boldsymbol{s}_{1|T} = \boldsymbol{s}_{1|0} + \boldsymbol{\Sigma}_{1|0} \boldsymbol{q}_0$ with $\boldsymbol{q}_0$ obtained from the recursion in Eq. (11.68).

Covariance Matrices of Smoothed Disturbances

The covariance matrix of the smoothed disturbance can also be obtained using Theorem 11.1. Specifically,

$$\begin{aligned}
\text{Var}(\boldsymbol{e}_t | F_T) &= \text{Var}(\boldsymbol{e}_t | F_{t-1}, \boldsymbol{v}_t, \ldots, \boldsymbol{v}_T) \\
&= \text{Var}(\boldsymbol{e}_t | F_{t-1}) - \sum_{j=t}^{T} \text{Cov}(\boldsymbol{e}_t, \boldsymbol{v}_j) \boldsymbol{V}_j^{-1} [\text{Cov}(\boldsymbol{e}_t, \boldsymbol{v}_j)]'.
\end{aligned}$$

Note that $\text{Cov}(\boldsymbol{e}_t, \boldsymbol{v}_j) = E(\boldsymbol{e}_t \boldsymbol{v}_j')$, which is given in Eq. (11.74). Thus, we have

$$\begin{aligned}
\text{Var}(\boldsymbol{e}_t | F_T) = \boldsymbol{H}_t &- \boldsymbol{H}_t (\boldsymbol{V}_t^{-1} + \boldsymbol{K}_t' \boldsymbol{Z}_{t+1}' \boldsymbol{V}_{t+1}^{-1} \boldsymbol{Z}_{t+1} \boldsymbol{K}_t \\
&+ \boldsymbol{K}_t' \boldsymbol{L}_{t+1}' \boldsymbol{Z}_{t+2}' \boldsymbol{V}_{t+2}^{-1} \boldsymbol{Z}_{t+2} \boldsymbol{L}_{t+1} \boldsymbol{K}_t \\
&+ \cdots + \boldsymbol{K}_t' \boldsymbol{L}_{t+1}' \cdots \boldsymbol{L}_{T-1}' \boldsymbol{Z}_T' \boldsymbol{V}_T^{-1} \boldsymbol{Z}_T \boldsymbol{L}_{T-1} \cdots \boldsymbol{L}_{t+1} \boldsymbol{K}_t) \boldsymbol{H}_t \\
= \boldsymbol{H}_t &- \boldsymbol{H}_t (\boldsymbol{V}_t^{-1} + \boldsymbol{K}_t' \boldsymbol{M}_t \boldsymbol{K}_t) \boldsymbol{H}_t \\
= \boldsymbol{H}_t &- \boldsymbol{H}_t \boldsymbol{N}_t \boldsymbol{H}_t,
\end{aligned}$$

where $\boldsymbol{N}_t = \boldsymbol{V}_t^{-1} + \boldsymbol{K}_t' \boldsymbol{M}_t \boldsymbol{K}_t$, where $\boldsymbol{M}_t$ is given in Eq. (11.70). Similarly,

$$\text{Var}(\boldsymbol{\eta}_t | F_T) = \text{Var}(\boldsymbol{\eta}_t) - \sum_{j=t}^{T} \text{Cov}(\boldsymbol{\eta}_t, \boldsymbol{v}_t) \boldsymbol{V}_t^{-1} [\text{Cov}(\boldsymbol{\eta}_t, \boldsymbol{v}_t)]^{-1},$$

where $\text{Cov}(\boldsymbol{\eta}_t, \boldsymbol{v}_j) = E(\boldsymbol{\eta}_t \boldsymbol{v}_j')$, which is given before when we derived the formula for $\boldsymbol{\eta}_{t|T}$. Consequently,

$$\begin{aligned}
\text{Var}(\boldsymbol{\eta}_t | F_T) &= \boldsymbol{Q}_t - \boldsymbol{Q}_t \boldsymbol{R}_t' (\boldsymbol{Z}_{t+1}' \boldsymbol{V}_{t+1}^{-1} \boldsymbol{Z}_{t+1} + \boldsymbol{L}_{t+1}' \boldsymbol{Z}_{t+2}' \boldsymbol{V}_{t+2}^{-1} \boldsymbol{Z}_{t+2} \boldsymbol{L}_{t+1} \\
&\quad + \cdots + \boldsymbol{L}_{t+1}' \cdots \boldsymbol{L}_{T-1}' \boldsymbol{Z}_T' \boldsymbol{V}_T^{-1} \boldsymbol{Z}_T \boldsymbol{L}_{T-1} \cdots \boldsymbol{L}_{t+1}) \boldsymbol{R}_t \boldsymbol{Q}_t \\
&= \boldsymbol{Q}_t - \boldsymbol{Q}_t \boldsymbol{R}_t' \boldsymbol{M}_t \boldsymbol{R}_t \boldsymbol{Q}_t.
\end{aligned}$$

In summary, the disturbance smoothing algorithm is as follows:

$$\begin{aligned}
\boldsymbol{e}_{t|T} &= \boldsymbol{H}_t(\boldsymbol{V}_t^{-1}\boldsymbol{v}_t - \boldsymbol{K}_t'\boldsymbol{q}_t),\\
\boldsymbol{\eta}_{t|T} &= \boldsymbol{Q}_t\boldsymbol{R}_t'\boldsymbol{q}_t,\\
\boldsymbol{q}_{t-1} &= \boldsymbol{Z}_t'\boldsymbol{V}_t^{-1}\boldsymbol{v}_t + \boldsymbol{L}_t'\boldsymbol{q}_t, \qquad (11.80)\\
\mathrm{Var}(\boldsymbol{e}_t|F_T) &= \boldsymbol{H}_t - \boldsymbol{H}_t(\boldsymbol{V}_t^{-1} + \boldsymbol{K}_t'\boldsymbol{M}_t\boldsymbol{K}_t)\boldsymbol{H}_t,\\
\mathrm{Var}(\boldsymbol{\eta}_t|F_T) &= \boldsymbol{Q}_t - \boldsymbol{Q}_t\boldsymbol{R}_t'\boldsymbol{M}_t\boldsymbol{R}_t\boldsymbol{Q}_t,\\
\boldsymbol{M}_{t-1} &= \boldsymbol{Z}_t'\boldsymbol{V}_t^{-1}\boldsymbol{Z}_t + \boldsymbol{L}_t'\boldsymbol{M}_t\boldsymbol{L}_t, \quad t = T, \ldots, 1,
\end{aligned}$$

where $\boldsymbol{q}_T = \boldsymbol{0}$ and $\boldsymbol{M}_T = \boldsymbol{0}$.

11.5 MISSING VALUES

For the general state-space model in Eqs. (11.24) and (11.25), we consider two cases of missing values. First, suppose that similar to the local trend model in Section 11.1 the observations $\boldsymbol{y}_t$ at $t = \ell + 1, \ldots, \ell + h$ are missing. In this case, there is no new information available at these time points and we set

$$\boldsymbol{v}_t = \boldsymbol{0}, \quad \boldsymbol{K}_t = \boldsymbol{0}, \quad \text{for} \quad t = \ell + 1, \ldots, \ell + h.$$

The Kalman filter in Eq. (11.62) can then proceed as usual. That is,

$$\boldsymbol{s}_{t+1|t} = \boldsymbol{d}_t + \boldsymbol{T}_t\boldsymbol{s}_{t|t-1}, \quad \boldsymbol{\Sigma}_{t+1|t} = \boldsymbol{T}_t\boldsymbol{\Sigma}_{t|t-1}\boldsymbol{T}_t' + \boldsymbol{R}_t\boldsymbol{Q}_t\boldsymbol{R}_t',$$

for $t = \ell + 1, \ldots, \ell + h$. Similarly, the smoothed state vectors can be computed as usual via Eq. (11.72) with

$$\boldsymbol{q}_{t-1} = \boldsymbol{T}_t'\boldsymbol{q}_t, \quad \boldsymbol{M}_{t-1} = \boldsymbol{T}_t'\boldsymbol{M}_t\boldsymbol{T}_t,$$

for $t = \ell + 1, \ldots, \ell + h$.

In the second case, some components of $\boldsymbol{y}_t$ are missing. Let $\boldsymbol{y}_t^* = \boldsymbol{J}\boldsymbol{y}_t$ be the vector of observed data at time t, where $\boldsymbol{J}$ is an indicator matrix identifying the observed data. More specifically, rows of $\boldsymbol{J}$ are a subset of the rows of the $k \times k$ identity matrix. In this case, the observation equation (11.25) of the model can be transformed as

$$\boldsymbol{y}_t^* = \boldsymbol{c}_t^* + \boldsymbol{Z}_t^*\boldsymbol{s}_t + \boldsymbol{e}_t^*,$$

where $\boldsymbol{c}_t^* = \boldsymbol{J}\boldsymbol{c}_t$, $\boldsymbol{Z}_t^* = \boldsymbol{J}\boldsymbol{Z}_t$, and $\boldsymbol{e}_t^* = \boldsymbol{J}\boldsymbol{e}_t$ with covariance matrix $\mathrm{Var}(\boldsymbol{e}_t^*) = \boldsymbol{H}_t^* = \boldsymbol{J}\boldsymbol{H}_t\boldsymbol{J}'$. The Kalman filter and state-smoothing recursion continue to apply except that the modified observation equation is used at time t. Consequently, the ease in handling missing values is a nice feature of the state-space model.

11.6 FORECASTING

Suppose that the forecast origin is t and we are interested in predicting $\boldsymbol{y}_{t+j}$ for $j = 1, \ldots, h$, where $h > 0$. Also, we adopt the minimum mean squared error forecasts. Similar to the ARMA models, the j-step ahead forecast $\boldsymbol{y}_t(j)$ turns out to be the expected value of $\boldsymbol{y}_{t+j}$ given F_t and the model. That is, $\boldsymbol{y}_t(j) = E(\boldsymbol{y}_{t+j}|F_t)$. In what follows, we show that these forecasts and the covariance matrices of the associated forecast errors can be obtained via the Kalman filter in Eq. (11.62) by treating $\{\boldsymbol{y}_{t+1}, \ldots, \boldsymbol{y}_{t+h}\}$ as missing values, that is, case one of Section 11.5.

Consider the 1-step ahead forecast. From Eq. (11.25),

$$\boldsymbol{y}_t(1) = E(\boldsymbol{y}_{t+1}|F_t) = \boldsymbol{c}_{t+1} + \boldsymbol{Z}_{t+1}\boldsymbol{s}_{t+1|t},$$

where $\boldsymbol{s}_{t+1|t}$ is available via the Kalman filter at the forecast origin t. The associated forecast error is

$$\boldsymbol{e}_t(1) = \boldsymbol{y}_{t+1} - \boldsymbol{y}_t(1) = \boldsymbol{Z}_{t+1}(\boldsymbol{s}_{t+1} - \boldsymbol{s}_{t+1|t}) + \boldsymbol{e}_{t+1}.$$

Therefore, the covariance matrix of the 1-step ahead forecast error is

$$\text{Var}[\boldsymbol{e}_t(1)] = \boldsymbol{Z}_{t+1}\boldsymbol{\Sigma}_{t+1|t}\boldsymbol{Z}'_{t+1} + \boldsymbol{H}_{t+1}.$$

This is precisely the covariance matrix $\boldsymbol{V}_{t+1}$ of the Kalman filter in Eq. (11.62). Thus, we have showed the case for $h = 1$.

Now, for $h > 1$, we consider 1-step to h-step ahead forecasts sequentially. From Eq. (11.25), the j-step ahead forecast is

$$\boldsymbol{y}_t(j) = \boldsymbol{c}_{t+j} + \boldsymbol{Z}_{t+j}\boldsymbol{s}_{t+j|t}, \tag{11.81}$$

and the associated forecast error is

$$\boldsymbol{e}_t(j) = \boldsymbol{Z}_{t+j}(\boldsymbol{s}_{t+j} - \boldsymbol{s}_{t+j|t}) + \boldsymbol{e}_{t+j}.$$

Recall that $\boldsymbol{s}_{t+j|t}$ and $\boldsymbol{\Sigma}_{t+j|t}$ are, respectively, the conditional mean and covariance matrix of $\boldsymbol{s}_{t+j}$ given F_t. The prior equation says that

$$\text{Var}[\boldsymbol{e}_t(j)] = \boldsymbol{Z}_{t+j}\boldsymbol{\Sigma}_{t+j|t}\boldsymbol{Z}'_{t+j} + \boldsymbol{H}_{t+j}. \tag{11.82}$$

Furthermore, from Eq. (11.24),

$$\boldsymbol{s}_{t+j+1|t} = \boldsymbol{d}_{t+j} + \boldsymbol{T}_{t+j}\boldsymbol{s}_{t+j|t},$$

which in turn implies that

$$\boldsymbol{s}_{t+j+1} - \boldsymbol{s}_{t+j+1|t} = \boldsymbol{T}_{t+j}(\boldsymbol{s}_{t+j} - \boldsymbol{s}_{t+j|t}) + \boldsymbol{R}_{t+j}\boldsymbol{\eta}_{t+j}.$$

Consequently,

$$\mathbf{\Sigma}_{t+j+1|t} = \boldsymbol{T}_{t+j}\mathbf{\Sigma}_{t+j|t}\boldsymbol{T}'_{t+j} + \boldsymbol{R}_{t+j}\boldsymbol{Q}_{t+j}\boldsymbol{R}'_{t+j}. \tag{11.83}$$

Note that $\text{Var}[\boldsymbol{e}_t(j)] = \boldsymbol{V}_{t+j}$ and Eqs. (11.81)–(11.83) are the recursion of the Kalman filter in Eq. (11.62) for $t+j$ with $j = 1, \ldots, h$ when $\boldsymbol{v}_{t+j} = \mathbf{0}$ and $\boldsymbol{K}_{t+j} = \mathbf{0}$. Thus, the forecast $\boldsymbol{y}_t(j)$ and the covariance matrix of its forecast error $\boldsymbol{e}_t(j)$ can be obtained via the Kalman filter with missing values.

Finally, the prediction error series $\{\boldsymbol{v}_t\}$ can be used to evaluate the likelihood function for estimation and the standardized prediction errors $\boldsymbol{D}_t^{-1/2}\boldsymbol{v}_t$ can be used for model checking, where $\boldsymbol{D}_t = \text{diag}\{\boldsymbol{V}_t(1,1), \ldots, \boldsymbol{V}_t(k,k)\}$ with $\boldsymbol{V}_t(i,i)$ being the (i,i)th element of $\boldsymbol{V}_t$.

11.7 APPLICATION

In this section, we consider some applications of the state-space model in finance and business. Our objectives are to highlight the applicability of the model and to demonstrate the practical implementation of the analysis in S-Plus with *SsfPack*.

Example 11.2. Consider the CAPM for the monthly simple excess returns of General Motors (GM) stock from January 1990 to December 2003; see Chapter 9. We use the simple excess returns of the S&P 500 composite index as the market returns. Our illustration starts with a simple market model

$$r_t = \alpha + \beta r_{M,t} + e_t, \quad e_t \sim N(0, \sigma_e^2) \tag{11.84}$$

for $t = 1, \ldots, 168$. This is a fixed-coefficient model and can easily be estimated by the ordinary least squares (OLS) method. Denote the GM stock return and the market return by `gm` and `sp`, respectively. The result is given below.

```
> fit=OLS(gm~sp)
> summary(fit)
Call:
OLS(formula = gm ~ sp)
Coefficients:
              Value Std. Error t value Pr(>|t|)
(Intercept) 0.0020 0.0063     0.3151  0.7531
         sp 1.0457 0.1453     7.1964  0.0000

Regression Diagnostics:
         R-Squared 0.238
Adjusted R-Squared 0.233
Durbin-Watson Stat 2.029

Residual Diagnostics:
              Stat P-Value
```

```
Jarque-Bera  2.537  0.281
  Ljung-Box 24.207  0.337

Residual standard error: 0.0813
```

Thus, the fitted model is

$$r_t = 0.02 + 1.0457 r_{M,t} + e_t, \quad \hat{\sigma}_e = 0.0813.$$

Based on the residual diagnostics, the model appears to be adequate for the GM stock returns with adjusted $R^2 = 23.3\%$.

As shown in Section 11.3, model (11.84) is a special case of the state-space model. We then estimate the model using *SsfPack*. The result is as follows:

```
> reg.m=function(parm,mX=NULL){
+ parm=exp(parm)    % log(sigma.e) used to ensure positiveness.
+ ssf.reg=GetSsfReg(mX)
+ ssf.reg$mOmega[3,3]=parm[1]
+ CheckSsf(ssf.reg)
+ }
> c.start=c(0.1)
> reg.fit=SsfFit(c.start,gm,"reg.m",mX=X.mtx)
RELATIVE FUNCTION CONVERGENCE
> sqrt(exp(reg.fit$parameters))
[1] 0.08129934
>
% Next, perform smoothing
> ssf.reg$mOmega[3,3]=exp(reg.fit$parameters)
> reg.s=SsfMomentEst(gm,ssf.reg,task="STSMO")
> reg.s$state.moment[10,]     % use 10th row to avoid impact
          state.1  state.2    % of the starting value.
[10,] 0.001985928 1.045712
% Next, obtain standard errors of estimates
> sqrt(reg.s$state.variance[10,])
      state.1    state.2
 0.006301927 0.1453096
```

As expected, the result is in total agreement with that of the OLS method.

Finally, we entertain the time-varying CAPM of Section 11.3.1. The estimation result, including time plot of the smoothed response variable, is given below. The command `SsfCondDens` is used to compute the smoothed estimates of the state vector and observation without variance estimation.

```
> tv.capm = function(parm,mX=NULL){ % Setup the model
+ parm=exp(parm)  %parameterize in log for positiveness.
+ Phi.t = rbind(diag(2),rep(0,2))
+ Omega=diag(parm)
```

```
+ JPhi=matrix(-1,3,2)
+ JPhi[3,1]=1
+ JPhi[3,2]=2
+ Sigma=-Phi.t
+ ssf.tv=list(mPhi=Phi.t,
+ mOmega=Omega,
+ mJPhi=JPhi,
+ mSigma=Sigma,
+ mX=mX)
+ CheckSsf(ssf.tv)
+ }
> tv.start=c(0,0,0)    %starting values
> tv.mle=SsfFit(tv.start,gm,"tv.capm",mX=X.mtx) %estimation
> sigma.mle=sqrt(exp(tv.mle$parameters))
> sigma.mle
  1.168806e-05 0.0007428207  0.08129916
% Smoothing
> smoEst.tv=SsfCondDens(gm,tv.capm(tv.mle$parameters,
+ mX=X.mtx),task="STSMO")
> names(smoEst.tv)
[1] "state"     "response" "task"
> par(mfcol=c(2,2))  %plotting
> plot(gm,type='l',ylab='excess return')
> title(main='(a) Monthly simple excess returns')
> plot(smoEst.tv$response,type='l',ylab='rtn')
> title(main='(b) Expected returns')
> plot(smoEst.tv$state[,1],type='l',ylab='value')
> title(main='(c) Alpha(t)')
> plot(smoEst.tv$state[,2],type='l',ylab='value')
> title(main='(d) Beta(t)')
```

Note that estimates of σ_η and σ_ε are 1.17×10^{-5} and 0.74×10^{-3}, respectively. These estimates are close to zero, indicating that α_t and β_t of the time-varying market model are essentially constant for the GM stock returns. This is in agreement with the fact that the fixed-coefficient market model fits the data well. Figure 11.5 shows some plots for the time-varying CAPM fit. Part (a) is the monthly simple excess returns of GM stock from January 1990 to December 2003. Part (b) is the expected returns of GM stock, that is, $r_{t|T}$, where $T = 168$ is the sample size. Parts (c) and (d) are the time plots of the estimates of α_t and β_t. Given the tightness in the vertical scale, these two time plots confirm the assertion that a fixed-coefficient market model is adequate for the monthly GM stock return.

Example 11.3. In this example we reanalyze the series of quarterly earnings per share of Johnson and Johnson from 1960 to 1980 using the unobserved component model; see Chapter 2 for details of the data. The model considered is

$$y_t = \mu_t + \gamma_t + e_t, \quad e_t \sim N(0, \sigma_e^2), \tag{11.85}$$

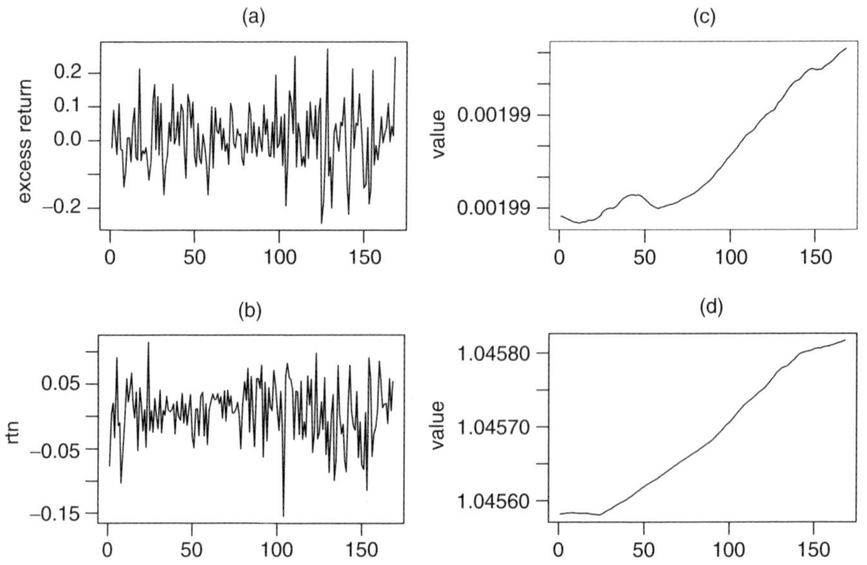

Figure 11.5. Time plots of some statistics for a time-varying CAPM applied to the monthly simple excess returns of General Motors stock. The S&P 500 composite index return is used as the market return: (a) monthly simple excess return, (b) expected returns $\boldsymbol{r}_{t|T}$, (c) α_t estimate, and (d) β_t estimate.

where y_t is the logarithm of the observed earnings per share, μ_t is the local trend component satisfying

$$\mu_{t+1} = \mu_t + \eta_t, \quad \eta_t \sim N(0, \sigma_\eta^2),$$

and γ_t is the seasonal component that satisfies

$$(1 + B + B^2 + B^3)\gamma_t = \omega_t, \quad \omega_t \sim N(0, \sigma_\omega^2),$$

that is, $\gamma_t = -\sum_{j=1}^{3} \gamma_{t-j} + \omega_t$. This model has three parameters σ_e, σ_η, and σ_ω and is a simple unobserved component model. It can be put in a state-space form as

$$\begin{bmatrix} \mu_{t+1} \\ \gamma_{t+1} \\ \gamma_t \\ \gamma_{t-1} \end{bmatrix} = \begin{bmatrix} 1 & 0 & 0 & 0 \\ 0 & -1 & -1 & -1 \\ 0 & 1 & 0 & 0 \\ 0 & 0 & 1 & 0 \end{bmatrix} \begin{bmatrix} \mu_t \\ \gamma_t \\ \gamma_{t-1} \\ \gamma_{t-2} \end{bmatrix} + \begin{bmatrix} 1 & 0 \\ 0 & 1 \\ 0 & 0 \\ 0 & 0 \end{bmatrix} \begin{bmatrix} \eta_t \\ \omega_t \end{bmatrix},$$

where the covariance matrix of $(\eta_t, \omega_t)'$ is diag$\{\sigma_\eta^2, \sigma_\omega^2\}$, and $y_t = [1, 1, 0, 0]\boldsymbol{s}_t + e_t$; see Section 11.3. This is a special case of the structural time series in *SsfPack* and can easily be specified using the command `GetSsfStsm`. Performing the maximum likelihood estimation, we obtain $(\hat{\sigma}_e, \hat{\sigma}_\eta, \hat{\sigma}_\omega) = (0.00143, 0.2696, 0.1712)$.

```
> jnj=scan(file='q-jnj.txt')
> y=log(jnj)
% Estimation
> jnj.m=function(parm){
+ parm=exp(parm)
+ jnj.sea=GetSsfStsm(irregular=parm[1],level=parm[2],
+ seasonalDummy=c(parm[3],4))
+ CheckSsf(jnj.sea)
+ }
>
> c.start=c(0,0,0)  % Starting values
> jnj.est=SsfFit(c.start,y,"jnj.m")
> names(jnj.est)
 [1] "parameters" "objective" "message" "grad.norm"
 [5] "iterations" "f.evals"   "g.evals" "hessian"
 [9] "scale"      "aux"       "call"
> jnjest=sqrt(exp(jnj.est$parameters))
> jnjest
[1] 0.001429867 0.269622976 0.171221806  % Estimates
% Next, specify the model with estimates
> jnj.ssf=GetSsfStsm(irregular=jnjest[1],level=jnjest[2],
+ seasonalDummy=c(jnjest[3],4))
> CheckSsf(jnj.ssf)
$mPhi:
     [,1] [,2] [,3] [,4]
[1,]    1    0    0    0
[2,]    0   -1   -1   -1
[3,]    0    1    0    0
[4,]    0    0    1    0
[5,]    1    1    0    0
$mOmega:
        [,1]    [,2] [,3] [,4]      [,5]
[1,] 0.07270 0.00000    0    0         0
[2,] 0.00000 0.02932    0    0         0
[3,] 0.00000 0.00000    0    0         0
[4,] 0.00000 0.00000    0    0         0
[5,] 0.00000 0.00000    0    0 2.044e-06
$mSigma:
     [,1] [,2] [,3] [,4]
[1,]   -1    0    0    0
[2,]    0   -1    0    0
[3,]    0    0   -1    0
[4,]    0    0    0   -1
[5,]    0    0    0    0
$mDelta:
     [,1]
[1,]    0
[2,]    0
[3,]    0
```

```
[4,]    0
[5,]    0
$mJPhi:
[1] 0
$mJOmega:
[1] 0
$mJDelta:
[1] 0
$mX:
[1] 0
$cT:
[1] 0
$cX:
[1] 0
$cY:
[1] 1
$cSt:
[1] 4
attr(, "class"):
[1] "ssf"   %below: smoothed components
> jnj.smo=SsfMomentEst(y,jnj.ssf,task="STSMO")
> up1=jnj.smo$state.moment[,1] +
+  2*sqrt(jnj.smo$state.variance[,1])
> lw1=jnj.smo$state.moment[,1] -
+  2*sqrt(jnj.smo$state.variance[,1])
> max(up1)  %obtain range for plotting
[1] 3.067664
> min(lw1)
[1] -1.063997
> up=jnj.smo$state.moment[,2] +
+  2*sqrt(jnj.smo$state.variance[,2])
> lw=jnj.smo$state.moment[,2] -
+  2*sqrt(jnj.smo$state.variance[,2])
> max(up)
[1] 0.5909587
> min(lw)
[1] -0.6157968
> par(mfcol=c(2,1)) %plotting
> plot(tdx,jnj.smo$state.moment[,1],type='l',xlab='year',
+ ylab='value',ylim=c(-1.1,3.1))
> lines(tdx,up1,lty=2)
> lines(tdx,lw1,lty=2)
> title(main='(a) Trend component')
> plot(tdx,jnj.smo$state.moment[,2],type='l',xlab='year',
+ ylab='value',ylim=c(-.62,0.6))
> lines(tdx,up,lty=2)
> lines(tdx,lw,lty=2)
> title(main='(b) Seasonal component')
% Filtering and smoothing
```

```
> jnj.fil=KalmanFil(y,jnj.ssf,task="STFIL")
> jnj.smo=KalmanSmo(jnj.fil,jnj.ssf)
> plot(tdx,jnj.fil$mOut[,1],type='l',xlab='year',
+  ylab='resi')
> title(main='(a) 1-Step forecast error')
> plot(tdx,jnj.smo$response.residuals[2:85],type='l',
+ xlab='year',ylab='resi')
> title(main='(b) Smoothing residual')
```

Figure 11.6 shows the smoothed estimates of the trend and seasonal components, that is, $\mu_{t|T}$ and $\gamma_{t|T}$ with $T = 84$, of the data. Of particular interest is that the seasonal pattern seems to evolve over time. Also shown are 95% pointwise confidence regions of the unobserved components. Figure 11.7 shows the residual plots, where part (a) gives the 1-step ahead forecast errors computed by Kalman filter and part (b) is the smoothed response residuals of the fitted model. Thus, state-space modeling provides an alternative approach for analyzing seasonal time series. It should be noted that the estimated components in Figure 11.6 are not unique. They depend on the model specified and constraints used. In fact, there are infinitely many ways to decompose an observed time series into unobserved components. For instance, one can use a different specification for the seasonal component,

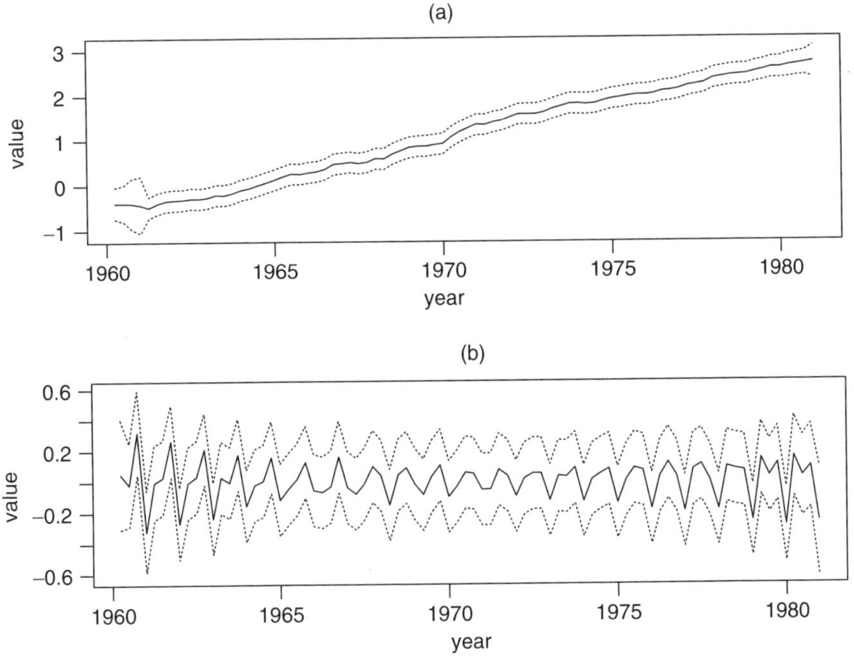

Figure 11.6. Smoothed components of fitting model (11.85) to the logarithm of quarterly earnings per share of Johnson and Johnson Company from 1960 to 1980: (a) trend component and (b) seasonal component. Dotted lines indicate pointwise 95% confidence regions.

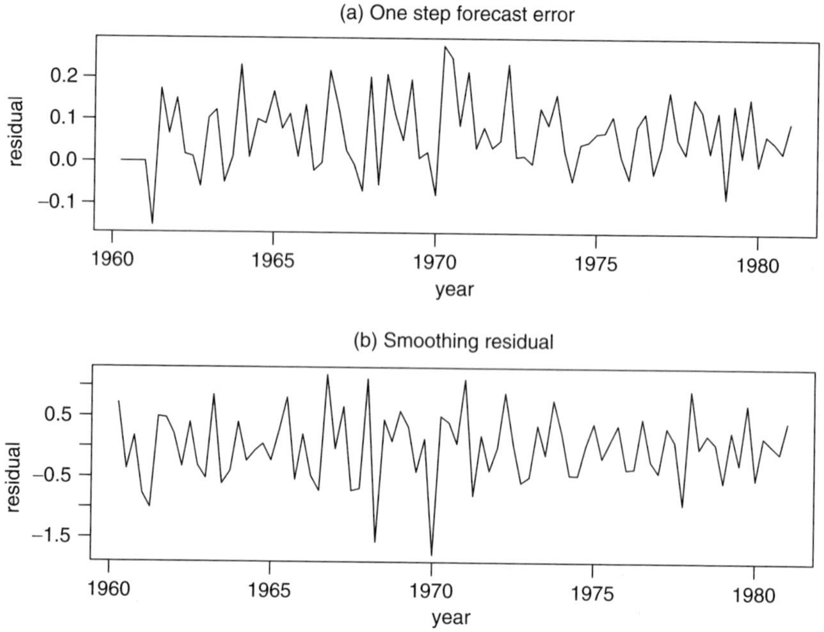

Figure 11.7. Residual series of fitting model (11.85) to the logarithm of quarterly earnings per share of Johnson and Johnson Company from 1960 to 1980: (a) 1-step ahead forecast error v_t and (b) smoothed residuals of response variable.

for example, `seasonalTrig` in *SsfPack*, to obtain another decomposition for the earnings series of Johnson and Johnson. Thus, care must be exercised in interpreting the estimated components. However, for forecasting purposes, the choice of decomposition does not matter provided that the chosen one is a valid decomposition.

EXERCISES

11.1. Consider the ARMA(1,1) model $y_t - 0.8y_{t-1} = a_t + 0.4a_{t-1}$ with $a_t \sim N(0, 0.49)$. Convert the model into a state-space form using (a) Akaike's method, (b) Harvey's approach, and (c) Aoki's approach.

11.2. The file `aa-rv-20m.txt` contains the realized daily volatility series of Alcoa stock returns from January 2, 2003 to May 7, 2004; see the example in Section 11.1. The volatility series is constructed using 20-minute intradaily log returns.

(a) Fit an ARIMA(0,1,1) model to the log volatility series and write down the model.

(b) Estimate the local trend model in Eqs. (11.1) and (11.2) for the log volatility series. What are the estimates of σ_e and σ_η? Obtain time plots for the filtered and smoothed state variables with pointwise 95% confidence interval.

11.3. Consider the monthly simple excess returns of Pfizer stock and the S&P 500 composite index from January 1990 to December 2003. The excess returns are in `m-pfesp-ex9003.txt` with Pfizer stock returns in the first column.

(a) Fit a fixed-coefficient market model to the Pfizer stock return. Write down the fitted model.

(b) Fit a time-varying CAPM to the Pfizer stock return. What are the estimated standard errors of the innovations to the α_t and β_t series? Obtain time plots of the smoothed estimates of α_t and β_t.

11.4. Consider the AR(3) model

$$x_t = \phi_1 x_{t-1} + \phi_2 x_{t-2} + \phi_3 x_{t-3} + a_t, \quad a_t \sim N(0, \sigma_a^2),$$

and suppose that the observed data are

$$y_t = x_t + e_t, \quad e_t \sim N(0, \sigma_e^2),$$

where $\{e_t\}$ and $\{a_t\}$ are independent and the initial values of x_j with $j \le 0$ are independent of e_t and a_t for $t > 0$.

(a) Convert the model into a state-space form.

(b) If $E(e_t) = c$, which is not zero, what is the corresponding state-space form for the system?

11.5. The file `m-ppiaco.txt` contains year, month, day, and U.S. Producer Price Index (PPI) from January 1947 to August 2004. The index is for all commodities and not seasonally adjusted. Let $z_t = \ln(Z_t) - \ln(Z_{t-1})$, where Z_t is the observed monthly PPI. It turns out that an AR(3) model is adequate for y_t if the minor seasonal dependence is ignored. Let y_t be the sample-mean corrected series of z_t.

(a) Fit an AR(3) model to y_t and write down the fitted model.

(b) Suppose that y_t has independent measurement errors so that $y_t = x_t + e_t$, where x_t is an AR(3) process and $\text{Var}(e_t) = \sigma_e^2$. Use a state-space form to estimate parameters, including the innovational variances to the state and σ_e^2. Write down the fitted model and obtain a time plot of the smoothed estimate of x_t. Also, show the time plot of filtered response residuals of the fitted state-space model.

REFERENCES

Akaike, H. (1975). Markovian representation of stochastic processes by canonical variables. *SIAM Journal on Control* **13**: 162–173.

Aoki, M. (1987). *State Space Modeling of Time Series*. Springer-Verlag, New York.

Anderson, B. D. O. and Moore, J. B. (1979). *Optimal Filtering*. Prentice Hall, Englewood Cliffs, NJ.

Chan, N. H. (2002). *Time Series: Applications to Finance*. Wiley, Hoboken, NJ.

de Jong, P. (1989). Smoothing and interpolation with the state space model. *Journal of the American Statistical Association* **84**: 1085–1088.

Durbin, J. and Koopman, S. J. (2001). *Time Series Analysis by State Space Methods*. Oxford University Press, Oxford, UK.

Hamilton, J. (1994). *Time Series Analysis*. Princeton University Press, Princeton, NJ.

Harvey, A. C. (1993). *Time Series Models*, 2nd edition. Harvester Wheatsheaf, Hemel Hempstead, UK.

Kalman, R. E. (1960). A new approach to linear filtering and prediction problems. *Journal of Basic Engineering, Transactions ASMA Series D* **82**: 35–45.

Kim, C. J. and Nelson, C. R. (1999). *State Space Models with Regime Switching*. Academic Press, New York.

Kitagawa, G. and Gersch, W. (1996). *Smoothness Priors Analysis of Time Series*. Springer-Verlag, New York.

Koopman, S. J. (1993). Disturbance smoother for state space models. *Biometrika* **80**: 117–126.

Koopman, S. J., Shephard, N. and Doornik, J. A. (1999). Statistical algorithms for models in state-space form using *SsfPack* 2.2. *Econometrics Journal* **2**: 113–166. Also, http://www.ssfpack.com/.

Shumway, R. H. and Stoffer, D. S. (2000). *Time Series Analysis and Its Applications*. Springer-Verlag, New York.

West, M. and Harrison, J. (1997). *Bayesian Forecasting and Dynamic Models*, 2nd edition. Springer-Verlag, New York.

CHAPTER 12

Markov Chain Monte Carlo Methods with Applications

Advances in computing facilities and computational methods have dramatically increased our ability to solve complicated problems. The advances also extend the applicability of many existing econometric and statistical methods. Examples of such achievements in statistics include the Markov chain Monte Carlo (MCMC) method and data augmentation. These techniques enable us to make some statistical inference that was not feasible just a few years ago. In this chapter, we introduce the ideas of MCMC methods and data augmentation that are widely applicable in finance. In particular, we discuss Bayesian inference via Gibbs sampling and demonstrate various applications of MCMC methods. Rapid developments in the MCMC methodology make it impossible to cover all the new methods available in the literature. Interested readers are referred to some recent books on Bayesian and empirical Bayesian statistics (e.g., Carlin and Louis, 2000; Gelman, Carlin, Stern, and Rubin, 2003).

For applications, we focus on issues related to financial econometrics. The demonstrations shown in this chapter represent only a small fraction of all possible applications of the techniques in finance. As a matter of fact, it is fair to say that Bayesian inference and the MCMC methods discussed here are applicable to most, if not all, of the studies in financial econometrics.

We begin the chapter by reviewing the concept of a *Markov process*. Consider a stochastic process $\{X_t\}$, where each X_t assumes a value in the space $\boldsymbol{\Theta}$. The process $\{X_t\}$ is a Markov process if it has the property that, given the value of X_t, the values of X_h, $h > t$, do not depend on the values X_s, $s < t$. In other words, $\{X_t\}$ is a Markov process if its conditional distribution function satisfies

$$P(X_h|X_s, s \le t) = P(X_h|X_t), \quad h > t.$$

If $\{X_t\}$ is a discrete-time stochastic process, then the prior property becomes

$$P(X_h|X_t, X_{t-1}, \ldots) = P(X_h|X_t), \quad h > t.$$

Analysis of Financial Time Series, Second Edition By Ruey S. Tsay

Let $\boldsymbol{A}$ be a subset of $\boldsymbol{\Theta}$. The function

$$P_t(\boldsymbol{\theta}, h, \boldsymbol{A}) = P(X_h \in \boldsymbol{A} | X_t = \boldsymbol{\theta}), \quad h > t$$

is called the transition probability function of the Markov process. If the transition probability depends on $h - t$, but not on t, then the process has a stationary transition distribution.

12.1 MARKOV CHAIN SIMULATION

Consider an inference problem with parameter vector $\boldsymbol{\theta}$ and data $\boldsymbol{X}$, where $\boldsymbol{\theta} \in \boldsymbol{\Theta}$. To make inference, we need to know the distribution $P(\boldsymbol{\theta}|\boldsymbol{X})$. The idea of Markov chain simulation is to simulate a Markov process on $\boldsymbol{\Theta}$, which converges to a stationary transition distribution that is $P(\boldsymbol{\theta}|\boldsymbol{X})$.

The key to Markov chain simulation is to create a Markov process whose stationary transition distribution is a specified $P(\boldsymbol{\theta}|\boldsymbol{X})$ and run the simulation sufficiently long so that the distribution of the current values of the process is close enough to the stationary transition distribution. It turns out that, for a given $P(\boldsymbol{\theta}|\boldsymbol{X})$, many Markov chains with the desired property can be constructed. We refer to methods that use Markov chain simulation to obtain the distribution $P(\boldsymbol{\theta}|\boldsymbol{X})$ as Markov chain Monte Carlo (MCMC) methods.

The development of MCMC methods took place in various forms in the statistical literature. Consider the problem of "missing value" in data analysis. Most statistical methods discussed in this book were developed under the assumption of "complete data" (i.e., there is no missing value). For example, in modeling daily volatility of an asset return, we assume that the return data are available for all trading days in the sample period. What should we do if there is a missing value?

Dempster, Laird, and Rubin (1977) suggest an iterative method called the EM algorithm to solve the problem. The method consists of two steps. First, if the missing value were available, then we could use methods of complete-data analysis to build a volatility model. Second, given the available data and the fitted model, we can derive the statistical distribution of the missing value. A simple way to fill in the missing value is to use the conditional expectation of the derived distribution of the missing value. In practice, one can start the method with an arbitrary value for the missing value and iterate the procedure for many times until convergence. The first step of the prior procedure involves performing the maximum likelihood estimation of a specified model and is called the M-step. The second step is to compute the conditional expectation of the missing value and is called the E-step.

Tanner and Wong (1987) generalize the EM algorithm in two ways. First, they introduce the idea of iterative simulation. For instance, instead of using the conditional expectation, one can simply replace the missing value by a random draw from its derived conditional distribution. Second, they extend the applicability of EM algorithm by using the concept of data augmentation. By data augmentation, we mean adding auxiliary variables to the problem under study. It turns out that many of the simulation methods can often be simplified or speeded up by data augmentation; see the application sections of this chapter.

12.2 GIBBS SAMPLING

Gibbs sampling (or Gibbs sampler) of Geman and Geman (1984) and Gelfand and Smith (1990) is perhaps the most popular MCMC method. We introduce the idea of Gibbs sampling by using a simple problem with three parameters. Here the word *parameter* is used in a very general sense. A missing data point can be regarded as a parameter under the MCMC framework. Similarly, an unobservable variable such as the "true" price of an asset can be regarded as N parameters when there are N transaction prices available. This concept of parameter is related to data augmentation and becomes apparent when we discuss applications of the MCMC methods.

Denote the three parameters by θ_1, θ_2, and θ_3. Let $\boldsymbol{X}$ be the collection of available data and M the entertained model. The goal here is to estimate the parameters so that the fitted model can be used to make inference. Suppose that the likelihood function of the model is hard to obtain, but the three conditional distributions of a single parameter given the others are available. In other words, we assume that the following three conditional distributions are known:

$$f_1(\theta_1|\theta_2, \theta_3, \boldsymbol{X}, M), \quad f_2(\theta_2|\theta_3, \theta_1, \boldsymbol{X}, M), \quad f_3(\theta_3|\theta_1, \theta_2, \boldsymbol{X}, M), \tag{12.1}$$

where $f_i(\theta_i|\theta_{j\neq i}, \boldsymbol{X}, M)$ denotes the conditional distribution of the parameter θ_i given the data, the model, and the other two parameters. In application, we do not need to know the exact forms of the conditional distributions. What is needed is the ability to draw a random number from each of the three conditional distributions.

Let $\theta_{2,0}$ and $\theta_{3,0}$ be two arbitrary starting values of θ_2 and θ_3. The Gibbs sampler proceeds as follows:

1. Draw a random sample from $f_1(\theta_1|\theta_{2,0}, \theta_{3,0}, \boldsymbol{X}, M)$. Denote the random draw by $\theta_{1,1}$.
2. Draw a random sample from $f_2(\theta_2|\theta_{3,0}, \theta_{1,1}, \boldsymbol{X}, M)$. Denote the random draw by $\theta_{2,1}$.
3. Draw a random sample from $f_3(\theta_3|\theta_{1,1}, \theta_{2,1}, \boldsymbol{X}, M)$. Denote the random draw by $\theta_{3,1}$.

This completes a Gibbs iteration and the parameters become $\theta_{1,1}$, $\theta_{2,1}$, and $\theta_{3,1}$.

Next, using the new parameters as starting values and repeating the prior iteration of random draws, we complete another Gibbs iteration to obtain the updated parameters $\theta_{1,2}$, $\theta_{2,2}$, and $\theta_{3,2}$. We can repeat the previous iterations for m times to obtain a sequence of random draws:

$$(\theta_{1,1}, \theta_{2,1}, \theta_{3,1}), \ldots, (\theta_{1,m}, \theta_{2,m}, \theta_{3,m}).$$

Under some regularity conditions, it can be shown that, for a sufficiently large m, $(\theta_{1,m}, \theta_{2,m}, \theta_{3,m})$ is approximately equivalent to a random draw from the joint distribution $f(\theta_1, \theta_2, \theta_3|\boldsymbol{X}, M)$ of the three parameters. The regularity conditions are weak; they essentially require that for an arbitrary starting value $(\theta_{1,0}, \theta_{2,0}, \theta_{3,0})$, the prior Gibbs iterations have a chance to visit the full parameter space. The actual convergence theorem involves using the Markov chain theory; see Tierney (1994).

In practice, we use a sufficiently large n and discard the first m random draws of the Gibbs iterations to form a Gibbs sample, say,

$$(\theta_{1,m+1}, \theta_{2,m+1}, \theta_{3,m+1}), \ldots, (\theta_{1,n}, \theta_{2,n}, \theta_{3,n}). \tag{12.2}$$

Since the previous realizations form a random sample from the joint distribution $f(\theta_1, \theta_2, \theta_3|\boldsymbol{X}, M)$, they can be used to make inference. For example, a point estimate of θ_i and its variance are

$$\widehat{\theta}_i = \frac{1}{n-m}\sum_{j=m+1}^{n} \theta_{i,j}, \quad \widehat{\sigma}_i^2 = \frac{1}{n-m-1}\sum_{j=m+1}^{n} (\theta_{i,j} - \widehat{\theta}_i)^2. \tag{12.3}$$

The Gibbs sample in Eq. (12.2) can be used in many ways. For example, if we are interested in testing the null hypothesis $H_o : \theta_1 = \theta_2$ versus the alternative hypothesis $H_a : \theta_1 \neq \theta_2$, then we can simply obtain the point estimate of $\theta = \theta_1 - \theta_2$ and its variance as

$$\widehat{\theta} = \frac{1}{n-m}\sum_{j=m+1}^{n} (\theta_{1,j} - \theta_{2,j}), \quad \widehat{\sigma}^2 = \frac{1}{n-m-1}\sum_{j=m+1}^{n} (\theta_{1,j} - \theta_{2,j} - \widehat{\theta})^2.$$

The null hypothesis can then be tested by using the conventional t-ratio statistic $t = \widehat{\theta}/\widehat{\sigma}$.

Remark. The first m random draws of a Gibbs sampling, which are discarded, are commonly referred to as the *burn-in* sample. The burn-ins are used to ensure that the Gibbs sample in Eq. (12.2) is indeed close enough to a random sample from the joint distribution $f(\theta_1, \theta_2, \theta_3|\boldsymbol{X}, M)$. □

Remark. The method discussed before consists of running a single long chain and keeping all random draws after the burn-ins to obtain a Gibbs sample. Alternatively, one can run many relatively short chains using different starting values and a relatively small n. The random draw of the last Gibbs iteration in each chain is then used to form a Gibbs sample. □

From the prior introduction, Gibbs sampling has the advantage of decomposing a high-dimensional estimation problem into several lower dimensional ones via full conditional distributions of the parameters. At the extreme, a high-dimensional problem with N parameters can be solved iteratively by using N univariate conditional distributions. This property makes the Gibbs sampling simple and widely applicable. However, it is often not efficient to reduce all the Gibbs draws into a univariate problem. When parameters are highly correlated, it pays to draw them jointly. Consider the three-parameter illustrative example. If θ_1 and θ_2 are highly correlated, then one should employ the conditional distributions $f(\theta_1, \theta_2|\theta_3, \boldsymbol{X}, M)$

and $f_3(\theta_3|\theta_1, \theta_2, \boldsymbol{X}, M)$ whenever possible. A Gibbs iteration then consists of (a) drawing jointly (θ_1, θ_2) given θ_3 and (b) drawing θ_3 given (θ_1, θ_2). For more information on the impact of parameter correlations on the convergence rate of a Gibbs sampler, see Liu, Wong, and Kong (1994).

In practice, convergence of a Gibbs sample is an important issue. The theory only states that the convergence occurs when the number of iterations m is sufficiently large. It provides no specific guidance for choosing m. Many methods have been devised in the literature for checking the convergence of a Gibbs sample. But there is no consensus on which method performs best. In fact, none of the available methods can guarantee 100% that the Gibbs sample under study has converged for all applications. Performance of a checking method often depends on the problem at hand. Care must be exercised in a real application to ensure that there is no obvious violation of the convergence requirement; see Carlin and Louis (2000) and Gelman et al. (2003) for convergence checking methods. In application, it is important to repeat the Gibbs sampling several times with different starting values to ensure that the algorithm has converged.

12.3 BAYESIAN INFERENCE

Conditional distributions play a key role in Gibbs sampling. In the statistical literature, these conditional distributions are referred to as *conditional posterior distributions* because they are distributions of parameters given the data, other parameter values, and the entertained model. In this section, we review some well-known posterior distributions that are useful in using MCMC methods.

12.3.1 Posterior Distributions

There are two approaches to statistical inference. The first approach is the classical approach based on the maximum likelihood principle. Here a model is estimated by maximizing the likelihood function of the data, and the fitted model is used to make inference. The other approach is Bayesian inference that combines prior belief with data to obtain posterior distributions on which statistical inference is based. Historically, there were heated debates between the two schools of statistical inference. Yet both approaches have proved to be useful and are now widely accepted. The methods discussed so far in this book belong to the classical approach. However, Bayesian solutions exist for all of the problems considered. This is particularly so in recent years with the advances in MCMC methods, which greatly improve the feasibility of Bayesian analysis. Readers can revisit the previous chapters and derive MCMC solutions for the problems considered. In most cases, the Bayesian solutions are similar to what we had before. In some cases, the Bayesian solutions might be advantageous. For example, consider the calculation of value at risk in Chapter 7. A Bayesian solution can easily take into consideration the parameter uncertainty in VaR calculation. However, the approach requires intensive computation.

Let $\boldsymbol{\theta}$ be the vector of unknown parameters of an entertained model and $\boldsymbol{X}$ be the data. Bayesian analysis seeks to combine knowledge about the parameters with the data to make inference. Knowledge of the parameters is expressed by specifying a *prior* distribution for the parameters, which is denoted by $P(\boldsymbol{\theta})$. For a given model, denote the likelihood function of the data by $f(\boldsymbol{X}|\boldsymbol{\theta})$. Then by the definition of conditional probability,

$$f(\boldsymbol{\theta}|\boldsymbol{X}) = \frac{f(\boldsymbol{\theta}, \boldsymbol{X})}{f(\boldsymbol{X})} = \frac{f(\boldsymbol{X}|\boldsymbol{\theta})P(\boldsymbol{\theta})}{f(\boldsymbol{X})}, \tag{12.4}$$

where the marginal distribution $f(\boldsymbol{X})$ can be obtained by

$$f(\boldsymbol{X}) = \int f(\boldsymbol{X}, \boldsymbol{\theta})\, d\boldsymbol{\theta} = \int f(\boldsymbol{X}|\boldsymbol{\theta})P(\boldsymbol{\theta})\, d\boldsymbol{\theta}.$$

The distribution $f(\boldsymbol{\theta}|\boldsymbol{X})$ in Eq. (12.4) is called the *posterior distribution* of $\boldsymbol{\theta}$. In general, we can use Bayes' rule to obtain

$$f(\boldsymbol{\theta}|\boldsymbol{X}) \propto f(\boldsymbol{X}|\boldsymbol{\theta})P(\boldsymbol{\theta}), \tag{12.5}$$

where $P(\boldsymbol{\theta})$ is the prior distribution and $f(\boldsymbol{X}|\boldsymbol{\theta})$ is the likelihood function. From Eq. (12.5), making statistical inference based on the likelihood function $f(\boldsymbol{X}|\boldsymbol{\theta})$ amounts to using a Bayesian approach with a constant prior distribution.

12.3.2 Conjugate Prior Distributions

Obtaining the posterior distribution in Eq. (12.4) is not simple in general, but there are cases in which the prior and posterior distributions belong to the same family of distributions. Such a prior distribution is called a *conjugate* prior distribution. For MCMC methods, use of conjugate priors means that a closed-form solution for the conditional posterior distributions is available. Random draws of the Gibbs sampler can then be obtained by using the commonly available computer routines of probability distributions. In what follows, we review some well-known conjugate priors. For more information, readers are referred to textbooks on Bayesian statistics (e.g., DeGroot 1990, Chapter 9).

RESULT 1. Suppose that $x_1, \ldots, x_n$ form a random sample from a normal distribution with mean μ, which is unknown, and variance σ^2, which is known and positive. Suppose that the prior distribution of μ is a normal distribution with mean μ_o and variance σ_o^2. Then the posterior distribution of μ given the data and prior is normal with mean μ_* and variance σ_*^2 given by

$$\mu_* = \frac{\sigma^2\mu_o + n\sigma_o^2\bar{x}}{\sigma^2 + n\sigma_o^2} \quad \text{and} \quad \sigma_*^2 = \frac{\sigma^2\sigma_o^2}{\sigma^2 + n\sigma_o^2},$$

where $\bar{x} = \sum_{i=1}^{n} x_i/n$ is the sample mean.

In Bayesian analysis, it is often convenient to use the *precision* parameter $\eta = 1/\sigma^2$ (i.e., the inverse of the variance σ^2). Denote the precision parameter of the prior distribution by $\eta_o = 1/\sigma_o^2$ and that of the posterior distribution by $\eta_* = 1/\sigma_*^2$. Then Result 1 can be rewritten as

$$\eta_* = \eta_o + n\eta \quad \text{and} \quad \mu_* = \frac{\eta_o}{\eta_*} \times \mu_o + \frac{n\eta}{\eta_*} \times \bar{x}.$$

For the normal random sample considered, data information about μ is contained in the sample mean $\overline{x}$, which is the sufficient statistic of μ. The precision of $\overline{x}$ is $n/\sigma^2 = n\eta$. Consequently, Result 1 says that (a) precision of the posterior distribution is the sum of the precisions of the prior and the data, and (b) the posterior mean is a weighted average of the prior mean and sample mean with weight proportional to the precision. The two formulas also show that the contribution of the prior distribution is diminishing as the sample size n increases.

A multivariate version of Result 1 is particularly useful in MCMC methods when linear regression models are involved; see Box and Tiao (1973).

Result 1a. Suppose that $\boldsymbol{x}_1, \ldots, \boldsymbol{x}_n$ form a random sample from a multivariate normal distribution with mean vector $\boldsymbol{\mu}$ and a known covariance matrix $\boldsymbol{\Sigma}$. Suppose also that the prior distribution of $\boldsymbol{\mu}$ is multivariate normal with mean vector $\boldsymbol{\mu}_o$ and covariance matrix $\boldsymbol{\Sigma}_o$. Then the posterior distribution of $\boldsymbol{\mu}$ is also multivariate normal with mean vector $\boldsymbol{\mu}_*$ and covariance matrix $\boldsymbol{\Sigma}_*$, where

$$\boldsymbol{\Sigma}_*^{-1} = \boldsymbol{\Sigma}_o^{-1} + n\boldsymbol{\Sigma}^{-1} \quad \text{and} \quad \boldsymbol{\mu}_* = \boldsymbol{\Sigma}_*(\boldsymbol{\Sigma}_o^{-1}\boldsymbol{\mu}_o + n\boldsymbol{\Sigma}^{-1}\overline{\boldsymbol{x}}),$$

where $\overline{\boldsymbol{x}} = \left(\sum_{i=1}^n \boldsymbol{x}_i\right)/n$ is the sample mean, which is distributed as a multivariate normal with mean $\boldsymbol{\mu}$ and covariance matrix $\boldsymbol{\Sigma}/n$. Note that $n\boldsymbol{\Sigma}^{-1}$ is the precision matrix of $\overline{\boldsymbol{x}}$ and $\boldsymbol{\Sigma}_o^{-1}$ is the precision matrix of the prior distribution.

A random variable η has a gamma distribution with positive parameters α and β if its probability density function is

$$f(\eta|\alpha, \beta) = \frac{\beta^\alpha}{\Gamma(\alpha)}\eta^{\alpha-1}e^{-\beta\eta}, \quad \eta > 0,$$

where $\Gamma(\alpha)$ is a gamma function. For this distribution, $E(\eta) = \alpha/\beta$ and $\text{Var}(\eta) = \alpha/\beta^2$.

Result 2. Suppose that $x_1, \ldots, x_n$ form a random sample from a normal distribution with a given mean μ and an unknown precision η. If the prior distribution of η is a gamma distribution with positive parameters α and β, then the posterior distribution of η is a gamma distribution with parameters $\alpha + (n/2)$ and $\beta + \sum_{i=1}^n (x_i - \mu)^2/2$.

A random variable θ has a beta distribution with positive parameters α and β if its probability density function is

$$f(\theta|\alpha, \beta) = \frac{\Gamma(\alpha+\beta)}{\Gamma(\alpha)\Gamma(\beta)}\theta^{\alpha-1}(1-\theta)^{\beta-1}, \quad 0 < \theta < 1.$$

The mean and variance of θ are $E(\theta) = \alpha/(\alpha+\beta)$ and $\text{Var}(\theta) = \alpha\beta/[(\alpha+\beta)^2(\alpha+\beta+1)]$.

Result 3. Suppose that $x_1, \ldots, x_n$ form a random sample from a Bernoulli distribution with parameter θ. If the prior distribution of θ is a beta distribution with given positive parameters α and β, then the posterior of θ is a beta distribution with parameters $\alpha + \sum_{i=1}^{n} x_i$ and $\beta + n - \sum_{i=1}^{n} x_i$.

RESULT 4. Suppose that $x_1, \ldots, x_n$ form a random sample from a Poisson distribution with parameter λ. Suppose also that the prior distribution of λ is a gamma distribution with given positive parameters α and β. Then the posterior distribution of λ is a gamma distribution with parameters $\alpha + \sum_{i=1}^{n} x_i$ and $\beta + n$.

RESULT 5. Suppose that $x_1, \ldots, x_n$ form a random sample from an exponential distribution with parameter λ. If the prior distribution of λ is a gamma distribution with given positive parameters α and β, then the posterior distribution of λ is a gamma distribution with parameters $\alpha + n$ and $\beta + \sum_{i=1}^{n} x_i$.

A random variable X has a negative binomial distribution with parameters m and λ, where $m > 0$ and $0 < \lambda < 1$, if X has a probability mass function

$$p(n|m, \lambda) = \begin{cases} \binom{m+n-1}{n} \lambda^m (1-\lambda)^n & \text{if } n = 0, 1, \ldots, \\ 0 & \text{otherwise.} \end{cases}$$

A simple example of negative binomial distribution in finance is how many MBA graduates a firm must interview before finding exactly m "right candidates" for its m openings, assuming that the applicants are independent and each applicant has a probability λ of being a perfect fit. Denote the total number of interviews by Y. Then $X = Y - m$ is distributed as a negative binomial with parameters m and λ.

RESULT 6. Suppose that $x_1, \ldots, x_n$ form a random sample from a negative binomial distribution with parameters m and λ, where m is positive and fixed. If the prior distribution of λ is a beta distribution with positive parameters α and β, then the posterior distribution of λ is a beta distribution with parameters $\alpha + mn$ and $\beta + \sum_{i=1}^{n} x_i$.

Next, we consider the case of a normal distribution with an unknown mean μ and an unknown precision η. The two-dimensional prior distribution is partitioned as $P(\mu, \eta) = P(\mu|\eta)P(\eta)$.

RESULT 7. Suppose that $x_1, \ldots, x_n$ form a random sample from a normal distribution with an unknown mean μ and an unknown precision η. Suppose also that the conditional distribution of μ given $\eta = \eta_o$ is a normal distribution with mean μ_o and precision $\tau_o \eta_o$ and the marginal distribution of η is a gamma distribution with positive parameters α and β. Then the conditional posterior distribution of μ given $\eta = \eta_o$ is a normal distribution with mean μ_* and precision η_*,

$$\mu_* = \frac{\tau_o \mu_o + n\bar{x}}{\tau_o + n} \quad \text{and} \quad \eta_* = (\tau_o + n)\eta_o,$$

where $\overline{x} = \left(\sum_{i=1}^{n} x_i\right)/n$ is the sample mean, and the marginal posterior distribution of η is a gamma distribution with parameters $\alpha + (n/2)$ and β_*, where

$$\beta_* = \beta + \frac{1}{2}\sum_{i=1}^{n}(x_i - \overline{x})^2 + \frac{\tau_o n(\overline{x} - \mu_o)^2}{2(\tau_o + n)}.$$

When the conditional variance of a random variable is of interest, an inverted chi-squared distribution (or inverse chi-squared) is often used. A random variable Y has an inverted chi-squared distribution with v degrees of freedom if $1/Y$ follows a chi-squared distribution with the same degrees of freedom. The probability density function of Y is

$$f(y|v) = \frac{2^{-v/2}}{\Gamma(v/2)} y^{-(v/2+1)} e^{-1/(2y)}, \quad y > 0.$$

For this distribution, we have $E(Y) = 1/(v-2)$ if $v > 2$ and $\text{Var}(Y) = 2/[(v-2)^2(v-4)]$ if $v > 4$.

RESULT 8. Suppose that $a_1, \ldots, a_n$ form a random sample from a normal distribution with mean zero and variance σ^2. Suppose also that the prior distribution of σ^2 is an inverted chi-squared distribution with v degrees of freedom (i.e., $(v\lambda)/\sigma^2 \sim \chi_v^2$, where $\lambda > 0$). Then the posterior distribution of σ^2 is also an inverted chi-squared distribution with $v + n$ degrees of freedom—that is, $\left(v\lambda + \sum_{i=1}^{n} a_i^2\right)/\sigma^2 \sim \chi_{v+n}^2$.

12.4 ALTERNATIVE ALGORITHMS

In many applications, there are no closed-form solutions for the conditional posterior distributions. But many clever alternative algorithms have been devised in the statistical literature to overcome this difficulty. In this section, we discuss some of these algorithms.

12.4.1 Metropolis Algorithm

This algorithm is applicable when the conditional posterior distribution is known except for a normalization constant; see Metropolis and Ulam (1949) and Metropolis et al. (1953). Suppose that we want to draw a random sample from the distribution $f(\boldsymbol{\theta}|\boldsymbol{X})$, which contains a complicated normalization constant so that a direct draw is either too time-consuming or infeasible. But there exists an approximate distribution for which random draws are easily available. The Metropolis algorithm generates a sequence of random draws from the approximate distribution whose distributions converge to $f(\boldsymbol{\theta}|\boldsymbol{X})$. The algorithm proceeds as follows:

1. Draw a random starting value $\boldsymbol{\theta}_0$ such that $f(\boldsymbol{\theta}_0|\boldsymbol{X}) > 0$.
2. For $t = 1, 2, \ldots$,
   (a) Draw a candidate sample $\boldsymbol{\theta}_*$ from a *known* distribution at iteration t given the previous draw $\boldsymbol{\theta}_{t-1}$. Denote the known distribution by $J_t(\boldsymbol{\theta}_t|\boldsymbol{\theta}_{t-1})$,

which is called a *jumping distribution* in Gelman et al. (2003). It is also referred to as a *proposal distribution*. The jumping distribution must be symmetric—that is, $J_t(\boldsymbol{\theta}_i|\boldsymbol{\theta}_j) = J_t(\boldsymbol{\theta}_j|\boldsymbol{\theta}_i)$ for all $\boldsymbol{\theta}_i$, $\boldsymbol{\theta}_j$, and t.

(b) Calculate the ratio

$$r = \frac{f(\boldsymbol{\theta}_*|\boldsymbol{X})}{f(\boldsymbol{\theta}_{t-1}|\boldsymbol{X})}.$$

(c) Set

$$\boldsymbol{\theta}_t = \begin{cases} \boldsymbol{\theta}_* & \text{with probability } \min(r, 1), \\ \boldsymbol{\theta}_{t-1} & \text{otherwise.} \end{cases}$$

Under some regularity conditions, the sequence $\{\boldsymbol{\theta}_t\}$ converges in distribution to $f(\boldsymbol{\theta}|\boldsymbol{X})$; see Gelman et al. (2003).

Implementation of the algorithm requires the ability to calculate the ratio r for all $\boldsymbol{\theta}_*$ and $\boldsymbol{\theta}_{t-1}$, to draw $\boldsymbol{\theta}_*$ from the jumping distribution, and to draw a random realization from a uniform distribution to determine the acceptance or rejection of $\boldsymbol{\theta}_*$. The normalization constant of $f(\boldsymbol{\theta}|\boldsymbol{X})$ is not needed because only a ratio is used.

The acceptance and rejection rule of the algorithm can be stated as follows: (i) if the jump from $\boldsymbol{\theta}_{t-1}$ to $\boldsymbol{\theta}_*$ increases the conditional posterior density, then accept $\boldsymbol{\theta}_*$ as $\boldsymbol{\theta}_t$; (ii) if the jump decreases the posterior density, then set $\boldsymbol{\theta}_t = \boldsymbol{\theta}_*$ with probability equal to the density ratio r, and set $\boldsymbol{\theta}_t = \boldsymbol{\theta}_{t-1}$ otherwise. Such a procedure seems reasonable.

Examples of symmetric jumping distributions include the normal and Student-t distributions for the mean parameter. For a given covariance matrix, we have $f(\boldsymbol{\theta}_i|\boldsymbol{\theta}_j) = f(\boldsymbol{\theta}_j|\boldsymbol{\theta}_i)$, where $f(\boldsymbol{\theta}|\boldsymbol{\theta}_o)$ denotes a multivariate normal density function with mean vector $\boldsymbol{\theta}_o$.

12.4.2 Metropolis–Hasting Algorithm

Hasting (1970) generalizes the Metropolis algorithm in two ways. First, the jumping distribution does not have to be symmetric. Second, the jumping rule is modified to

$$r = \frac{f(\boldsymbol{\theta}_*|\boldsymbol{X})/J_t(\boldsymbol{\theta}_*|\boldsymbol{\theta}_{t-1})}{f(\boldsymbol{\theta}_{t-1}|\boldsymbol{X})/J_t(\boldsymbol{\theta}_{t-1}|\boldsymbol{\theta}_*)} = \frac{f(\boldsymbol{\theta}_*|\boldsymbol{X})J_t(\boldsymbol{\theta}_{t-1}|\boldsymbol{\theta}_*)}{f(\boldsymbol{\theta}_{t-1}|\boldsymbol{X})J_t(\boldsymbol{\theta}_*|\boldsymbol{\theta}_{t-1})}.$$

This modified algorithm is referred to as the Metropolis–Hasting algorithm. Tierney (1994) discusses methods to improve computational efficiency of the algorithm.

12.4.3 Griddy Gibbs

In financial applications, an entertained model may contain some nonlinear parameters (e.g., the moving-average parameters in an ARMA model or the GARCH parameters in a volatility model). Since conditional posterior distributions of nonlinear parameters do not have a closed-form expression, implementing a Gibbs sampler in this situation may become complicated even with the Metropolis–Hasting algorithm. Tanner (1996) describes a simple procedure to obtain random draws in a Gibbs sampling when the conditional posterior distribution is univariate. The method is called the *Griddy Gibbs sampler* and is widely applicable. However, the method could be inefficient in a real application.

Let θ_i be a scalar parameter with conditional posterior distribution $f(\theta_i|\boldsymbol{X}, \boldsymbol{\theta}_{-i})$, where $\boldsymbol{\theta}_{-i}$ is the parameter vector after removing θ_i. For instance, if $\boldsymbol{\theta} = (\theta_1, \theta_2, \theta_3)'$, then $\boldsymbol{\theta}_{-1} = (\theta_2, \theta_3)'$. The Griddy Gibbs proceeds as follows:

1. Select a grid of points from a properly selected interval of θ_i, say, $\theta_{i1} \leq \theta_{i2} \leq \cdots \leq \theta_{im}$. Evaluate the conditional posterior density function to obtain $w_j = f(\theta_{ij}|\boldsymbol{X}, \boldsymbol{\theta}_{-i})$ for $j = 1, \ldots, m$.
2. Use $w_1, \ldots, w_m$ to obtain an approximation to the inverse cumulative distribution function (CDF) of $f(\theta_i|\boldsymbol{X}, \boldsymbol{\theta}_{-i})$.
3. Draw a uniform (0,1) random variate and transform the observation via the approximate inverse CDF to obtain a random draw for θ_i.

Some remarks on the Griddy Gibbs are in order. First, the normalization constant of the conditional posterior distribution $f(\theta_i|\boldsymbol{X}, \boldsymbol{\theta}_{-i})$ is not needed because the inverse CDF can be obtained from $\{w_j\}_{j=1}^m$ directly. Second, a simple approximation to the inverse CDF is a discrete distribution for $\{\theta_{ij}\}_{j=1}^m$ with probability $p(\theta_{ij}) = w_j / \sum_{v=1}^m w_v$. Third, in a real application, selection of the interval $[\theta_{i1}, \theta_{im}]$ for the parameter θ_i must be checked carefully. A simple checking procedure is to consider the histogram of the Gibbs draws of θ_i. If the histogram indicates substantial probability around θ_{i1} or θ_{im}, then the interval must be expanded. However, if the histogram shows a concentration of probability inside the interval $[\theta_{i1}, \theta_{im}]$, then the interval is too wide and can be shortened. If the interval is too wide, then the Griddy Gibbs becomes inefficient because most of w_j would be zero. Finally, the Griddy Gibbs or Metropolis–Hasting algorithm can be used in a Gibbs sampling to obtain random draws of some parameters.

12.5 LINEAR REGRESSION WITH TIME SERIES ERRORS

We are ready to consider some specific applications of MCMC methods. Examples discussed in the next few sections are for illustrative purposes only. The goal here is to highlight the applicability and usefulness of the methods. Understanding these examples can help readers gain insights into applications of MCMC methods in finance.

The first example is to estimate a regression model with serially correlated errors. This is a topic discussed in Chapter 2, where we use SCA to perform the estimation. A simple version of the model is

$$y_t = \beta_0 + \beta_1 x_{1t} + \cdots + \beta_k x_{kt} + z_t,$$
$$z_t = \phi z_{t-1} + a_t,$$

where y_t is the dependent variable, x_{it} are explanatory variables that may contain lagged values of y_t, and z_t follows a simple AR(1) model with $\{a_t\}$ being a sequence of independent and identically distributed normal random variables with mean zero and variance σ^2. Denote the parameters of the model by $\boldsymbol{\theta} = (\boldsymbol{\beta}', \phi, \sigma^2)'$, where $\boldsymbol{\beta} = (\beta_0, \beta_1, \ldots, \beta_k)'$, and let $\boldsymbol{x}_t = (1, x_{1t}, \ldots, x_{kt})'$ be the vector of all regressors at time t, including a constant of unity. The model becomes

$$y_t = \boldsymbol{x}_t'\boldsymbol{\beta} + z_t, \quad z_t = \phi z_{t-1} + a_t, \quad t = 1, \ldots, n, \tag{12.6}$$

where n is the sample size.

A natural way to implement Gibbs sampling in this case is to iterate between regression estimation and time series estimation. If the time series model is known, we can estimate the regression model easily by using the least squares method. However, if the regression model is known, we can obtain the time series z_t by using $z_t = y_t - \boldsymbol{x}_t'\boldsymbol{\beta}$ and use the series to estimate the AR(1) model. Therefore, we need the following conditional posterior distributions:

$$f(\boldsymbol{\beta}|\boldsymbol{Y}, \boldsymbol{X}, \phi, \sigma^2), \quad f(\phi|\boldsymbol{Y}, \boldsymbol{X}, \boldsymbol{\beta}, \sigma^2), \quad f(\sigma^2|\boldsymbol{Y}, \boldsymbol{X}, \boldsymbol{\beta}, \phi),$$

where $\boldsymbol{Y} = (y_1, \ldots, y_n)'$ and $\boldsymbol{X}$ denotes the collection of all observations of explanatory variables.

We use conjugate prior distributions to obtain closed-form expressions for the conditional posterior distributions. The prior distributions are

$$\boldsymbol{\beta} \sim N(\boldsymbol{\beta}_o, \boldsymbol{\Sigma}_o), \quad \phi \sim N(\phi_o, \sigma_o^2), \quad \frac{v\lambda}{\sigma^2} \sim \chi_v^2, \tag{12.7}$$

where again $\sim$ denotes distribution, and $\boldsymbol{\beta}_o$, $\boldsymbol{\Sigma}_o$, λ, v, ϕ_o, and σ_o^2 are known quantities. These quantities are referred to as hyperparameters in Bayesian inference. Their exact values depend on the problem at hand. Typically, we assume that $\boldsymbol{\beta}_o = \boldsymbol{0}$, $\phi_o = 0$, and $\boldsymbol{\Sigma}_o$ is a diagonal matrix with large diagonal elements. The prior distributions in Eq. (12.7) are assumed to be independent of each other. Thus, we use independent priors based on the partition of the parameter vector $\boldsymbol{\theta}$.

The conditional posterior distribution $f(\boldsymbol{\beta}|\boldsymbol{Y}, \boldsymbol{X}, \phi, \sigma^2)$ can be obtained by using Result 1a of Section 12.3. Specifically, given ϕ, we define

$$y_{o,t} = y_t - \phi y_{t-1}, \quad \boldsymbol{x}_{o,t} = \boldsymbol{x}_t - \phi \boldsymbol{x}_{t-1}.$$

Using Eq. (12.6), we have

$$y_{o,t} = \boldsymbol{\beta}'\boldsymbol{x}_{o,t} + a_t, \quad t = 2, \ldots, n. \tag{12.8}$$

Under the assumption of $\{a_t\}$, Eq. (12.8) is a multiple linear regression. Therefore, information of the data about the parameter vector $\boldsymbol{\beta}$ is contained in its least squares estimate

$$\widehat{\boldsymbol{\beta}} = \left(\sum_{t=2}^{n} \boldsymbol{x}_{o,t}\boldsymbol{x}_{o,t}'\right)^{-1} \left(\sum_{t=2}^{n} \boldsymbol{x}_{o,t} y_{o,t}\right),$$

which has a multivariate normal distribution

$$\widehat{\boldsymbol{\beta}} \sim N\left[\boldsymbol{\beta}, \quad \sigma^2 \left(\sum_{t=2}^{n} \boldsymbol{x}_{o,t}\boldsymbol{x}_{o,t}'\right)^{-1}\right].$$

Using Result 1a, the posterior distribution of $\boldsymbol{\beta}$, given the data, ϕ, and σ^2, is multivariate normal. We write the result as

$$(\boldsymbol{\beta}|\boldsymbol{Y}, \boldsymbol{X}, \phi, \sigma) \sim N(\boldsymbol{\beta}_*, \boldsymbol{\Sigma}_*), \tag{12.9}$$

where the parameters are given by

$$\boldsymbol{\Sigma}_*^{-1} = \frac{\sum_{t=2}^n \boldsymbol{x}_{o,t}\boldsymbol{x}'_{o,t}}{\sigma^2} + \boldsymbol{\Sigma}_o^{-1}, \quad \boldsymbol{\beta}_* = \boldsymbol{\Sigma}_* \left(\frac{\sum_{t=2}^n \boldsymbol{x}_{o,t}\boldsymbol{x}'_{o,t}}{\sigma^2}\widehat{\boldsymbol{\beta}} + \boldsymbol{\Sigma}_o^{-1}\boldsymbol{\beta}_o \right).$$

Next, consider the conditional posterior distribution of ϕ given $\boldsymbol{\beta}$, σ^2, and the data. Because $\boldsymbol{\beta}$ is given, we can calculate $z_t = y_t - \boldsymbol{\beta}'\boldsymbol{x}_t$ for all t and consider the AR(1) model

$$z_t = \phi z_{t-1} + a_t, \quad t = 2, \ldots, n.$$

The information of the likelihood function about ϕ is contained in the least squares estimate

$$\widehat{\phi} = \left(\sum_{t=2}^n z_{t-1}^2 \right)^{-1} \left(\sum_{t=2}^n z_{t-1} z_t \right),$$

which is normally distributed with mean ϕ and variance $\sigma^2(\sum_{t=2}^n z_{t-1}^2)^{-1}$. Based on Result 1, the posterior distribution of ϕ is also normal with mean ϕ_* and variance σ_*^2, where

$$\sigma_*^{-2} = \frac{\sum_{t=2}^n z_{t-1}^2}{\sigma^2} + \sigma_o^{-2}, \quad \phi_* = \sigma_*^2 \left(\frac{\sum_{t=2}^n z_{t-1}^2}{\sigma^2}\widehat{\phi} + \sigma_o^{-2}\phi_o \right). \tag{12.10}$$

Finally, turn to the posterior distribution of σ^2 given $\boldsymbol{\beta}$, ϕ, and the data. Because $\boldsymbol{\beta}$ and ϕ are known, we can calculate

$$a_t = z_t - \phi z_{t-1}, \quad z_t = y_t - \boldsymbol{\beta}'\boldsymbol{x}_t, \quad t = 2, \ldots, n.$$

By Result 8 of Section 12.3, the posterior distribution of σ^2 is an inverted chi-squared distribution—that is,

$$\frac{v\lambda + \sum_{t=2}^n a_t^2}{\sigma^2} \sim \chi^2_{v+(n-1)}, \tag{12.11}$$

where χ_k^2 denotes a chi-squared distribution with k degrees of freedom.

Using the three conditional posterior distributions in Eqs. (12.9)–(12.11), we can estimate Eq. (12.6) via Gibbs sampling as follows:

1. Specify the hyperparameter values of the priors in Eq. (12.7).
2. Specify arbitrary starting values for $\boldsymbol{\beta}$, ϕ, and σ^2 (e.g., the ordinary least squares estimate of $\boldsymbol{\beta}$ without time series errors).
3. Use the multivariate normal distribution in Eq. (12.9) to draw a random realization for $\boldsymbol{\beta}$.

4. Use the univariate normal distribution in Eq. (12.10) to draw a random realization for ϕ.
5. Use the chi-squared distribution in Eq. (12.11) to draw a random realization for σ^2.

Repeat steps 3–5 for many iterations to obtain a Gibbs sample. The sample means are then used as point estimates of the parameters of model (12.6).

Example 12.1. As an illustration, we revisit the example of U.S. weekly interest rates of Chapter 2. The data are the 1-year and 3-year Treasury constant maturity rates from January 5, 1962 to September 10, 1999 and are obtained from the Federal Reserve Bank of St. Louis. Because of unit-root nonstationarity, the dependent and independent variables are:

1. $c_{3t} = r_{3t} - r_{3,t-1}$, which is the weekly change in 3-year maturity rate,
2. $c_{1t} = r_{1t} - r_{1,t-1}$, which is the weekly change in 1-year maturity rate,

where the original interest rates r_{it} are measured in percentages. In Chapter 2, we employed a linear regression model with an MA(1) error for the data. Here we consider an AR(2) model for the error process. Using the traditional approach, we obtain the model

$$c_{3t} = 0.0002 + 0.782c_{1t} + z_t, \quad z_t = 0.205z_{t-1} - 0.068z_{t-2} + a_t, \qquad (12.12)$$

where $\widehat{\sigma_a} = 0.067$. Standard errors of the coefficient estimates of Eq. (12.12) are 0.0017, 0.008, 0.023, and 0.023, respectively. Except for a marginally significant residual ACF at lag 6, the prior model seems adequate.

Writing the model as

$$c_{3t} = \beta_0 + \beta_1 c_{1t} + z_t, \quad z_t = \phi_1 z_{t-1} + \phi_2 z_{t-2} + a_t, \qquad (12.13)$$

where $\{a_t\}$ is an independent sequence of $N(0, \sigma^2)$ random variables, we estimate the parameters by Gibbs sampling. The prior distributions used are

$$\boldsymbol{\beta} \sim N(\mathbf{0}, 4\boldsymbol{I}_2), \quad \boldsymbol{\phi} \sim N[\mathbf{0}, \text{diag}(0.25, 0.16)], \quad (v\lambda)/\sigma^2 = (10 \times 0.1)/\sigma^2 \sim \chi^2_{10},$$

where $\boldsymbol{I}_2$ is the 2×2 identity matrix. The initial parameter estimates are obtained by the ordinary least squares method (i.e., by using a two-step procedure of fitting the linear regression model first, then fitting an AR(2) model to the regression residuals). Since the sample size 1966 is large, the initial estimates are close to those given in Eq. (12.12). We iterated the Gibbs sampling for 2100 iterations but discard results of the first 100 iterations. Table 12.1 gives the posterior means and standard errors of the parameters. Figure 12.1 shows the histogram of the marginal posterior distribution of each parameter.

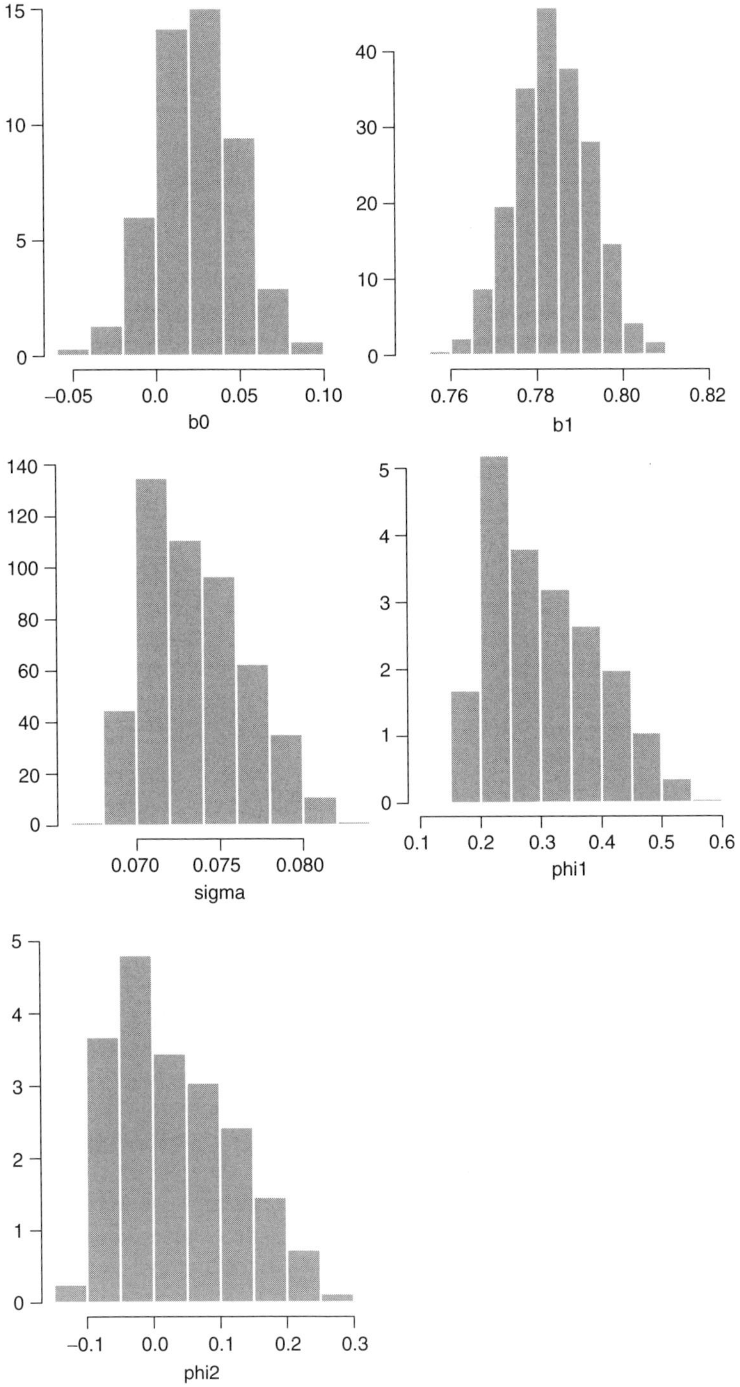

Figure 12.1. Histograms of Gibbs draws for the model in Eq. (12.13) with 2100 iterations. The results are based on the last 2000 draws. Prior distributions and starting parameter values are given in the text.

Table 12.1. Posterior Means and Standard Errors of Model (12.13) Estimated by a Gibbs Sampling with 2100 Iterations[a]

Parameter	β_0	β_1	ϕ_1	ϕ_2	σ
Mean	0.025	0.784	0.305	0.032	0.074
Standard error	0.024	0.009	0.089	0.087	0.003

[a]The results are based on the last 2000 iterations, and the prior distributions are given in the text.

We repeated the Gibbs sampling with different initial values but obtained similar results. The Gibbs sampling appears to have converged. From Table 12.1, the posterior means are close to the estimates of Eq. (12.12) except for the coefficient of z_{t-2}. However, the posterior standard errors of ϕ_1 and ϕ_2 are relatively large, indicating uncertainty in these two estimates. The histograms of Figure 12.1 are informative. In particular, they show that the distributions of $\widehat{\phi}_1$ and $\widehat{\phi}_2$ have not converged to the asymptotic normality; the distributions are skewed to the right. However, the asymptotic normality of $\widehat{\beta}_0$ and $\widehat{\beta}_1$ seems reasonable.

12.6 MISSING VALUES AND OUTLIERS

In this section, we discuss MCMC methods for handling missing values and detecting additive outliers. Let $\{y_t\}_{t=1}^n$ be an observed time series. A data point y_h is an additive outlier if

$$y_t = \begin{cases} x_h + \omega & \text{if } t = h, \\ x_t & \text{otherwise,} \end{cases} \tag{12.14}$$

where ω is the magnitude of the outlier and x_t is an outlier-free time series. Examples of additive outliers include recording errors (e.g., typos and measurement errors). Outliers can seriously affect time series analysis because they may induce substantial biases in parameter estimation and lead to model misspecification.

Consider a time series x_t and a fixed time index h. We can learn a lot about x_h by treating it as a missing value. If the model of x_t were known, then we could derive the conditional distribution of x_h given the other values of the series. By comparing the observed value y_h with the derived distribution of x_h, we can determine whether y_h can be classified as an additive outlier. Specifically, if y_h is a value that is likely to occur under the derived distribution, then y_h is not an additive outlier. However, if the chance to observe y_h is very small under the derived distribution, then y_h can be classified as an additive outlier. Therefore, detection of additive outliers and treatment of missing values in time series analysis are based on the same idea.

In the literature, missing values in a time series can be handled by using either the Kalman filter or MCMC methods; see Jones (1980), Chapter 11, and McCulloch and Tsay (1994a). Outlier detection has also been carefully investigated; see Chang, Tiao, and Chen (1988), Tsay (1988), Tsay, Peña, and Pankratz (2000) and the references therein. The outliers are classified into four categories depending on the nature of their impacts on the time series. Here we focus on additive outliers.

12.6.1 Missing Values

For ease in presentation, consider an AR(p) time series

$$x_t = \phi_1 x_{t-1} + \cdots + \phi_p x_{t-p} + a_t, \tag{12.15}$$

where $\{a_t\}$ is a Gaussian white noise series with mean zero and variance σ^2. Suppose that the sampling period is from $t = 1$ to $t = n$, but the observation x_h is missing, where $1 < h < n$. Our goal is to estimate the model in the presence of a missing value.

In this particular instance, the parameters are $\boldsymbol{\theta} = (\boldsymbol{\phi}', x_h, \sigma^2)'$, where $\boldsymbol{\phi} = (\phi_1, \ldots, \phi_p)'$. Thus, we treat the missing value x_h as an unknown parameter. If we assume that the prior distributions are

$$\boldsymbol{\phi} \sim N(\boldsymbol{\phi}_o, \boldsymbol{\Sigma}_o), \quad x_h \sim N(\mu_o, \sigma_o^2), \quad \frac{v\lambda}{\sigma^2} \sim \chi_v^2,$$

where the hyperparameters are known, then the conditional posterior distributions $f(\boldsymbol{\phi}|\boldsymbol{X}, x_h, \sigma^2)$ and $f(\sigma^2|\boldsymbol{X}, x_h, \boldsymbol{\phi})$ are exactly as those given in the previous section, where $\boldsymbol{X}$ denotes the observed data. The conditional posterior distribution $f(x_h|\boldsymbol{X}, \boldsymbol{\phi}, \sigma^2)$ is univariate normal with mean μ_* and variance σ_h^2. These two parameters can be obtained by using a linear regression model. Specifically, given the model and the data, x_h is only related to $\{x_{h-p}, \ldots, x_{h-1}, x_{h+1}, \ldots, x_{h+p}\}$. Keeping in mind that x_h is an unknown parameter, we can write the relationship as follows:

1. For $t = h$, the model says

$$x_h = \phi_1 x_{h-1} + \cdots + \phi_p x_{h-p} + a_h.$$

Letting $y_h = \phi_1 x_{h-1} + \cdots + \phi_p x_{h-p}$ and $b_h = -a_h$, the prior equation can be written as

$$y_h = x_h + b_h = \phi_0 x_h + b_h,$$

where $\phi_0 = 1$.

2. For $t = h + 1$, we have

$$x_{h+1} = \phi_1 x_h + \phi_2 x_{h-1} + \cdots + \phi_p x_{h+1-p} + a_{h+1}.$$

Letting $y_{h+1} = x_{h+1} - \phi_2 x_{h-1} - \cdots - \phi_p x_{h+1-p}$ and $b_{h+1} = a_{h+1}$, the prior equation can be written as

$$y_{h+1} = \phi_1 x_h + b_{h+1}.$$

3. In general, for $t = h + j$ with $j = 1, \ldots, p$, we have

$$x_{h+j} = \phi_1 x_{h+j-1} + \cdots + \phi_j x_h + \phi_{j+1} x_{h-1} + \cdots + \phi_p x_{h+j-p} + a_{h+j}.$$

Let $y_{h+j} = x_{h+j} - \phi_1 x_{h+j-1} - \cdots - \phi_{j-1} x_{h+1} - \phi_{j+1} x_{h-1} - \cdots - \phi_p x_{h+j-p}$ and $b_{h+j} = a_{h+j}$. The prior equation reduces to

$$y_{h+j} = \phi_j x_h + b_{h+j}.$$

Consequently, for an AR(p) model, the missing value x_h is related to the model, and the data in $p + 1$ equations

$$y_{h+j} = \phi_j x_h + b_{h+j}, \quad j = 0, \ldots, p, \tag{12.16}$$

where $\phi_0 = 1$. Since a normal distribution is symmetric with respect to its mean, a_h and $-a_h$ have the same distribution. Consequently, Eq. (12.16) is a special simple linear regression model with $p + 1$ data points. The least squares estimate of x_h and its variance are

$$\widehat{x}_h = \frac{\sum_{j=0}^{p} \phi_j y_{h+j}}{\sum_{j=0}^{p} \phi_j^2}, \quad \text{Var}(\widehat{x}_h) = \frac{\sigma^2}{\sum_{j=0}^{p} \phi_j^2}.$$

For instance, when $p = 1$, we have $\widehat{x}_h = [\phi_1/(1 + \phi_1^2)](x_{h-1} + x_{h+1})$, which is referred to as the filtered value of x_h. Because a Gaussian AR(1) model is time reversible, equal weights are applied to the two neighboring observations of x_h to obtain the filtered value.

Finally, using Result 1 of Section 12.3, we obtain that the posterior distribution of x_h is normal with mean μ_* and variance σ_*^2, where

$$\mu_* = \frac{\sigma^2 \mu_o + \sigma_o^2 \left(\sum_{j=0}^{p} \phi_j^2\right) \widehat{x}_h}{\sigma^2 + \sigma_o^2 \left(\sum_{j=0}^{p} \phi_j^2\right)}, \quad \sigma_*^2 = \frac{\sigma^2 \sigma_o^2}{\sigma^2 + \sigma_o^2 \sum_{j=0}^{p} \phi_j^2}. \tag{12.17}$$

Missing values may occur in patches, resulting in the situation of multiple consecutive missing values. These missing values can be handled in two ways. First, we can generalize the prior method directly to obtain a solution for multiple filtered values. Consider, for instance, the case that x_h and x_{h+1} are missing. These missing values are related to $\{x_{h-p}, \ldots, x_{h-1}; x_{h+2}, \ldots, x_{h+p+1}\}$. We can define a dependent variable y_{h+j} in a similar manner as before to set up a multiple linear regression with parameters x_h and x_{h+1}. The least squares method is then used to obtain estimates of x_h and x_{h+1}. Combining with the specified prior distributions, we have a bivariate normal posterior distribution for $(x_h, x_{h+1})'$. In Gibbs sampling, this approach draws the consecutive missing values jointly. Second, we can apply the result of a single missing value in Eq. (12.17) multiple times within a Gibbs iteration. Again consider the case of missing x_h and x_{h+1}. We can employ the conditional posterior distributions $f(x_h|\boldsymbol{X}, x_{h+1}, \boldsymbol{\phi}, \sigma^2)$ and $f(x_{h+1}|\boldsymbol{X}, x_h, \boldsymbol{\phi}, \sigma^2)$

separately. In Gibbs sampling, this means that we draw the missing value one at a time.

Because x_h and x_{h+1} are correlated in a time series, drawing them jointly is preferred in a Gibbs sampling. This is particularly so if the number of consecutive missing values is large. Drawing one missing value at a time works well if the number of missing values is small.

Remark. In the previous discussion, we assumed $h - p \geq 1$ and $h + p \leq n$. If h is close to the end points of the sample period, the number of data points available in the linear regression model must be adjusted. □

12.6.2 Outlier Detection

Detection of additive outliers in Eq. (12.14) becomes straightforward under the MCMC framework. Except for the case of a patch of additive outliers with similar magnitudes, the simple Gibbs sampler of McCulloch and Tsay (1994a) seems to work well; see Justel, Peña, and Tsay (2001). Again we use an AR model to illustrate the problem. The method applies equally well to other time series models when the Metropolis–Hasting algorithm or the Griddy Gibbs is used to draw values of nonlinear parameters.

Assume that the observed time series is y_t, which may contain some additive outliers whose locations and magnitudes are unknown. We write the model for y_t as

$$y_t = \delta_t \beta_t + x_t, \quad t = 1, \ldots, n, \tag{12.18}$$

where $\{\delta_t\}$ is a sequence of independent Bernoulli random variables such that $P(\delta_t = 1) = \epsilon$ and $P(\delta_t = 0) = 1 - \epsilon$, ϵ is a constant between 0 and 1, $\{\beta_t\}$ is a sequence of independent random variables from a given distribution, and x_t is an outlier-free AR(p) time series,

$$x_t = \phi_0 + \phi_1 x_{t-1} + \cdots + \phi_p x_{t-p} + a_t,$$

where $\{a_t\}$ is a Gaussian white noise with mean zero and variance σ^2. This model seems complicated, but it allows additive outliers to occur at every time point. The chance of being an outlier for each observation is ϵ.

Under the model in Eq. (12.18), we have n data points, but there are $2n + p + 3$ parameters—namely, $\boldsymbol{\phi} = (\phi_0, \ldots, \phi_p)'$, $\boldsymbol{\delta} = (\delta_1, \ldots, \delta_n)'$, $\boldsymbol{\beta} = (\beta_1, \ldots, \beta_n)'$, σ^2, and ϵ. The binary parameters δ_t are governed by ϵ and the β_t are determined by the specified distribution. The parameters $\boldsymbol{\delta}$ and $\boldsymbol{\beta}$ are introduced by using the idea of data augmentation with δ_t denoting the presence or absence of an additive outlier at time t, and β_t is the magnitude of the outlier at time t when it is present.

Assume that the prior distributions are

$$\boldsymbol{\phi} \sim N(\boldsymbol{\phi}_o, \boldsymbol{\Sigma}_o), \quad \frac{v\lambda}{\sigma^2} \sim \chi^2_v, \quad \epsilon \sim \text{Beta}(\gamma_1, \gamma_2), \quad \beta_t \sim N(0, \xi^2),$$

where the hyperparameters are known. These are conjugate prior distributions. To implement Gibbs sampling for model estimation with outlier detection, we need to consider the conditional posterior distributions of

$$f(\boldsymbol{\phi}|\boldsymbol{Y}, \boldsymbol{\delta}, \boldsymbol{\beta}, \sigma^2), \quad f(\delta_h|\boldsymbol{Y}, \boldsymbol{\delta}_{-h}, \boldsymbol{\beta}, \boldsymbol{\phi}, \sigma^2), \quad f(\beta_h|\boldsymbol{Y}, \boldsymbol{\delta}, \boldsymbol{\beta}_{-h}, \boldsymbol{\phi}, \sigma^2),$$
$$f(\epsilon|\boldsymbol{Y}, \boldsymbol{\delta}), \quad f(\sigma^2|\boldsymbol{Y}, \boldsymbol{\phi}, \boldsymbol{\delta}, \boldsymbol{\beta}),$$

where $1 \leq h \leq n$, $\boldsymbol{Y}$ denotes the data and $\boldsymbol{\theta}_{-i}$ denotes that the ith element of $\boldsymbol{\theta}$ is removed.

Conditioned on $\boldsymbol{\delta}$ and $\boldsymbol{\beta}$, the outlier-free time series x_t can be obtained by $x_t = y_t - \delta_t \beta_t$. Information of the data about $\boldsymbol{\phi}$ is then contained in the least squares estimate

$$\widehat{\boldsymbol{\phi}} = \left(\sum_{t=p+1}^{n} \boldsymbol{x}_{t-1}\boldsymbol{x}'_{t-1}\right)^{-1} \left(\sum_{t=p+1}^{n} \boldsymbol{x}_{t-1}x_t\right),$$

where $\boldsymbol{x}_{t-1} = (1, x_{t-1}, \ldots, x_{t-p})'$, which is normally distributed with mean $\boldsymbol{\phi}$ and covariance matrix

$$\widehat{\boldsymbol{\Sigma}} = \sigma^2 \left(\sum_{t=p+1}^{n} \boldsymbol{x}_{t-1}\boldsymbol{x}'_{t-1}\right)^{-1}.$$

The conditional posterior distribution of $\boldsymbol{\phi}$ is therefore multivariate normal with mean $\boldsymbol{\phi}_*$ and covariance matrix $\boldsymbol{\Sigma}_*$, which are given in Eq. (12.9) with $\boldsymbol{\beta}$ being replaced by $\boldsymbol{\phi}$ and $\boldsymbol{x}_{o,t}$ by $\boldsymbol{x}_{t-1}$. Similarly, the conditional posterior distribution of σ^2 is an inverted chi-squared distribution—that is,

$$\frac{v\lambda + \sum_{t=p+1}^{n} a_t^2}{\sigma^2} \sim \chi^2_{v+(n-p)},$$

where $a_t = x_t - \boldsymbol{\phi}'\boldsymbol{x}_{t-1}$ and $x_t = y_t - \delta_t \beta_t$.

The conditional posterior distribution of δ_h can be obtained as follows. First, δ_h is only related to $\{y_j, \beta_j\}_{j=h-p}^{h+p}$, $\{\delta_j\}_{j=h-p}^{h+p}$ with $j \neq h$, $\boldsymbol{\phi}$, and σ^2. More specifically, we have

$$x_j = y_j - \delta_j \beta_j, \quad j \neq h.$$

Second, x_h can assume two possible values: $x_h = y_h - \beta_h$ if $\delta_h = 1$ and $x_h = y_h$ otherwise. Define

$$w_j = x_j^* - \phi_0 - \phi_1 x_{j-1}^* - \cdots - \phi_p x_{j-p}^*, \quad j = h, \ldots, h+p,$$

where $x_j^* = x_j$ if $j \neq h$ and $x_h^* = y_h$. The two possible values of x_h give rise to two situations:

- Case I: $\delta_h = 0$. Here the hth observation is not an outlier and $x_h^* = y_h = x_h$. Hence, $w_j = a_j$ for $j = h, \ldots, h+p$. In other words, we have

$$w_j \sim N(0, \sigma^2), \quad j = h, \ldots, h+p.$$

- Case II: $\delta_h = 1$. Now the hth observation is an outlier and $x_h^* = y_h = x_h + \beta_h$. The w_j defined before is contaminated by β_h. In fact, we have

$$w_h \sim N(\beta_h, \sigma^2) \quad \text{and} \quad w_j \sim N(-\phi_{j-h}\beta_h, \sigma^2), \quad j = h+1, \ldots, h+p.$$

If we define $\psi_0 = -1$ and $\psi_i = \phi_i$ for $i = 1, \ldots, p$, then we have $w_j \sim N(-\psi_{j-h}\beta_h, \sigma^2)$ for $j = h, \ldots, h+p$.

Based on the prior discussion, we can summarize the situation as follows:

1. Case I: $\delta_h = 0$ with probability $1 - \epsilon$. In this case, $w_j \sim N(0, \sigma^2)$ for $j = h, \ldots, h+p$.
2. Case II: $\delta_h = 1$ with probability ϵ. Here $w_j \sim N(-\psi_{j-h}\beta_h, \sigma^2)$ for $j = h, \ldots, h+p$.

Since there are n data points, j cannot be greater than n. Let $m = \min(n, h+p)$. The posterior distribution of δ_h is therefore

$$P(\delta_h = 1|\boldsymbol{Y}, \boldsymbol{\delta}_{-h}, \boldsymbol{\beta}, \boldsymbol{\phi}, \sigma^2)$$
$$= \frac{\epsilon \exp\left[-\sum_{j=h}^{m}(w_j + \psi_{j-h}\beta_h)^2/(2\sigma^2)\right]}{\epsilon \exp\left[-\sum_{j=h}^{m}(w_j + \psi_{j-h}\beta_h)^2/(2\sigma^2)\right] + (1-\epsilon)\exp\left[-\sum_{j=h}^{m} w_j^2/(2\sigma^2)\right]}. \tag{12.19}$$

This posterior distribution is simply to compare the weighted values of the likelihood function under the two situations with weight being the probability of each situation.

Finally, the posterior distribution of β_h is as follows.

- If $\delta_h = 0$, then y_h is not an outlier and $\beta_h \sim N(0, \xi^2)$.
- If $\delta_h = 1$, then y_h is contaminated by an outlier with magnitude β_h. The variable w_j defined before contains information of β_h for $j = h$, $h+1, \ldots, \min(h+p, n)$. Specifically, we have $w_j \sim N(-\psi_{j-h}\beta_h, \sigma^2)$ for $j = h, h+1, \ldots, \min(h+p, n)$. The information can be put in a linear regression framework as

$$w_j = -\psi_{j-h}\beta_h + a_j, \quad j = h, h+1, \ldots, \min(h+p, n).$$

Consequently, the information is embedded in the least squares estimate

$$\widehat{\beta}_h = \frac{\sum_{j=h}^{m} -\psi_{j-h}w_j}{\sum_{j=h}^{m}\psi_{j-h}^2}, \quad m = \min(h+p, n),$$

which is normally distributed with mean β_h and variance $\sigma^2/\left(\sum_{j=h}^{m}\psi_{j-h}^2\right)$. By Result 1, the posterior distribution of β_h is normal with mean β_h^* and variance σ_{h*}^2, where

$$\beta_h^* = \frac{-\left(\sum_{j=h}^{m}\psi_{j-h}w_j\right)\xi^2}{\sigma^2 + \left(\sum_{j=h}^{m}\psi_{j-h}^2\right)\xi^2}, \quad \sigma_{h*}^2 = \frac{\sigma^2\xi^2}{\sigma^2 + \left(\sum_{j=h}^{m}\psi_{j-h}^2\right)\xi^2}.$$

Example 12.2. Consider the weekly change series of U.S. 3-year Treasury constant maturity interest rate from March 18, 1988 to September 10, 1999 for 600 observations. The interest rate is in percentage and is a subseries of the dependent variable c_{3t} of Example 12.1. The time series is shown in Figure 12.2a. If AR models are entertained for the series, the partial autocorrelation function suggests an AR(3) model and we obtain

$$c_{3t} = 0.227c_{3,t-1} + 0.006c_{3,t-2} + 0.114c_{3,t-2} + a_t, \quad \widehat{\sigma}^2 = 0.0128,$$

where standard errors of the coefficients are 0.041, 0.042, and 0.041, respectively. The Ljung–Box statistics of the residuals show $Q(12) = 11.4$, which is insignificant at the 5% level.

Next, we apply the Gibbs sampling to estimate the AR(3) model and to detect simultaneously possible additive outliers. The prior distributions used are

$$\boldsymbol{\phi} \sim N(\mathbf{0}, 0.25\boldsymbol{I}_3), \quad \frac{v\lambda}{\sigma^2} = \frac{5 \times 0.00256}{\sigma^2} \sim \chi_5^2, \quad \gamma_1 = 5, \quad \gamma_2 = 95, \quad \xi^2 = 0.1,$$

where $0.00256 \approx \widehat{\sigma}^2/5$ and $\xi^2 \approx 9\widehat{\sigma}^2$. The expected number of additive outliers is 5%. Using initial values $\epsilon = 0.05$, $\sigma^2 = 0.012$, $\phi_1 = 0.2$, $\phi_2 = 0.02$, and $\phi_3 = 0.1$, we run the Gibbs sampling for 1050 iterations but discard results of the first 50 iterations. Using posterior means of the coefficients as parameter estimates, we obtain the fitted model

$$c_{3t} = 0.252c_{3,t-1} + 0.003c_{3,t-2} + 0.110c_{3,t-2} + a_t, \quad \widehat{\sigma}^2 = 0.0118,$$

where posterior standard deviations of the parameters are 0.046, 0.045, 0.046, and 0.0008, respectively. Thus, the Gibbs sampling produces results similar to that of the maximum likelihood method. Figure 12.2b shows the time plot of posterior probability of each observation being an additive outlier, and Figure 12.2c plots the posterior mean of outlier magnitude. From the probability plot, some observations have high probabilities of being an outlier. In particular, $t = 323$ has a probability of 0.83 and the associated posterior mean of outlier magnitude is -0.304. This point corresponds to May 20, 1994 when the c_{3t} changed from 0.24 to -0.34 (i.e., about a 0.6% drop in the weekly interest rate within two weeks). The point with second highest posterior probability of being an outlier is $t = 201$, which is January 17, 1992. The outlying posterior probability is 0.58 and the estimated outlier size is 0.176. At this particular time point, c_{3t} changed from -0.02 to 0.33, corresponding to a jump of about 0.35% in the weekly interest rate.

Remark. Outlier detection via Gibbs sampling requires intensive computation, but the approach performs a joint estimation of model parameters and outliers. Yet the traditional approach to outlier detection separates estimation from detection. It is much faster in computation but may produce spurious detections when multiple outliers are present. For the data in Example 12.2, the SCA program also identifies $t = 323$ and $t = 201$ as the two most significant additive outliers. The estimated outlier sizes are -0.39 and 0.36, respectively. □

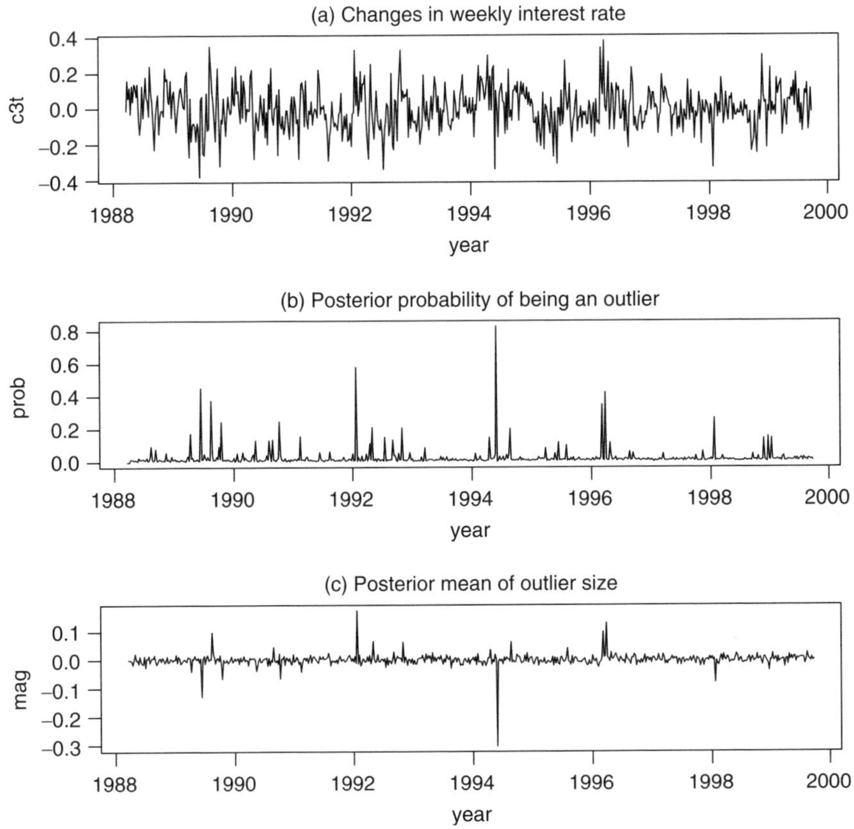

Figure 12.2. Time plots of weekly change series of U.S. 3-year Treasury constant maturity interest rate from March 18, 1988 to September 10, 1999: (a) the data, (b) the posterior probability of being an outlier, and (c) the posterior mean of outlier size. The estimation is based on a Gibbs sampling with 1050 iterations with the first 50 iterations as burn-ins.

12.7 STOCHASTIC VOLATILITY MODELS

An important financial application of MCMC methods is the estimation of stochastic volatility models; see Jacquier, Polson, and Rossi (1994) and the references therein. We start with a univariate stochastic volatility model. The mean and volatility equations of an asset return r_t are

$$r_t = \beta_0 + \beta_1 x_{1t} + \cdots + \beta_p x_{pt} + a_t, \quad a_t = \sqrt{h_t}\epsilon_t, \tag{12.20}$$

$$\ln h_t = \alpha_0 + \alpha_1 \ln h_{t-1} + v_t, \tag{12.21}$$

where $\{x_{it} | i = 1, \ldots, p\}$ are explanatory variables available at time $t-1$, the β_j are parameters, $\{\epsilon_t\}$ is a Gaussian white noise sequence with mean 0 and variance 1, $\{v_t\}$ is also a Gaussian white noise sequence with mean 0 and variance σ_v^2, and $\{\epsilon_t\}$ and $\{v_t\}$ are independent. The log transformation is used to ensure that h_t is positive for all t. The explanatory variables x_{it} may include lagged values of the return (e.g., $x_{it} = r_{t-i}$). In Eq. (12.21), we assume that $|\alpha_1| < 1$ so that the log volatility process $\ln h_t$ is stationary. If necessary, a higher order AR(p) model can be used for $\ln h_t$.

Denote the coefficient vector of the mean equation by $\boldsymbol{\beta} = (\beta_0, \beta_1, \ldots, \beta_p)'$ and the parameter vector of the volatility equation by $\boldsymbol{\omega} = (\alpha_0, \alpha_1, \sigma_v^2)'$. Suppose that $\boldsymbol{R} = (r_1, \ldots, r_n)'$ is the collection of observed returns and $\boldsymbol{X}$ is the collection of explanatory variables. Let $\boldsymbol{H} = (h_1, \ldots, h_n)'$ be the vector of unobservable volatilities. Here $\boldsymbol{\beta}$ and $\boldsymbol{\omega}$ are the "traditional" parameters of the model and $\boldsymbol{H}$ is an auxiliary variable. Estimation of the model would be complicated via the maximum likelihood method because the likelihood function is a mixture over the n-dimensional $\boldsymbol{H}$ distribution as

$$f(\boldsymbol{R}|\boldsymbol{X}, \boldsymbol{\beta}, \boldsymbol{\omega}) = \int f(\boldsymbol{R}|\boldsymbol{X}, \boldsymbol{\beta}, \boldsymbol{H}) f(\boldsymbol{H}|\boldsymbol{\omega})\, d\boldsymbol{H}.$$

However, under the Bayesian framework, the volatility vector $\boldsymbol{H}$ consists of augmented parameters. Conditioning on $\boldsymbol{H}$, we can focus on the probability distribution functions $f(\boldsymbol{R}|\boldsymbol{H}, \boldsymbol{\beta})$ and $f(\boldsymbol{H}|\boldsymbol{\omega})$ and the prior distribution $p(\boldsymbol{\beta}, \boldsymbol{\omega})$. We assume that the prior distribution can be partitioned as $p(\boldsymbol{\beta}, \boldsymbol{\omega}) = p(\boldsymbol{\beta}) p(\boldsymbol{\omega})$; that is, prior distributions for the mean and volatility equations are independent. A Gibbs sampling approach to estimating the stochastic volatility in Eqs. (12.20) and (12.21) then involves drawing random samples from the following conditional posterior distributions:

$$f(\boldsymbol{\beta}|\boldsymbol{R}, \boldsymbol{X}, \boldsymbol{H}, \boldsymbol{\omega}), \quad f(\boldsymbol{H}|\boldsymbol{R}, \boldsymbol{X}, \boldsymbol{\beta}, \boldsymbol{\omega}), \quad f(\boldsymbol{\omega}|\boldsymbol{R}, \boldsymbol{X}, \boldsymbol{\beta}, \boldsymbol{H}).$$

In what follows, we give details of practical implementation of the Gibbs sampling used.

12.7.1 Estimation of Univariate Models

Given $\boldsymbol{H}$, the mean equation in (12.20) is a nonhomogeneous linear regression. Dividing the equation by $\sqrt{h_t}$, we can write the model as

$$r_{o,t} = \boldsymbol{x}_{o,t}' \boldsymbol{\beta} + \epsilon_t, \quad t = 1, \ldots, n, \tag{12.22}$$

where $r_{o,t} = r_t/\sqrt{h_t}$ and $\boldsymbol{x}_{o,t} = \boldsymbol{x}_t/\sqrt{h_t}$, with $\boldsymbol{x}_t = (1, x_{1t}, \ldots, x_{pt})'$ being the vector of explanatory variables. Suppose that the prior distribution of $\boldsymbol{\beta}$ is multivariate normal with mean $\boldsymbol{\beta}_o$ and covariance matrix $\boldsymbol{A}_o$. Then the posterior distribution of $\boldsymbol{\beta}$ is also multivariate normal with mean $\boldsymbol{\beta}_*$ and covariance matrix $\boldsymbol{A}_*$. These two quantities can be obtained as before via Result 1a and they are

$$A_*^{-1} = \sum_{t=1}^{n} \boldsymbol{x}_{o,t} \boldsymbol{x}_{o,t}' + \boldsymbol{A}_o^{-1}, \quad \boldsymbol{\beta}_* = \boldsymbol{A}_* \left(\sum_{t=1}^{n} \boldsymbol{x}_{o,t} r_{o,t} + \boldsymbol{A}_o^{-1} \boldsymbol{\beta}_o \right),$$

where it is understood that the summation starts with $p+1$ if r_{t-p} is the highest lagged return used in the explanatory variables.

The volatility vector $\boldsymbol{H}$ is drawn element by element. The necessary conditional posterior distribution is $f(h_t|\boldsymbol{R}, \boldsymbol{X}, \boldsymbol{H}_{-t}, \boldsymbol{\beta}, \boldsymbol{\omega})$, which is produced by the normal distribution of a_t and the lognormal distribution of the volatility,

$$\begin{aligned} f(h_t|\boldsymbol{R}, \boldsymbol{X}, \boldsymbol{\beta}, \boldsymbol{H}_{-t}, \boldsymbol{\omega}) & \\ &\propto f(a_t|h_t, r_t, \boldsymbol{x}_t, \boldsymbol{\beta}) f(h_t|h_{t-1}, \boldsymbol{\omega}) f(h_{t+1}|h_t, \boldsymbol{\omega}) \\ &\propto h_t^{-0.5} \exp[-(r_t - \boldsymbol{x}_t'\boldsymbol{\beta})^2/(2h_t)] h_t^{-1} \exp[-(\ln h_t - \mu_t)^2/(2\sigma^2)] \\ &\propto h_t^{-1.5} \exp[-(r_t - \boldsymbol{x}_t'\boldsymbol{\beta})^2/(2h_t) - (\ln h_t - \mu_t)^2/(2\sigma^2)], \end{aligned} \tag{12.23}$$

where $\mu_t = [\alpha_0(1-\alpha_1) + \alpha_1(\ln h_{t+1} + \ln h_{t-1})]/(1+\alpha_1^2)$ and $\sigma^2 = \sigma_v^2/(1+\alpha_1^2)$. Here we have used the following properties: (a) $a_t|h_t \sim N(0, h_t)$; (b) $\ln h_t | \ln h_{t-1} \sim N(\alpha_0 + \alpha_1 \ln h_{t-1}, \sigma_v^2)$; (c) $\ln h_{t+1} | \ln h_t \sim N(\alpha_0 + \alpha_1 \ln h_t, \sigma_v^2)$; (d) $d \ln h_t = h_t^{-1} dh_t$, where d denotes differentiation; and (e) the equality

$$(x-a)^2 A + (x-b)^2 C = (x-c)^2 (A+C) + (a-b)^2 AC/(A+C),$$

where $c = (Aa + Cb)/(A+C)$ provided that $A + C \neq 0$. This equality is a scalar version of Lemma 1 of Box and Tiao (1973, p. 418). In our application, $A = 1$, $a = \alpha_0 + \ln h_{t-1}$, $C = \alpha_1^2$, and $b = (\ln h_{t+1} - \alpha_0)/\alpha_1$. The term $(a-b)^2 AC/(A+C)$ does not contain the random variable h_t and, hence, is integrated out in the derivation of the conditional posterior distribution. Jacquier, Polson, and Rossi (1994) use the Metropolis algorithm to draw h_t. We use Griddy Gibbs in this section, and the range of h_t is chosen to be a multiple of the unconditional sample variance of r_t.

To draw random samples of $\boldsymbol{\omega}$, we partition the parameters as $\boldsymbol{\alpha} = (\alpha_0, \alpha_1)'$ and σ_v^2. The prior distribution of $\boldsymbol{\omega}$ is also partitioned accordingly (i.e., $p(\boldsymbol{\omega}) = p(\boldsymbol{\alpha}) p(\sigma_v^2)$). The conditional posterior distributions needed are

- $f(\boldsymbol{\alpha}|\boldsymbol{Y}, \boldsymbol{X}, \boldsymbol{H}, \boldsymbol{\beta}, \sigma_v^2) = f(\boldsymbol{\alpha}|\boldsymbol{H}, \sigma_v^2)$: Given $\boldsymbol{H}$, $\ln h_t$ follows an AR(1) model. Therefore, the result of AR models discussed in the previous two sections applies. Specifically, if the prior distribution of $\boldsymbol{\alpha}$ is multivariate normal with mean $\boldsymbol{\alpha}_o$ and covariance matrix C_o, then $f(\boldsymbol{\alpha}|\boldsymbol{H}, \sigma_v^2)$ is multivariate normal with mean $\boldsymbol{\alpha}_*$ and covariance matrix $\boldsymbol{C}_*$, where

$$\boldsymbol{C}_*^{-1} = \frac{\sum_{t=2}^n \boldsymbol{z}_t \boldsymbol{z}_t'}{\sigma_v^2} + \boldsymbol{C}_o^{-1}, \quad \boldsymbol{\alpha}_* = \boldsymbol{C}_* \left(\frac{\sum_{t=2}^n \boldsymbol{z}_t \ln h_t}{\sigma_v^2} + \boldsymbol{C}_o^{-1} \boldsymbol{\alpha}_o \right),$$

  where $\boldsymbol{z}_t = (1, \ln h_{t-1})'$.
- $f(\sigma_v^2|\boldsymbol{Y}, \boldsymbol{X}, \boldsymbol{H}, \boldsymbol{\beta}, \boldsymbol{\alpha}) = f(\sigma_v^2|\boldsymbol{H}, \boldsymbol{\alpha})$: Given $\boldsymbol{H}$ and $\boldsymbol{\alpha}$, we can calculate $v_t = \ln h_t - \alpha_0 - \alpha_1 \ln h_{t-1}$ for $t = 2, \ldots, n$. Therefore, if the prior distribution of σ_v^2 is $(m\lambda)/\sigma_v^2 \sim \chi_m^2$, then the conditional posterior distribution of σ_v^2 is an inverted chi-squared distribution with $m + n - 1$ degrees of freedom; that is,

$$\frac{m\lambda + \sum_{t=2}^n v_t^2}{\sigma_v^2} \sim \chi_{m+n-1}^2.$$

Remark. Formula (12.23) is for $1 < t < n$, where n is the sample size. For the two end data points h_1 and h_n, some modifications are needed. A simple approach is to assume that h_1 is fixed so that the drawing of h_t starts with $t = 2$. For $t = n$, one uses the result $\ln h_n \sim (\alpha_0 + \alpha_1 \ln h_{n-1}, \sigma_v^2)$. Alternatively, one can employ a forecast of h_{n+1} and a backward prediction of h_0 and continue to apply the formula. Since h_n is the variable of interest, we forecast h_{n+1} by using a 2-step ahead forecast at the forecast origin $n - 1$. For the model in Eq. (12.21), the forecast of h_{n+1} is

$$\widehat{h}_{n-1}(2) = \alpha_0 + \alpha_1(\alpha_0 + \alpha_1 \ln h_{n-1}).$$

The backward prediction of h_0 is based on the time reversibility of the model

$$(\ln h_t - \eta) = \alpha_1(\ln h_{t-1} - \eta) + v_t,$$

where $\eta = \alpha_0/(1 - \alpha_1)$ and $|\alpha_1| < 1$. The model of the reversed series is

$$(\ln h_t - \eta) = \alpha_1(\ln h_{t+1} - \eta) + v_t^*,$$

where $\{v_t^*\}$ is also a Gaussian white noise series with mean zero and variance σ_v^2. Consequently, the 2-step backward prediction of h_0 at time $t = 2$ is

$$\widehat{h}_2(-2) = \alpha_1^2(\ln h_2 - \eta). \qquad \square$$

Remark. Formula (12.23) can also be obtained by using results of a missing value in an AR(1) model; see Section 12.6.1. Specifically, assume that $\ln h_t$ is missing. For the AR(1) model in Eq. (12.21), this missing value is related to $\ln h_{t-1}$ and $\ln h_{t+1}$ for $1 < t < n$. From the model, we have

$$\ln h_t = \alpha_0 + \alpha_1 \ln h_{t-1} + a_t.$$

Define $y_t = \alpha_0 + \alpha_1 y_{t-1}$, $x_t = 1$, and $b_t = -a_t$. Then we obtain

$$y_t = x_t \ln h_t + b_t. \tag{12.24}$$

Next, from

$$\ln h_{t+1} = \alpha_0 + \alpha_1 \ln h_t + a_{t+1},$$

we define $y_{t+1} = \ln h_{t+1} - \alpha_0$, $x_{t+1} = \alpha_1$, and $b_{t+1} = a_{t+1}$ and obtain

$$y_{t+1} = x_{t+1} \ln h_{t+1} + b_{t+1}. \tag{12.25}$$

Now Eqs. (12.24) and (12.25) form a special simple linear regression with two observations and an unknown parameter $\ln h_t$. Note that b_t and b_{t+1} have the same distribution because $-a_t$ is also $N(0, \sigma_v^2)$. The least squares estimate of $\ln h_t$ is then

$$\widehat{\ln h_t} = \frac{x_t y_t + x_{t+1} y_{t+1}}{x_t^2 + x_{t+1}^2} = \frac{\alpha_0(1 - \alpha_1) + \alpha_1(\ln h_{t+1} + \ln h_{t-1})}{1 + \alpha_1^2},$$

which is precisely the conditional mean of $\ln h_t$ given in Eq. (12.23). In addition, this estimate is normally distributed with mean $\ln h_t$ and variance $\sigma_v^2/(1+\alpha_1^2)$. Formula (12.23) is simply the product of $a_t \sim N(0, h_t)$ and $\widehat{\ln h_t} \sim N[\ln h_t, \sigma_v^2/(1+\alpha_1^2)]$ with the transformation $d\ln h_t = h_t^{-1}dh_t$. This regression approach generalizes easily to other AR(p) models for $\ln h_t$. We use this approach and assume that $\{h_t\}_{t=1}^p$ are fixed for a stochastic volatility AR(p) model. □

Remark. Starting value of h_t can be obtained by fitting a volatility model of Chapter 3 to the return series. □

Example 12.3. Consider the monthly log returns of the S&P 500 index from January 1962 to December 1999 for 456 observations. Figure 12.3 shows the time plot of the return measured in percentage. If GARCH models are entertained for the series, we obtain a Gaussian GARCH(1,1) model

$$\begin{aligned} r_t &= 0.658 + a_t, \quad a_t = \sqrt{h_t}\epsilon_t, \\ h_t &= 3.349 + 0.086a_{t-1}^2 + 0.735h_{t-1}, \end{aligned} \qquad (12.26)$$

where t-ratios of the coefficients are all greater than 2.52. The Ljung–Box statistics of the standardized residuals and their squared series fail to indicate any model inadequacy.

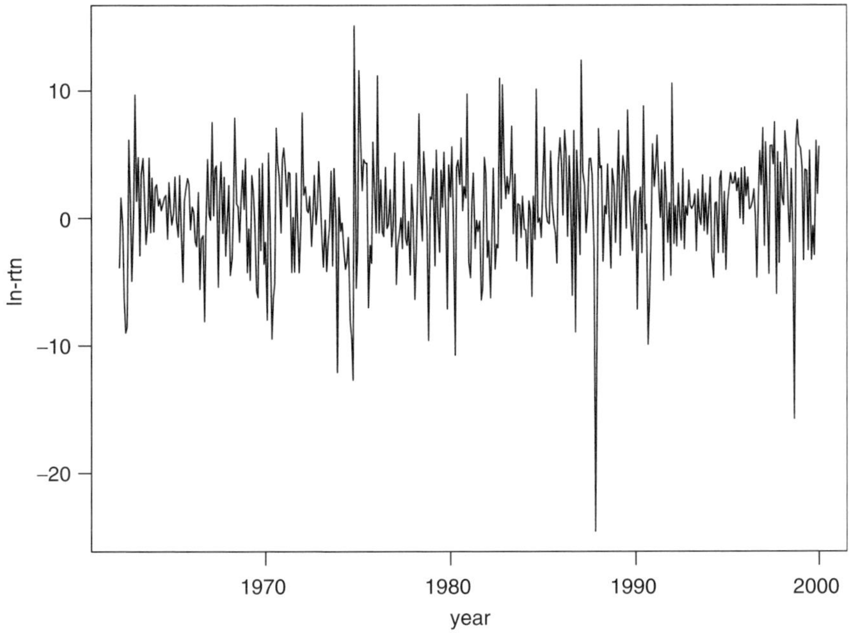

Figure 12.3. Time plot of monthly log returns of the S&P 500 index from 1962 to 1999.

Next, consider the stochastic volatility model

$$r_t = \mu + a_t, \quad a_t = \sqrt{h_t}\epsilon_t,$$
$$\ln h_t = \alpha_0 + \alpha_1 \ln h_{t-1} + v_t, \tag{12.27}$$

where the v_t are iid $N(0, \sigma_v^2)$. To implement the Gibbs sampling, we use the prior distributions

$$\mu \sim N(0, 9), \quad \boldsymbol{\alpha} \sim N[\boldsymbol{\alpha}_o, \text{diag}(0.09, 0.04)], \quad \frac{5 \times 0.2}{\sigma_v^2} \sim \chi_5^2,$$

where $\boldsymbol{\alpha}_o = (0.4, 0.8)'$. For initial parameter values, we use the fitted values of the GARCH(1,1) model in Eq. (12.26) for $\{h_t\}$ and set $\sigma_v^2 = 0.5$ and $\mu = 0.66$, which is the sample mean. In addition, h_t is drawn by using the Griddy Gibbs with 500 grid points and the range of h_t is $(0, 1.5s^2)$, where s^2 is the sample variance of the log return r_t.

We ran the Gibbs sampling for 5100 iterations but discarded results of the first 100 iterations. Figure 12.4 shows the density functions of the prior and posterior distributions of the four coefficient parameters. The prior distributions used are relatively noninformative. The posterior distributions are concentrated especially for μ and σ_v^2. Figure 12.5 shows the time plots of fitted volatilities. The upper panel shows the posterior mean of h_t over the 5000 iterations for each time point

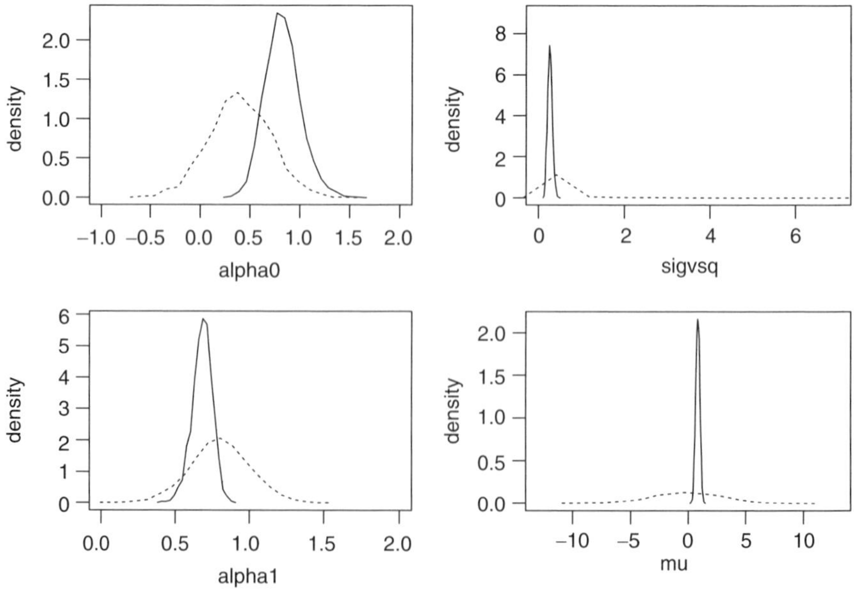

Figure 12.4. Density functions of prior and posterior distributions of parameters in a stochastic volatility model for the monthly log returns of the S&P 500 index. The dashed line denotes prior density and the solid line the posterior density, which is based on results of Gibbs sampling with 5000 iterations. See the text for more details.

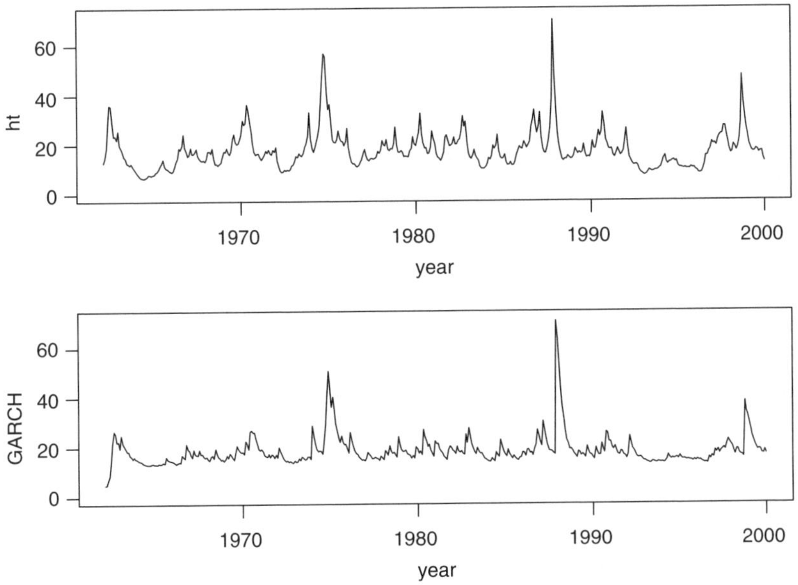

Figure 12.5. Time plots of fitted volatilities for monthly log returns of the S&P 500 index from 1962 to 1999. The upper panel shows the posterior means of a Gibbs sampler with 5000 iterations. The lower panel shows the results of a GARCH(1,1) model.

whereas the lower panel shows the fitted values of the GARCH(1,1) model in Eq. (12.26). The two plots exhibit a similar pattern.

The posterior mean and standard error of the four coefficients are as follows:

Parameter	μ	α_0	α_1	σ_v^2
Mean	0.836	0.831	0.685	0.265
Standard error	0.177	0.183	0.069	0.056

The posterior mean of α_1 is 0.685, which is smaller than that obtained by Jacquier, Polson, and Rossi (1994) who used daily returns of the S&P 500 index. But it confirms the strong serial dependence in the volatility series. Finally, we have used different initial values and 3100 iterations for another Gibbs sampler; the posterior means of the parameters change slightly, but the series of posterior means of h_t are stable.

12.7.2 Multivariate Stochastic Volatility Models

In this subsection, we study multivariate stochastic volatility models using the Cholesky decomposition of Chapter 10. We focus on the bivariate case, but the methods discussed also apply to the higher dimensional case. Based on the Cholesky decomposition, the innovation $\boldsymbol{a}_t$ of a return series $\boldsymbol{r}_t$ is transformed into $\boldsymbol{b}_t$ such that

$$b_{1t} = a_{1t}, \quad b_{2t} = a_{2t} - q_{21,t} b_{1t},$$

where b_{2t} and $q_{21,t}$ can be interpreted as the residual and least squares estimate of the linear regression

$$a_{2t} = q_{21,t}a_{1t} + b_{2t}.$$

The conditional covariance matrix of $\boldsymbol{a}_t$ is parameterized by $\{g_{11,t}, g_{22,t}\}$ and $\{q_{21,t}\}$ as

$$\begin{bmatrix} \sigma_{11,t} & \sigma_{12,t} \\ \sigma_{21,t} & \sigma_{22,t} \end{bmatrix} = \begin{bmatrix} 1 & 0 \\ q_{21,t} & 1 \end{bmatrix} \begin{bmatrix} g_{11,t} & 0 \\ 0 & g_{22,t} \end{bmatrix} \begin{bmatrix} 1 & q_{21,t} \\ 0 & 1 \end{bmatrix}, \tag{12.28}$$

where $g_{ii,t} = \text{Var}(b_{it}|F_{t-1})$ and $b_{1t} \perp b_{2t}$. Thus, the quantities of interest are $g_{11,t}$, $g_{22,t}$, and $q_{21,t}$.

A simple bivariate stochastic volatility model for the return $\boldsymbol{r}_t = (r_{1t}, r_{2t})'$ is as follows:

$$\boldsymbol{r}_t = \boldsymbol{\beta}_0 + \boldsymbol{\beta}_1\boldsymbol{x}_t + \boldsymbol{a}_t, \tag{12.29}$$

$$\ln g_{ii,t} = \alpha_{i0} + \alpha_{i1}\ln g_{ii,t-1} + v_{it}, \quad i = 1, 2, \tag{12.30}$$

$$q_{21,t} = \gamma_0 + \gamma_1 q_{21,t-1} + u_t, \tag{12.31}$$

where $\{\boldsymbol{a}_t\}$ is a sequence of serially uncorrelated Gaussian random vectors with mean zero and conditional covariance matrix $\boldsymbol{\Sigma}_t$ given by Eq. (12.28), $\boldsymbol{\beta}_0$ is a two-dimensional constant vector, $\boldsymbol{x}_t$ denotes the explanatory variables, and $\{v_{1t}\}$, $\{v_{2t}\}$, and $\{u_t\}$ are three independent Gaussian white noise series such that $\text{Var}(v_{it}) = \sigma^2_{iv}$ and $\text{Var}(u_t) = \sigma^2_u$. Again log transformation is used in Eq. (12.30) to ensure the positiveness of $g_{ii,t}$.

Let $\boldsymbol{G}_i = (g_{ii,1}, \ldots, g_{ii,n})'$, $\boldsymbol{G} = [\boldsymbol{G}_1, \boldsymbol{G}_2]$, and $\boldsymbol{Q} = (q_{21,1}, \ldots, q_{21,n})'$. The "traditional" parameters of the model in Eqs. (12.29)–(12.31) are $\boldsymbol{\beta} = (\boldsymbol{\beta}_0, \boldsymbol{\beta}_1)$, $\boldsymbol{\omega}_i = (\alpha_{i0}, \alpha_{i1}, \sigma^2_{iv})$ for $i = 1, 2$, and $\boldsymbol{\gamma} = (\gamma_0, \gamma_1, \sigma^2_u)$. The augmented parameters are $\boldsymbol{Q}$, $\boldsymbol{G}_1$, and $\boldsymbol{G}_2$. To estimate such a bivariate stochastic volatility model via Gibbs sampling, we use results of the univariate model in the previous subsection and two additional conditional posterior distributions. Specifically, we can draw random samples of:

1. $\boldsymbol{\beta}_0$ and $\boldsymbol{\beta}_1$ row by row using the result (12.22);
2. $g_{11,t}$ using Eq. (12.23) with a_t being replaced by a_{1t};
3. $\boldsymbol{\omega}_1$ using exactly the same methods as those of the univariate case with a_t replaced by a_{1t}.

To draw random samples of $\boldsymbol{\omega}_2$ and $g_{22,t}$, we need to compute b_{2t}. But this is easy because $b_{2t} = a_{2t} - q_{21,t}a_{1t}$ given the augmented parameter vector $\boldsymbol{Q}$. Furthermore, b_{2t} is normally distributed with mean 0 and conditional variance $g_{22,t}$.

It remains to consider the conditional posterior distributions

$$f(\boldsymbol{\varpi}|\boldsymbol{Q}, \sigma^2_u), \quad f(\sigma^2_u|\boldsymbol{Q}, \boldsymbol{\varpi}), \quad f(q_{21,t}|\boldsymbol{A}, \boldsymbol{G}, \boldsymbol{Q}_{-t}, \boldsymbol{\gamma}),$$

where $\boldsymbol{\varpi} = (\gamma_0, \gamma_1)'$ is the coefficient vector of Eq. (12.31) and $\boldsymbol{A}$ denotes the collection of $\boldsymbol{a}_t$, which is known if $\boldsymbol{R}$, $\boldsymbol{X}$, $\boldsymbol{\beta}_0$, and $\boldsymbol{\beta}_1$ are given. Given $\boldsymbol{Q}$ and σ^2_u, model

(12.31) is a simple Gaussian AR(1) model. Therefore, if the prior distribution of $\boldsymbol{\varpi}$ is bivariate normal with mean $\boldsymbol{\varpi}_o$ and covariance matrix $\boldsymbol{D}_o$, then the conditional posterior distribution of $\boldsymbol{\varpi}$ is also bivariate normal with mean $\boldsymbol{\varpi}_*$ and covariance matrix $\boldsymbol{D}_*$, where

$$\boldsymbol{D}_*^{-1} = \frac{\sum_{t=2}^n z_t z_t'}{\sigma_u^2} + \boldsymbol{D}_o^{-1}, \quad \boldsymbol{\varpi}_* = \boldsymbol{D}_* \left(\frac{\sum_{t=2}^n z_t q_{21,t}}{\sigma_u^2} + \boldsymbol{D}_o^{-1} \boldsymbol{\varpi}_o \right),$$

where $z_t = (1, q_{21,t-1})'$. Similarly, if the prior distribution of σ_u^2 is $(m\lambda)/\sigma_u^2 \sim \chi_m^2$ then the conditional posterior distribution of σ_u^2 is

$$\frac{m\lambda + \sum_{t=2}^n u_t^2}{\sigma_u^2} \sim \chi_{m+n-1}^2,$$

where $u_t = q_{21,t} - \gamma_0 - \gamma_1 q_{21,t-1}$. Finally,

$$\begin{aligned} f(q_{21,t}|\boldsymbol{A}, \boldsymbol{G}, \boldsymbol{Q}_{-t}, \sigma_u^2, \boldsymbol{\varpi}) \\ &\propto f(\boldsymbol{b}_{2t}|g_{22,t}) f(q_{21,t}|q_{21,t-1}, \boldsymbol{\varpi}, \sigma_u^2) f(q_{21,t+1}|q_{21,t}, \boldsymbol{\varpi}, \sigma_u^2) \\ &\propto g_{22,t}^{-0.5} \exp[-(a_{2t} - q_{21,t}a_{1t})^2/(2g_{22,t})] \exp[-(q_{21,t} - \mu_t)^2(2\sigma^2)], \end{aligned} \quad (12.32)$$

where $\mu_t = [\gamma_0(1 - \gamma_1) + \gamma_1(q_{21,t-1} + q_{21,t+1})]/(1 + \gamma_1^2)$ and $\sigma^2 = \sigma_u^2/(1 + \gamma_1^2)$. In general, μ_t and σ^2 can be obtained by using the results of a missing value in an AR(p) process. It turns out that Eq. (12.32) has a closed-form distribution for $q_{21,t}$. Specifically, the first term of Eq. (12.32), which is the conditional distribution of $q_{21,t}$ given $g_{22,t}$ and $\boldsymbol{a}_t$, is normal with mean a_{2t}/a_{1t} and variance $g_{22,t}/(a_{1t})^2$. The second term of the equation is also normal with mean μ_t and variance σ^2. Consequently, by Result 1 of Section 12.3, the conditional posterior distribution of $q_{21,t}$ is normal with mean μ_* and variance σ_*^2, where

$$\frac{1}{\sigma_*^2} = \frac{a_{1t}^2}{g_{22,t}} + \frac{1 + \gamma_1^2}{\sigma_u^2}, \quad \mu_* = \sigma_*^2 \left(\frac{1 + \gamma_1^2}{\sigma_u^2} \times \mu_t + \frac{a_{1t}^2}{g_{22,t}} \times \frac{a_{2t}}{a_{1t}} \right)$$

where μ_t is defined in Eq. (12.32).

Example 12.4. In this example, we study bivariate volatility models for the monthly log returns of IBM stock and the S&P 500 index from January 1962 to December 1999. This is an expanded version of Example 12.3 by adding the IBM returns. Figure 12.6 shows the time plots of the two return series. Let $\boldsymbol{r}_t = (\text{IBM}_t, \text{SP}_t)'$. If time-varying correlation GARCH models with Cholesky decomposition of Chapter 10 are entertained, we obtain the model

$$\boldsymbol{r}_t = \boldsymbol{\beta}_0 + \boldsymbol{a}_t, \quad (12.33)$$

$$g_{11,t} = \alpha_{10} + \alpha_{11} g_{11,t-1} + \alpha_{12} a_{1,t-1}^2, \quad (12.34)$$

$$g_{22,t} = \alpha_{20} + \alpha_{21} a_{1,t-1}^2, \quad (12.35)$$

$$q_{21,t} = \gamma_0, \quad (12.36)$$

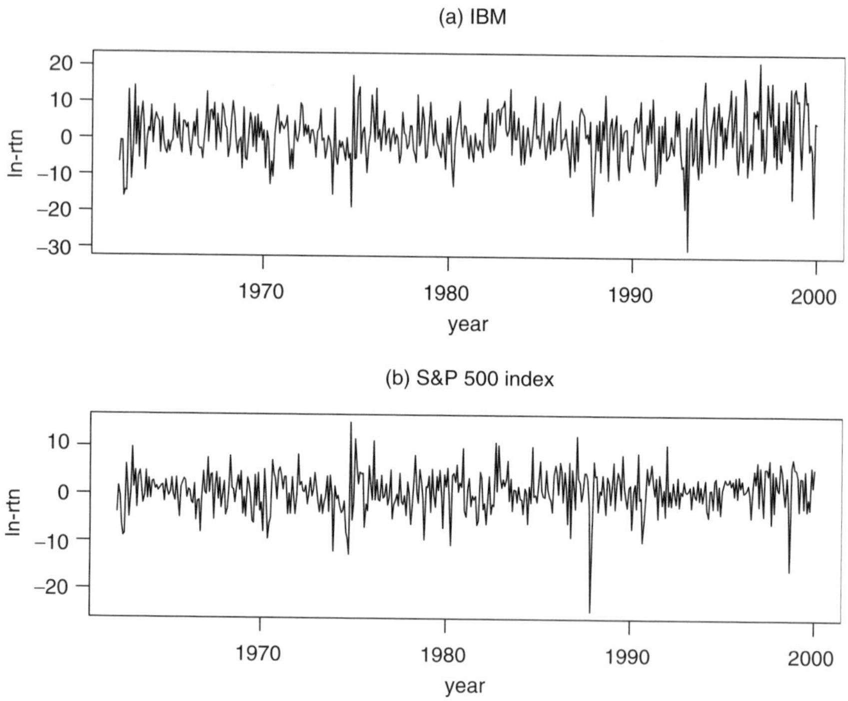

Figure 12.6. Time plots of monthly log returns of (a) IBM stock and (b) the S&P 500 index from 1962 to 1999.

where the estimates and their standard errors are given in Table 12.2(a). For comparison purpose, we employ the same mean equation in Eq. (12.33) and a stochastic volatility model similar to that in Eqs. (12.34)–(12.36). The volatility equations are

$$\ln g_{11,t} = \alpha_{10} + \alpha_{11} \ln g_{11,t-1} + v_{1t}, \quad \mathrm{Var}(v_{1t}) = \sigma_{1v}^2, \tag{12.37}$$

$$\ln g_{22,t} = \alpha_{20} + v_{2t}, \quad \mathrm{Var}(v_{2t}) = \sigma_{2v}^2, \tag{12.38}$$

$$q_{21,t} = \gamma_0 + u_t, \quad \mathrm{Var}(u_t) = \sigma_u^2. \tag{12.39}$$

The prior distributions used are

$$\beta_{i0} \sim N(0.8, 4), \quad \boldsymbol{\alpha}_1 \sim N[(0.4, 0.8)', \mathrm{diag}(0.16, 0.04)], \quad \alpha_{20} \sim N(5, 25),$$

$$\gamma_0 \sim N(0.4, .04), \quad \frac{10 \times 0.1}{\sigma_{1v}^2} \sim \chi_{10}^2, \quad \frac{5 \times 0.2}{\sigma_{2v}^2} \sim \chi_5^2, \quad \frac{5 \times 0.2}{\sigma_u^2} \sim \chi_5^2.$$

These prior distributions are relatively noninformative. We ran the Gibbs sampling for 1300 iterations but discarded results of the first 300 iterations. The random samples of $g_{ii,t}$ were drawn by Griddy Gibbs with 400 grid points in the intervals $[0, 1.5s_i^2]$, where s_i^2 is the sample variance of the log return r_{it}. Posterior means and

Table 12.2. Estimation of Bivariate Volatility Models for Monthly Log Returns of IBM Stock and the S&P 500 Index from January 1962 to December 1999

(a) Bivariate GARCH(1,1) Model with Time-Varying Correlations

Parameter	β_{01}	β_{02}	α_{10}	α_{11}	α_{12}	α_{20}	α_{21}	γ_0
Estimate	1.04	0.79	3.16	0.83	0.10	10.59	0.04	0.35
Standard error	0.31	0.20	1.67	0.08	0.03	0.93	0.02	0.02

(b) Stochastic Volatility Model

Parameter	β_{01}	β_{02}	α_{10}	α_{11}	σ^2_{1v}	α_{20}	σ^2_{2v}	γ_0	σ^2_u
Posterior mean	0.86	0.84	0.52	0.86	0.08	1.81	0.39	0.39	0.08
Standard error	0.30	0.18	0.18	0.05	0.03	0.11	0.06	0.03	0.02

[a]The stochastic volatility models are based on the last 1000 iterations of a Gibbs sampling with 1300 total iterations.

standard errors of the "traditional" parameters of the bivariate stochastic volatility model are given in Table 12.2(b).

To check for convergence of the Gibbs sampling, we ran the procedure several times with different starting values and numbers of iterations. The results are stable. For illustration, Figure 12.7 shows the scatterplots of various quantities for two different Gibbs samples. The first Gibbs sample is based on $300 + 1000$ iterations, and the second Gibbs sample is based on $500 + 3000$ iterations, where $M + N$ denotes that the total number of Gibbs iterations is $M + N$, but results of the first M iterations are discarded. The scatterplots shown are posterior means of $g_{11,t}$, $g_{22,t}$, $g_{21,t}$, $\sigma_{22,t}$, $\sigma_{21,t}$, and the correlation $\rho_{21,t}$. The line $y = x$ is added to each plot to show the closeness of the posterior means. The stability of the Gibbs sampling results is clearly seen.

It is informative to compare the GARCH model with time-varying correlations in Eqs. (12.33)–(12.36) with the stochastic volatility model. First, as expected, the mean equations of the two models are essentially identical. Second, Figure 12.8 shows the time plots of fitted volatilities for IBM stock return. Figure 12.8a is for the GARCH model, and Figure 12.8b shows the posterior mean of the stochastic volatility model. The two models show similar volatility characteristics; they exhibit volatility clusterings and indicate an increasing trend in volatility. However, the GARCH model produces higher peak volatility values. Third, Figure 12.9 shows the time plots of fitted volatilities for the S&P 500 index return. The GARCH model produces an extra volatility peak around 1993. This additional peak does not appear in the univariate analysis shown in Figure 12.5. It seems that for this particular instance the bivariate GARCH model produces a spurious volatility peak. This spurious peak is induced by its dependence on IBM returns and does not appear in the stochastic volatility model. Indeed, the fitted volatilities of the S&P 500 index return by the bivariate stochastic volatility model are similar to that of the univariate analysis. Fourth, Figure 12.10 shows the time plots of fitted

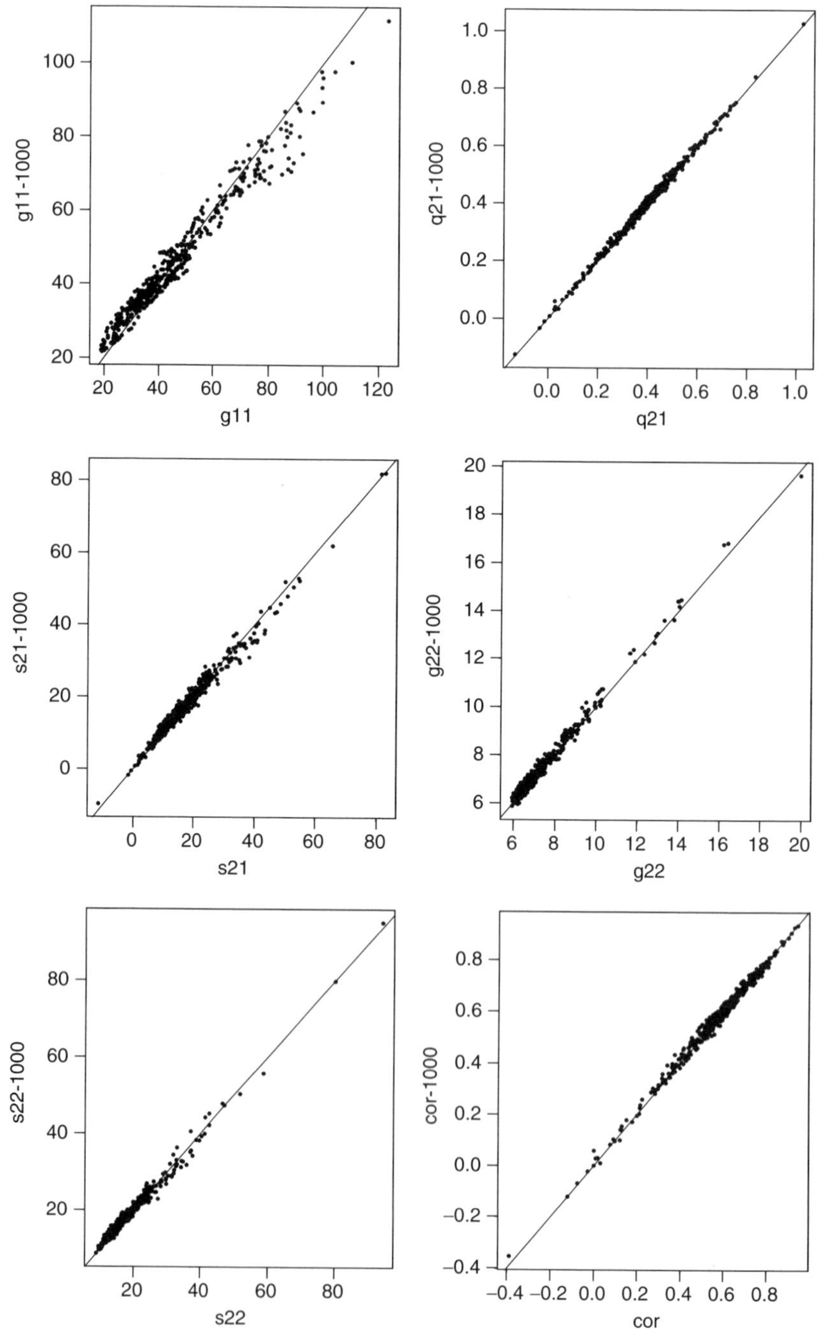

Figure 12.7. Scatterplots of posterior means of various statistics of two different Gibbs samples for the bivariate stochastic volatility model for monthly log returns of IBM stock and the S&P 500 index. The x-axis denotes results based on $500 + 3000$ iterations and the y-axis denotes results based on $300 + 1000$ iterations. The notation is defined in the text.

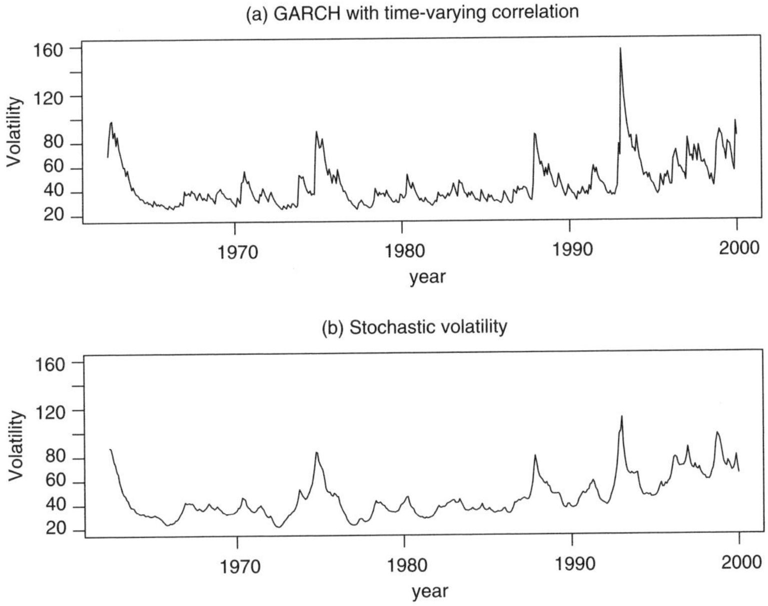

Figure 12.8. Time plots of fitted volatilities for monthly log returns of IBM stock from 1962 to 1999: (a) a GARCH model with time-varying correlations and (b) a bivariate stochastic volatility model estimated by Gibbs sampling with $300 + 1000$ iterations.

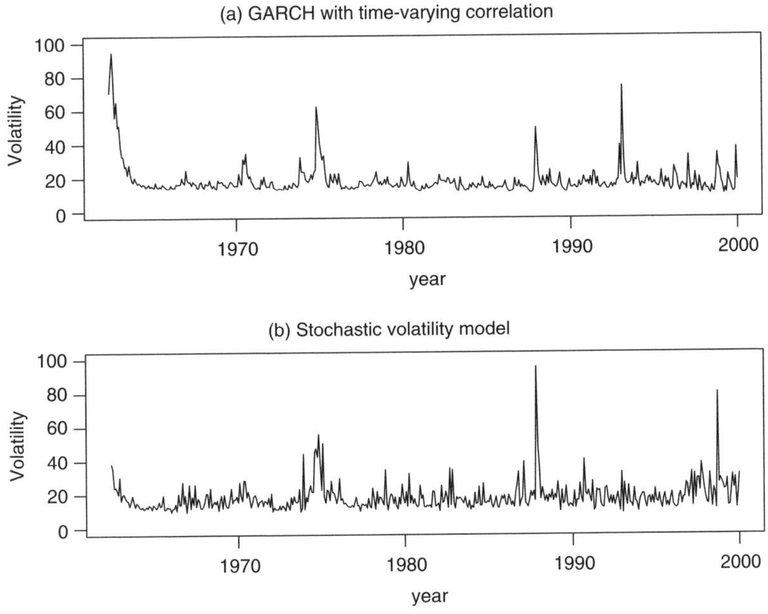

Figure 12.9. Time plots of fitted volatilities for monthly log returns of the S&P 500 index from 1962 to 1999: (a) a GARCH model with time-varying correlations and (b) a bivariate stochastic volatility model estimated by Gibbs sampling with $300 + 1000$ iterations.

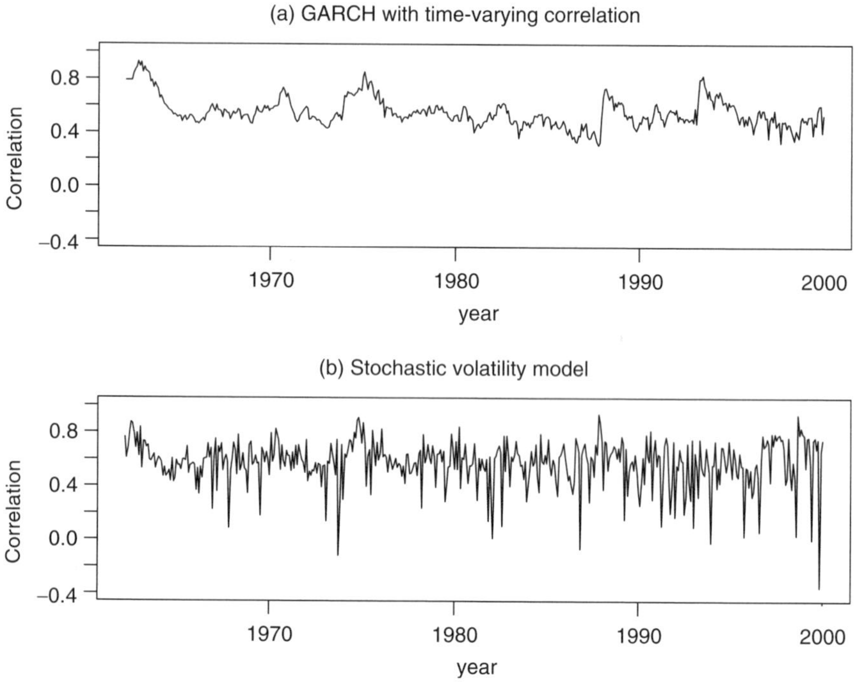

Figure 12.10. Time plots of fitted correlation coefficients between monthly log returns of IBM stock and the S&P 500 index from 1962 to 1999: (a) a GARCH model with time-varying correlations and (b) a bivariate stochastic volatility model estimated by Gibbs sampling with $300 + 1000$ iterations.

conditional correlations. Here the two models differ substantially. The correlations of the GARCH model are relatively smooth and positive with mean value 0.55 and standard deviation 0.11. However, the correlations produced by the stochastic volatility model vary markedly from one month to another with mean value 0.57 and standard deviation 0.17. Furthermore, there are isolated occasions on which the correlation is negative. The difference is understandable because $q_{21,t}$ contains the random shock u_t in the stochastic volatility model.

Remark. The Gibbs sampling estimation applies to other bivariate stochastic volatility models. The conditional posterior distributions needed require some extensions of those discussed in this section, but they are based on the same ideas. □

12.8 A NEW APPROACH TO SV ESTIMATION

In this section, we discuss an alternative procedure to estimate stochastic volatility models. This approach makes use of the technique of *forward filtering and backward sampling* (FFBS) within the Kalman filter framework to improve the efficiency of Gibbs sampling. It can dramatically reduce the computing time by drawing the volatility process jointly with the help of a mixture of normal distributions. In fact, the approach can be used to estimate many stochastic diffusion models with leverage effects and jumps.

For ease in presentation, we reparameterize the univariate stochastic volatility model in Eqs. (12.20) and (12.21) as

$$r_t = \boldsymbol{x}_t'\boldsymbol{\beta} + \sigma_0 \exp\left(\frac{z_t}{2}\right)\epsilon_t, \tag{12.40}$$

$$z_{t+1} = \alpha z_t + \eta_t, \tag{12.41}$$

where $\boldsymbol{x}_t = (1, x_{1t}, \ldots, x_{pt})'$, $\boldsymbol{\beta} = (\beta_0, \beta_1, \ldots, \beta_p)'$, $\sigma_0 > 0$, $\{z_t\}$ is a zero-mean log volatility series, and $\{\epsilon_t\}$ and $\{\eta_t\}$ are bivariate normal distributions with mean zero and covariance matrix

$$\boldsymbol{\Sigma} = \begin{bmatrix} 1 & \rho\sigma_\eta \\ \rho\sigma_\eta & \sigma_\eta^2 \end{bmatrix}.$$

The parameter ρ is the correlation between ϵ_t and η_t and represents the *leverage effect* of the asset return r_t. Typically, ρ is negative signifying that a negative return tends to increase the volatility of an asset price.

Compared with the model in Eqs. (12.20) and (12.21), we have $z_t = \ln(h_t) - \ln(\sigma_0^2)$ and $\sigma_0^2 = \exp\{E[\ln(h_t)]\}$. That is, z_t is a mean-adjusted log volatility series. This new parameterization has some nice characteristics. For example, the volatility series is $\sigma_0 \exp(z_t/2)$, which is always positive. More importantly, η_t is the innovation of z_{t+1} and is independent of z_t. This simple time shift enables us to handle the leverage effect. If one postulates $z_t = \alpha z_{t-1} + \eta_t$ for Eq. (12.41), then η_t and ϵ_t cannot be correlated, because a nonzero correlation implies that z_t and ϵ_t are correlated in Eq. (12.40), which would lead to some identifiability issues.

Remark. Alternatively, one can write the stochastic volatility model as

$$r_t = \boldsymbol{x}_t'\boldsymbol{\beta} + \sigma_0 \exp\left(\frac{z_{t-1}}{2}\right)\epsilon_t,$$

$$z_t = \alpha z_{t-1} + \eta_t,$$

where $(\epsilon_t, \eta_t)'$ is a bivariate normal distribution as before. Yet another equivalent parameterization is

$$r_t = \boldsymbol{x}_t'\boldsymbol{\beta} + \exp\left(\frac{z_{t-1}^*}{2}\right)\epsilon_t,$$

$$z_t^* = \alpha_0 + \alpha z_{t-1}^* + \eta_t,$$

where $E(z_t^*) = \alpha_0/(1-\alpha)$ is not zero. □

Parameters of the stochastic volatility model in Eqs. (12.40) and (12.41) are $\boldsymbol{\beta}, \sigma_0, \alpha, \rho, \sigma_\eta$, and $\boldsymbol{z} = (z_1, \ldots, z_n)'$, where n is the sample size. For simplicity, we assume z_1 is known. To estimate these parameters via MCMC methods, we need their conditional posterior distributions. In what follows, we discuss the needed conditional posterior distributions.

1. Given z and σ_0 and a normal prior distribution, $\boldsymbol{\beta}$ has the same conditional posterior distribution as that in Section 12.7.1 with $\sqrt{h_t}$ replaced by $\sigma_0 \exp(z_t/2)$; see Eq. (12.22).

2. Given z and σ_η^2, α is a simple AR(1) coefficient. Thus, with an approximate normal prior, the conditional posterior distribution of α is readily available; see Section 12.7.1.

3. Given $\boldsymbol{\beta}$ and z, we define $v_t = (r_t - \boldsymbol{x}_t'\boldsymbol{\beta})\exp(-z_t/2) = \sigma_0\epsilon_t$. Thus, $\{v_t\}$ is a sequence of iid normal random variables with mean zero and variance σ_0^2. If the prior distribution of σ_0^2 is $(m\lambda)/\sigma_0^2 \sim \chi_m^2$, then the conditional posterior distribution of σ_0^2 is an inverted chi-squared distribution with $m+n$ degrees of freedom; that is,

$$\frac{m\lambda + \sum_{t=1}^n v_t^2}{\sigma_0^2} \sim \chi_{m+n}^2.$$

4. Given $\boldsymbol{\beta}$, σ_0, z, and α, we can easily obtain the bivariate innovation $\boldsymbol{b}_t = (\epsilon_t, \eta_t)'$ for $t = 2, \ldots, n$. The likelihood function of (ρ, σ_η^2) is readily available as

$$\begin{aligned}\ell(\rho, \sigma_\eta^2) &= \prod_{t=2}^n f(\boldsymbol{b}_t|\boldsymbol{\Sigma}) \propto |\boldsymbol{\Sigma}|^{-(n-1)/2}\exp\left(-\frac{1}{2}\sum_{t=2}^n \boldsymbol{b}_t'\boldsymbol{\Sigma}^{-1}\boldsymbol{b}_t\right)\\ &\propto |\boldsymbol{\Sigma}|^{-(n-1)/2}\exp\left[-\frac{1}{2}tr\left(\boldsymbol{\Sigma}^{-1}\sum_{t=2}^n \boldsymbol{b}_t\boldsymbol{b}_t'\right)\right],\end{aligned}$$

where $tr(\boldsymbol{A})$ denotes trace of the matrix $\boldsymbol{A}$. However, this joint distribution is complicated because one cannot separate ρ and σ_η^2. We adopt the technique of Jacquier, Polson, and Rossi (2004) and reparameterize the covariance matrix as

$$\boldsymbol{\Sigma} = \begin{bmatrix} 1 & \rho\sigma_\eta \\ \rho\sigma_\eta & \sigma_\eta^2 \end{bmatrix} = \begin{bmatrix} 1 & \varphi \\ \varphi & \omega + \varphi^2 \end{bmatrix},$$

where $\omega = \sigma_\eta^2(1-\rho^2)$. It is easy to see that $|\boldsymbol{\Sigma}| = \omega$ and

$$\boldsymbol{\Sigma}^{-1} = \frac{1}{\omega}\begin{bmatrix} \varphi^2 & -\varphi \\ -\varphi & 1 \end{bmatrix} + \begin{bmatrix} 1 & 0 \\ 0 & 0 \end{bmatrix} \equiv \frac{1}{\omega}\boldsymbol{S} + \begin{bmatrix} 1 & 0 \\ 0 & 0 \end{bmatrix},$$

where $\boldsymbol{S}$ contains φ only. Let $\boldsymbol{e} = (\epsilon_2, \ldots, \epsilon_n)'$ and $\boldsymbol{\eta} = (\eta_2, \ldots, \eta_n)'$ be the innovations of the model in Eqs. (12.40) and (12.41). The likelihood function then becomes (keeping terms related to parameters only)

$$\ell(\varphi, \omega) \propto \omega^{-(n-1)/2}\exp\left(-\frac{1}{2\omega}tr(\boldsymbol{S}\boldsymbol{R})\right),$$

where $\boldsymbol{R} = \sum_{t=2}^n \boldsymbol{b}_t\boldsymbol{b}_t' = (\boldsymbol{e}, \boldsymbol{\eta})'(\boldsymbol{e}, \boldsymbol{\eta})$, which is the 2×2 cross-product matrix of the innovations. For simplicity, we use conjugate priors such that ω is inverse gamma (IG) with hyperparameters $(\gamma_0/2, \gamma_1/2)$: that is, $\omega \sim \text{IG}(\gamma_0/2, \gamma_1/2)$ and $\varphi|\omega \sim N(0, \omega/2)$. Then, after some algebraic manipulation, the joint posterior distribution of (φ, ω) can be decomposed into a normal and an inverse gamma distribution. Specifically,

$$\varphi \sim N[\tilde{\varphi}, \omega/(2 + \boldsymbol{e}'\boldsymbol{e})],$$

where $\tilde{\varphi} = \boldsymbol{e}'\boldsymbol{\eta}/(2 + \boldsymbol{e}'\boldsymbol{e})$, and

$$\omega \sim \text{IG}[(n + 1 + \gamma_0)/2, \{\gamma_1 + \boldsymbol{\eta}'\boldsymbol{\eta} - (\boldsymbol{e}'\boldsymbol{\eta})^2/(2 + \boldsymbol{e}'\boldsymbol{e})\}/2].$$

In Gibbs sampling, once φ and ω are available, we can obtain ρ and σ_η^2 easily because $\sigma_\eta^2 = \omega + \varphi^2$ and $\rho = \varphi/\sigma_\eta$. Note that the probability density function of an IG(α, β) random variable ω is

$$f(\omega|\alpha, \beta) = \frac{\beta^\alpha}{\Gamma(\alpha)}\omega^{-(\alpha+1)}\exp\left(-\frac{\beta}{\omega}\right), \quad \text{for } \omega > 0,$$

where $\alpha > 2$ and $\beta > 0$.

5. Finally, we consider the joint distribution of the log volatility z given the data and other parameters. From Eq. (12.40), we have

$$\frac{(r_t - \boldsymbol{x}_t'\boldsymbol{\beta})^2}{\sigma_0^2} = \exp(z_t)\epsilon_t^2.$$

Therefore, letting $y_t = \ln[(r_t - \boldsymbol{x}_t'\boldsymbol{\beta})^2/\sigma_0^2]$, we obtain

$$y_t = z_t + \epsilon_t^*, \tag{12.42}$$

where $\epsilon_t^* = \ln(\epsilon_t^2)$. Since $\epsilon_t^2 \sim \chi_1^2$, ϵ_t^* is not normally distributed. Treating Eq. (12.42) as an observation equation and Eq. (12.41) as the state equation, we have the form of a state-space model except that ϵ_t^* is not Gaussian; see Eqs. (11.25) and (11.24) of Chapter 11. To overcome the difficulty associated with non-normality, Kim, Shephard, and Chib (1998) use a mixture of seven normal distributions to approximate the distribution of ϵ_t^*. Specifically, we have

$$f(\epsilon_t^*) \approx \sum_{i=1}^{7} p_i N(\mu_i, \varpi_i^2),$$

where p_i, μ_i, and ϖ_i^2 are given in Table 12.3. See also, Chib, Nardari, and Shephard (2002).

To demonstrate the adequacy of the approximation, Figure 12.11 shows the density function of ϵ_t^* (solid line) and that of the mixture of seven normals (dashed line) in Table 12.3. These densities are obtained using simulations with 100,000 observations. From the plot, the approximation by the mixture of seven normals is very good.

Why is it important to have a Gaussian state-space model? The answer is that such a Gaussian model enables us to draw the log volatility series z jointly and

Table 12.3. Seven Components of Normal Distributions

Component i	Probability p_i	Mean μ_i	Variable ϖ_i^2
1	0.00730	−11.4004	5.7960
2	0.10556	−5.2432	2.6137
3	0.00002	−9.8373	5.1795
4	0.04395	1.5075	0.1674
5	0.34001	−0.6510	0.6401
6	0.24566	0.5248	0.3402
7	0.25750	−2.3586	1.2626

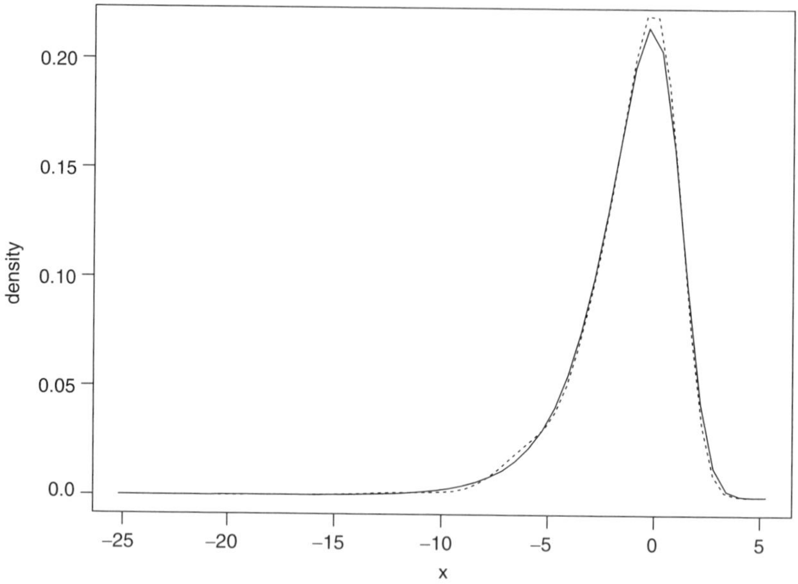

Figure 12.11. Density functions of $\log(\chi_1^2)$, solid line, and that of a mixture of seven normal distributions, dashed line. Results are based on 100,000 observations.

efficiently. To see this, consider the following special Gaussian state-space model, where η_t and e_t are uncorrelated (i.e., no leverage effects):

$$z_{t+1} = \alpha z_t + \eta_t, \qquad \eta_t \sim_{\text{iid}} N(0, \sigma_\eta^2), \tag{12.43}$$

$$y_t = c_t + z_t + e_t, \quad e_t \sim_{\text{ind.}} N(0, H_t) \tag{12.44}$$

where, as will be seen later, (c_t, H_t) assumes the value (μ_i, ϖ_i^2) of Table 12.3 for some i. For this special state-space model, we have the Kalman filter algorithm

$$v_t = y_t - y_{t|t-1} = y_t - c_t - z_{t|t-1},$$
$$V_t = \Sigma_{t|t-1} + H_t,$$

$$
\begin{aligned}
z_{t|t} &= z_{t|t-1} + \Sigma_{t|t-1} V_t^{-1} v_t, \\
\Sigma_{t|t} &= \Sigma_{t|t-1} - \Sigma_{t|t-1} V_t^{-1} \Sigma_{t|t-1}, \\
z_{t+1|t} &= \alpha z_{t|t}, \\
\Sigma_{t+1|t} &= \alpha^2 \Sigma_{t|t} + \sigma_\eta^2,
\end{aligned}
\tag{12.45}
$$

where $V_t = \text{Var}(v_t)$ is the variance of the 1-step ahead prediction error v_t of y_t given $F_{t-1} = (y_1, \ldots, y_{t-1})$, and $z_{j|i}$ and $\Sigma_{j|i}$ are, respectively, the conditional expectation and variance of the state variable z_j given F_i. See the Kalman filter discussion of Chaper 11.

Forward Filtering and Backward Sampling (FFBS)

Let $p(z|F_n)$ be the joint conditional posterior distribution of z given the return data and other parameters, where for simplicity the parameters are omitted from the condition set. We can partition the distribution as

$$
\begin{aligned}
p(z|F_n) &= P(z_2, z_3, \ldots, z_n|F_n) \\
&= p(z_n|F_n) p(z_{n-1}|z_n, F_n) p(z_{n-2}|z_{n-1}, z_n, F_n) \ldots p(z_2|z_3, \ldots, z_n, F_n) \\
&= p(z_n|F_n) p(z_{n-1}|z_n, F_n) p(z_{n-2}|z_{n-1}, F_n) \ldots p(z_2|z_3, F_n),
\end{aligned}
\tag{12.46}
$$

where the last equality holds because z_t in Eq. (12.43) is a Markov process so that conditioned on z_{t+1}, z_t is independent of z_{t+j} for $j > 1$.

From the Kalman filter in Eq. (12.45), we obtain that $p(z_n|F_n)$ is normal with mean $z_{n|n}$ and variance $\Sigma_{n|n}$. Next, consider the second term $p(z_{n-1}|z_n, F_n)$ of Eq. (12.46). We have

$$
p(z_{n-1}|z_n, F_n) = p(z_{n-1}|z_n, F_{n-1}, y_n) = p(z_{n-1}|z_n, F_{n-1}, v_n), \tag{12.47}
$$

where $v_n = y_n - y_{n|n-1}$ is the 1-step ahead prediction error of y_n. From the state-space model in Eqs. (12.43) and (12.44), z_{n-1} is independent of v_n. Therefore,

$$
p(z_{n-1}|z_n, F_n) = p(z_{n-1}|z_n, F_{n-1}). \tag{12.48}
$$

This is an important property because it implies that we can derive the posterior distribution $p(z_{n-1}|z_n, F_n)$ from the joint distribution of (z_{n-1}, z_n) given F_{n-1} via Theorem 11.1 of Chapter 11. First, the joint distribution is bivariate normal under the Gaussian assumption. Second, the conditional mean and covariance matrix of (z_{n-1}, z_n) given F_{n-1} are readily available from the Kalman filter algorithm in Eq. (12.45). Specifically, we have

$$
\begin{bmatrix} z_{n-1} \\ z_n \end{bmatrix}_{F_{n-1}} \sim N\left(\begin{bmatrix} z_{n-1|n-1} \\ z_{n|n-1} \end{bmatrix}, \begin{bmatrix} \Sigma_{n-1|n-1} & \alpha \Sigma_{n-1|n-1} \\ \alpha \Sigma_{n-1|n-1} & \Sigma_{n|n-1} \end{bmatrix} \right), \tag{12.49}
$$

where the covariance is obtained by (i) multiplying z_{n-1} by Eq. (12.43) and (ii) taking conditional expectation. Note that all quantities involved in Eq. (12.49) are available from the Kalman filter. Consequently, by Theorem 11.1, we have

$$p(z_{n-1}|z_n, F_n) \sim N(\mu^*_{n-1}, \Sigma^*_{n-1}), \tag{12.50}$$

where

$$\begin{aligned}
\mu^*_{n-1} &= z_{n-1|n-1} + \alpha \Sigma_{n-1|n-1} \Sigma^{-1}_{n|n-1}(z_n - z_{n|n-1}), \\
\Sigma^*_{n-1} &= \Sigma_{n-1|n-1} - \alpha^2 \Sigma^2_{n-1|n-1} \Sigma^{-1}_{n|n-1}.
\end{aligned}$$

Next, for the conditional posterior distribution $p(z_{n-2}|z_{n-1}, F_n)$, we have

$$\begin{aligned}
p(z_{n-2}|z_{n-1}, F_n) &= p(z_{n-2}|z_{n-1}, F_{n-2}, y_{n-1}, y_n) \\
&= p(z_{n-2}|z_{n-1}, F_{n-2}, v_{n-1}, v_n) \\
&= p(z_{n-2}|z_{n-1}, F_{n-2}).
\end{aligned}$$

Consequently, we can obtain $p(z_{n-2}|z_{n-1}, F_n)$ from the bivariate normal distribution of $p(z_{n-2}, z_{n-1}|F_{n-2})$ as before. In general, we have

$$p(z_t|z_{t+1}, F_n) = p(z_t|z_{t+1}, F_t), \quad \text{for } 1 < t < n.$$

Furthermore, from the Kalman filter, $p(z_t, z_{t+1}|F_t)$ is bivariate normal as

$$\begin{bmatrix} z_t \\ z_{t+1} \end{bmatrix}_{F_t} \sim N\left(\begin{bmatrix} z_{t|t} \\ z_{t+1|t} \end{bmatrix}, \begin{bmatrix} \Sigma_{t|t} & \alpha \Sigma_{t|t} \\ \alpha \Sigma_{t|t} & \Sigma_{t+1|t} \end{bmatrix} \right). \tag{12.51}$$

Consequently,

$$p(z_t|z_{t+1}, F_t) \sim N(\mu^*_t, \Sigma^*_t),$$

where

$$\begin{aligned}
\mu^*_t &= z_{t|t} + \alpha \Sigma_{t|t} \Sigma^{-1}_{t+1|t}(z_{t+1} - z_{t+1|t}), \\
\Sigma^*_t &= \Sigma_{t|t} - \alpha^2 \Sigma^2_{t|t} \Sigma^{-1}_{t+1|t}.
\end{aligned}$$

The prior derivation implies that we can draw the volatility series z jointly by a recursive method using quantities readily available from the Kalman filter algorithm. That is, given the initial values $z_{1|0}$ and $\Sigma_{1|0}$, one uses the Kalman filter in Eq. (12.45) to process the return data forward, then applies the recursive backward method to draw a realization of the volatility series z. This scheme is referred to as *forward filtering and backward sampling* (FFBS); see Carter and Kohn (1994) and Frühwirth-Schnatter (1994). Because the volatility $\{z_t\}$ is serially correlated, drawing the series jointly is more efficient.

Remark. The FFBS procedure applies to general linear Gaussian state-space models. The main idea is to make use of the Markov property of the model and the structure of the state-transition equation so that

$$p(\boldsymbol{S}_t|\boldsymbol{S}_{t+1}, F_n) = p(\boldsymbol{S}_t|\boldsymbol{S}_{t+1}, F_t, v_{t+1}, \ldots, v_n) = p(\boldsymbol{S}_t|\boldsymbol{S}_{t+1}, F_t),$$

where $\boldsymbol{S}_t$ denotes the state variable at time t and v_j is the 1-step ahead prediction error. This identity enables us to apply Theorem 11.1 to derive a recursive method to draw the state vectors jointly. □

Return to the estimation of the SV model. As in Eq. (12.42), let $y_t = \ln[(r_t - \boldsymbol{x}_t'\boldsymbol{\beta})^2/\sigma_0^2]$. To implement FFBS, one must determine c_t and H_t of Eq. (12.44) so that the mixture of normals provides a good approximation to the distribution of ϵ_t^*. To this end, we augment the model with a series of independent indicator variables $\{I_t\}$, where I_t assumes a value in $\{1, \ldots, 7\}$ such that $P(I_t = i) = p_{it}$ with $\sum_{i=1}^{7} p_{it} = 1$ for each t. In practice, conditioned on $\{z_t\}$, we can determine c_t and H_t as follows. Let

$$q_{it} = \Phi[(y_t - z_t - \mu_i)/\varpi_i], \quad \text{for } i = 1, \ldots, 7,$$

where μ_i and ϖ_i are the mean and standard error of the normal distributions given in Table 12.3 and $\Phi(.)$ denotes the cumulative distribution function of the standard normal random variable. These probabilities q_{it} are the likelihood function of I_t given y_t and z_t. The probabilities p_i of Table 12.3 form a prior distribution of I_t. Therefore, the posterior distribution of I_t is

$$p_{it} = \frac{p_i q_{it}}{\sum_{j=1}^{7} p_j q_{jt}}, \quad i = 1, \ldots, 7.$$

We can draw a realization of I_t using this posterior distribution. If the random draw is $I_t = j$, then we define $c_t = \mu_j$ and $H_t = \varpi_j^2$. In summary, conditioned on the return data and other parameters of the model, we employ the approximate linear Gaussian state-space model in Eqs. (12.43) and (12.44) to draw jointly the log volatility series $\boldsymbol{z}$. It turns out that the resulting Gibbs sampling is efficient in estimating univariate stochastic volatility models.

On the other hand, the square transformation involved in Eq. (12.42) fails to retain the correlation between η_t and ϵ_t if it exists, making the approximate state-space model in Eqs. (12.43) and (12.44) incapable of estimating the leverage effect. To overcome this inadequacy, Artigas and Tsay (2004) propose using a time-varying state-space model that maintains the leverage effect. Specifically, when $\rho \neq 0$, we have

$$\eta_t = \rho\sigma_\eta\epsilon_t + \eta_t^*,$$

where η_t^* is a normal random variable independent of ϵ_t and $\text{Var}(\eta_t^*) = \sigma_\eta^2(1 - \rho^2)$. The state-transition equation of Eq. (12.43) then becomes

$$z_{t+1} = \alpha z_t + \rho\sigma_\eta\epsilon_t + \eta_t^*.$$

Substituting $\epsilon_t = (1/\sigma_0)(r_t - \boldsymbol{x}_t'\boldsymbol{\beta})\exp(-z_t/2)$, we obtain

$$\begin{aligned} z_{t+1} &= \alpha z_t + \frac{\rho\sigma_\eta(r_t - \boldsymbol{x}_t'\boldsymbol{\beta})}{\sigma_0}\exp(-z_t/2) + \eta_t^* \\ &= G(z_t) + \eta_t^* \end{aligned} \tag{12.52}$$

where $G(z_t) = \alpha z_t + \rho\sigma_\eta(r_t - \boldsymbol{x}_t'\boldsymbol{\beta})\exp(-z_t/2)/\sigma_0$. This is a nonlinear transition equation for the state variable z_t. The Kalman filter in Eq. (12.45) is no longer applicable. To overcome this difficulty, Artigas and Tsay (2004) use a time-varying linear Kalman filter to approximate the system. Specifically, the last two equations of Eq. (12.45) are modified as

$$\begin{aligned} z_{t+1|t} &= G(z_{t|t}), \\ \Sigma_{t+1|t} &= g(z_{t|t})^2\Sigma_{t|t} + \sigma_\eta^2(1-\rho^2), \end{aligned} \tag{12.53}$$

where $g(z_{t|t}) = \partial G(x)/\partial x|_{x=z_{t|t}}$ is the first-order derivative of $G(z_t)$ evaluated at the smoothed state $z_{t|t}$.

Example 12.5. To demonstrate the FFBS procedure, we consider the monthly log returns of the S&P 500 index from January 1962 to November 2004 for 515 observations. Figure 12.12 shows the time plots of the logged S&P 500 index and the log return series. The original data were obtained from Yahoo Finance Web site. Let r_t be the monthly log return series. We consider two stochastic volatility models in the form:

$$\begin{aligned} r_t &= \mu + \sigma_o \exp(z_t/2)\epsilon_t, & \epsilon_t &\sim_{\text{iid}} N(0,1), \\ z_{t+1} &= \alpha z_t + \eta_t, & \eta_t &\sim_{\text{iid}} N(0,\sigma_\eta^2). \end{aligned} \tag{12.54}$$

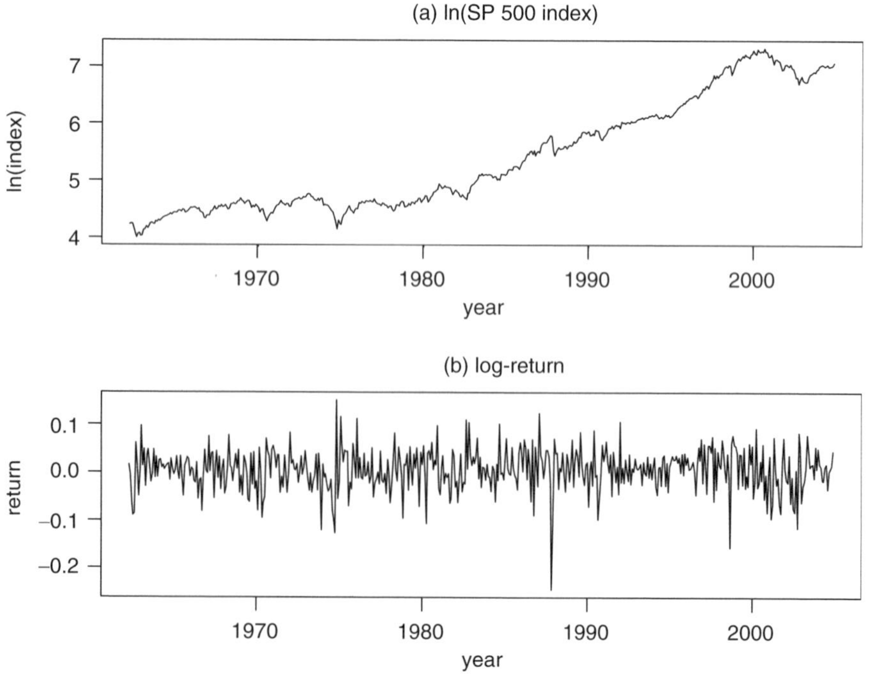

Figure 12.12. Time plots of monthly S&P 500 index from January 1962 to November 2004: (a) log index series and (b) log return series.

Table 12.4. Estimation of Stochastic Volatility Model in Eq. (12.54) for the Monthly Log Returns of the S&P 500 Index from January 1962 to November 2004 Using Gibbs Sampling with the FFBS Algorithm[a]

Parameter	μ	σ_o	α	σ_η	ρ
		With Leverage Effect			
Estimate	0.0081	0.0764	−0.0616	2.5639	−0.3892
Standard error	0.0274	0.0255	0.1186	0.3924	0.0292
		Without Leverage Effect			
Estimate	0.0080	0.0775	−0.0613	2.5827	
Standard error	0.0279	0.0266	0.1164	0.3783	

[a]The results are based on 2000 + 8000 iterations with the first 2000 iterations as burn-ins.

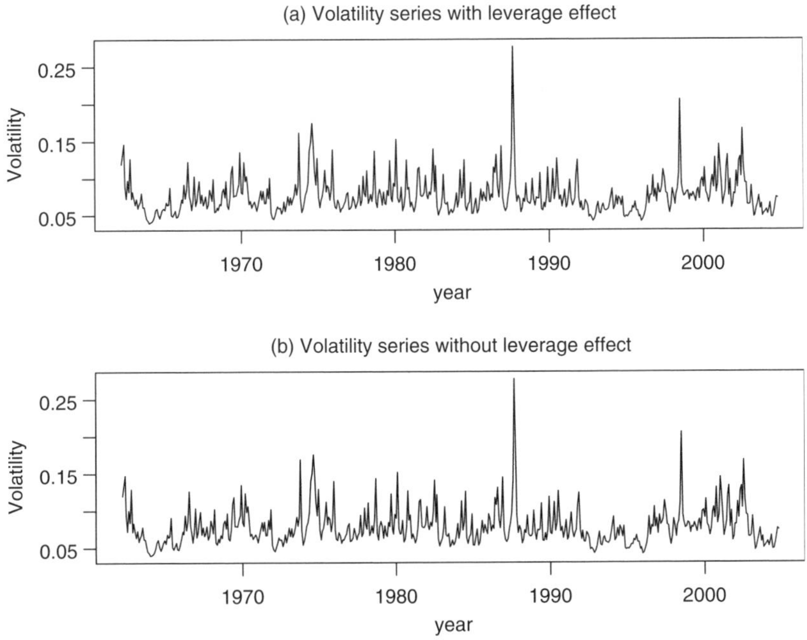

Figure 12.13. Estimated volatility of monthly log returns of the S&P 500 index from January 1962 to November 2004 using stochastic volatility models: (a) with leverage effect (b) without leverage effect.

In model 1, $\{\epsilon_t\}$ and $\{\eta_t\}$ are two independent Gaussian white noise series. That is, there is no leverage effect in the model. In model 2, we assume that $\text{corr}(\epsilon_t, e_t) = \rho$, which denotes the leverage effect.

We estimate the models via the FFBS procedure using a program written in Matlab. The Gibbs sampling was run for 2000 + 8000 iterations with the first 2000 iterations as burn-ins. Table 12.4 gives the posterior means and standard errors of the parameter estimates. In particular, we have $\hat{\rho} = -0.39$, which is close to the value commonly seen in the literature. Figure 12.13 shows the time plots of the posterior means of the estimated volatility. As expected, the two volatility series are very close. Compared with the results of Example 12.3, which uses a shorter series, the estimated volatility series exhibit similar patterns and are in the same magnitude. Note that the volatility shown in Figure 12.5 is conditional variance of percentage log returns whereas the volatility in Figure 12.13 is the conditional standard error of log returns.

12.9 MARKOV SWITCHING MODELS

The Markov switching model is another econometric model for which MCMC methods enjoy many advantages over the traditional likelihood method. McCulloch and Tsay (1994b) discuss a Gibbs sampling procedure to estimate such a model when the volatility in each state is constant over time. These authors applied the procedure to estimate a Markov switching model with different dynamics and mean levels for different states to the quarterly growth rate of U.S. real gross national product, seasonally adjusted, and obtained some interesting results. For instance, the dynamics of the growth rate are significantly different between periods of economic "contraction" and "expansion." Since this chapter is concerned with asset returns, we focus on models with volatility switching.

Suppose that an asset return r_t follows a simple two-state Markov switching model with different risk premiums and different GARCH dynamics:

$$r_t = \begin{cases} \beta_1\sqrt{h_t} + \sqrt{h_t}\epsilon_t, & h_t = \alpha_{10} + \alpha_{11}h_{t-1} + \alpha_{12}a_{t-1}^2 \quad \text{if } s_t = 1, \\ \beta_2\sqrt{h_t} + \sqrt{h_t}\epsilon_t, & h_t = \alpha_{20} + \alpha_{21}h_{t-1} + \alpha_{22}a_{t-1}^2 \quad \text{if } s_t = 2, \end{cases} \tag{12.55}$$

where $a_t = \sqrt{h_t}\epsilon_t$, $\{\epsilon_t\}$ is a sequence of Gaussian white noises with mean zero and variance 1, and the parameters α_{ij} satisfy some regularity conditions so that the unconditional variance of a_t exists. The probability transition from one state to another is governed by

$$P(s_t = 2|s_{t-1} = 1) = e_1, \quad P(s_t = 1|s_{t-1} = 2) = e_2, \tag{12.56}$$

where $0 < e_i < 1$. A small e_i means that the return series has a tendency to stay in the ith state with expected duration $1/e_i$. For the model in Eq. (12.55) to be identifiable, we assume that $\beta_2 > \beta_1$ so that state 2 is associated with higher risk premium. This is not a critical restriction because it is used to achieve uniqueness in labeling the states. A special case of the model results if $\alpha_{1j} = \alpha_{2j}$ for all j so that the model assumes a GARCH model for all states. However, if $\beta_i\sqrt{h_t}$ is replaced by β_i, then model (12.55) reduces to a simple Markov switching GARCH model.

Model (12.55) is a Markov switching GARCH-M model. For simplicity, we assume that the initial volatility h_1 is given with value equal to the sample variance of r_t. A more sophisticated analysis is to treat h_1 as a parameter and estimate it jointly with other parameters. We expect the effect of fixing h_1 will be negligible in most applications, especially when the sample size is large. The "traditional" parameters of the Markov switching GARCH-M model are $\boldsymbol{\beta} = (\beta_1, \beta_2)'$, $\boldsymbol{\alpha}_i = (\alpha_{i0}, \alpha_{i1}, \alpha_{i2})'$ for $i = 1$ and 2, and the transition probabilities $\boldsymbol{e} = (e_1, e_2)'$. The state vector $\boldsymbol{S} = (s_1, s_2, \ldots, s_n)'$ contains the augmented parameters. The volatility vector $\boldsymbol{H} = (h_2, \ldots, h_n)'$ can be computed recursively if h_1, $\boldsymbol{\alpha}_i$, and the state vector $\boldsymbol{S}$ are given.

Dependence of the return on volatility in model (12.55) implies that the return is also serially correlated. The model thus has some predictivity in the return. However, states of the future returns are unknown and a prediction produced by the model is necessarily a mixture of those over possible state configurations. This often results in high uncertainty in point prediction of future returns.

Turn to estimation. The likelihood function of model (12.55) is complicated as it is a mixture over all possible state configurations. Yet the Gibbs sampling approach only requires the following conditional posterior distributions:

$$f(\boldsymbol{\beta}|\boldsymbol{R}, \boldsymbol{S}, \boldsymbol{H}, \boldsymbol{\alpha}_1, \boldsymbol{\alpha}_2), \quad f(\boldsymbol{\alpha}_i|\boldsymbol{R}, \boldsymbol{S}, \boldsymbol{H}, \boldsymbol{\alpha}_{j\neq i}),$$

$$P(\boldsymbol{S}|\boldsymbol{R}, h_1, \boldsymbol{\alpha}_1, \boldsymbol{\alpha}_2), \quad f(e_i|\boldsymbol{S}), \quad i = 1, 2,$$

where $\boldsymbol{R}$ is the collection of observed returns. For simplicity, we use conjugate prior distributions discussed in Section 12.3—that is,

$$\beta_i \sim N(\beta_{io}, \sigma_{io}^2), \quad e_i \sim \text{Beta}(\gamma_{i1}, \gamma_{i2}).$$

The prior distribution of parameter α_{ij} is uniform over a properly specified interval. Since α_{ij} is a nonlinear parameter of the likelihood function, we use the Griddy Gibbs to draw its random realizations. A uniform prior distribution simplifies the computation involved. Details of the prior conditional posterior distributions are given below:

1. The posterior distribution of β_i only depends on the data in state i. Define

$$r_{it} = \begin{cases} r_t/\sqrt{h_t} & \text{if } s_t = i, \\ 0 & \text{otherwise.} \end{cases}$$

Then we have

$$r_{it} = \beta_i + \epsilon_t, \quad \text{for} \quad s_t = i.$$

Therefore, information of the data on β_i is contained in the sample mean of r_{it}. Let $\bar{r}_i = \left(\sum_{s_t=i} r_{it}\right)/n_i$, where the summation is over all data points in state i and n_i is the number of data points in state i. Then the conditional posterior distribution of β_i is normal with mean β_i^* and variance σ_{i*}^2, where

$$\frac{1}{\sigma_{i*}^2} = n_i + \frac{1}{\sigma_{io}^2}, \quad \beta_i^* = \sigma_{i*}^2 \left(n_i \bar{r}_i + \beta_{io}/\sigma_{io}^2\right), \quad i = 1, 2.$$

2. Next, the parameters α_{ij} can be drawn one by one using the Griddy Gibbs method. Given h_1, $\boldsymbol{S}$, $\boldsymbol{\alpha}_{v\neq i}$, and α_{iv} with $v \neq j$, the conditional posterior distribution function of α_{ij} does not correspond to a well-known distribution, but it can be evaluated easily as

$$f(\alpha_{ij}|.) \propto -\frac{1}{2}\left(\ln h_t + \frac{(r_t - \beta_i\sqrt{h_t})^2}{h_t}\right), \quad \text{if} \quad s_t = i,$$

where h_t contains α_{ij}. We evaluate this function at a grid of points for α_{ij} over a properly specified interval. For example, $0 \le \alpha_{11} < 1 - \alpha_{12}$.

3. The conditional posterior distribution of e_i only involves $\boldsymbol{S}$. Let ℓ_1 be the number of switches from state 1 to state 2 and ℓ_2 be the number of switches from state 2 to state 1 in $\boldsymbol{S}$. Also, let n_i be the number of data points in state i. Then by Result 3 of conjugate prior distributions, the posterior distribution of e_i is Beta($\gamma_{i1} + \ell_i$, $\gamma_{i2} + n_i - \ell_i$).

4. Finally, elements of $\boldsymbol{S}$ can be drawn one by one. Let $\boldsymbol{S}_{-j}$ be the vector obtained by removing s_j from $\boldsymbol{S}$. Given $\boldsymbol{S}_{-j}$ and other information, s_j can assume two possibilities (i.e., $s_j = 1$ or $s_j = 2$), and its conditional posterior distribution is

$$P(s_j|.) \propto \prod_{t=j}^{n} f(a_t|\boldsymbol{H})P(s_j|\boldsymbol{S}_{-j}).$$

The probability

$$P(s_j = i|\boldsymbol{S}_{-j}) = P(s_j = i|s_{j-1}, s_{j+1}), \quad i = 1, 2$$

can be computed by the Markov transition probabilities in Eq. (12.56). In addition, assuming $s_j = i$, one can compute h_t for $t \ge j$ recursively. The relevant likelihood function, denoted by $L(s_j)$, is given by

$$L(s_j = i) \equiv \prod_{t=j}^{n} f(a_t|\boldsymbol{H}) \propto \exp(f_{ji}), \quad f_{ji} = \sum_{t=j}^{n} -\frac{1}{2}\left(\ln(h_t) + \frac{a_t^2}{h_t}\right),$$

for $i = 1$ and 2, where $a_t = r_t - \beta_1\sqrt{h_t}$ if $s_t = 1$ and $a_t = r_t - \beta_2\sqrt{h_t}$ otherwise. Consequently, the conditional posterior probability of $s_j = 1$ is

$$P(s_j = 1|.) = \frac{P(s_j = 1|s_{j-1}, s_{j+1})L(s_j = 1)}{P(s_j = 1|s_{j-1}, s_{j+1})L(s_j = 1) + P(s_j = 2|s_{j-1}, s_{j+1})L(s_j = 2)}.$$

The state s_j can then be drawn easily using a uniform distribution on the unit interval [0, 1].

Remark. Since s_j and s_{j+1} are highly correlated when e_1 and e_2 are small, it is more efficient to draw several s_j jointly. However, the computation involved in enumerating the possible state configurations increases quickly with the number of states drawn jointly. □

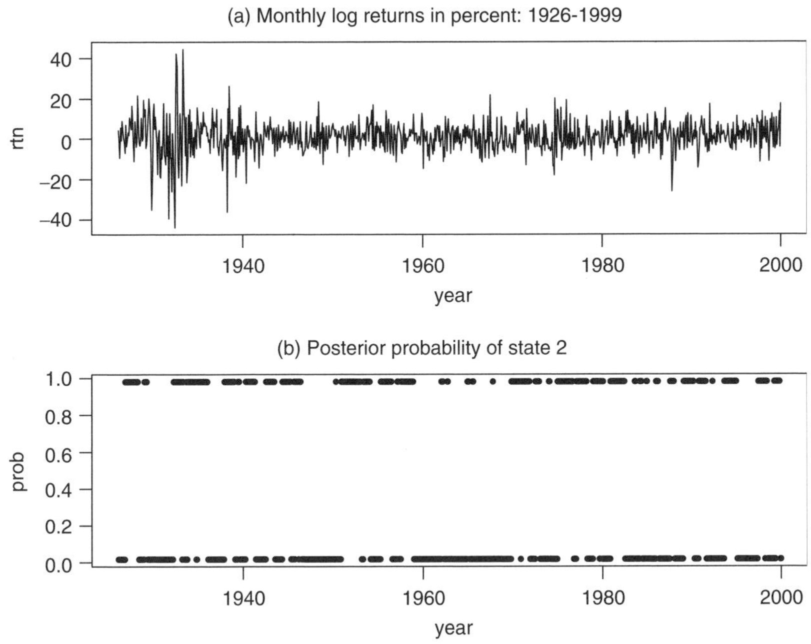

Figure 12.14. (a) Time plot of the monthly log returns, in percentages, of GE stock from 1926 to 1999. (b) Time plot of the posterior probability of being in state 2 based on results of the last 2000 iterations of a Gibbs sampling with 5000 + 2000 total iterations. The model used is a two-state Markov switching GARCH-M model.

Example 12.6. In this example, we consider the monthly log stock returns of General Electric Company from January 1926 to December 1999 for 888 observations. The returns are in percentages and shown in Figure 12.14a. For comparison purposes, we start with a GARCH-M model for the series and obtain

$$\begin{aligned} r_t &= 0.182\sqrt{h_t} + a_t, \quad a_t = \sqrt{h_t}\epsilon_t, \\ h_t &= 0.546 + 1.740h_{t-1} - 0.775h_{t-2} + 0.025a_{t-1}^2, \end{aligned} \tag{12.57}$$

where r_t is the monthly log return and $\{\epsilon_t\}$ is a sequence of independent Gaussian white noises with mean zero and variance 1. All parameter estimates are highly significant with p-values less than 0.0006. The Ljung–Box statistics of the standardized residuals and their squared series fail to suggest any model inadequacy. It is reassuring to see that the risk premium is positive and significant. The GARCH model in Eq. (12.57) can be written as

$$(1 - 1.765B + 0.775B^2)a_t^2 = 0.546 + (1 - 0.025B)\eta_t,$$

where $\eta_t = a_t^2 - h_t$ and B is the back-shift operator such that $Ba_t^2 = a_{t-1}^2$. As discussed in Chapter 3, the prior equation can be regarded as an ARMA(2,1) model with nonhomogeneous innovations for the squared series a_t^2. The AR polynomial can be factorized as $(1 - 0.945B)(1 - 0.820B)$, indicating two real characteristic roots with magnitudes less than 1. Consequently, the unconditional variance of r_t is finite and equal to $0.546/(1-1.765+0.775) \approx 49.64$.

Turn to Markov switching models. We use the following prior distributions:

$$\beta_1 \sim N(0.3, 0.09), \quad \beta_2 \sim N(1.3, 0.09), \quad \epsilon_i \sim \text{Beta}(5, 95).$$

The initial parameter values used are (a) $e_i = 0.1$, (b) s_1 is a Bernoulli trial with equal probabilities and s_t is generated sequentially using the initial transition probabilities, and (c) $\boldsymbol{\alpha}_1 = (1.0, 0.6, 0.2)'$ and $\boldsymbol{\alpha}_2 = (2, 0.7, 0.1)'$. Gibbs samples of α_{ij} are drawn using the Griddy Gibbs with 400 grid points, equally spaced over the following ranges: $\alpha_{i0} \in [0, 6.0]$, $\alpha_{i1} \in [0, 1]$, and $\alpha_{i2} \in [0, 0.5]$. In addition, we implement the constraints $\alpha_{i1} + \alpha_{i2} < 1$ for $i = 1, 2$. The Gibbs sampler is run for $5000 + 2000$ iterations but only results of the last 2000 iterations are used to make inference.

Table 12.5 shows the posterior means and standard deviations of parameters of the Markov switching GARCH-M model in Eq. (12.55). In particular, it also contains some statistics showing the difference between the two states such as $\theta = \beta_2 - \beta_1$. The difference between the risk premiums is statistically significant at the 5% level. The differences in posterior means of the volatility parameters between the two states appear to be insignificant. Yet the posterior distributions of volatility parameters show some different characteristics. Figures 12.15 and 12.16 show the histograms of all parameters in the Markov switching GARCH-M model.

Table 12.5. A Fitted Markov Switching GARCH-M Model for the Monthly Log Returns of GE Stock from January 1926 to December 1999[a]

			State 1		
Parameter	β_1	e_1	α_{10}	α_{11}	α_{12}
Posterior mean	0.111	0.089	2.070	0.844	0.033
Posterior standard error	0.043	0.012	1.001	0.038	0.033
			State 2		
Parameter	β_2	e_2	α_{20}	α_{21}	α_{22}
Posterior mean	0.247	0.112	2.740	0.869	0.068
Posterior standard error	0.050	0.014	1.073	0.031	0.024
			Difference Between States		
Parameter	$\beta_2 - \beta_1$	$e_2 - e_1$	$\alpha_{20} - \alpha_{10}$	$\alpha_{21} - \alpha_{11}$	$\alpha_{22} - \alpha_{12}$
Posterior mean	0.135	0.023	0.670	0.026	−0.064
Posterior standard error	0.063	0.019	1.608	0.050	0.043

[a]The numbers shown are the posterior means and standard deviations based on a Gibbs sampling with $5000 + 2000$ iterations. Results of the first 5000 iterations are discarded. The prior distributions and initial parameter estimates are given in the text.

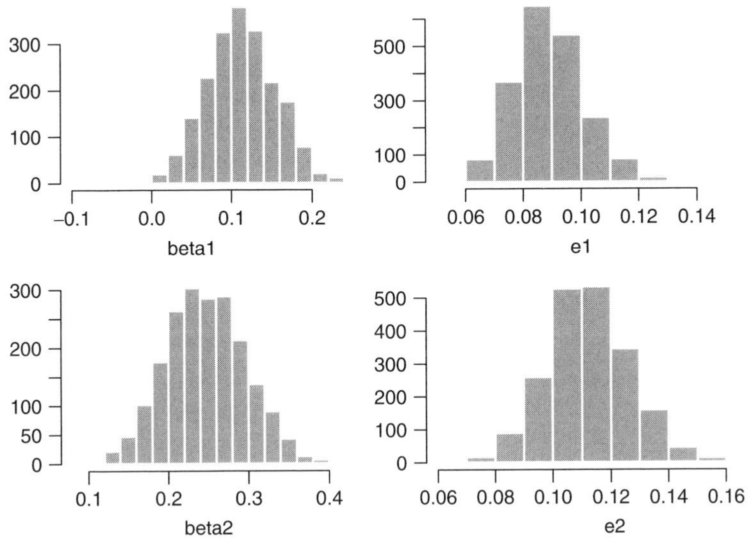

Figure 12.15. Histograms of the risk premium and transition probabilities of a two-state Markov switching GARCH-M model for the monthly log returns of GE stock from 1926 to 1999. The results are based on the last 2000 iterations of a Gibbs sampling with 5000 + 2000 total iterations.

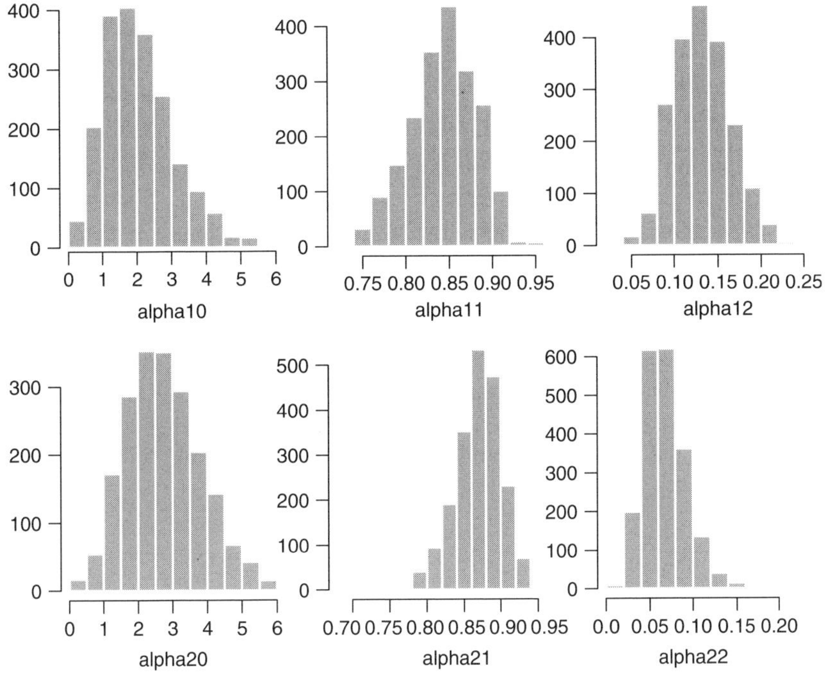

Figure 12.16. Histograms of volatility parameters of a two-state Markov switching GARCH-M model for the monthly log returns of GE stock from 1926 to 1999. The results are based on the last 2000 iterations of a Gibbs sampling with 5000 + 2000 total iterations.

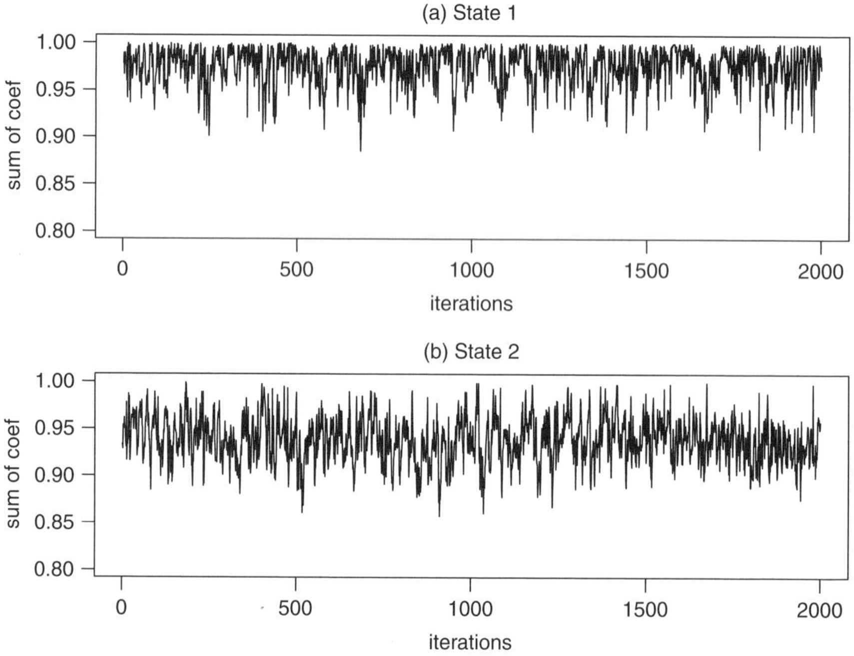

Figure 12.17. Time plots of the persistent parameter $\alpha_{i1} + \alpha_{i2}$ of a two-state Markov switching GARCH-M model for the monthly log returns of GE stock from 1926 to 1999. The results are based on the last 2000 iterations of a Gibbs sampling with 5000 + 2000 total iterations.

They exhibit some differences between the two states. Figure 12.17 shows the time plot of the persistent parameter $\alpha_{i1} + \alpha_{i2}$ for the two states. It shows that the persistent parameter of state 1 reaches the boundary 1.0 frequently, but that of state 2 does not. The expected durations of the two states are about 11 and 9 months, respectively. Figure 12.14b shows the posterior probability of being in state 2 for each observation.

Finally, we compare the fitted volatility series of the simple GARCH-M model in Eq. (12.57) and the Markov switching GARCH-M model in Eq. (12.55). The two fitted volatility series (Figure 12.18) show similar patterns and are consistent with the behavior of the squared log returns. The simple GARCH-M model produces a smoother volatility series with lower estimated volatilities.

12.10 FORECASTING

Forecasting under the MCMC framework can be done easily. The procedure is simply to use the fitted model in each Gibbs iteration to generate samples for the forecasting period. In a sense, forecasting here is done by using the fitted model to simulate realizations for the forecasting period. We use the univariate

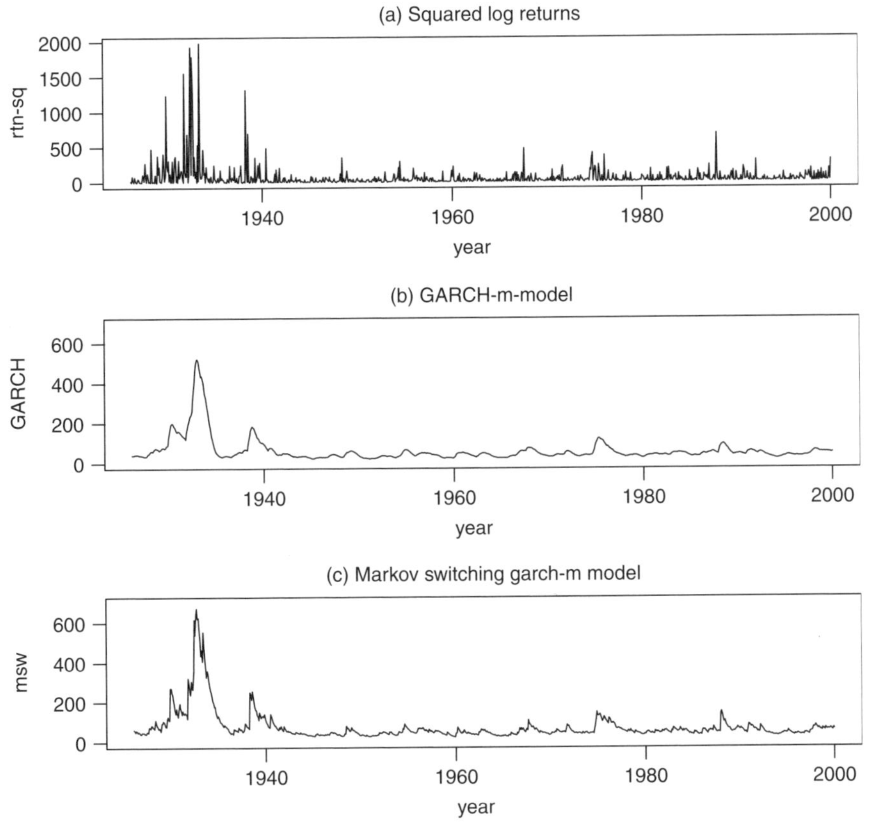

Figure 12.18. Fitted volatility series for the monthly log returns of GE stock from 1926 to 1999: (a) the squared log returns, (b) the GARCH-M model in Eq. (12.57), and (c) the two-state Markov switching GARCH-M model in Eq. (12.55).

stochastic volatility model to illustrate the procedure; forecasts of other models can be obtained by the same method.

Consider the stochastic volatility model in Eqs. (12.20) and (12.21). Suppose that there are n returns available and we are interested in predicting the return r_{n+i} and volatility h_{n+i} for $i = 1, \ldots, \ell$, where $\ell > 0$. Assume that the explanatory variables x_{jt} in Eq. (12.20) are either available or can be predicted sequentially during the forecasting period. Recall that estimation of the model under the MCMC framework is done by Gibbs sampling, which draws parameter values from their conditional posterior distributions iteratively. Denote the parameters by $\boldsymbol{\beta}_j = (\beta_{0,j}, \ldots, \beta_{p,j})'$, $\boldsymbol{\alpha}_j = (\alpha_{0,j}, \alpha_{1,j})'$, and $\sigma^2_{v,j}$ for the jth Gibbs iteration. In other words, at the jth Gibbs iteration, the model is

$$r_t = \beta_{0,j} + \beta_{1,j}x_{1t} + \cdots + \beta_{p,j}x_{pt} + a_t, \tag{12.58}$$

$$\ln h_t = \alpha_{0,j} + \alpha_{1,j} \ln h_{t-1} + v_t, \quad \text{Var}(v_t) = \sigma^2_{v,j}. \tag{12.59}$$

We can use this model to generate a realization of r_{n+i} and h_{n+i} for $i = 1, \ldots, \ell$. Denote the simulated realizations by $r_{n+i,j}$ and $h_{n+i,j}$, respectively. These realizations are generated as follows:

- Draw a random sample v_{n+1} from $N(0, \sigma^2_{v,j})$ and use Eq. (12.59) to compute $h_{n+1,j}$.
- Draw a random sample ϵ_{n+1} from $N(0, 1)$ to obtain $a_{n+1,j} = \sqrt{h_{n+1,j}}\epsilon_{n+1}$ and use Eq. (12.58) to compute $r_{n+1,j}$.
- Repeat the prior two steps sequentially for $n + i$ with $i = 2, \ldots, \ell$.

If we run a Gibbs sampling for $M + N$ iterations in model estimation, we only need to compute the forecasts for the last N iterations. This results in a random sample for r_{n+i} and h_{n+i}. More specifically, we obtain

$$\{r_{n+1,j}, \ldots, r_{n+\ell,j}\}_{j=1}^N, \quad \{h_{n+1,j}, \ldots, h_{n+\ell,j}\}_{j=1}^N.$$

These two random samples can be used to make inference. For example, point forecasts of the return r_{n+i} and volatility h_{n+i} are simply the sample means of the two random samples. Similarly, the sample standard deviations can be used as the standard deviations of forecast errors. To improve the computational efficiency in volatility forecast, importance sampling can be used; see Gelman, Carlin, Stern, and Rubin (2003).

Example 12.7 (Example 12.3 Continued). As a demonstration, we consider the monthly log return series of the S&P 500 index from 1962 to 1999. Table 12.6 gives the point forecasts of the return and its volatility for five forecast horizons starting with December 1999. Both the GARCH model in Eq. (12.26) and the stochastic volatility model in Eq. (12.27) are used in the forecasting. The volatility forecasts of the GARCH(1,1) model increase gradually with the forecast horizon to the unconditional variance $3.349/(1 - 0.086 - 0.735) = 18.78$. The volatility

Table 12.6. Volatility Forecasts for the Monthly Log Return of the S&P 500 Index

Horizon	1	2	3	4	5
			Log Return		
GARCH	0.66	0.66	0.66	0.66	0.66
SVM	0.53	0.78	0.92	0.88	0.84
			Volatility		
GARCH	17.98	18.12	18.24	18.34	18.42
SVM	19.31	19.36	19.35	19.65	20.13

[a]The data span is from January 1962 to December 1999 and the forecast origin is December 1999. Forecasts of the stochastic volatility model are obtained by a Gibbs sampling with 2000 + 2000 iterations.

forecasts of the stochastic volatility model are higher than those of the GARCH model. This is understandable because the stochastic volatility model takes into consideration the parameter uncertainty in producing forecasts. In contrast, the GARCH model assumes that the parameters are fixed and given in Eq. (12.26). This is an important difference and is one of the reasons that GARCH models tend to underestimate the volatility in comparison with the implied volatility obtained from derivative pricing.

Remark. Besides the advantage of taking into consideration parameter uncertainty in forecast, the MCMC method produces in effect a predictive distribution of the volatility of interest. The predictive distribution is more informative than a simple point forecast. It can be used, for instance, to obtain the quantiles needed in value at risk calculation. □

12.11 OTHER APPLICATIONS

The MCMC method is applicable to many other financial problems. For example, Zhang, Russell, and Tsay (2000) use it to analyze information determinants of bid and ask quotes, McCulloch and Tsay (2001) use the method to estimate a hierarchical model for IBM transaction data, and Eraker (2001) and Elerian, Chib, and Shephard (2001) use it to estimate diffusion equations. The method is also useful in value at risk calculation because it provides a natural way to evaluate predictive distributions. The main question is not whether the methods can be used in most financial applications, but how efficient the methods can become. Only time and experience can provide an adequate answer to the question.

EXERCISES

12.1. Suppose that x is normally distributed with mean μ and variance 4. Assume that the prior distribution of μ is also normal with mean 0 and variance 25. What is the posterior distribution of μ given the data point x?

12.2. Consider the linear regression model with time series errors in Section 12.5. Assume that z_t is an AR(p) process (i.e., $z_t = \phi_1 z_{t-1} + \cdots + \phi_p z_{t-p} + a_t$). Let $\boldsymbol{\phi} = (\phi_1, \ldots, \phi_p)'$ be the vector of AR parameters. Derive the conditional posterior distributions of $f(\boldsymbol{\beta}|\boldsymbol{Y}, \boldsymbol{X}, \boldsymbol{\phi}, \sigma^2)$, $f(\boldsymbol{\phi}|\boldsymbol{Y}, \boldsymbol{X}, \boldsymbol{\beta}, \sigma^2)$, and $f(\sigma^2|\boldsymbol{Y}, \boldsymbol{X}, \boldsymbol{\beta}, \boldsymbol{\phi})$ assuming that conjugate prior distributions are used: that is,

$$\boldsymbol{\beta} \sim N(\boldsymbol{\beta}_o, \boldsymbol{\Sigma}_o), \quad \boldsymbol{\phi} \sim N(\boldsymbol{\phi}_o, \boldsymbol{A}_o), \quad (v\lambda)/\sigma^2 \sim \chi^2_v.$$

12.3. Consider the linear AR(p) model in Section 12.6.1. Suppose that x_h and x_{h+1} are two missing values with a joint prior distribution being multivariate normal with mean $\boldsymbol{\mu}_o$ and covariance matrix $\boldsymbol{\Sigma}_o$. Other prior distributions are the same as that in the text. What is the conditional posterior distribution of the two missing values?

12.4. Consider the monthly log returns of General Motors stock from 1950 to 1999 with 600 observations: (a) build a GARCH model for the series, (b) build a stochastic volatility model for the series, and (c) compare and discuss the two volatility models.

12.5. Build a stochastic volatility model for the daily log return of Cisco Systems stock from January 1991 to December 1999. You may download the data from the CRSP database or the file `d-csco9199.txt`. Use the model to obtain a predictive distribution for 1-step ahead volatility forecast at the forecast origin December 1999. Finally, use the predictive distribution to compute the value at risk of a long position worth $1 million with probability 0.01 for the next trading day.

12.6. Build a bivariate stochastic volatility model for the monthly log returns of General Motors stock and the S&P 500 index for the sample period from January 1950 to December 1999. Discuss the relationship between the two volatility processes and compute the time-varying beta for GM stock.

REFERENCES

Artigas, J. C. and Tsay, R. S. (2004). Effective estimation of stochastic diffusion models with leverage effects and jumps. Working paper, Graduate School of Business, University of Chicago.

Box, G. E. P. and Tiao, G. C. (1973). *Bayesian Inference in Statistical Analysis*. Addison-Wesley, Reading, MA.

Carter, C. K. and Kohn, R. (1994). On Gibbs sampling for state space models. *Biometrika* **81**: 541–553.

Chang, I., Tiao, G. C., and Chen, C. (1988). Estimation of time series parameters in the presence of outliers. *Technometrics* **30**: 193–204.

Carlin, B. P. and Louis, T. A. (2000). *Bayes and Empirical Bayes Methods for Data Analysis*, 2nd edition. Chapman and Hall, London.

Chib, S., Nardari, F., and Shephard, N. (2002). Markov chain Monte Carlo methods for stochastic volatility models. *Journal of Econometrics* **108**: 281–316.

DeGroot, M. H. (1990). *Optimal Statistical Decisions*. McGraw-Hill, New York.

Dempster, A. P., Laird, N. M., and Rubin, D. B. (1977). Maximum likelihood from incomplete data via the EM algorithm (with discussion). *Journal of the Royal Statistical Society Series B* **39**: 1–38.

Elerian, O., Chib, S. and Shephard, N. (2001). Likelihood inference for discretely observed nonlinear diffusions. *Econometrica* **69**: 959–993.

Eraker, B. (2001). Markov chain Monte Carlo analysis of diffusion with application to finance. *Journal of Business & Economic Statistics* **19**: 177–191.

Frühwirth-Schnatter, S. (1994). Data augmentation and dynamic linear models. *Journal of Time Series Analysis* **15**: 183–202.

Gelfand, A. E. and Smith, A. F. M. (1990). Sampling-based approaches to calculating marginal densities. *Journal of the American Statistical Association* **85**: 398–409.

Gelfand, A. E., Hills, S. E., Racine-Poon, A., and Smith, A. F. M. (1990). Illustration of Bayesian inference in normal data models using Gibbs sampling, *Journal of the American Statistical Association* **85**: 972–985.

Gelman, A., Carlin, J. B., Stern, H. S., and Rubin, D. B. (2003). *Bayesian Data Analysis*, 2nd edition. Chapman and Hall/CRC Press, London.

Geman, S. and Geman, D. (1984). Stochastic relaxation, Gibbs distributions, and the Bayesian restoration of images. *IEEE Transactions on Pattern Analysis and Machine Intelligence* **6**: 721–741.

Hasting, W. K. (1970). Monte Carlo sampling methods using Markov chains and their applications. *Biometrika* **57**: 97–109.

Jacquier, E., Polson, N. G., and Rossi, P. E. (1994). Bayesian analysis of stochastic volatility models (with discussion). *Journal of Business & Economic Statistics* **12**: 371–417.

Jacquier, E., Polson, N. G., and Rossi, P. E. (2004). Bayesian analysis of stochastic volatility models with fat-tails and correlated errors. *Journal of Econometrics* **122**: 185–212.

Jones, R. H.(1980). Maximum likelihood fitting of ARMA models to time series with missing observations. *Technometrics* **22**: 389–395.

Justel, A., Peña, D., and Tsay, R. S. (2001). Detection of outlier patches in autoregressive time series. *Statistica Sinica* **11**: 651–673.

Kim, S., Shephard, N., and Chib, S. (1998). Stochastic volatility: Likelihood inference and comparison with ARCH models. *Review of Economic Studies* **65**: 361–393.

Liu, J., Wong, W. H., and Kong, A. (1994). Correlation structure and convergence rate of the Gibbs samplers I: Applications to the comparison of estimators and augmentation schemes. *Biometrika* **81**: 27–40.

McCulloch, R. E. and Tsay, R. S. (1994a), Bayesian analysis of autoregressive time series via the Gibbs sampler. *Journal of Time Series Analysis* **15**: 235–250.

McCulloch, R. E. and Tsay, R. S. (1994b). Statistical analysis of economic time series via Markov switching models. *Journal of Time Series Analysis* **15**: 523–539.

McCulloch, R. E. and Tsay, R. S. (2001). Nonlinearity in high-frequency financial data and hierarchical models. *Studies in Nonlinear Dynamics and Econometrics* **5**: 1–17.

Metropolis, N. and Ulam, S. (1949). The Monte Carlo method. *Journal of the American Statistical Association* **44**: 335–341.

Metropolis, N., Rosenbluth, A. W., Rosenbluth, M. N., Teller, A. H., and Teller, E. (1953). Equation of state calculations by fast computing machines. *Journal of Chemical Physics* **21**: 1087–1092.

Tanner, M. A. (1996). *Tools for Statistical Inference: Methods for the Exploration of Posterior Distributions and Likelihood Functions*, 3rd edition. Springer-Verlag, New York.

Tanner, M. A. and Wong, W. H. (1987). The calculation of posterior distributions by data augmentation (with discussion). *Journal of the American Statistical Association* **82**: 528–550.

Tierney, L. (1994). Markov chains for exploring posterior distributions (with discussion). *Annals of Statistics* **22**: 1701–1762.

Tsay, R. S. (1988). Outliers, level shifts, and variance changes in time series. *Journal of Forecasting* **7**: 1–20.

Tsay, R. S., Peña, D., and Pankratz, A. (2000). Outliers in multivariate time series. *Biometrika* **87**: 789–804.

Zhang, M. Y., Russell, J. R., and Tsay, R. S. (2000). Determinants of bid and ask quotes and implications for the cost of trading. Working paper, Statistics Research Center, Graduate School of Business, University of Chicago.

Index

WILEY SERIES IN PROBABILITY AND STATISTICS

ESTABLISHED BY WALTER A. SHEWHART AND SAMUEL S. WILKS

The ***Wiley Series in Probability and Statistics*** is well established and authoritative. It covers many topics of current research interest in both pure and applied statistics and probability theory. Written by leading statisticians and institutions, the titles span both state-of-the-art developments in the field and classical methods.

Reflecting the wide range of current research in statistics, the series encompasses applied, methodological and theoretical statistics, ranging from applications and new techniques made possible by advances in computerized practice to rigorous treatment of theoretical approaches.

This series provides essential and invaluable reading for all statisticians, whether in academia, industry, government, or research.

† ABRAHAM and LEDOLTER · Statistical Methods for Forecasting
AGRESTI · Analysis of Ordinal Categorical Data
AGRESTI · An Introduction to Categorical Data Analysis
AGRESTI · Categorical Data Analysis, *Second Edition*
ALTMAN, GILL, and McDONALD · Numerical Issues in Statistical Computing for the Social Scientist
AMARATUNGA and CABRERA · Exploration and Analysis of DNA Microarray and Protein Array Data
ANDĚL · Mathematics of Chance
ANDERSON · An Introduction to Multivariate Statistical Analysis, *Third Edition*
* ANDERSON · The Statistical Analysis of Time Series
ANDERSON, AUQUIER, HAUCK, OAKES, VANDAELE, and WEISBERG · Statistical Methods for Comparative Studies
ANDERSON and LOYNES · The Teaching of Practical Statistics
ARMITAGE and DAVID (editors) · Advances in Biometry
ARNOLD, BALAKRISHNAN, and NAGARAJA · Records
* ARTHANARI and DODGE · Mathematical Programming in Statistics
* BAILEY · The Elements of Stochastic Processes with Applications to the Natural Sciences
BALAKRISHNAN and KOUTRAS · Runs and Scans with Applications
BARNETT · Comparative Statistical Inference, *Third Edition*
BARNETT and LEWIS · Outliers in Statistical Data, *Third Edition*
BARTOSZYNSKI and NIEWIADOMSKA-BUGAJ · Probability and Statistical Inference
BASILEVSKY · Statistical Factor Analysis and Related Methods: Theory and Applications
BASU and RIGDON · Statistical Methods for the Reliability of Repairable Systems
BATES and WATTS · Nonlinear Regression Analysis and Its Applications
BECHHOFER, SANTNER, and GOLDSMAN · Design and Analysis of Experiments for Statistical Selection, Screening, and Multiple Comparisons
BELSLEY · Conditioning Diagnostics: Collinearity and Weak Data in Regression

*Now available in a lower priced paperback edition in the Wiley Classics Library.
†Now available in a lower priced paperback edition in the Wiley–Interscience Paperback Series.

† BELSLEY, KUH, and WELSCH · Regression Diagnostics: Identifying Influential Data and Sources of Collinearity
BENDAT and PIERSOL · Random Data: Analysis and Measurement Procedures, *Third Edition*
BERRY, CHALONER, and GEWEKE · Bayesian Analysis in Statistics and Econometrics: Essays in Honor of Arnold Zellner
BERNARDO and SMITH · Bayesian Theory
BHAT and MILLER · Elements of Applied Stochastic Processes, *Third Edition*
BHATTACHARYA and WAYMIRE · Stochastic Processes with Applications
† BIEMER, GROVES, LYBERG, MATHIOWETZ, and SUDMAN · Measurement Errors in Surveys
BILLINGSLEY · Convergence of Probability Measures, *Second Edition*
BILLINGSLEY · Probability and Measure, *Third Edition*
BIRKES and DODGE · Alternative Methods of Regression
BLISCHKE AND MURTHY (editors) · Case Studies in Reliability and Maintenance
BLISCHKE AND MURTHY · Reliability: Modeling, Prediction, and Optimization
BLOOMFIELD · Fourier Analysis of Time Series: An Introduction, *Second Edition*
BOLLEN · Structural Equations with Latent Variables
BOROVKOV · Ergodicity and Stability of Stochastic Processes
BOULEAU · Numerical Methods for Stochastic Processes
BOX · Bayesian Inference in Statistical Analysis
BOX · R. A. Fisher, the Life of a Scientist
BOX and DRAPER · Empirical Model-Building and Response Surfaces
* BOX and DRAPER · Evolutionary Operation: A Statistical Method for Process Improvement
BOX, HUNTER, and HUNTER · Statistics for Experimenters: Design, Innovation, and Discovery, *Second Editon*
BOX and LUCEÑO · Statistical Control by Monitoring and Feedback Adjustment
BRANDIMARTE · Numerical Methods in Finance: A MATLAB-Based Introduction
BROWN and HOLLANDER · Statistics: A Biomedical Introduction
BRUNNER, DOMHOF, and LANGER · Nonparametric Analysis of Longitudinal Data in Factorial Experiments
BUCKLEW · Large Deviation Techniques in Decision, Simulation, and Estimation
CAIROLI and DALANG · Sequential Stochastic Optimization
CASTILLO, HADI, BALAKRISHNAN, and SARABIA · Extreme Value and Related Models with Applications in Engineering and Science
CHAN · Time Series: Applications to Finance
CHARALAMBIDES · Combinatorial Methods in Discrete Distributions
CHATTERJEE and HADI · Sensitivity Analysis in Linear Regression
CHATTERJEE and PRICE · Regression Analysis by Example, *Third Edition*
CHERNICK · Bootstrap Methods: A Practitioner's Guide
CHERNICK and FRIIS · Introductory Biostatistics for the Health Sciences
CHILÈS and DELFINER · Geostatistics: Modeling Spatial Uncertainty
CHOW and LIU · Design and Analysis of Clinical Trials: Concepts and Methodologies, *Second Edition*
CLARKE and DISNEY · Probability and Random Processes: A First Course with Applications, *Second Edition*
* COCHRAN and COX · Experimental Designs, *Second Edition*
CONGDON · Applied Bayesian Modelling
CONGDON · Bayesian Statistical Modelling
CONOVER · Practical Nonparametric Statistics, *Third Edition*
COOK · Regression Graphics
COOK and WEISBERG · Applied Regression Including Computing and Graphics

*Now available in a lower priced paperback edition in the Wiley Classics Library.
†Now available in a lower priced paperback edition in the Wiley–Interscience Paperback Series.

COOK and WEISBERG · An Introduction to Regression Graphics
CORNELL · Experiments with Mixtures, Designs, Models, and the Analysis of Mixture Data, *Third Edition*
COVER and THOMAS · Elements of Information Theory
COX · A Handbook of Introductory Statistical Methods
* COX · Planning of Experiments
CRESSIE · Statistics for Spatial Data, *Revised Edition*
CSÖRGŐ and HORVÁTH · Limit Theorems in Change Point Analysis
DANIEL · Applications of Statistics to Industrial Experimentation
DANIEL · Biostatistics: A Foundation for Analysis in the Health Sciences, *Eighth Edition*
* DANIEL · Fitting Equations to Data: Computer Analysis of Multifactor Data, *Second Edition*
DASU and JOHNSON · Exploratory Data Mining and Data Cleaning
DAVID and NAGARAJA · Order Statistics, *Third Edition*
* DEGROOT, FIENBERG, and KADANE · Statistics and the Law
DEL CASTILLO · Statistical Process Adjustment for Quality Control
DEMARIS · Regression with Social Data: Modeling Continuous and Limited Response Variables
DEMIDENKO · Mixed Models: Theory and Applications
DENISON, HOLMES, MALLICK and SMITH · Bayesian Methods for Nonlinear Classification and Regression
DETTE and STUDDEN · The Theory of Canonical Moments with Applications in Statistics, Probability, and Analysis
DEY and MUKERJEE · Fractional Factorial Plans
DILLON and GOLDSTEIN · Multivariate Analysis: Methods and Applications
DODGE · Alternative Methods of Regression
* DODGE and ROMIG · Sampling Inspection Tables, *Second Edition*
* DOOB · Stochastic Processes
DOWDY, WEARDEN, and CHILKO · Statistics for Research, *Third Edition*
DRAPER and SMITH · Applied Regression Analysis, *Third Edition*
DRYDEN and MARDIA · Statistical Shape Analysis
DUDEWICZ and MISHRA · Modern Mathematical Statistics
DUNN and CLARK · Basic Statistics: A Primer for the Biomedical Sciences, *Third Edition*
DUPUIS and ELLIS · A Weak Convergence Approach to the Theory of Large Deviations
* ELANDT-JOHNSON and JOHNSON · Survival Models and Data Analysis
ENDERS · Applied Econometric Time Series
† ETHIER and KURTZ · Markov Processes: Characterization and Convergence
EVANS, HASTINGS, and PEACOCK · Statistical Distributions, *Third Edition*
FELLER · An Introduction to Probability Theory and Its Applications, Volume I, *Third Edition,* Revised; Volume II, *Second Edition*
FISHER and VAN BELLE · Biostatistics: A Methodology for the Health Sciences
FITZMAURICE, LAIRD, and WARE · Applied Longitudinal Analysis
* FLEISS · The Design and Analysis of Clinical Experiments
FLEISS · Statistical Methods for Rates and Proportions, *Third Edition*
† FLEMING and HARRINGTON · Counting Processes and Survival Analysis
FULLER · Introduction to Statistical Time Series, *Second Edition*
FULLER · Measurement Error Models
GALLANT · Nonlinear Statistical Models
GEISSER · Modes of Parametric Statistical Inference
GEWEKE · Contemporary Bayesian Econometrics and Statistics
GHOSH, MUKHOPADHYAY, and SEN · Sequential Estimation

*Now available in a lower priced paperback edition in the Wiley Classics Library.
†Now available in a lower priced paperback edition in the Wiley–Interscience Paperback Series.

GIESBRECHT and GUMPERTZ · Planning, Construction, and Statistical Analysis of Comparative Experiments
GIFI · Nonlinear Multivariate Analysis
GIVENS and HOETING · Computational Statistics
GLASSERMAN and YAO · Monotone Structure in Discrete-Event Systems
GNANADESIKAN · Methods for Statistical Data Analysis of Multivariate Observations, *Second Edition*
GOLDSTEIN and LEWIS · Assessment: Problems, Development, and Statistical Issues
GREENWOOD and NIKULIN · A Guide to Chi-Squared Testing
GROSS and HARRIS · Fundamentals of Queueing Theory, *Third Edition*
† GROVES · Survey Errors and Survey Costs
* HAHN and SHAPIRO · Statistical Models in Engineering
HAHN and MEEKER · Statistical Intervals: A Guide for Practitioners
HALD · A History of Probability and Statistics and their Applications Before 1750
HALD · A History of Mathematical Statistics from 1750 to 1930
† HAMPEL · Robust Statistics: The Approach Based on Influence Functions
HANNAN and DEISTLER · The Statistical Theory of Linear Systems
HEIBERGER · Computation for the Analysis of Designed Experiments
HEDAYAT and SINHA · Design and Inference in Finite Population Sampling
HELLER · MACSYMA for Statisticians
HINKELMANN and KEMPTHORNE · Design and Analysis of Experiments, Volume 1: Introduction to Experimental Design
HINKELMANN and KEMPTHORNE · Design and Analysis of Experiments, Volume 2: Advanced Experimental Design
HOAGLIN, MOSTELLER, and TUKEY · Exploratory Approach to Analysis of Variance
HOAGLIN, MOSTELLER, and TUKEY · Exploring Data Tables, Trends and Shapes
* HOAGLIN, MOSTELLER, and TUKEY · Understanding Robust and Exploratory Data Analysis
HOCHBERG and TAMHANE · Multiple Comparison Procedures
HOCKING · Methods and Applications of Linear Models: Regression and the Analysis of Variance, *Second Edition*
HOEL · Introduction to Mathematical Statistics, *Fifth Edition*
HOGG and KLUGMAN · Loss Distributions
HOLLANDER and WOLFE · Nonparametric Statistical Methods, *Second Edition*
HOSMER and LEMESHOW · Applied Logistic Regression, *Second Edition*
HOSMER and LEMESHOW · Applied Survival Analysis: Regression Modeling of Time to Event Data
† HUBER · Robust Statistics
HUBERTY · Applied Discriminant Analysis
HUNT and KENNEDY · Financial Derivatives in Theory and Practice
HUSKOVA, BERAN, and DUPAC · Collected Works of Jaroslav Hajek—with Commentary
HUZURBAZAR · Flowgraph Models for Multistate Time-to-Event Data
IMAN and CONOVER · A Modern Approach to Statistics
† JACKSON · A User's Guide to Principle Components
JOHN · Statistical Methods in Engineering and Quality Assurance
JOHNSON · Multivariate Statistical Simulation
JOHNSON and BALAKRISHNAN · Advances in the Theory and Practice of Statistics: A Volume in Honor of Samuel Kotz
JOHNSON and BHATTACHARYYA · Statistics: Principles and Methods, *Fifth Edition*
JOHNSON and KOTZ · Distributions in Statistics

*Now available in a lower priced paperback edition in the Wiley Classics Library.
†Now available in a lower priced paperback edition in the Wiley–Interscience Paperback Series.

JOHNSON and KOTZ (editors) · Leading Personalities in Statistical Sciences: From the Seventeenth Century to the Present
JOHNSON, KOTZ, and BALAKRISHNAN · Continuous Univariate Distributions, Volume 1, *Second Edition*
JOHNSON, KOTZ, and BALAKRISHNAN · Continuous Univariate Distributions, Volume 2, *Second Edition*
JOHNSON, KOTZ, and BALAKRISHNAN · Discrete Multivariate Distributions
JOHNSON, KOTZ, and KEMP · Univariate Discrete Distributions, *Third Edition*
JUDGE, GRIFFITHS, HILL, LÜTKEPOHL, and LEE · The Theory and Practice of Econometrics, *Second Edition*
JUREČKOVÁ and SEN · Robust Statistical Procedures: Aymptotics and Interrelations
JUREK and MASON · Operator-Limit Distributions in Probability Theory
KADANE · Bayesian Methods and Ethics in a Clinical Trial Design
KADANE AND SCHUM · A Probabilistic Analysis of the Sacco and Vanzetti Evidence
KALBFLEISCH and PRENTICE · The Statistical Analysis of Failure Time Data, *Second Edition*
KASS and VOS · Geometrical Foundations of Asymptotic Inference
† KAUFMAN and ROUSSEEUW · Finding Groups in Data: An Introduction to Cluster Analysis
KEDEM and FOKIANOS · Regression Models for Time Series Analysis
KENDALL, BARDEN, CARNE, and LE · Shape and Shape Theory
KHURI · Advanced Calculus with Applications in Statistics, *Second Edition*
KHURI, MATHEW, and SINHA · Statistical Tests for Mixed Linear Models
* KISH · Statistical Design for Research
KLEIBER and KOTZ · Statistical Size Distributions in Economics and Actuarial Sciences
KLUGMAN, PANJER, and WILLMOT · Loss Models: From Data to Decisions, *Second Edition*
KLUGMAN, PANJER, and WILLMOT · Solutions Manual to Accompany Loss Models: From Data to Decisions, *Second Edition*
KOTZ, BALAKRISHNAN, and JOHNSON · Continuous Multivariate Distributions, Volume 1, *Second Edition*
KOTZ and JOHNSON (editors) · Encyclopedia of Statistical Sciences: Volumes 1 to 9 with Index
KOTZ and JOHNSON (editors) · Encyclopedia of Statistical Sciences: Supplement Volume
KOTZ, READ, and BANKS (editors) · Encyclopedia of Statistical Sciences: Update Volume 1
KOTZ, READ, and BANKS (editors) · Encyclopedia of Statistical Sciences: Update Volume 2
KOVALENKO, KUZNETZOV, and PEGG · Mathematical Theory of Reliability of Time-Dependent Systems with Practical Applications
LACHIN · Biostatistical Methods: The Assessment of Relative Risks
LAD · Operational Subjective Statistical Methods: A Mathematical, Philosophical, and Historical Introduction
LAMPERTI · Probability: A Survey of the Mathematical Theory, *Second Edition*
LANGE, RYAN, BILLARD, BRILLINGER, CONQUEST, and GREENHOUSE · Case Studies in Biometry
LARSON · Introduction to Probability Theory and Statistical Inference, *Third Edition*
LAWLESS · Statistical Models and Methods for Lifetime Data, *Second Edition*
LAWSON · Statistical Methods in Spatial Epidemiology
LE · Applied Categorical Data Analysis
LE · Applied Survival Analysis
LEE and WANG · Statistical Methods for Survival Data Analysis, *Third Edition*

*Now available in a lower priced paperback edition in the Wiley Classics Library.
†Now available in a lower priced paperback edition in the Wiley–Interscience Paperback Series.

LEPAGE and BILLARD · Exploring the Limits of Bootstrap
LEYLAND and GOLDSTEIN (editors) · Multilevel Modelling of Health Statistics
LIAO · Statistical Group Comparison
LINDVALL · Lectures on the Coupling Method
LINHART and ZUCCHINI · Model Selection
LITTLE and RUBIN · Statistical Analysis with Missing Data, *Second Edition*
LLOYD · The Statistical Analysis of Categorical Data
LOWEN and TEICH · Fractal-Based Point Processes
MAGNUS and NEUDECKER · Matrix Differential Calculus with Applications in Statistics and Econometrics, *Revised Edition*
MALLER and ZHOU · Survival Analysis with Long Term Survivors
MALLOWS · Design, Data, and Analysis by Some Friends of Cuthbert Daniel
MANN, SCHAFER, and SINGPURWALLA · Methods for Statistical Analysis of Reliability and Life Data
MANTON, WOODBURY, and TOLLEY · Statistical Applications Using Fuzzy Sets
MARCHETTE · Random Graphs for Statistical Pattern Recognition
MARDIA and JUPP · Directional Statistics
MASON, GUNST, and HESS · Statistical Design and Analysis of Experiments with Applications to Engineering and Science, *Second Edition*
McCULLOCH and SEARLE · Generalized, Linear, and Mixed Models
McFADDEN · Management of Data in Clinical Trials
* McLACHLAN · Discriminant Analysis and Statistical Pattern Recognition
McLACHLAN, DO, and AMBROISE · Analyzing Microarray Gene Expression Data
McLACHLAN and KRISHNAN · The EM Algorithm and Extensions
McLACHLAN and PEEL · Finite Mixture Models
McNEIL · Epidemiological Research Methods
MEEKER and ESCOBAR · Statistical Methods for Reliability Data
MEERSCHAERT and SCHEFFLER · Limit Distributions for Sums of Independent Random Vectors: Heavy Tails in Theory and Practice
MICKEY, DUNN, and CLARK · Applied Statistics: Analysis of Variance and Regression, *Third Edition*
* MILLER · Survival Analysis, *Second Edition*
MONTGOMERY, PECK, and VINING · Introduction to Linear Regression Analysis, *Third Edition*
MORGENTHALER and TUKEY · Configural Polysampling: A Route to Practical Robustness
MUIRHEAD · Aspects of Multivariate Statistical Theory
MULLER and STOYAN · Comparison Methods for Stochastic Models and Risks
MURRAY · X-STAT 2.0 Statistical Experimentation, Design Data Analysis, and Nonlinear Optimization
MURTHY, XIE, and JIANG · Weibull Models
MYERS and MONTGOMERY · Response Surface Methodology: Process and Product Optimization Using Designed Experiments, *Second Edition*
MYERS, MONTGOMERY, and VINING · Generalized Linear Models. With Applications in Engineering and the Sciences
† NELSON · Accelerated Testing, Statistical Models, Test Plans, and Data Analyses
† NELSON · Applied Life Data Analysis
NEWMAN · Biostatistical Methods in Epidemiology
OCHI · Applied Probability and Stochastic Processes in Engineering and Physical Sciences
OKABE, BOOTS, SUGIHARA, and CHIU · Spatial Tesselations: Concepts and Applications of Voronoi Diagrams, *Second Edition*
OLIVER and SMITH · Influence Diagrams, Belief Nets and Decision Analysis
PALTA · Quantitative Methods in Population Health: Extensions of Ordinary Regressions

*Now available in a lower priced paperback edition in the Wiley Classics Library.
†Now available in a lower priced paperback edition in the Wiley–Interscience Paperback Series.

PANKRATZ · Forecasting with Dynamic Regression Models
PANKRATZ · Forecasting with Univariate Box-Jenkins Models: Concepts and Cases
* PARZEN · Modern Probability Theory and Its Applications
PEÑA, TIAO, and TSAY · A Course in Time Series Analysis
PIANTADOSI · Clinical Trials: A Methodologic Perspective
PORT · Theoretical Probability for Applications
POURAHMADI · Foundations of Time Series Analysis and Prediction Theory
PRESS · Bayesian Statistics: Principles, Models, and Applications
PRESS · Subjective and Objective Bayesian Statistics, *Second Edition*
PRESS and TANUR · The Subjectivity of Scientists and the Bayesian Approach
PUKELSHEIM · Optimal Experimental Design
PURI, VILAPLANA, and WERTZ · New Perspectives in Theoretical and Applied Statistics
† PUTERMAN · Markov Decision Processes: Discrete Stochastic Dynamic Programming
QIU · Image Processing and Jump Regression Analysis
* RAO · Linear Statistical Inference and Its Applications, *Second Edition*
RAUSAND and HØYLAND · System Reliability Theory: Models, Statistical Methods, and Applications, *Second Edition*
RENCHER · Linear Models in Statistics
RENCHER · Methods of Multivariate Analysis, *Second Edition*
RENCHER · Multivariate Statistical Inference with Applications
* RIPLEY · Spatial Statistics
RIPLEY · Stochastic Simulation
ROBINSON · Practical Strategies for Experimenting
ROHATGI and SALEH · An Introduction to Probability and Statistics, *Second Edition*
ROLSKI, SCHMIDLI, SCHMIDT, and TEUGELS · Stochastic Processes for Insurance and Finance
ROSENBERGER and LACHIN · Randomization in Clinical Trials: Theory and Practice
ROSS · Introduction to Probability and Statistics for Engineers and Scientists
† ROUSSEEUW and LEROY · Robust Regression and Outlier Detection
* RUBIN · Multiple Imputation for Nonresponse in Surveys
RUBINSTEIN · Simulation and the Monte Carlo Method
RUBINSTEIN and MELAMED · Modern Simulation and Modeling
RYAN · Modern Regression Methods
RYAN · Statistical Methods for Quality Improvement, *Second Edition*
SALTELLI, CHAN, and SCOTT (editors) · Sensitivity Analysis
* SCHEFFE · The Analysis of Variance
SCHIMEK · Smoothing and Regression: Approaches, Computation, and Application
SCHOTT · Matrix Analysis for Statistics, *Second Edition*
SCHOUTENS · Levy Processes in Finance: Pricing Financial Derivatives
SCHUSS · Theory and Applications of Stochastic Differential Equations
SCOTT · Multivariate Density Estimation: Theory, Practice, and Visualization
* SEARLE · Linear Models
SEARLE · Linear Models for Unbalanced Data
SEARLE · Matrix Algebra Useful for Statistics
SEARLE, CASELLA, and McCULLOCH · Variance Components
SEARLE and WILLETT · Matrix Algebra for Applied Economics
SEBER and LEE · Linear Regression Analysis, *Second Edition*
† SEBER · Multivariate Observations
† SEBER and WILD · Nonlinear Regression
SENNOTT · Stochastic Dynamic Programming and the Control of Queueing Systems
* SERFLING · Approximation Theorems of Mathematical Statistics
SHAFER and VOVK · Probability and Finance: It's Only a Game!

*Now available in a lower priced paperback edition in the Wiley Classics Library.
†Now available in a lower priced paperback edition in the Wiley–Interscience Paperback Series.

SILVAPULLE and SEN · Constrained Statistical Inference: Inequality, Order, and Shape Restrictions
SMALL and McLEISH · Hilbert Space Methods in Probability and Statistical Inference
SRIVASTAVA · Methods of Multivariate Statistics
STAPLETON · Linear Statistical Models
STAUDTE and SHEATHER · Robust Estimation and Testing
STOYAN, KENDALL, and MECKE · Stochastic Geometry and Its Applications, *Second Edition*
STOYAN and STOYAN · Fractals, Random Shapes and Point Fields: Methods of Geometrical Statistics
STYAN · The Collected Papers of T. W. Anderson: 1943–1985
SUTTON, ABRAMS, JONES, SHELDON, and SONG · Methods for Meta-Analysis in Medical Research
TANAKA · Time Series Analysis: Nonstationary and Noninvertible Distribution Theory
THOMPSON · Empirical Model Building
THOMPSON · Sampling, *Second Edition*
THOMPSON · Simulation: A Modeler's Approach
THOMPSON and SEBER · Adaptive Sampling
THOMPSON, WILLIAMS, and FINDLAY · Models for Investors in Real World Markets
TIAO, BISGAARD, HILL, PEÑA, and STIGLER (editors) · Box on Quality and Discovery: with Design, Control, and Robustness
TIERNEY · LISP-STAT: An Object-Oriented Environment for Statistical Computing and Dynamic Graphics
TSAY · Analysis of Financial Time Series, *Second Edition*
UPTON and FINGLETON · Spatial Data Analysis by Example, Volume II: Categorical and Directional Data
VAN BELLE · Statistical Rules of Thumb
VAN BELLE, FISHER, HEAGERTY, and LUMLEY · Biostatistics: A Methodology for the Health Sciences, *Second Edition*
VESTRUP · The Theory of Measures and Integration
VIDAKOVIC · Statistical Modeling by Wavelets
VINOD and REAGLE · Preparing for the Worst: Incorporating Downside Risk in Stock Market Investments
WALLER and GOTWAY · Applied Spatial Statistics for Public Health Data
WEERAHANDI · Generalized Inference in Repeated Measures: Exact Methods in MANOVA and Mixed Models
WEISBERG · Applied Linear Regression, *Third Edition*
WELSH · Aspects of Statistical Inference
WESTFALL and YOUNG · Resampling-Based Multiple Testing: Examples and Methods for *p*-Value Adjustment
WHITTAKER · Graphical Models in Applied Multivariate Statistics
WINKER · Optimization Heuristics in Economics: Applications of Threshold Accepting
WONNACOTT and WONNACOTT · Econometrics, *Second Edition*
WOODING · Planning Pharmaceutical Clinical Trials: Basic Statistical Principles
WOODWORTH · Biostatistics: A Bayesian Introduction
WOOLSON and CLARKE · Statistical Methods for the Analysis of Biomedical Data, *Second Edition*
WU and HAMADA · Experiments: Planning, Analysis, and Parameter Design Optimization
YANG · The Construction Theory of Denumerable Markov Processes
* ZELLNER · An Introduction to Bayesian Inference in Econometrics
ZHOU, OBUCHOWSKI, and McCLISH · Statistical Methods in Diagnostic Medicine

*Now available in a lower priced paperback edition in the Wiley Classics Library.
†Now available in a lower priced paperback edition in the Wiley–Interscience Paperback Series.